CASES AND COMMENTARY

ON

THE LAW OF TRUSTS

AUSTRALIA
The Law Book Company Ltd.
Sydney : Melbourne : Brisbane

CANADA AND U.S.A.
The Carswell Company Ltd.
Agincourt, Ontario

INDIA
N. M. Tripathi Private Ltd.
Bombay

ISRAEL
Steimatzky's Agency Ltd.
Jerusalem : Tel Aviv : Haifa

MALAYSIA—SINGAPORE—BRUNEI
Malayan Law Journal (Pte) Ltd.
Singapore

NEW ZEALAND
Sweet & Maxwell (N.Z.) Ltd.
Wellington

PAKISTAN
Pakistan Law House
Karachi

NATHAN AND MARSHALL

CASES AND COMMENTARY
ON
THE LAW OF TRUSTS

SIXTH EDITION

By

D. J. HAYTON
LL.B.(Newcastle), M.A.(Cantab.)
Of the Inner Temple and Lincoln's Inn, Barrister
Fellow of Jesus College Cambridge
Lecturer in Law in the University of Cambridge

LONDON
STEVENS & SONS
1975

First Edition	(1939)	By J. A. Nathan
Second Edition	(1951)	By O. R. Marshall
Third Edition	(1955)	,,
Fourth Edition	(1961)	,,
Second Impression	(1966)	,,
Fifth Edition	(1967)	,,
Second Impression	(1971)	,,
Sixth Edition	(1975)	By D. J. Hayton

Published by
Stevens & Sons Limited of
11 New Fetter Lane, London
and printed in Great Britain
by The Eastern Press Limited
of London and Reading

SBN   Hardback   420   43690   1
        Paperback   420   43700   2

PREFACE

It will be seen that *A Casebook on Trusts* has now become *Cases and Commentary on the Law of Trusts*. This recognises the approach that I have developed as new editor of the book, Sir Roy Marshall having moved on to high administrative positions. I have accelerated the trend of former editions towards the conversion of the book more into an independent text on the law of trusts. Conventional textbooks have their uses, but as aids to learning and as media for developing new ideas and exhibiting the fruits of research they have obvious limitations. Conventional casebooks, too, have their limitations.

The present edition is intended to cater for university and professional examinations and, so far as possible within the limits of space and time afforded for this edition, to remedy the deficiencies of conventional textbooks and casebooks. It aims to have a practical outlook and to show what trust law is all about with as little ceremony as possible. On another plane it aims to encourage readers to broaden their perspective, to develop their analytical faculties and to think critically for themselves. It is hoped that after this book has been read and digested it will afford a greater insight into trust law than any corresponding work.

Many changes have been made in this edition. Over fifty old cases have been omitted, about thirty new cases find a place, and, for the first time, room is found for certain materials (*e.g.* excerpts from articles, casenotes, books, annual reports of the Charity Commissioners) and for certain problems designed to stimulate thought. A large part of the Charities Act 1960 also appears, owing to its absence from Sweet & Maxwell's *Property Statutes*, which is otherwise so useful for statutory materials relevant to a trust course. Some of such materials, however, do appear in this book for purposes of continuity and ease of exposition. Most cases that have been omitted in their own right will generally be found to be fully discussed in cases that are now included. It must be admitted, though, that owing to the escalation of printing costs, I have been forced by considerations of space to be much more brutal than I would have wished in omitting cases altogether and in inserting reduced extracts from new cases and materials. If others feel that I have been too brutal, then letters or reviews to this effect would be appreciated in order that such pressure may persuade those who matter that a larger, dearer work would be sufficiently viable for the next edition.

The old Chapter 1, " The Nature of Equitable Interests arising under Trusts " has been scrapped in favour of an introductory chapter concerned with showing what a trust looks like and what trusts are used for. This necessarily entails a brief review of tax law. A brief outline of the law on wills and intestacies is also included, as my experience has been

v

that this helps to simplify problems that students would otherwise find an added complexity when dealing with aspects of trust law, such as resulting trusts and secret trusts: moreover, an introduction to the law of succession is no bad thing when otherwise many students would leave university with little knowledge of what laymen believe all lawyers know.

Chapter 2, though having to suffer from pruning more than any other chapter, deals additionally with bailment, agency and loans, whilst Chapter 3 is little changed. Chapter 4 is substantially changed to take account of *Re Gulbenkian's W.T., McPhail* v. *Doulton, Re Baden's Deed Trusts (No. 2), Re Manisty's Settlement, Re Denley's Trust Deed* and *Re Recher's W.T.* Perpetuity, in the forms of the rules against remoteness of vesting and the rule against inalienability, is also dealt with in Chapter 4 (instead of the old Chapter 6 on Charitable Trusts): the details of the rules against remoteness have been omitted as they are traditionally dealt with in land law books, though vital to the law of trusts.

Chapter 5 contains much new matter and is particularly concerned with clarifying the problems faced over the possible enforcement of incompletely constituted trusts, as this is an area always found difficult by all but the very best students. A new section 3 has been added to deal with attempts by settlors to deprive their creditors by using trusts.

Chapter 6 loses its section on " Perpetuity " and is more concerned with distinguishing charitable trusts from ordinary trusts (a distinction bedevilled by the tax advantages of charitable status) and with the administration of charitable trusts. Chapter 7 has been simplified owing to the new categorisation of " presumed " and " automatic " resulting trusts by Megarry J. in *Re Vandervell's Trusts* and the new contractual approach exemplified in certain types of circumstances by *Re West Sussex Constabulary Widows Fund* and *Re Sick and Funeral Society.*

Chapter 8 has been rearranged and contains much new matter. It is in this area of the constructive trust that there is likely to be most growth in trust law in the foreseeable future. Chapter 9 contains new sections on " Special Types of Trustee " and on the maxim, " Equity will not allow a trust to fail for want of a trustee."

Chapter 10 now merits a general introduction followed by the section on " Conflict of Interest and Duty " since a fiduciary's duty of loyalty is an overriding one, always to be borne in mind in the administration of a trust. The temptation to go to town on the Variation of Trusts Act 1958 was resisted on the grounds that it must have a low priority for the allocation of space in a book for students when it is essentially an area for practitioners with a good knowledge of tax law: *Re Holt's S.T.,* however, had to be given space.

Chapter 11 has retained its structure though the pre-1939 law on limitation of actions has been omitted *Re Lucking's W.T.* finds a place for itself there.

During proof-setting, the re-election of the February Labour Government in October 1974 and the subsequent publication of the Finance Bill on December 10 have resolved the uncertainty surrounding the introduction of—and the details of—the new capital transfer tax (" C.T.T.") directed at the avoidance of estate duty by *inter vivos* gifts and at discouraging the wealthy from transferring their wealth before the introduction of the projected wealth tax. At manuscript stage it was only possible to give the briefest of outlines (see page 20) but as C.T.T. is of especial significance I have thought it advisable to update and fill out the position as follows. (The following summary should be omitted until pages 17–20 have been read.)

Estate duty will no longer apply for deaths occurring after March 12, 1975. Instead C.T.T. will be charged on the value of the deceased's estate and the tax will come out of that estate. *Inter vivos* gratuitous transfers of value have been subject to C.T.T. since March 26, 1974, though *inter vivos* gifts which, on a death before March 13, 1975 are brought into charge under the estate duty rules, are exempt from C.T.T.

C.T.T. is chargeable on *inter vivos* gratuitous transfers as they occur and on a cumulative basis, a notional transfer on death of the whole of the deceased's estate being the final cumulation. The rates of C.T.T., like the estate duty rates, are progressively higher on successive slices of the cumulative total of chargeable transfers. However, the rates for lifetime transfers made more than three years before death are half the rates for transfers taking effect on, or within three years of, death up to a cumulative total of £100,000. At £300,000 the rates are the same having become progressivly more alike in the £100,000 to £300,000 region. No C.T.T. is payable until a £15,000 cumulative total is reached when a 5 per cent. or 10 per cent. rate, as the case may be, applies to the £15,000 to £20,000 slice. The rate reaches 75 per cent. at the £2m. mark.

Transfers between spouses in life and on death are exempt, though treated as separate persons for C.T.T. purposes. Transfers made out of a person's taxable income as part of his normal expenditure and leaving him sufficient income to maintain his usual standard of living are exempt. Transfers made in consideration of marriage are exempt up to £2,500 if the donor is a party to the marriage or his or her lineal ancestor and up to £1,000 if the donor is anyone else. Transfers made by a person in any one tax year (and not otherwise exempt) are exempt up to a value of £1,000. The last three exemptions apply only to *inter vivos* transfers and not to property passing on death or to transfers out of settled property. Finally, transfers to charities or to political parties are exempt except to the extent that they each exceed £100,000 where the transfers were made on or within one year of death.

The amount to be brought into charge is measured by the loss to the transferor consequential upon the transfer. The loss to the transferor includes the C.T.T. payable by him, C.T.T. being primarily his liability. Thus, on a gift of £30,000 the transferor is treated as having made a grossed up chargeable gift of £31,285 on which £1,285 C.T.T. is payable. This grossing up is done both for calculating C.T.T. rates and for assessing the cumulative total of the transferor's gifts for otherwise if the transferor's C.T.T. were not included in his chargeable gifts he would diminish the amount of his cumulative chargeable estate on death by the amount of C.T.T. on his *inter vivos* gifts. However, if the transferee agrees to pay and does pay the C.T.T. then the gift is treated as a net gift of £30,000 in respect of which £1,125 C.T.T. is payable by the transferee. Since the transferor is not paying the C.T.T. there is no question of him obtaining an unfair advantage by diminishing his chargeable estate by the amount of the C.T.T. " Loss to the transferor," significantly, is calculated without taking into account any expenses incidental to the gift (*e.g.*, stamp duty, legal costs) or any liability to capital gains tax arising in respect of the gift. Incidentally, on a death no charge to capital gains tax arises since C.T.T. alone is then payable: instead, the original base value for capital gains tax is given a " free " uplift to the value at the date of death.

When property is first settled on trustees the C.T.T. charge is on the same basis as for outright gifts whether *inter vivos* or testamentary. Once property has been settled the application of C.T.T. depends on whether or not there is currently a beneficiary with an interest in possession entitled to receive the income or otherwise enjoy the settled property (*e.g.* a life tenant as opposed to a beneficiary under a discretionary trust).

A beneficiary with an interest in possession is treated as if he were the current owner of the settled property. A C.T.T. charge arises if he disposes of his interest or if his interest terminates wholly or partly under provisions in the settlement (*e.g.*, on remarriage or on exercise of a power of appointment or advancement) except that no C.T.T. charge arises where a person becomes absolutely entitled to the property in which he had an interest in possession. Where the interest is sold, deduction of the purchase money is allowed in arriving at the chargeable value. Otherwise, the chargeable value is equal to the value of the property in which the interest subsisted, *e.g.* £1m. in the case of a life interest in settled property worth £1m., or £½m. if the life interest were only in half the income arising from the settled property. C.T.T. will be chargeable as if the life tenant had made a personal gift of the settled property or part thereof on the termination or disposal of his interest therein. His cumulative total for C.T.T. may thus be increased dramatically; however, C.T.T. payable in respect of the settled property is primarily the responsibility of the trustees.

Where no one has any entitlement in possession to the income or enjoyment of the settled property (*e.g.* discretionary trusts) there is a special periodic charge at ten-year intervals and C.T.T. is charged on actual or nominal distributions of capital out of the settled property to beneficiaries. An actual distribution occurs where capital leaves the settlement *e.g.* upon exercise of a power of appointment of £30,000 to B absolutely whereupon the trustees are liable to pay C.T.T. on a grossed up amount unless B agrees to pay and does pay C.T.T. on the net amount. A notional distribution occurs when a person becomes entitled to an interest in possession in property formerly without such an interest *e.g.* after an accumulation period expires or upon an exercise of a power of appointment conferring a life interest in a third of the property upon B. Notional distributions are not liable to grossing up. If the trust was already in existence on March 26, 1974, the charge to C.T.T. is computed as if the trust were an individual and the distributions were gifts by him. For such a trust transitional relief is available for distributions made before April 1, 1980, so that only a small percentage of the C.T.T. otherwise arising is payable *i.e.* only 10 per cent. before April 1, 1976, 12½ per cent. before April 1, 1977, 15 per cent. before April 1, 1978, 17½ per cent. before April 1, 1979, 20 per cent. before April 1, 1980. For later trusts the rate of C.T.T. in respect of distributions up to the amount of the actual initial settled capital is the over-all rate that would have been charged on a gift of that amount by the settlor when he made the initial settlement on the hypothesis that he survived his settlement by three years: distributions in excess of the initial capital fall into the higher cumulative slices as further gifts by the settlor would have done.

The periodic charge is to fall on every tenth anniversary of the date on which the discretionary trusts commenced, starting with anniversaries on or after April 1, 1980. The charge amounts to 30 per cent. of the C.T.T. that would have been chargeable if the whole capital held on the discretionary trusts had been distributed, subject to proportional abatement for any property so held only for nine or fewer years. For foreign managed trusts the charge is payable annually and no transitional relief is available.

It is possible to avoid this periodic charge by settling property not on discretionary trusts but to similar effect, *e.g.* for B for life, subject to an overriding discretionary power in the trustees to pay so much of the income and capital as they see fit to such member sof class C to Z as they see fit; on capital being appointed, though, this will rank as a *pro tanto* chargeable actual termination of B's defeasible life interest in possession.

Exceptionally, in the case of accumulation and maintenance settlements where income is to be accumulated so far as not applied for the maintenance, education or benefit of one or more beneficiaries who, on or before attaining a specified age, not exceeding 25 years, are to become entitled to settled property or to an interest in possession in settled property, the periodic charge will not apply and distributions to these beneficiaries will be exempt from the usual distribution charge to C.T.T. Property held for charitable purposes only is similarly exempt.

Protective trusts also receive favoured treatment in that upon the actual termination of the principal beneficiary's determinable interest when it is replaced by a discretionary trust no C.T.T. is chargeable; and once the discretionary trust is in operation actual or notional distributions for the benefit of the principal beneficiary are ignored for C.T.T. purposes. The periodic charge is also deferred until either a capital distribution (other than for the principal beneficiary's benefit) is made or the trust period terminates (usually on the principal beneficiary's death): the amount on which C.T.T. is then chargeable is the whole of the settled property where the trust period has terminated; otherwise it is the proportion of the settled property represented by the capital distribution occasionining the deferred charge.

I have endeavoured to set out the law in accordance with the sources available, as on January 1, 1975 except that the Preface has been updated to take account of the Finance Act 1975 passed on March 13, 1975. Useful articles on section 172 of the Law of Property Act 1925 and the criminal liability of trustees may now be found respectively in (1975) 91 L.Q.R. 86 (B. Langstaff) and (1975) 39 Conv. 29 (R. Brazier).

It remains for me to express my heartfelt appreciation to the publishers for their thoroughness in preparing this book for publication and for producing the index and the tables of cases and statutes.

DAVID HAYTON.

STONE BUILDINGS,
  LINCOLN'S INN.
April 3, 1975.

ACKNOWLEDGMENTS

THE author and publishers wish to thank the following for permission to reprint material from the books and periodicals indicated:

Butterworth Law Publishers Ltd.:
    The All England Law Reports.
    Underhill's *Law of Trusts and Trustees* (12th ed.).
    Pettit's *Equity and the Law of Trusts* (2nd ed.).

Pitman Publishing Ltd.:
    Keeton, *The Law of Trusts* (9th ed.).

Little, Brown & Co. (Boston):
    Scott, *Abridgment of The Law of Trusts* (3rd ed., 1960).

CONTENTS

TABLE OF CASES

Capitals and figures in italic type denote cases which are digested or quoted from in the text of the work.

TABLE OF STATUTES

ABBREVIATIONS

Goff & Jones: Goff & Jones, *The Law of Restitution* (1st ed.).

Hanbury: Hanbury & Maudsley's *Modern Equity* (9th ed. by R. H. Maudsley).

Lewin: *Lewin on Trusts* (16th ed. by W. J. Mowbray).

Maudsley & Burn: Maudsley & Burn, *Trust and Trustees: Cases and Materials* (1st ed.).

Megarry & Wade: Megarry & Wade, *The Law of Real Property* (3rd ed.).

Pettit: Pettit, *Equity and the Law of Trusts* (2nd ed.).

Snell: Snell, *Equity* (27th ed. by R. E. Megarry and P. V. Baker).

Underhill: Underhill, *Law of Trusts and Trustees* (12th ed. by R. T. Oerton).

Waters: Waters, *The Constructive Trust* (1st ed.).

Wolstenholme & Cherry: Wolstenholme & Cherry, *Conveyancing Statutes* (13th ed. by J. T. Farrand).

CHAPTER 1

INTRODUCTION

WHAT is the law of trusts about? It is about the preservation of family wealth. It is about settling property on trustees so as to minimise liability to the various taxes: generally no one with capital over £80,000 should be without a trust and many people with less capital will find a trust useful. It is about tying up property so that it can be enjoyed by a succession of people. It is about protecting family wealth from the depredations of creditors and of particular members of the family with extravagant, reckless dispositions. It is about arranging for the family wealth to be distributed according to the ever-changing needs of the family, taking into account the ever-changing fiscal laws over periods of up to 120 years.[1] It is about providing secretly for mentally defective dependants, for mistresses, for illegitimate children or for causes with which an open association is not desired. It is about the furtherance of charitable causes for unlimited periods or the furtherance of private causes for limited periods. It is about providing pensions for retired employees and their dependants. Indeed, it is customary for really wealthy people who wish to minimise their tax liabilities and be philanthropic to have three trusts: a family trust, a pensions trust for retired employees of the family companies and their dependants, and a charitable trust.

The trust concept is amazingly flexible and can be used for virtually any purpose imaginable. The above purposes are the main ones that spring to mind. The concept has proved particularly useful in the field of conveyancing so that whenever land is owned by two or more persons that land must be held on a trust for sale.[2] Maitland has quite rightly characterised the trust concept as " the greatest and most distinctive achievement performed by Englishmen in the field of jurisprudence." [3] No lawyer can claim to provide a proper service for his clients without a thorough grasp of trust law and its potentialities.

What then is a trust? It is as difficult to define as it is to define a " contract," " tort," or " crime." However, three definitions are now set out to provide a rough and ready introduction to trust law.

Scott, Trusts, 3rd ed., paras. 2, 3

" Even if it were possible to frame an exact definition of a legal concept, the definition would not be of great practical value. A definition cannot properly be used as though it were a major premise so that rules governing conduct can be deduced from it. Our law, at least, has not grown in that way. When the rules have been arrived at from other sources, it may be

---

[1] This is by using a royal lives perpetuity clause rather than the 80-year period specified in s. 1 of the Perpetuities and Accumulations Act 1964. See Chap. 4, *infra*.
[2] ss. 34–36 of the Law of Property Act 1925. Trustees hold property as joint tenants so that on the death of one trustee the property automatically passes to the surviving trustees by virtue of the *ius accrescendi*. On the death of the last surviving trustee his personal representatives take over his function until the appointment of new trustees: Trustee Act 1925, ss. 18, 36.
[3] *Selected Essays*, p. 129.

1

possible to attempt to frame a definition. But the definition results from
the rules, and not the rules from the definition.

All that one can properly attempt to do is to give such a description of
a legal concept that others will know in a general way what one is talking
about. It is possible to state the principal distinguishing characteristics of
the concept so that others will have a general idea of what the writer means.
With this in mind, those responsible for the Restatement of Trusts proposed
the following definition or description of an express trust. It is ' a fiduciary
relationship with respect to property, subjecting the person by whom the
title to property is held to equitable duties to deal with the property for the
benefit of another person, which arises as a result of a manifestation of an
intention to create it.' In this definition or description the following
characteristics are to be noticed: (1) a trust is a relationship; (2) it is a
relationship of a fiduciary character; (3) it is a relationship with respect to
property, not one involving merely personal duties; (4) it involves the existence of equitable duties imposed upon the holder of the title to the property
to deal with it for the benefit of another; and (5) it arises as a result of a
manifestation of an intention to create the relationship."

Underhill's Law of Trusts, 12th ed., p. 3

" A trust is an equitable obligation, binding a person (who is called a
trustee) to deal with property over which he has control (which is called the
trust property), for the benefit of persons (who are called beneficiaries or
cestuis que trust), of whom he may himself be one, and any one of whom
may enforce the obligation. Any act or neglect on the part of a trustee
which is not authorised or excused by the terms of the trust instrument, or
by law, is called a breach of trust." [4]

Keeton's Law of Trusts, 10th ed., p. 5

" A trust . . . is the relationship which arises wherever a person called the
trustee is compelled in equity to hold property, whether real or personal, and
whether by legal or equitable title, for the benefit of some persons (of whom
he may be one and who are termed beneficiaries) or for some object
permitted by law, in such a way that the real benefit of the property accrues,
not to the trustee, but to the beneficiaries or other objects of the trust."

It will thus be seen that the trust property is vested in the trustees to be
managed wholly for the benefit of the beneficiaries. Since the opportunities
for trustees to take advantage of their position are so great equity has imposed very strict rigorous duties upon trustees.[5] Indeed, so onerous have
these duties become that properly drawn trust instruments greatly relax the
standards that equity would otherwise demand: were it not for such relaxation few individuals or companies would be prepared to act as trustees. It
should be noted that so long as illegality or public policy or uncertainty [6]
does not intervene then draftsmen of trust instruments have a free hand to
vary or negative trust principles. In so far as the draftsman has not made
the consent of someone other than the trustees requisite before certain things

---

[4] Approved by Cohen J. in *Re Marshall's Will Trusts* [1945] Ch. 217, 219 and by
    Romer L.J. in *Green* v. *Russell* [1959] 2 Q.B. 226, 241.
[5] See Chap. 10, *infra*.
[6] See Chap. 4, *infra*.

are done the trustees have an independent, unfettered discretion in the running of the trust though, of course, the income and capital managed by the trustees must be held according to the terms of the trust for the relevant beneficiaries.

The interests of the beneficiaries are paramount and the trustees must do their best to hold the balance evenly between those beneficiaries (with life interests) interested in income and those beneficiaries (with absolute interests in remainder) interested in capital.[7] Indeed, the trustees have a paternalistic function of protecting each beneficiary against himself. Even if all the beneficiaries interested in a particular trust are each *sui juris* and wish the trustees to do a certain thing the trustees can refuse if they consider that some of the beneficiaries are not objectively acting in their own best interests [8]: however, if all the beneficiaries are between them absolutely entitled to the trust property and are each *sui juris* then under the *Saunders* v. *Vautier* [9] principle, the beneficiaries can call for the trust property to be vested in them (or their nominees) by the trustees, so terminating the trust.

Since the beneficiaries' interests are paramount the trustees cannot (in the absence of authorisation in the trust instrument) invest trust moneys as they might invest their own and speculate a little: they have to play " safe " and invest in a limited, " safe " portion of the securities market as set out in the Trustee Investments Act 1961.[10] On the other hand, whilst trustees when selling their own houses might feel bound to honour the commercial morality code and reject out of hand a higher offer when they had orally agreed, subject to contract, to sell to a purchaser who had just submitted his part of the contract to them, trustees, when selling trust property in such circumstances, must not reject the higher offer without probing it with a view to acceptance.[11]

To turn the spotlight from the trustees to the beneficiaries there has been much controversy [12] over the nature of the interest of a beneficiary under a trust based upon the differences between a right *in personam* and a right *in rem*. An examination of the controversy is useful so far is it throws light upon the nature of a beneficiary's equitable interest. If by right *in personam* is meant a right against a specified person or persons and by right *in rem* a right against all the world, then equitable interests arising under trusts are wider than *in personam* but not quite *in rem*: they prevail over the whole world except a bona fide purchaser of a legal estate for value without notice (" equity's darling ") or a purchaser who complies with the overreaching requirements of the Law of Property Act 1925 or the Settled Land Act 1925. If, on the other hand, by right *in personam* is meant the right of the beneficiary to compel administration of the trust according to its terms, and by right *in rem* is meant the right of the beneficiary to say that he is the owner of 'the property in which his equitable interest exists then his

---

[7] See Chap. 10, *infra.*
[8] *Re Brockbank* [1949] Ch. 206.
[9] *Saunders* v. *Vautier* (1841) 4 Beav. 115, *infra*, p. 523, *Re Smith* [1928] Ch. 915 *infra*, p. 177.
[10] See Chap. 10, *infra.*
[11] *Buttle* v. *Saunders* [1950] W.N. 255.
[12] Hart (1899) 15 L.Q.R. 294; A. W. Scott (1917) 17 Col.L.R. 269; H. Stone (1917) 17 Col.L.R. 467; H. G. Hanbury (1929) 45 L.Q.R. 198–199; V. Latham (1954) 32 Can.B.R. 520; D. W. M. Waters (1967) 45 Can.B.R. 219; *Baker* v. *Archer-Shee* [1927] A.C. 844; *Re Cuff Knox* [1963] I.R. 263.

rights are usually *in personam* though they may be *in rem*. Thus, a beneficiary under a trust of land is not entitled to distrain for rent due from a tenant to whom the trustee has granted a lease.[13] On the other hand, in some circumstances the beneficiary is regarded as the real owner of the assets constituting the trust fund so as to be liable to tax in respect of the income produced by those assets.[14] Further circumstances where a beneficiary has a right *in rem* are where he can invoke the principle of *Saunders* v. *Vautier*[15] to call for the trustees to vest the trust property in him and where he can exercise the tracing remedy.[16]

A beneficiary's interest will be one of two basic types. He will either have a fixed entitlement to income or capital of the trust (*e.g.* a life interest or an interest in remainder) or he will have no fixed entitlement to anything, merely having a hope (*spes*) that the trustees will from time to time give him some of the income or capital of the trust (*i.e.* he will merely be an object of a discretionary trust).[17] Trust instruments thus begin by setting out the sorts of interests that the beneficiaries are to have and laying down any contingencies that beneficiaries may have to satisfy; then, they set out any special powers of the settlor or the trustees to affect the beneficial interests under the trusts; finally, a host of administrative powers are conferred upon the trustees in such a way as to relax or abrogate the vigorous duties and standards that trust law would otherwise impose.

As seeing something for yourself is so much better than any description there now follows a typical trust instrument. Read it now and read it at later stages when the significance of its administrative clauses will be more apparent. The trust in question is a discretionary trust as its flexibility makes it a very popular form of trust.

Standard Discretionary Trust

THIS SETTLEMENT is made the —— day of —— 1975

BETWEEN —— of —— (hereinafter call " the Settlor ") of the one part and —— of —— and —— of —— (hereinafter called " the Original Trustees ")[18] of the other part

WHEREAS:

(A) The Settlor is desirous of making irrevocable provision for the Specified Class as herein defined [and for charity[19]] in manner hereinafter appearing

(B) With the intention of making such provision the Settlor has prior to the execution hereof transferred to the Original Trustees the assets specified in the Second Schedule hereto and is desirous of declaring such trusts thereof as hereinafter appear

(C) The Settlor may hereafter pay or transfer further assets to or

---

13 *Schalit* v. *Joseph Nadler Ltd.* [1933] 2 K.B. 79.
14 *Baker* v. *Archer-Shee* [1927] A.C. 844.
15 (1841) 4 Beav. 115, *infra*, p. 523.
16 See Chap. 8, section 7.
17 See Chap. 5, section 2.
18 As to the identity of the Trustees see clause 8 (*a*).
19 Delete reference to charity if settlor does not wish to benefit charity.

into the control of the Trustees hereof to be held by them on the trusts of this Settlement

Now THIS DEED WITNESSETH as follows:

1. (1) THE perpetuity period applicable to this Settlement under the rule against perpetuities shall be the period of eighty years from the execution of this deed

(2) IN this Settlement and the Schedules hereto the following expressions shall have the following meanings that is to say:

(a) " the Trustees " means the Original Trustees or other the trustees or trustee for the time being of this Settlement and " Trustee " has a corresponding meaning;

(b) subject to any and every exercise of the powers conferred by Clause 5 hereof " the Specified Class " has the meaning attributed to it in the First Schedule hereto;

(c) " the Appointed Day " means the day on which shall expire the period of eighty years less three days from the execution of this Deed;

(d) " The Trust Fund " means and includes:

(i) the said assets specified in the Second Schedule hereto;

(ii) All assets paid or transferred to or into the control of and accepted by the Trustees as additions to the Trust Fund; and

(iii) the assets from time to time representing the said assets specified in the Second Schedule hereto and the said additions to the Trust Fund or any part or parts thereof respectively

(e) " Spouse " means a party to a marriage which is for the time being subsisting and does not include a party to a former marriage which has terminated by death or divorce or otherwise

[(f) [20] " charity " means any institution whether corporate or not (including a trust) which is established for exclusively charitable purposes and " charities " bears a corresponding meaning]

(g) " the Nominating Beneficiaries " means such of the persons referred to in the First Schedule hereto as are for the time being members of the Specified Class and *sui juris*

2. THE Trustees shall stand possessed of the Trust Fund UPON TRUST at their discretion to retain the same (so far as not consisting of cash) in its existing form of investment or to sell the same or any part or parts thereof and to invest or apply the net proceeds of any sale and any other capital moneys in or upon any kind of investment or for any of the purposes hereinafter authorised with power at any time and from time to time to vary such investments or applications for others of any nature hereby authorised

---

[20] Delete sub-clause (f) if charities are not intended to benefit.

3. (1) [21] THE Trustees shall stand possessed of the Trust Fund and the income thereof UPON TRUST for all or such one or more exclusively of the others or other of the members of the Specified Class if more than one in such shares and either absolutely or at such age or time or respective ages or times upon and with such limitations conditions and restrictions and such trusts and powers (including discretionary trusts and powers over income and capital exercisable by any person or persons other than the Settlor or any Spouse of the Settlor whether similar to the discretionary trusts and powers herein contained or otherwise) and with such provisions (including provisions for maintenance and advancement and the accumulation of income for any period or periods authorised by law and provisions for investment and management of any nature whatsoever and provisions for the appointment of separate trustees of any appointed fund) and generally in such manner as the Trustees (being not less than two in number or being a corporate trustee) shall in their absolute discretion from time to time by any deed or deeds revocable or irrevocable appoint PROVIDED THAT:

    (i) no such appointment shall invalidate any payment or application of capital or income previously made under the trusts or powers herein elsewhere contained; and

    (ii) every appointment shall be made and every interest limited thereunder shall vest in interest (if at all) not later than the Appointed Day and no appointment shall be revoked later than the Appointed Day

[(2) [22] Subject to any appointment previously made by the Trustees under the powers hereinbefore contained the Trustees may in their absolute discretion and without prejudice to the generality of the said powers at any time and from time to time before the Appointed Day:

    (a) pay or transfer the whole or any part or parts of the income or capital of the Trust Fund to any charity or charities or apply the same for any exclusively charitable purpose or purposes;

    (b) revocably or irrevocably in writing appoint that the whole or any part or share of the income of the Trust Fund or any annual or other periodic sum out of the said income shall during any period or periods ending before the Appointed Day be paid to any charity or charities;

    (c) enter into any covenant or other arrangement with any charity or charities to enable or facilitate the recovery of any tax by such charity or charities in respect of any such payment transfer or appointment (as aforesaid)

PROVIDED ALWAYS that the receipt of the person purporting or appearing to be the treasurer or other proper officer of any charity or (in the case of a charitable trust) of the persons purporting or appearing to be

---

[21] Delete numeral (1) if sub-clause (2) deleted.
[22] Delete sub-clause (2) if charities are not intended to benefit.

the trustees thereof shall be a good discharge to the Trustees for any capital or income paid or transferred to such charity without the necessity for the Trustees to see further to the application thereof]

4. (1) IN default of and subject to and until any or every exercise of the powers conferred on the Trustees by the preceding clause hereof the Trustees shall until the Appointed Day hold the income of the Trust Fund upon the trusts and with and subject to the powers and provisions following namely:

(a) During the period of twenty-one years from the execution of this Deed the Trustees shall have power to pay or apply the whole or any part or parts of such income as it arises to or for the maintenance and support or otherwise for the benefit of all or such one or more exclusively of the others or other of the persons who shall for the time being be living and members of the Specified Class if more than one in such shares and in such manner as the Trustees shall in their absolute discretion without being liable to account for the exercise of such discretion think fit

(b) Subject to any and every exercise of the last-mentioned power the Trustees shall during the said period of twenty-one years accumulate the whole or the balance (as the case may be) of the said income by investing the same in any manner hereby authorised and shall hold the accumulations so made as an accretion to the capital of the Trust Fund for all purposes

(c) After the expiration of the said period of twenty-one years the Trustees shall until the Appointed Day pay or apply the whole of the annual income of the Trust Fund as it arises to or for the maintenance and support or otherwise for the benefit of all or such one or more exclusively of the others or other of the persons who shall for the time being be living and members of the Specified Class if more than one in such shares and in such manner as the Trustees shall in their absolute discretion without being liable to account for the exercise of such discretion think fit

(2) In default of and subject to any or every exercise of the said powers conferred on the Trustees by the preceding clause hereof the Trustees shall stand possessed of the Trust Fund on the Appointed Day UPON TRUST for such persons as shall be then living and members of the Specified Class if more than one in equal shares per capita absolutely

(3) Any income or capital of the Trust Fund which but for this present sub-clause would be undisposed of by this Deed shall be held by the Trustees Upon Trust for [[23] ――― and his/her executors

---

[23] The beneficiaries under this ultimate trust should not be the settlor or his spouse or anyone whom he might marry.

administrators and assigns absolutely] [24] [——— and ——— and their respective executors administrators and assigns in equal shares absolutely] [25] [——— (as a registered charity) absolutely and in the event of the failure of this present trust then for charitable purposes generally] [26]

5. THE Trustees (being not less than two in number or being a corporate trustee) may from time to time and at any time before the Appointed Day by any deed or deeds:

(a) declare that any person or class or description of person shall cease to be a member or members of the Specified Class and thereupon such person or class or description of person shall cease to be a member or members of the Specified Class in the same manner as if he she or they had originally been expressly excluded therefrom but without prejudice to any previous payment of capital or income to such person or any member of such class or description of person or application thereof for his her or their benefit PROVIDED that the removal of any such person or class or description of person as aforesaid shall not prejudice modify or affect any appointment of capital or income then already made [AND PROVIDED ALSO [27] that the removal of any such person or class or description of person as aforesaid shall not prejudice modify or affect the trust in favour of [——— and his/her executors administrators and assigns] [28] [——— and ——— and their executors administrators and assigns] [29] contained in sub-clause (3) of the last preceding clause hereof]

(b) declare that any person or persons (not being the Settlor or a Spouse of the Settlor or one of the Trustees) previously nominated in writing in that behalf by any one or more of the Nominating Beneficiaries shall thenceforth be included in the Specified Class and thereupon such person or persons shall become a member or members of the Specified Class for all the purposes hereof PROVIDED that (subject to obtaining any necessary Exchange Control consents) the Trustees shall have an absolute discretion whether or not to make any such declaration in relation to any person or persons nominated as aforesaid and PROVIDED FURTHER that any addition of any such person or persons to the Specified Class shall not prejudice modify or affect any appointment of capital or income then already made

---

[24] These are alternatives, so delete as appropriate.
[25] *Ibid.*
[26] *Ibid.*
[27] This proviso is not required if the ultimate trust in clause 4 (3) is in favour of charity.
[28] Delete as appropriate, for these are alternatives.
[29] *Ibid.*

(c) wholly or partially release or restrict all or any of the powers and discretions conferred upon them (including this present power) whether in relation to the whole Trust Fund or any part or parts thereof or the income thereof respectively

6. WHENEVER the Trustees shall determine to apply any income for the benefit of an infant the Trustees may either themselves so apply that income or for that purpose may pay the same to any parent guardian or other person for the time being having the care or custody of such infant (other than the Settlor or any Spouse of the Settlor) without being responsible for seeing to the further application thereof

7. (1) MONEYS to be invested under this Settlement may be invested or otherwise applied on the security of or in the purchase or acquisition of real or personal property (including the purchase or acquisition of chattels and the effecting or maintaining of policies of insurance or assurance) rights or interests of whatsoever kind and wheresoever situate including any stocks funds shares securities or other investments of whatsoever nature and wheresoever whether producing income or not and whether involving liability or not or on personal loan with or without interest and with or without security to any person (other than the Settlor or any Spouse of the Settlor) anywhere in the world including loans to any member of the Specified Class and the Trustees may grant indulgence to or release any debtor (other than as aforesaid) and give and take guarantees to and from any person (other than as aforesaid) with or without consideration and may enter into profit sharing agreements and give and take options with or without consideration and accept substitution of any security for other security or of one debtor for another debtor to the intent that the Trustees (subject as herein provided) shall have the same unrestricted powers of investing and using moneys and transposing investments and altering the user of moneys arising under these presents as if they were absolutely entitled thereto beneficially and section 6 (1) of the Trustee Investments Act 1961 shall not apply to these presents

(2) IT IS HEREBY EXPRESSLY DECLARED that without prejudice to the generality of the foregoing sub-clause and without prejudice to any powers conferred by law the Trustees shall (subject to the terms of any appointment made under the powers hereinbefore contained) have the following additional powers exercisable until the Appointed Day namely:

(a) The Trustees may:

(i) at any time or times lay out any part or parts of the Trust Fund in the purchase or acquisition of and paying the expenses of purchasing or acquiring and making improvements in or repairs to or on any land and buildings of freehold leasehold or of any other tenure or interest of whatsoever description situate in any part of the world whether or not in

the occupation of or intended for occupation by any member
or members of the Specified Class;

(ii) at any time or times lay out any part or parts of the
Trust Fund in the purchase of household furniture plate linen
china cutlery and articles of household use ornament or equip-
ment or any other chattels whatsoever for the use or enjoyment of any member or members of the Specified Class
whether occupying a building purchased as aforesaid or
otherwise

(b) (i) any land purchased by the Trustees shall if situate in
England or Wales be assured to the Trustees upon trust for
sale with power to postpone sale and if situate elsewhere be
assured to the Trustees either with or without any trust for
sale as the Trustees shall think fit but nevertheless with power
to sell the same;

(ii) in relation to any land situate outside England and
Wales the powers and indemnities given to the Trustees in
relation to land in England by English law shall apply as if
expressed in this Deed and the net rents and profits thereof
shall be applicable in like manner as if they arose from land
in England;

(iii) the Trustees shall stand possessed of any land so
purchased and the net proceeds of sale thereof and other
capital moneys arising under this Settlement upon the trusts
and with and subject to the powers and provisions (including
power to purchase land) upon with and subject to which the
money laid out in the purchase of such land would have been
held if the same had not been so laid out;

(iv) until the sale of any land purchased as aforesaid the
Trustees may permit any member or members of the Specified
Class to occupy the same upon such terms (if any) as to payment or non-payment of rent rates taxes and other expenses
and outgoings and as to repair and decoration and for such
period or periods before the Appointed Day as the Trustees
may think fit;

(v) the Trustees shall be indemnified out of the Trust Fund
against all costs rents covenants obligations and outgoings
relating to any land purchased as aforesaid or for which the
Trustees may be liable in respect of the said premises or the
said purchase

(c) Any household furniture or other chattels purchased by the
Trustees as aforesaid may be handed over to any member or
members of the Specified Class for his or her or their use or
enjoyment for any period before the Appointed Day upon and
subject to such terms and conditions (if any) as to maintaining

such inventory or inventories (if any) and as to insurance and preservation as the Trustees shall think fit

(d) (i) The Trustees shall be at liberty to borrow money (otherwise than from the Settlor or any Spouse of the Settlor) for any of the purposes of this Settlement (including the provision of money to give effect to any appointment authorised hereunder or for the purpose of effecting or maintaining any policies or purchasing or subscribing for any shares or stocks securities properties options rights or interests or other property of whatsoever description) and they may pledge or mortgage the whole or any part of the Trust Fund or the future income thereof by way of security for any such loan and no lender shall be obliged to enquire as to the purpose for which any loan is required or whether the money borrowed exceeds any such requirement

(ii) The Trustees may pledge or mortgage the whole or any part of the Trust Fund by way of principal collateral or other security or by way of guarantee to secure any bank overdraft or other moneys borrowed by any member or members of the Specified Class *Provided* that neither the Settlor nor any Spouse of the Settlor is the lender or one of the lenders in respect of or has any interest in such overdraft or other moneys and *Provided* further that no person other than a member or members of the Specified Class is liable for the repayment thereof

(e) The Trustees may at any time or times enter into any compromise or arrangement with respect to or may release all or any of their rights as shareholders stockholders or debenture stockholders or creditors of any company and whether in connection with a scheme of reconstruction or amalgamation or otherwise and may accept in or towards satisfaction of all or any of such rights such consideration as they shall in their discretion think fit whether in the form of shares stock debenture stock cash obligations or securities of the same or of any other company or companies or in any other form whatsoever

(f) (i) The Trustees may effect purchase or acquire any policy or policies assuring payment to the Trustees in the event of the death of any person of such sum as the Trustees in their absolute discretion (having regard to any prospective liability for tax that may arise in respect of the Trust Fund or any part thereof on the death of such person) may think fit or any endowment or sinking fund policy or policies of whatsoever nature and may pay any premium or premiums thereon out of income or capital

(ii) Without prejudice to the last-mentioned powers or to any powers vested in them under the general law the Trustees may from time to time apply any part or parts of the income or capital of the Trust Fund in or towards payment of the premium or premiums on any policy or policies in which any one or more of the members of the Specified Class shall (whether under this Settlement or any other deed or otherwise) have any beneficial interest whether vested or contingent and whether indefeasible or defeasible PROVIDED ALWAYS that no person except one or more of the members of the Specified Class shall have any beneficial interest whatsoever in the said policy or policies and so that (subject to the said proviso) the Trustees shall have power if they think fit to effect any such policy or policies on any life or lives in which any one or more of the members of the Specified Class shall have an insurable interest

(iii) PROVIDED ALWAYS that no income shall be paid or applied under the foregoing powers after the expiration of twenty-one years from the execution hereof if such payment or application would involve an accumulation of the said income

(iv) In relation to any policy held by them hereunder the Trustees shall have all the powers of a beneficial owner including (without prejudice to the generality of such powers) power to surrender any such policy or to convert the same into a paid up policy or into any other form of assurance or otherwise or to exercise any option thereunder or to sell mortgage charge or otherwise realise or dispose of the same

(g) The Trustees may exercise all voting rights appertaining to any investments comprised in the Trust Fund in as full free and absolute a manner as if they were absolute owners of such investments and in particular but without prejudice to the generality of the foregoing provisions shall be at liberty to exercise such voting rights either by voting or by abstaining from voting so as to ensure or further the appointment or reappointment of any one or more of their number to be directors secretaries or employees of any company in which any part of the Trust Fund may for the time being be invested or of any subsidiary of any such company and any Trustee receiving from any such company or subsidiary any fees salary bonuses or commissions for services rendered to such company or subsidiary shall be entitled to retain the same for his own benefit and shall not be required to account therefor to any person interested hereunder

(h) The Trustees shall have the powers of appropriation and other incidental powers conferred on a personal representative by Section 41 of the Administration of Estates Act 1925 but without the necessity of obtaining the consent of any person to the exercise thereof

(i) The Trustees may apportion as they think fit any funds subject to different trusts which may have become blended and (without prejudice to the jurisdiction of the Court) may determine as they shall consider just whether any money is to be considered as capital or income and whether any expense ought to be paid out of capital or income and all other questions and matters of doubt of whatsoever description arising in the execution of the trusts of these presents and none of the Trustees and no person having formerly been one of the Trustees and no estate of any deceased Trustee shall be liable for or for the consequences of any act done or omitted to be done or for any payment made or omitted to be made in pursuance of any such determination notwithstanding that such determination shall subsequently be held to have been wrongly made

(j) The Trustees may in addition and without prejudice to any powers to employ agents or attorneys conferred by law employ and remunerate on such terms and conditions as they shall think fit any Solicitors Brokers or other agents or advisers (being in each case a person firm or corporation other than and excluding the Settlor and any Spouse of the Settlor) for the purpose of transacting all or any business of whatever nature or doing any act or giving any advice requiring to be transacted done or given in relation to the trusts hereof including any business act or advice which a trustee not being in any profession or business could have transacted done or given personally and any such Solicitor Broker or other agent or adviser shall be entitled to retain any such remuneration or his share thereof notwithstanding that he or any partner of his is a trustee or the sole trustee hereof or is a member officer or employee of or is otherwise interested in any body corporate which is a trustee or the sole trustee hereof and notwithstanding that such agent or adviser is a body corporate of which one or more of the Trustees is a member officer or employee or in which one or more of the Trustees is otherwise interested And the Trustees shall not be responsible for the default of any such Solicitor Broker or other agent or adviser or for any loss occasioned by the employment thereof

(k) The Trustees may deposit any moneys deeds securities or investments (including shares and securities to bearer) held by them as trustees with any banker or any person firm or cor-

poration (other than and excluding the Settlor and any Spouse
of the Settlor) whether in the United Kingdom or abroad for
safe custody or receipt of dividends and may pay out of the
income or capital of such part of the Trust Fund as they shall
think proper any sum payable for such deposit and custody

(l) Assets of the Trust may be held in the names of any two or
more of the Trustees and the Trustees may vest such assets in
a stakeholder or in a nominee or nominees anywhere in the
world (other than the Settlor or any Spouse of the Settlor) on
behalf of the Trustees and entrust or concur in entrusting the
realisation and re-investment of such assets to such stakeholder
nominee or nominees upon such terms as the Trustees may
deem reasonable

(m) The Trustees may embark upon or carry on whether alone or
in partnership or as a joint venture with any other person or
persons (except the Settlor or any Spouse of the Settlor) or
corporation or corporations at the expense of the Trust Fund
and the income thereof any trade or business whatsoever
including (without prejudice to the generality of the foregoing)
any forestry timber farming development insurance banking
or other agricultural commercial industrial financial or professional trade or business whatsoever and may assist or finance
to any extent the commencement or carrying on of any trade
or business by any other or others (except as aforesaid)

8. THE following provisions shall apply to the trusteeship hereof:

(a) The statutory powers of appointing trustees shall apply hereto
and shall be exercisable by [the Settlor] [30] during [his/her] [31]
life PROVIDED that neither the Settlor nor any Spouse of the
Settlor shall be appointed a trustee of these presents

(b) The above-mentioned statutory powers shall be extended so as
to authorise the appointment of any person (other than the
Settlor or any Spouse of the Settlor) or corporation whatsoever
to be a trustee hereof notwithstanding that such person or
corporation may be resident domiciled or situate (whether
temporarily or permanently) outside the United Kingdom and
notwithstanding that as a result of any such appointment or
appointments all of the Trustees may be so resident domiciled
or situate   And the fact that a Trustee remains out of the
United Kingdom for more than twelve months shall not be
grounds for removing such Trustee

(c) Any Trustee engaged in any profession or business shall be
entitled to charge and be paid all professional or other charges
made by him or his firm for business done by him or his firm

---

[30] Amend as appropriate.
[31] *Ibid.*

in relation to the execution of the trusts hereof whether or not in the ordinary course of his profession or business and whether or not of a nature requiring the employment of a professional or business person

(d) Any corporation appointed to be a trustee hereof shall have the powers rights and benefits as to remuneration or otherwise as at or prior to its appointment may be agreed in writing between such corporation and the person or persons (or corporation or corporations) making such appointment

9. THE following provisions shall apply to the powers and discretions of the Trustees hereunder:

(1) Any Trustee may concur in exercising any such power or discretion notwithstanding that he may have a direct or other personal interest in the mode or result of exercising the same Provided that at least one of the Trustees has no such direct or other personal interest

(2) The Trustees shall not be concerned to see to the insurance preservation repair or renewal of any freehold leasehold or other property household furniture or other chattels occupied used or enjoyed by any member of the Specified Class and in the professed execution of the trusts and powers hereof no Trustee shall be liable for any loss to the trust premises arising by reason of any improper investment or application of the Trust Fund or any part thereof made in good faith

(3) Every discretion hereby conferred upon the Trustees shall be an absolute and unfettered discretion and the Trustees shall not be required to furnish to any beneficiary hereunder any reason or justification for the manner in which any such discretion may be exercised

(4) No power or discretion hereunder to which the rule against perpetuities applies shall be exercisable after the Appointed Day

10. NOTWITHSTANDING anything hereinbefore or in the Schedules hereto contained:

(a) the Trust Fund and the income thereof shall be possessed and enjoyed to the entire exclusion of the Settlor and of any benefit to the Settlor by contract or otherwise;

(b) no part of the Trust Fund or the income thereof shall be paid lent or applied for the benefit of the Settlor or any Spouse of the Settlor nor shall any power or discretion hereunder be exercised so as to confer any benefit on the Settlor or any Spouse of the Settlor in any circumstances whatsoever

11. THIS Settlement and the dispositions hereby made are intended to be and are irrevocable

IN WITNESS whereof the parties hereto have hereunto set their respective hands and seals the day and year first before written

THE FIRST SCHEDULE [32] hereinbefore referred to

The Specified Class [33] consists (subject to any exercise of the powers contained in Clause 5 of the foregoing Deed) of the following persons namely:

[(1) the children and remoter issue of the Settlor whether living at the date hereof or born hereafter;

(2) any person who shall (whether before or after the date hereof) have married any of such children or remoter issue of the Settlor as aforesaid (whether or not such marriage shall for the time being be subsisting);

(3) A.B. (the brother of the Settlor);

(4) the children and remoter issue of the said A.B. whether living at the date hereof or born hereafter;

(5) any person who shall (whether before or after the date hereof) have married any of such children or remoter issue of the said A.B. as aforesaid (whether or not such marriage shall for the time being be subsisting);

(6) any adopted child of the Settlor or of any of such children or remoter issue of the Settlor as aforesaid and the children and remoter issue of any such adopted child;

(7) any person who shall (whether before or after the date hereof) have married any such adopted child or any child or remoter issue of any such adopted child as aforesaid (whether or not such marriage shall for the time being be subsisting)

Provided that for the purposes of this present definition a person shall be deemed to be the adopted child of another person only if he or she shall be recognised as the adopted child of such other person by the Law of England for the time being in force.]

THE SECOND SCHEDULE [34] hereinbefore referred to

Fiscal Considerations

The emphasis placed in the above discretionary trust on excluding " the settlor and his spouse " straightaway reflects many important fiscal considerations. Indeed, without an understanding of the main fiscal considerations it is most difficult to understand why certain sorts of trusts are created and why certain clauses are inserted in trust instruments. Just as a swimmer's environment is water so a trust's environment is a fiscal system.

---

[32] This Schedule has been completed by way of example.

[33] If any member of the Specified Class is resident outside the Scheduled Territories Exchange Control consent will be required for the making of the settlement.

[34] This Second Schedule will contain details of the assets to be settled: as the assets are set out in this last schedule the assets to be settled need not be finalised till the last minute when they may be added to the earlier engrossment of the settlement. If any of the assets are foreign currency securities Exchange Control consent will be required for the making of the settlement. Consent might be given only if clause 8 (b) were replaced by a prohibition on non-resident trustees.

Except for very simple fixed trusts, no one should take on the office of trustee without a fair knowledge of the fiscal laws.

Clearly, a proper understanding of the fiscal laws would require the writing of a whole book on the subject.[35] Necessarily, space allows of only a superficial treatment here. It is hoped that this will not do more harm than good as some prognosticate.[36] Readers should first be warned that the following account concerns the 1974–75 tax year when a capital transfer tax payable by donors is proposed to be introduced in the Autumn Budget of 1974 and of which few details are public at the time of writing, and that with annual Finance Acts any detailed account of the law soon becomes out of date, though the basic structure can remain unchanged for long periods. A wealth tax is also proposed to be introduced in 1976 by the 1974 Labour Government though few details are known at the time of writing.

Capital gains tax

If a gain is made on disposal of some piece of property the gain will be treated as a capital gain subject to capital gains tax unless the gain is an income gain subject to income tax,[37] *e.g.* a profit made on the sale of trading stock. A disposal occurs where the property is actually sold or disposed of by way of gift or settlement, when disposal will be for the notional market value in the absence of any actual sale at market value. Thus the settlor on settling his property will have to pay capital gains tax on the notional gain then arising.[38] Capital gains tax is levied at a flat rate of 30 per cent. on the chargeable gains of the year of assessment less allowable losses. Individuals (but *not* trustees) may take advantage of the " half income rule ": where the gain does not exceed £5,000 half the gain may be added to the taxpayer's income and charged to income tax as the top slice thereof.[39] The fact that the half income rule is not available to trustees means that on disposals by the trustees in the course of managing the trust property the flat rate will have to be paid: this is no real deterrent to creating settlements as settlors usually have sufficient income to make the half income rule unavailable if they retained the property themselves instead of vesting it in trustees. The trustees will also be liable to capital gains tax where a beneficiary becomes absolutely entitled (*e.g.* by satisfying a 25 years of age contingency) as against the trustees to any trust property [40] (otherwise than on the death of a beneficiary with a life interest). Thereafter, since the trustees will have become bare trustees, the trustees' acts are treated as acts of the beneficiary so that on any subsequent disposal only the beneficiary will be chargeable.[41] Of course, once the trustees have become bare trustees the actual transfer to the beneficiary of what is his absolutely is not a chargeable disposal.

---

[35] For introductory works see Hepker's *Modern Approach to Tax Law,* Pinson's *Revenue Law,* Beattie's *Elements of Estate Duty,* Lawton & Sumption's *Tax Planning.* For detailed reference see Simon's *Taxes, British Tax Encyclopaedia,* Potter & Monroe's *Tax Planning,* Harris & Hewson's *Life Assurance and Tax Planning,* Dymond's *Death Duties.*

[36] Snell's Preface, p. vi.

[37] ss. 20, 21 and para. 2 of Sched. 6 to the Finance Act 1965.

[38] ss. 22, 25 of the F.A. 1965.

[39] s. 21 of the F.A. 1965. The other half is ignored.

[40] s. 25 of the F.A. 1965.

[41] s. 22 (5) of the F.A. 1965.

On a death no charge to capital gains tax arises since estate duty is payable on the value of the property at the deceased's death. However, that value is treated as the new base value of the property for purposes of calculating the gain made on any subsequent chargeable disposal [42]: there is thus a " free uplift " of the original base value of the property to take into account the fact that estate duty has been paid on the difference between the original base value and the value at the date of death.

Finally, the well-known exemption from capital gains tax of an individual's only or main residence need not be lost on settling a house. The exemption extends to gains made on a disposal by trustees if the house were used as the only or main residence of a person entitled to occupy it under the terms of the settlement or entitled to the whole income from it or its proceeds of sale [43]: Settled Land Act settlements and trusts for sale are both covered.

Estate duty

When a person dies estate duty is payable on the aggregate value of all property (exceeding £15,000) passing on his death.[44] Property " passing on his death " [45] includes *inter alia* (a) property of which the deceased was at the time of his death competent to dispose (known as his " free estate," *i.e.* his absolutely owned property including his interests in co-owned property), (b) settled property in which the deceased had an interest (*e.g.* a life interest) or where the deceased was the object of a discretionary trust or where the deceased was the settlor and a trust or power to accumulate the trust income terminated on his death, (c) property given away by the deceased more than seven [46] years before his death so long as bona fida possession and enjoyment of the property had been assumed and retained by the donee to the entire exclusion of the deceased and of any benefit to him by contract or otherwise.

The extent of the charge to estate duty in case (b) above is the whole capital of the settled property if the deceased had a life interest. If the deceased had been one of the objects of a discretionary trust the charge extends to a proportion of the capital corresponding to the proportion of the income received by the deceased in the material period.[47] Thus if D in the seven years preceding his death had received a tenth of the total trust income in that period then one tenth of the capital would be deemed to have passed on his death. Of course, if the trustees had wisely thought that D was getting on in years and liable to die in just over seven years and so had refrained from paying D any income in the seven years before his death then no part of the trust capital would be deemed to pass on D's death.

It is vital to appreciate that all property passing on death has to be

---

[42] s. 25 of the F.A. 1965.
[43] s. 29 (9) of the F.A. 1965; extra-statutory concession D3 in Inland Revenue Booklet I.R.I.
[44] F.A. 1894, s. 1.
[45] F.A. 1894, s. 2.
[46] One year in the case of gifts to charities but such gifts may be exempt altogether under F.A. 1972, s. 121 if not exceeding £50,000.
[47] F.A. 1969, s. 37. Before 1969 no duty at all was payable upon the death of any member of the class of objects (other than the last surviving member) since under trust law no member (but the last member) had any entitlement to anything so that no dutiable " interest " existed until F.A. 1969, s. 36, substituted a new s. 2 (1) (*b*) of the F.A. 1894.

aggregated [48] and the greater the chargeable total the higher the estate rate becomes.[49] Thus, if D had a free estate of £30,000 and a life interest in a trust fund of £480,000 the estate rate would be based on a dutiable estate of £510,000. His executors would pay the x per cent. rate on the £30,000 and the trustees of the settlement would pay the x per cent. rate on the £480,000. If D's widow were the next life tenant then the " surviving spouse " exemption [50] would apply so that the settlement would be ignored in the estate duty computation arising on *her* death: settled property (including property settled by D in his will) on which duty has been paid [51] since the date of the settlement on the death of one spouse is not liable to duty again on the death of the survivor so long as the survivor was not competent to dispose of the capital in his or her own favour. If D's free estate had not exceeded £15,000 then it could have been treated as a non-aggregable estate by itself [52] and not subject to duty as below the £15,000 floor at which duty becomes payable: the £480,000 settled fund would then have borne duty at the rate applicable to a £480,000 estate.

Gifts, whether direct or by way of settlement, are a useful vehicle for saving estate duty. If the donor survives for the seven year period there is total exemption and graduated relief is available to reduce the dutiable value of the property by 15, 30 and 60 per cent. in the fifth, sixth and seventh years respectively.[53] Irrespective of the seven year period gifts made in consideration of marriage are to some extent exempt.[54] The exemption applies to the first £5,000 only of a gift by a parent or remoter ancestor of one of the parties and the first £1,000 only of a gift by other donors. A marriage might thus attract a total exemption of £22,000 if two fathers, one mother, one grandfather, and two uncles all gave the maximum amounts.

Exemption from estate duty also applies to property given *inter vivos* or by will to charity up to a limit of £50,000 and property given *inter vivos* or by will to or devolving upon the deceased's surviving spouse up to a limit of £15,000.[55] This last exemption is very useful so that if D leaves the whole of his £30,000 estate to his widow, £15,000 of that falls within the exemption and the remaining £15,000 is below the floor at which estate duty becomes payable so that no estate duty at all is paid. There is a further exemption for gifts made out of D's income as part of his normal expenditure so long as they leave D with sufficient income after tax to maintain his usual standard of living.[56]

This last exemption is particularly useful in enabling premiums to be paid on gifted assurance policies on D's life when the proceeds of such policies will not be dutiable on D's death. Insurance policies as well as assurance policies are much used in connection with estate duty saving schemes. Thus, if trustees fear that their settlor may die within seven years of making the settlement they can insure against the estate duty risk but they must be careful to pay the premiums purely out of accumulated income [57]

---

[48] F.A. 1894, s. 4.
[49] F.A. 1969, s. 35 (2).
[50] F.A. 1894, s. 5 (2) as restricted by F. (1909–10) A. 1910, s. 55 and F.A. 1914, s. 14.
[51] Or would have been paid but for the smallness of the estate or F.A. 1972, s. 121.
[52] F.A. 1894, s. 16 (3), F.A. 1972, s. 120 (3)
[53] F.A. 1968, s. 35 (2).
[54] F.A. 1968, s. 36, F.A. 1963, s. 58.
[55] F.A. 1972, s. 121 and Sched. 26.
[56] F.A. 1968, s. 37.   [57] F.A. 1957, s. 38 (14).

of the settlement for otherwise the proceeds of the policy will rank as part of the dutiable settled property.

Of course, a sale is not a potentially dutiable gift for the seven year period but sales to relatives are treated as gifts unless it can be shown that full consideration in money or money's worth was given to the deceased for his own use or benefit.[58] If the full consideration provided by the relative was an annuity for the deceased's life (dutiable value nil on death) this does not count as consideration.[59] Annuities coupled with life assurance policies can be useful in estate duty saving schemes if bona fide. However, if millionaire, D, on his deathbed borrows £1 million on the security of his assets to spend it on an annuity on his life from the X Co., gives the annuity to his sole relative, R, who is forthwith paid the first £10,000 annual sum payable under the annuity and who then pays the £10,000 to the X Co. as the first premium on a policy on D's life for £960,000 (the X Co. not bothering with a medical examination) R cannot get away with an assertion that the gifted property was the annuity on D's life (value nil at D's death) so as to take the £960,000 duty free.

Capital Transfer Tax

In a White Paper Cmnd. 5705 (August 1974) there is a broad outline of this new tax which is to be set out in detail in the 1974 Autumn Finance Bill of the Labour Government. Capital transfer tax is to apply to gratuitous transfers of capital whether *inter vivos* or on death. It is to catch *inter vivos* transfers as from March 26, 1974, and it is to replace estate duty from a date to be fixed in the Autumn Bill not earlier than the date of publication of such Bill. Gifts taken into account in determining estate duty liability on a death in this interim period are to be exempt from the lifetime charge. Capital transfer tax is to be at progressive rates charged on the cumulative total of gifts made during a person's lifetime with the further final cumulation passing on death. Capital transfer tax is to be the primary liability of the donor or his personal representatives though there will be rights of recovery from donees. There is to be a charge on all capital taken out of a settlement and on the termination or transfer of the whole or part of an interest in possession under a trust. As from a date to be fixed in the Autumn Bill there is also to be a periodic charge on the capital of discretionary and accumulation trusts. Trustees will be liable for any tax chargeable but there will also be rights of recovery from beneficiaries and, if the trustees are resident outside the United Kingdom, from settlors. Spouses are to be chargeable as separate individuals but gifts between them while they are both alive and property left by one to the other on death will be exempt from capital transfer tax. Exemptions will also exist for small gifts, wedding gifts within limits, gifts made out of income as part of the donor's normal expenditure, and gifts to charities within limits. It seems that capital transfer tax and capital gains tax are to operate independently of each other. For further details please see Preface.

Income tax

(1) *The settlor's position.* For 1974–75 tax is charged at the " basic rate " of 33 per cent. and (a) in respect of total incomes exceeding £4,500 at pro-

---

[58] F.A. 1940, s. 44.   [59] F.A. 1940, s. 44 (1A).

gressively higher rates from 38 per cent. up to 83 per cent. and (b) in respect of investment income exceeding £1,000 at the additional rate of 15 per cent. Since the rate of tax paid on income progressively increases as the amount of income increases a substantial tax saving could be achieved by a wealthy man hiving off the top slice of his income (*e.g.* to an individual or charity not taxable at the higher rates of tax or at all) either by transferring the capital yielding that slice of income to trustees of a settlement (for individuals or charities) or by covenanting with trustees to pay them that slice of income for a period that can exceed six years. However, complex anti-avoidance provisions prevent such possibilities being abused, especially where the persons benefited are spouses and children to whom the settlor in any case has an obligation to support.

(a) Income settlements. " Seven-year covenants " should be a relatively familiar device: deeds of covenant are only effective to make the settlor's income that of the covenantees if the period can exceed six years and the deed is irrevocable in that no one has power to diminish the covenanted payment or do anything whereby part of the income may be applied to or for the benefit of the settlor or his spouse.[60] However, if the settlement is in favour of the settlor's unmarried infant child or children the covenanted income is deemed to be the settlor's whether the income is distributed to the children or accumulated.[61] If the settlor retains any interest [62] in the covenanted income then if any income is accumulated by the trustees in a year of assessment this undistributed income is treated as the settlor's income. Since 1965 seven-year covenants have only been effective to save basic rate liability to tax and not higher rate liability except that higher rate liability may also be saved in respect of (a) payments made for full consideration under a partnership agreement to a retired partner or his widow or dependants, (b) payments made for full consideration by the purchaser of a business to the vendor or his widow or dependants, and (c) payments made by one party to a marriage by way of provision for the other divorced or separated spouse.[63] Where trustees have power to accumulate covenanted income then if the income is held by the trustees on a discretionary trust or contingently for beneficiaries [64] no relief is given on account of tax paid by the trustees in respect of the undistributed income,[65] so that if the income is distributed to the beneficiaries in a later year they cannot obtain any repayment of tax to which they might otherwise be entitled by reason of their own low rate of tax liability: trustees will thus often wish to make as full a distribution as possible before April 5 in each year (the end of the year of assessment).

(b) Capital settlements. If a settlor wishes to transfer part of his income-

---

[60] Income & Corporation Taxes Act 1970, ss. 445, 446, 448.

[61] I.C.T.A. 1970, ss. 437, 438. In the Chancellor's Budget Speech, March 1974, it was made clear that for 1975–1976 the Labour Party intends to revive the provisions in s. 15 Finance Act 1968 and attack grandparents' and other relatives' settlements, by making all unearned income of unmarried infants not regularly working rank as the income of the infants' parents though the parents be not the settlors.

[62] I.C.T.A. 1970, s. 447 which also provides for certain limited policy exceptions where a retained interest is not deemed a retained interest.

[63] I.C.T.A. 1970, s. 457.

[64] If a beneficiary has a vested interest then the income belongs to him and he is assessable to tax whether or not he actually receives the income: *Hamilton-Russell's Executors* v. *I.R.C.* (1943) 25 T.C. 200.

[65] I.C.T.A. 1970, s. 450 (3).

yielding capital to trustees to save income tax then stringent conditions must be satisfied. The settlement must be irrevocable in that no one must have power to determine the settlement or diminish the settled property to the benefit of the settlor or the settlor's spouse.[66] If the settlement is in favour of the settlor's unmarried infant child or children then any income paid to or for the benefit of such a child is treated as the settlor's income,[67] *but* accumulated income is not so treated [68]: incidentally, any supposed capital advances made to a child out of accumulated income are treated as distributions of income (taxable as the settlor's) except to the extent that they exceed the aggregate available income [69] for distribution. If a settlor retains any interest in any income arising under the settlement or in any of the settled property then if any income is accumulated by the trustees it is treated as the settlor's [70]: the income cannot be allowed to accumulate and so pass as capital to the settlor at some later date.

Special draconic provisions tackle accumulation settlements where the trustees might lend money to the settlor so that the settlor obtained these non-taxable capital sums in place of the heavily taxable income he would have received from the settled property if he had not settled it. Capital sums paid by trustees or by any body corporate connected with the settlement to the settlor or his spouse are treated as income of the settlor for that year to the extent of the net income accumulated under the settlement in that year and previous years [71] (to the extent not already deemed the settlor's income under other statutory provisions). The capital sum has to be grossed up at the basic rate and the additional 15 per cent. rate and that amount is then liable as income of the settlor in the year of payment. If the capital sum is greater than the net accumulations of income to date the balance can be carried forward indefinitely so that any accumulations in future years are treated as the settlor's income of those years until the capital sum is wiped out. Unfortunately, the width of the provision is such as to be a terrifying trap for the unwary.[72]

(2) *The trustees' position.* They are liable to pay tax on trust income at the basic rate (33 per cent.) *plus* the additional rate (15 per cent.).[73] They cannot claim the personal reliefs available to individuals to reduce the total taxable income but they are not assessable to the higher rates of tax (applicable to total incomes exceeding £4,500).

(3) *The beneficiary's position.* If he has a vested right to the income (*e.g.* a life interest) [74] he is taxed whether or not he actually received the income.[75] If he has only a contingent or discretionary interest and the income is accumulated and not applied for his benefit then he cannot be assessed to tax thereon. If, however, income to which he is not entitled is

---

[66] I.C.T.A. 1970, ss. 446, 448.
[67] I.C.T.A. 1970, s. 437. See also note 61, *supra.*
[68] I.C.T.A. 1970, s. 438 (2).
[69] I.C.T.A. 1970, s. 438 (2) (*b*).
[70] I.C.T.A., s. 444.
[71] I.C.T.A., s. 451.
[72] J. Silberrad [1970] B.T.R. 380. On this and on retention of an interest by a settlor within I.C.T.A. 1970, s. 447 see *I.R.C.* v. *Wachtel* [1971] Ch. 573.
[73] F.A. 1973, ss. 16, 17; F.A. 1974, s. 5.
[74] Note also the vested right to income that arises on attaining majority under Trustee Act 1925, s. 31.
[75] *Hamilton-Russell's Executors* v. *I.R.C.* [1943] 1 All E.R. 474; (1943) 25 T.C. 200.

actually paid to him under an exercise of the trustees' discretions then of course he will be assessable. He will actually receive the income net of the basic and additional rate tax deducted by the trustees [76] : accordingly, he may be able to reclaim some of this tax if his personal financial resources are low enough to make him assessable only at some lower rate.

Capital sums paid to the beneficiary (*e.g.* pursuant to a power of advancement or of appointment) are of course not liable to income tax but the Revenue are astute to characterise regular payments out of capital as being in the nature of income payments to keep up the beneficiary's standard of living and so liable to income tax.[77] Genuine capital payments, however, may involve a charge to capital gains tax and may involve a liability to estate duty if an inconvenient death occurs. These potential liabilities are to be replaced by a liability to capital transfer tax in the Autumn Finance Bill 1974.

Practical conclusions

Ensure that the settlement is " irrevocable " [78] and that the settlor and his spouse are excluded from any benefit in any circumstances whatsoever [79] : the settlor's widow or widower may benefit.[80] Do not allow the settlor or his spouse to be a trustee or borrow money from the settlement. Ensure that the separateness of spouses for capital transfer tax is taken advantage of in conjunction with other exemptions and privileges.

Relevant Aspects of the Law Relating to Wills and Intestacy

In a study of trust law there are many occasions when points relating to wills or intestacies crop up. A general outline knowledge of the laws applicable thereto is thus useful before embarking on a detailed study of trust law.[81]

Basically, a will must be in writing signed at the end by the testator (or by some other person in his presence and by his direction).[82] The testator's signature has to be made or acknowledged by him in the presence of two witnesses both with the testator at the same time. The witnesses must then sign their names in the testator's presence. The document will be intended to take effect only on the testator's death.[83] Thus, if S by deed settles £50,000 upon trust for himself for life and then for R absolutely, the formalities for a will are not applicable since S's settlement takes effect immediately, giving R a present vested interest in remainder and entitling S only to the income from the £50,000 for the rest of his life. If S had made a will bequeathing £50,000 to R absolutely S could use in his lifetime not only the income from the £50,000 but also the whole £50,000: he could also revoke his will and bequeath the £50,000 to X instead. Incidentally, personal property is said to be bequeathed and real property to be devised by will.

Gifts by will may fail to take effect by reason *inter alia* of ademption, abatement, lapse, or the beneficiary being an attesting witness or the spouse

---

[76] F.A. 1973, s. 17.
[77] *Cunard's Trustees* v. *I.R.C.* [1946] 1 All E.R. 154.
[78] I.C.T.A. 1970, ss. 439, 445, 446.
[79] Though some " long-stop " circumstances may be permissible: I.C.T.A. 1970, ss. 447 (2), 457 (6).
[80] *Vestey's Executors* v. *I.R.C.* [1949] W.N. 233.
[81] For further reference the following books are useful: *Theobald on Wills*, S. J. Bailey's *Law of Wills*, A. R. Mellows' *Law of Succession*.
[82] Wills Act 1837, s. 9.   [83] *Att.-Gen.* v. *Jones and Bartlett* (1817) 3 Price 368.

thereof.[84] Ademption occurs if T specifically leaves some property such as "my Ming dynasty vase" or "my house Blackacre" but no longer has the property when he dies: the legacy or devise is adeemed and the legatee or devisee receives nothing. Abatement is a little less drastic: if T's debts are such that the Ming vase and Blackacre forming part of T's estate at T's death have to be sold but that a surplus remains after using the proceeds to pay off the debts then a rateable proportion will pass to the legatee and devisee. General legacies such as "I bequeath £5,000 to A, £3,000 to B and £1,000 to C" must first abate to their entire extent before resort can be had to specific gifts.[85]

Lapse occurs if a legatee or devisee predeceases the testator unless the legatee or devisee was a child (or other issue) of the testator and left issue alive at the testator's death [86]: in such an exceptional case the gift is effective in favour of the legatee/devisee's estate.[87] Where lapse occurs the gift fails and will fall into any residuary gift of the testator (*e.g.* "I leave all the residue of my property not otherwise hereinbefore disposed of to R"). Necessarily, if it is the residuary legatee, R, who has predeceased the testator and occasioned the lapse then the gifted property must be undisposed of and so pass to the next of kin under the intestacy rules applicable on the partial intestacy of the testator. Similarly, if a trust in a will fails, the property purportedly subject to the trust will pass under the residuary gift unless the trust was of the residuary property when the property will pass to the next of kin under the intestacy rules.

If it is uncertain whether or not a beneficiary predeceased the testator (*e.g.* where they are both killed by a bomb or in a car or plane crash) the younger is presumed to have survived the elder under the *commorientes* rule in section 184 of the Law of Property Act 1925. Exceptionally, where an intestate and his spouse die in circumstances which make it uncertain which survived the other section 184 does not apply: they are each presumed to have predeceased each other [88] for otherwise the elder intestate's property would pass to the younger's estate and thence to the younger's family, so leaving the intestate's family out in the cold.

This brings us to the intestacy rules but first it should be noted that, whilst a testator in his will can appoint "executors" to administer the testator's estate and who will obtain "probate" of the will, where a person dies intestate his closest relatives have to take out "letters of administration" and act as "administrators": the phrase "personal representatives" covers both executors and administrators. A testator's will, if professionally drafted, will usually begin by giving everything to the executors on a trust for sale, and on an intestacy statute [89] directs the administrators to hold the intestate's property on a trust for sale.

---

84 Wills Act 1837, s. 15 as restricted by Wills Act 1968 for which see Chap. 8, s. 5 (iv), *infra*, p. 413.

85 The order in which property has to be resorted to to pay debts etc. is laid down in Part II, 1st Sched. to the Administration of Estates Act 1925.

86 Wills Act 1837, s. 33. Illegitimate issue count: Family Law Reform Act 1969, s. 16.

87 It may well be that the living issue who save the gift obtain no benefit. The persons entitled to the estate are ascertained as at the date of the real death of the legatee/devisee: *Re Basioli* [1953] Ch. 367, *Re Hurd* [1941] Ch. 196.

88 Administration of Estates Act 1925, s. 46 (3).

89 Administration of Estates Act 1925, s. 33.

Where an intestate is survived by a spouse and issue [90] the spouse takes the intestate's personal chattels absolutely and the net sum of £15,000 free of death duties and costs [91]: the residue is held on " the statutory trusts " for the issue subject to the spouse having a life interest [92] in half the residue. If the intestate is survived by a spouse and one or more of the following, that is to say, a parent, a brother or sister of the whole blood, or issue of such a brother or sister, but leaves no issue, then, the spouse takes the personal chattels absolutely and the net sum of £40,000 free of death duties and costs: half any residue is held for the surviving spouse absolutely and the other half is held for the surviving parents or parent or, if there is no surviving parent, it is held on " the statutory trusts " for the brothers and sisters of the whole blood. If the intestate leaves a spouse and no issue and no parent or brother or sister of the whole blood and no issue of such brother or sister then the surviving spouse takes everything.

If the intestate leaves issue, but no surviving spouse, everything is held on " the statutory trusts " for the issue. If the intestate leaves no spouse and no issue any surviving parent or parents of the intestate take the assets absolutely. If, in such circumstances, there is no such surviving parent the intestate's relatives are entitled in the following order so that if any member of one class takes a vested interest he excludes all members of subsequent classes:

(i) the brothers and sisters of the whole blood on " the statutory trusts,"
(ii) brothers and sisters of the half blood on " the statutory trusts,"
(iii) grandparents,
(iv) uncles and aunts of the whole blood on " the statutory trusts,"
(v) uncles and aunts of the half blood on " the statutory trusts." In default the Crown (or the Duchy of Lancaster or of Cornwall) takes everything as *bona vacantia*.

If property is held on the statutory trusts, *e.g.* for issue, this means that the property is held upon trust equally for all the intestate's children living at his death who have attained or subsequently attain 18 years of age or who marry under that age: if a child predeceased the intestate, but left issue living or conceived at the death of the intestate, then such issue stand in the parent's shoes and take his share if they go on to attain 18 years of age or marry thereunder.[93] Thus, if an intestate widower dies leaving a 40-year old son (with two daughters of his own) and two grandchildren aged 20 and 15, being the children of a deceased son of the intestate, then the 40-year old son takes one half of the intestate's property, and the two grandchildren acquire interests in the other half. The elder grandchild takes one quarter of the property absolutely whilst the other quarter is held for the younger grandchild contingent upon his attaining 18 or marrying thereunder: if he should

---

[90] " Issue " includes illegitimate issue: Family Law Reform Act 1969, s. 14. Indeed, unless s. 15 of that Act is excluded any disposition (by will or deed) referring to various relatives (*e.g.* child, nephew) covers both legitimate and illegitimate relatives.

[91] The rules are in A.E.A. 1925, s. 46 and the current amount of the statutory legacies in 1972 S.I. No. 716.

[92] The surviving spouse has a right to have the personal representatives purchase or redeem the life interest by paying over its capital value: Administration of Estates Act 1925, s. 47A. She also has a right to compel the personal representatives to appropriate the matrimonial home at a proper valuation towards satisfaction of her interest under the intestacy: Intestates' Estates Act 1952, s. 5.

[93] Administration of Estates Act 1925, s. 47 (1).

die before then his elder brother would then obtain the whole half share that would have passed to his father had he not predeceased the intestate.

Finally, mention may be made of the fact that if a testator's will or the intestacy rules fail to make reasonable provision for the maintenance of the testator's or intestate's dependants then an application under the Inheritance (Family Provision) Act 1938 [94] can be made to the court for the court to order reasonable provision to be made out of the deceased's net estate. " Net estate " means all the property of which a deceased person had power to dispose by his Will (*otherwise than by virtue of a special power of appointment*) less the amount of his funeral testamentary and administration expenses, *debts* and *liabilities* and estate duty payable out of his estate on his death.[95] It follows that *inter vivos* settlements may be used to avoid the effect of the Act.[96]

---

[94] As amended by Family Provision Act 1966.
[95] Inheritance Family Provision Act, s. 5.
[96] E. G. Tyler's Family Provision (1st ed.), pp. 24 *et seq.* *Cf. Schaefer* v. *Schaefer* [1972] 1 All E.R. 621 (P.C.) and cases there cited.

CHAPTER 2

DISTINCTION BETWEEN TRUSTS AND OTHER RELATIONSHIPS

Introduction

IT will be hoped that Chapter 1 has given some positive indication of the nature of a trust. However, as Sir Francis Bacon stated in his Reading upon the Statute of Uses, " The nature of a use is best discerned by considering what it is not, and then what it is, for it is in the nature of all human science and knowledge to proceed most safely by negatives and exclusives to what is affirmative and inclusive." Historically, Sir Francis' " use " is the modern " trust." [1]

English law allows many ways of providing for someone to deal with property for the benefit of another e.g., agency, bailment, contract, trusts. Where an ambiguous benevolent intent is shown then it can be very difficult to determine which type of relationship was in the donor's mind. It is necessary to examine the donor's expressed wishes in the context of the surrounding circumstances for indications as to the consequences expected to flow from his actions and to see whether or not these indicia are more appropriate to a trust relationship rather than an agency, bailment, contract, etc. relationship.

Section 1. Trust and Bailment

Pettit: Equity and the Law of Trusts (2nd ed.), p. 17

" Blackstone [2] has caused some confusion by defining bailment as ' a delivery of goods in trust, upon a contract expressed or implied, that the trust shall be faithfully executed on the part of the bailee '. It may well be that the bailee is, in a popular sense, entrusted with the goods lent, hired out, deposited for safe custody, or whatever it may be; there is, however, no trust in the technical sense and the concepts are distinct. It is indeed better to define bailment as a delivery of personal chattels upon a condition, express or implied, that they shall be redelivered to the bailor, or according to his directions, when the purpose of the bailment has been carried out. Bailment was a recognised common law institution, while trusts, of course, were only recognised by courts of equity. Apart from historical and procedural differences, bailment only applies to personal property, while the trust concept applies to all kinds of property. The essential difference is, perhaps, that the bailee has, as it is said, only a special property in or special ownership of the goods bailed, the general property or general ownership remaining in the bailor, while the trustee is the full owner. Consequently the bailee cannot, as a rule,[3] pass a title to the goods which will be valid as against the

---

[1] See Snell, pp. 89–98, Hanbury, pp. 85–98, Pettitt, pp. 16–29.
[2] *Commentaries*, Book II, p. 451; Maitland's *Equity Lecture IV*.
[3] There are important exceptions e.g., under Factors Act 1889; sale in market overt; estoppel.

bailor, but a trustee can pass a good title to someone who acquires legal ownership *bona fide* for value without notice of the trust."

Section 2. Trust and Agency

Trustees and agents have certain fiduciary obligations in common. They are under a duty not to let their personal interests conflict with their duties under the terms of the agency or trust. They have a duty to act for the benefit of the beneficiaries or principal respectively and not to make any unauthorised profits. They are also under a duty not to delegate responsibilities and they have a duty to keep proper accounts.

There are many differences. A trustee (other than a Settled Land Act trustee) must have title to property vested in him. An agent need have no control over any property belonging to his principal. He may often have possession of such property but it is rare for him to have title to such property. Moreover, in all such cases the agent is subject to the control of his principal. A trustee is not subject to the control of the beneficiaries: his duty is to deal with property in accordance with the terms of the trust and the beneficiaries can only compel him to perform that duty.[4] If the settlor of a trust is compared with a principal the settlor cannot give the trustees directions nor can he terminate the trust unless there is an express power to such effect reserved in the trust instrument.[5] However, a principal can direct his agent all the time and can terminate the agency at will. An agent acting within the scope of his authority has power to subject his principal to liabilities in contract and tort: a trustee has no such power. A principal can bring an action against a third party for injury to his property whilst in the agent's hands: a beneficiary (or settlor) cannot sue a third party for injury to trust property. An agent contracting with a third party and disclosing his agency is not personally liable: a trustee disclosing his trusteeship is personally liable in such circumstances as he is treated as acting as a principal, though he has a right of indemnity against the trust property.[6]

Usually there is no contractual relationship between trustees and beneficiaries only a proprietary relationship, the trustees holding legal or equitable interests in property on trust for the beneficiaries equitably entitled under the trusts. Agency, on the other hand, normally arises by contract between principal and agent. As the beneficiaries are the equitable beneficial owners of the trust property they can trace the trust property into the hands of a bankrupt trustee so that such property is not available as part of the trustee's assets for the benefit of the trustee's creditors generally.[7] However, an ordinary agent is only liable to a personal claim to account to his principal for money obtained in the course of the agency so that the principal is not treated as the owner of such money and so cannot trace against the agent's assets so as to obtain priority over the agent's creditors upon bankruptcy of the agent. Exceptionally, the tracing remedy is available against an agent if he has entered into a special fiduciary relationship with his principal as where it has been agreed that he will keep separate his own money or property from that obtained on his principal's behalf.[8]

---

[4] *Re Brockbank* [1948] Ch. 206, *infra*, p. 451.   [5] *Mallott* v. *Wilson* [1903] 2 Ch. 494.
[6] Trustee Act 1925, s. 30 (2); *Hardoon* v. *Belilios* [1901] A.C. 118, *infra*, p. 609.
[7] See Chap. 8 *infra*.
[8] See Goff and Jones, p. 41 and cases there cited plus *Cohen* v. *Cohen* (1929) 42 C.L.R. 91.

Section 3. Trusts and Contracts [9]

The general rule is that only a party to a contract is entitled to sue upon it; but a beneficiary under a trust is entitled to compel its performance even though he was not a party to its creation. This rule was established in *Tweddle* v. *Atkinson* [10] and adopted by the House of Lords in *Dunlop* v. *Selfridge* [11] and affirmed by them in *Scruttons* v. *Midland Silicones* [12] and assumed to be good law by them in *Beswick* v. *Beswick* [13] and by the Privy Council in *New Zealand Shipping Co. Ltd.* v. *A. M. Satterthwaite & Co. Ltd.*[14] However, the operation of the doctrine of privity of contract [15] is qualified by rules of equity and statute.

The general position is that equity will allow C to obtain the benefit of a contract made between A and B if A contracted expressly or impliedly as trustee of the benefit of the contract for C.[16] It must be shown that A intended to create a trust which was to benefit C: this involves the construction of the contract and an examination of the special circumstances surrounding the contract. On the present state of the authorities it is difficult to forecast exactly what are the circumstances when a court will find a trust to be established but the courts have become increasingly reluctant [17] to find that persons like A intended to contract as trustees, if only because this renders the contract between A and B incapable of being varied without C's consent, a result not often contemplated by A. All too often the courts rightly adjudge the claim to a trust relationship to be a transparent device to evade the privity of contract doctrine. Of course, subsequent to his contract with B (or a covenant by B necessarily in a deed under seal) A may create a trust of the benefit of the contract or covenant for C either by declaring himself trustee of the chose in action or by assigning it to T as trustee for C. Indeed, if A wishes to settle a chose in action upon C he may covenant with T to pay £60,000 to T with intent that the benefit of such covenant shall be held by T upon trust for C: *Fletcher* v. *Fletcher*.[18]

Where a trust is held to exist then C can enforce it and obtain his due

---

[9] See Corbin (1930) 46 L.Q.R. 12; Glanville Williams (1944) 7 M.L.R. 123; Scamell, 8 *Current Legal Problems* 131; Dowrick (1956) 19 M.L.R. 374; Elliott (1956) 20 Conv.(N.S.) 43, 114; Andrews (1959) 23 Conv.(N.S.) 179; Elliott (1960) 76 L.Q.R. 100; Hornby (1962) 79 L.Q.R. 228; Jones [1965] C.L.J. 46; Matheson (1966) 29 M.L.R. 397; Treitel (1966) 29 M.L.R. 567; M. A. Millner (1967) 16 I.C.L.Q. 446–463; Treitel's *Law of Contract* (3rd ed.), pp. 557–572; Cheshire and Fifoot's *Law of Contract* (8th ed.), pp. 430–442.

[10] (1861) 1 B. & S. 393; 30 L.J.Q.B. 265.

[11] [1915] A.C. 847.

[12] [1962] A.C. 440.

[13] [1968] A.C. 58.   [14] [1974] 1 All E.R. 1015

[15] The attempts of Lord Denning M.R. in *Smith & Snipes Hall Farm Ltd.* v. *R. Douglas Catchment Board* [1949] 2 K.B. 500, *Drive Yourself Hire Co. Ltd.* v. *Strutt* [1954] 1 Q.B. 250 and *Beswick* v. *Beswick* [1966] Ch. 538 to treat the doctrine of privity of contract as a procedural rule or as ousted by section 56 of the Law of Property Act 1925 are audacious if not outrageous. The s. 56 argument was decisively rejected in the House of Lords and the other point was abandoned by counsel on appeal.

[16] *Lloyd's* v. *Harper* (1880) 16 Ch.D. 290; *Harmer* v. *Armstrong* [1934] Ch. 65; *Walford's Case* [1919] A.C. 801; *Gregory and Parker* v. *Williams* (1817) 3 Mer. 582; *Tomlinson* v. *Gill* (1756) Amb. 330; *Re Gordon* [1940] Ch. 851; *Royal Exchange Assurance* v. *Hope* [1928] Ch. 179; *Re Webb* [1941] Ch. 225.

[17] *Re Engelbach's Estate* [1924] 2 Ch. 348; *Vandepitte* v. *Preferred Accident Insurance Co. of New York* [1933] A.C. 70; *Re Sinclair's Life Policy* [1938] Ch. 799; *Re Schebsman* [1944] Ch. 83; *Green* v. *Russell* [1959] 2 Q.B. 226; *Beswick* v. *Beswick* [1966] Ch. 538.

[18] (1844) 4 Hare 67; 14 L.J.Ch. 66; 8 Jur.(O.S.) 1040.

benefit from the contract or covenant. It matters not that C is a volunteer
not having provided any consideration. The creation of trusts is dealt with
fully in Chapter 4 *infra*.

Statutes also create exceptions to the rule that only a party to a contract
can sue upon it. The most important examples are:

Section 56 of the Law of Property Act 1925

This provides that " A person may take an immediate or other interest
in land or other property, or the benefit of any condition, right of entry,
covenant or agreement over or respecting land or other property, although
he may not be named as a party to the conveyance or other instrument."

This section replaced section 5 of the Real Property Act 1845. Its
object was to abolish a technical rule which distinguished between a covenant in a deed poll and one in a deed *inter partes*.[19] Covenants in a deed
poll could be enforced by non-parties (in fact, a deed poll has only
one party, *i.e.,* the person executing the deed); but not so [20] covenants in
deeds *inter partes*. The effect of section 56 is to allow a non-executing party
to enforce the agreement. The section does not create third party rights: it
merely enables rights created independently of it to be enforced.[21] Before
the section can come to his aid the third party must show that the
agreement was made with him and did not merely confer a benefit on him.[22]
In *Beswick* v. *Beswick* [23] three members of the House of Lords considered
that the history of the section meant that the words " land or other property " had to be construed as " land or other real property " whilst the
other two members considered that the section was limited to deeds *inter
partes*.

Section 11 of the Married Women's Property Act 1882

" . . . A policy of assurance effected by any man on his own life, and
expressed to be for the benefit of his wife, or of his children, or of his wife
and children, or any of them, or by any woman on her own life, and
expressed to be for the benefit of her husband, or of her children, or of
her husband and children, or any of them, shall create a trust in favour of
the objects therein named, and the moneys payable under any such policy
shall not, so long as any object of the trust remains unperformed, form part
of the estate of the insured, or be subject to his or her debts [except where
the policy was effected and premiums were paid with intent to defeat
creditors]."

The section applies to endowment policies [24] and accident insurance
policies.[25] Where the wife is unnamed the policy enures for the benefit of a

---

19 See *Chelsea & Walham Green Building Society* v. *Armstrong* [1957] Ch. 853,
Beswick v. *Beswick* [1968] A.C. 58.
20 If a deed were made between A of the first part, B of the second part, C of the
third part and D of the fourth part and A covenanted with B, C, D and the other
owners of part of the estate formerly known as the Fitzalan Estate then if X were
one of such other owners he could not enforce the covenant as he was not a party
to the deed. After the 1845 Act (replaced by s. 56) X could enforce the covenant.
21 *Beswick* v. *Beswick* [1968] A.C. 58.
22 See *White* v. *Bijou Mansions Ltd.* [1937] Ch. 610, 624, 625; [1938] Ch. 351, 365;
Re Sinclair's Life Policy [1938] Ch. 799; *Re Foster* [1938] 3 All E.R. 357; *Strom-
dale & Ball Ltd.* v. *Burden* [1952] Ch. 233; *Re Miller's Agreement* [1947] Ch. 615;
Beswick v. *Beswick* [1968] A.C. 58.
23 [1968] A.C. 58.
24 *Re Ioakimidis' Policy Trusts* [1925] Ch. 403.   25 *Re Gladitz* [1937] Ch. 588.

second wife and her children,[26] but where the wife is named she has an absolute vested interest in the policy, and if she predeceases her husband the policy moneys are payable on her husband's death to her personal representatives.[27] Unless the policy provides otherwise the beneficiaries will take jointly.[28]

Section 148 (4) of the Road Traffic Act 1972 [29]

" Notwithstanding anything in any enactment, a person issuing a policy of insurance under section 145 of this Act shall be liable to indemnify the persons or classes of persons specified in the policy in respect of any liability which the policy purports to cover in the case of those persons or classes of persons."

Fundamental differences

The many attempts to persuade courts that a trust relationship existed in order to evade the privity of contract doctrine must not be allowed to obscure the really fundamental differences between the concepts of contract and trust. A contract is a creature of the common law and creates a personal right against the other party. It requires consideration (or a deed) and is based upon agreement. A trust is equitable and creates a proprietary interest in the beneficiaries. It is based upon the intention of the settlor. Consideration is not required and is not usual except in marriage settlements. A deed is often required not to provide for the absence of consideration but to ensure that the trust property is effectively vested in the trustees. Different limitation periods apply to actions for breach of contract and breach of trust.

It is possible for a person to contract or covenant to create a trust when the rights of the " beneficiaries " will depend upon whether or not they can compel the " settlor " to constitute the trust: unless they have given consideration or are parties to the covenant they will not be able to do so, for " equity will not assist volunteers." This matter is discussed fully in Chapter 4 *infra*.

Finally, in special circumstances it is possible for the concepts of trust and contract to overlap where a trust arises as the result of an agreement for valuable consideration with the trustee: *Barclays Bank Ltd.* v. *Quistclose Investments Ltd., infra*.

BARCLAYS BANK LTD. v. QUISTCLOSE INVESTMENTS LTD.
House of Lords [1970] A.C. 567; [1968] 3 W.L.R. 1097; [1968] 3 All E.R. 651.

Although Rolls Razor Ltd. had declared a dividend on its shares it could not pay the dividend without a loan of £209,719 8s. 6d. which Quistclose agreed to make " for the purpose of paying the final dividend on July 24 next." A cheque for this sum was paid into a separate account at the Bank, with whom it was agreed by confirming letter of

---

[26] *Re Browne's Policy* [1903] 1 Ch. 188.
[27] *Cousins* v. *Mutual Reserve Fund Life Association* [1892] 1 Q.B. 147.
[28] *Re Davies' Policy* [1892] 1 Ch. 90.
[29] Re-enacting s. 206 (3) of the Road Traffic Act 1960 itself re-enacting s. 36 (4) of the Road Traffic Act 1930.

July 15 that the account would "only be used to meet the dividend due on July 24."

Before the dividend was paid Rolls Razor went into liquidation. The Bank wished to set the £209,719 8s. 6d. against Rolls Razor's overdraft whilst Quistclose claimed that the sum was held on trust for Quistclose. Quistclose succeeded.

LORD WILBERFORCE: "Two questions arise, both of which must be answered favourably to the respondents if they are to recover the money from the appellants. The first is whether, as between the respondents and Rolls Razor, Ltd., the terms on which the loan was made were such as to impress on the sum of £209,719 8s. 6d. a trust in their favour in the event of the dividend not being paid. The second is whether, in that event, the appellants had such notice of the trust or of the circumstances giving rise to it as to make the trust binding on them.

"It is not difficult to establish precisely on what terms the money was advanced by the respondents to Rolls Razor, Ltd. There is no doubt that the loan was made specifically in order to enable Rolls Razor, Ltd., to pay the dividend. There is equally, in my opinion, no doubt that the loan was made only so as to enable Rolls Razor, Ltd., to pay the dividend and for no other purpose. This follows quite clearly from the terms of the letter of Rolls Razor, Ltd., to the appellants of July 15, 1964, which letter, before transmission to the appellants, was sent to the respondents under open cover in order that the cheque might be (as it was) enclosed in it. The mutual intention of the respondents and of Rolls Razor, Ltd., and the essence of the bargain, was that the sum advanced should not become part of the assets of Rolls Razor, Ltd., but should be used exclusively for payment of a particular class of its creditors, namely, those entitled to the dividend. A necessary consequence from this, by process simply of interpretation, must be that if, for any reason, the dividend could not be paid, the money was to be returned to the respondents: the word 'only' or 'exclusively' can have no other meaning or effect.

"That arrangements of this character for the payment of a person's creditors by a third person, give rise to a relationship of a fiduciary character or trust, in favour, as a primary trust, of the creditors, and secondarily, if the primary trust fails, of the third person, has been recognised in a series of cases over some 150 years.

"In *Toovey* v. *Milne* [30] part of the money advanced was, on the failure of the purpose for which it was lent (viz., to pay certain debts) repaid by the bankrupt to the person who had advanced it. On action being brought by the assignee of the bankrupt to recover it, the plaintiff was nonsuited and the nonsuit was upheld on a motion for a retrial. In his judgment ABBOTT C.J., said [31]:

---

[30] (1819) 2 B. & Ald. 683.   [31] (1819) 2 B. & Ald. at p. 684.

' I thought at the trial, and still think, that the fair inference from the facts proved was that this money was advanced for a special purpose, and that, being so clothed with a specific trust, no property in it passed to the assignee of the bankrupt. Then the purpose having failed, there is an implied stipulation, that the money shall be repaid. That has been done in the present case; and I am of opinion that that repayment was lawful, and that the nonsuit was right.'

The basis for the decision was thus clearly stated, viz., that the money advanced for the specific purpose did not become part of the bankrupt's estate. This case has been repeatedly followed and applied (see *Edwards* v. *Glynn*[32]; *Re Rogers, Ex p. Holland and Hannen*[33]; *Re Drucker (No. 1), Ex p. Basden*[34]; and *Re Hooley, Ex p. Trustees*[35]). *Re Rogers* was a decision of a strong Court of Appeal. In that case, the money provided by the third party had been paid to the creditors before the bankruptcy. Afterwards the trustee in bankruptcy sought to recover it. It was held that the money was advanced to the bankrupt for the special purpose of enabling his creditors to be paid, was impressed with a trust for the purpose and never became the property of the bankrupt. LINDLEY L.J., decided the case on principle but said that if authority was needed it would be found in *Toovey* v. *Milne*[36] and other cases. BOWEN L.J., said that the money came to the bankrupt's hands impressed with a trust and did not become the property of the bankrupt divisible amongst his creditors, and the judgment of KAY L.J., was to a similar effect.

" These cases have the support of longevity, authority, consistency and, I would add, good sense. But they are not binding on your lordships and it is necessary to consider such arguments as have been put why they should be departed from or distinguished.

" It is said, first, that the line of authorities mentioned above stands on its own and is inconsistent with other, more modern, decisions. Those are cases in which money has been paid to a company for the purpose of obtaining an allotment of shares (see *Moseley* v. *Cressey's Co.*[37]; *Stewart* v. *Austin*[38]; and *Re Nanwa Gold Mines, Ltd., Ballantyne* v. *Nanwa Gold Mines, Ltd.*[39]). I do not think it necessary to examine these cases in detail, nor to comment on them, for I am satisfied that they do not affect the principle on which this appeal should be decided. They are merely examples which show that, in the absence of some special arrangement creating a trust (as was shown to

[32] (1859) 2 E. & E. 29.
[33] (1891) 8 Morr. 243.
[34] [1902] 2 K.B. 237.
[35] (1915) 84 L.J.K.B. 181. See also *Re Kayford Ltd. (In Liquidation), The Times*, October 9, 1974.
[36] (1819) 2 B. & Ald. 683.
[37] (1865) L.R. 1 Eq. 405.
[38] (1866) L.R. 3 Eq. 299.
[39] [1955] 3 All E.R. 219.

exist in *Re Nanwa Gold Mines, Ltd.*), payments of this kind are made on the basis that they are to be included in the company's assets. They do not negative the proposition that a trust may exist where the mutual intention is that they should not be included.

" The second, and main, argument for the appellants was of a more sophisticated character. The transaction, it was said, between the respondents and Rolls Razor, Ltd., was one of loan, giving rise to a legal action of debt. This necessarily excluded the implication of any trust, enforceable in equity, in the respondents' favour: a transaction may attract one action or the other, it could not admit of both.

" My lords, I must say that I find this argument unattractive. Let us see what it involves. It means that the law does not permit an arrangement to be made by which one person agrees to advance money to another, on terms that the money is to be used exclusively to pay debts of the latter, and if, and so far as not so used, rather than becoming a general asset of the latter available to his creditors at large, is to be returned to the lender. The lender is obliged, in such a case, because he is a lender, to accept, whatever the mutual wishes of lender and borrower may be, that the money he was willing to make available for one purpose only shall be freely available for others of the borrower's creditors for whom he has not the slightest desire to provide.

" I should be surprised if an argument of this kind—so conceptualist in character—had ever been accepted. In truth it has plainly been rejected by the eminent judges who from 1819 onwards have permitted arrangements of this type to be enforced, and have approved them as being for the benefit of creditors and all concerned. There is surely no difficulty in recognising the co-existence in one transaction of legal and equitable rights and remedies: when the money is advanced, the lender acquires an equitable right to see that it is applied for the primary designated purpose (see *Re Rogers* [40] where both LINDLEY and KAY L.JJ., explicitly recognised this): when the purpose has been carried out (i.e., the debt paid) the lender has his remedy against the borrower in debt: if the primary purpose cannot be carried out, the question arises if a secondary purpose (i.e., repayment to the lender) has been agreed, expressly or by implication: if it has, the remedies of equity may be invoked to give effect to it, if it has not (and the money is intended to fall within the general fund of the debtor's assets) then there is the appropriate remedy for recovery of a loan. I can appreciate no reason why the flexible interplay of law and equity cannot let in these practical arrangements, and other variations if desired: it would be to the discredit of both systems if they could not. In the present case the intention to create a secondary trust for the benefit of the lenders, to arise if the primary trust, to pay the dividend,

---

[40] (1891) 8 Morr. 243

could not be carried out, is clear and I can find no reason why the law should not give effect to it.

" I pass to the second question, that of notice. I can deal with this briefly because I am in agreement with the manner in which it has been disposed of by all three members of the Court of Appeal.[41] I am prepared, for this purpose, to accept, by way of assumption, the position most favourable to the appellants, i.e., that it is necessary to show that the appellants had notice of the trust, or of the circumstances giving rise to the trust, at the time when they received the money, viz., on July 15, 1964, and that notice on a later date, even though they had not in any real sense given value when they received the money or thereafter changed their position, will not do. It is common ground, and I think right, that a mere request to put the money into a separate account is not sufficient to constitute notice. But on July 15, 1964, the appellants, when they received the cheque, also received the covering letter of that date which I have set out above; previously there had been the telephone conversation between Mr. Goldbart and Mr. Parker, to which I have also referred. From these there is no doubt that the appellants were told that the money had been provided on loan by a third person and was to be used only for the purpose of paying the dividend. This was sufficient to give them notice that it was trust money and not assets of Rolls Razor, Ltd.: the fact, if it be so, that they were unaware of the lenders' identity (though the respondents' name as drawers was on the cheque) is of no significance. I may add to this, as having some bearing on the merits of the case, that it is quite apparent from earlier documents that the appellants were aware that Rolls Razor, Ltd., could not provide the money for the dividend and that this would have to come from an outside source and that they never contemplated that the money so provided could be used to reduce the existing overdraft. They were in fact insisting that other or additional arrangements should be made for that purpose. As was appropriately said by RUSSELL L.J.,[42] it would be giving a complete windfall to the appellants if they had established a right to retain the money.

" In my opinion, the decision of the Court of Appeal was correct on all points and the appeal should be dismissed." *Appeal dismissed.*

Section 4. Trusts and the Office of Personal Representative [43]

The authority of personal representatives to deal with pure personalty is joint and several; in respect of freehold and leasehold land it seems that one of two or more personal representatives can enter into a valid contract of sale (so long as he does not purport to act for the other representatives without their knowledge) but that the land cannot be conveyed without the

---

[41] [1968] 1 All E.R. 613.
[42] [1968] 1 All E.R. at p. 626C.
[43] See B. S. Ker, " Personal Representative or Trustee " (1955) 19 Conv.(N.S.) 199.

concurrence of the other representatives or an order of the court.[44] The authority of trustees to deal with all types of property is, and always has been, joint.[45] In the Trustee Act 1925, by virtue of section 68 (17) " trustee," where the context admits, includes a personal representative.

A personal representative who has completed administration of a deceased's estate becomes a trustee thereof and in that capacity can appoint new or additional trustees: *Re Cockburn's Will Trusts, infra*. Such an appointment makes the new or additional trustee a trustee of the trusts of the estate; but if the trust property consists of land, the legal estate therein remains outstanding in the personal representative until he executes a written assent in favour of the trustees: *Re King's Will Trust, infra*. The significance of this last decision may be seen in the following example. E and F complete the administration of T's estate and under T's will they are to hold the residuary estate (which includes Blackacre) on trust for sale for A for life, remainder for B absolutely. Five years later E dies. F then purports as surviving trustee to appoint T and U additional trustees with himself. Four years later F dies. T and U as trustees then sell Blackacre to P. Later P contracts to sell to Q, who objects to P's title. The objection is valid. The legal estate is in F's personal representatives and not P since E and F never executed a written assent of Blackacre in favour of themselves in their new capacity as trustees. They could thus not take advantage of sections 36 and 40 of the Trustee Act 1925.

Re COCKBURN'S WILL TRUSTS

Chancery Division [1957] Ch. 438; [1957] 3 W.L.R. 212; 101 S.J. 534

By his will dated November 28, 1928, the testator, Sir James Stanhope Cockburn, appointed three persons to be the executors and trustees thereof, and declared that references to his trustees should include them and the survivors or survivor of them or other the trustees or trustee for the time being of his will except where such construction was precluded by the context. The will contained a wide discretionary power of appropriation exercisable by the trustees. No person was nominated by the will for the purpose of appointing new trustees.

The testator died on April 1, 1947. Two of the persons named in

---

[44] Administration of Estates Act 1925, ss. 2 (2), 3 (1), 54; *Fountain Forestry Ltd.* v. *Edwards* [1974] 2 All E.R. 280, where since the one personal representative had purported to contract for himself and the other personal representative (when the other had no knowledge of this and had refused to ratify the contract) there was no contract to be enforced, the first personal representative being open to an action for breach of warranty of authority only.

[45] It can be crucial whether a person disposing of property is a personal representative or a trustee. In *Attenborough* v. *Solomon* [1913] A.C. 76, T died in 1878 leaving his property to A. A. S. and J. D. S. to be his executors and trustees to hold the property after payment of debts and expenses upon certain trusts. The estate accounts were settled in 1879. In 1892 A. A. S. pledged some of the estate silver to secure a personal loan of £65. This was not discovered till 1908, after the death of A. A. S. The pledgee threatened to sell the silver unless it was immediately redeemed. T's representatives claimed that the pledgee had no right to retain the silver as A. A. S. at the date of the pledge had ceased to hold the silver as executor and instead held it as trustee with J. D. S. The pledge was thus invalid as the authority of trustees is joint only. The House of Lords upheld this claim.

the will as executors and trustees died during the lifetime of the testator and the third renounced probate.

On July 24, 1947, letters of administration with the will annexed were granted to James Francis Cockburn and Claude John Ledstone Lewis. The testator's widow, who had certain interests during her life under the will, died on May 20, 1953.

It being desirable that the residuary estate should be divided by a proper scheme of appropriation, the administrators were advised that they were probably not entitled, in their capacity as such, to exercise the discretionary power conferred by the testator on the trustees for the time being of the will, and that it was impracticable, in the events which had happened, to appoint new trustees without the assistance of the court.

A summons was, therefore, taken out by one of the administrators to determine (*inter alia*) whether the administrators were trustees for the purposes of the will and at liberty to exercise the powers and discretion thereby conferred on the trustees for the time being of the will.

DANCKWERTS J.: " The question which I am asked to decide is whether the administrators of the estate, having cleared the estate and completed the administration in the ordinary way (the testator having been dead for about ten years) are in a position to appoint new trustees of the will, and whether those new trustees, when so appointed by them, will continue to exercise the powers which are conferred by the will upon the trustees for the time being of the will. I feel no doubt about the matter at all. Whether persons are executors or administrators, once they have completed the administration in due course, they become trustees holding for the beneficiaries either on an intestacy or under the terms of the will, and are bound to carry out the duties of trustees, though in the case of personal representatives they cannot be compelled to go on indefinitely acting as trustees, and are entitled to appoint new trustees in their place and thus clear themselves from those duties which were not expressly conferred on them under the terms of the testator's will and which, for that purpose, they are not bound to accept.

" It seems to me that, if they do not appoint new trustees to proceed to execute the trusts of the will, they will become trustees in the full sense. Further, it seems to me that they have the power, under the trusts conferred by section 36 of the Trustee Act 1925, to appoint new trustees of the will to act in their place. That seems to me to have been clearly established by the decision of Sargant J. in *Re Ponder*.[46]

" My attention has been called to the observations made in *Harvell* v. *Foster*[47] which are obiter so far as they cast any doubt on the decision of Sargant J., and which, with all respect, I should have thought

---

[46] [1921] 2 Ch. 59.
[47] [1954] 2 Q.B. 367. There a testator had died leaving his estate to his 18-year-old

were not justified. The point in *Harvell* v. *Foster* [47] was a very different
one. It was whether a personal representative, who had not duly completed his duties as personal representative, was under any liability to
the persons who were interested in the estate in his capacity of
administrator. I should have thought that there was no doubt that the
answer was that, if he did not duly perform his duties, he was under
such a liability. But that does not seem to me to have anything to do
with the question whether a personal representative, who has completed
his duties in a proper way, is or is not in a position to appoint new
trustees. I feel no doubt whatever—and it has been recognised for a
great number of years—that a personal representative in that position
can appoint new trustees, and I so propose to declare. I therefore declare
in the present case that the plaintiff and the first defendant are in a
position to appoint trustees of the testator's will, who will be in a
position to exercise the powers and discretions conferred upon the
trustees of the will by the terms of the will and codicil." [48]

Re KING'S WILL TRUSTS

Chancery Division [1964] Ch. 542; [1964] 2 W.L.R. 913; 108 S.J. 335;
    [1964] 1 All E.R. 833

The testatrix by her will appointed H. B. Curwen, C. T. Highett and
B. L. Johnston to be executors and the two first-mentioned of them to
be trustees. The testatrix died on November 21, 1939, and H. B.
Curwen and C. T. Highett proved her will on March 4, 1940. On
February 12, 1951, C. T. Highett died, leaving H. B. Curwen as sole
surviving executor and trustee. In 1952 the executors' administration
account was brought in, and on June 20, 1953, H. B. Curwen appointed
B. L. Johnston to be a trustee of the will jointly with himself in respect
of the freehold land and other property described in the deed of appointment as being subject to the trusts of the will. H. B. Curwen died on
May 2, 1958, and his will was proved by his executors, G. E. Curwen
and H. D. Carter. On March 13, 1959, B. L. Johnston appointed R. H.
Asshiton to be a trustee of the will of the testatrix jointly with himself.
G. E. Curwen died on November 13, 1959, and B. L. Johnston died on
November 23, 1962. In these circumstances H. D. Carter became
under section 7 of the Administration of Estates Act 1925 the sole
surviving personal representative of the testatrix by representation and
R. H. Asshiton became the sole surviving trustee of the trusts of her

---

daughter whom he had appointed his sole executrix. As she was an infant her husband took out letters of administration. He entered into the then usual administration bond (now replaced by a requirement for sureties only by s. 8 of the
Administration of Estates Act 1971 substituting a new s. 167 of the Supreme
Court of Judicature Act 1925) with the daughter's solicitors joining as sureties.
After the solicitors had cleared the estate they transferred the residue to the hus-
band-administrator to hold for his wife when she became 21. The husband absconded with most of the money so on attaining 21 the wife claimed the deficiency
from the solicitor-sureties. They were held liable on the footing that the husband's
breaches of duty were *qua* administrator and not *qua* trustee.

[48] See (1957) 73 L.Q.R. 450 (R. E. M.). See also *Re Aldhous* [1955] 1 W.L.R. 459.

will. There had, however, never been any assent to the vesting of the above-mentioned freehold land unless the deed of appointment dated June 20, 1953, operated as such an assent. The question therefore arose as to the persons in whom the legal estate in the said land was vested.

PENNYCUICK J.: "... An assent is the instrument or act whereby a personal representative effectuates a testamentary disposition by transferring the subject-matter of the disposition to the person entitled to it. An assent in relation to land is governed by section 36 of the Administration of Estates Act 1925, which, so far as now material, is in the following terms: '... (4) An assent to the vesting of a legal estate shall be in writing, signed by the personal representative, and shall name the person in whose favour it is given and shall operate to vest in that person the legal estate to which it relates; and an assent not in writing or not in favour of a named person shall not be effectual to pass a legal estate. ...'

" Subsection (4) presents no difficulty where the person entitled to the estate or interest is someone other than the personal representative himself. It has been suggested that where the personal representative is also entitled in some other capacity, for example, as trustee of the will, as beneficiary or otherwise, to the estate or interest he may come to hold the estate or interest in that other capacity without any written assent.

" ... in my judgment, the contention is not well founded. ... The first sentence of subsection (4) ... contemplates that ... a person may by assent vest an estate in himself in another capacity, and such vesting, of course, necessarily implies that he is divesting himself of the estate in his original capacity. It seems to me impossible to regard the same operation as lying outside the negative provision contained in the second sentence of the subsection. To do so involves making a distinction between the operation of divesting and vesting the legal estate and that of passing the legal estate. I do not think that this highly artificial distinction is legitimate. On the contrary, the second sentence appears to me to be intended as an exact counterpart to the first.

" Mr. Micklem [49] rested his contention primarily on section 40 [50] of the Trustee Act 1925 [paragraphs (a) and (b) of subsection (1) of which provide in effect that a deed of appointment of new trustees executed after 1925 shall operate as if it contained a vesting declaration extending *inter alia* to any estate or interest in land subject to the trust without the necessity for any separate conveyance or transfer of that estate or interest]. This argument is that ... where a person, X, has the dual capacity of a personal representative and a trustee and after the completion of administration X appoints a trustee, Y, to act jointly with himself as trustee, the deed of appointment of Y operates as if it

[49] Counsel for the plaintiff.
[50] For the terms of this section, see p. 457, *post*.

had contained a declaration by X vesting in X and Y all the estates and interests with respect to which X could have made a declaration, and these estates and interests include, it is said, the legal estate vested in him as personal representative. So, here, it is said that the deed of appointment containing such a declaration is an assent in writing signed by the personal representative. . . .

" That is an ingenious argument, but I do not think that it is well founded. . . . paragraphs (*a*) and (*b*) ought . . . to be construed only as being applicable to estates and interests which form part of the existing trust property. I do not think that where an estate or interest is vested in the existing trustee in some other capacity, for example, as here, a legal estate vested in him as personal representative, the estate or interest can fairly be brought within the words merely by reason of the fact that in the other capacity he has become bound to transfer the estate or interest to the trustees of the trust. The interest which does vest in such a case is not the estate or interest itself, *i.e.,* here the legal estate, but the right to insist on a transfer by the personal representative of the estate or interest. Again, I think that it may be said that the instrument, *i.e.,* the deed of appointment, executed by the trustee in that capacity could not aptly be described as having been signed by the personal representative within the meaning of section 36 (4) of the Administration of Estates Act 1925. . . ." *Declaration that the legal estate remained vested in the personal representative of the testatrix, H. D. Carter.*[51]

The office of personal representative (" P.R.") is different from that of a trustee in several respects. The function of a P.R. is to collect all the deceased's assets, pay off all debts and expenses and then to distribute the assets to the beneficiaries under the will or intestacy. His duty is owed to the estate as a whole so that he is under no duty to consider the effect of the exercise of his administrative powers so as to keep an even hand between those interested in income and those interested in capital.[52] A trustee has a continuing function to hold property on the terms of his trust. Until P.R.s assent to assets passing to the beneficiaries the whole legal and equitable ownership is vested in the P.R.s—the beneficiaries merely have a right to compel due administration of the estate though this right is a chose in

---

[51] This decision is inconsistent with the opinions of some text-writers and with the previous practice of some conveyancers. If correct, it produces the inconvenient result that some titles hitherto assumed to be valid are now technically defective: see R. R. A. Walker (1954) 80 L.Q.R. 328; J. F. Garner (1964) 28 Conv.(N.S.) 298. The Law Society's Working Party on Conveyancing therefore recommend in their Third Interim Report that where a personal representative is entitled to property under a will as trustee, beneficiary or in some other capacity, a conveyancing instrument executed by him and intended to pass the legal estate shall operate as an assent to vest the property in himself in his other capacity, and shall also be effective for its intended conveyancing purpose. The Working Party also recommend legislation to validate those titles now rendered defective by the decision: see (1967) 64 L.S.Gaz. 63. See further Farrand's *Contract and Conveyance* (2nd ed.), pp. 112–119, for a detailed examination of the position.

[52] *Re Hayes' W.T.* [1971] 1 W.L.R. 758.

action capable of transmission under a beneficiary's will: *Re Leigh's W.T.*[53] Under a trust the beneficiaries have the beneficial equitable interest in the trust property, the trustees merely having nominal ownership of the trust property. Exceptionally, a sole P.R. acting as such (unlike a sole trustee other than a trust corporation) can give a valid receipt for capital moneys arising on a trust for sale of land.[54] P.R.s can only be appointed by will or by the court whereas the Trustee Act 1925 confers wide powers of appointing new trustees.[55]

Section 5. Trusts and Powers

The essence of a trust is the intention to impose an obligation: that of a power to confer an option. This gives rise to the following distinctions:

(a) The court will enforce a trust to divide property among a class; it will not compel the exercise of a power to do so: *Brown* v. *Higgs.*[56] The court will, however, compel the exercise of a power in the nature of a trust, where the donor has manifested an intention that in any event the property shall go to the objects of the power: *Burrough* v. *Philcox*[57]; but nothing short of this will suffice: *Re Weekes' Settlement.*[58] Sometimes, instead of treating the power as a power coupled with a duty to exercise it, which the court will exercise on *McPhail* v. *Doulton* principles[59] if the donee of the power fails to exercise it, the court treats the power as a mere power but implies a trust for the objects of the power equally in default of exercise of the power.[60] The significance of such treatment is that a mere power not held by a donee qua trustee can be released, unlike a trust power, and a trust in default of appointment for persons equally is subject to a stricter test of certainty than a trust power (otherwise known as a discretionary trust).

---

[53] [1970] Ch. 277; and see P. V. Baker (1970) 86 L.Q.R. 20 for a stimulating note on the implications of the decision.

[54] Law of Property Act 1925, s. 27 (2).

[55] See Chap. 9.

[56] (1803) 8 Ves. 561; *McPhail* v. *Doulton* [1971] A.C. 424, 456, 457, *infra*, p. 79.

[57] (1840) 5 My. & Cr. 72; 41 E.R. 305. Here T died leaving life interests to his two children with remainders to their issue but if there were no issue (as happened) then the survivor of the two children was to have power to dispose of the property by will " amongst my nephews and nieces, or their children, either all to one of them or to as many of them as my surviving child shall think proper." There was no gift in default. Lord Cottenham L.C. held that the nephews and nieces or their children were intended to take the property subject only to a power of selection given to the survivor of T's children. Thus, on failure to exercise the power the nephews and nieces or their children all benefited since the power was in the nature of a trust.

[58] Property was left by T to T's husband for life with a " power to dispose of all such property by will amongst our children in accordance with the power granted to him as regards the other property which I have under my marriage settlements." There was no gift over in default of appointment and T's husband died intestate without having exercised the power. The surviving children claimed the property in equal shares. Romer J. rejected the claim on the ground that T did not intend that the children should definitely take the property if her husband failed to exercise the power.

[59] *Infra*, p. 79. See Chap. 4, s. 3, *infra*.

[60] *Wilson* v. *Duguid* (1883) 24 Ch.D. 244; *Re Arnold's Trusts* [1947] Ch. 131: *Re Wills' Trust Deeds* [1964] Ch. 219; A. J. Hawkins (1968) 84 L.Q.R. 64; M. G. Unwin (1962) 26 Conv.(N.S.) 92.

(b) The objects of a fixed trust (*e.g.,* to divide a million pounds equally between all employees and former employees of the X Co. Ltd. and any persons with whom such persons have resided at any time and the relatives of any such persons) must be certain in the sense of it being possible to draw up a comprehensive list of all the objects if the trust is to be valid. A power in the nature of a trust (or a discretionary trust to use a synonymous term) and an ordinary power are both valid so long as it is possible to say of any particular person who presents himself whether he certainly is or is not an object of the power (or discretionary trust). This is fully dealt with in Chapter 4, section 3, *infra.* The distinction between a discretionary trust and an ordinary power can be seen in the following example: " I leave all my property to my trustees to distribute the income from it during the Perpetuity Period hereinbefore specified between such of my issue as they shall see fit from time to time but they shall have power if they see fit to distribute up to half of such income amongst such of my nephews and nieces as they shall see fit." The issue are objects of a discretionary trust: the nephews and nieces are objects of a power.

(c) The lack of someone to enforce a trust is fatal to its validity save in the cases mentioned below, *infra,* pp. 108–109; the validity of a power does not depend upon the existence of someone capable of compelling its exercise.

Note [61]

Mere powers are voluntary, trusts imperative.[62] The question, therefore, is " When is a power not a mere power, but a power in the nature of a trust? " The general principle is that everything depends upon the intention of the settlor, which will be ascertained by the courts in accordance with ordinary rules of construction. More specifically the following propositions [63] can be stated:

(1) If there is a gift over in default of appointment, the power is a mere power,[64] even where the gift over is void for some reason.[65]

(2) A residuary gift in favour of the donee of the power is not a gift over for this purpose.[66]

(3) If it is to deprive a power of the character of a trust, the gift over must be in default of appointment, and not for any other event. Thus in the absence of a gift in default of appointment, a gift over on the failure of the appointees or any of them to reach a specified age will not necessarily prevent the power from being coupled with a trust.[67]

(4) Where there is no gift over in default of appointment, the power may

---

[61] See generally (1962) 26 Conv.(N.S.) 92 (M. G. Unwin).
[62] An apparent exception exists in the case of trusts of imperfect obligation in that they are unenforceable at the suit of a beneficiary; *infra,* pp. 108–109.
[63] It should be noted that general powers of appointment are never considered to be in the nature of trusts, since there is no class of persons in whose favour the trust could operate. The question, therefore, arises only in connection with special powers of appointment.
[64] *e.g., Re Mills* [1930] 1 Ch. 654.
[65] *Re Sprague* (1880) 43 L.T. 236; *Re Sayer* [1957] Ch. 423.
[66] *Re Brierley* (1894) 43 W.R. 36.
[67] *Re Llewellyn's Settlement* [1921] 2 Ch. 281.

be coupled with a trust or it may not, according to the true intention of the settlor.[68]

Section 6. Trusts and Conditions [69]

The remaining sections of this chapter are concerned with the situation where a testator, A, leaves property to B and requires B to make some payment to C or perform some obligation in favour of C. In the context of the will there are five possible constructions open to a court.

A's words may be treated as:

(1) Merely indicating his motive for making the gift so that B takes an absolute beneficial interest, *e.g.*, " to my wife B that she may support herself and the children acording to their needs."

(2) Intended to create a trust in favour of C.[70]

(3) Creating a condition which binds B. The disadvantage of such a construction is that in the case of a devise of freehold land subject to a condition subsequent, if the condition is broken then A's heir before 1838 or the specific devisee of A's right of entry or A's residuary divisee after 1837 [71] or in the case of a partial intestacy A's heir before 1926 or A's next-of-kin after 1925 has the right to enter and determine B's estate and thereby determine the interest intended for C. For C not to lose his interest the court would have to construe A's words as creating a trust or a charge or a personal obligation binding B.

(4) Creating a charge on the property given to B so that B takes the property beneficially subject to the charge.

(5) Creating a personal obligation binding B to C (exceptionally it might be possible to find that both a charge and a personal obligation were present though such a claim failed in *Re Lester, infra*).

If A gives property to B subject to the occurrence of a certain event (condition precedent) or upon a condition the occurrence of which is intended to cause the transfer of the property to C (condition subsequent) the following is the result:

If a condition precedent attached to realty is impossible, contrary to public policy, or illegal, both the devise and the condition are void: *Re Turton*.[72]

If a condition precedent attached to personalty is *physically* impossible (*e.g.*, a condition to drink up the ocean) the gift takes effect notwithstanding the condition: *Re Wolffe*.[73] The result is the same where the performance

---

[68] *Burrough* v. *Philcox* (1840) 5 My & Cr. 72; *Re Weekes' Settlement, supra*; *Re Combe* [1925] Ch. 210; *Re Perowne* [1951] Ch. 785; *Re Scarisbrick* [1951] Ch. 622; *Re Arnold's Trusts* [1947] Ch. 131.

[69] On ss. 6, 7 and 8, see Thomas, " Conditions in Favour of Third Parties " (1952) 11 C.L.J. 240.

[70] See Chap. 4, *infra*.

[71] Wills Act 1837, s. 3; Megarry and Wade, p. 81; *Re Oliver, infra*.

[72] [1926] Ch. 96. For a statement of the realty/personalty rules see *Re Elliott* [1952] Ch. 217, 220–222.

[73] [1953] 1 W.L.R. 1211.

of the condition is rendered impossible by the act of the testator: *Darby* v. *Langworthy*,[74] or by operation of law: *Re Thomas*.[75]

If the condition is subsequent and is impossible, uncertain, contrary to public policy or illegal, the interest given to B becomes absolute and C has no right: *Egerton* v. *Earl Brounlow*.[76]

If A gives property to B on condition that he pay something out of it in favour of C, then if B performs the condition, he keeps the remainder of the property absolutely: *Attorney-General* v. *The Cordwainers' Company, infra*. On the other hand, if the court construes the obligation to which B is subject as a trust, then B will be bound to give the benefit to C notwithstanding the impossibility of performing the obligation precisely according to its terms: *Re Frame*,[76a] and may have to hold the remainder of the property on a resulting trust for the settlor.

ATT.-GEN. v. THE CORDWAINERS' COMPANY

Master of the Rolls (1833) 3 My. & K. 534; 40 E.R. 203

John Fysher, by his will dated March 31, 1547, after bequeathing certain legacies to charitable and other purposes, devised unto the master, wardens, fellowship and company of the craft or mystery of cordwainers within the City of London and to their successors for evermore, his house " The Sign of the Falcon " to hold the same for the use and performance of his will, that is to say, to pay to his brother David Fysher an annuity of £6 during his life and after the death of the said David Fysher to pay to Mary Fysher, David's wife, an annuity of 40s. during her life; and to distribute in alms within the parish of St. Dunstan's, £5 sterling, by 12d. a house, to every poor householder and to such as shall be most needy and poor, by the discretion of the churchwardens of St. Dunstan's; and to distribute in alms among poor people, strangers and others coming out of other places and parishes the sum of 6s. 8d. After certain other directions the testator devised certain other estates to David Fysher with remainder to Nicholas Parnell in fee subject as to such remainder in fee to the payment of £4 per year for certain charitable purposes, and after giving certain other pecuniary legacies, the testator proceeded as follows: " And all the residue of my goods not bequeathed I hereby give and bequeath to David Fysher, my brother, whom I make my sole executor of this my last will and testament. And I admit for my overseer and supervisor Robert Fleetwood, being of the King's High Court of Chancery; provided always, that if the said master, wardens, fellowship and company of the craft or mystery of cordwainers aforesaid, do not well and truly perform, fulfil and keep all and singular the thing and things above said by them to be observed, performed, fulfilled and kept, but do cease in doing of the same by the space of one year, contrary to this my last will and testament, that then it shall be lawful for my said brother David Fysher,

---

[74] (1774) 3 B.P.C. 359.
[76] (1853) 4 H.L. 1.
[75] [1930] 2 Ch. 67.
[76a] [1939] Ch. 700; *cf. Re Brace* [1954] 1 W.L.R. 955.

and his heirs, into all the said lands, tenements, and other the premises with the appurtenances to enter, and the said premises to keep, have hold, and enjoy, to him his heirs and assigns for ever; and the said master, wardens, fellowship and company, to be clearly expelled, discharged, and put out of the premises."

The estate devised to the Cordwainers' Company consisted at the date of the will of the Falcon Inn let at a yearly rent of £6 and two other messuages let respectively at £5 and £1 6s. 8d. By 1833 the annual rental had increased to the sum of £358. The Cordwainers' Company distributed the sums of £5 and 6s. 8d. annually among the poor of the parish of St. Dunstan's and other poor as directed by the will; and they also paid some other small sums amounting to £2 17s. 6d. to the minister, churchwardens and officers of the parish of St. Dunstan's, and after making such payments they applied the surplus of the rents to the general corporate purposes of the company.

The information prayed that the Cordwainers' Company might be declared to be trustees of the rents and profits of the messuages and premises devised to them; that an account of rents might be taken against the company, and that the surplus rents might be applied in augmentation of the sums of £5 and 6s. 8d. given to the charitable uses and purposes mentioned in the will, either in the whole or rateably with the other sums mentioned therein; or that some other proportional or reasonable augmentation of the sums directed to be paid for charitable purposes might be made out of the increased rents, in performance and advancement of the charitable intentions of the testator; and that a proper scheme might be settled by the Master.[77]

The defendants by their answer insisted that they were devisees of the estates in question, subject only to the payment of the fixed and limited sums which the testator had directed to be paid; and that they had a right, as their predecessors had always done, to apply the surplus rents to the uses and purposes of the company.

Upon the construction of the will two questions were raised: first, whether the testator intended to devote to charitable purposes the whole income of the estates devised to the company; secondly, if the whole income were not so devoted, whether the objects of the charity were entitled to an increase in the sums given to them; proportioned to the amounts of increased rents.

LEACH M.R.: " The first question is whether this testator intended the corporation to take as mere trustees, or whether he intended to give them any beneficial interest. The next consideration is whether, if the corporation were to take as trustees, they were to be trustees for mere charitable purposes.

" It does not appear to me that the words of this devise do constitute

---

[77] *Cf. Re Lepton's W.T.* [1972] Ch. 276.

this corporation mere trustees. The estate is absolutely given to them; not upon trust, but for the use, interest, and performance of the testator's will. It is rather a gift upon condition, than a gift upon trust. They are to take the estate so devised to them, upon condition that they perform the duties which by the terms of the will are imposed upon them. Those duties are not for mere charitable purposes. Half the property that this testator disposes of is disposed of to his brother; an annuity of £6 is given to his brother for life; and after his brother's death there is no disposition of this annuity, except that £2 a year are given to his widow if she survived him. These are not charitable purposes. It is plain that a beneficial estate was intended to be given to the Cordwainers' Company, because the testator expressly declares that, if the condition upon which this estate is devised to the corporation be not performed, the brother shall enter and defeat the estate given to the Cordwainers' Company. Defeat what estate? An estate given to them in mere trust, from which they were to derive no benefit? Is it to be supposed that this was considered by the testator in the nature of a penalty? The imposition of a penalty for non-performance of the condition implies a benefit, if the condition be performed, and is inconsistent with any other intention, than that the testator meant to give a beneficial interest to the company upon the terms of complying with the directions contained in his will. There is therefore, no trust, either express or implied, for charitable purposes further than to the extent of the special charge imposed; and, upon all the principles applied in this court to such a case, this information must be dismissed. . . ."

Section 7. Trusts and Charges

A charge differs from a trust in the following respects [78]:

   (a) Once the party subject to the charge has fulfilled the charge he holds the property beneficially: *Re Oliver, infra: aliter* a trustee who may have to hold the property on a resulting trust: *Re West, infra.*

   (b) A trustee who occupies trust property must account for rents and profits: *aliter* a person holding property subject to a charge: *Re Oliver, infra.*

Re OLIVER

Chancery Division (1890) 62 L.T. 533

John Oliver, by his will dated August 26, 1879, gave various specific and general bequests and certain annuities, included among which was

---

[78] But a charge is similar to a trust in the following respects:
   (a) Neither a person subject to a charge nor a trustee is under a personal obligation to make up any deficiency caused by insufficiency of assets: *Re Cowley* (1885) 53 L.T. 494.
   (b) Both a charge and a trust create equitable interests which give way to the bona fide purchaser for value of the legal estate without notice: *Parker* v. *Judkin* [1931] 1 Ch. 475. For charges see Settled Land Act 1925, s. 1 (1) (v).

an annuity of £52 a year to his sister Mary Glew during her life, and the testator charged that annuity upon his estate at Barnby-in-the-Willows.

The testator gave his real estate at North and South Collingham and his residuary real estate to his nephew John Beckett, his heirs and assigns for ever, he also paying thereout the following legacies: £1,000 to the trustees of the will to be held by them upon certain trusts; £1,000 to the four daughters of his late niece Mary Holroyd in equal shares; £200 to his niece Sarah Woodruff. The testator directed that these legacies were to be paid at the end of six months after the death of his sister Mary Glew, and he directed his trustees to stand possessed of the sum of £1,000 directed by his will to be paid to them and charged on his Collingham estate upon certain trusts.

Mary Glew died on June 23, 1884.

The testator died on June 16, 1887.

After the death of the testator John Beckett was in possession and receipt of the rents and profits of the testator's real estate in North and South Collingham.

An action was brought for the administration of the real and personal estate of the testator, and an order was made for the sale of the North and South Collingham property.

A summons was taken out in the action asking that John Beckett might, in his account of the rents and profits of the testator's real estate, be charged with an occupation rent in respect of so much of the real estate at North and South Collingham as was in his occupation at the date of the testator's death for the period between that date and the date of completion of the sale of the real estate on October 11, 1889.

CHITTY J.: ". . . [The answer to the question asked in the summons] depends upon whether, on the true construction of the testator's will, John Beckett is a trustee of the property for the legatees, or whether he is the owner of the property subject to a charge in respect of the legacies. In the latter case the legatees would not be entitled to call upon John Beckett to account for the back rents and profits received by him. On behalf of the legatees it is contended that the testator's nephew is a trustee for them, and that everything he received he must account for. Now, this is a conveyancer's will; that is to say, the will is in a form generally used by conveyancers. The reason why I make that observation will appear when I state the terms of the will. [His Lordship stated the terms of the will, and continued:] The words ' he paying thereout the following legacies ' are prima facie words of condition, and in this case the condition is a condition subsequent. That is shown by the direction that the legacies shall be paid at the end of six calendar months after the death of the annuitant, the testator's sister, Mary Glew. Consequently, John Beckett, who is immediately entitled to the benefit of the devise, does not have to pay the legacies until six months after the death of the testator's sister. Therefore he would enter into receipt of the rent and profits of the property for six months before he would be bound to pay the legacies. Now, there is a well-known rule of construction that a devise upon condition that the devisee makes certain payments within a given time will, as a general rule, be construed as a trust and not as a condition, because, if construed as a condition, the only person who takes advantage of the condition being unperformed, when the devise is by will, is the testator's own heir. ' The right of entry for breach of a condition subsequent could not be reserved in favour of a stranger, but only of the grantor or his heirs; and the effect of entry by him, or them, after breach, was to defeat altogether the estate which had before passed to the grantee; so that that grantor or his heirs were *in* as of their former seisin.' [79] If it was held that the devise must be construed as importing a condition and nothing else, the person entitled to receive the payments would lose the payments, because, if the payments were not made within a given time, the heir of the testator would enter and take the estate, and take it free. It was to get over that objection that it has been said that generally the right construction is to hold that the devise creates a trust and not a condition. It has been termed a trust without any particular regard to the language, a legal effect being given so as to enable the person entitled to get the payments. It is upon that class of cases, to which I have referred only in general terms, that the argument has been based that here the devise is not a condition, and is therefore a trust. But it is equally plain, for ordinary purposes, that the effect of the devise is to create a charge, and not a trust. Now, I proceed to consider whether it is a trust or a charge. On the face of the will, when the testator intends to create a trust, he knows how to do it. [His Lordship discussed the provisions of the will, and continued:] The testator imposes a trust upon one of the persons who takes beneficially, and if the matter stood there I should find some difficulty in deciding that this was a charge and not a trust. But the testator is entitled to explain his own meaning, and he says in so many words, in a subsequent part of his will, that the trustees shall stand possessed of the £1,000 which he has 'charged on my Collingham estate.' I see no reason to say that the testator does not know the meaning of his own will. On the contrary, I think that the testator has shown that he is well acquainted with what he has done before. Therefore, upon the true construction of this will, I think that the legacies constitute a charge and only a charge. Unquestionably a difficulty arises on that part of the will where the testator says, ' he also paying thereout the following legacies.' But there are the subsequent words by which he explains that they are a charge. Those words ' he paying thereout' are only words upon which it turns whether there is a charge or a trust. But the testator has given, in respect of those words,

---

[79] Stephen's *Commentaries* (9th ed.), Vol. 1, p. 299.

a 'dictionary' explaining their effect. These legacies are consequently simply a charge on the North and South Collingham estate, as I am satisfied, looking at the will as a whole. I hold, therefore, that the devisee is not liable to account for the back rents and profits."

Section 8. Trusts and Personal Obligations

If A gives property to B subject to or in consideration of a payment thereout in favour of C, the court may construe this as imposing a personal obligation on B to make the necessary payment. In that case C's rights are personal against B and not against the property given to B; C's rights are equitable but they do not arise under a trust; and B's obligations may be greater than those of a trustee, for he is required to perform the obligation even if it costs him more than the value of the property received.[80]

Re LESTER

Chancery Division [1942] Ch. 324; 111 L.J.Ch. 197; 58 T.L.R. 250; 86 S.J. 168; [1942] 1 All E.R. 646

By his will dated February 9, 1927, the testator bequeathed the remainder of his shares in two companies to his son Albert William Lester, subject to the payment by him to another son, Alfred John Lester, during his life of the sum of £8 a week, and after the death of Alfred John Lester to the payment of £6 a week to his widow during her life or until her remarriage, and after the death of the survivor of Alfred John Lester and his wife or after her remarriage, as the case may be, to the payment to their daughter, Dorothy Louise Lester, during her lifetime or until her marriage, of the sum of £2 a week.

The testator died on December 21, 1940. Albert William Lester, who was also one of the executors of the will, took out this summons asking whether a charge was created by the will, on the shares, in favour of the annuitants. He admitted that once he had assented to the legacy, the words of the will imposed a personal obligation on him to make the prescribed payments.

SIMONDS J.: "Various authorities have been cited to me and the result of them is, in my judgment, that it must be a question of construction in each case whether an obligation or a charge is created or whether both are created. I find it difficult to construe such words as those in this case as creating both a personal obligation and a charge. There may be words which create both, as in *Welby* v. *Rockliffe*[81] and *Wright* v. *Wilkin*,[82] where the language does not admit fairly of any other conclusion than that there was both a personal obligation and a charge. In *Rees* v. *Engelback*[83] the language was such as to create a personal obliga-

---

[80] As happened in *Re Hodge* [1940] Ch. 260.
[81] (1830) 1 Russ. & My. 571.
[82] (1860) 7 Jur.(N.S.) 441.
[83] (1871) L.R. 12 Eq. 225.

tion, and there are two Irish cases, *Re M'Mahon* [84] and *Duffy* v. *Duffy*,[85] where language was used which was apt to impose a personal obligation but not to create a charge.   In *Rees* v. *Engelback* [86] the testator had devised his business to his trustees on trust to allow his son to carry it on ' upon the terms and conditions following '—*i.e.*, that he should pay certain annuities, and the only question was whether his son, having accepted the legacy, had incurred a personal liability; and the Vice-Chancellor said [87]: ' Now, upon the authority of the case of *Messenger* v. *Andrews*,[88] and even without the authority of that case, upon very plain principles of justice and law, the defendant, who admits that he has enjoyed the benefit given to him by a will upon the conditions expressed in it, is under a personal liability, which can be enforced in this court, of fulfilling those conditions.'   It is true that in the bill the plaintiff had claimed a declaration that the annuities were by the will charged on the business, but that question was not ventilated.   In *Re Hodge* [89] a testatrix devised to her husband, who was her executor and sole residuary legatee, certain freehold property in consideration of his paying her sister £2 a week for life.   There it will be observed that a condition was introduced by the words ' in consideration of,' and the judge came to the conclusion that there was a personal obligation on the husband, if he accepted the devise.   I think there is very little difference between a bequest ' in con-sideration of ' and a bequest ' subject to ' the payment by the legatee of certain sums.   In either case the words are apt to create a personal obligation.   On the other hand, where there is no reference to the legatee as the person by whom the payment is to be made, but the property is merely given subject to the payment of a certain sum, it may well be that the effect is to create a charge on the property but not to impose a personal obligation on the legatee.   The distinction is a fine but, I think, a real one.   Here where it is rightly, in my view, conceded that a personal obligation is imposed on the legatee to make the payment, I see no ground for saying that in addition a charge is created.

"I must refer to two other cases that were cited to me.   In *Re Cowley* [90] a testator gave all his interest in certain leasehold premises to his son, subject to payment of all his debts, funeral and testamentary expenses.   The son accepted the bequest and it was held that he must be deemed to have accepted it, but was not personally liable to pay the debts, funeral or testamentary expenses.   In his judgment Kay J. says [91]: ' In the absence of authority, I am not prepared to say that the gift of

84 [1901] 1 I.R. 489.
85 [1920] 1 I.R. 122.
86 (1871) L.R. 12 Eq. 225.
87 *Ibid.* p. 237.
88 (1828) 4 Russ. 478.
89 [1940] Ch. 260.
90 (1885) 53 L.T. 494.
91 *Ibid.* p. 495.

specific legacies contained in the present will, " subject to payment of debts, funeral and testamentary expenses " means anything but that the testator gives this property and the other property subject to payment of his debts, funeral and testamentary expenses. It does not seem to me at all intended that, whether or not the property is enough, the legatee is to pay the debts.' From the passage that follows it is clear that the learned judge is assuming that the words under consideration were apt to create a charge on the property of the debts, funeral and testamentary expenses. He goes on: ' It is commonly expressed in very different terms—" he paying the debts." Here I take the words only as amounting to a charge by the testator between that property and the other property. I think that the testator's son must be deemed to have elected to accept the legacies, subject to payment of the debts, funeral and testamentary expenses, but that he is not personally liable to pay such debts, funeral or testamentary expenses, or any part thereof.' The opening word ' It ' in the passage last cited means ' the intention that, whether or not the property is enough, the legatee is to pay the debts.' The learned judge does not in so many words say that in that case a charge would not be created, but he is clearly contrasting the two cases of charge and personal liability. The other case is *Re Oliver*.[92] There the testator gave his real estate at North and South Collingham and his residuary estate to his nephew, ' he also paying thereout the following legacies . . . ,' but later referred to the legacies as ' charged on my Collingham estate.' Chitty J. held that the words ' he also paying thereout the following legacies . . .' would by themselves have been apt to create a trust (he does not use the words ' personal obligation '), but as the testator had referred to the legacies as ' charged ' on the Collingham estate, he was constrained to hold that a charge only, not a trust, was created. He was, I think, clearly of the opinion that such an expression could not carry the double burden of creating a charge and imposing a personal obligation. So also in the present case, since it is clear that a personal obligation is imposed on the legatee, on his assenting to the legacy, I should not be justified in saying that the words in question also create a charge on the subject-matter of the legacy."

---

[92] (1890) 62 L.T. 533; *supra*, p. 46.

CHAPTER 3

CLASSIFICATION AND FORMALITIES OF TRUSTS

Section 1. Classification of Trusts [1]

TRUSTS are basically classified as express, implied, resulting or constructive. Classification is significant in that no formalities are required for implied resulting or constructive trusts [2] whilst a person, who, owing to an incapacity such as minority, is incapable of being appointed an express trustee may nevertheless become a trustee by operation of law.[3]

Although there is no authoritative classification for the purpose of this work the following classification is adopted:

Express trust: a trust where the settlor has expressed his intention to create a trust whether using the word " trust " or other informal words.

Implied trust: a resulting trust.

Resulting trust [4]: a presumed resulting trust, where A transfers property to B gratuitously such that B is rebuttably presumed to hold on trust for A, or an automatic resulting trust, where A transfers property to B on trusts which for some reason leave some or all of the beneficial interest undisposed of so B automatically holds on a resulting trust for A to the extent of the undisposed of beneficial interest.

Constructive trust [5]: a trust automatically imposed by equity in special cases where the conduct of an owner of property makes it unconscionable for him to hold the property for his own benefit.

It should be noted, however, that " constructive trust " is sometimes used to cover automatic resulting trusts, and " implied trust " to cover resulting and constructive trusts or to cover only presumed resulting trusts or even only informally expressed " express trusts." [6] Needless to say this has created problems for parliamentary draftsmen.[7]

Section 2. Formalities of Trusts

Formalities are required for (a) the declaration of express *inter vivos* trusts of land, (b) the *inter vivos* disposition of equitable interests in both land and pure personalty, and (c) contracts for the disposition of any interest in land. These requirements do not affect the creation or operation of resulting, implied or constructive trusts. Express trusts or dispositions by will must be in writing conforming with the Wills Act 1837.

Statutory provisions

The relevant provisions of the Law of Property Act 1925 are:

Section 53 (1) (b): " a declaration of trust respecting any land or any interest therein must be manifested and proved by some writing signed by some person who is able to declare such trust . . ."

---

1 Snell, pp. 98–99; Hanbury, pp. 98–102; Pettit, pp. 43–47; Underhill, pp. 9–12; Lewin, pp. 6–8.
2 s. 53 (2) of the L.P.A. 1925, *infra*.   3 *Re Vinogradoff* [1935] W.N. 68.
4 *Per* Megarry J. in *Re Vandervell's Trusts* [1974] 1 All E.R. 47, 68–69; Chap. 7, *infra*.   5 Chap. 8, *infra*.
6 *Cp. Soar* v. *Ashwell* [1893] 2 Q.B. 390; *Cook* v. *Fountain* (1676) 3 Swan. 585; *Re Llanover Estates* [1926] Ch. 626; *Lloyd* v. *Spillit* (1740) Barn. Ch. 384, 388.
7 *e.g.*, L.P.A. 1925, s. 53 (2) and T.A. 1925, s. 68 (17).

This replaces section 7 of the Statute of Frauds 1677, but omits the sanction that oral declarations of trusts " shall be utterly void and of none effect." " Void " had been and still is assumed to mean " unenforceable." The person able to declare the trust within the meaning of the section is the beneficial owner: see *Tierney* v. *Wood* [8]; *Kronheim* v. *Johnson*.[9]

Section 53 (1) (c): " a disposition of an equitable interest or trust subsisting at the time of the disposition, must be in writing signed by the person disposing of the same, or by his agent thereunto lawfully authorised in writing or by will." [10]

This replaces section 9 of the Statute of Frauds 1677, substituting for the words " *all grants and assignments* " the single word " *disposition*," and omitting the sanction that oral dispositions " shall be utterly void and of none effect." Since the subsection makes writing an essential requirement of a disposition and not merely evidence of it unlike s. 53 (1) (*b*), " void " has always been regarded as meaning what it says.

Section 53 (2): " This section does not affect the creation or operation of resulting, implied or constructive trusts."

This replaces section 8 of the Statute of Frauds 1677, which was in terms limited to trusts of lands which " may arise or result by the implication or construction of law, or be transferred or extinguished by an act or operation of law." Constructive trusts will be imposed where someone tries to take unfair advantage of the absence of the requisite formalities for " equity will not allow a statute to be used as an engine of fraud ": *Bannister* v. *Bannister, infra*.

Section 40: " (1) No action may be brought upon any contract for the sale or other disposition of land or any interest in land, unless the agreement upon which such action is brought, or some memorandum or note thereof, is in writing, and signed by the party to be charged or by some other person thereunto by him lawfully authorised.

" (2) This section . . . does not affect the law relating to part performance . . ."

This replaces in part section 4 of the Statute of Frauds 1677, and gives statutory recognition to the equitable doctrine of part-performance." [11]

For testamentary dispositions compliance with section 9 of the Wills Act 1837 set out *infra*, p. 396 is vital.

Importance of formal requirements

Formal requirements are important because the validity and consequences of a transaction may depend on compliance with a particular form. Thus although oral transactions cannot attract stamp duty, a written instrument, which operates as the completion of a pre-existing oral contract,

---

[8] (1854) 19 Beav. 330.   [9] (1877) 7 Ch.D. 60, 66.
[10] Where the disponee is to hold as trustee there is no need for the writing to contain particulars of the trust: *Re Tyler* [1967] 1 W.L.R. 1269. The disposition may be in two or more interconnected documents, only one of which is signed: *Re Danish Bacon Co. Staff Pension Fund Trusts* [1971] 1 W.L.R. 248. For the inapplicability of s. 53 (1) (*c*) to disclaimers and to variation of trusts by the court under the Variation of Trusts Act 1958 see respectively *Re Paradise Motor Co.* [1968] 1 W.L.R. 1125 and *Re Holt's Settlement* [1969] 1 Ch. 100, *infra*, p. 533.
[11] The act of part performance must be unequivocally referable to some contract between the parties and consistent with the contract alleged: *Maddison* v. *Aldeson* (1883) 8 App.Cas. 467; *Wakeham* v. *Mackenzie* [1968] 1 W.L.R. 1175; *Steadman* v. *Steadman* [1974] 3 W.L.R. 56, criticised (1974) 90 L.Q.R. 433.

will do so: *Oughtred* v. *I.R.C., infra.* And the choice of an inappropriate form may result in the failure of a trust or disposition with catastrophic tax consequences for a settlor: *Vandervell* v. *I.R.C., infra.*

Complexity of present law

The excessive complexity of the present law can be seen from the following examples:

T1 and T2 hold property on trust for A:

(i) A declares himself a trustee of his interest for himself for life, with remainder to B. This is a declaration of trust within section 53 (1) (*b*), which must be evidenced in writing, where the property is land, unless the trust falls into one of the excepted categories of resulting, implied or constructive trusts: *Bannister* v. *Bannister, infra.* Where the property is pure personalty, the declaration may be oral.

(ii) A declares himself a trustee of his interest for B absolutely. This is probably not a declaration of trust within section 53 (1) (*b*), but a disposition of A's entire equitable interest within section 53 (1) (*c*), which requires to be in writing whether the property is land or pure personalty: *Grainge* v. *Wilberforce.*[12]

(iii) A directs T1 and T2 to hold the property on trust for himself for life, with remainder to B, or on trust for B absolutely. In either case such a direction amounts to a disposition within section 53 (1) (*c*) and requires to be in writing where the property is pure personalty [13]: *Grey* v. *I.R.C., infra,* and undoubtedly also where it is land. According to *Tierney* v. *Wood* [14] such a direction is also a declaration of trust within section 53 (1) (*b*) and requires to be evidenced in writing, where the property is land. *Sed quaere,* since in neither case does A hold anything on trust: see *Grey* v. *I.R.C., infra.*

(iv) A directs T1 and T2 to transfer their legal and his equitable interest in pure personalty to B. Such a direction has been held not to be a disposition of the equitable interest within section 53 (1) (*c*): *Vandervell* v. *I.R.C., infra.* The same would presumably apply where the property is land.

(v) A assigns his equitable interest to B or to C and D on trust for B or to C and D on trust for A himself for life, with remainder to B. Such an assignment is a disposition within section 53 (1) (*c*) and requires to be in writing whether the property is land or pure personalty.

(vi) A contracts with B to transfer his interest to him. Such a contract requires to be evidenced in writing to comply with section 40 where A's interest is land or exists under a trust for sale of land: *Cooper* v. *Critchley.*[15] No evidence in writing is required where A's interest exists in pure personalty.

Special problems exist in the case of gifts to unincorporated associations with a changing membership.[16]

---

12 (1889) 5 T.L.R. 436.
13 But where the property was held on a *resulting* trust for A, see the surprising decision of the Court of Appeal in *Re Vandervell's Trust (No.* 2) [1974] 3 W.L.R. 256.
14 (1854) 19 Beav. 330; see also *Timpson's Executors* v. *Yerbury* [1936] 1 K.B. 645; *Re Chrimes* [1917] 1 Ch. 30; *Re Wale* [1956] 1 W.L.R. 1346.
15 [1955] Ch. 431.
16 *Neville Estates Ltd.* v. *Madden* [1962] Ch. 832, 849; Morris & Leach, *The Rule Against Perpetuities,* pp. 313–318; Ford, *Unincorporated Non-Profit Associations,* pp. 5–8, 21–23.

GREY v. INLAND REVENUE COMMISSIONERS

House of Lords [1960] A.C. 1; [1959] 3 W.L.R. 759; 103 S.J. 896; [1959] 3 All E.R. 603; [1959] T.R. 311 (Viscount Simonds, Lords Radcliffe, Cohen, Keith of Avonholm and Reid)

On February 1, 1955, Mr. Hunter, as settlor, transferred 18,000 shares of £1 each to the appellants as nominees for himself. The appellants were the trustees of six settlements, which Mr. Hunter had previously created. On February 18, 1955, Mr. Hunter orally directed the trustees to divide the 18,000 shares into six parcels of 3,000 shares each and to appropriate the parcels to the trusts of the six settlements, one parcel to each settlement.

On March 25, 1955, the trustees executed six deeds of declaration of trust (which Mr. Hunter also executed in order to testify to the oral direction previously given by him) declaring that since February 18, 1955, they held each of the parcels of 3,000 shares on the trusts of the relevant settlement. The Commissioners of Inland Revenue assessed the deeds of declaration of trust to *ad valorem* stamp duty. The trustees appealed. Upjohn J.,[17] allowing the appeal, held that under section 9 of the Statute of Frauds (now replaced by section 53 (1) (*c*) of the Law of Property Act 1925) a declaration of trust of an equitable interest did not require writing, that a direction to trustees to hold on new trusts was equivalent to a declaration of trust, and that the Law of Property Act had not altered the law. It followed that the oral direction of February 18, 1955, was effectual to pass the equitable interest in the shares, and accordingly the six deeds of March 25, 1955, were not chargeable with *ad valorem* duty. The Commissioners appealed to the Court of Appeal, which held [18] by a majority (Morris and Ormerod L.JJ., Lord Evershed M.R. dissenting) that the word " disposition " in section 53 (1) (*c*) of the Law of Property Act was wide enough to cover every method by which a beneficial interest in X was substituted for a beneficial interest in Y. Accordingly, there was no effectual disposition until the deeds of March 25, 1955, and *ad valorem* duty was chargeable. The trustees appealed to the House of Lords.

LORD RADCLIFFE: " My Lords, if there is nothing more in this appeal than the short question whether the oral direction that Mr. Hunter gave to his trustees on February 18, 1955, amounted in any ordinary sense of the words to a ' disposition of an equitable interest or trust subsisting at the time of the disposition,' I do not feel any doubt as to my answer. I think that it did. Whether we describe what happened in technical or in more general terms, the full equitable interest in the eighteen thousand shares concerned, which at that time was his, was (subject to any statutory invalidity) diverted by his direction from his

---

[17] [1958] Ch. 375. [18] [1958] Ch. 690.

ownership into the beneficial ownership of the various equitable owners, present and future, entitled under his six existing settlements.

" But that is not the question which has led to difference of opinion in the courts below. Where opinions have differed is on the point whether his direction was a ' disposition ' within the meaning of section 53 (1) (c) of the Law of Property Act 1925, the argument for giving it a more restricted meaning in that context being that section 53 is to be construed as no more than a consolidation of three sections of the Statute of Frauds, sections 3, 7 and 9. So treated, ' disposition,' it is said, is merely the equivalent of the former words of section 9, ' grants and assignments,' except that testamentary disposition has to be covered as well, and a direction to a trustee by the equitable owner of the property prescribing new trusts on which it is to be held is a declaration of trust but not a grant or assignment. The argument concludes, therefore, that neither before January 1, 1926, nor since did such a direction require to be in writing signed by the disponor or his agent in order to be effective.

" In my opinion, it is a very nice question whether a parol declaration of trust of this kind was or was not within the mischief of section 9 of the Statute of Frauds. The point has never, I believe, been decided and perhaps it never will be. Certainly it was long established as law that while a declaration of trust respecting land or any interest therein required writing to be effective a declaration of trust respecting personalty did not. Moreover, there is warrant for saying that a direction to his trustee by the equitable owner of trust property prescribing new trusts of that property was a declaration of trust. But it does not necessarily follow from that that such a direction, if the effect of it was to determine completely or *pro tanto* the subsisting equitable interest of the maker of the direction, was not also a grant or assignment for the purposes of section 9 and therefore required writing for its validity. Something had to happen to that equitable interest in order to displace it in favour of the new interests created by the direction: and it would be at any rate logical to treat the direction as being an assignment of the subsisting interest to the new beneficiary or beneficiaries or, in other cases, a release or surrender of it to the trustee.

" I do not think, however, that that question has to be answered for the purposes of this appeal. It can only be relevant if section 53 (1) of the Law of Property Act 1925 is treated as a true consolidation of the three sections of the Statute of Frauds concerned and as governed, therefore, by the general principle, with which I am entirely in agreement, that a consolidating Act is not to be read as effecting changes in the existing law unless the words it employs are too clear in their effect to admit of any other construction. If there is anything in the judgments of the majority of the Court of Appeal which is inconsistent with this principle I must express my disagreement with them. But, in my opinion, it is impossible to regard section 53 of the Law of Property Act 1925 as a consolidating enactment in this sense. It is here that the premises upon which Upjohn J. and the Master of the Rolls founded their conclusions are, I believe, unsound.

" The Law of Property Act 1925 itself was, no doubt, strictly a consolidating statute. But what it consolidated was not merely the Law of Property Act 1922, a statute which had itself effected massive changes in the law relating to real property and conveyancing, but also the later Law of Property (Amendment) Act 1924. The Statute of Frauds sections had not been touched by the Act of 1922; but they were in effect repealed and re-enacted in altered form by the operation of section 3 of the Act of 1924 and the provisions of Schedule III to that Act. The Schedule is divided into two Parts, the contents of Part I being described simply as ' Amendments ' and the contents of Part II being headed by the description ' Provisions facilitating consolidation . . .' I suppose that the authors of the Act of 1924 understood what was the significance of the division of Schedule III into these two Parts under their different headings. I cannot say that I do. Each Part, when examined, is seen to contain numerous amendments of various previous statutes relating to real property and conveyancing, apart from the Act of 1922 itself, and in this sort of matter I cannot see how one can satisfactorily measure the degrees of substance involved in the various changes. The point is that they were avowedly changes. It is paragraph 15 of Part II of Schedule III which deals with the Statute of Frauds: and though the introductory words do seem to suggest that the sections concerned are only being re-enacted in different words, it is apparent, when they are read through, that this is not so and that alterations of more or less moment are in fact being made. This new wording is what is carried into section 53 of the Act of 1925.

" For these reasons, I think that there is no direct link between section 53 (1) (c) of the Act of 1925 and section 9 of the Statute of Frauds. The link was broken by the changes introduced by the amending Act of 1924, and it was those changes, not the original statute, that section 53 must be taken as consolidating. If so, it is inadmissible to allow the construction of the word ' disposition ' in the new Act to be limited or controlled by any meaning attributed to the words ' grant ' or ' assignment ' in section 9 of the old Act. I agree that the appeal should be dismissed." [19] *Appeal dismissed.*

OUGHTRED v. INLAND REVENUE COMMISSIONERS

House of Lords [1960] A.C. 206; [1959] 3 W.L.R. 898; 103 S.J. 896; [1959] 3 All E.R. 623; [1959] T.R. 319 (Lords Keith of Avonholm, Denning and Jenkins; Lords Radcliffe and Cohen dissenting)

[19] See (1958) 74 L.Q.R. 180 (P. V. B. commenting on the decision of Upjohn J.); *ibid.* 487 (R. E. M. and P. V. B. commenting on the decision of the Court of Appeal); J. G. Monroe, " After Grey and Oughtred " [1960] B.T.R. 17 (commenting on the decision of the House of Lords); [1960] C.L.J. 31 (J. W. A. Thornely, a general and valuable review).

The trustees of a settlement held the legal title in 200,000 shares in a company called William Jackson & Son Ltd. in trust for the appellant, Mrs. Oughtred, for life and after her death for her son Peter. The appellant also owned 72,700 shares in her own right. On June 18, 1956, an oral agreement was made between the appellant and her son to the effect that on the 26th of the same month she would transfer to him the 72,700 shares and in exchange he would make her the absolute beneficial owner of the settled shares by giving up to her his beneficial reversionary interests.[20] The oral agreement was followed by the execution of three documents all dated June 26, 1956, namely, (1) a deed of release made between the appellant of the first part, Peter of the second part and the trustees of the settlement of the third part which recited that the 200,000 shares were now held in trust for the appellant absolutely and that it was intended to transfer them to her, and gave the trustees a general release in respect of their trusteeship, but was executed only by the appellant and Peter; (2) a transfer by the appellant of the 72,700 shares to nominees for Peter expressed to be made in consideration of 10s.; and (3) a deed of transfer expressed to be made in consideration of 10s. by which the trustees transferred the 200,000 shares to the appellant.

The matter came before Upjohn J.[21] on an appeal by way of case stated by the Commissioners of Inland Revenue under section 13 of the Stamp Act of 1891 at the request of the appellant. The Commissioners had assessed the stamp duty chargeable on the third transfer mentioned above at £663 10s., made up of £663 *ad valorem* transfer on sale duty together with the fixed duty of 10s. on the transfer of the legal interest in the 200,000 shares to the appellant.

Upjohn J. allowed the appeal, holding that the transfer in question was not chargeable with *ad valorem* duty and declaring that it was chargeable with the fixed duty of 10s. only. In his opinion a vendor under a specifically enforceable contract of sale became a constructive trustee for the purchaser. Accordingly Peter became a constructive trustee for the appellant from the date of the oral agreement on June 18, 1956. The appellant obtained an equitable interest under the oral constructive trust. Hence there was no document to attract *ad valorem* duty. The Commissioners appealed to the Court of Appeal,[22] which allowed the appeal and held that the transfer in question was chargeable with the *ad valorem* duty of £663, but not with the fixed duty of 10s. In their opinion, whether or not there was a constructive trust, the transfer in question was the completion of the oral contract and was liable to *ad valorem* duty for that reason. They rejected the claim to the fixed duty of 10s. on the ground that as Peter had not executed the transfer, it

---

20 The idea was to save estate duty as otherwise on the appellant's death duty would be payable on the aggregated value of the settled property and the appellant's free estate. Nowadays, capital transfer tax would apply.
21 [1958] Ch. 383.
22 [1958] Ch. 678.

could not be regarded at one and the same time as the transfer on sale of Peter's equitable interest and the transfer (not on sale) of the legal interest in the shares. The appellant appealed.

LORD JENKINS: " The provisions of the Stamp Act 1891 directly relevant to the claim are these: section 1 (which contains the charge of stamp duties) provides that the stamp duties ' upon the several instruments specified in Schedule 1 to this Act shall be the several duties in the said schedule specified. . . .' Section 54 provides as follows: ' For the purposes of this Act the expression " conveyance on sale " includes every instrument . . . whereby any property, or any estate or interest in any property, upon the sale thereof is transferred to or vested in a purchaser, or any other person on his behalf or by his direction.'
" Schedule 1 imposes under the head of charge ' Conveyance or transfer on sale of any property' (except as therein mentioned) *ad valorem* duty upon ' the amount or value of the consideration for the sale '; and under the head of charge ' Conveyance or transfer of any kind not hereinbefore described ' a fixed duty of 10s."
[His Lordship referred to section 53 (1) (*c*) and (2) of the Law of Property Act 1925, and continued:] " The question, then, is whether, upon the true construction of section 54 of the Act of 1891 and having regard to the terms and effect of the oral agreement and the nature of the interests with respect to which that agreement was made, the disputed transfer was an instrument whereby property in the shape of the settled shares or any estate or interest in that property was transferred ' upon the sale thereof ' to a purchaser in the person of the appellant.
" . . . It is said, and said truly, that stamp duty is imposed on instruments, not transactions, and that a transaction of sale carried out without bringing into existence an instrument which has the effect of transferring to or vesting in the purchaser the property sold attracts no duty: see *per* Lord Esher M.R. in *Inland Revenue Commissioners* v. *Angus,* where he said [23]: ' The first thing to be noticed is that the thing which is made liable to the duty is an " instrument." If a contract of purchase and sale, or a conveyance by way of purchase and sale, can be, or is, carried out without an instrument, the case is not within the section, and no tax is imposed. It is not the transaction of purchase and sale which is struck at; it is the instrument whereby the purchase and sale are effected which is struck at. And if anyone can carry through a purchase and sale without an instrument, then the legislature have not reached that transaction. The next thing is that it is not every instrument which may be brought into being in the course of a transaction of purchase and sale which is struck at. It is the instrument " whereby any property upon the sale thereof is legally or equitably transferred." The taxation is confined to the instrument whereby the property is transferred. The transfer must be made by the instrument. If a transfer requires something more

[23] (1889) 23 Q.B.D. 579, 589.

than an instrument to carry it through, then the transaction is not struck
at, and the instrument is not struck at because the property is not
transferred by it.'

" It is said further that, in the present case, the disputed transfer
transferred nothing beyond a bare legal estate, because, in accordance
with the well-settled principle applicable to contracts of sale between
contract and completion, the appellant became under the oral agreement
beneficially entitled in equity to the settled shares, subject to the due
satisfaction by her of the purchase consideration, and, accordingly, the
entire beneficial interest in the settled shares had already passed to her
at the time of the execution of the disputed transfer, and there was
nothing left upon which the disputed transfer could operate except the
bare legal estate.

" The Commissioners of Inland Revenue seek to meet this argument
by reference to section 53 (1) (*c*) of the Law of Property Act 1925. They
contend that, as the agreement of June 18, 1956, was an oral agreement,
it could not, in view of section 53 (1) (*c*), effect a disposition of a subsisting equitable interest or trust, and, accordingly, that Peter's subsisting equitable interest under the trusts of the settlement, in the shape
of his reversionary interest, remained vested in him until the execution
of the disputed transfer, which, in these circumstances, operated as a
transfer on sale to the appellant of Peter's reversionary interest and
additionally as a transfer not on sale to the appellant of the legal interest
in the settled shares. It was by this process of reasoning that the commissioners arrived at the opinion expressed in the case stated that the
disputed transfer attracted both the *ad valorem* duty exigible on a transfer
on sale of the reversionary interest and also the fixed duty of 10s. This
argument is attacked on the appellant's side by reference to subsection (2)
of section 53 of the Act of 1925, which excludes the creation or operation
of resulting, implied or constructive trusts from the provisions of
subsection (1). It is said that, inasmuch as the oral agreement was an
agreement of sale and purchase, it gave rise, on the principle to which I
have already adverted, to a constructive trust of the reversionary interest
in favour of the appellant, subject to performance by her of her obligation to transfer to Peter the free shares forming the consideration for the
sale. It is said that this trust, being constructive, was untouched by
section 53 (1) (*c*) in view of the exemption afforded by section 53 (2),
and that the appellant's primary argument still holds good.

" I find it unnecessary to decide whether section 53 (2) has the effect
of excluding the present transaction from the operation of section 53 [24]

---

[24] Lord Radcliffe took the view that s. 53 (1) (*c*) was excluded whilst Lords Cohen
and Denning took the view that s. 53 (1) (*c*) applied. Lord Keith merely concurred
with Lord Jenkins. The relevant dicta of Lords Cohen and Denning are as follows:
Lord Denning (at p. 233): " I do not think the oral agreement was effective to
transfer Peter's reversionary interest to his mother. I should have thought that
the wording of s. 53 (1) (*c*) clearly made a writing necessary to effect a transfer:
and s. 53 (2) does not do away with that necessity." Lord Cohen (at p. 230):
" Before your Lordships Mr. Wilberforce was prepared to agree that on the

(1) (*c*), for, assuming in the appellant's favour that the oral contract did have the effect in equity of raising a constructive trust of the settled shares for her untouched by section 53 (1) (*c*), I am unable to accept the conclusion that the disputed transfer was prevented from being a transfer of the shares to the appellant on sale because the entire beneficial interest in the settled shares was already vested in the appellant under the con-structive trust, and there was, accordingly, nothing left for the disputed transfer to pass to the appellant except the bare legal estate. The con-structive trust in favour of a purchaser which arises on the conclusion of a contract for sale is founded upon the purchaser's right to enforce the contract in proceedings for specific performance. In other words, he is treated in equity as entitled by virtue of the contract to the property which the vendor is bound under the contract to convey to him. This interest under the contract is, no doubt, a proprietary interest of a sort, which arises, so to speak, in anticipation of the execution of the transfer for which the purchaser is entitled to call. But its existence has never (so far as I know) been held to prevent a subsequent transfer, in perform-ance of the contract, of the property contracted to be sold from consti-tuting for stamp duty purposes a transfer on sale of the property in question. Take the simple case of a contract for the sale of land. In such a case a constructive trust in favour of the purchaser arises on the con-clusion of the contract for sale, but (so far as I know) it has never been held on this account that a conveyance subsequently executed in perform-ance of the contract is not stampable *ad valorem* as a transfer on sale. Similarly, in a case like the present one, but uncomplicated by the exist-ence of successive interests, a transfer to a purchaser of the investments comprised in a trust fund could not, in my judgment, be prevented from constituting a transfer on sale for the purposes of stamp duty by reason of the fact that the actual transfer had been preceded by an oral agree-ment for sale.

" In truth, the title secured by a purchaser by means of an actual transfer is different in kind from, and may well be far superior to, the special form of proprietary interest which equity confers on a purchaser in anticipation of such transfer.

" This difference is of particular importance in the case of property such as shares in a limited company. Under the contract, the purchaser is, no doubt, entitled in equity as between himself and the vendor to the beneficial interest in the shares, and (subject to due payment of the purchase consideration) to call for a transfer of them from the vendor as trustee for him. But it is only on the execution of the actual transfer that he becomes entitled to be registered as a member, to attend and vote at meetings, to effect transfers on the register, or to receive dividends otherwise than through the vendor as his trustee.

---

making of the oral agreement Peter became a constructive trustee of his equitable reversionary interest for the appellant, but he submitted that nonetheless s. 53 (1) (*c*) applied and accordingly Peter could not assign that equitable interest to the appellant except by a disposition in writing. My Lords, with that I agree."

" The parties to a transaction of sale and purchase may, no doubt, choose to let the matter rest in contract. But if the subject-matter of a sale is such that the full title to it can only be transferred by an instrument, then any instrument they execute by way of transfer of the property sold ranks for stamp duty purposes as a conveyance on sale, notwithstanding the constructive trust in favour of the purchaser which arose on the conclusion of the contract. . . ." *Appeal dismissed.*[25]

VANDERVELL v. INLAND REVENUE COMMISSIONERS

House of Lords [1967] 2 A.C. 291 (Lords Pearce, Upjohn and Wilberforce; Lords Reid and Donovan dissenting)

In 1958 the taxpayer, G. A. Vandervell, decided to give £150,000 to the Royal College of Surgeons to found a Chair of Pharmacology. The taxpayer was chairman, managing director and principal shareholder of Vandervell Products Ltd., whose capital structure included three classes of ordinary shares: first 500,000 voting shares held by the taxpayer; secondly, 100,000 " A " non-voting shares held by a bank as trustee for the taxpayer; and, thirdly, 2,600,000 " B " non-voting shares, of which 2,053,308 were held by Vandervell Trustees Ltd. as trustees of a family settlement, and the remainder were held by the taxpayer. To effect his gift the taxpayer caused the bank to transfer the 100,000 " A " non-voting shares to the College and declared and paid dividends thereon to the amount of £145,000. He also required the College to give Vandervell Trustees Ltd. an option to purchase the shares for £5,000 which that company exercised after the dividends had been paid to the College.

The taxpayer was assessed to surtax on the basis that the dividends were required to be treated as his income on the ground that he had not divested himself absolutely of the shares in favour of the College, and consequently did not enjoy the exemption from surtax provided for by section 415 (1) (*d*) and (2) of the Income Tax Act 1952.

The Commissioners of Inland Revenue based their claim to surtax on two grounds: first, that section 53 (1) (*c*) of the Law of Property Act 1925 was applicable but had not been complied with, since the taxpayer had not made a separate written disposition to the College of his equitable interest in the shares; and, secondly, that the option which Vandervell Trustees Ltd. received from the College was held by that company neither beneficially nor on the trusts of the family settlement, but on trust for the taxpayer.

---

[25] See J. G. Monroe, " After Grey and Oughtred " [1960] B.T.R. 17; [1960] C.L.J. 31 (J. W. A. Thornely). This case has been said to be authority for the view that " an instrument may be liable to *ad valorem* duty as a conveyance or transfer on sale when it operates as the completion of a pre-existing bargain although the property transferred by the instrument is not the same property as that which was the subject of the earlier bargain provided that the former does in truth and in reality ' represent ' the latter ": *Henty & Constable Ltd.* v. *I.R.C.* [1961] 1 W.L.R. 1504, 1510 (Lord Denning M.R.).

On the second point their Lordships (Lords Reid and Donovan dissenting) held (affirming the decision of the Court of Appeal [26] and of Plowman J.) that the option was vested in Vandervell Trustees Ltd. either on trusts to be subsequently declared or on trusts which were at present undefined and on either basis the result was that it was held on a resulting trust for the taxpayer, whose assessment to surtax had therefore been properly made.

The following extracts from the speeches in the House of Lords concern the first point, namely whether the transfer by the bank of the legal title to the shares carried with it the equitable interest of the tax-payer without any separate written disposition by him.

LORD UPJOHN: ". . . the object of the section, as was the object of the old Statute of Frauds, is to prevent hidden oral transactions in equitable interests in fraud of those truly entitled, and making it diffi-cult, if not impossible, for the trustees to ascertain who are in truth the beneficiaries. When the beneficial owner, however, owns the whole beneficial estate and is in a position to give directions to his bare trustee with regard to the legal as well as the equitable estate there can be no possible ground for invoking the section where the beneficial owner wants to deal with the legal estate as well as the equitable estate.

"I cannot agree with Diplock L.J. that prima facie a transfer of the legal estate carries with it the absolute beneficial interest in the property transferred; this plainly is not so, *e.g.*, the transfer may be on a change of trustee; it is a matter of intention in each case. If, however, the intention of the beneficial owner in directing the trustee to transfer the legal estate to X is that X should be the beneficial owner, I can see no reason for any further document or further words in the document assigning the legal estate also expressly transferring the beneficial interest; the greater includes the less. X may be wise to secure some evidence that the beneficial owner intended him to take the beneficial interest in case his beneficial title is challenged at a later date but it certainly cannot, in my opinion, be a statutory requirement that to effect its passing there must be some writing under section 53 (1) (*c*).

"Counsel for the Crown admitted that where the legal and beneficial estate was vested in the legal owner and he desired to transfer the whole legal and beneficial estate to another he did not have to do more than transfer the legal estate and he did not have to comply with section 53 (1) (*c*); and I can see no difference between that case and this.

"As I have said, that section is, in my opinion, directed to cases where dealings with the equitable estate are divorced from the legal estate and I do not think any of their Lordships in *Grey* v. *I.R.C.*[27] and *Oughtred* v. *I.R.C.*[28] had in mind the case before your Lordships.

---

[26] [1966] Ch. 261; [1965] 2 All E.R. 37.
[27] [1960] A.C. 1.   [28] [1960] A.C. 206.

To hold the contrary would make assignments unnecessarily complicated; if there had to be assignments in express terms of both legal and
equitable interests that would make the section more productive of
injustice than the supposed evils it was intended to prevent. . . ."

LORD DONOVAN: ". . . If, owning the entire estate, legal and
beneficial, in a piece of property, and desiring to transfer that entire
estate to another, I do so by means of a disposition which *ex facie*
deals only with the legal estate, it would be ridiculous to argue that
section 53 (1) (*c*) has not been complied with, and that therefore the
legal estate alone had passed. The present case, it is true, is different
in its facts in that the legal and equitable estates in the shares were in
separate ownership; but when the taxpayer, being competent to do so,
instructed the bank to transfer the shares to the College, and made
it abundantly clear that he wanted to pass, by means of that transfer,
his own beneficial, or equitable, interest, plus the bank's legal interest,
he achieved the same result as if there had been no separation of the
interests. The transfer thus made pursuant to his intentions and instructions was a disposition, not of the equitable interest alone, but of the
entire estate in the shares. In such a case I see no room for the operation
of section 53 (1) (*c*). . . ."

LORD WILBERFORCE: ". . . On November 14, 1958, the taxpayer's
solicitor received from the bank a blank transfer of the shares, executed
by the bank, and the share certificate. So at this stage the taxpayer
was the absolute master of the shares and only needed to insert his
name as transferee in the transfer and to register it to become the
full legal owner. He was also the owner in equity. On November
19, 1958, the solicitor . . . on behalf of the taxpayer, who intended
to make a gift, handed the transfer to the College, which, in due
course, sealed it and obtained registration of the shares in the College's
name. The case should then be regarded as one in which the taxpayer himself has, with the intention to make a gift, put the College
in a position to become the legal owner of the shares, which the
College in fact became. If the taxpayer had died before the College
had obtained registration, it is clear on the principle of *Re Rose* [29]
that the gift would have been complete, on the basis that he had
done everything in his power to transfer the legal interest, with an
intention to give, to the College. No separate transfer, therefore, of
the equitable interest ever came to or needed to be made and there
is no room for the operation of the subsection. What the position
would have been had there simply been an oral direction to the legal
owner (*viz.*, the bank) to transfer the shares to the College, followed
by such a transfer, but without any document in writing signed by the

---

[29] [1949] Ch. 78; *post*, pp. 138–143.

taxpayer as equitable owner, is not a matter which calls for consideration here.[30] . . ."

BANNISTER v. BANNISTER

Court of Appeal [1948] W.N. 261; 92 S.J. 377; [1948] 2 All E.R. 133
(Scott and Asquith L.JJ. and Jenkins J.)

One of the terms of an oral contract of sale of two cottages—Nos. 30 and 31, Maryland Cottages, Mountnessing, Essex—was that the purchaser would allow the vendor to live in one of the cottages as long as she liked rent-free. The conveyance made no mention of this undertaking. The purchaser paid £250 for the cottages which the evidence showed to be worth £400. Subsequently the purchaser brought an action against the vendor for the recovery of possession of No. 30, which the vendor occupied, in order to be able to sell it with vacant possession. His Honour Judge Pratt at Brentwood County Court found as a fact that the vendor would not have sold the cottages to the purchaser at such a bargain price but for the purchaser's undertaking, that there was no fraud on the purchaser's part at the time of the conveyance, but that there was nevertheless a constructive trust under which the purchaser held No. 30 in trust for the vendor during her life. He accordingly dismissed the claim for possession and the purchaser appealed.

SCOTT L.J.: " The conclusion thus reached by the learned county court judge was attacked in this court on substantially the following three grounds: First, it was said that the oral undertaking found by the learned county court judge to have formed part of the agreement—namely, that the plaintiff would let the defendant stay in No. 30 as long as she liked rent-free—did not, as a matter of construction of the language used, amount to a promise that the defendant should retain a life interest in No. 30, but amounted merely to a promise that the plaintiff would allow the defendant to remain in No. 30 rent-free as his tenant at will. Secondly, it was said that, even if the terms of the oral undertaking were such as to amount to a promise that the defendant should retain a life interest in No. 30, a tenancy at will free of rent was, nevertheless, the greatest interest she could claim in view of the absence of writing and the provisions of sections 53 and 54 of the Law of Property Act 1925. Thirdly, it was said that a constructive trust in favour of the defendant (which the absence of writing admittedly would not defeat) could only be raised by findings to the effect that there was actual fraud on the part of the plaintiff and that the property was sold and conveyed to him on the faith of an express oral declaration of trust which it would be fraudulent in him to deny. It was, accordingly, submitted that the learned county court judge's conclusion that there was a constructive trust could not stand since it was negatived by his findings that there

---

[30] See valuable surveys by Gareth Jones [1966] C.L.J. 19–25 and S. M. Spencer (1967) 31 Conv.(N.S.) 175–181.

was no fraud in the case and by the absence of any evidence of anything amounting to an express oral declaration of trust.

"In support of the first of these three objections reliance was placed on *Buck* v. *Howarth*,[31] in which a King's Bench Divisional Court held that the occupant of a house who had been told by a predecessor in title of the freeholder 'that he could live in the house until he died' (an oral and, it would seem, a purely voluntary promise) was given an uncertain interest in the premises and that the law would presume a tenancy at will, with the result that proceedings under the Small Tenements Recovery Act 1838 could be taken. That was, obviously, a very different case from the present one and we find ourselves unable to derive any assistance from it. The promise was a purely voluntary one, and any court would naturally have been slow to construe it as intended to confer a life interest, even if it was literally capable of that construction. Moreover, whatever the words may have meant, the case clearly fell within section 54 of the Law of Property Act 1925, under which interests in land created by parol have the force and effect of interests at will only. There was, of course, no question of a resulting trust as there might have been if the occupant of the house had been a former owner who had sold the freehold on the faith of a similar promise. In the present case the defendant did, on the facts found sell and convey the property on the faith of the oral undertaking and would not otherwise have done so, and the undertaking must be assumed to have been regarded as reserving to her a benefit worth at least £150 or three-eighths of the contemporary market value of the property without vacant possession. We, therefore, see no reason why the words of the undertaking should not be given the most favourable construction, from the defendant's point of view, of which they are properly capable. Similar words in deeds and wills have frequently been held to create a life interest determinable (apart from the special considerations introduced by the Settled Land Act 1925) on the beneficiary ceasing to occupy the premises: see, *e.g.*, *Re Carne's Settled Estate* [32] and *Re Boyer's Settled Estates.*[33]   In our view, that is the meaning which should, in the circumstances of the present case, be placed on the words of the oral undertaking found by the learned county court judge to have been given by the plaintiff. We are, accordingly, of opinion that the first objection fails, though the interest promised to the defendant by the plaintiff must, we think, be taken to have been a life interest determinable on her ceasing to occupy No. 30 and not a life interest simpliciter as held by the learned county court judge.

"As will be seen from what is said below, the second objection (based on want of writing) in effect stands or falls with the third, and it will, therefore, be convenient to deal with that next. It is, we think, clearly a mistake to suppose that the equitable principle on which a

---

[31] [1947] 1 All E.R. 342.
[32] [1899] 1 Ch. 324.   [33] [1916] 2 Ch. 404.

constructive trust is raised against a person who insists on the absolute character of a conveyance to himself for the purpose of defeating a beneficial interest, which, according to the true bargain, was to belong to another, is confined to cases in which the conveyance itself was fraudulently obtained. The fraud which brings the principle into play arises as soon as the absolute character of the conveyance is set up for the purpose of defeating the beneficial interest, and that is the fraud to cover which the Statute of Frauds or the corresponding provisions of the Law of Property Act 1925 cannot be called in aid in cases in which no written evidence of the real bargain is available. Nor is it, in our opinion, necessary that the bargain on which the absolute conveyance is made should include any express stipulation that the grantee is in so many words to hold as trustee. It is enough that the bargain should have included a stipulation under which some sufficiently defined beneficial interest in the property was to be taken by another. The above propositions are, we think, clearly borne out by the cases to which we were referred of *Booth* v. *Turle*,[34] *Chattock* v. *Muller*,[35] *Re Duke of Marlborough*[36] and *Rochefoucauld* v. *Boustead*.[37] We see no distinction in principle between a case in which property is conveyed to a purchaser on terms that the entire beneficial interest in some part of it is to be retained by the vendor (as in *Booth* v. *Turle*[38]) and a case, like the present, in which property is conveyed to a purchaser on terms that a limited beneficial interest in some part of it is to be retained by the vendor. We are, accordingly, of opinion that the third ground of objection to the learned county court judge's conclusion also fails. His finding that there was no fraud in the case cannot be taken as meaning that it was not fraudulent in the plaintiff to insist on the absolute character of the conveyance for the purpose of defeating the beneficial interest which he had agreed the defendant should retain. The conclusion that the plaintiff was fraudulent, in this sense, necessarily follows from the facts found, and, as indicated above, the fact that he may have been innocent of any fraudulent intent in taking the conveyance in absolute form is for this purpose immaterial. The failure of the third ground of objection necessarily also destroys the second objection based on want of writing and the provisions of sections 53 and 54 of the Law of Property Act 1925. . . ." *Appeal dismissed.*[39]

PROBLEMS

1. Is the approach to Law of Property Act 1925, s. 53 in *Re Holt's Settlement, infra,* p. 533 consistent with the majority view in *Oughtred* v. *I.R.C., supra,* p. 57.

---

[34] (1873) L.R. 16 Eq. 182.   [35] (1878) 8 Ch.D. 177.
[36] [1894] 2 Ch. 133.
[37] [1897] 1 Ch. 196.
[38] *Supra* note 34.
[39] Followed by the Court of Appeal in *Binions* v. *Evans* [1972] Ch. 359. See further *Hodgson* v. *Marks* [1971] Ch. 892; *Ottoway* v. *Norman* [1972] Ch. 698, *infra,* p. 397; [1973] C.L.J. 123 (R. J. Smith); [1973] *Current Legal Problems* 17 (A. J. Oakley).

2. T1 and T2 hold property on trust for X. What formalities are required if:

    (i) X assigns his equitable interest to Y or to A and B on trust for Y;

    (ii) X directs T1 and T2 to hold the property on trust for Y;

    (iii) X contracts with Y to transfer his equitable interest to him;

    (iv) X declares himself a trustee of his interest for Y?

Does it matter if the property is land or personalty? Does it matter if the property were held on resulting trust for X?

CHAPTER 4

THE ESSENTIALS OF A TRUST

To create a trust the appropriate formalities must be observed and the
" three certainties " must be present *i.e.*, certainty of intention, certainty of
subject-matter and certainty of objects. Charitable trusts fall into a special
category and are dealt with in Chapter 6.

Section 1. Certainty of Intention: Precatory Trusts

Normally, the intention is clear by use of the word " trust " or some other
imperative formula. However, on the assumption that there is certainty of
subject-matter [1] and of objects,[2] the court will hold a " precatory " trust to
have been created if it considers that the precatory expressions used, studied
in relation to the document as a whole, impose an obligation.

Re WILLIAMS, WILLIAMS v. WILLIAMS

Court of Appeal [1897] 2 Ch. 12; 66 L.J.Ch. 485; 76 L.T. 600; 45 W.R.
519; 41 S.J. 452 (Lindley, A. L. Smith and Rigby L.JJ.)

A testator bequeathed his residuary real and personal estate
" unto my wife Lucy her heirs executors administrators and assigns
absolutely, in the fullest confidence that she will carry out my wishes
in the following particulars namely that she pays the premiums due and
to become due during her life in respect of the policy for £1,000 on
her own life and that she by her will leaves the moneys to become
due and payable under such policy and also the moneys to become
payable . . . under the £300 policy on my life to my daughter Lucy if
she survives my wife in trust for her sole and separate use. . . . "
The testator appointed his wife to be one of the executors and trustees
of his will. The testator's widow by her will gave the proceeds of the
policy on the testator's life to the daughter, and the proceeds of the
policy on her own life she bequeathed to another.

An originating summons raised the question whether the widow
was under any obligation with respect to the policy on her own life if
she accepted the benefits given to her by her husband's will (which she
had done). Romer J. held that she (the widow) took for her own benefit
all the property given to her by her husband's will. The daughter
appealed.

LINDLEY L.J.: " . . . There can be no doubt that equitable obligations,
whether trusts or conditions, can be imposed by any language which is
clear enough to show an intention to impose an obligation, and is

[1] *Wynne* v. *Hawkins* (1782) 1 Bro.C.C. 179, 180; Lord Eldon in *Morice* v. *Bishop of
  Durham* (1805) 10 Ves. 522, 536; *Briggs* v. *Penny* (1851) 3 Mac. & G. 546, 554;
  Fox v. *Fox* (1859) 27 Beav. 301, 302, Romilly M.R.; *infra*, p. 72.
[2] *Infra*, p. 73.

69

definite enough to enable the court to ascertain what the precise obligation is and in whose favour it is to be performed. There is also abundant
authority for saying that if property is left to a person in confidence
that he will dispose of it in a particular way as to which there is no
ambiguity, such words are amply sufficient to impose an obligation.
Nothing can be plainer than Lord Eldon's statement to this effect in
Wright v. *Atkyns.*[3] The books are full of cases decided in accordance
with this doctrine: see *Shovelton* v. *Shovelton,*[4] *Curnick* v. *Tucker,*[5]
Le Marchant v. *Le Marchant,*[6] in all of which the devise or bequest
was to the devisee or legatee absolutely. See also other cases cited in
Lewin on Trusts.[7] But still in each case the whole will must be looked at;
and unless it appears from the whole will that an obligation was intended
to be imposed, no obligation will be held to exist; yet, moreover, in some
of the older cases obligations were inferred from language which in
modern times would be thought insufficient to justify such an inference.

"It would, however, be an entire mistake to suppose that the old
doctrine of precatory trusts is abolished. Trusts—*i.e.*, equitable obligations to deal with property in a particular way—can be imposed by any
language which is clear enough to show an intention to impose them.

"The term 'precatory' only has reference to forms of expression.
Not only in wills but in daily life an expression may be imperative in
its real meaning, although couched in language which is not imperative
in form. A request is often a polite form of command. A trust is really
nothing except a confidence reposed by one person in another, and
enforceable in a court of equity. In one sense it is true to say that a
trust of property cannot be created by a person who is not entitled to
that property. But there is no difficulty in disposing of one's own
property upon condition, express or implied, that the person who takes
it shall do something himself, *e.g.*, shall dispose of his property in a
particular way indicated by the owner of the property which he accepts.
Moreover, a condition of this kind is enforceable in equity, and need
not amount to a common law condition—*i.e.*, a condition involving a
forfeiture of the property taken subject to the condition—if that condition is not performed.

"Instances of conditions enforceable in equity will be found in
Messenger v. *Andrewes,*[8] *Re Skingley,*[9] *Wright* v. *Wilkin.*[10] The whole
equitable doctrine of election, when a testator disposes of property
not his own, is based upon the principle that a court of equity will
enforce performance of implied conditions on which property is given
and accepted.

---

[3] (1823) Turn. & R. 143, 157.
[4] (1863) 32 Beav. 143.
[5] (1874) L.R. 17 Eq. 320.
[6] (1874) L.R. 18 Eq. 414.
[7] 9th ed., p. 137.
[8] (1828) 4 Russ. 478.
[9] (1851) 3 Mac. & G. 221.
[10] (1862) 2 B. & S. 232.

"Having made these preliminary observations, I return to the testator's will. He has in terms given his property to his wife absolutely in the confidence that she will herself leave the policy moneys by her will to her daughter, and he has appointed his wife and another person to be executors and trustees without indicating any duty which they are to perform as trustees as distinguished from executors. These circumstances show, and I think conclusively show, that he did not intend his wife to be tenant for life only of the £300 policy. The £1,000 policy not being payable until her own death, she cannot be tenant for life of that.

"The legal effect of a devise of real estate to a person in fee in confidence that he will leave it by will to somebody else was considered and to a great extent settled by the House of Lords in the celebrated case of *Wright* v. *Atkyns*.[11] . . . Lord St. Leonards in his work on the *Law of Property*, published in 1849, wrote as follows (see p. 375): ' The law as to the operation of words of recommendation, confidence, request, or the like, attached to an absolute gift, has in late times varied from the earlier authorities.[12] In nearly every recent case the gift has been held to be uncontrolled by the request or recommendation made, or confidence expressed. This undoubtedly simplifies the law, and it is not an unwholesome rule, that if a testator really means his recommendation to be imperative, he should express his intention in a mandatory form; but this conclusion was not arrived at without a considerable struggle.' The more modern authorities, from *Lambe* v. *Eames* [13] to *Re Hamilton*,[14] show how strong the tendency now is to recognise this sensible rule.

"The particularity with which the testator has stated what his wishes were removes all difficulty in giving effect to those wishes if they are expressed in language which is shown by the will to be intended to be imperative; but such particularity does not supply the want of imperative language. The testator has employed the same language with respect to his own policy as with respect to his wife's. He has shown no intention of imposing an obligation on her in respect of one of them and not in respect of the other. I feel great difficulty in holding that he has not left his own policy to her absolutely free from all trust and condition, and the difficulty of making any distinction between the two policies forces me to the conclusion that the widow is not put to her election as regards her own policy. I might not have come to this conclusion if he had not dealt with both policies in the same way, for to put her to her election as to her property does not fetter her enjoyment of his. The case is in my opinion one of great difficulty, and I am quite aware that there are decisions in the books which if followed would be in the daughter's favour. But our task is to construe the will before us, and other cases are useless for that purpose except

---

[11] (1823) Turn. & R. 143.

[12] The rule established by the earlier authorities is stated by Leach V.-C. in *Eade* v. *Eade* (1820) 5 Madd. 118, 121, as follows: " *A request or recommendation will raise a trust*, if the objects and the property are described with such certainty that the court can execute it."

[13] (1871) L.R. 6 Ch. 597.   [14] [1895] 2 Ch. 370.

so far as they establish some principle of law. There is no principle except to ascertain the intention of the testator from the words he has used, and to ascertain and give effect to the legal consequences of that intention when ascertained.

"Having given the case my best attention, I have arrived at the conclusion that the testator has not used language sufficiently clear to impose upon his widow an obligation to leave either policy to his daughter. I believe, further, that he has refrained from language imperative in its terms, such as upon trust or upon condition, and that he used the language which he did because he really intended to trust his widow's discretion with respect to his daughter, and not to provide for his daughter himself by putting a legal fetter on his widow's power of disposition of her own policy or of the property which he left her. I read the will as expressing a wish that his daughter should have both policies unless his widow should see reason for otherwise disposing of them, and I do not find in the will a command to his widow to leave the policies to his daughter if his widow should think right to dispose of them otherwise.

"The appeal ought, I think, to be dismissed." *Appeal dismissed.*[15]

Section 2. Certainty of Subject-matter [16]

SPRANGE v. BARNARD

Master of the Rolls (1789) 2 Bro.C.C. 585

A testatrix provided as follows: "This is my last will and testament at my death, for my husband Thomas Sprange, to bewill to him the sum of £300, which is now in the joint stock annuities, for his sole use; and, at his death, *the remaining part of what is left, that he does not want for his own wants and use,* to be divided between my brother John Crapps, my sister Wickenden, and my sister Bauden, to be equally divided between them." The stock being vested in trustees, Thomas Sprange

---

[15] *Re Williams* is really no authority on precatory trusts (for the husband could not create a trust of his wife's property), although a question of precatory trust might have been raised with respect to the policy on the husband's life if *that* had been bequeathed by the wife to someone other than the daughter; but the case contains a statement of the principles which govern such trusts. See also Stuart V.-C. in *Lomax* v. *Ripley* (1855) 3 Sm. & Giff. 48, 78; *Re Conolly* [1910] 1 Ch. 219, 221–222; *Comiskey* v. *Bowring-Hanbury* [1905] A.C. 84; *Re Barton* (1932) 48 T.L.R. 205 *Re Adams and the Kensington Vestry* (1884) 27 Ch.D. 394; *Commissioner of Stamp Duties* v. *Julliffe* (1920) 28 C.L.R. 178. For an abortive attempt to create a precatory trust by the use of the word "request," see *Re Johnson* [1939] 2 All E.R. 458; for a successful one, see *Re Steele's Will Trusts* [1948] Ch. 603, where it was held that a rather unusual formula for disposing of jewellery which Page-Wood V.-C. in *Shelley* v. *Shelley* (1868) L.R. 6 Eq. 540 had held to create a trust was also apt to create a trust since it was likely that the professional draftsman had the earlier decision in mind: (1968) 32 Conv.N.S. 361 (P. St. John Langan).

[16] See also *Cruwys* v. *Colman* (1804) 9 Ves. 319, 323; *Horwood* v. *West* (1823) 1 Sim. & St. 389; *Curtis* v. *Rippon* (1820) 5 Madd. 434; *Cowman* v. *Harrison* (1852) 17 Jur.(o.s.) 313; *Palmer* v. *Simmonds* (1854) 2 Drew. 221, 227; *Flint* v. *Hughes* (1843) 1 L.T.(o.s.) 311; *Boyce* v. *Boyce* (1849) 16 Sim. 476; generally (1940) 4 M.L.R. 20 (Glanville Williams).

applied to them for payment, but they refused; whereupon he filed
this bill.

ARDEN M.R.: ". . . The words are a bequest of the £300 South
Sea annuities to his [Thomas Sprange's] sole use; and '. . . at his death,
the remaining part of what is left, that he does not want for his own
wants,' to the brother and sisters. The husband has taken out administration and filed his bill for the sum. It is contended, for the persons
to whom it is given in remainder, that he shall only have it for his
life, and that the words are strictly mandatory on him to dispose of
it in a certain way; but it is only to dispose of what he has no occasion
for: therefore the question is whether he may not call for the whole;
and it seems to be perfectly clear on all the authorities that he may.
I agree with the doctrine in *Pierson* v. *Garnet*,[17] following the cases of
Harland v. *Trigg* [18] and *Wynne* v. *Hawkins*,[19] *that the property, and
the person to whom it is to be given, must be certain* in order to raise a
trust. Now here the property is wasting, as it is only what shall remain
at his death . . .[20] It is contended that the court ought to impound
the property; but it appears to me to be a trust which would be impossible
to be executed. I must therefore declare him to be absolutely entitled
to the £300, and decree it to be transferred to him. The costs to come
out of the £300." [21]

Section 3. Certainty of Objects and Administrative Workability

Prior to the radical decision in *McPhail* v. *Doulton, infra,* a distinction had
to be drawn between trusts and powers for certainty purposes. Since trusts,
even if discretionary, *have* to be carried out by trustees it must be possible
in default for the courts to enforce and control the trust: for this reason
there must be no linguistic or semantic uncertainty in the expression of the
objects nor can the objects be such that the trust is administratively un-

---

[17] (1787) 2 Bro.C.C. 226.

[18] (1782) 1 Bro.C.C. 142.

[19] (1782) 1 Bro.C.C. 179.

[20] This should read: " Now here the property, so far from being certain, is only what
shall remain at his death ": 29 E.R. 322. In regard to such property see the vali-
dating " floating trust " approach in the case of secret trusts and mutual wills:
Ottaway v. *Norman* [1972] Ch. 698, *infra*, p. 397, indorsing dicta in *Birmingham* v.
Renfrew (1937) 57 C.L.R. 666, 689, *infra*, p. 423.

[21] See also *In the Estate of Last* [1958] P. 137; bequest to the testatrix' brother of
" everything I have. . . . At his death anything that is left, that came from me to
go to my late husband's grandchildren." Held by Karminski J. that in spite of the
words " anything that is left " the testatrix intended to give a life interest only to
her brother, with the result that on his death the grandchildren were entitled.
Quaere whether the result would have been the same if during his lifetime the
brother had applied to the court for the determination of the question whether
the bequest to him was absolute; *Bromley* v. *Tryon* [1952] A.C. 265, where the
House of Lords upheld a *defeasance clause* which provided that if X became entitled
to the possession or the receipt of the rents and profits of a specified estate, or
the bulk thereof, his interest in the settled estate should determine; *Re Golay* [1965]
2 All E.R. 660; 81 L.Q.R. 481 (R. E. M.); bequest of " a reasonable income "
sufficiently certain. *Cf.* " reasonable price " or " reasonable rent " in *Talbot* v.
Talbot [1968] Ch. 1; *Smith* v. *Morgan* [1971] 1 W.L.R. 803; *Brown* v. *Gould*
[1972] Ch. 53; *Kings Motors Ltd.* v. *Lax* [1970] 1 W.L.R. 426.

workable.   It was considered that if trustees failed to carry out a discretionary trust then since it would be invidious and injudicial for the courts
to distinguish between the possible discretionary beneficiaries the court
would have to act on the maxim. "Equality is equity" and distribute the
trust assets equally.   It followed that for an equal division it must be
possible to draw up a comprehensive list of the beneficiaries.   Accordingly,
trusts failed for uncertainty if such a list could not be drawn up.[22]

On the other hand, where powers are concerned, so long as the trustees
consider whether or not to exercise the powers and do not go beyond the
scope of the powers the courts cannot intervene unless the trustees can be
shown to have acted mala fide or capriciously.   It is purely up to the
trustees whether or not they exercise the powers so all that is required is that
they are in a proper position to consider the exercise of the powers, *i.e.* if
they can say with certainty of any given person that he is or is not within
the scope of the power: *Re Gulbenkian's S.T., infra*, rejecting the view expressed in the Court of Appeal that it suffices if the trustees can say of any
one person with certainty that he is within the scope of the power though
uncertainty may exist in respect of other persons.   Accordingly, a power
fails for uncertainty only if the court cannot with certainty determine
whether any given individual is or is not within the scope of the power.

In *McPhail* v. *Doulton, infra*, the House of Lords held by a 3 : 2 majority
that the *Gulbenkian* test for powers is also the appropriate test for discretionary trusts as it was possible for the court to carry out a discretionary
trust by distributing the trust assets not equally amongst all possible
beneficiaries (surely the last thing the settlor ever intended) but in such
proportions as appropriate in all the circumstances.   The case was then
remitted for determination whether on this basis the trust was valid or void
for uncertainty.   In *Re Baden's Deed Trusts (No. 2), infra*, the Court of
Appeal unanimously held the trust valid, but the difference of approach to
applying the new test between (1) Sachs and Megaw L.JJ. and (2) Stamp
L.J. heralds further difficulties to be resolved at some future date by the
House of Lords: see (1972) 36 Conv. 351.

It should be noted that the old comprehensive list test still applies to
fixed trusts, *e.g.* a trust of £100,000 to be divided equally between the
employees of the Z Co. Ltd., and their dependents and relatives.   The
Gulbenkian test applies to discretionary trusts and to powers.   In this connection when reading cases it is important to note that "trust powers,"
"powers in the nature of a trust" and "discretionary trusts" are essentially
synonymous.   What are really powers are variously called "mere powers,"
"bare powers" or "collateral powers."   They may be "general powers"
if the donor has power to appoint to anyone or "special powers" if the
donor has power to appoint to a restricted class.

Nowadays, powers to add persons to the number of possible beneficiaries
under discretionary trusts are quite common in order to provide flexibility
for dealing with tax changes or changes in personal circumstances.   In
Blausten v. *I.R.C.*[23] a power for trustees with the previous consent in
writing of the settlor to appoint anyone other than the settlor into a specified

---

[22] *I.R.C.* v. *Broadway Cottages Trust* [1955] Ch. 20. For the effect of *McPhail* v.
   Doulton see generally (1971) 87 L.Q.R. 31 (J. W. Harris); (1974) 37 M.L.R. 245.
[23] [1972] Ch. 256, 271-273.

class of beneficiaries was held valid by the Court of Appeal as a power "not to introduce anyone in the world to the class but only anyone proposed by the trustees and approved by the settlor."[24] In *Re Manisty's Settlement*, *infra*, Templeman J. went so far as to hold valid a power to add anyone in the world other than members of an "Excepted Class" as defined in the settlement.

His judgment indicates that the test of administrative workability might well invalidate some provisions cast in the form of a trust which could be valid if cast in the form of a power. The basis for this lies in Lord Wilberforce's speech in *McPhail* v. *Doulton* making it clear that a wider and more comprehensive range of inquiry is called for in the case of discretionary trusts than in the case of powers since in the former there is a duty to carry out the trusts, which the court will itself perform if necessary, while in the latter all the trustees have to do is consider whether or not to exercise the powers. In the case of powers Templeman J. stated,[25] "the only 'control' exercisable by the court is the removal of the trustees and the only 'due administration' which can be 'directed' is an order requiring the trustees to consider the exercise of the power, and, in particular a request from a person within the ambit of the power."

At present the authority of *Re Manisty's Settlement* is a little doubtful so it is safest to couch the power to add as a power for the trustees to add to the class of beneficiaries anyone from a list of persons submitted to them by any existing beneficiary.[26]

Re GULBENKIAN'S SETTLEMENT TRUSTS

House of Lords [1970] A.C. 508; [1968] 3 W.L.R. 1127; [1968] 3 All E.R. 785.

Settlements were made including a special power for trustees to appoint in favour of Nubar Gulbenkian " and any wife and his children or remoter issue . . . and any person . . . in whose house or apartment or in whose company or under whose care or control or by or with whom [he] may from time to time be employed or residing," and with trusts in default of appointment.

The House of Lord unanimously upheld the power and (Lord Donovan reserving his opinion) rejected *obiter* the broad view expressed in the Court of Appeal [27] that a power was valid if any one person clearly fell within the scope of the power. The leading speech was given by Lord Upjohn.

LORD UPJOHN: "In a very careful argument counsel for the appellants advanced a number of points which he submitted showed there were fourteen cases where the trustees would have an impossible task to execute, but these alleged impossibilities can be classified I

---

[24] *Ibid.* 272.
[25] [1974] Ch. 17, 27–28. See p. 102 *infra*. Also (1974) 38 Conv. 269.
[26] If the list were to be submitted by the settlor it would be open to the Estate Duty Office to argue that this created a dutiable gift situation owing to the Finance Act 1940, s. 44. A beneficiary will normally do as the settlor wishes anyway.
[27] [1968] Ch. 126.

think under four headings; uncertainty on the meaning of—(i)
' residing '; (ii) persons ' with whom ' the son is residing; (iii) persons
' in whose company ' the son is residing; and (iv) persons ' under whose
care or control ' the son is residing.

My lords, on this matter I agree entirely with the Court of Appeal.[28]
Many difficult and borderline cases may occur in any one of these
situations. But mere difficulty is nothing to the point. If the trustees
feel difficulty or even doubt on the point the Court of Chancery is
available to solve it for them. It solves many such problems every
year. I cannot for myself see any insuperable difficulty arising in the
solution of any given state of affairs which would make it necessary to
hold that the relevant clause as I have construed it fails to comply with
the test. Of course I have not overlooked *Sifton* v. *Sifton*,[29] but that
was the entirely different case of a divesting clause. In my opinion,
this clause is not void for uncertainty, and the Court of Appeal[30] were
quite right to overrule the decision of Harman J., in *Re Gresham's
Settlements*,[31] where he held that a similar clause was void on that
ground.

My lords, that is sufficient to dispose of the appeal, but, as I have
mentioned earlier, the reasons of two members of the Court of Appeal
went further and have been supported by counsel for the respondents
with much force and so must be examined.

Lord Denning M.R.,[32] propounded a test in the case of powers
collateral, namely, that if you can say of one particular person meaning thereby, apparently, any one person only that he is clearly within
the category the whole power is good though it may be difficult to say
in other cases whether a person is or is not within the category, and
he supported that view by reference to authority. Winn L.J., said[33]
that where there was not a complete failure by reason of ambiguity
and uncertainty the court would give effect to the power as valid
rather than hold it defeated since it will not have wholly failed, which
put—though more broadly—the view expressed by Lord Denning M.R.
Counsel for the respondents in his second line of argument relied on
these observations as a matter of principle but he candidly admitted
that he could not rely on any authority. Moreover, Lord Denning
M.R., expressed the view[34] that the different doctrine with regard to
trust powers should be brought into line with the rule with regard to
conditions precedent and powers collateral. So I propose to make
some general observations on this matter.

If a donor (be he a settlor or testator) directs trustees to make

---

28 *Ibid.*
29 [1938] A.C. 656.
30 [1968] Ch. 126.
31 [1956] 2 All E.R. 193.
32 [1968] Ch. 126, 133, 134.
33 [1968] Ch. 126, 138.
34 [1968] Ch. 126, 138.

some specified provision for " John Smith," then to give legal effect to that provision it must be possible to identify " John Smith." If the donor knows three John Smiths then by the most elementary principles of law neither the trustees nor the court in their place can give effect to that provision; neither the trustees nor the court can guess at it. It must fail for uncertainty unless of course admissible evidence is available to point to a particular John Smith as the object of the donor's bounty.

Then, taking it one stage further, suppose the donor directs that a fund, or the income of a fund, should be equally divided between members of a class. That class must be as defined as the individual; the court cannot guess at it. Suppose the donor directs that a fund be divided equally between ' my old friends,' then unless there is some admissible evidence that the donor has given some special ' dictionary ' meaning to that phrase which enables the trustee to identify the class with sufficient certainty, it is plainly bad as being too uncertain. Suppose that there appeared before the trustees (or the court) two or three individuals who plainly satisfied the test of being among ' my old friends ' the trustees could not consistently with the donor's intentions accept them as claiming the whole or any defined part of the fund. They cannot claim the whole fund for they can show no title to it unless they prove they are the only members of the class which of course they cannot do, and so, too, by parity of reasoning they cannot claim any defined part of the fund and there is no authority in the trustees or the court to make any distribution among a smaller class than that pointed out by the donor. The principle is, in my opinion, that the donor must make his intention sufficiently plain as to the object of his trust and the court cannot give effect to it by misinterpreting his intentions by dividing the fund merely among those present. Secondly, and perhaps it is the most hallowed principle, the Court of Chancery, which acts in default of trustees, must know with sufficient certainty the objects of the beneficence of the donor so as to execute the trust. Then, suppose the donor does not direct an equal division of his property among the class but gives a power of selection to his trustees among the class; exactly the same principles must apply. The trustees have a duty to select the donees of the donor's bounty from among the class designated by the donor; he has not entrusted them with any power to select the donees merely from among known claimants who are within the class, for that is constituting a narrower class and the donor has given them no power to do this.

So if the class is insufficiently defined the donor's intentions must in such cases fail for uncertainty. Perhaps I should mention here that it is clear that the question of certainty must be determined as of the date of the document declaring the donor's intention (in the case of a will, his death). Normally the question of certainty will arise because of the ambiguity of definition of the class by reason of the language employed by the donor, but occasionally owing to some of the curious settlements executed in recent years it may be quite impossible to construct even with all the available evidence anything like a class capable of definition (*Re Sayer Trust* [35]), though difficulty in doing so will not defeat the donor's intentions (*Re Hain's Settlement* [36]).   But I should add this: if the class is sufficiently defined by the donor the fact that it may be difficult to ascertain the whereabouts or continued existence of some of its members at the relevant time matters not.   The trustees can apply to the court for directions to pay a share into court.

But when mere or bare powers are conferred on donees of the power (whether trustees or others) the matter is quite different.   As I have already pointed out, the trustees have no duty to exercise it in the sense that they cannot be controlled in any way.   If they fail to exercise it then those entitled in default of its exercise are entitled to the fund.   Perhaps the contrast may be put forcibly in this way: in the first case it is a mere power to distribute with a gift over in default; in the second case it is a trust to distribute among the class defined by the donor with merely a power of selection within that class.   The result is in the first case even if the class of appointees among whom the donees of the power may appoint is clear and ascertained and they are all of full age and sui juris, nevertheless they cannot compel the donees of the power to exercise it in their collective favour.   If, however, it is a trust power, then those entitled are entitled (if they are of full age and sui juris) to compel the trustees to pay the fund over to them, unless the fund is income and the trustees have power to accumulate for the future.

Again the basic difference between a mere power and a trust power is that in the first case trustees owe no duty to exercise it and the relevant fund or income falls to be dealt with in accordance with the trusts in default of its exercise, whereas in the second case the trustees *must* exercise the power and in default the court will.   It is briefly summarised in 30 *Halsbury's Laws* (3rd Edn.), p. 241, para. 445:

> '. . . the court will not . . . compel trustees to exercise a purely discretionary power given to them; but will restrain the trustees from exercising the power improperly, and if it is coupled with a duty . . . can compel the trustees to perform their duty.'

It is a matter of construction whether the power is a mere power or a trust power and the use of inappropriate language is not decisive (*Wilson* v. *Turner* [37]).

So, with all respect to the contrary view, I cannot myself see how, consistently with principle, it is possible to apply to the execution of a trust power the principles applicable to the permissible exercise by the

---

[35] [1957] Ch. 423.
[36] [1961] 1 All E.R. 848.
[37] (1883) 22 Ch.D. 521, 525.

donees, even if the trustees of mere powers; that would defeat the intention of donors completely.

But with respect to mere powers, while the court cannot compel the trustees to exercise their powers, yet those entitled to the fund in default must clearly be entitled to restrain the trustees from exercising it save among those within the power. So the trustees, or the court, must be able to say with certainty who is within and who is without the power. It is for this reason that I find myself unable to accept the broader proposition advanced by Lord Denning M.R., and Winn L.J., mentioned earlier, and agree with the proposition as enunciated in *Re Gestetner* [38] and the later cases.

My lords, I would dismiss these appeals." *Appeals dismissed.*

McPHAIL v. DOULTON

House of Lords [1971] A.C.; [1970] 2 W.L.R. 1110; [1970] 2 All E.R. 228.

The facts and the issues appear clearly in the following speech of Lord Wilberforce with which Lord Reid and Viscount Dilhorne concurred though dissenting speeches were delivered by Lords Hodson and Guest.

LORD WILBERFORCE: " My Lords, this appeal is concerned with the validity of a trust deed dated July 17, 1941, by which Mr. Bertram Baden established a fund for the benefit, broadly, of the staff of the respondent company Matthew Hall & Co. Ltd. Mr. Baden died in 1960 and the appellants are the executors of his will. They claim that the trust deed is invalid and that the assets transferred to the trustees by their testator revert to his estate. The trusts established by the deed are of a general type which has recently become common, the beneficiaries including a wide class of persons among whom the trustees are given discretionary powers or duties of distribution. It is the width of the class which in this, and in other cases before the courts, has given rise to difficulty and to the contention that the trusts are too indefinite to be upheld.

The trust deed begins with a recital that the settlor desired to establish a fund for providing benefits for the staff of the company and their relatives or dependants. The critical clauses are as follows:

'9. (a) The Trustees shall apply the net income of the Fund in making at their absolute discretion grants to or for benefit of any of the officers and employees or ex-officers or ex-employees of the Company or to any relatives or dependants of any such persons in such amounts at such times and on such conditions (if any) as they think fit and any such grant may at their discretion be made by payment to the beneficiary or to any institution or person to be applied for his or her benefit and in the latter case

---
[38] [1953] Ch. 672.

the Trustees shall be under no obligation to see to the application of the money,

'(b) The Trustees shall not be bound to exhaust the income of any year or other period in making such grants as aforesaid and any income not so applied shall be dealt with as provided by clause 6 (a) hereof.

'[Clause 6 (a). All moneys in the hands of the Trustees and not required for the immediate service of the Fund may be placed in a deposit or current account with any Bank or Banking house in the name of the Trustees or may be invested as hereinafter provided.]

'(c) The Trustees may realise any investments representing accumulations of income and apply the proceeds as though the same were income of the Fund and may also (but only with the consent of all the Trustees) at any time prior to the liquidation of the Fund realise any other part of the capital of the Fund which in the opinion of the Trustees it is desirable to realise in order to provide benefits for which the current income of the Fund is insufficient.

'10. All benefits being at the absolute discretion of the Trustees, no person shall have any right title or interest in the Fund otherwise than pursuant to the exercise of such discretion, and nothing herein contained shall prejudice the right of the Company to determine the employment of any officer or employee.'

Clause 11 defines a perpetuity period within which the trusts are, in any event, to come to an end and clause 12 provides for the termination of the fund. On this event the trustees are directed to apply the fund in their discretion in one or more of certain specified ways of which one is in making grants as if they were grants under clause 9 (a). . . .

In this House, the appellants contended, and this is the first question for consideration, that the provisions of clause 9 (a) constitute a trust and not a power. If that is held to be the correct result, both sides agree that the case must return to the Chancery Division for consideration, on this footing, whether this trust is valid. But here comes a complication. In the present state of authority, the decision as to validity would turn on the question whether a complete list (or on another view a list complete for practical purposes) can be drawn up of all possible beneficiaries. This follows from the Court of Appeal's decision in *Inland Revenue Comrs.* v. *Broadway Cottages Trust* [39] as applied in later cases by which, unless this House decides otherwise, the Court of Chancery would be bound. The respondents invite your Lordships to review this decision and challenge its correct-

---

[39] [1955] Ch. 20.

ness. So the second issue which arises, if clause 9 (a) amounts to a trust, is whether the existing test for its validity is right in law and if not, what the test ought to be.

Before dealing with these two questions some general observations, or reflections, may be permissible. It is striking how narrow and in a sense artificial is the distinction, in cases such as the present, between trusts or as the particular type of trust is called, trust powers, and powers. It is only necessary to read the learned judgments in the Court of Appeal [40] to see that what to one mind may appear as a power of distribution coupled with a trust to dispose of the undistributed surplus, by accumulation or otherwise, may to another appear as a trust for distribution coupled with a power to withhold a portion and accumulate or otherwise dispose of it. A layman and, I suspect, also a logician, would find it hard to understand what difference there is.

It does not seem satisfactory that the entire validity of a disposition should depend on such delicate shading. And if one considers how in practice reasonable and competent trustees would act, and ought to act, in the two cases, surely a matter very relevant to the question of validity, the distinction appears even less significant. To say that there is no obligation to exercise a mere power and that no court will intervene to compel it, whereas a trust is mandatory and its execution may be compelled, may be legally correct enough, but the proposition does not contain an exhaustive comparison of the duties of persons who are trustees in the two cases. A trustee of an employees' benefit fund, whether given a power or a trust power, is still a trustee and he would surely consider in either case that he has a fiduciary duty; he is most likely to have been selected as a suitable person to administer it from his knowledge and experience, and would consider he has a responsibility to do so according to its purpose. It would be a complete misdescription of his position to say that, if what he has is a power unaccompanied by an imperative trust to distribute, he cannot be controlled by the court if he exercised it capriciously, or outside the field permitted by the trust (*cf. Farwell on Powers* [41]). Any trustee would surely make it his duty to know what is the permissible area of selection and then consider responsibly, in individual cases, whether a contemplated beneficiary was within the power and whether, in relation to other possible claimants, a particular grant was appropriate.

Correspondingly a trustee with a duty to distribute, particularly among a potentially very large class, would surely never require the preparation of a complete list of names, which anyhow would tell him little that he needs to know. He would examine the field, by class and category; might indeed make diligent and careful enquiries, depending on how much money he had to give away and the means at his disposal, as to the composition and needs of particular categories and of

---

[40] [1969] 2 Ch. 388.
[41] 3rd ed., 1916, p. 524.

individuals within them; decide on certain priorities or proportions, and then select individuals according to their needs or qualifications. If he acts in this manner, can it really be said that he is not carrying out the trust?

Differences there certainly are between trusts (trust powers) and powers, but as regards validity should they be so great as that in one case complete, or practically complete ascertainment is needed, but not in the other? Such distinction as there is would seem to lie in the extent of the survey which the trustee is required to carry out; if he has to distribute the whole of a fund's income, he must necessarily make a wider and more systematic survey than if his duty is expressed in terms of a power to make grants. But just as, in the case of a power, it is possible to underestimate the fiduciary obligation of the trustee to whom it is given, so, in the case of a trust (trust power), the danger lies in overstating what the trustee requires to know or to enquire into before he can properly execute his trust. The difference may be one of degree rather than of principle; in the well-known words of Sir George Farwell (*Farwell on Powers* [42]) trusts and powers are often blended, and the mixture may vary in its ingredients.

With this background I now consider whether the provisions of clause 9 (a) constitute a trust or a power. I do so briefly because this is not a matter on which I or, I understand, any of your Lordships have any doubt. Indeed, a reading of the judgments of Goff J. [43] and of the majority in the Court of Appeal [44] leaves the strong impression that, if it had not been for their leaning in favour of possible validity and the state of the authorities, these learned judges would have found in favour of a trust. Naturally read, the intention of the deed seems to me clear: clause 9 (a), whose language is mandatory ('shall'), creates, together with a power of selection, a trust for distribution of the income, the strictness of which is qualified by clause 9 (b) which allows the income of any one year to be held up and (under clause 6 (a)) either placed, for the time, with a bank, or, if thought fit, invested. Whether there is, in any technical sense an accumulation, seems to me in the present context a jejune enquiry; what is relevant is that clause 9 (c) marks the difference between 'accumulations' of income and the capital of the fund: the former can be distributed by a majority of the trustees, the latter cannot. As to clause 10, I do not find in it any decisive indication. If anything it seems to point in favour of a trust, but both this and other points of detail are insignificant in the face of the clearly expressed scheme of clause 9. I therefore agree with Russell L.J. and would to that extent allow the appeal, declare that the provisions of clause 9 (a) constitute a trust and remit the case to the Chancery Division for determination whether on this basis clause

[42] 3rd ed., 1916, p. 10.
[43] [1967] 1 W.L.R. 1457.
[44] [1969] 2 Ch. 388.

9 is (subject to the effects of section 164 of the Law of Property Act 1925) valid or void for uncertainty.

This makes it necessary to consider whether, in so doing, the court should proceed on the basis that the relevant test is that laid down in the *Broadway Cottages* case [45] or some other test. That decision gave the authority of the Court of Appeal to the distinction between cases where trustees are given a *power* of selection and those where they are bound by a *trust* for selection. In the former case the position, as decided by this House, is that the power is valid if it can be said with certainty whether any given individual is or is not a member of the class and does not fail simply because it is impossible to ascertain every member of the class. (The *Gulbenkian* case [46].) But in the latter case it is said to be necessary, for the trust to be valid, that the whole range of objects (I use the language of the Court of Appeal) should be ascertained or capable of ascertainment.

The respondents invited your Lordships to assimilate the validity test for trusts to that which applies to powers. Alternatively, they contended that in any event the test laid down in the *Broadway Cottages* case was too rigid, and that a trust should be upheld if there is sufficient practical certainty in its definition for it to be carried out, if necessary with the administrative assistance of the court, according to the expressed intention of the settlor. I would agree with this, but this does not dispense from examination of the wider argument. The basis for the *Broadway Cottages* case principle is stated to be that a trust cannot be valid unless, if need be, it can be executed by the court, and (though it is not quite clear from the judgment where argument ends and decision begins) that the court can only execute it by ordering an equal distribution in which every beneficiary shares. So it is necessary to examine the authority and reason for this supposed rule as to the execution of trusts by the court.

Assuming, as I am prepared to do for present purposes, that the test of validity is whether the trust can be executed by the court, it does not follow that execution is impossible unless there can be equal division. As a matter of reason, to hold that a principle of equal division applies to trusts such as the present is certainly paradoxical. Equal division is surely the last thing the settlor ever intended; equal division among all may, probably would, produce a result beneficial to none. Why suppose that the court would lend itself to a whimsical execution? And as regards authority, I do not find that the nature of the trust, and of the court's powers over trusts, calls for any such rigid rule. Equal division may be sensible and has been decreed, in cases of family trusts for a limited class, here there is life in the maxim 'equality is equity,' but the cases provide numerous examples where

[45] [1955] Ch. 20.
[46] [1970] A.C. 508.

this has not been so, and a different type of execution has been ordered, appropriate to the circumstances.

Moseley v. *Moseley*[47] is an early example, from the time of equity's architect, where the court assumed power (if the executors did not act) to nominate from the sons of a named person as it should think fit and most worthy and hopeful, the testator's intention being that the estate should not be divided. In *Clarke* v. *Turner*,[48] on a discretionary trust for relations, the court decreed conveyance to the heir at law judging it '... most reputable for the family, that the heir at law should have it.' In *Warburton* v. *Warburton*[49] on a discretionary trust to distribute between a number of the testator's children, the House of Lords affirmed a decree of Lord Keeper Wright that the eldest son and heir, regarded as necessitous, should have a double share, the court exercising its own discretionary judgment against equal division.

These are examples of family trusts but in *Richardson* v. *Chapman*[50] the same principle is shown working in a different field. There was a discretionary trust of the testator's ' options' (*viz.* rights of presentation to the benefices or dignities in the Church) between a number of named or specified persons, including present and former chaplains and other domestics; also ' my worthy friends and acquaintance, particularly ... the Reverend Doctor Richardson.' The House of Lords (reversing Lord Keeper Henley) set aside a ' corrupt' presentation and ordered the trustees to present Dr. Richardson as the most suitable person. The grounds of decision in this House, in accordance with the prevailing practice, were not reported, but it may be supposed that the reported argument was accepted that where the court sets aside the act of the trustee, it can at the same time decree the proper act to be done, not by referring the matter to the trustee's discretion, but by directing him to perform as a mere instrument the thing decreed.[51] This shows that the court can in a suitable case execute a discretionary trust according to the perceived intention of the truster. It is interesting also to see that it does not seem to have been contended that the trust was void because of the uncertainty of the words ' my worthy friends and acquaintance.' There was no doubt that Dr. Richardson came within the designation. In the time of Lord Eldon L.C., the Court of Chancery adopted a less flexible practice; in *Kemp* v. *Kemp*[52] Sir Richard Arden M.R. commenting on *Warburton* v. *Warburton* (' a very extraordinary case ') said that the court now disclaims the right to execute a power (i.e. a trust power) and gives the fund equally. But I do not think that this change

47 (1673) Rep.temp.Finch 53.
48 (1694) Freem.Ch. 198.
49 (1702) 4 Bro.Parl.Cas. 1.
50 (1760) 7 Bro.Parl.Cas. 318.
51 (1760) 7 Bro.Parl.Cas. 318, 326, 327.
52 (1801) 5 Ves. 849.

of attitude, or practice, affects the principle that a discretionary trust can, in a suitable case, be executed according to its merits and otherwise than by equal division. I prefer not to suppose that the great masters of equity, if faced with the modern trust for employees, would have failed to adapt their creation to its practical and commercial character. Lord Eldon L.C. himself, in *Morice* v. *Bishop of Durham*,[53] laid down clearly enough that a trust fails if the object is insufficiently described or if it cannot be carried out, but these principles may be fully applied to trust powers without requiring a complete ascertainment of all possible objects. His earlier judgment in the leading, and much litigated, case of *Brown* v. *Higgs*,[54] shows that he was far from fastening any rigid test of validity on trust powers. After stating the distinction, which has ever since been followed, between powers, which the court will not require the donee to execute, and powers in the nature of a trust, or trust powers, he says of the latter that if the trustee does not discharge it, the court will, to a certain extent, discharge the duty in his room and place. To support this, he cites *Harding* v. *Glyn*[55] an early case where the court executed a discretionary trust for 'relations' by distributing to the next of kin.

I dwell for a moment on this point because, not only was *Harding* v. *Glyn* described by Lord Eldon L.C. as having been treated as a clear authority in his experience for a long period, but the principle of it was adopted in several nineteenth century authorities. When the *Broadway Cottages Trust* case[56] came to be decided in 1955, these cases were put aside as anomalous[57] but I think they illustrate the flexible manner in which the court, if called on, executes trust powers for a class. At least they seem to prove that the supposed rule as to equal division does not rest on any principle inherent in the nature of a trust. They prompt one to ask why a practice, or rule, which has been long followed and found useful in 'relations' cases, should not also serve in regard to 'employees,' or 'employees and their relatives,' and whether a decision which says the contrary is acceptable.

I now consider the modern English authorities, particularly those relied on to show that complete ascertainment of the class must be possible before it can be said that a discretionary trust is valid. *Re Ogden, Brydon* v. *Samuel*[58] is not a case which I find of great assistance. The argument seems to have turned mainly on the question whether the trust was a purpose trust or a trust for ascertained objects. The latter was held to be the case and the court then held that all the objects of the discretionary gift could be ascertained. It is a weak authority for the requirement of complete ascertainment.

---

[53] (1805) 10 Ves. 522.
[54] (1803) 8 Ves. 561.
[55] (1739) 1 Atk. 469.
[56] [1955] Ch. 20.
[57] [1955] Ch. 20, 33, 35.
[58] [1953] Ch. 678.

The modern shape of the rule derives from *Re Gestetner (decd.)*, *Barnett* v. *Blumka*[59] where the judgment of Harman J., to his later regret, established the distinction between discretionary powers and discretionary trusts. The focus of this case was on powers. The judgment first establishes a distinction between, on the one hand, a power collateral, or appurtenant, or other power[60] '... which does not import a trust on the conscience of the donee' and on the other hand a trust imposing a duty to distribute. As to the first, the learned judge said[60]: '... I do not think it can be the law that it is necessary to know of all the objects in order to appoint to any one of them.' As to the latter he used these words[61]:

> '... it seems to me there is much to be said for the view that he must be able to review the whole field in order to exercise his judgment properly.'

He then considered authority on the validity of powers, the main stumbling block in the way of his own view being some words used by Fry J. in *Blight* v. *Hartnoll*,[62] which had been adversely commented on in *Farwell on Powers*, and I think it worthwhile quoting the words of his conclusion. He said[63]:

> 'The settlor had good reason to trust the persons whom he appointed as trustees, I have no doubt, but I cannot see that there is here such a duty as makes it essential for these trustees, before parting with any income or capital, to survey the whole field and consider whether A is more deserving of bounty than B. That is a task which is, and which much have been known to the settlor to be impossible, having regard to the ramifications of the persons who might be members of this class.
>
> 'If, therefore, there is no duty to distribute, but only a duty to consider, it does not seem to me that there is any authority binding on me to say that this whole trust ... is bad. In fact, as has been admitted, there is no difficulty in ascertaining whether any given postulant is a member of the specified class; if that could not be ascertained, the matter would be quite different, but of John Doe or Richard Roe it can be postulated whether he is or is not eligible to receive the settlor's bounty. There being no uncertainty in that sense, I am reluctant to introduce a notion of uncertainty in the other sense by saying that the trustees must survey the world from China to Peru when there are perfectly good objects of the class ... in England.'

Subject to one point which was cleared up in this House in *Re Gulbenkian's Settlement Trusts*,[64] all of this, if I may say so, seems

---

[59] [1953] Ch. 672.
[60] [1953] Ch. 672, 684.
[61] [1953] Ch. 672, 685.
[62] (1881) 19 Ch. 294, 300, 301.
[63] [1953] Ch. 672, 688.		[64] [1970] A.C. 508.

impeccably good sense, and I do not understand the learned judge to have later repented of it. If the judgment was in any way the cause of future difficulties, it was in the indication given—not by way of decision, for the point did not arise—that there was a distinction between the kind of certainty required for powers and that required for trusts. There is a difference perhaps but the difference is a narrow one, and if one is looking to reality one could hardly find better words than those I have just quoted to describe what trustees, in either case, ought to know. A second look at this case, while fully justifying the decision, suggests to me that it does not discourage the application of a similar test for the validity of trusts.

So I come to *Inland Revenue Comrs.* v. *Broadway Cottage Trusts.*[65] This was certainly a case of trust, and it proceeded on the basis of an admission, in the words of the judgment, ' that the class of " beneficiaries " is incapable of ascertainment.' In addition to the discretionary trust of income, there was a trust of capital for all the beneficiaries living or existing at the terminal date. This necessarily involved equal division and it seems to have been accepted that it was void for uncertainty since there cannot be equal division among a class unless all the members of the class are known. The Court of Appeal[65] applied this proposition to the discretionary trust of income, on the basis that execution by the court was only possible on the same basis of equal division. They rejected the argument that the trust could be executed by changing the trusteeship, and found the relations cases of no assistance as being in a class by themselves. The court could not create an arbitrarily restricted trust to take effect in default of distribution by the trustees. Finally they rejected the submission that the trust could take effect as a power; a valid power could not be spelt out of an invalid trust.

My Lords, it will have become apparent that there is much in this which I find out of line with principle and authority, but before I come to a conclusion on it, I must examine the decision of this House in *Re Gulbenkian's Settlement Trusts* on which the appellants placed much reliance as amounting to an endorsement of the *Broadway Cottages* case. But is this really so? That case was concerned with a power of appointment coupled with a gift over in default of appointment. The possible objects of the power were numerous and were defined in such wide terms that it could certainly be said that the class was unascertainable. The decision of this House was that the power was valid if it could be said with certainty whether any given individual was or was not a member of the class and did not fail simply because it was impossible to ascertain every member of the class. In so deciding, their Lordships rejected an alternative submission, to which countenance had been given in the Court of Appeal[66] that it was

65 [1955] Ch. 20.
66 [1968] Ch. 126.

enough that one person should certainly be within the class. So, as a matter of decision, the question now before us did not arise or nearly arise. However the opinions given were relied on, and strongly, as amounting to an endorsement of the 'complete ascertainment' test as laid down in the *Broadway Cottages* case.[67]

My Lords, I comment on this submission with diffidence, because three of those who were party to the decision are present here today, and will express their own views. But with their assistance, and with respect for their views, I must endeavour to appraise the appellants' argument. My noble and learned friend Lord Reid's opinion can hardly be read as an endorsement of the *Broadway Cottages* case. It is really the opinion of my noble and learned friend Lord Upjohn which has to be considered. Undoubtedly the main part of that opinion, as one would expect, was concerned to deal with the clause in question, which required careful construction, and with the law as to powers of appointment among a numerous and widely defined class. But having dealt with these matters the opinion continues with some general observations. I have considered these with great care and interest; I have also had the advantage of considering a detailed report of the argument of counsel on both sides who were eminent in this field. I do not find that it was contended on either side that the *Broadway Cottages* case was open to criticism—neither had any need to do so. The only direct reliance on it appears to have been to the extent of the fifth proposition,[68] which was relevant as referring to powers, but does not touch this case. It is consequently not surprising that my noble and learned friend Lord Upjohn nowhere expresses his approval of this decision and indeed only cites it, in the earlier portion, in so far as it supports a proposition as to powers. Whatever dicta therefore the opinion were found to contain, I could not, in a case where a direct and fully argued attack has been made on the *Broadway Cottages* case, regard them as an endorsement of it and I am sure that my noble and learned friend, had he been present here, would have regarded the case at any rate open to review. In fact I doubt very much whether anything his Lordship said was really directed to the present problem. I read his remarks as dealing with the suggestion that trust powers ought to be entirely assimilated to conditions precedent and powers collateral.[69] . . . What he is concerned with is to point to the contrast between powers and trusts which lies in the facultative nature of the one and the mandatory nature of the other, the conclusion being the rejection of the 'broader' proposition as to powers accepted by two members of the Court of Appeal. With this

---

[67] [1955] Ch. 20.

[68] [1955] Ch. 20, 31.

[69] Here Lord Wilberforce referred to passages of Lord Upjohn's speech already extracted in the case preceding this one. See pp. 78–79, *supra*.

in mind it becomes clear that the sentence so much relied on by the appellants will not sustain the weight they put on it. This is [70]:

> ' The trustees have a duty to select the donees of the donor's bounty from among the class designated by the donor; he has not entrusted them with any power to select the donees merely from among known claimants who are within the class, for that is constituting a narrower class and the donor has given them no power to do this.'

What this does say, and I respectfully agree, is that, in the case of a trust, the trustees must select from the class. What it does not say, as I read it, or imply, is that in order to carry out their duty of selection they must have before them, or be able to get, a complete list of all possible objects.

So I think that we are free to review the *Broadway Cottages* case.[71] The conclusion which I would reach, implicit in the previous discussion, is that the wide distinction between the validity test for powers and that for trust powers, is unfortunate and wrong, that the rule recently fastened on the courts by the *Broadway Cottages* case ought to be discarded, and that the test for the validity of trust powers ought to be similar to that accepted by this House in *Re Gulbenkian's Settlement Trusts* for powers, namely that the trust is valid if it can be said with certainty that any given individual is or is not a member of the class.

I am interested, and encouraged, to find that the conclusion I had reached by the end of the argument is supported by distinguished American authority. Professor Scott in his well-known book on Trusts [72] discusses the suggested distinction as regards validity between trusts and powers and expresses the opinion that this would be ' highly technical.' Later in the Second Restatement of Trusts [73] (which Restatement aims at stating the better modern view and which annotates the *Broadway Cottages* case) a common test of invalidity is taken, whether trustees are ' authorised ' or ' directed '; this is that the class must not be so indefinite that it cannot be ascertained whether any person falls within it. The reporter is Professor Austin Scott. In his Abridgement,[74] Professor Scott maintains the same position:

> ' It would seem . . . that if a power of appointment among the members of an indefinite class is valid, the mere fact that the testator intended not merely to confer a power but to impose a duty to make such an appointment should not preclude the making of such an appointment. It would seem to be the height of technicality . . .'

---

[70] [1968] 3 All E.R. at 793, [1968] 3 W.L.R. at 1138.
[71] [1955] Ch. 20.
[72] 1939, Vol. 1, s. 122, p. 613.
[73] 1959, s. 122.
[74] Abridgement of the Law of Trusts, 1960, s. 122.

Assimilation of the validity test does not involve the complete assimilation of trust powers with powers. As to powers, I agree with my
noble and learned friend Lord Upjohn in *Re Gulbenkian's Settlement*
that although the trustees may, and normally will, be under a fiduciary
duty to consider whether or in what way they should exercise their
power, the court will not normally compel its exercise. It will intervene if the trustees exceed their powers, and possibly if they are proved
to have exercised it capriciously. But in the case of a trust power, if
the trustees do not exercise it, the court will; I respectfully adopt as to
this the statement in Lord Upjohn's opinion.[75] I would venture to
amplify this by saying that the court, if called on to execute the trust
power, will do so in the manner best calculated to give effect to the
settlor's or testator's intentions. It may do so by appointing· new
trustees, or by authorising or directing representative persons of the
classes of beneficiaries to prepare a scheme of distribution, or even,
should the proper basis for distribution appear, by itself directing the
trustees so to distribute. The books give many instances where this has
been done and I see no reason in principle why they should not do so
in the modern field of discretionary trusts (see *Brunsden* v. *Wool-
redge*,[76] *Supple* v. *Lowson*,[77] *Liley* v. *Hey*[78] and Lewin on Trusts[79]).
Then, as to the trustees' duty of enquiry or ascertainment, in each case
the trustees ought to make such a survey of the range of objects or
possible beneficiaries as will enable them to carry out their fiduciary
duty (*cf. Liley* v. *Hey*). A wider and more comprehensive range of
enquiry is called for in the case of trust powers than in the case of
powers.

Two final points: first, as to the question of certainty, I desire to
emphasise the distinction clearly made and explained by Lord
Upjohn,[80] between linguistic or semantic uncertainty which, if unresolved by the court, renders the gift void, and the difficulty of
ascertaining the existence or whereabouts of members of the class, a
matter with which the court can appropriately deal on an application
for directions. There may be a third case where the meaning of the
words used is clear but the definition of beneficiaries is so hopelessly
wide as not to form 'anything like a class' so that the trust is
administratively unworkable or in Lord Eldon L.C.'s words one that
cannot be executed (*Morice* v. *Bishop of Durham*[81]). I hestitate to
give examples for they may prejudice future cases, but perhaps 'all
the residents of Greater London' will serve. I do not think that a
discretionary trust for 'relatives' even of a living person· falls within
this category. . . ."

---

75 [1970] A.C. 508, 525. See p. 78 *supra*.
76 (1765) Amb. 507.
77 (1773) Amb. 729.
78 (1842) 1 Hare 580.
79 16th ed., 1964, p. 630.
80 [1970] A.C. 508, 524. See p. 77 *supra*.   81 (1805) 10 Ves. at 527.

Appeal allowed. Declaration that the provisions of clause 9 (a) constituted a trust. Case remitted for determination whether on this basis clause 9 was (subject to the effects of section 164 of the Law of Property Act 1925) valid or void for uncertainty.

Re BADEN'S DEED TRUSTS (No. 2)

Court of Appeal [1973] Ch. 9; [1972] 3 W.L.R. 250; [1972] 2 All E.R. 1304.

Upon remittance Brightman J.[82] and the Court of Appeal held the power valid but there was a difference of approach in applying the test for certainty as shown by the following excerpts from the reserved judgments of the Court of Appeal.

SACHS L.J.: " . . . Once the class of persons to be benefited is conceptually certain it then becomes a question of fact to be determined on evidence whether any postulant has on enquiry been proved to be within it; if he is not so proved then he is not in it. That position remains the same whether the class to be benefited happens to be small (such as 'first cousins') or large (such as 'members of the X Trade Union' or 'those who have served in the Royal Navy'). The suggestion that such trusts could be invalid because it might be impossible to prove of a given individual that he was *not* in the relevant class is wholly fallacious—and only the persuasiveness of counsel for the defendant executors has prevented me from saying that the contention is almost unarguable."

MEGAW L.J.: " . . . The main argument of counsel for the defendant executors was founded on a strict and literal interpretation of the words in which the decision of the House of Lords in *Re Gulbenkian's Settlement Trust* [83] was expressed. That decision laid down the test for the validity of powers of selection. It is relevant for the present case, because in the previous excursion of this case to the House of Lords [84] it was held that there is no relevant difference in the test of validity, whether the trustees are given a power of selection or, as was held by their Lordships to be the case in this trust deed, a trust for selection. The test in either case is what may be called the *Gulbenkian* test. The *Gulbenkian* test, as expressed by Lord Wilberforce [85] (and again in almost identical words in a later passage [86]) is this:

'. . . the power is valid if it can be said with certainty whether any given individual is or is not a member of the class and does not fail simply because it is impossible to ascertain every member of the class.'

---

[82] [1972] Ch. 607. Would *Re Saxone Shoe Co. Ltd.'s Trust Deed* [1962] 1 W.L.R. 943 be decided differently nowadays?
[83] [1970] A.C. 508.
[84] [1971] A.C. 424.
[85] [1971] A.C. 424, 450.
[86] [1971] A.C. 424, 454.

The executors' argument concentrates on the words ' or is not ' in the first of the two limbs of the sentence quoted above: ' if it can be said with certainty whether any given individual is *or is not* a member of the class.' It is said that those words have been used deliberately, and have only one possible meaning; and that, however startling or drastic or unsatisfactory the result may be—and counsel for the defendant executors does not shrink from saying that the consequence is drastic—this court is bound to give effect to the words used in the House of Lords' definition of the test. It would be quite impracticable for the trustees to ascertain in many cases whether a particular person was *not* a relative of an employee. The most that could be said is: ' There is no proof that he is a relative.' But there would still be no ' certainty ' that such a person was not a relative. Hence, so it is said, the test laid down by the House of Lords is not satisfied, and the trust is void. For it cannot be said with certainty, in relation to any individual, that he is not a relative.

I do not think it was contemplated that the words ' or is not ' would produce that result. It would, as I see it, involve an incon-sistency with the latter part of the same sentence: ' does not fail simply because it is impossible to ascertain every member of the class.' The executors' contention, in substance and reality, is that it *does* fail ' simply because it is impossible to ascertain every member of the class.'

The same verbal difficulty, as I see it, emerges also when one considers the words of the suggested test which the House of Lords expressly rejected. That is set out by Lord Wilberforce in a passage [87] immediately following the sentence which I have already quoted. The rejected test was in these terms: ' . . . it is said to be necessary . . . that the whole range of objects . . . shall be ascertained or capable of ascertainment.' Since that test was rejected, the resulting affirmative proposition, which by implication must have been accepted by their Lordships, is this: a trust for selection will not fail simply because the whole range of objects cannot be ascertained. In the present case, the trustees could ascertain, by investigation and evidence, many of the objects; as to many other theoretically possible claimants, they could not be certain. Is it to be said that the trust fails because it cannot be said with certainty that such persons are not members of the class? If so, is that not the application of the rejected test; the trust failing because ' the whole range of objects cannot be ascertained? '

In my judgment, much too great emphasis is placed in the executors' argument on the words ' or is not.' To my mind, the test is satisfied if, as regards at least a substantial number of objects, it can be said with certainty that they fall within the trust; even though, as regards a substantial number of other persons, if they ever for some

---

[87] [1971] A.C. 424, 450. See p. 83 *supra*.

fanciful reason fell to be considered, the answer would have to be, not ' they are outside the trusts,' but ' it is not proven whether they are in or out.' What is a ' substantial number ' may well be a question of common sense and of degree in relation to the particular trust: particularly where, as here, it would be fantasy, to use a mild word, to suggest that any practical difficulty would arise in the fair, proper and sensible administration of this trust in respect of relatives and dependants.

I do not think that this involves, as counsel for the defendant executors suggested, a return by this court to its former view which was rejected by the House of Lords in the *Gulbenkian* case.[88] If I did so think, I should, however reluctantly, accept his argument and its consequences. But as I read it, the criticism in the House of Lords of the decision of this court in that case related to this court's acceptance of the view that it would be sufficient if it could be shown that *one single person* fell within the scope of the power or trust. The essence of the decision of the House of Lords in the *Gulbenkian* case, as I see it, is *not* that it must be possible to show with certainty that any given person is *or is not* within the trust; but that it is not, or may not be, sufficient to be able to show that one individual person is within it. If it does not mean that, I do not know where the line is supposed to be drawn, having regard to the clarity and emphasis with which the House of Lords has laid down that the trust does not fail because the whole range of objects cannot be ascertained. I would dismiss the appeal."

STAMP L.J.: ". . . Counsel for the defendant executors, fastening on those words, ' if it can be said with certainty that any given individual is or is not a member of the class,' submitted in this court that a trust for distribution among officers and employees or ex-officers or ex-employees or any of their relatives or dependants does not satisfy the test. You may say with certainty that any given individual is or is not an officer, employee, ex-officer or ex-employee. You may say with certainty that a very large number of given individuals are relatives of one of them; but, so the argument runs, you will never be able to say with certainty of many given individuals that they are not. I am bound to say that I had thought at one stage of counsel's able argument that this was no more than an exercise in semantics and that the phrase on which he relies indicated no more than that the trust was valid if there was such certainty in the definition of membership of the class that you could say with certainty that some individuals were members of it; that it was sufficient that you should be satisfied that a given individual presenting himself has or has not passed the test and that it matters not that having failed to establish his membership—here his relationship—you may, perhaps wrongly,

[88] [1970] A.C. 508.

reject him. There are, however, in my judgment serious difficulties in the way of a rejection of counsel's submission.

The first difficulty, as I see it, is that the rejection of counsel's submission involves holding that the trust is good if there are individuals—or even one—of whom you can say with certainty that he is a member of the class. That was the test adopted by and the decision of the Court of Appeal in the *Gulbenkian* case [89] where what was under consideration was a power of distribution among a class conferred on trustees as distinct from a trust for distribution: but when the *Gulbenkian* case came before the House of Lords that test was decisively rejected and the more stringent test on which counsel for the defendant executors insists was adopted. Clearly Lord Wilberforce in expressing the view that the test of validity of a discretionary trust ought to be similar to that accepted by the House of Lords in the *Gulbenkian* case did not take the view that it was sufficient that you could find individuals who were clearly members of the class; for he himself remarked, towards the end of his speech as to the trustees' duty of enquiring or ascertaining, that in each case the trustees ought to make such a survey of the range of objects or possible beneficiaries as will enable them to carry out their fiduciary duty. It is not enough that trustees should do nothing but distribute the fund among those objects of the trust who happen to be at hand or present themselves. Lord Wilberforce, after citing that passage which I have already quoted from the speech of Lord Upjohn in the *Gulbenkian* case,[90] put it more succinctly by remarking that what this did say (and he agreed) was that the trustes must select from the class, but that passage did not mean (as had been contended) that they must be able to get a complete list of all possible objects. I have already called attention to Lord Wilberforce's opinion that the trustees ought to make such a survey of the range of objects or possible beneficiaries as will enable them to carry out their fiduciary duty, and I ought perhaps to add that he indicated that a wider and more comprehensive range of enquiry is called for in the case of what I have called discretionary trusts than in the case of fiduciary powers. But, as I understand it, having made the appropriate survey, it matters not that it is not complete or fails to yield a result enabling you to lay out a list or particulars of every single beneficiary. Having done the best they can, the trustees may proceed on the basis similar to that adopted by the court where all the beneficiaries cannot be ascertained and distribute on the footing that they have been: see, for example, *Re Benjamin*.[91] What was referred to as 'the complete ascertainment test' laid down by this court in the *Broadway Cottages* case [92] is rejected. So also is

[89] [1968] Ch. 126.
[90] [1970] A.C. 508, 524.
[91] [1902] 1 Ch. 723.
[92] [1955] Ch. 20.

the test laid down by this court in the *Gulbenkian* case.[93] Validity or invalidity is to depend on whether you can say of any individual—and the accent must be on that word ' any,' for it is not simply the individual whose claim you are considering who is spoken of—that he ' is or is not a member of the class,' for only thus can you make a survey of the range of objects or possible beneficiaries.

If the matter rested there, it would in my judgment follow that, treating the word " relatives " as meaning descendants from a common ancestor, a trust for distribution such as is here in question would not be valid. Any ' survey of the range of objects or possible beneficiaries ' would certainly be incomplete, and I am able to discern no principle on which such a survey could be conducted or where it should start or finish. The most you could do, so far as regards relatives, would be to find individuals who are clearly members of the class—the test which was accepted in the Court of Appeal, but rejected in the House of Lords, in the *Gulbenkian* case.[94] The matter does not, however, rest there. . . . *Harding* v. *Glyn* [95] is authority endorsed by the decision of the House of Lords [96] that a discretionary trust for " relations " was a valid trust to be executed by the court by distribution to the next-of-kin. The class of beneficiaries thus becomes a clearly defined class and there is no difficulty in determining whether a given individual is within it or without it.

Does it then make any difference that here the discretionary trust for relations was a reference not to the relations of a deceased person but of one who was living? I think not. The next-of-kin of a living person are as readily ascertainable at any given time as the next-of-kin of one who is dead."

Appeal dismissed. Leave to appeal to the House of Lords refused.

Re MANISTY'S SETTLEMENT

Chancery Division [1974] Ch. 17; [1973] 3 W.L.R. 341; [1973] 2 All E.R. 1203.

Clause 4 (a) (iii) of a settlement executed in 1971 by Edward Manisty conferred on the trustees power to declare that any person(s), corporation(s) or charity(ies) (other than a member of the Excepted Class or one of the Trustees) should thenceforth for a specified period (not extending beyond the closing date) be included in the class of beneficiaries. The trustees purported to add the settlor's mother and any person who should be the widow (as opposed to wife) of the settlor.[97] The Excepted Class consisted of the settlor, the wife for the

[93] [1968] Ch. 126.
[94] [1968] Ch. 126; on appeal [1970] A.C. 508.
[95] (1739) 1 Atk. 469.
[96] [1971] A.C. 424, 452.
[97] The settlor's mother and widow are safe for tax purposes whilst the members of the excepted class are excepted from being beneficiaries for if they were beneficiaries this could be ruinous from a tax point of view.

time being of the settlor, any other person or corporation settling
property on the trusts of the settlement and the spouse of any such
other settlor.

Doubts having arisen as to the validity of the power the trustees
took out an originating summons to determine the question.

TEMPLEMAN J. (in a reserved judgment): " The power to add
beneficiaries and to benefit the persons so added is exercisable in
favour of anyone in the world except the settlor, his wife, the other
members of the Excepted Class for the time being and the trustees,
other than the settlor's brother Henry who was one of the original
beneficiaries. This is not a general power exercisable in favour of
anyone, nor a special power exercisable in favour of a class, but an
intermediate power exercisable in favour of anyone, with certain
exceptions.

." Counsel for the fourth and fifth defendants submits that an
intermediate power cannot be conferred on trustees because of
principles of non-delegation and uncertainty. The argument based on
the principle of non-delegation [98] stems from the proposition that a
testator must not delegate to other persons the right to make a will
for him. It is, however, established by authority that a testator, and
a fortiori a settlor, may create powers of disposition exercisable by
individuals or by trustees without thereby infringing any rule
against delegation. If delegation is the vice then delegation to an
individual is as bad as delegation to a trustee. But in *Re Park* [99]
Clauson J. held valid an intermediate power conferred by a testator
on an individual to appoint to anyone in the world, except the donee
of the power. If delegation is the vice then delegation to trustees by
means of a special power is as bad as delegation to trustees by means
of an intermediate power. But in *Re Gulbenkian's Settlement Trusts* [1]
the House of Lords held valid a special power conferred by a settlor
on trustees to benefit the settlor's son and his associates. To make
assurance double sure, in *Re Abrahams' Will Trusts* [2] Cross J. held
valid an intermediate power conferred by a testator on trustees to
appoint to anyone in the world except the trustees, and he expressly
rejected the argument based on the principle of non-delegation. I
conclude that the settlor in the present case was not precluded by the
doctrine of non-delegation from conferring an intermediate power on
his trustees.

" The argument based on uncertainty is that the trustees are under
a duty to consider from time to time whether and how to exercise their
powers, and that they cannot perform that duty, and a court cannot judge the performance of that duty, if the power is too wide.

[98] The width of the exceptions to the supposed principle of non-delegation to which
so much lip-service has been paid serves to cast doubt upon the existence of the
principle: see 5th ed. hereof, p. 113.
[99] [1932] 1 Ch. 580.
[1] [1970] A.C. 508.   [2] [1969] 1 Ch. 463, 474–476.

An intermediate power, it is said, is wider than any special power and is practically unlimited, and is therefore too wide, uncertain and invalid.

"Invalidity, based on uncertainty, was the subject of *Re Gulbenkian's Settlement Trusts*,[3] relating to special powers in favour of a class, and *McPhail* v. *Doulton*,[4] relating to discretionary trusts in favour of a class. Those authorities establish that such a power or trust is valid if it can be said with certainty that any given individual is or is not a member of the class. The principle of the rule thus established does not strike down an intermediate power provided that, having regard to the definition of excepted persons, it can be said with certainty that any given individual is or is not an object of the power. The principle for which counsel for the second defendant contends may be adopted from the summary of the effect of *Re Gulbenkian's Settlement Trusts* to be found in the dissenting speech of Lord Guest in *McPhail* v. *Doulton*[5] where he said:

'In the case of a power it is only necessary for the trustees to know whether a particular individual does or does not come within the ambit of the power.'

Counsel for the second defendant says, applying that principle to the present case, the definition of Excepted Class being certain, it follows that there is no uncertainty about the power.

"*Gulbenkian* and *McPhail* v. *Doulton* also establish, or rather reiterate, the rule that trustees of a power must consider from time to time whether and how to exercise the power, for in the words of Lord Reid in *Gulbenkian*[6]:

'A settlor or testator who entrusts a power to his trustees must be relying on them in their fiduciary capacity so they cannot simply push aside the power and refuse to consider whether it ought in their judgment to be exercised. And they cannot give money to a person who is not within the classes of persons designated by the settlor: the construction of the power is for the court.'

"In *McPhail* v. *Doulton*[7] Lord Wilberforce, referring to special powers, suggested:

'Any trustee would surely make it his duty to know what is the permissible area of selection and then consider responsibly, in individual cases, whether a contemplated beneficiary was within the power and whether, in relation to other possible claimants, a particular grant was appropriate.'

---

[3] [1970] A.C. 508.
[4] [1971] A.C. 424.
[5] [1971] A.C. 424, 445.
[6] [1970] A.C. 508, 518.
[7] [1971] A.C. 424, 449.

He added,[8] referring to special powers and to discretionary trusts in favour of a class, that ' in each case the trustees ought to make such a survey of the range of objects or possible beneficiaries as will enable them to carry out their fiduciary duty.'

" It is said that if a power is too wide the trustees cannot perform the duty reiterated in *Gulbenkian* and *McPhail* v. *Doulton* of considering from time to time whether and how to exercise the power and the court cannot determine whether or not the trustees are in breach of their duty. In my judgment, however, the mere width of a power cannot make it impossible for trustees to perform their duty nor prevent the court from determining whether the trustees are in breach. . . .

" I conclude from *Gestetner*,[9] *Gulbenkian*,[10] *McPhail* v. *Doulton* [11] and *Baden* (*No. 2*),[12] that a power cannot be uncertain merely because it is wide in ambit.

" An alternative argument against the validity of an intermediate power conferred on trustees is that a power which is not confined to individuals or to classes recognised by the court is too vague. An intermediate power which does not attempt to classify the beneficiaries but only specifies or classifies excepted persons is therefore, it is said, too vague. It is admitted that it may be difficult to define or describe those classes which would not be recognised by the court, and are therefore also too vague, but the example suggested by Lord Wilberforce in *McPhail* v. *Doulton* [13] of ' all the residents of Greater London ' is given as an instance of a class which would not be so recognised.

" The submission that an intermediate power is too vague because the beneficiaries are not limited to specified individuals or recognised classes is in the final analysis based on the same reasoning as the attack on wide discretionary trusts which was rejected in *Baden* (*No.* 2).[14] The argument is that an intermediate power where the beneficiaries are not limited to specified individuals or recognised classes precludes the trustees from considering in a sensible manner whether and how to exercise the power, and prevents the court from judging whether the trustees have surveyed the field of objects and have properly considered whether and how to exercise the power.

" Implicit in this argument are two assertions, first, that the terms of a special power in favour of recognised classes necessarily provide some guidance to the trustees with regard to the proper mode of considering how to exercise the power, and secondly, that the terms of a special power in favour of recognised classes enable the court to judge

---

[8] [1971] A.C. 424, 457.
[9] [1953] Ch. 672.
[10] [1970] A.C. 508.
[11] [1971] A.C. 424.
[12] [1973] Ch. 9.
[13] [1971] A.C. 424, 457.
[14] [1972] Ch. 607; [1973] Ch. 9.

whether the trustees are in breach of their duty. In my judgment neither assertion is well founded.

" Some powers may give an indication of the expectations of the settlor. In *Gulbenkian* [15] it was plain that the trustees were expected to have regard to the best interests of Mr. Nubar Gulbenkian. There are similar powers where all the beneficiaries are equal but some are more equal than others. But in *Gestetner* [16] it was impossible to derive any assistance from the terms of the power, save that the trustees, it could be assumed, were expected to have regard to the considerations which might move the settlor to confer bounty on the beneficiaries. A similar expectation may be implied from an intermediate power, and in the present case if the settlement is read as a whole the expectations of the settlor are not difficult to discern. In *Gestetner* the terms of the power did not in themselves indicate how employees were to be compared with relations, charities, individuals and other classes of beneficiaries. The terms of the power in themselves did not indicate whether and on what grounds one employee might be considered, whether by reference to services rendered to Gestetner Ltd. or to the settlor or by reference to age, health or any other criterion. The terms of the power did not in themselves indicate whether and on what grounds one relation out of many was to be considered, whether by reference to his proximity to the settlor, poverty, educational requirements or any other circumstances. The terms of a special power do not necessarily indicate in themselves how the trustees are to consider the exercise of the power. That consideration is confided to the absolute discretion of the trustees.

" The court cannot insist on any particular consideration being given by the trustees to the exercise of the power. If a settlor creates a power exercisable in favour of his issue, his relations and the employees of his company, the trustees may in practice for many years hold regular meetings, study the terms of the power and the other provisions of the settlement, examine the accounts and either decide not to exercise the power or to exercise it only in favour, for example, of the children of the settlor. During that period the existence of the power may not be disclosed to any relation or employee and the trustees may not seek or receive any information concerning the circumstances of any relation or employee. In my judgment it cannot be said that the trustees in those circumstances have committed a breach of trust and that they ought to have advertised the power or looked beyond the persons who are most likely to be the objects of the bounty of the settlor. [17] The trustees are, of course, at liberty to make further enquiries, but cannot be compelled to do so at the behest of any beneficiary. The court cannot judge the adequacy of the

---

[15] [1970] A.C. 508.
[16] [1953] Ch. 672.
[17] But see *Re Baden* [1973] Ch. 9. Could the trustees not be directed to advertise?

consideration given by the trustees to the exercise of the power, and it cannot insist on the trustees applying a particular principle or any principle in reaching a decision.

" If a person within the ambit of the power is aware of its existence he can require the trustees to consider exercising the power and in particular to consider a request on his part for the power to be exercised in his favour. The trustees must consider this request, and if they decline to do so or can be proved to have omitted to do so, then the aggrieved person may apply to the court which may remove the trustees and appoint others in their place. This, as I understand it, is the only right and only remedy of any object of the power: see, for example, *Gestetner*,[18] where Harman J. said that the trustees—

> ' are not entitled entirely to relase the power. That means that they are bound to consider at all times during which the trust is to continue whether or no they are to distribute any, and, if so, what, part of the fund, and to whom they should distribute it. To that extent I have no doubt that there is a duty on these trustees, and that a member of the specified class might, if he could show that the trustees had deliberately refused to consider any question of the want or suitability of any member of the class, procure their removal . . . there is no obligation on the trustees to do more than consider from time to time the merits of such persons of the specified class as are known to them, and, if they consider them meritorious, to give them something. The settlor had good reason to trust the persons whom he appointed as trustees, I have no doubt, but I cannot see that there is here such a duty as makes it essential for these trustees, before parting with any income or capital, to survey the whole field and consider whether A is more deserving of bounty than B. That is a task which is, and which must have been known to the settlor to be impossible, having regard to the ramifications of the persons who might be members of this class.'

Similarly, in the case of an intermediate power the settlor has no doubt good reason to trust the persons whom he appoints trustees. In my judgment the reasoning is parallel.

" The court may also be persuaded to intervene by removing the trustees if the trustees act ' capriciously,' that is to say, act for reasons which I apprehend could be said to be irrational, perverse or irrelevant to any sensible expectation of the settlor; for example, if they chose a beneficiary by height or complexion or by the irrelevant fact that he was a resident of Greater London.

" A special power does not show the trustees how to consider the exercise of the power in a sensible manner and does not by its terms enable the court to judge whether the power is being considered in a

---

[18] [1953] Ch. 672, 688.

proper manner. The conduct and duties of trustees of an intermediate power, and the rights and remedies of any person who wishes the power to be exercised in his favour, are precisely similar to the conduct and duties of trustees of special powers and the rights and remedies of any person who wishes a special power to be exercised in his favour. In practice, the considerations which weigh with the trustees will be no different from the considerations which will weigh with the trustees of a wide special power. In both cases reasonable trustees will endeavour, no doubt, to give effect to the intention of the settlor in making the settlement and will derive that intention not from the terms of the power necessarily or exclusively, but from all the terms of the settlement, the surrounding circumstances and their individual knowledge acquired or inherited. In both cases the trustees have an absolute discretion and cannot be obliged to take any form of action, save to consider the exercise of the power and a request from a person who is within the ambit of the power. In practice, requests to trustees armed with an intermediate power are unlikely to come from anyone who has no claim on the bounty of the settlor. In practice, requests to trustees armed with a special power in favour, for example, of issue, relations and employees of a company, are unlikely to come from anyone who has no claim on the bounty of the settlor, or has no plausible grounds for being given a benefit from property derived from the settlor. The only difference between an intermediate power and a special power for present purposes is that a settlor by means of a special power cannot be certain that he has armed his trustees against all developments and contingencies. A settlor who creates a special power exercisable in favour of issue, relations and employees may later regret that the trustees have no power to benefit adopted issue, widows and other persons from outside the ambit of the power. Hence the recent popularity, as I am informed, of intermediate powers which arm the trustees with a weapon which will enable them to consider all developments, and all future mishaps and disasters.

"Logically, in my judgment, there is no reason to bless a special power which prescribes the ambit of the power by classifying beneficiaries and at the same time to outlaw an intermediate power which prescribes the ambit of the power by classifying excepted persons.

"It may well be that there are some classes of special power which will not be recognised by the court, but this possibility does not affect the validity of intermediate powers. The objection to the capricious exercise of a power may well extend to the creation of a capricious power. A power to benefit ' residents of Greater London ' is capricious because the terms of the power negative any sensible intention on the part of the settlor. If the settlor intended and expected the trustees would have regard to persons with some claim on his bounty or some interest in an institution favoured by the settlor, or if the settlor had any other sensible intention or expectation, he would not have required the trustees to consider only an accidental conglomeration of persons who have no discernible link with the settlor or with any institution. A capricious power negatives a sensible consideration by the trustees of the exercise of the power. But a wide power, be it special or intermediate, does not negative or prohibit a sensible approach by the trustees to the consideration and exercise of their powers.

"If there is no logical objection to intermediate powers it remains to be considered whether the authorities, for historical or other reasons, forbid the conferment of intermediate powers on trustees. In *Morice* v. *The Bishop of Durham* [19] a trust for ' such objects of benevolence and liberality as the trustee in his own discretion shall most approve ' was held to be invalid and Lord Eldon L.C. said this:

> ' As it is a maxim, that the execution of a trust shall be under the controul of the Court, it must be of such a nature, that it can be under that controul; so that the administration of it can be reviewed by the Court; or, if the trustee dies, the Court itself can execute the trust: a trust therefore, which, in case of mal-administration could be reformed; and a due administration directed; and then, unless the subjects and the objects can be ascertained, upon principles, familiar in other cases, it must be decided, that the Court can neither reform mal-administration, nor direct a due administration.'

The decision in that case does not touch the present controversy. In a trust where the objects are described by vague adjectives such as ' benevolent ' and ' liberal ' the trust breaks the rule that the trustees and the court must be able to determine with certainty whether a particular individual or a particular object is within the ambit of the power. Nor does an intermediate power break the principles laid down by Lord Eldon L.C. in the passage which I have read because, in relation to a power exercisable by the trustees at their absolute discretion, the only ' control ' exercisable by the court is the removal of the trustees, and the only ' due administration ' which can be ' directed ' is an order requiring the trustees to consider the exercise of the power, and in particular a request from a person within the ambit of the power. This control and direction may be exercised by the court in relation to a power, whether special or intermediate.

"In *Re Park* [20] Clauson J. held that an intermediate power exercisable by an individual was valid, but he said [21]:

> ' It is clearly settled that if a testator creates a trust he must mark out the metes and bounds which are to fetter the trustees or, as has been said, the trust must not be too vague for the Court to

---

[19] (1805) 10 Ves.Jun. 522, 539, 540; [1803–13] All E.R.Rep. 451, 458.
[20] [1932] 1 Ch. 580.					[21] [1932] 1 Ch. 580, 583.

enforce, and that is why a gift to trustees for such purposes as they may in their discretion think fit is an invalid trust; there are no metes and bounds within which the trust can be defined, and unless the trust can be defined the Court cannot enforce it.'

" If the object of metes and bounds is to enable the trustees and the court to determine whether an individual is or is not a beneficiary then an intermediate power satisfies that test. If the requirement of certainty is the same as that mentioned by Lord Eldon L.C. in *Morice* v. *The Bishop of Durham* [22] this passage from the judgment of Clauson J. does not affect powers, whether special or intermediate, where the only ' enforcement ' allowed to the court is enforcement of the right of any person within the ambit of the power to require the trustees to consider the exercise of the power and his request. If the passage means more than this, it nevertheless does not in terms apply to powers, and even in relation to trusts may be required to be reconsidered in the light of the consequences of the decision of the majority of the House of Lords in *McPhail* v. *Doulton*. [23]

" In *Re Abrahams' Will Trusts* [24] Cross J. considered *Re Park* and decided that an intermediate power exercisable by trustees was valid. Counsel for the fourth and fifth defendants points out that *Re Abrahams' Will Trusts* was decided before the decision of the House of Lords in *Gulbenkian*, [25] but it is plain that the judgment of Cross J. is not inconsistent with *Gulbenkian* and he discussed the nature of a power and the duty of the trustees in words which anticipated both *Gulbenkian* and *McPhail* v. *Doulton*. The learned judge said [26]:

' It is not a trust imposed on them; it is a mere power. It is a fiduciary power given to them in the capacity of trustees and they cannot release it. They must retain it unless and until they exercise it, and consider from time to time whether they ought to exercise it.'

The learned judge clearly did not envisage that the trustees' function, to which he alluded in terms anticipating *Gulbenkian* and *McPhail* v. *Doulton*, would be difficult or impossible for trustees to carry out in connection with an intermediate power, and clearly did not envisage that the court would find any difficulty in carrying out its limited function with regard to the exercise by the trustees of powers.

" In *McPhail* v. *Doulton* [27] Lord Wilberforce referred first to ' linguistic or semantic uncertainty which, if unresolved by the court, renders the gift void ' and secondly to—

' the difficulty of ascertaining the existence or whereabouts of

[22] (1805) 10 Ves.Jun. 522, 539, 540.
[23] [1971] A.C. 424.
[24] [1969] 1 Ch. 463, 474.
[25] [1970] A.C. 508.
[26] [1969] 1 Ch. 463, 474, 475.
[27] [1971] A.C. 424, 457.

members 'of the class, a matter with which the court can appropriately deal on an application for directions.'

Then he said this[28]:

'There may be a third case where the meaning of the words used is clear but the definition of beneficiaries is so hopelessly wide as not to form "anything like a class" so that the trust is administratively unworkable or in Lord Eldon L.C.'s words one that cannot be executed.'

And he cited *Morice* v. *The Bishop of Durham.*[29]   He continued:

'I hesitate to give examples for they may prejudice future cases, but perhaps "all the residents of Greater London" will serve.   I do not think that a discretionary trust for "relatives" even of a living person falls within this category.'

"In these guarded terms Lord Wilberforce appears to refer to trusts which may have to be executed and administered by the court and not to powers where the court has a very much more limited function.   Moreover, a capricious power exercisable in favour of 'residents of Greater London' may, as I have already outlined, well be uncertain.   The settlor neither gives the trustees an unlimited power which they can exercise sensibly, nor a power limited to what may be described a 'sensible' class, but a power limited to a class, membership of which is accidental and irrelevant to any settled purpose or to any method of limiting or selecting beneficiaries.

"Finally, in *Blausten* v. *Inland Revenue Comrs.*,[30] there are passages which are admittedly obiter to the decision of Buckley L.J., in which the learned Lord Justice accepted the validity of an intermediate power exercisable by trustees with the consent of the settlor but was clearly not disposed to accept the validity of an intermediate power exercisable by trustees at their sole discretion.   The full consequences and implications of *Gestetner*,[31] *Gulbenkian*,[32] *McPhail* v. *Doulton*[33] and *Baden* (*No. 2*)[34] do not, however, appear to have been fully explored for the assistance of Buckley L.J. and that is not surprising in view of the fact that the Court of Appeal reached its conclusions on grounds which did not involve a final pronouncement on the validity of intermediate powers.

"In the result, I conclude that I am not constrained by authority to strike down a power which a settlor, disposing of his own property under skilled advice, wishes to confer on his trustees."

Declaration accordingly.

---

28 [1971] A.C. 424, 457.
29 (1805) Ves.Jun. 522, 527.
30 [1972] 1 Ch. 256, 271.
31 [1953] Ch. 672.
32 [1970] A.C. 508.
33 [1971] A.C. 424.
34 [1972] Ch. 607; affd. [1973] Ch. 9.

Section 4. Compliance with the Rules against Perpetuity

Trusts are often said to be void for perpetuity without it being made clear whether the trusts are void for infringing the rule against remoteness of vesting, directed at interests commencing at too remote a time, or for infringing the rule against inalienability, directed at vested interests which can go on for too long, so tying up trust property for too long.

The rule against remoteness is dealt with at length in property text-books [35] and need not be dealt with here. It suffices that in Gray's words [36] the rule is, "No interest is good unless it *must* vest, if at all, not later than twenty-one years after some life in being at the creation of the interest." An outside possibility that the interest *might* vest outside the period could invalidate the interest. After the Perpetuities and Accumulation Act 1964 it became possible to "wait and see" until it became clear that an interest in fact must vest outside the period before invalidating the interest. The Act also replaced causally relevant lives in being by a list of statutory lives in being and allowed an eighty-year period specifically to be chosen instead as the perpetuity period. Today, it is customary to choose the eighty-year period or to use a royal lives clause, *i.e.,* "within twenty-one years of the death of the last survivor of all the descendants of King George V now living." The 1964 Act only affects instruments taking effect after July 16, 1964, and, in the case of instruments made in the exercise of a special power of appointment, only applies where the instrument creating the power took effect after July 16, 1964: the perpetuity period for special powers, unlike that for general powers, runs not from the date of the appointment but from the date of the instrument creating the power. It is noteworthy that the rule against remoteness cannot be evaded by imposing a condition that the last person within the perpetuity period to receive the capital absolutely must resettle the capital upon certain trusts for his issue or forfeit the capital: such a condition is void for repugnancy as being repugnant to the absolute nature of the gift, an absolute owner having as one of the vital incidents of ownership the right to dispose freely of his property.[37]

To explain the rule against inalienability it is easiest to consider some examples. T by will leaves £25,500 to trustees to hold £15,000 upon trust to pay the income to T's wife, W, £10,000 upon trust to pay the income to the old Bugfordians' Association for defraying its clubhouse expenses and £500 upon trust to use the income to provide a cup annually for the Association's best dinghy sailor.

The £15,000 trust is valid since W is absolutely entitled to her life interest which she may alienate as she wishes and since it lasts only for W's lifetime.[38] The £10,000 trust is void since the income is tied up indefinitely: it would make no difference if the £10,000 had been left directly to the

---

[35] Megarry & Wade, Chap. 5; Cheshire, Chap. 5; *Morris & Leach on Perpetuities.*

[36] *Rule Against Perpetuities*, 4th ed., s. 201.

[37] *Re Wenger's Settlement* (1963) 107 S.J. 981; *Re Brown* [1954] Ch. 39.

[38] *Re Macaulay's Estate* [1943] Ch. 422; *Leahy* v. *Att.-Gen. for New South Wales* [1959] A.C. 457, *infra.* Alienability of the life entitlement to income is the crucial factor, for a trust created under T's will conferring a life interest upon T's first grandchild to attain twenty-one is valid although such grandchild could well live longer than the perpetuity period, terminating twenty-one years from the death of the survivor of his parents, so tying up the capital of the trust for longer than the perpetuity period.

Association for defraying its clubhouse expenses ("the receipt of the treasurer for the time being, being a sufficient discharge for my executors") since the treasurer or other officials would have to hold the capital on trust for defraying maintenance expenses. Similarly, the £500 trust is void,[39] since its income is tied up indefinitely. It makes no difference that the actual capital may be transposed from one investment to another. It is the fact that the income is rendered inalienable as it must always be used in a certain way that infringes the rule against inalienability. It must be said, however, that this inalienability of the income has the effect of rendering the capital inalienable as it must always be retained in one form or another to give effect to the income trusts, but this applies equally to W's life interest which does not infringe the rule against inalienability as we have seen.

The rule against inalienability may thus be said to be the rule that an interest under a trust is void if the terms of the trust compel the income to be used for specific purposes such that the interest in income is rendered inalienable for a period that may exceed the perpetuity period consisting of causally relevant lives plus twenty-one years. Normally, as in the £10,000 and £500 examples above, there are no causally relevant lives, so the courts [40] have referred in terms to a twenty-one-year period, but there seems no reason in principle why the usual perpetuity period should not apply [41] if there were causally relevant lives as there would be if a "royal lives clause" were used. It is vital to note that the rule against inalienability was expressly left unaffected by the Perpetuities and Accumulation Act 1964 [42] : there is thus no "wait and see" available nor the eighty-year perpetuity period.

Of course, if a trust is concerned with a trust or power to accumulate (*e.g.*, a children's settlement) then it is crucial to restrict the accumulation to one of the six periods allowed by section 164 of the Law of Property Act 1925 and the very useful section 13 of the 1964 Act:

(a) the life of the grantor or settlor;

(b) twenty-one years from the death of the grantor, settlor or testator;

(c) the duration of the minority or respective minorities of any person(s) living or *en ventre sa mère* at the death of the grantor, settlor or testator;

(d) the duration of the minority or respective minorities only of any person(s) who under the limitations of the instrument directing the accumulations would, for the time being, if of full age, be entitled to the income directed to be accumulated;

(e) twenty-one years from the date of the making of the disposition;

(f) the duration of the minority or respective minorities of any person(s)· in being at that date.

If an excessive accumulation infringes the perpetuity period it is void *in toto*.[43] If within the perpetuity period it is cut down to the nearest

---

[39] *Re Nottage* [1895] 2 Ch. 649; *Re Gwyon* [1930] 1 Ch. 255.

[40] *e.g.*, *Re Hooper* [1932] 1 Ch. 38; *Pirbright* v. *Salwey* [1896] W.N. 86.

[41] This seems to have been assumed in *Re Astor's S.T.* [1952] Ch. 534. See also *Re Chardon* [1928] Ch. 464; *Re Denley's Trust Deed* [1969] 1 Ch. 373.

[42] s. 15 (4).

[43] *Curtis* v. *Lukin* (1842) 5 Beav. 147.

appropriate period of the six permitted, and only the excess is void.[44] This can have nasty estate duty repercussions if the appropriate period is the settlor's life.[45]

Section 5. The Beneficiary Principle [46]

Over the past twenty-five years an off-shoot of the principle that the courts of equity will not recognise as valid any trust which they cannot properly administer has taken on a particularly lively lease of life. This requirement can be stated as, " There must be somebody in whose favour the court can decree performance " [47] or " A trust to be valid must be for the benefit of individuals." [48]   It follows that a trust for purposes (other than charitable purposes when the Attorney-General can sue: see later) is invalid as emphasised in *Re Astor's S.T., infra*,[49] in *Re Endacott* [50] where the Court of Appeal warmly endorsed *Re Astor's S.T.*, in *Re Shaw* [51] and in *Leahy* v. *Att.-Gen. for New South Wales, infra*,[52] unless the attainment of the trust purposes is sufficiently for the benefit of individuals that they have *locus standi* to apply to the court to enforce the trust: *Re Denley's Trust Deed, infra*.[53]   In this last case Goff J. opined that the beneficiary principle only invalidates purpose trusts which are abstract or impersonal.   However, he failed to deal adequately with *Leahy* v. *Att.-Gen. for New South Wales* (though strictly distinguishable on the footing that there there was no restriction to the perpetuity period) and in so far as his judgment suggests that a factual interest in performance of a trust may suffice for *locus standi* it appears to conflict with *Shaw* v. *Lawless* [54] and *Gandy* v. *Gandy*.[55] The employees in *Denley* had *locus standi*, it is submitted, as licensees under a deed (analogous to contractual licensees) sufficient to give them standing to seek a court order compelling performance of the trust if the trustees happened to refuse to carry out the trust.

It would appear that the beneficiary principle, like the certainty principle,[56] is intended to enable the courts positively to carry out trusts if the trustees fail to do so, so that someone with a positive interest in seeing trusts properly performed will have *locus standi* to satisfy the beneficiary principle whilst someone having a negative interest in preventing trust moneys from being misapplied will not have *locus standi* to satisfy the beneficiary principle.   After all, there will almost always be some living person in the background (*e.g.,* a residuary legatee or the next-of-kin) with an interest in applying to the courts in the case of failure on the part of

---

44 *Re Watt's W.T.* [1936] 2 All E.R. 1555, 1562; *Re Ransome* [1957] Ch. 348, 361.
45 Finance Act 1894, s. 2 (1) (*b*) (iv); *Re Browne's S.T.* [1946] 1 All E.R. 411.
46 Scott (1945) 58 Harv.L.R. 458; Sheridan (1953) 17 Conv.(N.S.) 46; Marshall (1953) 6 C.L.P. 151; Sheridan (1958) 4 U. of W.A.L.Rev. 235; Lovell (1970) 34 Conv. (N.S.) 77; Harris (1971) 87 L.Q.R. 31; McKay (1973) 37 Conv.(N.S.) 420.
47 Sir William Grant M.R., *Morice* v. *Bishop of Durham* (1804) 9 Ves. 399, 405.
48 Lord Parker, *Bowman* v. *Secular Society Ltd.* [1917] A.C. 406, 441.
49 p. 110.
50 [1960] Ch. 232.
51 [1957] 1 W.L.R. 729.
52 p. 114.
53 p. 124.
54 (1838) 5 Cl. & Fin. 129.
55 (1885) 30 Ch.D. 57. See McKay (1973) 37 Conv.(N.S.) 420, 426–427.
56 *McPhail* v. *Doulton* [1971] A.C. 424, 440, 456.

trustees to carry out abstract impersonal purposes, but his existence will not validate such purpose trusts.[57]

For the present the ambit of the beneficiary principle is unclear. However, it does appear that powers (as opposed to trusts) to carry out abstract impersonal purposes can be valid,[58] though the courts refuse to allow a trust to take effect as though it were a power in order to enable the purposes to be carried out.[59] Although a strong case[60] can be made out against such a refusal, especially when some purpose trusts represent desirable social experiments falling outside the realm of charity and when, in principle, equity should give effect to a settlor's intentions unless they are capricious, harmful or illegal, it is likely[61] that the House of Lords would endorse the conventional view and leave it to Parliament to change the law if it wishes.[62]

It is thus up to draftsmen to carry out their clients' intentions by using powers, in the hope that the chosen trustees will be likely to exercise the powers, or by using trusts in a special manner expressly limited to a royal lives plus twenty years' perpetuity period, e.g., £50,000 upon trust to T1, T2 to apply the income therefrom for the following purpose . . . until one day from the end of the " perpetuity period " whereupon if the income has been so used, then capital to X Co Ltd.[63] or £50,000 upon trust to T1, T2 to pay income therefrom to A. Charity Co. Ltd. for A. Charity Co. Ltd. to dispose of as it wishes for so long as the following purpose . . . shall happen to be carried out but as soon as such purpose shall not be carried out then to pay income to B. Charity Co. Ltd. for B. Charity Co. Ltd. to dispose of as it wishes for so long as the said purpose shall happen to be carried out [and so on to Z. Charity Co. Ltd.].[64]

In certain cases such deviousness will be unnecessary, for the Court of Appeal[65] has accepted that there are some anomalous cases where trusts infringing the beneficiary principle have been held valid, but these cases are not to be extended at all. These anomalous cases are (1) trusts for the erection or maintenance of monuments or graves,[66] (2) trusts for the saying

---

[57] *e.g., Re Astor's S.T.* [1952] Ch. 534; *Re Shaw* [1957] 1 W.L.R. 729; *Leahy* v. *Att.-Gen. for N.S.W.* [1959] A.C. 457.

[58] *Re Douglas* (1887) 35 Ch.D. 472; *Gott* v. *Nairne* (1876) 3 Ch.D. 278; *Re Shaw* [1957] 1 W.L.R. 729.

[59] *Re Shaw* [1957] 1 W.L.R. 729, 746; *Re Endacott* [1960] Ch. 232, 246.

[60] Ames (1892) 5 Harv.L.R. 389; Scott (1945) 58 Harv.L.R. 548; Morris & Leach's *Perpetuities* (2nd ed.), pp. 319–321.

[61] *Cf.* the refusal to treat trusts like powers for certainty purposes: *I.R.C.* v. *Broadway Cottages Trust* [1955] Ch. 20, 36.

[62] *e.g.,* as in s. 16 of the Ontario Perpetuities Act 1966, *infra.*

[63] X. Co. Ltd. has an equitable interest . contingent upon performance of the trust probably giving it *locus standi* to compel due execution of the trust. A company has legal personality enabling it to enforce trusts just like human beneficiaries.

[64] *Re Chardon* [1928] Ch. 464; *Re Chambers* [1950] Ch. 267; the alienability of the determinable interest in income satisfies the rule against inalienability. Gifts over, other than from one charity to another, may now be invalidated for infringing the rule against remoteness by virtue of the Perpetuities and Accumulation Act 1964, s. 12.

[65] *Re Endacott* [1960] Ch. 232.

[66] *Pirbright* v. *Salwey* [1896] W.N. 86; *Re Hooper* [1932] 1 Ch. 38; *Trimmer* v. *Danby* (1856) 25 L.J.Ch. 424; *Mussett* v. *Bingle* [1876] W.N. 170. Maintenance of private graves may be possible for 99 years under the Parish Council and Burial Authorities (Miscellaneous Provisions) Act 1970, s. 1.

of masses if they are not charitable,[67] (3) trusts for the maintenance of particular animals,[68] (4) miscellaneous cases, *e.g.*, trusts for the promotion and furtherance of fox hunting.[69]

Trusts for unincorporated associations appear[70] to be subject to the beneficiary principle. Special consideration has to be given to the construction of gifts or trusts for such associations as this is all-important in determining whether the beneficiary principle or the rules against remoteness or inalienability are infringed.

Take a gift by will to the X. Society. Depending upon the nature of the gift (*e.g.*, £100, £50,000 or 500 acres), the type of society (*e.g.*, an " inward-looking " social club or an " outward-looking " organisation promoting some external purpose), the rules of the society (*e.g.*, the members can dissolve the society at any time and divide the assets or only when the members fall below ten) and the number and nature of its members, the following possibilities appear (as apparent from *Re Recher's W.T., infra*[71]) though any terms attached to the gift will, of course, be of crucial significance.

(1) The gift is for charitable purposes and thus valid.[72]
(2) There is an absolute gift to the members of the society at the testator's death as joint tenants so any member can sever his share and claim.[73]
(3) There is a gift to the existing members but as an accretion to the funds of the society subject to the contract made between the members qua members. Any member's share will not be severable but will accrue to other members on his death or resignation even if such members become members after the gift.[74] The beneficiary principle is satisfied and unless the terms of the gift or the society's rules preclude the members at any one time from dividing the gift between themselves the rule against inalienability is satisfied. The rule against remoteness has no application whether on the footing that the members have contracted not to exercise their right of severance or on the footing that a special kind of co-ownership exists not carrying with it a right of severance.[75]

---

67 *Bourne* v. *Keane* [1919] A.C. 815, 874–875; owing to the absence of the element of public benefit doubts have been cast on the solitary decision *Re Caus* [1934] Ch. 162 holding that trusts for masses are charitable: *Gilmour* v. *Coats* [1949] A.C. 426, 451–452, 454.
68 *Re Dean* (1889) 41 Ch.D. 552; *Pettingall* v. *Pettingall* (1842) 11 L.J.Ch. 176.
69 *Re Thompson* [1934] Ch. 342.
70 *Leahy* v. *Att.-Gen. for New South Wales* [1959] A.C. 457, 478–479, 484–485; *Re Cain* [1950] V.L.R. 382, 389.
71 [1972] Ch. 526; Morris & Leach's *Perpetuities* (2nd ed.), pp. 313 *et seq.*
72 *Re Benfield* [1968] 1 W.L.R. 846.
73 *Re Smith* [1914] 1 Ch. 937; *Re Ogden* [1933] Ch. 678; *Cocks* v. *Manners* (1871) L.R. 12 Eq. 574.
74 *Neville Estates Ltd.* v. *Madden* [1962] Ch. 832, 849; *Re Recher's W.T.* [1972] Ch. 526; *Re Clarke* [1901] 2 Ch. 110; *Re Drummond* [1914] 2 Ch. 90 approved by House of Lords in *Macauley* v. *O'Donnell* [1943] 1 Ch. 453n but disapproved in *Leahy* v. *Att.-Gen. for N.S.W.* [1959] A.C. 457, 479–480.
75 The rule against remoteness does not apply to contractual as opposed to proprietary relationships: *Hutton* v. *Watling* [1948] Ch. 26; *Worthing Corporation* v. *Heather* [1906] 2 Ch. 532; but see Perpetuities and Accumulations Act 1964, s. 10. Nor does it apply to the relationship between co-owners: *Re Smith* [1914] 1 Ch. 937, 948; *Re Goode* [1960] V.R. 117, 124. But how does a club member's equit-

(4) There is a gift to the existing and future members of the society beneficially. This is void for infringing the rule against remoteness.[76]

(5) There is a gift to the existing members (or officers) as trustees for the accomplishment of a purpose.[77] If the purpose is abstract or impersonal then it infringes the beneficiary principle as well as the rule against inalienability. If the purpose satisfies the beneficiary principle as being for the benefit of future members then the rule against remoteness is infringed as well as the rule against inalienability (unless, of course, the gift were restricted to the perpetuity period).

These matters of construction are also relevant in determining the destination of gifts or legacies to an unincorporated society when the society dissolves itself after the date of the gift or legacy or had dissolved itself at a prior date.[78]

Re ASTOR'S SETTLEMENT TRUSTS, ASTOR v. SCHOLFIELD

Chancery Division [1952] Ch. 534; [1952] 1 T.L.R. 1003; 96 S.J. 246; [1952] 1 All E.R. 1067

In February 1945, Lord Astor settled substantially all the issued shares of the Observer Ltd., the proprietors of the *Observer* and other newspapers, upon trust to apply the income during a specified period not obnoxious to the rule against perpetuities for all or any of a number of public but not exclusively charitable purposes, such application to be at the discretion of the trustees, but subject to the direction of the settlor. At the expiration of the period the trust funds were to be held upon trust for a person not yet ascertainable absolutely and beneficially. The objects and purposes for which the income was to be applied included the improvement of good understanding between nations, the preservation of the independence and integrity of newspapers, the promotion of the freedom, independence and integrity of the Press, the protection of newspapers (particularly country or provincial newspapers) from being absorbed by combines, the restoration and maintenance of the independence of the editors of and writers in newspapers, the securing for the public of means of ascertaining by whom any newspaper is actually owned or controlled, and the establishment of any charitable public or benevolent schemes for (1) the improvement of newspapers or journalism, or (2) the relief of persons or their families actually or formerly engaged in journalism or in the newspaper business or any branch thereof, or (3) for any of the objects previously mentioned. Some time after this settlement it was pointed out to Lord Astor that the trusts of

---

able interest pass on resignation to the other members without signed writing within L.P.A. 1925, s. 53? See Ford's *Unincorporated Non-Profit Associations*, pp. 5–7, 21–23.

[76] *Re Recher's W.T.* [1972] Ch. 526, *infra*, p. 129.

[77] *Leahy* v. *Att.-Gen. for New South Wales* [1959] A.C. 457; *Carne* v. *Long* (1860) 2 De G.F. & J. 75.

[78] See Chap. 6 section 4, *infra*, p. 295.

income during the specified period might be void and that the trust at the end of the specified period would fail if the ultimate beneficiary could not then be ascertained. On August 20, 1951, Lord Astor settled upon charitable trusts any beneficial interest which he might have in the trust funds settled by the 1945 settlement in the event of that settlement being held void. Roxburgh J. confirmed the apprehension felt by Lord Astor's advisers as to the validity of the 1945 trust by holding it to be void.

ROXBURGH J.: " The question upon which I am giving this reserved judgment is whether the non-charitable trusts of income during ' the specified period ' declared by . . . the settlement of 1945 are void. [Counsel for the trustees of the 1951 settlement and for the Attorney-General] have submitted that they are void on two grounds: (1) that they are not trusts for the benefit of individuals; (2) that they are void for uncertainty. Lord Parker considered the first of these two questions in his speech in *Bowman* v. *Secular Society Ltd.*,[79] and I will cite two important passages. The first is [80] ' The question whether a trust be legal or illegal or be in accordance with or contrary to the policy of the law only arises when it has been determined that a trust has been created, and is then only part of the larger question whether the trust is enforceable. For, as will presently appear, trusts may be unenforceable and therefore void, not only because they are illegal or contrary to the policy of the law, but for other reasons.' The second is [81]: ' A trust to be valid must be for the benefit of individuals, which this is certainly not, or must be in that class of gifts for the benefit of the public which the courts in this country recognise as charitable in the legal as opposed to the popular sense of that term.'

" Commenting on those passages, [counsel for the trustees of the 1945 settlement] observed that *Bowman* v. *Secular Society Ltd.* arose out of a will and he asked me to hold that Lord Parker intended them to be confined to cases arising under a will. But they were, I think, intended to be quite general in character. Further, counsel pointed out that Lord Parker made no mention of the exceptions or apparent exceptions which, undoubtedly, exist, and from this he asked me to infer that no such general principle can be laid down. The question is whether those cases are to be regarded as exceptional and anomalous or whether they are destructive of the supposed principle. I must later analyse them. But I will first consider whether Lord Parker's propositions can be attacked from a base of principle.

" The typical case of a trust is one in which the legal owner of property is constrained by a court of equity so to deal with it as to give effect to the equitable rights of another. These equitable rights have been

[79] [1917] A.C. 406.
[80] *Ibid.* 437.
[81] *Ibid.* 441.

hammered out in the process of litigation in which a claimant on equitable grounds has successfully asserted rights against a legal owner or
other person in control of property. Prima facie, therefore, a trustee
would not be expected to be subject to an equitable obligation unless
there was somebody who could enforce a correlative equitable right
and the nature and extent of that obligation would be worked out in
proceedings for enforcement. This is what I understand by Lord
Parker's first proposition. At an early stage, however, the courts were
confronted with attempts to create trusts for charitable purposes which
there was no equitable owner to enforce. Lord Eldon explained, in
Att.-Gen. v. *Brown*,[82] how this difficulty was dealt with: ' It is the duty
of a court of equity, a main part, originally almost the whole, of its
jurisdiction, to administer trusts; to protect not the visible owner, who
alone can proceed at law, but the individual equitably, though not
legally, entitled. From this principle has arisen the practice of administering the trust of a public charity: persons possessed of funds appropriated to such purposes are within the general rule; but no one being
entitled by an immediate and peculiar interest to prefer a complaint,
who is to compel the performance of their obligations, and to enforce
their responsibility? It is the duty of the King, as *parens patriae*, to
protect property devoted to charitable uses; and that duty is executed
by the officer who represents the Crown for all forensic purposes. On
this foundation rests the right of the Attorney-General in such cases to
obtain by information the interposition of a court of equity. . . .'

    " But if the purposes are not charitable, great difficulties arise both
in theory and in practice. In theory, because, having regard to the
historical origins of equity, it is difficult to visualise the growth of equitable obligations which nobody can enforce, and in practice, because it
is not possible to contemplate with equanimity the creation of large
funds devoted to non-charitable purposes which no court and no
department of state can control, or, in the case of maladministration,
reform. Therefore, Lord Parker's second proposition would prima
facie appear to be well founded. Moreover, it gains no little support
from the practical considerations that no officer has ever been constituted
to take, in the case of non-charitable purposes, the position held by the
Attorney-General in connection with charitable purposes, and no case
has been found in the reports in which the court has ever directly
enforced a non-charitable purpose against a trustee. Indeed, where,
as in the present case, the only beneficiaries are purposes and an at
present unascertainable person, it is difficult to see who could initiate
such proceedings. If the purposes are valid trusts, the settlors have
retained no beneficial interest and could not initiate them. It was
suggested that the trustees might proceed *ex parte* to enforce the trusts
against themselves. I doubt that, but at any rate nobody could enforce
the trusts against them. This point, in my judgment, is of importance,

---

[82] (1818) 1 Swan. 265, 290.

because in most of the cases which are put forward to disprove Lord Parker's propositions, the court had indirect means of enforcing the execution of the non-charitable purpose.

" These cases I must now consider. First of all, there is a group relating to horses, dogs, graves and monuments, among which I was referred to *Pettingall* v. *Pettingall*,[83] *Mitford* v. *Reynolds*,[84] *Re Dean*,[85] *Pirbright* v. *Salwey*[86] and *Re Hooper*.[87] ...

" Let me, then sum up the position so far. On the one side, there are Lord Parker's two propositions with which I began. These were not new, but merely re-echoed what Sir William Grant had said, as Master of the Rolls, in *Morice* v. *Bishop of. Durham*[88] as long ago as 1804: ' There must be somebody in whose favour the court can decree performance.' The position was recently restated by Harman J. in *Re Wood*[89]: ' a gift on trust must have a *cestui que trust*,' and this seems to be in accord with principle. On the other side is a group of cases relating to horses and dogs, graves and monuments—matters arising under wills and intimately connected with the deceased—in which the courts have found means of escape from these general propositions, and also *Re Thompson* and *Re Price*, which I have endeavoured to explain. *Re Price* belongs to another field. The rest may, I think, properly be regarded as anomalous and exceptional and in no way destructive of the proposition which traces descent from or through Sir William Grant, through Lord Parker, to Harman J. Perhaps the late Sir Arthur Underhill was right in suggesting that they may be concessions to human weakness or sentiment.[90] They cannot, in my judgment, of themselves (and no other justification has been suggested to me) justify the conclusion that a court of equity will recognise as an equitable obligation affecting the income of large funds in the hands of trustees a direction to apply it in furtherance of enumerated non-charitable purposes in a manner which no court or department can control or enforce. I hold that the trusts here in question are void on the first of the grounds submitted by [counsel for the trustees of the settlement of 1951 and counsel for the Attorney-General].

" The second ground upon·which the relevant trusts are challenged is uncertainty. If (contrary to my view) an enumeration of purposes outside the realm of charities can take the place of an enumeration of beneficiaries, the purposes must, in my judgment, be stated in phrases which embody definite concepts, and the means by which the trustees are to try to attain them must also be prescribed with a sufficient degree of certainty. The test to be applied is stated by Lord Eldon L.C. in

[83] (1842) 11 L.J.Ch. 176.
[84] (1848) 16 Sim. 105.
[85] (1889) 41 Ch.D. 552.
[86] [1896] W.N. 86.
[87] [1932] 1 Ch. 38.
[88] (1804) 9 Ves. 399, 405.
[89] [1949] Ch. 498, 499.
[90] See Underhill's *Law of Trusts and Trustees*, 11th ed., pp. 103–104.

Morice v. *Bishop of Durham* [91] as follows: ' As it is a maxim, that the execution of a trust shall be under the control of the court, it must be of such a nature, that it can be under that control; so that the administration of it can be reviewed by the court; or, if the trustee dies, the court itself can execute the trust: a trust therefore, which, in case of maladministration, could be reformed; and a due administration directed; and then, unless the subject and the objects can be ascertained, upon principles, familiar in other cases, it must be decided, that the court can neither reform maladministration, nor direct a due administration.' [92] [His Lordship then examined the clauses of the 1945 settlement and came to the conclusion that they were too vague to be enforced and that the court had no power to bring certainty by formulating a scheme.] He then concluded: ' Accordingly in my judgment, the trusts for the application of income during " the specified period " are also void for uncertainty. But while I have reached my decision on two separate grounds, both, I think, have their origin in a single principle, namely, that a court of equity does not recognise as valid a trust which it cannot both enforce and control. This seems to me to be good equity and good sense.' "
Trust held void.

LEAHY v. ATTORNEY-GENERAL FOR NEW SOUTH WALES

Privy Council [1959] A.C. 457; [1959] 2 W L.R. 722; 103 S.J. 391; [1959] 2 All E.R. 300 (Viscount Simonds, Lords Morton of Henryton, Cohen, Somervell of Harrow and Denning)

By clause 3 of his will the testator, Francis George Leahy, provided as follows: "As to my property known as ' Elmslea ' situated at Bungendore aforesaid and the whole of the land comprising the same and the whole of the furniture contained in the homestead thereon upon trust for such order of nuns of the Catholic Church or the Christian Brothers as my executors and trustees shall select and I again direct that the selection of the order of nuns or brothers as the case may be to benefit under this clause of my will shall be in the sole and absolute discretion of my said executors and trustees."

An originating summons was taken out by the trustees in the Supreme Court of New South Wales to determine *inter alia* the effect of the disposition made by clause 3 of the will.

Counsel for the trustees argued that the disposition made thereby was good as it stood. Once the trustees selected the recipient of the gift, whether an order of nuns or the Christian Brothers, the selected body became absolutely entitled to the gift. No question of uncertainty or perpetuity was therefore involved and the gift was valid. It should be observed that this argument, if successful, would enable the trustees to select as the recipient an order of nuns which was not

---
[91] (1805) 10 Ves. 522, 539.   [92] See also *Re Macduff* [1896] 2 Ch. 451, *per* Lindley L.J.

charitable in the legal sense of that term. The phrase "order of nuns" included "contemplative" as well as "active" orders, the former of which were not charitable.[93] Counsel for the trustees, accordingly, argued, in the alternative, that, if the disposition made by clause 3 was not valid as it stood, it was nevertheless saved from invalidity by section 37D of the Conveyancing Act 1919–54.[94] That section provided as follows: "(1) No trust shall be held to be invalid by reason that some non-charitable and invalid purpose as well as some charitable purpose is or could be deemed to be included in any of the purposes to or for which an application of the trust funds or any part thereof is by such trust directed or allowed. (2) Any such trust shall be construed and given effect to in the same manner in all respects as if no application of the trusts funds or any part thereof to or for any such non-charitable and invalid purpose had been or could be deemed to have been so directed or allowed." It should be observed that this argument, if successful, would not enable the trustees to select as the recipient a "contemplative," and therefore non-charitable, order of nuns. The area of choice would be restricted to "active" orders.

On appeal to the High Court of Australia (Dixon C.J., McTiernan, Williams, Webb and Kitto JJ.), that court affirmed the order of Myers J. in regard to the disposition made by clause 3, holding (by a majority)[90] that an absolute gift was thereby established in favour of the selected beneficiary and (unanimously) that in any case it was saved by section 37D.

The testator's widow and children appealed to Her Majesty in Council.

VISCOUNT SIMONDS: "The disposition made by clause 3 must now be considered. As has already been pointed out, it will in any case be saved by the section so far as orders other than contemplative orders are concerned, but the trustees are anxious to preserve their right to select such orders. They can only do so if the gift is what is called an absolute gift to the selected order, an expression which may require examination.

"Upon this question there has been a sharp division of opinion in the High Court. Williams and Webb JJ. agreed with Myers J. that the disposition by clause 3 was valid. They held that it provided for an immediate gift to the particular religious community selected by the trustees and that it was immaterial whether the order was charitable or not because the gift was not a gift in perpetuity. 'It is given,' they said

---

[93] See *Gilmour* v. *Coats* [1949] A.C. 426; *infra*, p. 249.
[94] New South Wales. See also s. 131 of the Property Law Act 1928 (Victoria); s. 2 of The Trustee Amendment Act 1935 (New Zealand); s. 24, Charities Act 1964 (Northern Ireland); (1946) 62 L.Q.R. 23 (E. H. Coghill); *ibid.* 339 (R. Else Mitchell); E. H. Coghill (1950) 24 Austr. L.J. 239; *cf.* the terms of the Charitable Trusts Validation Act 1954; *infra*, p. 275. See generally M. C. Cullitty (1967) 16 I.C.L.Q. 464–490.

(and these are the significant words), ' to the individuals comprising the community selected by the trustees at the date of the death of the testator. It is given to them for the benefit of the community.' Kitto J. reached the same conclusion. He thought that the selected order would take the gift immediately and absolutely, and could expend immediately the whole of what is received. ' There is,' he said, ' no attempt to create a perpetual endowment.' A different view was taken by the Chief Justice and McTiernan J. After an exhaustive examination of the problem and of the relevant authorities, they concluded that the provision made by clause 3 was intended as a trust operating for the furtherance of the purpose of the order as a body of religious women or, in the case of the Christian Brothers, as a teaching order. ' The membership of any order chosen,' they said, ' would be indeterminate and the trust was intended to apply to those who should become members at any time. There was no intention to restrain the operation of the trust to those presently members or to make the alienation of the property a question for the governing body of the order chosen or any section or part of that order.' They therefore held that unless the trust could be supported as a charity it must fail.

"The brief passages that have been cited from the judgments in the High Court sufficiently indicate the question that must be answered and the difficulty of solving it. It arises out of the artificial and anomalous conception of an unincorporated society which, though it is not a separate entity in law, is yet for many purposes regarded as a continuing entity and, however inaccurately, as something other than an aggregate of its members. In law a gift to such a society simpliciter (i.e., where, to use the words of Lord Parker in *Bowman* v. *Secular Society Ltd.*,[95] neither the circumstances of the gift nor the directions given nor the objects expressed impose on the donee the character of a trustee) is nothing else than a gift to its members at the date of the gift as joint tenants or tenants in common. It is for this reason that the prudent conveyancer provides that a receipt by the treasurer or other proper officer of the recipient society for a legacy to the society shall be a sufficient discharge to executors. If it were not so, the executors could only get a valid discharge by obtaining a receipt from every member. This must be qualified by saying that by their rules the members might have authorised one of themselves to receive a gift on behalf of them all.

"It is in the light of this fundamental proposition that the statements, to which reference has been made, must be examined. What is meant when it is said that a gift is made to the individuals comprising the community and the words are added ' it is given to them for the benefit of the community ' ? If it is a gift to individuals, each of them is entitled to his distributive share (unless he has previously bound himself by the rules of the society that it shall be devoted to some other purpose). It is difficult to see what is added by the words ' for the benefit of the

---

[95] [1917] A.C. 406, 437.

community.' If they are intended to import a trust, who are the beneficiaries? If the present members are the beneficiaries, the words add nothing and are meaningless. If some other persons or purposes are intended, the conclusion cannot be avoided that the gift is void. For it is uncertain and beyond doubt tends to a perpetuity.

" The question then appears to be whether, even if the gift to a selected order of nuns is prima facie a gift to the individual members of that order, there are other considerations arising out of the terms of the will, or the nature of the society, its organisation and rules, or the subject-matter of the gift, which should lead the court to conclude that though prima facie the gift is an absolute one (absolute both in quality of estate and in freedom from restriction) to individual nuns, yet it is invalid because it is in the nature of an endowment and tends to a perpetuity or for any other reason. This raises a problem which is not easy to solve as the divergent opinions in the High Court indicate.

" The prima facie validity of such a gift (by which term their Lordships intend a bequest or demise [96]) is a convenient starting-point for the examination of the relevant law. For, as Lord Tomlin (sitting at first instance in the Chancery Division) said in *Re Ogden*,[97] a gift to a voluntary association of persons for the general purposes of the association is an absolute gift and prima facie a good gift. He was echoing the words of Lord Parker in *Bowman's* case [98] that a gift to an unincorporated association for the attainment of its purposes ' may . . . be upheld as an absolute gift to its members.' These words must receive careful consideration, for it is to be noted that it is because the gift can be upheld as a gift to the individual members that it is valid, even though it is given for the general purposes of the association. If the words ' for the general purposes of the association' were held to import a trust, the question would have to be asked, what is the trust and who are the beneficiaries? A gift can be made to persons (including a corporation) but it cannot be made to a purpose or to an object: so, also, a trust may be created for the benefit of persons as *cestuis que trust* but not for a purpose or object unless the purpose or object be charitable. For a purpose or object cannot sue, but, if it be charitable, the Attorney-General can sue to enforce it. (Upon this point something will be added later.) It is therefore by disregarding the words ' for the general purposes of the association' (which are assumed not to be charitable purposes) and treating the gift as an absolute gift to individuals that it can be sustained. The same conclusion had been reached fifty years before in *Cocks* v. *Manners*,[99] where a bequest of a share of residue to the ' Dominican Convent at Carisbrooke (payable to the superior for the time being)' was held a valid gift to the individual members of that society. In that case no difficulty was created by the addition of words which might suggest that the community as a whole, not its members

---

[96] This appears to be a misprint for " devise."
[98] [1917] A.C. 406, 442.
[97] [1933] Ch. 678, 681.
[99] (1871) L.R. 12 Eq. 574.

individually, should be the beneficiary. So also with *Re Smith.*[1] There
the bequest was to 'the society or institution known as the Franciscan
Friars of Clevedon [in the] County of Somerset' absolutely. Joyce J.
had no difficulty in construing this as a gift individually to the small
number of persons who had associated themselves together at Clevedon
under monastic vows. Greater difficulty must be felt when the gift is
in such terms that though it is clearly not contemplated that the
individual members shall divide it amongst themselves, yet it is prima
facie a gift to the individuals and, there being nothing in the constitution
of the society to prohibit it, they can dispose of it as they think fit. Of
this type of case *Re Clarke*[2] may be taken as an example. There the
bequest was to the committee for the time being of the Corps of Commissionaires in London to aid in the purchase of their barracks, or in
any other way beneficial to the Corps. The judge (Byrne J.) was able
to uphold this as a valid gift on the ground that all the members of
the association could join together to dispose of the funds or the
barracks. He assumed (however little the testator may have intended it)
that the gift was to the individual members in the name of the society
or of the committee of the society. This might be regarded as an extreme
case had it not been followed by *Re Drummond.*[3] In that case a testator
devised and bequeathed his residuary real and personal estate to his
trustees upon trust for sale and conversion and to stand possessed of the
proceeds upon trust for the Old Bradfordians' Club, London (being a
club instituted by Bradford Grammar School old boys), the receipt of
the treasurer for the time being of the club to be a sufficient discharge
to his trustees. By a codicil the testator declared that he desired that the
said moneys should be used by the club for such purpose as the committee for the time being might determine, the object and intent of the
bequest being to benefit old boys of the Bradford Grammar School
residing in London or members of the club, and to enable the committee,
if possible, to acquire premises to be used as a club-house for the use of
the members, with various other powers, including the founding of
scholarships, as the committee for the time being should think best
in the interests of the club or the school. Eve J. said[4] that he could not
hold, as the result of the will and codicil together, that the residuary
gift to the Old Bradfordians' Club was a gift to the members individually,
but there was in his opinion a trust and there was abundant authority
for holding that it was not such a trust as would render the legacy void
as tending to a perpetuity. He cited only *Re Clarke*, though other cases
had been referred to in argument, and he ignored that Byrne J. had been
able to reach his conclusion in that case just because he regarded the
gift as a gift to the individual members of the Corps who could together
dispose of its assets as they thought fit. The judge added that the legacy
was not subject to any trust which would prevent the committee of the

[1] [1914] 1 Ch. 937.   [2] [1901] 2 Ch. 110.
[3] [1914] 2 Ch. 90.   [4] *Ibid.* 97.

club from spending it in any manner they might think fit for the benefit of the class intended. There was therefore a valid gift to the club for such purposes as the committee should determine for the old boys or members of the club. Their Lordships have thought it desirable to state *Drummond's* case at some length both because it provides an interesting contrast to cases that will be referred to later and was itself an authority relied on by Farwell J. in *Re Taylor* [5] and by Cohen J. (as he then was) in *Re Price*.[6] In the former case, the judge observed [7] that *Re Clarke* showed that a gift to a fund for a voluntary body of persons may be perfectly valid unless the rules governing that fund or the purpose for which the institution was created prevent the members from dealing with it, both capital and income, in any way they please. It does not appear that he was making any distinction between a gift to a voluntary body of persons and a gift to a fund for such a body. Two other cases had in the meantime been decided to which reference may be made. In *Re Prevost* [8] a testator had devised and bequeathed the whole of his residuary estate to the trustees of the London Library to be held by them upon trust for the general purposes of that institution, including the benefit of the staff. This case, too, came before Eve J., who held that the gift was valid upon the ground that it was a gift to the trustees of the library upon trust to be expended in carrying out the objects of the society according to its rules and that, inasmuch as there was nothing in the terms of the gift or in the rules of the library to prevent the expenditure of the corpus of the property, the gift did not fail for perpetuity. Here there was no question of a gift to an unincorporated society which was to be regarded as a gift to its individual members and capable of being dealt with by them as they should think fit. The judge nevertheless regarded it as falling within the class of case of which *Cocks* v. *Manners* was the leading authority. Nearer to *Cocks* v. *Manners*, and nearer too to the present case, was *Re Ray's Will Trusts*.[9] In that case a testatrix, who was a nun in a convent, by her will gave all her property to the person who at the time of her death should be, or should act as, the abbess of the convent. The will was witnessed by two nuns belonging to the convent, one of whom was subsequently elected abbess and held that office at the time of the death of the testatrix. The substantial question was whether the gift was invalidated by section 15 of the Wills Act 1837, and it was held not to be so invalidated because the gift was not to the abbess personally but in trust for, and as an addition to, the funds of the community. As to this Clauson J. made the following observations which state the point at issue [10]: ' Another perfectly lawful form of gift would be a gift of a legacy to the controlling officer of a society in his capacity of officer, to be dealt with as he would deal with other funds with which, as such officer of a voluntary society, it would

5 [1940] Ch. 481.
6 [1943] Ch. 422.
7 [1940] Ch. 481, 488.
9 [1936] Ch. 520.

8 [1930] 2 Ch. 383.
10 *Ibid*. 524.

be his duty to deal. Again, that would be a gift which the court will recognise as a good gift, subject only to this point, which sometimes causes difficulty, that if the frame of the gift indicates that the legacy is not to be used at once and immediately for the purposes of the voluntary society, but is to be set aside and invested and the income only to be used, the capital being preserved as an endowment of the voluntary society, the court will not give effect to the gift because it infringes the rule that no gift except a charitable gift is to be a perpetuity, and a gift thus to endow a voluntary society necessarily creates a perpetuity.'

" The cases that have been referred to (and many others might have been referred to in the courts of Australia, England and Ireland) are all cases in which gifts have been upheld as valid either on the ground that, where a society has been named as legatee, its members could demand that the gift should be dealt with as they should together think fit; or on the ground that a trust had been established (as in *Re Drummond*) which did not create a perpetuity. It will be sufficient to mention one only of the cases in which a different conclusion has been reached, before coming to a recent decision of the House of Lords which must be regarded as of paramount authority. In *Carne* v. *Long* [11] the testator devised his mansion-house after the death of his wife to the trustees of the Penzance Public Library to hold to them and their successors for ever, for the use, benefit, maintenance and support of the said library. It appeared that the library was established and kept on foot by the subscriptions of certain inhabitants of Penzance, that the subscribers were elected by ballot and the library managed by officers chosen from amongst themselves by the subscribers, that the property in the books and everything else belonging to the library was vested in trustees for the subscribers and that it was provided that the institution should not be broken up so long as ten members remained. It was urged that the gift was to a number of private persons and there were in truth no other beneficiaries. But Campbell L.C. rejected the plea in words which, often though they have been cited, will bear repetition [12]: ' If the devise had been in favour of the existing members of the society, and they had been at liberty to dispose of the property as they might think fit, then it might, I think, have been a lawful disposition and not tending to a perpetuity. But looking to the language of the rules of this society, it is clear that the library was intended to be a perpetual institution, and the testator must be presumed to have known what the regulations were.' This was, perhaps, a clear case where both from the terms of the gift and the nature of the society a perpetuity was indicated.

" Their Lordships must now turn to the recent case of *Re Macaulay's Estate*,[13] which appears to be reported only in a footnote to *Re Price*.[14]

11 (1860) 2 De G.F. & J. 75.
12 *Ibid.* 79.
13 [1943] Ch. 435n.
14 [1943] Ch. 422.

There the gift was to the Folkestone Lodge of the Theosophical Society absolutely for the maintenance and improvement of the Theosophical Lodge at Folkestone. It was assumed that the donee ' the Lodge ' was a body of persons. The decision of the House of Lords in July 1933, to which both Lord Buckmaster and Lord Tomlin were parties, was that the gift was invalid. A portion of Lord Buckmaster's speech may well be quoted. He had previously referred to *Re Drummond* and *Carne v. Long*. ' A group of people,' he said, ' defined and bound together by rules and called by a distinctive name can be the subject of gift as well as any individual or incorporated body. The real question is what is the actual purpose for which the gift is made. There is no perpetuity if the gift is for the individual members for their own benefit, but that, I think, is clearly not the meaning of this gift. Nor again is there a perpetuity if the society is at liberty in accordance with the terms of the gift to spend both capital and income as they think fit. . . . If the gift is to be for the endowment of the society to be held as an endowment and the society is according to its form perpetual, the gift is bad: but, if the gift is an immediate beneficial legacy, it is good.' In the result he held the gift for the maintenance and improvement of the Theosophical Lodge at Folkestone to be invalid. Their Lordships respectfully doubt whether the passage in Lord Buckmaster's speech in which he suggests the alternative ground of validity, *viz.*, that the society is at liberty in accordance with the terms of the gift to spend both capital and income as they think fit, presents a true alternative. It is only because the society, *i.e.*, the individuals constituting it, are the beneficiaries that they can dispose of the gift. Lord Tomlin came to the same conclusion. He found in the words of the will ' for the maintenance and improvement ' a sufficient indication that it was the permanence of the Lodge at Folkestone that the testatrix was seeking to secure and this, he thought, necessarily involved endowment. Therefore a perpetuity was created. A passage from the judgment of Lord Hanworth M.R. (which has been obtained from the records) may usefully be cited. He said: ' The problem may be stated in this way. If the gift is in truth to the present members of the society described by their society name so that they have the beneficial use of the property and can, if they please, alienate and put the proceeds in their own pocket, then there is a present gift to individuals which is good: but if the gift is intended for the good not only of the present but of future members so that the present members are in the position of trustees and have no right to appropriate the property or its proceeds for their personal benefit, then the gift is invalid. It may be invalid by reason of there being a trust created, or it may be by reason of the terms that the period allowed by the rule against perpetuities would be exceeded.'

" It is not very clear what is intended by the dichotomy suggested in the last sentence of the citation, but the penultimate sentence goes to the root of the matter. At the risk of repetition their Lordships would point out that if a gift is made to individuals, whether under their own names or in the name of their society, and the conclusion is reached that they are not intended to take beneficially, then they take as trustees. If so, it must be ascertained who are the beneficiaries. If, at the death of the testator, the class of beneficiaries is fixed and ascertained or ascertainable within the limit of the rule against perpetuities, all is well. If it is not so fixed and not so ascertainable, the trust must fail. Of such a trust, no better example could be found than a gift to an order for the benefit of a community of nuns, once it is established that the community is not confined to living and ascertained persons. A wider question is opened if it appears that the trust is not for persons but for a non-charitable purpose. As has been pointed out, no one can enforce such a trust. What follows? *Ex hypothesi*, the trustees are not themselves the beneficiaries, yet the trust fund is in their hands and they may or may not think fit to carry out their testator's wishes. If so, it would seem that the testator has imperfectly exercised his testamentary power; he has delegated it, for the disposal of his property lies with them, not with him. Accordingly, the subject-matter of the gift will be undisposed of or fall into the residuary estate, as the case may be. Their Lordships do not ignore that from this fundamental rule there has from time to time been a deviation: see, for example, *Re Dean*,[15] *Re Thompson* [16]: and that attempts have been made to explain or justify such cases (see, in particular, *Gray on the Rule against Perpetuities* (4th ed.), p. 776 *et seq.*). But the rule as stated in *Morice* v. *Bishop of Durham* [17] (*per* Sir William Grant M.R.[18]) (*per* Lord Eldon L.C.) continues to supply the guiding principle. It may be difficult to reconcile this principle with the decision of *Drummond's* case, but the judge did treat that case as governed by *Cocks* v. *Manners* and, if so, must have assumed that when the will trustees had got the trust fund in their hands they could be compelled by the members of the Old Bradfordians' Club or of the school to apply it as they thought fit. But it is difficult to see how he made such an assumption or arrived at the conclusion that no perpetuity had been created. No similar difficulty arises in regard to the observations of Lord Buckmaster and Lord Tomlin, which have already been cited. The effect is the same, whether the gift is to A, B and C or to a society of A, B and C and no others, upon such terms that they can spend both capital and income as they think fit.

"It is significant of the fine distinctions that are made in these cases that, in *Re Price*, the judge, to whose attention *Re Macaulay's Estate* had been called, held that a gift of a share of residue to the Anthroposophical Society in Great Britain ' to be used at the discretion of the Chairman and Executive Council of the Society for carrying on the teachings of the founder, Dr. Rudolf Steiner,' was a valid gift.

---

15 (1889) 41 Ch.D. 552.
16 [1934] Ch. 342.
17 (1804) 9 Ves. 399.
18 (1805) 10 Ves. 522.

" Before turning once` more and finally to the terms of the present gift, their Lordships must mention the case of *Re Cain*.[19] In that case, Dean J. has made an exhaustive examination of the relevant case-law which must prove of great value in similar cases.

" It must now be asked, then, whether in the present case there are sufficient indications to displace the prima facie conclusion that the gift made by clause 3 of the will is to the individual members of the selected order of nuns at the date of the testator's death so that they can together dispose of it as. they think fit. It appears to their Lordships that such indications are ample.

" In the first place, it is not altogether irrelevant that the gift is in terms upon trust for a selected order. It is true that this can in law be regarded as a trust in favour of each and every member of the order. But at least the form of the gift is not to the members, and it may be questioned whether the testator understood the niceties of the law. In the second place, the members of the selected order may be numerous, very numerous perhaps, and they may be spread over the world. If the gift is to the individuals it is to all the members who were living at the death of the testator, but only to them. It is not easy to believe that the testator intended an ' immediate beneficial legacy ' (to use the words of Lord Buckmaster) to such a body of beneficiaries. In the third place, the subject-matter of the gift cannot be ignored. It appears from the evidence filed in the suit that Elmslea is a grazing property of about 730 acres, with a furnished homestead containing twenty rooms and a number of outbuildings. With the greatest respect to those judges who have taken a different view, their Lordships do not find it possible to regard all the individual members of an order as intended to become the beneficial owners of such a property. Little or no evidence has been given about the organisation and rules of the several orders, but it is at least permissible to doubt whether it is a common feature of them that all their members regard themselves or are to be regarded as having the capacity of (say) the Corps of Commissionaires (see *Re Clarke*) to put an end to their association and distribute its assets. On the contrary, it seems reasonably clear that, however little the testator understood the effect in law of a gift to an unincorporated body of persons by their society name, his intention was to create a trust not merely for the benefit of the existing members of the selected order but for its benefit as a continuing society and for the furtherance of its work.

". . . Their Lordships, therefore, humbly advise Her Majesty that the appeal should be dismissed, but that the gift made by clause 3 of the will is valid by reason only of the provisions of section 37D of the Conveyancing Act 1919–54, and that the power of selection thereby given to the trustees does not extend to contemplative orders of nuns." *Appeal dismissed.*

---

[19] [1950] V.L.R. 382.

Re DENLEY'S TRUST DEED

Chancery Division [1969] 1 Ch. 373; [1968] 3 W.L.R. 457; [1968] 3 All
E.R. 65.

In 1936 land was conveyed by a company to trustees so that until
the expiration of twenty-one years from the death of the last survivor
of certain specified persons the land should under clause 2 (c) of a
trust deed " be maintained and used as and for the purpose of a
recreation or sports ground primarily for the benefit of the employees
of the company and secondarily for the benefit of such other person
or persons (if any) as the trustees may allow to use the same."
Various questions arose as to this clause and other clauses so the
trustees took out an originating summons to have them resolved. The
main question was dealt with as follows in a reserved judgment:

GOFF J. " It was decided in *Re Astor's Settlement Trusts, Astor* v.
Scholfield [20] that a trust for a number of non-charitable purposes was
not merely unenforceable but void on two grounds; first that they
were not trusts for the benefit of individuals, which I will refer to as
' the beneficiary principle,' and, secondly, for uncertainty.

Counsel for the first defendant has argued that the trust in clause 2
(c) in the present case is either a trust for the benefit of individuals, in
which case he argues that they are an unascertainable class and therefore the trust is void for uncertainty, or it is a purpose trust, that is a
trust for providing recreation, which he submits is void on the
beneficiary principle, or alternatively it is something of a hybrid having
the vices of both kinds.

I think that there may be a purpose or object trust, the carrying
out of which would benefit an individual or individuals, where that
benefit is so indirect or intangible or which is otherwise so framed as
not to give those persons any locus standi to apply to the court to
enforce the trust, in which case the beneficiary principle would, as it
seems to me, apply to invalidate the trust, quite apart from any
question of uncertainty or perpetuity. Such cases can be considered
if and when they arise. The present is not, in my judgment, of that
character, and it will be seen that clause 2 (d) of the trust deed
expressly states that, subject to any rules and regulations made by the
trustees, the employees of the company shall be entitled to the use and
enjoyment of the land.

Apart from this possible exception, in my judgment the beneficiary
principle of *Re Astor*,[21] which was approved in *Re Endacott (decd.),
Endacott* v. *Corpe*,[22] see particularly by Harman L.J.,[23] is confined to
purpose or object trusts which are abstract or impersonal. The

[20] [1952] Ch. 534.
[21] [1952] Ch. 534.
[22] [1960] Ch. 232.
[23] [1960] Ch. 232, 250.

objection is not that the trust is for a purpose or object per se, but that there is no beneficiary or cestui que trust. The rule is so expressed in *Lewin on Trusts* (16th ed.), p. 17, and, in my judgment, with the possible exception which I have mentioned, rightly so. In *Re Wood, Barton* v. *Chilcott*,[24] Harman J. said:

> ' There has been an interesting argument on the question of perpetuity, but it seems to me, with all respect to that argument, that there is an earlier obstacle which is fatal to the validity of this bequest, namely, that a gift on trust must have a cestui que trust, and there being here no cestui que trust the gift must fail.'

Again, in *Leahy* v. *Att.-Gen. of New South Wales*,[25] Viscount Simonds, delivering the judgment of the Privy Council, said:

> ' A gift can be made to persons (including a corporation) but it cannot be made to a purpose or to an object: so, also [and these are the important words] a trust may be created for the benefit of persons as cestuis que trust but not for a purpose or object unless the purpose or object be charitable. For a purpose or object cannot sue, but, if it be charitable, the Attorney-General can sue to enforce it.'

Where, then, the trust, though expressed as a purpose, is directly or indirectly for the benefit of an individual or individuals, it seems to me that it is in general outside the mischief of the beneficiary principle.

I am fortified in this conclusion by the dicta of Lord Evershed M.R. and Harman L.J. in *Re Harpur's Will Trusts, Haller* v. *Att.-Gen.*[26] It is fair to say that there are two matters which, in my view, weaken those passages; first, of course, that *Re Astor*[27] and *Re Endacott*[28] were not cited, and, secondly, so far as Lord Evershed M.R. is concerned, that he prefaced his remarks by saying that the argument had satisfied him, and one sees that the examples given in argument were all powers, not trusts,[29] and this does not appear to be due to incomplete reporting, because counsel for the Attorney-General in his reply said[30] that all the examples given by counsel for the next-of-kin were of powers and not trusts. On the other hand, the instance given by Lord Evershed M.R.,[31] which he referred to as an illustration given, which must mean given in the argument, is clearly couched as a trust, albeit discretionary.

Be this as it may, these are weighty dicta, because they were directed to a point specifically taken and pressed in the argument. It was urged that section 2 of the Charitable Trusts (Validation) Act

---

[24] [1949] Ch. 498, 501.
[25] [1959] A.C. 457, 478.
[26] [1962] Ch. 78, 91, 96.
[27] [1952] Ch. 534.
[28] [1960] Ch. 232.
[29] [1962] Ch. 78, 84.
[30] [1962] Ch. 78, 86.
[31] [1962] Ch. 78, 91.

1954 clearly envisages a valid 'imperfect trust provision,' and that there could not be any such valid provision unless the word 'purposes' in the definition in section 1 (1) were so construed as to include institutions.[32] Lord Evershed M.R.[33] said that if the premise were right he would be strongly disposed so to construe the section, but he rejected the premise, saying this:

> 'But the argument in this court has satisfied me that there may well be provisions for purposes, as distinct from provisions for distribution among institutions, which would be imperfect trust provisions within the definition but which, none the less, being valid, could be saved by section 2 (1) from the impact of section 1 (2). An illustration was given of a gift upon trust to apply income during a limited period of, say, ten years for certain named purposes such as the trustees think fit, some of the purposes being charitable and some not charitable. It seems to me that such a gift would by the ordinary law be valid. It is no less clear, as I think, that a provision in that form would be an imperfect trust provision within the definition of the section. It, therefore, is, as I think, no longer true to say that failure to bring a gift of this class into the scope of section 1 is inevitably to give no effect to section 2.'

The passage in the judgment of Harman L.J. is perhaps not quite as reinforced, because he would not (as he described it) have twisted the language of section 1 (1) even if the premise were right, but still he too rejected it, and he said [34]:

> 'I do not feel impressed by that argument because, in my judgment, there are gifts to objects which would be hit by section 1 (1) although perfectly valid and which, therefore, need the protection of section 2 (1). That being so, the motive for the suggested restating of the language does not seem to me to have any particular force.'

Read without any qualification, these observations would, I think, with the greatest respect, be too wide, because 'named purposes' or 'objects' would cover abstract objects, which would be void under the operation of the beneficiary principle, but it is difficult to think that those two learned judges, and in particular Harman L.J., who had in 1959 in *Re Endacott* [35] applauded the orthodox sentiments expressed by Roxburgh J. in *Re Astor*,[36] were in 1962 unmindful of the beneficiary principle. In my judgment, therefore, these dicta, and especially that of Harman L.J., clearly show that in their view there

[32] [1962] Ch. 78, 82, 91.
[33] [1962] Ch. 78, 91.
[34] [1962] Ch. 78, 96.
[35] [1960] Ch. 232, 250.
[36] [1952] Ch. 534.

are purpose or object trusts which escape the operation of that principle.

Some further support for my conclusion is, I think, to be found in *Re Aberconway's Settlement Trusts, McLaren* v. *Aberconway*,[37] where it was assumed that a trust for the upkeep and development of certain gardens which were part of a settled estate was valid. Since the majority of the Court of Appeal decided that the gift over in the event which had happened, namely, the sale of the greater part of the garden, was not invalidated by section 106 of the Settled Land Act 1925 and had therefore taken effect, the question whether the trust was in any event invalid was only indirectly relevant and was not argued, but even so it is, I think, not without significance that in the very next year after *Re Astor*[38] was decided, Sir Raymond Evershed M.R. appears to have had no doubt in his mind that a provision which he described[39] as

'This trust is for a very special and particular object, not, as I assume, a charitable object, but a public object of somewhat similar character,'

that is to say, clearly a purpose trust, and which earlier on the same page he had said might no doubt be regarded as being indirectly for the benefit of the tenant for life, was a valid trust.

Moreover, in the court below[40] Danckwerts J., who thought that the gift over was invalidated, did unquestionably assume the validity of the trust, and so did Denning L.J. in his dissenting judgment,[41] where he said:

'It seems to me, on that evidence, that the trusts which were originally intended by the Garden settlement can be carried out now in the retained part. The only modification necessary in the trusts is to make them apply to the retained part instead of the whole gardens. That is, I think, quite permissible.'

I also derive assistance from what was said by North J. in *Re Bowes, Earl of Strathmore* v. *Vane*.[42] That was a bequest of a sum of money on trust to expend the same in planting trees for shelter on certain settled estates. It happened that there was a father and a son of full age, tenant for life in possession and tenant in tail in remainder respectively; so that, subject to the son disentailing, they were together absolutely entitled, and the actual decision was that they could claim the money, but North J. said[43]:

---

[37] [1953] Ch. 647.
[38] [1952] Ch. 534.
[39] [1953] Ch. 647, 665.
[40] [1952] W.N. 526.
[41] [1953] Ch. 647, 669.
[42] [1896] 1 Ch. 507.
[43] [1896] 1 Ch. 507, 510.

'If it were necessary to uphold it, the trees can be planted upon the whole of it until the fund is exhausted. Therefore, there is nothing illegal in the gift itself . . .';

and [44]: 'I think there clearly is a valid trust to lay out money for the benefit of the persons entitled to the estate.'

The trust in the present case is limited in point of time so as to avoid any infringement of the rule against perpetuities and, for the reasons which I have given, it does not offend against the beneficiary principle; and unless, therefore, it be void for uncertainty, it is a valid trust.

There is, however, one other aspect of uncertainty which has caused me some concern; that is, whether this is in its nature a trust which the court can control, for, as Lord Eldon L.C. said in *Morice* v. *Bishop of Durham* [45]:

'As it is a maxim that the execution of a trust shall be under the control of the court, it must be of such a nature that it can be under that control; so that the administration of it can be reviewed by the court; or, if the trustee dies, the court itself can execute the trust: a trust, therefore, which, in case of mal-administration could be reformed; and a due administration directed; and then, unless the subject and the objects can be ascertained upon principles familiar in other cases, it must be decided that the court can neither reform mal-administration nor direct a due administration.'

The difficulty which I have felt is that there may well be times when some of the employees wish to use the sports club for one purpose while others desire to use it at the same time for some other purpose of such nature that the two cannot be carried on together. The trustees could, of course, control this by making rules and regulations under clause 2 (d) of the trust deed, but they might not. In any case, the employees would probably agree amongst themselves, but I cannot assume that they would. If there were an impasse, the court could not resolve it, because it clearly could not either exercise the trustees' power to make rules or settle a scheme, this being a non-charitable trust: see *Re Astor.* [46]

In my judgment, however, it would not be right to hold the trust void on this ground. The court can, as it seems to me, execute the trust both negatively by restraining any improper disposition or use of the land, and positively by ordering the trustees to allow the employees and such other persons (if any) as they may admit to use the land for the purpose of a recreation or sports ground. Any difficulty there might be in practice in the beneficial enjoyment of the land by those

[44] [1896] 1 Ch. 507, 511.
[45] (1805) 10 Ves. 522, 539.
[46] [1952] Ch. 534.

entitled to use it is, I think, really beside the point. The same kind of problem is equally capable of arising in the case of a trust to permit a number of persons—for example, all the unmarried children of a testator or settlor—to use or occupy a house or to have the use of certain chattels; nor can I assume that in such cases agreement between the parties concerned would be more likely, even if that be a sufficient distinction, yet no-one would suggest, I fancy, that such a trust would be void.

In my judgment, therefore, the provisions of clause 2 (c) are valid."

Re RECHER'S W.T.

Chancery Division [1972] Ch. 526; [1971] 3 W.L.R. 321; [1971] 3 All E.R. 401.

By will dated May 23, 1957, T gave a share of her residuary estate to what the learned judge interpreted as " The London and Provincial Anti-Vivisection Society " which had ceased to exist as such on January 1, 1957. T died in 1962. In a reserved judgment considera- tion was first given to the question whether the gift would have been valid if the unincorporated society had continued its separate existence to T's death:

BRIGHTMAN J.: "... I accept the third defendant's submission that the gift in clause 7 (b) (4) of the will is not a gift to the persons who were the members of the London and Provincial Society at the testa- trix's death, as joint tenants or as tenants in common beneficially, so as to entitle any member to a distributive share. It would be absurd to suppose that the testatrix intended, as soon as the gift fell into possession, that any such member should be entitled, as of right, to demand an aliquot share. Indeed, there is no one joined in these proceedings who would be interested to argue for such construction, and rightly so. Nor do I think that the gift was intended to take effect in favour of present and future members beneficially.

" I turn to the submission that, as a matter of construction, clause 7 (b) (4) of the will ought to be read as a gift in trust ' for the purposes of ' the London and Provincial Society. If so read, it is clear beyond argument that the gift must fail; it is sufficient to cite two sentences from the decision in *Leahy* v. *Att.-Gen. of New South Wales* [47]:

 ' A gift can be made to persons (including a corporation) but it cannot be made to a purpose or to an object; so, also, a trust may be created for the benefit of persons as cestuis que trustent, but not for a purpose or object unless the purpose or object be charitable. For a purpose or object cannot sue, but, if it be charitable, the Attorney-General can sue to enforce it.'

[47] [1959] A.C. 457, 478.

It is argued that I am compelled to read clause 7 (b) (4) as a gift in trust for the purposes of the London and Provincial Society and to decide that it is therefore void. The general proposition relied on is that where one has a gift to an unidentified institution bearing a name suggesting charitable purposes, particularly if found in the company of a number of gifts to identified charitable institutions, the court may save the unidentified gift by assuming that the testator's bounty is not directed towards the particular institutions named by him but is directed towards a purpose. Reference was made to the decisions in *Re Davis, Hannen* v. *Hillyer*,[48] *Re Knox, Fleming* v. *Carmichael*[49] and *Re Satterthwaite's Will Trusts, Midland Bank Executor & Trustee Co. Ltd.* v. *Royal Veterinary College*,[50] as examples of this process. By parity of reasoning, it is said, clause 7 (4) must be read as a gift in trust for the purposes of the London and Provincial Society, although the inevitable result of that construction is to avoid the intended gift. The gift to the London and Provincial Society accompanied gifts to five other animal societies. The testatrix described all six of the clause 7 beneficiaries as charities, and repeated this description in clause 9. She plainly, it is said, had purposes and not institutions in mind.

I appreciate the force of this argument, but I am not tempted to succumb to it. So far as I am aware, the principle invoked by the third defendant has only been applied by the court to avoid the failure of an unidentified gift. I do not know that it has ever been called into play when it would destroy an identified gift. I can well understand that a court of construction may be disposed to read absent words into a will in order to give what effect it can to an equivocal gift. It would, however, be perverse to read absent words into a will in such a way as to defeat, in the process, the intention of the deceased. As a matter of construction, therefore, I do not read clause 7 (4) as a gift in trust for the purposes of the London and Provincial Society.

Having reached the conclusion that the gift in question is not a gift to the members of the London and Provincial Society at the date of death, as joint tenants or tenants in common so as to entitle a member as of right to a distributive share, nor an attempted gift to present and future members beneficially, and is not a gift in trust for the purpose of the society, I must now consider how otherwise, if at all, it is capable of taking effect.

As I have already mentioned, the rules of the London and Provincial Society do not purport to create any trusts except insofar as the honorary trustees are not beneficial owners of the assets of the society, but are trustees on trust to deal with such assets according to the directions of the committee.

---

[48] [1902] 1 Ch. 876.
[49] [1937] Ch. 109.
[50] [1966] 1 W.L.R. 277.

A trust for non-charitable purposes, as distinct from a trust for individuals, is clearly void because there is no beneficiary. It does not, however, follow that persons cannot band themselves together as an association or society, pay subscriptions and validly devote their funds in pursuit of some lawful non-charitable purpose. An obvious example is a members' social club. But it is not essential that the members should only intend to secure direct personal advantages to themselves. The association may be one in which personal advantages to the members are combined with the pursuit of some outside purpose. Or the association may be one which offers no personal benefit at all to the members, the funds of the association being applied exclusively to the pursuit of some outside purpose. Such an association of persons is bound, I would think, to have some sort of constitution; *i.e.* the rights and liabilities of the members of the association will inevitably depend on some form of contract *inter se*, usually evidenced by a set of rules. In the present case it appears to me clear that the life members, the ordinary members and the associate members of the London Provincial Society were bound together by a contract *inter se*. Any such member was entitled to the rights and subject to the liabilities defined by the rules. If the committee acted contrary to the rules, an individual member would be entitled to take proceedings in the courts to compel observance of the rules or to recover damages for any loss he had suffered as a result of the breach of contract. As and when a member paid his subscription to the association, he would be subjecting his money to the disposition and expenditure thereof laid down by the rules. That is to say, the member would be bound to permit, and entitled to require, the honorary trustees and other members of the society to deal with that subscription in accordance with the lawful directions of the committee. Those directions would include the expenditure of that subscription, as part of the general funds of the association, in furthering the objects of the association. The resultant situation, on analysis, is that the London and Provincial Society represented an organisation of individuals bound together by a contract under which their subscriptions became, as it were, mandated towards a certain type of expenditure as adumbrated in rule 1. Just as the two parties to a bipartite bargain can vary or terminate their contract by mutual assent, so it must follow that the life members, ordinary members and associate members of the London and Provincial Society could, at any moment of time, by unanimous agreement (or by majority vote if the rules so prescribe), vary or terminate their multi-partite contract. There would be no limit to the type of variation or termination to which all might agree. There is no private trust or trust for charitable purposes or other trust to hinder the process. It follows that if all members agreed, they could decide to wind up the London and Provincial Society and divide the net assets among themselves beneficially. No one would have any locus standi to stop them so doing. The contract is the same as any other contract and concerns only those who are parties to it, that is to say, the members of the society.

The funds of such an association may, of course, be derived not only from the subscriptions of the contracting parties but also from donations from non-contracting parties and legacies from persons who have died. In the case of a donation which is not accompanied by any words which purport to impose a trust, it seems to me that the gift takes effect in favour of the existing members of the association as an accretion to the funds which are the subject-matter of the contract which such members have made *inter se*, and falls to be dealt with in precisely the same way as the funds which the members themselves have subscribed. So, in the case of a legacy. In the absence of words which purport to impose a trust, the legacy is a gift to the members beneficially, not as joint tenants or as tenants in common so as to entitle each member to an immediate distributive share, but as an accretion to the funds which are the subject-matter of the contract which the members have made *inter se*.

In my judgment the legacy in the present case to the London and Provincial Society ought to be construed as a legacy of that type, that is to say, a legacy to the members beneficially as an accretion to the funds subject to the contract which they had made *inter se*. Of course, the testatrix did not intend the members of the society to divide her bounty between themselves, and doubtless she was ignorant of that remote but theoretical possibility. Her knowledge or absence of knowledge of the true legal analysis of the gift is irrelevant. The legacy is accordingly in my view valid, subject only to the effect of the events of January 1, 1957.

A strong argument has been presented to me against this conclusion and I have been taken through most, if not all, of the cases which are referred to in *Leahy's* case [51] as well as later authorities. It has been urged upon me that if the gift is not a purpose gift, there is no half-way house between, on the one hand, a legacy to the members of the London and Provincial Society at the date of death, as joint tenants beneficially, or as tenants in common beneficially, and, on the other hand, a trust for members which is void for perpetuity because no individual member acting by himself can ever obtain his share of the legacy. I do not see why the choice should be confined to these two extremes. If the argument were correct it would be difficult, if not impossible, for a person to make a straightforward donation, whether *inter vivos* or by will, to a club or other non-charitable association which the donor desires to benefit. This conclusion seems to me contrary to common sense.

---

[51] [1959] A.C. 457.

I do not propose to undertake a lengthy review of the cases. In *Re Clarke, Clarke* v. *Clarke* [52] the well-known case dealing with the Corps of Commissionaires, Byrne J. said:

'It is, I think, established by the authorities that a gift to a perpetual institution not charitable is not necessarily bad. The test, or one test, appears to be, will the legacy when paid be subject to any trust which will prevent the existing members of the association from spending it as they please? If not, the gift is good.'

In *Re Ray's Will Trusts, Public Trustee* v. *Barry* [53] Clauson J. said:

' Another perfectly lawful form of gift would be a gift of a legacy to the controlling officer of a society in his capacity of officer, to be dealt with as he would deal with other funds with which, as such officer of a voluntary society, it would be his duty to deal. Again, that would be a gift which the Court will recognize as a good gift, subject only to this point, which sometimes causes difficulty, that if the frame of the gift indicates that the legacy is not to be used at once and immediately for the purposes of the voluntary society, but is to be set aside and invested and the income only to be used, the capital being preserved as an endowment of the voluntary society, the Court will not give effect to the gift because it infringes the rule that no gift except a charitable gift is to be a perpetuity, and a gift thus to endow a voluntary society necessarily creates a perpetuity.'

There are similar observations in the judgment of Farwell J. in *Re Taylor, Midland Bank Executor & Trustee Co. Ltd.* v. *Smith.* [54] I find this passage in *Leahy's* case [55]:

' For, as Lord Tomlin (sitting at first instance in the Chancery Division) said in *Re Ogden, Brydon* v. *Samuel,* [56] a gift to a voluntary association of persons for the general purposes of the association is an absolute gift and, prima facie, a good gift. He was echoing the words of Lord Parker of Waddington in *Bowman's* case [57] that a gift to an unincorporated association for the attainment of its purposes " may . . . be upheld as an absolute gift to its members." '

Finally, I cite and gratefully adopt the following passage which forms part of the judgment of Cross J. in *Neville Estates Ltd.* v. *Madden* [58]:

' I turn now . . . to the legal issues involved. The question of the construction and effect of gifts to or in trust for unincor-

---

[52] [1901] 2 Ch. 110, 114.
[53] [1936] Ch. 520, 524.
[54] [1940] Ch. 481.
[55] [1959] A.C. 478.
[56] [1933] Ch. 678 at 681.
[57] *i.e., Bowman* v. *Secular Society Ltd.* [1917] A.C. 406, 442.
[58] [1962] Ch. 832, 849.

porated associations was recently considered by the Privy Council in *Leahy* v. *Att.-Gen. of New South Wales.*[59]   The position as I understand it, is as follows.   Such a gift may take effect in one or other of three quite different ways.   In the first place, it may, on its true construction, be a gift to the members of the association at the relevant date as joint tenants, so that any member can sever his share and claim it whether or not he continues to be a member of the association.   Secondly, it may be a gift to the existing members not as joint tenants, but subject to their respective contractual rights and liabilities towards one another as members of the association.   In such a case a member cannot sever his share.   It will accrue to the other members on his death or resignation, even though such members include persons who became members after the gift took effect.   If this is the effect of the gift, it will not be open to objection on the score of perpetuity, unless there is something in its terms or in the rules of the association which precludes the members at any given time from dividing the subject of the gift between them on the footing that they are solely entitled to it in equity.   Thirdly, the terms or circumstances of the gift or the rules of the association may show that the property in question is not to be at the disposal of the members for the time being, but is to be held in trust so that it or its income may be enjoyed by the association or its members from time to time.   In this case . . . the gift will fail unless the association is a charitable body.'

[He went on to hold that the gift lapsed owing to the dissolution of the Society on January 1, 1957.]

REFORM ?

Section 16 of the Ontario Perpetuities Act 1966

(1) A trust for a specific non-charitable purpose that creates no enforceable equitable interest in a specific person shall be construed as a power to appoint the income or the capital, as the case may be, and, unless the trust is created for an illegal purpose or a purpose contrary to public policy, the trust is valid so long as, and to the extent that it is exercised either by the original trustee or his successor, within a period of twenty-one years, notwithstanding that the limitation creating the trust manifested an intention, either expressly or by implication, that the trust should or might continue for a period in excess of that period, but, in the case of such a trust that is expressed to be of perpetual duration, the court may declare the limitation to be void if the court is of opinion that by so doing the result would more closely approximate to the intention of the creator of the trust than the period of validity provided by this section.

(2) To the extent that the income or capital of a trust for a specific non-charitable purpose is not fully expended within a period of twenty-one

---

[59] [1959] A.C. 457.

years, or within any annual or other recurring period within which the
limitation creating the trust provided for the expenditure of all or a specified portion of the income or the capital, the person or persons, or his or
their successors, who would have been entitled to the property comprised
in the trust if the trust had been invalid from the time of its creation, are
entitled to such unexpended income or capital.

PROBLEMS

1. A testator who died in January 1975 by his will made the following
bequests:

   (i) £10,000 to Alan and at his death the remaining part of what is left
      that he does not want for his own use to be divided equally between
      Xerxes and Yorick;

  (ii) £50,000 to my trustees Tom and Tim to distribute amongst such
      of the inhabitants of Greater London as they shall in their unfettered
      discretion think fit;

 (iii) £100,000 to my said trustees to distribute amongst Brian, Charles,
      David, Ellen, Oswald, Peter, Quentin and Roger and such of my
      other business associates and old friends as they shall see fit;

 (iv) residue to my son Simon trusting that he will see to it that my old
      friends shall have the contents of my wine cellar and in case of
      any doubts he shall have power to designate who are my business
      associates and old friends.[60]

Consider the validity of these bequests.

2. "*Re Denley's Trust Deed* is blatantly out of line with previous
authority." Discuss.

3. Tina by will left ten £10,000 legacies to ten specific legatees who were
collectively referred to in her will as "my Beneficiaries." One of them was
Eric whom she had appointed "Executor" of her will. She left her residuary
estate (worth £50,000) to "my life-long true friend Eric, whose judgment I
know I can absolutely rely on, to distribute it amongst such of my Beneficiaries in such proportions as he shall see fit."

Tina has just died and Eric seeks your advice as to whether he can keep
all or any part of the residuary estate.

---

[60] See *Re Coxen* [1948] Ch. 747, 761–762; *Re Raven* [1915] 1 Ch. 673.

CHAPTER 5

EXPRESS PRIVATE TRUSTS

Section 1. Completely and Incompletely Constituted Trusts [1]

THERE are two ways of completely constituting a trust: (1) by the settlor transferring the property intended to be the subject-matter of the trust to persons as trustees upon certain trusts, or (2) by the settlor declaring that he himself will hold certain of his property as trustee upon certain trusts.

I. CREATION OF EXPRESS TRUSTS BY AN EFFECTUAL TRANSFER UPON TRUST [1]

A voluntary transfer is ineffectual both at law and in equity where something remains to be done by the transferor in order to render the transfer effectual. When, however, the transferor has done everything which it is necessary for him to do to render the transfer effectual, but something remains to be done by a third party, the transfer, though invalid at law, is nevertheless valid in equity.

MILROY v. LORD

Court of Appeal in Chancery (1862) 4 De G.F. & J. 264; 31 L.J.Ch. 798; 7 L.T. 178; 8 Jur. 806 (Turner and Knight-Bruce L.JJ.)

Thomas Medley executed a voluntary deed [2] purporting to assign fifty shares in the Louisiana Bank to Samuel Lord upon trust for the benefit of the plaintiffs. The shares were transferable only by entry in the books of the bank; *but no such transfer was ever made.* Samuel Lord held at the time a general power of attorney authorising him to transfer Thomas Medley's shares, and Thomas Medley, after the execution of the settlement, gave him a further power of attorney authorising him to receive the dividends on the bank shares. Thomas Medley lived three years after the execution of the deed, during which period the dividends were received by Samuel Lord and remitted by him to the plaintiffs, sometimes directly and sometimes through Thomas Medley.

Shortly after the execution of the deed, the settlor had delivered to Samuel Lord the certificates for the shares; and on the death of the settlor, Samuel Lord gave up the certificates to the settlor's executor. The shares stood in the settlor's name before and at the time of his death.

Stuart V.-C. held that a trust had been created for the plaintiffs but was reversed upon an appeal by the executor.

TURNER L.J.: "Under the circumstances of this case, it would be difficult not to feel a strong disposition to give effect to this settlement

---

[1] For the formalities required for the creation of trusts, see *supra,* pp. 52–68.
[2] The deed (apparently executed in Louisiana) was expressed to be made in consideration of one dollar.

to the fullest extent, and certainly I have spared no pains to find the means of doing so, consistently with what I apprehend to be the law of the court; but, after full and anxious consideration, I find myself unable to do so. *I take the law of this court to be well settled, that, in order to render a voluntary settlement valid and effectual, the settlor must have done everything which, according to the nature of the property comprised in the settlement, was necessary to be done in order to transfer the property and render the settlement binding upon him. He may, of course, do this by actually transferring the property to the persons for whom he intends to provide, and the provision will then be effectual, and it will be equally effectual if he transfers the property to a trustee for the purposes of the settlement, or declares that he himself holds it in trust for those purposes* [3] *; and if the property be personal, the trust may, as I apprehend, be declared either in writing or by parol; but, in order to render the settlement binding, one or other of these modes must, as I understand the law of this court, be resorted to, for there is no equity in this court to perfect an imperfect gift. The cases, I think, go further to this extent: that if the settlement is intended to be effectuated by one of the modes to which I have referred, the court will not give effect to it by applying another of those modes. If it is intended to take effect by transfer, the court will not hold the intended transfer to operate as a declaration of trust,* [4] *for then every imperfect instrument would be made effectual by being converted into a perfect trust.* These are the principles by which, as I conceive, this case must be tried.

"Applying, then, these principles to the case, there is not here any transfer either of the one class of shares or of the other [5] to the objects of the settlement, and the question therefore must be whether a valid and effectual trust in favour of those objects was created in the defendant Samuel Lord or in the settlor himself as to all or any of these shares. Now it is plain that it was not the purpose of this settlement, or the intention of the settlor, to constitute himself a trustee of the bank shares. The intention was that the trust should be vested in the defendant Samuel Lord, and I think therefore that we should not be justified in holding that by the settlement, or by any parol declaration made by the settlor, he himself became a trustee of these shares for the purposes of the settlement. By doing so we should be converting the settlement or the parol declaration to a purpose wholly different from that which was intended to be effected by it and, as I have said, creating a perfect trust out of an imperfect transaction. . . .

"The more difficult question is whether the defendant Samuel Lord did not become a trustee of these shares. Upon this question I have felt considerable doubt; but in the result, I have come to the conclusion that no perfect trust was ever created in him. The shares,

---

[3] See Sect. 1 (II), *infra.*
[4] See Sect. 1 (III), *infra.*
[5] A similar question arose in the case with reference to a second set of shares.

it is clear, were never legally vested in him; and the only ground on which he can be held to have become a trustee of them is that he held a power of attorney under which he might have transferred them into his own name; but he held that power of attorney as the agent of the settlor; and if he had been sued by the plaintiffs as trustee of the settlement for an account under the trust, and to compel him to transfer the shares into his own name as trustee, I think he might well have said: ' These shares are not vested in me; I have no power over them except as the agent of the settlor, and without his express directions I cannot be justified in making the proposed transfer, in converting an intended into an actual settlement.' A court of equity could not, I think, decree the agent of the settlor to make the transfer, unless it could decree the settlor himself to do so, and it is plain that no such decree could have been made against the settlor. In my opinion, therefore, this decree cannot be maintained as to the fifty Louisiana bank shares. . . .

" Upon the hearing of the appeal it was contended for the plaintiffs, that so far as they might fail in recovering any of the shares in question, they were entitled to recover the value of them against the estate of Thos. Medley. I am not sure that this point can properly be considered to be open upon these pleadings, but whether it be so or not, I agree with my learned brother that the plaintiffs' claim in this respect cannot be maintained. There is no express covenant in the settlement, and whatever might be done as to implying a covenant to do no act in derogation of the settlement, it would, I think, be going too far to imply a covenant to perfect it. If there be a breach of any implied covenant by the delivery of the certificates [by Samuel Lord] to [the executor of Thos. Medley] the plaintiffs' remedy sounds in damages, and they may pursue that remedy at law; for which purpose, if the plaintiffs desire it, there may be inserted in the decree a direction that they be at liberty to use the name of the defendant Lord, of course upon the usual terms of indemnifying him. . . ." [6]

Re ROSE, ROSE v. INLAND REVENUE COMMISSIONERS

Court of Appeal [1952] Ch. 499; [1952] 1 T.L.R. 1577; [1952] 1 All E.R. 1217; [1952] T.R. 175; 31 A.T.C. 138 (Evershed M.R., Jenkins and Morris L.JJ.)

The transferor, Eric Hamilton Rose, was the registered owner of a number of shares in a company known as Leweston Estates Co. On

---

[6] With this case contrast *Kekewich* v. *Manning* (1851) 1 De G.M. & G. 176. A and B held property on trust for A for life, remainder to B. B then *assigned* her beneficial interest by deed to C on trust for D. It was held that a trust had been constituted in favour of D, for the property (an equitable trust interest) had been effectually transferred to the trustee C.

March 30, 1943, he executed two transfers [7] in respect of two blocks of these shares, one in favour of his wife, and the other in favour of his wife and another person to be held by them upon certain trusts. The transfers were registered by Leweston Estates Co. on June 30, 1943. The transferor died more than five years after executing the instruments of transfer but less than five years after the transfers were registered. The question was whether in these circumstances the two blocks of shares should be taken into account for the purpose of assessing estate duty. The relevant taxing provisions were contained in section 2 (1) (c) of the Finance Act 1894 and Schedule XI, Part II, to the Finance Act 1946, according to which if the shares were taken under a voluntary disposition made by a person more than five years before his death and purporting to operate as an immediate gift, no duty would be leviable unless the donee failed to assume bona fide possession and enjoyment of the shares immediately the gift was made, and thenceforward retained possession to the entire exclusion of the donor.

Roxburgh J.[8] decided the question, which arose in both cases, adversely to the Inland Revenue Commissioners, who appealed unsuccessfully to the Court of Appeal.

EVERSHED M.R. read the transfer, which was in the following form: "I Eric Hamilton Rose of Leweston Manor Sherborne in the County of Dorset, Esquire, in consideration of the love and affection I have for my wife, Rosamond Mary Rose of Leweston Manor Sherborne aforesaid (hereinafter called the said 'transferee') do hereby transfer to the said transferee 10,000 (ten thousand) shares of £1 each Nos. 3 to 10,002 inclusive in the undertaking called the Leweston Estates Company to hold unto the said transferee subject to the several conditions on which I held the same at the time of the execution thereof; and I, the said transferee, do hereby agree to accept and take the said shares subject to the conditions aforesaid." He then continued:
"There are certain observations which may be made upon that document. The first is this: it was in form in exact correspondence with the requirements of the company's regulations, for in article 29, dealing with the transfer of shares, it is provided that 'shares in the company shall be transferred in the following form or as near thereto as circumstances will permit'. . . .' The form which followed was that which Mr. Rose adopted. On its execution the deed of transfer was beyond question delivered to the transferee, together with the certificate relative to those shares.
"It follows, therefore, that so far as lay in his power the transferor Mr. Rose did all that he could—he followed carefully and precisely the obligations imposed on a proposing transferor by the article—to divest

---

[7] One was a gratuitous transfer, and the other was expressed to be for a nominal consideration.
[8] [1951] 2 All E.R. 959.

himself then and there in favour of his wife of all his interest, legal and equitable, in the shares.

" The next thing to notice . . . is this. The company was unlimited, and this form of transfer differed, therefore, in one respect from the forms of transfer sometimes found in the case of limited companies, in that it contained what was in effect (because it was under seal) a covenant by Mrs. Rose to accept and take the shares subject to the conditions . . . imposed on shareholders by the regulations of the company, and it was executed not only by the transferor but also by the transferee . . .

" The burden of the case presented by the Crown may be briefly put as it was formulated by counsel. This document, he said, on the face of it, was intended to operate and operated, if it operated at all, as a transfer. If for any reason it was at its date incapable of so operating it is not legitimate, either by reference to the expressed intention in the document or on well-established principles of law, to extract from it a wholly different transaction, *i.e.*, to make it take effect, not as a transfer, but as a declaration of trust. Now I agree that on the face of the document it was obviously intended (if you take the words used) to operate, and operate immediately, as a transfer . . . of rights. To some extent at least, it is said, it could not possibly do so. To revert to the illustration which has throughout been taken, if the company had declared a dividend during his interregnum, it is not open to question that the company must have paid that dividend to the donor. So that *vis-à-vis* the company this document did not and could not operate to transfer to Mrs. Rose the right against the company to claim and receive that dividend. Shares, it is said by counsel for the Crown, are property of a peculiar character consisting, as it is sometimes put, of a bundle of rights, *i.e.*, rights against or in the company. It has followed from counsel's argument that, if such a dividend had been paid, Mr. Rose could, consistently with the document to which he has set his hand and seal, have retained that dividend, and if he had handed it over to his wife it would have been an independent gift. I think myself that such a conclusion is startling. Indeed, I venture to doubt whether to anybody but a lawyer such a conclusion would even be comprehensible, at least without a considerable amount of explanation. That again is not conclusive, but I confess that I approach a matter of this kind with a preconceived notion that a conclusion that offends common sense so much as this would prima facie do ought not to be the right conclusion. Jenkins L.J. carried the illustration a stage further. He said: Suppose, on the Crown's view, the donor, retaining, pending registration, full rights over these shares (for counsel for the Crown argued that this document not only did not transfer the legal estate, but that it transferred no interest or estate whatever), repented of his generosity and told the company not to register the transfer. Supposing the wife went to the company and the directors of the company had nevertheless said that they were willing to register the transfer. Let it be then further supposed that the donor proceeded to take action to restrain the company by injunction from registering the transfer. If the donor, in truth, retained at that time a proprietary interest the court would be bound to protect it by granting an injunction. That, indeed, was perhaps too startling for counsel, for he said that he thought the court would not grant an injunction and that, the document having at least operated as a gift of a piece of paper, *viz.*, the share certificate, the donor could not be heard then to claim the court's assistance so as to restrain the company from doing that which possession, as upon gift, of the certificate and of this transfer enabled the donee to require the company to do. I do not pursue these examples, but it seems to follow from testing this matter by such extreme cases that the assertion that nothing whatever passed under this deed except the right to possess, as . . . physical things, two pieces of paper is not right. [His Lordship then examined *Milroy* v. *Lord*[9] and after quoting the passage from that case italicised *supra*, p. 137, continued:] Those last few sentences form the gist of the Crown's argument, and on it is founded the broad, general proposition that if a document is expressed as, and on the face of it intended to operate as, a transfer, it cannot in any respect take effect by way of trust—so far I understand the argument to go. In my judgment, that statement is too broad and involves too great a simplification of the problem, and is not warranted by authority. I agree that if a man purporting to transfer property executes documents which are not apt to effect that purpose, the court cannot then extract from those documents some quite different trans- action and say that they were intended merely to operate as a declaration of trust which *ex facie* they were not; but if a document is apt and proper to transfer the property—is, in truth, the appropriate way in which the property must be transferred—then it does not seem to me to follow from the statement of Turner L.J. that, as a result, either during some limited period or otherwise, a trust may not arise, for the purpose of giving effect to the transfer. The simplest case will, perhaps, provide an illustration. If a man executes a document transferring all his equitable interest, say, in shares, that document, operating and intended to operate as a transfer, will give rise to and take effect as a trust, for the assignor will then be a trustee of the legal estate in the shares for the person in whose favour he has made an assignment of his beneficial interest. And for my part I do not think that *Milroy* v. *Lord* is an authority which compels this court to hold that in this case, where, in the terms of Turner L.J.'s judgment, the settlor did everything which, according to the nature of the property comprised in the settlement, was necessary to be done by him in order to transfer the property, the result necessarily negatives the conclusion that, pending registration, the settlor was a trustee of the legal interest for the transferee.

"The view of the limitations of *Milroy* v. *Lord* which I have tried

---

[9] (1862) 4 De G.F. & J. 264; *supra*, p. 136.

to express was much better expressed by Jenkins J. in the recent case which also bears the name of *Re Rose* [10] (though that is a coincidence). It is true that the main point, the essential question to be determined, was whether there had been a transfer *eo nomine* of certain shares within the meaning of a will. The testator in that case, Rose, by his will had given a number of shares to one Hook, but the gift was subject to this qualification: 'If such . . . shares have not been transferred to him previously to my death.' The question was: Had the shares been transferred to him in these circumstances? He had executed (as had this Mr. Rose) a transfer in appropriate form, and handed the transfer and the certificate to Hook, but, at the time of his death, the transfer had not been registered. It was said, therefore, that there had been no transfer, and (following the argument of counsel for the Crown) there had been no passing to Hook of any interest, legal or beneficial, whatever, by the time the testator died. If that view were right, then, of course, Hook would be entitled to the shares under the will. But Jenkins J. went a little more closely into the matter because it was obvious that on one view of it, if it were held that there was a 'transfer' within the terms of the will, though the transfer was inoperative in the eye of the law and not capable of being completed after the death, then Mr. Hook suffered the misfortune of getting the shares neither by gift *inter vivos* nor by testamentary benefaction. Therefore Jenkins J. considered *Milroy* v. *Lord* and in regard to it he used this language [11]: ' I was referred on that to the well-known case of *Milroy* v. *Lord* and also to the recent case of *Re Fry*.[12] Those cases, as I understand them, turn on the fact that the deceased donor had not done all in his power, according to the nature of the property given, to vest the legal interest in the property in the donee. In such circumstances it is, of course, well settled that there is no equity to complete the imperfect gift. If any act remains to be done by the donor to complete the gift at the date of the donor's death, the court will not compel his personal representatives to do that act and the gift remains incomplete and fails. In *Milroy* v. *Lord* the imperfection was due to the fact that the wrong form of transfer was used for the purpose of transferring certain bank shares. The document was not the appropriate document to pass any interest in the property at all.' Then he refers to *Re Fry*, which is another illustration, and continued: ' In this case, as I understand it, the testator had done everything in his power to divest himself of the shares in question to Mr. Hook. He had executed a transfer. It is not suggested that the transfer was not in accordance with the company's regulations. He had handed that transfer together with the certificate to Mr. Hook. There was nothing else the testator could do.'

"I venture respectfully to adopt the whole of the passage I have

---

[10] [1949] Ch. 78.
[11] *Ibid.* 89.
[12] [1946] Ch. 312. For inessential irregularities see *Re Paradise Motor Co.* [1968] 1 W.L.R. 1125.

read which, in my judgment, is a correct statement of the law. If that be so, then it seems to me that it cannot be asserted on the authority of *Milroy* v. *Lord*, and I venture to think it also cannot be asserted as a matter of logic and good sense or principle, that because, by the regulations of the company, there had to be a gap before Mrs. Rose could, as between herself and the company, claim the rights which the shares gave her *vis-à-vis* the company, Mr. Rose was not in the meantime a trustee for her of all his rights and benefits under the shares. That he intended to pass all those rights, as I have said, seems to me too plain for argument. I think the matter might be put, perhaps, in a somewhat different fashion though it reaches the same end. Whatever might be the position during the period between the execution of this document and the registration of the shares, the transfers were on June 30, 1943, registered. After registration, the title of Mrs. Rose was beyond doubt complete in every respect, and if Mr. Rose had received a dividend between execution and registration and Mrs. Rose had claimed to have that dividend handed to her, what would Mr. Rose's answer have been? It could no longer be that the purported gift was imperfect; it had been made perfect. I am not suggesting that the perfection was retroactive. But what else could he say? How could he, in the face of his own statement under seal, deny the proposition that he had, on March 30, 1943, transferred the shares to his wife? By the phrase ' transfer the shares ' surely must be meant transfer to her ' the shares and all my right, title and interest thereunder.' Nothing else could sensibly have been meant. Nor can he, I think, make much of the fact that this was a voluntary settlement on his part. Being a case of an unlimited company, as I have said, Mrs. Rose had herself to undertake by covenant to accept the shares subject to their burdens—in other words to relieve Mr. Rose of his liability as a corporator. I find it unnecessary to pursue the question of consideration, but it is, I think, another feature which would make exceedingly difficult, and sensibly impossible, the assertion on Mr. Rose's part of any right to retain any such dividend. . . ."

Held, therefore, that the transfer was valid and effectual in equity from March 30, 1943, and accordingly the shares were not assessable for estate duty. *Appeal dismissed.*

Note

A gift of shares is, therefore, valid in equity if (1) the transferor has executed the form of transfer required by the company's articles [13] and (2) has done everything else which it is necessary for him to do to make the transfer effective and binding upon him.[14] The gift is effective at law when registration of the transfer is made, and until this is done a transferor who complies with (1) and (2) above is a trustee for the transferee.

---

[13] In *Milroy* v. *Lord* (*supra*) the form used was a deed poll; in *Antrobus* v. *Smith* (1805) 12 Ves. 39, unsealed writing, both of which were inappropriate forms according to the company's articles.
[14] In *Re Fry* [1946] Ch. 312 it would have been necessary for the donor to execute confirmatory transfers.

The identical principle applies to a gift of a debt. If, therefore, the donor makes an absolute written assignment of the debt,[15] the gift is good in equity, though it will not be valid at law until written notice is received by the debtor.[16] A voluntary oral assignment on the other hand would be ineffective both at law and in equity.[17]

The same applies to a gift of an equitable interest. If the donor has made a written assignment, whether of the whole or a part of the equitable interest,[18] and done everything else which was required of him, the gift is good. This was so in *Kekewich* v. *Manning*,[19] where the donor made a voluntary assignment by deed of his equitable interest in a trust fund. On the other hand, in *Re McArdle*,[20] even if the court had been able to construe the transaction as a gift, as distinct from a promise to give, it would still have failed since, though the gift was in writing, the donors had not done everything else necessary to perfect it. It was still necessary for them to authorise the executors to pay and, this not having been done, the gift was ineffectual.

Legal estates in freehold or leasehold property must be transferred by deed or in the case of registered land by a transfer form which is subsequently registered.

Personal chattels must be transferred by delivery or by deed. It is noteworthy that money is not effectively given by the donor giving his cheque for the money.[21]

II. CREATION OF AN EXPRESS TRUST BY AN EFFECTUAL DECLARATION OF TRUST

In each case where a declaration of trust is relied on the court must be satisfied that a *present irrevocable* declaration of trust has been made complying with the requisite formalities.[22]

JONES v. LOCK

Lord Chancellor (1865) L.R. 1 Ch.App. 25; 35 L.J.Ch. 177; 13 L.T. 514; 11 Jur. 913; 14 W.R. 149

Robert Jones had a son aged nine months. One day at home, in the presence of the father, mother and child, the child's nurse said to the father: "You have come back from Birmingham and have not brought baby anything." To this the father replied that he had given baby a pair of boots, and would now make him a handsome present. He then produced a cheque for £900, saying: "Look you here, I give this to

---

[15] As required by s. 136 of the Law of Property Act 1925.
[16] *Holt* v. *Heatherfield Trust* [1942] 2 K.B 1.
[17] *Cf. Tibbits* v. *George* (1836) 5 A. & E. 107.
[18] As required by s. 53 (1) (c) of the Law of Property Act 1925; see *Letts* v. *I.R.C.* [1957] 1 W.L.R. 201, discussed by J. C. Hall, "Gift of Part of a Debt" [1959] C.L.J. 99, 102.
[19] (1851) 1 De G.M. & G. 176; such an assignment may take the form of a written direction to the trustees to hold on trust for the third party; *Grey* v. *I.R.C.*, *supra*, p. 55; *Re Wale* [1956] 1 W.L.R. 1346. [20] [1951] Ch. 669.
[21] *Re Swinburne* [1926] Ch. 38; *Re Owen* [1949] W.N. 202 [1949] 1 All E.R. 901.
[22] Neville J. in *Re Cozens* [1913] 2 Ch. 478, 486; Romilly M.R. in *Grant* v. *Grant* (1865) 34 Beav. 623, 626.

baby; it is for himself, and I am going to put it away for him, and will give him a great deal more along with it." He then placed the cheque in the child's hand, whereupon his wife said: " Don't let him tear it "; to which he answered: " Never mind if he does; it is his own, and he may do what he likes with it." Taking the cheque away from the child, he said to the nurse: " Now, Lizzie, I am going to put this away for my own son." He then put it in his safe.

This cheque had in fact been drawn in favour of the father, since when the father had informed his solicitor of his intention of adding £100 to it and investing the whole sum of £1,000 for his son. A few days later he spoke to his solicitor as follows: " I·shall come to your office on Monday to alter my will, that I may take care of my son." He died the very same day, and the solicitor, who was one of his executors, having found the cheque in the safe, obtained payment in favour of the estate.

Held, by the Vice-Chancellor, that there had been a declaration of trust in favour of the son. Legatees under the will of Robert Jones appealed.

LORD CRANWORTH L.C.: " This is a special case, in which I regret to say that I cannot bring myself to think that, either on principle or on authority, there has been any gift or any valid declaration of trust. No doubt a gift may be made by any person *sui juris* and *compos mentis*, by conveyance of a real estate or by delivery of a chattel; and there is no doubt also that, by some decisions, unfortunate I must think them, a parol declaration of trust of personalty may be perfectly valid even when voluntary. If I give any chattel that, of course, passes by delivery, and if I say, expressly or impliedly, that I constitute myself a trustee of personalty, that is a trust executed, and capable of being enforced without consideration. I do not think it necessary to go into any of the authorities cited before me; they all turn upon the question whether what has been said was a declaration of trust or an imperfect gift. In the latter case the parties would receive no aid from a court of equity if they claimed as volunteers. But when there has been a declaration of trust, then it will be enforced, whether there has been consideration or not. Therefore the question in each case is one of fact; has there been a gift or not, or has there been a declaration of trust or not? I should have every inclination to sustain this gift, but unfortunately I am unable to do so. The case turns on the very short question whether Jones intended to make a declaration that he held the property in trust for the child; and I cannot come to any other conclusion than that he did not. I think it would be of very dangerous example if loose conversations of this sort, in important transactions of this kind, should have the effect of declarations of trust . . .

" It was all quite natural, but the testator would have been very much surprised if he had been told that he had parted with the £900, and could no longer dispose of it. It all turns upon the facts, which do not lead me to the conclusion that the testator meant to deprive himself of all property in the note, or to declare himself a trustee of the money for the child. I extremely regret this result, because it is obvious that, by the act of God, this unfortunate child has been deprived of a provision which his father meant to make for him. . . ." *Appeal allowed.*[23]

Note

A declaration of trust, to be effectual, need not be literal. It is not necessary for an intending declarant to say: "I declare myself a trustee." What is necessary is some form of expression which shows clearly that he intended to constitute himself trustee, or to constitute another a beneficiary.[24]

Neville J., in *Re Cozens*,[25] referred to a "present irrevocable declaration of trust." The distinction is apparently between these declarations: "I declare a trust for X to arise on my death" and "I declare that on my death I will declare a trust for X." The latter is a mere promise to create a trust in the future, an example being *Bayley* v. *Boulcott*.[26] The former would operate as a declaration of trust in favour of the declarant for life, remainder to X, an example being *Kelly* v. *Walsh*.[27]

An interesting example of a declaration of trust occurred in *Re Ralli's Will Trusts*.[28] H, the owner of a reversionary interest under the will of her deceased father covenanted with the trustees of her marriage settlement to settle all her existing and after-acquired property upon certain trusts which failed and ultimately upon trusts for the benefit of the children of H's sister who were volunteers. A clause in the marriage settlement declared that all property comprised within the terms of the covenant should be subject in equity to the trusts of the settlement pending transfer to the trustees. H never assigned the reversionary interest to the trustees. Buckley J. held (p. 298) that the reversionary interest being existing property of H at the time of her declaration of trust there was a valid trust of the interest. It would appear that if her reversionary interest had only been acquired by her subsequently to her settlement so as to be after-acquired property then no trust of the interest would have arisen as declarations of trust in respect of after-acquired property are ineffective at law and in equity.[29]

---

23 So also *Dipple* v. *Corles* (1853) 11 Hare 183; *Re Mills* (1859) 7 W.R. 372; *Re Glover* (1862) 2 J. & H. 186; *Heartley* v. *Nicholson* (1875) L.R. 19 Eq. 233; *Re Shield* (1885) 53 L.T. 5; *Adams* v. *Lopdell* (1890) 25 L.R.Ir. 311 323–324; *North* v. *Medley* (1891) 8 T.L.R. 141; *Allan* v. *Inland Revenue* [1925] N.I. 50; 133 L.T. 9.
24 See *Ex p. Pye* (1811) 18 Ves. 140, 149–150; *Wheatley* v. *Purr* (1837) 1 Keen 551; *Thorpe* v. *Owen* (1842) 5 Beav. 224; *Moore* v. *Darton* (1851) 4 De G. & Sm. 517; *Wilcocks* v. *Hannyngton* (1855) 5 Ir.Ch.R. 38, 44–46; *Steele* v. *Waller* (1860) 28 Beav. 466; *Parker* v. *Stones* (1868) 38 L.J.Ch. 46; *Armstrong* v. *Timperon* [1871] W.N. 4; *Miller* v. *Harrison* (1871) Ir.R. 5 Eq. 324, 341 *et seq.*; *Kelly* v. *Walsh* (1878) 1 L.R.Ir. 275, 281–282; *Hartopp* v. *Hartopp* (1887) 3 T.L.R. 384; *Re Davison* (1893) 31 L.R.Ir. 249, 257; affd. [1894] 1 Ir.R. 56; *New's Trustee* v. *Hunting* [1897] 2 Q.B. 19; affd. [1899] A.C. 419.
25 [1913] 2 Ch. 478, 486.
26 (1828) 4 Russ. 345.
27 (1878) 1 L.R.Ir. 275; see also *Re Smith* (1890) 64 L.T. 13.
28 [1964] Ch. 288; distinguishing *Re Anstis* (1886) 31 Ch.D. 596, and as an independent ground of the decision applying the rule in *Strong* v. *Bird* (1874) L.R. 18 Eq. 315, *infra*, p. 172.
29 *Williams* v. *C.I.R.* [1965] N.Z.L.R. 395, *infra*, p. 164.

III. Ineffectual Transfers not Saved by being Regarded as Effectual Declarations

However clearly there may have been an intention to create a (voluntary) trust by transfer, if the intending transferor has used an ineffectual method of transfer, this will not be construed into a declaration of trust.

RICHARDS v. DELBRIDGE

Master of the Rolls (1874) L.R. 18 Eq. 11; 43 L.J.Ch. 459; 22 W.R. 584

A grandfather was possessed of leasehold business premises. He indorsed and signed on the lease a memorandum as follows: " This deed and all thereto belonging I give to R. from this time forth, with all the stock-in-trade." Shortly afterwards he delivered the lease to R.'s mother on behalf of R. (who was his grandson, an infant). The grandfather died, his will making no specific reference to the business premises, but disposing of his furniture and effects.

A bill was filed claiming that the indorsement on the lease by the testator and the delivery of it by him to R.'s mother on behalf of R. created a valid trust in favour of R. R., the plaintiff, contended that though there is no equity to perfect an imperfect gift, yet where there is a clear intention to create a trust the court will hold that an instrument, though informal, constitutes a declaration of trust; citing *Richardson* v. *Richardson* [30] and *Morgan* v. *Malleson*.[31]

JESSEL M.R.: " This bill is warranted by the decisions in *Richardson* v. *Richardson* and *Morgan* v. *Malleson*; but, on the other hand, we have the case of *Milroy* v. *Lord* [32] before the Court of Appeal, and the more recent case of *Warriner* v. *Rogers*.[33] . . . The two first-mentioned cases are wholly opposed to the two last. That being so, I am not at liberty to decide the case otherwise than in accordance with the decision of the Court of Appeal. It is true the judges appear to have taken different views of the construction of certain expressions, but I am not bound by another judge's view of the construction of particular words; and there is no case in which a different principle is stated from that laid down by the Court of Appeal. Moreover, if it were my duty to decide the matter for the first time, I should lay down the law in the same way.

" The principle is a very simple one. A man may transfer his property, without valuable consideration, in one of two ways: he may either do such acts *as amount in law to a conveyance or assignment*

---

[30] (1867) L.R. 3 Eq. 686.
[31] (1870) L.R. 10 Eq. 475.
[32] (1862) 4 De G.F. & J. 264; *supra*, p. 136.
[33] (1873) L.R. 16 Eq. 340.

of the property, and thus completely divest himself of the legal [34] ownership, in which case the person who by those acts acquires the property
takes it beneficially, or on trust, as the case may be; or the legal owner
of the property may, by one or other of the modes recognised as
amounting to a valid declaration of trust, *constitute himself a trustee*
and, without an actual transfer of the legal title, may so deal with the
property as to deprive himself of its beneficial ownership, and declare
that he will hold it from that time forward on trust for the other person.
It is true he need not use the words ' I declare myself a trustee,' but he
must do something which is equivalent to it, and use expressions which
have that meaning; for however anxious the court may be to carry out
a man's intention, it is not at liberty to construe words otherwise than
according to their proper meaning.

"The cases in which the question has arisen are nearly all cases in
which a man, by documents insufficient to pass a legal interest, has
said: ' I give or grant certain property to A B.' Thus, in *Morgan* v.
Malleson the words were: ' I hereby give and make over to Dr. Morris
an India bond '; and in *Richardson* v. *Richardson* the words were:
' grant, convey, and assign.' In both cases the judges held that the
words were effectual declarations of trust. In the former case Lord
Romilly considered that the words were the same as these: ' I undertake
to hold the bond for you,' which would undoubtedly have amounted
to a declaration of trust.

"The true distinction appears to me to be plain and beyond dispute:
for a man to make himself a trustee there must be an expression of
intention to become a trustee, whereas words of present gift show an
intention to give over property to another, and not retain it in the
donor's hands for any purpose, fiduciary or otherwise.

"In *Milroy* v. *Lord* Turner L.J., after referring to the two modes
of making a voluntary settlement valid and effectual, adds these words:
' The cases, I think, go further, to this extent, that if the settlement is
intended to be effectuated by one of the modes to which I have referred,
the court will not give effect to it by applying another of those modes.
If it is intended to take effect by transfer, the court will not hold the
intended transfer to operate as a declaration of trust, for then every
imperfect instrument would be made effectual by being converted into
a perfect trust.'

"It appears to me that that sentence contains the whole law on the
subject. If the decisions of Lord Romilly and of Vice-Chancellor Wood
[in *Morgan* v. *Malleson* and *Richardson* v. *Richardson*, respectively]
were right, there never could be a case where an expression of a present
gift would not amount to an effectual declaration of trust, which would
be carrying the doctrine on that subject too far. . . ."

---

[34] Or equitable; but the formalities required for a transfer or declaration by an
equitable owner may differ from those required by a legal owner: see *supra*, pp.
52–68.

Held, therefore, no trust had been created; for the assignment not under seal was ineffectual to transfer a chattel real, and the court will not construe an ineffectual transfer into a declaration of trust, however clearly there may have been an intention to create a trust.[35]

IV. THE IMPORTANCE OF THE DISTINCTION BETWEEN COMPLETELY AND INCOMPLETELY CONSTITUTED TRUSTS

If a trust in your favour is completely constituted, either by a transfer upon trust or by a declaration of trust, you claim as *cestui que trust*, and it is immaterial that you are a volunteer. Moreover, in order to be effectual, a declaration of trust must manifest a clear intention on the part of the settlor to constitute himself trustee, and a transfer upon trust must be made by a method of transfer which is appropriate to pass the property in question. If the transfer is ineffectual both at law and in equity, it will not be construed by the court to take effect as a declaration.

If, on the other hand, something remains to be done in order to render a promised or intended trust or gift in your favour completely constituted, then you cannot enforce the promise if you are a volunteer[36]; for "Equity will not assist a volunteer."[37] You are not, however, a volunteer if either you have given value or you can bring yourself within a marriage consideration: *Pullan* v. *Koe* (*infra*). In such a case you can sue the settlor in your own right joining the trustees as co-defendants if they refuse to sue.[38] Trusts in wills are special in that they are all completely constituted though executory.

A promise to create a trust made before and in consideration of marriage is regarded in equity as having been made for value. If the trust is created after marriage and contains a recital that it was made in pursuance of an ante-nuptial promise to create the trust, it is also regarded as having been made for value.[39] It appears, however, that only the parties to, and the issue of, a marriage are within the marriage consideration[40]; although, exceptionally, children of a former marriage or a possible second marriage —or even illegitimate children—may come within a marriage consideration if their interests are inseparable from those of the issue of the marriage.[41]

---

[35] These principles are discussed and applied in numerous cases other than those specifically dealt with in the preceding part of this chapter. For such cases dealing with various subject matters, please see 5th ed. hereof p. 130, n. 34.

[36] See *Re D'Angibau* (1880) 15 Ch.D. 228; *Paul* v. *Paul* (1882) 20 Ch.D. 742; *Pullan* v. *Koe* [1913] 1 Ch. 9; *Re Plumptre's Marriage Settlement* [1910] 1 Ch. 609; *Re Kay's Settlement* [1939] Ch. 329; *Re Cook's S.T.* [1965] Ch. 902.

[37] Equity will assist beneficiaries who are not volunteers if they seek to have a trust completely constituted even though volunteers will thereby be benefited, *e.g.*, where someone within a marriage consideration and having a life interest sues to have property brought into a settlement the court will order this and will not exclude volunteers taking under the settlement when the life interest determines, since the covenant sued upon is enforced in its entirety: *Davenport* v. *Bishopp* (1843) 2 Y. & C.C.C. 451, affd. (1846) 1 Ph. 698.

[38] *Vandepitte* v. *Preferred Accident Insurance Co. of New York* [1933] A.C. 70, 79; *Harmer* v. *Armstrong* [1934] Ch. 65.

[39] *Re Holland* [1902] 2 Ch. 360.

[40] See *De Mestre* v. *West* [1891] A.C. 264; *Att.-Gen.* v. *Jacobs Smith* [1895] 2 Q.B. 341; *Re D'Avigdor-Goldsmid* [1957] Ch. 1038, 1053 (reversed on other grounds [1953] A.C. 347); *I.R.C.* v. *Rennell* [1964] A.C. 173; *Re Cook's S.T.* [1965] Ch. 902.

[41] *Newstead* v. *Searles* (1737) 1 Atk. 265; *Clark* v. *Wright* (1861) 6 H. & N. 849; *Re Cook's S.T.* [1965] Ch. 902, 917; Family Law Reform Act 1969.

However, although you are a volunteer you can recover full damages at common law for breach of covenant if you are a covenantee: *Cannon* v. *Hartley* [42] (*infra*).

Normally, though, the covenant will not be with you but with the trustees. Can they not sue as covenantees and recover damages at common law which they could then hold on trust for you? This is a vexed question.[43] It should first be observed that in certain special circumstances it may not be necessary to resort to such action as there will already be a completely constituted trust of the benefit of the covenant which may thus be enforced by you on ordinary trust principles, *e.g.*, if the settlor covenanted to transfer £50,000 to T1 and T2 to the intent that they should hold the benefit of the covenant as a chose in action for the benefit of various beneficiaries including yourself or where the circumstances are so special that such an intention can be inferred (as where your father is a respectable pillar of society and you are his illegitimate son for whom he secretly executed a deed in which he covenanted with trustees that his personal representatives should within one year of his death transfer to them the sum of £50,000 to hold upon trust for you absolutely upon attaining the age of twenty-one).[44] However, if the covenant were to settle after-acquired property [45] there could be no completely constituted trust of the benefit of it as the subject-matter is too uncertain: a *spes* of future property cannot be assigned and is incapable of being the subject-matter of a trust though a contract to assign a *spes* of future property is enforceable once the property materialises [46] (as for example in the case of settlements made in consideration of marriage).

Thus, if the settlor covenanted to transfer all property he might acquire under his father's will to T1 and T2 to hold upon trust for you and upon his father's death the settlor refused to transfer more than a quarter of such property, what is the position? It is quite clear [47] that the settlor cannot change his mind and recover that quarter, but can the trustees sue the settlor for damages at common law for breach of his covenant with them?

The difficulty is that such a straightforward action would indirectly assist you though you were a mere volunteer, and equity, which prevails where there is any conflict with the common law, has the maxim, " Equity will not assist a volunteer." Moreover, if the trustees do not first obtain the leave of the court to take proceedings on behalf of the trust they will be at personal risk as to the costs of the proceedings if such are unsuccessful unless they can establish that the costs were properly incurred.[48] If they try to establish this the court puts itself " in the position in which the court

---

42 [1949] Ch. 213; L.P.A. 1925, s. 56.
43 D. W. Elliott (1960) 76 L.Q.R. 100; J. A. Hornby (1962) 78 L.Q.R. 228; D. Matheson (1966) 29 M.L.R. 397; J. D. Davies [1967] *Annual Survey of Commonwealth Law*, pp. 287–297; W. A. Lee (1969) 85 L.Q.R. 313.
44 *Fletcher* v. *Fletcher* (1844) 4 Hare 67, *infra*, p. 167.
45 Difficult questions of construction can arise as to the scope of such covenants: *Re Peel's Settlement* [1964] 1 W.L.R. 1232 and cases there cited.
46 *Re Tilt* (1896) 74 L.T. 163; *Re Ellenborough* [1903] 1 Ch. 697; *Re Cook's S.T.* [1965] Ch. 902; *Re Brooks' S.T.* [1939] Ch. 993; *Williams* v. *Commissioners of Inland Revenue* [1965] N.Z.L.R. 395 (*infra*); *Holroyd* v. *Marshall* (1862) 10 H.L.C. 191; *Re Lind* [1915] 2 Ch. 345; *Collyer* v. *Isaacs* (1881) 19 Ch.D. 342.
47 *Re Bowden* [1936] Ch. 71; *Re Adlard* [1954] Ch. 29.
48 *Re Beddoe* [1893] 1 Ch. 547.

would have been had an application been made to the court, as it ought to have been made if it was intended to throw the costs of the proceedings on the estate, before commencing the action which has been brought and tried." [49]

If the trustees do seek the leave of the court, as they should, they will be directed that they ought not to sue.[50] Since this is well established there is no need for the trustees to seek leave and they will have a complete defence if you sought to sue them for breach of trust for not suing for damages.[51] Though the cases establishing that the trustees will be directed not to sue concern after-acquired property covenants, they appear [52] to be based on the principle that the enforcement of the covenants would be to give volunteers by indirect means relief they could not obtain by any direct procedure and would in effect be to enforce the settlement in favour of volunteers and "Equity will not assist volunteers." The position should thus be the same for other covenants such as covenants to transfer specific items of property or specific sums of money except that in these cases there is an outside chance that there might be a completely constituted trust of the benefit of the covenant. The chance is very much an outside one because when a settlor covenants to transfer £50,000 to T1 and T2 upon trust for various beneficiaries he normally has no intention of creating a trust of the benefit of the covenant, only an intention to create a trust of the £50,000 as and when it is transferred to the trustees.[53]

In practice it is most unlikely that trustees would ever sue a settlor for damages for breach of covenant where there was no completely constituted trust of the covenant. However, if they did, upon being indemnified as to costs by an interested volunteer, what are their chances of success if they tried for summary judgment under R.S.C., Ord. 14 in the Chancery Division?

It would appear that since the maxim is "Equity will not assist a volunteer" and is not "Equity will frustrate a volunteer suing at law" the action would prima facie succeed.[54] Moreover, since a beneficiary-covenantee would recover full damages [55] prima facie trustee-covenantees should recover full damages and not nominal damages.[56] But trustees are only entitled to full damages because the beneficiaries under the trust have suffered real damage, and to suffer real damage the beneficiaries must have

---

[49] *Per* Neville J. in *Re Yorke* [1911] 1 Ch. 370.

[50] *Re Pryce* [1917] 1 Ch. 234; *Re Kay* [1939] Ch. 329; *Re Cook's S.T.* [1965] Ch. 902.

[51] *Re Ralli's W.T.* [1964] Ch. 288, 301, 302; *Gandy* v. *Gandy* (1885) 30 Ch.D. 57.

[52] See *Re Pryce* [1917] 1 Ch. 234; *Re Kay* [1939] Ch. 329; *Re Ralli's W.T.* [1964] Ch. 301, 302.

[53] However, there is some slight authority for the view that if the settlement contained a covenant for further assurance, this is some evidence that the settlor seriously intended the trustees to hold the benefit of the covenant for further assurance upon trust for volunteer beneficiaries: *Re Cavendish-Browne's S.T.* [1916] W.N. 341 and cases there cited and *Milroy* v. *Lord* (1862) 4 De G.F. and J. 264 at 273, 278, *supra*, p. 138.

[54] See *Ward* v. *Audland* (1845) 8 Beav. 201, 211, 213 followed by action at law in (1847) 16 M. and W. 862; dicta in *Milroy* v. *Lord* (1862) 4 De G.F. and J. 264 at 273, 278 encouraging pursuit of remedy at law; *Cannon* v. *Hartley* [1949] Ch. 213. Equity would only intervene if undue influence or oppressive unconscionable conduct were involved.

[55] *Cannon* v. *Hartley* [1949] Ch. 213; *Williamson* v. *Codrington* (1750) 1 Ves.Sen. 511; *Cox* v. *Barnard* (1850) 8 Hare 810.

[56] *Re Parkin* [1892] 3 Ch. 510; *Re Cavendish-Browne's S.T.* [1916] W.N. 341.

had an equitable interest under the trust capable of being damaged. However, where a trust is incompletely constituted a volunteer has no equitable interest but only a *spes* and he cannot complain if his hopes are unfulfilled. Since the volunteer has no equitable interest there must be a resulting trust [57] in favour of the settlor of anything that the trustees recover by way of common law damages: the trustees cannot for example by acquiring £50,000 damages for breach of a covenant to pay them £50,000 themselves completely constitute the trust as this is something that only a settlor can do: cf. *Re Brooks' S.T.*,[58] *infra*. It follows that since the settlor is under the resulting trust a *sui juris* absolutely entitled beneficiary he must under the *Saunders* v. *Vautier* [59] principle be able to terminate the trust and prevent the trustees from launching upon such a pointless exercise as a suit against himself for damages. In practice, it would seem that as soon as the settlor makes it clear to the trustees that he does not want them to sue him, that is an end of the matter.[60] It must be admitted, however, that the position is far from certain.

PULLAN v. KOE

Chancery Division [1913] 1 Ch. 9; 82 L.J.Ch. 37.

A marriage settlement of 1859 contained a covenant by the husband and wife to settle the wife's after-acquired property of the value of £100 or upwards.

In 1879 the wife received £285 and paid it into her husband's banking account, on which she had power to draw. Part of it was shortly after invested in two bearer bonds which remained at the bank till the husband's death in 1909 and were now in his executors' possession:

Held, that the moment the wife received the £285 it was specifically

---

[57] *Cf.* resulting trust of £500 in *Re Tilt* (1896) 74 L.T. 163.

[58] [1939] Ch. 993. For an exception under the *Strong* v. *Bird* principle, see *Re Ralli's W.T.* [1964] Ch. 288.   The inadequately reported case of *Re Cavendish-Browne's S.T.* [1916] W.N. 341 where trustees recovered full damages for breach of a covenant for further assurance by a settlor in favour of volunteers is difficult to support except on the footing that there was a completely constituted trust of that covenant or, possibly on the footing that such a covenant amounted to a mandate to the trustees to constitute the trust on the part of the settlor which it was inequitable to allow the settlor to revoke and to raise a resulting trust in his favour.

[59] (1841) 4 Beav. 115.

[60] In *Hirachand Punamchand* v. *Temple* [1911] 2 K.B. 330, where plaintiff moneylenders accepted a lesser sum from the defendant's father in satisfaction of a debt and then sued the defendant for the balance, it is noteworthy that Vaughan Williams L.J. held that any money recovered would be held in trust for the defendant's father and " there might have been a defence in a court of law on the ground that any money recoverable by the plaintiffs was recoverable by them merely as trustees for [the father] and that, under the circumstances disclosed by the correspondence, the relations between father and son were such that it was impossible to suppose that the father wished to insist on payment by the son " (p. 337) and Fletcher-Moulton L.J. stated that, " if there be any difficulty in formulating a defence at common law I have no hesitation in saying that a court of equity would have regarded the plaintiffs as disentitled to sue except as trustees for the father, and would have restrained them from suing " (p. 342). However, see also *Morley* v. *Moore* [1936] 2 K.B. 359 which seems to depend upon the court's dislike for " knock for knock " insurance agreements and is distinguishable on the footing that the debt of £33 2s. 8d. was indivisible or that in the circumstances the court could not see that the insurance company beneficiary had the slightest right to direct the assured trustee not to sue the wrongdoer (p. 366).

bound by the covenant and was consequently subject in equity to a trust enforceable in favour of all persons within the marriage consideration, and therefore, notwithstanding the lapse of time, the trustees were entitled on behalf of those persons to follow and claim the bonds as trust property, though their legal remedy on the covenant was statute-barred.

SWINFEN EADY J. (in a reserved judgment): " The defence of laches and acquiescence was given up by the defendants, but they insisted that, although they still retained the bonds, they were under no liability to the plaintiffs. They put their case in this way—that the plaintiff trustees could not follow the bonds into their hands, that the only liability of the husband was upon his covenant, and the claim of the trustees was for damages only, and that as this claim accrued in 1879 it was long since barred by the Statutes of Limitation.

" Having regard to the authority of the wife in respect of the banking account, and to the difficulty of ascertaining now the exact extent of it (the old papers of Messrs. Parsons & Co. being no longer available), there is some doubt as to whether these bonds were in the husband's lifetime in his sole possession or under his sole control, but having regard to the allegations in the statement of claim I must deal with the case upon the footing that the bonds were in the possession of the husband at his death. He received the bonds, purchased with his wife's money, with full notice of the trusts of the settlement, and knowing that the £285 and the bonds purchased with part of it were bound by the covenant, and moreover he gave no value, but is in the position of a volunteer. The trustees having traced the property into his hands are entitled to claim it from his executors.

" It was contended that the bonds never in fact became trust property, as both the wife and husband were only liable in damages for breach of covenant, and that the case was different from cases where property which has once admittedly become subject to the trusts of an instrument has been improperly dealt with, and is sought to be recovered. In my opinion as soon as the £285 was paid to the wife it became in equity bound by and subject to the trusts of the settlement. The trustees could have claimed that particular sum, could have obtained at once the appointment of a receiver of it, if they could have shown a case of jeopardy, and, if it had been invested and the investment could be traced, could have followed the money and claimed the investment.

" This point was dealt with by Jessel M.R. in *Smith* v. *Lucas*,[61] where he said: ' What is the effect of such a covenant in equity? It has been said that the effect in equity of the covenant of the wife, as far as she is concerned, is that it does not affect her personally, but

[61] 18 Ch.D. 531, 543.

that it binds the property: that is to say, it binds the property under the doctrine of equity that that is to be considered as done which ought to be done. That is in the nature of specific performance of the contract no doubt. If therefore, this is a covenant to settle the future-acquired property of the wife, and nothing more is done by her, the covenant will bind the property.'

"Again in *Collyer* v. *Isaacs* [62] Jessel M.R. said: ' A man can contract to assign property which is to come into existence in the future, and when it has come into existence, equity, treating as done that which ought to be done, fastens upon that property, and the contract to assign thus becomes a complete assignment. If a person contract for value, *e.g.*, in his marriage settlement, to settle all such real estate as his father shall leave him by will, or purports actually to convey by the deed all such real estate, the effect is the same. It is a contract for value which will bind the property if the father leaves any property to his son.'

" The property being thus bound, these bonds became trust property, and can be followed by the trustees and claimed from a volunteer.

" Again the trustees are entitled to come into a Court of Equity to enforce a contract to create a trust, contained in a marriage settlement, for the benefit of the wife and the issue of the marriage, all of whom are within the marriage consideration. The husband covenanted that he and his heirs, executors, and administrators should, as soon as circumstances would admit, convey, assign, and surrender to the trustees the real or personal property to which his wife should become beneficially entitled. The trustees are entitled to have that covenant specifically enforced by a Court of Equity. In *In re D'Angibau* [63] and in *In re Plumptre's Marriage Settlement* [64] it was held that the Court would not interfere in favour of volunteers, not within the marriage consideration, but here the plaintiffs are the contracting parties and the object of the proceeding is to benefit the wife and issue of the marriage."

CANNON v. HARTLEY

Chancery Division [1949] Ch. 213

By a deed of separation made on January 23, 1941, between the defendant of the first part, his wife of the second part and the plaintiff, their daughter, of the third part, the defendant covenanted, *inter alia*, " If and whenever during the lifetime of the wife or the daughter the husband shall become entitled . . . under the will or codicil . . . of either of his parents . . . to àny money or property exceeding in net amount or value £1,000, he will forthwith at his own expense . . .

---

[62] 19 Ch.D. 342, 351.
[63] 15 Ch.D. 228, 242.   [64] [1910] 1 Ch. 609, 616.

settle one-half of such money or property upon trust for himself for life and for the wife for life after his death and subject thereto in trust for the daughter absolutely..." In 1944 the defendant became entitled, subject to a prior life interest therein of his mother, to a quarter share of a fund of approximately £50,000. The defendant's wife died in 1946. The defendant refused to execute a settlement in accordance with the said covenant. On a claim by the plaintiff for damages for breach of the covenant:

Held, that the plaintiff was entitled to damages.

ROMER J.: " The question with which I have now to deal follows on my finding that the reversionary interest to which the defendant became entitled under his father's will was caught by clause 7 of the deed of separation. It has been argued on behalf of the defendant that the plaintiff, not having given any consideration for this covenant by her father, is not only unable to apply to a court of equity for the enforcement of the covenant by way of specific performance, but that she is also disqualified from suing at common law for damages for breach of the covenant.

" It is, of course, well established that in such a case as this a volunteer cannot come to a court of equity and ask for relief which is peculiar to the jurisdiction of equity, *viz.*, specific performance; but for my part I thought it was reasonably clear that, the document being under seal, the covenantee's claim for damages would be entertained, and that is still my belief. . . .

" But the defendant relies (and this appears to be the foundation of his defence) upon some observations made by Eve J. in *In re Pryce*,[65] and on the subsequent decision of Simonds J. in *In re Kay's Settlement*.[66] I think the point of the observations of Eve J. in *In re Pryce* [65] appear sufficiently in *In re Kay's Settlement*.[66] The headnote of that case is: ' A voluntary settlement executed by a spinster contained a covenant in the usual form to settle any after-acquired property, with certain exceptions. The settlor afterwards married and had three children. Having become entitled under a will to a legacy and a share of residue which fell within the covenant, and a share in an appointed fund, she was asked by the trustees of the settlement to settle this property, but refused to do so: Held, on an application by the trustees for directions, that the children, being volunteers, had no right to enforce the covenant, and therefore the trustees ought to be directed not to take any proceedings to enforce the covenant, by action for damages for breach, or otherwise.'

" Simonds J., after referring to the facts of the case, said at p. 338: ' It is in these circumstances that the trustees have issued this summons, making as parties to it, first, the settlor herself and, secondly,

---

[65] [1917] 1 Ch. 234.
[66] [1939] Ch. 329, 338.

her infant children, who are beneficiaries under the settlement. But, be it observed, though beneficiaries, her children are, for the purpose of this settlement, to be regarded as volunteers, there being no marriage consideration, which would have entitled them to sue, though they are parties to this application. The trustees ask whether, in the event which has happened of the settlor having become entitled to certain property, they should take proceedings against her to compel performance of the covenant or to recover damages on her failure to implement it.

" I am bound to say that that does not seem to me to be a very happy form of proceeding, though perhaps it is difficult to see how else the trustees should act. It is to be observed that one of the persons made a party is the very person as to whom the trustees ask the question whether she should be sued. She, the settlor, has appeared by Mr. Evershed and has contended, as she was entitled to contend, that the only question before the court was whether the trustees ought to be directed to take such proceedings; that is to say, she contended that the only question before the court was precisely that question which Eve J. had to deal with in *In re Pryce*. She has said that the question before me is not primarily whether, if she were sued, such an action would succeed (as to which she might have a defence, I know not what), but whether, in the circumstances as they are stated to the court, the trustees ought to be directed to take proceedings against her.

" As to that, the argument before me has been, on behalf of the children of the marriage, beneficiaries under the settlement, that, although it is conceded that the trustees could not successfully take proceedings for specific performance of the agreements contained in the settlement, yet they could successfully, and ought to be directed to, take proceedings at law to recover damages for the non-observance of the agreements contained in the settlement, first, the covenant for further assurance of the appointed share of the first-mentioned £20,000 and, secondly, the covenant with regard to the after-acquired property. In the circumstances I must say that I felt considerable sympathy for the argument which was put before me by Mr. Winterbotham on behalf of the children, that there was, at any rate, on the evidence before the court today, no reason why the trustees should not be directed to take proceedings to recover what damages might be recoverable at law for breach of the agreements entered into by the settlor in her settlement. But on a consideration of *In re Pryce* it seemed to me that so far as this court was concerned the matter was concluded and that I ought not to give any directions to the trustees to take the suggested proceedings.

" In *In re Pryce* the circumstances appear to me to have been in no wise different from those which obtain in the case which I have to consider. In that case there was a marriage settlement made in 1887.

It contained a covenant to settle the wife's after-acquired property. In 1904 there was a deed of gift under which certain interests in reversion belonging to the husband were assured by him absolutely to his wife. The husband was also entitled to a one-third share in certain sums appointed to him by the will of his father in exercise of a special power of appointment contained in a deed of family arrangement. The share of the £9,000 fell into possession in 1891 on the death of his father, and was paid to him, unknown to the trustees of his marriage settlement, and spent. The interests given by the husband to the wife and his share of the £4,700 came into possession in 1916 on the death of the husband's mother, and were outstanding in the trustees of his parent's settlement and of the deed of family arrangement respectively. The husband died in 1907, and there was no issue of the marriage. Subject to his widow's life interest in both funds, the ultimate residue of the wife's fund was held in trust for her statutory next-of-kin, and the husband's fund was held in trust for him absolutely. The widow was also tenant for life under her husband's will. The trustees of the marriage settlement in that case took out a summons ' to have it determined whether these interests and funds were caught by the provisions of the settlement, and, if so, whether they should take proceedings to enforce them.' In those proceedings, apparently, the plaintiffs were the trustees of the marriage settlement, and the only defendant appears to have been the widow of the settlor; that is to say, there were no other parties to the proceedings to whose beneficial interest it was to argue in favour of the enforceability and enforcement of the covenant, but the trustees no doubt argued in favour of their interests, as it was their duty to do. Eve J., in a considered judgment, held that although the interests to which I have referred were caught by the covenant of the wife and the agreement by the husband respectively, yet the trustees ought not to take any steps to recover any of them. In the case of the wife's fund he said that her next of kin were volunteers, who could neither maintain an action to enforce the covenant nor for damages for breach of it, and that the court would not give them by indirect means what they could not obtain by direct procedure; therefore he declined to direct the trustees to take proceedings either to have the covenant specifically enforced or to recover damages at law. The learned judge, as I have said, took time to consider his judgment. Many of the cases which have been cited to me, though not all of them apparently, were cited to him, and after deciding that no steps should be taken to enforce specific performance of the covenant he used these words: ' The position of the wife's fund is somewhat different, in that her next of kin would be entitled to it on her death; but they are volunteers, and although the court would probably compel fulfilment of the contract to settle at the instance of any persons within the marriage consideration—see *per* Cotton L.J. in *In re D'Angibau* [67] and in their favour will treat the outstanding property as subjected to an enforceable trust— *Pullan* v. *Koe* [68] " volunteers have no right whatever to obtain specific performance of a mere covenant which has remained as a covenant and has never been performed ": see *per* James L.J. in *In re D'Angibau*. Nor could damages be awarded either in this court, or, I apprehend, at law, where, since the Judicature Act, 1873, the same defences would be available to the defendant as would be raised in an action brought in this court for specific performance or damages.'

" That is the exact point which has been urged on me with great insistence by Mr. Winterbotham. Whatever sympathy I might feel for his argument, I am not justified in departing in any way from this decision, which is now twenty-one years old. The learned judge went on: ' In these circumstances, seeing that the next-of-kin could neither maintain an action to enforce the covenant nor for damages for breach of it, and that the settlement is not a declaration of trust constituting the relationship of trustee and cestui que trust between the defendant and the next of kin, in which case effect could be given to the trusts even in favour of volunteers, but is a mere voluntary contract to create a trust, ought the court now for the sole benefit of these volunteers to direct the trustees to take proceedings to enforce the defendant's covenant? I think it ought not; to do so would be to give the next of kin by indirect means relief they cannot obtain by any direct procedure, and would in effect be enforcing the settlement as against the defendant's legal right to payment and transfer from the trustees of the parents' marriage settlement.' It is true that in those last words the learned judge does not specifically refer to an action for damages, but it is clear that he has in his mind directions both with regard to an action for specific performance and an action to recover damages at law—or, now, in this court. In those circumstances it appears to me that I must follow the learned judge's decision and I must direct the trustees not to take any steps either to compel performance of the covenant or to recover damages through her failure to implement it."

" Now it appears to me that neither *In re Pryce* [69] nor *In re Kay's Settlement* [70] is any authority for the proposition which has been submitted to me on behalf of the defendant. In neither case were the claimants parties to the settlement in question, nor were they within the consideration of the deed. When volunteers were referred to in *In re Pryce* it seems to me that what Eve J. intended to say was that they were not within the class of non-parties, if I may use that expression, to whom Cotton L.J. recognised in *In re D'Angibau* [71] that the court would afford assistance. In the present case the plaintiff, although a

---

[67] 15 Ch.D. 228, 242, 246.
[68] [1913] 1 Ch. 9.
[69] [1917] 1 Ch. 234.
[70] [1939] Ch. 329.
[71] 15 Ch.D. 228.

volunteer, is not only a party to the deed of separation but is also a direct covenantee under the very covenant upon which she is suing. She does not require the assistance of the court to enforce the covenant for she has a legal right herself to enforce it. She is not asking for equitable relief but for damages at common law for breach of covenant.

" For my part, I am quite unable to regard *In re Pryce*, which was a different case dealing with totally different circumstances, or anything which Eve J. said therein, as amounting to an authority negativing the plaintiff's right to sue in the present case. I think that what Eve J. was pointing out in *In re Pryce* was that the next of kin who were seeking to get an indirect benefit had no right to come to a court of equity because they were not parties to the deed and were not within the consideration of the deed and, similarly, they would have no right to proceed at common law by an action for damages, as the court of common law would not entertain a suit at the instance of volunteers who were not parties to the deed which was sought to be enforced, any more than the court of equity would entertain such a suit.

" It was suggested to me in argument that in such a case as the present, where the covenant is to bring in after-acquired property, an action for damages for breach of that covenant is in effect the same as a suit for specific performance of a covenant to settle. I myself think that the short answer to that is that the two things are not the same at all. The plaintiff here is invoking no equitable relief; she is merely asking for monetary compensation for a breach of covenant.

" I shall accordingly direct an inquiry as to the damages sustained by the plaintiff for breach by the defendant of the covenant with the plaintiff contained in clause 7 of the deed of separation and the plaintiff will have her costs of the action, the costs of the inquiry to be reserved." *Judgment for the plaintiff.*

Re COOK'S S.T.

Chancery Division [1965] Ch. 902; [1965] 2 W.L.R. 179; [1964] 3 All E.R. 898.

Sir Herbert as life tenant and his son, Sir Francis, as remainderman agreed that certain settled property (including a Rembrandt) should become Sir Francis' absolutely subject to Sir Francis re-settling some of the property (not the Rembrandt) and covenanting with the trustees of the resettlement that in case any of certain pictures (including the Rembrandt) should be sold during Sir Francis' lifetime the net proceeds of sale should be paid over to the trustees to be held by them on the resettlement trusts in favour of Sir Francis' children. A settlement was executed pursuant to this agreement.

Sir Francis gave the Rembrandt to his wife who desired to sell it.

The trustees, therefore, took out a summons as to whether or not upon any sale of the Rembrandt the trustees wou' be obliged to take steps to enforce the covenant.

Held, (1) Since Sir Francis' children were volunteers they could not enforce the covenant so that the trustees would be directed not to enforce the covenant on the principles in *Re Pryce* [72] and *Re Kay* [73] but (2) that in any case the covenant operated only upon a sale by Sir Francis and not by his wife.

As to (1):

BUCKLEY J.: " . . . Counsel appearing for Sir Francis, submitted that as a matter of law the covenant . . . is not enforceable against him by the trustees of the settlement. . . ." [He] submits that the covenant was a voluntary and executory contract to make a settlement in a future event and was not a settlement of a covenant to pay a sum of money to the trustees. He further submits that, as regards the covenant, all the beneficiaries under the settlement are volunteers with the consequence that not only should the court not direct the trustees to take proceedings on the covenant but also that it should positively direct them not to take proceedings. He relies on *Re Pryce, Nevill* v. *Pryce* [72] and *Re Kay's Settlement, Broadbent* v. *Macnab.* [73]

" Counsel for the second and third defendants have contended that, on the true view of the facts, there was an immediate settlement of the obligation created by the covenant, and not merely a covenant to settle something in the future. It was said, as counsel for the second defendant put it, that, by the agreement, Sir Herbert bought the rights arising under the covenant for the benefit of the cestuis que trust under the settlement and that, the covenant being made in favour of the trustees, these rights became assets of the trust. He relied on *Fletcher* v. *Fletcher,* [74] *Williamson* v. *Codrington* [75] and *Re Cavendish Browne's Settlement Trusts, Horner* v. *Rawle.* [76] I am not able to accept this argument. The covenant with which I am concerned did not, in my opinion, create a debt enforceable at law, that is to say, a property right, which, although to bear fruit only in the future and on a contingency, was capable of being made the subject of an immediate trust, as was held to be the case in *Fletcher* v. *Fletcher.* Nor is this covenant associated with property which was the subject of an immediate trust, as in *Williamson* v. *Codrington.* Nor did the covenant relate to property which then belonged to the covenantor, as in *Re Cavendish Browne's Settlement Trusts.* In contrast to all these cases, this covenant on its true construction is, in my opinion, an executory contract to settle a particular fund or particular funds of

[72] [1917] 1 Ch. 234.
[73] [1939] Ch. 329.
[74] (1844) 4 Hare, 67.
[75] (1750) 1 Ves.Sen. 511.
[76] (1916) 61 S.J. 27.

money which at the date of the covenant did not exist and which might never come into existence. It is analogous to a covenant to settle an expectation or to settle after-acquired property. The case, in my judgment, involves the law of contract, not the law of trusts.

"Accordingly, the second and third defendants are not in my judgment entitled to require the trustees to take proceedings to enforce the covenant, even if it is capable of being construed in a manner favourable to them."

Re BROOKS' SETTLEMENT TRUSTS

Chancery Division [1939] 1 Ch. 993.

By the terms of a marriage settlement the income of the settled fund was directed to be paid to the wife during her life and subject to that trust the fund was to be held in trust for such of her issue as she might by deed or will appoint; in default of any such appointment the fund was to be held in trust for all her children who being sons should attain the age of twenty-one years or being daughters should attain that age or marry in equal shares. In 1929 one of her children, A. T., executed a voluntary settlement whereby he assigned to Lloyds Bank as trustees " all the part or share, parts or shares and other interest whether vested or contingent to which the settlor is now or may here-after become entitled whether in default of appointment, or under any appointment hereafter to be made or on failure of any such appoint-ment of and in the trust property " subject to the marriage settlement. By an appointment in pursuance of the power executed in 1939, his mother appointed him a sum of £3,517 and released her life interest. Thereupon Lloyds Bank Ltd., who had by then become trustees of the marriage settlement as well as the voluntary settlement took out a summons asking whether they should pay A. T. the £3,517.

Held, that A. T. was entitled to require payment of the sum appointed, and could not be compelled to permit the Bank to retain the £3,517. [*Cf. Re Ralli's W.T.* [1964] Ch. 288.]

FARWELL J.: " When one looks at the voluntary settlement, at first sight the answer would seem to be quite clearly that the trustees' duty was to retain the sum of £3,517 as part of the funds which the son had voluntarily settled, and the language of the voluntary settlement would seem to leave no doubt on that score, because the settlor assigned to the bank ' all the part or share parts or shares and other interest whether vested or contingent to which the settlor is now or may hereafter become entitled whether in default of appointment or under any appointment hereafter to be made or on failure of any such appointment of and in the trust property which is now or may at any time hereafter become subject to the trusts of the wife's settle-ment.' One would say, looking at the language of the settlement, that it would be difficult to find words more apt to embrace in the voluntary settlement all the interests which the son had then or might thereafter have under the marriage settlement and that accordingly the answer should be that it is the duty of the trustees to retain this as part of the voluntary settlement fund. But, when one considers the legal position in this matter, a different aspect seems to appear. If the matter could be tested simply as one of construction, the answer would appear to be in favour of the trustees of the voluntary settlement; but the question is not one of construction only, and I have to consider whether the attempt to assign that which the son has now become entitled to by virtue of the exercise of the power is enforceable against him.

" The legal position in the case of a special power of appointment is not in any doubt at all. Referring to *Farwell on Powers*, 3rd ed., p. 310, I find this statement of principle, which will be found in exactly the same language in earlier editions of the book, and therefore is not in any way the creation of the editor: ' The exercise of a power of appointment divests (either wholly or partially according to the terms of the appointment) the estates limited in default of appointment and creates a new estate, and that, too, whether the property be real or personal.' Then there is a reference to a decision in the *Duke of Northumberland* v. *Inland Revenue Commissioners*,[77] where this statement was adopted by Hamilton J., as he then was. The effect of this is that in the case of a special power the property is vested in the persons who take in default of appointment, subject, of course, to any prior life interest, but liable to be divested at any time by a valid exercise of the power, and the effect of such an exercise of the power is to defeat wholly or *pro tanto* the interests which up to then were vested in the persons entitled in default of appointment and to create new estates in those persons in whose favour the appointment had been made. That being so, it is, in my judgment, impossible to say that until an appointment has been made in favour of this son that son had any interest under his mother's settlement other than an interest as one of the people entitled in default of appointment; he had an interest in that; but that interest was liable to be divested, and, if an appointment was made (as in fact it was made) in favour of the son, then to that extent the persons entitled in default were defeated and he was given an interest in the funds which he had never had before and which came into being for the first time when the power was exercised. No doubt it is quite true to say that the appointment has to be read in to the marriage settlement, but, in my judgment, that is not sufficient ground for saying that at the time when this voluntary settlement was made the son had any interest at all in the fund other than his vested interest in default of appointment; for the rest, he had

[77] [1911] 2 K.B. 343, 354.

nothing more than a mere expectancy, the hope that at some date his mother might think fit to exercise the power of appointment in his favour, but, until she did so choose, he had nothing other than his interest in default of appointment to which he could point and say: ' That is a fund to which I shall become entitled in future or to which I am contingently entitled.' Apart from this he was not contingently entitled at all; he had no interest whatever in the fund until the appointment had been executed.

" If that be the true view, as I believe it to be, the result must be that, whatever the language of the settlement may be, the settlor under the voluntary settlement was purporting to assign to the trustees something to which he might in certain circumstances become entitled in the future, but to which he was not then entitled in any sense at all, and if that be so, then it is plain on the authorities that the son cannot be compelled to hand over or to permit the trustees to retain this sum and that he is himself entitled to call upon them to pay it over to him.

" There are two cases to which I have been referred. One of them is a decision of Buckley J. (as he then was) in a case of *In re Ellenborough. Towry Law* v. *Burne.*[78] The headnote in that case is this: ' The decision in *Meek* v. *Kettlewell*[79] that the voluntary assignment of an expectancy, even though under seal, will not be enforced by a Court of Equity, has not been overruled by *Kekewich* v. *Manning.*'[80] What Buckley J. said was this[78]: ' The question is whether a volunteer can enforce a contract made by deed to dispose of an expectancy. It cannot be and is not disputed that if the deed had been for value the trustees could have enforced it. If value be given, it is immaterial what is the form of assurance by which the disposition is made, or whether the subject of the disposition is capable of being thereby disposed of or not. An assignment for value binds the conscience of the assignor. A Court of Equity as against him will compel him to do that which ex hypothesi he has not yet effectually done. Future property, possibilities, and expectancies are all assignable in equity for value: *Tailby* v. *Official Receiver.*[81] But when the assurance is not for value, a Court of Equity will not assist a volunteer, the reason for that being, that, since it is merely a voluntary act and not an act for consideration at all, the conscience of the assignor is not affected so as in equity to prevent him from saying: ' I am not going to hand over this property to which now for the first time I have become entitled.' Then Buckley J. cites a passage from *Meek* v. *Kettlewell* and points out that that is not overruled by the latter decision of the Court of Appeal in *Kekewich* v. *Manning*, and that the rule is still binding. If that be the true view, it must follow that this particular interest, which

---

[78] [1903] 1 Ch. 697, 700.
[79] (1842) 1 Hare 464.
[80] (1851) 1 De G.M. & G. 176.
[81] (1888) 13 App.Cas. 523.

for the first time came into being when the appointment was made, is not caught by the settlement.

" The other case to which I was referred was one before Romer J. (as he then was), *Lovett* v. *Lovett.*[82] There the facts were not dissimilar from those in the case that I am considering. Romer J. seems to me to have decided it principally as a question of construction and partly upon the question of estoppel. So far as it is a decision on pure construction, it cannot help me in this case; but I think that, though the learned judge appears to have based it on construction, it is an authority for saying that the view which I take in this case is the true one. Notwithstanding the fact that the language of this voluntary settlement as a matter of construction is wide enough to comprise this interest, the principle of law which I have stated makes it impossible to enforce the settlement to that extent and prevents the settlor from being compelled by this Court to transfer or permit the trustees to retain this money as part of the funds subject thereto.

" I regret to have to come to this conclusion, because I think it is quite plainly contrary to what was intended at the date when the voluntary settlement was executed, but none the less I feel compelled by the principles to which I have referred to hold that the answer to the summons must be that the trustees ought to pay to the defendant the sum in question on the footing that that settlement does not operate as a valid assignment or declaration of trust in respect thereof. I make that declaration accordingly."

WILLIAMS v. COMMISSIONERS OF INLAND REVENUE

New Zealand Court of Appeal [1965] N.Z.L.R. 395.

Williams, who had a life interest under a trust, executed a voluntary deed, in which " the assignor by way of gift hereby assigns to the assignee for the religious purposes of the Parish of the Holy Trinity Gisborne for the four years commencing on June 30, 1960 the first £500 of the net income which shall accrue to the assignor personally while he lives in each of the said four years from the Trust. . . . And the assignor hereby declares that he is trustee for the sole use and benefit of the assignee for the purpose aforesaid of so much (if any) of the said income as may not be capable of assignment (or may come to his hands)."

The question arose whether Williams had effectively divested himself of his interest in the £500 so as not to be liable for income tax on it. The New Zealand Court of Appeal held that he had not.

TURNER J. (delivering the judgment of North P. and himself) said: " Mr. Thorp, for the appellant, submitted that what was assigned by this document was a defined share in the existing life estate of the assignor in the trust property, and hence that the deed of assignment

---
[82] [1898] 1 Ch. 82.

took effect, as at its date, to divest the assignor of the annual sums of £500 so that he did not thereafter derive them for taxation purposes in the years under consideration. For the respondent Commissioner it was contended that the deed was ineffective to divest the assignor of the sums, and that its effect was no more than that of an order upon the trustees still revocable by the assignor until payment.

" The life interest of the appellant in the trust was at the date of the execution of the deed an existing equitable interest. This cannot be doubted, and it was so conceded by the learned Solicitor-General. Being an existing interest, it was capable in equity of immediate effective assignment. Such an assignment could be made without consideration, if it immediately passed the equitable estate: *Kekewich* v. *Manning*.[83] There is no doubt that if the deed before us had purported to assign, not ' the first £500,' but the whole of the appellant's life interest under the trust, such an assignment would have been good in equity.

" But while equity will recognise a voluntary assignment of an existing equitable interest, it will refuse to recognise in favour of a volunteer an assignment of an interest, either legal or equitable, not existing at the date of the assignment, but to arise in the future. Not yet existing, such property cannot be owned, and what may not be owned may not be effectively assigned: *Holroyd* v. *Marshall*.[84] If, not effectively assigned, it is made the subject of an agreement to assign it, such an agreement may be good in equity, and become effective upon the property coming into existence but if, and only if, the agreement is made for consideration (as in *Spratt* v. *Commissioner of Inland Revenue*[85]), for equity will not assist a volunteer: *In re Ellenborough, Towry Law* v. *Burne*.[86]

" The deed on which this appeal is founded was not made for consideration. The simple question is therefore—was that which it purported to assign (*viz.* ' the first five hundred pounds of the net income which shall accrue ') an existing property right, or was it a mere expectancy, a future right not yet in existence? If the former, counsel agree that the deed was effective as an immediate assignment: if the latter, it is conceded by Mr. Thorp that it could not in the circumstances of this case have effect.

" What then was it that the assignor purported to assign? What he had was the life interest of a *cestui que trust* in a property or partnership adventure vested in or carried on by trustees for his benefit. Such a life interest exists in equity as soon as the deed of trust creating it is executed and delivered. Existing, it is capable of immediate assignment. We do not doubt that where it is possible to assign a right completely it is possible to assign an undivided interest in it. The

---

[83] (1851) 1 De G.M. & G. 176; 42 E.R. 519.
[84] (1862) 10 H.L.C. 191, 210; 11 E.R. 999, 1006 *per* Lord Westbury L.C.
[85] [1964] N.Z.L.R. 272. [86] [1903] 1 Ch. 697.

learned Solicitor-General was therefore right, in our opinion, in conceding that if here, instead of purporting to assign ' the first £500 of the income,' the assignor had purported to assign (say) an undivided one-fourth share in his life estate, then he would have assigned an existing right, and in the circumstances effectively.

" But in our view, as soon as he quantified the sum in the way here attempted, the assignment became one not of a share or a part of his right, but of moneys which should arise from it. Whether the sums mentioned were ever to come into existence in whole or in part could not at the date of assignment be certain. In any or all of the years designated the net income might conceivably be less than five hundred pounds; in some or all of them the operations of the trust might indeed result in a loss. The first £500 of the net income, then, might or might not (judging the matter on the date of execution of the deed) in fact have any existence.

" We accordingly reject Mr. Thorp's argument that what was here assigned was a part or share of the existing equitable right of the assignor. He did not assign part of his right to income; he assigned a right to a part of the income, a different thing. The £500 which was the subject of the purported assignment was five hundred pounds *out of the net income*. There could be no such income for any year until the operations of that year were complete, and it became apparent what debits were to be set off against the gross receipts. For these reasons we are of opinion that what was assigned here was money; and that was something which was not presently owned by the assignor. He had no more than an expectation of it, to arise, it is true, from an existing equitable interest—but that interest he did not purport to assign. . . .

" It was argued in the alternative by Mr. Thorpe, but somewhat-faintly that if the document were not effective as an assignment it was effective as a declaration of trust, and that this result was sufficient to divest the appellant of the enjoyment of the annual sums so that he did not derive them as income. It will be recalled in this regard that the text of the deed includes an express declaration of trust. Mr. Thorp's submission was that this express declaration is effective even if the assignment fails. We agree that there may be circumstances in which a purported assignment, ineffective for insufficiency of form or perhaps through lack of notice, may yet perhaps be given effect by equity by reason of the assignor having declared himself to be a trustee; but it is useless to seek to use this device in the circumstances of the present case. Property which is not presently owned cannot presently be impressed with a trust any more than it can be effectively assigned; property which is not yet in existence may be the subject of a present agreement to impress it with a trust when it comes into the hands of the donor; but equity will not enforce such an agreement at the instance of the *cestui que trust* in the absence of consideration: *Ellison* v. *Ellison* [87]; *Brennan* v. *Morphet* [88]; cf. *Underhill's Law of Trusts and Trustees*, 11th ed. 43. For the same reasons therefore as apply in this case to the argument on assignment, Mr. Thorp's second alternative submission must also fail."

FLETCHER v. FLETCHER

Vice-Chancellor (1844) 4 Hare 67; 14 L.J.Ch. 66; 8 Jur.(o.s.) 1040.

The bill was filed by Jacob, a natural son of the testator, Ellis Fletcher, demanding payment by the defendants, who were the executors of Ellis Fletcher, of the sum of £60,000 from the assets (and interest calculated from a date twelve months after the death of the testator). The claim was founded upon a voluntary deed executed by the testator some years before his death and discovered for the first time some years after his death. The deed had been retained by the testator in his own possession and, so far as appeared, he had not communicated its contents either to the trustees or to the beneficiaries.

The indenture in question was expressed to be made on September 1, 1829, between Ellis Fletcher of the one part and five trustees therein named of the other part; and it recited that Ellis Fletcher, being desirous of making provision for his two natural sons, John and Jacob, who were at that time eleven and six years old respectively, thereby covenanted for himself, his heirs, executors and administrators, with the said trustees, their heirs, executors, administrators and assigns, that if either or both of the sons should survive the testator, the latter's heirs, etc., would pay to the trustees, their heirs, etc., the sum of £60,000 within twelve months of the death of the testator to be held upon the following trusts: if both sons were alive at the testator's death and attained the age of twenty-one the trustees were to hold the money on trust for them both in equal shares as tenants in common; if only one son fulfilled these conditions the money was to be held on trust for him alone. In the event of either or both of the sons surviving the testator but neither attaining the age of twenty-one, the money was to fall back into residue. It was further provided that if either or both of the sons should be living but under twenty-one on the death of the testator the trustees were to invest the £60,000 or the appropriate part thereof, and apply the interest to the maintenance and education of the infant or infants. The trustees were given a power to raise and apply sums not exceeding £10,000 each for their preferment and advancement.

Until every person or persons became absolutely entitled under the trusts the trustees were to accumulate the income for the benefit of

---

[87] (1802) 6 Ves.Jun. 656, 662; 31 E.R. 1243, 1246 *per* Lord Eldon L.C.
[88] (1908) 6 C.L.R. 22, 30 *per* Griffith C.J.

that person or those persons who eventually became entitled under the trusts.

The deed contained the usual clauses enabling the trustees to give receipts and for indemnifying them.

Both sons survived the testator but John died without attaining the age of twenty-one. Jacob accordingly claimed that he had become solely entitled to the £60,000 and interest under the indenture of covenant, and asked that the defendants, the executors, might be decreed to pay him what was due to him.

The executors admitted assets. The surviving trustees named in the indenture of covenant, by their answer, said that they had not accepted or acted in the trusts of the indenture; and they declined to accept or act in such trusts, unless the court should be of opinion that they were bound so to act; they also declined to take proceedings either at law or in equity, or to permit their names to be used for the purpose of recovering the said sum of £60,000, except under the order and upon being indemnified by the decree of the court; and they declined to receive the said sum, or to hold it upon the trusts of the indenture, unless under such decree; but they stated that they were willing to act as the court should direct.

At the close of the argument, Wigram V.-C. said:

" It is not denied that, if the plaintiff in this case had brought an action in the name of the trustees, he might have recovered the money; and it is not suggested that, if the trustees had simply allowed their name to be used in the action, their conduct could have been impeached. There are two classes of cases, one of which is in favour of, and the other, if applicable, against, the plaintiff's claim. The question is to which of the two classes it belongs.

" In trying the equitable question I shall assume the validity of the instrument at law. If there was any doubt of that it would be reasonable to allow the plaintiff to try the right by suing in the name of the surviving trustee. The first proposition relied upon against the claim in equity was that equity will not interfere in favour of a volunteer. That proposition, though true in many cases, has been too largely stated. A court of equity, for example, will not, in favour of a volunteer, enforce the performance of a contract *in specie*. That it will, however, sometimes act in favour of a volunteer is proved by the common case of a volunteer on a bond who may prove his bond against the assets. Again, where the relation of trustee and *cestui que trust* is constituted, as where property is transferred from the author of the trust into the name of a trustee, so that he has lost all power of disposition over it, and the transaction is complete as regards him, the trustee, having accepted the trust, cannot say he holds it, except for the purposes of the trust; and the court will enforce the trust at the suit of a volunteer. According to the authorities I cannot, I admit, do anything to perfect the liability of the author of the trust if it is not already perfect. This covenant, however, is already perfect. The covenantor is liable at law, and the court is not called upon to do any act to perfect it. One question made in argument has been whether there can be a trust of a covenant the benefit of which shall belong to a third party; but I cannot think there is any difficulty in that. Suppose, in the case of a personal covenant to pay a certain annual sum for the benefit of a third person, the trustee were to bring an action against the covenantor; would he be afterwards allowed to say he was not a trustee? If he cannot do so after once acknowledging the trust, then there is a case in which there is a trust of a covenant for another. In the case of *Clough* v. *Lambert* [89] the question arose; the point does not appear to have been taken during the argument, but the Vice-Chancellor of England was of opinion that the covenant bound the party; that the *cestui que trust* was entitled to the benefit of it; and that the mere intervention of a trustee made no difference. The proposition, therefore, that in no case can there be a trust of a covenant is clearly too large, and the real question is whether the relation of trustee and *cestui que trust* is established in the present case.

" There is another class of cases: *Brackenbury* v. *Brackenbury*,[90] *Cecil* v. *Butcher*,[91] and others, in which it was doubted whether, if the author of a voluntary deed retains it in his possession, the court will interfere in favour of the volunteer to have it delivered up; but these are cases which I think hardly affect the present question.

" It was then said that this was an agreement by A and B for the benefit of C, a stranger to both; and that, according to the cases of which *Colyear* v. *Lady Mulgrave* [92] is an example, C, the stranger, could not enforce the agreement. But where the transaction is of such a nature that there is no doubt of the intention of A, while dealing with his own property, to constitute B a trustee for C, and B has accepted the trust, may not C be in a condition to compel B to enforce the legal right which the trust deed confers upon him? If the trustees have in this case accepted the trust I think the decision in *Clough* v. *Lambert* applies; and if they have not accepted the trust I scarcely think that fact can make a difference. It is an extraordinary proposition that, nothing being wanted to perfect the liability of the estate to pay the debt, the plaintiff has no right in equity to obtain the benefit of the trust."

WIGRAM V.-C.: " The objections made to the relief sought by the plaintiff under the covenant in the trust deed of September 1829 were three: first, that the covenant was voluntary; secondly, that it was executory; and, thirdly, that it was testamentary, and had not been proved as a will. For the purpose of considering these objections I

---

[89] (1839) 10 Sim. 174.
[91] (1821) 2 J. & W. 565.
[90] (1820) 2 J. & W. 391.
[92] (1836) 2 Keen 81.

shall first assume that the surviving trustee of the deed of September 1829 might recover upon the covenant at law; and upon that assumption the only questions will be, first, whether I shall assist the plaintiff in this suit so far as to allow him the use of the name of the surviving trustee, upon the latter being indemnified, a course which the trustee does not object to if the court shall direct it; and, secondly, whether I shall further facilitate the plaintiff's proceeding at law by ordering the production of the deed of covenant for the purposes of the trial.

" Now, with regard to the first objection, for the reasons which I mentioned at the close of the argument, I think the proposition insisted upon, that because the covenant was voluntary therefore the plaintiff could not recover in equity, was too broadly stated. I referred to the case of a volunteer by specialty claiming payment out of assets, and to the case of one claiming under a voluntary trust, where a fund has been transferred. The rule against relief to volunteers cannot, I conceive, in a case like that before me, be stated higher than this, that a court of equity will not, in favour of a volunteer, give to a deed any effect beyond what the law will give to it. But if the author of the deed has subjected himself to a liability at law, and the legal liability comes regularly to be enforced in equity, as in the cases before referred to, the observation that the claimant is a volunteer is of no value in favour of those who represent the author of the deed. If, therefore, the plaintiff himself were the covenantee,[93] so that he could bring the action in his own name, it follows, from what I have said, that in my opinion he might enforce payment out of the assets of the covenantor in this case. Then, does the interposition of the trustee of this covenant make any difference? I think it does not. Upon this part of the case I have asked myself the question, proposed by Vice-Chancellor Knight-Bruce in *Davenport* v. *Bishopp*,[94] whether, if the surviving trustee chose to sue, there would be any equity on the part of the estate to restrain him from doing so [95]; or, which is the same question, in principle, whether in a case in which the author of the deed has conferred no discretion on the trustees (upon which supposition the estate is liable at law) the right of the plaintiff is to depend upon the caprice of the trustee, and to be kept in suspense until the Statute of Limitations might become a bar to an action by the trustee. Or, in the case of new trustees being appointed (perhaps by the plaintiff himself, there being a power to appoint new trustees), supposing his own nominees to be willing to sue, the other trustees might refuse to sue. I think the answer to these and like questions must be in the negative. The testator has bound himself absolutely. There is a debt created and existing. I give no assistance against the testator. I only deal with him as he has dealt by himself, and, if in such a case the trustee will

---

[93] A case of this type is *Cannon* v. *Hartley* [1949] Ch. 213.
[94] (1843) 2 Y. & C.C.C. 451.　　　　　　[95] See (1960) 76 L.Q.R. 100 (Elliott).

not sue without the sanction of the court, I think it is right to allow the *cestui que trust* to sue for himself, in the name of the trustee, either at law, or in this court, as the case may require. The rights of the parties cannot depend upon mere accident and caprice. Having come to this conclusion upon abstract reasoning, it was satisfactory to me to find that this view of the case is not only consistent with, but is supported by, the cases of *Clough* v. *Lambert*[96] and *Williamson* v. *Codrington*.[97] If the case, therefore, depended simply upon the covenant being voluntary my opinion is that the plaintiff would be entitled to use the name of the trustee at law, or to recover the money in this court, if it were unnecessary to have the right decided at law, and, where the legal right is clear, to have the use of the deed, if that use is material.

" The second question is whether, taking the covenant to be executory, the title of the plaintiff to relief is affected by that circumstance. The question is answered by what I have already said. Its being executory makes no difference, whether the party seeks to recover at law in the name of the trustee, or against the assets in this court.

" The third question is whether the plaintiff is precluded from relief in this court, on the ground suggested that this is a testamentary paper ... There is, therefore, no ground for the argument that the interest is testamentary.

" The only other question arises from the circumstance of the instrument having been kept in the possession of the party—does that affect its legal validity? In the case of *Dillon* v. *Coppin*[98] I had occasion to consider that subject, and I took pains to collect the cases upon it. The case of *Doe* v. *Knight*[99] shows that, if an instrument is sealed and delivered, the retainer of it by the party in his possession does not prevent it from taking effect. No doubt the intention of the parties is often disappointed by holding them to be bound by deeds which they have kept back, but such unquestionably is the law. ...

" Declare that the deed of September 1, 1829, constitutes a debt at law, and decree payment of the principal and interest on the same to the plaintiff out of the assets of the testator, deducting thereout as in part-payment thereof any sums which have been applied for his maintenance during his minority."

---

[96] (1839) 10 Sim. 174.
[98] (1839) 4 Myl. & Cr. 647, 660.
[97] (1750) 1 Ves.Sen. 511.
[99] (1826) 5 B. & C. 671.

V. Exceptions to the Rule that Equity will not Assist a Volunteer

To these general principles there seem to be three equitable and two statutory exceptions.

1. *Equitable exceptions*

    (a) The rule in *Strong* v. *Bird* [1-3]

    A expresses a present intention of making a gift to B, and that intention continues unchanged up to the death of A; but it is not accompanied by an actual transfer to B. If A appoints B his executor, or if B becomes A's administrator, B can hold the property beneficially. A's intention must continue unchanged,[4] and must be an intention of present gift, not of future gift or of testamentary benefaction.[5] Though the gift to B was incomplete up to the time of A's death, it is completed by the vesting of the property in B, as executor or administrator.[6] *Strong* v. *Bird* itself concerned the waiver of a debt in favour of a donee-executor, but the case has been applied by analogy to imperfect gifts of all types of property (including realty since the coming into operation of the Land Transfer Act 1897 [7]). A similar principle applies where A makes an imperfect gift of a reversionary interest under C's will to B upon trust and B subsequently becomes a trustee of C's will and thereby acquires the legal title to the property.[8]

    (b) *Donationes mortis causa* [9]

    Cases of *donationes mortis causa* sometimes provide an exception to the rule that equity will not perfect an imperfect gift. A *donatio mortis causa* must comply with the following essential requirements:

    (i) The donor must have made the gift in contemplation though not necessarily in expectation of death.

    (ii) He must have delivered the subject-matter of the gift to the donee or transferred to him the means or part of the means of getting at that subject-matter.

    (iii) The circumstances must have been such as to establish that the gift was to be absolute and complete only on the donor's death. A condition to this effect need not be expressed and will normally be implied from the fact that the gift was made when the donor was ill.[10]

Since, in the case of a chose in action, physical delivery is impossible, it follows that the title of the donee will not be completely vested at the death of the donor. The question is, therefore, whether the donee can, as a

---

[1-3] (1874) L.R. 18 Eq. 315.

[4] *Re Wale* [1956] 1 W.L.R. 1346; see also *Re Eiser's W.T.* [1937] 1 All E.R. 244 (donor forgave debt to donee-executor and subsequently took security: had this amounted to a change of mind?).

[5] *Re Freeland* [1952] Ch. 110.

[6] *Re Stewart* [1908] 2 Ch. 251; *Re Innes* [1910] 1 Ch. 188; *Re Greene* [1949] Ch. 333.

[7] *Re James, James* v. *James* [1935] Ch. 449. It makes no difference that the donee is one of several executors or administrators.

[8] *Re Ralli's W.T.* [1964] Ch. 288. But see p. 161, *supra.*   [9] See Snell, pp. 366–372.

[10] See *Re Lillingston* [1952] 2 All E.R. 184; *Re Mustapha* (1891) 8 T.L.R. 160; *cf. Lord Advocate* v. *M'Court* (1893) 20 R. (Ct. of Sess.) 488.

volunteer, compel the personal representatives of the donor to complete the gift. Equity will not grant its assistance to the donee in every such case; it will do so only in those cases in which the donor has delivered to the donee a document which is an index of title to the chose in action, *i.e.*, a document the possession or production of which is necessary in order to entitle the possessor or producer to payment of the money as property purported to be given.[11] It is not necessary that the document should contain all the terms on which the subject-matter of the chose in action is held.[12] In the case of a bank deposit book, delivery of the book is sufficient to pass the money in the deposit account if the bank insists on production of the book before paying out. Delivery of title deeds to land or of share certificates is incapable of amounting to a *d.m.c.* of the land[13] or of the shares.[14] Delivery of a donor's own cheque cannot amount to a *d.m.c.* of the sum represented by the cheque.[15]

(c) Equitable estoppel

In some circumstances equity will prevent an owner of land, who has made an imperfect gift of some estate or interest in it, from asserting his title against the donee. The equity of the donee exists where he has expended money on the land in the mistaken belief that he has or will acquire an interest in it and the owner, knowing of the mistake, stood by and allowed the expenditure to be incurred. This type of equity has a wider sphere of operation than an estoppel of the ordinary kind, and in some cases nothing short of a conveyance of the owner's estate or interest to the donee will be sufficient to satisfy the equity.[16]

2. *Statutory exceptions*

The Settled Land Act 1925 provides two further exceptions to the rule.

(a) Conveyance to an infant

First, although after 1925 an infant cannot hold a legal estate in land, an attempt to transfer a legal estate to him is not wholly ineffective. It operates as an agreement for value by the grantor to execute a settlement in favour of the infant, and in the meantime to hold the land in trust for him.[17]

---

[11] *Moore* v. *Darton* (1851) 4 De G. & Sm. 517; *Re Dillon* (1890) 44 Ch.D. 76; *Birch* v. *Treasury Solicitor* [1951] Ch. 298.

[12] *Birch* v. *Treasury Solicitor* [1951] Ch. 298; disapproving dicta in *Re Weston* [1902] 1 Ch. 680 and *Delgoffe* v. *Fader* [1939] Ch. 922.

[13] *Duffield* v. *Elwes* (1827) 1 Bli.N.S. 497, 530, 539, 543.

[14] *Ward* v. *Turner* (1752) 2 Ves.Sen. 431; *Moore* v. *Moore* (1874) L.R. 18 Eq. 474; *Re Weston* [1902] 1 Ch. 680; but what if also a share transfer form is properly executed and handed over: *Staniland* v. *Willott* (1850) 3 Mac. & G. 664; *Re Craven's Estate* [1937] Ch. 423.

[15] *Re Beaumont* [1902] 1 Ch. 889; *Re Leaper* [1916] 1 Ch. 579; *Re Swinburne* [1926] Ch. 38.

[16] See Snell, pp. 565–568; *Dillwyn* v. *Llewellyn* (1862) 4 De G.F. & J. 517; *Ramsden* v. *Dyson* (1866) L.R. 1 H.L. 129; *Plimmer* v. *Wellington Corporation* (1884) 9 App.Cas. 699; *Hopgood* v. *Brown* [1955] 1 W.L.R. 213; *Armstrong* v. *Sheppard & Short Ltd.* [1959] 2 Q.B. 384; *Chalmers* v. *Pardoe* [1963] 1 W.L.R. 677; *Inwards* v. *Baker* [1965] 2 Q.B. 29; *Ward* v. *Kirkland* [1966] 1 W.L.R. 601; *Ives (E. R.) Investments Ltd.* v. *High* [1967] 2 Q.B. 379; *Thomas* v. *Thomas* [1956] N.Z.L.R. 785.

[17] Settled Land Act 1925, s. 27 (1); Law of Property Act 1925, s. 1 (6).

(b) Imperfect settlement by an instrument *inter vivos*

Secondly, section 4 of the Settled Land Act 1925 requires a settlement *inter vivos* to be created by a proper vesting deed and trust instrument. An instrument other than a vesting deed will not operate to pass the legal estate, but by virtue of the statute it will operate as a trust instrument. The trustees may then execute the proper vesting deed, and must do so on the request of the tenant for life or statutory owner.[18]

PROBLEMS

1. Under the terms of a voluntary settlement made five years ago Prudence, a spinster, covenanted under seal with the trustees of the settlement and her brother Montague:

   (a) to pay £10,000 to the trustees on trust for Prudence's illegitimate son Roger absolutely;
   (b) to transfer a freehold property, Peyton Plains, to Montague;
   (c) to transfer 9,000 I.C.I. ordinary shares to the trustees on trust for any husband Prudence might marry for life, with remainder to the children of such marriage and in default thereof for Prudence's next of kin as if she had never married.

Two years ago Prudence married Alfonso who has recently left her. Prudence has not performed these covenants and seeks your advice as the trustees of the settlement have now died and Alfonso is the executor of the last surviving trustee.

2. Five years ago, 26-year-old Sheila executed a voluntary settlement whereby she assigned to Barclays Bank as her trustee all property to which she might become entitled under anybody's will or intestacy and she covenanted with the Bank to transfer to it upon the trusts of the settlement the sum of £30,000 to which she would become entitled under another trust if she attained 30.

Last year Sheila's mother died by her will appointing Barclays Bank her executor and leaving £20,000 to Sheila. After receiving the £30,000 on attaining 30 Sheila, who then banked with Lloyds Bank, sent off her cheque for that sum in favour of Barclays Bank but stopped the cheque before it was met and sent off a cheque for £10,000 in its place. This cheque was cashed.

Sheila now claims to be entitled to recover this £10,000 and to be under no obligation to pay the £20,000 balance. She further demands that Barclays Bank pay her the £20,000 due to her under her mother's will. Advise the Bank.

Would it make any difference if Sheila had died last month having appointed Barclays Bank executor of her will and having left everything to her husband, Barry, whom she had married last year and who persisted with her claims and demands?

3. On Albert's hundredth birthday he asked his three children to visit him in bed as he felt most unwell.

To Maud he said, " Here is a large envelope for you but don't open it

---

[18] Settled Land Act 1925, s. 9.

till you've left me." To George he said, " Here is my share certificate for 4,000 ordinary shares in P.Q Ltd., together with a transfer in your favour which I've signed. You can also have my car." To Emma he said, " I feel awful. If I die I want you to have everything else including this house and all my furniture. All the necessary papers are in this deed box underneath my bed. Here is the only key."

Albert died in his sleep that very night. His will appointed George his executor and left everything equally amongst his children.

In Maud's envelope were a cheque for £2,000 and the deeds of some freehold land and on the last conveyance to Albert he had written, " I hold this for Maud." In the deed box Emma found several share certificates, Albert's Trustee Saving Bank passbook showing a balance of £1,000, and a receipt acknowledging that the Bank had the safe custody of the title deeds to the house. George was unable to get himself registered in respect of the 4,000 shares as the directors refused to register him and were entitled to do so under the company's articles.

Advise Albert's executor on the distribution of Albert's estate.

4. Is the following approach to completely and incompletely constituted trusts a sound one?

(1) Has a trust been completely constituted by a declaration of trust or by property having been effectively given to trustees bearing in mind that the strict rules as to gifts have been attenuated by *Strong* v. *Bird* principles and *donatio mortis causa* principles?

(2) If a trust is incompletely constituted is the beneficiary seeking to enforce the trust
   (a) a covenantee,
   (b) someone who gave consideration for the settlor's covenant,
   (c) someone within the marriage consideration if the settlement was made in consideration of marriage?

(3) If a beneficiary cannot enforce the trust can the trustees as covenantees sue at common law and hold the damages on trust—but for whom?

Section 2. Discretionary and Protective Trusts [19]

If a settlor wishes to provide for B by creating a trust for the benefit of B (*e.g.*, conferring a life interest upon B) he ought to consider whether his intention will best be carried out by conferring a distinct fixed interest upon B. After all, if B becomes bankrupt his life interest like his other property will pass to his trustee in bankruptcy for the benefit of his creditors. Moreover, B himself could sell his life interest and lose the proceeds on a gambling holiday so as then to be unprovided for.

If, however, B were merely an object of a discretionary trust [20] B would have no right to any of the trust income: he would merely have a hope

---

[19] See generally Sheridan, " Discretionary Trusts " (1957) 21 Conv.(N.S.) 55; " Protective Trusts," *ibid.* 110; A. J. Hawkins (1967) 31 Conv.(N.S.) 117.

[20] For the nature of an interest under a discretionary trust see *Gartside* v. *I.R.C.* [1968] A.C. 553; *Re Weir's Settlement* [1969] Ch. 657 (reversed [1971] Ch. 145 on grounds not affecting these principles); *McPhail* v. *Doulton* [1971] A.C. 424. For an example of a draft discretionary settlement see *supra*, p. 4.

that the trustees' discretion would be exercised in his favour. The essence of a discretionary trust is, of course, the complete discretion of the trustees as to the amount of income, if any, to be paid to the various objects of the trust. If the trustees have no power to retain income for accumulation the whole income has to be distributed though only amongst such of the objects and in such proportions as the trustees see fit.[21] Only if all the objects of the discretionary trust are each *sui juris* and between themselves absolutely entitled to the income and capital of the trust and call for the trustees to transfer the trust property to them (or to their nominee) do the trustees' discretions determine: *Re Smith, infra*.

If B is made an object of a discretionary trust and then assigns his interest or becomes bankrupt his assignee or trustee in bankruptcy has no more right than he to demand payment from the trustees. If the trustees do exercise their discretion in favour of B by paying money to him or delivering goods to him then B's assignee or trustee in bankruptcy is entitled to the money or goods.[22] Indeed, where the trustees have had notice of the assignment or bankruptcy but have still paid money to B they have been held liable to his assignee or trustee in bankruptcy for the money so paid.[23] It seems, however, that if the trustees spend trust money on the maintenance of B by paying third parties for food, clothes or accommodation for B then the assignee or trustee in bankruptcy will have no claim.[24]

Discretionary trusts thus have the advantage of protecting beneficiaries from themselves, besides the obvious advantages of flexibility and of lesser liability to estate duty than fixed trusts conferring life interests and reversionary interests. However, there is the disadvantage that such trusts create uncertainty for a beneficiary as he has no fixed entitlement as he would have, say, if he had a life interest.

To tackle this disadvantage there arose the protective trust[25] conferring upon a beneficiary a life (or lesser) interest determinable upon the bankruptcy of B or upon any other event which would deprive B of the right to receive all the income of the trust whereupon a discretionary trust springs up in favour of B and his next of kin. It has long been established that whilst a condition or proviso for forfeiture of an interest on bankruptcy or attempted alienation of the interest is void a limitation of an interest to last until bankruptcy or attempted alienation is valid.[26] The justification for such a distinction[27] is that a limitation merely sets a natural limit to an interest whilst a condition or proviso cuts down an interest before it reaches its natural limit: if such a condition or proviso is void for being contrary

---

21 *Re Gourju's W.T.* [1943] Ch. 24; *Re Gulbenkian's Settlements (No. 2)* [1970] Ch. 408; *Re Allen Meyrick's W.T.* [1966] 1 W.L.R. 499.

22 *Re Coleman* (1888) 39 Ch.D. 443.

23 *Re Neil* (1890) 62 L.T. 649; *Re Bullock* (1891) 60 L.J.Ch. 341 though *Re Ashby* [1892] 1 Q.B. 872 has created some uncertainty by indicating that an assignee or a trustee in bankruptcy can only claim to the extent to which sums paid are in excess of the amount necessary for B's maintenance.

24 *Re Coleman* (1888) 39 Ch.D. 443, 451; *Re Allen-Meyrick's W.T.* [1966] 1 W.L.R. 499.

25 See the statutory form invoked by use of the phrase " protective trusts " set out in the Trustee Act 1925, s. 33, *infra*, p. 180.

26 *Brandon* v. *Robinson* (1811) 18 Ves. 429; *Rochford* v. *Hackman* (1852) 9 Hare 475; *Re Leach* [1912] 2 Ch. 422.

27 Generally see *Megarry & Wade*, pp. 75–83, Glanville Williams (1943), 59 L.Q.R. 343.

to a course of devolution prescribed by law, in cutting down the natural length of an interest to prevent creditors obtaining the benefit of the interest, or for being repugnant to the nature of the alienable interest granted, then the whole natural interest is available for creditors and for alienation. A limitation, however, creates a determinable interest lasting until the limiting event happens and such interest itself is the whole natural interest. The conceptual difference between conditional and determinable interests might be stated as the difference between giving someone a twelve-inch ruler subject to being cut down to a six-inch ruler in certain conditions and giving someone a six-inch ruler in the first place.

Protective trusts are now normally created by use of the shorthand phrase "protective trusts" which invokes the detailed trusts set out in section 33 of the Trustee Act 1925, *infra*. It is also quite common in the cause of fiscal flexibility to insert some express provision enabling the protected life tenant during the currency of his determinable life interest if he obtains the written aproval of the trustees to enter into arrangements with the other beneficiaries under the settlement for dividing up the trust funds or otherwise rearranging the beneficial interests as if he had an absolute life interest. Indeed, the protected life tenant (especially, if he is the settlor) may be given a general power of appointment exercisable only with the written consent of the trustees (for this purpose being a trust corporation or not less than two persons other than or in addition to the protected life tenant) so as to be able to vary the beneficial or administrative provisions of the settlement or even completely to revoke the settlement.[28] For the reasons set out in an extract *infra* from a case note by R.E.M. on *Re Richardson's W.T.*, *infra* it has also become not uncommon to create a series of protective trusts, *e.g.*, one set until a beneficiary is thirty, another from thirty to forty, a third from forty to fifty and another for the rest of his life.

As will be seen upon examining section 33 of the Trustee Act 1925 a protective trust contains three parts: (1) a life or lesser interest determinable on certain events; (2) a forfeiture clause specifying the determining events; (3) a discretionary trust which arises after forfeiture.

Re SMITH, PUBLIC TRUSTEE v. ASPINALL

Chancery Division [1928] Ch. 915; 97 L.J.Ch. 441; 140 L.T. 369.

The testator, who died on July 30, 1905, by his will dated March 31, 1905, directed his trustees to stand possessed of one-fourth of his residuary estate upon trust during the life of the defendant Mrs. Aspinall at their absolute discretion and in such manner as they should think fit "to pay or apply the whole or any part of the annual income of such one-fourth and the investments thereof or if they shall think fit from time to time any part of the capital thereof unto or for the maintenance and

---

[28] Such a general power falls to be treated as a special power for perpetuity purposes so that the perpetuity period runs not from the date of the exercise of the power of appointment but from the date of the settlement creating the power: *Re Earl of Coventry's Indentures* [1974] Ch. 77; Perpetuities and Accumulations Act 1964, s. 7.

personal support or benefit of the said Lilian Aspinall or as to the income thereof but not as to the capital for the maintenance education support or benefit of all or any one or more of the children of the said Lilian Aspinall and either themselves so to apply the same or to pay the same for that purpose to any other person or persons without seeing to the application thereof. And during the period of twenty-one years from my death if the said Lilian Aspinall shall live so long to accumulate the surplus if any of such income at compound interest by investing the same and the resulting income thereof in any of the investments aforesaid by way of addition to the capital of such fund as aforesaid and so as to be subject to the same trusts as are hereby declared concerning the same and during the remainder of the life of the said Lilian Aspinall in case she shall survive the said period of twenty-one years to pay or apply such surplus income (if any) to the person or persons or for the purposes to whom and for which the same would for the time being be payable or applicable if the said Lilian Aspinall were then dead. And after the death of the said Lilian Aspinall as regards both capital and income both original and accumulated in trust for the child or children of the said Lilian Aspinall who either before or after her decease shall being a son or sons attain the age of twenty-one years or being a daughter or daughters attain that age or marry and if more than one in equal shares." Mrs. Aspinall had three children, all of whom attained the age of twenty-one years, and one of whom died before the proceedings in this summons. Mrs. Aspinall was of an age when it was quite impossible that she should have any further issue. In those circumstances Mrs. Aspinall, the two surviving children and the legal personal representatives of the deceased child all joined in executing a mortgage dated April 13, 1923, to the defendants the Legal and General Assurance Company, which took the form of an assignment to the assurance company of all the interests that Mrs. Aspinall and the three children took under the will in any event.

This summons was taken out by the Public Trustee (who was the sole trustee of the will of the testator) for the determination of the question whether he was bound to pay the whole of the income of the one-fourth share of the testator's residuary estate, which was settled by the will upon trust for the benefit of Mrs. Aspinall and her children, to the defendant society, until the discharge of the mortgage, or whether he was at liberty, in his discretion (notwithstanding the notice dated February 6, 1928, given to him by the solicitors of the defendant society, to pay all income then due or to become due in respect of the share of Mrs. Aspinall under the will direct to the society as mortgagees), to apply all or any part of the income or capital of the share for the maintenance or personal support or benefit of Mrs. Aspinall.

ROMER J.: " The question I have to determine is whether the Legal and General Assurance Company are now entitled to call upon the trustees to pay the whole of the income to them. It will be observed from what I have said that the whole of this share is now held by the trustees upon trusts under which they are bound to apply the whole income and eventually pay over or apply the whole capital to Mrs. Aspinall and the three children or some or one of them. So far as the income is concerned they are obliged to pay it or apply it for her benefit or to pay it or apply it for the benefit of the children. So far as regards the capital, they have a discretion to pay it, and to apply it for her benefit and subject to that, they must hold it upon trust for the children. Mrs. Aspinall, the two surviving children and the representatives of the deceased child are between them entitled to the whole fund. In those circumstances it appears to me, notwithstanding the discretion which is reposed in the trustees, under which discretion they could select one or more of the people I have mentioned as recipients of the income, and might apply part of the capital for the benefit of Mrs. Aspinall and so take it away from the children, that the four of them, if they were all living, could come to the court and say to the trustees: 'Hand over the fund to us.' It appears to me that that is in accordance with the decision of the Court of Appeal in a case of *Re Nelson*,[29] of which a transcript of the judgments has been handed to me, and is in accordance with principle. What is the principle? As I understand it it is this. Where there is a trust under which trustees have a discretion as to applying the whole or part of a fund to or for the benefit of a particular person, that particular person cannot come to the trustees, and demand the fund; for the whole fund has not been given to him but only so much as the trustees think fit to let him have. But when the trustees have no discretion as to the amount of the fund to be applied, the fact that the trustees have a discretion as to the method in which the whole of the fund shall be applied for the benefit of the particular person does not prevent that particular person from coming and saying: 'Hand over the fund to me.' That appears to be the result of the two cases which were cited to me: *Green* v. *Spicer* [30] and *Younghusband* v. *Gisborne*.[31]

"Now this third case arises. What is to happen where the trustees have a discretion whether they will apply the whole or only a portion of the fund for the benefit of one person, but are obliged to apply the rest of the fund, so far as not applied for the benefit of the first-named person, to or for the benefit of a second-named person? There, two people together are the sole objects of the discretionary trust and, between them, are entitled to have the whole fund applied to them or for their benefit. It has been laid down by the Court of Appeal in the case to which I have referred that, in such a case as that, you treat all the people put together just as though they formed one person, for whose benefit the trustees were directed to apply the whole of a particular fund. The case before the Court of Appeal was this: A testator had directed his

---

[29] [1928] Ch. 920n.
[30] (1830) 1 Russ. & My. 395. [31] (1844) 1 Coll.C.C. 400.

trustees to stand possessed of one-third of his residuary estate upon
trust during the lifetime of the testator's son Arthur Hector Nelson:
' to apply the income thereof for the benefit of himself and his wife
and child or children or of any of such persons to the exclusion of the
others or other of them as my trustees shall think fit.' What happened
was something very similar to what happened in the case before me.
Hector Nelson, his wife and the only existing child of the marriage
joined together in asking the trustees to hand over the income to them,
and it was held by the Court of Appeal that the trustees were obliged
to comply with the request, in other words, to treat all those persons
who were the only members of the class for whose benefit the income
could be applied as forming together an individual for whose benefit
a fund has to be applied by the trustees without any discretion as to
the amount so to be applied.

"I only want to add this out of respect to Mr. Sanger's [32] argument.
Where there is a trust to apply the whole or such part of a fund as
trustees think fit to or for the benefit of A, and A has assigned his interest
under the trust, or become bankrupt, although his assignee or his trustee
in bankruptcy stand in no better position than he does and cannot
demand that the fund shall be handed to them, yet they are in a position
to say to A: 'Any money which the trustees do in the exercise of their
discretion pay to you passes by the assignment or under the bankruptcy.'
But they cannot say that in respect of any money which the trustees have
not paid to A or invested in purchasing goods or other things for A, but
which they apply for the benefit of A in such a way that no money
or goods ever gets into the hands of A. That depends on a perfectly
different principle which in no way assists Mr. Sanger in his argument
in the present case.[33]

"There will, consequently, be a declaration that, in the events which
have happened, the plaintiff is bound to pay the whole of the income
of the one-fourth to the defendant society during the lifetime of Mrs.
Aspinall, or until the mortgage is discharged."

The Trustee Act 1925

Section 33.—(1) Where any income, including an annuity or other periodical
income payment, is directed to be held on protective trusts for the benefit of
any person (in this section called " the principal beneficiary ") for the period
of his life or for any less period, then, during that period (in this section
called the " trust period ") the said income shall, without prejudice to any
prior interest, be held on the following trusts, namely:

---

[32] Counsel for Mrs. Aspinall.
[33] The cases on this point are not altogether free from ambiguity. They are: *Re
Coleman* (1888) 39 Ch.D. 443 (C.A.) (beneficiary assigned interest under discretionary
trust: assignee gave notice to trustees: *held*, trustees *must* pay assignee); *Re Ashby*
[1892] 1 Q.B. 872 (beneficiary became bankrupt: *held*, trustee in bankruptcy entitled
only to sums *paid* to the bankrupt in excess of what was necessary for his
support); *Re Bullock* (1891) 64 L.T. 736 (*held*, trustees may *apply* income for
benefit of beneficiary). *Quaere* can they apply the *whole* or only so much as is
needed for his *support*?

(i) Upon trust for the principal beneficiary during the trust period or until he, whether before or after the termination of any prior interest, does or attempts to do or suffers any act or thing, or until any event happens, other than an advance under any statutory or express power,[34] whereby, if the said income were payable during the trust period to the principal beneficiary absolutely during that period, he would be deprived of the right to receive the same or any part thereof, in any of which cases, as well as on the termination of the trust period, whichever first happens, this trust of the said income shall fail or determine;

(ii) If the trust aforesaid fails or determines during the subsistence of the trust period, then, during the residue of that period, the said income shall be held upon trust for the application thereof for the maintenance or support, or otherwise for the benefit, of all or any one or more exclusively of the other or others of the following persons (that is to say)—

(a) the principal beneficiary and his or her wife or husband, if any, and his or her children or more remote issue, if any; or

(b) if there is no wife or husband or issue of the principal beneficiary in existence, the principal beneficiary and the persons who would, if he were actually dead, be entitled to the trust property or the income thereof or to the annuity fund, if any, or arrears of the annuity, as the case may be;

as the trustees in their absolute discretion, without being liable to account for the exercise of such discretion, think fit.

(2) This section does not apply to trusts coming into operation before the commencement of this Act, and has effect subject to any variation [35] of the implied trusts aforesaid contained in the instrument creating the trust.

(3) Nothing in this section operates to validate any trust which would, if contained in the instrument creating the trust, be liable to be set aside.[36]

Re RICHARDSON'S WILL TRUSTS

Chancery Division [1958] Ch. 504; [1958] 2 W.L.R. 414; 102 S.J. 176; [1958] 1 All E.R. 538

By his will the testator gave £2,000 to his trustees to hold the income on protective trusts for the benefit of his grandson Douglas William

---

[34] See *Re Hodgson* [1913] 1 Ch. 34; *Re Shaw's Settlement* [1951] Ch. 833; *Re Rees* [1954] Ch. 202; *cf. Re Stimpson's Trusts* [1931] 2 Ch. 77, which should now be confined to its own facts, *viz.*, where an express advancement clause is lacking and where no use is made of s. 33 of the Trustee Act. Even so, it must be regarded as of doubtful authority.

[35] See, *e.g.*, *Re Wittke* [1944] Ch. 166: bequest of residue upon protective trusts for testatrix's sister, no period being specified, but trustees being given a power to pay capital to the sister from time to time. *Held* by Vaisey J. that a protected life interest had been created, for, had an absolute interest been given, it would have been open to the sister to call for an immediate transfer of the capital, which would have been inconsistent with the power given to the trustees.

[36] This preserves *inter alia* the rule that although a settler may validly create in favour of another person a life interest determinable by bankruptcy, such a limitation in favour of himself is void against his trustee in bankruptcy. See *Re Burroughs-Fowler* [1916] 2 Ch. 251; *Re Detmold* (1889) 40 Ch.D. 585 (where a determining event, other than bankruptcy, occurred, and it was held that the life interest determined). See section 3, *infra*.

Llewellyn Evans during his life and until he attained the age of thirty-five in accordance with section 33 of the Trustee Act 1925. If, on attaining that age, the grandson had not attempted to do or suffer any act or thing or no event had happened (other than any advance under any statutory or express power) whereby he would then or at any time thereafter have been deprived of the right to receive the capital or income or any part thereof, he was to receive the capital absolutely. If, on the other hand, he had made such attempt or sufferance or such event had happened, then he was to receive the income on protective trusts for the rest of his life. If he died before attaining the age of thirty-five or the protective trusts for his benefit after his attaining that age came into operation, then on his death the capital was to go to his children, who attained the age of twenty-one, if more than one in equal shares.

On November 15, 1954, the grandson's wife obtained a decree absolute of divorce against him. On June 3, 1955, an order was made in the Probate, Divorce and Admiralty Division charging the grandson's interest under the will with a payment of £50 per annum interim maintenance in favour of his wife. On October 24, 1955, the grandson attained the age of thirty-five. On August 27, 1956, he was adjudicated bankrupt.

The Public Trustee (who was the sole trustee of the will) took out a summons to have determined (1) whether the capital (a) vested in the grandson, Douglas William Llewellyn Evans, on his attaining the age of thirty-five (in which case his trustee in bankruptcy would now be entitled to it) or (b) by reason of the order of June 3, 1955, the grandson forfeited his interest therein; (2) if the grandson had forfeited his interest in the capital, whether the capital was held (a) during the remainder of his life on the discretionary trusts provided for in section 33 (1) (ii) of the Trustee Act 1925 and after his death on the trusts in the testator's will expressed to take effect in the event of the protective trusts for his benefit after his attaining the age of thirty-five having come into operation, or (b) upon some other trusts.

DANCKWERTS J.: " In considering whether there has been a forfeiture, the first question is: What was the effect of the order of June 3, 1955, on the footing that it was never completed by the execution of any deed? The matter has been very well argued before me, and I have been taken through a number of cases. I am satisfied, upon three decisions, that clearly the effect of that order in itself was to create an equitable charge, if that were possible, upon the interest of Douglas William Llewellyn Evans under his grandfather's will. The cases in question are *Waterhouse* v. *Waterhouse*,[37] *Maclurcan* v. *Maclurcan*[38] and *Hyde* v. *Hyde*.[39] In the last of those cases Barnard J. applied what previously had been no more really than the dicta of the Court of Appeal in the *Waterhouse* case and in *Maclurcan* v. *Maclurcan* that an order referring

---

[37] [1893] P. 284.
[38] (1897) 77 L.T. 474.
[39] [1948] P. 198.

to specific property, in the manner of this order which I have to consider, did upon its date create an equitable charge upon the property to which reference therein was made.

" That being so, the next thing to consider is: What was the effect of that order which created that equitable charge? There are two portions of the will which involve the question of forfeiture. First of all, there is the part which invokes section 33 of the Trustee Act 1925 before the grandson had attained the age of thirty-five, and then the part which describes what is to happen upon his attaining that age. As to the first part, the trusts of the will before he attains the age of thirty-five years must be taken to be expressed in this form: ' Upon trust for the principal beneficiary '—that is, the grandson—' during the trust period or until he . . . does or attempts to do or suffers any act or thing, or until any event happens (other than any advance under any statutory or express power) whereby, if the said income were payable during the trust period to the principal beneficiary absolutely during that period, he would be deprived of the right to receive the same or any part thereof.' It seems to me that the effect of the order was to create, or attempt to create, an equitable charge on his interest under the testator's will. When this order was made, if he had been absolutely entitled, he would have been deprived of the right to receive part of the income, because part of the income was to be payable to his former wife to the extent of £50 a year. Consequently, it seems to me that there was a forfeiture at that date; but in any case under the express terms of the will he never succeeded in attaining his absolute interest, and the protective trusts which were to take effect during the rest of his life in accordance with section 33 of the Trustee Act 1925 came into effect because the direction was, if such event had happened, that the protective trusts were to come into effect, and the fund in question is referred to as the fund of which ' he would then or at any time thereafter be deprived of the right to receive the capital or income or any part thereof.' When, therefore, the order of the Divorce Division was made on June 3, 1955, an event happened whereby he would either then or at some time thereafter ' be deprived of the right to receive the capital or income ' or any part of it.

" An argument was put forward on behalf of the trustee in bankruptcy that I must construe the order made by the registrar of the Divorce Division, in accordance with the numerous cases on the subject which have come before the court, in such a way as to give effect to the order and avoid any forfeiture. It was argued that the proper way to construe the order was as a direction that upon attaining the age of thirty-five years, then, and not until then, the charge was to be operated upon the interests of the grandson under his grandfather's will. It seems to me that I am unable to do that. I have to deal with the order as I find it. Undoubtedly, on its terms, and on the cases to which I have been referred in which orders of this kind have been construed in the

Probate and Divorce Division, the effect of such an order is to attempt at any rate to create an immediate charge. Of course, the result of the forfeiture provision in the will is that that attempt is unsuccessful, but that is the way in which the forfeiture provisions in the will operate. An event operates by which—if only there had been an absolute interest taken by the person in question—he would have been deprived of the income; but, owing to the forfeiture provision followed by the discretionary trust, he is in fact not necessarily deprived of the income but has received discretionary payments from the trustees under the protective trusts which follow. Consequently, I have come to the conclusion that, in the events which have happened in this case, by the time that Douglas William Llewellyn Evans became bankrupt his interest under the will had been forfeited, and a discretionary trust had come into effect. Consequently, the trustee in bankruptcy cannot take anything under the testator's will.

"Mr. Rossdale, on behalf of the trustees in bankruptcy, wished to argue as to the effect of sections 40 and 42 of the Bankruptcy Act 1914 on the order of June 3, 1955; but, in my view, it is not open to me to consider this matter in the absence of the bankrupt's former wife, and, accordingly, I express no opinion upon that matter at all.

"I will make a declaration that by reason of the order dated June 3, 1955, the life interest of Douglas William Llewellyn Evans under the terms of the testator's will was determined, and that he did not become entitled to an absolute interest upon the attainment by him of the age of thirty-five years, and that on the true construction of the will, and in the events which have happened, during the life of Douglas William Llewellyn Evans, the plaintiff as trustee holds the trusts of the property during the rest of the life of Douglas William Llewellyn Evans and the income thereof upon the discretionary trusts laid down in section 33 (1) (i) of the Trustee Act 1925, and after the death of the said Douglas William Llewellyn Evans as to the capital and income thereof upon the trusts in the testator's said will expressed then to take effect if the protective trusts for his benefit after his attaining the age of thirty-five years should come into operation."

R. E. Megarry (1958) 74 L.Q.R. 184

" This sequence of events points a moral for draftsmen. Hitherto the normal course of drafting has been to give a life interest simply ' on protective trusts,' with or without variations. The result is that a single mistaken act by the beneficiary may deprive him of his determinable life interest and reduce him for the rest of his life to the status of merely one of the beneficiaries of a discretionary trust. *Re Richardson* suggests that there may be advantages in setting up a series of protective trusts, *e.g.*, one set until the beneficiary is twenty-five, another from twenty-five to thirty-five, a third from thirty-five to forty-five, and another for the rest of his life. The result would be that a youthful indiscretion at, say, twenty-two, would not irretrievably condemn the beneficiary to the mere hopes of a beneficiary under a discretionary trust, dependent upon the exercise of the trustees' discretion, but would give him a fresh start when he was twenty-five. Again, a bankruptcy at the age of thirty would not *per se* mean that when he was twice that age he would still have not an income as of right, but a mere hope of a well-exercised discretion. Indeed, instead of relating the stages to the age of the beneficiary, they might be related to a period of time (*e.g.*, five years) after the occurrence of any event which had made the initial trust pass from Stage 1 to Stage 2. England lacks the device of the spendthrift trust in the American sense, but it is far from clear that the fullest possible use is being made of the existing machinery of protective and discretionary trusts."

Whether the interest of the beneficiary is determined in the events which have happened is a question of construction of the forfeiture clause in each particular case. It is sometimes said that forfeiture clauses should be construed in favour of the principal beneficiary, but it must be remembered that he is not the sole object of the testator's bounty, and that there are other persons upon whom the testator intended to confer a benefit.[40] It is only if, after construing the clause, a doubt remains that this should be resolved in favour of the principal beneficiary, for "the burden is upon those who allege a forfeiture to satisfy the court that a forfeiture has occurred." [41]

The forfeiture clause contained in section 33 of the Trustee Act 1925 is very wide, for it includes not only the acts and omissions of the principal beneficiary, but also the happening of any event which deprives him of his right to receive the income or any part thereof. Such an event was the Trading with the Enemy Act 1939 and orders made thereunder, whereby the property of those resident in enemy territory vested in the Custodian of Enemy Property.[42] It was otherwise with express forfeiture clauses which were drafted in narrower terms. Thus in *Re Hall, Public Trustee* v. *Montgomery* [43] forfeiture was to occur "if the annuitant should alienate or charge her annuity or become bankrupt or do or suffer any act or thing whereby the said annuity or any part thereof would or might become vested in or payable to any other person." It was held by Uthwatt J. that the clause was directed to the forfeiture of the annuity in the event of the annuitant doing *personally* certain classes of things whereby she would be deprived of her annuity. Accordingly, the Trading with the Enemy Act 1939 did not bring about a forfeiture.

Apart from these special cases, involving the application of the Trading with the Enemy Act to protective trusts, the following events have been held to cause a forfeiture:

Re Balfour's Settlement [44]: the impounding by the trustees of part of the income of the principal beneficiary to repair a breach of trust

---

40 *Re Sartoris's Estate* [1892] 1 Ch. 11, 16.

41 *Re Baring's Settlement Trusts* [1940] Ch. 737 (Morton J.).

42 *e.g.*, Trading with the Enemy (Custodian) Order 1939 (S.R. & O. 1939 No. 1198). Later orders contained a proviso that vesting in the custodian should not take place if it would cause a forfeiture (*e.g.*, S.R. & O. 1945 No. 887).

43 [1944] Ch. 46; so too *Re Furness, Wilson* v. *Kenmare (No.* 1) [1944] 1 All E.R. 575; *Re Harris* [1945] Ch. 316; *Re Pozot's Settlement Trusts* [1952] Ch. 427.

44 [1938] Ch. 928.

committed by them in paying part of the trust fund to him at his own instigation.

Re Walker, Public Trustee v. *Walker* [45]: the bankruptcy of the principal beneficiary, even if this had occurred before the trust first came into operation.

Re Baring's Settlement Trusts [46]: an order of sequestration of the income for contempt of court, even though the contempt is subsequently purged.

Re Dennis's Settlement Trusts [47]: the execution by the principal beneficiary of a deed of variation relinquishing his right to part of the income in certain events.

Re Richardson's W.T., [48] *supra*: an order of the court attempting to impose a charge which though ineffectual for that purpose was sufficient to bring about a forfeiture.

On the other hand no forfeiture occurred in the following cases:

Re Tancred's Settlement [49]: the appointment by the principal beneficiary of an attorney to receive the income, even though the attorney's expenses are to be deducted from the income, and the balance paid over to the principal beneficiary.

Re Mair [50]: the making by the court of an order under section 57 of the Trustee Act 1925 authorising capital moneys to be raised to enable the principal beneficiary to pay certain pressing liabilities: section 57 is an overriding section whose provisions are read into every settlement. *Cf. Re Salting,* [51] where the scheme sanctioned by the court under section 57 involved the doing of certain acts by the principal beneficiary—and *his* omission to do them caused a forfeiture. The scheme provided for the life tenant to pay premiums on insurance policies with a proviso that the trustees were to pay the premiums out of his income if the premiums were not duly paid: his failure to pay was held to create a forfeiture.

Re Westby's Settlement [52]: the charge of a lunacy percentage upon the estate of a lunatic under section 148 (3) of the Lunacy Act 1890, since the fees payable were to be regarded as management expenses, and, even if a charge was created by the section, it was not such an incumbrance as was contemplated for the forfeiture clause. [53]

Re Longman [54]: a testatrix left the income of her residuary estate on certain trusts for her son under which he would forfeit his interest if he should " commit permit or suffer any act default or process whereby the said income or any part thereof would or might but for this present proviso become vested in or payable to any other person." The son authorised the trustee to pay his creditors specified sums out of a particular

45 [1939] Ch. 974. 46 [1940] Ch. 737.
47 [1942] Ch. 283; see (1942) 58 L.Q.R. 312.
48 See also *Edmonds* v. *Edmonds* [1965] 1 W.L.R. 58 (attachment of earnings order to secure former wife's maintenance held to cause forfeiture of husband's protected interest in pension fund).
49 [1903] 1 Ch. 715.
50 [1935] Ch. 562.
51 [1932] 2 Ch. 57.
52 [1950] Ch. 296; overruling *Re Custance's Settlements* [1946] Ch. 42; see also *Re Oppenheim's Will Trusts* [1950] Ch. 633.
53 The same result is now achieved, independently of the cases, by the Law Reform (Miscellaneous Provisions) Act 1949, s. 8.
54 [1955] 1 W.L.R. 197.

future dividend due on shares forming part of the residuary estate. The son later withdrew this authority, and the company afterwards did not declare a dividend. It was held by Danckwerts J. that the withdrawal of authority would not by itself prevent forfeiture [55]; but the failure to declare a dividend did, since the income of the residuary estate never included anything to which the authority could possibly have attached.

General Accident Fire and Life Assurance Corporation Ltd. v. *I.R.C.*[56]: order of the court diverting income from husband to wife and taking effect in priority to the protective trusts was held by the Court of Appeal not to create a forfeiture. Although the case turned on a narrow ground of construction of section 33 it seems better to treat it on the same basis as *Re Mair, supra* (order under section 57 of the Trustee Act): all protective trusts must be read as subject to the court's jurisdiction to make orders under section 57 of the Trustee Act and sections 24 and 31 of the Matrimonial Causes Act 1973.

An order of the court may sometimes do more than cause a forfeiture: it may destroy the protected life interest and discretionary trusts altogether. This happened in *Re Allsopp's Marriage Settlement Trusts*[57]; where an express protective trust was created by a marriage settlement in 1916 with discretionary trusts after forfeiture. In 1928 on the dissolution of the marriage the court made an order varying the marriage settlement by *extinguishing* the rights of the husband as if he were already dead. Vaisey J. held that the husband's protected life interest was extinguished for all purposes and the discretionary trusts were so closely connected with the life interest that they also were destroyed.

The effect of the forfeiture is to determine the principal beneficiary's life interest and to bring the discretionary trusts into operation. Thus in *Re Gourju's Will Trusts*,[58] the Trading with the Enemy Act 1939 and orders made thereunder having brought about a forfeiture of the principal beneficiary's interests, and the discretionary trusts having arisen, it was held by Simonds J. that income which had accrued due before the forfeiture was payable to the Custodian of Enemy Property, but income which accrued due after that event, was to be held on the discretionary trusts for the benefit of the objects, and that since the Act contemplated a continuous benefit to those objects, the trustees were not to retain the income, but were to apply it for the objects as and when it came in, subject to such reasonable exceptions as the exigencies of the case demanded.[59] Thus the trustees could not accumulate the income so as to pay it at the end of the war to the principal beneficiary (a woman marooned in German occupied Nice).

Section 3. Attempts by a Settlor to deprive his Creditors

Although a settlor may validly create in favour of another person a life interest determinable upon bankruptcy such a limitation in favour of him-

---

[55] See *Re Baker* [1904] 1 Ch. 157.
[56] [1963] 1 W.L.R. 1207; (1963) 27 Conv.(N.S.) 517 (F. R. Crane).
[57] [1959] Ch. 81. [58] [1943] Ch. 24.
[59] As to the position if the trustees fail to exercise their discretion, see Sheridan, " Protective Trusts " (1957) 21 Conv.(N.S.) 110, 116; Walford, *ibid.* 323; Sheridan, *ibid.* 324; A. J. Hawkins (1967) 31 Conv.(N.S.) 117.

self is void against his trustee in bankruptcy though effective between himself and the other beneficiaries under the settlement; *Re Burroughs-Fowler, infra.* Where there are several determinable events including bankruptcy then the occurrence before bankruptcy of some other determinable event is, however, valid against the trustee in bankruptcy.[60] A settlement upon discretionary trusts where the settlor is one of the discretionary objects is prima facie valid but may be impeached under section 172 of the Law of Property Act 1925 or section 42 of the Bankruptcy Act 1914, *infra.*

These sections are broad enough to catch many dispositions by a settlor in favour of third parties. Section 172 operates independently of any bankruptcy of the settlor and runs as follows:

"(1) Save as provided in this section every conveyance of property made . . . with intent to defraud creditors shall be voidable at the instance of any person thereby prejudiced.

(2) This section does not affect the operation of a disentailing assurance or the law of bankruptcy.

(3) This section does not extend to any estate or interest in property conveyed for valuable consideration and in good faith or upon good consideration and in good faith to any person not having, at the time of the conveyance, notice of the intent to defraud creditors."

The burden of proof under section 172 (1) lies on the person seeking to avoid the conveyance and that under section 172 (3) lies on the transferee.[61]

Certain problems of interpretation have arisen owing to the fact that in *Re Eichholz*[62] Harman J. and counsel overlooked the fact that the Law of Property Act 1925 is not a consolidating statute as regards the Statute of Elizabeth 1571 (which it replaces and which was concerned with avoiding conveyances to defraud creditors) but only as regards the Law of Property (Amendment) Act 1924 "which substantially altered the Statute of Elizabeth."[63] Harman J. had to consider whether a "conveyance" within section 172 included an oral transaction when the 1571 Statute concerned any transaction "by writing or otherwise" but section 205 (1) (ii) of the Law of Property Act 1925 assumes that a conveyance of necessity implies a transaction in writing in defining "conveyance," unless the context otherwise requires, as including "a mortgage, charge, lease, assent, vesting declaration, vesting instrument, disclaimer, release and every other assurance of property or of an interest therein by any instrument, except a will." He held that since the 1925 Act was a consolidating statute it was "not to be taken as making an alteration in the law unless the words admit of no other interpretation,"[64] so that even though the language of section 172 was "strikingly different"[65] from that of the 1571 statute a conveyance must be deemed to include in this context an oral transaction. Although such a conclusion can be supported on policy grounds as plugging a loophole for oral transactions, such as an oral gift of a valuable chattel perfected by delivery of the chattel, it is of doubtful authority[66] especially when section

---

[60] *Detmold* (1889) 40 Ch.D. 585.
[61] *Lloyds Bank Ltd.* v. *Marcan* [1974] 1 W.L.R. 370.
[62] [1959] Ch. 708.
[63] *Lloyds Bank Ltd.* v. *Marcan* [1973] 2 All E.R. 359, 367 *per* Pennycuick V.-C.
[64] [1959] Ch. 708, 725.　　　　　　　　　　　　　[65] *Ibid.*, 726.
[66] In *Thomson* v. *Nicholson* [1939] V.L.R. 157 a section of a statute of the state of Victoria in identical terms to s. 172 was held not to include an oral transaction.

42 of the Bankruptcy Act 1914 can to a large extent deal with the alleged loophole.

Re Eichholz is further unsatisfactory in that there it seems to have been assumed without argument that section 172 (3) only protects a person who takes property for valuable consideration, presumably on the footing that the 1571 statute used the words " upon good consideration " which were judicially interpreted [67] to mean " upon valuable consideration." However, section 172 clearly uses " valuable " and " good " consideration in contradistinction to each other so that either type of consideration will suffice under section 172 (3) as indicated by Pennycuick V.-C. in *Lloyds Bank Ltd.* v. *Marcan*.[68] Valuable consideration consists of money or money's worth or marriage whilst good consideration consists of natural love and affection for relatives.

Whether the settlor intended to defraud his creditors is, of course, a question of fact in all the circumstances of the case. What is required is some proof of dishonesty or sharp practice [69] and in the case of a voluntary conveyance where the settlor cannot pay his debts without the property conveyed such dishonesty is almost irrebuttably presumed.[70] It will also be presumed where immediately before engaging in a speculative venture a man voluntarily settles all his property on his wife and family.[71] Creditors can take advantage of the section whether or not their debts existed before the conveyance in question.[72]

Despite the presence of an intention to defraud, a transferee will be protected under section 172 (3) if he can show that he had no actual or constructive notice [73] of the intent to defraud and that there has been a conveyance for valuable or for good consideration, in either case in good faith. This good faith though gramatically that of the settlor cannot be so for *ex hypothesi* the settlor intended to defraud creditors [74]: presumably it is the good faith of the transferee alone.

Where a settlement falls foul of section 172 it is not wholly cancelled if there is a possibility that a surplus may exist after payment of all creditors prejudiced by the settlement: the trustees are directed to join in and concur in all acts necessary for making the settled property available for creditors.[75] The settlement is thus set aside *pro tanto*.

A fraudulent conveyance ranks as an act of bankruptcy within section 1 (1) (*b*) of the Bankruptcy Act 1914 for a period of three months from such conveyance.[75] If in this period a bankruptcy petition is presented and the settlor adjudicated bankrupt the settlement will be avoided by the

[67] *Twyne's Case* (1602) 3 Co.Rep. 80b; *Mathews* v. *Feaver* (1786) 1 Cox Eq.Cas. 278; *Re David & Adlard* [1914] 2 K.B. 694.
[68] [1973] 2 All E.R. 359, 368.
[69] *Lloyds Bank Ltd.* v. *Marcan* [1973] 3 All E.R. 754, *infra*.
[70] *Freeman* v. *Pope* (1870) 5 Ch.App. 538; *cf. Re Wise* (1886) 17 Q.B.D. 290; Underhill, pp. 152–155; dicta of Cairns L.J. in *Lloyds Bank Ltd.* v. *Marcan* [1973] 3 All E.R. 754, 761 go too far.
[71] *Mackay* v. *Douglas* (1872) L.R. 14 Eq. 106; *Re Butterworth* (1882) 19 Ch.D. 588.
[72] *Re Butterworth* (1882) 19 Ch.D. 588.
[73] *Lloyds Bank Ltd.* v. *Marcan* [1973] 2 All E.R. 359, 369; *Re Fasey* [1892] 3 Ch. 382.
[74] Snell, pp. 127–128; see also *Lloyds Bank Ltd.* v. *Marcan* [1973] 2 All E.R. 359, 369.
[75] *Ideal Bedding Co.* v. *Holland* [1907] 2 Ch. 157.
[76] B.A. 1914, s. 4 (1) (*c*).

relation back of the trustee in bankruptcy's title to the day of the act of bankruptcy.[77]

Once a settlor has been adjudicated bankrupt then settlements made up to ten years earlier may be avoided in circumstances detailed in section 42 of the bankruptcy Act 1914,[78] *infra*, where no proof of intent to deprive creditors is required.

Finally, under section 37 of the Matrimonial Causes Act 1973 the Family Division has jurisdiction to set aside certain dispositions made within three years of the application to the court with the intention of defeating a spouse's claim to financial relief.

Re BURROUGHS-FOWLER

Chancery Division [1916] 2 Ch. 251.

ADJOURNED SUMMONS. By an antenuptial settlement dated March 24, 1905, freeholds and leaseholds belonging to W. J. Fowler, the intended husband, were conveyed to the trustees upon trust to sell with the consents therein mentioned and " to pay the rents profits and income thereof to the said W. J. Fowler or to permit him to receive the same during his life or until he shall be outlawed or be declared bankrupt or become an insolvent debtor within the meaning of some Act of Parliament for the relief of insolvent debtors or shall do or suffer something whereby the said rents profits and income or some part thereof respectively might if absolutely belonging to him become vested in or payable to some other person or persons. And from and immediately after the death of the said W. J. Fowler or other the determination of the trust for his benefit in his lifetime to pay the said rents profits and income unto the " wife if she should survive him during her life for her separate use without power of anticipation, and after the death of the survivor upon the usual trusts for the children of the marriage.

Some time after the solemnisation of the marriage the husband took the name of Burroughs-Fowler.

On May 13, 1915, the husband was adjudicated bankrupt. The official receiver at Oxford was appointed trustee in the bankruptcy and offered for sale the husband's life interest under the settlement, but the intending purchaser objected that the debtor's life interest remained defeasible if the debtor should do or suffer any of the other specified acts of forfeiture.

The trustee took out this summons against the wife, the husband, and the trustee for the determination of the question to what estate, right or interest in the income and capital of the trust funds and property he could make a good title in favour of a purchaser.

PETERSON J.: " In this case I am required to solve a puzzle which arises out of a clause relating to a protected life interest under a

---

[77] B.A. 1914, s. 37.   [78] See, generally, *Williams on Bankruptcy*.

marriage settlement dated March 24, 1905. Under that settlement W. J. Fowler (who afterwards took the name of Burroughs-Fowler), on the occasion of his marriage with his then intended wife, settled certain property belonging to him. The property was conveyed to the trustees in trust for conversion and investment of the proceeds, and the trust premises were to be held by the trustees upon the following trusts ": [His Lordship read the trusts above set out and continued:] " The marriage took place a few days after the execution of the settlement, and on May 13, 1915, the husband was adjudicated bankrupt. The trustee in bankruptcy has entered into negotiations for the sale of the bankrupt's interest under the settlement, and the question which has arisen is what is the interest which has vested in the trustee and of which the trustee is now able to dispose.

" Now the limitation until the settlor is declared bankrupt is void against the trustee in bankruptcy, and therefore, so far as the trustee in bankruptcy is concerned, the words relating to the bankruptcy and insolvency of the settlor must be treated as if they were omitted altogether from the clause. But on the other hand the provision as to bankruptcy and insolvency is not void as between the husband and the wife; for it was decided in *In re Johnson* [79] that, while the provision for the cessation of the life interest on bankruptcy was void as against the trustee in bankruptcy, it was effective for the purpose of producing a forfeiture as between the person who had the protected life interest and the persons interested in remainder. What, then, is the result? It is said that the result may be that the trustee in bankruptcy will be in a position to dispose of more than was vested in the bankrupt himself. That would be so in any case, because, so far as the trustee is concerned, the provisions for terminating the protected life interest upon bankruptcy are void. It seems to me that the true view is that, so far as the trustee in bankruptcy is concerned, the provisions as to bankruptcy and insolvency must be treated as excluded from the settlement, and the trustee is therefore in a position to deal with the interest of the husband under the settlement, whatever it may be, as if those provisions were excluded. So far, however, as the wife is concerned the forfeiture by reason of the bankruptcy has already taken place, and, therefore, it is no longer possible for the husband hereafter to do or suffer something which would determine his interest. The result is that the trustee in bankruptcy is in possession of the life interest of the bankrupt, which is now incapable of being affected by any subsequent forfeiture."

LLOYDS BANK LTD. v. MARCAN

Court of Appeal [1973] 3 All E.R. 254 (Russell, Cairns L.JJ., Goulding J.)

RUSSELL L.J.: " This is an appeal by Mrs. Marcan, the second

---
[79] [1904] 1 K.B. 134.

defendant, from a decision of Pennycuick V.-C. which is reported below.[80]   Reference to the reports may be made for the details of the case, which is an unusual one.   Pennycuick V.-C. decided that the lease of the dwelling-house and market garden granted by Mr. Marcan, the first defendant, to his wife pursuant to and within his statutory powers as mortgagor was a conveyance made by him with intent to defraud the bank, the mortgagee, within section 172 of the Law of Property Act 1925; further that Mrs. Marcan knew of that intent and that accordingly the lease was voidable at the instance of the bank. He made accordingly an order against both Mr. and Mrs. Marcan for possession.

   " Some facts are clear.   (1) The bank was seeking possession in these proceedings against Mr. Marcan with a view to enforcing its security by sale with vacant possession.   (2) Mr. Marcan sought means to deprive the bank of ability to obtain vacant possession because he wanted to remain with his wife and family in their home and with the market garden business.   (3) After taking advice, he and his wife entered into the 20 year lease in question in order to achieve those objects, after the proceedings demanding possession from Mr. Marcan had been initiated and had been adjourned after a first hearing by the master.   (4) On the evidence, the bank would sell with vacant possession at a greater figure than if it sold subject to the lease to Mrs. Marcan.   (5) Mr. Marcan did not know this and therefore did not know that his conduct would thus prejudice the amount which the bank would obtain towards payment off of his debt.   On the other hand, it is clearly, and was accepted to be, the right inference that Mr. Marcan must have appreciated that the bank, in seeking vacant possession in the course of realising their security, attached value to vacant possession.   (6) The terms of the lease were in accordance with Mr. Marcan's statutory powers of leasing under section 99 of the Law of Property Act 1925, and in particular the ' best rent' requirement. (7) If Mr. Marcan had a relevant intent, Mrs. Marcan knew of it; though it was faintly suggested before us that this was not shown.

   " Several points were taken in argument.   It was first said that the lease, being within the statutory powers forming part of the bargain involved in the mortgage between the bank and Mr. Marcan, could not in any event be asserted by the bank as within section 172 of the 1925 Act; and perhaps more particularly in that by appointment of a receiver the bank could at any time have deprived Mr. Marcan of his statutory powers of leasing and chose not to do so.   I cannot accept this.   It cannot be said that it was part of the bargain that Mr. Marcan should be at liberty to exercise his power to lease so as, and with the intent, to defraud the bank, or (to put it another way) that it was part of the bargain that the statute which empowered leasing should

---

[80] [1973] 1 W.L.R. 339.

be part of the bargain but that the other statute—section 172—should not be.

"The next criticism of the judgment below was as follows. The judge found [80] that Mr. Marcan—

> 'intended to deprive the bank of timely recourse to the property charged . . . and that such an intention is an intention to defraud the bank within the meaning of section 172 (1).'

This, it was argued, would deprive the section of any content of fraud in any sense, having regard to the express finding that, since Mr. Marcan did not know that the value of the property would be less without vacant possession, Pennycuick V.-C. held [81] that 'the element of depreciation by the mere grant of a lease cannot . . . be material in determining Mr. Marcan's intention.' Moreover, it was argued that a passage in the judgment below [82] indicated that Pennycuick V.-C. considered that perfectly innocent hindrance or delay to a creditor could come within section 172, notwithstanding the liberal content of the Statute of Elizabeth of 1571,[83] of words indicating dishonesty and fraud: the enactment is set out in full in the report of *Re Eichholz (decd.)*.[84]

"I am not sure what is meant by a perfectly innocent defeat, hindrance or delay. It must be remembered that in every case under this section the debtor has done something which in law he has power and is entitled to do; otherwise it would never reach the section. If he disposes of an asset which would be available to his creditors with the intention of prejudicing them by putting it (or its worth) beyond their reach, he is in the ordinary case acting in a fashion not honest in the context of the relationship of debtor and creditor. And in cases of voluntary disposition that intention may be inferred.

"Here we have this situation. A part of the bundle of rights in the bank's secured debt was a right to possession. True, possession may be of two kinds: the receipt of rents if the property is let, and vacant possession if not. Here the situation was, at the time of the lease, that the bank was seeking vacant possession, and, as I have indicated, the debtor must have appreciated that the bank was seeking vacant possession because the bank considered that to obtain vacant possession was of value to it in realising its security and obtaining repayment of the debt. The intention of Mr. Marcan is perfectly plain: the lease to his wife was designed expressly to deprive the bank of the ability to obtain the vacant possession to which the bank plainly attributed value, and to diminish to that extent the strength of the bank's position as creditor. To take that action at that juncture in my

---

[81] [1973] 1 W.L.R. 339, 347.
[82] [1973] 1 W.L.R. 339, 344.
[83] 13 Eliz. 1, c. 5.
[84] [1959] Ch. 708.

judgment was, in the context of the relationship of debtor and creditor, less than honest: it was sharp practice, and not the less so because he was advised that he had power to grant the lease. It was in my judgment a transaction made with intent to defraud the bank within section 172 of the Law of Property Act 1925, and would have been within the Statute of Elizabeth. I would accordingly uphold the decision of Pennycuick V.-C."

CAIRNS L.J.: " My mind fluctuated much during the argument of this appeal and it is only by a narrow margin and with some reluctance that I agree that the appeal should be dismissed. Both under the Statute of Elizabeth of 1571 and under section 172 of the Law of Property Act 1925 it is clear from the words of the enactment that fraud has to be established before a transaction can be avoided. In my opinion, fraud involves dishonesty and I cannot go with Pennycuick V.-C.[85] in his observation that the word ' defraud ' in section 172—

> ' is not intended to be confined to cases of fraud in the ordinary modern sense of that word, *i.e.* as involving actual deceit or dishonesty.'

It is clear enough that deceit is not a necessary element, but in my view dishonest intention is, at any rate when the conveyance is for consideration. That is shown by *Copis* v. *Middleton,*[86] *Wood* v. *Dixie,*[87] *Alton* v. *Harrison,*[88] *Re Johnson* [89] and *Re David & Adlard.*[90]

" Other cases make it clear that if the conveyance is voluntary it is easier to infer a dishonest intention than when it is made for consideration or even that no dishonest intention need then be established: see *Freeman* v. *Pope,*[91] *Ideal Bedding & Co. Ltd.* v. *Holland,*[92] *Re Eichholz (decd.).*[93]

" It does however appear that a conveyance for good consideration will be regarded as fraudulent if made with the deliberate intention of hindering creditors and for the benefit of the debtor himself rather than as a bona fide family arrangement or an arrangement which merely prefers one set of creditors to another set. To that effect was *Re Fasey,*[94] decided by a very strong Court of Appeal (Lord Sterndale M.R., Warrington and Atkin L.JJ.).

" In the present case the debtor let the property at a rent which was honestly fixed; he was unaware (as Pennycuick V.-C. found) that the land would be worth more with vacant possession than when sub-

---

85 [1973] 1 W.L.R. 339, 344
86 (1818) 2 Madd. 410.
87 (1845) 7 Q.B. 892.
88 (1869) 4 Ch.App. 622.
89 (1881) 20 Ch.D. 389.
90 [1914] 2 K.B. 694.
91 (1870) 5 Ch.App. 538.
92 [1907] 2 Ch. 157.
93 [1959] Ch. 708.   94 [1923] 2 Ch. 1.

ject to the lease; he acted at least in part for the sake of his wife and family; and he took legal advice before granting the lease. These facts tend to support the view that he acted honestly.

" The elements which in the end persuade me that he acted with intent to defraud his creditors are that he granted the lease at a time when he knew that the bank was seeking possession; that he must have known that it would have been more convenient for the bank to have vacant possession than merely to have possession of the rents and profits; and that while his wife was the grantee of the lease it was obviously for his own benefit that he wished her to be in possession rather than the bank.

" I accordingly agree that the appeal must be dismissed."

Bankruptcy Act 1914

42. Avoidance of certain settlements.—(1) Any settlement of property, not being a settlement made before and in consideration of marriage, or made in favour of a purchaser or incumbrancer in good faith and for valuable consideration, or a settlement made on or for the wife or children of the settlor of property which has accrued to the settlor after marriage in right of his wife, shall, if the settlor becomes bankrupt within two years after the date of the settlement, be void [95] against the trustee in the bankruptcy, and shall, if the settlor becomes bankrupt at any subsequent time within ten years after the date of the settlement, be void against the trustee in the bankruptcy, unless the parties claiming under the settlement can prove that the settlor was, at the time of making the settlement, able to pay all his debts without the aid of the property comprised in the settlement, and that the interest of the settlor in such property passed to the trustee of such settlement on the execution thereof.

(2) Any covenant or contract made by any person (hereinafter called the settlor) in consideration of his or her marriage, either for the future payment of money for the benefit of the settlor's wife or husband, or children, or for the future settlement on or for the settlor's wife or husband or children, of property, wherein the settlor had not at the date of the marriage any estate or interest, whether vested or contingent, in possession or remainder, and not being money or property in right of the settlor's wife or husband, shall, if the settlor is adjudged bankrupt and the covenant or contract has not been executed at the date of the commencement of his bankruptcy, be void against the trustee in the bankruptcy, except so far as it enables the persons entitled under the covenant or contract to claim for dividend, in the settlor's bankruptcy under or in respect of the covenant or contract, but any such claim to dividend shall be postponed until all claims

---

[95] Void means voidable: *Re Brall* [1893] 2 Q.B. 381; *Re Carter and Kenderdine's Contract* [1897] 1 Ch. 776; *Re Hart* [1912] 3 K.B. 6. Thus a purchaser for value is protected provided that before the trustee in bankruptcy applied to the court to have the settlement set aside the purchaser acquired title in good faith without notice of an act of bankruptcy or of any intention to defeat creditors: notice of the voluntary settlement does not of course amount to notice of such intention. Any avoidance is only to the extent necessary for satisfying the settlor's debts and bankruptcy costs: *Re Parry* [1904] 1 K.B. 129.

of the other creditors for valuable consideration in money or money's worth have been satisfied.

(3) Any payment of money (not being payment of premiums on a policy of life assurance) or any transfer of property made by the settlor in pursuance of such a covenant or contract as aforesaid shall be void against the trustee in the settlor's bankruptcy, unless the persons to whom the payment or transfer was made prove either—

    (a) that the payment or transfer was made more than two years before the date of the commencement of the bankruptcy; or;

    (b) that at the date of the payment or transfer the settlor was able to pay all his debts without the aid of the money so paid or the property so transferred; or

    (c) that the payment or transfer was made in pursuance of a covenant or contract to pay or transfer money or property expected to come to the settlor from or on the death of a particular person named in the covenant or contract and was made within three months after the money or property came into the possession or under the control of the settlor;

but, in the event of any such payment or transfer being declared void, the persons to whom it was made shall be entitled to claim for dividend under or in respect of the covenant or contract in like manner as if it had not been executed at the commencement of the bankruptcy.

(4) "Settlement"[96] shall, for the purposes of this section, include any conveyance or transfer of property.

PROBLEM

Sharp transferred various assets to trustees to be held on trust for Sharp himself for life or until he should become bankrupt or his property should otherwise become available to his creditors. On any such event occurring the trustees were directed to pay the income to Sharp's wife for her life. Subject to those trusts the trustees were to hold on trust for Sharp's children absolutely in equal shares.

Eight years after making the settlement Sharp was adjudicated bankrupt when he had a wife and two adult children.

Advise Sharp's trustee in bankruptcy as to the position if he wishes (1) to sell or (2) to retain Sharp's interest under the settlement. What consequences might ensue in the event of Sharp being discharged from bankruptcy after (a) his interest was sold or (b) his interest was retained?

---

[96] The section " applies only to such conveyances or transfers as are in the nature of settlements in the sense of being dispositions of property by a person to be held and preserved for the enjoyment of some other person. The retention of the property in some sense must be contemplated and not its immediate alienation or consumption. But it is not necessary . . . that there should be any actual restriction of the power of alienation by the donee " *per* Wright J. in *Re Tankard* [1899] 2 Q.B. 57, 59.

CHAPTER 6

CHARITABLE (OR PUBLIC) TRUSTS [1]

Section 1. The Advantages of Charity

UNITED KINGDOM [2] charities do not pay income tax on their investment income which is applicable to charitable purposes only and is in fact applied solely for those purposes.[3] They can recover tax paid by donors in respect of seven-year covenants drawn up in their favour. Where trading income is concerned, however, they are only exempt from tax if either the trade is exercised in the course of the actual carrying out of a primary purpose of the charity or the work in connection with the trade is mainly carried out by beneficiaries of the charity.[4]

Charities do not pay capital gains tax in respect of gains made upon disposals by them [5] and individuals are encouraged to make *inter vivos* gifts to charities since no charge to capital gains tax arises upon such gifts.[6] Where estate duty is concerned testamentary gifts to charities are exempt to an aggregate limit of £50,000 [7] whilst gifts to charities are totally exempt if made more than one year (instead of the usual seven years) before the donor's death to the entire exclusion of the donor from all benefit by contract or otherwise.[8] In the case of rates charities can obtain relief as of right in respect of half the normal liability to rates for premises wholly or mainly used for charitable purposes and some discretionary relief in respect of the other half.[9] It is only in the sphere of value added tax that charities have little privilege.[10] Indeed, in the introduction of VAT little attention

---

[1] *Tudor on Charities* is the authoritative legal work though all books on trusts have chapters specially devoted to charitable trusts. Keeton and Sheridan's *Modern Law of Charities* can also be useful. To view charities in a broader perspective see Benedict Nightingale's *Charities* published in 1973 by Allen Lane, and Ben Whitaker's *The Foundations* published in 1974 by Eyre-Methuen.

[2] *Camille and Henry Dreyfus Foundation Inc.* v. *I.R.C.* [1956] A.C. 39.

[3] Income and Corporation Taxes Act 1970, s. 360, replacing Income Tax Act 1952, ss. 447, 448. See *I.R.C.* v. *Educational Grants Association Ltd.* [1967] Ch. 123 *infra*, p. 241; *Drexler Ofrex Foundation Trustees* v. *I.R.C.* [1966] Ch. 675; *Campbell* v. *I.R.C.* [1970] A.C. 77. The position is the same for charitable companies paying corporation tax: I.C.T.A. 1970, s. 250.

[4] I.C.T.A. 1970, s. 360; G. N. Glover [1972] B.T.R. 346. If substantial trading is being carried on which is not within the exemption the charity may form a company to run the trade and have the company covenant to pay its net profits to the charity for a period capable of exceeding 6 years: the company then deducts the payment as a charge on income for the purposes of corporation tax: I.C.T.A. 1970, s. 248 (5), (8), (9).

[5] Finance Act 1965, s. 35; I.C.T.A. 1970, s. 265 (2).

[6] Finance Act 1972, s. 119.

[7] Finance Act 1972, s. 121 and 26th Sched.

[8] Finance (1909–10) Act 1910, s. 59 (3), as substituted by Finance Act 1969, Sched. 17 Pt. III, para. 6 (*b*). For capital transfer tax see Preface.

[9] General Rate Act 1967, ss. 40, 41; G. N. Glover [1971] B.T.R. 86; Charity Commissioners' Report for 1972, paras. 93–95; *Commissioner of Valuation for Northern Ireland* v. *Fermanagh Protestant Board of Education* [1969] 1 W.L.R. 475 (H.L.). It is vital that the premises be wholly or mainly used for charitable purposes: *Oxfam* v. *Birmingham City Council, The Times,* June 10, 1974.

[10] For educational and medical activities see Finance Act 1972, Sched. 5, Groups 6 and 7; Customs and Excise Notice 701, p. 71. S.I. 1973 No. 385 zero rates the supply of goods given to charities established for the relief of distress and also all goods exported by charities. Now see VAT (Consolidation) Order 1974.

seems to have been paid to its detrimental effects upon charities so that it is likely that special treatment will come to be afforded to charities as pressure mounts against the Government.

The fiscal advantages of charities are such that about £90 million tax is lost to the Exchequer each year and about £12 million rates is lost to the rating authorities each year.[11] By making up the loss the taxpayer and the ratepayer are subsidising all sorts of charities and so have a direct personal interest in the integrity and efficiency of charities: as one man's philanthropy is another man's tax burden it is only right that legal safeguards should exist to ensure that there is proper philanthropy properly carried out.

Charities have further advantages in that they are not subject to the rule against inalienability [12] and they enjoy one limited exemption from the rule against remoteness. At common law a gift over from one person to another that might possibly take effect outside the perpetuity period was void.[13] However, a gift over from one charity to another charity was valid, the property being treated as belonging to charity throughout so as not to be caught by the rule against remoteness.[14] If the gift were a gift over from a charity to a non-charity [15] or from a non-charity to a charity [16] then the rule against remoteness applied. Since the Perpetuities and Accumulations Act 1964 came into force it is now possible in these two latter instances to wait and see [17] when the gift over takes effect: if it takes effect within the perpetuity period then it is good, if not it is bad and the first gift becomes absolute, no longer subject to defeasance or determination.[18] Of course, the validity of gifts over from one charity to another charity is unaffected by the 1964 Act.

Furthermore, the trust requirement of certainty of objects has no application to charitable trusts so long as the settlor manifested a general charitable intention to enable a *cy-près* scheme to be formulated for giving effect to his intention as nearly as possible.[19] The *cy-près* doctrine is peculiar to charitable trusts and will be dealt with at the end of this chapter.

At this stage it might usefully be noted that a charity will often take the form of a charitable trust with individual or corporate trustees but it may take the form of a company incorporated under the Companies Act 1948

---

11 See Nightingale's *Charities* pp. 35–36. At present, there are over 112,000 charities in the U.K. Using 1970 figures the largest U.K. charity by assets is the Wellcome Trust with about 60 million dollars compared with the largest U.S.A. Foundation, the Ford Foundation with about 2,902 million dollars, the largest West German foundation, the Volkswagenwerk Stiftung, with about 376 million dollars, the largest Portugese foundation, the Calouste Gulbenkian Foundation, with 280 million dollars, and the largest Canadian Foundation, J. W. McConnell Foundation, with 172 million dollars : see Whitaker's *Foundations*.

12 *e.g.*, *Re Banfield* [1968] 1 W.L.R. 846 compared with *Re Warre's W.T.* [1953] 1 W.L.R. 725 or *Re Gwyon* [1903] 1 Ch. 255.

13 *Re Frost* (1889) 43 Ch.D. 246.

14 *Christ's Hospital* v. *Grainger* (1849) 1 Mac. & G. 400; *Re Tyler* [1891] 3 Ch. 252.

15 *Re Bowen* [1893] 2 Ch. 491.

16 *Re Dalziel* [1943] Ch. 277; *Re Peel's Release* [1921] 2 Ch. 218.

17 Perpetuities and Accumulations Act 1964, s. 3.

18 P.A.A. 1964 s. 12 treats determinable interests in the same way as conditional interests.

19 If the trust is one the administration of which the court could not undertake and control and no exclusively charitable intent appears so as to found a *cy-près* scheme then the trust fails: *Re Hummultenberg* [1923] 1 Ch. 237 (legacy to the treasurer of the London Spiritualistic Alliance for the purpose of establishing a college for the training of suitable persons as mediums).

with charitable provisions in its memorandum and articles of association. Such provisions will not be trusts in the strict equitable sense but will be trusts for the purposes of the Charities Act 1960 (concerned with the proper administration of charities) by virtue of section 46 thereof. Earlier, section 45 defines a charity as " any institution, corporate or not, which is established for charitable purposes and is subject to the control of the High Court in the exercise of the court's jurisdiction with respect to charities." A gift to a company which is incorporated under the Companies Acts, so that its general property is held for charitable purposes without the intervention of trusts, is usually treated as intended to be held as an addition to the company's general property and not upon trusts unless the donor uses express words importing a trust.[20] Although a company can always change its objects clause in its memorandum under section 5 of the Companies Act 1948 it cannot thereby cease to be a charity and so free its general property for non-charitable purposes: section 30 (2) of the Charities Act 1960. Of course, where property was gifted upon express trusts then the company must always give effect to those trusts unless and until a *cy-près* scheme is finalised.

Section 2. The Scope of Charity [21]

I. INTRODUCTORY

(a) *The spirit and intendment of the 1601 preamble*

Before the Statute of Charitable Uses 1601, the Court of Chancery exercised jurisdiction in matters relating to charity, but notions of what was a charity were imprecise. The preamble to that statute contained a list of charitable objects which the courts used as " an index or chart " for the decision of particular cases, with the result that, in addition to the objects enumerated in the preamble, other objects analogous to them or within the spirit and intendment of the preamble came to be regarded as charitable: see *Scottish Burial Reform and Cremation Society* v. *Glasgow Corporation, infra.*

The enumerated objects were: " The relief of aged, impotent and poor people; the maintenance of sick and maimed soldiers and mariners, schools of learning, free schools, and scholars in universities; the repair of bridges, ports, havens, causeways, churches, sea banks and highways; the education and preferment of orphans; the relief, stock, or maintenance for houses of correction; the marriage of poor maids; the supportation aid and help of young tradesmen, handicraftsmen and persons decayed; the relief or redemption of prisoners or captives; the aid or ease of any poor inhabitants concerning payment of fifteens, setting out of soldiers and other taxes."

The Statute of Charitable Uses 1601 was repealed by the Mortmain and Charitable Uses Act 1888, but section 13 (2) of the latter Act expressly preserved the preamble to the former statute, and on the basis of its continued existence Lord Macnaghten in *Commissioners of Income Tax* v.

---

[20] *Re Finger's W.T.* [1972] Ch. 286 and see Charity Commissioners' Report for 1971, paras. 22–30.

[21] See Bentwick (1936) 49 L.Q.R. 520; Brunyate (1945) 61 L.Q.R. 268; Keeton (1949) 2 C.L.P. 86; Cross (1956) 72 L.Q.R. 187; Sheridan (1957) 13 Malayan L.J. 86; Nightingale's *Charities*, pp. 34–68.

Pemsel enunciated his famous fourfold classification of charity: "Charity in its legal sense comprises four principal divisions: trusts for the relief of poverty; trusts for the advancement of education; trusts for the advancement of religion; and trusts for other purposes beneficial to the community, not falling under any of the preceding heads."

The Mortmain and Charitable Uses Act 1888, and with it the preamble to the Statute of Charitable Uses 1601, were repealed by section 38 (1) of the Charities Act 1960, section 38 (4) of which went on to provide: "Any reference in any enactment or document to a charity within the meaning, purview and interpretation of the Charitable Uses Act 1601, or of the preamble to it, shall be construed as a reference to a charity within the meaning which the word bears as a legal term according to the law of England and Wales."

This provision is not free from obscurity,[22] but the courts treat the somewhat ossificatory classification to which the preamble gave rise as still surviving in the decided cases.[23]

(b) *Public benefit* [24]

A valid charitable trust must also promote some public benefit unless it is within Lord Macnaghten's first category of trusts for the relief of poverty.[25] This exception is anomalous but well established in the House of Lords: *Dingle* v. *Turner, infra.*

The public benefit test does not require a benefit available to all the public: it suffices that the possibility of benefiting is conferred upon some section of the public such that the trust is a public one as opposed to a private one. The House of Lords in *Oppenheim* v. *Tobacco Securities Trust Co. Ltd., infra,* used the personal nexus test put forward in *Re Compton* [26] to distinguish between public trusts and private trusts: they held that except in "poverty" trusts no class of beneficiaries can constitute a section of the public if the distinguishing quality which links them together is relationship to a particular individual either through a common ancestor or a common employer. Thus a trust for the education of children of employees or former employees of British American Tobacco Co. Ltd. or any of its subsidiary or allied companies was not a valid charitable trust though there were over 110,000 current employees. If the trust had been for children of those employed or formerly employed in the tobacco industry it would have been valid as it would if confined to children of those engaged in the tobacco industry in a particular county or town.[27]

The weaknesses of the personal nexus test are revealed in the dissenting speech of Lord MacDermott in *Oppenheim, infra,* and with whose broad approach the House of Lords were in agreement obiter in *Dingle* v. *Turner, infra,* where Lord Cross indicated that whether or not the potential bene-

---

22 See Marshall (1961) 24 M.L.R. 444.
23 *e.g., Re Hopkins W.T., infra; Incorporated Council of Law Reporting* v. *Att.-Gen., infra,* p. 225.
24 S. G. Maurice (1951) 15 Conv.(N.S.) 328; G. H. L. Fridman (1953) 31 Can.B.R. 537; P. S. Atiyah (1958) 21 M.L.R. 138; Nathan Committee Report (1952) Cmd. 8710.
25 *Oppenheim* v. *Tobacco Securities Trust Co. Ltd., infra; Gilmour* v. *Coats, infra; I.R.C.* v. *Baddeley* [1955] A.C. 572.
26 [1945] Ch. 123.
27 [1951] A.C. 297, 318; *Re Morgan* [1955] 1 W.L.R. 718.

ficiaries can fairly be said to constitute a section of the public is a question of degree in all the circumstances of the case and that much must depend upon the purpose of the trusts.[28] Indeed, the cases reveal that minute public benefit is required for religious trusts,[29] a substantial amount of public benefit is required for educational trusts [30] and, possibly, slightly more public benefit still is required for trusts for other purposes beneficial to the community.[31]

Owing to the conflicting views expressed in the Lords in *Oppenheim* and in *Dingle* v. *Turner* lower courts will face an unenviable dilemma when the case arises that compels a choice between the two views. In its favour the broad approach at least concerns itself with the substance of the matter and is not unduly preoccupied with form as is the narrow personal nexus approach. The narrow formal approach, though conducive to certainty, also leads to artificial manipulation of the legal forms so as to obtain fiscal advantages.

Indeed, the law of charitable trusts is bedevilled by the fact that such trusts enjoy not just immunity from the rules against uncertainty and inalienability but also automatically fiscal privileges. The two questions of the validity of the trust and of exemption from rates and taxes are joined together in an unholy and unnatural union. It is most noticeable that in " Chancery " cases, where the validity of a trust is attacked by the residuary legatee or next of kin, there are many doubtful first instance cases in favour of charity, whereas in " Revenue " cases, where exemption from taxes is the real bone of contention, there are many appellate cases restricting the scope of charity.[32] Is it too much to ask that fresh consideration should be given to the recommendations of the Radcliffe Commission on Taxation [33] that the question whether a trust should be regarded as a charitable trust for the purpose of general validity as a trust should be separated from the question whether it should enjoy any fiscal privileges? [34] It is noteworthy that in *Dingle* v. *Turner* the Lords disagreed over the influence of fiscal considerations in an application of a broad public benefit test. It would seem that Lords Simon and Cross thought that fiscal considerations would require a case like *Oppenheim* to be decided the same way today.

Most charities have to be registered with the Charity Commissioners under the Charities Act 1960 [35] so that in the vast majority of instances it

---

28 D. J. Hayton (1972) 36 Conv.(N.S.) 209; Gareth Jones (1974) C.L.J. 63. For comments of Lord Cross see *Carter* v. *Race Relations Board* [1973] A.C. 868, 907.

29 *Re Watson* [1973] 1 W.L.R. 1472; *Thornton* v. *Howe* (1862) 31 Beav. 14; *Dingle* v. *Turner*, dicta, *infra*.

30 *Oppenheim* v. *Tobacco Securities Trust Ltd.*, *infra*; *I.R.C.* v. *Educational Grants Association Ltd.*, *infra*.

31 *I.R.C.* v. *Baddeley* [1955] A.C. 572; *Williams' Trustees* v. *I.R.C.*, *infra*; indeed, it may be that, whilst purposes within Lord Macnaghten's first three categories are charitable in whatever part of the world they are carried on, purposes within the fourth category will be charitable only if there is some benefit to the U.K. community: Charity Commissioners' Report 1963, para. 72, but see D. M. E. Evans, (1965) 29 Conv.(N.S.) 123.

32 See Cross (1956) 72 L.Q.R. 187.

33 (1955) Cmd. 9474.

34 Scottish law treats the questions separately: *Wink's Executors* v. *Tallent*, 1947 S.C. 470, (1953) 69 L.Q.R. 517; *I.R.C.* v. *Glasgow Police Athletic Association* [1953] A.C. 380.

35 s. 4; appeal to the courts is possible under s. 5 (3) though the cost of appeal is a deterrent: between 1960 and 1971 only one appeal resulted from 1,380 refusals of charitable status (*New Law Journal Annual Charities Review* 1974, p. 34).

is the Charity Commissioners who alone determine the issue of charity or not. They produce Annual Reports showing what their practice is in interpreting the case law. As to be expected they feel it their duty to err on the side of a conservative restrictive interpretation. This has brought them much criticism especially from recently established philanthropic bodies which to a greater or lesser extent pursue political ends. However, some of the criticism would be better directed at the anomalous state of the law for as the Commissioners write in their defence, " The law is, of course, what it is and we cannot change it." [36]

Trusts for political purposes have always been held non-charitable trusts on the basis that the courts have no means of judging whether a proposed change in the law would or would not be for the public benefit [37] and the law could not stultify itself by holding that it was for the public benefit that the law itself should be changed.[38] It may be that political purposes comprise not only attempts to change the law by legislation but also attempts to influence government foreign policy. Thus the following bodies are not registered as charities: the National Anti-Vivisection Society, National Council for Civil Liberties, Campaign against Racial Discrimination, Martin Luther King Fund, Anti-Apartheid Movement, Human Rights Society, South African Defence and Aid Fund, United Nations Association, Amnesty, and the Disablement Income Group. However, if a body, particularly a long established one, which exists for much wider charitable purposes,[39] incidentally puts pressure on the public and politicians this does not affect the charitable status of the body *e.g.*, the RSPCA fighting vivisection, the British Legion fighting for better pensions for ex-servicemen, Guide Dogs for the Blind resisting purchase tax and VAT on dog food, the Society for the Relief and Discharge of Persons imprisoned for Small Debts lobbying for reform of the law allowing such imprisonment, the National Association for Mental Health in their MIND campaign organising and presenting a petition to Parliament. Certain registered charities such as the Child Poverty Action Group and Shelter have been walking the tightrope so precariously as to lead the Charity Commissioners to publish some guidance in their 1969 Annual Report, *infra*.

Since the essence of any living law and of any healthy democracy is change, it is difficult to see why trusts for political purposes should not be capable of being valid charitable trusts, though whether trusts for purely party political purposes should attract fiscal advantages is rather doubtful and raises wider issues. Relaxation or abrogation of the vitiating political factor could usefully be part and parcel of reforms separating the fiscal advantages of charities from their other advantages.

---

[36] 1971 Report, para. 10.

[37] *Bowman* v. *Secular Society* [1917] A.C. 406, 442 *per* Lord Parker.

[38] *National Anti-Vivisection Society* v. *I.R.C.*, *infra*. See also *Bonar Law Memorial Trust* v. *I.R.C.* (1933) 49 T.L.R. 220 (Conservative); *Re Ogden* [1933] Ch. 678 (Liberal); *Re Hopkinson* [1949] W.N. 29 (Socialist); *Re Strakosch* [1949] Ch. 529 (appeasing racial feeling); *Re Bushnell, The Times,* December 9, 1974.

[39] These purposes do not in practice have to be much wider in the case of respectable long established charities like the Anti-Slavery Society, the Lords Day Observance Society and the Howard League for Penal Reform. By way of contrast the Humanist Trust, the National Secular Society and the Sexual Law Reform Society are not charities. Surprisingly, the Upper Teesdale Defence Fund was registered as a charity though its *raison d'être* seemed to be to oppose a Private Bill in Parliament: but see pp. 207–208, *infra*.

For the present, bodies that are sufficiently hard-pressed to need relief on rates and taxes are not prepared to risk the costs of fighting the decisions of the Charity Commissioners in the Law Courts, especially when it is possible to hive off part of their funds for such activities as are certainly charitable, *e.g.*, Amnesty with its Prisoners of Conscience Fund for relieving the poverty of such prisoners and their families, the National Council for Civil Liberties with its Cobden Trust for educational activities, the Martin Luther King Fund with its Martin Luther King Foundation for educational activities, and UNA and the Anti-Apartheid Movement also have their own separate education trusts.

SCOTTISH BURIAL REFORM AND CREMATION SOCIETY LTD. v. GLASGOW CORPORATION

House of Lords [1968] A.C. 138; [1967] 3 W.L.R. 1132; [1968] 3 All E.R. 215.

The appellants were a non-profit making limited company with a main object of promoting inexpensive and sanitary methods of disposal of the dead, in particular promoting cremation. For rating purposes they claimed a declaration that they were a charity, it being common ground that English law determined the issue.

On appeal from the Court of Session the House of Lords held that the appellants were a charity within Lord Macnaghten's fourth category of charitable purposes and indicated the approach adopted by the courts as follows:

LORD REID: "... The appellants must also show, however, that the public benefit is of a kind within the spirit and intendment of the statute of Elizabeth. The preamble specifies a number of objects which were then recognised as charitable. But in more recent times a wide variety of other objects have come to be recognised as also being charitable. The courts appear to have proceeded first by seeking some analogy between an object mentioned in the preamble and the object with regard to which they had to reach a decision. Then they appear to have gone farther, and to have been satisfied if they could find an analogy between an object already held to be charitable and the new object claimed to be charitable. This gradual extension has proceeded so far that there are few modern reported cases where a bequest or donation was made or an institution was being carried on for a clearly specified object which was for the benefit of the public at large and not of individuals, and yet the object was held not to be within the spirit and intendment of the statute of Elizabeth. Counsel in the present case were invited to search for any case having even the remotest resemblance to this case in which an object was held to be for the public benefit but not yet to be within that spirit and intendment; but no such case could be found.

" There is, however, another line of cases where the bequest did not clearly specify the precise object to which it was to be applied, but left a discretion to trustees or others to choose objects within a certain field.   There the courts have been much more strict, so that if it is possible that those entrusted with the discretion could, without infringing the testator's directions, apply the bequest in any way which would not be charitable (for example, because it did not benefit a sufficiently large section of the public) then the claim that the bequest is charitable fails.   That line of cases, however, can have no application to the present case, and it is easy to fall into error if one tries to apply to a case like the present judicial observations made in a case where there was a discretion which could go beyond objects strictly charitable.   In the present case the appellants make a charge for the services which they provide.   It has never been held, however, that objects, otherwise charitable, cease to be charitable if beneficiaries are required to make payments for what they receive.   It may even be that public demand for the kind of service which the charity provides becomes so large that there is room for a commercial undertaking to come in and supply similar services on a commercial basis; but no authority and no reason has been put forward for holding that when that stage is reached the objects and activities of the non-profit earning charitable organisation cease to be charitable.

" If, then, all that is necessary to bring the objects and activities of the appellants within the spirit and intendment of the preamble to the statute of Elizabeth is to find analogous decided cases, I think that there is amply sufficient analogy with the series of cases dealing with burial.   I would therefore allow this appeal."

Lord Wilberforce: " ... Were, then, the appellants established for charitable purposes only?   I interpret their objects clause as meaning that the appellants were formed for a general and a particular purpose: the general purpose was to promote methods of disposal of the dead which should be inexpensive and sanitary; the particular purpose (to which the appellants have in fact confined themselves) to promote the method known as cremation.   It is this combination of purposes which has to be examined in order to see whether it satisfies the legal test of charitable purposes.

" On this subject, the law of England, though no doubt not very satisfactory and in need of rationalisation, is tolerably clear.   The purposes in question, to be charitable, must be shown to be for the benefit of the public, or the community, in a sense or manner within the intendment of the preamble to the statute, 43 Eliz. 1 c. 4.   The latter requirement does not mean quite what it says: for it is now accepted that what must be regarded is not the wording of the preamble itself, but the effect of decisions given by the courts as to its scope, decisions which have endeavoured to keep the law as to charities moving according as new social needs arise or old ones become obsolete or satisfied.

Lord Macnaghten's grouping of the heads of recognised charity in *Income Tax Special Purposes Comrs.* v. *Pemsel*[40] is one that has proved to be of value and there are many problems which it solves. But three things may be said about it, which its author would surely not have denied: first that, since it is a classification of convenience, there may well be purposes which do not fit neatly into one or other of the headings: secondly, that the words used must not be given the force of a statute to be construed, and thirdly, that the law of charity is a moving subject which may well have evolved even since 1891.

"With this in mind, approach may be made to the question whether the provision of facilities for the disposal of human remains, whether, generally, in an inexpensive and sanitary manner, or, particularly, by cremation, can be considered as within the spirit of the statute. Decided cases help us, at any rate to the point of showing that trusts for the repair or maintenance of burial grounds connected with a church are charitable. This was, if not decided, certainly assumed in *Vaughan* v. *Thomas*,[41] as it had been earlier assumed in *Att.-Gen.* v. *Blizard*.[42]

"More explicitly, in *Re Manser, Att.-Gen.* v. *Lucas*,[43] a trust for keeping in good order burial grounds for members of the Society of Friends was considered charitable. The opinion of Warrington J. was [44] that such trusts could be brought within the heading " advancement of religion "—" I think one naturally connects the burial of the dead with religion " he said.[45] Then in *Re Eighmie, Colbourne* v. *Wilks*,[46] a trust for the maintenance of a cemetery owned and managed by a local authority was held charitable. The cemetery was an extension of a closed churchyard, so that the decision can be regarded as a logical step rather than a new departure. Now what we have to consider is whether to take the further step of holding charitable the purpose of providing burial, or facilities for the disposal of mortal remains, without any connection with a church, by an independent body. I have no doubt that we should. I would regard the earlier decisions as falling on the borderline between trusts for the advancement of religion and trusts otherwise beneficial to the community. One may say either that burial purposes fall within both, or that the categories themselves shade one into the other. So I find no departure in principle in saying that purposes such as the present—which, though the appellants in fact provide the means for religious observance, should be regarded as independent of any religious basis—are to be treated as equally within the charitable class." *Appeal allowed.*

---

[40] [1891] A.C. 531, 583.
[41] (1886) 33 Ch.D. 187.
[42] (1855) 21 Beav. 233.
[43] [1905] 1 Ch. 68.
[44] [1905] 1 Ch. 68, 73.
[45] [1905] 1 Ch. 68, 74.
[46] [1935] Ch. 524.

10. It is a well-established principle of charity law that a trust for the attainment of a political object is not a valid charitable trust and that any purpose with the object of influencing the legislature is a political purpose. Thus no organisation can be a charity and at the same time include among its purposes the object of bringing influence to bear directly or indirectly on Parliament to change the general law of the land. If the governing instrument of an organisation were to give it power, other than in a way merely ancillary to some charitable purpose, to play a part in bringing political pressure to bear, that by itself would throw serious doubt on the organisation's claim to be a charity. Thus it is very unlikely that it will lie within any charity's purposes and powers to sponsor action groups or bring pressure to bear on the government to adopt or alter a particular line of action. In the past it was recognised that such activity lay well ouside the true field of charity although, as will be mentioned below, there are other more traditional approaches to Parliament and to the government that have long been accepted as perfectly proper for a charity. Today, however, it seems that the limitations on action of this kind are not always recognised by those responsible for running charities.

11. Those trustees who feel that their charity should become involved in the political field frequently seek to justify such action as coming within the field of " education." In our report for 1966 we mentioned the misuse of this word in the governing instruments of some organisations applying for registration as charities. Increasingly we are confronted by attempts to represent as educational a variety of activities which are primarily of a propagandist nature and which accordingly cannot be accepted as coming within the meaning of the " advancement of education " as it is used in charity law. There is a similar tendency for those registered charities which have as a subsidiary object the education of the public in the particular aspect of charity with which the organisation is concerned (for instance the need for the relief of poverty in under-developed countries) to overstep the boundary of what might properly be described as education and pass outside their declared purposes into the field of propaganda. There is obvious difficulty in determining exactly where this boundary lies but if a charity with general objects, such as the relief of poverty or distress, issues literature urging the government to take a particular course or organises sympathisers to apply pressure for that purpose to their elected representatives, we think it is clear that the boundary has been overstepped.

12. We would emphasise that it is not for us to judge whether the object of a propagandist or political activity is morally or socially right or wrong although we can appreciate the reasons why some charities feel a moral obligation to attempt to influence policies. We are concerned simply with the law of charity and with seeking to ensure that funds which are impressed with charitable trusts are used for the purposes of those trusts and not for other purposes which could not be recognised as charitable. However small the proportion of the income of a charity which may be used in this way, we believe that the charity will be led into difficulties if it appears to be giving its support to any objects that are not strictly within its charitable purposes.

13. We have, where it has seemed to us to be necessary, brought these considerations to the notice of individual charities. We are aware, however, that there may be other charities, which have perhaps not yet discussed their problems with us, and which are hesitating about promoting their objects by activities which might perhaps be considered to be political activities. We believe that it might help charities to realise what they have power to do if we point the contrast by giving some examples of such activities which we believe can justifiably be regarded as being proper for a charity. These examples fall into three classes, the first and third of which present little difficulty. The first class comprises those examples in which it is the government itself which is investigating or has propounded proposals for changes in the law. Government officials frequently seek advice and infor- mation from those who are responsible for running charities and the charities quite properly respond. Similarly by publishing a green or white paper the government may impliedly invite comments from the public generally and a charity may justifiably avail itself of such an invitation to make any comments which may appear to be useful. Again when a parliamentary bill has been published a charity will be justified in supplying relevant information to a Member of either House and such arguments to be used in debate as it believes will assist the furtherance of its purposes. So also there can be other cases, not involving legislation, in which a charity is entitled to persuade a Member to support its cause in Parliament, for instance, where the question arises whether a government grant is to be made or continued to a particular charity.

14. The second class of examples, which includes those in which the charity itself or with others wishes to put forward proposals for changes in the law, can be more difficult to justify. It is probably unobjectionable for a charity to present to a government department a reasoned memoran- dum advocating changes in the law provided that in doing so the charity is acting in furtherance of its purposes. On the other hand, a charity can only spend its funds on the promotion of public general legislation if in doing so it is exercising a power that is merely ancillary to its charitable purposes. But here again difficulty arises in defining the boundary between what is merely ancillary and what amounts to adopting a new purpose in itself. A charity would be well advised to seek advice either from its legal advisers or from us before undertaking any such activities.

15. Finally, the third class of examples comprises cases where, although Parliament is involved, it appears to us that the reason for approaching it is not to be regarded as political. This, for instance, includes legislation that is only intended to confer enabling powers, such as the Sharing of Church Buildings Act which is mentioned in paragraphs 36 to 39 of this report. By supporting the passage of this Act the various charities involved were seeking to obtain wider powers to carry out their purposes. Similarly, virtually all private bills are free from taint of political activities. A private bill is in the nature of litigation as much as of legislation and the action of supporting or opposing such a bill resembles a court action and nearly always has no political tinge. We feel, therefore, that the principle laid down by the courts that a political object is not a charitable purpose should not be extended in such a way as to deny to a charity that right to promote

or oppose private legislation which is enjoyed by public and private bodies in general. Thus in every session some charities, with our consent under section 19 (7) of the Charities Act, promote private bills which may set out to alter the constitution of the charity or to give it powers which only Parliament can confer. An example of such a bill in the present session is the National Trust Bill. The case mentioned in paragraphs 23 and 24 of this report provides an example of a charity which in order to realise its charitable purposes played a part in opposing a private bill.

16. There are two general points which we should like to mention in concluding this section of our report. First, if the trustees of a charity do stray into the field of political activity their action will be in breach of trust and those responsible for the action could be called on at law to recoup to the charity any of its funds which have been spent outside its purposes. Moreover a charity is not entitled to tax relief on income which is not applied to charitable purposes. But the fact that political action had been taken in the name of the charity would not affect its status as a charity nor constitute a reason for removing it from the register of charities. If, however, doubt had been cast on the correctness of the original registration, removal might be considered by us or by the High Court on an appeal by any other body interested. Secondly we think it should also be borne in mind that if charities step outside the sphere of activities to which the law confines them they may not only prejudice the support they receive from some people, who could resent the new activities, but they may also eventually endanger the privileged position which charities as a whole have been accorded by the state. The attempts now being made in the United States to curtail the privileges enjoyed by charitable foundations there result in part from allegations that some of those foundations have been using their funds for purposes which are essentially political.

II. Trusts for the Relief of Poverty

This group of charitable trusts has its origins in that part of the preamble to the Statute of Charitable Uses 1601 which speaks of " the relief of aged, impotent and poor people." It has been held that these words must be read disjunctively so that a trust is charitable if the beneficiaries fall within any one of the enumerated categories.[47] In *Re Cottam's Will Trusts*,[48] however, the provision of flats at economic rents for the aged was held charitable mainly because it was possible to discover an intention to benefit aged persons of small means.

" Poverty " is a relative term and the expression " poor people " is not necessarily confined to the destitute poor[49]: it includes persons who have to " go short " in the ordinary acceptation of that term, due regard being had to their station in life and so forth[50]; but the " working classes " do not *ipso facto* constitute a section of the poor.[51]

---

[47] Age: *Re Robinson* [1951] Ch. 198; *Re Glyn's W.T.* [1950] 2 All E.R. 1150n.; *Re Bradbury* [1950] 2 All E.R. 1150n.; impotence: *Re Elliott* (1910) 102 L.T. 528; *Re Hillier* [1944] 1 All E.R. 480; *Re Lewis* [1955] Ch. 104. *Quaere*: if so, is a trust for aged millionaires charitable? See (1951) 67 L.Q.R. 164 (R. E. M.); (1955) 71 L.Q.R. 16 (R. E. M.); (1958) 21 M.L.R. 140–141 (Atiyah).

[48] [1955] 1 W.L.R. 1299. See also *Re Payling's W.T.* [1969] 1 W.L.R. 1595.

[49] See 78 S.J. 377; 82 S.J. 882.

[50] *Re Coulthurst* [1951] Ch. 661, 666 (Evershed M.R.); *I.R.C.* v. *Baddeley* [1955] A.C. 572, 585 (Lord Simonds).   [51] *Re Sanders' W.T.* [1954] Ch. 265.

If a trust may be brought under any of the other three heads, then it is no objection that it may incidentally benefit the rich as well as the poor; but if it cannot be brought under any head save that of the relief of poverty, then the benefits contemplated by the trust must be directed exclusively to that end: *Re Gwyon.*

Trusts for the relief of poverty form an exception to the principle that every charitable trust must be for the public benefit. The exception covers both the poor relations of a named person [52] and the poor employees of a particular employer and their families: *Dingle* v. *Turner, infra.* However, there must be a primary intent to relieve poverty, though amongst a particular class of person. If the primary intent is to benefit particular persons (*e.g.*, A, B, C and their children if they are ever in needy circumstances) the trust is a private one and not charitable.[53]

DINGLE v. TURNER

House of Lords [1972] A.C. 601; [1972] 2 W.L.R. 523; [1972] 1 All E.R. 878.

The facts sufficiently appear in Lord Cross' speech, *infra.*

VISCOUNT DILHORNE: " My Lords, I have had the advantage of reading the opinions of my noble and learned friends, Lord Cross of Chelsea and Lord MacDermott. I agree with Lord Cross that this appeal should be dismissed and with the reasons he gives for that conclusion.

" With Lord MacDermott, I too do not wish to extend my concurrence to what my noble and learned friend Lord Cross has said with regard to the fiscal privileges of a legal charity. Those privileges may be altered from time to time by Parliament and I doubt whether their existence should be a determining factor in deciding whether a gift or trust is charitable.

" I agree that the costs of all the parties should be paid out of the fund."

LORD MACDERMOTT: " My Lords, the conclusion I have reached on the facts of this case is that the gift in question constitutes a public trust for the relief of poverty which is charitable in law. I would therefore dismiss the appeal.

" I do not find it necessary to state my reasons for this conclusion in detail. In the first place, the views which I have expressed at some length in relation to an educational trust in *Oppenheim* v. *Tobacco Securities Trust Co. Ltd.*[54] seem to me to apply to this appeal and to mean that it fails. It would, of course, be otherwise if the case just cited purported to rule the point now in issue. But that is not so, for it clearly left that point undecided and open for further consideration.

---

[52] *Isaac* v. *De Friez* (1754) Amb. 595; *White* v. *White* (1802) 7 Ves. 423; *Att.-Gen.* v. *Price* (1810) 17 Ves. 371; *Re Scarisbrick* [1951] Ch. 662.
[53] *Re Scarisbrick* [1951] Ch. 662; *Re Cohen* [1973] 1 W.L.R. 415.
[54] [1951] A.C. 297. See pp. 236–241, *infra.*

And, secondly, I have had the advantage of reading the opinion prepared by my noble and learned friend, Lord Cross of Chelsea, and find myself in agreement with his conclusion for the reasons he has given. In particular, I welcome his commentary on the difficulties of the phrase ' a section of the public.' But I would prefer not to extend my concurrence to what my noble and learned friend goes on to say respecting the fiscal privileges of a legal charity. This subject may be material on the question whether what is alleged to be a charity is sufficiently altruistic in nature to qualify as such, but beyond that, and without wishing to express any final view on the matter, I doubt if these consequential privileges have much relevance to the primary question whether a given trust or purpose should be held charitable in law.

"I agree with the order as to costs proposed by my noble and learned friend."

LORD HODSON: " My Lords, I agree with my noble and learned friend, Lord Cross of Chelsea, that this appeal should be dismissed and with his reasons for that conclusion. With this reservation: that I share the doubts expressed by my noble and learned friends, Lord MacDermott and Viscount Dilhorne, as to the relevance of fiscal considerations in deciding whether a gift or trust is charitable."

LORD SIMON OF GLAISDALE: " My Lords, I have had the advantage of reading the opinion of my noble and learned friend, Lord Cross of Chelsea, with which I agree. I too would dismiss this appeal, and make the same recommendation as to costs."

LORD CROSS OF CHELSEA: " My Lords, by his will dated January 10, 1950, Frank Hanscomb Dingle (whom I will call ' the testator ') after appointing Lloyds Bank Ltd., his wife Annie Dingle and his solicitor Henry Elliot Turner to be his executors and trustees made the following—among other—dispositions. By clause 5 he gave to his trustees his ordinary and preference shares in E. Dingle & Co. Ltd. on trust to pay the income arising therefrom to his wife for her life and after her death to hold the same in trust for such person or persons as she should by will or codicil appoint but without any trust in default of appointment. By clause 8 (*a*) he directed his trustees to pay the income of his residuary estate after payment thereout of his debts, funeral and testamentary expenses to his wife for her life. By clause 8 (*b*), (*c*), (*d*), (*e*) and (*f*) he directed his trustees to raise various sums out of his residuary estate after the death of his wife. Clause 8 (*e*) was in the following terms:

'(*e*) To invest the sum of Ten thousand pounds in any of the investments for the time being authorised by law for the investment of trust funds in the names of three persons (hereinafter referred to as "the Pension Fund Trustees") to be nominated for the purpose by the persons who at the time at which my Executors assent to this bequest are directors of E. Dingle & Company Limited and the Pension Fund Trustees shall hold the said sum and the investments for the time being representing the same (hereinafter referred to as "the Pensions Fund") UPON TRUST to apply the income thereof in paying pensions to poor employees of E. Dingle & Company Limited or of any other company to which upon any reconstruction or amalgamation the goodwill and the assets of E. Dingle & Company Limited may be transferred who are of the age of Sixty years at least or who being of the age of Forty five years at least are incapacitated from earning their living by reason of some physical or mental infirmity PROVIDED ALWAYS that if at any time the Pension Fund Trustees shall for any reason be unable to apply the income of the Pensions Fund in paying such pensions to such employees as aforesaid the Pension Fund Trustees shall hold the Pensions Fund and the income thereof UPON TRUST for the aged poor in the Parish of St. Andrew, Plymouth.'

Finally by clause 8 (*g*) the testator directed his trustees to hold the ultimate residue of his estate on the trusts set out in clause 8 (*e*).

"The testator died on January 10, 1950. His widow died on October 8, 1966, having previously released her testamentary power of appointment over her husband's shares in E. Dingle & Co. Ltd., which accordingly fell into the residuary estate. When these proceedings started in July 1970, the value of the fund held on the trusts declared by clause 8 (*e*) was about £320,000 producing a gross income of about £17,800 per annum.

"E. Dingle and Co. Ltd. was incorporated as a private company on January 20, 1935. Its capital was owned by the testator and one John Russell Baker and it carried on the business of a departmental store. At the time of the testator's death the company employed over 600 persons and there was a substantial number of ex-employees. On October 23, 1950, the company became a public company. Since the testator's death its business has expanded and when these proceedings started it had 705 full-time and 189 part-time employees and was paying pensions to 89 ex-employees.

"The trustees took out an originating summons in the Chancery Division on July 30, 1970, asking the court to determine whether the trusts declared by clause 8 (*e*) were valid and if so to determine various subsidiary questions of construction—as, for example, whether part-time employees or employees of subsidiary companies were eligible to receive benefits under the trust. To this summons they made defendants (1) representatives of the various classes of employees or ex-employees, (2) those who would be interested on an intestacy if the trusts failed, and (3) Her Majesty's Attorney-General. It has been common ground throughout that the trust at the end of clause 8 (*e*) for the aged poor in the Parish of St. Andrew Plymouth is dependent on the preceding trust for poor employees of the company so that although it will catch any surplus income which the trustees do not apply for the benefit of poor employees it can have no application if the preceding trust is itself void.

" By his judgment given on April 2, 1971, Megarry J. held, *inter alia,* following the decision of the Court of Appeal in *Gibson* v. *South American Stores (Gath & Chaves) Ltd.,*[55] that the trust declared by clause 8 (*e*) was a valid charitable trust but, on the application of the appellant, Betty Mary Dingle, one of the persons interested under an intestacy, he granted a certificate under section 12 of the Administration of Justice Act 1969 enabling her to apply to this House directly for leave to appeal against that part of his judgment, and on May 17, 1971, the House gave her leave to appeal.

" Your Lordships, therefore, are now called on to give to the old ' poor relations ' cases and the more modern ' poor employees ' cases that careful consideration which, in his speech in the *Oppenheim* case[56] Lord Morton of Henryton said that they might one day require.

" The contentions of the appellant and the respondents may be stated broadly as follows. The appellant says that in the *Oppenheim* case this House decided that in principle a trust ought not to be regarded as charitable if the benefits under it are confined either to the descendants of a named individual or individuals or the employees of a given individual or company and that although the ' poor relations ' cases may have to be left standing as an anomalous exception to the general rule because their validity has been recognised for so long, the exception ought not to be extended to ' poor employees ' trusts which had not been recognised for long before their status as charitable trusts began to be called in question. The respondents, on the other hand, say, first, that the rule laid down in the *Oppenheim* case with regard to educational trusts ought not to be regarded as a rule applicable in principle to all kinds of charitable trust and, secondly, that in any case it is impossible to draw any logical distinction between ' poor relations ' trusts and ' poor employees ' trusts, and, that as the former cannot be held invalid today after having been recognised as valid for so long, the latter must be regarded as valid also.

" By a curious coincidence within a few months of the decision of this House in the *Oppenheim* case the cases on gifts to ' poor relations ' had to be considered by the Court of Appeal in *Re Scarisbrick, Cockshott* v. *Public Trustee.*[57] Most of the cases on this subject were decided in the eighteenth or early nineteenth centuries and are very

---

[55] [1950] Ch. 177.
[56] [1951] A.C. 297, 313.
[57] [1951] Ch. 622.

inadequately reported but two things at least were clear. First, that it never occurred to the judges who decided them that in the field of 'poverty' a trust could not be a charitable trust if the class of beneficiaries was defined by reference to descent from a common ancestor. Secondly, that the courts did not treat a gift or trust as necessarily charitable because the objects of it had to be poor in order to qualify, for in some of the cases the trust was treated as a private trust and not a charity. The problem in *Re Scarisbrick* was to determine on what basis the distinction was drawn. Roxburgh J.—founding himself on some words attributed to Sir William Grant M.R. in *Att.-Gen.* v. *Price* [58]—had held that the distinction lay in whether the gift took the form of a trust under which capital was retained and the income only applied for the benefit of the objects, in which case the gift was charitable, or whether the gift was one under which the capital was immediately distributable among the objects, in which case the gift was not a charity. The Court of Appeal rejected this ground of distinction. They held that in this field the distinction between a public or charitable trust and a private trust depended on whether as a matter of construction the gift was for the relief of poverty amongst a particular description of poor people or was merely a gift to particular poor persons, the relief of poverty among them being the motive of the gift. The fact that the gift took the form of a perpetual trust would no doubt indicate that the intention of the donor could not have been to confer private benefits on particular people whose possible necessities he had in mind; but the fact that the capital of the gift was to be distributed at once did not necessarily show that the gift was a private trust. The appellant in the instant case, while of course submitting that the judges who decided the old cases were wrong in not appreciating that no gift for the relief of poverty among persons tracing descent from a common ancestor could ever have a sufficiently 'public' quality to constitute a charity, did not dispute the correctness of the analysis of those cases made by the Court of Appeal in *Re Scarisbrick*.

[His Lordship then reviewed the earlier cases leading up to *Gibson* v. *S. American Stores*.]

"The facts in *Gibson* v. *South American Stores* (*Gath & Chaves*) *Ltd.* [59]—the case followed by Megarry J. in this case—were that a company had vested in trustees a fund derived solely from its profits to be applied at the discretion of the directors in granting gratuities, pensions or allowances to persons—

'who . . . are or shall be necessitous and deserving and who for the time being are or have been in the company's employ . . . and the wives widows husbands widowers children parents and other

---

[58] [1803–13] All E.R. Rep. 467; (1810) 17 Ves. 371.
[59] [1950] Ch. 177.

dependants of any person who for the time being is or would if living have been himself or herself a member of the class of beneficiaries.'

The Court of Appeal held that this trust was a valid charitable trust but it did so without expressing a view of its own on the question of principle involved, because the case of *Re Laidlaw* [60] which was unearthed in the course of the hearing showed that the Court of Appeal had already accepted the decision in *Re Gosling* [61] as correct.

    " In *Oppenheim* v. *Tobacco Securities Trust Co. Ltd.* [62] this House had to consider the principle laid down by the Court of Appeal in *Re Compton.* [63] There the trustees of a fund worth over £125,000 were directed to apply its income and also if they thought fit all or any part of the capital—

> ' in providing for or assisting in providing for the education of children of employees or former employees of British-American Tobacco Co., Ltd. . . . or any of its subsidiary or allied companies. . . .'

There were over 110,000 such employees. The majority of your Lordships—namely Lord Simonds (in whose judgment Lord Oaksey concurred), Lord Normand and Lord Morton of Henryton—in holding that the trust was not a valid charitable trust gave unqualified approval to the *Compton* principle. They held, that is to say, that although the ' poverty ' cases might afford an anomalous exception to the rule, it was otherwise a general rule applicable to all charitable trusts that no class of beneficiaries can constitute a ' section of the public ' for the purpose of the law of charity if the distinguishing quality which links them together is relationship to a particular individual either through common descent or common employment. My noble and learned friend, Lord MacDermott, on the other hand, in his dissenting speech, while not challenging the correctness of the decisions in *Re Compton* or in the *Hobourn Aero* case [64] said that he could not regard the principle stated by Lord Greene M.R. as a criterion of general applicability and conclusiveness. He said [65]:

> ' . . . I see much difficulty in dividing the qualities or attributes which may serve to bind human beings into classes into two mutually exclusive groups, the one involving individual status and purely personal, the other disregarding such status and quite impersonal. As a task this seems to me no less baffling and elusive than the problem to which it is directed, namely, the

---

[60] (January 11, 1935) unreported, the decision (and not the reasoning) only being available.
[61] (1900) 48 W.R. 300.
[62] [1951] A.C. 297.
[63] [1945] Ch. 123.
[64] [1946] Ch. 194.
[65] [1951] A.C. 297, 317.

determination of what is and what is not a section of the public
for the purposes of this branch of the law.'

He thought that the question whether any given trust was a public or
a private trust was a question of degree to be decided in the light of
the facts of the particular case and that viewed in that light the trust
in the *Oppenheim* case was a valid charitable trust.

" In *Re Cox (decd.), Baker* v. *National Trust Co. Ltd., Public
Trustee for Ontario (Province)* v. *National Trust Co. Ltd.*[66] a Canadian
testator directed his trustees to hold the balance of his residuary
estate on trust to pay its income in perpetuity for charitable purposes
only, the persons to benefit directly in pursuance of such charitable
purposes being such as were or had been employees of a certain company and/or the dependants of such employees. This disposition
raised, of course, a question of construction—namely whether ' charitable purposes ' was simply a compendious mode of referring to any
purposes a trust to promote which would be charitable providing that
the beneficiaries were the public or a section of the public or whether
the words meant such purposes only as having regard to the class of
beneficiaries named could be the subject of a valid charitable trust. It
was only on the latter construction that the question whether *Gibson*
v. *South American Stores*[67] was rightly decided would arise and in
fact both the courts below and the Privy Council held that the former
construction was the right one. It is, however, to be observed that
the Court of Appeal in Ontario unanimously held that even if the
second construction was right the trust would still fail for want of any
possible purposes since the ' poor relations ' cases formed a class apart
and the ' poor employees ' cases could not stand with the decision in
the *Oppenheim* case. The Privy Council expressly refrained from
expressing any opinion on this point. . . .

" After this long—but I hope not unduly long—recital of the
decided cases I turn to consider the arguments advanced by the
appellant in support of the appeal. For this purpose I will assume
that the appellant is right in saying that the *Compton*[68] rule ought in
principle to apply to all charitable trusts and that the ' poor relations '
cases, the ' poor members ' cases and the ' poor employees ' cases are
all anomalous—in the sense that if such cases had come before the
courts for the first time after the decision in *Re Compton* the trusts
in question would have been held valid as ' private ' trusts.

" Even on that assumption—as it seems to me—the appeal must
fail. The status of some of the ' poor relations ' trusts as valid charitable trusts was recognised more than 200 years ago and a few of those
then recognised are still being administered as charities today. In *Re
Compton*[69] Lord Greene M.R. said that it was ' quite impossible ' for

---

[66] [1955] A.C. 627.
[67] [1950] Ch. 177.
[68] [1945] Ch. 123.

[69] [1945] Ch. 123, 139.

the Court of Appeal to overrule such old decisions and in the *Oppen-heim case* [70] Lord Simonds in speaking of them remarked on the unwisdom of—

' [casting] doubt on decisions of respectable antiquity in order to introduce a greater harmony into the law of charity as a whole.'

Indeed counsel for the appellant ventured to suggest that we should overrule the ' poor relations ' cases. His submission was that which was accepted by the Court of Appeal in Ontario in *Re Cox (decd.)* [71] —namely that while the ' poor relations ' cases might have to be left as long standing anomalies there was no good reason for sparing the ' poor employees ' cases which only date from *Re Gosling* [72] decided in 1900 and which have been under suspicion ever since the decision in *Re Compton* in 1945. But the ' poor members ' and the ' poor em-ployees ' decisions were a natural development of the ' poor relations ' decisions and to draw a distinction between different sorts of ' poverty ' trusts would be quite illogical and could certainly not be said to be introducing ' greater harmony ' into the law of charity. Moreover, although not as old as the ' poor relations ' trusts, ' poor employees ' trusts have been recognised as charities for many years; there are now a large number of such trusts in existence; and assuming, as one must, that they are properly administered in the sense that benefits under them are only given to people who can fairly be said to be, according to current standards, ' poor persons ' to treat such trusts as charities is not open to any practical objection. So as it seems to me it must be accepted that wherever else it may hold sway the *Compton* rule has no application in the field of trusts for the relief of poverty and that there the dividing line between a charitable trust and a private trust lies where the Court of Appeal drew it in *Re Scarisbrick*. [73]

" The *Oppenheim* case was a case of an educational trust and although the majority evidently agreed with the view expressed by the Court of Appeal in the *Hobourn Aero* case, [74] that the *Compton* rule was of universal application outside the field of poverty, it would no doubt be open to this House without overruling *Oppenheim* to hold that the scope of the rule was more limited. If ever I should be called on to pronounce on this question—which does not arise in this appeal —I would as at present advised be inclined to draw a distinction between the practical merits of the *Compton* rule and the reasoning by which Lord Greene M.R. sought to justify it. That reasoning— based on the distinction between personal and impersonal relationships —has never seemed to me very satisfactory and I have always—if I may say so—felt the force of the criticism to which my noble and

---

70 [1951] A.C. 297, 309.
71 [1951] O.R. 205.
72 (1900) 48 W.R. 300.
73 [1951] Ch. 622.
74 [1946] Ch. 194.

learned friend Lord MacDermott subjected it in his dissenting speech
in the *Oppenheim* case.[75] For my part I would prefer to approach the
problem on far broader lines. The phrase ' a section of the public ' is
in truth a vague phrase which may mean different things to different
people. In the law of charity judges have sought to elucidate its meaning by contrasting it with another phrase ' a fluctuating body of private
individuals.' But I get little help from the supposed contrast for as I
see it one and the same aggregate of persons may well be describable
both as a section of the public and as a fluctuating body of private
individuals. The ratepayers in the Royal Borough of Kensington and
Chelsea, for example, certainly constitute a section of the public; but
would it be a misuse of language to describe them as a ' fluctuating
body of private individuals ' ? After all, every part of the public is
composed of individuals and being susceptible of increase or decrease
is fluctuating. So at the end of the day one is left where one started
with the bare contrast between ' public ' and ' private.' No doubt
some classes are more naturally describable as sections of the public
than as private classes while other classes are more naturally
describable as private classes than as sections of the public. The blind,
for example, can naturally be described as a section of the public; but
what they have in common—their blindness—does not join them
together in such a way that they could be called a private class. On
the other hand, the descendants of Mr. Gladstone might more reasonably be described as a ' private class ' than as a section of the public,
and in the field of common employment the same might well be said
of the employees in some fairly small firm. But if one turns to large
companies employing many thousands of men and women most of
whom are quite unknown to one another and to the directors the
answer is by no means so clear. One might say that in such a case the
distinction between a section of the public and a private class is not
applicable at all or even that the employees in such concerns as ICI or
GEC are just as much ' sections of the public ' as the residents in
some geographical area. In truth the question whether or not the
potential beneficiaries of a trust can fairly be said to constitute a
section of the public is a question of degree and cannot be by itself
decisive of the question whether the trust is a charity. Much must
depend on the purpose of the trust. It may well be that, on the one
hand, a trust to promote some purpose, prima facie charitable, will
constitute a charity even though the class of potential beneficiaries
might fairly be called a private class and that, on the other hand, a
trust to promote another purpose, also prima facie charitable, will not
constitute a charity even though the class of potential beneficiaries
might seem to some people fairly describable as a section of the public.

" In answering the question whether any given trust is a charitable
trust the courts—as I see it—cannot avoid having regard to the fiscal

---

[75] [1951] A.C. 297.

privileges accorded to charities. As counsel for the Attorney-General remarked in the course of the argument the law of charity is bedevilled by the fact that charitable trusts enjoy two quite different sorts of privilege. On the one hand, they enjoy immunity from the rules against perpetuity and uncertainty and although individual potential beneficiaries cannot sue to enforce them the public interest arising under them is protected by the Attorney-General. If this was all there would be no reason for the courts not to look favourably on the claim of any ' purpose ' trust to be considered as a charity if it seemed calculated to confer some real benefit on those intended to benefit by it whoever they might be and if it would fail if not held to be a charity. But that is not all. Charities automatically enjoy fiscal privileges which with the increased burden of taxation have become more and more important and in deciding that such and such a trust is a charitable trust the court is endowing it with a substantial annual subsidy at the expense of the taxpayer. Indeed, claims of trusts to rank as charities are just as often challenged by the Revenue as by those who would take the fund if the trust was invalid. It is, of course, unfortunate that the recognition of any trust as a valid charitable trust should automatically attract fiscal privileges, for the question whether a trust to further some purpose is so little likely to benefit the public that it ought to be declared invalid and the question whether it is likely to confer such great benefits on the public that it should enjoy fiscal immunity are really two quite different questions. The logical solution would be to separate them and to say—as the Radcliffe Commission proposed—that only some charities should enjoy fiscal privileges. But as things are, validity and fiscal immunity march hand in hand and the decisions in the *Compton*[76] and *Oppenheim*[77] cases were pretty obviously influenced by the consideration that if such trusts as were there in question were held valid they would enjoy an undeserved fiscal immunity. To establish a trust for the education of the children of employees in a company in which you are interested is no doubt a meritorious act; but however numerous the employees may be the purpose which you are seeking to achieve is not a public purpose. It is a company purpose and there is no reason why your fellow taxpayers should contribute to a scheme which by providing ' fringe benefits ' for your employees will benefit the company by making their conditions of employment more attractive. The temptation to enlist the assistance of the law of charity in private endeavours of this sort is considerable—witness the recent case of the Metal Box scholarships—*Inland Revenue Comrs.* v. *Educational Grants Association Ltd.*[78]—and the courts must do what they can to discourage such

---

[76] [1945] Ch. 123.
[77] [1951] A.C. 297.
[78] [1967] Ch. 993, *infra*, p. 241.

attempts. In the field of poverty the danger is not so great as in the field of education—for while people are keenly alive to the need to give their children a good education and to the expense of doing so, they are generally optimistic enough not to entertain serious fears of falling on evil days much before they fall on them. Consequently the existence of company ' benevolent funds,' the income of which is free of tax does not constitute a very attractive ' fringe benefit.' This is a practical justification—although not, of course, the historical explanation—for the special treatment accorded to poverty trusts in charity law. For the same sort of reason a trust to promote some religion among the employees of a company might perhaps safely be held to be charitable provided that it was clear that the benefits were to be purely spiritual. On the other hand, many ' purpose ' trusts falling under Lord Macnaghten's fourth head [79] if confined to a class of employees would clearly be open to the same sort of objection as educational trusts. As I see it, it is on these broad lines rather than for the reasons actually given by Lord Greene M.R. that the *Compton* rule can best be justified.

"My Lords, for the reasons given earlier in this speech I would dismiss this appeal; but as the view was expressed in the *Oppenheim* case that the question of the validity of trusts for poor relations and poor employees ought some day to be considered by this House and as the fund in dispute in this case is substantial, your Lordships may perhaps think it proper to direct that the costs of all parties to the appeal be paid out of it." *Appeal dismissed.*

III. TRUSTS FOR THE ADVANCEMENT OF EDUCATION

This group of charitable trusts has its origins in those parts of the preamble to the Statute of Charitable Uses 1601 which speak of " the maintenance of schools of learning, free schools and scholars in universities " and " the education and preferment of orphans."

Education is not confined to matters formally taught in schools and universities. It includes the promotion or encouragement of the arts and graces of life: see *Re Shaw's Will Trusts* [80] (" the teaching, promotion and encouragement in Ireland of self-control, elocution, oratory, deportment, the arts of personal contact, of social intercourse, and the other arts of public, private, professional and business life "); *Royal Choral Society* v. *I.R.C.* [81] (choral singing in London); *Re Levien* [82] (organ music); *Re Delius* [83] (the music of the composer Delius); and *Re Dupree's Deed Trusts* [84] (encouragement of chess-playing among young people in Portsmouth).

[79] See *Income Tax Special Purposes Comrs.* v. *Pemsel* [1891] A.C. 531, 583.
[80] [1952] Ch. 163.
[81] [1943] 2 All E.R. 101; contrast *Associated Artists Ltd.* v. *I.R.C.* [1956] 1 W.L.R. 752 (production of artistic dramatic works).
[82] [1955] 1 W.L.R. 964.
[83] [1957] Ch. 299; contrast *Re Pinion* [1965] Ch. 85 (bequest of worthless works of art to found a museum); *Sutherland's Trustees* v. *Verschoyle*, 1968 S.L.T. 43.
[84] [1945] Ch. 16.

The decision of Harman J. in *Re Shaw* [85] (where George Bernard Shaw had bequeathed funds for pursuing inquiries into a new 40 letter alphabet) appeared to render doubtful the validity of trusts for the advancement of research, at any rate where no element of teaching was involved; but the decision of Wilberforce J. in *Re Hopkins' Will Trusts, infra,*[86] removes most of the doubts.

The promotion of sport as such is not a charitable object: see *Re Nottage* [87] (yacht-racing); *Re Clifford* [88] (angling); *Re Patten* [89] (cricket); *Re King* [90] (general sport); *I.R.C.* v. *City of Glasgow Police Athletic Association* [91] (all forms of athletic sports and general pastimes); *I.R.C.* v. *Baddeley* [92] (moral, social and physical training and recreation). In certain circumstances trusts for similar objects may now be charitable by virtue of the Recreational Charities Act 1958, *infra.*[93] On the other hand, where the promotion of sport is ancillary to a charitable object, it will itself be charitable: *Re Mariette* [94] (sport in a school—educational), *Re Gray* [95] (sport in a regiment—general public benefit in promoting the efficiency of the Army).

The promotion of a particular type of political education [96] is not charitable; and some forms of education may not be for the public benefit: *Re Hummeltenberg* [97] (training of spiritualistic mediums).

A trust for the education of beneficiaries who are ascertained by reference to some personal tie (*e.g.,* of blood or contract), such as the relations of a particular individual, the members of a particular family, the employees of a particular firm, or the members of a particular association, lacks the element of public benefit and is not charitable: *Oppenheim* v. *Tobacco Securities Trust Co. Ltd., infra*; *I.R.C.* v. *Educational Grants Association Ltd., infra.*

Re HOPKINS' WILL TRUSTS

Chancery Division [1965] Ch. 669; [1964] 3 W.L.R. 840; 108 S.J. 601; [1964] 3 All E.R. 46.

By her will dated November 21, 1957, the testatrix, Miss Evelyn May Hopkins, who died on April 7, 1961, bequeathed a part of her residuary estate on trust for the Francis Bacon Society Inc., of 50A, Old Brompton Road, London, S.W.7, " to be earmarked and applied

[85] [1957] 1 W.L.R. 729.
[86] See (1965) 29 Conv.(N.S.) 368 (Newark and Samuels).
[87] [1895] 2 Ch. 649.
[88] (1911) 106 L.T. 14.
[89] [1929] 2 Ch. 276.
[90] [1931] W.N. 232.
[91] [1953] A.C. 380.
[92] [1955] A.C. 572.
[93] pp. 220–5; see (1959) 23 Conv.(N.S.) 365, 386–389 (Waters); on the pre-1958 position, see (1956) 9 C.L.P. 39 (Marshall).
[94] [1915] 2 Ch. 284.
[95] [1925] Ch. 362; but this has been doubted in *I.R.C.* v. *City of Glasgow Police Athletic Association* [1953] A.C. 380, 391, 401.
[96] *Bonar Law Memorial Trust* v. *I.R.C.* (1933) 49 T.L.R. 220; *Re Hopkinson* [1949] 1 All E.R. 346; *cf. Re Scowcroft* [1898] 2 Ch. 638 which nowadays should be regarded as of doubtful authority; and see *Re McDougall* [1957] 1 W.L.R. 81 (study of methods of government is a charitable object).
[97] [1923] 1 Ch. 237.

towards finding the Bacon-Shakespeare manuscripts. . . ." The society's main objects both at the date of her will and when she died were: "(1) to encourage the study of the works of Francis Bacon as philosopher, lawyer, statesman and poet; also his character, genius and life; his influence on his own and succeeding times, and the tendencies and results of his writings; (2) to encourage the general study of the evidence in favour of Francis Bacon's authorship of the plays commonly ascribed to Shakespeare, and to investigate his connection with other works of the Elizabethan period." A summons was taken out for the determination *inter alia* of the question whether the bequest was held on valid charitable trusts.

WILBERFORCE J.: ". . . . Before I come to the legal question whether [the gift is charitable] it is convenient to deal with an argument put forward on behalf of the next-of-kin that the bequest is made for a purpose so manifestly futile that it does not even qualify for consideration as a possible charitable gift. This argument is relevant and is similar in substance whichever of the two interpretations of the bequest is correct. Its validity depends upon the evidence which has been filed, which I will now examine. Let me say at once that no determination of the authorship of the 'Shakespeare' plays, or even of any subsidiary question relating to it, falls to be made in the present proceedings. The court is only concerned, at this point, with the practicability and later with the legality of carrying Miss Hopkins' wishes into effect, and it must decide this, one way or the other, upon the evidence of the experts which is before it.

" On this evidence, should the conclusion be reached that the search for the Bacon-Shakespeare manuscripts is so manifestly futile that the court should not allow this bequest to be spent upon it as upon an object devoid of the possibility of any result? I think not. The evidence shows that the discovery of any manuscript of the plays is unlikely; but so are many discoveries before they are made (one may think of the Codex Sinaiticus, or the tomb of Tutankhamen, or the Dead Sea Scrolls); I do not think that that degree of improbability has been reached which justifies the court in placing an initial interdict on the testatrix's benefaction.

" I come, then, to the only question of law: is the gift of a charitable character? The society has put its case in the alternative under the two headings of education and of general benefit to the community and has argued separately for each. This compartmentalisation is derived from the accepted classification into four groups of the miscellany found in the Statute of Elizabeth (43 Eliz. 1, c. 4). That statute, preserved as to the preamble only by the Mortmain and Charitable Uses Act 1888, lost even that precarious hold on the Statute Book when the Act of 1888 was repealed by the Charities Act 1960, but the somewhat ossificatory classification to which it gave rise survives in the decided cases. It is unsatisfactory because the frontiers of 'educational purposes' (as of the other divisions) have been extended and are not easy to trace with precision, and because, under the fourth head, it has been held necessary for the court to find a benefit to the public within the spirit and intendment of the obsolete Elizabethan statute. The difficulty of achieving that, while at the same time keeping the law's view of what is charitable reasonably in line with modern requirements, explains what Lord Simonds accepted as the case-to-case approach of the courts: see *National Anti-Vivisection Society* v. *Inland Revenue Commissioners.*[98] There are, in fact, examples of accepted charities which do not decisively fit into one rather than the other category. Examples are institutes for scientific research (see the *National Anti-Vivisection* case, *per* Lord Wright* [99]), museums (see *Re Pinion* [1]), the preservation of ancient cottages (*Re Cranstoun* [2]), and even the promotion of Shakespearian drama (*Re Shakespeare Memorial Theatre Trust* [3]). The present may be such a case.

" Accepting, as I have the authority of Lord Simonds for so doing, that the court must decide each case as best it can, on the evidence available to it, as to benefit, and within the moving spirit of decided cases, it would seem to me that a bequest for the purpose of search, or research, for the original manuscripts of England's greatest dramatist (whoever he was) would be well within the law's conception of charitable purposes. The discovery of such manuscripts, or of one such manuscript, would be of the highest value to history and to literature. It is objected, against this, that as we already have the text of the plays, from an almost contemporary date, the discovery of a manuscript would add nothing worth while. This I utterly decline to accept. Without any undue exercise of the imagination, it would surely be a reasonable expectation that the revelation of a manuscript would contribute, probably decisively, to a solution of the authorship problem, and this alone is benefit enough. It might also lead to improvements in the text. It might lead to more accurate dating.

" Is there any authority, then, which should lead me to hold that a bequest to achieve this objective is not charitable? By Mr. Fox, for the next-of-kin, much reliance was placed on the decision on Bernard Shaw's will, the ' British Alphabet ' case (*Re Shaw, decd.* [4]). Harman J. held that the gift was not educational because it merely tended to the increase of knowledge and that it was not within the fourth charitable category because it was not itself for a beneficial purpose but for the purpose of persuading the public by propaganda that it was beneficial. The gift was very different from the gift here. But the judge did say

98 [1948] A.C. 31; 63 T.L.R. 424; [1947] 2 All E.R. 217 (H.L.).
99 [1948] A.C. 31, 42.
1 [1963] 3 W.L.R. 778, 783.
2 [1932] 1 Ch. 537; 48 T.L.R. 226.
3 [1923] 2 Ch. 398; 39 T.L.R. 676.
4 [1957] 1 W.L.R. 729.

this [5]: ' If the object be merely the increase of knowledge, that is not in itself a charitable object unless it be combined with teaching or education '; and he referred to the House of Lords decision *Whicker* v. *Hume*,[6] where, in relation to a gift for advancement of education and learning, two of the Lords read ' learning ' as equivalent to ' teaching,' thereby in his view implying that learning, in its ordinary meaning, is not a charitable purpose.

" This decision certainly seems to place some limits upon the extent to which a gift for research may be regarded as charitable. Those limits are that either it must be ' combined with teaching or education,' if it is to fall under the third head, or it must be beneficial to the community in a way regarded by the law as charitable, if it is to fall within the fourth category. The words ' combined with teaching or education,' though well explaining what the judge had in mind when he rejected the gift in *Shaw's* case,[7] are not easy to interpret in relation to other facts. I should be unwilling to treat them as meaning that the promotion of academic research is not a charitable purpose unless the researcher were engaged in teaching or education in the conventional meaning; and I am encouraged in this view by some words of Lord Greene M.R. in *Re Compton*.[8] The testatrix there had forbidden the income of the bequest to be used for research, and Lord Greene M.R. treated this as a negative definition of the education to be provided. It would, he said, exclude a grant to enable a beneficiary to conduct research on some point of history or science. This shows that Lord Greene M.R. considered that historic research might fall within the description of ' education.' I think, therefore, that the word ' education ' as used by Harman J. in *Re Shaw, decd., Public Trustee* v. *Day*[9] must be used in a wide sense, certainly extending beyond teaching, and that the requirement is that, in order to be charitable, research must either be of educational value to the researcher or must be so directed as to lead to something which will pass into the store of educational material, or so as to improve the sum of communicable knowledge in an area which education may cover— education in this last context extending to the formation of literary taste and appreciation (compare *Royal Choral Society* v. *Inland Revenue Commissioners*[10]). Whether or not the test is wider than this, it is, as I have stated it, amply wide enough to include the purposes of the gift in this case.

" As regards the fourth category, Harman J. is evidently leaving it open to the court to hold, on the facts, that research of a particular kind may be beneficial to the community in a way which the law regards as charitable, ' beneficial ' here not being limited to the production of

---

[5] *Ibid*. 737.
[6] (1858) 7 H.L.C. 124 (H.L.).
[7] [1957] 1 W.L.R. 729.
[8] [1945] Ch. 123, 127.
[9] [1957] 1 W.L.R. 729.
[10] [1943] 2 All E.R. 101 (C.A.).

material benefit (as through medical or scientific research) but including at least benefit in the intellectual or artistic fields.

" So I find nothing in this authority to prevent me from finding that the gift falls under either the third or fourth head of the classification of charitable purposes.

" On the other side there is *Re British School of Egyptian Archaeology*,[11] also a decision of Harman J., a case much closer to the present. The trusts there were to excavate, to discover antiquities, to hold exhibitions, to publish works and to promote the training and assistance of students—all in relation to Egypt. Harman J. held that the purposes were charitable, as being educational. The society was one for the diffusion of a certain branch of knowledge, namely, knowledge of the ancient past of Egypt; and it also had a direct educational purpose, namely, to train students. The conclusion reached that there was an educational charity was greatly helped by the reference to students, but it seems that Harman J. must have accepted that the other objects —those of archaeological research—were charitable, too. They were quite independent objects on which the whole of the society's funds could have been spent, and the language ' the school has a direct educational purpose, namely, to train students ' seems to show that the judge was independently upholding each set of objects.

" Mr. Fox correctly pointed out that in that case there was a direct obligation to diffuse the results of the society's research and said that it was this that justified the finding that the archaeological purposes were charitable. I accept that research of a private character, for the benefit only of the members of a society, would not normally be educational —or otherwise charitable—as did Harman J.,[12] but I do not think that the research in the present case can be said to be of a private character, for it is inherently inevitable, and manifestly intended, that the result of any discovery should be published to the world. I think, therefore, that the *British School of Egyptian Archaeology* case [13] supports the society's contentions.

" A number of other authorities were referred to as illustrating the wide variety of objects which have been accepted as educational or as falling under the fourth category but, since none of them is close to the present, I shall not refer to them. They are well enough listed in the standard authorities.

" One final reference is appropriate: to *Re Shakespeare Memorial Trust*.[14] The scheme there was for a number of objects which included the performance of Shakespearian and other classical English plays, and stimulating the art of acting. I refer to it for two purposes, first, as an example of a case where the court upheld the gift either as educational

---

[11] [1954] 1 W.L.R. 546.
[12] *Ibid*. 551.
[13] *Ibid*. 546.
[14] [1923] 2 Ch. 398.

or as for purposes beneficial to the community—an approach which commends itself to me here—and, secondly, as illustrative of the educational and public benefit accepted by the court as flowing from a scheme designed to spread the influence of Shakespeare as the author of the plays. This gift is not that, but it lies in the same field, for the improving of our literary heritage, and my judgment is for upholding it. . . ."

INCORPORATED COUNCIL OF LAW REPORTING FOR ENGLAND AND WALES v. ATTORNEY-GENERAL

Court of Appeal [1972] Ch. 73; [1971] 3 W.L.R. 853; [1971] 3 All E.R. 1029.

The Charity Commissioners refused to register the Council as a charity so it appealed to the courts under section 5 (3) of the Charities Act 1960. Foster J. held that the Council was a charity within Lord Macnaghten's fourth category but not his second category.

On appeal, Sachs and Buckley L.JJ. affirmed the charitable status of the Council but as falling within the second category. Russell L.J. considered that the second category was inapplicable but that the fourth category was applicable. Sachs and Buckley L.JJ. stated that if they had not found the second category to be applicable then they would have found the fourth category applicable. The judgment of Sachs L.J. follows immediately whilst the judgment of Russell L.J. follows later in this chapter at p. 265.

SACHS L.J.: " The right of the Incorporated Council of Law Reporting to be registered as a charity under section 4 of the Charities Act 1960 depends on whether it is one ' which is established for charitable purposes ' (see the definition of ' charity ' in s. 45 (1)). By section 46 ' charitable purposes ' is defined as meaning ' purposes which are exclusively charitable according to the law of England and Wales.' For the best part of four centuries the question whether the purposes of any given trust or institution are charitable has been decided by reference to the preamble of the Charitable Uses Act 1601 —' the Statute of Elizabeth I.' Since 1891 the courts have followed the guidance given in the classic speech of Lord Macnaghten in *Income Tax Special Purposes Comrs.* v. *Pemsel* [15] where it is stated that ' " Charity " in its legal sense comprises four principal divisions.' In every case since then the issue has been whether the purposes of any given trust or institution fell within one of those divisions. The result of the present case depends on whether the purposes of the council fall within the second—' trusts for the advancement of education,' or alternatively within the fourth—' trusts for other purposes beneficial to the community ' not falling within any of the other heads.

" To come to a conclusion whether those purposes fall within either

---

[15] [1891] A.C. 531.

of the two above divisions—and, in particular, whether it falls within
the fourth—it is necessary to have regard to what, since the judgment
of Sir William Grant M.R. in *Morice* v. *Bishop of Durham* [16] in 1804,
has been termed ' the spirit and intendment ' of the above preamble,
words commonly regarded as having the same meaning as ' the equity
of the statute.' It so happens that there are available to us through
judgments given in open court the contents of two documents substantially contemporaneous with the Statute of Elizabeth I which
throw useful light both as to the spirit and intendment of that statute
in relation to administration of the law in general and to the word
' education ' in reference thereto: the charters of an Inn of Chancery
(Clifford's Inn) [17] and an Inn of Court (Inner Temple) [18] dated respectively 1618 and 1608. It is, however, preferable first to approach
each of the questions that arise in the instant case apart from what can
be learnt from these documents.

"Before considering more closely what are the answers to these
questions with the aid of the education to be derived from studying
the judgments in the 41 reports cited to us and the mass of learning
shown to have been devoted, at any rate, over the last two centuries
to the relevant problems, it is convenient at the outset to mention
some points which have often been repeated in those judgments.
First, the word ' charity ' is ' of all words in the English language . . .
one which more unmistakeably has a technical meaning in the strictest
sense of the term . . . peculiar to the law ' (*per* Lord Macnaghten in
Pemsel's case [19]), one that is ' wide and elastic ' (*per* Lord Ash-
bourne [20]), and one that can include something quite outside the
ordinary meaning the word has in popular speech (*cf.* Lord Cozens-
Hardy M.R., *Re Wedgwood, Allen* v. *Wedgwood* [21]). It is thus
necessary to eliminate from one's mind a natural allergy, stemming
simply from the popular meaning of ' charity ', to the idea that law
reporting might prove to be a charitable activity. Secondly, it is clear
that the mere fact that charges on a commercial scale are made for
services rendered by an institution does not of itself bar that institution
from being held to be charitable—so long, at any rate, as all the
profits must be retained for its purposes and none can enure to the
benefit of its individual members (*cf. Scottish Burial Reform and
Cremation Society Ltd.* v. *Glasgow City Corpn.* [22]). Thirdly, that there
have, over at any rate the past century, been a number of references
to the oddity that the tests by which the courts decide whether an

[16] (1804) 9 Ves. 399, 405.
[17] For the charter, as set out and discussed in the judgment of Sir Richard Henn
Collins M.R. in *Smith* v. *Kerr* [1902] 1 Ch. 774, see the end of the report.
[18] For the charter, as set out and discussed in the judgment of the Deputy Judge of
the Mayor's and City of London Court in *Thomson* v. *Trustees of the Honourable Society of the Inner Temple* (May 30, 1967), see the end of the report.
[19] [1891] A.C. 531, 581.
[20] In *Re Cranston, Webb* v. *Oldfield* [1898] 1 I.R. 431, 442.
[21] [1915] 1 Ch. 113, 117. [22] [1968] A.C. 138.

institution is charitable depend entirely on the preamble of the Statute of Elizabeth I. The most recent is one opining that this state of affairs was ' almost incredible to anyone not familiar with this branch of the English law ' (*per* Lord Upjohn in the *Scottish Burial* case [23]). To this I will return later.

" Turning now to the points of substance argued before us, there came *in limine* the question as to what material we were entitled to look at to determine whether the purposes of the council were charitable. Counsel for the Crown contended that in substance the court could and should only look at paragraph 3 of the memorandum of association and in particular at its important first sub-paragraph:

> ' The Objects for which the Association is established are:
> 1. The preparation and publication, in a convenient form, at a moderate price, and under gratuitous professional control, of Reports of Judicial Decisions of the Superior and Appellate Courts in England.'

This contention involved the proposition that we could neither look at any of the facts to which the trial judge [24] referred under the heading of ' the historical background ' nor at any available evidence as to what at any time since July 1870 had been the use to which the Law Reports are put. That in effect would mean looking at paragraph 3 (1) as if it were situate in a vacuum. That cannot be right.

" Moreover he went on to submit that (a) the courts cannot look at the motives of the founders in order to show the purposes of an institution—at any rate, when those purposes as otherwise ascertained might be shown not to be charitable, and (b) the absence in the opening phrase of paragraph 3 of general words such as ' for the purpose of the advancement and promotion of the science of law ' was fatal to the council's claim even if on the facts it was shown that that was the exclusive purpose of their activities and that that purpose was charitable. Whilst the first of those submissions was correct (*cf. Keren Kayemeth Le Jisroel Ltd.* v. *Inland Revenue Comrs.* [25] *per* Lawrence L.J.), the second was not. The courts look at the substance of what is being effected.

" A further question discussed was whether the use of the words ' is established ' in the section 45 (1) definition of ' charity ' is to bind the court to look only at facts as existing at the date the 1960 Act came into force, or whether the court could or should look at the facts as at the date of the incorporation of the council. It makes no practical difference in the present case whether one looks at the circumstances of 1870 or of 1970, but to my mind it is the foundation date that matters when considering whether an institution is established for charitable purposes.

" Whilst appreciating what has been said as to the courts not being

---

[23] [1968] A.C. 138, 151.
[24] [1971] Ch. 626.
[25] [1931] 2 K.B. 465, 484.

permitted, where plain language is used in a charter or memorandum, to admit extrinsic evidence as to its construction, it is yet plain from the course adopted by the courts in many cases that they are entitled to and do look at the circumstances in which the institution came into existence and at the sphere in which it operates to enable a conclusion to be reached on whether its purposes are charitable. Such matters were likewise regularly taken into account over the 117 years of the operation of Scientific Societies Act 1843, when the issue was whether buildings belonged ' to any Society instituted for purposes of science, literature or the fine arts exclusively '.

" The necessity for this course is all the more obvious when the purposes of an ancient institution become the subject of examination, remembering that if it started as a charity it so remains. An example of the above approach is to be found in *Smith* v. *Kerr* [26] (the Clifford's Inn case) where at first instance Cozens-Hardy J. fully examined the circumstances affecting Clifford's Inn, and Sir Richard Henn Collins M.R. on appeal [27] followed the same course, to ascertain the purpose to which the funds were to be applied. (The question whether in fact it has applied or is applying some of its funds to non-charitable purposes is, of course, a separate issue which arises when tax or rate exemptions are under consideration.)

" As to the circumstances in which the council came into existence and the sphere in which it has since operated, the facts are admirably marshalled in the affidavit of Professor Goodhart with the accustomed lucidity of that eminent jurist. Reference can also be made to the 1853 Report [28] of the Society for Promoting the Amendment of the Law, an extract from page 4 of which is aptly cited in the judgment of Foster J. [29] In the main the relevant circumstances and sphere are within judicial knowledge and need no detailed exposition in this judgment. The kernel of the matter is the vital function of judge-made law in relation not only to the common law and to equity, but to declaring the meaning of statutory law. No one—layman or lawyer —can have reasonably full knowledge of how the law affects what he or his neighbours are doing without recourse to reports of judicial decisions as well as to the statutes of the realm.

" What in that state of affairs is the purpose of law reports? There is in substance only one purpose. To provide essential material for the study of the law—in the sense of acquiring knowledge of what the law is, how it is developing and how it applies to the enormous range of human activities which it affects.

" At this juncture it is apposite to recall that the profession of the law is a learned profession. It was one of the earliest to be recognised

---

[26] [1900] 2 Ch. 511, *affd.* [1902] 1 Ch. 774.
[27] [1902] 1 Ch. 774.
[28] Law Reporting Reform.
[29] [1971] Ch. 626, 640.

as such, well before the Statute of Elizabeth I: to establish that point there is no need to have recourse to examples of this recognition such as the traditional House of Commons appellation 'honourable and *learned*' to members of the profession. Similarly it is plainly correct to speak of law as a science and of its study as a study of science in the same way as one speaks of the study of medicine or chemistry. If further exemplification were needed of the categories of learning and science the pursuit of which have been held to be charitable, one can turn to the names of the institutions listed in *Tudor on Charities* [30]: there one finds such divers names as the Royal Literary Society, the British School of Egyptian Archaeology, and the Institution of Civil Engineers. That the law is such a science happens to be illustrated by Sir Frederick Pollock's celebrated essay on ' The Science of Case-Law ' [31]; but this merely provides from within the profession an authoritative view which plainly accords in principle both with the decisions affecting the above cited institutions and that under the Scientific Societies Act 1843 (see *Westminster City Council* v. *Royal United Service Institution* [32]). It may at this point be of relevance to note that Lord Macnaghten's phrase ' advancement of education ' has consistently been taken to be an *enlargement* of the phrase ' advancement of learning ' used by Sir Samuel Romilly for his second division of charities in *Morice* v. *Bishop of Durham* [33]: in other words, there can be no question but that the latter is included in the former, as is illustrated by the authorities.

" Against that background I turn to the question whether the council's purposes are educational. It would be odd indeed and contrary to the trend of judicial decisions if the institution and maintenance of a library for the study of a learned subject or of something rightly called a science did not at least prima facie fall within the phrase ' advancement of education,' whatever be the age of those frequenting it. The same reasoning must apply to the provision of books forming the raw material for that study, whether they relate to chemical data or to case histories in hospitals; and I can find no good reason for excluding case law as developed in the courts. If that is the correct approach, then when the institution is one whose individual members make no financial gain from the provision of that material and is one which itself can make no use of its profits except to provide further and better material, why is the purpose not charitable?

" On behalf of the Attorney-General the only point taken against this conclusion was that the citation of the reports in court cannot be educational—in part, at any rate, because of the theory that the judges are deemed to have complete knowledge of the law. For the Crown

---

[30] 6th ed., p. 29.
[31] See Pollock, *Essays in Jurisprudence and Ethics* (1882), p. 237.
[32] [1938] 2 All E.R. 545, 549.
[33] (1805) 10 Ves. 522, 531.

the main contention was that the use by the legal profession of the reports was in general (not merely when in court) a use the purpose of which was to earn professional remuneration—a use for personal profit; and that it followed that the purpose of the council was not charitable.

"Taking the latter point first, it is, of course, the fact that one of the main, if not the main, uses to which law reports are put is by members of the legal profession who study their contents so as to advise clients and plead on their behalf; those reports are as essential to them in their profession as the statutes; without them they would be ill equipped to earn professional fees. Does it follow, as submitted by counsel for the Crown, that a main purpose of the reports is the advancement of professional interests and thus not charitable? The argument put thus is attractive, not least to those who, like myself, are anxious not to favour or to seem to favour their one-time profession. But the doctor must study medical research papers to enable him to treat his patients and earn his fees; and it would be difficult indeed to say that because doctors thus earn their emoluments the printing and sale of such papers by a non-profit making institution could not be held to be for the advancement of education in medicine.

"Where the purpose of producing a book is to enable a specified subject, and a learned subject at that, to be studied, it is, in my judgment, published for the advancement of education, as this, of course, includes as regards the Statute of Elizabeth I the advancement of learning. That remains its purpose despite the fact that professional men—be they lawyers, doctors or chemists—use the knowledge acquired to earn their living. One must not confuse the results flowing from the achievement of a purpose with the purpose itself, any more than one should have regard to the motives of those who set that purpose in motion.

"As to the point that the citation of reports to the judiciary is fatal to the council's claim, this, if independent of the contention concerning professional user to earn fees, seems to turn on the suggestion that as the judges are supposed to know the law the citations cannot be educative. That, however, is an unrealistic approach. It ignores the fact that citation of authority by the Bar is simply a means by which there is brought to the attention of the judge the material he has to study to decide the matter in hand; in this country he relies on competent counsel to quote the extracts relevant to any necessary study of law on the points in issue, instead of having to embark on the time-consuming process of making the necessary researches himself. Indeed, it verges on the absurd to suggest that the courteous facade embodied in the traditional phrase ' as, of course, your Lordships know ' can be used to attempt to conceal the fact that no judge can possibly be aware of all the contents of all the law reports that show the continuing development of our ever changing laws. The Law

Reports (including vol. 1 of the Weekly Law Reports) for 1970 alone contain some 5,200 pages; incidentally, if one confined one's views to the three volumes of the Weekly Law Reports there would still remain over 4,000 pages. For my part I feel no diffidence in expressing my indebtedness to counsel in the instant case, as I have done in other cases this term dealing with other subjects, for educating me in the law of charitable purposes by the citation of the 41 authorities previously mentioned.

"For these reasons I reject the contention that the user of the Law Reports by the legal profession for earning fees of itself results in the purposes of the council not being charitable and thus return to the question whether they are charitable on the footing that their substantially exclusive purpose is to further the study of the law in the way already discussed. Such a purpose must in my judgment be charitable unless the submission that the advancement of learning is not an advancement of education within the spirit and intendment of the preamble is upheld; but for the reasons already given that submission plainly fails. Accordingly, having regard to the fact that the members of the council cannot themselves gain from its activities, its purposes in my judgment fall within the second of Lord Macnaghten's divisions.

"Despite the above conclusion, it seems desirable to consider as compactly as is practicable whether had the council's purpose not fallen within the second division it would nonetheless have come withing the fourth as being beneficial to the community. The Charity Commission, after a year's consideration of the council's application to be registered as a charity, wrote a letter dated December 6, 1967, which contained the following phrase:

> 'The Commissioners did not dispute that the advancement of the administration of law was a charitable purpose.'

The Attorney-General supports that view: the Crown opposes it. Foster J.[34] rejected the Crown's contention.

"Being myself convinced that the correct approach is that which the learned first instance judge [35] referred to as Lord Wilberforce's wider test (see *Scottish Burial* case [36])—a test that clearly also attracted Lord Reid [37] with whom Lord Guest [38] agreed—I do not propose to consider the instant case on the basis of analogies. The analogies or 'stepping stones' approach was rightly conceded on behalf of the Attorney-General not to be essential; its artificiality has been demonstrated in the course of the consideration of the numerous authorities put before us. On the other hand, the wider test—advancement of purposes beneficial to the community or objects of general public utility—has an admirable breadth and flexibility which enables it to

---

[34] [1971] Ch. 626.
[35] [1971] Ch. 626, 647.
[36] [1968] A.C. 138, 156.
[37] [1968] A.C. 138, 146, 147.
[38] [1968] A.C. 138, 148.

be reasonably applied from generation to generation to meet changing circumstances; it has thus such patent advantages that for my part I appreciate the wisdom of the legislature in refraining from providing a detailed definition of charitable purposes in the 1960 Act and preferring to allow the existing law to be applied. Any statutory definition might well merely produce a fresh spate of litigation and provide a set of undesirable artificial distinctions. There is indeed much to be said for flexibility in such matters.

" The first question to be considered in relation to the wider test is whether the advancement of the administration of the law in its broad sense (which would include the elucidation, proper application, and betterment of the law) is something beneficial to the community. To pose that question to one whose function it is to administer the law provokes unease and a tendency to lean over backwards to avoid giving an affirmative reply. But such a mental posture is no more conducive to a balanced view than to elegance. Looking at the issue squarely and attempting to use the eyes of the generality of subjects of either Elizabeth I or Elizabeth II there is, however, manifestly only one answer—of course it is beneficial to the community. The answer being eminently a matter of first impression derived from an overall view of the preamble coupled with the general trend of some centuries of decisions, no useful purpose can be served by citation of specific authorities. It is an impression formed without reference to the contents of either of the two previously mentioned charters, to which I will, however, return.

" Next comes the question whether the particular purpose of the council's activities sufficiently contributes to that advancement. Does it benefit a sufficiently wide section of the community? As satisfactory administration of the law in practice depends on there being a proper system of law reporting, it can well be said that the whole community benefits from the purposes of the council: but even if the benefits were confined to those who have to make judicial decisions and to the members of the legal profession advising clients and appearing for them in court, nonetheless a sufficiently large section of the community would derive the relevant benefits.

" Adopting the test propounded by my brother Russell L.J., I next turn to consider whether there is any reason for excluding these benefits from the range of those that are capable of being classified as charitable, and can find no such reason.

" Finally as regards this head comes the question whether the contribution is made in a charitable manner. This point having been fully discussed in the judgments of my brethren to an effect with which I agree it is not necessary to go over the ground again. In my judgment, the way in which the council operates qualifies it for inclusion among charities as defined by the 1960 Act once it is shown that its purposes can properly be said to be charitable if operated in a charitable manner.

" Accordingly if, contrary to my view, the purposes of the council do not fall within the second division, they are nonetheless charitable because they would then fall within the fourth.

OPPENHEIM v. TOBACCO SECURITIES TRUST CO. LTD.

House of Lords [1951] A.C. 297; [1951] 1 T.L.R. 118; [1951] 1 All E.R. 31 (Lord Simonds, Normand, Oaksey and Morton; Lord Mac-Dermott dissenting) [39]

Certain investments were held by the respondents, Tobacco Securities Trust Co. Ltd., on trust to apply the income in providing for the education of children of employees or former employees of British-American Tobacco Co. Ltd. . . . or any of its subsidiary or allied companies without any limit of time being specified. It was clear in these circumstances that the trust would be void for perpetuity unless it were charitable. Both Roxburgh J. in the Chancery Division, and the Court of Appeal, declared the trust void on the ground that it lacked public benefit, following *Re Compton* [40] and *Re Hobourn Aero Component Ltd.'s Air Raid Distress Fund.* [41] On appeal to the House of Lords:

LORD SIMONDS: " It is a clearly established principle of the law of charity that a trust is not charitable unless it is directed to the public benefit. This is sometimes stated in the proposition that it must benefit the community or a section of the community. Negatively it is said that a trust is not charitable if it confers only private benefits. In the recent case of *Gilmour* v. *Coats* [42] this principle was reasserted. It is easy to state and has been stated in a variety of ways, the earliest statement that I find being in *Jones* v. *Williams*,[43] in which Lord Hardwicke L.C. is briefly reported as follows [44]: ' Definition of charity: a gift to a general public use, which extends to the poor as well as to the rich. . . .' With a single exception, to which I shall refer, this applies to all charities. We are apt now to classify them by reference to Lord Macnaghten's decision in *Income Tax Special Purposes Commissioners* v. *Pemsel*,[45] and, as I have elsewhere pointed out, it was at one time suggested that the element of public benefit was not essential except for charities falling within the fourth class, ' other purposes beneficial to the community.' This is certainly wrong except in the anomalous case of trusts for the relief of poverty, with which I must specifically deal. In the case of trusts for educational purposes the condition of public benefit must be satisfied. The difficulty lies in determining what is sufficient to satisfy the test, and there is little to help your Lordships to solve it.

---

[39] See also *Davies* v. *Perpetual Trustee Co.* [1959] A.C. 439; 75 L.Q.R. 292.
[40] [1945] Ch. 123.
[41] [1946] Ch. 194.
[42] [1949] A.C. 426.
[43] (1767) Amb. 651.
[44] *Ibid.* 652.
[45] [1891] A.C. 531, 583.

"If I may begin at the bottom of the scale, a trust established by a father for the education of his son is not a charity. The public element, as I will call it, is not supplied by the fact that from that son's education all may benefit. At the other end of the scale the establishment of a college or university is beyond doubt a charity. 'Schools of learning and free schools, and scholars of universities' are the very words of the preamble to the [Charitable Uses Act 1601 (43 Eliz. 1, c. 4)]. So also the endowment of a college, university or school by the creation of scholarships or bursaries is a charity, and nonetheless because competition may be limited to a particular class of persons. It is on this ground, as Lord Greene M.R. pointed out in *Re Compton*, that the so-called 'founder's kin' cases can be rested. The difficulty arises where the trust is not for the benefit of any institution either then existing or by the terms of the trust to be brought into existence, but for the benefit of a class of persons at large. Then the question is whether that class of persons can be regarded as such a 'section of the community' as to satisfy the test of public benefit. These words 'section of the community' have no special sanctity, but they conveniently indicate (1) that the possible (I emphasise the word 'possible') beneficiaries must not be numerically negligible, and (2) that the quality which distinguishes them from other members of the community, so that they form by themselves a section of it, must be a quality which does not depend on their relationship to a particular individual. It is for this reason that a trust for the education of members of a family or, as in *Re Compton*, of a number of families cannot be regarded as charitable. A group of persons may be numerous, but, if the nexus between them is their personal relationship to a single *propositus* or to several *propositi*, they are neither the community nor a section of the community for charitable purposes.

"I come, then, to the present case where the class of beneficiaries is numerous, but the difficulty arises in regard to their common and distinguishing quality. That quality is being children of employees of one or other of a group of companies. I can make no distinction between children of employees and the employees themselves. In both cases the common quality is found in employment by particular employers. The latter of the two cases, by which the Court of Appeal held itself to be bound, the *Hobourn* case, is a direct authority for saying that such a common quality does not constitute its possessors a section of the public for charitable purposes. In the former case, *Re Compton*, Lord Greene M.R. had by way of illustration placed members of a family and employees of a particular employer on the same footing, finding neither in common kinship nor in common employment the sort of nexus which is sufficient. My Lords, I am so fully in agreement with what was said by Lord Greene in both cases, and by my noble and learned friend, then Morton L.J., in the *Hobourn* case, that I am in danger of repeating without improving upon their words. No one who has been versed for many years in this difficult and very artificial branch of the law can be unaware of its illogicalities, but I join with my noble and learned friend in echoing the observations which he cited [46] from the judgment of Russell L.J. in *Re Grove-Grady*,[47] and I agree with him that the decision in *Re Drummond* [48] . . . ' imposed a very healthy check upon the extension of the legal definition of charity.' It appears to me that it would be an extension, for which there is no justification in principle or authority, to regard common employment as a quality which constitutes those employed a section of the community. It must not, I think, be forgotten that charitable institutions enjoy rare and increasing privileges, and that the claim to come within that privileged class should be clearly established. With the single exception of *Re Rayner*,[49] which I must regard as of doubtful authority, no case has been brought to the notice of the House in which such a claim as this has been made, where there is no element of poverty in the beneficiaries, but just this and no more, that they are the children of those in a common employment.

" Learned counsel for the appellant sought to fortify his case by pointing to the anomalies that would ensue from the rejection of his argument. For, he said, admittedly those who follow a profession or calling—clergymen, lawyers, colliers, tobacco-workers and so on—are a section of the public; how strange then it would be if, as in the case of railwaymen, those who follow a particular calling are all employed by one employer. Would a trust for the education of railwaymen be charitable,[50] but a trust for the education of men employed on the railways by the Transport Board not be charitable? And what of service of the Crown, whether in the civil service or the armed forces? Is there a difference between soldiers and soldiers of the King? My Lords, I am not impressed by this sort of argument and will consider on its merits if the occasion should arise, the case where the description of the occupation and the employment is in effect the same, where in a word, if you know what a man does, you know who employs him to do it. It is to me a far more cogent argument, as it was to my noble and learned friend in the *Hobourn* case, that, if a section of the public is constituted by the personal relation of employment, it is impossible to say that it is not constituted by a thousand as by 100,000 employees, and if by a thousand, then by a hundred, and, if by a hundred, then by ten. I do not mean merely that there is a difficulty in drawing the line, though that, too, is significant. I have it also in mind that, though the actual number of employees at any one moment might be small, it might increase to any extent, just as, being large, it might decrease to any extent. If the number of employees is the test of validity, must the

---

[46] [1946] Ch. 194, 208. [47] [1929] 1 Ch. 557, 582.
[48] [1914] 2 Ch. 90.
[49] (1920) 89 L.J.Ch. 369.
[50] As to this see *Hall* v. *Derby Sanitary Authority* (1885) 16 Q.B.D. 163.

court take into account potential increase or decrease, and, if so, as at what date?

"I would end, my Lords, where I began—by saying that I concur in the reasoning of the Court of Appeal in the *Hobourn* case, but there are certain points in the arguments for the appellants about which I should say a few words. It was urged by counsel for the Attorney-General, who was allowed to address the House, that there was here a valid charitable trust created, since there was no private person who could sue to enforce the trust. I am not persuaded that this would be so, if the trust were otherwise enforceable. But, in any case, the test is not a valid one. If this trust is charitable, the Attorney-General can sue to enforce it. It does not follow that it is charitable because no one else can sue to enforce it. I would also, as I have previously indicated, say a word about the so-called ' poor relations ' cases. I do so only because they have once more been brought forward as an argument in favour of a more generous view of what may be charitable. It would not be right for me to affirm or to denounce or to justify these decisions. I am concerned only to say that the law of charity, so far as it relates to ' the relief of aged, impotent, and poor people ' (I quote from the [Charitable Uses Act 1601]) and to poverty in general, has followed its own line, and that it is not useful to try to harmonise decisions on that branch of the law with the broad proposition on which the determination of this case must rest. It is not for me to say what fate might await those cases if in a poverty case this House had to consider them. But, as was observed by Lord Wright in *Admiralty Commissioners* v. *Valverda (Owners)*,[51] while ' this House has, no doubt, power to overrule even a long-established course of decisions of the courts, provided it has not itself determined the question ' . . . yet ' in general this House will adopt this course only in plain cases, where serious inconvenience or injustice would follow from perpetuating an erroneous construction or ruling of law.' I quote with respect those observations to indicate how unwise it would be to cast any doubt upon decisions, of respectable antiquity in order to introduce a greater harmony into the law of charity as a whole."

LORD MACDERMOTT (dissenting)[52]: " . . . The question is whether it is of a public nature, whether, in the words of Lord Wrenbury in *Verge* v. *Somerville*,[53] ' it is for the benefit of the community or of an appreciably important class of community.' The relevant class here is that from which those to be educated are to be selected. The appellant contends that this class is public in character; the respondent bank (as personal representative of the last surviving settlor) denies this and says that the class is no more than a group of private individuals.

---

51 [1938] A.C. 173, 194; the proviso has now been abandoned: see [1966] 3 All E.R. 77; *Oldendorff & Co. G.m.b.H.* v. *Tradax Export* [1973] 3 W.L.R. 382.
52 See (1951) 67 L.Q.R. 162 (R. E. M.); *ibid.* 164 (A. L. G.).
53 [1924] A.C. 496, 499.

" Until comparatively recently the usual way of approaching an issue of this sort, at any rate where educational trusts were concerned, was, I believe, to regard the facts of each case and to treat the matter very much as one of degree. No definition of what constituted a sufficient section of the public for the purpose was applied, for none existed; and the process seems to have been one of reaching a conclusion on a general survey of the circumstances and considerations regarded as relevant rather than of making a single, conclusive test. The investigation left the course of the dividing line between what was and what was not a section of the community unexplored, and was concluded when it had gone far enough to establish to the satisfaction of the court whether or not the trust was public; and the decision as to that was, I think, very often reached by determining whether or not the trust was private.

" If it is still permissible to conduct the present inquiry on these broad if imprecise lines, I would hold with the appellant. The numerical strength of the class is considerable on any showing. The employees concerned number over 110,000, and it may reasonably be assumed that the children, who constitute the class in question, are no fewer. The large size of the class is not, of course, decisive but in my view it cannot be left out of account when the problem is approached in this way. Then it must be observed that the *propositi* are not limited to those presently employed. They include former employees (not reckoned in the figure I have given) and are, therefore, a more stable category than would otherwise be the case. And, further, the employees concerned are not limited to those in the service of the ' British American Tobacco Co. Ltd. or any of its subsidiary or allied companies '—itself a description of great width—but include the employees, in the event of the British American Tobacco Co. Ltd. being reconstructed or merged on amalgamation, of the reconstructed or amalgamated company or any of its subsidiary companies. No doubt the settlors here had a special interest in the welfare of the class they described, but, apart from the fact that this may serve to explain the particular form of their bounty, I do not think it material to the question in hand. What is material, as I regard the matter, is that they have chosen to benefit a class which is, in fact, substantial in point of size and importance and have done so in a manner which, to my mind, manifests an intention to advance the interests of the class described as a class rather than as a collection or succession of particular individuals. . . .

" The respondent bank, however, contends that the inquiry should be of quite a different character to that which I have been discussing. It advances as the sole criterion a narrower test derived from the decisions of the Court of Appeal in *In re Compton*,[54] and in *In re Hobourn Aero Components Ltd.'s Air Raid Distress Fund.*[55] The

---

[54] [1945] Ch. 123.
[55] [1946] Ch. 194.

basis and nature of this test appear from the passage in the judgment of the court in *In re Compton*,[56] where Lord Greene M.R., says: ' In the case of many charitable gifts it is possible to identify the individuals who are to benefit, or who at any given moment constitute the class from which the beneficiaries are to be selected. This circumstance does not, however, deprive the gift of its public character. Thus, if there is a gift to relieve the poor inhabitants of a parish the class to benefit is readily ascertainable. But they do not enjoy the benefit, when they receive it, by virtue of their character as individuals but by virtue of their membership of the specified class. In such a case the common quality which unites the potential beneficiaries into a class is essentially an impersonal one. It is definable by reference to what each has in common with the others, and that is something into which their status as individuals does not enter. Persons claiming to belong to the class do so not because they are A.B., C.D. and E.F., but because they are poor inhabitants of the parish. If, in asserting their claim, it were necessary for them to establish the fact that they were the individuals A.B., C.D. and E.F., I cannot help thinking that on principle the gift ought not to be held to be a charitable gift, since the introduction into their qualification of a purely personal element would deprive the gift of its necessary public character. It seems to me that the same principle ought to apply when the claimants, in order to establish their status, have to assert and prove, not that they themselves are A.B., C.D. and E.F., but that they stand in some specified relationship to the individuals A.B., C.D. and E.F., such as that of children or employees. In that case, too, a purely personal element enters into and is an essential part of the qualification, which is defined by reference to something, *i.e.*, personal relationship to individuals or an individual which is in its essence non-public.'

    " The test thus propounded focuses upon the common quality which unites those within the class concerned and asks whether that quality is essentially impersonal or essentially personal. If the former, the class will rank as a section of the public and the trust will have the element common to and necessary for all legal charities; but, if the latter, the trust will be private and not charitable. It is suggested in the passage just quoted, and made clear beyond doubt in *In re Hobourn*,[57] that in the opinion of the Court of Appeal employment by a designated employer must be regarded for this purpose as a personal and not as an impersonal bond of union. In this connection and as illustrating the discriminating character of what I may call ' the *Compton*[58] test ' reference should be made to that part of the judgment of the learned Master of the Rolls in *In re Hobourn*,[59] in which he speaks

---

[56] [1945] Ch. 123, 129–30.
[57] [1946] Ch. 194.
[58] [1945] Ch. 123.
[59] [1946] Ch. 194, 206.

of the decision in *Hall* v. *Derby Borough Urban Sanitary Authority.*[60]
The passage runs thus:

> ' That related to a trust for railway servants. It is said that if
> a trust for railway servants can be a good charity, so too a trust
> for railway servants in the employment of a particular railway
> company is a good charity. That is not so. The reason, I think,
> is that in the one case the trust is for railway servants in general
> and in the other case it is for employees of a particular company,
> a fact which limits the potential beneficiaries to a class ascertained
> on a purely personal basis.'

" My Lords, I do not quarrel with the result arrived at in the
Compton and *Hobourn* cases, and I do not doubt that the *Compton*
test may often prove of value and lead to a correct determination.
But, with the great respect due to those who have formulated this test,
I find myself unable to regard it as a criterion of general applicability
and conclusiveness. In the first place I see much difficulty in dividing
the qualities or attributes, which may serve to bind human beings into
classes, into two mutually exclusive groups, the one involving individual status and purely personal, the other disregarding such status and
quite impersonal. As a task this seems to me no less baffling and
elusive than the problem to which it is directed, namely, the determination of what is and what is not a section of the public for the
purposes of this branch of the law. After all, what is more personal
than poverty or blindness or ignorance? Yet none would deny that a
gift for the education of the children of the poor or blind was charitable; and I doubt if there is any less certainty about the charitable
nature of a gift for, say, the education of children who satisfy a specified examining body that they need and would benefit by a course of
special instruction designed to remedy their educational defects.

" But can any really fundamental distinction, as respects the personal or impersonal nature of the common link, be drawn between
those employed, for example, by a particular university and those whom
the same university has put in a certain category as the result of
individual examination and assessment? Again, if the bond between
those employed by a particular railway is purely personal, why should
the bond between those who are employed as railway men be so
essentially different? Is a distinction to be drawn in this respect
between those who are employed in a particular industry before it is
nationalized and those who are employed therein after that process has
been completed and one employer has taken the place of many? Are
miners in the service of the National Coal Board now in one category
and miners at a particular pit or of a particular district in another?
Is the relationship between those in the service of the Crown to be
distinguished from that obtaining between those in the service of some

---

[60] 16 Q.B.D. 163.

other employer? Or, if not, are the children of, say, soldiers or civil servants to be regarded as not constituting a sufficient section of the public to make a trust for their education charitable?

" It was conceded in the course of the argument that, had the present trust been framed so as to provide for the education of the children of those engaged in the tobacco industry in a named county or town, it would have been a good charitable disposition, and that even though the class to be benefited would have been appreciably smaller and no more important than is the class here. That concession follows from what the Court of Appeal has said. But if it is sound and a personal or impersonal relationship remains the universal criterion I think it shows, no less than the queries I have just raised in indicating some of the difficulties of the problem, that the *Compton* test is a very arbitrary and artificial rule. This leads me to the second difficulty that I have regarding it. If I understand it aright it necessarily makes the quantum of public benefit a consideration of little moment; the size of the class becomes immaterial and the need of its members and the public advantage of having that need met appear alike to be irrelevant. To my mind these are considerations of some account in the sphere of educational trusts for, as already indicated, I think the educational value and scope of the work actually to be done must have a bearing on the question of public benefit.

" Finally, it seems to me that, far from settling the state of the law on this particular subject, the *Compton* test is more likely to create confusion and doubt in the case of many trusts and institutions of a character whose legal standing as charities has never been in question. I have particularly in mind gifts for the education of certain special classes such, for example, as the daughters of missionaries, the children of those professing a particular faith or accepted as ministers of a particular denomination, or those whose parents have sent them to a particular school for the earlier stages of their training. I cannot but think that in cases of this sort an analysis of the common quality binding the class to be benefited may reveal a relationship no less personal than that existing between an employer and those in his service. Take, for instance, a trust for the provision of university education for boys coming from a particular school. The common quality binding the members of that class seems to reside in the fact that their parents or guardians all contracted for their schooling with the same establishment or body. That the school in such a case may itself be a charitable foundation seems altogether beside the point and quite insufficient to hold the *Compton* test at bay if it is well founded in law.

" My Lords, counsel for the appellant and for the Attorney-General adumbrated several other tests for establishing the presence or absence of the necessary public element. I have given these my careful consideration and I do not find them any more sound or satis-

factory than the *Compton* test. I therefore return to what I think was
the process followed before the decision in *Compton's* case, and, for the
reasons already given, I would hold the present trust charitable and
allow the appeal. I have only to add that I recognize the imperfections
and uncertainties of that process. They are as evident as the difficulties
of finding something better. But I venture to doubt if it is in the power
of the courts to resolve those difficulties satisfactorily as matters stand. It
is a long cry to the age of Elizabeth and I think what is needed is a fresh
start from a new statute." *Appeal dismissed.*

I.R.C. v. EDUCATIONAL GRANTS ASSOCIATION LTD.

Chancery Division [1967] Ch. 123; [1966] 3 W.L.R. 724; [1966] 3 All
E.R. 708

The Revenue appealed from a decision of the Special Commissioners of Income Tax that the respondents were a charity entitled to
exemption from income tax under section 447 (1) (*b*) of the Income
Tax Act 1952 (now section 360 (1) (*c*) of the Income and Corporation
Taxes Act 1970).

The respondents were a company limited by guarantee formed for
the advancement of education. However, the promoters of the company and its management were very much connected with Metal Box
Ltd. Virtually all the income came from a seven-year deed of covenant executed by Metal Box Ltd. Care was taken that details of the
company's objects did not leak out except to the higher ranks of
Metal Box employees and their associates. Between 75 and 85 per
cent. of payments were for the benefit of children of Metal Box
employees.

The Revenue conceded that the respondents were established for
charitable purposes only and so the case turned upon whether or not
the payments had been applied to charitable purposes only.

Pennycuick J. allowed the appeal holding that the absence of
public benefit had the consequence that the payments had not been
applied to charitable purposes only. The Court of Appeal [61] in short
extempore judgments affirmed his decision but without pursuing his
doubts over *Re Koettgen.* The reserved judgment of Pennycuick J.
appears below as illuminating the issues more clearly than the Court
of Appeal decision.

PENNYCUICK J.: " I will next read the relevant part of section 447
of the Income Tax Act 1952.

' (1) Exemption shall be granted . . . (*b*) . . . from tax chargeable under Sch. D in respect of any yearly interest or other
annual payment, forming part of the income of any body of
persons or trust established for charitable purposes only, or which,

[61] [1967] Ch. 993.

according to the rules or regulations established by Act of Parliament, charter, decree, deed of trust or will, are applicable to charitable purposes only, and so far as the same are applied to charitable purposes only.'

I will, for brevity, refer to the relevant provision in section 447 as ' the subsection.'

" I propose, in the first place, to state what seems to me to be the proper construction and effect of the subsection in the common case where an object or trust is expressed in wide and general terms, for example, the advancement of education; next, to consider certain contentions advanced by counsel on either side; and, finally, to apply the subsection to the facts of the present case.

" It will be observed that the subsection imposes two distinct requirements: (i) the income must form part of the income of a body of persons or trust established for charitable purposes only, or must, according to the rules established by the relevant instrument, be applicable to charitable purposes only; and (ii) the exemption is available only so far as the income is applied to charitable purposes only. The first requirement depends on the construction of the relevant instrument; the second requirement depends on what is in fact done with the income as it arises from time to time. I will, for convenience, consider these requirements in their application to a corporate body, since that is the case now before me. They apply equally, mutatis mutandis, in the case of a trust created by a will or settlement.

" The first step is to construe the constituent instrument of the corporation, normally its memorandum of association. If one finds that all its expressed objects (leaving aside merely ancillary objects) are exclusively for charitable purposes, the first requirement is satisfied. In this connection, however, it is of the first importance to bear in mind that, with one or two qualifications not now in point, an object is not charitable unless it is directed to the public benefit: see, as regards education, *Oppenheim* v. *Tobacco Securities Trust Co. Ltd.*[62] and in particular the speech of LORD SIMONDS.[63] I will read only one sentence:

' It is a clearly established principle of the law of charity that a trust is not charitable unless it is directed to the public benefit.'

So a charitable object is, by definition, an object for the public benefit. Where the objects are expressed in general terms—*e.g.,* ' the advancement of education '—it is unnecessary and would be unusual to add specifically the words, ' for the public benefit '; but the object can only be regarded as charitable if those words are implied. The advancement of education for private benefit, or in part for public benefit and in part for private benefit, is not an exclusively charitable purpose.

" The second step is to consider how the income has in fact been

---

[62] [1951] A.C. 297.   [63] [1951] A.C. 297, 305.

applied. The words ' or charitable purposes only ' are repeated in the second requirement, but on analysis it seems clear that, where the first requirement is satisfied, then, so long as the income is expended at all (in contra-distinction to being accumulated), the second requirement must equally be satisfied if the application is within the powers of the corporation. If the purposes of the corporation are exclusively charitable, any application within those purposes must necessarily be charitable, too. Nevertheless, the repetition of the words, ' for charitable purposes only ' in the second requirement is striking. Here again, the element of public benefit is of the first importance. The objects of the corporation, in order that they may be exclusively charitable, must be confined to objects for the public benefit. Equally, the application of the income, if it is to be within those objects, must be for the public benefit. Conversely, the application of income otherwise than for the public benefit must be outside the objects and *ultra vires*. For example, under an object for the advancement of education, once that is accepted as an exclusively charitable object, the income must be applied for the advancement of education by way of public benefit. An application of income for the advancement of education by way of private benefit would be *ultra vires*, and nonetheless so by reason that, in the nature of things, the members of a private class are included in the public as a whole. This may perhaps explain the repetition of the words ' for charitable purposes only ' in the second requirement of the subsection.

" Counsel for the taxpayers advanced a simple and formidable argument: *viz*. (i) the taxpayers are established for specified educational purposes; (ii) those purposes are admittedly charitable purposes, so the first requirement is satisfied; (iii) the income has been applied for the specified educational purposes; and (iv) therefore the income has been applied for charitable purposes, and the second requirement is satisfied. It seems to me that this argument leaves out of account the element of public benefit. It is true that it is claimed by the taxpayers and admitted by the Crown that the educational purposes specified in the taxpayers' memorandum are charitable purposes, but this by definition implies that the purposes are for the public benefit. In order that the second requirement may be satisfied, it must equally be shown that their income has been applied not merely for educational purposes as expressed in the memorandum but for those educational purposes by way of public benefit. An application of income by way of private benefit would be *ultra vires*. It is not open to the taxpayers first to set up a claim which can only be sustained on the basis that the purposes expressed in the memorandum are for the public benefit, and then, when it comes to the application of the income, to look only to the purposes expressed in the memorandum, leaving the element of public benefit out of account. This point may be illustrated by considering the familiar example of a case in which a fund is settled on trust for the advancement of education in general terms and the income is applied for the education of the settlor's children. Counsel for the taxpayer does not shrink from the conclusion that such an application comes within the terms of the trust and satisfies the second requirement of the subsection. I think that it does neither.

" I understand from counsel for the taxpayers that he advanced the foregoing contention—and, I think, only this contention—before the Special Commissioners, although it is not very clearly reflected in their findings. The Special Commissioners were evidently much preoccupied by the case of *Re Koettgen*,[64] to which I shall refer in a moment. It was substantially the only argument which counsel for the taxpayers advanced before me as to the construction of the section.

" Counsel for the Crown based his argument on construction broadly on the lines which I have indicated above as being correct. He devoted much of his argument to repelling the application of the *Koettgen* case to the present one. In the *Koettgen* case a testatrix bequeathed her residuary estate on trust ' for the promotion and furtherance of commercial education. . . .' The will provided that

> ' The persons eligible as beneficiaries under the fund shall be persons of either sex who are British born subjects and who are desirous of educating themselves or obtaining tuition for a higher commercial career but whose means are insufficient or will not allow of their obtaining such education or tuition at their own expense. . . .'

The testatrix further directed that in selecting the beneficiaries

> ' It is my wish that the . . . trustees shall give a preference to any employees of J.B. & Co. (London), Ltd., or any members of the families of such employees; failing a sufficient number of beneficiaries under such description then the persons eligible shall be any persons of British birth as the . . . trustees may select provided that the total income to be available for benefiting the preferred beneficiaries shall not in any one year be more than seventy-five per cent. of the total available income for that year.'

In the event of the failure of those trusts there was a gift over to a named charity. It was admitted that the trust was for the advancement of education, but it was contended for the charity that having regard to the direction to prefer a limited class of persons the trusts were not of a sufficiently public nature to constitute valid charitable trusts. It was held that the gift to the primary class from whom the trustees could select beneficiaries contained the necessary element of benefit to the public, and that it was when that class was ascertained that the validity of the trust had to be determined; so that the subsequent

---

[64] [1954] Ch. 252.

direction to prefer, as to 75 per cent. of the income, a limited class did not affect the validity of the trust, which was accordingly a valid and effective charitable trust. *Oppenheim* v. *Tobacco Securities Trust Co. Ltd.*,[65] was distinguished. That, I think, accurately represents the effect of what the judge decided.

"The other case considered by the Special Commissioners was *Caffoor (Trustees of the Abdul Gaffoor Trust)* v. *Comr. of Income Tax, Colombo* [66] in the Privy Council. In that case by the terms of a trust deed executed in Ceylon in 1942 the trust income after the death of the grantor was to be applied by the board of trustees, the appellants, in their absolute discretion for all or any of a number of purposes, which included ' (2) (b) the education instruction or training in England or elsewhere abroad of deserving youths of the Islamic Faith ' in any department of human activity. The recipients of the benefits were to be selected by the board from the following classes of persons and in the following order: (i) male descendants along either the male or female line of the grantor or of any of his brothers or sisters failing whom youths of the Islamic Faith born of Muslim parents of the Ceylon Moorish community permanently resident in Colombo or elsewhere in Ceylon. It was held that in view of what was in effect the absolute priority to the benefit of the trust income which was conferred on the grantor's own family by clause 2 (b) (i) of the trust deed this was a family trust and not a trust of a public character solely for charitable purposes, and the income thereof was accordingly not entitled to the exemption claimed. *Re Compton, Powell* v. *Compton*,[67] *Oppenheim* v. *Tobacco Securities Trust Co. Ltd.*[68] and *Re Koettgen* [69] were considered. In his speech, Lord Radcliffe, giving the decision of the Privy Council, made the following comments [70] on the *Koettgen* case:

> ' It was argued with plausibility for the appellants that what this trust amounted to was a trust whose general purpose was the education of deserving young people of the Islamic Faith, and that its required public character was not destroyed by the circumstances that a preference in the selection of deserving recipients was directed to be given to members of the grantor's own family. Their lordships go with the argument so far as to say that they do not think that a trust which provides for the education of a section of the public necessarily loses its charitable status or its public character merely because members of the founder's family are mentioned explicitly as qualified to share in the educational benefits or even, possibly, are given some kind of preference in the

[65] [1951] A.C. 297.
[66] [1961] A.C. 584.
[67] [1945] Ch. 123.
[68] [1951] A.C. 297.
[69] [1954] Ch. 252.
[70] [1961] A.C. 297, 603.

selection. They part with the argument, however, because they do not consider that the trust which is now before them comes within the range of any such qualified exception.'

Lord Radcliffe went on to say that, there, the grantor's own family had, in effect, absolute priority. Then he said:

'In the Supreme Court judgment, much consideration was given to the English decision *Re Koettgen, Westminster Bank, Ltd.* v. *Family Welfare Association Trustees Ltd.* the facts of which have much in common with those of the present case.'

He then set out the effect of the *Koettgen* case, and proceeded [71]:

'It is not necessary for their lordships to say whether they would have put the same construction on the will there in question as the learned judge did, or whether they regard the distinction which he made as ultimately maintainable. The decision edges very near to being inconsistent with *Oppenheim's* case, but it is sufficient to say that the construction of the gift which was there adopted does not tally with the construction which their lordships are bound to place on the trust which is now before them. Here, the effect of the wording of para. 2 (b) (i) is to create a primary disposition of the trust income in favour of the family of the grantor.'

I am not concerned with the construction placed by Upjohn J. on the particular will before him in the *Koettgen* case. I will assume that the effect of the will was as he construed it, *i.e.*, that it constituted a primary public class and then directed that the trustees should give preference to employees of a named company and their families, those employees being necessarily members of the whole public class. Upjohn J., held the trust to be charitable. In the *Caffoor* case, Lord Radcliffe gave a very guarded and qualified assent to that principle. The decision in *Koettgen's* case is concerned with the character of a trust on the construction of the relevant instrument, and not with the application of income. Its relevance in the latter connection is presumably that, if in the instrument creating a trust for a public class a private class whose members are included in the public class can be mentioned specifically and accorded a preference, then a preferential application of income for the benefit of a private class whose members are comprised in a public class is a proper execution of a trust for the public class. This is a long step, and I do not feel obliged to take it.

" The position as regards the two requirements of the subsection is different at least in this respect, that a trust for public benefit with preference for a private class confers on the public an interest in every particle of income as it will arise in the future; the payment of income

---
[71] [1961] A.C. 297, 604.

to members of a private class excludes the public once and for all from any interest in the income so paid.

"'I think it right, however, to add that for myself I find considerable difficulty in the *Koettgen* decision. I should have thought that a trust for the public with preference for a private class comprised in the public might be regarded as a trust for the application of income at the discretion of the trustees between charitable and non-charitable objects. However, I am not concerned here to dispute the validity of the *Koettgen* decision. I only mention the difficulty which I feel as affording some additional reason for not applying the *Koettgen* decision by analogy in connection with the second requirement of the subsection.

"I return now to the present case. The taxpayers have claimed that the purposes of the taxpayers are exclusively charitable, which imports that the purposes must be for the public benefit. The Crown have admitted that claim. I have then to consider whether the taxpayers have applied their income within their expressed objects and by way of public benefit. There is no doubt that the application has been within their expressed objects, but has it been by way of the public benefit? In order to answer this question, I must, I think, look at the individuals and institutions for whose benefit the income has been applied, and seek to discern whether these individuals and institutions possess any, and, if so, what, relevant characteristics by virtue of which the income has been applied for their benefit. One may for this purpose look at the minutes of the council, circular letters and so forth. Counsel for the Crown at one time appeared to suggest that one might look at the actual intention of the members of the council. I do not think that that is so.

"When one makes this enquiry, one finds that between 75 per cent. and 85 per cent. of the income of the taxpayers has been expended on the education of children connected with Metal Box Co. Ltd. The taxpayers are intimately connected with Metal Box Co. Ltd., in the many respects found in the Case Stated. They derive most of their income from Metal Box Co. Ltd. The council of management, as the Special Commissioners found, has followed a policy of seeking applications for grants from employees and ex-employees of Metal Box Co. Ltd., though these applications are not, of course, always successful. The inference is inescapable that this part of the taxpayer's income— *i.e.*, 75 per cent. to 85 per cent.—has been expended for the benefit of these children by virtue of a private characteristic: *i.e.*, their connection with Metal Box Co. Ltd. Such an application is not by way of public benefit. It is on all fours with an application of 75 per cent. to 85 per cent. of the income of a trust fund on the education of a settlor's children. It follows, in my judgment, that, as regards the income which has been applied for the education of children of Metal Box Co. Ltd's. employees, the taxpayers have failed to satisfy the second requirement in the subsection, and that the claim for relief fails. No reason has been suggested why the taxpayers should not obtain relief in respect of income applied for the benefit of institutions and outside individuals; see the words " so far as " in the section.

" I recognise that this conclusion involves a finding that the council of management has acted *ultra vires* in applying the income of the taxpayers as it has done, albeit within the expressed objects of the taxpayers' memorandum. This conclusion follows from the basis on which the taxpayers have framed their objects and based their claim. It is of course open to a comparable body to frame its objects so as to make clear that its income may be applied for private as well as public purposes, but in that case it may not obtain tax relief. It does not seem to me that such a body can have it both ways. I propose, therefore, to allow this appeal." *Appeal allowed.*

Note

The doubts over *Re Koettgen* seem with respect to be well justified. After all, if *Re Koettgen* is correct it means that a settlor can successfully create a trust in favour of charity to which he attaches a direction that a specified portion of the income shall be applied in perpetuity to private non-charitable purposes. Should not the direction be regarded as repugnant to the primary trust for charity? Alternatively, if the fund is regarded as comprised of two definite parts, should not the charitable part be held valid and the non-charitable part void; but if the amount to be attributed to each part is indefinite, would not the vice of uncertainty render the whole trust void?

IV. TRUSTS FOR THE ADVANCEMENT OF RELIGION

This group of charitable trusts has its origin in that part of the preamble to the Statute of Charitable Uses 1601 which speaks of " the repair of churches "; but its scope extends to religious work generally, provided the work is exclusively religious [72] and contains an element of public benefit: *Gilmour* v. *Coats, infra.* The element of public benefit may be very small: *Re Watson* [73] where a trust " for the continuance of the work of God as it has been maintained by H and myself since 1942 by God's enabling . . ." was held charitable. The work consisted principally in the free distribution of tracts written by H. They were of no intrinsic merit but displayed a religious tendency and were fundamentalist in inspiration. They were of no utility except in confirming in their religious opinions the members of the " in-group " within which they were produced. Essentially, *Thornton* v. *Howe* [74] was followed where a trust for the publication of Joanna

---

[72] See *Dunne* v. *Byrne* [1912] A.C. 407; *Re Davies* (1933) 49 T.L.R. 5; *Farley* v. *Westminster Bank* [1939] A.C. 430; cf. *Re Garrard* [1907] 1 Ch. 382; *Re Simson* [1946] Ch. 299; *Re Norman* [1947] Ch. 349; *Re Eastes* [1948] Ch. 257; *Re Flinn* [1948] Ch. 241; *Re Rumball* [1955] 1 W.L.R. 1037; 71 L.Q.R. 465 (R. E. M.).

[73] [1973] 1 W.L.R. 1472; (1974) 90 L.Q.R. 4.

[74] (1862) 31 Beav. 14, 20 showing that the courts are ready to assume public benefit unless the doctrines are adverse to the very foundations of all religion, and that they are subversive of all morality.

Southcott's works was held charitable; she claimed that she was with child by the Holy Ghost and would give birth to a second Messiah.

If a gift is made to an ecclesiastic in his official name and by virtue of his office, then if no purposes are expressed in the gift the gift is for the charitable purposes inherent in the office.[75] However, if the purposes of the gift are expressed in terms not confining them to purposes charitable *stricto sensu* then the charitable character of the trustee will not make the gift charitable.[76]

GILMOUR v. COATS

House of Lords [1949] A.C. 426; [1949] L.J.R. 1034; 65 T.L.R. 234; 93 S.J. 355; [1949] 1 All E.R. 848 (Lords Simonds, du Parcq, Normand, Morton and Reid)

The income of a trust fund was to be applied to the purposes of a Carmelite convent, if those purposes were charitable. The convent was comprised of an association of strictly cloistered and purely contemplative nuns who were concerned with prayers and meditation, and who did not engage in any activities for the benefit of people outside the convent. In the view of the Roman Catholic Church, however, their prayers and meditation caused the intervention of God for the benefit of members of the public, and their life inside the convent provided an example of self-denial and concentration on religious matters which was beneficial to the public. It was held by Jenkins J.[77] that the trust was not a charitable one, and his decision was affirmed by the Court of Appeal.[78] The prioress of the convent appealed.

LORD SIMONDS: ". . . I need not go back beyond the case of *Cocks* v. *Manners*,[79] which was decided nearly eighty years ago by Wickens V.-C. In that case the testatrix left her residuary estate between a number of religious institutions, one of them being the Dominican convent at Carisbrooke, a community not differing in any material respect from the community of nuns now under consideration. The learned judge, who was, I suppose, as deeply versed in this branch of the law as any judge before or since (for he had been for many years junior counsel to the Attorney-General in equity cases), used these words,[80] which I venture to repeat, though they have already been cited in the courts below: ' On the Act [the statute of Elizabeth] unaffected

---

[75] *Re Spensley's W.T.* [1954] Ch. 233; *Re Rumball* [1956] Ch. 105; V. T. H. Delany (1960) 24 Conv.(N.S.) 306.
[76] *Re Simson* [1946] Ch. 299 (gift to vicar " for his work in the parish " charitable); *Farley* v. *Westminster Bank* [1939] A.C. 430 (gift to vicar and churchwardens " for parish work " not charitable); *Re Stratton* [1931] 1 Ch. 197 (gift to vicar " for parochial institutions or purposes " not charitable).
[77] [1947] 2 All E.R. 422.
[78] [1948] Ch. 430.
[79] (1871) L.R. 12 Eq. 574.
[80] *Ibid.* 585.

by authority I should certainly hold that the gift to the Dominican convent is neither within the letter nor the spirit of it; and no decision has been referred to which compels me to adopt a different conclusion. A voluntary association of women for the purpose of working out their own salvation by religious exercises and self-denial seems to me to have none of the requisites of a charitable institution, whether the word " charitable " is used in its popular sense or in its legal sense. It is said, in some of the cases, that religious purposes are charitable, but that can only be true as to religious services tending directly or indirectly towards the instruction or the edification of the public; an annuity to an individual, so long as he spent his time in retirement and constant devotion, would not be charitable, nor would a gift to ten persons, so long as they lived together in retirement and performed acts of devotion, be charitable. Therefore the gift to the Dominican convent is not, in my opinion, a gift on a charitable trust.'

" No case, said the learned Vice-Chancellor, had been cited to compel him to come to a contrary conclusion, nor has any such case been cited to your Lordships. Nor have my own researches discovered one. But since that date the decision in *Cocks* v. *Manners* has been accepted and approved in numerous cases.

" Apart from what I have called the final argument, which I will deal with later, the contention of the appellant rests, not on any change in the lives of the members of such a community as this, nor, from a wider aspect, on the emergence of any new conception of the public good, but solely on the fact that for the first time certain evidence of the value of such lives to a wider public together with new arguments based on that evidence has been presented to the court. Never before, it was urged, has the benefit to be derived from intercessory prayer and from edification been brought to the attention of the court; if it had been, the decision in *Cocks* v. *Manners* would, or at least should, have been otherwise.

" My Lords, I would speak with all respect and reverence of those who spend their lives in cloistered piety, and in this House of Lords spiritual and temporal, which daily commences its proceedings with intercessory prayers, how can I deny that the Divine Being may in His Wisdom think fit to answer them? But, my Lords, whether I affirm or deny, whether I believe or disbelieve, what has that to do with the proof which the court demands that a particular purpose satisfies the test of benefit to the community? Here is something which is manifestly not susceptible of proof. But, then it is said, this is a matter not of proof but of belief, for the value of intercessory prayer is a tenet of the Catholic faith, therefore, and in such a prayer there is benefit to the community. But it is just at this ' therefore ' that I must pause. It is, no doubt, true that the advancement of religion is, generally speaking, one of the heads of charity, but it does not follow from this that the court must accept as proved whatever a particular church believes. The faithful must embrace their faith believing where they cannot prove : the court can act only on proof. A gift to two or ten or a hundred cloistered nuns in the belief that their prayers will benefit the world at large does not from that belief alone derive validity any more than does the belief of any other donor for any other purpose. The importance of this case leads me to state my opinion in my own words but, having read again the judgment of the learned Master of the Rolls, I will add that I am in full agreement with what he says on this part of the case.

" I turn to the second of the alleged elements of public benefit, edification by example, and I think that this argument can be dealt with very shortly. It is, in my opinion, sufficient to say that this is some-thing too vague and intangible to satisfy the prescribed test. The test of public benefit has, I think, been developed in the last two centuries. Today it is beyond doubt that that element must be present. No court would be rash enough to attempt to define precisely or exhaustively what its content must be. But it would assume a burden which it could not discharge if now for the first time it admitted into the category of public benefit something so indirect, remote, imponderable and, I would add, controversial as the benefit which may be derived by others from the example of pious lives. The appellant called in aid the use by Wickens V.-C. of the word ' indirectly ' in the passage that I have cited from his judgment in *Cocks* v. *Manners*, but I see no reason to suppose that that learned judge had in mind any such question as your Lordships have to determine.

" I must now refer to certain cases on which the appellant relied. They consist of a number of cases in the Irish courts and *Re Caus*,[81] a decision of Luxmoore J. A consideration of the Irish cases shows that it has there been decided that a bequest for the saying of masses, whether in public or in private, is a good charitable bequest: see, *e.g.*, *Att.-Gen.* v. *Hall*[82] and *O'Hanlon* v. *Logue*.[83] And in *Re Caus* Luxmoore J. came to the same conclusion. I would expressly reserve my opinion on the question whether these decisions should be sustained in this House. So important a matter should not be decided except on a direct consideration of it. It is possible that, particularly in regard to the celebration of masses in public, good reason may be found for supporting a gift for such an object as both a legal and a charitable purpose. But it follows from what I have said in the earlier part of this opinion that I am unable to accept the view, which at least in the Irish cases is clearly expressed, that in intercessory prayer and edification that public benefit which is the condition of legal charity is to be found. It is, perhaps, significant that even in Ireland, where in regard to the say-ing of masses the law has thus been established, there is no consensus of opinion that a gift to a community of contemplative nuns is charitable :

---

[81] [1934] Ch. 162.
[82] [1897] 2 I.R. 426.
[83] [1906] 1 I.R. 247.

see *Munster and Leinster Bank* v. *Att.-Gen.*,[84] *Re Maguire* [85] and *Re Keogh.*[86] From the judgment of Black J. in the first-cited case I would quote these words,[87] which succinctly express my own view: ' There are perhaps few forms of human activity, good in themselves, but solely designed to benefit individuals associated for the purposes of securing that benefit, which may not have some repercussions or consequential effects beneficial to some section of the general community; and unless a further and sweeping inroad is to be made on the rule against perpetuities, the line must be drawn somewhere. *Cocks* v. *Manners* has drawn it.' Of the decision of Luxmoore J. in *Re Caus*, I would only say that his *ratio decidendi* is expressly stated to be,[88] ' first, that it (*i.e.,* a gift for the saying of masses) enables a ritual act to be performed which is recognised by a large proportion of Christian people to be the central act of their religion, and, secondly, that it assists in the endowment of priests whose duty it is to perform the ritual act.' The decision, therefore, does not assist the appellant's argument in the present case and I make no further comments on it.

    " It remains, finally, to deal with an argument which, as I have said, was not presented to the Court of Appeal but appears in the prioress's formal case. It is that the element of public benefit is supplied by the fact that qualification for admission to membership of the community is not limited to any group of persons but is open to any woman in the wide world who has the necessary vocation. Thus, it is said, just as the endowment of a scholarship open to public competition is a charity, so also a gift to enable any woman (or, presumably, any man) to enter a fuller religious life is a charity. To this argument, which, it must be admitted, has a speciously logical appearance, the first answer is that which I have indicated earlier in this opinion. There is no novelty in the idea that a community of nuns must, if it is to continue, from time to time obtain fresh recruits from the outside world. That is why a perpetuity is involved in a gift for the benefit of such a community, and it is not to be supposed that, to mention only three masters of this branch of the law, Wickens V.-C., Lord Lindley or Lord Macnaghten failed to appreciate the point. Yet, by direct decision or by way of emphatic example, a community such as this is by them regarded as the very type of religious institution which is not charitable. I know of no consideration applicable to this case which would justify this House in unsettling a rule of law which has been established so long and by such high authority. But that is not the only, nor, indeed, the most cogent, reason why I cannot accede to the appellant's argument. It is a trite saying that the law is life, not logic. But it is, I think, conspicuously true of the law of charity that it has been built up, not logically,

---

[84] [1940] I.R. 19.
[85] [1943] I.R. 238.
[86] [1945] I.R. 13.
[87] [1940] I.R. 19, 30–31.
[88] [1934] Ch. 162, 170.

but empirically. It would not, therefore, be surprising to find that, while in every category of legal charity some element of public benefit must be present, the court had not adopted the same measure in regard to different categories, but had accepted one standard in regard to those gifts which are alleged to be for the advancement of religion, and it may be yet another in regard to the relief of poverty. To argue by a method of syllogism or analogy from the category of education to that of religion ignores the historical process of the law. Nor would there be lack of justification for the divergence of treatment which is here assumed. For there is a legislative and political background peculiar to so-called religious trusts, which has, I think, influenced the development of the law in this matter. Thus, even if the simple argument that, if education is a good thing, then the more education the better, may appear to be irrefutable, to repeat that argument substituting ' religion ' for ' education ' is to ignore the principle, which I understand to be conceded, that not all religious purposes are charitable purposes. It was, no doubt, this consideration which led Wickens V.-C. to say [89] that a gift to a Dominican convent was ' one of the last gifts which the legislature which passed the Act would have thought of including in it.' Upon this final argument I would add this observation. I have stressed the empirical development of the law of charity and your Lordships may detect some inconsistency in an attempt to rationalise it. But it appears to me that it would be irrational to the point of absurdity, on the one hand, to deny to a community of contemplative nuns the character of a charitable institution, but, on the other, to accept as a charitable trust a gift which had no other object than to enable it to be maintained in perpetuity by recruitment from the outside world.

"Finally, I would say this. I have assumed for the purpose of testing this argument that it is a valid contention that a gift for the advancement of education is necessarily charitable if it is not confined within too narrow limits. But that assumption is itself difficult to justify. It may well be that the generality of the proposition is subject to at least two limitations. The first of them is implicit in the decision of Russell J. in *Re Hummeltenberg.*[90] The second is one that is not in the nature of things likely to occur, but if it can be imagined that it was made a condition of a gift for the advancement of education that its beneficiaries should lead a cloistered life and communicate to no one, and leave no record of the fruits of this study, I do not think that the charitable character of the gift could be sustained." [91] *Appeal dismissed.*

---

[89] (1871) L.R. 12 Eq. 574, 585.

[90] [1923] 1 Ch. 237 (administrative unworkability).

[91] The Nathan Committee on Charitable Trusts rejected the suggestion of the representatives of the Roman Catholic Church that trusts for the advancement of religion should be defined to include " the advancement of religion by those means which that religion believes and teaches are means by which it does advance it ": (1952) Cmnd. 8710, paras. 129-130: see also *Re Warre's W.T.* [1953] 1 W.L.R. 725. The Charities Act 1960 has not altered the law as illustrated in *Gilmour* v. *Coats.*

V. Trusts for Other Purposes Beneficial to the Community

This group of charitable trusts has its origin in the remaining charitable purposes enumerated in the preamble to the Statute of Charitable Uses 1601, and like the other groups it includes purposes within the spirit and intendment of those enumerated.

Thus a trust for the benefit of animals generally may be charitable, provided there is a benefit to the community in the execution of its terms: *Att.-Gen.* v. *Plowden, infra.*[92]

Trusts to abolish vivisection, which were once held charitable, are now invalid because (a) the advantages that would accrue from the abolition of vivisection are not commensurate with those that are derived from its continuance and (b) vivisection is permitted by legislation and "the law could not stultify itself by holding that it was for the public benefit that the law itself should be changed": *National Anti-Vivisection Society* v. *I.R.C., infra, sed quaere* as to (b). The case also emphasises that it is the opinion of the court and not of the settlor that determines whether or not the trust is beneficial to the community.[93]

Public benefit is an essential requirement of all charitable trusts except those for the relief of poverty.[94] The degree of benefit required for this residual group is certainly much greater than that required for religion and, from what was said by Lords Simonds and Somervell in *I.R.C.* v. *Baddeley*, may be greater than that required for education: Lord Reid, however, dissented and Lords Porter and Tucker left the point open.[95]

A purpose is not *ipso facto* charitable because it benefits the community in one way or another: it must also fall within the spirit and intendment of the instances enumerated in the Statute of Charitable Uses 1601: *Williams' Trustees* v. *I.R.C., infra*[96]; and a trust which is not a charitable trust cannot be changed into a charitable one by limiting the area in which it is to operate: *ibid.*

ATT.-GEN. v. PLOWDEN

Court of Appeal [1929] 1 Ch. 557; 167 L.T. 136 (Hanworth M.R. and Russell L.J., Lawrence L.J. dissenting)[97]

By her will, Mrs. Grove-Grady directed her trustees to hold her residuary real and personal estate on trust "for the founding and establishing forthwith or as soon as may be after my decease if not

---

[92] *Re Moss* [1949] W.N. 93 also.

[93] The American view set out in *Restatement of the Law of Trusts* (2nd ed.) para. 374, comment 1 is, "The Courts do not take sides or attempt to decide which of two conflicting views of promoting the social interest of the community is the better adapted to the purpose, even though the views are opposed to each other." Thus trusts for both armament and disarmament and vivisection and anti-vivisection should be charitable.

[94] See (1951) 15 Conv.(N.S.) 328 (S. G. Maurice); (1953) 31 Can.B.R. 537 (G. H. L. Fridman); (1938) 31 M.L.R. 138 (P. S. Atiyah); *Dingle* v. *Turner, supra,* p. 209.

[95] See note upon Recreational Charities Act 1958, *infra.*

[96] For a hard case which was held not to fall within the spirit and intendment of the statute, see *Re Cole* [1958] Ch. 877; 74 L.Q.R. 481 (R. E. M.); reluctantly followed in *Re Sahal's W.T.* [1958] 1 W.L.R. 1243.

[97] The decision was affirmed by the House of Lords, subject to a variation agreed on a compromise. See [1931] W.N. 89.

already founded in my lifetime (without the acquisition of any interest in land which cannot lawfully be acquired and held for charitable purposes) and the thereafter upholding and maintaining of a charitable institution to be called ' The Beaumont Animals Benevolent Society.' . . . Provided that all members of the committee and of the governing body and all officials . . . shall be and always have been declared anti-vivisectionists and opponents of all sport involving the pursuit or death of any stag . . . or any other animal." The objects were the acquisition (with authority) of land for the purpose of providing a refuge or refuges for the preservation of all animals, birds or other creatures not human, where they might be safe from human molestation, and the founding and supporting or providing of hospitals or homes for animals having no declared vivisectionist connected with the management. The residuary estate was valued at some £200,000. The trustees took out an originating summons to determine whether the trust was charitable.

Held, by Romer J., that the trust was charitable, in that the prevention of cruelty and suffering to the lower animals is an object which benefits the community by tending to promote public morality. The next-of-kin appealed successfully.

RUSSELL L.J.: " There can be no doubt that upon the authorities as they stand a trust in perpetuity for the benefit of animals may be a valid charitable trust if in the execution of the trust there is *necessarily* involved benefit to the public; for if this be a necessary result of the execution of the trust, the trust will fall within Lord Macnaghten's fourth class in *Pemsel's* case [98]—namely, ' trusts for other purposes beneficial to the community.'

" So far as I know there is no decision which upholds a trust in perpetuity in favour of animals upon any other ground than this, that the execution of the trust in the manner defined by the creator of the trust must produce some benefit to mankind. I cannot help feeling that in some instances matters have been stretched in favour of charities almost to bursting point; and that a decision benevolent to one doubtful charity has too often been the basis of a subsequent decision still more benevolent in favour of another.

" The cases have accordingly run to fine distinctions, and speaking for myself I doubt whether some dispositions in favour of animals held to be charitable under former decisions could be held charitable today. For instance, anti-vivisection societies, which were held to be charities by Chitty J. in *Re Foveaux* [99] and were described by him as near the borderline, might possibly in the light of later knowledge in regard to the benefits accruing to mankind from vivisection be held not to be charities. The difficulty arises when you apply the test of benefit to the public to each particular case. The will of Mrs. Grove-Grady

[98] [1891] A.C. 531, 583.
[99] [1895] 2 Ch. 501. See *National Anti-Vivisection Soc.* v. *I.R.C., infra,* p. 257.

is no exception, for it presents a very difficult problem. . . . The testatrix calls the proposed institution a 'charitable institution'—but this will not make the trust valid if in law the institution is not charitable. To ascertain this we must ascertain the objects of the institution and the purposes for which the moneys may consistently with the terms of the trust be applied. . . . It comes down to this, that the residuary estate may be applied in acquiring a tract of land, in turning it into an animal sanctuary, and keeping a staff of employees to ensure that no human being shall ever molest or destroy any of the animals there. Is that a good charitable trust within the authorities?

"In my opinion it is not. It is merely a trust to secure that all animals within the area shall be free from molestation or destruction by man. It is not a trust directed to ensure absence or diminution of pain or cruelty in the destruction of animal life. If this trust is carried out according to its tenor, no animal within the area may be destroyed by man, no matter how necessary that destruction may be in the interests of mankind or in the interests of the other denizens of the area or in the interests of the animal itself; and no matter how painlessly such destruction may be brought about. It seems to me impossible to say that the carrying out of such a trust necessarily involves benefit to the public. Beyond perhaps hearing of the existence of the enclosure the public does not come into the matter at all. Consistently with the trust the public could be excluded from entering the area or even looking into it. . . .

"It was, however, argued before us that a trust merely for the protection and benefit of animals must be a good charity, and for this proposition reliance was placed on the decision of this court in *Re Wedgwood*.[1] . . . If the argument on this point means that it is unnecessary to find a benefit to the community as an ingredient of the charitable trust, in other words that a gift for the benefit of animals simpliciter which involves no such benefit is a good charity, the answer is that *Re Wedgwood* decides no such thing. All the members of the court discovered in the trust a benefit to the community. Unless such a benefit is involved in the trust, you could not bring the case within Lord Macnaghten's fourth class in *Pemsel's* case. If the argument is this, that *Re Wedgwood* lays down as a principle that every trust for the protection and benefit of any animals necessarily involves a benefit to the community and is therefore charitable, again the answer is that *Re Wedgwood* lays down no such principle. . . .

"I think Romer J. erred in this case in attributing too wide an effect

1 [1915] 1 Ch. 113. In that case a testatrix gave her residuary estate upon (a secret) trust for the protection and benefit of animals. She had assented to the trustee's suggestion that helping forward the movement for the humane slaughtering of animals and the movement to provide municipal abattoirs should be within the scope of what she contemplated, but gave the trustee a free hand as to the mode in which he would give effect to her object. It was held by the Court of Appeal that the trust was charitable.

to the decision in *Re Wedgwood*. He takes the view, I think, that the case decided, or that the decision involves, that every gift for the benefit of the lower animals must tend to promote public morality, and must therefore be charitable. As indicated above, I do not take this view. I think the decision covers a much narrower field and is based upon the expressed desire of the testatrix to diminish cruelty, out of which the court felt itself able to find that benefit to the community must necessarily follow from the execution of the trust. . . ." *Appeal allowed.*

NATIONAL ANTI-VIVISECTION SOCIETY v. INLAND REVENUE COMMISSIONERS

House of Lords [1948] A.C. 31; 177 L.T. 226; [1947] L.J.R. 1112; 63 T.L.R. 424; [1947] 2 All E.R. 217 (Lords Simon, Wright, Simonds and Normand; Lord Porter dissenting)

The question was whether the appellant society was a body established for charitable purposes only within the meaning of section 37 of the Income Tax Act 1918 and accordingly entitled to exemption from income tax upon the income of its investments. The Special Commissioners for the purposes of the Income Tax Acts held that they were so entitled, but this decision was reversed by Macnaghten J.,[2] whose judgment was upheld by the Court of Appeal [3] (Mackinnon and Tucker L.JJ., Greene M.R. dissenting). The society appealed unsuccessfully.

LORD SIMONDS: " . . . The first point is whether a main purpose of the society is of such a political character that the court cannot regard it as charitable. The second point is whether the court, for the purpose of determining whether the object of the society is charitable, may disregard the finding of fact that any assumed public benefit in the direction of the advancement of morals and education was far outweighed by the detriment to medical science and research and, consequently, to the public health, which would result if the society succeeded in achieving its objects, and that, on balance, the object of the society, so far from being for the public benefit, was gravely injurious thereto.

"My Lords, on the first point the learned Master of the Rolls cites in his judgment [4] a passage from the speech of Lord Parker in *Bowman* v. *Secular Society Ltd.*[5]: ' . . . a trust for the attainment of political objects has always been held invalid, not because it is illegal . . . but because the court has no means of judging whether a proposed change in the law will or will not be for the public benefit . . .' Lord Parker is here considering the possibility of a valid charitable trust, and nothing

---

[2] [1945] 2 All E.R. 529.
[3] [1946] K.B. 185.
[4] [1946] K.B. 185, 207.
[5] [1917] A.C. 406, 442.

else, and when he says ' has always been held invalid ' he means ' has always been held not to be a valid charitable trust.' The learned Master of the Rolls found this authoritative statement upon a branch of the law, with which no one was more familiar than Lord Parker, to be inapplicable to the present case for two reasons, first, because he felt difficulty in applying the words to ' a change in the law which is in common parlance a " non-political " question ' and, secondly, because he thought they could not in any case apply when the desired legislation is ' merely ancillary to the attainment of what is *ex hypothesi* a good charitable object.'

"My Lords, if I may deal with this second reason first, I cannot agree that in this case an alteration in the law is merely ancillary to the attainment of a good charitable object. In a sense, no doubt, since legislation is not an end in itself, every law may be regarded as ancillary to the object which its provisions are intended to achieve. But that is not the sense in which it is said that a society has a political object. Here the finding of the commissioners is itself conclusive. ' We are satisfied,' they say, ' that the main object of the society is the total abolition of vivisection . . . and (for that purpose) the repeal of the Cruelty to Animals Act 1876, and the substitution of a new enactment prohibiting vivisection altogether.' This is a finding that the main purpose of the society is the compulsory abolition of vivisection by Act of Parliament. What else can it mean? And how else can it be supposed that vivisection is to be abolished? Abolition and suppression are words that connote some form of compulsion. It can only be by Act of Parliament that that element can be supplied. Upon this point I must with respect differ both from the learned Master of the Rolls and from Chitty J., whose decision in *Re Foveaux* [6] I shall later consider. Coming to the conclusion that it is a main object, if not the main object, of the society to obtain an alteration of the law, I ask whether that can be a charitable object, even if its purposes might otherwise be regarded as charitable.

"My Lords, I see no reason for supposing that Lord Parker, in the cited passage, used the expression ' political objects ' in any narrow sense or was confining it to objects of acute political controversy. On the contrary, he was, I think, propounding familiar doctrine, nowhere better stated than in a textbook which has long been regarded as of high authority, but appears not to have been cited for this purpose to the courts below (as it certainly was not to your Lordships), *Tyssen on Charitable Bequests.* The passage [7] is worth repeating at length : ' It is a common practice for a number of individuals amongst us to form an association for promoting some change in the law, and it is worth our while to consider the effect of a gift to such an association. It is clear that such an association is not of a charitable nature. However desirable

6 [1895] 2 Ch. 501.
7 1st ed., 1898, p. 176.

the change may really be, the law could not stultify itself by holding that it was for the public benefit that the law itself should be changed. Each court in deciding on the validity of a gift must decide on the principle that the law is right as it stands. On the other hand, such a gift could not be held void for illegality.'

" Lord Parker uses slightly different language, but means the same thing, when he says that the court has no means of judging whether a proposed change in the law will or will not be for the public benefit. It is not for the court to judge and the court has no means of judging. The same question may be looked at from a slightly different angle. One of the tests, and a crucial test, whether a trust is charitable lies in the competence of the court to control and reform it. I would remind your Lordships that it is the King as *parens patriae* who is the guardian of charity, and that it is the right and duty of his Attorney-General to intervene and inform the court if the trustees of a charitable trust fall short of their duty. So too it is his duty to assist the court, if need be, in the formulation of a scheme for the execution of a charitable trust. But, my Lords, is it for a moment to be supposed that it is the function of the Attorney-General, on behalf of the Crown, to intervene and demand that a trust shall be established and administered by the court, the object of which is to alter the law in a manner highly preju- dicial, as he and His Majesty's Government may think, to the welfare of the state? This very case would serve as an example if upon the footing that it was a charitable trust it became the duty of the Attorney-General on account of its maladministration to intervene. There is, undoubtedly, a paucity of judicial authority on this point. It may fairly be said that *De Themmines* v. *De Bonnevale*,[8] to which Lord Parker referred in *Bowman's* case, turned on the fact that the trust there in question was held to be against public policy. In *Commissioners of Inland Revenue* v. *Temperance Council*[9] the principle was clearly recognised by Rowlatt J. as it was in *Re Hood*.[10] But in truth the reason of the thing appears to me so clear that I neither expect nor require much authority. I conclude upon this part of the case that a main object of the society is political and for that reason the society is not established for charitable purposes only. I would only add that I would reserve my opinion upon the hypo- thetical example of a private enabling Act, which was suggested in the course of the argument. I do not regard *Re Villers-Wilkes*[11] as a decision that a legacy which had for its main purpose the passing of such an Act is charitable.

" The second question raised in this appeal . . is of wider im- portance, and I must say at once that I cannot reconcile it with my conception of a court of equity, that it should take under its care and administer a trust, however well intentioned its creator, of which

---

[8] (1828) 5 Russ. 288.
[9] (1926) 136 L.T. 27.
[10] [1931] 1 Ch. 240, 250, 252.
[11] (1895) 72 L.T. 323.

the consequence would be calamitous to the community. [His Lordship made a brief review of the origin of the equitable jurisdiction in matters of charity, and continued:]

" My Lords, this then being the position, that the court determined 'one by one' whether particular named purposes were charitable, applying always the overriding test whether the purpose was for the public benefit, and that the King as *parens patriae* intervened *pro bono publico* for the protection of charities, what room is there for the doctrine, which has found favour with the learned Master of the Rolls, and has been so vigorously supported at the Bar of the House, that the court may disregard the evils that will ensue from the achievement by the society of its ends? It is to me a strange and bewildering idea that the court must look so far and no farther, must see a charitable purpose in the intention of the society to benefit animals, and thus elevate the moral character of men, but must shut its eyes to the injurious results to the whole human and animal creation. I will readily concede that, if the purpose is within one of the heads of charity forming the first three classes in the classification which Lord Macnaghten borrowed from Sir Samuel Romilly's argument in *Morice* v. *Bishop of Durham*,[12] the court will easily conclude that it is a charitable purpose. But even here to give the purpose the name of 'religious' or 'educational' is not to conclude the matter. It may yet not be charitable if the religious purpose is illegal or the educational purpose is contrary to public policy. Still there remains the overriding question: Is it *pro bono publico*? It would be another strange misreading of Lord Macnaghten's speech in *Pemsel's* case [13] (one was pointed out in *Re Macduff* [14]) to suggest that he intended anything to the contrary. I would rather say that, when a purpose appears broadly to fall within one of the familiar categories of charity, the court will assume it to be for the benefit of the community and therefore charitable unless the contrary is shown, and further that the court will not be astute in such a case to defeat upon doubtful evidence the avowed benevolent intention of a donor. But, my Lords, the next step is one that I cannot take. Where upon the evidence before it the court concludes that, however well intentioned the donor, the achievement of his object will be greatly to the public disadvantage, there can be no justification for saying that it is a charitable object. If and so far as there is any judicial decision to the contrary, it must, in my opinion, be regarded as inconsistent with principle and be overruled. This proposition is clearly stated by Russell J. in *Re Hummeltenberg*.[15] ' In my opinion,' he said,[16] ' the question whether a gift is or may be operative for the public benefit is a question to be answered by the court by forming an opinion upon

[12] (1805) 10 Ves. 522.
[13] [1891] A.C. 531, *supra.*
[14] [1896] 2 Ch. 451.
[15] [1923] 1 Ch. 237, *supra.*
[16] *Ibid.* 242.

the evidence before it.' This statement of that very learned judge follows immediately upon some observations on the cases of *Re Foveaux* and *Re Cranston*,[17] which were the mainstay of the appellant's argument.

"My Lords, what I have said is enough to conclude this case. But there is an important passage in the judgment of the Master of the Rolls which I ought not to ignore. ' I do not see,' he says,[18] ' how at this time of day it can be asserted that a particular exemplification of those objects is not beneficial merely because in that particular case the achievement of those objects would deprive mankind of certain consequential benefits, however important those benefits may be. If this were not so, it would always be possible, by adducing evidence which was not before the court on the original occasion, to attack the status of an established charitable object to the great confusion of trustees and all others concerned. Many existing charities would no doubt fail if such a criterion were to be adopted.' I venture with great respect to think that this confuses two things. A purpose regarded in one age as charitable may in another be regarded differently. I need not repeat what was said by Jessel M.R. in *Re Campden Charities*. A bequest in the will of a testator dying in 1700 might be held valid upon the evidence then before the court, but, upon different evidence, held invalid if he died in 1900. So, too, I conceive that an anti-vivisection society might at different times be differently regarded. But this is not to say that a charitable trust, when it has once been established, can ever fail. If, by a change in social habits and needs, or, it may be, by a change in the law, the purpose of an established charity becomes superfluous or even illegal, or if, with increasing knowledge, it appears that a purpose once thought beneficial is truly detrimental to the community, it is the duty of trustees of an established charity to apply to the court or, in suitable cases, to the Charity Commissioners, or, in educational charities,[18a] to the Minister of Education, and ask that a *cy-près* scheme may be established. And I can well conceive that there might be cases in which the Attorney-General would think it his duty to intervene to that end. A charity once established does not die, though its nature may be changed. But it is wholly consistent with this that in a later age the court should decline to regard as charitable a purpose to which in an earlier age that quality would have been ascribed, with the result that (unless a general charitable intention could be found) a gift for that purpose would fail. I cannot share the apprehension of the Master of the Rolls that great confusion will be caused if the court declines to be bound by the beliefs and knowledge of a past age in considering whether a particular purpose is today for the benefit of the community. But if it is so, then I say that it is the lesser of two evils. . . ." *Appeal dismissed.*

---

[17] [1898] 1 I.R. 431.
[18] [1946] K.B. 185, 205. [18a] Not after February 1, 1974: S.I. 1973 No. 1661.

WILLIAMS' TRUSTEES v. INLAND REVENUE COMMISSIONERS

House of Lords [1947] A.C. 447; 176 L.T. 462; 63 T.L.R. 352; [1947] 1 All E.R. 513 (Lords Simon, Wright, Porter, Simonds and Normand)

A trust was established for the purpose of maintaining an institute " for the benefit of Welsh people resident in or near or visiting London with a view to creating a centre in London for promoting the moral, social, spiritual and educational welfare of Welsh people, and fostering the study of the Welsh language and of Welsh history, literature, music and art." [19] The trust property consisted of two blocks of property, one of which was let out to tenants, and the other occupied by the London Welsh Association Ltd. This association had been incorporated for substantially the same purposes as those contained in the deed of trust which are set out above. The trustees applied the rents of the first block and made certain gifts to the association intending that they should be directed to the following purposes: public lectures and debates, a music club, literary and educational classes, the maintenance of the headquarters' premises, badminton and table-tennis clubs, dances, whist- and bridge-drives, an annual dinner and garden-party, a weekly social and dance, and the provision of a central information bureau. The trustees admitted that the purposes of the association were not exclusively charitable, but contended that they themselves were trustees of a trust established for charitable purposes only, and that in applying the rents of the first block of trust property to the purposes of the association they had applied them to charitable purposes only and that accordingly they were entitled to exemption from income tax in respect of the rents of that property.[20]

The Court of Appeal held [21] that on the true construction of the trust deed the property was not vested in the trustees for charitable purposes only, and on the facts the rents applied to the purpose of the association were not applied for charitable purposes only. The trustees appealed unsuccessfully.

LORD SIMONDS: ". . . it is just because the purpose of the trust deed in this case is said to be beneficial to the community or a section of the community, and for no other reason, that its charitable character is asserted. It is not alleged that the trust is (1) for the benefit of the community and (2) beneficial in a way which the law regards as

---

[19] These purposes might today be regarded as charitable by the Recreational Charities Act 1958, *infra*, p. 268, and might therefore satisfy one of the two criteria of a valid charitable trust. It would still be necessary to prove the existence of the other criterion, namely, an element of public benefit. *Williams' Trustees* v. *I.R.C.* remains an important authority on the latter requirement.

[20] See s. 37 (1) of the Income Tax Act 1918, later ss. 447, 448 of the Income Tax Act 1952 and now Income and Corporation Taxes Act 1970, s. 360.

[21] [1945] 2 All E.R. 236 (Scott, Lawrence and Morton L.JJ.).

charitable. Therefore, as it seems to me, in its mere statement the claim is imperfect and must fail.

"My Lords, the cases in which the question of charity has come before the courts are legion, and no one who is versed in them will pretend that all the decisions, even of the highest authority, are easy to reconcile, but I will venture to refer to one or two of them . . . In *Houston* v. *Burns* [22] the question was as to the validity of a gift ' for such public benevolent or charitable purposes in connection with the parish of Lesmahagow or the neighbourhood ' as might be thought proper. This was a Scottish case, but upon the point now under consideration there is no difference between English and Scottish law. It was argued that the limitation of the purpose to a particular locality was sufficient to validate the gift, that is to say, though purposes beneficial to the community might fail, yet purposes beneficial to a localised section of the community were charitable. That argument was rejected by this House. If the purposes are not charitable *per se*, the localisation of them will not make them charitable. It is noticeable that Lord Finlay L.C. expressly overrules a decision or dictum of Lord Romilly to the contrary effect in *Dolan* v. *MacDermot*. [23] . . .

"My Lords, I must mention another aspect of this case, which was discussed in the Court of Appeal and in the argument at your Lordships' Bar. It is not expressly stated in the preamble to the statute, but it was established in the Court of Chancery and, so far as I am aware, the principle has been consistently maintained, that a trust to be charitable must be of a public character. It must not be merely for the benefit of particular private individuals. If it is it will not be in law a charity, though the benefit taken by those individuals is of the very character stated in the preamble. The rule is thus stated by Lord Wrenbury in *Verge* v. *Somerville* [24] ' To ascertain whether a gift constitutes a valid charitable trust so as to escape being void on the ground of perpetuity, a first inquiry must be whether it is public—whether it is for the benefit of the community or of an appreciably important class of the community. The inhabitants of a parish or town, or any particular class of such inhabitants, may for instance be the objects of such a gift, but private individuals, or a fluctuating body of private individuals, cannot.' It is, I think, obvious that this rule, necessary as it is, must often be difficult of application, and so the courts have found. Fortunately, perhaps, though Lord Wrenbury put it first, the question does not arise at all if the purpose of the gift, whether for the benefit of a class of inhabitants or of a fluctuating body of private individuals, is not itself charitable. I may, however, refer to a recent case in this House which in some aspects resembles the present case. In *Keren* v. *Inland Revenue Commissioners* [25] a company had been formed which had as its main

---

[22] [1918] A.C. 337.
[23] (1867) L.R. 5 Eq. 60, 62.
[24] [1924] A.C. 496, 499.
[25] [1932] A.C. 650.

object (to put it shortly) the purchase of land in Palestine, Syria or other parts of Turkey in Asia and the peninsula of Sinai for the purpose of settling Jews on such lands. In its memorandum it took numerous other powers which were to be exercised only in such a way as should, in the opinion of the company, be conducive to the attainment of the primary object. No part of the income of the company was distributable among its members. It was urged that the company was established for charitable purposes for numerous reasons, with only one of which I will trouble your Lordships, namely, that it was established for the benefit of the community or of a section of the community, whether the association was for the benefit of Jews all over the world, or of the Jews repatriated in the Promised Land. Lord Tomlin,[26] dealing with the argument that I have just mentioned on the footing that if benefit to a ' community ' could be established the purpose might be charitable, proceeded to examine the problem in that aspect and sought to identify the community. He failed to do so, finding it neither in the community of all Jews throughout the world nor in that of the Jews in the region presented for settlement. It is perhaps unnecessary to pursue the matter. Each case must be judged on its own facts and the dividing-line is not easily drawn, but the difficulty of finding the community in the present case, when the definition of ' Welsh people ' in the first deed is remembered, would not, I think, be less than that of finding the community of Jews in *Keren's* case.

"At an early stage in this opinion I said that cases on the law of charity are not easy to reconcile. I would not be taken as suggesting that there is any doubt about the present case. I agree with the judges of the Court of Appeal that, on the construction which they have adopted of the trust deed—and it is the only possible construction—the property is not vested in the appellants for charitable purposes only. It is clear, as I have already said, that they have not applied the income for charitable purposes only, and I do not doubt that they have applied it strictly in accordance with their trust. ' Matters,' said Russell L.J., ' have been stretched in favour of charities almost to bursting point ': see *Re Grove-Grady*.[27] That point would be reached if your Lordships held that this trust deed has a purpose which falls within the spirit and intendment of the preamble. It clearly does not, and, if it does not, let the community be what you will, let the purpose be as beneficial as you like, here is no charity.

"My Lords, it would not be right for me in a case which raises in such a general form the broad question of charitable trusts to ignore a line of authorities relied on by the appellants. More accurately, I think, there are two lines of authorities which are apt to converge and cross each other. There is first the class of case of which *Re Smith*[28] is typical.

[26] *Ibid.* 659.
[27] [1929] 1 Ch. 557, 582, *supra*, p. 255.
[28] [1932] 1 Ch. 153.

In that case the testator gave his residuary estate 'unto my country England for its own use and benefit absolutely' [*sic*]. This was held to be a good charitable trust. Here no particular purpose or benefit was defined. Secondly, there is the type of case of which *Goodman* v. *Saltash* [29] may be regarded as the prototype. There Lord Selborne L.C. used the words so often cited in the reports: 'A gift subject to a condition or trust for the benefit of the inhabitants of a parish or town or of any particular class of such inhabitants is (as I understand the law) a charitable trust.' In the one class of case there is no particularity of benefit and the widest range of beneficiary, in the other the beneficiaries are localised and the nature of the benefit defined. How are these cases to be reconciled with the decisions of this House to which I earlier referred? In *Tudor on Charities* it is said [30]: 'It is hard to avoid the conclusion that the foregoing cases, which establish that gifts for the benefit of particular districts are charitable, are anomalous. They cannot be related to the Statute of Elizabeth, and they logically involve the proposition that purposes which are not charitable in the world at large are charitable if confined to a specified locality, for public or benevolent purposes are not charitable, while there is nothing to prevent the trustees of a fund given for the benefit of a parish from spending it upon public or benevolent purposes, and yet the gift of such a fund is charitable. Nevertheless, the gift for public purposes in a particular parish is not charitable.' Your Lordships may think that this sounds like a cry of despair and, in truth, there is some ground for it, but I would suggest that it is possible to justify as charitable a gift to 'my country England' on the ground that, where no purpose is defined, a charitable purpose is implicit in the context. It is at least not excluded by the express prescription of 'public' purposes. Where the gift is localised, but the nature of the benefit is defined, no reconstruction is possible except on the assumption that the particular purpose was in each case regarded as falling within the spirit and intendment of the preamble to the Statute of Elizabeth, though I find it difficult to ascribe this quality to the benefit taken by the freemen of Saltash. If this affords no solution of the problem, I can only invite your Lordships to maintain the principles which have consistently been asserted in this House over the last fifty years in this difficult and intricate branch of the law. . . ." *Appeal dismissed*.

INCORPORATED COUNCIL OF LAW REPORTING FOR ENGLAND AND WALES v. ATTORNEY-GENERAL

Court of Appeal [1972] Ch. 73; [1971] 3 W.L.R. 853; [1971] 3 All E.R. 1029

This decision, as already seen,[31] turned primarily upon Lord

---

[29] (1882) 7 App.Cas. 633, 642.
[30] 5th ed., p. 45. See also *Re Strakosch* [1949] Ch. 529
[31] *Supra*, p. 225.

Macnaghten's secondary category but the following extract from the judgment of Russell L.J. illuminates the present approach of the court to Lord Macnaghten's fourth category (which Sachs and Buckley L.JJ. were prepared to find applicable as well as the second category).

RUSSELL L.J.: "... I come now to the question whether, if the main purpose of the Association is (as I think it is) to further the sound development and administration of the law in this country, and if (as I think it is) that is a purpose beneficial to the community or of general public utility, that purpose is charitable according to the law of England and Wales. On this point the law is rooted in the Statute of Elizabeth,[32] a statute whose object was the oversight and reform of abuses in the administration of property devoted by donors to purposes which were regarded as worthy of such protection as being charitable. The preamble to the statute listed certain examples of purposes worthy of such protection. These were from an early stage regarded merely as examples, and have through the centuries been regarded as examples or guide-posts for the courts in the differing circumstances of a developing civilisation and economy. Sometimes recourse has been had by the courts to the instances given in the preamble in order to see whether in a given case sufficient analogy may be found with something specifically stated in the preamble, or sufficient analogy with some decided case in which already a previous sufficient analogy has been found. Of this approach perhaps the most obvious example is the provision of crematoria by analogy with the provision of burial grounds by analogy with the upkeep of churchyards by analogy with the repair of churches. On other occasions a decision in favour or against a purpose being charitable has been based in terms on a more general question whether the purpose is or is not within 'the spirit and intendment' of the Elizabethan statute and in particular its preamble. Again (and at an early stage in development) whether the purpose is within 'the equity' or within 'the mischief' of the statute. Again whether the purpose is charitable 'in the same sense' as purposes within the purview of the statute. I have much sympathy with those who say that these phrases do little of themselves to elucidate any particular problem. 'Tell me,' they say, 'what you define when you speak of spirit, intendment, equity, mischief, the same sense, and I will tell you whether a purpose is charitable according to law. But you never define. All you do is sometimes to say that a purpose is none of these things. I can understand it when you say that the preservation of sea walls is for the safety of lives and property, and therefore by analogy the voluntary provision of lifeboats and fire brigades are charitable. I can even follow you as far as crematoria. But these other generalities teach me nothing.' I say I have much sympathy for such an approach; but it seems to me to be unduly and improperly

---

[32] 1601, 43 Eliz. 1, c. 4.

restrictive. The Statute of Elizabeth was a statute to reform abuses; in such circumstances and in that age the courts of this country were not inclined to be restricted in their implementation of Parliament's desire for reform to particular examples given by the statute, and they deliberately kept open their ability to intervene when they thought necessary in cases not specifically mentioned, by applying as the test whether any particular case of abuse of funds or property was within the ' mischief ' or the ' equity ' of the statute.

" For myself I believe that this rather vague and undefined approach is the correct one, with analogy its handmaid, and that when considering Lord Macnaghten's fourth category in *Pemsel's* case [33] of ' other purposes beneficial to the community ' (or as phrased by Sir Samuel Romilly [34] ' objects of general public utility ') the courts, in consistently saying that not all such are necessarily charitable in law, are in substance accepting that if a purpose is shown to be so beneficial or of such utility it is prima facie charitable in law, but have left open a line of retreat based on the equity of the statute in case they are faced with a purpose (*e.g.*, a political purpose) which could not have been within the contemplation of the statute even if the then legislators had been endowed with the gift of foresight into the circumstances of later centuries.

" In a case such as the present, in which in my view the object cannot be thought otherwise than beneficial to the community and of general public utility, I believe the proper question to ask is whether there are any grounds for holding it to be outside the equity of the statute; and I think the answer to that is here in the negative. I have already touched on its essential importance to our rule of law. If I look at the somewhat random examples in the preamble to the statute I find in the repair of bridges, havens, causeways, sea banks and highways examples of matters which if not looked after by private enterprise must be a proper function and responsibility of government, which would afford strong ground for a statutory expression by Parliament of anxiety to prevent misappropriation of funds voluntarily dedicated to such matters. It cannot I think be doubted that if there were not a competent and reliable set of reports of judicial decisions, it would be a proper function and responsibility of government to secure their provision for the due administration of the law. It was argued that the specific topics in the preamble that I have mentioned are all concerned with concrete matters, and that so also is the judicially accepted opinion that the provision of a court house is a charitable purpose. But whether the search be for analogy or for the equity of the statute this seems to me to be too narrow or refined an approach. I cannot accept that the provision, in order to facilitate the proper administration of the law, of the walls and other physical

---

[33] [1891] A.C. 531, 583.
[34] In *Morice* v. *Bishop of Durham* (1805) 10 Ves. 522, 531.

facilities of a court house is a charitable purpose, but that the dissemination by accurate and selective reporting of knowledge of a most important part of the law to be there administered is not.

" In my judgment accordingly the purpose for which the Association is established is exclusively charitable in the sense of Lord Macnaghten's fourth category."

VI. The Provision of Facilities for Recreation in the Interests of Social Welfare

The Recreational Charities Act 1958 [35]

Section 1.—(1) Subject to the provisions of this Act, it shall be and be deemed always to have been charitable to provide, or assist in the provision of, facilities for recreation or other leisure-time occupation, if the facilities are provided in the interests of social welfare:

Provided that nothing in this section shall be taken to derogate from the principle that a trust or institution to be charitable must be for the public benefit.

(2) The requirement of the foregoing subsection that the facilities are provided in the interests of social welfare shall not be treated as satisfied unless—

(a) the facilities are provided with the object of improving the conditions of life for the persons for whom the facilities are primarily intended; and

(b) either—

(i) those persons have need of such facilities as aforesaid by reason of their youth, age, infirmity or disablement, poverty or social and economic circumstances; or

(ii) the facilities are to be available to the members or female members of the public at large.

(3) Subject to the said requirement, subsection (1) of this section applies in particular to the provision of facilities at village halls, community centres and women's institutes, and to the provision and maintenance of grounds and buildings to be used for purposes of recreation or leisure-time occupation, and extends to the provision of facilities for those purposes by the organising of any activity.

[Section 2 makes special provision for trusts for miners' welfare; section 3 makes it clear that the Act does not restrict the purposes which are charitable independently of the Act, makes provision for saving past transactions, and extends the ordinary time-limits for claiming repayment of income tax and excess stamp duty; and section 4 enables the Parliament of Northern Ireland to enact similar legislation in relation to the law of charity in Northern Ireland.]

---

[35] See S. G. Maurice, " Recreational Charities " (1959) 23 Conv.(n.s.) 15; (1958) 21 M.L.R. 534 (L. Price).

Note

The Act was passed to remedy a defect in the law revealed by the House of Lords in *I.R.C.* v. *Baddeley*.[36] The short issue in that case was whether a conveyance of land to trustees should be stamped at a reduced rate under section 13 of the Stamp Act 1891, on the ground that the trusts upon which it was held were exclusively charitable. The objects of the trusts were " the moral, social and physical well-being of persons resident in West Ham and Leyton who for the time being were or were likely to become members of the Methodist Church and who were of insufficient means otherwise to enjoy the advantages provided." The method by which the objects were to be attained was " by the provision of facilities for moral, social and physical training and recreation and by promoting and encouraging all forms of such activities." The House of Lords by a majority (Lords Simonds, Porter, Tucker and Somervell; Lord Reid dissenting) held that the objects were not exclusively charitable. The word " social" included worthy objects of benevolence which were not charitable in the legal sense and the trust accordingly failed.[37] Lord Simonds also held[38] that " a trust cannot qualify as a charity within the fourth class in *Pemsel's* case (*i.e.*, as being of general public utility) if the beneficiaries are a class of persons not only confined to a particular area but selected from within it by reference to a particular creed." Lord Somervell appeared to agree with this. Lords Porter and Tucker expressed no opinion on the point and Lord Reid dissented.[39]

The Act established two criteria for the validity of a recreational charity: first, the trust must be for the public benefit; and, secondly, the facilities must be provided in the interests of social welfare. The second criterion itself has two elements: the first is constant, namely, that the object of providing the facilities must be to improve the conditions of life of the beneficiaries; but the second may be satisfied in alternative ways— by showing *either* that the beneficiaries have need of the facilities by reason of the factors enumerated in the Act, *or* that the facilities are available to the members or female members of the public at large.

The Act is not free from difficulties of interpretation. For example, what is the test of " public benefit" to be applied? If it is Lord Simonds' test for trusts of general public utility, a trust like that in *I.R.C.* v. *Baddeley* would still not be charitable. Moreover, the " social welfare" criterion would not be satisfied in that the beneficiaries did not have need of the facilities by reason of the factors comprised in the Act. Similarly, *Williams* v. *I.R.C.*[40] may be unaffected on the footing that the London Welsh factor is not a sufficient qualifying factor. There would even be some difficulty forcing *I.R.C.* v. *Glasgow Police Athletic Association*[41] (police recreation held not charitable) within the Act as police are not normally considered as

[36] [1955] A.C. 572. The provision of a recreation ground for the inhabitants of a particular area is, however, charitable: *Re Morgan* [1955] 1 W.L.R. 738.
[37] See *Williams' Trustees* v. *I.R.C.* [1947] A.C. 447, *supra*.
[38] [1955] A.C. 572, 592. See *Tudor on Charities*, 6th ed., p. 114.
[39] Citing *Verge* v. *Somerville* [1924] A.C. 496; and *Goodman* v. *Mayor of Saltash* (1882) 7 App.Cas. 633.
[40] [1947] A.C. 447, *supra*.   [41] [1953] A.C. 380.

persons needing recreational facilities by reason of age or social and economic circumstances. *Cf. Re Denley's Trust Deed, supra,* p. 124.

There have been no contested decisions on the scope of the Act. In *Wynn and Others* v. *Skegness U.D.C.*[42] a convalescent home and holiday centre for North Derbyshire mineworkers was conceded to be within the terms of the Act but Ungoed-Thomas J. discussed some of the difficulties inherent in the Act.

VII. THE PURPOSE OF THE TRUST MUST BE EXCLUSIVELY CHARITABLE

If, consistently with its terms, a trust may be applied exclusively for purposes which are not charitable, it is a non-charitable trust notwithstanding that, consistently with its terms, it may be applied exclusively for purposes which are charitable.

CHICHESTER DIOCESAN FUND AND BOARD OF FINANCE (INCORPORATED) v. SIMPSON

House of Lords [1944] A.C. 341; 113 L.J.Ch. 225; 171 L.T. 141; 60 T.L.R. 492; 88 S.J. 246; [1944] 2 All E.R. 60 (Viscount Simon, Lords Macmillan, Porter and Simonds; Lord Wright dissenting)

The testator, Caleb Diplock, left his residuary estate to the executors of his will upon trust " for such charitable institution or institutions or other charitable or benevolent object or objects as his executors might in their absolute discretion select." After the estate had been wound up and the residue distributed among several charities, the testator's next-of-kin claimed that the residuary gift was void for uncertainty. Farwell J. held that the residuary bequest was valid, but his decision was reversed by the Court of Appeal. The charities concerned appealed to the House of Lords.

LORD PORTER: " My Lords, it is common ground and undoubted law that, in construing a will, the object of the court is to try to ascertain the intention of the testator, but it is the expressed intention which must govern. The principle is succinctly expressed by Lindley L.J., as he then was, in *Re Morgan* [43]: ' Now, I do not see why, if we can tell what a man intends, and can give effect to his intention *as expressed*, we should be driven out of it by other cases or decisions in other cases.' The italics are mine. In construing what the testator has said, it is permissible to consider that he did not intend to die intestate: see *per* Lord St. Leonards in *Grey* v. *Pearson*.[44] But technical words must be interpreted in their technical sense and ' charity ' or ' charitable ' are technical words in English law and must be so construed unless it can be seen from the wording of the will as a whole that they are used in some other than their technical sense. For this purpose and in order to discover the testator's intention it is the duty of the court to take into consideration

---

[42] [1967] 1 W.L.R. 52.
[43] [1893] 3 Ch. 222, 227, 228.
[44] (1857) 6 H.L.C. 61, 99.

the whole of the terms of the will and not to confine itself to the disputed words or their immediate context.

"In the present case the words whose interpretation is contested are 'charitable or benevolent.' It is admitted on behalf of the appellants that, if the word 'benevolent' stood alone, it would be too vague a term and the gift would be void: see *James* v. *Allen* [45]; but it is said that, when coupled with the word 'charitable' even by the disjunctive 'or,' it either takes its colour from its associate, or is merely exegetical, and the phrase is used as implying either that 'charitable' and 'benevolent' are the same thing or that 'benevolent' qualifies 'charitable' so as to limit the gift to objects which are both charitable and benevolent.

"In my view, the words so coupled do not naturally bear any of the meanings suggested. The addition of 'benevolent' to 'charitable' on the face of it suggests an alternative purpose and I do not see why in this collocation 'benevolent' should be read as 'charitable benevolent.' Nor do I think that it can be said to be merely exegetical. Prima facie, these are alternative objects, and, even if they were not, the word 'charitable,' to be exegetical of 'benevolent,' should follow and not precede it. The wording should be 'benevolent or charitable,' meaning 'benevolent, *i.e.*, charitable,' not 'charitable or benevolent,' meaning 'charitable, *i.e.*, benevolent.' In the latter case the gift might still be said to be given to too wide a class, *viz.*, to benevolent and not to charitable objects. In truth, however anxious though one may be to strain the language used so as to benefit charities only, the weight of authority is too great to be readily overthrown.

"Two matters of principle in the interpretation of wills are firmly established. (1) The testator must make his own will and not leave his executors to make their choice of the objects of his bounty, subject to this, that a general gift of charity will be upheld. (2) It is not, however, enough that he should leave property under a disposition in pursuance of which his assets may be disposed of to charities or for some other purpose, not even though his executors in fact apply them only to charitable purposes. 'The question is,' said Grant M.R. in *James* v. *Allen*,[46] 'what authority would this court have to say that the property must not be applied to purposes however so benevolent, unless they also come within the technical denomination of charitable purposes. If it might, consistently with the will, be applied to other than strictly charitable purposes, the trust is too indefinite for the court to execute.' The same principle is enunciated in *Hunter* v. *Attorney-General*,[47] where Lord Davey, in saying that the charitable purposes must not be mixed up with other purposes of such an indefinite nature that the court cannot execute them, gives as illustrations of such mixing the conjunction of '"charitable

---

[45] (1817) 3 Mer. 17.
[46] *Ibid.* 19.
[47] [1899] A.C. 309, 323.

or benevolent," or "charitable or philanthropic," or "charitable or pious." '

" The various tribunals in England which have expressed their views as to this combination have all tended the same way. So long ago as 1836 Lord Cottenham L.C. expressed the opinion in *Ellis* v. *Selby* [48] that a gift to ' charitable or other purposes ' was void. Similar opinions are to be found in *Attorney-General for New Zealand* v. *Brown*,[49] in *Houston* v. *Burns*,[50] and in *Attorney-General for New Zealand* v. *New Zealand Insurance Co. Ltd.*,[51] to quote but three from among those discussed in your Lordships' House or in the Privy Council. Indeed, in *Williams* v. *Kershaw* [52] a bequest of property for benevolent charitable and religious purposes was held void because it was considered that the testator could not have intended the recipient purposes to be ber volent and charitable and religious all at the same time, and, therefore, that ' and ' must be read disjunctively. I need not refer at length to the numerous cases decided in courts of first instance and in the Court of Appeal expressing a view similar to that contained in those quoted. If, however, the authorities be extended beyond those decided in a final court of appeal, the exact combination ' charitable or benevolent ' is to be found and was held void in *Re Jarman's Estate*.[53] Nor is the force of these and the many other authorities to the same effect weakened by the fact that a bequest for charitable *and* benevolent purposes has been held a valid gift: see *Re Best*,[54] since the conjunction in that case is effected by using ' and,' not ' or.' Nor by the decisions in *Attorney-General for New Zealand* v. *Brown*, where the wording was ' charitable benevolent religious and educational institutions societies associations and objects,' and in *Re Bennett*,[55] where the wording was ' for the benefit of the schools, and charitable institutions, and poor, and other objects of charity or any other public objects.' In each of these last two cases it was held the complex phrases used must properly be construed so that ' benevolent ' or ' public,' as the case might be, took its colour from charitable and must be read as *ejusdem generis* with it. In so complex a form of words the *ejusdem generis* rule might well be prayed in aid, whereas in a simpler form it might be inapplicable.

" In truth, however, the terms in which other wills are framed are but a loose guide to the construction of that in question. Each will must be interpreted in the light of its own wording. No doubt, the testator in the present case wished his estates to go to objects of a benevolent character or, as Goddard L.J. has it,[56] to ' charity in the

---

48 (1836) 1 My. & Cr. 286, 299.
49 [1917] A.C. 393.
50 [1918] A.C. 337, 341.
51 (1936) 53 T.L.R. 37.
52 (1835) 5 Cl. & F. 111n.
53 (1878) 8 Ch.D. 584.
54 [1904] 2 Ch. 354.
55 [1920] 1 Ch. 305.
56 [1941] Ch. 253, 267.

popular sense ': but ' charity ' in that sense is not coterminous with
' charity ' in the technical sense, and I can find nothing in the wording of
the will to lead to a different result. The fact that in another clause of
this will the testator gave certain specific legacies leads nowhere, and
a gift in the case of institutions limited to charitable ones, followed by a
gift to ' other charitable or benevolent objects,' to my mind suggests a
widening of his beneficence in the latter case rather than a general
charitable intent, if ' charity ' be used in its technical sense. The
appellants, however, gain their strongest support from the Scottish
decisions. In those cases ' societies or institutions of a benevolent or
charitable nature ': *Hay's Trustees* v. *Baillie* [57]; ' such charities or benevolent or beneficent institutions ': *Paterson's Trustees* v. *Paterson* [58];
and ' charitable or philanthropic institutions ': *Mackinnon's Trustees*
v. *Mackinnon*,[59] have all been held valid charitable trusts, while in
Reid's Trustees v. *Cattanach's Trustees*,[60] a bequest in the form ' poor
persons in Eskdale or such charitable educational or benevolent societies
or public institutions in Scotland ' failed only, it appears, because of the
addition of ' public institutions.' In all the cases where the gift was held
good, the *ratio decidendi* appears to have been that the testator was
designating one class of recipients, *i.e.*, charities, not two or more separate
classes of beneficiary. But Scottish law differs from English law on this
point, probably because it approaches the subject from a different angle.
In the first place the statute 43 Eliz. 1, c. 4, the benevolently interpreted
preamble of which forms the basis for determining what are charities in
English law, never applied to Scotland, and, in the second, charities,
speaking generally, are not controlled by the Scots courts. The ambit
of ' charity ' in Scotland may be narrower than it is in England. At any
rate, Lord Moncreiff thought so, as appears from his dissenting judgment
in *Macintyre* v. *Grimond's Trustees*,[61] afterwards approved in your
Lordships' House.[62] Whether it be narrower or not, it differs, and I do
not think your Lordships can obtain any satisfactory guidance from the
decisions in the Scottish courts in a case where the validity of a gift in
an English will depends on its charitable nature. I find myself in accord
with the judgment of the Master of the Rolls and agree that the appeal
should be dismissed." *Appeal dismissed.*

Note

There are some exceptions to the rule that a trust cannot be charitable
unless its purposes are exclusively charitable.

[57] 1908 S.C. 1224.
[58] 1909 S.C. 485.
[59] 1909 S.C. 1041.
[60] 1929 S.C. 727.
[61] (1904) 6 F. 285, 293.
[62] [1905] A.C. 124, 127.

(i) *Incidental Purposes*

If the main purpose of a corporation or trust is charitable and the only elements in its constitution and operations, which are non-charitable, are merely incidental to that main purpose, the corporation and trust are established for charitable purposes only.[63] If the non-charitable object is itself a main object, neither the corporation nor the trust is established for charitable purposes only; but there is this difference between them: the corporation remains validly constituted, but the trust is void.[64]

(ii) *Apportionment*

Where a trustee is directed to apportion between charitable and non-charitable objects the trust is always good as to the charitable objects. The trust will be valid *in toto* if the non-charitable objects are certain and valid,[65] and, in the absence of apportionment by the trustee, the court will divide the fund equally between both classes of objects in accordance with the maxim that "equality is equity."[66] If the non-charitable objects are uncertain, the trust will be good as to the charitable objects only[67]: in either case it is immaterial whether the charitable objects themselves are or are not certain, for an exclusively charitable trust does not fail for uncertainty.[68]

If there is no direction to apportion, and if the trust is partly for a non-charitable purpose, and then to apply the remainder to a charitable purpose, some cases decide that where the court is satisfied that an inquiry is practicable as to the portion required for the non-charitable purpose, it will direct such an inquiry and uphold the charitable part of the gift.[69] If, on the other hand, such an inquiry is impracticable, it will divide the fund into equal shares, the share applicable to non-charitable purposes falling into residue.[70] Other cases, however, have held that the whole of the gift goes to charity, independently of the question whether the portion which would otherwise have been required for the non-charitable purpose is ascertainable.[71] Yet another case decides that if the non-charitable part of the gift cannot be carried out without also performing the charitable part the whole gift will be valid.[72]

In *Re Coxen*,[73] Jenkins J. (as he then was) emphasised that, where the amount applicable to the non-charitable purpose cannot be quantified, the

---

63 *Royal College of Surgeons of England* v. *National Provincial Bank Ltd.* [1952] A.C. 631; *Re Coxen* [1948] Ch. 747.
64 *Oxford Group* v. *I.R.C.* [1949] W.N. 343; *Chichester Diocesan Fund and Board of Finance (Incorporated)* v. *Simpson* [1944] A.C. 341, *supra*; *Associated Artists Ltd.* v. *I.R.C.* [1956] 1 W L.R. 752.
65 *Re Douglas* (1887) 35 Ch.D. 472; but see *Re Endacott* [1960] Ch. 232; and pp. 107–108, *supra*.
66 *Salusbury* v. *Denton* (1857) 3 K. & J. 529.
67 *Re Clarke* [1923] 2 Ch. 407.
68 The *cy-près* doctrine is available.
69 *Re Rigley* (1867) 36 L.J.Ch. 147; *Re Vaughan* (1886) 33 Ch.D. 187.
70 *Adnam* v. *Cole* (1843) 6 Beav. 353; *Hoare* v. *Osborne* (1866) L.R. 1 Eq. 585; *cf. Fowler* v. *Fowler* (1864) 33 Beav. 616, where the whole gift failed.
71 *Fisk* v. *Att.-Gen.* (1867) L.R. 4 Eq. 521; *Hunter* v. *Bullock* (1872) L.R. 14 Eq. 45; *Dawson* v. *Small* (1874) L.R. 18 Eq. 114; *Re Williams* (1877) 5 Ch.D. 735; *Re Birkett* (1878) 9 Ch.D. 576; *Re Rogerson* [1901] 1 Ch. 715; *cf. Re Porter* [1925] Ch. 746.
72 *Re Eighmie* [1935] Ch. 524   73 [1948] Ch. 747, 752.

whole gift fails for uncertainty. He pointed out, however, that there were two exceptions to this general rule: first, an exception of a general character to the effect that, where, as a matter of construction, the gift to charity was a gift of the entire fund subject to the payments thereout required for the non-charitable purpose, the amount set free by the failure of the non-charitable gift was caught by, and passed under, the charitable gift [74]; and, secondly, an exception of a more limited character, applicable in the " tomb " cases, to the effect that where there is a primary trust (imposing a merely honorary obligation [75]) to apply the income in perpetuity to the repair of a tomb not in a church, followed by a charitable trust in terms extending only to the balance of the income, the established rule is to ignore the invalid trust for the repair of the tomb and treat the whole income as given to charity.

(iii) *The Charitable Trusts (Validation) Act 1954*

(a) **Relevant provisions**

Validation and modification of imperfect trust instruments

Section 1.—(1) In this Act, " imperfect trust provision " means any provision declaring the objects for which property is to be held or applied, and so describing those objects that, consistently with the terms of the provision, the property could be used exclusively for charitable purposes, but could nevertheless be used for purposes which are not charitable.

(2) Subject to the following provisions of this Act, any imperfect trust provision contained in an instrument taking effect before the sixteenth day of December, nineteen hundred and fifty-two,[76] shall have, and be deemed to have had, effect in relation to any disposition or covenant to which this Act applies—

(*a*) as respects the period before the commencement of this Act,[77] as if the whole of the declared objects were charitable; and

(*b*) as respects the period after that commencement as if the provision had required the property to be held or applied for the declared objects in so far only as they authorise use for charitable purposes.

(3) A document inviting gifts of property to be held or applied for objects declared by the document shall be treated for the purposes of this section as an instrument taking effect when it is first issued.

(4) In this Act, " covenant " includes any agreement, whether under seal or not, and " covenantor " is to be construed accordingly.

Dispositions and covenants to which the Act applies

Section 2.—(1) Subject to the next following subsection, this Act applies to any disposition of property to be held or applied for objects declared by an imperfect trust provision, and to any covenant to make such a disposition, where apart from this Act the disposition or covenant is invalid

---

[74] *Cf. Hancock* v. *Watson* [1902] A.C. 14; *infra*, p. 319.

[75] *Re Morton's W.T.* [1948] 2 All E.R. 842; *Re Dalziel* [1943] Ch. 277, 278; *Tudor on Charities*, 6th ed., pp. 135–137, 197.

[76] The date on which the Report of the Nathan Committee on Charitable Trusts was presented to Parliament. The Act gives effect to certain recommendations of that Committee (Cmnd. 8710 (1952); Chap. 12).

[77] July 30, 1954.

under the law of England and Wales, but would be valid if the objects were exclusively charitable.

[Subsection (2) excepts from the operation of the Act any disposition under which property or income therefrom was paid or distributed before December 16, 1952, on the footing that the imperfect trust provision was void.]

(3) A disposition in settlement or other disposition creating more than one interest in the same property shall be treated for the purposes of this Act as a separate disposition in relation to each of the interests created.

[Section 3 [78] saves the rights of persons entitled by reason of the invalidity of a disposition, unless the rights accrued more than six years before December 16, 1952; forbids the enforcement of such rights after July 30, 1955, unless the rights were acknowledged by, or concealed through the fraud of the trustees; contains saving provisions where persons are under disability or have future interests; and preserves certain rights against trustees who dispose of property in disregard of express notice of an adverse claim. Section 4 left unaffected orders or judgments made or given or liability to tax incurred before December 16, 1952; but permitted orders or judgments made or given between that date and July 30, 1954, to be reopened within six months after the latter date. Section 5 empowered the Parliament of Northern Ireland to enact similar legislation and section 6 made the Act and any Northern Ireland legislation binding on the Crown.]

(b) **Comment**

The effect of the Act may be summarised as follows: Where consistently with the terms of a trust which took effect before December 16, 1952, the trust property could be used exclusively for charitable purposes, but could, nevertheless, be used for purposes which are not charitable, then for the period before July 30, 1954, the trust is deemed to have had effect as if all the declared objects were charitable, and for the period after that date, the trust is deemed to require the property to be applied for the declared objects in so far only as they are charitable. The provisions of such trusts are called " imperfect trust provisions " and the Act applies to dispositions of property held under such trusts, where apart from the Act the disposition would be invalid, but would be valid if the objects were exclusively charitable. But the Act does not apply if before December 16, 1952, the property has been disposed of in favour of persons entitled by reason of the invalidity of the trust. The Act is limited in effect; but likely to remain important for many years, particularly with regard to the construction of trusts of reversionary interests created before, but falling into possession after, December 16, 1952.[79]

The language of the Act [80] is more complicated and obscure than similar legislation from other Commonwealth countries, which is generally not circumscribed by the same limitations.[81] It has given rise to the following problems:

---

[78] See *Re Thomas' W.T.* [1969] 3 All E.R. 1492.

[79] See, *e.g.*, *Re Wykes* [1961] Ch 229.

[80] For an analysis, see two articles by S. G. Maurice (1954) 18 Conv.(N.S.) 532 and (1962) 26 Conv.(N.S.) 200.

[81] See (New South Wales) Conveyancing Act 1938, s. 37D, interpreted in *Leahy* v. *Att.-Gen. for N.S.W.* [1959] A.C. 457, 474–476; (Victoria) Property Law Act 1928, s. 131; (New Zealand) Trustee Amendment Act 1935, s. 2; (Western Australia)

1. Where an appeal is made for funds for three purposes, two of which are not charitable, and the third (worthy causes) includes both charitable and non-charitable objects, it is clear that section 1 (1) does not apply to the fund as a whole, since it could not be used in its entirety exclusively for charitable purposes: see *Re Gillingham Bus Disaster Fund.*[82] Is there, however, a separate disposition for the third purpose within section 2 (3)? At first instance Harman J. held not: the letter making the appeal was not a disposition, and, even if it were, it did not create different interests in the same property—one for each of the named purposes. On appeal Evershed M.R. and Romer L.J. considered that dispositions were made by contributors in response to the appeal, but agreed with Harman J. that the dispositions did not create separate interests in the same property. Ormerod L.J. considered section 2 (3) to be applicable.

2. Must the dichotomy of purposes (charitable and non-charitable) be expressed or can it be implied? In *Re Gillingham Bus Disaster Fund* Harman J. held that the failure to mention charity as one of the objects of the trust was fatal to the claim in support of validation. On appeal Evershed M.R. thought that the use of a phrase such as " worthy causes," which had within it the notion of charity, *might* come within the terms of section 1 (1); Romer L.J. thought that the operation of the section was confined to cases where one, at least, of the objects was charitable, so that it would apply to the formula " charitable or benevolent," but not " philanthropic or benevolent "; and Ormerod L.J. thought that the phrase *did* come within the section since it included on its face both charitable and non-charitable purposes. In *Re Harpur's W.T.*[83] Cross J. purported to follow the view of Harman J. that the section applied only to a gift which was *expressed* to be for charitable as well as non-charitable purposes; but in *Re Wykes*[84] Buckley J., after reviewing in a classic judgment the course of the decision in *Re Gillingham Bus Disaster Fund* and the history and scope of the Act, held, following the view of Ormerod L.J. in that case, that the Act applied to a trust for the division of a fund among " benevolent or welfare purposes "; and in *Re Saxone Shoe Co. Ltd.'s Trust Deed*[85] Cross J. decided to follow Buckley J. There must, however, be a reference, express or implied, to charitable and non-charitable purposes, for it seems clear that the Act would not apply to a trust for unspecified purposes, *e.g.,* " such purposes as my trustees think fit."

3. Does the Act apply where the potential beneficiaries do not constitute a section of the public for the purposes of the law of charity, but a trust in their favour would nevertheless be valid if applied for the benefit of such of them as were poor: *e.g.,* " a trust for welfare purposes for the benefit of the employees of a particular company "? In *Re Wykes* Buckley J. held that since, consistently with the terms of the trust, the whole fund could be applied exclusively for charitable purposes, *i.e.,* the

---

Trustees Act 1962, s. 102; (Northern Ireland) Charities Act 1964, s. 24; (1946) 62 L.Q.R. 23 (E. H. Coghill); *ibid.* 339 (R. Else Mitchell); (1950) 24 Austr.L.J. 239 (E. H. Coghill); M. C. Cullity (1967) 16 I.C.L.Q. 464.

[82] [1958] Ch. 300 (Harman J.); affirmed [1959] Ch. 62 (C.A.: Evershed M.R. and Romer L.J., Ormerod L.J. dissenting); see [1959] C.L.J. 41 (S. J. Bailey); [1958] 74 L.Q.R. 190; *ibid.* 489 (P. S. Atiyah).

[83] [1961] Ch. 38; affirmed [1962] Ch. 78.

[84] [1961] Ch. 229.

[85] [1962] 1 W.L.R. 943.

relief of poverty, the Act applied; and in *Re Mead's Trust Deed* [86] Cross J. came to the same conclusion. On the other hand, in *Re Saxone Shoe Co. Ltd.'s Trust Deed,* where there was neither an express nor an implied reference to charitable purposes (trust for any purposes the trustees should consider to be for the benefit of employees and former employees of a particular company and their dependants), Cross J. held that the case fell outside the Act, which did not apply to a private discretionary trust as opposed to a trust for the promotion of quasi-charitable purposes.

4. It seems clear that the Act does not apply to a trust for institutions [87] or individuals [88] as distinct from a trust for purposes.

VIII. A NEW DEFINITION OF CHARITY?

B. Nightingale, Charities,[89] pp. 61–67

" The idea of a new definition of charity, or rather *a* definition to substitute for the present accumulation of case-law, has often been raised. The Royal Commission on Taxation thought that there would be " no insuperable difficulty " in working one out; several witnesses argued for one before the Nathan Committee; and the committee itself suggested that Lord Macnaghten's classification should be written into charitable law, as a version of it had been when charitable purposes were mentioned in an earlier War Damage Act. The government of the day disagreed, and probably rightly, since such an addition would only have formalised what was the practice already, and left the case-law untouched. As a result, there was no definition at all in the 1960 Act. " Charity," it declared, " means any institution, corporate or not, which is established for charitable purposes and is subject to the control of the High Court in the exercise of the court's jurisdiction with respect to charities ": a tautology denounced in the Commons as a " confession of failure ".

There are good reasons for caution, however. Construct too wide a definition, and you may find that the National Front or the Communist Party are eligible as charities. Construct too detailed a one, and you may exclude important social needs that only subsequently become apparent. As the Nathan Committee saw, any new definition would have to be at once precise and flexible, and that is hard to achieve. Lawyers have admitted in the Commons that they have tried to construct one and failed. Recently, the Society of Labour Lawyers set up a committee to investigate the subject, but it " could not solve the fundamental problem of how you would distinguish between those charities we thought ought to be assisted by the state and those which should not ": the committee was abandoned.

But there have been suggestions. In 1945, in a widely quoted article, John Brunyate suggested that the courts were ignoring important decisions. One, in 1882, emerged from a curious case in which the right of the

---

[86] [1961] 1 W.L.R. 1244 (a trust to provide a convalescent home for members of a trade union and a home for poor retired members).

[87] *Re Harpur's W.T.* [1962] Ch. 78.

[88] *Re Saxone Shoe Co. Ltd.'s Trust Deed* [1962] 1 W.L.R. 943.

[89] Published in 1973 by Allen Lane. See also Charity Law Reform Committee statement in *New Law Journal Annual Charities Review* 1974, pp. 26 *et seq.* where a completely new category of organisation is suggested: the Non-Profit-Distribution Organisation.

tenement dwellers of Saltash to dredge in the river for oysters was held to be a charitable trust, lasting forever. The only reason for giving charitable status to such a practice was, simply, that it benefited the public. Indeed, " public benefit " and that alone should be the test of what constitutes a charity, argued Brunyate, quoting a neat ruling of 1915 in his support: " any gift which proceeds from a philanthropic or benevolent motive or which is intended to benefit an appreciably important class of our fellow-creatures . . . and which will confer the supposed benefit without contravening law or morals, will be charitable ". He might also have invoked a much older and even simpler ruling: that of Lord Camden who defined charity in 1767 as a " gift to a general public use, which extends to the poor as well as the rich ". These judgments, taken together, certainly suggest that there is an alternative tradition of reasoning in relation to charities, which judges could have followed rather than complicate matters by emphasising the statute of Elizabeth and piling analogy on analogy.

The definition of charity Brunyate proposes, then, is any purpose " in the general enlightened opinion of the time for the benefit of the community, although such benefit be intangible "; and other legal critics have supported him. In 1956, Geoffrey Cross asked why Macnaghten's " purposes beneficial to the community " shouldn't be taken at face value, and not limited to those analogous with the 1601 preamble; and the same year, in an article that has attracted too little attention, John Willcock argued that Elizabethan statute and Macnaghten rules alike should be rejected for three main categories: trusts which benefit the public as a whole directly, trusts which benefit directly a limited class of persons and the public as a whole indirectly, and trusts which benefit a limited class and don't benefit the public at all, " but which fulfil a moral obligation which the public as a whole feel ".

There are objections to be made to this. Is medical research, for instance, exactly an " obligation "? If something is an " obligation ", shouldn't we demand that the state, not charity, fulfil it? Again, can we really trust the " public as a whole "? They would seem to feel little obligation towards addicts, unmarried mothers, ex-prisoners, even the mentally sick. On the other hand, the " enlightened opinion of the time " would feel an obligation not only for these, but for such near-charities as the National Council of Civil Liberties, Amnesty and the Anti-Apartheid Movement. Perhaps we need to reconcile Brunyate's phrase with Willcock's fuller classification. Somewhere here may be the basis for a new definition.

But it would still have to be interpreted. Professor Keeton, for one, opposes even a liberal definition on the grounds that judges would eventually become as technical, legalistic, fixated on verbal subtlety, inflexible and negative as he believes they are now. In charitable cases they are, in essence, making important decisions on a branch of public policy. They are deciding the channels into which philanthropy can flow with the greatest effect: " unfortunately, the most recent decisions give little sign of an increasing breadth of view on the part of the judiciary ". And Keeton presses the attack further, describing the present system as " a hit or miss process " and confirming the suggestion of a tacit bias: " otherwise a number of decisions which appear in our law books seem quite irreconcilable ". Why not, he asks, remove the power to decide what is and is not charitable from the courts and give it to a special tribunal, acting on a definition broadly couched and embodied in an Act of Parliament? The " definition " he proposes would be some variation on the expression " social welfare ", which is already written into an Act which expounds the range of " recreational charities ". This system he calls " a matter for serious consideration ", as indeed it is. But it was suggested in 1962, and there is no evidence that it has been seriously considered since.

Nor have we exhausted the number of areas that continue to cause the courts difficulties. There are more anomalous decisions that those who wish to relieve them of the burden of charity can adduce. As the examples quoted earlier indicate, they have had trouble defining poverty; they have had trouble deciding when an organisation exists primarily for the benefit of some closed group, and is therefore not charitable, and when it exists for a sufficient section of the public, and is   Disaster funds are charitable, even though there may be only two or three beneficiaries from the very start. Yet a few years ago, a trust for the education of the children of 110,000-odd employees and ex-employees of a tobacco firm was held not to be charitable: the element of public benefit was absent. It has been pointed out that the decision meant that a trust for the education of the inhabitants of Bournville would be charitable, but that one for the education of the children of the employees of Cadbury's would not be, even though the beneficiaries might be identical.

In any case, the public schools, which in practice exist for the children of the upper and middle classes only, continue to be regarded as charitable, in spite of the recommendation of the Newsom Commission that they should be deprived of their status unless they become much more " integrated ". They were performing a charitable function in a technical sense only: it was " a plain anomaly " that they should receive a subsidy from the taxpayer and ratepayer which amounted to £2,380,000 in 1965–6, excluding relief on tax payable on income from investments. This, added Newsom, meant that the fee-payer was being subsidised, too. But the government took no action, and similarly ignored a half-facetious suggestion in the House that it should divert Eton's endowment—originally for poor, needy children of good character and decent life—to primary schools.

But if " public benefit " has caused the courts trouble, " vagueness " has caused more. In a notorious decision only a few years ago, £250,000 was lost for charity because the will in question wanted it to be used for " charitable or benevolent " purposes. If it had said " charitable *and* benevolent ", the gift would have been good. But the court held that the two words were not synonymous in meaning, that the money could be spent on " benevolent " purposes that were not charitable, and the gift was therefore void. It was absolutely clear that the testator himself wished his legacy to benefit humanity, whatever the niceties of wording: his wish was stultified on a mere technicality, and, as Tudor points out, the same would happen in a similarly expressed trust today. There are other cases which suggest that, as Keeton says, the courts seem positively to try to think of activities that might disqualify an organisation from being a charity. There are times when the very last thing they seem to consider is the social merits of the case. So absorbed are they in the question of what *is* a charity that they don't ask what *ought* to be one.

But, equally, it would be foolish to underestimate the difficulties a tribunal would face, however informed its members, and however representative of donors, recipients, and the social services. It would still have to interpret " purposes beneficial to the community ", or something of the sort. How far would, and should, it favour (say) pressure-groups catering for minorities and not yet well established? The bias of this chapter has been towards secular, libertarian organisations. But there. is, of course, no reason why such preferences should carry the day. It is perfectly possible that a tribunal might have quite other ones, and might prove less generous than the courts towards charities. The Royal Commission on Taxation complained of the " undue width " of objects considered charitable: many appeared to have no connection with popular ideas of charity. It wanted a new definition, and " a more restrictive one ". In a reservation, a minority of members went further, arguing that some of the tax privileges of such charities as remained should be withdrawn. A tribunal, with its eye firmly on the value of charitable status, might well endorse this view.

In some ways this would be unfortunate. It has not been sufficiently remarked that designation as a charity has two quite different implications for an organisation. On the one hand, it brings financial gain and the benefit of perpetuity; on the other, it places it under the jurisdiction and control of the Charity Commission. Both results are entirely automatic, regardless of the quality or potential of the organisation. Now, we may agree that it is right that an effective, useful organisation should get tax advantages, and wrong that a dubiously useful one should also get them. But we are unlikely to agree that it is right that a useful organisation should submit to official control and scrutiny, and wrong that an ineffective one should also do so. It is clearly in the public interest that there should still be a check on the activities of a poor organisation, whether subsidised by the taxpayer or not. The absurdity of the present situation is that so much weight is placed on a mere definition. The magic word " charity " is uttered, and the implications for an organisation are enormous; the word is withheld, and it is neglected. We have seen numerous examples of organisations trying to qualify for the advantages of registration. One can also imagine organisations so phrasing their constitutions as to avoid charitable status for their own, dark reasons.

But could not the two, seemingly contradictory, results of registration be separated? There seems no reason why a tribunal should not accept an organisation as a charity, or, having discovered its existence, actually *force* it to become one—and then deny it the traditional advantages. Alternatively, the Charity Commissioners, who would retain their custodial functions, could themselves continue to adjudicate on charitable status in the old way. Then, and only then, would the tribunal or (presumably) system of regional tribunals appear, to give tax and rate exemption certificates to those organisations which deserved public subsidy. If they wished, they could also give them to voluntary organisations that had been denied status under the existing law. The criterion would be social merit, as it is in Sweden, where they find it perfectly possible to discriminate between organisations of " especially high public utility " and those of lesser utility, and to give them larger or smaller tax concessions according to their place on the scale.

Defining "social merit" or "public utility" would, of course, be just one of the difficulties that would remain. Could the tribunals really adjudicate over the thousands of tiny, local, unevenly effective local charities that claim little tax relief, but do have the privilege of perpetuity and thus may perceive permanent endowments? While there is no good reason why the public should continue to subsidise many of them, it would surely be wrong to force them to realise previously untouchable assets and condemn them to extinction. The right to perpetuity would presumably continue unchanged and, to make the work of the tribunals more manageable, their approval would be necessary only for those charities which occupied buildings, and were therefore subject to rates, and those which stood to get back more than (say) £50 in tax relief. This would certainly take the heat out of the argument over a new "definition", since it would deprive definition of its importance. Something of the sort seems worth consideration."

Section 3. Administration of Charities

Overall supervision of charities is carried on by the Charity Commissioners [90] under the powers conferred on them by the Charities Act 1960: the more significant provisions of the Act are set out *infra*, except for sections 13 and 14 which appear in the next part of this chapter concerned with the *cy-près* powers of the Commissioners and of the courts.

In exceptional cases the Attorney-General may authorise trustees to make *ex gratia* payments out of charitable funds to persons outside the class of charitable beneficiaries and to whom it would be morally wrong to refuse such payments.[91] Normally trustees must be most careful to restrict their payments to the specific purposes of their charity as is shown by *Baldry* v. *Feintuck* discussed in the following extract from paragraphs 19–22 of the Commissioners' 1972 Report.

1972 Annual Report

Baldry v. Feintuck and Others [1972] 1 W.L.R. 552

19. This case throws some interesting light on the duties and powers of charity trustees in the application of their funds. Sussex University was founded by Royal charter in 1961, its objects being to advance learning and knowledge by teaching and research and to enable students to obtain

---

[90] The Commissioners established 870 schemes in 1972. See their 1970 Report for a review of the first 10 years operation of the 1960 Act, their 1966 Report, paras. 18–26 for the way the commission works and paras. 27–41 for their approach to registering prospective charities. Under s. 1 of the Education Act 1973 jurisdiction over educational charities has been transferred from the Department of Education to the Charity Commissioners as from February 1, 1974.

[91] *Re Snowden* [1970] Ch. 700 (very substantial gift of shares by will was adeemed and its value fell into residue giving charitable residuary legatees ten times the value of their intended legacies: it was held they could make *ex gratia* payments to the adeemed legatees).

the advantages of university education. Article 15 of the charter provided that there should be a students' union of the university, the constitution, powers and functions of which should be prescribed in the ordinances. The council of the university made an ordinance in December 1967 establishing the constitution of the union. The aims of the union included: (*a*) to encourage and develop the corporate life of the union in cultural, social and athletic fields, and (*e*) to maintain and extend friendly relations with other students' unions and with the general public. The constitution also established a governing body called the council and an administrative body called the executive committee consisting of eight student officers elected by the union and one officer nominated by the senate of the university. The constitution further required that any amendments of the constitution should be carried at a council meeting and ratified at a general meeting of the union by a two-thirds majority in each case before taking effect, any such amendments being reported to the senate and the council of the university. The union had been treated by the Inland Revenue as established for exclusively charitable purposes and its charitable status was not a point in issue.

20. In the autumn of 1971 the annual general meeting of the union purported to ratify the adoption of a new constitution which had previously been approved at a meeting of the union council and also to adopt a budget for 1971–72. The objects of the union were redefined in the new constitution as being the promotion of any matter whatsoever of interest to its members. The budget in its final form included two disputed payments, a proposed contribution to War on Want and a proposed contribution to a fund for financing a political campaign of protest against the Government's policy of ending certain free milk supplies for school children.

21. The first point was whether the union had power to make such an alteration to its constitution. The Judge, Mr. Justice Brightman, said that the union was clearly an educational charity and the officers who had power to dispose of the union's funds were, clearly, trustees of those funds for charitable educational purposes. It was not, therefore, open to the union, by a purported amendment to the union's constitution, to authorise the use of the union's funds for the purpose of promoting any object which may happen to interest the members of the union regardless of whether such object was charitable and educational or not. In his view this is what the new constitution was seeking to do but it was a result which no charitable body such as the union was capable of achieving. Accordingly, the definition of the union's objects set out in the original constitution was still subsisting, because such original objects had never been displaced. But even if that interpretation of the new constitution was erroneous and the new object was valid, the Judge considered that it must, by necessary implication, be construed in the context of the educational purposes of Sussex University, and it would still follow that the objects of the union were confined to charitable educational purposes.

22. Regarding the two disputed payments, the Judge was unable to accept the argument that students should be able to use a reasonable amount

of the union's funds in support of those views which, after discussion, they desired to advocate. The educational process included research, discussion, debate and reaching a corporate conclusion on social and economic problems, but, in the judge's view, the provision of money to finance the adoption outside the university of that corporate conclusion did not form any part of the educational process. If members of the union wished to express their views financially, the money should come from their own personal funds and not from the trust money. Thus, although War on Want was a charity, it was not an educational charity, and far less an educational charity connected with students' welfare at Sussex University, and the judge held that it was not open to one charity to subscribe to the funds of another charity unless the recipient charity is expressly or by implication a purpose or object of the donor charity. With regard to the proposed Milk Campaign Fund, this was, admittedly, a political purpose and it was, therefore, inevitably not a charitable purpose, educational or otherwise, because political purposes were not charitable. It followed, therefore, that the charitable funds of the union could not lawfully be used for setting up such a fund.

Charities Act 1960

The Charity Commissioners

1.—(1) There shall continue to be a body of Charity Commissioners for England and Wales, and they shall have such functions as are conferred on them by this Act in addition to any functions under any other enactment not repealed by this Act.

(2) The provisions of the First Schedule to this Act shall have effect with respect to the constitution and proceedings of the Commissioners and other matters relating to the Commissioners and their officers and servants.

(3) The Commissioners shall (without prejudice to their specific powers and duties under other enactments) have the general function of promoting the effective use of charitable resources by encouraging the development of better methods of administration, by giving charity trustees information or advice on any matter affecting the charity and by investigating and checking abuses.

(4) It shall be the general object of the Commissioners so to act in the case of any charity (unless it is a matter of altering its purposes) as best to promote and make effective the work of the charity in meeting the needs designated by its trusts; but the Commissioners shall not themselves have power to act in the administration of a charity.

(5) The Commissioners shall, as soon as possible after the end of every year, make to the Secretary of State a report on their operations during that year, and he shall lay a copy of the report before each House of Parliament.

The official custodian for charities

3.—(1) There shall be an " official custodian for charities ", whose function it shall be to act as trustee for charities in the cases provided for by this Act; and the official custodian for charities shall be by that name a corporation sole having perpetual succession and using an official seal, which shall be officially and judicially noticed.

(2) Such officer of the Commissioners as they may from time to time designate shall be the official custodian for charities.

(3) The official custodian for charities shall perform his duties in accordance with such general or special directions as may be given him by the Commissioners, and his expenses (except those re-imbursed to him or recovered by him as trustee for any charity) shall be defrayed by the Commissioners.

Register of charities

4.—(1) There shall be a register of charities which shall be established and maintained by the Commissioners and in which there shall be entered such particulars as the Commissioners may from time to time determine of any charity there registered.

(2) There shall be entered in the register every charity not excepted by subsection (4) below; and a charity so excepted may be entered in the register at the request of the charity, but (whether or not it was excepted at the time of registration) may at any time, and shall at the request of the charity, be removed from the register.

(3) Any institution which no longer appears to the Commissioners to be a charity shall be removed from the register, with effect, where the removal is due to any change in its purposes or trusts, from the date of that change; and there shall also be removed from the register any charity which ceases to exist or does not operate.

(4) The following charities are not required to be registered, that is to say,—

(a) any charity comprised in the Second Schedule to this Act (in this Act referred to as an " exempt charity ");
(b) any charity which is excepted by order or regulations;
(c) any charity having neither any permanent endowment, nor any income from property amounting to more than fifteen pounds a year, nor the use and occupation of any land;

and no charity is required to be registered in respect of any registered place of worship.

(5) With any application for a charity to be registered there shall be supplied to the Commissioners copies of its trusts (or, if they are not set out in any extant document, particulars of them), and such other documents or information as may be prescribed or as the Commissioners may require for the purpose of the application.

(6) It shall be the duty—

(a) of the charity trustees of any charity which is not registered nor excepted from registration to apply for it to be registered, and to supply the documents and information required by subsection (5) above; and
(b) of the charity trustees (or last charity trustees) of any institution which is for the time being registered to notify the Commissioners if it ceases to exist, or if there is any change in its trusts, or in

the particulars of it entered in the register, and to supply to the Commissioners particulars of any such change and copies of any new trusts or alterations of the trusts;

and any person who makes default in carrying out any of the duties imposed by this subsection may be required by order of the Commissioners to make good that default.

Effect of, and claims and objections to, registration

5.—(1) An institution shall for all purposes other than rectification of the register be conclusively presumed to be or have been a charity at any time when it is or was on the register of charities.

(2) Any person who is or may be affected by the registration of an institution as a charity may, on the ground that it is not a charity, object to its being entered by the Commissioners in the register, or apply to them for it to be removed from the register; and provision may be made by regulations as to the manner in which any such objection or application is to be made, prosecuted or dealt with.

(3) An appeal against any decision of the Commissioners to enter or not to enter an institution in the register of charities, or to remove or not to remove an institution from the register, may be brought in the High Court by the Attorney General, or by the persons who are or claim to be the charity trustees of the institution, or by any person whose objection or application under subsection (2) above is disallowed by the decision.

(4) If there is an appeal to the High Court against any decision of the Commissioners to enter an institution in the register, or not to remove an institution from the register, then until the Commissioners are satisfied whether the decision of the Commissioners is or is not to stand, the entry in the register shall be maintained, but shall be in suspense and marked to indicate that it is in suspense; and for the purposes of subsection (1) above an institution shall be deemed not to be on the register during any period when the entry relating to it is in suspense under this subsection.

(5) Any question affecting the registration or removal from the register of an institution may, notwithstanding that it has been determined by a decision on appeal under subsection (3) above, be considered afresh by the Commissioners and shall not be concluded by that decision, if it appears to the Commissioners that there has been a change of circumstances or that the decision is inconsistent with a later judicial decision, whether given on such an appeal or not.

General power to institute inquiries

6.—(1) The Commissioners may from time to time institute inquiries with regard to charities or a particular charity or class of charities, either generally or for particular purposes:

Provided that no such inquiry shall extend to any exempt charity.

(2) The Commissioners may either conduct such an inquiry themselves or appoint a person to conduct it and make a report to them.[92]

---

[92] See *Jones* v. *Att.-Gen.* [1973] 3 W.L.R. 608; 1971 Report, paras. 90–96; 1972 Report, paras. 80–81; 1973 Report, paras. 87–97.

(3) For the purposes of any such inquiry the Commissioners may by order, and a person appointed by them to conduct the inquiry may by precept, require any person (subject to the provisions of this section)—

    (*a*) to furnish accounts and statements in writing with respect to any matter in question at the inquiry, being a matter on which he has or can reasonably obtain information, or to return answers in writing to any questions or inquiries addressed to him on any such matter, and to verify any such accounts, statements or answers by statutory declaration;

    (*b*) to attend at a specified time and place and give evidence or produce documents in his custody or control which relate to any matter in question at the inquiry.

(4) For the purposes of any such inquiry evidence may be taken on oath, and the person conducting the inquiry may for that purpose administer oaths, or may instead of administering an oath require the person examined to make and subscribe a declaration of the truth of the matters about which he is examined.

Local authority's index of local charities

10.—(1) The council of a county or of a borough may maintain an index of local charities or of any class of local charities in the council's area, and may publish information contained in the index, or summaries or extracts taken from it.

(2) A council proposing to establish or maintaining under this section an index of local charities or of any class of local charities shall, on request, be supplied by the Commissioners free of charge with copies of such entries in the register of charities as are relevant to the index or with particulars of any changes in the entries of which copies have been supplied before; and the Commissioners may arrange that they will without further request supply a council with particulars of any such changes.

(3) An index maintained under this section shall be open to public inspection at all reasonable times.

Reviews of local charities by local authority

11.—(1) The council of a county or of a borough may, subject to the following provisions of this section, initiate, and carry out in co-operation with the charity trustees, a review of the working of any group of local charities with the same or similar purposes in the council's area, and may make to the Commissioners such report on the review and such recommendations arising from it as the council after consultation with the trustees think fit.

(2) A council having power to initiate reviews under this section may co-operate with other persons in any review by them of the working of local charities in the council's area (with or without other charities), or may join with other persons in initiating and carrying out such a review.

(3) No review initiated by a council under this section shall extend to any charity without the consent of the charity trustees, nor to any ecclesiastical charity.

Concurrent jurisdiction with High Court for certain purposes

18.—(1) Subject to the provisions of this Act, the Commissioners may by order exercise the same jurisdiction and powers as are exercisable by the High Court in charity proceedings for the following purposes, that is to say:—

(a) establishing a scheme for the administration of a charity;

(b) appointing, discharging or removing a charity trustee or trustee for a charity, or removing an officer or servant;

(c) vesting or transferring property, or requiring or entitling any person to call for or make any transfer of property or any payment.

(2) Where the court directs a scheme for the administration of a charity to be established, the court may by order refer the matter to the Commissioners for them to prepare or settle a scheme in accordance with such directions (if any) as the court sees fit to give, and any such order may provide for the scheme to be put into effect by order of the Commissioners as if prepared under subsection (1) above and without any further order of the court.

(3) The Commissioners shall not have jurisdiction under this section to try or determine the title at law or in equity to any property as between a charity or trustee for a charity and a person holding or claiming the property or an interest in it adversely to the charity, or to try or determine any question as to the existence or extent of any charge or trust.

(4) Subject to the following subsections, the Commissioners shall not exercise their jurisdiction under this section as respects any charity, except—

(a) on the application of the charity; or

(b) on an order of the court under subsection (2) above.

(5) In the case of a charity not having any income from property amounting to more than fifty pounds a year, and not being an exempt charity, the Commissioners may exercise their jurisdiction under this section on the application—

(a) of the Attorney General; or

(b) of any one or more of the charity trustees, or of any person interested in the charity, or of any two or more inhabitants of the area of the charity, if it is a local charity.

(6) Where in the case of a charity, other than an exempt charity, the Commissioners are satisfied that the charity trustees ought in the interests of the charity to apply for a scheme, but have unreasonably refused or neglected to do so, the Commissioners may apply to the Secretary of State for him to refer the case to them with a view to a scheme, and if, after giving the charity trustees an opportunity to make representations to him, the Secretary of State does so, the Commissioners may proceed accordingly without the application required by subsection (4) or (5) above:

Provided that the Commissioners shall not have power in a case where they act by virtue of this subsection to alter the purposes of a charity, unless forty years have elapsed from the date of its foundation.

(7) The Commissioners may on the application of any charity trustee

or trustee for a charity exercise their jurisdiction under this section for the purpose of discharging him from his trusteeship.

(8) Before exercising any jurisdiction under this section otherwise than on an order of the court, the Commissioners shall give notice of their intention to do so to each of the charity trustees, except any that cannot be found or has no known address in the United Kingdom or who is party or privy to an application for the exercise of the jurisdiction; and any such notice may be given by post and, if given by post, may be addressed to the recipient's last known address in the United Kingdom.

(9) The Commissioners shall not exercise their jurisdiction under this section in any case (not referred to them by order of the court) which, by reason of its contentious character, or of any special question of law or of fact which it may involve, or for other reasons, the Commissioners may consider more fit to be adjudicated on by the court.

(10) An appeal against any order of the Commissioners under this section may be brought in the High Court by the Attorney General.

(11) An appeal against any order of the Commissioners under this section may also, at any time within the three months beginning with the day following that on which the order is published, be brought in the High Court by the charity or any of the charity trustees, or by any person removed from any office or employment by the order (unless he is removed with the concurrence of the charity trustees or with the approval of the special visitor, if any, of the charity):

Provided that no appeal shall be brought under this subsection except with a certificate of the Commissioners that it is a proper case for an appeal or with the leave of one of the judges of the High Court attached to the Chancery Division.

(12) Where an order of the Commissioners under this section establishes a scheme for the administration of a charity, any person interested in the charity shall have the like [93] right of appeal under subsection (11) above as a charity trustee, and so also, in the case of a charity which is a local charity in any area, shall any two or more inhabitants of the area and the parish council of any rural parish comprising the area or any part of it; but a parish council shall not exercise their right of appeal without the consent of the parish meeting.

Power to act for protection of charities

20.—(1) Where the Commissioners are satisfied as the result of an inquiry instituted by them under section six of this Act—

(*a*) that there has been in the administration of a charity any misconduct or mismanagement; and

(*b*) that it is necessary or desirable to act for the purpose of protecting the property of the charity or securing a proper application for the purposes of the charity of that property or of property coming to the charity;

---

[93] See, *Childs* v. *Att.-Gen.* [1973] 1 W.L.R. 497 for the incorporation of the proviso to subs. (11).

then for that purpose the Commissioners may of their own motion do all
or any of the following things : —

    (i) they may by order remove any trustee,[94] charity trustee, officer,
        agent or servant of the charity who has been responsible for or
        privy to the misconduct or mismanagement or has by his conduct
        contributed to it or facilitated it;

    (ii) they may make any such order as is authorised by subsection (1) of
        section sixteen of this Act with respect to the vesting in or transfer
        to the official custodian for charities of property held by or in trust
        for the charity;

    (iii) they may order any bank or other person who holds money or
        securities on behalf of the charity or of any trustee for it not to
        part with the money or securities without the approval of the
        Commissioners;

    (iv) they may, notwithstanding anything in the trusts of the charity, by
        order restrict the transactions which may be entered into, or the
        nature or amount of the payments which may be made, in the
        administration of the charity without the approval of the Com-
        missioners.

(2) The references in subsection (1) above to misconduct or mismanagement shall (notwithstanding anything in the trusts of the charity) extend to
the employment for the remuneration or reward of persons acting in the
affairs of the charity, or for other administrative purposes, of sums which
are excessive in relation to the property which is or is likely to be applied
or applicable for the purposes of the charity.

(3) The Commissioners may also remove a charity trustee by order
made of their own motion—

    (a) where the trustee has been convicted of felony, or is a bankrupt or
        a corporation in liquidation, or is incapable of acting by reason of
        mental disorder within the meaning of the Mental Health Act, 1959;

    (b) where the trustee has not acted, and will not declare his willingness
        or unwillingness to act;

    (c) where the trustee is outside England and Wales or cannot be found
        or does not act, and his absence or failure to act impedes the proper
        administration of the charity.

(4) The Commissioners may by order made of their own motion appoint
a person to be a charity trustee—

    (a) in place of a charity trustee removed by them under this section or
        otherwise;

    (b) where there are no charity trustees, or where by reason of vacancies
        in their number or the absence of incapacity of any of their number
        the charity cannot apply for the appointment;

    (c) where there is a single charity trustee, not being a corporation aggre-
        gate, and the Commissioners are of opinion that it is necessary to
        increase the number for the proper administration of the charity;

    (d) where the Commissioners are of opinion that it is necessary for the
        proper administration of the charity to have an additional charity

---

[94] See *Jones* v. *Att.-Gen.* [1973] 3 W.L.R. 608.

trustee, because one of the existing charity trustees who ought nevertheless to remain a charity trustee either cannot be found or does not act or is outside England and Wales.

(5) The powers of the Commissioners under this section to remove or appoint charity trustees of their own motion shall include power to make any such order with respect to the vesting in or transfer to the charity trustees of any property as the Commissioners could make on the removal or appointment of a charity trustee by ·them under section eighteen of this Act.

(6) Any order under this section for the removal or appointment of a charity trustee or trustee for a charity, or for the vesting or transfer of any property, shall be of the like effect as an order made under section eighteen of this Act.

(7) Subsections (10) and (11) of section eighteen of this Act shall apply to orders under this section as they apply to orders under that, save that where the Commissioners have by order removed a trustee, charity trustee, officer, agent, or servant of a charity under the power conferred by subsection (1) of this section, an appeal against such an order may be brought by any person so removed without a certificate of the Commissioners and without the leave of one of the judges of the High Court attached to the Chancery Division.

(8) The power of the Commissioners under subsection (1) above to remove a trustee, charity trustee, officer, agent or servant of a charity shall include power to suspend him from the exercise of his office or employment pending the consideration of his removal (but not for a period longer than three months), and to make provision as respects the period of the suspension for matters arising out of it, and in particular for enabling any person to execute any instrument in his name or otherwise act for him and, in the case of a charity trustee, for adjusting any rules governing the proceedings of the charity trustees to take account of the reduction in the number capable of acting.

(9) Before exercising any jurisdiction under this section, the Commissioners shall give notice of their intention to do so to each of the charity trustees, except any that cannot be found or has no known address in the United Kingdom; and any such notice may be given by post and, if given by post, may be addressed to the recipient's last known address in the United Kingdom.

Power to authorise dealings with charity property, etc.

23.—(1) Subject to the provisions of this section, where it appears to the Commissioners that any action proposed or contemplated in the administration of a charity is expedient in the interests of the charity, they may by order sanction that action, whether or not it would otherwise be within the powers exercisable by the charity trustees in the administration of the charity; and anything done under the authority of such an order shall be deemed to be properly done in the exercise of those powers.

Power to advise charity trustees

24.—(1) The Commissioners may on the written application of any charity trustee give him their opinion or advice on any matter affecting the performance of his duties as such.

(2) A charity trustee or trustee for a charity acting in accordance with the opinion or advice of the Commissioners given under this section with respect to the charity shall be deemed, as regards his responsibility for so acting, to have acted in accordance with his trust, unless, when he does so, either—

(*a*) he knows or has reasonable cause to suspect that the opinion or advice was given in ignorance of material facts; or

(*b*) the decision of the court has been obtained on the matter or proceedings are pending to obtain one.

Taking of legal proceedings

28.—(1) Charity proceedings [95] may be taken with reference to a charity either by the charity, or by any of the charity trustees, or by any person interested in the charity, or by any two or more inhabitants of the area of the charity, if it is a local charity, but not by any other person.

(2) Subject to the following provisions of this section, no charity proceedings relating to a charity (other than an exempt charity) shall be entertained or proceeded with in any court unless the taking of the proceedings is authorised by order of the Commissioners.

(3) The Commissioners shall not, without special reasons, authorise the taking of charity proceedings where in their opinion the case can be dealt with by them under the powers of this Act.

(4) This section shall not require any order for the taking of proceedings in a pending cause or matter or for the bringing of any appeal.

(5) Where the foregoing provisions of this section require the taking of charity proceedings to be authorised by an order of the Commissioners, the proceedings may nevertheless be entertained or proceeded with if after the order had been applied for and refused leave to take the proceedings was obtained from one of the judges of the High Court attached to the Chancery Division.

(6) Nothing in the foregoing subsections shall apply to the taking of proceedings by the Attorney General, with or without a relator.

(7) Where it appears to the Commissioners, on an application for an order under this section or otherwise, that it is desirable for legal proceedings to be taken with reference to any charity (other than an exempt charity) or its property or affairs, and for the proceedings to be taken by the Attorney General, the Commissioners shall so inform the Attorney General, and send him such statements and particulars as they think necessary to explain the matter.

(8) In this section "charity proceedings" means proceedings in any court in England or Wales brought under the court's jurisdiction with respect

---

[95] " Charity proceedings " as defined in s. 28 (8) do not cover proceedings by way of construction of a will or of a conveyance to determine whether or not the will or conveyance is effective to create a charitable trust: *Re Belling* [1967] Ch. 425; *Hauxwell* v. *Barton-upon-Humber U.D.C.* [1973] 3 **W.L.R.** 41.

to charities, or brought under the court's jurisdiction with respect to trusts in relation to the administration of a trust for charitable purposes.

Restrictions on dealing with charity property

29.—(1) Subject to the exceptions provided for by this section, no property forming part of the permanent endowment of a charity shall, without an order of the court or of the Commissioners, be mortgaged or charged by way of security for the repayment of money borrowed, nor, in the case of land in England or Wales, be sold, leased or otherwise disposed of.

(2) Subsection (1) above shall apply to any land which is held by or in trust for a charity and is or has at any time been occupied for the purposes of the charity, as it applies to land forming part of the permanent endowment of a charity; but a transaction for which the sanction of an order under subsection (1) above is required by virtue only of this subsection shall, notwithstanding that it is entered into without such an order, be valid in favour of a person who (then or afterwards) in good faith acquires an interest in or charge on the land for money or money's worth.

(3) This section shall apply notwithstanding anything in the trusts of a charity, but shall not require the sanction of an order—

(a) for any transaction for which general or special authority is expressly given (without the authority being made subject to the sanction of an order) by any statutory provision contained in or having effect under an Act of Parliament or by any scheme legally established; or

(b) for the granting of a lease for a term ending not more than twenty-two years after it is granted, not being a lease granted wholly or partly in consideration of a fine; or

(c) for any disposition of an advowson.

(4) This section shall not apply to an exempt charity, nor to any charity which is excepted by order or regulations.

Charitable companies

30.—(1) Where a charity may be wound up by the High Court under the Companies Act, 1948, a petition for it to be wound up under that Act by any court in England or Wales having jurisdiction may be presented by the Attorney General, as well as by any person authorised by that Act.

(2) Where a charity is a company or other body corporate, and has power to alter the instruments establishing or regulating it as a body corporate, no exercise of that power which has the effect of the body ceasing to be a charity shall be valid so as to affect the application of any property acquired under any disposition or agreement previously made otherwise than for full consideration in money or money's worth, or of any property representing property so acquired, or of any property representing income which has accrued before the alteration is made, or of the income from any such property as aforesaid.

Manner of executing instruments

34.—(1) Charity trustees [96] may, subject to the trusts of the charity, confer on any of their body (not being less than two in number) a general authority, or an authority limited in such manner as the trustees think fit, to execute in the names and on behalf of the trustees assurances or other deeds or instruments for giving effect to transactions to which the trustees are a party; and any deed or instrument executed in pursuance of an authority so given shall be of the same effect as if executed by the whole body.

(2) An authority under subsection (1) above—

    (a) shall suffice for any deed or instrument if it is given in writing or by resolution of a meeting of the trustees, notwithstanding the want of any formality that would be required in giving an authority apart from that subsection ;

    (b) may be given so as to make the powers conferred exercisable by any of the trustees, or may be restricted to named persons or in any other way;

    (c) subject to any such restriction, and until it is revoked, shall, notwithstanding any change in the charity trustees, have effect as a continuing authority given by and to the persons who from time to time are of their body.

(3) In any authority under this section to execute a deed or instrument in the names and on behalf of charity trustees there shall, unless the contrary intention appears, be implied authority also to execute it for them in the name and on behalf of the official custodian for charities or of any other person, in any case in which the charity trustees could do so.

(4) Where a deed or instrument purports to be executed in pursuance of this section, then in favour of a person who (then or afterwards) in good faith acquires for money or money's worth an interest in or charge on property or the benefit of any covenant or agreement expressed to be entered into by the charity trustees, it shall be conclusively presumed to have been duly executed by virtue of this section.

Transfer and evidence of title to property vested in trustees

35.—(1) Where, under the trusts of a charity, trustees of property held for the purposes of the charity may be appointed or discharged by resolution of a meeting of the charity trustees, members or other persons, a memorandum declaring a trustee to have been so appointed or discharged shall be sufficient evidence of that fact, if the memorandum is signed either at the meeting by the person presiding or in some other manner directed by the meeting, and is attested by two persons present at the meeting.

(2) A memorandum evidencing the appointment or discharge of a trustee under subsection (1) above, if executed as a deed, shall have the like operation under section forty of the Trustee Act, 1925 (which relates to vesting declarations as respects trust property in deeds appointing or discharging trustees), as if the appointment or discharge were effected by the deed.

---

[96] Charities are not limited to four trustees (Trustee Act 1925, s. 34) and charitable trustees may act by majority: *Re Whiteley* [1910] 1 Ch. 600.

Settled Land Act 1925

Charitable and public trusts

29.—(1) For the purposes of this section, all land vested or to be vested in trustees on or for charitable, ecclesiastical, or public trusts or purposes shall be deemed to be settled land, and the trustees shall, without constituting them statutory owners, have in reference to the land, all the powers which are by this Act conferred on a tenant for life and on the trustees of a settlement.

In connexion only with the exercise of those powers, and not so as to impose any obligation in respect of or to affect—

(a) the mode of creation or the administration of such trusts; or

(b) the appointment or number of trustees of such trusts;

the statute or other instrument creating the trust or under which it is administered shall be deemed the settlement, and the trustees shall be deemed the trustees of the settlement, and, save where the trust is created by a will coming into operation after the commencement of this Act, a separate instrument shall not be necessary for giving effect to the settlement.

Any conveyance of land held on charitable, ecclesiastical or public trusts shall state that the land is held on such trusts, and, where a purchaser has notice that the land is held on charitable, ecclesiastical, or public trusts, he shall be bound to see that any consents or orders requisite for authorising the transaction have been obtained.

Section 4. The Cy-Près Doctrine [97]

As the next chapter shows where a private trust is initially ineffective or subsequently fails there arises a resulting trust for the settlor or his estate if he is dead. If a charitable trust is initially impracticable or impossible, but the settlor had a general charitable intention,[98] then the trust property will be applied *cy-près* under a scheme formulated by the Charity Commissioners or the court, *i.e.*, it will be applied to some other charitable purposes as nearly as possible resembling the original purposes. If an effective charitable trust subsequently becomes impracticable or impossible then the trust property will be applied *cy-près* irrespective of the question of general charitable intention[99]: the settlor or, if he is dead, his residuary legatee or next of kin are forever excluded once the property has been effectually dedicated to charity.

Since 1960 section 14 of the Charities Act, *infra*, may be relied upon in special circumstances to establish general charitable intention and section 13, *infra*, has relaxed the requirements of impracticability or impossibility.

Initial lapse

As Wilberforce J. (as he then was) has observed,[1] " The courts have gone very far in the decided cases to resist the conclusion that a legacy to a

---

[97] See Sheridan & Delany's *The Cy-Près Doctrine* (J. D. Davies (1960) 76 L.Q.R. 598); Nathan Report (1952 Cmd. 8710), Chap. 9.

[98] If no general charitable intent exists then a resulting trust arises in accordance with general principle, *e.g.*, *Re Rymer, infra, Re Stemson* [1970] Ch. 16.

[99] Assuming the gift is an absolute one or made absolute by Perpetuities and Accumulations Act 1964, s. 12.

[1] *Re Roberts* [1963] 1 W.L.R. 406, 412.

charitable institution lapses, and a number of very refined arguments have been found acceptable with a view to avoiding that conclusion." This is because,[2] " Charity is always favoured by equity " and it is usually easier for the courts to find that no lapse has occurred rather than that lapse has occurred but that a general charitable intention is present to save the legacy for charity.

Essentially, charitable gifts can be construed in one of three ways and it is this question of construction that will normally be decisive of the lapse issue.[3] The gift may be construed as a gift to a particular charitable institution for the purposes thereof—and for no other purpose. In such a case if the institution ceases to exist before the testator's death the gift lapses: *Re Rymer, infra.*[4]

However, *Re Rymer* has been more honoured in being distinguished than in being followed as two other possible constructions are available for the court to save a gift. The gift may be construed as really being a gift for a particular charitable purpose so that the existence of the particular institution is not essential for the gift's validity if the purpose can be carried out by other means [5]: whilst institutions die, purposes live for ever (though they may become impossible or impracticable): *Re Finger's W.T., infra.* In this respect a gift to an unincorporate institution must necessarily be construed as a purpose gift whilst a gift to a corporate institution is construed as a gift to the corporate institution as part of its general funds without the imposition of any purpose trust unless there is something in the context of the will to justify the imposition of a purpose trust: *Re Finger's W.T.*[6]

Alternatively, the gift may be construed as a gift to augment the endowed funds of a named charity in which case though the named charity may have ceased to exist the gift will accrue to whichever charity holds the named charity's funds under some scheme or amalgamation: *Re Lucas, infra.*[7] However, if the named charity is liable to dissolution under its own constitution and chooses to dissolve itself so that its surplus funds on its winding up are transferred to some other charity the gift will lapse [8] unless this other charity can invoke the purpose construction: the testator made the gift to the named charity for the purpose of being held on the trusts and subject

---

[2] *Per* Lord Hanworth in *Re Watt* [1932] 2 Ch. 243n, 246.

[3] See J. B. E. Hutton (1969) 32 M.L.R. 283; R. B. M. Cotterell (1972) 36 Conv.(N.S.) 198; J. Martin (1974) 38 Conv.(N.S.) 187.

[4] Also *Re Stemson's W.T.* [1970] Ch. 16.

[5] *e.g., Re Watt* [1932] 2 Ch. 243n and *Re Roberts* [1963] 1 W.L.R. 406 where prima facie gifts to charitable institutions were construed as gifts for purposes. In the former a residuary gift to the " Southwark Diocesan Society " which ceased to exist before the testator's death took effect in favour of the " South London Church Fund and Southwark Diocesan Board of Finance " which was carrying on the same purposes as the earlier body. In the latter case a residuary gift to " the Sheffield Boys Working Home (Western Bank, Sheffield) " which had been sold before the testator's death took effect by way of a scheme directed by the court to carry out the purposes of that Home.

[6] If the unincorporate body has special statutory powers making it a quasi-corporation the corporation presumption applies: *Re Edis' Trusts* [1972] 2 All E.R. 769, 777.

[7] The principle was earlier established in *Re Faraker*. The question of endowed funds is immaterial if the gift is construed as a gift for purposes despite the contrary views of Plowman J. in *Re Slatter's W.T.* [1964] Ch. 512; see Hutton (1969) 32 M.L.R. 297, Farrand (1964) 28 Conv.(N.S.) 314.

[8] *Re Stemson's W.T.* [1970] Ch. 16.

to the powers contained in that charity's constitution so that the gift follows the surplus funds.[9]

If matters of construction cannot save the gift then the gift lapses unless the court can find a general charitable intention present. There have been many judicial statements on the meaning of the phrase: *e.g.*, Kay J. in *Re Taylor* [10]: " If upon the whole scope and intent of the will you discover the paramount object of the testator was to benefit not a particular institution but to effect a particular form of charity independently of any special institution or mode, then, although he may have indicated the mode in which he desires that to be carried out, you are to regard the primary paramount intention chiefly, and if the particular mode for any reason fails, to use the phrase familiar to us, execute that *cy-près*, that is, carry out the general paramount intention indicated without which his intention itself cannot be effected." Also Buckley J. in *Re Lysaght* [11]: " A general charitable intention ... may be said to be a paramount intention on the part of a donor to effect some charitable purpose which the court can find a method of putting into operation, notwithstanding that it is impracticable to give effect to some direction by the donor which is not an essential part of his true intention—not, that is to say, of his paramount intention.

" In contrast, a particular charitable intention exists when the donor means his charitable disposition to take effect if, but only if, it can be carried into effect in a particular specified way, for example, in connection with a particular school to be established at a particular place,[12] or by establishing a home in a particular house. ..." [13]

Where the gift is to an institution described by a particular name and the institution has never existed, a general charitable intent is presumed if the name imports a charitable object [14]; but the presumption may be easily rebutted if the will also includes a residuary gift in favour of charity.[15] On the other hand, the court is assisted in discovering a general charitable intention if the gift to the non-existent institution is of a share of residue and the other residuary legatees are charities.[16]

Where the gift is to an institution which exists at the testator's death but has ceased to exist before the legacy is paid, the fund has become devoted to charity and will be applied *cy-près*.[17]

Initial Failure

Whilst a legacy to an institution can lapse like a legacy to a pre-deceasing beneficiary, a legacy for a purpose does not lapse in the usual sense though it may be impossible or impracticable to carry out the purpose. If the purpose thus fails *ab initio* then the legacy fails unless there is a general

---

[9] This will be difficult to establish: *Re Roberts* [1963] 1 W.L.R. 406.

[10] (1888) 58 L.T. 538, 543.

[11] [1966] Ch. 191.

[12] *Re Wilson* [1913] 1 Ch. 314.

[13] *Re Packe* [1918] 1 Ch. 437.

[14] *Re Davis* [1902] 1 Ch. 876; *Re Harwood* [1936] Ch. 285.

[15] *Re Goldschmidt* [1957] 1 W.L.R. 524; 73 L.Q.R. 166 (V. T. H. Delany).

[16] *Re Knox* [1937] Ch. 109. See also *Re Satterthwaite's W.T.* [1966] 1 W.L.R. 277; and contrast *Re Jenkins' W.T.* [1966] 2 W.L.R. 615.

[17] *Re Slevin* [1891] 2 Ch. 236, *infra*; *Re Moon's W.T.* (1948) 64 T.L.R. 123, where the gift to the institution was to take effect after a life interest, during which the institution was discontinued.

charitable intention.[18]   If it is an *inter vivos* gift that fails a resulting trust arises in the absence of any general charitable intention.[19]

The time for determining whether failure has occurred is the date of the testator's death. If it is necessary an inquiry will be directed "whether at the date of the death of the testator it was practicable to carry his intentions into effect or whether at the said date there was any reasonable prospect that it would be practicable to do so at some future time."[20]   Where a future gift to charity is defeasible, an inquiry as to its practicability should be undertaken on the footing that the gift will not be defeated but will take effect at some future time as an interest in possession.[21]

Subsequent Failure

If at the testator's death the designated charity existed or it was not impossible or impracticable to carry out the designated charitable purposes then the gifted property has become charitable property to the perpetual exclusion of the testator's residuary legatee or next of kin[22]: *Re Slevin, infra.* Accordingly, the *cy-près* doctrine is available upon any subsequent failure: there is no need to prove any general charitable intent.[23]   The same is true of *inter vivos* gifts effectively dedicated to charity.

Impossibility and Impracticability

Before section 13 of the Charities Act 1960, *infra*, was enacted failure occurred when the purposes of the trust became impossible[24] or impracticable[25] or there was a surplus after the purposes had been carried out.[26] "Impracticable" appears to have become liberally interpreted over the years

---

18 *Re Wilson* [1913] 1 Ch. 314 (to endow a school at a particular place where there was no reasonable chance of such a school being established); *Re Good's W.T.* [1950] 2 All E.R. 653 (funds insufficient for erection and upkeep of rest-homes); *Re Ulverston and District New Hospital Building Trusts* [1956] Ch. 622 (funds always insufficient for required purpose); *Re Mackenzie* [1962] 2 All E.R. 890 (trust to provide bursaries for education at secondary schools rendered impossible by provision of free education by state); *Re Lysaght* [1966] Ch. 191 (gift to Royal College of Surgeons on trust to provide studentships for persons not of Jewish or Catholic faith failed as the College was not prepared to act as trustees of such a trust and Buckley J., rather remarkably, held that this was the rare type of case where the identity of the trustees was vital to the trust. He further held that a paramount charitable intent was present so that a *cy-près* scheme could be directed omitting the offending religious conditions. This reveals the flexibility of *cy-près* applications which can even provide remedies in special circumstances).

19 In a case like *Re Ulverston* [1956] Ch. 622, section 14 of the Charities Act 1960 would now provide the necessary general charitable intent.

20 *Re Wright* [1954] Ch. 347; *Re White* [1955] Ch. 188.

21 *Re Tacon* [1958] Ch. 447.

22 Assuming the gift is an absolute one or made absolute by Perpetuities and Accumulations Act 1964, s. 12.

23 *Re Moon's W.T.* [1948] 1 All E.R. 300; *Re Wokingham Fire Brigade Trusts* [1951] Ch. 373; *Re North Devon Relief Fund Trusts* [1953] 1 W.L.R. 1260; *Re Wright* [1954] Ch. 347; *Re King* [1923] 1 Ch. 243; *Re Robertson* [1930] 2 Ch. 71; *Re Royce* [1940] Ch. 514; *Re Raine* [1956] Ch. 417.

24 *Att.-Gen.* v. *City of London* (1790) 3 Bro.L.C. 171 (teaching Christianity to natives near Harvard U.S.A.).

25 *Ironmonger's Co.* v. *Att.-Gen.* (1844) 10 C.L. 8 F. 908 (redemption of British slaves in Turkey or Barbary).   The Charity Commissioners' Annual Reports are full of interesting examples.

26 *Re Campden Charities* (1881) 18 Ch.D. 310, *Re Robertson* [1930] 2 Ch. 71; *Re Raine* [1956] Ch. 417.

so as to include "highly undesirable," [27] but failure did not occur merely because performance in another way would be more beneficial or more suitable.[28] Section 13 now consolidates and extends the circumstances in which the *cy-près* doctrine may be available.

Section 14, *infra*, further provides that in certain circumstances the *cy-près* doctrine shall be available, without proof of general charitable intent, in the case of property given for specific *charitable* purposes which fail. The idea is to prevent resulting trusts arising in favour of anonymous donors contributing in the course of street collections etc. to specific charitable appeals.[29]

Re RYMER

Court of Appeal [1895] 1 Ch. 19; 64 L.J.Ch. 86; 71 L.T. 590 (Lord Herschell L.C., Lindley and A. L. Smith L.JJ.)

Rymer bequeathed £5,000 " to the rector for the time being of St. Thomas' seminary for the education of priests in the diocese of Westminster for the purposes of such seminary." At the date of the will the seminary was carried on at Hammersmith but it ceased to exist shortly before Rymer's death. Its students were transferred to a Birmingham seminary.

The court (affirming Chitty J.) held that the legacy lapsed and there was no general charitable intention to enable a *cy-près* application.

LINDLEY L.J.: " I think the result at which Mr. Justice Chitty has arrived is right. I have attended to and followed the arguments both of Mr. Cozens-Hardy and of Mr. Ingle Joyce, and in a great many of those arguments I concur. I think, with Mr. Joyce, that it does not do to approach a will of this kind by a short cut by saying there is a lapse, and there is an end of it. It is begging the question whether there is a lapse or not. You must construe the will and see what the real object of the language which you have to interpret is. I will not read the words of this gift again; I have read them very often, and studied them with care. I cannot arrive at the conclusion at which the Appellant's counsel ask me to arrive, that this is in substance and in truth a bequest of £5,000 for the education of the priests in the diocese of Westminster. I do not think it is. It is a gift of £5,000 to a particular seminary for the purposes thereof, and I do not think it is possible to get out of that. I think the context shows it. I refer to the masses, the choice of candidates, and so on. If once you get thus far the question arises, Does that seminary exist? The answer is, It

---

27 *Re Dominion Students' Hall Trust* [1947] Ch. 183 (scheme removing provision barring coloured students from a Hall for Dominion students).
28 *Re Weir Hospital* [1910] 2 Ch. 124 (houses left for use as hospital—site not suitable—so scheme for home for nurses—but held by C.A. to be *ultra vires* the Charity Commissioners as site not wholly impracticable); *Philpott* v. *St. George's Hospital* (1859) 27 Beav. 107, 111 *per* Romilly M.R.
29 *e.g., Re Ulverston* [1956] Ch. 622.

does not. Then you arrive at the result that there is a lapse; and if there is a lapse, is there anything in the doctrine of *cy-près* to prevent the ordinary doctrine of lapse from applying? I think not. Once you arrive at the conclusion that there is a lapse, then all the authorities which are of any value show that the residuary legatee takes the lapsed gift. We are asked to overrule that doctrine, laid down by Vice-Chancellor Kindersley in *Clark* v. *Taylor* [30] and followed in *Fisk* v. *Attorney-General*.[31] I think that the doctrine is perfectly right. There may be a difficulty in arriving at the conclusion that there is a lapse. But when once you arrive at the conclusion that a gift to a particular seminary or institution, or whatever you may call it, is 'for the purposes thereof,' and for no other purpose—if you once get to that, and it is proved that that institution or seminary, or whatever it is, has ceased to exist in the lifetime of the testator, you are driven to arrive at the conclusion that there is a lapse, and then the doctrine of *cy-près* is inapplicable. That is in accordance with the law, and in accordance with all the cases that can be cited. I quite agree that in coming to that conclusion you have to consider whether the mode of attaining the object is only machinery, or whether the mode is not the substance of the gift. Here it appears to me the gift to the seminary is the substance of the whole thing. It is the object of the testator. I think that is plain from the language used.

"Those are the short grounds of my judgment. I do not comment upon the decisions, because the Lord Chancellor has done that sufficiently."

Re FINGER'S WILL TRUSTS

Chancery Division [1972] Ch. 286; [1971] 3 W.L.R. 775; [1971] 3 All E.R. 1050

By her 1930 will the testatrix bequeathed her residuary estate in equal shares to eleven charitable institutions, two being named as the "National Radium Commission" and the "National Council for Maternity for Child Welfare 117 Piccadilly London". The Radium Commission was an unincorporated body created at the same time as the National Radium Trust: they voluntarily wound themselves up at the request of the Minister of Health when the National Health Service Acts came into effect.

The National Council for Maternity and Child Welfare was a corporate body existing at the date of the will but in 1948 it wound itself up voluntarily and transferred its surplus assets to the National Association for Maternity and Child Welfare, a similar organisation. In 1965 the testatrix died.

[30] 1 Drew. 642.
[31] L.R. 4 Eq. 521.

GOFF J. (in a reserved judgment): "Both gifts, therefore, fail unless they can be supported as purpose gifts, in which case they will be applicable by way of scheme for the indicated purpose, and if either or both cannot so stand there remains a final question, whether the will discloses a general charitable intention, in which case of course the share or shares will be applicable by scheme *cy-près*, failing which there is an intestacy.

"If the matter were *res integra* I would have thought that there would be much to be said for the view that the status of the donee, whether corporate or unincorporate, can make no difference to the question whether as a matter of construction a gift is absolute or on trust for purposes. Certainly, drawing such a distinction produces anomalous results. In my judgment, however, on the authorities a distinction between the two is well established, at all events in this court.

"I refer first to *Re Vernon's Will Trusts*[32] where Buckley J. said[33]:

'Every bequest to an unincorporated charity by name without more must take effect as a gift for a charitable purpose. No individual or aggregate of individuals could claim to take such a bequest beneficially. If the gift is to be permitted to take effect at all, it must be as a bequest for a purpose, *i.e.*, that charitable purpose which the named charity exists to serve. A bequest which is in terms made for a charitable purpose will not fail for lack of a trustee but will be carried into effect either under the sign manual or by means of a scheme. A bequest to a named unincorporated charity, however, may on its true interpretation show that the testator's intention to make the gift at all was dependent on the named charitable organisation being available at the time when the gift takes effect to serve as the instrument for applying the subject-matter of the gift to the charitable purpose for which it is by inference given. If so and the named charity ceases to exist in the lifetime of the testator, the gift fails (*Re Ovey, Broadbent* v. *Barrow*[34]). A bequest to a corporate body, on the other hand, takes effect simply as a gift to that body beneficially, unless there are circumstances which show that the recipient is to take the gift as a trustee. There is no need in such a case to infer a trust for any particular purpose. The objects to which the corporate body can properly apply its funds may be restricted by its constitution, but this does not necessitate inferring as a matter of construction of the testator's will a direction that the bequest is to be held in trust to be applied for those purposes: the natural construction is that the bequest is made to

---

[32] [1972] Ch. 300n.
[33] *Ibid.* 303.
[34] (1885) 29 Ch.D. 560.

the corporate body as part of its general funds, that is to say, beneficially and without the imposition of any trust. That the testator's motive in making the bequest may have undoubtedly been to assist the work of the incorporated body would be insufficient to create a trust.'

That was, of course, obiter in drawing the distinction but it was part of the decision so far as corporations are concerned, and he would clearly have held that there was a lapse, but for the escape which he found in the principle of *Re Faraker, Faraker* v. *Durell* [35] and *Re Lucas (decd.), Sheard* v. *Mellor*.[36] It has been submitted that the decision based on the application or analogy of those cases was wrong, but I need not go into that because that was a case of statutory interference under the National Health Service Act 1946, whereas the two charities with which I am concerned were wound up by themselves under powers in their respective constitutions, and it was held by Plowman J. in *Re Stemson's Will Trusts, Carpenter* v. *Treasury Solicitor*,[37] distinguishing *Re Vernon*,[38] that *Re Faraker* and *Re Lucas* do not in any event apply to such a case. That point, therefore, is not open before me, although counsel for the third defendant has reserved it for argument elsewhere should this case go higher.

"As I read the dictum in *Re Vernon* Buckley J.'s view was that in the case of an unincorporated body the gift is *per se* a purpose trust and, provided that the work is still being carried on, will have effect given to it by way of scheme notwithstanding the disappearance of the donee in the lifetime of the testator, unless there is something positive to show that the continued existence of the donee was essential to the gift. Then Buckley J. put his dictum into practice and decided *Re Morrison, Wakefield* v. *Falmouth*,[39] on that very basis, for there was nothing in that case beyond the bare fact of a gift to a dissolved unincorporated committee. In the case of a corporation, however, *Re Vernon* shows that the position is different as there has to be something positive in the will to create a purpose trust at all.

"In the relevant part of his judgment in *Re Meyers (decd.), London Life Association* v. *St. George's Hospital*,[40] Harman J. was not dealing with lapse at all but with a different question, namely, who could give a good receipt. Lapse was argued on two special grounds, first, because there was a direction that the gift was to be added to the invested funds of the respective hospitals, and by virtue of the Act the old corporations no longer had any such funds, and, secondly, that the old corporations had ceased to have any trustees who could give a receipt; both of which he rejected. He then commenced the second part of his judgment [41] with these words, ' Supposing there is no lapse '

---

[35] [1912] 2 Ch. 488.
[36] [1948] Ch. 424, *infra*, p. 306.
[37] [1970] Ch. 16.
[38] See [1972] Ch. 300.
[39] (1967) 111 S.J. 758.
[40] [1951] Ch. 534.
[41] [1951] Ch. 534, 539.

and went on to consider the competing claims of the old corporations and the new statutory bodies. Even so, two passages in the judgment appear to me clearly to recognise the distinction to which I have referred and to justify the analysis of *Re Meyers* (*decd.*) made by Buckley J. in *Re Vernon.* Those passages read as follows [42]:

'In other words, where there is a gift to an unincorporated body of that sort it is not given to the mere bricks and mortar or to the beds or the carpets but for the purpose for which the work is carried on. The judge held that the new body, namely, the hospital management committee appropriate to that locality, were carrying on that work and were therefore the proper recipients of the legacy involved in that case. . . . It seems to me that it would be contrary to common sense not to give a like construction to all the gifts in this clause and not to give the like kind of effect to them. Feeling as I do, and holding as I do, in the case of the unincorporated hospitals, that the gift must be construed as a gift for the work of the hospitals in question, and finding as I do find that in the case of the incorporated hospitals that work is to be carried on in every case by the governors or the hospital management committee appropriate to the locality, I must in this case find that the gifts are to the new body so constituted under the Act.'

I was much pressed in argument to the contrary of this conclusion with the decision of Wilberforce J. in *Re Roberts* (*decd.*), *Stenton* v. *Hardy*,[43] and particularly where he said [44]:

'The mere fact that a gift is given to an unincorporated charity does not seem to me to be enough to enable me to come to the conclusion that it is a gift for charitable purposes. . . .'

That, however, must be taken in the context of the question which he had just previously posed for himself:

'Is this a gift to a particular institution at a particular place, or should it be treated as a gift for charitable purposes, the purposes for which the home was originally established? '

He was not, as I understand it, considering whether this was a purpose gift; he assumed—and if I may say so rightly—that it was. That case was not a gift to a named unincorporated body but to a home, which describes something having a physical existence and in such a case the conclusion that it is a purpose gift is almost, if not absolutely, inescapable, and the hospital cases themselves rest on that basis. Nor was he considering whether there is any distinction between corporate and unincorporated bodies.

" The most that can be said of this passage is that it suggests perhaps that in both cases Wilberforce J. would look for some positive

---

[42] [1951] Ch. 534, 539, 541.
[43] [1963] 1 W.L.R. 406.
[44] [1963] 1 W.L.R. 406, 414.

indication that the purposes were general and not tied to the particular body or institution but in fact he reached the conclusion that it was general without any real context affirmatively to show that. He said [45]:

> ' I have enough to know that there was a charity in existence with premises acquired in 1889 and funds acquired later and I do not think I can accept the conclusion that the trusts relating to the funds were set out in the 1889 deed. How much the testatrix knew of all this is a matter of speculation, but I think that the gift of the testatrix in her will was for the purposes of an institution, and it was not so exclusively tied up with a particular home physically located on the premises used by the home as to enable me to say that, when the trusts of the physical home ceased to exist, the charity ended.'

In my judgment, therefore, there is nothing in this case seriously conflicting with *Re Vernon, Re Meyers* and *Re Morrison*.

"Accordingly I hold that the bequest to the National Radium Commission being a gift to an unincorporated charity is a purpose trust for the work of the commission which does not fail but is applicable under a scheme, provided (1) there is nothing in the context of the will to show—and I quote from *Re Vernon*—that the testatrix's intention to make the gift at all was dependent on the named charitable organisation being available at the time when the gift took effect to serve as the instrument for applying the subject-matter of the gift to the charitable purpose for which it was by inference given; (2) *that* charitable purpose still survives; but that the gift to the National Council for Maternity and Child Welfare 177 Piccadilly London being a gift to a corporate body fails, notwithstanding the work continues, unless there is a context in the will to show that the gift was intended to be on trust for that purpose and not an absolute gift to the corporation.

"I take first the National Radium Commission and I find in this will no context whatever to make that body of the essence of the gift. There was much argument what, on the true construction of the charter, were the objects of the National Radium Trust, but having regard to the construction which I have placed on the will the real question, as I see it, is, what were the purposes of the Radium Commission, and those are set out in article 5 of the supplemental charter of July 20, 1939, substituting a new article 7 for the original article 7 contained in the principal charter.

"The evidence of Anne Brenda Farthing in her affidavit sworn on November 27, 1970, satisfies me that with the possible exception of the function of maintaining a central record and statistical office the whole of the work formerly carried on by the commission has been, and is now being, carried on by or under the aegis of the Minister of Health

---

[45] [1963] 1 W.L.R. 406, 415.

and his successor the Secretary of State for Social Services. In my judgment, therefore, this is a valid gift for the purposes of the Radium Commission as specified in article 7 of the supplemental charter of July 20, 1939, and I direct that a scheme be settled for the administration of the gift.

" I turn to the other gift and here I can find no context from which to imply a purpose trust. Counsel for the Attorney-General relied on *Re Meyers*,[46] but there the context was absolutely compelling. There were many gifts to hospitals and the case dealt only with the hospitals, and whilst hospitals are not identical, this did mean that all were of the same type and character. Morever, not only were those gifts both to incorporated and unincorporated hospitals but in some of the corporate cases the name used by the testator was that by which the hospital was generally known to the public but was not the exact title of the corporation.

" In the present case there are at best three different groups of charities not one; they are not in fact grouped in the order in which they appear in the will, and the particular donees within the respective groups are not all of the same type or character. Further, and worse, two do not fit into any grouping at all, and for what it is worth they come first in the list. In my judgment, therefore, this case is not comparable with *Re Meyers*[46] and I cannot find a context unless I am prepared, which I am not, to say that the mere fact that residue is given to a number of charities, some of which are incorporated and others not, is of itself a sufficient context to fasten a purpose trust on the corporation. In my judgment, therefore, the bequest to the National Council for Maternity and Child Welfare fails.

" Finally, I must consider, however, whether the share passes on intestacy or whether the will discloses a general charitable intention. Here, of course, I was at once presented with *Re Harwood, Coleman* v. *Innes*,[47] and I feel the force of the argument on behalf of the next of kin based on that case, although I confess that I have always felt the decision in that case to be rather remarkable. However, Farwell J. did not say that it was impossible to find a general charitable intention where there is a gift to an identifiable body which has ceased to exist but only that it would be very difficult. Moreover, I observe that in *Re Roberts*[48] Wilberforce J. said this about *Re Harwood*:

' Lastly, there is *Re Harwood, Coleman* v. *Innes*, a decision of Farwell J., where there was a gift to a very particular society for a very special purpose, the Wisbech Peace Society, where it was not difficult to come to the conclusion that the society having disappeared the gift lapsed. Though I gladly accept what Farwell J., said,[49] that where the gift was to a particular charity carefully

[46] [1951] Ch. 534.
[47] [1936] Ch. 285.
[48] [1963] 1 W.L.R. 404, 416.   [49] [1936] Ch. 285, 287.

identified, it would be very difficult for the court to find a general charitable intent if the named charity had ceased to exist at the testator's death, one must consider that in relation to the circumstances of the charity and the information which can be found whether in fact the particular charity has ceased to exist.'

In the present case the circumstances are very special. First, of course, apart from the life interest given to the mother and two small personal legacies the whole estate is devoted to charity, and that is, I think, somewhat emphasised by the specific dedication to charity in the preface:

> ' And after payment of the said legacies my Trustees shall hold the balance then remaining of my residuary estate upon trust to divide the same in equal shares between the following charitable institutions and funds.'

Again, I am, I think, entitled to take into account the nature of the council, which as I have said was mainly, if not exclusively, a co-ordinating body. I cannot believe that this testatrix meant to benefit that organisation and that alone. Finally, I am entitled to place myself in the armchair of the testatrix and I have evidence that she regarded herself as having no relatives.

"Taking all these matters into account, in my judgment I can and ought to distinguish *Re Harwood* and find, as I do, a general charitable intention. Accordingly, this share is applicable *cy-près*, and I understand the Attorney-General is willing that it should be paid to the association. That seems to me manifestly the proper thing to do, and therefore I shall order by way of scheme, the Attorney-General not objecting, that this share be paid to the proper officer of the association to be held on trust to apply the same for its general purposes."
Order accordingly.

Re LUCAS

Court of Appeal [1948] Ch. 424; [1948] 2 All E.R. 22 (Lord Greene M.R., Somervell L.J., Jenkins J.).

A testatrix by her will dated October 12, 1942, after bequeathing (*inter alia*) a legacy of 500*l*. " to the Crippled Children's Home, Lindley Moor, Huddersfield " devised and bequeathed also three twenty-seconds of her residuary estate to " the Crippled Children's Home." In 1916 a home called " The Huddersfield Home for Crippled Children " was built on Lindley Moor. On October 17, 1941, this home was closed and a scheme for the future administration of its assets was made by the charity commissioners. Under that scheme the charity thereby created was to be known as " The Huddersfield Charity for Crippled Children " and the trustees were directed to apply the income (after payment of expenses of management) " in or towards sending poor crippled children to holiday or convalescent homes." The testatrix died on December 18, 1943, and her will was proved on April 14, 1944. A summons was taken out by the trustees of the will to determine whether the bequests were valid or failed by lapse, owing to the closing of the home at Lindley Moor in the lifetime of the testatrix. Roxburgh J. held[50] that the bequests lapsed and the Attorney-General appealed successfully.

The judgment of the court was read by LORD GREENE M.R.: " In these circumstances the question arose whether the gifts made by the testatrix to ' the Crippled Children's Home, Lindley Moor, Hudders-field' took effect as gifts to the Huddersfield Charity for Crippled Children (that is to say to the charity established by the trust deed of March 29, 1915, in the reconstituted form in which it was continued under the scheme); or lapsed as gifts made for a particular charitable purpose which had wholly failed with the closing of the home at Lindley Moor, with the result that the legacy so given fell into residue and the share of residue so given was undisposed of by the will and passed as on intestacy.

" It is settled by authority binding upon this court that so long as there are funds held in trust for the purposes of a charity the charity continues in existence and is not destroyed by any alteration in its constitution or objects made in accordance with law, as for example by a scheme under the Charitable Trusts Acts: (see *In re Faraker*[51]). There is no doubt that the facts stated above regarding the charity established by the trust deed of March 29, 1915, in the present case are such as to bring it well within this principle. Accordingly, if the gifts made by the testatrix were upon their true construction gifts to the charity, that is to say gifts simply in augmentation of the funds held by the trustees of the trust deed of March 29, 1915, for the objects of the Huddersfield Home for Crippled Children as defined by the deed, they took effect as gifts to that same charity in the reconstituted form in which it was continued under the scheme, that is to say as gifts in augmentation of the funds held by the trustees appointed by the scheme for the modified objects thereby prescribed.

" On the other hand, it is equally well settled that (in the absence of general charitable intention which is not in question here) a gift for a particular charitable purpose which has wholly failed is subject to the ordinary doctrine of lapse: (see *In re Rymer*[52]). Accordingly if the testatrix's gifts were on their true construction gifts for the up-keep of the premises at Lindley Moor as a home for crippled children and for no other purpose, they lapsed with the consequences indicated above, as gifts for a particular charitable purpose which had wholly

[50] [1943] 1 Ch. 175.
[51] [1912] 2 Ch. 488.
[52] [1895] 1 Ch. 19.

failed in the lifetime of the testatrix, and indeed before the date of the will, with the expiry of the lease and consequent closing of the home.

" The learned judge was therefore perfectly right in holding, as he did, that the case turns upon this short question of construction.

" His conclusion upon it was to the effect that the gifts were on their true construction gifts for the upkeep of the particular home, and not gifts by way of addition to the endowment of the charity, and accordingly lapsed on the second of the two principles stated above.

" We think it is pertinent to consider what the position would have been if the home at Lindley Moor had in fact remained subject to the trusts of the trust deed of March 29, 1915, and in use in accordance with its provisions, down to a date subsequent to the death of the testatrix. If in this assumed state of affairs the court had been called to decide the destination of the testatrix's gifts to ' The Crippled Children's Home, Lindley Moor, Huddersfield,' we think it is reasonably plain that the court, upon evidence that there was a charity called ' The Huddersfield Home for Crippled Children,' established by the trust deed of March 29, 1915, with the objects therein mentioned, and carrying on a home for crippled children at the address specified by the testatrix, would have held that the description given by the testatrix was a mere misdescription of ' The Huddersfield Home for Crippled Children,' and would accordingly have construed the gifts as equivalent to gifts expressed to be made simply to ' The Huddersfield Home for Crippled Children.' On being apprised of the constitution of the charity, the court would, we think, have held further that the gifts took effect as gifts to the trustees for the time being of the trust deed of March 29, 1915. If the court had further been called on to decide on what trusts the trustees would hold the gifts when received, we think the answer would necessarily have been ' Upon the trusts of the trust deed as an addition to the funds subjects to those trusts.' This conclusion would, we think, have followed from the absence of any words in the will to indicate that the gifts were to be held for some special or restricted purpose as distinct from the general purposes of the charity. No such indication could have been collected from the references to crippled children and to a home in the inaccurate description used by the testatrix, in as much as the correct description itself contains similar references. In a word, the court would we think have properly construed the gift as a gift to the trustees of the charity for the general purposes of the charity.

" If that would have been the right construction of the gifts on the footing that the home at Lindley Moor had remained in use under the provisions of the trust deed until after the death of the testatrix, it must in our view still be the right construction in the events which acually happened. The fact that the home had actually been closed before the date of the will, and the testatrix's apparent ignorance of that fact, cannot alter the meaning of the language which she used. The effect in the events which have happened of the gifts as so construed is determined, so far as this court is concerned, by *In re Faraker*.[53]

" For these reasons we hold that the appeal should be allowed and that the order of Roxburgh J. should be varied by substituting for the declaration therein contained a declaration to the effect that the gifts in question constitute valid and effectual charitable bequests and that the trustees of the Huddersfield Charity for Crippled Children are entitled to such bequests by way of addition to the endowment of such charity, and by omitting the inquiry and directions consequential thereon." *Appeal allowed.*

Re SLEVIN

Court of Appeal [1891] 2 Ch. 236; 60 L.J.Ch. 439; 64 L.T. 311; 39 W.R. 578; 7 T.L.R. 394 (Lindley, Bowen and Kay L.JJ.)

The testator gave a number of legacies to various persons, using the introductory words " I bequeath the pecuniary legacies following." He then gave a number of legacies to various institutions, churches and bodies, using the introductory words " I bequeath the following charitable legacies." Included among the last-mentioned legacies was one to an orphanage voluntarily maintained by a lady at her own expense which was in existence at the testator's death but was discontinued shortly afterwards and before the assets of his estate were administered. Stirling J. held that the legacy was not applicable *cy-près*. The Attorney-General appealed.

KAY L.J.: " This case raises a question which seems only to have occurred in two instances in the books, namely, whether a charitable bequest to an institution which comes to an end after the death of the testator, but before the legacy is paid over, fails for the benefit of the residuary legatee, as in the case of a lapse. . . .

" The orphanage did come to an end before the legacy was paid over. In the case of a legacy to an individual, if he survived the testator it could not be argued that the legacy would fall into the residue. Even if the legatee died intestate and without next-of-kin, still the money was his, and the residuary legatee would have no right whatever against the Crown. So, if the legatee were a corporation which was dissolved after the testator's death, the residuary legatee would have no claim.

" Obviously it can make no difference that the legatee ceased to exist immediately after the death of the testator. The same view must be applicable whether it was a day, or month, or year, or as might well happen, ten years after; the legacy not having been paid either from delay occasioned by the administration of the estate or owing to part of

---

[53] [1912] 2 Ch. 488.

the estate not having been got in. The legacy became the property of
the legatee upon the death of the testator, though he might not, for some
reason, obtain the receipt of it till long after. When once it became the
absolute property of the legatee, that is equivalent to saying that it
must be provided for; and the residue is only what remains after making
such provision. It does not for all purposes cease to be part of the
testator's estate until the executors admit assets and appropriate and
pay it over; but that is merely for their convenience and that of the
estate. The rights as between the particular legatee and the residue are
fixed at the testator's death.

"These propositions are so obvious that it would seem impossible
to dispute them without some authority to the contrary. Is there any
such authority? [He found no such authority.]

"In the present case we think that the Attorney-General must
succeed, not on the ground that there is such a general charitable
intention that the fund should be administered *cy-près* even if the
charity had failed in the testator's lifetime, but because, as the charity
existed at the testator's death, this legacy became the property of that
charity, and on its ceasing to exist its property falls to be administered
by the Crown, who will apply it, according to custom, for some
analogous purpose of charity: *Att.-Gen.* v. *Ironmongers' Co.*[54]; *Wilson*
v. *Barnes*[55]; *Tyssen on Charitable Bequests.*[56]" *Appeal allowed.*

Charities Act 1960

Occasions for applying property cy-près

13.—(1) Subject to subsection (2) below, the circumstances in which the
original purposes of a charitable gift can be altered to allow the property
given or part of it to be applied *cy-près* shall be as follows[57]:

(a) where the original purposes, in whole or in part,—

(i) have been as far as may be fulfilled; or
(ii) cannot be carried out, or not according to the directions given and to the spirit of the gift; or

(b) where the original purposes provide a use for part only of the property available by virtue of the gift; or

(c) where the property available by virtue of the gift and other property applicable for similar purposes can be more effectively used in conjunction, and to that end can suitably, regard being had to the spirit of the gift, be made applicable to common purposes; or

(d) where the original purposes were laid down by reference to an area which then was but has since ceased to be a unit for some other purpose, or by reference to a class of persons or to an area which has for any reason since ceased to be suitable, regard being had to the spirit of the gift, or to be practical in administering the gift; or

[54] (1834) 2 My. & K. 576. [55] (1886) 38 Ch.D. 507.
[56] p. 440.
[57] The section is available for initial and subsequent failure, subs. (2) preserving the requirement of general charitable intention for cases of initial failure.

(*e*) where the original purposes,[58] in whole or in part, have, since they were laid down,—

       (i) been adequately provided for by other means; or

       (ii) ceased,[59] as being useless or harmful to the community or for other reasons, to be in law charitable; or

       (iii) ceased in any other way to provide a suitable and effective method of using the property available by virtue of the gift, regard being had to the spirit of the gift.[60]

(2) Subsection (1) above shall not affect the conditions which must be satisfied in order that property given for charitable purposes may be applied *cy-près*, except in so far as those conditions require a failure of the original purposes.

(3) References in the foregoing subsections to the original purposes of a gift shall be construed, where the application of the property given has been altered or regulated by a scheme or otherwise, as referring to the purposes for which the property is for the time being applicable.

(5) It is hereby declared that a trust for charitable purposes places a trustee under a duty, where the case permits and requires the property or some part of it to be applied *cy-près*, to secure its effective use for charity by taking steps to enable it to be so applied.

Application cy-près of gifts of donors unknown or disclaiming

14.—(1) Property given for specific charitable purposes which fail shall be applicable *cy-près* as if given for charitable purposes generally, where it belongs—

(*a*) to a donor who, after such advertisements and inquiries as are reasonable,[61] cannot be identified or cannot be found; or

(*b*) to a donor who has executed a written disclaimer of his right to have the property returned.[62]

(2) For the purposes of this section property shall be conclusively presumed (without any advertisement or inquiry) to belong to donors who cannot be identified, in so far as it consists—

(*a*) of the proceeds of cash collections made by means of collecting boxes or by other means not adapted for distinguishing one gift from another; or

(*b*) of the proceeds of any lottery, competition, entertainment, sale or

---

[58] " The original purposes " are apt to apply to the trusts as a whole where the trust is for payment of a fixed annual sum out of the income of a fund to charity A and payment of the residue of the income to charity B: the phrase is not read severally in relation to the trust for payment of the fixed annual sum and the trust for payment of residuary income: *Re Lepton's Charity* [1972] Ch. 276.

[59] See Lord Simonds in *National Anti-Vivisection Society* v. *I.R.C.* [1948] A.C. 31, 64, 65.

[60] This broad head is very useful indeed. The phrase " spirit of the gift " was recommended by the Nathan Committee (Cmd. 8710, para. 365) who borrowed it from s. 116 of the Education (Scotland) Act 1946 where it appears as " the spirit of the intention of the founders as embodied either (i) in the original deed constituting the endowment where it is still the governing instrument, or (ii) in any scheme affecting the endowment." See also *Re Lepton's Charity* [1972] Ch. 276.

[61] See *Re Henry Wood National Memorial Trusts* [1966] 1 W.L.R. 1601.

[62] Apart from this provision disclaimer might have resulted in the property being *bona vacantia*.

similar money-raising activity, after allowing for property given to provide prizes or articles for sale or otherwise to enable the activity to be undertaken.

(3) The court may by order direct that property not falling within subsection (2) above shall for the purposes of this section be treated (without any advertisement or inquiry) as belonging to donors who cannot be identified, where it appears to the court either—

    (*a*) that it would be unreasonable, having regard to the amounts likely to be returned to the donors, to incur expense with a view to returning the property; or

    (*b*) that it would be unreasonable, having regard to the nature, circumstances and amount of the gifts, and to the lapse of time since the gifts were made, for the donors to expect the property to be returned.

(4) Where property is applied *cy-près* by virtue of this section, the donor shall be deemed to have parted with all his interest at the time when the gift was made; but where property is so applied as belonging to donors who cannot be identified or cannot be found, and is not so applied by virtue of subsection (2) or (3) above,—

    (*a*) the scheme shall specify the total amount of that property; and

    (*b*) the donor of any part of that amount shall be entitled, if he makes a claim not later than twelve months after the date on which the scheme is made, to recover from the charity for which the property is applied a sum equal to that part, less any expenses properly incurred by the charity trustees after that date in connection with claims relating to his gift; and

    (*c*) the scheme may include directions as to the provision to be made for meeting any such claim.

(5) For the purposes of this section, charitable purposes shall be deemed to " fail " where any difficulty in applying property to those purposes makes that property or the part not applicable *cy-près* available to be returned to the donors.

(6) In this section, except in so far as the context otherwise requires, references to a donor include persons claiming through or under the original donor, and references to property given include the property for the time being representing the property originally given or property derived from it.

(7) This section shall apply to property given for charitable purposes, notwithstanding that it was so given before the commencement of this Act.

PROBLEMS

1. Are the following trusts charitable, and, if not, are they otherwise valid?

    (i) To apply the income from £50,000 amongst such of my relations, with preference for my nephews and nieces, as my trustees may consider to be poor.

    (ii) £40,000 to my trustees to invest and apply the income therefrom in educating the children of needy employees or ex-employees of London Transport for 21 years whereupon the income shall be used to provide an English Public School education for such children living in Oxford as my trustees shall determine provided that in either case no person of the Roman Catholic faith shall be so assisted.

(iii) A £500,000 trust set up by I.C.I. Ltd. and Barclays Bank for the income to be used at the trustees' discretion in assisting towards the education of the children or grandchildren of any persons employed or formerly employed by I.C.I. Ltd. or Barclays Bank or any of their subsidiary or associated companies.

2. In 1975 a public appeal for funds to establish a recreation and sports centre for the Sheffield City Police was launched. £20,000 was donated by Hank Badman, £8,000 was obtained from street collections, £1,000 profit was made out of a pop festival in aid of the appeal and £2,000 was donated anonymously. It has now proved completely impossible to obtain any suitable site. What should be done with the moneys? [63]

3. By his will dated April 1, 1969, Oscar O'Flaherty bequeathed £10,000 to the Society for the Relief of Poverty among Ulster Liberationists. In 1974 that Society was amalgamated with the Society for the Relief of Poverty among Ulster Freedom Fighters. Oscar has just died. Advise his executors.

4. By his will Alan left his residuary estate to Tim and Tom " upon trust to apply the income therefrom to such of the adult residents of Greater London as my Trustees in their absolute discretion shall think fit having due regard to the need to combat the stress, squalor and expense of residing in Greater London provided that my Trustees shall have power to add as further possible beneficiaries adult residents of any other city in the United Kingdom where the stress, squalor and expense are in my Trustees' absolute discretion comparable to that of Greater London provided further that one day before the expiration of the period of eighty years from my death (which period I hereby specify as the perpetuity period applicable hereto) the aforesaid Trust shall determine and the capital shall be distributed equally *per stirpes* amongst those who shall then be my statutory next of kin."

Alan has just died and Tim and Tom seek advice on the validity of the Trust.

---

[63] Consider again after reading the next chapter.

CHAPTER 7

RESULTING TRUSTS

MEGARRY J. has recently classified resulting trusts as either being "automatic resulting trusts" or "presumed resulting trusts": *Re Vandervell's Trusts, infra.* The former arise automatically wherever some or all of the beneficial interest has not been effectively exhausted by the express trusts. The latter are presumed to arise where property is bought by X in Y's name or gratuitously transferred by X to Y in which case Y will rebuttably be presumed to hold the property on trust for X. Resulting trusts are exempt from the formal requirements of the Law of Property Act 1925, s. 53 and, in particular, take on significance where spouses or relatives contribute towards property without any writing being used to set out the relative size of each contributor's interest in the property.

Re VANDERVELL'S TRUSTS (No. 2)

Chancery Division [1974] 1 All E.R. 47

This is the third of a line of cases concerning the late Mr. Vandervell's affairs, the earlier two [1] having gone to the Lords as is likely with this case. It also seems likely that there will be two further cases.[2] The misfortunes of Mr. Vandervell are a lawyer's nightmare.

In the first Vandervell case the Lords held that a valuable option held by a company trustee was held by the company on a resulting trust for Mr. Vandervell, owing to the absence of express trusts, so surtax was payable in respect of dividends declared in respect of the shares to which the option related, since Mr. Vandervell had not divested himself absolutely of all interest in the shares within Income Tax Act 1952, s. 415.

In this case Mr. Vandervell's personal representatives claimed from the trustee company (which had exercised the option) the substantial dividends received by the company since exercising the option on the basis that they were held on a resulting trust. The company adduced new evidence to show *inter alia* that no resulting trust arose—but without avail.

MEGARRY J. (in a reserved judgment): "It seems to me that the relevant points on resulting trusts may be put in a series of propositions which, so far as not directly supported, appear at least to be consistent with Lord Wilberforce's speech, and reconcilable with the true intent of Lord Upjohn's speech, though it may not be with all his words on a

---

[1] *Vandervell* v. *I.R.C.* [1967] 2 A.C. 291; *Vandervell Trustees Ltd.* v. *White* [1971] A.C. 912.

[2] *Re Vandervell's Trusts* [1974] 1 All E.R. 47, 57, 58.

literal reading. The propositions are the broadest of generalisations, and do not purport to cover the exceptions and qualifications that doubtless exist. Nevertheless, these generalisations at least provide a starting point for the classification of a corner of equity which might benefit from some attempt at classification. The propositions are as follows.

"(1) If a transaction fails to make any effective disposition of any interest it does nothing. This is so at law and in equity, and has nothing to do with resulting trusts.

"(2) Normally the mere existence of some unexpressed intention in the breast of the owner of the property does nothing: there must at least be some expression of that intention before it can effect any result. To yearn is not to transfer.

"(3) Before any doctrine of resulting trust can come into play, there must at least be some effective transaction which transfers or creates some interest in property.

"(4) Where A effectually transfers to B (or creates in his favour) any interest in any property, whether legal or equitable, a resulting trust for A may arise in two distinct classes of case. For simplicity, I shall confine my statement to cases in which the transfer or creation is made without B providing any valuable consideration, and where no presumption of advancement can arise; and I shall state the position for transfers without specific mention of the creation of new interests.

"(a) The first class of case is where the transfer to B is not made on any trust. If, of course, it appears from the transfer that B is intended to hold on certain trusts, that will be decisive, and the case is not within this category; and similarly if it appears that B is intended to take beneficially. But in other cases there is a rebuttable presumption that B holds on a resulting trust for A. The question is not one of the automatic consequences of a dispositive failure by A, but one of presumption: the property has been carried to B, and from the absence of consideration and any presumption of advancement B is presumed not only to hold the entire interest on trust, but also to hold the beneficial interest for A absolutely. The presumption thus establishes both that B is to take on trust and also what that trust is. Such resulting trusts may be called ' presumed resulting trusts.'

"(b) The second class of case is where the transfer to B is made on trusts which leave some or all of the beneficial interest undisposed of. Here B automatically holds on a resulting trust for A to the extent that the beneficial interest has not been carried to him or others. The resulting trust here does not depend on any intentions or presumptions, but is the automatic consequence of A's failure to dispose of what is vested in him. Since *ex hypothesi* the transfer is on trust, the resulting trust does not establish the trust but merely carries back to A the beneficial interest that has not been disposed of. Such resulting trusts may be called ' automatic resulting trusts.'

" (5) Where trustees hold property in trust for A, and it is they who, at A's direction, make the transfer to B, similar principles apply, even though on the face of the transaction the transferor appears to be the trustees and not A. If the transfer to B is on trust, B will hold any beneficial interest that has not been effectually disposed of on an automatic resulting trust for the true transferor, A. If the transfer to B is not on trust, there will be a rebuttable presumption that B holds on a resulting trust for A.

" I turn to the speech of Lord Wilberforce. At the outset [3] he stated his concurrence with the view taken below, based on Mr. Vandervell's failure to divest himself of all interest in the option, and said that but for the division of opinion in the House he would have thought it sufficient to express his concurrence. He then turned to the facts, and after discussing them at some length, he rejected the contention that the option had become subject to the trusts of the children's settlement. He did this because it was not the intention of Mr. Vandervell or Mr. Robins ' at the time the option was exercised that this should be so.' [4] I think that the word ' exercised ' probably should be read as ' granted ', for there does not seem to have been any evidence before this House as to the intentions which Mr. Vandervell or Mr. Robins had when the option was exercised in 1961; and, I may add, the reference to the Law Reports to the alternative ' numbered 3 above ' [5] is plainly not to the arabic (3) [6] but to the roman (iii).[7] Lord Wilberforce held that on the evidence the defendant company held the option not beneficially, subject to some understanding or gentleman's agreement, but on ' trusts which were undefined, or in the air '.[8] He then referred to the decision of the Court of Appeal [9] as being one where, starting from the fact that the defendant company took the option as a volunteer, the court thought that the presumption of a resulting trust arose and was not displaced. Lord Wilberforce then said [10]:

> " ' For my part, I prefer a slightly different and simpler approach. The transaction has been investigated on the evidence of the settlor and his agent and the facts have been found. There is no need, nor room, as I see it, to invoke a presumption. The conclusion, on the facts found, is simply that the option was vested in the trustee company as a trustee on trusts, not defined at the time, possibly to be defined later. The equitable, or beneficial interests, however, cannot remain in the air: the consequence in

[3] [1967] 2 A.C. 291, 324.
[4] [1967] 2 A.C. 291, 327.
[5] [1967] 2 A.C. at 327.   [6] [1967] 2 A.C. 291, 326.
[7] [1967] 2 A.C. 291, 325.   [8] [1967] 2 A.C. 291, 328.
[9] [1966] Ch. 261.   [10] [1967] 2 A.C. 291, 329.

law must be that it remains in the settlor. There is no need to
consider some of the more refined intellectualities of the doctrine
of resulting trust, nor to speculate whether, in possible circumstances, the shares might be applicable for the taxpayer's benefit:
he had, as the direct result of the option and of the failure to
place the beneficial interest in it securely away from him, not
divested himself absolutely of the shares which it controlled.'

" Now as its seems to me this passage shows Lord Wilberforce as
rejecting the application of what I have called the ' presumption ' class
of resulting trust and accepting that the case falls into what I have
called the ' automatic ' class. The grant of the option to the defendant
company was, as he had held, on trust. There was thus no need, nor,
indeed, any reason to consider whether the option was granted to the
defendant company beneficially, or whether there was any presumption
of a resulting trust, for that question had been foreclosed by the
decision that the defendant company did not take beneficially but held
on trust. The only question was whether Mr. Vandervell had ever
effectually disposed of the beneficial interest that the defendant company, holding on trust, must hold on a resulting trust for him unless
and until an effective trust for some other beneficiary was constituted.
This had not been done, and so the defendant company continued to
hold on a resulting trust for Mr. Vandervell.

" If one bears in mind Lord Wilberforce's speech and the principles
that I have tried to state it seems to me that when one looks again at
Lord Upjohn's speech it is at least possible to read it as supporting
what seems to me to be the right analysis of the case, namely, that the
true grantor of the option was Mr. Vandervell, that the option was
granted to the defendant company on trust, that no effective trusts
were ever declared, and so the defendant company held the option on
an automatic resulting trust for Mr. Vandervell. Indeed, that is what
I think he was laying down. The question is whether, on the evidence
before me I ought to reach any other conclusion." [" No " was the
answer given to this by the learned judge.]

Reversed by the Court of Appeal, [1974] 3 W.L.R. 256: but leave to
appeal to the House of Lords was granted.

Section 1. Automatic Resulting Trusts

These trusts arise in favour of the settlor where his property has been subjected to express trusts which fail whether for failure of marriage consideration, uncertainty, lapse, disclaimer, perpetuity, illegality or for any other
reason.[11] If the illegal purpose is effected before the settlor repents this

---

[11] *Hodgson* v. *Marks* [1971] Ch. 892, 933 *per* Russell L.J. but his remarks about
failure of express trusts for lack of form being just the occasion for implication of
a resulting trust cannot be taken at face value but must be read in the special
circumstances of the case; *Re Ames' Settlement* [1946] Ch. 217 though see now
sections 16 and 24 of the Matrimonial Causes Act 1973. If the settlor were a
testator then the property results to the testator's estate: if the property were speci-

will prevent the enforcement of the resulting trust.[12] Resulting trusts also
arise if settlors fail to dispose of the whole beneficial interest under the
trusts.[13] Usually, the imposition of a resulting trust creates the situation
which the settlor would have intended to arise if asked—that is why the
phrase "implied trust" is sometimes used in such situations. However,
fiscal considerations these days often make a trust in favour of the settlor
in a particular eventuality the very last thing intended by the settlor.[14]

Whether or not the settlor has failed to dispose effectively of the entire
beneficial interest is often a difficult question of construction. In *Re
Andrew's Trust* [15] a fund was subscribed for the education of a deceased
clergyman's children, and when they had attained full age and completed
their education a surplus remained. Instead of holding that there was a
resulting trust for the subscribers, the court held that the fund should be
divided equally among the children, treating the fund as having been subscribed for the benefit of the children generally with particular reference to
their education. Contrast the resulting trust in *Re Abbott Fund, infra.* In
Re Foord [16] where a testator left his estate to his sister absolutely on trust
to pay his wife an annuity, and the estate income exceeded the annuity, the
sister was held beneficially entitled to the balance so as to exclude any
resulting trust. Contrast the resulting trust in *Re West.*[17]

Where a donor has parted with his money out and out in pursuance of
some contract this suffices to prevent any resulting trust arising. Thus, in
the case of a society, formed to raise funds by subscriptions from its members for the purpose of providing for widows of deceased members, which
had surplus funds after the death of the last widow there could be no
resulting trust for the deceased members' estates. Each member parted
absolutely with his money in return for contractual benefits for his widow.
Each member had received all that he had contracted for so the surplus
passed as *bona vacantia* to the Crown.[18] Similarly, no resulting trust
should arise where donors part absolutely with their money for tickets con-
tractually entitling them to participate in raffles, sweepstakes, beetle drives,
whist drives, discotheques or to watch live entertainment, and the purposes
for which such moneys have been raised fail to exhaust the moneys: *Re
West Sussex Constabulary's Benevolent Fund Trusts, infra.*

Where no contractual element is present then it is very difficult where
money is raised for certain purposes to show that the donors had a general
intention to part with their money out and out beyond all recall rather than
merely part with their money *sub modo* to the intent that their particular
wishes only should be carried into effect. However, where street

---

fically devised or bequeathed it falls into residue, whilst if the property were comprised in the residuary gift the property passes to the next of kin under the intestacy rules set out in the Administration of Estates Act 1925 as amended.

12 *Re Great Berlin Steamboat Co.* (1884) 26 Ch.D. 616; *Gascoigne* v. *Gascoigne*
[1918] 1 K.B. 223; *Chethiar* v. *Chethiar* [1962] A.C. 294; *Perpetual Executors
Association of Australia Ltd.* v. *Wright* (1917) 23 C.L.R. 185; *Petherpermal Chetty*
v. *Muniandi Servai*, L.R. 35 Ind.App. 98.
13 *Re Gillingham Bus Disaster Fund, infra*; *Re Abbott Trust, infra*; *Re West*,
[1900] 1 Ch. 84.
14 *Re Vandervell's Trusts (No. 2)* [1974] 3 All E.R. 205.
15 [1905] 2 Ch. 48.
16 [1922] 2 Ch. 519.
17 [1900] 1 Ch. 84.
18 *Cunnack* v. *Edwards* [1896] 2 Ch. 679.

collections are concerned, with thousands of anonymous donors, the courts are becoming increasingly ready to find a general intention to part with money out and out so as to exclude any resulting trusts: *cf. Re Gillingham Bus Disaster Fund, infra,* and *Re West Sussex Constabulary's Benevolent Fund Trusts, infra.* If no resulting trust arises, then the money will pass as *bona vacantia* to the Crown.[19]

Members' clubs raise special considerations where these bodies are dissolved. Instead of a resulting trust arising or property passing as *bona vacantia* to the Crown the property will pass to the members as of the date of dissolution equally *per capita* or, it seems in the case of friendly or mutual benefit societies with rules contemplating advantages related to contributions, rateably *per* contributions. Members make contributions to the club or society for their own benefit and obtain contractual rights under the rules of the club or society. In the absence of special rules governing a dissolution, it is only fit and proper that existing members at the dissolution should take equally *per capita,* equal enjoyment being the ethic behind members' clubs, except that in the friendly and mutual benefit society cases distribution should be rateably *per* contributions where such societies contemplate advantages related to contributions but otherwise should be *per capita*: *Re The Sick and Funeral Society of St. John's Sunday School, infra.*[20]

It should be noted that what appears to be a failure to exhaust the beneficial interest so as to invoke a resulting trust may not be the case owing to the doctrine of acceleration.[21] Thus, if T by will leaves property to A for life and after A's death to B absolutely and A disclaims his interest B's interest is accelerated so as to take effect immediately: there is no resulting trust of the income of the property until A's death.

Finally, no resulting trust in favour of the settlor or his estate arises where the rule in *Hancock* v. *Watson*[22] applies. This is the rule " that if you find an absolute gift to a legatee in the first instance, and trusts are engrafted or imposed on that absolute interest which fail, either from lapse or invalidity or any other reason, then the absolute gift takes effect so far as the trusts have failed to the exclusion of the residuary legatee or next of kin as the case may be."[23] The rule is equally applicable to *inter vivos* settlements.[24]

Re ABBOTT FUND, SMITH v. ABBOTT

Chancery Division [1900] 2 Ch. 326; 69 L.J.Ch. 539; 48 W.R. 541

A sum of about £248, which had been collected by the late Dr. Fawcett for the benefit of two members of the late Dr. Abbott's family,

---

[19] Generally see Ing's *Bona Vacantia* (1971).

[20] Also *Re St. Andrew's Allotment Association* [1969] 1 W.L.R. 229; These two cases and *Re William Denby Sick Fund* [1971] 2 All E.R. 1196, 1201 reveal that the old view that rights to funds of a members' club are founded in trust has been superseded by the sounder view that such rights are founded in contract.

[21] *Re Davies* [1957] 1 W.L.R. 922; *Re Harker* [1969] 1 W.L.R. 1125 (rightly not following *Re Davies* on the impact of acceleration upon the class closing rules); *Re Hodge* [1943] Ch. 300; A. M. Pritchard [1973] C.L.J. 246.

[22] [1902] A.C. 14.

[23] *Per* Lord Davey [1902] A.C. 14, 22.

[24] *Att.-Gen.* v. *Lloyds Bank* [1935] A.C. 382; *Re Burton's S.T.* [1955] Ch. 348.

had been placed by Dr. Fawcett to the credit of two accounts headed " The Abbott Fund " and " The Abbott Fund, Treasurer, Dr. Rowland Morris Fawcett." Dr. Fawcett died shortly afterwards without having drawn on either of these accounts, but the matter was taken up by the plaintiff, who issued a circular appealing for annual subscriptions for the benefit of the same two persons, the circular stating that the fund which had been collected by Dr. Fawcett was insufficient. Large sums were received in response to the circular; the executors of Dr. Fawcett transferred the Abbott fund to the plaintiff and another as trustees; payments were made to the two beneficiaries; both the beneficiaries died in 1899; and there was now a surplus in the hands of the trustees. An originating summons was taken out to determine who was entitled to the surplus, the defendants being the personal representative of the two beneficiaries and one of the subscribers chosen to represent the subscribers as a class. In response to the learned judge's request for further information, the plaintiff stated that the circular had been sent to the majority of the contributors to the fund collected by Dr. Fawcett, but that no annual statement of accounts showing how far the Fawcett fund was being drawn upon had been sent to those contributors.

It was argued for the defendant personal representative that the various subscriptions had been made as absolute gifts for the benefit of the two beneficiaries during their joint lives and then for the survivor, so that the surplus now accrued to the estate of the survivor.

STIRLING J.: " The difficulty in this case arises from the fact that there is no declaration of trust. The case is one which not infrequently happens, as I have reason to believe. The late Dr. Fawcett, a gentleman well known in Cambridge, collected a sum of upwards of £248 for the purpose of being applied for the relief of two ladies who were deaf and dumb. These two ladies had been provided by their father with ample means of livelihood, but had been deprived of it by the defalcations of a gentleman whom he had appointed a trustee. We have no information as to the terms on which this fund was handed over to Dr. Fawcett. After his death, which took place before 1891, the matter was taken up by a gentleman still living, the plaintiff, Mr. Hamblin Smith. He issued a circular stating what had been done by Dr. Fawcett. [His Lordship read the circular, and also the statement which had been made by Mr. Smith in answer to his Lordship's request for further information, and continued:] It seems to me, having regard to that statement, that I may treat the fund which was collected by Dr. Fawcett as really applicable to the same purpose, for that is the effect of it, as that which was subscribed in response to the circular issued by Mr. Smith. The ladies are both dead, and the question is whether, so far as this fund had not been applied for their benefit, there is a resulting trust of it for the subscribers. I cannot believe that it was ever intended to become the absolute property of the ladies so that they should be in a position to demand a transfer of it to themselves, or so that if they became bankrupt the trustee in the bankruptcy should be able to claim it. I believe it was intended that it should be administered by Mr. Smith, or the trustees who had been nominated in pursuance of the circular. I do not think the ladies ever became absolute owners of this fund. I think that the trustee or trustees were intended to have a wide discretion as to whether any, and if any what, part of the fund should be applied for the benefit of the ladies and how the application should be made. That view would not deprive them of all right in the fund, because if the trustees had not done their duty—if they either failed to exercise their discretion or exercised it improperly—the ladies might successfully have applied to the court to have the fund administered according to the terms of the circular. In the result, therefore, there must be a declaration that there is a resulting trust of the moneys remaining unapplied for the benefit of the subscribers to the Abbott fund." *Declaration accordingly.*

Re GILLINGHAM BUS DISASTER FUND

Chancery Division [1958] Ch. 300; [1957] 3 W.L.R. 1069; 101 S.J. 974; [1958] 1 All E.R. 37

In 1951 the Mayors of Gillingham, Rochester and Chatham wrote a letter to the Press inviting subscriptions for a fund to be devoted, " among other things, to defraying the funeral expenses [of the boys killed in the disaster], caring for boys who may be disabled, and then to such worthy cause or causes in memory of the boys who lost their lives, as the Mayors may determine." Named and anonymous donors contributed to the fund, part of which could not be applied for the designated purposes. The trusts not being charitable and not having been made so by the Charitable Trusts Validation Act 1954,[25] the cy-près doctrine was inapplicable. The question therefore was whether the remaining part of the fund was repayable to the donors or went to the Crown as *bona vacantia.*

HARMAN J.: " . . . The general principle must be that where money is held upon trust and the trusts declared do not exhaust the fund it will revert to the donor or settlor under what is called a resulting trust. The reasoning behind this is that the settlor or donor did not part with his money absolutely out-and-out but only *sub modo* to the intent that his wishes as declared by the declaration of trust should be carried into effect. When, therefore, this has been done any surplus still belongs to him. This doctrine does not, in my judgment, rest on any evidence of the state of mind of the settlor, for in the vast majority of cases no doubt he does not expect to see his money back: he has created a trust which so far as he can see will absorb the whole of it.

---

[25] *Supra,* pp. 275–278.

The resulting trust arises where that expectation is for some unforeseen reason cheated of fruition, and is an inference of law based on after-knowledge of the event.

[His Lordship referred to *Re Abbott* [26] and to *Re Hobourn Aero Components Air Raid Distress Fund*,[27] in both of which a resulting trust had been held to arise, but the Crown had not made any claim to the surplus funds as *bona vacantia*. He then continued:] I was referred to two cases where a claim was made to *bona vacantia* and succeeded. The first of these was *Cunnack* v. *Edwards*.[28] This was a case of a society formed to raise a fund by subscriptions and so forth from the members to provide for widows of deceased members. Upon the death of the last widow of a member it was found that there was a surplus. It was held by the Court of Appeal that no question of charity arose, that there was no resulting trust in favour of the subscribers, but that the surplus passed to the Crown as *bona vacantia*. [His Lordship then quoted passages from the judgments of A. L. Smith [29] and Rigby [30] L.JJ., and continued:]

" The *ratio decidendi* seems to have been that having regard to the constitution of the fund no interest could possibly be held to remain in the contributor who had parted with his money once and for all under a contract for the benefit of his widow. When this contract had been carried into effect the contributor had received all that he had contracted to get for his money and could not ask for any more.

" A similar result was reached in the case of *Smith* v. *Cooke*,[31] cited by A. L. Smith L.J.,[32] though it does not appear from the report what the result was. Another case cited to me was *Braithwaite* v. *Attorney-General*.[33] Here again it was held that there was no room for a resulting trust and the claim to *bona vacantia* succeeded. The opponents there, it appears, were the last two surviving annuitants. Their claim was rejected on the ground that they had had or were having everything for which the contract provided. The claim of the Attorney-General on behalf of charity was rejected, it being held that there was no charity. A different result was reached by Kekewich J. in *Re Buck*,[34] but it was on the ground that the society was a charity and the money was therefore directed to be applied *cy-près*.

" In addition there were cited to me the three hospital cases: *Re Welsh Hospital (Netley) Fund*,[35] *Re Hillier's Trusts* [36] and *Re Ulverston*

---

26 [1900] 2 Ch. 326; *supra*, p. 319.
27 [1946] Ch. 86.
28 [1896] 2 Ch. 679.
29 *Ibid*. 683.
30 *Ibid*. 689.
31 [1891] A.C. 297.
32 [1896] 2 Ch. 679, 683.
33 [1909] 1 Ch. 510.
34 [1896] 2 Ch. 727.
35 [1921] 1 Ch. 655.
36 [1954] 1 W.L.R. 9, 700 (C.A.).

and District New Hospital Building Trusts.[37] In the first of these cases
P. O. Lawrence J. held that all subscribers to the hospital must be taken
to have parted with their money with a general intention in favour
of charity. This was the only contest in the case, between the subscribers on the one hand and charity on the other. In *Hillier's* case [38]
Upjohn J., at first instance, found that certain categories of subscribers
were entitled to have their money back but that others, namely, those
who had contributed to collections at entertainments and so forth, had
no such right. The Court of Appeal varied this order [39] and declared
that the whole fund should go to charity but without prejudice to the
right of any individual to prove that he had no general intention but
only the particular intention in favour of one hospital. In the *Ulverston*
case the Court of Appeal decided that the whole fund had been collected
with only one object and not for general charitable purposes and that,
so far as money had been received from identifiable sources, there was
a resulting trust. No claim to *bona vacantia* was there made, and
Jenkins L.J., in explaining the position in *Re Hillier's Trusts*, said
this [40]: 'I appreciate that anonymous contributors cannot expect their
contributions back in any circumstances, at all events so long as they
remain anonymous. I appreciate also the justice of the conclusion that
anonymous contributors must be regarded as having parted with their
money out-and-out, though I would make a reservation in the case of
an anonymous contributor who was able to prove conclusively that he
had in fact subscribed some specified amount to the fund. If the
organisers of a fund designed exclusively and solely for some particular
charitable purpose send round a collecting-box on behalf of the fund,
I fail to see why a person who had put £5 into the box, and could prove
to the satisfaction of the court he had done so, should not be entitled
to have his money back in the event of the failure of the sole and
exclusive charitable purpose for which his donation was solicited and
made.'

   " Jenkins L.J., in the course of his judgment,[41] threw out the suggestion that donations from unidentifiable donors might in such a case
be treated as *bona vacantia*.

   " It was argued for the Crown that the subscribers to this fund must
be taken to have parted with their money out-and-out, and that there
was here, as in *Cunnack* v. *Edwards* and *Braithwaite* v. *Att.-Gen.*, no
room for a resulting trust. But there is a difference between those cases
and this in that they were cases of contract and this is not. Further,
it seems to me that the hospital cases are not of great help because the
argument centred round general charitable intent, a point which cannot
arise unless the immediate object be a charity. I have already held

---

[37] [1956] Ch. 622.
[38] [1954] 1 W.L.R. 9.
[39] *Ibid.* 711.
[40] [1956] Ch. 622, 633.
[41] *Ibid.*

there is no such question here. In my judgment the nearest case is the *Hobourn* case, which, however, is no authority for the present because no claim for *bona vacantia* was made.

"In my judgment the Crown has failed to show that this case should not follow the ordinary rule merely because there was a number of donors who, I will assume, are unascertainable. I see no reason myself to suppose that the small giver who is anonymous has any wider intention than the large giver who can be named. They all give for the one object. If they can be found by inquiry the resulting trust can be executed in their favour. If they cannot I do not see how the money could then, with all respect to Jenkins L.J., change its destination and become *bona vacantia*. It will be merely money held upon a trust for which no beneficiary can be found. Such cases are common and where it is known that there are beneficiaries the fact that they cannot be ascertained does not entitle the Crown to come in and claim. The trustees must pay the money into court like any other trustee who cannot find his beneficiary. I conclude, therefore, that there must be an inquiry for the subscribers to this fund." *Declaration accordingly.*

Re WEST SUSSEX CONSTABULARY'S BENEVOLENT FUND TRUSTS

Chancery Division [1971] Ch. 1; [1970] 2 W.L.R. 848; [1970] 1 All E.R. 544

In 1930 a fund was set up to provide for widows and orphans of deceased members. The W. Sussex Constabulary amalgamated with other forces in 1968 so that it was doubtful as to how its funds were to be dealt with. The funds came from (1) contributions of past and present members; (2) entertainments, raffles, sweepstakes, collecting boxes; (3) donations and legacies.

In a reserved judgment Goff J. held that (3) were held on resulting trusts for the donors whilst (1) and (2) were *bona vacantia*.

GOFF J.: "... I now have to determine what is [the fund's] destination in those circumstances.

"First it was submitted that it belongs exclusively and in equal shares to all those persons now living who were members on December 31, 1967, and the personal representatives of all the then members since deceased, to all of whom I will refer collectively as 'the surviving members.' That argument is based on the analogy of the members' club cases, and the decisions in *Re Printers and Transferrers Amalgamated Trades Protection Society*,[42] *Re Lead Co.'s Workmen's Fund Society, Lowes* v. *Governor and Co. for Smelting Down Lead with Pit and Sea Coal* [43] and the Irish case, *Tierney* v. *Tough*.[44]

---

[42] [1899] 2 Ch. 184.
[43] [1904] 2 Ch. 196.
[44] [1914] 1 I.R. 142.

" The *ratio decidendi* of the first two of those cases was that there was a resulting trust, but that would not give the whole fund to the surviving members unless rule 10 could somehow be made to carry to them the contributions of the former members despite the failure of the purposes of the fund, as was pointed out by Sir Charles O'Connor M.R. in *Tierney's* case,[45] and unless, indeed, the moneys raised from outside sources also could somehow be made to accrue to the surviving members. I agree with Ungoed-Thomas J. that the *ratio decidendi* of *Tierney's* case is to be preferred: see *Re St. Andrew's Allotment Association's Trusts, Sargeant* v. *Probert.*[46]

" This brings one back to the principle of the members' clubs, and I cannot accept that as applicable, for these reasons. First, it simply does not look like it. This was nothing but a pensions or dependent relatives fund not at all akin to a club. Secondly, in all the cases where the surviving members have taken, with the sole exception of *Tierney's* case, the club, society or organisation existed for the benefit of the members for the time being exclusively, whereas in the present case as in *Cunnack* v. *Edwards,*[47] only third parties could benefit. Moreover, in *Tierney's* case the exception was minimal and discretionary and can, I think, fairly be disregarded. Finally, this very argument was advanced and rejected by Chitty J. in the *Cunnack* case [48] at first instance, and was abandoned on the hearing of the appeal.

" That judgment also disposes of the further argument that the surviving members had power to amend the rules under rule 14 and could, therefore, have reduced the fund into possession and so ought to be treated as the owners of it or the persons for whose benefit it existed at the crucial moment. They had the power but they did not exercise it, and it is now too late.

" Then it was argued that there is a resulting trust, with several possible consequences. If this be the right view there must be a primary division into three parts, one representing contributions from former members, another contributions from the surviving members, and the third moneys raised from outside sources. The surviving members then take the second, and possibly by virtue of rule 10 the first also. Rule 10 is as follows:

' Any member who voluntarily terminates his membership shall forfeit all claim against the Fund except in the case of a member transferring to a similar Fund of another force in which instance the contributions paid by the member to the West Sussex Constabulary's Widows, Children and Benevolent (1930) Fund may be paid into the Fund of the force to which the member transfers.'

---

[45] [1914] 1 I.R. 147, 155.
[46] [1969] 1 W.L.R. 229, 238.
[47] [1896] 2 Ch. 679.
[48] [1895] 1 Ch. 489, 496.

Alternatively, the first may belong to the past members on the footing that rule 10 is operative so long only as the fund is a going concern, or may be *bona vacantia*. The third is distributable in whole or in part between those who provided the money, or again is *bona vacantia*.

"In my judgment the doctrine of resulting trust is clearly inapplicable to the contributions of both classes. Those persons who remained members until their deaths are in any event excluded because they have had all they contracted for, either because their widows and dependants have received or are in receipt of the prescribed benefits, or because they did not have a widow or dependants. In my view that is inherent in all the speeches in the Court of Appeal in *Cunnack* v. *Edwards*.[49] Further, whatever the effect of rule 10 may be on the contribution of those members who left prematurely, they and the surviving members alike are also unable to claim under a resulting trust, because they put up their money on a contractual basis and not one of trust: see *per* Harman J., in *Re Gillingham Bus Disaster Fund, Bowman* v. *Official Solicitor*.[50]

"The only case which has given me difficulty on this aspect of the matter is *Re Hobourn Aero Components Ltd.'s Air-Raid Distress Fund, Ryan* v. *Forrest*,[51] where in somewhat similar circumstances it was held there was a resulting trust. The argument postulated, I think, the distinction between contract and trust but in another connection, namely whether the fund was charitable.[52] There was in that case a resolution to wind up but that was not, at all events as expressed, the *ratio decidendi* (see *per* Cohen J.[53]) but as his Lordship observed there was no argument for *bona vacantia*. Moreover no rules or regulations were ever made and although in fact £1 per month was paid or saved for each member serving with the forces, there were no prescribed contractual benefits. In my judgment that case is therefore distinguishable.

"Accordingly, in my judgment all the contributions of both classes are *bona vacantia*, but I must make a reservation with respect to possible contractual rights. In *Cunnack* v. *Edwards* and *Braithwaite* v. *Att.-Gen.*,[54] all the members had received or provision had been made for all the contractual benefits. Here the matter has been cut short.

"Those persons who died whilst still in membership cannot, I conceive, have any rights, because in their case the contract has been fully worked out, and on a contractual basis I would think that members who retired would be precluded from making any claim by rule 10, although that is perhaps more arguable. The surviving mem-

[49] [1896] 2 Ch. 679.
[50] [1958] Ch. 300, 314.
[51] [1946] Ch. 86.
[52] [1946] Ch. 89, 90.
[53] [1946] Ch. 97.
[54] [1909] 1 Ch. 510

bers, on the other hand, may well have a right in contract on the ground of frustration or total failure of consideration, and that right may embrace contributions made by past members, although I do not see how it could apply to moneys raised from outside sources. I have not, however, heard any argument based on contract and therefore the declarations I propose to make will be subject to the reservation which I will later formulate. This will not prevent those parts of the fund which are *bona vacantia* from being paid over to the Crown as it has offered to give a full indemnity to the trustees.

" I must now turn to the moneys raised from outside sources. Counsel for the Attorney-General made an overriding general submission that there could not be a resulting trust of any of the outside moneys because in the circumstances it is impossible to identify the trust property. No doubt something could be achieved by complicated accounting, but this, he submitted, would not be identification but notional reconstruction. I cannot accept that argument. In my judgment in a case like this the present equity will cut the gordian knot by simply dividing the ultimate surplus in proportion to the sources from which it has arisen. Chitty J. in *Cunnack* v. *Edwards* [55] at first instance, was prepared to order an inquiry notwithstanding the difficulty that it involved going back over many years and despite the fact that the early records were not available, but that was a difficulty of ascertaining the original contributions, not of working out surpluses or interest calculations year by year. Similarly it was not suggested that any such operation ought to be carried out, or that the necessity for it prevented the doctrine of resulting trust being applied in the *Printers'* case. [56] Yet in both those cases, although the matter was not further complicated by outside contributions, the problem of interest on invested funds and of contributions and expenditure made at different times must have presented itself. Again in the *Printers'* case fines and forfeitures were ignored.

" There may be cases of tolerable simplicity where the court will be more refined, but in general where a fund has been raised from mixed sources interest has been earned over the years and income and possibly capital expenditure has been made indiscriminately out of the fund as an entirety, and when the venture comes to an end, prematurely or otherwise, the court will not find itself baffled but will cut the gordian knot as I have said.

" Then counsel divided the outside moneys into three categories: first, the proceeds of entertainments, raffles and sweepstakes; secondly, the proceeds of collecting boxes; and thirdly, donations including legacies, if any, and he took particular objections to each. I agree that there cannot be any resulting trust with respect to the first category.

---

[55] [1895] 1 Ch. 489, 497, 498.
[56] [1899] 2 Ch. 184.

I am not certain whether Harman J. meant to decide otherwise in the *Gillingham Bus Disaster* case.[57] The statement of facts [58] refers to ' street collections and so forth.' There is mention of whist drives and concerts in the argument,[59] but the judge himself did not speak of anything other than gifts. If he did, however, I must respectfully decline to follow his judgment in that regard, for whatever may be the true position with regard to collecting boxes, it appears to me to be impossible to apply the doctrine of resulting trust to the proceeds of entertainments and sweepstakes and such-like money raising operation for two reasons. First, the relationship is one of contract and not of trust. The purchaser of a ticket may have the motive of aiding the cause or he may not. He may purchase a ticket merely because he wishes to attend the particular entertainment or to try for the prize, but whichever it be he pays his money as the price of what is offered and what he receives. Secondly, there is in such cases no direct contribution to the fund at all. It is only the profit, if any, which is ultimately received, and there may even be none. In any event the first category cannot be any more susceptible to the doctrine than the second to which I now turn.

" Here one starts with the well-known dictum of P. O. Lawrence J. in *Re Welsh Hospital (Netley) Fund, Thomas* v. *Att.-Gen.*[60]:

> ' So far as regards the contributors to entertainments, street collections, etc., I have no hesitation in holding that they must be taken to have parted with their money out and out. It is inconceivable that any person paying for a concert ticket or placing a coin in a collecting box presented to him in the street should have intended that any part of the money so contributed should be returned to him when the immediate object for which the concert was given or the collection made had come to an end. To draw such an inference would be absurd on the face of it.'

This was adopted by Upjohn J. in *Re Hillier, Hillier* v. *Att.-Gen.*,[61] where the point was actually decided.

" [The analysis of Upjohn J.] was approved by Denning L.J. in the same case in the Court of Appeal,[62] although it is true that he went on to say that the law makes a presumption of charity:

> ' Let me first state the law as I understand it in regard to money collected for a specific charity by means of a church collection, a flag day, a whist drive, a dance, or some such activity. When a man gives money on such an occasion, he gives it, I think, beyond recall. He parts with his money out and out.'

---

57 [1958] Ch. 300.
58 [1958] Ch. 300, 304.
59 [1958] Ch. 300, 309.
60 [1921] 1 Ch. 655, 660, 661
61 [1954] 1 W.L.R. 9.
62 [1954] 1 W.L.R. 700, 714.

" In *Re Ulverston & District New Hospital Building Fund, Birkett
v. Barrow and Furness Hospital Management Committee*,[63] Jenkins
L.J. threw out a suggestion that there might be a distinction in the
case of a person who could prove that he put a specified sum in a
collecting box, and in the *Gillingham* case [64] Harman J. after noting
this, decided that there was a resulting trust with respect to the proceeds of collections. He said [65]:

> ' In my judgment the Crown has failed to show that this case
> should not follow the ordinary rule merely because there was a
> number of donors who, I will assume, are unascertainable. I see
> no reason myself to suppose that the small giver who is anony-
> mous has any wider intention than the large giver who can be
> named. They all give for the one object. If they can be found
> by inquiry the resulting trust can be executed in their favour. If
> they cannot I do not see how the money could then, with all
> respect to Jenkins L.J., change its destination and become *bona
> vacantia*. It will be merely money held on a trust for which no
> beneficiary can be found. Such cases are common, and where it
> is known that there are beneficiaries, the fact that they cannot be
> ascertained does not entitle the Treasury Solicitor to come in and
> claim. The trustees must pay the money into court like any other
> trustee who cannot find his beneficiary. I conclude, therefore,
> that there must be an inquiry for the subscribers to this fund.'

It will be observed that Harman J. considered that the *Welsh Hospital
(Netley)* case,[66] *Re Hillier* [67] and *Re Ulverston* [68] did not help him
greatly because they were charity cases. It is true that they were and,
as will presently appear, in my view that is very significant in relation
to the third category, but I do not think it was a valid objection with
respect to the second, and for my part I cannot reconcile the decision
of Upjohn J. in *Re Hillier* with that of Harman J. in the *Gillingham*
case. As I see it, therefore, I have to choose between them. On the
one hand it may be said that Harman J. had the advantage which
Upjohn J. had not of considering the suggestion made by Jenkins L.J.
On the other that, with all respect, seems to me somewhat fanciful and
unreal. I agree that all who put their money into collecting boxes
should be taken to have the same intention, but why should they not
all be regarded as intending to part with their money out and out,
absolutely, in all circumstances? I observe that P.O. Lawrence J.
used very strong words. He said any other view was inconceivable and
absurd on the face of it. That commends itself to my humble judg-

[63] [1956] Ch. 622, 633.
[64] [1958] Ch. 300.
[65] [1958] Ch. 300, 314.
[66] [1921] 1 Ch. 655.
[67] [1954] 1 W.L.R. 9.
[68] [1956] Ch. 622.

ment, and I, therefore, prefer and follow the judgment of Upjohn J. in *Re Hillier*.

That brings me to the third category. [His Lordship referred to *Re Hillier*.]

" Therefore, where, as in the present case, the object was neither equivocal nor charitable, I can see no justification for infecting the third category with the weaknesses of the first and second, and I cannot distinguish this part of the case from *Re Abbott Fund Trusts, Smith* v. *Abbott*.[69]

" I will hear counsel on the form of order and in any case will direct a minute to be signed and circulated, but in general I direct two inquiries. (1) What donations of specific amounts other than through collecting boxes but including legacies were at any time given to the fund and by whom, and whether any living donors have since died and, if so, who are their personal representatives and who are the personal representatives of any testators by whom such legacies were bequeathed. (2) What is the total amount of: (a) the contributions made by the members since the inception of the fund; (b) the proceeds of entertainments, sweepstakes, collections and any similar money raising activities; and (c) such donations including legacies. I then direct the total net assets after payment of costs to be divided between these three portions *pro rata*.

" And I make the following declarations: first, that the portion attributable to donations and legacies is held on a resulting trust for the donors or their estates and the estates of the respective testators; and secondly, that the remainder of the fund is *bona vacantia*. These declarations are, however, without prejudice to: (1) any claim which may be made in contract by any person or the personal representatives of any person who was at any time a member; and (2) any right or claim of the trustees to be indemnified against any such claim out of the whole fund including the portion attributable to donations and legacies.

" Finally there will, of course, be general liberty to apply."
Declarations accordingly.

Re THE SICK AND FUNERAL SOCIETY OF ST. JOHN'S SUNDAY SCHOOL

Chancery Division [1973] Ch. 51; [1972] 2 W.L.R. 902; [1972] 2 All E.R. 439.

The Society was formed to provide benefits for its members who fell into two classes, adult members and child members, the latter paying contributions at half the rate and receiving allowances and death benefit at half the rate. On the voluntary winding up of the

---

[69] [1900] 2 Ch. 326.

Society one question that arose related to the proportions in which the assets should be divided amongst members.

MEGARRY J.: " ... Is each member entitled to an equal share, or is there to be a division into full shares and half shares, with those paying ½d. a week entitled only to a half share, and those paying 1d. a week a full share? Or is the basis of distribution to be proportionate to the amounts respectively contributed by each member? The first step, in my view, is to decide between the first two contentions on the one hand and the third on the other; is the proper basis that of division *per capita*, whether in full or half shares, or that of division in proportion to the amounts contributed? In discussing this, I speak, of course, in general terms, and subject to any other basis for division that is to be discerned in the rules or any other source.

" The authorities are in a curious state. In *Re Printers and Trans-ferrers Amalgamated Trades Protection Society* [70] Byrne J. applied the amounts-contributed basis to a trade union, putting matters on the footing of a resulting trust, and directing division on that basis among the members existing at the time of the resolution for dissolution. In *Re Lead Co.'s Workmen's Fund Society* [71] Warrington J. followed this decision in the case of an unregistered friendly society. In these cases payments for forfeitures, fines, sick benefits and so on, were disregarded. In *Tierney* v. *Tough*,[72] another case of an unregistered friendly society, Sir Charles O'Connor M.R. was critical of the application of the law relating to resulting trusts to such cases. Despite his criticism, however, he directed division on the basis of the amounts contributed. On the other hand, in the case of clubs, *Brown* v. *Dale* [73] supports the *per capita* basis, although it is so shortly reported as to provoke more questions than it answers. *Feeney and Shannon* v. *MacManus*,[74] another club case, also supports the same basis. The case is a little remarkable in that the headnote proclaims that *Tierney* v. *Tough* was ' applied '; and it appears [75] that the basis of the decision was not so much that equal division was right, but that equality was necessary because ascertaining the proportionate contributions was an impossibility. Finally, in *Re St. Andrew's Allotment Association's Trusts*,[76] concerning an allotment association, Ungoed-Thomas J. considered these cases, together with *Re Blue Albion Cattle Society*,[77] where Cross J. had applied the *per capita* basis to a cattle-breeding society. In the *St. Andrew's* case [78] Ungoed-Thomas J. said:

[70] [1899] 2 Ch. 184.
[71] [1904] 2 Ch. 196.
[72] [1914] 1 I.R. 142.
[73] (1878) 9 Ch.D. 78.
[74] [1937] I.R. 23.
[75] [1937] I.R. 23, 33.
[76] [1969] 1 W.L.R. 229.
[77] [1966] C.L.Y. 1294; (1966) *The Guardian*, May 28.
[78] [1969] 1 W.L.R. 229, 238, 239.

' If the true principle is the one laid down in *Tierney* v. *Tough*, and that principle certainly seems to me preferable to the principle of the resulting trust adopted in *Re Printers and Transferrers Amalgamated Trades Protection Society*, then it would seem to me that prima facie the assets are distributable between members at the relevant date *per capita*. It is conceivable that a basis for distinguishing the friendly and mutual benefit society cases may be that whereas the club cases contemplate enjoyment *ab initio* and equality, the friendly society cases contemplate advantages related to contributions.'

The reference to the principle laid down in *Tierney* v. *Tough* must, I think, be to the comments of Sir Charles O'Connor M.R. which rejected the concept of resulting trust, rather than to the actual decision, which was on the basis of the proportionate contributions that flow from the concept of resulting trust.

" It seems to me, with all respect, that much of the difficulty arises from confusing property with contract. A resulting trust is essentially a property concept; any property that a man does not effectually dispose of remains his own. If, then, there is a true resulting trust in respect of an unexpended balance of payments made to some club or association, there will be a resulting trust in respect of that unexpended balance, and the beneficiaries under that trust will be those who made the payments. If any are dead, the trust will be for their estates; death does not deprive a man of his beneficial interest. Yet in what I may call ' the resulting trust cases,' the beneficiaries who were held to be entitled were the members living at the time of the dissolution, to the exclusion of those who had died or otherwise ceased to be members. If, then, there was any resulting trust, it must be a trust modified in some way, perhaps by some unexplained implied term, that distinguishes between the quick and the dead. It cannot be merely an ordinary resulting trust.

" On the other hand, membership of a club or association is primarily a matter of contract. The members make their payments, and in return they become entitled to the benefits of membership in accordance with the rules. The sums they pay cease to be their individual property, and so cease to be subject to any concept of resulting trust. Instead, they become the property, through the trustees of the club or association, of all the members for the time being, including themselves. A member who, by death or otherwise, ceases to be a member thereby ceases to be the part owner of any of the club's property: those who remain continue owners. If, then, dissolution ensues, there must be a division of the property of the club or association among those alone who are owners of that property, to the exclusion of former members. In that division, I cannot see what relevance there can be in the respective amounts of the contributions. The newest member, who has made a single payment when he joined only a year ago, is as much a part owner of the property of the club or association as a member who has been making payments for 50 years. Each has had what he has paid for; the newest member has had the benefits of membership for a year or so and the oldest member for 50 years. Why should the latter, who for his money has had the benefits of membership for 50 times as long as the former, get the further benefit of receiving 50 times as much in the winding up?

" I have, of course, been speaking in the broadest of outlines; but I must say that the view taken on principle by Sir Charles O'Connor M.R.[79] and by Ungoed-Thomas J.[80] seem to me to be preferable to the other view, despite certain difficulties in the basis of distinction between the club cases and the others tentatively suggested by Ungoed-Thomas J. in the passage that I have read. Accordingly, I reject the basis of proportionate division in favour of equality, or division *per capita*. But then the second question arises, namely, whether the principle of equality prevails not only when there is no more than one class of members but when there are two or more classes. Is the proposed division into shares and half shares sound, or ought it to be rejected in favour of equality throughout?

" On the footing that the rules of a club or association form the basis of the contract between all the members, I must look at the rules of the society to see whether they indicate any basis other than that of equality. It seems to me that they do. Those aged from 5 to 12 years old pay contributions at half the rate (rule 9), and correspondingly their allowances (rule 12) and death benefit (rule 14) are also paid at half the rate. Where the rules have written into them the basis of inequality among different classes of members in relation to the principal contractual burdens and benefits of membership, it seems to me to follow that this inequality ought also to be applied to the surplus property of the society. A distinction between classes of members is quite different from a distinction between individual members of the same class based on the amounts contributed by each member. At any given moment one can say that the rights and liabilities of all the members of one class differ in the same way from the rights and liabilities of all the members of the other class, irrespective of the length of membership or anything else. It was indeed suggested that the words ' two classes of subscribers ' in rule 9 did not mean that there were two classes of members, the word ' subscribers ' being in contrast with the word ' member ' used in the next sentence. But the rules are too ill drafted for any such inferences to be drawn and rule 5, providing for special meetings of the committee when requested by three ' subscribers,' and a general meeting if required by twenty of the

---

[79] In *Tierney* v. *Tough* [1914] 1 I.R. 142.
[80] In *Re St. Andrew's Allotment Association's Trusts* [1969] 1 All E.R. 147, 154; [1969] 1 W.L.R. 229, 238, 239.

' members,' strongly suggests that the terms are used interchangeably. At any rate, I have heard no sensible explanation of the distinction.

"It may indeed be that there will be cases in which the distinction between one class and another is not so clear-cut as in the case before me, where there are only two classes and the ratio of burden and benefits between the two classes is a simple two to one. A members' club may have several classes of members, such as town members, country members, junior members and senior members. Some ratio of burden may emerge from comparing the different rates of subscription without there being any clear-cut ratio of benefits, in that there is no more than the expectation that, for instance, geography may mean that, as a group, country members will use the club facilities less than town members, and so on; and lower subscriptions for junior members may be more a tribute to stresses on junior budgets and the need to recruit young blood than any acceptance of a probable lesser use of the club facilities. These cases can be left until they arise. I shall say no more than that a comparison of the rates of subscription or dues or other payments in each class may well provide a prima facie guide, subject to modification by other elements, as to how far the members of each class may be regarded as owning the assets of the club from time to time. However that may be, the distinction in the case before me is, as I have indicated, plain and clear-cut, and I do not see why I should be deterred from giving effect to it by the possibility of other and more arguable cases. My answer to question 2 is accordingly in sense (b)." [On a *per capita* basis one share for each full member and one half share for each child member.]

Section 2. Presumed Resulting Trusts

A. Presumption of a Resulting Trust

These trusts arise in X's favour where X purchases property but in Y's name or in the name of X and Y or where X and Y purchase property in Y's name. They may also arise in cases where X gratuitously transfers his interest in property to others.

It should be realised that where X and Y are married to each other the effect of the doctrine of resulting trusts and of the presumption of advancement [81] has become rather uncertain owing in particular to the desire of Lord Denning's division of the Court of Appeal to do what is "just in all the circumstances of the case." [82] Indeed, at times it appears that constructive trusts are being utilised for this purpose without it being made

---

[81] *Infra*, p. 339, operating in favour of the donor's wife, children or persons to whom the donor stands in *loco parentis*.

[82] *Per* Lord Denning in *Davis* v. *Vale* [1971] 1 W.L.R. 1022, 1027; *Heseltine* v. *Heseltine* [1971] 1 W.L.R. 342; *Hazell* v. *Hazell* [1972] 1 W.L.R. 301; *Hargrave* v. *Newton* [1971] 1 W.L.R. 1611. For a valuable survey see Cretney's *Principles of Family Law*, Chap. 6. Also, Lesser (1973) 23 Univ. of Toronto L.J. 148.

clear that constructive and not resulting trusts are being so utilised.[83] This unfortunate situation has arisen because the House of Lords [84] in their two leading decisions on resulting trusts and the matrimonial home revealed such a diversity of approach, making the proper *rationes* very difficult to ascertain, that it left the way open for the Court of Appeal to pay lip-service to the Lords whilst often ignoring the fundamental majority views of the Lords.[85]

Whilst strict property law and trust law should apply beforehand,[86] on granting a decree of divorce or nullity or judicial separation the court may under section 24 of the Matrimonial Causes Act 1973 [87] make (a) an order that a party to the marriage shall transfer to the other party, to any child of the family or to someone as trustee for the child such property as may be specified being property to which the first-mentioned party is entitled (b) an order that a party to the marriage should settle certain of his property for the benefit of the other party and of the children (c) an order varying any ante-nuptial or post-nuptial settlement [88] made on the parties to the marriage (d) an order extinguishing or reducing the interest of either of the parties under any such settlement. In considering what order to make the court must have regard *inter alia* to the contributions made by each of the parties to the welfare of the family, including any contributions made by looking after the home or caring for the family: section 25 (*f*) of the Matrimonial Causes Act 1973.[89]

It should be noted that in the law of resulting trusts such a contribution does not rank as a contribution to the purchase price.[90] What is required is payment towards the deposit or the mortgage instalments or some understanding that one spouse's earnings will be used for household expenses so as to relieve the other's earnings for payment of mortgage instalments.[91] Although the general rule is that " in the absence or agreement or estoppel, a person who does work on the property of another, or expends money on improving it, has no claim upon the property," [92] by virtue of section 37

---

[83] *Heseltine* v. *Heseltine, supra, Cooke* v. *Head* [1972] 1 W.L.R. 518 where a mistress was treated as if she had been a wife despite *Diwell* v. *Farnes* [1959] 1 W.L.R. 624; A. J. Oakley [1973] C.L.P. 17, *infra.* For the position of a mistress see further *Richards* v. *Dove* [1974] 1 All E.R. 888.

[84] *Pettitt* v. *Pettitt* [1970] A.C. 777; *Gissing* v. *Gissing* [1971] A.C. 886; J. G. Miller, 86 L.Q.R. 98; Bromley's *Family Law* (4th ed.), Chap. 14 and supplement; Dymond's *Death Duties* (15th ed.), pp. 448 *et seq.*

[85] *Hazell* v. *Hazell* [1972] 1 W.L.R. 301, J. M. Eekelaar (1972) 88 L.Q.R. 333, S. M. Cretney (1971) 115 S.J. 615, Bagnall J. in *Cowcher* v. *Cowcher* [1972] 1 W.L.R. 425 doing his best to lay down principles reconciling subsequent Court of Appeal decisions with the two earlier Lords' decisions.

[86] *Gissing* v. *Gissing* [1971] A.C. 886; *Cowcher* v. *Cowcher (supra).*

[87] Replacing Matrimonial Proceedings and Property Act 1970, s. 4.

[88] This covers property co-owned in equity: *Cook* v. *Cook* [1962] P. 235; *Ulrich* v. *Ulrich* [1968] 1 W.L.R. 180.

[89] Replacing Matrimonial Proceedings and Property Act 1970, s. 5.

[90] *Gissing* v. *Gissing* [1971] A.C. 886; *Kowalczuk* v. *Kowalczuk* [1973] 1 W.L.R. 930.

[91] *Gissing* v. *Gissing* [1971] A.C. 886, 896, 897, 903, 908, 909; *Cowcher* v. *Cowcher* [1972] 1 W.L.R. 425; but see *Hazell* v. *Hazell* [1972] 1 W.L.R. 301, 88 L.Q.R. 333. If the wife works in the husband's business for small wages or none she will be regarded as having an interest in a house purchased out of the profits of the business: *Re Cummins* [1972] Ch. 62.

[92] Snell, p. 523.

of the Matrimonial Proceedings and Property Act 1970 as between spouses where one contributes in money or money's worth to the improvement of the other's real or personal property, then, if the contribution is of a substantial nature [93] the one is treated (subject to any express or implied agreement to the contrary) as having thereby acquired a share or an enlarged share in the property. In default of agreement the share will be such as in all the circumstances seems just to the court.[94]

The decisions on purchases in another's name and analogous transactions may be grouped as in (a) to (f), *infra*.

(a) *Purchase in the name of another*

X purchases property (real or personal) in the name of Y. Ordinarily, if X wishes to make a gift to Y, he will purchase the property in his own name and then convey it to Y. Here he has paid the purchase-money, but has required his vendor to convey to Y. Y is then presumed in equity to hold the property on a resulting trust for X.[95]

(b) *Purchase by one in joint names of himself and another*

X purchases property (real or personal) in the *joint* names of himself *and* Y. As in (a) above, X has paid the purchase-money, but instead of requiring his vendor to convey to Y alone, he takes a conveyance to himself and Y jointly. Here again equity presumes that X and Y hold the property on a resulting trust for X.[96] Where X is the husband of Y, the presumption of advancement (*infra*, p. 339) arises so as prima facie to give Y an equal beneficial interest in the property.

(c) *Joint purchase in name of one*

X *and* Y jointly purchase property (real or personal) in the name of Y alone. Both X and Y have contributed towards the purchase-money, but the conveyance is taken in the name of Y alone.[97] There will be a presumption that it was the intention of X and Y to constitute X a proportionate beneficiary.[98] Where, however, the relationship between X and Y is that of husband and wife, the presumption of a proportionate distribution may be displaced in favour of a presumption of equality. The court tries to

---

[93] See *Harnett* v. *Harnett*, *The Times*, Nov. 23, 1973, C.A.; *Kowalczuk* v. *Kowalczuk* [1973] 1 W.L.R. 930 which indicates as does *Griffiths* v. *Griffiths* [1974] 1 All E.R. 932 that reliance should not be placed on s. 37 of the 1970 Act and Married Women's Property Act 1882, s. 17 where, what are now, ss. 23, 24, 25 of the Matrimonial Causes Act 1973 are available. Further see *Re Nicholson Deceased* [1974] 1 W.L.R. 476 and [1975] New L.J. 20 (V. Chapman).

[94] It is to be hoped that matrimonial property will be removed from the realm of resulting trusts by the implementation of proposals of the Law Commission for equal ownership in the absence of express agreement to the contrary: see Law Com. Published Working Paper No. 52 (1973).

[95] *Gascoigne* v. *Thwing* (1685) 1 Vern. 366, *semble*; *Ambrose* v. *Ambrose* (1716) 1 P.Wms. 321; *Loyd* v. *Read* (1719) 1 P.Wms. 607; *Withers* v. *Withers* (1752) Amb. 151; *Re Howes* (1905) 21 T.L.R. 501; *cf. Nicholson* v. *Mulligan* (1869) Ir.R. 3 Eq. 308; see *Crow* v. *Pettingill* (1869) 38 L.J.Ch. 186; *Vandervell* v. *I.R.C.* [1967] 2 A.C. 179.

[96] *Benger* v. *Drew* (1721) 1 P.Wms. 781; *Rider* v. *Kidder* (1805) 10 Ves. 360.

[97] Contribution to payment of rent and outgoings does not amount to contribution to purchase price so that where one of three students takes a yearly tenancy in his name and all three contribute to rent and outgoings and then the one buys up the 62-year leasehold reversion this is not held on a resulting trust subject to the other two indemnifying the one against the price of the reversion: *Savage* v. *Dunningham* [1973] 3 W.L.R. 471.

[98] *Wray* v. *Steele* (1814) 2 V. & B. 388; *The Venture* [1908] P. 218; *Bull* v. *Bull* [1955] 1 Q.B. 234.

ascertain what was in the parties' minds at the time of the acquisition of the property and makes an order which, on the break-up of the marriage, gives effect to their intention at that time.[99] Where the purchase is made in the name of the wife alone the presumption of advancement (*infra*, p. 339) arises, though it is fairly easily rebuttable in favour of the principle of equality, at any rate where there is a joint asset of a single family involved.[1] Where the purchase is made in the name of the husband alone and the wife has made no contribution to the purchase-money, of course the husband is entitled to the exclusion of the wife.[2]

Section 17 of the Married Women's Property Act 1882, which enables the court to make such orders as it thinks fit in any question between husband and wife as to the title to property, does not permit the court to vary agreed or established titles to property. It is a procedural section and does not alter substantive rights.[3]

(d) *Transfer from one to another*

X gratuitously *transfers* property into the name of Y. In (a), (b) and (c) above the transaction was a *purchase*; here it is a *transfer*. Property already stands in the name of X, who gratuitously transfers it into the name of Y. If X is the father of Y or stands *in loco parentis* (*patris*) or other sufficient relationship to Y, there will be a rebuttable[4] presumption of advancement in favour of Y.[5]

But if X and Y are *strangers*, *i.e.*, if there is no special relationship between them, the position before 1926 was evidently uncertain, according

---

[99] See *Re Rogers' Question* [1948] 1 All E.R. 328 (proportionate distribution); *Jones* v. *Maynard* [1951] Ch. 572 (equality); *Rimmer* v. *Rimmer* [1953] 1 Q.B. 63; 69 L.Q.R. 11 (R. E. M.) (equality: Court of Appeal applying " palm-tree justice " and differing from the county court judge and registrar); *Fribance* v. *Fribance* [1957] 1 All E.R. 357; 20 M.L.R. 281 (O. M. Stone) (equality); *Macdonald* v. *Macdonald* [1957] 2 All E.R. 690 (equality: principle in *Rimmer* v. *Rimmer*, *supra*, applicable even where proceedings are not brought under s. 17 of the Married Women's Property Act 1882); *Wilson* v. *Wilson* [1963] 2 All E.R. 447 (equality); *Davis* v. *Vale* [1971] 1 W.L.R. 1022 (equality); *Falconer* v. *Falconer* [1970] 1 W.L.R. 1333 (equality, after wife obtained site value of land); *Hargrave* v. *Newton* [1971] 1 W.L.R. 1011 (equality); *Cowcher* v. *Cowcher* [1972] 1 W.L.R. 425 (2:1); *Hazell* v. *Hazell* [1972] 1 W.L.R. 301 (4:1); *Pettitt* v. *Pettitt* [1970] A.C. 777; *Gissing* v. *Gissing* [1971] A.C. 886; *Re Nicholson* [1974] 1 W.L.R. 476; *Burke* v. *Burke* [1974] 1 W.L.R. 1063.

[1] See *Jones* v. *Maynard* [1951] Ch. 572, 575; *Silver* v. *Silver* [1958] 1 W.L.R. 259; 74 L.Q.R. 165; 21 M.L.R. 419 (Alan Milner); *Richards* v. *Richards* [1958] 3 All E.R. 513; *Falconer* v. *Falconer* [1970] 1 W.L.R. 1333; and see Married Women's Property Act 1964: money derived from any allowance made by a husband for the expenses of the matrimonial home or for similar purposes, or any property acquired out of that money, is to be treated as belonging equally to husband and wife in the absence of a contrary agreement. For the position of a mistress contrast *Diwell* v. *Farnes* [1959] 1 W.L.R. 624, 75 L.Q.R. 296 with *Cooke* v. *Head* [1972] 1 W.L.R. 518. See also *Richards* v. *Dove* [1974] 1 All E.R. 888. See generally (1956) 20 Conv.(N.S.) 467 (A. G. Guest); (1959) 37 Can.B.R. 473 (A. Milner); (1959) 22 M.L.R. 241 (O. Kahn Freund); (1966) 30 Conv.(N.S.) 354 (F. W. Taylor and H. K. Bevan); (1971) 115 S.J. 615 (S. M. Cretney); (1970) 86 L.Q.R. 98.

[2] *Allen* v. *Allen* [1961] 3 All E.R. 385, 386 (Evershed M.R.) *Kowalczuk* v. *Kowalczuk* [1973] 1 W.L.R. 930.

[3] *National Provincial Bank Ltd.* v. *Ainsworth* [1965] A.C. 1175; *Pettitt* v. *Pettitt* [1970] A.C. 777; *Cowcher* v. *Cowcher* [1972] 1 W.L.R. 425.

[4] *Kilpin* v. *Kilpin* (1834) 1 My. & K. 520 (stock); *Re Gooch* (1890) 62 L.T. 384 (shares); *Shephard* v. *Cartwright* [1955] A.C. 431.

[5] *Crabb* v. *Crabb* (1834) 1 My. & K. 511 (stock); *Currant* v. *Jago* (1844) 1 Coll. 261 (cash); *May* v. *May* (1863) 33 Beav. 81 (land); *cf. Jennings* v. *Selleck* (1687) 1 Vern. 467 and *Hepworth* v. *Hepworth* (1870) L.R. 11 Eq. 10.

to whether the property was real or personal.[6] Today the point appears to be settled, at any rate if the property is land, by section 60 (3) of the Law of Property Act 1925, which provides: "In a voluntary conveyance a resulting trust for the grantor shall not be implied merely by reason that the property is not expressed to be conveyed for the use or benefit of the grantee." By section 205 (1) (ii) of the Act the expression "conveyance" includes a "mortgage, charge, lease . . . and every other assurance of property or of an interest therein by any instrument, except a will," unless the context otherwise requires; and by section 205 (1) (xx) the expression "property" includes any interest in property real *or* personal, unless the context otherwise requires. The context of section 60 appears, however, to restrict the meaning of "property" in subsection (3) to land. For other property the better opinion is that the stranger, Y, will hold the property rebuttably upon a resulting trust for X.[7]

(e) *Transfer into joint names of transferor and another*

X gratuitously transfers property into the *joint* names of himself and Y. As in (d) above, property already stands in the name of X, but instead of transferring it into the *sole* name of Y, he gratuitously transfers it into the *joint* names of himself and Y. There will be a presumption of a resulting trust in favour of X.[8] A modern illustration is *Young* v. *Sealey*,[9] in which X opened a joint banking account with Y, but during her life X retained complete control of the account, and Y neither paid anything into nor drew anything out of it. On X's death Y took the legal title by survivorship. Did he, however, hold it on trust for X's estate? Romer J. held that the presumption of a trust in favour of X's estate arose, but that this was rebutted by the evidence of Y as to X's intentions. Romer J. rejected the argument that the intended gift was void as an attempt to make a post-mortem gift otherwise than in accordance with the Wills Act. In his view, there were previous cases[10] of a similar nature, in which the point had passed *sub silentio*, but it should now be taken to be settled in favour of Y. If X and Y are married then the presumption of advancement applies: *Re Figgis, infra.*

(f) *Joint purchase and joint mortgage*

Where X and Y jointly purchase property in their joint names or jointly advance money on mortgage in their joint names, and X dies, Y takes the legal title to the whole by survivorship but is often treated as a tenant in common in equity and holds the share of the purchase or mortgage money advanced by X on trust for X's estate.[11]

---

[6] See conflicting authorities and dicta cited in White and Tudor, 9th ed., Vol. 2, p. 762 (but some of the cases there cited relate to *purchases*); Snell, pp. 180–181.
[7] Snell, p. 181.
[8] See *Owens* v. *Greene* [1932] Ir.R. 225; *Doyle* v. *Byrne* (1922) 56 Ir.L.T. 125; *Re Vinogradoff* [1935] W.N. 68, a rather extreme case as is *Re Muller* [1953] N.Z.L.R. 879.
[9] [1949] Ch. 278; *Re Reid* (1921) 50 Ont.L.R. 595; *Russell* v. *Scott* (1936) 55 C.L.R. 440.
[10] See the observations of Jessel M.R. in *Marshal* v. *Cruttwell* (1875) L.R. 20 Eq. 328, 329.
[11] See Snell, pp. 36 and 37; *Re Jackson* (1887) 34 Ch.D. 732; and see *Cobb* v. *Cobb* [1955] 2 All E.R. 696 (C.A.), Law of Property Act 1925, s. 111.

B. PRESUMPTION OF ADVANCEMENT

Where a special relationship exists between X and Y there is no presumption of resulting trust but a presumption of advancement. The principle is stated by Lord Eldon in *Murless* v. *Franklin* [12] as follows: "The general rule that on a purchase by one man in the name of another, the nominee is a trustee for the purchaser, is subject to exception where the purchaser is under a species of natural obligation to provide for the nominee."

The presumption of advancement always arises where X is the father of Y or stands *in loco parentis* (*patris*) to Y,[13] or is the husband of Y.[14] It does not arise where X is merely cohabiting with Y,[15] nor where X is the wife of Y.[16]

It was apparently held in *Sayre* v. *Hughes* [17] and *Re Grimes* [18] that a presumption of advancement arises also where X is the *mother* of Y, at any rate if she is a *widowed* mother. This is supported by a dictum in *Garrett* v. *Wilkinson* [19]; but *Re De Visme* [20] and *Bennet* v. *Bennet* [21] are to the opposite effect. The ground of the decision in these two cases was that whether the father is alive or not, the mother is under no equitable obligation which will raise the presumption of advancement. If the matter is purely one of equitable obligation it makes no difference that section 42 (1) of the National Assistance Act 1948 [22] has imposed upon a married woman who has property a statutory obligation to maintain her husband and children.

C. REBUTTING THE PRESUMPTIONS

Both the presumption of a resulting trust and the presumption of advancement can be rebutted by evidence within the limits laid down by the House of Lords in *Shephard* v. *Cartwright*.[23] That case reaffirms the rule that evidence of subsequent acts, though not admissible in favour of the party doing the acts, is admissible against him. It appears, however, that acquiescence by a child, in whose name a purchase has been made, in the receipt by his father during his life of the rents or the income of the property does not rebut the presumption of advancement,[24] at any rate where the child has not already been fully advanced [25]; for if the child is an infant

---

[12] (1818) 1 Swans. 13, 17.
[13] *Shephard* v. *Cartwright* [1955] A.C. 431; *Beckford* v. *Beckford* (1774) Lofft 490 (illegitimate child). *Semble* the presumption arises in respect of more than one advance made by X to Y: *Hepworth* v. *Hepworth* (1870) L.R. 11 Eq. 10.
[14] *Thornley* v. *Thornley* [1893] 2 Ch. 229; *Dunbar* v. *Dunbar* [1909] 2 Ch. 639; *Silver* v. *Silver* [1958] 1 W.L.R. 259; *cf. Richards* v. *Richards* [1958] 3 All E.R. 513; *Moate* v. *Moate* [1948] 2 All E.R. 486 (intended husband: marriage afterwards solemnised).
[15] *Rider* v. *Kidder* (1805) 10 Ves. 360.
[16] *Re Curtis* (1885) 52 L.T. 244; *Mercier* v. *Mercier* [1903] 2 Ch. 98.
[17] (1868) L.R. 5 Eq. 376.
[18] [1937] Ir.R. 470.
[19] (1848) 2 De G. & Sm. 244, 246.
[20] (1863) 2 De G.J. & S. 17.
[21] (1879) 10 Ch.D. 474.
[22] Replacing s. 14 (4) of the Poor Law Act 1930.
[23] [1955] A.C. 431.
[24] *Commissioner of Stamp Duties* v. *Byrnes* [1911] A.C. 386; compare, however, Wickens V.-C. in *Stock* v. *McAvoy* (1872) L.R. 15 Eq. 55, 59; *Northern Canadian Trust Co.* v. *Smith* [1947] 3 D.L.R. 135.
[25] *Grey* v. *Grey* (1677) 2 Swans. 594; and see *Hepworth* v. *Hepworth* (1870) L.R. 11 Eq. 10.

it is natural that the father should receive the profits, while if the child is an adult, it is an act of good manners on his part not to dispute their reception by his father. But the retention of the title deeds by the father with a contemporaneous declaration by him that the transaction was not a gift is sufficient to rebut the presumption of advancement,[26] though retention of the title deeds without such a declaration may be insufficient.[27] Nowadays, it seems that the presumptions are readily rebutted by comparatively slight evidence.[28]

One further point must be mentioned. Evidence is never admitted where its admission would be contrary to public policy. Thus, where a husband put property in his wife's name without intending to "advance" her but in order to defeat his creditors, evidence was not admitted to rebut the presumption of advancement and the wife was allowed to keep the property.[29] A similar result was reached where the object of the advancement was the evasion of a foreign tax.[30]

Re FIGGIS

Chancery Division [1969] 1 Ch. 123; [1968] 2 W.L.R. 1173; [1968] 1 All E.R. 999.

Mr. Figgis at his death had a deposit and a current account in the joint names of his wife and himself. His wife had a separate account of her own. Mr. Figgis operated the joint accounts as if they were his own except for periods of absence abroad or illness.

By his will Mr. Figgis directed that any estate duty payable by reason of his death on "any gifts made by me in my lifetime to my wife" should be paid out of residue.

Megarry J. in a reserved judgment held that the presumption of advancement had not been rebutted but that the credit balances on the joint accounts were not "gifts."

MEGARRY J.: "... When the husband died a sum of £5,705 18s. 10d. stood to the credit of a current account in the joint names of husband and wife in the Mincing Lane branch of the Midland Bank Ltd.; and a further sum of £10,700 stood to the credit of a deposit account in the joint names of husband and wife at the same branch. The second question is whether these sums form part of the husband's estate or part of the wife's. If they form part of the wife's estate (and not otherwise) the third question arises. That is whether clause 7 of the will requires any estate duty in respect of these moneys to be paid out of the husband's estate. Clause 7 of the will reads as follows:

---

26 *Warren* v. *Gurney* [1944] 2 All E.R. 472.
27 *Scawin* v. *Scawin* (1841) 1 Y. & C.C.C. 65.
28 *Pettitt* v. *Pettitt* [1970] A.C. 777, 813, 824; *Falconer* v. *Falconer* [1970] 1 W.L.R. 1333; *Heseltine* v. *Heseltine* [1971] 1 W.L.R. 742.
29 *Gascoigne* v. *Gascoigne* [1918] 1 K.B. 223. Compare *Heseltine* v. *Heseltine* [1971] 1 W.L.R. 742.
30 *Re Emery's Investment Trusts* [1959] 2 W.L.R. 461. See also *Chettiar* v. *Chettiar* [1962] A.C. 294.

'I direct that any estate or other duties payable by reason of my death on any gifts made by me in my lifetime to my wife or Margaret shall be paid out of my residuary estate and not by my wife or Margaret.'

The reference there to Margaret is to Mrs. Parker. With both the husband and wife dead, there has been an understandable difficulty in ascertaining the full facts relating to these accounts, particularly as the joint current account was opened over fifty years ago. I feel no doubt, however, that the executors, who are the same under each will, have done all that is possible to elicit the facts, and I must do the best I can with the material available.

" The history of the joint current account is as follows. On July 11, 1912, the husband, who was then a tea and rubber broker, opened a current account in his sole name with the Mincing Lane branch. He married the wife on November 27, 1915, when he was serving in the army. On August 9, 1917, he opened the joint current account here in question in the names of himself and the wife, and transferred to it the credit balance in his own current account. Thereafter he had no current account in his sole name anywhere; and for the rest of his life he operated this joint current account as his own. Indeed, apart from a short-lived deposit account, the only sole bank account he had after 1917 was a post office savings bank account which had been dormant for many years before his death. When the current account was opened the husband and wife each signed one of the bank's printed forms. . . .

" As regards the wife, on October 9, 1929, she opened a current account in her sole name with the Beckenham Junction branch of the bank. On February 13, 1953, she transferred this account to the Mincing Lane branch.

" I turn to the deposit accounts. The huband seems to have had such an account in his sole name from the end of 1942 until some time in 1944, when it was closed. The joint deposit account was opened on June 22, 1949, by the husband transferring £14,000 from the joint current account. The wife also had a deposit account in her sole name at the Mincing Lane branch, and this was opened on February 13, 1953, by a transfer of £3,000 from the joint deposit account. She also had a dormant post office savings bank account in her sole name. All the accounts were substantially in credit when the husband died. Ignoring the post office savings bank accounts, the position was thus that for over ten years before the husband's death there had been a joint deposit account and a joint current account. In addition, the wife had a deposit account and a current account in her sole name. The husband, on the other hand, had no account in his sole name.

" The husband was a man who was clearly meticulous in money

matters. There was put in evidence an account book in his writing
which ran from December, 1954, until a little over two months before
his death. It records on the left-hand side cheques and payments by
the bank under what I assume to be standing orders. On the right-
hand side there are detailed records of payments which he had made
down to the smallest items such as shillings and pence for fares, sweets,
matches and papers. From entries in this book and the other evidence,
I obtain the impression of a man of settled and detailed financial habits.
In the words of Mrs. Parker, his adopted daughter,

> ' For as long as I can remember it was the husband's habit to
> keep control of all household expenditure. Larger bills he paid
> himself by cheque. For smaller items he would give cash to the
> wife for which she was expected to account to him.'

She also says that the husband did not consider that women were
capable of dealing with business matters, and that soon after his
marriage he had unsuccessfully tried to persuade the wife to transfer
to him the shares which she then owned. He seems also, again unsuccessfully, to have attempted to induce his wife to let him manage
her financial affairs. Even during his last illness he persisted in trying
to make out and sign all the necessary cheques; and he refused to
part with his cheque book. To this episode I must return in due
course. Nevertheless, though careful in money matters, he was far
from being mean or ungenerous. In 1960 he gave Mrs. Parker a house
and investments costing nearly £20,000; and in 1964 he gave to her and
his wife investments of a total value of over £28,000. His accounts
record many other gifts of relatively small amounts.

" I am satisfied from the evidence that, subject to two qualifications,
the husband throughout operated the joint current account and the
joint deposit account as if they were his own, and that the wife left
them severely alone. For over thirty-five years she operated the
current account which stood in her sole name; and this was fed by her
investments, by assets from the estates of her father and mother, and
by transfers from the joint current account. In 1929 the husband
gave the bank a standing order to transfer £21 a month from the joint
current account to the wife's current account. This was reduced to
£15 in 1931, and to £10 in 1942, at which figure it remained unchanged
until the husband's death. With two qualifications, the wife never
operated either of the joint accounts. These qualifications were both
in respect of the joint current account, and are as follows. First, while
the husband was abroad on active service during the first world war
it seems probable that the wife operated the joint current account, and
that the husband's purpose in opening this account was to enable the
wife to draw money while he was away. After the war the husband
was in India for a while and it is possible that the wife operated the
account then; but this is mere surmise.

" Second, during the husband's last illness, the husband, as I have already mentioned, refused to part with his cheque book. He also refused to permit Mrs. Parker to make out the cheques so that he need only sign his name. There were three cheques for household and other expenses which he was unable to complete. Mrs. Parker took these to the Kingswood branch of the bank, where the husband had established drawing arrangements on August 16, 1962, and the manager told her that as the account was a joint account the wife could sign the cheques; and the wife then did so. The manager also obtained a new cheque book because, in Mrs. Parker's words,

> '... the wife was afraid to try to take and use the husband's cheque book. She would not agree to draw money from her own bank account for household expenses.'

" On those facts I turn to the law. Counsel for the first defendant contends that this is a case in which the presumption of advancement applies, so that the wife's estate is entitled to the balances in the two accounts. Counsel for the second defendant, supported by counsel for the third defendant, argues on the other hand that the presumption stands rebutted. The leading case is the decision of Sir George Jessel M.R. in *Marshal* v. *Crutwell*.[31] In that case the presumption of advancement was held to be applicable to a joint bank account, though on the facts it was decided that the presumption had been rebutted. The headnote reads as follows:

> ' The husband of the plaintiff being in failing health transferred his banking account from his own name into the joint names of himself and his wife, and directed the bankers to honour cheques drawn either by himself or his wife; and he afterwards paid in considerable sums to this account. All cheques were afterwards drawn by the plaintiff at the direction of her husband, and the proceeds were applied in payment of household and other expenses. The husband never explained to the plaintiff what his intention was in transferring the account, but he was stated by the bank manager to have remarked at the time of the transfer that the balance of the account would belong to the survivor of himself and his wife. After the death of her husband (which took place a few months after the transfer) the plaintiff claimed to be entitled to the balance: *Held*, that the transfer of the account was not intended to be a provision for the plaintiff, but merely a mode of conveniently managing her husband's affairs; and consequently that she was not entitled.'

The concluding passage of the judgment of Sir George Jessel M.R. is as follows [32]:

---

[31] (1875), L.R. 20 Eq. 328.
[32] (1875), L.R. 20 Eq. 328, 330, 331.

... taking into view all the circumstances (as I understand I am bound to do), as a juryman, I think the circumstances show that this was a mere arrangement for convenience, and that it was not intended to be a provision for the wife in the event which might happen, that at the husband's death there might be a fund standing to the credit of the banking account. I take into account the circumstance that the wife could draw upon the fund in the husband's lifetime, so that it would not necessarily be a provision for her after his death; and also the circumstance that the amount of the fund at his death must be altogether uncertain; and, having regard to the rule which is now binding on me, that I must infer from the surrounding circumstances what the nature of the transaction was, I come to the conclusion that it was not intended to be a provision for the wife, but simply a mode of conveniently managing the testator's affairs, and that it leaves the money therefore still his property.'

That case was distinguished in *Re Harrison, Day* v. *Harrison.*[33] The headnote reads as follows:

'A husband, in 1908, transferred the money standing to a current account at his bank in his own name into the joint names of himself and his wife. He did not inform his wife of the joint account, and always drew cheques on the account himself. He died in November, 1919. The wife never drew any cheque on the account until shortly before his death, when he was in failing health and unable to attend to business. The bank manager then informed her of the joint account, and advised her to draw a cheque, which she did. The husband had also from time to time made deposits in the joint names of himself and his wife, and in August, 1919, consolidated them into one deposit in the joint names. The wife never knew of this deposit until after her husband's death. There was then found among his papers an envelope endorsed with the wife's initials and containing the deposit receipt and a document in which he said: "I would like this paying away at once if possible as under," with a list of names with amounts against them: *Held*, that the moneys standing to the credit of both the current account and the deposit account belonged to the wife as survivor, and that the document did not raise any presumption that the husband regarded the deposit as his own property.'

In that case Russell J. carefully compared the facts of *Marshal* v. *Crutwell*[34] with those of the case before him and said[35]:

'None of the circumstances mentioned by Sir George Jessel

---

[33] (1920), 90 L.J.Ch. 186.
[34] (1875), L.R. 20 Eq. 328.
[35] (1920), 90 L.J.Ch. 186, 191.

exist in the present case. Many of those which do exist point in the opposite direction. There was no motive of convenience here in creating a joint account. One cheque only was drawn against the account by the wife, and that was drawn in very exceptional circumstances which are explained by the bank manager in his evidence. If I am to infer from the surrounding circumstances what the motive of the transaction was, I hold that it was intended by the husband that the moneys standing on current account in the joint names were intended to belong to the survivor. The case for the defendants as regards the deposit account is much more difficult than that as regards the current account, and I can see nothing to displace the wife's claim. I hold, therefore, that the moneys standing to the credit of both accounts belong to the wife.'

The applicability of the presumption of advancement to a joint bank account seems undoubted; and so the question here is whether that presumption has been rebutted. Counsel for the second defendant relied on the facts of the case as establishing that the joint current account was opened merely for convenience within the doctrine of *Marshal* v. *Crutwell*, and that throughout it was treated by both husband and wife as belonging to the husband alone. The husband opened the account so that the wife could draw on it while he was abroad during the first world war, and this, he said, characterised the account throughout its life. The joint deposit account, which was opened by a transfer from the joint current account, had the same origin in convenience, he added. He also put some emphasis on the wife's acquiescence over a long period in the husband treating the joint accounts as his own.

"I am not persuaded by these contentions. The difficulties in ascertaining a man's intentions are great enough when there is a plentitude of evidence. Here there is a paucity. Convenience may well have been one reason why the husband opened the joint current account in 1917; but after his return from France some fifty years ago until he lay on his deathbed I cannot see any evidence of convenience. The case is very different from *Marshal* v. *Crutwell*.[36] There the joint account was opened by the husband less than six months before his death, when he had for some time been in failing health; every cheque on that joint account was drawn by the wife, and not by the husband. Here it cannot be said what was in the husband's mind when he opened the joint current account. If convenience was one consideration, as I think that it was, that does not mean that the husband had no thought of the account forming a provision for his wife if he were to be killed. At a time when a bloody war had lasted for over three years, he was leaving a bride of less than two years standing and facing the risks of that war; and although one is in the

---

[36] (1875) L.R. 20 Eq. 328.

sphere of inference and speculation, I should be slow to hold that an account opened in such circumstances was opened merely for convenience. If the husband had intended to make arrangements for mere convenience, there was indeed no need for him to open a joint account. He could simply have given instructions to the bank to honour cheques drawn on the current account that he had in his sole name. Furthermore, I bear in mind the husband's carefulness in money matters. Once the war was over he might have been expected to terminate the joint current account and to resume a current account in his own name, if all that he had intended was to make convenient arrangements. The more careful the man, the more significant the long subsistence of the joint account seems to be.

" I regard the joint deposit account as being *a fortiori*. In any case, the mere fact that it was opened with moneys taken from the joint current account could not, I think, suffice to stamp it with the quality of the joint current account, even if that had been opened merely for convenience. Furthermore, in the nature of things a deposit account is far less appropriate than a current account as a provision made for convenience. Certainly in *Marshal* v. *Crutwell* the account seems to have been a current account; and to counsel for the second defendant and counsel for the third defendant I would say, with Russell J. in *Re Harrison* [37]:

> ' The case for the defendants as regards the deposit account is much more difficult than that as regards the current account, and I can see nothing to displace the wife's claim.'

I will add this: even if initially the joint current account was opened merely for convenience, I do not think that this character is stamped on the account immutably. Whatever may be the position with an unchanging asset, a current account fluctuates from day to day, and the wife can be advanced only to the extent of what remains after the husband has drawn his last cheque. If after the account is opened the husband changes his intention, I see no reason why effect should not be given to that change. An account initially opened for mere convenience may thus later become an advancement for the wife. Here, as the years slipped by and there was no longer any convenience to serve, I think that any considerations of convenience that there were in the initial opening faded into significance. I attach little weight to the cast of the husband as he lay on his deathbed, for he was old and ill; but the wife's fear of using his cheque book, and the fact that it was the bank manager and not the wife who told Mrs. Parker that the wife could sign cheques on the joint current account, seem to me to suggest that by 1966 all considerations of convenience had gone. The husband could hardly have forgotten that the account was a joint account, for the names of both husband and wife were printed on the

---

[37] (1920) 90 L.J.Ch. 186, 191.

cheques, and doubtless also on the bank statements.   Long before his death, in my judgment, the main or only reason for the account standing in the joint names of the husband and wife was to benefit the wife. The fact that the husband had always used the joint current account as if it were his own seems to me to emphasise rather than detract from the significance of the joint names.   Accordingly, I hold that the balance standing to the credit of each joint account forms part of the estate of the wife, and I answer question 2 in that sense.

" This decision makes it necessary for me to answer the third question, relating to the liability of the husband's estate to discharge the estate duty on the balance in the joint accounts.   I have already read clause 7 of the will.   The question is whether this applies to these balances.

" In the case of an advancement consisting of a certain and unchanging asset there will usually be no difficulty of this kind.   But an active bank account is very different.   Moneys are paid in and moneys are drawn out.   Nobody has suggested anything but that what the wife could take by way of advancement would be the balance remaining at the husband's death.   When, then, is such an advancement made?   Were the gifts of the balances " gifts made by me in my lifetime "?

" Counsel for the first defendant has contended that clause 7 does apply.   In response to a question from the bench he roundly asserted that as soon as a cheque was paid into the joint account it thereupon constituted a gift to the wife.   True, he said, it was a gift liable to be diminished by the husband exercising his power to draw on the account, so that in the end the wife would get only the balance remaining; but subject to that power, each deposit in the account constituted a gift instanter, and so each deposit (or what remained of it) satisfied clause 7 as being a gift ' made by me in my lifetime.'   Counsel for the first defendant supported his argument by reference to the case of *Young* v. *Sealey* [38] and *Russell* v. *Scott.* [39]   In *Young* v. *Sealey,* the headnote reads as follows [40]

> ' Money belonging to the deceased intestate was paid by her into joint banking accounts in the name of herself and her nephew, the defendant, but during her lifetime she alone made payments and withdrawals.   The evidence was that she intended the beneficial, as well as the legal interest to pass on her death to the defendant, whom she had always regarded with affection.   On her death intestate, *Held*, notwithstanding that the beneficial interest in the dispositions made by the deceased passed only on her death, they were not invalid by reason of failure to comply with the requirements of the Wills Act, 1837.'...

---

[38] [1949] Ch. 278.
[39] (1936) 55 C.L.R. 440.
[40] [1949] Ch. 278.

"In *Russell* v. *Scott*,[41] the headnote provides little help on the subject with which I am concerned. It reads as follows:

'An elderly lady and her nephew opened a joint account in the Commonwealth Savings Bank by the transfer of a large sum from an account in the lady's name. The nephew, who assisted his aunt in all her matters of business, did not contribute to the account, which was kept in funds by payments from the aunt's investments. The account was used solely for the purpose of supplying the aunt's needs. Moneys for this purpose were withdrawn by the nephew as required, the withdrawal slips being signed by both the aunt and the nephew. When the account was opened the aunt told the nephew and others that any balance remaining in the account at her death would belong to the nephew, and it was found as a fact that the aunt intended her nephew to take beneficially whatever balance stood to the credit of the account at her death. Upon his aunt's death the nephew claimed the balance of the account. *Held*, that the presumption of a resulting trust in favour of the aunt and her estate was rebutted; the nephew's legal right by survivorship to the balance of the account prevailed and was not the subject of any resulting trust.'

"What had happened in that case was that in the court below Nicholas J. had held that the nephew could not take because the provision was testamentary in nature and had not been made in accordance with the statutory requirements for wills; this, of course, was substantially the point raised in *Young* v. *Sealey* a dozen years later. The High Court of Australia reversed that decision. Starke J. said,[42] citing certain authorities:

'A person who deposits money in a bank on a joint account vests the right to the debt or the chose in action in the persons in whose names it is deposited, and it carries with it the legal right to title by survivorship . . . The vesting of the right and title to the debt or chose in action takes effect immediately, and is not dependent upon the death of either of the persons in whose names the money has been deposited. In short it is not a testamentary disposition.'

Dixon J. and Evatt J. in a joint judgment, said,[43] in commenting on *Owens* v. *Green* [44]:

'. . . by placing the money in the joint names, the deceased did then and there and by that act give a present right of survivorship.'

"It appears to me that there is some difficulty in defining the precise way in which the doctrine of advancement operates in the case of bank accounts. It seems quite unreal to regard each deposit in the

---

41 (1936), 55 C.L.R. 440.
42 (1936) 55 C.L.R. 440, 448.
43 (1936) 55 C.L.R. 440, 455.   44 [1932] I.R. 225.

account as an advancement, subject to diminution by the drawing of subsequent cheques. A husband who over fifty years has paid into a joint account some £10,000 a year, and at his death has drawn out all but £1,000, would on this analysis have made gifts of £500,000 to his wife, only to take back £499,000 of what he has given. This may be the law; it might even be equity; but it is indisputably remarkable. On the other hand, a gift of whatever stands to the credit of the bank account at the husband's death runs the peril of being accounted testamentary in nature, so as to require due execution as a will.

" It may be that the correct analysis is that there is an immediate gift of a fluctuating and defeasible asset consisting of the chose in action for the time being constituting the balance in the bank account. But whether that is right or wrong (and the subject is worthy of academic disputation), I am happy to regard it as a problem that I need not attempt to resolve in this case. For here my duty is but to construe the words of the will. First, there are the words ' any gifts '. I take these words to refer to gifts in the ordinary sense of that word. As I have already mentioned, there were ordinary gifts of substantial amounts which the husband made in his lifetime to his wife and Mrs. Parker, and for these the clause was plainly apt. Whatever might have been thought by a learned equity lawyer, had he been the testator, I cannot believe that when the husband paid money into the joint account he regarded himself as making a gift to the wife, any more than he regarded himself as diminishing gifts already made whenever he drew a cheque on that account. Nor do I think that moneys which became indefeasibly the wife's only, *eo instanti* with the husband's death can fairly be said to fall within the phrase ' gifts made by me during my lifetime.'

" There is also the context in which the phrase appears. Clause 7 of the will is concerned with ' any estate or other duties payable by reason of my death on any gifts made by me in my lifetime.' I doubt very much whether the Inland Revenue or anyone else would contemplate that every sum paid into the joint account by the husband within five years of his death ought to be considered for the purposes of a possible liability for estate duty. In short, I hold that clause 7 is confined in its operation to gifts in the ordinary sense of the word, and does not extend, in counsel for the second defendant's phrase, to amorphous rights in a joint account. Accordingly, I answer ' No ' to question 3." *Declarations accordingly.*[45]

PROBLEMS

1. The Ravers Anonymous Club which is not a charitable organisation has just dissolved itself one week after having received £10,000 donated by

---

[45] Generally see M. C. Cullity " Joint Bank Accounts with Volunteers " (1969) 85 L.Q.R. 530.

Sir Launcelot Hellfire for the purposes of the Club and one month after having received £1,000 from certain raffles and sweepstakes and £150 from collections taken at a public meeting called to publicise the Club. What should be done with these sums?

2. The Black Sheep Club was formed in 1884 to encourage the breeding and improvement of Black Sheep and also to provide sick benefits for the widows of members. The members paid an annual subscription of £5. Funds were also raised from annual covenants from well-wishers, from collections made at the annual show and from the profits of an annual dance and monthly beetle drives. The Club has been inactive since 1968. There are four surviving members and one widow of a deceased member. Its assets amount to £10,000. Advise as to the distribution of the Club's assets.

3. Six years before her death Miss Spry opened a current account with Barclays Bank in the joint names of herself and her nephew, Neal Smug. Both of them called on the manager when they came to open the joint account. Miss Spry told the manager that as she was getting frail her nephew would look after her banking matters for her. She also said that if she died before her nephew he could keep any credit balance in the account at her death. It was arranged that cheques drawn by either Miss Spry or Neal would be honoured.

As had been envisaged only Miss Spry contributed moneys to the joint account and at her death a credit balance of £2,000 remained. Who is entitled to this if Miss Spry by will had left everything to four specified charities equally?

CHAPTER 8

CONSTRUCTIVE TRUSTS [1]

A constructive trust arises whenever the title to property is in X, but the beneficial interest is, by operation of the rules of equity, in Y.[2] It usually arises independently of any intention on the part of X to create a trust, but sometimes, as in cases of secret trusts,[3] that intention exists, but is expressed in disregard of the formal requirements of statute, or, as in the case of mutual wills,[4] the intention is originally expressed with due regard to those requirements, is later revoked in accordance therewith but nevertheless remains effectual in equity.

In some cases the constructive trustee has the same duties of administration to perform as an express trustee, as where a trustee of a lease renews it for his own benefit,[5] or where trust property, in which successive interests subsist, comes into the hands of a purchaser with notice. In many cases, however, the constructive trustee has no duties of administration to perform, but merely a duty to make the property or its product available to the claimant, as where a volunteer receives trust money without knowledge of the trust and innocently mixes it with his own.[6] In such circumstances, the constructive trust appears to be a remedial and not a substantive institution.[7]

The scope of constructive trusts appears to be wider in the United States of America than in England. The American *Restatement of Restitution* states the principle in this way [8]: "Where a person holding title to property is subject to an equitable duty to convey it to another on the ground that he would be unjustly enriched if he were permitted to retain it, a constructive trust arises." Despite strong and persuasive advocacy in its support [9] and certain dicta of Lord Denning in recent cases [10] this broad generalisation cannot yet be regarded as part of English law [11] which affords relief, on the ground of constructive trust, in specific situations, the limits of which are not fixed by reference to any satisfactory conceptual theory.

---

[1] See A. W. Scott, " Constructive Trusts " (1955) 71 L.Q.R. 39; R. H. Maudsley, " Proprietary Remedies for the Recovery of Money " (1959) 75 L.Q.R. 234, 236–237; Sealy, " Fiduciary Relationships " [1962] C.L.J. 69, and " Some Principles of Fiduciary Obligation " [1963] C.L.J. 119; Waters, *The Constructive Trust* (1965); Goff and Jones' *Law of Restitution*, pp. 36–38; A. J. Oakley [1973] C.L.P. 17, *infra*.
[2] *cf. Hardoon* v. *Belilios* [1901] A.C. 118, 123, *per* Lord Lindley.
[3] s. 5, *infra*.
[4] s. 6, *infra*.
[5] s. 2, *infra*.
[6] s. 7, *infra*.
[7] Pound, " The Progress of the Law " (1920) 33 H.L.R. 420, 421.
[8] (1936) s. 160.
[9] See, for example, *Nelson* v. *Larholt* [1948] K.B. 339, 342–343 (Denning J.); Lord Denning, " The Recovery of Money " (1949) 65 L.Q.R. 37; Lord Wright, *Legal Essays and Addresses*, at p. 26; Winfield (1937) 53 L.Q.R. 447; (1938) 54 L.Q.R. 529; Winfield, *Province of the Law of Tort*, p. 139.
[10] *Hussey* v. *Palmer* [1972] 1 W.L.R. 1286, 1290; *Binions* v. *Evans* [1972] Ch. 359, 368 discussed by A. J. Oakley in [1973] C.L.P. 17 *infra*.
[11] *Reading* v. *Att.-Gen.* [1951] A.C. 507, 513 (Lord Porter); P. V. Baker (1973) 89 L.Q.R. 2; A. J. Oakley [1973] C.L.P. 17; *Carl Zeiss Stiftung* v. *Herbert Smith* [1969] 2 Ch. 276.

Section 1. The Frustration of Fraudulent or Unconscionable Conduct

A. J. Oakley, Current Legal Problems 1973, p. 17

HAS THE CONSTRUCTIVE TRUST BECOME A GENERAL EQUITABLE REMEDY?

"THE English law of constructive trusts has not fired the imagination of judges or writers." So wrote Professor Waters in 1964 as the opening sentence of his monograph *The Constructive Trust*.[12] No such statement could be made today. The constructive trust has, in recent years, been taken up and used by the courts for a variety of purposes; so much so that there is a certain amount of truth in the recent judicial comment that a constructive trust 'is a trust imposed by law whenever justice and good conscience require it.... It is an equitable remedy by which the court can enable an aggrieved party to obtain restitution.'[13] How far do such statements accurately reflect the recent practice of the courts? How far are these recent developments desirable? This paper will attempt to suggest an answer to these questions.

INTRODUCTION

"Some general discussion of the constructive trust may be useful by way of introduction. No clear view emerges from the decided cases as to the nature of a constructive trust. It seems, however, to be generally accepted that a constructive trust arises irrespective of the intention of the parties, being imposed by the court because of the conduct of the parties. Thus, it is a creature of law, arising by operation of law. What is clear is that the attitude of English law towards the constructive trust is very different from that of the American jurisdiction. This difference has been expressed in a number of ways. Professor R. H. Maudsley has stated, in an oft-quoted passage, that 'English law has always thought of the constructive trust as an institution, a type of trust.'[14] The American jurisdictions, on the other hand, are said to regard the constructive trust as 'purely a remedial institution.'[15] This terminology, however, causes some difficulty since it creates the impression that English law does not, in any sense, regard the constructive trust as a remedy. While it may indeed be accurate to state that English law does not regard the constructive trust as a remedy in the sense that it regards the injunction as a remedy, it can hardly be said that a plaintiff who seeks the imposition of a constructive trust is not seeking a remedy. The effective distinction between the English and the American approaches may, perhaps, rather be expressed in this way. English law demands, as a prerequisite of the imposition of a constructive trust, that some legal wrong should have been committed by the party upon whom the trust is to be imposed. The American courts, on the other hand, will impose a constructive trust in order to enable a party to recover 'that which is unfairly

---

[12] D. W. M. Waters, *The Constructive Trust* (1964), p. 1.
[13] *Per* Lord Denning M.R. in *Hussey* v. *Palmer* [1972] 1 W.L.R. 1286, at 1290.
[14] In (1959) 75 L.Q.R. 234, 237.
[15] These are the words of Roscoe Pound in 33 Harv.L.R. 420, 421 (1920).

withheld from him to the benefit of the withholder.' [16]   A plaintiff need show only that the defendant has been unjustly enriched at his expense.

"It has long been argued that the English courts should adopt the American approach and impose a constructive trust in order to prevent unjust enrichment.   Certainly, in principle, there is no reason why the categories of situations in which English courts will impose a constructive trust should be regarded as closed.   However, the effects of the imposition of a constructive trust are such as to render it an inappropriate instrument for dealing out justice *inter partes*.   The imposition of a constructive trust places upon the trustee a considerable liability.   He will be obliged to account, with interest, for the property of which he is declared to be a constructive trustee.   In the event of his bankruptcy, the beneficiaries will be entitled to priority over his general creditors.   Further, they will be able to trace the trust property or its product into the hands of any transferee, subject to the defence of bona fide purchase for value without notice.[17] The constructive trust, therefore, is a remedy which has far-reaching ramifications not only for the person on whom it is imposed but also for third parties.   Its indiscriminate invocation and imposition is highly undesirable. The constructive trust should not be invoked by the courts as some sort of instant remedy to prevent what the court regards as an unjust result in an individual case.   Therefore, it is submitted that the categories of situations in which English courts will impose a constructive trust should be extended only where the courts are prepared to lay down a new principle which will apply generally.   Such a principle should not be established without the fullest consideration of the effects thus produced upon the general law and upon the interests of the general creditors of the trustee.   In particular, such a principle should not be established by deciding an individual case on grounds applicable only to that particular case.

"It might be expected that some general principle, which would be of some guidance in determining when a constructive trust should be imposed, could be extracted from those situations which English law recognises as giving rise to a constructive trust.   This is, unfortunately, not the case.   No clear principle can be enunciated as the basis of the doctrine of constructive trusts.   However, attempts, unquestionably contradictory and for the most part unsuccessful, have been made to elicit from the cases some consistent golden thread.   It has been argued [18] that this golden thread is the principle of unjust enrichment, that a constructive trust is imposed in order to prevent the unjust enrichment of the trustee at the expense of the beneficiary. Another view, enunciated by Edmund Davies L.J. in *Carl Zeiss Stiftung* v. *Herbert Smith* (*No. 2*),[19] is that the golden thread is a 'want of probity' in the trustee.   However, as the law now stands, it is impossible to state that any general application of either of these concepts has occurred.   Such concepts, therefore, can only be of initial assistance in determining when a constructive trust should be imposed; they should in no way detract from

---

[16] Waters, *op. cit.*, p. 12.   Many examples of the American courts imposing a constructive trust for this reason are cited by Professor Waters.

[17] The rules of tracing property into its product are expounded and criticised in Chap. 2 of R. Goff and G. Jones, *The Law of Restitution* (1966).

[18] By the authors of *The Law of Restitution*, who state their conception of the principle of unjust enrichment in Chap. 1 of that work.

[19] [1969] 2 Ch. 276, 301.

or impinge upon the fundamental principle that a constructive trust should only be imposed where the courts are prepared to lay down a new principle which will apply generally.

"The recent developments in the law will now be examined with this principle borne in mind.

THE EFFECT OF RECENT DECISIONS

"There is little unanimity as to precisely which trusts may properly be described as constructive trusts. Widely diverging views have been expressed as to whether certain types of trusts (secret trusts, for example) are or are not constructive trusts. There are, however, certain types of situations which are generally recognised as giving rise to a constructive trust; one of these categories of accepted constructive trusts is where a trust is imposed to frustrate fraudulent or unconscionable conduct. It is this category which the courts have extended to enable the constructive trust to be used as a general equitable remedy. What situations fall within this category of constructive trusts?

"Since the eighteenth century, it has been a rule of equity that a person who obtains property from another through undue influence will be held to be a constructive trustee of that property for the person from whom he has obtained it.[20]

"In the same way, the courts will impose a constructive trust in accordance with the principle enunciated in *Cleaver* v. *Mutual Reserve*.[21] This principle was expressed in simple terms by Fry L.J.: ' it is,' he said,[22] ' against public policy to allow a criminal to claim any benefit by virtue of his crime.' In accordance with this principle, the courts will impose a constructive trust upon a criminal who has received the property of his victim. Such a trust will be imposed for the benefit of the persons otherwise entitled to the property. Usually, however, the criminal or his representatives are prevented from ever obtaining the property. This occurred in *In the Estate of Crippen*.[23] Crippen murdered his wife, who died intestate. He was indicted for her murder, convicted, and hanged. The question now arose as to whether the beneficiary under his will was entitled to Mrs. Crippen's estate. Sir Samuel Evans P. held that Crippen could not take under his wife's intestacy; her estate, therefore, passed to her next of kin. It is clear that, had the property already reached the hands of Crippen's representatives, the court would have imposed upon them a constructive trust in favour of Mrs. Crippen's next of kin.

"These are the two classic situations in which the courts will impose a constructive trust upon a person whose conduct has been fraudulent or unconscionable. Conduct of a similar kind was the basis of the imposition of a constructive trust in *Bannister* v. *Bannister*.[24] The defendant owned two adjacent cottages which she was negotiating to sell to the plaintiff, her

---

20 This doctrine is generally thought to have been evolved by Lord Hardwicke L.C. in *Morris* v. *Burroughs* (1737) 1 Atk. 398. A full discussion of the rules relating to the recovery of benefits conferred under undue influence is contained in Chap. 9 of Goff and Jones (*op. cit.*).

21 [1892] 1 Q.B. 147. See also T. G. Youdan (1973) 89 L.Q.R. 235.

22 *Ibid.* 156. See also Earnshaw & Pace (1974) 37 M.L.R. 481.

23 [1911–12] P. 108.

24 [1948] W.N. 261, *supra*, p. 65.

brother-in-law. They agreed orally that she could continue to live in one of the two cottages rent-free for as long as she wished. However, the conveyance following the sale was a plain conveyance upon sale without any mention of the right of the defendant to so reside. Subsequently, the plaintiff gave the defendant notice to quit and brought an action claiming possession of the cottage. The defendant counterclaimed for a declaration that the plaintiff held the cottage on trust for her for her life. The plaintiff sought to rely on the absence of the writing which the Law of Property Act 1925 [25] requires for the creation of the interest claimed by the defendant. However, the Court of Appeal (Scott, Asquith L.JJ. and Jenkins J.) had no hesitation in rejecting the plaintiff's attempts to claim possession by this means. The judgment of the court, which was delivered by Scott L.J., was based fairly and squarely on the fraudulent conduct of the plaintiff.

> ' The fraud, which brings the principle on which a constructive trust is raised into play, arises as soon as the absolute character of the conveyance is set up for the purpose of defeating the beneficial interest, and that is the fraud to cover which the Statute of Frauds, or the corresponding provisions of the Law of Property Act 1925, cannot be called in aid in cases in which no written evidence of the real bargain is available.' [26]

The Court of Appeal, therefore, imposed a constructive trust upon the plaintiff and made the following declaration:

> '...the plaintiff holds [the cottage] in trust during the life of the defendant to permit the defendant to occupy the same for so long as she may desire to do so and subject thereto in trust for the plaintiff. A trust in this form has the effect of making the beneficiary a tenant for life within the meaning of the Settled Land Act 1925, and consequently, there is very little practical difference between such a trust and a trust for life *simpliciter.*' [27]

"This decision has been generally regarded as establishing the proposition that a constructive trust will be imposed to prevent a person unconscionably relying on the absence of written evidence to defeat the interest of another. Such a proposition is entirely consistent with the earlier authorities.... *Bannister* v. *Bannister* has since been cited [28] as authority for a much wider proposition, namely, that the courts will impose a constructive trust wherever the result would, otherwise, be inequitable.

"This broad principle has also been based upon a remark by Lord Diplock in *Gissing* v. *Gissing.*[29] His lordship said this:

> ' A resulting, implied or constructive trust—and it is unnecessary for present purposes to distinguish between these three classes of trust— is created by a transaction between the trustee and the *cestui que trust*

---

[25] s. 54 (1) of the Law of Property Act 1925 establishes that " All interest in land created by parol and not put in writing and signed by the persons so creating the same, or by their agents thereunto lawfully authorised in writing, have notwithstanding any consideration having been given for the same, the force and effect of interests at will only."

[26] [1948] W.N. 261, 264.

[27] *Ibid.* 261, 265.

[28] By Lord Denning M.R. in *Binions* v. *Evans* [1972] Ch. 359, 368.

[29] [1971] A.C. 886, 905.

in connection with the acquisition by the trustee of a legal estate in land, whenever the trustee has so conducted himself that it would be inequitable to deny to the *cestui que trust* a beneficial interest in the land acquired.'

" This statement, when thus isolated from its context, does indeed appear to support the proposition for which it has been cited as authority in several subsequent decisions,[30] namely, that the courts will impose a constructive trust in order to do justice *inter partes* wherever the result would, otherwise, be inequitable. That Lord Diplock placed an immediate limitation on his statement in the following sentence has, generally, been ignored. His lordship continued:

' And he will be held so to have conducted himself if by his words or conduct he has induced the *cestui que trust* to act to his own detriment in the reasonable belief that by so acting he was acquiring a beneficial interest in the land.'

" *Gissing* v. *Gissing* was a case in which the House of Lords reviewed and restated the law relating to the acquisition by spouses of beneficial interests over matrimonial property. One of the fundamental propositions which was laid down by the House of Lords in this decision (and in the earlier decision of the House in *Pettitt* v. *Pettitt*[31]) was that rights of property are not to be determined according to what is reasonable and fair or just in all the circumstances. This proposition was expressly asserted by four of the members of the House in *Pettitt* v. *Pettitt*[32] and is also fundamental to the decision in *Gissing* v. *Gissing*. The fundamental nature of this principle was emphatically stated by Bagnall J. in *Cowcher* v. *Cowcher*[33] where he said:

' In any individual case the application of [*Pettitt* v. *Pettitt* and *Gissing* v. *Gissing*] may produce a result which appears unfair. So be it; in my view that is not an injustice. I am convinced that in determining rights, particularly property rights, the only justice that can be attained by mortals, who are fallible and are not omniscient, is justice according to law; the justice that flows from the application of sure and settled principles to proved or admitted facts. So in the field of equity the length of the Chancellor's foot has been measured or is capable of measurement. This does not mean that equity is past childbearing; simply that its progeny must be legitimate—by precedent

---

30 Lord Diplock's dictum was expressly cited in support of this proposition by the Court of Appeal in *Heseltine* v. *Heseltine* [1971] 1 W.L.R. 342 *per* Lord Denning M.R. at 344 and in *Binions* v. *Evans* [1972] Ch. 359 *per* Lord Denning M.R. at 368. The Court of Appeal has adopted this broad principle in seven other cases: *Falconer* v. *Falconer* [1970] 1 W.L.R. 1333 *per* Lord Denning at 1336; *Davis* v. *Vale* [1971] 1 W.L.R. 1022 *per* Lord Denning M.R. at 1026; *Re Cummins* [1972] Ch. 62 *per* Lord Denning M.R. at 68; *Hargrave* v. *Newton* [1971] 1 W.L.R. 1611 *per* Lord Denning M.R. at 1613; *Hazell* v. *Hazell* [1972] 1 W.L.R. 301 *per* Lord Denning M.R. at 305; *per* Megaw L.J. at 306; *Cooke* v. *Head* [1972] 1 W.L.R. 518 *per* Lord Denning M.R. at 522; and *Hussey* v. *Palmer* [1972] 1 W.L.R. 1286 *per* Lord Denning M.R. at 1890.
31 [1970] A.C. 777.
32 By Lord Reid at 793, by Lord Morris of Borth-y-Gest at 801, 803, 805, by Lord Hodson at 809, and by Lord Diplock at 825. The principle is also implicit in the judgment of Lord Upjohn.
33 [1972] 1 W.L.R. 425.

out of principle. It is well that this should be so; otherwise no lawyer could safely advise on his client's title and every quarrel would lead to a law suit.'

" This principle, which is crucial for the maintenance of that certainty which should be the hallmark of every system of laws, has, however, been ignored in subsequent cases in favour of the interpretation placed on the remarks of Lord Diplock, to which previous reference has been made. This has occurred in five decisions of the Court of Appeal relating to matrimonial property, the field of law with which *Pettitt* v. *Pettitt* and *Gissing* v. *Gissing* were principally concerned.[34] Further, the Court of Appeal has extended the principle that a constructive trust will be imposed wherever the result would, otherwise, be inequitable into other fields.[35]

" *Heseltine* v. *Heseltine* [36] is an illustration of the attitude of the Court of Appeal towards the determination of the beneficial interests in matrimonial property. In this case, the plaintiff wife had very considerable means of her own. She had contributed four-fifths of the purchase price of the matrimonial home, which had been conveyed into the name of the husband. She had, at various times, transferred to her husband out of her own capital sums totalling £40,000, relying entirely on his advice that this would save estate duty if she predeceased him. She also transferred to him a further £20,000 for the sole purpose of enabling him to raise the securities necessary to become a ' name ' at Lloyd's. During the marriage, the parties had purchased four houses, all of which had been conveyed into the name of the husband. What were the beneficial interests in these assets? The case came before the Court of Appeal (Lord Denning M.R., Karminski and Megaw L.JJ.). The principal judgment was delivered by the Master of the Rolls. He considered first the matrimonial home and said this [37]:

> ' This is a typical case where the matrimonial home was acquired by the joint resources of each, but was taken in the name of one only, *i.e.*, the husband. In the usual way the court imputes a trust under which the husband is to hold it for them both jointly in equal shares. But half-and-half is not an invariable division. If some other division is more fair, the court will adopt it: see *Gissing* v. *Gissing*.' [38]

" His lordship then held that the division of the proceeds of sale should be as to three-quarters to the wife and one-quarter to the husband. It is difficult to see how the approach taken by his lordship (though not, perhaps, the result reached) can be justified under the principles enunciated in *Gissing* v. *Gissing*. The House of Lords held [39] that if, under section 17 of the Married Women's Property Act 1882, a person claims an interest in property other than that of an absolute legal and beneficial owner, the claim

---

34 In *Falconer* v. *Falconer* [1970] 1 W.L.R. 1333; *Heseltine* v. *Heseltine* [1971] 1 W.L.R. 342; *Davis* v. *Vale* [1971] 1 W.L.R. 1022; *Hargrave* v. *Newton* [1971] 1 W.L.R. 1611; *Re Cummins* [1972] Ch. 62; and *Hazell* v. *Hazell* [1972] 1 W.L.R. 301.

35 In *Cooke* v. *Head* [1972] 1 W.L.R. 518; *Binions* v. *Evans* [1972] Ch. 359; and *Hussey* v. *Palmer* [1972] 1 W L.R. 1286.

36 [1971] 1 W.L.R. 342.

37 *Ibid.* 345.

38 [1971] A.C. 886.

39 *Per* Lord Reid at 896, *per* Viscount Dilhorne at 900, *per* Lord Pearson at 902, and *per* Lord Diplock at 904, 905.

must be determined in accordance with equitable principles relating to trusts. In particular, rights of property are not to be determined according to what is reasonable and fair or just in all the circumstances. Surely, therefore, the Court of Appeal should have decided this matter by considering the principles of resulting trusts, not by 'imputing a trust in the usual way.' It is well established that, where property is voluntarily transferred into the name of another, there is a presumption that the transferee holds the property upon a resulting trust for the transferor.[40] Equally, where property is conveyed to a person other than the purchaser or to some only of the purchasers, there is a presumption that the property is held upon a resulting trust for the purchaser(s).[41] Application of the principles of resulting trusts to the facts of *Heseltine* v. *Heseltine* would have led to a division of the proceeds of sale of the matrimonial home as to four-fifths to the wife and one-fifth to the husband [41]—a result admittedly not very different from that reached by the Court of Appeal. The advantage of such an approach, apart from the fact that the House of Lords has decided that it alone should be used, is that it is certain—parties can be safely advised as to their position, something which is totally impossible when the courts impute trusts according to their view of what is fair or just.

"His lordship then considered the £40,000.[42] He cited the dictum of Lord Diplock [43] to which reference has already been made and continued:

> 'What Lord Diplock said about land applies also to shares, money or chattels. If the conduct of the husband is such that it would be inequitable for him to claim the property beneficially as his own, then, although it is transferred into his name, the court will impose on him a trust to hold it for them both jointly, or for her alone, as the circumstances of the case may require. Applying this principle, it would plainly be inequitable that the husband should hold this £40,000 beneficially as his own.'

"His lordship, therefore, held that the husband held the £40,000 on trust for the wife. He then considered the £20,000 and the four houses and held that the same principles applied. The husband held the property on trust for his wife.[44] It is clear that the application of the principles of resulting trusts to the four houses would have produced the same result.[45] But the principles of resulting trusts have no application to either the £40,000 or the £20,000 The wife clearly intended to transfer the £40,000 to the husband absolutely—how, otherwise, could estate duty be avoided? Similarly, the beneficial interest in the £20,000 must have been transferred to the husband absolutely. How could the husband have been assisted to become a 'name' at Lloyd's by holding securities in which he had no beneficial interest? By imposing a trust for the benefit of the wife the court must, therefore, have been imposing a constructive trust in order to prevent a result which would, otherwise, have been inequitable. The imposition of such a trust cannot be justified either upon precedent or upon

---

40 See *Re Vinogradoff* [1935] W.N. 68. See pp. 334–340, *supra*.
41 See *Dyer* v. *Dyer* (1788) 2 Cox Eq.Cas. 92.
42 [1971] 1 W.L.R. 342, 346.
43 In *Gissing* v. *Gissing* [1971] A.C. 886, 905.
44 [1971] 1 W.L.R. 342, 347.
45 See *Dyer* v. *Dyer* (1788) 2 Cox Eq.Cas. 92.

principle. Precedent can only justify such a result if the wife could have brought her case within the doctrine of undue influence.[46] This was not attempted. Principle cannot justify the wife thus being given an advantage over the general creditors of her husband[47] and being permitted (as the court expressly held[48]) to trace the £40,000 into its products. It is submitted, therefore, that the imposition of a constructive trust in *Heseltine* v. *Heseltine* is unjustifiable.

" Subsequently, the Court of Appeal extended the principles enunciated in *Heseltine* v. *Heseltine* outside the area of matrimonial property to an analogous situation involving a man and his mistress. This occurred in *Cooke* v. *Head*.[49] The plaintiff was the mistress of the defendant. They decided to acquire some land on which to build a bungalow. The defendant paid all the outgoings save for a small amount, but the plaintiff helped him greatly in the actual task of building the bungalow, doing, in the words of the Master of the Rolls,[50] ' quite an unusual amount of work for a woman.' In fact, the parties never occupied the bungalow because they split up before it was completed. Subsequently, the defendant sold the bungalow. The plaintiff brought an action claiming a share in the proceeds. Plowman J. applied the principles of resulting trusts and, since the plaintiff had contributed one-twelfth of the outgoings, awarded her a one-twelfth interest in the proceeds. However, the Court of Appeal (Lord Denning M.R., Karminski and Orr L.JJ.) adopted a different approach. In the words of the Master of the Rolls[51]:

> ' It is now held that, whenever two parties by their joint efforts acquire property to be used for their joint benefit, the courts may impose or impute a constructive or resulting trust. The legal owner is bound to hold the property on trust for them both. This trust... applies to husband and wife, to engaged couples, and to man and mistress, and maybe to other relationships too.'[52]

" His lordship then went on to consider the contribution made by the plaintiff and held that she was entitled to a one-third interest in the proceeds.[53] It is clear that, on the principles of resulting trusts, the plaintiff was, as Plowman J. held, entitled to a one-twelfth interest in the proceeds. Had this been a case between husband and wife, the plaintiff could also have invoked section 37 of the Matrimonial Proceedings and Property Act 1970[54] to claim an enlarged interest by virtue of her contribution in money's worth to the improvement of the property. Be that as it may, it cannot be

---

[46] *Supra*, 20.
[47] The court, on the principles enunciated, would presumably have reached the same decision had the husband been bankrupt and liable to produce the securities to settle an insurance claim.
[48] [1971] 1 W.L.R. 342, *per* Lord Denning M.R. at 348, *per* Megaw L.J. at 352.
[49] [1972] 1 W.L.R. 518.
[50] *Ibid.* 519.
[51] *Ibid.* 520.
[52] It is unclear what other relationships the Master of the Rolls had in mind.
[53] [1972] 1 W.L.R. 518, 521–522.
[54] s. 37 provides that, where a spouse contributes in money or money's worth to the improvement of real or personal property in which either or both of the spouses have a beneficial interest, the spouse shall be treated as having acquired a share or an enlarged share in the beneficial interest of such an extent as may seem in all the circumstances just to any court hearing proceedings concerning the beneficial interest. See p. 336, *supra*.

denied that the court once again reached their decision by imposing a constructive trust in order to present a result which would, otherwise, in the view of the court, have been unjust. Apart from the fact that this approach renders the operation of the law uncertain and unpredictable, why should the plaintiff obtain an advantage over the general creditors of the defendant? It is submitted that in *Cooke* v. *Head* the imposition of a constructive trust in order to do justice *inter partes* is unjustifiable.

" The principle that a constructive trust will be imposed in order to prevent a result which would, otherwise, be inequitable was extended still further in *Binions and Another* v. *Evans*.[55] The husband of the defendant, Mrs. Evans, had been employed throughout his working life by the Tredegar Estate, who had permitted him to live rent-free in a cottage. After his death, the Estate entered into an agreement with Mrs. Evans under which, in return for keeping the property in good order, she was permitted to live there rent-free for the rest of her life. In 1970, the Estate sold the cottage to the plaintiffs, Mr. and Mrs. Binions. The property was sold ' subject to the tenancy . . . in favour of Mrs. Evans,' and it was found as a fact that the plaintiffs for this reason paid a lower price. Nevertheless, six months later, they gave Mrs. Evans notice to quit and subsequently claimed possession in the county court. This action reached the Court of Appeal (Lord Denning M.R., Megaw and Stephenson L.JJ.). Megaw and Stephenson L.JJ. found that the effect of the agreement between the Tredegar Estate and Mrs. Evans was the same as the effect of the agreement considered by the Court of Appeal in *Bannister* v. *Bannister*.[56] Mrs. Evans was thus a tenant for life within the meaning of the Settled Land Act 1925. In the words of Megaw L.J.[57]:

' I realise that the application of the Settled Land Act 1925 may produce some odd consequences, but no odder than those which were inherent in the decision in *Bannister* v. *Bannister*. I do not find anything in the possible, theoretical, consequences to lead me to the conclusion that *Bannister's* case should not be followed. The plaintiffs took with express notice of the agreement which constitutes, or gives rise to, the trust. They cannot turn [Mrs. Evans] out of the house against her will; for that would be a breach of the trust which binds them.'

" Their lordships, therefore, imposed a constructive trust in accordance with *Bannister* v. *Bannister*.

" The Master of the Rolls disagreed. He argued that Mrs. Evans was not a life tenant under the Settled Land Act. He held that the agreement had created a licence in favour of Mrs. Evans.[58] He imposed upon the plaintiffs a constructive trust ' for the simple reason that it would be utterly inequitable for the purchaser to turn the defendant out contrary to the stipulation subject to which he took the premises.'[59] Can the imposition of such a constructive trust be justified?

[55] [1972] Ch. 359.
[56] [1948] W.N. 261.
[57] [1972] Ch. 359, 370. See Stephenson L.J. to the same effect at p. 372.
[58] [1972] Ch. 359, 367.
[59] [1972] Ch. 359, 368.

" The Master of the Rolls cited *Bannister* v. *Bannister* as authority for his decision.... In addition, his lordship relied on two dicta, that statement of Lord Diplock [60] to which reference has already been made and a statement by Cardozo J. in *Beatty* v. *Guggenheim Exploration Co.*[61] that a 'constructive trust is the formula through which the conscience of equity finds expression.' It has already been shown that this statement of Lord Diplock has been taken out of its context and that the American and English attitudes to the constructive trust are very different....

" What of the approach taken by Megaw and Stephenson L.JJ., who imposed a constructive trust in accordance with *Bannister* v. *Bannister*? Since their lordships imposed a constructive trust having made a finding of unconscionable conduct on the part of the plaintiffs, this result seems to be in accordance with authority.

" It is submitted, therefore, that the imposition of a constructive trust in *Binions* v. *Evans* is only justifiable on the approach taken by Megaw and Stephenson L.JJ. The imposition of such a trust to protect a contractual licence cannot be justified [for it would be to let in by the back door contractual licences as property interests in defiance of the views expressed in *National Provincial Bank* v. *Ainsworth* [62] and in *Re A Debtor* [63] about it not being open to the courts to elevate contractual licences to the status of property interests].[64]

" In the most recent decision, *Hussey* v. *Palmer*,[65] it is even more apparent that the court is invoking the constructive trust as an equitable remedy to do justice *inter partes*. The plaintiff, Mrs. Hussey, sold her condemned house and was invited by her son-in-law and daughter to live with them. Because their house was rather small, they had an extension built for which Mrs. Hussey paid. Differences arose and, after some fifteen months, Mrs. Hussey left. Subsequently, she became very short of money and asked her son-in-law to repay to her the sum spent on the extension. When he refused, she brought an action against him. Initially, she claimed for money lent. However, the county court registrar, before whom the case came by consent, intimated a strong opinion that this was not a loan. Mrs. Hussey therefore submitted to a non-suit and started a fresh action claiming the sum under a resulting trust. This action failed before the county court judge who felt that there was, on the evidence, a loan, not a resulting trust. Mrs. Hussey appealed to the Court of Appeal (Lord Denning M.R., Phillimore and Cairns L.JJ.). The court held, by a majority, that there was a trust in respect of the house in favour of the plaintiff. The majority, the Master of the Rolls and Phillimore L.J., reached this result by invoking the doctrine of constructive trusts. The Master of the Rolls reviewed the facts and held that there was no loan. He then continued [66]:

> ' If there was no loan, was there a resulting trust? and, if so, what where the terms of the trust? Although the plaintiff alleged that there was a resulting trust, I should have thought that the trust in this case,

---

[60] In *Gissing* v. *Gissing* [1971] A.C. 886, 905.
[61] 225 N.Y. 380, at 395 (1919).
[62] [1965] A.C. 1175; [1964] Ch. 702.
[63] [1967] Ch. 573.
[64] (1972) 36 Conv.(N.S.) 278–279.
[65] [1972] 1 W.L.R. 1286; (1973) 89 L.Q.R. 2.
[66] [1972] 1 W.L.R. 1286, at 1289.

if there was one, was more in the nature of a constructive trust; but
this is more a matter of words than anything else. The two run
together.'

" His lordship, in that passage, equates resulting and constructive trusts.
This seems somewhat strange, since a resulting trust arises out of the presumed intentions of the parties, whereas a constructive trust is imposed by
the court quite irrespective of the intentions of the parties. His lordship then
continued (referring to what is generally regarded as a constructive trust):

' By whatever name it is described, it is a trust imposed by law whenever justice and good conscience require it. It is a liberal process,
founded on large principles of equity, to be applied in cases where the
defendant cannot conscientiously keep the property for himself alone,
but ought to allow another to have the property or a share in it. The
trust may arise at the outset when the property is acquired, or later on,
as the circumstances may require. It is an equitable remedy by which
the courts can enable an aggrieved party to obtain restitution.'

" His lordship then considered such decisions as *Heseltine* v. *Heseltine*,[67]
Cooke v. *Head* [68] and *Binions* v. *Evans* [69] and decided that ' the present case
is well within the principles of those cases.' His lordship therefore held
that:

' The court should, and will, impose or impute a trust by which
[the son-in-law] is to hold the property on terms under which, in the
circumstances which have happened, [Mrs. Hussey] has an interest in
the property proportionate to the £607 she put into it.' [70]

" Phillimore L.J. agreed.[71] Cairns L.J., however, dissented, holding that
the transaction was one of loan, not of resulting trust.[72] Such a view, of
course, would have necessitated Mrs. Hussey starting yet another action.
Nevertheless, such a result would have been preferable to the imposition of
a constructive trust. Apart from the fact that all the evidence points towards
the relationship being one of loan, why should a constructive trust be imposed upon the defendant in this case? Such a result gives Mrs. Hussey a
right to call for the sale of the house to obtain her interest. Further, the
Master of the Rolls stated that the payment of the sum expended would
suffice. But, on the terms of his order, Mrs. Hussey could claim not the
sum expended but the value of an interest in the house proportionate to the
relative expenditure of herself and her son-in-law—an interest which, in
present conditions, would be considerably larger. Would the court have
imposed a constructive trust if Mrs. Hussey had claimed in the alternative
for money lent and under a resulting trust?

" The Master of the Rolls also placed some reliance on the equitable
doctrine of acquiescence,[73] under which, as Lord Cranworth L.C. explained
in *Ramsden* v. *Dyson*,[74]

67 [1971] 1 W.L.R. 342.
68 [1972] 1 W.L.R. 518.
69 [1972] Ch. 359.
70 [1972] 1 W.L.R. 1286, 1291.
71 *Ibid.*
72 *Ibid.* 1292.
73 This doctrine is expounded in Goff and Jones, *op. cit.*, pp. 96–99.
74 (1866) L.R. 1 H.L. 129, 140.

' If a stranger begins to build on my land supposing it to be his own, and I, perceiving his mistake, abstain from setting him right, and leave him to persevere in his error, a court of equity will not allow me afterwards to assert my title to the land on which he has expended money on the supposition that the land was his own.'

" It is by no means clear that this doctrine is available both as a sword and as a shield, since Danckwerts L.J., in the most recent case, *Inwards* v. *Baker*,[75] took the view that the doctrine gave the improver no distinct cause of action against the owner. This view is, however, not entirely borne out by the older authorities and there is much to be said for the view that the improver should have a distinct cause of action. Even upon this assumption, however, it is doubtful whether the equitable doctrine of acquiescence can apply to the facts of *Hussey* v. *Palmer*. The doctrine only applies if the improver has made a mistake as to his own legal rights and if the owner of the land encouraged the improver in this mistake either directly or by a failure to assert his own legal right. It is doubtful whether Mrs. Hussey was mistaken as to her legal rights at the time the extension was built and, even if she was, her son-in-law does not appear to have encouraged her either directly or by inactivity. Further, even if the doctrine does apply to the facts, it is difficult to justify the imposition of a constructive trust. An equitable lien or charge would surely have sufficed.

" It is submitted, therefore, that there is no justification for the imposition of a constructive trust in *Hussey* v. *Palmer*.

THE RECENT DECISIONS ASSESSED

" In each of the recent decisions which have been considered, the Court of Appeal has imposed a constructive trust in order to prevent a result which would, otherwise, have been inequitable. It is clear that, in the field of matrimonial property, such practice is contrary to the most recent decisions of the House of Lords. This apart, the practice has, in principle, little to commend it; it makes the operation of the law totally uncertain and enables one spouse to acquire rights over property which could never have been obtained under existing equitable principles.[76] Outside the field of matrimonial property, the practice is even more undesirable, since the implications of the imposition of constructive trusts to do justice *inter partes* may well seriously undermine established principles of property law.[77] Recent developments in the field of constructive trusts in English law have been towards imposing a constructive trust only where there is some conscious unconscionable act by the trustee. Among the many examples of this approach are *Holder* v. *Holder*,[78] where an executor who purchased trust property was held not liable to account for it to the trust in the absence of actual abuse of position, and *Carl Zeiss Stiftung* v. *Herbert Smith (No. 2)*,[79] where it was stated that agents handling trust property in the ordinary course of their agency would be liable to account for that property to the trust only where they had actual notice of a breach of trust. The use of the

---

75 [1965] 2 Q.B. 29.
76 See *Heseltine* v. *Heseltine (supra)*.
77 See *Binions* v. *Evans (supra)*.
78 [1968] Ch. 353.
79 [1969] 2 Ch. 276.

constructive trust to do justice *inter partes* must, in some cases, involve the imposition of constructive trusts upon parties not in any way guilty of a legal wrong. The practice, therefore, is not in accordance with recent developments in English law. This is not to say that the categories of situations in which English courts will impose a constructive trust should not be extended. But they should only be extended where the courts are prepared to lay down a new principle which will apply generally. It is unsatisfactory for a constructive trust to be imposed whenever the courts feel, on their own individual ideas of justice, that such a remedy will bring about the ' right ' result.

"What, then, can be said by way of conclusion? It cannot be denied that the cases discussed in this paper have built up a formidable body of case law in support of the proposition that the constructive trust may be used to prevent a result which would, otherwise, be inequitable. Nevertheless, it is submitted that the imposition of a constructive trust on such a basis in these cases cannot be justified on the criteria that should be a prerequisite of the imposition of a constructive trust. It is to be hoped, therefore, that, should the House of Lords have an opportunity of considering these recent developments, some certainty will be restored to this area of the law."

Section 2. The Fiduciary as Constructive Trustee

If a trustee or other fiduciary by virtue of his fiduciary connection acquires an interest in property he must hold the interest acquired on trust for the estate, *e.g.*, a trustee renewing a lease in his favour to the exclusion of his beneficiaries,[80] an agent commissioned to buy a particular type of property buying it on his own behalf,[81] a director supposed to acquire certain types of contracts for his company taking up the contracts personally.[82]

A fiduciary is under very strict obligations not to profit from his fiduciary relationship.[83] If he does, then subject to certain exceptions, he must disgorge any benefit obtained by him " even though he acted honestly and in his principal's best interests, even though his principal benefited as well as he from his conduct, even though his principal could not otherwise have obtained the benefit, and even though the benefit was obtained through the use of the fiduciary's own assets and in consequence of his personal skill and judgment." [84] The benefit (or profit) is held by him as constructive trustee except that if he has only exploited a fiduciary position (as opposed to trust property) and has not deprived his principal or beneficiaries of property or diverted to himself property which might have come to the principal or to the trust, he will be accountable only in a personal action for the profit he has obtained.[85]

---

[80] *Keech* v. *Sandford* (1726) 2 Eq.Cas.Abr. 741.
[81] *James* v. *Smith* [1891] 1 Ch. 384; *Reiger* v. *Campbell-Stuart* [1939] Ch. 676; *Re Cape Breton* (1885) 29 Ch.D. 795, 803–804.
[82] *Cook* v. *Deeks* [1916] 1 A.C. 554.
[83] *Infra*, Chap. 10.
[84] Gareth Jones (1968) 84 L.Q.R. 472, 474; *Boardman* v. *Phipps, infra.*
[85] *Lister* v. *Stubbs* (1890) 45 Ch.D. 1. An agent received secret commissions which he invested. His principal sought an injunction restraining the agent from dealing with the investments or an order directing him to bring them into court. The C.A. rejected the claim since the secret commissions did not belong in equity to the principal: the agent was merely liable to account for the amount of the commissions. See Goff and Jones, pp. 459–460, Hanbury, p. 424, Gareth Jones (1968) 84 L.Q.R. 472, 477 as to whether this exception is justifiable.

The advantage of imposing a constructive trusteeship is that (1) it enables the plaintiff to recover not merely the property exploited by the fiduciary but also its fruits and (2) it confers priority over the fiduciary's general creditors, the property and its fruits being treated as belonging to the plaintiff throughout so as not to be available for the fiduciary's creditors. However, where the fiduciary is good for the money the plaintiff will usually be satisfied with making the fiduciary liable to account for his profits. In *Boardman* v. *Phipps, infra,* the plaintiff claimed (i) a declaration that the defendant fiduciaries held five-eighteenths of the shareholding obtained by them (through using confidential information, the property of the trust) as constructive trustees for him, (ii) an account of the profits made by the fiduciaries and (iii) an order that the fiduciaries should transfer to him the shares held by them as constructive trustees and should pay him five-eighteenths of the profit found to be due upon taking the account. Wilberforce J. gave the plaintiff the relief requested by him under (i) and (ii) but in respect of (iii) the matter was adjourned. Presumably, this was to allow the account of profits to be taken and the inquiry to be held as to the payment on a liberal scale to be made to the fiduciaries for their extraordinarily skilful work, whereupon the balance would be due to the plaintiff, who could then consider whether or not it would be worthwhile calling for the shares subject to satisfying the fiduciaries' lien for their outlay on the purchase of the shares. Appeals against the judgment failed in the Court of Appeal and the Lords, who held that since the fiduciaries were constructive trustees they were clearly liable to account for their profits: Wilberforce J.'s declaration of constructive trusteeship [86] and order for account of profits, subject to inquiry as to a liberal allowance for the fiduciaries' efforts, thus stood.

As the Lords were divided 3:2 (taking over five months to make up their minds) it may well be that in some future similar case a less strict approach to the fiduciary's duty of loyalty will be taken, especially if the policy of the law is analysed in more detail.[87]

KEECH v. SANDFORD [88]

Lord Chancellor (1726) 2 Eq.Cas.Abr. 741; Sel.Cas.Ch. 61

A person being possessed of a lease of the profits of a market devised his estate to a trustee in trust for his infant. Before the expiration of the term the trustee applied to the lessor for a renewal, for the benefit of the infant, which he refused, in regard that, it being only of

---

[86] It appears from the report in [1964] 2 All E.R. 187, 208, Pearson L.J. in [1965] Ch. 992, 1021, Lords Cohen and Guest in [1967] 2 A.C. 46 at 99 and 112 respectively that Wilberforce J. granted a declaration of constructive trust despite the report of Wilberforce J.'s order in [1964] 1 W.L.R. 993, 1018 relating to accountability only.

[87] See the cogent article of Gareth Jones, 84 L.Q.R. 472; also Chap. 10, s. 2, *infra*.

[88] The rule in *Keech* v. *Sandford* is derived from the principle that a trustee must not put himself in a position where his interest conflicts with his duty: in case of conflict, duty prevails over interest. Several instances of this principle occur in the administration of express trusts: *infra*, pp. 466–489. See Hart, " The Development of the Rule in *Keech* v. *Sandford* " (1905) 21 L.Q.R. 258; Cretney (1969) 33 Conv.(N.S.) 161.

the profits of a market, there could be no distress, and must rest singly in covenant, which the infant could not enter into.

There was clear proof of the refusal to renew for the benefit of the infant, on which the trustee gets a lease made to himself.

Bill is now brought (by the infant) to have the lease assigned to him, and for an account of the profits, on the principle that wherever a lease is renewed by a trustee or executor it shall be for the benefit of *cestui que use*, which principle was agreed on the other side, though endeavoured to be differenced on account of the express proof of refusal to renew to the infant.

LORD KING L.C.: "I must consider this as a trust for the infant, for I very well see, if a trustee, on the refusal to renew, might have a lease to himself, few trust estates would be renewed to *cestui que use*. Though I do not say there is fraud in this case, yet he should rather have let it run out than to have had the lease to himself. This may seem hard, that the trustee is the only person of all mankind who might not have the lease; but it is very proper that that rule should be strictly pursued, and not in the least relaxed; for it is very obvious what would be the consequences of letting trustees have the lease on refusal to renew to *cestui que use*."

So decreed, that the lease should be assigned to the infant, and that the trustee should be indemnified from any covenants comprised in the lease, and an account of the profits made since the renewal.[89]

Note

The rule applies whether the trustee obtains a renewal by virtue of a provision in the lease to that effect or whether he obtains it by virtue of the advantage which his position as sitting tenant gives him.[90] The principle applies not only to trustees and tenants for life,[91] but also to other fiduciaries such as mortgagees,[92] directors[93] and partners.[94] But unlike trustees and tenants for life the latter group of persons are not irrebuttably precluded from taking the renewal of a lease. In *Re Biss*,[95] a lease formed part of the personalty of an intestate, and after the lessor had refused to renew to

---

[89] For a modern instance, see *Re Jarvis* [1958] 1 W.L.R. 815. Testator gave to his two executors, subject to certain annuities, the tenancy of his shop with its goodwill and assets, but without authorising the executors to carry on the business. Owing to war damage, business had almost ceased at the shop, but one of the executors obtained a renewal of the tenancy and successfully restarted the business. Some years later the other executor claimed that there was a constructive trust of both tenancy and business. *Held* by Upjohn J. (i) the claim to the tenancy was not barred by laches (as to which, see *infra*, p. 654); the court was merely enforcing an equitable proprietary right in the premises; (ii) the claim to the business was barred: it was not open to the beneficiary to stand by to see whether the business was successful before making his claim (1958) 74 L.Q.R. 487 (R.E.M.).

[90] *Re Knowles' Will Trusts* [1948] 1 All E.R. 866.

[91] *James* v. *Dean* (1808) 15 Ves. 236; *Lloyd-Jones* v. *Clark-Lloyd* [1919] 1 Ch. 424; ss. 16, 107 of the Settled Land Act 1925.

[92] *Rushworth's Case* (1676) Freem.Ch. 13; *Leigh* v. *Burnett* (1885) 29 Ch.D. 231.

[93] *G. E. Smith Ltd.* v. *Smith* [1952] N.Z.L.R. 470; *Crittenden & Cowler Co.* v. *Cowler*, 72 New York State 701 (1901).

[94] *Featherstonhaugh* v. *Fenwick* (1810) 17 Ves. 298; *cf. Piddock* v. *Burt* [1894] 1 Ch. 343. [95] [1903] 2 Ch. 40.

the administratrix, one of her sons (helping her run the deceased's business at the premises) obtained a renewal for himself. It was held, however, to be unimpeachable, since he could show affirmatively that he acted bona fide and did not take advantage of the other persons interested. Romer L.J. said,[96] "where the person renewing the lease does not clearly occupy a fiduciary position" he "is only held to be a constructive trustee of the renewed lease if, in respect of the old lease, he occupied some special position and owed, by virtue of that position, a duty towards the other persons interested."

In *Protheroe* v. *Protheroe* [97] the Court of Appeal in a one-page extempore judgment of Lord Denning held that under the *Keech* v. *Sandford* principle there was "a long-established rule of equity" that a trustee purchasing the reversion upon a lease held by him *automatically* held the reversion upon the same trusts as the lease. *Sed quaere* as till then such constructive trusts of the reversion were only imposed where the lease was renewable by custom or contract (the purchase thus cutting off the right of renewal) or where the trustee obtained the reversion by virtue of his position *qua* leaseholder (*e.g.*, a landlord offering enfranchisement to all his leaseholders).[98] The reason for the distinction is that "whereas in the case of a renewal the trustee is in effect buying a part of the trust property, in the case of a reversion this is not so; it is a separate item altogether." [99] Of course, purchases of a reversion stand a very good chance of falling foul of the strict principles illustrated by *Boardman* v. *Phipps, infra.*

BOARDMAN AND ANOTHER v. PHIPPS

House of Lords [1967] 2 A.C. 46; [1966] 3 W.L.R. 1009; [1966] 3 All E.R. 721 (Lords Cohen, Hodson and Guest; Viscount Dilhorne and Lord Upjohn dissenting)

The respondent, Mr. J. A. Phipps, was one of the residuary legatees under the will of his father, Mr. C. W. Phipps, who died in 1944. The residuary estate included 8,000 out of 30,000 issued shares in a private company, Lester & Harris Ltd. By his will the testator left an annuity to his widow and subject thereto five-eighteenths of his residuary estate to each of his three sons and three-eighteenths to his only daughter. At the end of 1955 the trustees of the will were the testator's widow (who was senile and took no part in the affairs of the trust), his only daughter, Mrs. Noble, and an accountant, Mr. W. Fox. The first appellant, Mr. T. G. Boardman, was at all the material times solicitor to the trustees and also to the children of the testator (other than the respondent). The second appellant, Mr. T. E. Phipps, was the younger brother of the respondent and in the transactions which gave rise to this action

---

[96] *Ibid.* 61.

[97] [1968] 1 W.L.R. 519; followed in *Thompson's Trustee* v. *Heaton* [1974] 1 W.L.R. 605. See (1968) 84 L.Q.R. 309; (1974) 38 Conv.(N.S.) 288.

[98] *Bevan* v. *Webb* [1905] 1 Ch. 620; *Longton* v. *Wilsby* (1887) 76 L.T. 770; *Randall* v. *Russell* (1817) 3 Mer. 190; *Phillips* v. *Phillips* (1884) 29 Ch.D. 673; *Phipps* v. *Boardman* [1964] 1 W.L.R. 993, 1009; *Brenner* v. *Rose* [1973] 1 W.L.R. 443, 448, but *cf. Thompson's Trustee* v. *Heaton* [1974] 1 W.L.R. 605.

[99] *Phipps* v. *Boardman* (*ibid.*); *cf.* different treatment of renewals and reversions for purposes of rule against remoteness: *Woodall* v. *Clifton* [1905] 2 Ch. 257.

he was associated with and represented by the first appellant, Mr. Boardman.

In 1956 Mr. Boardman and Mr. Fox decided that the recent accounts of Lester & Harris Ltd. were unsatisfactory and with a view to improving the position the appellants attended the annual general meeting of the company in December 1956 with proxies obtained from two of the trustees, Mrs. Noble and Mr. Fox. They were not satisfied with the answers given at the meeting regarding the state of the company's affairs.

Shortly after this meeting the appellants decided with the knowledge of Mrs. Noble and Mr. Fox to try to obtain control of Lester & Harris Ltd. by themselves making an offer for all the outstanding shares in that company other than the 8,000 held by the trustees. The trustees had no power to invest in the shares of the company without the sanction of the court and Mr. Fox said in evidence that he would not have considered seeking such sanction. The appellants originally offered £2 5s. per share, which they later increased to £3, but by April 1957 they had received acceptances only in respect of 2,925 shares and it was clear that as things then stood they would not go through with their offer. This ended the first phase in the negotiations which ultimately led to the acquisition by the appellants of virtually all the outstanding shares in Lester & Harris Ltd. During this phase the appellants attended the annual general meeting as proxies of the two trustees and obtained information from the company as to the prices at which shares had recently changed hands; but they made the offer to purchase on their own behalf.

The second phase lasted from April 1957 to August 1958. Throughout this period Mr. Boardman carried on negotiations with the chairman of Lester & Harris Ltd. with a view to reaching agreement on the division of the assets of that company between the Harris family and the directors on the one hand and the Phipps family on the other. During this phase Mr. Boardman obtained valuable information as to the value of the company's assets and throughout he purported to act on behalf of the trustees. These negotiations proved abortive.

The third phase began in August 1958 with the suggestion by Mr. Boardman that he and Mr. T. E. Phipps should acquire for themselves the outstanding shares in the company. The widow died in November 1958 and a conditional agreement for the sale of the shares was made on March 10, 1959. On May 26, 1959, the appellants gave notices making the agreements unconditional to buy 14,567 shares held by the chairman of the company and his associates at £4 10s. per share. This, in addition to the earlier agreements to purchase 2,925 shares at £3 each and the purchase of a further 4,494 shares at £4 10s. each, made the appellants holders in all of 21,986 shares.

Thereafter the business of the company was reorganised, part of its assets was sold off at considerable profit, and substantial sums of capital, amounting in the aggregate to £5 17s. 6d. per share, were returned to the shareholders, whose shares were still worth at least £2 each after the return of capital. The appellants acted honestly throughout.

The respondent, like the other members of the Phipps family, was asked by Mr. Boardman whether he objected to the acquisition of control of the company by the appellants for themselves; but Mr. Boardman did not give sufficient information as to the material facts to succeed in the defence of consent on the part of the respondent. At first the respondent expressed his satisfaction but later he became antagonistic and issued a writ claiming (i) that the appellants held five-eighteenths of the above-mentioned 21,986 shares as constructive trustees for him [1] and (ii) an account of the profits made by the appellants out of the said shares. Wilberforce J. granted this relief [2] and his decision was affirmed by the Court of Appeal. [3] The appellants appealed to the House of Lords.

LORD COHEN: " . . . As Wilberforce J. said, [4] the mere use of any knowledge or opportunity which comes to the trustee or agent in the course of his trusteeship or agency does not necessarily make him liable to account. In the present case had the company been a public company and had the appellants bought the shares on the market, they would not, I think, have been accountable. The company, however, is a private company and not only the information but also the opportunity to purchase these shares came to them through the introduction which Mr. Fox gave them to the board of the company and, in the second phase, when the discussions related to the proposed split up of the company's undertaking, it was solely on behalf of the trustees that Mr. Boardman was purporting to negotiate with the board of the company. The question is this: when in the third phase the negotiations turned to the purchase of the shares at £4 10s. a share, were the appellants debarred by their fiduciary position from purchasing on their own behalf the 21,986 shares in the company without the informed consent of the trustees and the beneficiaries?

" Wilberforce J. [5] and, in the Court of Appeal, [6] both Lord Denning M.R. and Pearson L.J. based their decision in favour of the respondent on the decision of your Lordships' House in *Regal (Hastings) Ltd.* v. *Gulliver.* [7] I turn, therefore, to consider that case. Counsel for the respondent relied on a number of passages in the judgments of the learned Lords who heard the appeal, in particular on (i) a passage in

[1] The appellants would, of course, have a lien for their outlay on the purchase of the shares.
[2] [1964] 1 W.L.R. 993.
[3] [1965] Ch. 992 (Lord Denning M.R., Pearson and Russell L.JJ.).
[4] [1964] 1 W.L.R. 993, 1011.
[5] *Ibid.*
[6] [1965] Ch. 992.
[7] [1942] 1 All E.R. 378.

the speech of Lord Russell of Killowen where he said [8]: 'The rule of equity which insists on those, who by use of a fiduciary position make a profit, being liable to account for that profit, in no way depends on fraud, or absence of bona fides; or upon such questions or considerations as whether the profit would or should otherwise have gone to the plaintiff, or whether the profiteer was under a duty to obtain the source of the profit for the plaintiff, or whether he took a risk or acted as he did for the benefit of the plaintiff, or whether the plaintiff has in fact been damaged or benefited by his action. The liability arises from the mere fact of a profit having, in the stated circumstances, been made'; (ii) a passage in the speech of Lord Wright where he says [9]: 'That question can be briefly stated to be whether an agent, a director, a trustee or other person in an analogous fiduciary position, when a demand is made upon him by the person to whom he stands in the fiduciary relationship to account for profits acquired by him by reason of his fiduciary position, and by reason of the opportunity and the knowledge, or either, resulting from it, is entitled to defeat the claim upon any ground save that he made profits with the knowledge and assent of the other person. The most usual and typical case of this nature is that of principal and agent. The rule in such cases is compendiously expressed to be that an agent must account for net profits secretly (that is, without the knowledge of his principal) acquired by him in the course of his agency. The authorities show how manifold and various are the applications of the rule. It does not depend on fraud or corruption.' These paragraphs undoubtedly help the respondent but they must be considered in relation to the facts of that case. In that case the profit arose through the application by four of the directors of Regal for shares in a subsidiary company which it had been the original intention of the board should be subscribed for by Regal. Regal had not the requisite money available but there was no question of it being *ultra vires* Regal to subscribe for the shares. In the circumstances Lord Russell of Killowen said [10]: 'I have no hesitation in coming to the conclusion, upon the facts of this case, that these shares, when acquired by the directors, were acquired by reason, and only by reason, of the fact that they were directors of Regal, and in the course of their execution of that office.' He went on to consider whether the four directors were in a fiduciary relationship to Regal and concluded that they were. Accordingly, they were held accountable. Counsel for the appellants argued that the present case is distinguishable. He puts his argument thus. The question one asks is whether the information could have been used by the principal for the purpose for which it was used by his agents. If the answer to that question is no, the information was not used in the course of their duty as agents. In the present case the information could never have been used by the

8 *Ibid.* 386.
9 *Ibid.* 392.
10 *Ibid.* 387.

trustees for the purpose of purchasing shares in the company; therefore purchase of shares was outside the scope of the appellants' agency and they are not accountable.

" This is an attractive argument, but it does not seem to me to give due weight to the fact that the appellants obtained both the information which satisfied them that the purchase of the shares would be a good investment and the opportunity of acquiring them as a result of acting for certain purposes on behalf of the trustees. Information is, of course, not property in the strict sense of that word and, as I have already stated, it does not necessarily follow that, because an agent acquired information and opportunity while acting in a fiduciary capacity, he is accountable to his principals for any profit that comes his way as the result of the use he makes of that information and opportunity. His liability to account must depend on the facts of the case. In the present case much of the information came the appellants' way when Mr. Boardman was acting on behalf of the trustees on the instructions of Mr. Fox, and the opportunity of bidding for the shares came because he purported for all purposes except for making the bid to be acting on behalf of the owners of the 8,000 shares in the company. In these circumstances it seems to me that the principle of the *Regal* case applies and that the courts below came to the right conclusion.

" That is enough to dispose of the case but I would add that an agent is, in my opinion, liable to account for profits which he makes out of the trust property if there is a possibility of conflict between his interest and his duty to his principal. Mr. Boardman and Mr. Tom Phipps were not general agents of the trustees, but they were their agents for certain limited purposes. The information which they had obtained and the opportunity to purchase the 21,986 shares afforded them by their relations with the directors of the company—an opportunity they got as the result of their introduction to the directors by Mr. Fox—were not property in the strict sense but that information and that opportunity they owed to their representing themselves as agents for the holders of the 8,000 shares held by the trustees. In these circumstances they could not, I think, use that information and that opportunity to purchase the shares for themselves if there was any possibility that the trustees might wish to acquire them for the trust. Mr. Boardman was the solicitor whom the trustees were in the habit of consulting if they wanted legal advice. Granted that he would not be bound to advise on any point unless he were consulted, he would still be the person they would consult if they wanted advice. He would clearly have advised them that they had no power to invest in shares of the company without the sanction of the court. In the first phase he would also have had to advise on the evidence then available that the court would be unlikely to give such sanction: but the appellants learnt much more during the second phase. It may well be that even in third phase the answer of the court would have been the same but, in my opinion, Mr. Boardman would not have been able to give unprejudiced advice if he had been consulted by the trustees and was at the same time negotiating for the purchase of the shares on behalf of himself and Mr. Tom Phipps. In other words, there was, in my opinion, at the crucial date (March 1959) a possibility of a conflict between his interest and his duty.

" In making these observations I have referred to the fact that Mr. Boardman was the solicitor to the trust. Mr. Tom Phipps was only a beneficiary and was not as such debarred from bidding for the shares, but no attempt was made in the courts below to differentiate between them. Had such an attempt been made it would very likely have failed, as Mr. Tom Phipps left the negotiations largely to Mr. Boardman, and it might well be held that, if Mr. Boardman was disqualified from bidding, Mr. Tom Phipps could not be in a better position. Be that as it may, counsel for the appellants rightly did not seek at this stage to distinguish between the two. He did, it is true, say that Mr. Tom Phipps as a beneficiary would be entitled to any information that the trustees obtained. This may be so, but nonetheless I find myself unable to distinguish between the two appellants. They were, I think, in March 1959, in a fiduciary position *vis-à-vis* the trust. That fiduciary position was of such a nature that (as the trust fund was distributable) the appellants could not purchase the shares on their own behalf without the informed consent of the beneficiaries: it is now admitted that they did not obtain that consent. They are therefore, in my opinion, accountable to the respondent for his share of the net profits which they derived from the transaction.

" I desire to repeat that the integrity of the appellants is not in doubt. They acted with complete honesty throughout, and the respondent is a fortunate man in that the rigour of equity enables him to participate in the profits which have accrued as the result of the action taken by the appellants in March 1959 in purchasing the shares at their own risk. As the last paragraph of his judgment clearly shows, the trial judge evidently shared this view. He directed an inquiry as to what sum was proper to be allowed to the appellants or either of them in respect of their or his work and skill in obtaining the said shares and the profits in respect thereof. The trial judge concluded by expressing the opinion that payment should be on a liberal scale. With that observation I respectfully agree. . . ."

LORD HODSON: ". . . The proposition of law involved in this case is that no person standing in a fiduciary position, when a demand is made on him by the person to whom he stands in the fiduciary relationship to account for profits acquired by him by reason of his fiduciary position and by reason of the opportunity and the knowledge, or either, resulting from it, is entitled to defeat the claim on any ground save that he made profits with the knowledge and assent of the other person. . . .

" . . . it is said on behalf of the appellants that information as such is not necessarily property and it is only trust property which is relevant. I agree, but it is nothing to the point to say that in these times corporate trustees, *e.g.*, the Public Trustee and others, necessarily acquire a mass of information in their capacity of trustees for a particular trust and cannot be held liable to account if knowledge so acquired enables them to operate to their own advantage, or to that of other trusts. Each case must depend on its own facts, and I dissent from the view that information is of its nature something which is not properly to be described as property. We are aware that what is called 'know-how' in the commercial sense is property which may be very valuable as an asset. I agree with the learned judge [11] and with the Court of Appeal [12] that the confidential information acquired in this case, which was capable of being and was turned to account, can be properly regarded as the property of the trust. It was obtained by Mr. Boardman by reason of the opportunity which he was given as solicitor acting for the trustees in the negotiations with the chairman of the company, as the correspondence demonstrates. The end result was that, out of the special position in which they were standing in the course of the negotiations, the appellants got the opportunity to make a profit and the knowledge that it was there to be made. . . .

" *Regal (Hastings) Ltd.* v. *Gulliver* differs from this case mainly in that the directors took up shares and made a profit thereby, it having been originally intended that the company should buy these shares. Here there was no such intention on the part of the trustees. There is no indication that they either had the money or would have been ready to apply to the court for sanction enabling them to do so. On the contrary, Mr. Fox, the active trustee and an accountant who concerned himself with the details of the trust property, was not prepared to agree to the trustees buying the shares and encouraged the appellants to make the purchase. This does not affect the position. As *Keech* v. *Sandford* [13] shows, the inability of the trust to purchase makes no difference to the liability of the appellants, if liability otherwise exists. The distinction on the facts as to intention to purchase shares between this case and *Regal (Hastings) Ltd.* v. *Gulliver* is not relevant. The company (Regal) had not the money to apply for the shares on which the profit was made. The directors took the opportunity which they had presented to them to buy the shares with their own money and were held accountable. Mr. Fox's refusal as one of the trustees to take any part in the matter on behalf of the trust, so far as he was concerned, can make no difference. Nothing short of fully informed consent, which the

---

[11] [1964] 1 W.L.R. 993, 1008–1011.
[12] [1965] Ch. 992.
[13] (1726) Sel.Cas.Ch. 61; *supra*, p. 365.

learned judge found not to have been obtained, could enable the appellants in the position which they occupied, having taken the opportunity provided by that position, to make a profit for themselves. . . .

" The confidential information which the appellants obtained at a time when Mr. Boardman was admittedly holding himself out as solicitor for the trustees was obtained by him as representing the trustees, the holders of 8,000 shares of Lester & Harris Ltd. As Russell L.J. put it [14]: ' The substantial trust shareholding was an asset of which one aspect was its potential use as a means of acquiring knowledge of the company's affairs, or of negotiating allocations of the company's assets, or of inducing other shareholders to part with their shares.' Whether this aspect is properly to be regarded as part of the trust assets is, in my judgment, immaterial. The appellants obtained knowledge by reason of their fiduciary position, and they cannot escape liability by saying that they were acting for themselves and not as agents of the trustees. Whether or not the trust, or the beneficiaries in their stead, could have taken advantage of the information is immaterial, as the authorities clearly show. No doubt it was but a remote possibility that Mr. Boardman would ever be asked by the trustees to advise on the desirability of an application to the court in order that the trustees might avail themselves of the information obtained. Nevertheless, whenever the possibility of conflict is present between personal interest and the fiduciary position the rule of equity must be applied. . . ."

LORD GUEST: " . . . I take the view that from first to last Mr. Boardman was acting in a fiduciary capacity to the trustees. This fiduciary capacity arose in phase 1 and continued into phase 2, which glided into phase 3. In saying this I do not for one moment suggest that there was anything dishonest or underhand in what Mr. Boardman did. He has obtained a clean certificate below and I do not wish to sully it; but the law has a strict regard for principle in ensuring that a person in a fiduciary capacity is not allowed to benefit from any transactions into which he has entered with trust property. If Mr. Boardman was acting on behalf of the trust, then all the information that he obtained in phase 2 became trust property. The weapon which he used to obtain this information was the trust holding; and I see no reason why information and knowledge cannot be trust property. . . ."

LORD UPJOHN (dissenting): " . . . [*Regal* (*Hastings*) *Ltd.* v. *Gulliver* and *Keech* v. *Sandford* bear no relation to this case.]

" This case, if I may emphasise it again, is one concerned not with trust property or with property of which the persons to whom the fiduciary duty was owed were contemplating a purchase but, in contrast to the facts in *Regal*, with property which was not trust property or

---

[14] [1965] Ch. 992, 1031.

property which was ever contemplated as the subject-matter of a possible purchase by the trust. . . .

" [After quoting a passage from the judgment of Russell L.J. in the Court of Appeal which is also quoted by Lord Hodson and is set out *supra*, p. 374, his Lordship continued:] My Lords, I regard that proposition as untenable.

" In general, information is not property at all. It is normally open to all who have eyes to read and ears to hear. The true test is to determine in what circumstances the information has been acquired. If it has been acquired in such circumstances that it would be a breach of confidence to disclose it to another, then courts of equity will restrain the recipient from communicating it to another. In such cases such confidential information is often and for many years has been described as the property of the donor, the books of authority are full of such references; knowledge of secret processes, ' know-how,' confidential information as to the prospects of a company or of someone's intention or the expected results of some horse-race based on stable or other confidential information. But in the end the real truth is that it is not property in any normal sense, but equity will restrain its transmission to another if in breach of some confidential relationship.

" With all respect to the views of Russell L.J., I protest at the idea that information acquired by trustees in the course of their duties as such is necessarily part of the assets of trust property which cannot be used by the trustees except for the benefit of the trust. Russell L.J. referred to the fact that two out of three of the trustees could have no authority to turn over this aspect of trust property to the appellants except for the benefit of the trust; this I do not understand, for if such information is trust property not all the trustees acting together could do it, for they cannot give away trust property. . . .

" [After an elaborate analysis of the factors which in his opinion were required to make an agent liable to account, his Lordship concluded:] In *Barnes* v. *Addy*[15] Lord Selborne L.C. said: ' It is equally important to maintain the doctrine of trusts which is established in this court, and not to strain it by unreasonable construction beyond its due and proper limits. There would be no better mode of undermining the sound doctrines of equity than to make unreasonable and inequitable applications of them.' That, in my judgment, is applicable to this case.

" The trustees were not willing to buy more shares in the company. The active trustees were very willing that the appellants should do so themselves for the benefit of their large minority holding. The trustees, so to speak, lent their name to the appellants in the course of prolonged and difficult negotiations and, of course, the appellants thereby learnt much which would have otherwise been denied to them. The negotiations were in the end brilliantly successful. How successful Tom [*i.e.*,

---

[15] (1874) L.R. 9 Ch. 244, 251.

T. E. Phipps] was in his reorganisation of the company is apparent to all. They ought to be very grateful.

" In the long run the appellants have bought for themselves with their own money shares which the trustees never contemplated buying and they did so in circumstances fully known and approved of by the trustees. To extend the doctrines of equity to make the appellants accountable in such circumstances is, in my judgment, to make unreasonable and inequitable applications of such doctrines. . . ."
Appeal dismissed.

PROBLEM

Tom and Trevor, holding *inter alia* a lease with two years unexpired on trust for Brian for life, remainder for Brian's children equally, were trying to sell the lease as they were likely to receive a heavy dilapidations schedule for remedying at the expiry of the lease. They had tried to purchase the free-hold reversion for the trust but the landlord had refused. Tom's friend Joe, hearing of the predicament, had relieved the trust of the lease at the proper market price. Joe happened to play golf regularly with the land-lord and after persisting for four months was able to contract to purchase the freehold.

Joe, only having half the purchase price, went to see Tom and suggested that Tom put up the other half for he had been a good friend and without him Joe would never have heard of the property and obtained the opportunity to buy the freehold. Tom was only too happy to put up half the purchase price, delighted that Joe was letting him in on the deal rather than merely borrow the money from Tom or a bank. Shortly afterwards Joe and Tom sold the property with vacant possession making £25,000 profit each.

Brian seeks your advice.

Section 3. The Stranger as Constructive Trustee

A stranger may be a constructive trustee because (although not nominated as trustee) he has received trust property with actual or constructive notice that it is trust property transferred in breach of trust or because (not being a bona fide purchaser for value without notice) he acquires notice subsequent to such receipt.[16] Furthermore, " a person who, not being a trustee and not having authority from a trustee, takes upon himself to intermeddle with trust matters or do acts characteristic of the office of trustee, makes himself a trustee *de son tort*, a trustee of his own wrong, or, as such a person is also termed, a constructive trustee." [17] The distinguishing features of such a trustee *de son tort* [18] are that he does not claim to act in his own behalf but for the beneficiaries and his assumption to act is not of itself a ground of liability (save in the sense, of course, of liability to account and liability for any failure in the duty so assumed) and so his status as trustee precedes the occurrence which may be the subject of a claim against him.[19]

16 *Karak Rubber Co.* v. *Burden, infra*; Snell, pp. 186–187.
17 *Per* Danckwerts L.J. in *Carl Zeiss Stiftung* v. *Herbert Smith & Co.* [1969] 2 Ch. 276, 289 citing Halsbury's *Laws of England*, 3rd ed., para. 1550, p. 861 with approval.
18 *Cf.* executor *de son tort*, Tiley's *Casebook on Equity*, Chap. 19.
19 See *Selangor United Rubber Estates Ltd.* v. *Cradock (No. 3)* [1968] 1 W.L.R. 1555, 1579 *per* Ungoed-Thomas J.

In the above cases the trust property and its fruits will be held upon constructive trusts so affording the beneficiaries priority over the constructive trustee's general creditors if necessary.[20]

A person who has not become chargeable with trust property as a constructive trustee in the above ways may be personally liable to account to the beneficiaries if he assists with actual or constructive [21] knowledge in a dishonest and fraudulent design on the part of the trustees: *Karak Rubber Co.* v. *Burden* (*No.* 2), *infra.* Such a person originally was often not considered a constructive trustee since he often had no trust property that he could hold as trustee.[22] However, he clearly ought to be liable in equity to the beneficiaries and so had to be treated as a trustee of some sort. As it was his wrongful act that led to him being treated as a trustee he might as well be treated as a trustee "*de son tort.*" [23] The modern approach, however is to refer to him not as a trustee "*de son tort*" but as a constructive trustee thereby making him personally liable to account to the beneficiaries.[24] Of course, if in knowingly assisting the trustees to commit a breach of trust he also had some of the trust property transferred to him a constructive trust could be imposed on that property so as to give the beneficiaries priority over his general creditors.[25]

In this second category of constructive trusteeship imposed to make strangers to the trust (including agents of the trustees) liable to account there is some doubt as to the requisite amount of knowledge of the " dishonest and fraudulent design " that the stranger must have. It is clear that actual knowledge suffices and that it also suffices if the stranger closed his eyes with the deliberate intention of avoiding actual knowledge. According to Ungoed-Thomas J. in *Selangor* (*No.* 3) [26] it suffices if the stranger has " knowledge of circumstances which would indicate to an honest, reasonable man that such a design was being committed, or would put him on inquiry, which the stranger failed to make whether it was being committed." Brightman J. agreed with this view and applied it in *Karak Rubber* where he rejected the submission that it was necessary to show that there was want of probity on the part of the stranger.

Karak Rubber and its predecessor *Selangor* (*No.* 3) are rather unsatisfactory in that they make no proper attempt to deal with cases like *Mara* v. *Browne* [27] and *Williams-Ashman* v. *Price, infra.* These cases are authority for the view that agents acting as agents for trustees (so that no question arises of the agents purporting to act as trustees and so becoming liable as

[20] *Barnes* v. *Addy* (1874) L.R. 9 Ch. 244; *Selangor* (*No.* 3), *supra.*

[21] The requisite knowledge " is knowledge of circumstances which would indicate to an honest, reasonable man that such a design was being committed, or would put him on inquiry, which the stranger failed to make, whether it was being committed. Acts in the circumstances normal in the honest conduct of affairs do not indicate such a misapplication, though compatible with it; and answers to inquiries are prima facie to be presumed to be honest." *Per* Ungoed-Thomas J. at 1590.

[22] *Re Barney* [1892] 2 Ch. 265.

[23] *Cf. Bentley* v. *Robinson* (1859) 9 Ir.Ch.R. 479, 484.

[24] *Selangor* (*No.* 3) [1968] 1 W.L.R. 1555.

[25] *e.g. Wilson* v. *Moore* (1834) 1 My. & K. 337; *Att.-Gen.* v. *Leicester Corp.* (1844) 7 Beav. 176; *Andrews* v. *Bonsfield* (1847) 10 Beav. 511; *Alleyne* v. *Davey* (1854) 4 Ir.Ch.R. 199.

[26] [1968] 1 W.L.R. 1555, 1590.

[27] [1896] 1 Ch. 199 (C.A.).

trustees *de son tort*) only become liable to account as constructive trustees
if they are guilty of some fraudulent or dishonest conduct: thus the solicitor-
agents in both cases who had acted honestly though foolishly were not liable
as constructive trustees.

In *Selangor* (*No.* 3) Ungoed-Thomas J., renowned for his skill as a judge
of fact with a supreme ability for sniffing out anything smacking of dishonesty or sharp practice and for coming down indignantly on anyone even
slightly involved in such things rather than for pellucid exegeses of the law,
off-handedly treated the two cases as concerned only with the possibility of
making the solicitors liable as trustees *de son tort* for intermeddling.[28] In
Karak Rubber Co., Mara v. *Browne* was not cited whilst *Williams-Ashman*,
though cited, does not feature in Brightman J.'s judgment which discounts,
a little cavalierly, certain dicta of the Court of Appeal in *Carl Zeiss Stiftung*
v. *Herbert Smith*.[29] In particular, having heard much citation of authority
including the two cases in question, Edmund Davies L.J. summarised the
position as follows [30]: " (A) A solicitor or other agent who receives money
from his principal which belongs at law or in equity to a third party is not
accountable as a constructive trustee to that third party unless he has been
guilty of some wrongful act in relation to that money. (B) To act ' wrongfully ' he must be guilty of (i) knowingly participating in a breach of trust
by his principal; or (ii) intermeddling with the trust property otherwise than
merely as an agent and thereby becoming a trustee *de son tort*; or (iii)
receiving or dealing with the money knowing that his principal has no right
to pay it over or to instruct him to deal with it in the manner indicated; or
(iv) some dishonest act relating to the money. These are indeed but variants
or illustrations of the ' want of probity ' to which I have earlier referred."
Sachs L.J.[31] also favourably cited a passage from Underhill's *Law of
Trusts*,[32] " Where the agent of the trustees acts honestly and confines himself
to the duties of an agent then he will not be accountable to the beneficiaries
though they will have their remedy against the persons who are the real
trustees."

It is thought that constructive notice for the first category of constructive
trusteeship and constructive knowledge for the second category of constructive trusteeship may be distinguished as follows. For the first category
where an owner of property is compelled to hold it as trustee since the
property is trust property of which he has constructive notice it is fair to
make him trustee [33] since he will have the property or traceable assets
representing the property and he should have discovered the trusts by making
all those inspections and inquiries which ought reasonably to have been
made before acquiring the property: in the context of purchase of land for
example there is the standard intensive duty to make various inspections and
inquiries.

In the second category where an agent is assisting trustees in dealing with
trust property he is surely entitled to assume that the trustees clothed with
legal power and control over the trust property are acting properly in the

28 [1968] 1 W.L.R. 1555, 1579.
29 [1969] 2 Ch. 276; D. M. Gordon (1970) 44 Austr.L.J. 261.
30 *Ibid.* 303–304.
31 *Ibid.* 299.
32 11th ed. (1959), p. 599, now 12th ed., p. 676.
33 See *Selangor* (*No.* 3) [1968] 1 W.L.R. 1555, 1582, 1583.

instructions given to him.[34]   Accordingly, the agent is under no duty to make inspections and inquiries as to the trust documents and surrounding circumstances unless the instructions given to him are out of the ordinary in the context of his actual knowledge and experience so that he feels the ground so solid for suspecting that something " fishy " is going on that he ought to make further inquiries before carrying out the instructions.[35]   If he fails to make further inquiries in such circumstances then he ought to be burdened with constructive knowledge especially since it might be said that in equity there is then a lack of probity, *e.g.*, arguably on the part of Barclays Bank in *Karak Rubber* (though Brightman J. assumed there was no lack of probity) where the Bank appear to have been reckless not caring one way or another what Messrs. Burden and Cross were up to so long as the Bank's financial interest in obtaining £99,504 to meet the Bank's draft prevailed. Such element of self-interest was not present in *Williams-Ashman, infra* and making investments in companies pursuant to wide powers of investment in properly drawn trust instruments was (and is) a commonplace thing: the loan to the trustee's son, however, was a little out of the ordinary and, perhaps, the defendants should consider themselves lucky not to have been held accountable for that loan.[35a]   Bennett J. seems to have been concerned with the subjective state of mind of the defendants rather than with what the state of their minds ought objectively to have been in all the circumstances and seems to have considered that they did not think that there was solid ground for suspecting that something " fishy " was going on amounting to a breach of trust: as honest fools they were thus not accountable.[36]

Brightman J. in *Karak Rubber* clearly prefers an objective test and has no time for honest fools.   Whilst people who take on the onerous office of trustee are liable for breach of trust, though honest fools,[37] it does seem harsh to extend equity's strict approach to agents who have the double misfortune of being employed by trustees and of being foolish but who have the supreme virtue of being honest.

KARAK RUBBER CO. LTD. v. BURDEN (No. 2)

Chancery Division [1972] 1 W.L.R. 602; [1972] 1 All E.R. 1210.

Mr. Burden and Mr. Cross so manipulated bankers' drafts (including a Barclays Bank draft) and cheques that Karak's moneys were unlawfully used in the purchase of its own shares contrary to section 54 of the Companies Act 1948.   Karak thus lost over £99,000 just as Selangor United Rubber Estates Ltd. had similarly lost over £232,000 in another deal involving Mr. Burden.[38]

---

[34] See *Barnes* v. *Addy* (1874) 9 Ch.App. 244, 251, 252, endorsed by Danckwerts L.J. in *Carl Zeiss Stiftung* v. *Herbert Smith* [1969] 2 Ch. 276.

[35] *Cf.* the test applied for contractual liability by Brightman J. in *Karak Rubber Co.* v. *Burden (No.* 2) [1972] 1 W.L.R. 602 except that Brightman J.'s test was objective and not subjective.   [35a] Any interest rate is undisclosed.

[36] Of course the agents may be liable for negligent performance of their duties, *e.g.*, *Mara* v. *Browne* [1896] 1 Ch. 199 except that such an action would have been out of time.

[37] *e.g.*, *Re Lucking's W.T., infra*, p. 618.

[38] *Selangor (No.* 3) [1968] 1 W.L.R. 1555; *R.* v. *Sinclair* [1968] 1 W.L.R. 1246 (criminal conspiracy to cheat and defraud arising out of the *Selangor* circumstances).

Karak sued Barclays Bank for damages for breach of their contractual duty of care and for liability to account in equity as constructive trustees.

Brightman J. found that the bank had been present throughout the meeting where the manipulation had been effected in circumstances which were so unusual and so out of the ordinary course of business, when the sum involved (£99,504) was so large and the ground so solid for suspecting that someone was using Karak's money to finance its own take-over, that a reasonable banker would have made further inquiries before inviting or allowing B and C as directors of the bank's customer, Karak, to pay over £99,504 of Karak's moneys so off-setting the bank's draft (which the bank's manager was most anxious about). Such inquiries would in all probability have revealed the impropriety, so the bank was liable for breach of the contractual duty of care owed to Karak.

As full argument had been heard on the constructive trust issue, the learned judge in his reserved judgment dealt fully with the issue, holding a constructive trust to be established.

BRIGHTMAN J.: "... I must first touch on Karak's claim against the trustee in bankruptcy of Mr. Burden and Mr. Cross. These claims have not been actively fought. I deal with them at this stage because the quality of the conduct of Mr. Burden and Mr. Cross is decisive of the question whether the claim against Barclays Bank in constructive trusteeship is capable of succeeding; that claim is based on the existence of their fraud and dishonesty. Karak pleads that Mr. Burden and Mr. Cross procured that the amount of the Karak cheque should be misapplied in bad faith in providing out of Karak's money the purchase price of the 40,804 shares and the expenses incidental to that purchase. In my judgment, on the evidence I have heard, and quite apart from admissions by Mr. Burden and Mr. Cross to which I will refer later, it is plain beyond the possibility of argument to the contrary that Mr. Burden, in deliberate and conscious fraud, procured that £99,504 10s. 6d. of Karak's money, that is to say, the amount of the Karak cheque, should be misapplied in financing the purchase of the Karak shares so as to be lost to Karak, and that Mr. Cross, either knowingly or recklessly, was implicated in that fraudulent and dishonest design. I did not understand counsel on behalf of Barclays Bank to seek to argue otherwise.

" It is convenient to make an initial distinction between (i) a person who is a constructive trustee because (although not nominated as a trustee) he has received trust property with actual or constructive notice that it is trust property transferred in breach of trust, or because (not being a bona fide purchaser for value without notice) he acquires notice subsequent to such receipt and then deals with the property in a manner inconsistent with the trust, and (ii) a person who has not received and become chargeable with trust property in that manner but whom equity nevertheless fixes with liability as a constructive trustee on account of assistance which he has rendered to a breach of trust. This is not intended to be an exhaustive definition of constructive trusteeship, but to distinguish two categories thereof. There is included in the second category of constructive trusteeship the duly appointed agent of the trustees who is in receipt of trust property solely by virtue of the existence of such agency but who, by assisting in a breach of trust at the direction of trustees, is fixed with liability as a constructive trustee. The two categories are conveniently labelled in Snell's *Principles of Equity* [39] with the catch-phrases ' knowing receipt or dealing ' and ' knowing assistance,' which seem to me an admirable shorthand description of their different natures.

" The question of law which arises is: in what circumstances will a court of equity treat the second category of person as a trustee in order to provide an equitable remedy against that person on account of conduct which a court of equity considers unconscionable?

" It is common ground that directors of a company, although not trustees in the strictest sense of that expression, are to be considered and treated as trustees of money which comes to their hands or is under their control. The fact that they are to be considered and treated as trustees bears on the question whether the imposition of the equitable remedy of constructive trusteeship is available against those who have dealings with them. It is also common ground that a bank is not a trustee for its customer of the amount to his credit in his account. In the result, Mr. Burden and Mr. Cross are to be considered and treated as trustees in relation to the sum of money comprised in the Chartered cheque and paid into Karak's account with Barclays Bank, and Barclays Bank is to be considered and treated as the agent of such trustees.

" The conclusion of law reached by the learned judge in the *Selangor* case,[40] in relation to the second category of constructive trustees, was as follows: (1) strangers who act as the agents of trustees are liable as constructive trustees if they ' assist with knowledge in a dishonest and fraudulent design on the part of the trustees '; (2) [41]

> ' The knowledge required to hold a stranger liable as constructive trustee in a dishonest and fraudulent design, is knowledge of circumstances which would indicate to an honest, reasonable man that such a design was being committed or would put him on

---

[39] 26th ed., pp. 202, 203.
[40] [1968] 1 W.L.R. 1555, 1580.
[41] [1968] 1 W.L.R. 1555, 1590.

enquiry, which the stranger failed to make, whether it was being committed.'

(3) What is 'a dishonest and fraudulent design' is to be judged [42]:

> '... according to "the plain principles of a court of equity" ... The governing consideration is to give effect to equitable rights, where it is not inequitable to do so, and when knowledge of the existence of those rights is material to granting equitable relief. In general, at any rate, it is equitable that a person with actual notice or constructive notice of those rights should be fixed with knowledge of them. This is in a context of producing equitable results in a civil action and not in the context of criminal liability.'

These conclusions were reached after consideration of a large number of authorities, ranging in time from the decision of Leach V.-C. in 1819 in *Keane* v. *Robarts* [43] down to the decision of the Privy Council in *Bank of New South Wales* v. *Goulburn Valley Butter Co. Propietary Ltd.* [44]

"The formulation in the *Selangor* case [45] of the law applicable to the second category of constructive trusteeship is based on the judgment of Lord Selborne L.C. in 1874 in *Barnes* v. *Addy* [46] with which James and Mellish L.JJ. concurred. This was a case in which beneficiaries unsuccessfully sued solicitors who had been associated with the fraud of the trustee; it was found that the solicitors had no knowledge or suspicion of the fraud and that there was nothing to lead them to suppose that a fraud was intended. The test of liability (which it may be convenient to call the *Barnes* v. *Addy* formula), in the words of Lord Selborne L.C., was that [47]:

> 'they assist with knowledge in a dishonest and fraudulent design on the part of the trustees.'

This was paraphrased with approval by Lord Esher M.R. in *Soar* v. *Ashwell* [48] (a first category case) as:

> '. . . he has knowingly assisted a nominated trustee in a fraudulent and dishonest disposition of the trust property.'

The point on which the authorities were obscure, until the *Selangor* case,[49] was what degree of 'knowledge' was required to satisfy that test. A person may have knowledge of an existing fact because in a subjective sense he is actually aware of that fact. In an appropriate context a court of law may attribute knowledge of an existing fact to that person because in a subjective sense he has knowledge of circum-

---

42 [1968] 1 W.L.R. 1555, 1582, 1583.
43 (1819) 4 Madd. 332.
44 [1902] A.C. 543.
45 [1968] 1 W.L.R. 1555.
46 (1874) 9 Ch.App. 244.
47 (1874) 9 Ch.App. 244, 252.
48 [1893] 2 Q.B. 390, 394, 395; [1891–94] All E.R.Rep. 991, 994.
49 [1968] 1 W.L.R. 1555.

stances which would lead a postulated man to the conclusion that the fact exists or which would put a postulated man on enquiry whether the fact exists.

" The claim against the District Bank was that it knew, or as a reasonable banker ought to have known, that Selangor's money was being applied for the purpose of giving financial assistance in connection with the purchase by Cradock of Selangor stock. It was not pleaded that the District Bank ought to have made enquiries. The decision, which went against the District Bank on constructive trusteeship as it did in negligence, was based on proof of facts which would have brought home the knowledge of such misapplication to the mind of a reasonable banker.

" Counsel for Barclays Bank attacked the statement of law in the *Selangor* case principally on two grounds: (1) that it was inconsistent with the *ratio decidendi* of and was impliedly overruled by the decision of the Court of Appeal in *Carl Zeiss-Stiftung* v. *Herbert Smith & Co.*,[50] and (2) because important and decisive cases were not brought to the attention of the learned judge.

" It will be observed that, according to the *Selangor* case, an objective test is to be applied both in assessing the defendant's ' knowledge ' and in assessing the character of the ' design '. Counsel for Barclays Bank, in an argument of great penetration, accepted the objective test in relation to the ' design ' but not in relation to ' knowledge '. There is no such thing, he submitted, as constructive trusteeship of the category with which this case is concerned, based on the defendant's constructive knowledge of facts as distinct from his actual knowledge of facts or knowledge which has to be imputed to him because he has closed his eyes with the deliberate intention of avoiding actual knowledge; counsel bracketed actual knowledge with imputed knowledge in that special sense. He said that a defendant is not to be fixed with liability as a constructive trustee of the second category unless he has been guilty of a lack of probity, which he likened to moral obliquity or dishonesty or bad faith or fraud. The test is subjective to this extent, that the court must first assess the acts, the knowledge and the intention of the defendant, and by knowledge is meant actual or imputed knowledge but not constructive knowledge. These subjective matters are then to be submitted to the objective test of the accepted moral standard of the community and adjudged accordingly. In other words, the defendant is not liable as a constructive trustee if he had no actual or imputed knowledge of the design and did not intend to participate in it; on the other hand, he cannot successfully defend a claim by saying that he knew of the design but did not regard it as dishonest. Unless, it is submitted, a subjective test is applied to the acts, knowledge and intention of the defendant, it is not possible to

---

[50] [1969] 2 Ch. 276.

charge him with that lack of probity which is the foundation of a
stranger's liability as a constructive trustee. It is important to an
understanding of this argument to appreciate the special sense given to
the expression 'imputed knowledge', which in counsel's formulation
is brought about by the deliberate shutting of eyes so as to avoid actual
knowledge.

" The *Carl Zeiss* case [51] was a dispute between the Carl Zeiss company of Jena ('the East German foundation') and the Carl Zeiss
company of Würtemburg ('the West German foundation'). In the
main action the East German foundation claimed, *inter alia*, that the
assets of the West German foundation, including its property in
England, were held by that foundation in trust for the East German
foundation. The East German foundation later issued a writ against
the current and former solicitors of the West German foundation
claiming that when they were put in funds by their client, they had
notice, via the East German foundation's pleadings in the main action
and from other material, that such money belonged to the East
German foundation, and it was said that the solicitors were accountable accordingly. The matter came on for trial as a preliminary issue.

" The East German foundation based its claim on a submission
that a man who receives trust property which he knows or ought to
know is trust property and applies that property in a manner which he
knows or ought to know is inconsistent with the terms of the trust, is
accountable at the suit of the beneficiaries under that trust. The
submission failed, on the ground that the solicitors only had knowledge
of a disputed claim that the assets of the West German foundation
were trust property; they did not have knowledge that such assets were
in *fact* trust property. Danckwerts L.J. expressed his conclusion as
follows [52]:

> '. . . claims are not the same thing as facts. . . . What we
> have to deal with is the state of the defendants' knowledge (actual
> or imputed) at the date when they received payments of their
> costs and disbursements. At that date they cannot have had more
> than knowledge of the claims above mentioned. It was not
> possible for them to know whether they were well founded or
> not. . . . Consequently, it seems to me that the plaintiff's claim
> against the defendant solicitors must fail on the requisite condition
> of knowledge or notice.'

Sachs L.J. said [53]:

> 'First, and to my mind decisively, whatever be the nature of
> the knowledge or notice required, cognisance of what has been
> termed a " doubtful equity " is not enough.'

[51] [1969] 2 Ch. 276.
[52] [1969] 2 Ch. 276, 293.
[53] [1969] 2 Ch. 276, 296.

Later, after discussing the relevance of constructive notice in the sense of section 199 of the Law of Property Act 1925, he added [54]:

> ' As at present advised, I am inclined to the view that a further element has to be proved, at any rate in a case such as the present one. That element is one of dishonesty or of consciously acting improperly, as opposed to an innocent failure to make what a court may later decide to have been proper enquiry. That would entail both actual knowledge of the trust's existence and actual knowledge that what is being done is improperly in breach of that trust—though, of course, in both cases a person wilfully shutting his eyes to the obvious is in no different position than if he had kept them open.'

Then, after referring to the *Selangor* case and certain other authorities, he added [55]:

> ' Out of deference to the conclusions reached by Ungoed-Thomas J. and to the fact that the *Selangor* case is under appeal, it now seems best, however, for me not to state a final view in this matter, especially when the instant case concerns agents who may thus be in a different position from other strangers.'

It is plain that he was not expressing any decided opinion on this point. Lastly, I quote from the judgment of Edmund Davies L.J.[56]:

> ' The concept of " want of probity " appears to provide a useful touchstone in considering circumstances said to give rise to constructive trusts, and I have not found it misleading when applying it to the many authorities cited to this court. It is because of such a concept that evidence as to " good faith," " knowledge " and " notice " plays so important a part in the reported decisions. It is true that not every situation where probity is lacking gives rise to a constructive trust. Nevertheless, the authorities appear to show that nothing short of it will do.'

Then, after having cited two cases, he said that they were [57]—

> ' but two illustrations among many to be found in the reports of that want of probity which, to my way of thinking, is the hallmark of constructive trusts, however created.'

The *Selangor* case was certainly not expressly overruled by the *Carl Zeiss* case. It was not even referred to in the judgments of Danckwerts and Edmund Davies L.JJ. Nor do I think that it was overruled by necessary implication. Counsel for Barclays Bank submitted that Danckwerts L.J. used the expression ' imputed knowledge ' in his own sense of wilful shutting of eyes as distinct from knowledge which is to

---

[54] [1969] 2 Ch. 276, 298.
[55] [1969] 2 Ch. 276, 299.
[56] [1969] 2 Ch. 276, 301.
[57] [1969] 2 Ch. 276, 302.

be attributed to the defendant because a reasonable person would have drawn the inference or would have been put on enquiry. I do not read his words in that sense, nor does it seem consistent with his later reference to ' the requisite condition of knowledge or notice.'

"I agree with counsel that the judgment of Edmund Davies L.J. might be read as supporting his proposition. But in the end the *ratio decidendi* of that judgment appears to be the same as that of the other judgments, namely [58]:

> '. . . mere notice of a claim asserted by a third party is insufficient to render the agent guilty of a wrongful act in dealing with property derived from his principal in accordance with the latter's instructions unless the agent *knows* that the third party's claim is well founded and that the principal accordingly had no authority to give such instructions.'

Accordingly I reject the submission that the *Selangor* judgment on constructive trusteeship is inconsistent with the *ratio decidendi* of the *Carl Zeiss* case.

"In support of his proposition that lack of probity is an essential ingredient of the second category of constructive trusteeship, counsel for Barclays Bank also referred me to five pre-*Keane* v. *Robarts*[59] cases. These were *Nugent* v. *Gifford*,[60] *Mead* v. *Lord Orrery*,[61] *Scott* v. *Tyler*,[62] *Hill* v. *Simpson*[63] and *McLeod* v. *Drummond*.[64] It may well be that these cases are consistent with the proposition that fraud or what is tantamount to fraud must be found before an agent who has not intermeddled is rendered accountable as a constructive trustee. They are not, in my view, decisive against the relevance of an objective test, that is to say, whether the circumstances would have indicated a dishonest and fraudulent design to a reasonable man or have put him on enquiry. It must, I think, be remembered that equitable doctrines have developed over the passage of time and it would not be right to assume that principles expressed two centuries ago were being fully and exhaustively enunciated for all ages to come." [*Williams* v. *Williams*[65] was then considered in detail.]

"In my view, *Williams* v. *Williams* on a proper analysis was a case concerned with the first rather than the second category of constructive trusteeship. The claim against Mr. Cheese was that trust money was wrongfully in his hands by the direction of one who had no title thereto and that he proceeded to dispose of it in defiance of the beneficiaries' title of which he had been given due notice. That is not the

---

[58] [1969] 2 Ch. 276, 304.
[59] (1819) 4 Madd. 332.
[60] (1738) 1 Atk. 463.
[61] (1745) 3 Atk. 235.
[62] (1788) 2 Bro.C.C. 431.
[63] (1802) 7 Ves. 152.
[64] (1807) 14 Ves. 353.
[65] (1881) 17 Ch.D. 437.

type of case with which the second category of constructive trusteeship is concerned. The same observation applies to the *Carl Zeiss* case.

"I take this opportunity to record that I asked counsel for Karak
whether he based his claim to any extent on the first category of constructive trusteeship, having regard to the fact that the Karak cheque
was made payable to Barclays Bank and was endorsed by Barclays
Bank and credited to Minories, so that in that sense the trust money
passed through the hands of Barclays Bank. Counsel told me that the
claim against Barclays Bank in the context of constructive trusteeship
was based exclusively on the second category of constructive trusteeship, that is to say, on the *Barnes* v. *Addy* [66] formula, where it is
fundamental to find the existence of a dishonest and fraudulent design
on the part of the trustees.

"I respectfully agree with the explanation of the *Barnes* v. *Addy*
formula which I find in the *Selangor* judgment. If, as seems to be
established by the cases, an objective test of ' knowledge ' is rightly
applied in the context of the first category of constructive trusteeship
(see, for example, *Reckitt* v. *Barnett* [67] and *Nelson* v. *Larholt* [68]), I do
not myself see any particular logic in denying it a similar role in the
context of the second category of constructive trusteeship. To borrow
the words of Lord Cranworth, spoken admittedly in a different context, ' Constructive notice is as good as any notice, if it does amount
to notice.' [69]

"Applying the *Barnes* v. *Addy* formula, as explained in the
Selangor case, I reach the conclusion, for reasons already indicated in
dealing with the claim in negligence, that a reasonable banker would
have been put on enquiry as to the propriety of the Karak cheque and
that such enquiry would in all probability have revealed the impropriety. So I find the claim against Barclays Bank made good in equity
as in contract. I do not consider, because it is unnecessary, whether
the circumstances known to Mr. Cooper or Mr. Hockley would have
brought the dishonest and fraudulent design home to the mind of a
reasonable man, as distinct from putting him on enquiry."

WILLIAMS-ASHMAN v. PRICE and WILLIAMS

Chancery Division [1942] Ch. 219; [1942] 1 All E.R. 310.

In 1927 three persons including Dr. MacGowan settled over £900
on Dr. MacGowan and Mr. Streather upon trust to pay the income
to the incumbent for the time being of Holy Trinity Church, Kingsway,
London. Dr. MacGowan was then vicar of Holy Trinity. £900 was
invested on a mortgage of freehold property belonging to Miss Pullen.

---

[66] (1874) 9 Ch.App. 244.
[67] [1929] A.C. 176.
[68] [1948] 1 K.B. 339.
[69] In *Cookson* v. *Lee* (1853) 23 L.J.Ch. 473, 478.

The defendant firm of solicitors were responsible for preparing the trust deed and the mortgage and in particular the defendant Mr. Alfred Williams was concerned in these matters. The other defendant, Mr. Franklin, was Mr. Williams' managing clerk and a friend of Dr. MacGowan (" Dr. M.").

In 1936 Mr. Franklin (" Mr. F.") was asked by Dr. M. to arrange for repayment of £200 of the £900 lent on mortgage to Miss Pullen. The £200 was paid to the firm who were informed that Dr. M. was going to use the £200 for structural repairs to the vicarage costing £300 the remaining £100 being paid by Dr. M. himself. The firm then paid over the £200 to Dr. M. Very shortly afterwards Dr. M. paid Mr. F. £200 to be invested in shares of a company of which Mr. F. was a director, an unauthorised investment. The shares were taken in Dr. M.'s name.

Later in 1936 Mr. Streather died leaving Dr. M. sole trustee. In 1937 on instructions given by Dr. M., Mr. Williams required repayment of the £700 balance of the mortgage debt. The £700 was paid to the firm who, on further instructions, paid £300 to Dr. M.'s son by way of loan and invested the remaining £400 in the shares of the company in which Dr. M. had already invested the earlier £200: all these shares were taken in Dr. M.'s name.

In July 1939 Dr. M. died intestate and in October 1939 Mr. Williams found in the firm's safe the 1927 trust instrument. He wrote forthwith to one of the churchwardens of the Holy Trinity parish suggesting that the solicitors acting for the administrators of Dr. M.'s estate should be approached in the matter.

As a result the plaintiff, the current incumbent of Holy Trinity, sued the defendants to make good any deficiency in the £900 which resulted from applications and reinvestments of that sum in breach of the trusts declared by the 1927 deed. The £300 loan to the son was irrecoverable and the value of the shares had fallen.

BENNETT J.: (in a reserved judgment)... " As regards Mr. Alfred Williams and Mr. Franklin, no charge of bad faith was made against either of them. I saw them both in the witness box and came to the conclusion that each of them was an honest man and was trying to tell me the truth to the best of his recollection about the transactions which were being inquired into. I came to the conclusion that neither Mr. Williams nor Mr. Franklin was conscious of the fact that either Dr. MacGowan or Mr. Streather was committing a breach of trust. I feel sure that neither of them was assisting Dr. MacGowan or Mr. Streather to commit a breach of trust. Both of these defendants knew that the money which was lent to Miss Pullen was trust money. Mr. Alfred Williams at one time undoubtedly knew what the trusts were. Mr. Franklin said that he never knew exactly what the terms of the trust were. I feel sure that in 1936 and 1937 neither Mr. Alfred

Williams nor Mr. Franklin remembered what the terms of the trust were. They might easily have ascertained them, but neither took any steps to do so.

" The plaintiff alleges in para. 7 of the statement of claim that the sum of £200 paid by the defendant firm to Dr. MacGowan on August 18, 1936, was, by arrangement between Dr. MacGowan and the firm, repaid by Dr. MacGowan to Mr. Franklin to be invested in the Regional company. The evidence of Mr. Alfred Williams and Mr. Franklin has satisfied me that there never was any such arrangement between Dr. MacGowan and the firm, but that the investment was made by .Dr. MacGowan as the result of talks between himself and Mr. Franklin in which Mr. Alfred Williams took no part and of which he knew nothing. Moreover, the investment was made at Dr. MacGowan's own request and not as a result of pressure put on him by Mr. Franklin or requests made to him by Mr. Franklin. I have no ground for thinking that in regard to these investments Mr. Franklin was dealing otherwise than honestly and fairly with Dr. MacGowan.

" I will now consider the claims made by the plaintiff against the defendants respectively. The basis of all of them seems to be that in some way or another the defendants have made themselves accountable to the plaintiff as a beneficiary under the declaration of trust, either because they had in their hands money subject to the declaration of trust or because they had made themselves liable for breaches of trust as constructive trustees. . . .

" There now remains for determination the plaintiff's claim in respect of the balance of the trust fund, namely, the sum of £900 lent to Miss Pullen. Of this sum, £200 came into possession of the firm on behalf of the trustees in August of 1936 in the manner I have stated. The plaintiff seeks to make Mr. Franklin as well as the firm liable in respect of it, and I will first deal with the claim against Mr. Franklin.

" The ground upon which the plaintiff sought at the Bar to establish Mr. Franklin's liability was that when he received Dr. MacGowan's cheque for £200 he knew that he was receiving trust money subject to the declaration of trust and so became constructively a trustee of that sum for the persons beneficially interested in the trust fund of which it was part.

" This contention breaks down on the facts. Mr. Franklin has said in evidence (and I accept it) that whilst he knew that Pullen's mortgage was a mortgage vested in Dr. MacGowan and Mr. Streather as trustees, he did not at any time know what the trusts were. He said that he had been told by Dr. MacGowan that he had utilised money of his own in paying for structural repairs executed at No. 2 Gate Street. I have no grounds for disbelieving this statement. The question is not whether the doctor's statement was true but whether the doctor made it and whether Mr. Franklin believed it to be true. I accept Mr. Franklin's evidence that he believed the doctor's statement. The effect of Mr. Franklin's evidence is that when he received Dr. MacGowan's cheque for £200 with a request to invest it in the Regional company's shares he believed that he was receiving the doctor's money. He, therefore, never became a constructive trustee of the money, and the claim against him must fail.

" The case of the plaintiff against the firm was, if I rightly under- stood the arguments, put in two ways. The first contention was that the firm called the money in on the instructions of Dr. MacGowan alone and got possession of it as a consequence of those instructions. They then paid it over to Dr. MacGowan alone and so never got a good discharge from the two persons entitled to the money, namely, Dr. MacGowan and Mr. Streather.

" In support of this contention the decision of Bacon V.-C. in *Lee* v. *Sankey* [70] was relied on. The instructions to call in the money did come from Dr. MacGowan alone, but I do not see the relevance of this fact or its bearing on the liability of the defendant firm. The firm undoubtedly got the money into their possession. The question is whether the proper inference to be drawn from the documents is that the firm paid the £200 to Dr. MacGowan with the authority of Mr. Streather. I draw the inference from these documents that it was so paid, and, therefore, in my judgment the contention founded on *Lee* v. *Sankey* fails.

" The second contention put forward on behalf of the plaintiff in respect of this sum and also with respect to the £700, which was the balance of the mortgage debt, was that both these sums came into the possession of the defendant firm with knowledge acquired through Mr. Alfred Williams that they were trust moneys, and, therefore, that the firm owed a duty to the persons beneficially interested in the moneys to see that the moneys were dealt with in accordance with the trusts to which they were subject. It is clear that Mr. Alfred Williams knew that both sums of money were trust money. The question is whether that knowledge saddles either the firm or Mr. Alfred Williams with the responsibilities of a trustee. Does the knowledge of that fact give rise in equity to a duty to the persons beneficially interested in the trust money?

" The defendant firm contend that the answer to that question is in the negative. Their answer is based partly on fact and partly on law. They say that Mr. Alfred Williams acted honestly, and was not a party to any breach of trust by the express trustees, and that they (the firm) received the money as agents for principals and dealt with it in accordance with the directions of their principals. On those facts the firm contend that as a matter of law they never came under any

---

[70] L.R. 15 Eq. 204.

duty to the persons beneficially interested in the money. The line of difference between the parties seems to me to be very clearly marked. The plaintiff affirms that when an agent receives on behalf of a principal money which he knows to be trust money, he becomes a constructive trustee of that money and can only discharge himself by showing that the money was duly applied in accordance with the trust. The defendant firm contend that in those circumstances, so long as he acts honestly, an agent owes no duty to anyone except his principal, and that he only becomes liable as a constructive trustee if he intermeddles in the trust by dealing with or disposing of the trust money without his principal's instructions.

" The plaintiff's argument was based on a passage in Underhill's Law of Trusts and Trustees, 9th ed., p. 548, in these terms: ' Where trust funds come into the custody and under the control of a solicitor, or indeed of anyone else, with notice of the trusts, he can only discharge himself of liability by showing that the property was duly applied in accordance with the trusts.' The authority for this statement is a passage from the judgment of Stirling J. in *Blyth* v. *Fladgate*.[71] In *Morgan* v. *Stephens* [72] Stuart V.-C. says: ' If a trustee employs an agent, so long as the acts done by the person so employed are confined to mere agency on behalf of his employer the trustee, generally speaking the agent cannot be accountable as trustee. But where the agent obtains possession of the trust funds and his acts are not in strict conformity with his duty as agent, he ceases to be a mere agent.' Lord Selborne, in an oft cited passage from his judgment in *Barnes* v. *Addy*,[73] says that the responsibility of a trustee ' may no doubt be extended in equity to others who are not properly trustees if they are found either making themselves *trustees de son tort*, or actually participating in any fraudulent conduct of the trustee to the injury of the *cestui que trust*. But, on the other hand, strangers are not to be made constructive trustees merely because they act as the agents of trustees in transactions within their legal powers, transactions perhaps of which a court of equity may disapprove, unless those agents receive and become chargeable with some part of the trust property or unless they assist with knowledge in a dishonest and fraudulent design on the part of the trustees.'

" The authority, which, I think, is decisive of the present case is *Mara* v. *Browne*,[74] a decision of the Court of Appeal. There beneficiaries sought to make liable for breaches of trust two solicitors, Hugh Browne and Arthur Browne, who carried on business in partnership. The breaches of trust complained of were advances of trust money on eight mortgages suggested as securities by Hugh Browne which were alleged to be speculative, risky and not such as could be

---

[71] [1891] 1 Ch. 337.
[72] (1861) 3 Giff. 226, 236.
[73] L.R. 9 Ch. 244, 251.   [74] [1896] 1 Ch. 199, 251

justified by a trustee. The moneys so advanced amounted to £9,200 and before they were advanced they came into the hands of Hugh Browne and were paid by him into his own bank account. He then made the advances to the respective mortgagors on the authority of persons purporting to act as trustees of the settlement. The judge at the trial came to the conclusion that the investments were not proper for trustees to make and were breaches of trust, and with this conclusion of fact the Court of Appeal agreed, but the court exonerated the solicitors from liability on the ground that they never became constructive trustees. I will read a passage from the judgment of A. L. Smith L.J.[75] which states the ground on which the decision went:

> ' North J. found, and I agree with him, that eight of the mortgages taken for the trust funds were speculative and risky, and not such as could be justified by a trustee—in fact, these investments constituted breaches of trust. Although this might well render the trustees liable for a breach of trust, it certainly does not *per se* render their solicitor so liable. But it is said that the facts show that there should be imputed to Hugh Browne the character of a trustee, or, in other words, that he was a *trustee de son tort*, and upon this ground the learned judge has held him liable. It is not contended on behalf of the plaintiffs that Hugh Browne has been guilty of any fraudulent or dishonest conduct to the injury of the *cestui que trust*, nor, to use Lord Langdale's words in *Fyler* v. *Fyler* [76] did he, being a solicitor, " take advantage of his position to acquire a benefit for himself at the hazard, if not to the prejudice, of the trust "; but it was said that he had made himself a constructive trustee, which, so far as I know, is the same thing as a *trustee de son tort*. Now, what constitutes a *trustee de son tort*? It appears to me if one, not being a trustee and not having authority from a trustee, takes upon himself to intermeddle with trust matters or to do acts characteristic of the office of trustee, he may thereby make himself what is called in law a trustee of his own wrong—*i.e.*, a *trustee de son tort*, or, as it is also termed, a constructive trustee.'

" *Mara* v. *Browne* [77] seems to me to be a decision that an agent in possession of money which he knows to be trust money, so long as he acts honestly, is not accountable to the beneficiaries interested in the trust money unless he intermeddles in the trust by doing acts characteristic of a trustee and outside the duties of an agent. After all, the beneficiaries have their remedy against the persons who are the real trustees. I have stated that, in my opinion, Mr. Alfred Williams acted throughout the transactions honestly. Indeed, the

75 *Ibid.* 209.
76 (1841) 3 Beav. 550, 560
77 [1896] 1 Ch. 199.

contrary is not suggested. He acted throughout on the instructions of his principals. He never intermeddled in the trust. He has, I think, acted incautiously. Many people might take the view that he ought to have ascertained by reference to the declaration of trust what the trusts were before he did what he was asked to do first by Dr. MacGowan and Mr. Streather and afterwards, when Mr. Streather had died, by Dr. MacGowan alone. But considerations of this kind do not assist the plaintiff unless he can establish that when the money came into the possession of the firm, Mr. Alfred Williams or the firm came under a duty to him as a beneficiary interested in the trust fund. It is only if the plaintiff can establish the existence of such a duty that he can establish a liability on the firm arising out of the breaches of trust committed by the express trustees.

"The plaintiff is, I think, trying to use the passage from Stirling J.'s judgment and the statement from Underhill's Law of Trusts and Trustees to support a proposition which neither Stirling J. nor the late Sir Arthur Underhill could have had in mind when they used the words relied on.

"*Blyth* v. *Fladgate* [78] was plainly a case where the defendants, a firm of solicitors, were saddled with the liability of trustees because they had dealt with trust moneys in breach of trust and without instructions from their principals. The facts were that at a time when there was but one trustee of a marriage settlement, trust moneys had been invested in exchequer bills which had been deposited with the bankers of the solicitors and were so deposited when the sole trustee died. Afterwards, while there was no trustee, the bills were sold and the proceeds of sale were placed to the credit of the solicitors with their bankers and afterwards paid by the solicitors to a mortgagor who, as security for their repayment, executed a mortgage in favour of three persons who were subsequently appointed to be trustees of the settlement. The advance on this mortgage was held improper and a breach of trust, and for this breach the solicitors were held to be responsible as constructive trustees because, having in their possession money which they knew was trust money, they had made an improper investment of it without instructions from or the authority of any principal. Stirling J.'s observations must be read in relation to the facts with which he was dealing. In *Mara* v. *Browne* [79] the Court of Appeal laid down clearly the principles which govern the rights of the plaintiff and defendant firm in respect of the two sums of £200 and £700 received by the firm from Miss Pullen. On the facts, as I find them to be, the firm is not responsible to the plaintiff for the breaches of trust committed by the express trustees of the declaration of trust in respect of these two sums. The result is that the action fails and must be dismissed with costs." *Judgment for defendants.*

---

[78] [1891] 1 Ch. 337.   [79] [1896] 1 Ch. 199.

Section 4. The Vendor as Constructive Trustee [80]

When a vendor enters into a specifically enforceable contract for the sale of property he becomes a constructive trustee thereof for the purchaser until the contract is completed by a conveyance of the property.[81] When the purchaser has paid the purchase price then the vendor is a bare trustee for the absolutely entitled purchaser. Until then the trusteeship is a special modified trusteeship.

The vendor has to "use reasonable care to preserve the property in a reasonable state of preservation, and, so far as may be, as it was when the contract was made" or "to take reasonable care that the property is not deteriorated in the interval before completion."[82] This has much nuisance value to a purchaser upon whom a vendor has served a notice to complete [83] making time of the essence of the contract: the purchaser can claim that the notice was invalid because the vendor was not ready able and willing to complete the contract owing to breach of his fiduciary duty of preservation.[84] However, if the contract goes off the vendor cannot be liable to the purchaser for failing to preserve the property.[85]

Till completion the vendor is a quasi-trustee with a highly interested trusteeship: he has a paramount right to protect his own interest.[86] He is entitled to keep the rents and profits till the date fixed for completion [87] and to retain possession of the property until the contract is completed by payment of the price.[88] If he parts with possession to the purchaser before actual completion or even conveys the land he may fall back on his equitable lien to ensure that he is paid.[89]

Section 5. Secret Trusts

I. GENERAL

The doctrine of secret trusts [90] is a product of equity not allowing statutes

---

[80] J. T. Farrand's *Contract and Conveyance*, 2nd ed., Chap. 7; V. G. Wellings (1959) 23 Conv.(N.S.) 173; Water's *Constructive Trust*, Chap. 2; Barnsley's *Conveyancing Law and Practice*, pp. 227–230.

[81] *Wall* v. *Bright* (1820) 1 Jac. & W. 494, 503; *Royal British P.B.S.* v. *Bomash* (1887) 35 Ch.D. 390, 397; *Rayner* v. *Preston* (1881) 18 Ch.D. 1, 6; *Cumberland Consolidated Holdings Ltd.* v. *Ireland* [1946] K.B. 264; *Re Watford Corporation's Contract* [1943] Ch. 82, 85; *Lake* v. *Bayliss* [1974] 1 W.L.R. 1073.

[82] *Clarke* v. *Ramuz* [1891] 2 Q.B. 456, 460, 468; risk, however, passes to the purchaser after exchange of contracts in so far as concerns anything not caused by a breach of the vendor's duties: *Rayner* v. *Preston* (1881) 18 Ch.D. 1 (affected by Law of Property Act 1925, s. 47, now).

[83] Law Society Conditions of Sale (1973 Revision) Condition 19; National Conditions of Sale 1970, Condition 22.

[84] Purchasers have taken this point where squatters have managed to break into the property the subject of the contract: so far the cases appear to have been settled without the need to spend days in court arguing whether or not the vendor's precautions were reasonable.

[85] *Plews* v. *Samuel* [1904] 1 Ch. 464; *Ridout* v. *Fowler* [1904] 1 Ch. 658; [1904] 2 Ch. 93.

[86] *Shaw* v. *Foster* (1872) L.R. 5 H.L. 321, 338; *Re Watford Corporation's Contract* [1943] Ch. 82, 85.

[87] *Cuddon* v. *Tite* (1858) 1 Giff 395.

[88] *Gedge* v. *Montrose* (1858) 26 Beav. 45; *Phillips* v. *Silvester* (1872) L.R. 8 Ch. 173.

[89] *Nives* v. *Nives* (1880) 15 Ch.D. 649; *Re Birmingham* [1959] Ch. 523; *London & Cheshire Insurance Co. Ltd.* v. *Laplagrene* [1971] Ch. 499.

[90] Snell, pp. 106–111; Hanbury, pp. 155–170; Pettit, pp. 89–96; P. & M., pp. 41–52; Waters, pp. 57–62; Underhill, pp. 122, 125–130; (1915) 28 Harvard L.R. 237 (G.

to be used as an instrument of fraud.[91] It will already have been seen that statutes prescribe certain formalities for declarations of trust respecting land and for dispositions of equitable interests.[92] In addition, section 9 of the Wills Act 1837 prescribes special formalities for the validity of testamentary dispositions whilst the Administration of Estates Act 1925 lays down rules of intestate succession. All too often a person might be induced to die intestate leaving X as his intestate successor [93] or to leave property by will to X or to transfer land *inter vivos* to X on the secret oral understanding that X was to hold the property he received on trust for B. If X were allowed to retain the property beneficially, instead of taking merely as trustee, then this would be allowing statutes to be used as an instrument of fraud by X. Accordingly, equity treats X as a trustee despite the absence of the requisite formalities.

Secret trusts most commonly concern trusts engrafted on wills and in this context it is most important to distinguish between (1) fully secret trusts, (2) half-secret trusts, and (3) cases where the probate doctrine of incorporation by reference arises. Respective examples (where X has agreed to hold on trust for B) are (1) I devise Blackacre to X absolutely (2) I devise Blackacre to X for purposes which I have communicated to him and (3) I devise Blackacre to X for purposes which I have communicated to him by letter dated November 11, 1973. In this last example since the will refers to a written instrument, already existing at the date of the will, in such terms that the written instrument can be ascertained, the requirements of the doctrine of incorporation are satisfied [94] so that the incorporated document is admitted to probate as part of the testator's will, the will's compliance with the requirements of section 9 of the Wills Act being sufficient to cover the unattested written instrument referred to in the will. It will be seen that the application of the doctrine of incorporation renders the imposition of a secret trust unnecessary as the requisite formalities for an express trust are present, preventing any possibility of fraud upon X's part.

Testators, today, who do not want their testamentary wishes to become public by admission to probate as part of their will can take advantage of the doctrine of secret trusts to make provision for mistresses, illegitimate children, relatives whom they do not wish to appear to be helping or organisations which they do not wish to appear to be helping. Indecisive, aged testators can also leave everything by will absolutely to their solicitors, from time to time calling upon or phoning their solicitors with their latest wishes.

P. Costigan); (1937) 53 L.Q.R. 501 (W. S. Holdsworth); (1947) 12 Conv.(N.S.) 28 (J. G. Fleming); (1951) 67 L.Q.R. 314 (L. A. Sheridan); (1963) 27 Conv.(N.S.) 92 (J. A. Andrews).

[91] *McCormick* v. *Grogan* (1869) L.R. 4 H.L. 82; *Blackwell* v. *Blackwell* [1929] A.C. 318, *infra*, p. 406; *Bannister* v. *Bannister* [1948] W.N. 261, *supra*, p. 65.

[92] Law of Property Act 1925, s. 53, *supra*, pp. 52–53.

[93] *Sellack* v. *Harris* (1708) 2 Eq.Ca.Ab. 46.

[94] *In the goods of Smart* [1902] P. 238; *Re Jones* [1942] Ch. 328, restricted by *Re Edwards W.T.* [1948] Ch. 440; Tiley, p. 412; *Re Schintz's W.T.* [1951] Ch. 870; for a case on the borderline of half secret trusts and incorporation see *Guest* v. *Webb* [1965] V.R. 427; 1966 Annual Survey of Commonwealth Law, 346.

II. FULLY SECRET TRUSTS

A fully secret trust is one where neither the existence of the trust nor its terms are disclosed by the will or other instrument.[95]

If a testator makes a valid will bequeathing or devising property to X, apparently beneficially, and communicates to X his intention that X is to hold the property on certain trusts or subject to certain conditions or charges, which X accepts either expressly by promise or impliedly by silence, oral evidence is admissible to prove both the existence and the terms of the trust or conditions or charges which, if clearly proved, X will be compelled to carry out: *Ottaway* v. *Norman, infra.* Nothing short of an express or implied acceptance by X will raise a trust (or condition or charge): *Wallgrave* v. *Tebbs, infra.* Communication and acceptance must be of a definite obligation, not of a mere hope or confidence expressed by the testator.[96] Communication and acceptance [97] may be effected at any time during the life of the testator, whether before or after the execution of the will and communication may be made through an agent.[98] It may also be made by handing to X a sealed envelope containing the terms of the trust, and requiring X not to open it until after the testator's death: *Re Keen, infra.* If X is told in the testator's lifetime that he is to hold the property on trust, but is not informed of the terms of the trust, he holds the property on a resulting trust for the testator's residuary legatee or devisee, or if there is no such person, or if X himself is the residuary legatee or devisee, then for the testator's intestate successors: *Re Boyes, infra.* If X is not so told he takes the property beneficially as is also the case if X is told that he is to take the property subject to a condition (*stricto sensu*) or charge but is not informed of the terms of the condition or charge.

The Wills Act 1837

Section 9.[99] No will shall be valid unless it shall be in writing and ... signed at the foot or end thereof [1] by the testator, or by some other person in his presence and by his direction; and such signature shall be made or

---

[95] The cases in this Section concern trusts engrafted on wills; but secret trusts may arise in respect of *inter vivos* instruments: *Bannister* v. *Bannister* [1948] 2 All E.R. 133; *supra*, p. 65; and also where there is no instrument, as, *e.g.*, in cases of intestacy: *Sellack* v. *Harris* (1708) 2 Eq.Ca.Ab. 46. See also the broad dicta of Romer J. in *Re Gardner (No. 2)* [1923] 2 Ch. 227, 232–233, *infra*, p. 420.

[96] See *Att.-Gen.* v. *Chamberlain* (1904) 90 L.T. 581. Whether the obligation is technically a trust or a condition or a charge (see Chap. 2, ss. 6 and 7, *supra*) it seems that equity will intervene.

[97] The full extent of the property to be covered by the obligation must be communicated and accepted so that where a secret trust for a £5,000 legacy has been communicated to and accepted by the trustee and the legacy is increased by £5,000 in a further codicil but nothing said to the trustee the further £5,000 is not caught by the secret trust: *Re Colin Cooper* [1939] Ch. 580, 811. The further £5,000 is taken beneficially by the " trustee."

[98] *Moss* v. *Cooper* (1861) 1 J. & H. 352. If the agent were unauthorised but the legatee did not approach the testator to clarify the matter would this amount to acquiescence?

[99] Superseding the Statute of Frauds 1677, s. 5.

[1] " At the foot or end thereof ": amended by the Wills Act Amendment Act 1852, s. 1, to include a signature " at or after, or following, or under, or beside, or opposite to the end of the will whereby it is apparent on the face of the will that the testator intended by his signature to give effect thereto." For a hard case see *Re Beadle* [1974] 1 W.L.R. 417.

acknowledged by the testator in the presence of two or more witnesses present at the same time, and such witnesses shall attest and shall subscribe the will in the presence of the testator, but no form of attestation shall be necessary.

OTTAWAY v. NORMAN

Chancery Division [1972] Ch. 698; [1972] 2 W.L.R. 50; [1971] 3 All E.R. 1325.

A testator, Harry Ottaway, by will devised his bungalow (with fixtures, fittings and furniture) to his housekeeper Miss Hodges in fee simple and gave her a legacy of £1,500 and half the residue of his estate. It was alleged that Miss Hodges had orally agreed with the testator to leave the bungalow etc. by her will to the plaintiffs, who were the testator's son and daughter-in-law, Mr. and Mrs. William Ottaway, and that she had also orally agreed to leave to them whatever money was left at her death. By her will Miss Hodges left all her property away from the plaintiffs, who thus brought an action against Miss Hodges' executor, Mr. Norman, for a declaration that the appropriate parts of Miss Hodges' estate were held by him on trust for the plaintiffs.

Brightman J. upheld the plaintiffs' claim except in respect of the moneys.

BRIGHTMAN J.: "... It will be convenient to call the person on whom such a trust is imposed the 'primary donee' and the beneficiary under that trust the 'secondary donee.' The essential elements which must be proved to exist are: (i) the intention of the testator to subject the primary donee to an obligation in favour of the secondary donee; (ii) communication of that intention to the primary donee; and (iii) the acceptance of that obligation by the primary donee either expressly or by acquiescence. It is immaterial whether these elements precede or succeed the will of the donor. I am informed that there is no recent reported case where the obligation imposed on the primary donee is an obligation to make a will in favour of the secondary donee as distinct from some form of *inter vivos* transfer. But it does not seem to me that that can really be a distinction which can validly be drawn on behalf of the defendant in the present case. The basis of the doctrine of a secret trust is the obligation imposed on the conscience of the primary donee and it does not seem to me that there is any materiality in the machinery by which the donor intends that that obligation shall be carried out. ...

"Counsel for the defendant sought at one stage to deploy an argument that a person could never succeed in establishing a secret trust unless he could show that the primary donee was guilty of deliberate and conscious wrong doing of which he said there was no evidence in the case before me. That proposition, if correct, would lead to the surprising result that if the primary donee faithfully observed the obligation imposed on him there would not ever have been a trust at any time in existence. The argument was discarded and I think rightly. Counsel then fastened on the words ' clearest and most indisputable evidence ' and he submitted that an exceptionally high standard of proof was needed to establish a secret trust. I do not think that Lord Westbury's words mean more than this: that if a will contains a gift which is in terms absolute, clear evidence is needed before the court will assume that the testator did not mean what he said. It is perhaps analogous to the standard of proof which this court requires before it will rectify a written instrument, for there again a party is saying that neither meant what they have written.

" I find as a fact that Harry Ottaway intended that Miss Hodges should be obliged to dispose of the bungalow in favour of the plaintiffs at her death, that he communicated that intention to Miss Hodges and that Miss Hodges accepted the obligation. I find the same facts in relation to the furniture, fixtures and fittings which passed to Miss Hodges under clause 4 of Harry Ottaway's will. I am not satisfied that any similar obligation was imposed and accepted as regards any contents of the bungalow which had not devolved on Miss Hodges under clause 4 of Harry Ottaway's will.

" I turn to the question of money. In cross-examination William Ottaway said the trust extended to the house, furniture and money:

> ' Everything my father left to Miss Hodges was to be in the trust. The trust comprised the lot. She could use the money as she liked. She had to leave my wife and me whatever money was left.'

In cross-examination Mrs. Ottaway said that her understanding was that Miss Hodges was bound to make a will giving her and her husband the bungalow, contents and any money she had left. ' She could please herself about the money. She did not have to save it for us. She was free to spend it.' It seems to me that two questions arise. First as a matter of fact what did the parties intend should be comprised in Miss Hodges's obligation? All money which Miss Hodges had at her death, including money which she had acquired before Harry's death and money she acquired after his death from all sources? Or, only money acquired under Harry's will? Secondly, if such an obligation existed would it as a matter of law create a valid trust? On the second question I am content to assume for present purposes but without so deciding that if property is given to the primary donee on the understanding that the primary donee will dispose by his will of such assets, if any, as he may have at his command at his death in favour of the secondary donee, a valid trust is created in favour of the secondary donee which is in suspense during the lifetime of the primary donee, but attaches to the estate of the primary donee at the moment of the latter's death. There would seem to be at least some support for this proposition in an Australian case to which I was referred: *Birmingham* v. *Renfrew*.[2] I accept that the parties mentioned money on at least some occasions when they talked about Harry Ottaway's intentions for the future disposition of Ashcroft. I do not, however, find sufficient evidence that it was Harry Ottaway's intention that Miss Hodges should be compelled to leave all her money, from whatever source derived, to the plaintiffs. This would seem to preclude her giving even a small pecuniary legacy to any friend or relative. I do not think it is clear that Harry Ottaway intended to extract any such far-reaching undertaking from Miss Hodges or that she intended to accept such a wide obligation herself. Therefore the obligation, if any, is in my view to be confined to money derived under Harry Ottaway's will. If the obligation is confined to money derived under Harry Ottaway's will, the obligation is meaningless and unworkable unless it includes the requirement that she shall keep such money separate and distinct from her own money. I am certain that no such requirement was ever discussed or intended. If she had the right to mingle her own money with that derived from Harry, there would be no ascertainable property on which the trust could bite at her death. This aspect distinguishes this case from *Re Gardner*.[3]

" There is another difficulty. Does money in this context include only cash or cash and investments, or all moveable property of any description? The evidence is quite inconclusive. In my judgment the plaintiff's claim succeeds in relation to the bungalow and in relation to the furniture, fixtures and fittings which devolved under clause 4 of Harry Ottaway's will subject, of course, to normal wastage and fair wear and tear, but not to any other assets."

WALLGRAVE v. TEBBS

Vice-Chancellor (1855) 2 K. & J. 313; 25 L.J.Ch. 241; 26 L.T.(o.s.) 147; 20 J.P. 84; 4 W.R. 194; 2 Jur. 83

A testator bequeathed to the defendants, Mr. Tebbs and Mr. Martin, a legacy of £12,000 as joint tenants, and also devised some freehold properties in Chelsea and a field at Earl's Court " unto and to the use of Tebbs and Martin, their heirs and assigns, for ever, as joint tenants." The testator had in his lifetime contemplated devoting part of his property to charitable objects. One of his executors, G., had been asked by him to undertake a trust for that purpose, but had declined. After the will was made G. suggested that the testator should communicate to Tebbs and Martin the motives which had influenced him in selecting them as legatees and devisees. At the testator's request G. wrote a letter as a sketch for him to consider, and to sign if he approved of it. It was not in fact signed by the testator, and was not shown to the defendants

---

[2] (1937) 57 C.L.R. 666.   [3] [1920] 2 Ch. 523; [1920] All E.R.Rep. 723.

until after his death. It ran as follows: " You know what my wishes
were with regard to the Chelsea freeholds and the £12,000 and the
difficulties in my way of doing what I wished. I am confident, from
the Christian characters of Mr. Tebbs and Mr. Martin, that, if they are
not able to do what I would have done, they will make use of what I
have given them in such a way as seems to them best fitted to promote
the glory of God, and the welfare of our fellow sinners. I trust, however, that they will keep . . . hundred pounds for themselves. You know
that it was my intention to have built a church or chapel in my field
behind Smith Street, and to have endowed it out of the Chelsea
property; and to have built ten or twelve almshouses at Earl's Court,
in the field behind the terrace, with the money, and provided by weekly
payments for the living there of poor married couples or widows."

No undertaking, express or implied, on the part of the defendants
to carry out the testator's wishes was proved. They admitted that it
would be proper for them to make use of the property in a manner
consistent with the motives which had induced the testator to leave the
property to them, but claimed to be entitled in law to hold it
beneficially.

The plaintiffs (residuary legatees and devisees) unsuccessfully claimed
that a secret trust had been created which was rendered void by the
Statute of Mortmain.

WOOD V.-C.: " I have anxiously considered this case, and the more
so because I do not find that there is any authority by which it is
decided.[4] In *Russell* v. *Jackson* [5] Turner L.J., then Vice-Chancellor,
expressly guards himself from being supposed to give any opinion upon
the question now raised.

" But, although I do not find any decision in point, I find in
Addlington v. *Cann* [6] a clear indication of the opinion which Lord
Hardwicke would have entertained upon a question like the present;
and in *Muckleston* v. *Brown* [7] I find an equally clear indication that
the same view would have been taken by Lord Eldon. And I am satisfied that I ought not to be the first to overstep the clear line which
separates mere trusts from devises and bequests, which, on the face
of the will, are absolute, but which are alleged to have been in fact
given with an intention to evade the statute.

" Where a person, knowing that a testator in making a disposition
in his favour intends it to be applied for purposes other than his own
benefit, either *expressly promises*, or *by silence implies*, that he will
carry the testator's intention into effect, and the property is left to him
upon the faith of that promise or undertaking, it is in effect a case of
trust; and, in such a case, the court will not allow the devisee to set

---

[4] There were one or two earlier authorities: *Paine* v. *Hall* (1812) 18 Ves. 475; *Pod-
more* v. *Gunning* (1836) 7 Sim. 644.
[5] (1852) 10 Hare 204, 210.
[6] (1744) 3 Atk. 141.   [7] (1801) 6 Ves. 52.

up the Statute of Frauds—or rather the Statute of Wills, by which the Statute of Frauds is now, in this respect, superseded; and for this reason: the devisee by his conduct has induced the testator to leave him the property; and, as Turner L.J. says in *Russell* v. *Jackson*,[8] no one can doubt, that, if the devisee had stated that he would not carry into effect the intentions of the testator, the disposition in his favour would not have been found in the will. But in this the court does not violate the spirit of the statute: but for the same end, namely, prevention of fraud, it engrafts the trust on the devise, by admitting evidence which the statute would in terms exclude, in order to prevent a party from applying property to a purpose foreign to that for which he undertook to hold it.

" But the question here is totally different. Here there has been no such promise or undertaking on the part of the devisees. Here the devisees knew nothing of the testator's intention until after his death. That the testator desired, and was most anxious to have, his intentions carried out is clear. But, it is equally clear, that he has suppressed everything illegal. He has abstained from creating, either by his will or otherwise, any trust upon which this court can possibly fix. Upon the face of the will, the parties take indisputably for their own benefit. Can I possibly hold that the gift is void? If I knew perfectly well that a testator in making me a bequest, absolute on the face of the will, intended it to be applied for the benefit of a natural child, of whom he was not known to be the father, provided that intention *had not been communicated to me during the testator's life,* the validity of the bequests as an absolute bequest to me could not be questioned.

" It was argued, that, if the object of the gift had been not merely *malum prohibitum,* but *malum in se,* the devise must necessarily have been void. The answer is the same: the devise would have been void if the intention with which it was made had been known to the devisees during the life of the testator, and if they, by their conduct, had induced him to believe that they meant to carry that intention into effect. . . .

" In the present case there is no trust created. It is impossible for the court to look upon a document which is excluded by the Statute [of Wills]; and, such evidence being excluded, the case is reduced to one in which the testator has relied solely on the honour of the devisees, who, as far as this court is concerned, are left perfectly at liberty to apply the property to their own purposes. . . .

" Upon the face of this will the devisees are entitled to the property in question for their own absolute benefit. The statute prevents the court from looking at the paper-writing in which the testator's intentions are expressed; and the parties seeking to avoid the devise have failed to show that during the testator's lifetime, there was any bargain or understanding between the testator and the devisees, or any communication which could be construed into a trust, that they would apply the

---

[8] (1852) 10 Hare 204, 211.

property in such a manner as to carry the testator's intentions into effect. The devise, therefore, is a valid devise, and the bill must be dismissed.

" If no case similar to the present has yet been agitated, it is because the attempt has hitherto been looked upon as hopeless. I must, therefore, dismiss the bill with costs."

Re BOYES, BOYES v. CARRITT

Chancery Division (1884) 26 Ch.D. 531; 53 L.J.Ch. 654; 50 L.T. 581; 32 W.R. 630.

A testator, by a will drawn for him by his solicitor (Mr. Carritt), gave his property, which consisted of personal estate only, to Carritt absolutely, and appointed him executor. The testator had previously told Carritt that he wished him to hold the property according to directions which he would communicate by letter; and Carritt agreed. Such directions were not given by the testator, but after his death two unattested documents, both addressed to Carritt, were found, in which the testator stated his wish that Mrs. B should have the property. The testator's next-of-kin brought this action against Carritt, claiming a declaration that they were beneficially entitled. Carritt claimed to hold the property as trustee for Mrs. B.

It was argued for Mrs. B that the trust in her favour was completely constituted: the subject-matter was defined by the will, and the object by the unattested documents, with a transfer of the property to the trustee and an acceptance by him. The will might precede the communication to the trustee of the object of the trust: *Moss* v. *Cooper*.[9] If a trust was complete the fact that its object was not communicated to the trustee until after the testator's death would not destroy the trust: *Donaldson* v. *Donaldson*[10] and *Re Way's Trusts*[11, 12]; otherwise an accident, such as neglect to post a letter, might " vitiate a trust for the constitution of which everything possible had been done by the settlor."

KAY J.: " . . . Mr. Carritt admits that he is a trustee of all the property given to him by the will. He desires to carry out the wishes of the testator as expressed in the two letters, but of course he can only do so if they constitute a binding trust as against the next-of-kin.

" If it had been expressed on the face of the will that the defendant was a trustee, but the trusts were not thereby declared, it is quite clear that no trust afterwards declared by a paper not executed as a will could be binding: *Johnson* v. *Ball*[13]; *Briggs* v. *Penny*[14]; *Singleton* v.

---

9 1861) 1 J. & H. 352.
10 (1854) Kay 711.
11 (1864) 2 De G.J. & S. 365.
12 These two cases were not decisions on testamentary trusts, but on trusts *inter vivos*.
13 (1851) 5 De G. & Sm. 85.
14 (1851) 3 Mac. & G. 546.

Tomlinson.[15]   In such a case the legatee would be a trustee for the next-of-kin.

"There is another well-known class of cases where no trust appears on the face of the will, but the testator has been induced to make the will, or, having made it, has been induced not to revoke it, by a promise on the part of the devisee or legatee to deal with the property, or some part of it, in a specified manner.   In these cases the court has compelled discovery and performance of the promise, treating it as á trust binding the conscience of the donee, on the ground that otherwise a fraud would be committed, because it is to be presumed that if it had not been for such promise the testator would not have made or would have revoked the gift.   The principle of these decisions is precisely the same as in the case of an heir who has induced a testator not to make a will devising the estate away from him by a promise that if the estate were allowed to descend he would make a certain provision out of it for a named person: *Stickland* v. *Aldridge*[16]; *Wallgrave* v. *Tebbs*[17]; *McCormick* v. *Grogan.*[18]   But no case has ever yet decided that a testator can, by imposing a trust upon his devisee or legatee, *the objects of which he does not communicate to him,* enable himself to evade the Statute of Wills by declaring those objects in an unattested paper found after his death.

"The essence of all those decisions is that the devisee or legatee accepts a particular trust which thereupon becomes binding upon him, and which it would be a fraud in him not to carry into effect.

"If the trust was not declared when the will was made, it is essential, in order to make it binding, that it should be communicated to the devisee or legatee in the testator's lifetime and that he should accept that particular trust.   It may possibly be that he would be bound if the trust had been put in writing and placed in his hands in a sealed envelope, and he had engaged that he would hold the property given to him by the will upon the trust so declared, although he did not know the actual terms of the trust: *McCormick* v. *Grogan.*   But the reason is that it must be assumed that if he had not so accepted, the will would be revoked.   Suppose the case of an engagement to hold the property not upon the terms of any paper communicated to the legatee or put into his hands, but of any paper that might be found after the testator's death.

"The evidence in this case does not amount to that, but if it did the rule of law would intervene, which prevents a testator from declaring trusts in such a manner by a paper which was not executed as a will or codicil.   The legatee might be a trustee, but the trust declared by such an unattested paper would not be good.   For this purpose there is no difference whether the devisee or legatee is declared to

---

[15] (1878) 3 App.Cas. 404.
[16] (1804) 9 Ves. 516.
[17] (1855) 2 K. & J. 313; *supra*, p. 399.
[18] (1869) L.R. 4 H.L. 82.

be a trustee on the face of the will, or by an engagement with the testator not appearing on the will. The devisee or legatee cannot by accepting an indefinite trust enable the testator to make an unattested codicil.

" I cannot help regretting that the testator's intention of bounty should fail by reason of an informality of this kind, but in my opinion it would be a serious innovation upon the law relating to testamentary instruments if this were to be established as a trust in her favour.

" The defendant, however, having admitted that he is only a trustee, I must hold, on the authority of *Muckleston* v. *Brown*,[19] *Briggs* v. *Penny* and *Johnson* v. *Ball,* that he is a trustee of this property for the next-of-kin of the testator. I can only hope they will consider the claim which this lady has upon their generosity."

III. HALF-SECRET TRUSTS

A half-secret trust is one where the existence of the trust is disclosed by the will or other instrument but the terms are not.

If a testator makes a valid will bequeathing or devising property to X on trust, without specifying in the will the objects of the trust, but communicates the objects to X *before or at the time of* the execution of the will, which states that the objects have been so communicated, X will be compelled to carry out the trust for the specified objects[20]: *Blackwell* v. *Blackwell, infra.* If, however, the testator communicates the objects to X *after* the execution of the will, X will hold the property on trust, because the will has created a trust; but since the objects have not been effectively specified, the beneficial interest will belong to the testator's residuary legatee or devisee, or if there is no such person, or if X himself is the residuary legatee or devisee, to the testator's intestate successors: *Re Keen, infra.*

The supposed justification of this is that a testator cannot, through the medium of a valid will which imposes a trust but does not create the beneficial interests of that trust, reserve to himself a power to create the beneficial interests in an informal non-testamentary manner, so giving the go-by to the requirements of the Wills Act 1837. After all, as we have seen, in the case of the probate doctrine of incorporation of documents by reference the documents must exist prior to or contemporaneously with the execution of the will, for to allow otherwise would be to give the go-by to the Wills Act. However, the doctrine of incorporation by reference operates within the ambit of the statutory formalities, whilst the whole justification for secret trusts is to impose them just where the statutory formalities have not been satisfied: they operate outside the will and independently of the

---

19 (1801) 6 Ves. 52.

20 The full extent of the property to be covered by the obligation must be communicated so that if £5,000 is bequeathed on a half-secret trust accepted by the trustee and then a codicil increases that sum to £15,000 but the trustee is not informed of this increase, the surplus £10,000 will not be held on the half-secret trust but on trust for the residuary legatee or next-of-kin: *cf. Re Colin Cooper* [1939] Ch. 580, 611.

Wills Act.[21] Fully secret trusts, allowing communication of the trusts between execution of the will and the testator's death, allow the go-by to be given to the Wills Act, and since a will is ambulatory, being of no effect till death, there is logically no difference between declarations of trusts before and after the will. Logically, half-secret trusts in this respect should be assimilated to fully secret trusts, as in Ireland [22] and most American jurisdictions,[23] rather than have a different rule based upon a misplaced analogy with the doctrine of incorporation by reference. At present, there are the following differences between half-secret trusts and the probate doctrine of incorporation:

(i) In half-secret trusts the will need not specify the type of communication with any precision; in incorporation by reference the will must refer to the document to be incorporated with sufficient precision to enable it to be identified.[24]

(ii) In half-secret trusts the communication may be oral; in incorporation by reference the document to be incorporated must be in writing.

(iii) In half-secret trusts the testator must take the intended trustee into his confidence; in incorporation by reference the intended trustee need not be told of the document to be incorporated. Indeed, incorporation by reference may be effected in cases of absolute gift as well as in cases of trust.

(iv) In half-secret trusts the names of the beneficiaries are not made public; in incorporation by reference the incorporated document is admitted to probate and so made public.

(v) A beneficiary under a half-secret trust who witnesses the will does not forfeit his beneficial interest, whereas a beneficiary named in an incorporated document who witnesses the will does.[25]

(vi) The interest of a beneficiary under a half-secret trust who predeceases the testator does not lapse: in like circumstances that of a beneficiary named in an incorporated document does.[26]

One special requirement for half-secret trusts which is inapposite for fully secret trusts is that the communication of the trusts and the terms of the trust must not conflict with the wording of the will, for to allow otherwise would be to allow oral evidence to contradict the express words of the will: *Re Keen, infra.* Thus, leaving property to four persons " to be dealt with in accordance with my wishes which I have made known *to them* " is ineffective to create a half-secret trust unless the wishes were communicated

---

[21] *Re Young* [1951] Ch. 344; *Re Gardner (No.* 2) [1923] 2 Ch. 230; *Cullen* v. *Att.-Gen. for N. Ireland* (1866) L.R. 1 H.L. 190 at 198; *Blackwell* v. *Blackwell* [1929] A.C. 318, 340, 342.

[22] *Re Browne* [1944] Ir.R. 90; 67 L.Q.R. 413 (L. A. Sheridan).

[23] Scott, *Law of Trusts*, para. 55.8; *Restatement of Trusts*, para. 55 (*c*) (*h*).

[24] *In the goods of Smart* [1902] P. 258; *Re Jones* [1942] Ch. 328; *Re Edwards' W.T.* [1948] Ch. 440; *Re Schintz W.T.* [1957] Ch. 870; *Guest* v. *Webb* [1965] V.R. 427 (Victoria).

[25] *Re Young* [1951] Ch. 344, *infra*, p. 413. On the reasoning therein it would appear that a grandchild beneficiary taking under a half-secret trust in the will of his partially intestate grandfather might well not have to bring the benefit into hotchpot under s. 49 (1) (*a*) of the Administration of Estates Act 1925 whereas he would if benefiting under an incorporated document. Would a child beneficiary be caught by s. 47 (1) (iii) of the Act?

[26] *Re Gardner (No.* 2) [1923] Ch. 230.

to all four [27]: communication to less than four would only be effective if
the words " or any one or more of them " had been added.[28]   Furthermore,
if property is left by will to X as trustee, evidence is not admissible to show
that X was meant to have some part of that property beneficially.[29]

By way of contrast if the wording of the will gives property " to X
absolutely " or " to X relying on him, but not by way of trust, to carry out
my wishes . . ." then oral evidence is admissible to prove a secret trust,
contradicting the express words of the will, for to allow otherwise would be
to allow the possibility of the perpetration of fraud: *Re Spencer's Will.*[30]

BLACKWELL v. BLACKWELL

House of Lords [1929] A.C. 318; 98 L.J.Ch. 251; 140 L.T. 444; 45
    T.L.R. 208; 73 S.J. 92; affirming Chancery Division [1928] Ch.
    614; 97 L.J.Ch. 257; 139 L.T. 200; 44 T.L.R. 521; 73 S.J. 318
    (Lord Hailsham L.C., Viscount Sumner, Lords Buckmaster,
    Carson and Warrington)

A testator by a codicil bequeathed a legacy of £12,000 to five
persons upon trust to invest according to their discretion and " to apply
the income . . . for the purposes indicated by me to them." Before the
execution of the codicil the objects of the trust were communicated in
outline to four of the legatees and in detail to the fifth, and the trust
was accepted by all of them. The legatee to whom the communication
had been made in detail also made a memorandum, on the same day
as (though a few hours after) the execution of the codicil, of the testator's instructions. The plaintiffs (the residuary legatees) now claimed
a declaration that no valid trust in favour of the objects so communicated had been created, on the ground principally that parol evidence
was inadmissible to establish the purposes indicated by the testator:
Johnson v. *Ball.*[31]

Eve J. held, following *Re Fleetwood,*[32] that the evidence was admissible, and here proved a valid secret trust for the persons named by
the testator in his instructions to the legatees. The plaintiffs appealed.
The Court of Appeal affirmed the decision of Eve J., being of opinion

---

[27] *Re Spence* [1949] W.N. 237 following *Re Keen, infra.* Is this rule of construction
unwarranted on the footing that secret trusts arise outside the will as if there were
no reference contained in the will at all as *Re Young* [1951] Ch. 344 shows?
[28] " to them or either of them " was used in *Re Keen, infra.*
[29] *Re Rees* [1950] Ch. 204; *Re Tyler* [1967] 1 W.L.R. 1269; *Re Pugh's W.T.* [1967] 1
W.L.R. 1262; *Re Baillie* (1886) 2 T.L.R. 660. *Aliter* if property given under a
fully secret trust when the possibilities of trust, conditional gift and equitable
charge have to be examined: *Irvine* v. *Sullivan* (1869) L.R. 8 Eq. 673. See also
Re Armstrong (1969) 7 D.L.R. (3d) 36 (Nova Scotia).
[30] (1887) 57 L.T. 519; *Irvine* v. *Sullivan* (*supra*); *Re Falkiner* [1924] 1 Ch. 88; *Re
Stirling* [1954] 1 W.L.R. 763.
[31] (1851) 5 De G. & Sm. 85.
[32] (1880) 15 Ch.D. 594, where a testatrix by a codicil bequeathed to X all her personalty " to be applied as I have requested him to do." Before the execution of
the codicil she had stated to X the trusts on which she intended the property to be
held, and X made a memorandum of the details in her presence. Hall V.-C. held
that external evidence was admissible to prove the terms of the understanding
between X and the testatrix.

that the basis of Hall V.-C.'s decision in *Re Fleetwood* had been
adopted by the Court of Appeal in *Re Huxtable*.[33] The appellants
appealed unsuccessfully.

VISCOUNT SUMNER: " My Lords, I am satisfied that *Re Fleetwood*,
which is not distinguishable from the present case on the facts, was
affirmed by the Court of Appeal in *Re Huxtable* and that professional
opinion generally has accepted these decisions as correct. In argument, however, counsel for the appellants treated it as almost self-
evident that they conflicted with section 9 of the Wills Act, and counsel
for the respondents, while making no admission, elected to rely mainly
on the time that has passed and the probable volume of rights that
have arisen since these cases were decided and in consequence of them.
I do not think that this question ought to turn merely on the dates of
the decisions and the extent of their adoption in practice. It is a grave
thing to affirm a doctrine that violates the prescriptions of a statute,
and especially such a statute as the Wills Act, even though the error
is of long standing. In view of this, and also in deference to the reser-
vations of opinion expressed by Lords Dunedin and Parker of Waddington in *Le Page* v. *Gardom*[34] and Warrington L.J. in *Gardner's*
case,[35] I venture to examine this aspect of the matter.

" In itself the doctrine of equity, by which parol evidence is admissible to prove what is called ' fraud ' in connection with secret trusts,
and effect is given to such trusts when established, would not seem to
conflict with any of the Acts under which from time to time the legislature has regulated the right of testamentary disposition. A court of
conscience finds a man in the position of an absolute legal owner of a
sum of money, which has been bequeathed to him under a valid will,
and it declares that, on proof of certain facts relating to the motives and
actions of the testator, it will not allow the legal owner to exercise his
legal right to do what he will with his own. This seems to be a perfectly
normal exercise of general equitable jurisdiction. The facts commonly,
but not necessarily, involve some immoral and selfish conduct on the
part of the legal owner. The necessary elements, on which the question
turns, are intention, communication and acquiescence. The testator
intends his absolute gift to be employed as he and not as the donee
desires; he tells the proposed donee of this intention and, either by
express promise or by the tacit promise, which is satisfied by acquiescence, the proposed donee encourages him to bequeath the money in
the faith that his intentions will be carried out. The special circumstance that the gift is by bequest only makes this rule a special case of
the exercise of a general jurisdiction, but in its application to a bequest
the doctrine must in principle rest on the assumption that the will has
first operated according to its terms. It is because there is no one to

[33] [1902] 2 Ch. 793.
[34] (1915) 84 L.J.Ch. 749, 752, 753.
[35] [1920] 2 Ch. 523.

whom the law can give relief in the premises that relief, if any, must be sought in equity. So far, and in the bare case of a legacy absolute on the face of it, I do not see how the statute-law relating to the form of a valid will is concerned at all, and the expressions, in which the doctrine has been habitually described, seem to bear this out. For the prevention of fraud equity fastens on the conscience of the legatee a trust, a trust, that is, which otherwise would be inoperative; in other words it makes him do what the will in itself has nothing to do with; it lets him take what the will gives him and then makes him apply it as the court of conscience directs, and it does so in order to give effect to wishes of the testator which would not otherwise be effectual.

" To this, two circumstances must be added to bring the present case to the test of the general doctrine, first, that the will states on its face that the legacy is given on trust but does not state what the trusts are, and further contains a residuary bequest, and, second, that the legatees are acting with perfect honesty, seek no advantage to themselves, and only desire, if the court will permit them, to do what in other circumstances the court would have fastened it on their conscience to perform.

" Since the current of decisions down to *Re Fleetwood* and *Re Huxtable* has established that the principles of equity apply equally when these circumstances are present as in cases where they are not, the material question is whether and how the Wills Act affects this case. It seems to me that, apart from legislation, the application of the principle of equity which was made in *Fleetwood's* case and *Huxtable's* case was logical, and was justified by the same considerations as in the cases of fraud and absolute gifts. Why should equity forbid an honest trustee to give effect to his promise, made to a deceased testator, and compel him to pay another legatee, about whom it is quite certain that the testatator did not mean to make him the object of his bounty? In both cases the testator's wishes are incompletely expressed in his will. Why should equity, over a mere matter of words, give effect to them in one case and frustrate them in the other? No doubt the words ' in trust ' prevent the legatee from taking beneficially, whether they have simply been declared in conversation or written in the will, but the fraud, when the trustee, so called in the will, is also the residuary legatee, is the same as when he is only declared a trustee by word of mouth accepted by him. I recoil from interfering with decisions of long standing, which reject this anomaly, unless constrained by statute. . . .

" . . . I think the conclusion is confirmed, which the frame of section 9 of the Wills Act seems to me to carry on its face, that the legislation did not purport to interfere with the exercise of a general equitable jurisdiction, even in connection with secret dispositions of a testator, except in so far as reinforcement of the formalities required for a valid will might indirectly limit it. The effect, therefore, of a bequest being made in terms on trust, without any statement in the will to show what the trust is, remains to be decided by the law as laid down by the courts before and since the Act and does not depend on the Act itself.

"The limits, beyond which the rules as to unspecified trusts must not be carried, have often been discussed. A testator cannot reserve to himself a power of making future unwitnessed dispositions by merely naming a trustee and leaving the purposes of the trust to be supplied afterwards, nor can a legatee give testamentary validity to an unexecuted codicil by accepting an indefinite trust, never communicated to him in the testator's lifetime: *Johnson* v. *Ball, Re Boyes*,[36] *Riordan* v. *Banon*,[37] *Re Hetley*.[38] To hold otherwise would indeed be to enable the testator to 'give the go-by' to the requirements of the Wills Act, because he did not choose to comply with them. It is communication of the purpose to the legatee, coupled with acquiescence or promise on his part, that removes the matter from the provision of the Wills Act and brings it within the law of trusts, as applied in this instance to trustees, who happen also to be legatees. . . ." *Appeal dismissed.*

Re KEEN, EVERSHED v. GRIFFITHS

Court of Appeal [1937] Ch. 236; 106 L.J.Ch. 177; 156 L.T. 207; 53 T.L.R. 320; 81 S.J. 97; [1937] 1 All E.R. 452 (Wright M.R., Greene and Romer L.JJ.)

The testator by clause 5 of his will, dated August 11, 1932, gave to his executors and trustees, Captain Hazelhurst and Mr. Evershed, the sum of £10,000 free of duty "to be held upon trust and disposed of by them among such person, persons or charities as may be notified by me to them or either of them during my lifetime, and in default of such notification and so far as such notification shall not extend I declare that the said sum of £10,000 or such part thereof as shall not be disposed of in manner aforesaid shall fall into and form part of my residuary estate." Shortly before this, on March 31, 1932, the testator had made a will containing an identical gift. He had on that date handed to Mr. Evershed a sealed envelope containing the name of the intended beneficiary, but he had not disclosed its contents to Mr. Evershed, having directed in fact that it was not to be opened until after his death. In these circumstances Mr. Evershed regarded himself as having undertaken and as being bound to hold the £10,000 in accordance with the directions contained in the sealed envelope. When the new will was executed on August 11, 1932, no fresh directions were given, and Mr. Evershed still regarded himself as being bound by the previous communication. On the testator's death an originating summons was taken out to determine whether the £10,000 was held by Captain Hazelhurst and Mr. Evershed on trust for the intended bene-

---

[36] (1884) 26 Ch.D. 531, *supra*, p. 402.
[37] (1876) 10 I.R.Eq. 469.
[38] [1902] 2 Ch. 866.

ficiary or whether it fell into residue. It was held by Farwell J. that it fell into residue, and his decision was affirmed by the Court of Appeal.

LORD WRIGHT M.R.: " Farwell J. . . . decided adversely to the claims of the lady [the intended beneficiary] on the short ground that she could not prove that she was a person notified to the trustees by the testator during his lifetime within the words of clause 5 [of the will]. His opinion seems to be that the clause required the name and identity of the lady to be expressly disclosed to the trustees during the testator's lifetime, so that it was not sufficient to place these particulars in the physical possession of the trustees, or one of them, in the form of a memorandum which they were not to read till the testator's death.

" I am unable to accept this conclusion, which appears to me to put too narrow a construction on the word ' notified ' as used in clause 5 in all the circumstances of the case. To take a parallel, a ship which sails under sealed orders is sailing under orders though the exact terms are not ascertained by the captain till later. I note that the case of a trust, put into writing, which is placed in the trustees' hands in a sealed envelope, was hypothetically treated by Kay J. as possibly constituting a communication in a case of this nature.[39] This, so far as it goes seems to support my conclusion. The trustees had the means of know-ledge available whenever it became necessary and proper to open the envelope. I think Mr. Evershed was right in understanding that the giving of the sealed envelope was a notification within clause 5.

" This makes it necessary to examine the matter on a wider basis, and to consider the principles of law which were argued both before Farwell J. and this court, but which the judge found it merely necessary to mention. There are two main questions: first, how far parol evidence is admissible to define the trust under such a clause as this and, secondly, and in particular, how far such evidence, if admissible at all, would be excluded on the ground that it would be inconsistent with the true meaning of clause 5?

" It is first necessary to state what, in my opinion, is the true construction of the words of the clause.

" These words, in my opinion, can only be considered as referring to a definition of trusts which have not yet, at the date of the will, been established and which, between that date and the testator's death, may or may not be established. Mr. Roxburgh[40] has strenuously argued, basing himself in particular on the word ' may,' that the clause, even though it covers future dispositions, also includes a disposition antecedent to or contemporaneous with the execution of the will. I do not think that even so wide a construction of the word ' may ' would enable Mr. Roxburgh's contention to succeed, but, in any case, I do

---

[39] *Re Boyes* (1884) 26 Ch.D. 531, 536; *supra*, p. 402.
[40] Counsel for the appellant

not feel able to accept it. The words of the clause seem to me to refer only to something future and hypothetical, to something as to which the testator is reserving an option whether to do or not to do it.

" It must then be considered whether the first paragraph of the clause can be held valid as a testamentary disposition. It is said, on behalf of the residuary legatees, some of whom are infants, that it cannot, and that the only trust which takes effect is that which operates in their favour in the event of the provisions of the first part of the clause proving ineffective.

" The principles of law or equity relevant in a question of this nature have now been authoritatively settled or discussed by the House of Lords in *Blackwell* v. *Blackwell* [41] [in the case of half-secret trusts and *McCormick* v. *Grogan* [42] in the case of fully secret trusts. The Master of the Rolls then analysed the facts and decisions in those cases, and continued:] As, in my judgment, clause 5 should be considered as contemplating future dispositions, and as reserving to the testator the power of making such dispositions without a duly attested codicil, simply by notifying them during his lifetime, the principles laid down by Lord Sumner [in *Blackwell* v. *Blackwell*] must be fatal to the appellant's claim. Indeed, they would be equally fatal even on the construction for which Mr. Roxburgh contended, that the clause covered both anterior or contemporaneous notifications and future notifications. The clause would be equally invalid, but as already explained I cannot accept that construction. In *Blackwell* v. *Blackwell*,[43] *Re Fleetwood* [44] and *Re Huxtable* [45] the trusts had been specifically declared to some or all of the trustees, at or before the execution of the will, and the language of the will was consistent with that fact. There was, in these cases, no reservation of a future power to change the trusts, in whole or in part. Such a power would involve a power to change a testamentary disposition by an unexecuted codicil, and would violate section 9 of the Wills Act. This was so held in *Re Hetley*.[46] *Johnson* v. *Ball* [47] is, again, a somewhat different example of the rule against dispositions made subsequently to the date of the will in cases where the will in terms leaves the property on trust, and shows that the position may be different from the position where the will in terms leaves the gift absolutely. The trusts referred to, but undefined in the will, must be described in the will as established prior to, or at least contemporaneously with, its execution.

" But there is a still further objection which, in the present case, renders the appellant's claim unenforceable: the trusts which it is sought to establish by parol evidence would be inconsistent with the express terms of the will. That such an objection is fatal appears

[41] [1929] A.C. 318; *supra*, p. 406.
[42] (1869) L.R. 4 H.L. 82.
[43] [1929] A.C. 318.
[44] (1880) 15 Ch.D. 594.
[45] [1902] 2 Ch. 793.
[46] [1902] 2 Ch. 866.
[47] (1851) 5 De G. & Sm. 85.

from the cases already cited, such as *Re Huxtable*. In that case, an undefined trust of money for charitable purposes was declared in the will, as in respect of the whole corpus and, accordingly, evidence was held inadmissible that the charitable trust was limited to the legatee's life, so that he was free to dispose of the corpus after his death. Similarly in *Johnson* v. *Ball* the testator by the will left the property to trustees, upon the uses contained in a letter signed 'by them and myself': it was held that that evidence was not admissible to show that, though no such letter was in existence at the date of the will, the testator had made a subsequent declaration of trust; the court held that these trusts could not be enforced. Lord Buckmaster in *Blackwell's* case [48] described *Johnson* v. *Ball* as an authority pointing 'to a case where the actual trusts were left over after the date of the will to be subsequently determined by the testator.' That, in his opinion, would be a contravention of the Wills Act. I know of no authority which would justify such a contravention. Lord Buckmaster also quotes [49] the grounds on which Parker V.-C. based his decision as being both 'that the letter referred to in the will had no existence at the time when the will was made and that, supposing it referred to a letter afterwards signed, it is impossible to give effect to it as a declaration of the trusts since it would admit the document as part of the will and it was unattested.'

"In the present case, while clause 5 refers solely to a future definition, or to future definitions, of the trust, subsequent to the date of the will, the sealed letter relied on as notifying the trust was communicated (as I find the facts) before the date of the will. That it was communicated to one trustee only, and not to both, would not, I think, be an objection (see Lord Warrington's observation in the *Blackwell* case).[50] But the objection remains that the notification sought to be put in evidence was anterior to the will, and hence not within the language of clause 5, and inadmissible simply on that ground, as being inconsistent with what the will prescribes. . . ." *Appeal dismissed*.[51]

IV. THE BASIS OF SECRET TRUSTS

Before dealing with the basis of secret trusts it is as well to examine certain unusual secret trust situations.

---

[48] [1929] A.C. 318, 331.
[49] *Ibid.* 330.
[50] *Ibid.* 341.
[51] In *Re Bateman's W.T.* [1970] 1 W.L.R. 1463; [1970] 3 All E.R. 817, *Re Keen* was followed without argument where a testator had directed his trustees to set aside £24,000 and pay the income thereof "to such persons and in such proportions *as shall* be stated by me in a sealed letter to my trustees": "[The direction] clearly imports that the testator may, in the future after the date of the will, give a sealed letter to his trustees. It is impossible to confine the words to a sealed letter already so given. If that be the true construction of the wording it is not in dispute that the direction is invalid." *Per* Pennycuick V.-C. at pp. 1468 and 820, respectively.

(i) *Attestation of will by secret beneficiary*

Section 15 of the Wills Act 1837: " If any person shall attest the execution of any will to whom or to whose wife or husband any beneficial devise, legacy, estate, interest, gift, or appointment, of or affecting any real or personal estate (other than and except charges and directions for the payment of any debt or debts), shall be thereby given or made, such devise, legacy, estate, interest, gift, or appointment shall, so far only as concerns such person attesting the execution of such will, or the wife or husband of such person, or any person claiming under such person or wife or husband, be utterly null and void, and such person so attesting shall be admitted as a witness to prove the execution of such will, or to prove the validity or invalidity thereof, notwithstanding such devise, legacy, estate, interest, gift, or appointment mentioned in such will."

Section 1 of the Wills Act 1968: " For the purposes of section 15 of the Wills Act 1837 the attestation of a will by a person to whom or to whose spouse there is given or made any such disposition as is described in that section shall be disregarded if the will is duly executed without his attestation and without that of any other such person."

Re Young [1951] Ch. 344 (Danckwerts J.): bequest by a testator to his wife with a direction that on her death she should leave the property for the purposes which he had communicated to her. Before execution of will, direction given and accepted by wife that she would leave a legacy of £2,000 to testator's chauffeur. The chauffeur had witnessed the testator's will. *Held* that the chauffeur had not forfeited his legacy under section 15 of the Wills Act 1837 for " the whole theory of the formation of a secret trust is that the Wills Act has nothing to do with the matter because the forms required by the Wills Act are entirely disregarded, since the persons do not take by virtue of the gift in the will, but by virtue of the secret trusts imposed upon the beneficiary who does in fact take under the will."

Quaere whether persons taking under a fully secret trust would receive nothing if the trustee taking absolutely beneficially on the face of the will had witnessed the will or whether the admission of oral evidence to establish the trusteeship would carry the day: half-secret trustees taking as trustees on the face of the will clearly cannot infringe section 15 of the Wills Act 1837.[52]

(ii) *Trustee predeceasing testator*

Generally, a gift by will to X is said to lapse if X predeceases the testator and the gift fails.[53] If, however, the gift is to X on trust for B and B survives the testator then despite X's predecease the gift will not lapse for equity will not allow a trust to fail for want of a trustee: the testator's personal representative will take over as trustee.[54]

According to dicta of Cozens-Hardy L.J. in *Re Maddock*,[55] a case

---

[52] *Cf. Re Armstrong* (1969) 7 D.L.R. (3d) 36.
[53] Exceptionally, if issue predecease a testator leaving issue of their own surviving the testator the gift takes effect in favour of the estate of the deceased issue: Wills Act 1837, s. 33.
[54] *Sonley* v. *Clock Makers' Company* (1780) 1 Bro.C.C. 81; *Mallott* v. *Wilson* [1903] 2 Ch. 494; *Re Smirthwaite's Trusts* (1871) L.R. 11 Eq. 251; *Re Armitage* [1972] Ch. 438. See p. 463, *infra*.
[55] [1902] 2 Ch. 220, 231.

concerning a fully secret trust, " if the legatee renounces and disclaims, or dies in the lifetime of the testator, the persons claiming under the memorandum [*i.e.*, the secret trusts] can take nothing." This is based upon the view that the secret trusts only arise when the property intended to be the subject matter of the trust vests in someone under the terms of the will. It follows that if for some reason the property does not so vest then no trust arises.

Quaere whether the position should be the same for fully secret and half-secret trusts when in the latter case the person taking on the face of the will is expressly a trustee and equity will not allow a trust to fail for want of a trustee so that the property could be vested in the personal representatives upon the secret trusts.

(iii) *Trustee disclaiming after testator's death*

A beneficiary under a will can always disclaim a legacy or devise before acceptance and a person can always disclaim the office of trustee before acceptance.[56] If a person named as a half-secret trustee disclaimed the office then it would seem that the testator's personal representative would hold on the trusts for the secret beneficiaries. Where disclaimer by fully secret trustees is concerned although Cozens-Hardy L.J. opined in *Re Maddock* (*supra*) that no trusts would arise in such a case there are contrary dicta of Lord Buckmaster in *Blackwell* v. *Blackwell*[57]: " In the case where no trusts are mentioned the legatee might defeat the whole purpose by renouncing the legacy and the breach of trust would not in that case inure to his own benefit, but I entertain no doubt that the court having once admitted the evidence of the trust, would interfere to prevent its defeat." Lord Buckmaster's dicta presuppose the existence of a trust whereof the legatee is in breach and apply the maxim that equity will not allow a trust to fail for want of a trustee. Whether the trusts arose on the testator's death or at an earlier time is not stated by Lord Buckmaster. By analogy with mutual wills the testator's death might be the appropriate time, it being immaterial whether or not gifts were disclaimed.[58] Disclaimer might, however, be material if the testator's orally communicated intentions to the legatee were construed not as imposing trusts but as conferring a gift subject to a condition.[59]

(iv) *Trustee revoking acceptance before the testator's death*

Compare the three following examples:

(a) Testator, T, bequeaths £10,000 to X absolutely, having told X that he wants X to hold the money on trust for Y and Z. A year later X tells T that he is no longer prepared to hold the money

---

[56] *Re Sharman's W.T.* [1942] Ch. 311.

[57] [1929] A.C. 318, 328.

[58] *Cf. Re Hagger, infra*; see also *Blackwell* v. *Blackwell* [1929] A.C. 318, 341 *per* Lord Warrington: " It has long been settled that if a gift be made to a person in terms absolutely but in fact upon a trust communicated to the legatee and accepted by him, the legatee would be bound to give effect to the trust, on the principle that the gift may be presumed to have been made on the faith of his acceptance of the trust, and a refusal after the death of the testator to give effect to it would be a fraud on the part of the legatee." See also (1972) 36 Conv.(N.S.) 113 (R. Burgess).

[59] See Chap. 2, s. 6, *supra*.

on trust for anyone. Five years later T dies without having changed his will;

(b) The bequest as before but X tells T that he is no longer prepared to hold the money on trust for anyone only three days before T dies of a week-long illness;

(c) The bequest as before but T is incurably insane when informed by X as before and T remains so till his death.

Does X take the £10,000 beneficially in each case? Is X under any obligations before T's death?

(v) *Secret beneficiary predeceasing testator*

If T by will left property to X on trust expressly for B and B predeceased T the gift to B would lapse. One would have imagined that the result would be the same if T, having asked X to hold on trust for B, left property " to X absolutely " or " to X upon trusts that I have communicated to him." However, in *Re Gardner (No. 2)* [60] Romer L.J. held that B's interest did not lapse as B obtained an interest as soon as T communicated the terms of the trust to X and X accepted the trust. B's interest derived not from T's will (to which the rules regarding lapse would have applied) but under the agreement between T and X. " The rights of the parties appear to me to be exactly the same as though the husband (X), after the memorandum had been communicated to him by the testatrix (T) in the year 1909 had executed a declaration of trust binding himself to hold any property that should come to him upon his wife's (T's) partial intestacy upon trust as specified in the memorandum." [61] Such a declaration, however, does not create a properly constituted trust since the subject matter is future property. [62] It would appear that Romer J. must have considered that the vesting of the property in X completely constituted the trust [63] but on the terms of the memorandum. However, the interests of those taking under the memorandum only became vested proprietorial interests after T's death: until then the so-called interests only amounted to mere *spes* that T would not change her mind and make a new will or die insolvent and that X would not revoke his acceptance, so that ultimately X would receive property to hold on trust for them. Just as an *inter vivos* trust constituted by X in 1919 declaring himself trustee of certain property for the benefit of A, B and C equally would give B no interest, if at that date B were dead and so no longer an existing legal entity, so the trust arising in *Re Gardner* after T's death in 1919 could give B no interest, B being dead by that date. It makes no difference that whilst B was alive he might have had some sort of *spes* that if he lived long enough a trust might come into existence for his benefit at a later late. The authority of *Re Gardner* is thus doubtful.

---

[60] [1923] 2 Ch. 230.

[61] *Ibid.* at 233.

[62] *Re Ellenborough* [1903] 1 Ch. 697; *Re Northcliffe* [1925] Ch. 651; *Williams* v. *C.I.R.* [1965] N.Z.L.R. 395, *supra*, p. 164; *Brennan* v. *Morphett* (1908) 6 C.L.R. 22.

[63] *Cf. Re Ralli's W.T.* [1964] Ch. 288; *Re Adlard* [1954] Ch. 29.

(vi) *Bequest to two on a promise by one*

The orthodox position is laid down in *Re Stead* [64] by Farwell J.:

"If A induced B either to make, or to leave unrevoked, a will leaving property to A and C as tenants in common, by expressly promising or tacitly consenting, that he and C will carry out the testator's wishes and C knows nothing of the matter until after the testator's death, A is bound, but C is not bound: *Tee* v. *Ferris* [65]; the reason stated being, that to hold otherwise would be to enable one beneficiary to deprive the rest of their benefits by setting up a secret trust. If, however, the gift were to A and C as joint tenants, the authorities have established a distinction between those cases in which the will is made on the faith of an antecedent promise by A and those in which the will is left unrevoked on the faith of a subsequent promise. In the former case the trust binds both A and C: *Russell* v. *Jackson* [66]; *Jones* v. *Badley*,[67] the reason stated being that no person can claim an interest under a fraud committed by another; in the latter case A and not C is bound: *Burney* v. *Macdonald* [68] and *Moss* v. *Cooper*,[69] the reason stated being that the gift is not tainted with any fraud in procuring the execution of the will. Personally, I am unable to see any difference between a gift made on the faith of an antecedent promise and a gift left unrevoked on the faith of a subsequent promise to carry out the testator's wishes; but apparently a distinction has been made by the various judges who have had to consider the question. I am bound, therefore, to decide in accordance with these authorities. . . ."

However, Bryn Perrins in (1972) 88 L.Q.R. 225 examines these authorities to different effect, persuasively concluding that the only question to be asked is: was the gift to C induced by A's promise? If yes, C is bound; if no, he is not:

Bryn Perrins (1972) 88 L.Q.R. 225

"The reasons stated" by Farwell J. in *Re Stead* are at first sight contradictory. One consideration is that a person must not be allowed, by falsely setting up a secret trust, to deprive another of his benefits under the will. Apparently this is decisive if the parties are tenants in common but not if they are joint tenants. On the other hand one person must not profit by the fraud of another. Apparently this is decisive only if the parties are joint tenants and not if they are tenants in common. Yet again it is apparently only fraud in procuring the execution of a will that is relevant, and not fraud in inducing a testator not to revoke a will already made. All very,

---

[64] [1900] 1 Ch. 231, 241. The principles here discussed apply only to fully secret trusts. In the case of half-secret trusts, if the will permits communication to be made to one only of several trustees, a communication made before or at the time of the execution of the will to one only of the trustees binds all of them, the trust being a joint office: *Blackwell* v. *Blackwell* [1929] A.C. 318, *Re Spence* [1949] W.N. 237; *Ward* v. *Duncombe* [1893] A.C. 369.

[65] (1856) 2 K. & J. 357.

[66] (1852) 10 Hare 204.

[67] (1868) L.R. 3 Ch. 362.

[68] (1845) 15 Sim. 6.

[69] (1861) 1 J. & H. 352.

confusing, but add *Huguenin* v. *Baseley*[70] and the whole picture springs into focus and the confusion disappears. Returning to A and C, whether they are tenants in common or joint tenants, C is not bound *if his gift was not induced by the promise of A* because to hold otherwise would be to enable A to deprive C of his benefit by setting up a secret trust; but C is bound *if his gift was induced by the promise of A* because he cannot profit by the fraud of another; and if the trust was communicated to A after the will was made, then C takes free *if his gift was not induced by the promise of A* because if there is no inducement there is no fraud affecting C.

This, it is submitted, is what was decided by the cases cited in Farwell J.'s judgment.

In the light of the foregoing discussion of unusual secret trust situations it will be seen that the title of a beneficiary under a fully secret and a half-secret trust arises outside the will and is not testamentary.[71] To what extent such a trust is conditional and dependent upon the gift by will taking effect according to its terms *e.g.*, where a fully secret trustee witnesses the will, predeceases the testator or disclaims is not precisely clear. The position will only be clarified when the English courts make up their minds as to whether or not secret trusts are to be regarded traditionally as substantive trusts or progressively as remedial trusts not having to satisfy strict trust requirements.[72] However, it seems clear that section 9 of the Wills Act 1837 is irrelevant to the validity of secret trusts which depends solely on the existence of an obligation enforceable in equity in accordance with the principles already considered.

The next question is whether this equitable obligation arises under an express or constructive trust. If the former, then, in so far as it relates to land, it must be evidenced in writing to comply with section 53 (1) (*b*) of the Law of Property Act 1925[73]: if the latter, formal requirements are dispensed with, even as regards land, by virtue of section 53 (2) of the same Act.[74]

In the light of *Ottaway* v. *Norman*,[75] *Stickland* v. *Aldridge*[76] and *Bannister* v. *Bannister*,[77] where fully secret trusts of land were held valid despite the absence of writing, fully secret trusts are constructive trusts. In the light of *Re Baillie*,[78] where a half-secret trust of land was held invalid for the absence of writing it would appear that half-secret trusts are express trusts. Current opinion favours this view since the legatee is named as a trustee on the face of the will, having accepted the trusts declared to him by the testator. However, a case can be made out that since *Blackwell* v. *Blackwell*[79] equates half-secret trusts, within the limits of their validity, to

---

[70] (1807) 14 Ves. 273. This is authority for the principle, " No man may profit by the fraud of another." A widow was persuaded by Rev. Baseley, who managed her property, to settle some of it on him and his family. Later, she married Mr. Huguenin and sought to set aside the conveyance for undue influence. She succeeded, for Lord Eldon held that the Rev. Baseley's wife and children, though innocent, could not profit from Baseley's fraud and retain their vested interests.
[71] *e.g.*, *Re Gardner* [1923] 2 Ch. 230; *Re Young* [1951] Ch. 364.
[72] Waters, pp. 9–19, 56–62, *e.g.* the three " certainties."
[73] Replacing Statute of Frauds 1677, s. 7.
[74] Replacing Statute of Frauds 1677, s. 8.
[75] *Supra*, p. 397.
[76] (1804) 4 Ves.Jr. 516.
[77] *Supra*, p. 65.
[78] (1866) 2 T.L.R. 660.
[79] *Supra*, p. 406.

fully secret trusts, then, within those limits, the half-secret trust should likewise be constructive.[80]

On the other hand, it would appear that the real reason why fully and half-secret trusts are enforced despite the provisions of the Wills Act (those provisions being held irrelevant, the trusts arising outside the will) is in order to give effect to the wishes of the testator that would otherwise be ineffectual or to enforce an equitable obligation binding a man's conscience, affected by his acceptance of arrangements on the faith of which a will has been executed or left unrevoked.[81] However, the provisions of section 53 (1) (*b*) of the Law of Property Act 1925 are relevant to the formalities required for the evidencing of trusts of land. To obtain exemption from these formalities it is necesssary to prove a constructive trusteeship, which does not arise merely in order to give effect to trusts that otherwise would be ineffectual or merely to enforce equitable obligations binding a man's conscience, for otherwise the exemption would always apply, so making nonsense of the rule. It is necessary to prove that were it not for imposing a constructive trust a fraud would be committed by the alleged trustee obtaining a personal benefit. This can only occur in the case of fully secret trusts so they alone are constructive.

Section 6. Mutual Wills [82]

The term " mutual wills " is used to describe documents of a testamentary character made as the result of an agreement between husband and wife, or other persons, to create irrevocable interests in favour of ascertainable beneficiaries. The revocable nature of the wills under which the interests are created is fully recognised by the court of probate [83]; but, in certain circumstances, the court of equity will protect and enforce the interests created by the agreement despite the revocation of the will by one party after the death of the other without having revoked his will.

A typical case of mutual wills arises in the following circumstances: H(usband) and W(ife) agree to execute mutual wills leaving their respective properties to the survivor of them for life, with remainder to the same ultimate beneficiary (B). H dies, W makes a fresh will leaving her property away from B to her second husband (S).

In these circumstances, H's will is admitted to probate on his death and, under it, W gets a life interest and B an interest in remainder. On W's death, her second will is admitted to probate. Under it her property vests in her personal representatives upon trust, not for S, but to give effect to the terms of the agreement upon which the mutual wills were made, *i.e.*, upon trust for B.

---

[80] See the 5th ed. of this book, p. 286.

[81] *Blackwell* v. *Blackwell* [1929] A.C. 318, 334 *per* Viscount Sumner, at p. 342 *per* Lord Warrington. This basis is adhered to completely in the case of fully secret trusts but, illogically, only partially in the case of half-secret trusts since *Re Keen* makes it clear that half-secret trusts must be communicated not at any time in the testator's lifetime but only before or at the time of the execution of the will and the communication must conform to the terms of the will.

[82] Snell, pp. 182–184; Hanbury, pp. 228–233; Pettit, pp. 97–100; P. & M., pp. 144–149; Waters, pp. 62–65; Underhill, pp. 48–49; (1951) 14 M.L.R. 136 (J. D. B. Mitchell); (1970) 34 Conv.(N.S.) 230 (R. Burgess).

[83] *Re Heys* [1914] P. 192.

B's interest in W's property arises as soon as H dies. Hence it prevails over the interest of S therein by virtue of the maxim that "where the equities are equal the first in time prevails." Moreover, if B survives H but predeceases W his interest in W's property does not lapse but is payable to his personal representatives, and forms part of his estate: *Re Hagger, infra.* The better opinion is that B's interest arises irrespective of whether W disclaims her benefit under H's will.[84] It is the death [85] of H, no longer having the opportunity to revoke his own will, which renders the will of W irrevocable in equity, though, of course, it is always revocable at law.

The courts will not infer a trust merely because mutual wills are made in almost identical terms. There must be evidence of an agreement to create interests under the mutual wills which are intended to be irrevocable after the death of the first to die. Where there is no such evidence the fact that the survivor takes an absolute interest is a factor against the implication of an agreement: *Re Oldham.* Where, however, the evidence is clear, as, for example, where it is contained in recitals in the wills themselves, the fact that each testator gave the other an absolute interest with a substitutional gift in the event of the other's prior death does not prevent a trust from arising: *Re Green.*[86]

The principle is that the survivor becomes a trustee for the performance of the mutual agreement after the death of the first to die. Accordingly, if the agreement is too vague to be enforced, there will be no trust. Subject to this, however, the agreement can define the property, which is to be subject to the trust, in any way it pleases: *e.g.,* all the property of the survivor as it stands at the death of the first to die (or at the death of the survivor); or, more restrictively, it may bind some parts only of the respective properties of H and W, leaving the rest free from the trust and at the disposal of H and W, as the case may be.[87]

Before the death of the first to die the agreement is a contractual one made in consideration of the mutual promises of H and W for the benefit of B, who neither is a party to the contract nor supplies consideration.[88] Whether H would be in breach of the contract if he told W that he no longer intended to give effect to their arrangement, or if his will was automatically revoked by remarriage to someone else after divorcing W, or if he revoked his will without informing W but predeceased W, depends on the construction of the contract.[89] The contract might be construed as a contract not to depart from the terms of the arrangement without notice to the other party in the other party's lifetime. Even if H made a new will containing new arrangements without informing W, but predeceased W, it is difficult to see what W's measure of damages would be, especially since she would be free to rearrange her own will as she pleased.

---

[84] *Dufour* v. *Pereira* (1769) 1 Dick. 419, 421; *Stone* v. *Hoskins* [1905] P. 194, 197; *Re Hagger, infra,* p. 292; J. D. B. Mitchell, " Some Aspects of Mutual Wills " (1951) 14 M.L.R. 136, 138.

[85] *Quaere*: would incurable insanity on the part of H. have the same effect? Consider s. 103, Mental Health Act 1959.

[86] [1951] Ch. 148.

[87] See J. D. B. Mitchell, 14 M.L.R. 139 and R. Burgess (1972) 36 Conv.(N.S.) 113.

[88] *Dufour* v. *Pereira* (1769) 1 Dick. 419, 421; *Lord Walpole* v. *Lord Orford* (1797) 3 Ves. 402; *Gray* v. *Perpetual Trustee Co.* [1928] A.C. 391; *Birmingham* v. *Renfrew* (1937) 57 C.L.R. 666.

[89] *Cf. Dufour* v. *Pereira, supra* at 420; *Stone* v. *Hoskins* [1905] P. 194, 197.

If H died first, by his will carrying into effect the mutual arrangement, then, in order to protect B and to prevent W thwarting her obligations, a constructive trust is imposed since B is unable to bring an action for specific performance.[90] The terms of the trust, of course, depend upon the terms of the contract but since the trust is imposed by way of a remedy the trust can be an unusual sort of trust floating over W's assets during W's lifetime and crystallising on W's death: *Ottaway* v. *Norman, supra*; *Birmingham* v. *Renfrew, infra.*

Ottaway v. *Norman*, indeed, reveals how close the affinity is between mutual wills and secret trusts except that the arrangement giving rise to the subsequent imposition of a trust is, in the former case, contractual whilst, in the latter case it is voluntary, the testator, in essence, stating that he intends to give certain property by will to X, if X is prepared to deal with it in a certain way when he receives it, and the testator being under no obligation to leave the property to X. Both mutual wills and secret trusts exemplify the "long-established principle that if the owner of property makes a gift of it [by will or *inter vivos*] on the faith of a promise by the donee that he will deal with the property in a particular way, an obligation so to deal with it is placed upon the donee and can be enforced in the courts": *per* Romer J. in *Re Gardner* (*No.* 2).[91] The requirement for mutual wills sometimes expressed as the need for "an agreement not to revoke" the wills is more aptly expressed as the need for "acceptance of an obligation imposed by the other party" as the obligation may well allow the will of the survivor to be revoked so long as a new will is made giving effect to the agreed arrangements.[92] The acceptance of an obligation may be difficult to prove in husband and wife situations where there is less likely to be an intention to impose legal relationships, neither party making the gifts by will on the faith of a promise by the other to accept legal obligations, but instead, making the gifts without any strings attached, confidently assuming the other party will do as asked, *e.g., Gray* v. *Perpetual Trustee Co. Ltd.*[93]; *Re Oldham.*[94]

Re HAGGER, FREEMAN v. ARSCOTT

Chancery Division [1930] 2 Ch. 190; 99 L.J.Ch. 492; 143 L.T. 610

A husband and wife made a joint will in 1902 by which, after reciting that they had agreed to dispose of their property by that will and *that there was to be no alteration or revocation except by agreement*, they gave the whole of their estate at the death of the first spouse to die to their trustees to pay debts, expenses and legacies, and to pay the income to the survivor for life. By another clause they gave their property at Wandsworth on trust after the death of the survivor to sell the same, and to divide the proceeds in certain shares between nine beneficiaries, of whom Eleanor Palmer was one. By clause 8 of the

90 *Birmingham* v. *Renfrew* (1937) 57 C.L.R. 666.
91 [1923] 2 Ch. 230, 232.
92 *Cf. Re Oldham* [1925] Ch. 75 where Mrs. O after Mr. O's death had revoked her mutual will but made another in similar terms, when it was not suggested that there had been a breach of her agreement with Mr. O, the breach only allegedly occurring when she made yet another will but in different terms.
93 [1928] A.C. 391.   94 [1925] Ch. 75.

will they gave their residuary estate on trust after the death of the survivor for two other beneficiaries in equal shares.

The wife died in 1904, and the husband, who died in 1928 (and had since 1904 received the income of the whole estate), by his will made in 1921 gave " everything of which he was able to dispose " to his executors on trust for conversion, to pay debts and expenses, and to divide the residue between various persons, of whom some were not mentioned in the joint will. An originating summons was taken out to determine the effect of the two wills, probate having been granted to both.

Eleanor Palmer had died in 1923. On behalf of her personal representatives it was argued that the parties to the joint will had clearly intended the whole of their estate to be impressed with a trust on the first death, so that beneficiaries took under the joint will and not under the husband's will; hence the interest of Eleanor Palmer had not lapsed.

CLAUSON J.: " As a matter of construction it is clear that at the moment this document came into operation its effect was to confer a life interest on the survivor of the husband and wife and a vested interest in remainder, as to one-sixth of the Wandsworth property, on Eleanor Palmer.

" The wife died in 1904, and the joint will was proved as her will. The husband survived her, and during his lifetime Eleanor Palmer died. It has been argued that because of E. Palmer's death in the lifetime of the husband she took no interest in the Wandsworth property. It is admitted, however, that so far as that property could be shown to be the property of the wife, E. Palmer obtained a vested interest on the death of the wife, and there would be no lapse, but it was said that so far as the property could be shown to have belonged to the husband E. Palmer took no interest, because as regards his part of the property his document only became effective on his death, and that those administering it as the husband's will would have to look round to see who then took an interest in the property, and they would then find that E. Palmer's share had lapsed.

" It is perfectly clear that when the husband and wife made this joint will they contemplated that the property which they were pooling would all go to the same beneficiaries, whether in its inception it was the property of the husband or the property of the wife, and that if I fail to give effect to this, in so far as E. Palmer's share is concerned, I shall be departing from the intention of the parties. I am satisfied that the law does not compel me to depart from that intention, and I reach that conclusion on reading the judgment of Lord Camden in *Dufour* v. *Pereira*,[95] where he says: ' The instrument itself is the evidence of the agreement; and he, that dies first, does by his death carry the agreement on his part into execution. If the other then refuses, he is guilty of a fraud, can never unbind himself, and becomes a trustee of course.

---

[95] (1769) 1 Dick. 419, 421.

For no man shall deceive another to his prejudice. By engaging to do something that is in his power, he is made a trustee for the performance and transmits that trust to those that claim under him.'

" To my mind *Dufour* v. *Pereira* decides that where there is a joint will such as this on the death of the first testator the position as regards that part of the property which belong to the survivor is that the survivor will be treated in this court as holding the property on trust to apply it so as to carry out the effect of the joint will. As I read Lord Camden's judgment in *Dufour* v. *Pereira*, that would be so, even though the survivor did not signify his election to give effect to the will by taking benefits under it.[96] But in any case it is clear that Lord Camden has decided that if the survivor takes a benefit conferred on him by the joint will he will be treated as a trustee in this court, and he will not be allowed to do anything inconsistent with the provisions of the joint will. It is not necessary for me to consider the reasons on which Lord Camden based his judgment. The case must be accepted in this court as binding. Therefore I am bound to hold that from the death of the wife the husband held the property, according to the tenor of the will, subject to the trusts thereby imposed upon it, at all events if he took advantage of the provisions of the will. In my view he did take advantage of those provisions.

" The effect of the will was that the husband and wife agreed that the property should on the death of the first of them to die pass to trustees to hold on trusts inconsistent with the right of survivorship, and therefore the will effected a severance of the joint interest of the husband and wife. By the will they made a provision which was inconsistent with the survivor taking by survivorship. Therefore the property at the moment when, on the wife's death, it came within the ambit of the will ceased to be held by the two jointly, and the husband had no title to the wife's interest on her dying in his lifetime, save in so far as he took a life interest under the joint will. From the moment of the wife's death the Wandsworth property was held on trust for the husband for life with a vested interest in remainder as to one-sixth in E. Palmer. So far as the husband's interest in the property is concerned the will operated as a trust from the date of the wife's death. There is, accordingly, no lapse by reason of Eleanor Palmer's death in the husband's lifetime, but after the wife's death."

Held, therefore, that, being an agreement from which an intention could clearly be implied that a trust was to arise on the death of the first spouse to die, a trust of the Wandsworth property arose on the death of the wife in 1904, under which Eleanor Palmer took a vested interest in remainder. That interest having vested in possession on the death of the husband in 1928, it was now payable to Eleanor Palmer's personal representative.[97]

---

[96] See also *Stone* v. *Hoskins* [1905] P. 194, 197.
[97] See also *Walpole* v. *Orford* (1797) 3 Ves. 402; *Gray* v. *Perpetual Trustee Co.* [1928] A.C. 391.

Note

Certainty of subject matter of the mutual will or secret trust often gives rise to problems especially if the constructive trust is treated as a substantive trust and not as a remedy: what sort of interest does the survivor have in his own property and in the predeceased's property? A life interest with power to resort to capital or an absolute interest subject to some floating equitable obligation that crystallises on the survivor's death? *Ottaway* v. *Norman* [98] together with the following dicta of Dixon J. (as he then was) in *Birmingham* v. *Renfrew* [99] should be considered where the parties have not made their wishes clear:

DIXON J.: ". . . The purpose of an arrangement for corresponding wills must often be, as in this case, to enable the survivor during his life to deal as absolute owner with the property passing under the will of the party first dying. That is to say, the object of the transaction is to put the survivor in a position to enjoy for his own benefit the full ownership so that, for instance, he may convert it and expend the proceeds if he choose. But when he dies he is to bequeath what is left in the manner agreed upon. It is only by the special doctrines of equity that such a floating obligation, suspended, so to speak, during the lifetime of the survivor can descend upon the assets at his death and crystallize into a trust. No doubt gifts and settlements, *inter vivos*, if calculated to defeat the intention of the compact, could not be made by the survivor and his right of disposition, *inter vivos*, is, therefore, not unqualified. But, substantially, the purpose of the arrangement will often be to allow full enjoyment for the survivor's own benefit and advantage upon condition that at his death the residue shall pass as arranged."

PROBLEMS

1. Is a sound approach to gifts by will where secret trusts or mutual wills may be involved as follows:

(1) Appearance of (a) incorporation by reference (b) half-secret trust (c) fully secret trust (d) mutual wills?

(2) If (a) does the will refer to an ascertainable already existing document or does it attempt to incorporate a future document or an assortment of present and future documents?

(3) If (b) so that on the face of the will there really was an intent to create a binding obligation were the terms of the obligation (i) communicated before or after the will and, if before, were they (ii) communicated in accordance with the will (iii) to a person who accepted them and (iv) who does not take beneficially under the trust if the obligation was a trust and not a beneficial gift upon condition?

(4) If (c) so that there was an intention outside of the will to create a binding obligation were the terms of the obligation (i) communicated in the testator's lifetime (ii) to a person who accepted the obligation?

(5) If (d) so that the arrangements were communicated to each testator,

---

[98] *Supra*, p. 397 and see (1973) 36 M.L.R. 210.
[99] (1937) 57 C.L.R. 666, 689.

resulting in the alike wills, was there an acceptance that the survivor would be legally obliged to carry out the arrangements?

2. In 1968 Sag Gosht made his will as follows: "Whatever I die possessed of I give to my wife Bhuna." The will was witnessed by two of Sag's daughters, Pappadom and Chapathi. Shortly afterwards, Sag asked Bhuna if she would hold half the property she received under his will for their three daughters, Pappadom, Chapathi and Nan equally. Bhuna assented to this. In 1972 Nan ran away with a merchant seaman, Vindaloo. As a result Sag told Bhuna to keep Nan's share for herself. In 1974 Pappadom died, childless, and a week later Sag died after a long illness. How should his £15,000 estate be distributed? Would it make any difference if Bhuna disclaimed all benefits due to pass to her under the will and relied, instead, upon her rights under the intestacy rules?

3. H and W make wills in identical terms *mutatis mutandis* in pursuance of an agreement that they were each to leave their estates upon trust for sale for the survivor absolutely, the survivor being obliged to leave half of the estate he received to their nephews A and B equally. Each agreed not to withdraw from the arrangement without giving notice to the other. W died childless having left all her estate upon trust for sale for H absolutely.

H later married S and made a second will leaving half his property to A and B equally, one quarter to S absolutely and one quarter to S " upon trusts which have been communicated to her." In a sealed envelope given to S shortly before H made his second will there were directions that S was to hold the quarter share given to her as trustee on trust for X for life remainder to Y absolutely, whilst one month before his death H asked S to hold her absolute quarter share upon trust for Z and she agreed. H and S were involved in a bad car crash resulting in S predeceasing H by one day.

How should H's estate be distributed if the property received by H under W's will was worth £100,000 whilst the property passing under H's will was worth £60,000? Would it make any difference if 2 years after W's death and 7 years before his own death H had created a settlement of £40,000 on trust for X for life, remainder to Y absolutely? Would the position be any different if W's estate had been worth £30,000 and she had died intestate owing to her will failing to comply with the formalities required by the Wills Act 1837?

Section 7. Special Remedies of the Beneficiary against Recipients of the Trust Property: Claims in Personam and Claims in Rem [1]

I. Meaning of Claims in Personam and Claims in Rem

By a claim *in personam* is meant a claim enforceable against a defendant personally as distinct from a claim *in rem* enforceable against a particular fund or a particular piece of property in the hands or under the control of the defendant. In the former case the claim, if successful, will give rise

---

[1] The claim *in personam* against the trustee, as distinct from a recipient from the trustee, is considered in the chapter on Liability for Breach of Trust, *infra*, pp. 615 *et seq*. The claim *in rem* considered in this Section is available against the trustee as well as a recipient of the trust property from the trustee, subject to the differences discussed *infra*, pp. 431–433.

to a judgment imposing a personal liability on the defendant: in the latter the judgment will make available to the claimant a particular fund or piece of property in the hands of the defendant. It will not involve the defendant in any personal liability over and above that which is implicit in his being required to give up to the plaintiff either the entirety or a part of the fund which he has hitherto been claiming as his own. This usage of the terms *in personam* and *in rem* is distinct from the normal jurisprudential usage, according to which a right *in personam* is one which is available against a definite person or group of persons, and a right *in rem* is one available against the whole world generally.[2]

II. Claims in Personam

Until the decision of the Court of Appeal in *Re Diplock* [3] in 1948, and its affirmation by the House of Lords under the name of *Ministry of Health* v. *Simpson* [4] in 1951, it was generally assumed that where money belonging to A (the beneficial owner) was wrongfully and without A's authority paid by B (the trustee) to C, A's action to recover it would be an action in equity analogous to the common law action for money had and received,[5] and as such would be subject to the limitation that, if the mistake which induced B to part with the money was a mistake of law,[6] A's right of recovery would be lost *in limine*.[7] This assumption, however, is now proved to be wrong, at least in cases where B is a personal representative distributing the estate of a deceased person.

In *Re Diplock* the executors of a will distributed large sums to various charities in the belief that a direction in the will to apply the residuary estate " for such charitable institution or institutions or other charitable or benevolent object or objects " as they should in their absolute discretion select had created a valid charitable bequest. It was subsequently held by the House of Lords that this direction was void for uncertainty,[8] with the result that the money belonged in equity to the next-of-kin.

The next-of-kin brought an action against the executors in respect of the sums which had been distributed among the charities, and also sought to recover these sums direct from the charities themselves. The action against the executors was compromised with the approval of the court, and part of the money was ordered to be refunded by the executors to the next-of-kin. The subsequent history of the case is concerned with the claims of the next-of-kin to recover from the charities the sums received by them less the amounts received from the executors under the compromise. These claims fell under two heads: (a) claims *in personam* with which this section is concerned, and (b) claims *in rem* which will be discussed later.

---

[2] See Salmond, *Jurisprudence*, 12th ed., pp. 235–238. For an interesting case where it is not clear how the claims were formulated, see *G. L. Baker Ltd.* v. *Medway Building & Supplies Ltd.* [1958] 1 W.L.R. 1216; (1959) 22 M.L.R. 87 (P. H. Pettit).
[3] [1948] Ch. 465.
[4] [1951] A.C. 251.
[5] *Re Robinson* [1911] 1 Ch. 502; *Re Mason* [1928] Ch. 385; [1929] 1 Ch. 1; *Re Blake* [1932] 1 Ch. 54.
[6] See *Holt* v. *Markham* [1923] 1 K.B. 504; *Re Diplock* [1948] Ch. 465; *cf. Re Ainsworth* [1915] 2 Ch. 96; *Re Musgrave* [1916] 2 Ch. 417.
[7] *Re Diplock* [1947] Ch. 716 (Wynn-Parry J.).
[8] *Chichester Diocesan Fund* v. *Simpson* [1944] A.C. 341; *supra*, p. 270.

Wynn-Parry J. held [9] that the mistake which gave rise to the mis-
payment was a mistake of law and, applying the analogy of the common
law action for money had and received, came to the conclusion that the
claims *in personam* failed in their entirety. Before the Court of Appeal
two arguments were put forward in support of these claims: first, that,
by the terms of the letters which accompanied the payments made
by the executors, the charities were given notice of the invalidity of the
trusts declared of the residuary estate, or, at least, were put on inquiry as
regards their validity, so that, being pure volunteers, they were subjected
to a constructive trust of the money they received, in favour of the next-of-
kin; and, secondly, quite apart from any question of notice, that the
charities had received money which in equity belonged to the next-of-kin,
who, in the circumstances, could maintain a direct claim, recognised and
established by the court of equity, for its recovery.

The Court of Appeal rejected the first of the next-of-kin's arguments.
"In our judgment," said Lord Greene,[10] "persons in the position of the
respondents, themselves unversed in the law, are entitled in such circumstances as existed in the present case to assume that the executors are
properly administering their estate, and if, as is admitted in this case,
they took the money bona fide believing themselves to be entitled to it,
they should not have imposed on them the heavy obligations of trusteeship.
We do not think it necessary or desirable to attempt an exhaustive formulation of the law applicable as regards notice in case of payments to
legatees, save to say that every case of this kind will depend on its own
facts and that the principles applicable to such cases are not the same as
the principles in regard to notice of defects in title applicable to transfer
of land, where regular machinery has long since been established for
inquiry and investigation."

The next-of-kin's second argument was upheld. The Court of Appeal
rejected the analogy to the common law action for money had and
received. They pointed out that the common law action had a lineage
altogether independent of and in no sense derived from equity,[11] and
demonstrated the differences between common law and equity in this
respect. In distributing the residuary estate among the wrong persons it
was the executors who had made the mistake and not the next-of-kin,[12]
and since the executors were not acting as agents of the next-of-kin their

---

9 [1947] Ch. 716.
10 [1948] Ch. 465, 478–479.
11 The Court of Appeal considered that the common law action was based on an
implied promise. See, generally, Jackson, *History of Quasi-Contract*; Stoljar, *Law
of Quasi-Contracts*.
12 "It is difficult to see what relevance this distinction [*i.e.*, between mistake of fact
and of law] can have where a legatee does not plead his own mistake or his own
ignorance, but, having exhausted his remedy against the executor who has made
the wrongful payment, seeks to recover money from him who has been wrongfully
paid. To such a suit the executor was not a necessary party and there was no
means by which the plaintiff could find out whether his mistake was of law or of
fact or even whether his wrongful act was mistaken or deliberate. He could guess
and ask the court to guess, but he could prove nothing. I reject, therefore, the
suggestion that the equitable remedy in such circumstances was thus restricted [*i.e.*,
to cases where the mistake was one of fact]": *per* Lord Simonds L.C. [1951] A.C.
251, 270.

acts were incapable of ratification.[13] The analogy being discarded, there
was no reason why the action of the next-of-kin should fail on the ground
of mistake of law.

It was then contended that " the jurisdiction of equity " to enforce its
personal remedies " was subject to the limiting principle that equity acts
on the conscience of the defendant which is affected where (and only
where) the defendant has the necessary knowledge or the necessary
knowledge can be imputed to him." [14] The court, however, came to the
conclusion that in a case such as this the conscience of the defendants
would be affected simply on the ground of their having received more,
at the time, than they were entitled to.[15]

At this point it must be emphasised that the position of the bona fide
purchaser for value without notice remains inviolable. The difficulty centres
around the volunteer. If he takes with notice, then the full rigour of the
maxim that " Equity acts *in personam* " will avail against him. If he takes
more than he is entitled to without notice, then his conscience is affected,
presumably on the footing that he is a volunteer falling outside the benefit
of the cardinal principle of equity that equitable rights bind everyone except
a bona fide purchaser for value without notice. However, why should equity
enforce the personal claim against him irrespective of his conduct in the
intervening period, and of the possibility that he may have altered his
position in reliance upon the validity of the payment to him—and this not
necessarily *to his own personal benefit* (as, for example, by spending the
money on an investment which has become a total loss)? Should not the
plaintiff be left to his remedy *in rem*? Indeed, as we shall see later, as
the law stands this will entitle him to rank *pari passu* with the innocent
volunteer in relation to the amalgam acquired with his own and the volunteer's money. It is submitted that the innocent volunteer should as a general
rule be no worse off in respect of the claim *in personam* than he is in respect
of the claim *in rem*.[16] However, as we shall see later, the claim *in rem*
ignores the cardinal principle that a plaintiff's equitable rights prevail over
volunteers as they are not bona fide purchasers for value without notice.

The above considerations suggest that one must regard the right of a creditor, an unpaid legatee or the next-of-kin to obtain personal judgment against
a wrongly paid or overpaid legatee for a refund as exceptional and as
enforceable on broader grounds than those normally applied in a court of
equity. Indeed the Court of Appeal did not attempt to enlarge the scope
of this right beyond the situation which they were considering. And when
the case reached the House of Lords, their lordships were at pains to
emphasise that they were dealing with an equitable claim in respect of the

---

13 In *United Australia Ltd.* v. *Barclays Bank Ltd.* [1941] A.C. 1, 29, Lord Atkin considered that the common law action existed irrespective of the fiction of implied
promise and of that of agency and ratification. See also Lord Denning, " The
Recovery of Money " (1949) 65 L.Q.R. 35, 41; Goff & Jones, p. 46.

14 [1948] Ch. 465, 482.

15 *Ibid.* 488.

16 See Lord Denning, " The Recovery of Money " (1949) 65 L.Q.R. 37, 49–50; Dennis
Lloyd (1948) 26 Can.B.R. 1356, 1366–1367; Gareth Jones, " Change of Circum-
stances in Quasi-Contract " (1957) 73 L.Q.R. 48; but see P. F. P. Higgins, " *Re
Diplock*—A Reappraisal," 6 Western Australian Law Review 428–448, especially 446.
See also Goff & Jones, Chaps. 2, 30, 42.

administration of estates, and it did not follow that the relevant rules were the same as those applicable between one *cestui que trust* and another.[17]

In coming to the conclusion that the next-of-kin were entitled to succeed in regard to the claims *in personam,* the Court of Appeal relied upon a number of early authorities which they submitted to an elaborate and exhaustive analysis. The earliest was *Nelthrop* v. *Hill,*[18] in 1669, which, together with *Grove* v. *Banson*[19] and *Chamberlain* v. *Chamberlain,*[20] was cited in *Noel* v. *Robinson,*[21] a decision of Lord Nottingham, now regarded as the foundation of the equitable jurisdiction in this matter. In that case it was held that creditors and underpaid legatees could compel wrongly and overpaid legatees to refund where there was a deficiency of assets. Later authorities[22] limited this right to cases in which there was an original deficiency of assets, but "where the deficiency arose from later waste by the executor, then, on the principle of *vigilantibus non dormientibus succurrit lex,* there would be no right to a refund."[23] And *Orr* v. *Kaines*[24] established that the primary remedy was against the executor, "but if the executor is insolvent, then because 'there is no other way' the unpaid or underpaid legatee can directly compel the fully paid legatee to refund."[25]

The Court of Appeal found that these early authorities did not justify the conclusion that the intervention of equity was limited to cases in which knowledge could be imputed to the defendant that his title to the money paid to him might be defeasible in favour of other interested persons. "The test as regards conscience seems rather to be whether at the time when the payment was made the legatee received anything more than, at the time, he was properly entitled to receive."[26] Further, there was no limitation of the right of action to cases in which the estate was being administered by the court, nor was there any qualification in respect of the type of mistake which induced the executor to part with the money in favour of the overpaid legatees. "As regards the latter, it is no doubt true that so far as can be gathered from the reports, the over-payments that had been made arose from nothing more than a miscalculation of the assets available and might, therefore, fairly be regarded as due to mistakes of fact, but so far from suggesting that the nature of the mistake made was a relevant consideration, the authorities do not for the most part even indicate how it came about that the payments were made in fact."[27]

Later cases did nothing to qualify the results of these early authorities. In fact, *David* v. *Frowd*[28] was, if anything, an extension, for it equated the rights of the next-of-kin to those of the creditor and the legatee. It was regarded by the House of Lords as settling the practice of the Court

---

17 [1951] A.C. 251, especially 266, 273–274. But see *G. L. Baker Ltd.* v. *Medway Building & Supplies Ltd.* [1958] 1 W.L.R. 1216, discussed in *Eddis* v. *Chichester Constable* [1969] 1 W.L.R. 385, 389.
18 (1669) 1 Cas. in Ch. 135.
19 (1669) 1 Cas. in Ch. 148.
20 (1675) 1 Cas. in Ch. 256.
21 (1682) 1 Vern. 90.
22 *Newman* v. *Barton* (1690) 2 Vern. 205; *Anon* (1718) 1 P.Wms. 495; *Walcott* v. *Hall* (1788) 2 Bro.C.C. 305; *Fenwick* v. *Clarke* (1862) 4 De G.F. & J. 240.
23 [1948] Ch. 465, 487.
24 (1750) 2 Ves.Sen. 194.
25 [1948] Ch. 465, 487.
26 *Ibid.* 488.
27 *Ibid.* 489.						28 (1833) 1 My. & K. 200.

of Chancery, whatever may have been the position in the spiritual courts.[29] Moreover, though some of the later cases contained observations indicating an analogy between the claim in equity and the action at law for money had and received, these observations were found on analysis to be *obiter*. In *Re Rivers*[30] there was an exercise of " the equitable jurisdiction to order an overpaid beneficiary to refund "[31] notwithstanding that " there was no question of making an adjustment in due course of administration "[32]; in *Hilliard* v. *Fulford*[33] there was no question of a refund and so the consideration of the *Noel* v. *Robinson*[34] line of decisions did not arise; in *Re Hatch*[35] the observation of Sargant J. that the mistake must be one of fact was made without considering *Noel* v. *Robinson* and so could not be relied upon to militate against the next-of-kin's claim; and similar objections applied to *Re Mason*[36] and *Re Blake*.[37]

In the result, therefore, it was held:

(1) the claim in equity was available alike to an unpaid or underpaid creditor, legatee or next-of-kin;

(2) the claim of the next-of-kin was not defeated merely

(a) in the absence of administration by the court, or

(b) because the mistake under which the original payment was made was one of law rather than fact, or

(c) because the original recipient had no title at all and was a stranger to the estate, and in consequence would have to be dispossessed altogether in favour of the next-of-kin;

(3) the next-of-kin must first exhaust their remedy against the personal representatives, and in the subsequent action against the recipients they must give credit for the amount so received [38, 39];

(4) the claim lay for principal only and not for interest.[40]

(5) the appropriate limitation period was that under section 20 of the

---

[29] [1951] A.C. 251.
[30] [1920] 1 Ch. 320.
[31] [1948] Ch. 465, 496.
[32] *Ibid.* 497.
[33] (1876) 4 Ch.D. 389.
[34] (1682) 1 Vern. 90.
[35] [1919] 1 Ch. 351.
[36] [1929] 1 Ch. 1.
[37] [1932] 1 Ch. 54.
[38] This can be very hard on the personal representatives especially since as the law stands they cannot recover from the recipient money paid under a mistake of law (as opposed to fact): Goff & Jones, p. 87. To protect themselves they should take full advantage of the Trustee Act 1925, s. 27, and, if need be, act solely upon a court order, *e.g.*, a Benjamin order as in *Re Benjamin* [1902] 1 Ch. 723 (liberty to distribute estate on footing that B, of whom no one has heard for several years, predeceased testator).
[39] The court indicated that " prima facie and subject to discussion " the next-of-kin's proprietary claim as well as their personal claim against the recipients should be reduced and the sum recovered from the personal representatives divided rateably among the charities: [1948] Ch. 556. Basic principle suggests that the proprietary claim should not be reduced and the claimants should be allowed to recover their property, the personal representatives being subrogated to the claimants' rights to the extent that recovery of the property on top of the moneys recovered from the personal representatives would make a profit for the claimants. The court's solution benefits the recipients at the expense of the luckless personal representatives. A legislative solution could be to require the claimants to exhaust all their other remedies before suing the personal representatives: New Zealand Administration Act 1952, s. 30 B(5), Western Australia Trustee Act 1962, s. 65 (7).
[40] *Gittins* v. *Steele* (1818) 1 Swan. 199.

Limitation Act 1939, *i.e.*, 12 years " from the date when the right to receive the share or interest accrued " (normally one year from death).

III. CLAIMS IN REM

The particular advantages of claims *in rem* all follow from the fact that the property in question has throughout belonged to the plaintiff. Thus the defendant's bankruptcy has no effect on the claim. If the property has increased in value then this accrues to the plaintiff's advantage. If the plaintiff wishes to have the property preserved intact pending the hearing of his claim he may obtain an order for this under R.S.C., Ord. 50, r. 3. If the plaintiff's money was used with the defendant's money so as to earn any interest or dividends the plaintiff is entitled to a proportionate share of the interest or dividends.[41]

Differences between common law and equity

At common law the true owner of a chattel or money can follow it into the hands of a person who changes its form: " the product of or substitute for the original thing still follows the nature of the thing itself, as long as it can be ascertained to be such and the right only ceases when the means of ascertainment fail, which is the case when the subject is turned into money, and mixed and confounded in a general mass of the same description." [42] Thus, if D, having been lent P's car, sells it for £1,000 depositing the proceeds in a bank account freshly opened for the purpose and transferring £300 of these proceeds into his mistress's bank account freshly opened for the purpose, then P can follow the car's proceeds into the two bank accounts.[43] Money does not lose its identity at common law merely because it is paid into a bank account [44]: it only loses its identity when mixed with other moneys.[45] The common law right is enforced by a personal action for money had and received or for conversion and entitles the plaintiff to recover earmarked moneys or goods given to the defendant to sell for the plaintiff in priority to the defendant's general creditors if bankruptcy is involved.[46] Little is now heard of the common law right owing to its failure to deal with the mixing of moneys and the broad scope of the equitable right to trace.

In equity a plaintiff must base his claim on the existence of an equitable right to property and must show a fiduciary relationship between himself and the defendant or himself and a person who transferred the property to the defendant. The right of the beneficiaries to trace appears to depend

---

41 *Re Diplock* [1948] Ch. 465, 517, 557.
42 *Taylor* v. *Plumer* (1815) 3 M. & S. 562, 575 *per* Lord Ellenborough.
43 Assuming no other moneys are mixed with the £700 or £300.
44 *Banque Belge* v. *Hambrouck* [1921] 1 K.B. 321; *Transvaal & Delagoa Bay Investment Co. Ltd.* v. *Atkinson* [1944] 1 All E.R. 579, 583.
45 *Re Diplock* [1948] Ch. 465; *Sinclair* v. *Brougham* [1914] A.C. 398. But see M. Scott (1966) 7 Western Australia L.R. 463; F. O. B. Babafemi (1971) 34 M.L.R. 12; Stoljar's *Law of Quasi-Contract*, pp. 114–115.
46 *Scott* v. *Surman* (1742) Willes 400, 405; *Williams on Bankruptcy*, pp. 300–301. The right exists independently of any fiction of agency and rectification: Goff & Jones, p. 46; Denning (1949) 65 L.Q.R. 37, 41; *Taylor* v. *Plumer* (1815) 3 M. & S. 562, 567, 574. *Cf. Sinclair* v. *Brougham* [1914] A.C. 348, 441; *Re Diplock* [1948] Ch. 465, 518.

upon their ratification of the fiduciary's unauthorised dealings. Unlike the position at common law, there can be no doubt that equity regards " a composite fund as an amalgam constituted by the mixture of two or more funds, each of which ... " is " capable, in proper circumstances, of being resolved into its component parts." [47] The remedy in equity is *in rem*: it is not available at all against the bona fide purchaser for value without notice: it is available to a limited extent against the innocent volunteer.[48] It depends upon the continued existence of the *res* or its product.

The scope of the equitable remedy in rem

(1) Whenever a trustee, or a person who stands in a fiduciary relationship to the beneficiary, mixes trust money with his own, the beneficiary is entitled to a declaration of charge on the amalgam of which the trust money forms a component part.[49] The fiduciary relationship may be that of solicitor and client, bailor and bailee, principal and agent,[50] and it may arise from the receipt of trust property with knowledge, either actual or constructive, that it is trust property.[51] Where the amalgam has depreciated in value the beneficiary is entitled to be completely reimbursed in priority to the trustee or other fiduciary. Where the amalgam has appreciated in value the beneficiary is entitled to a share in it proportionate to his share in the amalgam when first formed.[52]

(2) It is not only a beneficiary who can follow trust funds, for in certain circumstances a trustee may do so. If X and Y are trustees, and Y deals improperly with trust funds, then X, even if he concurred in the breach of trust, may follow the trust funds.[53]

(3) There is, of course, no following of trust property into the hands of the bona fide purchaser for value without notice.[54]

---

[47] [1948] Ch. 465, 520.
[48] *Infra*, pp. 432–433.
[49] *Re Hallett's Estate* (1880) 13 Ch.D. 696.
[50] The agent must be a fiduciary agent: *Kirkham* v. *Peel* (1880) 43 L.T. 171, 172 *per* Jessel MR. limiting his judgment in *Re Hallett's Estate, supra.* Such an agent seems to be under a duty to keep his own money separate from his principal's money: Goff & Jones, p. 41; Sealy [1962] C.L.J. 69.
[51] The fiduciary obligation was the means historically of conferring jurisdiction upon the Chancery Courts but it has outlived its usefulness since the Judicature Acts 1873–1875. It is anomalous that tracing is not available where P's money is stolen by a stranger Q but is available if Q had been P's fiduciary agent who had stolen money entrusted to him by P. The tracing rationale is that it would be unjust if Q were bankrupt to allow Q's general creditors to benefit fortuitously at P's expense—this applies with equal force whatever the relationship between P and Q. The removal of the fiduciary relationship requirement would also save the courts from performing contortions in order to find some sort of fiduciary relationship, *e.g., Sinclair* v. *Brougham* [1914] A.C. 398; [1938] 6 C.L.J. 305 (Lord Wright). See Goff & Jones, pp. 41–43; Waters' *Constructive Trust*, pp. 67–72; Hanbury, pp. 423–424; F. O. B. Babafemi (1971) 34 M.L.R. 12; Maudsley (1959) 75 L.Q.R. 234. The American courts do not require a fiduciary relationship but only unjust enrichment.
[52] *Re Tilley's W.T.* [1967] Ch. 1179, *infra*; *Scott* v. *Scott* (1963) 109 C.L.R. 649. Indeed, it is arguable that the beneficiary should take the whole increase, preventing the trustee recovering more than the trustee's own moneys, for otherwise the trustee might be profiting from his fiduciary position enabling him to put the trust moneys with his own to take advantage of some opportunity that he would otherwise have lost.
[53] See *Price* v. *Blakemore* (1843) 6 Beav. 507; *Carson* v. *Sloane* (1884) 13 L.R.Ir. 139.
[54] *Thorndike* v. *Hunt* (1859) 3 De G. & J. 563; *Taylor* v. *Blakelock* (1886) 32 Ch.D. 560. Notice, of course, covers constructive notice.

(4) There is a limited right to follow trust property into the hands of a volunteer *who takes without notice*. The limitation is imposed because in this case the equities (*i.e.*, of the beneficiary and the volunteer) are said to be equal. Accordingly, where the amalgam has depreciated in value the claims of both beneficiary and volunteer will abate in proportion to the amounts of their contributions.[55] Correspondingly, any appreciation in value should be enjoyed rateably.[56] The attitude of equity may be thus summarised: " Just as a volunteer is not allowed by equity in the case, *e.g.*, of a conveyance of the legal estate of land to set up his legal title adversely to the claim of a person having an equitable interest in the land, so in the case of a mixed fund of money the volunteer must give such recognition as equity considers him in conscience (as a volunteer) bound to give to the interest of the equitable owner of the money which has been mixed with the volunteer's own. But this burden on the conscience of the volunteer is not such as to compel him to treat the claim of the equitable owner as paramount. That would be to treat the volunteer as strictly as if he himself stood in a fiduciary relationship to the equitable owner, which *ex hypothesi* he does not. The volunteer is under no greater duty of conscience to recognise the interest of the equitable owner than that which lies on a person having an equitable interest in one of two trust funds of ' money ' which have become mixed towards the equitable owner of the other. Such a person is not in conscience bound to give precedence to the equitable owner of the other of the two funds." [57]

Both *Sinclair* v. *Brougham* [58] and *Re Diplock* [59] come under this head. The contest in *Sinclair* v. *Brougham* was between shareholders and depositors in respect of a miscellaneous mass of assets distributable by the liquidator in the winding up of a building society. The deposits had been made and the assets used in connection with a banking business carried on in the name of the society, in excess of its powers. The Court of Appeal in *Re Diplock* [59] subjected the facts of *Sinclair* v. *Brougham* to an elaborate analysis. They pointed out that " if the directors had paid the money of a depositor into their own banking account, he would have had an action against them exactly similar to the action in *Hallett's* case,[60] and it would

---

[55] *Quaere* whether this puts the innocent volunteer in too favourable a position in the light of the cardinal principle of equity that equitable rights prevail except against a bona fide *purchaser for value* without notice. Scott (1949) 62 H.L.R. 1002, 1113; Goff & Jones, pp. 52–53; Babafemi (1971) 34 M.L.R. 12.

[56] *Re Diplock* [1948] Ch. 539; Goff & Jones, p. 52; *cf. Maudsley* (1959) 75 L.Q.R. 234, 251–252. If the cardinal principle of equity is applied subject to the defence of change of position (see *infra*, p. 436) so that the beneficiary prevails in the case of depreciation, then in the case of appreciation there is much to be said for the American solution giving the volunteer, whose initiative and industry has led to the fund increasing in value, the option of either paying the beneficiary's money with interest or letting the beneficiary have a proportionate share in the fund.

[57] [1948] Ch. 465, 524.

[58] [1914] A.C. 398.

[59] [1948] Ch. 465; the Court of Appeal made an exhaustive analysis of the scope of the claim *in rem*, although they had already held the wrongly paid recipients to be fully liable to refund under the claim *in personam*. One of their reasons for doing so was that if the House of Lords reversed them on the claim *in personam* it might like to have their views on the claim *in rem*. In fact the House of Lords upheld the Court of Appeal on the claim *in personam*, thinking its reasoning and conclusion to be unimpeachable, and it accordingly became unnecessary for their Lordships to discuss the claim *in rem*.

[60] (1880) 13 Ch.D. 696, *infra*, pp. 433–434, 441–443.

have been correctly said that the directors could not be heard to set up a title of their own to the money standing in the account adverse to the claim of the depositor. But nothing of the sort could be said if the directors paid the money into the account of the society at its bankers. Neither the conscience of the society nor of its liquidator (if it went into liquidation) could ever come into the picture on the basis of a fiduciary relationship, since the only parties to that relationship were the directors and the depositors. The society could not have been a party to it, since it had no power to accept the depositor's money. If, therefore, in such a case the depositor could claim a charge on the society's account with its bankers, the claim must have been based on some wider principle." [61] The court found this principle to be " that equity may operate on the conscience not merely of those who acquire a legal title in breach of some trust, express or constructive, or of some other fiduciary obligation, but of volunteers, provided that as a result of what has gone before, some equitable proprietary interest has been created and attaches to the property in the hands of the volunteer " [62] and subject to the limitation that neither party is entitled to priority over the other. " It would be inequitable for the volunteer to claim priority for the reason that he is a volunteer: it would be equally inequitable for the true owner of the money to claim priority over the volunteer, for the volunteer is innocent and cannot be said to act unconscionably if he claims equal treatment for himself. The mutual recognition of one another's rights is what equity insists on as a condition of giving relief." [63]

Re Diplock takes *Sinclair* v. *Brougham* a stage further, for in the latter case the depositors' money had been mixed by the directors who stood in a fiduciary position towards them, but in *Re Diplock* the mixing was done by the charities themselves, who, it was agreed, were innocent volunteers and owed no fiduciary duties to the next-of-kin. The Court of Appeal, however, while agreeing that a fiduciary relationship was necessary at some stage in order to bring into being " an equitable right of property," decided that once this had happened the existence of the fiduciary relationship was not necessary to support the right to "trace." "In our view there can be no difference in principle between a case where the mixing has been done by the volunteer, and a case where the mixing has been done previously by the fiduciary agent." [64]

The special position of current banking accounts

In *Re Hallett's Estate, infra,* the Court of Appeal by a majority held— reversing Fry J. and notwithstanding the authority of *Pennell* v. *Deffell* [65]— that where a trustee *mixes trust moneys with his own moneys,* as between

---

[61] [1948] Ch. 465, 530.

[62] *Ibid.* *Quaere* whether this is too restricted a view as suggested *supra,* p. 431. R. H. Maudsley, *loc. cit.,* suggests that the remedy should be available (a) where the plaintiff is legal and beneficial owner as well as where he is equitable owner (at pp. 241–243); (b) even where the plaintiff has no proprietary interest but only a quasi-contractual or equitable right to claim (at pp. 243–245). But he concedes that *Lister* v. *Stubbs* (1890) 45 Ch.D. 1 (C.A.), *supra,* p. 364 is, to some extent, an obstacle in the way of (b).

[63] [1948] Ch. 465, 539.

[64] [1948] Ch. 465, 534.

[65] (1853) 4 De G.M. & G. 372.

him and his beneficiary, the rule in *Clayton's* case [66] does *not* apply. In *Clayton's* case it was held that with reference to a *current account* there is a presumption that withdrawals are offset against payments in *in order of date*. "Presumably," said Grant M.R., "it is the sum first paid in that is first drawn out." If *Clayton's* case applied as between a trustee and his beneficiary where he mixes trust moneys with his own, the presumption might operate to the prejudice of his beneficiary by appropriating withdrawals for his own purposes to earlier payments in of trust moneys.[67] X, a trustee or a person in a fiduciary character, opens an account into which he pays in £10 of trust moneys, then £30 of his own, then £50 of trust moneys, then £20 of his own, and then withdraws £50 for private purposes. X, who has no other property, is indebted to a creditor to the extent of £20. If *Clayton's* case applied, there would be a presumption that the £50 withdrawn offset against earlier payments in; so that the first two payments in, plus £10 of the third payment in, would be exhausted, with the result that the beneficiary could only put his finger on £40 as trust money. But, by virtue of the decision in *Re Hallett's Estate, infra,* X is considered to have exhausted first of all his own moneys, which would then leave the beneficiary the whole trust fund of £60, and the trustee's creditor nothing. The creditor has been brought into this example because *Clayton's* case is logically of practical importance only if the trustee is insolvent, for neither creditor nor beneficiary would be worried about the order of appropriating withdrawals to a current account if the trustee had sufficent other property with which to satisfy his liabilities.[68] However, if it suits the beneficiary better (as where nothing is left in the current account but there is a valuable asset purchased with the first payment out of the mixed funds) he may claim that the first payment was of trust moneys so that the asset purchased belongs to the trust.[69]

The principle of *Re Hallett's Estate* is based on the principle of attributing an honest intention to the trustee wherever such an intention is attributable, or that *allegans suam turpitudinem non est audiendus*. But there is no principle which allows the beneficiary to claim that subsequent payments in of private moneys are presumed to replace earlier withdrawals in breach of trust [70]: X opens an account into which he pays in £20 of trust moneys on Monday, £30 of his own on Tuesday, £40 of trust moneys on Wednesday, and then withdraws £35 on Thursday for private purposes. As the matter stands, he is considered to have exhausted his own £30 first of all; but since there is now only £55 to the credit of the account, necessarily he has withdrawn £5 in breach of trust. If, then, on Friday he pays in £5 of his own, there is no presumption that that subsequent payment in of £5 of private moneys replaces the earlier withdrawal in breach of trust.

The question now arises whether the rule in *Clayton's* case applies *as between beneficiaries* of the same trustee under different trusts. X is trustee

---

[66] (1816) 1 Mer. 572, 608; see also *Bodenham* v. *Purchas* (1817) 2 B. & Ald. 39, 45; *Merriman* v. *Ward* (1860) 1 J. & H. 371; and *Hooper* v. *Keay* (1875) 1 Q.B.D. 178.
[67] *Re Tilley's W.T.* [1967] Ch. 1179, *infra,* [1968] C.L.J. 28.
[68] See *Re Oatway* [1903] 2 Ch. 356, *infra,* p. 439; *Re Wreford* (1897) 13 T.L.R. 153.
[69] "It is not a presumption that a trustee's drawings from the mixed fund must necessarily be treated as drawings of the trustee's own money where the beneficiary's claim is against the property bought by such drawings": *Re Tilley's W. T.* [1967] 2 All E.R. 303, 308.
[70] *Roscoe* v. *Winder* [1915] 1 Ch. 62. It depends on X's real intention.

of £20 for A, and of £40 for B. He opens an account into which he pays in the £20 on Monday, and the £40 on Tuesday, and then withdraws £30 for his own purposes on Wednesday. As between A and B, does *Clayton's* case apply, *i.e.*, does the sum withdrawn exhaust A's £20 first of all, and ultimately leave B with £30, or can A claim to have a share with B in what remains?   In *Re Hallett's Eestate*, there were three, not merely two, conflicting claims: the trustee's creditor, his beneficiary under one trust, and his beneficiary under another trust. Fry J. held that the rights of *all* parties must be governed by *Clayton's* case: *i.e.*, both (a) as between the trustee and the beneficiaries as a whole on the one hand; and (b) as between the two sets of beneficiaries themselves on the other. The Court of Appeal (as has been mentioned) reversed the learned judge as to (a) by holding that *Clayton's* case did not apply as between the trustee and the beneficiaries. As to (b), it so happened that it was unnecessary for the Court of Appeal to decide it, because if the court held (as it did hold) that *Clayton's* case did not apply as between the trustee and the beneficiaries, there would be sufficient assets to follow to satisfy both sets of beneficiaries. But, besides Fry J.'s decision as to (b), there are also dicta of Cotton L.J. in *Hancock* v. *Smith* [71] and of North J. in *Re Stenning* [72] to the same effect, namely, that as between beneficiaries of the same trustee under different trusts, the rule in *Clayton's* case does apply. So, in the example quoted in this paragraph, A would receive (from the account) nothing, while B would get most of his fund.[73]   Exactly the same principle is applied when the claimants are, not two beneficiaries under different trusts, but one beneficiary and one volunteer,[74] whose moneys have been mixed in a current account; but if a volunteer who has mixed trust money with his own subsequently unmixes it, equity will pay regard to the fact, and treat the right of the beneficiary to trace as being preserved.[75]

The rule in *Clayton's* case can apply only where there is *one unbroken account*,[76] and will not be extended beyond the case of a banking account. So, if X mixes money of his own with that of Y in his banking account and subsequently purchases stock, part of which he then sells, the equitable way of dealing with these sales is to regard each sum of stock withdrawn from the mass as having been made up in proportion to the respective contributions.[77]   The presumption raised by the rule is rebuttable by an expressed intention to the contrary, or special circumstances from which

---

[71] (1889) 41 Ch.D. 456, 461.
[72] [1895] 2 Ch. 433.
[73] Why should the loss not be borne rateably?   In the words of Judge Learned Hand in *Re Walter J. Schmidt & Co.* (1923) 298 Fed. 314, 316, " There is no reason in law or justice why [the fiduciary's] depredations upon the funds should not be borne equally between them.   To throw all the loss upon one, through the mere chance of his being earlier in time, is irrational and arbitrary, and is equally a fiction as the rule in *Clayton's* case.   When the law attempts a fiction it is, or at least it should be, for some purpose of justice.   To adopt it here is to apportion a common misfortune through a test which has no relation whatever to the justice of the case."   D. A. McConville (1963) 79 L.Q.R. 388, 401–402; P. F. P. Higgins (1965) 6 Western Australia L.R. 428, Goff & Jones, p. 54, Z. Chaffee (1950) 36 Cornell L.Q. 176.
[74] *Re Diplock* [1948] Ch. 465.
[75] *Ibid.* 551–552, dealing with the claim against the National Institute for the Deaf; reversed on an amended statement of facts; see *ibid.* 559.
[76] See *The Mecca* [1897] A.C. 286; Lord Selborne in *Re Sherry* (1884) 25 Ch.D. 692, 702.
[77] [1948] Ch. 465, 554–555.

such an intention could be implied.[78] There is, furthermore, no room
for the application of the rule as between trustee and beneficiary unless
the trustee mixes trust moneys with his own: *Hancock* v. *Smith*.[79] In that
case the account showed trust moneys only, with the result that the property
belonged to the beneficiaries in its entirety.

Loss of right to trace

(1) If property has reached hands of bona fide purchaser for value.[80]
(2) If plaintiff acquiesced in wrongful mixing or distribution.[81]
(3) If property has been dissipated so that tracing is physically impossible,
    e.g., trust moneys spent on world cruise, a party, extinguishing an
    unsecured debt.[82]
(4) If it would be inequitable to allow the plaintiff to trace in certain
    types of circumstances.[83] Thus if an innocent volunteer spends
    money on altering or improving his land there can be no declaration
    of charge and consequently no tracing for the method of enforcing
    a charge is by sale which would force the volunteer to exchange
    his land and buildings for money: an inequitable possibility, parti-
    cularly if the alterations had not enhanced the value of the property.
    If the innocent volunteer had altered or improved his property with
    money borrowed for the purpose on the security of the property
    and subsequently repaid the loan with trust money the plaintiff
    beneficiary is no better off than in the previous case for the same
    reason. The position is the same if the innocent volunteer's pro-
    perty was purchased subject to a mortgage and the trust money is
    used to pay off the mortgage so creating an unencumbered title for
    otherwise the volunteer might have to submit to a sale of his interest.

This defence of " inequitability " is closely circumscribed as the English
courts [84] have so far refused to recognise the general defence of change of
position so well established in America, namely, that if an innocent volunteer
had bona fide undertaken expenditure which would not have been incurred
but for the mistaken payment and which was of such a character that it
would be inequitable to enforce the plaintiff's claim then the plaintiff's claim
will fail. The Restatement of Restitution [85] defines the defence as follows:

> " (1) The right of a person to restitution from another because of a
> benefit received is terminated or diminished if, after the receipt of the
> benefit, circumstances have so changed that it would be inequitable to
> require the other to make full restitution.

---

[78] See Baggallay L.J. in *Re Hallett's Estate* (1880) 13 Ch.D. 696, 783; *Re British Red Cross* [1914] 2 Ch. 419.
[79] (1889) 41 Ch.D. 456.
[80] *Re Diplock* [1948] Ch. 465, 539; *Taylor* v. *Blakelock* (1886) 32 Ch.D. 560.
[81] *Blake* v. *Gale* (1886) 32 Ch.D. 571.
[82] *Re Diplock* [1948] Ch. 465, 521, 549.
[83] *Ibid.* 546–550. The reasons given for the special treatment afforded innocent volunteers in these circumstances are difficult to justify: R. H. Maudsley (1959) 75
L.Q.R. 240, 248–249. It is especially difficult to see why the plaintiff should not
be subrogated to the position of secured creditors paid off with his money: Goff
& Jones, pp. 54–55, 377.
[84] Goff & Jones, Chap. 42; *Baylis* v. *Bishop of London* [1913] 1 Ch. 127; *Ministry
of Health* v. *Simpson* [1951] A.C. 251, 276; (1957) 73 L.Q.R. 48 (Gareth Jones).
[85] Para. 142; see also para. 69.

(2) Change of circumstances may be a defense or a partial defense if the conduct of the recipient was not tortious and he was no more at fault for his receipt, retention or dealing with the subject matter than was the claimant."

The mere spending of money is insufficient to establish the defence, *e.g.*, spending on ordinary living expenses, payment of previous debts. It has to be shown that a change of position arose *as a result of* the particular payment, *e.g.*, causing the recipient to indulge in exceptional, irretrievable and detrimental expenditure.

The advantage of the existence of such a defence is that it produces a more logical and just system of law. To protect innocent volunteers the courts have formulated the strange principle that as between innocent volunteers and plaintiff beneficiaries any reduction of a mixed fund is to be borne proportionately. This breaks the cardinal principle of equity, that equitable rights bind everyone except bona fide purchasers of a legal estate for value without notice, which would confer priority upon the plaintiff beneficiaries over the innocent volunteers. It would be simpler to give effect to this cardinal principle subject to the defence of change of position. Where the personal claim against the wrong recipients of a deceased's estate is concerned the plaintiff's claim already does have priority over the innocent volunteers in accordance with cardinal equitable principle. This meant that the charities in *Re Diplock* though having the narrow " equitable " defence available to the proprietary claim were fully liable in the personal action.[86] It would have been more satisfactory if a general defence of change of position had been available.

Indeed, it must be admitted that English law is in a rather primitive state compared with the sophisticated approach of American law.[87]

Re TILLEY'S WILL TRUSTS

Chancery Division [1967] Ch. 1179; [1967] 2 W.L.R. 1533; [1967] 2 All E.R. 303

Tilley's will appointed his widow executrix and gave her a life interest in his estate with remainder to his son Charles and daughter Mabel equally. Tilley died in 1932 and his widow died in 1959 leaving £94,00, she having had a successful career as a property dealer. It so happened that she had mixed £2,237 of trust moneys with her own moneys but at all material times she had substantial moneys of her own or substantial overdraft facilities. Mabel died in 1955.

The plaintiff as Mabel's administrator claimed to be entitled to

---

[86] Charging orders upon land may be obtained under Administration of Justice Act 1956, s. 35 and R.S.C.O. 50 to enforce judgment debts so that the charities' lands could thereby ultimately be sold if the debts were not speedily satisfied, unless the fact that the proprietary claim failed on the grounds that this could lead to an inequitable sale of the charities' lands could be adduced as " sufficient cause shown to the contrary " within R.S.C.O. 50 so as to persuade the court not to impose any charging orders.

[87] See Restatement of Restitution paras. 160–162, 202–215, 126; Restatement of Trusts, para. 199; (1955) 71 L.Q.R. 39 (A. W. Scott).

half of the profits made by the widow in respect of properties purchased originally for £2,237.

UNGOED-THOMAS J.: " The plaintiff claims that Mabel's estate should, in virtue of Mabel's half interest in the estate, subject to the widow's life interest, have half of the proportion of the profits of the purchases made by the widow to the extent to which the defendants, as her legal personal representatives, cannot show that those properties were purchased out of the widow's personal moneys. The defendants, on the other hand, say that the plaintiff is entitled only to a charge on the defendants' bank account for half the trust moneys paid into that bank account with interest, *i.e.*, half the sum of £2,237, which is shown to have been paid into that bank account, and the interest on that amount.

" I come first to the law. The plaintiff relied on the statement of the law in *Lewin on Trusts* (16th ed.), at p. 223 and some of the cases cited in support of it. That statement reads:

'Wherever the trust property is placed, if a trustee amalgamates it with his own, his beneficiary will be entitled to every portion of the blended property which the trustee cannot prove to be his own.'

Lupton v. *White, White* v. *Lupton* [88] is the leading case for this proposition. In that case the defendant, an accounting party, had mixed the plaintiff's lead ore of unascertainable amount with his own lead ore, and the reference to the case of *Panton* v. *Panton* [89] shows that the same principle applies where moneys are similarly mixed. The principle is thus stated [90]:

'... to apply the great principle, familiar both at law and in equity, that, if a man, having undertaken to keep the property of another distinct, mixes it with his own, the whole must both at law and in equity be taken to be the property of the other, until the former puts the subject under such circumstances, that it may be distinguished as satisfactorily, as it might have been before that unauthorised mixture upon his part.'

Subsequently, in referring to *Armory* v. *Delamirie*,[91] the case in which a jeweller gave a trifle for a diamond ring found by a poor boy, the reason for the principle appears. The Lord Chancellor said [92]:

'... the Lord Chief Justice directed the jury to find, that the stone was of the utmost value they could find; upon this principle, that it was the defendant's own fault, by his own dishonest act, that the jury could not find the real value.'

[88] (1808) 15 Ves. 432.   [89] Undated, cited 15 Ves. 435, 440.
[90] *Lupton* v. *White* (1808) 15 Ves. 437.
[91] (1722) 1 Stra. 505.
[92] *Per* Lord Eldon L.C. in *Lupton* v. *White* (1808) 15 Ves. 440.

In *Gray* v. *Haig, Haig* v. *Gray*[93] Sir John Romilly M.R. followed *Lupton* v. *White*. The principle was followed and restated thus by Sir John Stuart V.-C. in *Cook* v. *Addison*[94]:

> ' It is a well-established doctrine in this court, that if a trustee or agent mixes and confuses the property which he holds in a fiduciary character with his own property, so as that they cannot be separated with perfect accuracy, he is liable for the whole. This doctrine was explained by Lord Eldon L.C. in *Lupton* v. *White*.'

The words in that passage ' so as that they cannot be separated with perfect accuracy ' are an essential part of Sir John Stuart's proposition, and indeed of the principle of *Lupton* v. *White*. If a trustee mixes trust assets with his own, the onus is on the trustee to distinguish the separate assets and, to the extent that he fails to do so, they belong to the trust. The *Lupton* v. *White* line of cases does not appear to me to go further than this. So the proposition in Lewin, which I have read, is limited to cases where the amalgam of mixed assets is such that they cannot be sufficiently distinguished and treated separately; it is based on the lack of evidence to do so being attributable to the trustee's fault.

" The defendants relied on *Re Hallett's Estate, Knatchbull* v. *Hallett, Cotterill* v. *Hallett*,[95] with a view to establishing that the trustee must be presumed to have drawn out his own moneys from the bank account of mixed moneys in priority to trust moneys, with the result that property bought by such prior drawings must be the trustee's exclusive personal property. In that case the claim was against a bank balance of mixed fiduciary and personal funds, and it is in the context of such a claim that it was held that the person in a fiduciary character drawing out money from the bank account must be taken to have drawn out his own money in preference to the trust money, so that the claim of the beneficiaries prevailed against the balance of the account. *Re Oatway, Hertslet* v. *Oatway*[96] was the converse of this decision in *Re Hallett's Estate*.

" In that case the claim was not against the balance left in the bank of such mixed moneys but against the proceeds of sale of shares which the trustee had purchased with moneys which, as in *Re Hallett's Estate*,[97] he had drawn from the bank account; but, unlike the situation in *Re Hallett's Estate*, his later drawings had exhausted the account, so that it was useless to proceed against the account. It was held that the beneficiary was entitled to the proceeds of sale of the shares, which were more than their purchase price but less than the

---

[93] (1855) 20 Beav. 219.
[94] (1869) L.R. 7 Eq. 466, 470.
[95] (1880) 13 Ch.D. 696.
[96] [1903] 2 Ch. 356.
[97] (1880) 13 Ch.D. 696.

trust moneys paid into the account.   The law is reviewed and the
principles are stated by Joyce J.[98]   He says:

> ' Trust money may be followed into land or any other property
> in which it has been invested; and when a trustee has, in making
> any purchase or investment, applied trust money together with
> his own, the *cestuis que trust* are entitled to a charge on the pro-
> perty purchased for the amount of the trust money laid out in the
> purchase or investment.   Similarly, if money held by any person
> in a fiduciary capacity be paid into his own banking account, it
> may be followed by the equitable owner, who, as against the
> trustee, will have a charge for what belongs to him upon the
> balance to the credit of the account.   If, then, the trustee pays in
> further sums, and from time to time draws out money by cheques,
> but leaves a balance to the credit of the account, it is settled that
> he is not entitled to have the rule in *Devaynes* v. *Noble, Baring*
> v. *Noble, Clayton's Case* [99] applied so as to maintain that the sums
> which have been drawn out and paid away so as to be incapable
> of being recovered represented *pro tanto* the trust money, and
> that the balance remaining is not trust money, but represents only
> his own moneys paid into the account.   *Brown* v. *Adams* [1] to the
> contrary ought not to be followed since the decision in *Re
> Hallett's Estate*.   It is, in my opinion, equally clear that when any
> of the money drawn out has been invested, and the investment
> remains in the name or under the control of the trustee, the rest
> of the balance having been afterwards dissipated by him, he cannot
> maintain that the investment which remains represents his own
> money alone, and that what has been spent and can no longer be
> traced and recovered was the money belonging to the trust.   In
> other words, when the private money of the trustee and that which
> he held in a fiduciary capacity have been mixed in the same bank-
> ing account, from which various payments have from time to time
> been made, then, in order to determine to whom any remaining
> balance or any investment that may have been paid for out of the
> account ought to be deemed to belong, the trustee must be debited
> with all the sums that have been withdrawn and applied to his
> own use so as to be no longer recoverable, and the trust money
> in like manner be debited with any sums taken out and duly
> invested in the names of the proper trustees.   The order of priority
> in which the various withdrawals and investments may have been
> respectively made is wholly immaterial.   I have been referring, of
> course, to cases where there is only one fiduciary owner or set of
> *cestuis que trust* claiming whatever may be left as against the
> trustee.   In the present case there is no balance left.   The only

---

[98] [1903] 2 Ch. 359–361.
[99] [1814–23] All E.R. Rep. 1; (1816) 1 Mer. 572.
[1] (1869) 4 Ch.App. 764.

investment or property remaining which represents any part of the mixed moneys paid into the banking account is the Oceana shares purchased for £2,137. Upon these, therefore, the trust had a charge for the £3,000 trust money paid into the account. That is to say, those shares and the proceeds thereof belong to the trust. It was objected that the investment in the Oceana shares was made at a time when Oatway's own share of the balance to the credit of the account (if the whole had been then justly distributed) would have exceeded £2,137, the price of the shares; that he was therefore entitled to withdraw that sum, and might rightly apply it for his own purposes; and that consequently the shares should be held to belong to his estate. To this I answer that he never was entitled to withdraw the £2,137 from the account, or, at all events, that he could not be entitled to take that sum from the account and hold it or the investment made therewith, freed from the charge in favour of the trust, unless or until the trust money paid into the account had been first restored, and the trust fund reinstated by due investment of the money in the joint names of the proper trustees, which never was done. The investment by Oatway, in his own name, of the £2,137 in Oceana shares no more got rid of the claim or charge of the trust upon the money so invested, than would have been the case if he had drawn a cheque for £2,137 and simply placed and retained the amount in a drawer without further disposing of the money in any way. The proceeds of the Oceana shares must be held to belong to the trust funds under the will of which Oatway and Maxwell Skipper were the trustees.'

So, contrary to the defendant's contention, it is not a presumption that a trustee's drawings from the mixed fund must necessarily be treated as drawings of the trustee's own money where the beneficiary's claim is against the property bought by such drawings. Further, *Re Oatway* [2] did not raise the question whether a beneficiary was entitled to any profit made out of the purchase of property by a trustee out of a fund consisting of his personal moneys which he mixed with the trust moneys, and so the judgment was not directed to, and did not deal with, that question.

"I return now to the judgments in *Re Hallett's Estate*.[3] Sir George Jessel M.R.[4] said:

'There is no doubt, therefore, that Mr. Hallett stood in a fiduciary position towards Mrs. Cotterill. Mr. Hallett, before his death, improperly sold the bonds and put the money to his general account at his bankers. It is not disputed that the money was at

---

[2] [1903] 2 Ch. 356.
[3] (1880) 13 Ch.D. 696.
[4] (1880) 13 Ch.D. 708.

his bankers mixed with his own money at the time of his death; that is, he had not drawn out that money from his bankers. In that position of matters Mrs. Cotterill claimed to be entitled to receive the proceeds, or the amount of the proceeds, of the bonds out of the money in the hands of Mr. Hallett's bankers at the time of his death, and that claim was allowed by the learned judge of the court below, and I think was properly so allowed.'

Later Sir George Jessel said [5]:

'The modern doctrine of equity as regards property disposed of by persons in a fiduciary position is a very clear and well-established doctrine. You can, if the sale was rightful, take the proceeds of the sale, if you can identify them. If the sale was wrongful, you can still take the proceeds of the sale, in a sense adopting the sale for the purpose of taking the proceeds, if you can identify them. There is no distinction, therefore, between a rightful and a wrongful disposition of the property, so far as regards the right of the beneficial owner to follow the proceeds. But it very often happens that you cannot identify the proceeds. The proceeds may have been invested, together with money belonging to the person in a fiduciary position, in a purchase. He may have bought land with it, for instance, or he may have bought chattels with it. What is the position of the beneficial owner as regards such purchases? I will, first of all, take his position when the purchase is clearly made with what I will call, for shortness, the trust money, although it is not confined, as I will show presently, to express trusts. In that case, according to the now well-established doctrine of equity, the beneficial owner has a right to elect either to take the property purchased, or to hold it as a security for the amount of the trust money laid out in the purchase, or, as we generally express it, he is entitled at his election either to take the property, or to have a charge on the property for the amount of the trust money. But where a trustee has mixed the money with his own, there is the distinction that the *cestui que trust* or beneficial owner can no longer elect to take the property. . . .'

Pausing there, what is apparently meant is that a beneficiary cannot take the whole property, which is the possibility with which Sir George Jessel had just before this been dealing. He went on [6]

'. . . because it is no longer bought with the trust money simply and purely, but with a mixed fund. He is, however, still entitled to a charge on the property purchased for the amount of the trust money laid out in the purchase, and that charge is quite independent of the amount laid out by the trustee. The moment

---

[5] (1880) 13 Ch.D. 708, 709.
[6] (1880) 13 Ch.D., 709.

you get a substantial portion of it furnished by the trustee, using the word 'trustee' in the sense I have mentioned, as including all persons in a fiduciary relation, the right to the charge follows.'

Here, as I read this judgment, it does not exclude the right of the beneficiary to claim a proportion of the mixed fund. There was no need in that case to go further than the charge claimed in the case. So again that question was not there considered.

"Later on Sir George Jessel said [7]:

'When we come to apply that principle to the case of a trustee who has blended trust moneys with his own, it seems to me perfectly plain that he cannot be heard to say that he took away the trust money when he had a right to take away his own money. . . . What difference does it make if, instead of putting the trust money into a bag, he deposits it with his banker, then pays in other money of his own, and then draws out some money for his own purposes? Could he say that he had actually drawn out anything but his own money? His money was there, and he had a right to draw it out, and why should the natural act of simply drawing out the money be attributed to anything except to his ownership of money which was at his bankers? '

But again this was said in relation to a claim seeking to make the account liable and not to a claim to make what was bought with the drawings liable.

"In *Sinclair* v. *Brougham* [8] the decision in *Re Hallett's Estate* was considered. Lord Parker of Waddington said [9]:

'The principle on which, and the extent to which, trust money can be followed in equity is discussed at length in *Re Hallett's Estate* by Sir George Jessel M.R. He gives two instances. First, he supposes the case of property being purchased by means of trust money alone. In such a case the beneficiary may either take the property itself or claim a lien on it for the amount of the money expended in the purchase. Secondly, he supposes the case of the purchase having been made partly with the trust money and partly with money of the trustee. [I shall come back to the next sentence later.] In such a case the beneficiary can only claim a charge on the property for the amount of the trust money expended in the purchase. The trustee is precluded by his own misconduct from asserting any interest in the property until such amount has been refunded. By the actual decision in the case, this principle was held applicable when the trust money had been paid into the trustee's banking account. I will add two further illustrations which have some bearing on the present case.

---

[7] (1880) 13 Ch.D., 727, 728.
[8] [1914] A.C. 398.
[9] [1914] A.C. 442.

Suppose the property is acquired by means of money, part of
which belongs to one owner and part to another, the purchaser
being in a fiduciary relationship to both. Clearly each owner has
an equal equity. Each is entitled to a charge on the property for
his own money, and neither can claim priority over the other. It
follows that their charges must rank *pari passu* according to their
respective amounts [again, I emphasise this]. Further, I think
that as against the fiduciary agent they could by agreement claim
to take the property itself, in which case they would become
tenants in common in shares proportioned to amounts for which
either could claim a charge.'

It seems to me that when Lord Parker says in the sentence, to which
I first called particular attention, that ' In such a case the beneficiary
can only claim a charge on the property for the amount of the trust
money expended in the purchase,' he is merely contrasting the charge
with the right to take the whole property which is the matter with
which he has just been dealing, and Lord Parker is not, as I see it,
addressing his mind to the question whether the beneficiary could
claim a proportion of the property corresponding to his own contribution to its purchase. This interpretation of the passage seems to me
to be the only interpretation which in principle is consistent with Lord
Parker's view expressed at the end of the passage which I quoted, and
to which I drew particular attention, where the purchase is made by
the trustee wholly out of moneys of two different beneficiaries. In that
case he says that they are not limited to charges for their respective
amounts, but are together entitled to the whole property. Nevertheless if each of two beneficiaries can, in co-operation with the other,
take the whole property which has resulted in profit from the trustee's
action in buying it with their money, why can they not do so if the
trustee himself has also paid some part of the purchase price? Moreover if two beneficiaries can do so why not one? Indeed, it was conceded in argument that the passage should be so interpreted as
suggested.

" In Snell's *Principles of Equity* (26th edn.), at p. 315 the law is
thus stated:

'Where the trustee mixes trust money with his own, the
equities are clearly unequal. Accordingly, the beneficiaries are
entitled to a first charge on the mixed fund, or on any land,
securities or other assets purchased with it. Thus if the trustee
purchases shares with part of the mixed fund, leaving enough of
it to repay the trust moneys, and then dissipates the balance, the
beneficiaries' charge binds the shares; for although under the rule
in *Re Hallett's Estate* the trustee is presumed to have bought the
shares out of his own money, the charge attached to the entire
fund, and could be discharged only by restoring the trust moneys.

Where the property purchased has increased in value, the charge will be not merely for the amount of the trust moneys but for a proportionate part of the increased value. Thus if the trustee purchases land with £500 of his own money and £1,000 of trust moneys, and the land doubles in value, he would be profiting from his breach of trust if he were entitled to all except £1,000; the beneficiaries are accordingly entitled to a charge on the land for £2,000.'

For the defendants it has been rightly admitted that, if a trustee wrongly uses trust money to pay the whole of the purchase price in respect of the purchase of an asset, a beneficiary can elect either to treat the purchased asset as trust property or to treat the purchased asset as security for the recouping of the trust money. It was further conceded that this right of election by a beneficiary also applies where the asset is purchased by a trustee in part out of his own money and in part out of the trust moneys, so that he may, if he wishes, require the asset to be treated as trust property with regard to that proportion of it which the trust moneys contributed to its purchase.

" Does this case fall within that principle?

" Estate properties were sold in June 1951, January and April 1952 and realised approximately £490, £750 and £735 respectively, making with the £261 already mentioned a total of approximately £2,237 trust capital received by Mrs. Tilley. It appears, however, and is not disputed, that from before the first of these sales, and at all relevant times thereafter, Mrs. Tilley's bank account was sufficiently in credit from her own personal contributions to it (without regard to any trust moneys credited to it) to pay for her later property purchases.

" The *Lupton* v. *White* [10] principle is not applicable to this bank account as the amount of trust moneys paid into the mixed bank account is distinguishable as £2,237 and can be readily separated from the widow's personal moneys. In the circumstances of this case there would be a charge on the properties purchased by the widow out of the bank account as security for repayment of the £2,237 trust moneys paid into her bank account in accordance with the principle in *Re Oatway*,[11] but that would be immaterial as the £2,237 is readily available out of the widow's estate.

" Can the beneficiary, however, claim the proportion of the proceeds of sale of 11, Church Street which £179 approximately bears to its purchase price of £1,000 and the proportion of the proceeds of sale of 17/17A, High Street for which £82 10s. bears to the purchase price of approximately £2,050 plus costs? These trust moneys bore a small proportion to the purchase price of the properties. The widow had ample overdraft facilities to pay the purchase price without relying on these trust sums at the time of the High Street purchase, for she had

---

[10] (1808) 15 Ves. 432.
[11] [1903] 2 Ch.D. 356.

an overdraft of over £22,000 apparently within her own overdraft facilities, and presumably properly secured, and this would make any contribution of £82 10s. negligible. She had throughout mixed her personal finances and those of her husband's estate, whether paying that estate's debts when it was without ready money or paying its proceeds of sale into her account. The £179 and £82 10s. were clearly not trust moneys deliberately taken by Mrs. Tilley out of the trust fund for the purpose of investing in property in her name. They merely avoided, to the extent of their amount, the use of Mrs. Tilley's ample overdraft facilities, and in the case of the £179 that advantage was lost after two months by her bank account showing a credit, although it went into debit again seventeen months later. Moreover no interest in these trust sums was lost to any other bene- ficiary, as the widow was herself a life tenant. All these considera- tions appear to me to indicate overwhelmingly that the widow was not deliberately using trust moneys to invest in or contribute towards or otherwise buy properties in her own name, and the whole course of dealing with the trust funds and the bank accounts and the pro- perties purchased and their history, which I have mentioned, indicate that what happened was that the widow mixed the trust moneys and her own in the bank account but did not rely on the trust moneys for any of the purchases. If, as it was suggested for the defendants, the correct test whether a beneficiary is entitled to adopt a purchase by a trustee to which his trust moneys have contributed and thus claim a due proportion of its profits, is a subjective test, depending on the trustee's intention to use the trust moneys to contribute to the purchase, then in my view there was no such intention and the bene- ficiary is not so entitled. My conclusion about the trustee's intention, however, is based not on any direct evidence but on the circumstantial evidence which I have mentioned. If, of course, a trustee deliberately uses trust money to contribute with his own money to buy property in his own name, then I would see no difficulty in enabling a beneficiary to adopt the purchase and claim a share of any resulting profits; but the subjective test does not appear to me to be exclusive, or indeed adequate, if it is the only test. It seems to me that if, having regard to all the circumstances of the case objectively considered, it appears that the trustee has in fact, whatever his intention, laid out trust moneys in or towards a purchase then the beneficiaries are entitled to the property purchased and any profits which it produces to the extent to which it has been paid for out of the trust moneys. Even by this objective test, it appears to me, however, that the trust moneys were not in this case so laid out. On a proper appraisal of all the facts of this particular case, the trustee's breach halted at the mixing of the funds in her bank account. Although properties bought out of those funds would, like the bank account itself, at any rate if the moneys in the bank account were inadequate, be charged with repayment of the trust moneys which then would stand in the same position as the bank account, yet the trust moneys were not invested in properties at all but merely went in reduction of the trustee's overdraft which was in reality the source of the purchase moneys.

" The plaintiff's claim therefore fails and he is entitled to no more than repayment of half the sum of £2,237, interest not being in issue. £2,237 is readily available which makes the existence of any charge for its security immaterial." *Order accordingly.*

PROBLEMS

1. Trevor who is a trustee deposits £6,000 of trust moneys in his personal current account which is £100 in credit though he has overdraft facilities limited to £1,000. On the following day he attends an auction of paintings and buys a painting which he has always wanted for £6,500. He pays for it by a cheque drawn on his personal account. A month later he opens a trustee account into which he pays £6,000. The painting is now worth £13,000. Advise the beneficiaries. Would your advice be different if a fire had destroyed the painting?

2. Shyster is sole trustee of two funds holding the first for Brian and Brian's children and the second for Charles and Charles' children. Shyster paid into his own current bank acount, which then had a credit balance of £800, dividends of £500 belonging to Brian's fund. He then paid into the same account £1,500, the proceeds of sale of investments belonging to Charles' fund. Subsequently, Shyster withdrew first, £700 which he invested in securities now worth £1,050, and then £1,000 with which he purchased a car now worth £600 after a crash. Shyster then went bankrupt leaving £1,100 remaining in the account.

Advise Brian and Charles. Would it make any difference if Shyster had not had a bank account but had placed all the above sums in a box under his bed, all the other facts remaining the same?

3. Tim, trustee of a trust arising under a will of which he is executor and trustee, pays £6,000 under a mistake of law to Roger. Roger spends £4,500 on a new swimming pool in his garden and £1,500 on a world cruise. Advise the beneficiaries. Would it make any difference if the trust had been an *inter vivos* trust?

CHAPTER 9

APPOINTMENT, RETIREMENT AND REMOVAL OF
TRUSTEES

Section 1. Appointment of Trustees

I. APPOINTMENT UNDER THE STATUTORY POWER

The Trustee Act 1925

SECTION 36.[1]—(1) Where a trustee,[2] either original or substituted, and
whether appointed by a court or otherwise, is dead, or remains out of the
United Kingdom for more than twelve months,[3] or desires to be discharged
from all or any of the trusts or powers reposed in or conferred on him,
or refuses or is unfit to act therein, or is incapable of acting therein, or is
an infant, then, subject to the restrictions imposed by this Act on the
number of trustees [4]—

  (a) the person or persons nominated for the purpose of appointing new
  trustees by the instrument, if any, creating the trust [5]; or

---

1 This section reproduces, with amendments and additions, the Trustee Act 1893, s.
10 (1) (3) and (4). Wolstenholme & Cherry's *Conveyancing Statutes*, 13th ed., by
J. T. Farrand, Vol. 4, provides a most useful commentary on all sections of the
Trustee Act.

2 " Trustee " is used as to exclude personal representatives. Accordingly, no power
is conferred to appoint executors.

3 It does not follow that there is an absolute bar to the appointment of non-resident trustees. " On the other hand, apart from exceptional circumstances, it is not
proper to make such an appointment, that is to say the court would not make such
an appointment; nor would it be right for the donees of the power to make such
an appointment out of court. If they did, presumably the court would be likely
to interfere at the instance of the beneficiaries. . . . The most obvious exceptional
circumstances are those in which the beneficiaries have settled permanently in some
country outside the U.K." *Per* Pennycuick V.-C. in *Re Whitehead's W.T.* [1971] 1
W.L.R. 833.

4 Maximum of 4 trustees except for charities: Trustee Act 1925, s. 34.

5 See *Re Wheeler* [1896] 1 Ch. 315: a decision on s. 10 (1) of the Trustee Act of
1893, which is in substance re-enacted by s. 36 (1) of the Act of 1925. In that case
the settlor, instead of nominating X the person to appoint new trustees generally—
as in *Re Walker and Hughes* (1883) 24 Ch.D. 698—nominated X to appoint new
trustees in certain specified events. One of the trustees became bankrupt and
absconded, whereupon he became "unfit" to act, but not "incapable" of acting.
The events specified by the settlor included the event of a trustee becoming "incapable," but not that of a trustee becoming "unfit." The question was whether the
proper person to nominate a new trustee was X, as being "the person or persons
nominated for the purpose of appointing new trustees by the instrument, if any,
creating the trust "—s. 36 (1) (a)—or whether the proper person was the surviving
or continuing trustees or trustee under s. 36 (1) (b). Kekewich J. held that if a
power of appointment contained in the instrument of trust is a limited one, and the
event which has actually happened is not one of the events contemplated by that
power, then the nominee is not "the person or persons nominated for the purpose
of appointing new trustees by the instrument, if any, creating the trust." Hence
the proper person to appoint a new trustee in *Re Wheeler* was to be found in s. 36
(1) (b). *Re Wheeler* was followed, with reluctance, by Neville J. in *Re Sichel* [1916]
1 Ch. 358. Since there does not seem to be anything in the relevant provisions of
the Act of 1925 which would alter the construction put upon the Act of 1893 by *Re
Wheeler*, the law on this point appears to remain the same.

448

(*b*) if there is no such person, or no such person able and willing to act, then the surviving or continuing [6] trustees or trustee for the time being, or the personal representatives of the last surviving or continuing trustee [7];

may, by writing,[8] appoint one or more other persons [9] (whether or not being the persons exercising the power) to be a trustee or trustees in the place of the trustee so deceased, remaining out of the United Kingdom, desiring to be discharged, refusing, or being unfit or being incapable, or being an infant, as aforesaid.

(2) Where a trustee has been removed under a power contained in the instrument creating the trust, a new trustee or new trustees may be appointed in the place of the trustee who is removed, as if he were dead, or, in the case of a corporation, as if the corporation desired to be discharged from the trust, and the provisions of this section shall apply accordingly, but subject to the restrictions imposed by this Act on the number of trustees.

(3) Where a corporation being a trustee is or has been dissolved, either before or after the commencement of this Act, then, for the purposes of this section and of any enactment replaced thereby, the corporation shall be deemed to be and to have been from the date of the dissolution incapable of acting in the trusts or powers reposed in or conferred on the corporation.

(4) The power of appointment given by subsection (1) of this section or any similar previous enactment to the personal representatives of a last surviving or continuing trustee shall be and shall be deemed always to have been exercisable by the executors for the time being (whether original or by representation) of such surviving or continuing trustee who have proved the will of their testator or by the administrators for the time being of such trustee without the concurrence of any executor who has renounced or has not proved.

(5) But a sole or last surviving executor intending to renounce, or all the executors where they all intend to renounce, shall have and shall be deemed always to have had power, at any time before renouncing probate, to exercise the power of appointment given by this section, or by any similar previous enactment, if willing to act for that purpose and without thereby accepting the office of executor.

(6) Where a sole trustee, other than a trust corporation, is or has been originally appointed to act in a trust, or where, in the case of any trust, there are not more than three trustees (none of them being a trust corporation) either original or substituted and whether appointed by the court or otherwise, then and in any such case—

---

[6] A continuing trustee is one who is to continue to act after completion of the intended appointment: *Re Coates to Parsons* (1886) 34 Ch.D. 370.

[7] Apart from this case executors cannot take advantage of the section to appoint trustees: persons appointed executors and trustees of wills of land must formally assent in favour of themselves qua trustees before they can take advantage of this section and section 40: *Re King's W.T.* [1964] Ch. 542. An executor who has not proved his testator's will can exercise the power but the trustee appointed in such circumstances can only prove his title by reference to a proper grant of representation so that such a grant is, in practice, vital: *Re Crowhurst Park* [1974] 1 W.L.R. 583.

[8] For the desirability of making the appointment by deed, see s. 40 of the Trustee Act 1925, *infra*.

[9] Not being infants: Law of Property Act 1925, s. 20. Corporations may be appointed.

(a) the person or persons nominated for the purpose of appointing new trustees by the instrument, if any, creating the trust; or

(b) if there is no such person, or no such person able and willing to act, then the trustee or trustees for the time being;

may, by writing, appoint another person or other persons [10] to be an additional trustee or additional trustees, but it shall not be obligatory to appoint any additional trustee, unless the instrument, if any, creating the trust, or any statutory enactment provides to the contrary, nor shall the number of trustees be increased beyond four by virtue of any such appointment.

(7) Every new trustee appointed under this section as well before as after all the trust property becomes by law, or by assurance, or otherwise, vested in him, shall have the same powers, authorities, and discretions, and may in all respects act as if he had been originally appointed a trustee by the instrument, if any, creating the trust.

(8) The provisions of this section relating to a trustee who is dead include the case of a person nominated trustee in a will but dying before the testator, and those relative to a continuing trustee include a refusing or retiring trustee, if willing to act in the execution of the provisions of this section.[11]

---

[10] It was held in *Re Power's Settlement Trusts* [1951] Ch. 1074 that while the donee of a power to appoint new trustees could appoint himself a trustee in substitution for a person ceasing to be a trustee under s. 36 (1) of the Trustee Act 1925, he could not appoint himself an additional trustee under s. 36 (6) thereof where no vacancy had arisen in the number of trustees. The reason for the difference lies in the wording of the subsections. S. 36 (1) authorises the appointment of " one or more other persons, whether or not being persons exercising the power." S. 36 (6) limits appointments of additional trustees to " another person or other persons." S. 36 (6) is new, but the formula " another person or other persons " was contained in s. 10 (1) of the Trustee Act 1893, the predecessor of s. 36 (1) of the Act of 1925. Under s. 10 (1) the courts had held that this formula did not authorise the donee of the power to appoint himself: *Re Sampson* [1906] 1 Ch. 435. In 1925 the legislature changed the formula in s. 36 (1) in the manner indicated and the fact that it thought it necessary to make the change " must be taken to have put, as it were, the imprimatur of Parliament on the judicial decisions ": [1951] Ch. 1074, 1079. Hence the retention of the formula in s. 36 (6) must be regarded as an indication that it was to have the meaning which had been given to it in s. 10 (1) of the Act of 1893.

[11] Express powers to appoint new trustees had been inserted in settlements before s. 31 of the Conveyancing Act 1881 conferred the statutory power, and one of the problems which had arisen with regard to express powers was whether a person who was not going to continue as a trustee after the new appointment was a continuing trustee for the purpose of making the appointment. *Stones* v. *Rowton* (1853) 17 Beav. 308 and *Travis* v. *Illingworth* (1865) 2 Dr. & Sm. 344, which decided that he was not, led to the difficulty that if a sole surviving trustee wished to retire, he was incapable of appointing a new trustee to take his place. Accordingly s. 31 (6) of the Conveyancing Act 1881 provided that a continuing trustee should include a refusing or retiring trustee if willing to act in the execution of the provisions of the section. S. 10 (4) of the Trustee Act 1893 and s. 36 (8) of the Trustee Act 1925 are to the same effect.

In *Re Stoneham's Settlement Trusts* [1953] Ch. 59, X and Y were the trustees of a settlement. Y remained out of the United Kingdom for a period longer than 12 months. X executed a deed retiring from the trust and appointing C and D to be trustees in place of himself and Y. Y challenged the validity of the new appointments on the ground that he was entitled to participate in making them. Danckwerts J. rejected his contention, first because he had been validly removed from the trust owing to his continuous absence from the United Kingdom for more than 12 months, even though the removal might have been against his will, and secondly because he was not a " continuing trustee " within the meaning of s. 36 (8) of the Act of 1925. He was not a " refusing or retiring " trustee but a trustee who had

(9) Where a trustee is incapable, by reason of mental disorder within the meaning of the Mental Health Act, 1959, of exercising his functions as trustee and is also entitled in possession to some beneficial interest in the trust property, no appointment of a new trustee in his place shall be made by virtue of paragraph (*b*) of subsection (1) of this section unless leave to make the appointment has been given by the authority having jurisdiction under Part VIII of the Mental Health Act 1959.[12]

It should be noted that the power of appointment of trustees is a fiduciary power exercisable by the current trustees having due regard to the interests of the trust and of the conflicting interests of the beneficiaries. Indeed, the trustees' function is a paternalistic one requiring them to protect the beneficiaries from themselves.[13] Thus if the beneficiaries are all *sui juris* and between them absolutely entitled they cannot compel the trustees under section 36 to appoint their nominee: the trustees are entitled to exercise their independent judgment. All that the beneficiaries can do is put an end to the existing settlement under the rule in *Saunders* v. *Vautier* [14] and then create a new settlement of which, as settlors, they will be able to appoint new trustees—but this may well have fiscal disadvantages.

Re BROCKBANK

Chancery Division [1948] Ch. 206; [1948] 1 All E.R. 287

VAISEY J.: " . . . . It is said that where all the beneficiaries concur, they may force a trustee to retire, compel his removal and direct the trustees, having the power to nominate their successors, to appoint as such successors such persons or person or corporation as may be indicated by the beneficiaries, and it is suggested that the trustees have no option but to comply.

" I do not follow this. The power of nominating a new trustee is a discretionary power, and, in my opinion is no longer exercisable and, indeed, can no longer exist if it has become one of which the exercise can be dictated by others. But then it is said that the beneficiaries could direct the trustees to transfer the trust property either to themselves absolutely, or to any other person or persons or corporation, upon trusts identical with or corresponding to the trusts of the testator's will. I agree, provided that the trustees are adequately protected against any possible claim for future death duties and are fully indemnified as regards their costs, charges and expenses. But the result of such a transaction (that is to say a transaction which involves the repetition of the former trusts) would be to establish a new settlement, with (as it seems to me) two consequences which would be to the disadvantage of the beneficiaries: First, it would probably attract an *ad valorem* stamp duty

---

been compulsorily removed from the trust and so his concurrence in the new appointments could be dispensed with: *Re Coates to Parsons* (1886) 34 Ch.D. 370 explained.

[12] As amended by the Mental Health Act 1959, s. 149 (1) and Sched. 7.

[13] *Head* v. *Gould* [1898] 2 Ch. 250.

[14] *Infra*, p. 523.

and, secondly, the benefit of the exemption from estate duty given by section 14 of the Finance Act 1914 on the death of the widow, as a surviving spouse, would be lost.

" It seems to me that the beneficiaries must choose between two alternatives. Either they must keep the trusts of the will on foot, in which case those trusts must continue to be executed by trustees duly appointed pursuant either to the original instrument or to the powers of section 36 of the Trustee Act 1925 and not by trustees arbitrarily selected by themselves; or they must, by mutual agreement, extinguish and put an end to the trusts, with the consequences which I have just indicated.

" The claim of the beneficiaries to control the exercise of the defendant's fiduciary power of making or compelling an appointment of the trustees is, in my judgment, untenable. The court itself regards such a power as deserving of the greatest respect and as one with which it will not interfere." [15]

II. APPOINTMENT BY THE COURT

The court has power to appoint new trustees under section 41 [16] of the Trustee Act 1925, *infra,* but application should not be made to the court where the power of appointing new trustees contained in section 36 (1) of the Act, *supra,* can be exercised [17]: *Re Gibbon's Trusts.*[18] The principles [19] which guide the court in making an appointment are set out in *Re Tempest, infra.* If non-resident trustees are to be appointed the beneficiaries must have a real and substantial connection with the country where the proposed trustees are resident: *Re Windeatt's W.T., infra.*

The Trustee Act 1925

Section 41 [20]—(1) The court may, whenever it is expedient to appoint a new trustee or new trustees, and it is found inexpedient, difficult or impracticable so to do without the assistance of the court, make an order appointing a new trustee or new trustees either in substitution for or in addition to any existing trustee or trustees, or although there is no existing trustee.

In particular and without prejudice to the generality of the foregoing provision, the court may make an order appointing a new trustee in substitution for a trustee who is convicted of felony or is incapable, by reason

---

[15] See M. Jump [1974] B.T.R. 68.

[16] Under the section a trustee may be displaced against his will: *Re Henderson* [1940] Ch. 764.

[17] *Aliter,* if it is uncertain whether the power under s. 36 (1) of the Act is exercisable: *Re May's Will Trusts* [1941] Ch. 109.

[18] (1882) 30 W.R. 287; 45 L.T. 756.

[19] As to what persons the court consider suitable or unsuitable to be appointed in particular cases, see Underhill, *Law of Trusts,* 12th ed., pp. 551–554.

[20] As amended by the Mental Health Act 1959, s. 149 (1) and Sched. 7. It will be noted that under the section the court cannot discharge a trustee without appointing a new trustee in his place.

of mental disorder within the meaning of the Mental Health Act 1959, of exercising his functions as trustee, or is a bankrupt, or is a corporation which is in liquidation or has been dissolved.

Re TEMPEST

Court of Appeal in Chancery (1866) L.R. 1 Ch. 485; 35 L.J.Ch. 632; 14 L.T. 688; 12 Jur.(N.S.) 539; 14 W.R. 850 (Turner and Knight-Bruce L.JJ.)

TURNER L.J.: " There are two questions raised by this appeal. First, whether the order of the Master of the Rolls ought to be reversed in so far as it appoints Mr. Petre to be a trustee of the testator's will; and, secondly, whether, assuming that the order ought to be reversed in this respect, Lord Camoys ought to be appointed the trustee. The first of these questions has not seemed to me to be altogether free from difficulty, and in my view of this case it is by no means an unimportant question. It involves, as I think, to no inconsiderable extent the principles on which this court ought to act in the appointment of new trustees.

" It was said in argument, and has been frequently said, that in making such appointments the court acts upon and exercises its discretion; and this, no doubt, is generally true; but the discretion which the court has and exercises in making such appointments is not, as I conceive, a mere arbitrary discretion, but a discretion in the exercise of which the court is, and ought to be, guided by some general rules and principles, and, in my opinion, the difficulty which the court has to encounter in these cases lies not so much in ascertaining the rules and principles by which it ought to be guided, as in applying those rules and principles to the varying circumstances of each particular case. The following rules and principles may, I think, safely be laid down as applying to all cases of appointments by the court of new trustees.

" First, the court will have regard to the wishes of the persons by whom the trust has been created, if expressed in the instrument creating the trust, or clearly to be collected from it.[21] I think this rule may be safely laid down, because if the author of the trust has in terms declared that a particular person, or a person filling a particular character, should not be a trustee of the instrument, there cannot, as I apprehend, be the least doubt that the court would not appoint to the office a person whose appointment was so prohibited, and I do not think that upon a question of this description any distribution can

---

[21] See also *Re Badger* [1915] W.N. 166; 84 L.J.Ch. 567: the court will not appoint an additional trustee against the wishes of a sole trustee appointed by the settlor, in the absence of allegations against his honesty, even at the unanimous request of the beneficiaries *in esse*, except where land is trust property since a valid receipt cannot be given by less than two trustees or a trust corporation: Law of Property Act 1925, s. 27 (2).

be drawn between express declarations and demonstrated intention. The analogy of the course which the court pursues in the appointment of guardians affords, I think, some support to this rule. The court in those cases attends to the wishes of the parents, however informally they may be expressed.

" Another rule which may, I 'think, safely be laid down is this— that the court will not appoint a person to be trustee with a view to the interest of some of the persons interested under the trust, in opposition either to the wishes of the testator or to the interests of others of the *cestuis que trusts.*[22]   I think so for this reason, that it is of the essence of the duty of every trustee to hold an even hand between the parties interested under the trust. Every trustee is in duty bound to look to the interests of all, and not of any particular member or class of members of his *cestuis que trusts.*[23]

" A third rule which, I think, may safely be laid down is that the court in appointing a trustee will have regard to the question whether his appointment will promote or impede the execution of the trust, for the very purpose of the appointment is that the trust may be better carried into execution. . . .[24]

" There cannot, I think, be any doubt that the court ought not to appoint a trustee whose appointment will impede the due execution of the trust; but, on the other hand, if the continuing or surviving trustee refuses to act with a trustee who may be proposed to be appointed . . . I think it would be going too far to say that the court ought, on that ground alone, to refuse to appoint the proposed trustee; for this would, as suggested in the argument, be to give the continuing or surviving trustee a veto upon the appointment of the new trustee. In such a case, I think it must be the duty of the court to inquire and ascertain whether the objection of the surviving or continuing trustee is well founded or not, and to act or refuse to act upon it accordingly. . . ."[25]

Re WINDEATT'S WILL TRUSTS

Chancery Division [1969] 1 W.L.R. 692; [1969] 2 All E.R. 324

PENNYCUICK J.: " . . . It is now proposed that two persons resident in Jersey be appointed trustees of the will in place of the third defendant who is at present the sole trustee, and that, after such appointment, the trust fund shall be transferred to the new trustees in Jersey to be held by them on the trusts of a new declaration of trust proposed to be made by them in Jersey. A draft of that declaration of trust is in evidence.

---

[22] This should be *cestuis que trust*: see C. Sweet (1910) 26 L.Q.R. 196.
[23] *Ibid.*
[24] A person will thus not be appointed if so to do would place him in a position in which his interest and duty would be likely to conflict: *Re Parsons* [1940] Ch. 973.
[25] The court may postpone an order for appointment of new trustees in order to protect the interests of the existing trustees, *e.g.*, where they may be accountable for payment of estate duty under Finance Act 1894, s. 8 (4): *Re Pauling S.T. (No. 2)* [1963] Ch. 576.

The trusts are drawn so as to correspond in all relevant respects with the trusts of the residuary estate of the testator. There is in evidence an affidavit of Lester Vivian Bailhache, who is an advocate practising in Jersey, has also been called to the English bar, and is the President of the Jersey Law Society. He goes in detail into the law of Jersey in relation to settlements, and he states in the most unqualified terms that in his opinion and that of the other advocates in Jersey the nature of whose practice requires them to consider the legality of setttlements, a settlement in the terms proposed will be effective as expressed under the law of Jersey: so it follows that, if the order which I am asked to make is made, the property will be under the control of Jersey trustees and held on trust which will be in all relevant respects the same as the existing trusts.

" I think it is clear that I have jurisdiction to make the order. I was referred to *Re Seale's Marriage Settlements.*[26] The headnote ran as follows:

'By a marriage settlement made in 1931 certain investments were settled on trust for the wife for life, after her death on trust for the husband for life upon protective trusts if he survived her, and after the death of the survivor on trust for the children or remoter issue of the marriage as the husband and wife jointly or the survivor of them should appoint, and in default of such appointment to the children of the marriage who, being male, attained the age of 21 years, or, being female, attained that age or married, if more than one in equal shares. At the date of the settlement the husband and wife were domiciled in England but they subsequently emigrated to Canada. There were three children of the marriage, one of whom had attained the age of 21 years. On a summons asking the court to appoint a Canadian corporation to be trustee of the settlement in place of the present English trustee and to approve, under section 1 of the Variation of Trust Act 1958 an arrangement whereby the trustee of the English settlement might transfer the property comprised in that settlement to the trustee of a Canadian settlement which was as similar to the English settlement as possible: *Held*, that, having regard to the fact that the court could approve an arrangement revoking all the trusts of a settlement, the court had jurisdiction to approve an arrangement, such as the present, which, in effect, revoked all the trusts of the English settlement in the event of the trust property becoming subject to the trusts of a settlement which would be recognised and enforced by some other jurisdiction.'

" This decision covers the matter of jurisdiction. I am told, also, that in at least two subsequent cases other judges have made comparable orders. The only difficulty results from *Re Weston's Settlements,*[27]

---

[26] [1961] Ch. 574. [27] [1969] Ch. 223.

before Stamp J., and before the Court of Appeal. In that case, the judge on the particular facts of the case exercised his discretion under the Act to refuse to sanction an arrangement, and the Court of Appeal affirmed his decision. The judge in *Re Weston* referred to *Re Seale*, as did the Court of Appeal, without disapproval. *Re Weston* went on its own facts entirely, which were extremely striking. The settlor there, with his family, had moved to Jersey only a very short time before the application to the court was made. It might well be inferred that the whole object of moving to Jersey was to escape a particular fiscal liability, and it appeared that their stay in that country might well be transitory. These facts are brought out in the judgment of Lord Denning, M.R., in the Court of Appeal [28]:

> ' But here the family had only been in Jersey three months when they presented this scheme to the court. The inference is irresistible: the underlying purpose was to go there in order to avoid tax. . . . I cannot help wondering how long these young people will stay in Jersey. It may be to their financial interest at present to make their home there permanently, but will they remain there once the capital gains are safely in hand, clear of tax? They may well change their minds and come back to enjoy their untaxed gains.'

Similarly, Harman L.J. said [29]:

> ' The two young men who alone may be considered cannot be said to have proved that they truly intend to make Jersey their home.'

It seems to me that *Re Weston's Settlements* was decided on its own particular facts, and on those facts it is a decision with which I am, if I may respectfully say so, in the most complete agreement. The facts of the case now before me are quite different. Here, the family has been in Jersey for 19 years and has made a genuine and permanent home in Jersey. The children were born there.

" There is no other reason why it would not be right to exercise the jurisdiction in the present case."

III.   POSITION OF A PURCHASER OF LAND OF WHICH NEW TRUSTEES HAVE BEEN APPOINTED

The Trustee Act 1925

Section 38.—(1) A statement, contained in any instrument coming into operation after the commencement of this Act by which a new trustee is appointed for any purpose connected with land, to the effect that a trustee has remained out of the United Kingdom for more than twelve months or refuses or is unfit to act, or is incapable of acting, or that he is not entitled to a beneficial interest in the trust property in possession, shall, in favour of a purchaser of a legal estate, be conclusive evidence of the matter stated.

---

[28] [1969] Ch. 245, 246.   [29] [1969] Ch. 247, 248.

(2) In favour of such purchaser any appointment of a new trustee depending on that statement, and any vesting declaration, express or implied, consequent on the appointment, shall be valid.

IV. VESTING OF TRUST PROPERTY IN NEW OR CONTINUING TRUSTEES

The Trustee Act 1925

Section 40.[30]—(1) Where by a deed a new trustee is appointed to perform any trust, then—

(a) if the deed contains a declaration by the appointor to the effect that any estate or interest in any land subject to the trust, or in any chattel so subject, or the right to recover or receive any debt or other thing in action so subject, shall vest in the persons who by virtue of the deed become or are the trustees for performing the trust, the deed shall operate,[31] without any conveyance or assignment, to vest in those persons as joint tenants and for the purposes of the trust the estate interest or right to which the declaration relates; and

(b) if the deed is made after the commencement of this Act and does not contain such a declaration, the deed shall, subject to any express provision to the contrary therein contained, operate as if it had contained such a declaration by the appointor extending to all the estates interests and rights with respect to which a declaration could have been made.

(2) Where by a deed a retiring trustee is discharged under the statutory power without a new trustee being appointed, then—

(a) if the deed contains such a declaration as aforesaid by the retiring and continuing trustees, and by the other person, if any, empowered to appoint trustees, the deed shall, without any conveyance or assignment, operate to vest in the continuing trustees alone, as joint tenants, and for the purposes of the trust, the estate, interest, or right to which the declaration relates; and

(b) if the deed is made after the commencement of this Act and does not contain such a declaration, the deed shall, subject to any express provision to the contrary therein contained, operate as if it had contained such a declaration by such persons as aforesaid extending to all the estates, interests and rights with respect to which a declaration could have been made.

(3) An express vesting declaration, whether made before or after the commencement of this Act, shall, notwithstanding that the estate, interest or right to be vested is not expressly referred to, and provided that the other statutory requirements were or are complied with, operate and be deemed always to have operated (but without prejudice to any express

---

[30] This section replaces, with amendments and the addition of subss. (1) (b), (2) (b) and (3), s. 12 of the Trustee Act 1893.

[31] Even when the estate, interest or right is not vested in the person making the appointment. *Cf.* s. 9 of the Law of Property Act 1925; but not as in *Re King's W.T.* [1964] Ch. 542, *supra*, p. 38, where the legal estate is held by the appointor in his capacity as personal representative, not having executed an assent in his favour as trustee. Entry on the register is needed for registered land.

provision to the contrary contained in the deed of appointment on discharge) to vest in the persons respectively referred to in subsections (1) and (2) of this section, as the case may require, such estates, interests and rights as are capable of being and ought to be vested in those persons.

(4) This section does not extend—

    (*a*) to land conveyed by way of mortgage for securing money subject to the trust, except land conveyed on trust for securing debentures or debenture stock;

    (*b*) to land held under a lease which contains any covenant, condition or agreement against assignment or disposing of the land without licence or consent, unless, prior to the execution of the deed containing expressly or impliedly the vesting declaration, the requisite licence or consent has been obtained, or unless, by virtue of any statute or rule of law, the vesting declaration, express or implied, would not operate as a breach of covenant or give rise to a forfeiture;

    (*c*) to any share, stock, annuity or property which is only transferable in books kept by a company or other body, or in manner directed by or under an Act of Parliament.

In this subsection " lease " includes an underlease and an agreement for a lease or underlease.

(5) For purposes of registration of the deed in any registry, the person or persons making the declaration expressly or impliedly, shall be deemed the conveying party or parties, and the conveyance shall be deemed to be made by him or them under a power conferred by this Act.

(6) This section applies to deeds of appointment or discharge executed on or after the first day of January, eighteen hundred and eighty-two.

Section 2. Retirement of Trustees

Where a trustee retires and a new trustee is appointed [32] to fill the vacancy, the retirement and new appointment are effected under section 36 (1) of the Trustee Act 1925, *supra*. Where a new trustee is not appointed to fill the vacancy, the retirement is effected under section 39, *infra*.

The Trustee Act 1925

Section 39.[33]—(1) Where a trustee is desirous of being discharged from the trust, and after his discharge there will be either a trust corporation or at least two individuals to act as trustees to perform the trust, then, if such trustee as aforesaid by deed declares that he is desirous of being dis-

---

[32] If no one else can be found the Public Trustee will usually be willing to act.

[33] This section reproduces, with amendments, s. 11 of the Trustee Act 1893. Independently of statute a trustee may retire (i) under a power of retirement contained in the trust instrument: *Camoys* v. *Best* (1854) 19 Beav. 414; (ii) by the consent of all the beneficiaries, the latter being *sui juris*: *Wilkinson* v. *Parry* (1828) 4 Russ. 472, 476; (iii) by authority of the court, to which the trustee has a right to apply to be discharged from the trust; but costs will depend on whether he has reasonable grounds for desiring to be discharged: *Coventry* v. *Coventry* (1837) 1 Keen 758; *Porter* v. *Watts* (1852) 21 L.J.Ch. 211; *Forshaw* v. *Higginson* (1855) 20 Beav. 485; *Gardiner* v. *Dounes* (1856) 22 Beav. 395; *Barker* v. *Peile* (1865) 2 Dr. & Sm. 340; *Re Chetwynd* [1902] 1 Ch. 692.

charged from the trust, and if his co-trustees and such other person, if any, as is empowered to appoint trustees, by deed consent to the discharge of the trustee, and to the vesting in the co-trustees alone of the trust property, the trustee desirous of being discharged shall be deemed to have retired from the trust, and shall, by the deed, be discharged therefrom under this Act, without any new trustee being appointed in his place.

(2) Any assurance or thing requisite for vesting the trust property in the continuing trustees alone shall be executed or done.

Section 3. Disclaimer by Trustees

A person appointed trustee may naturally *disclaim,* for " a man cannot have an estate put into him in spite of his teeth." The disclaimer of a trust by a person appointed trustee —

> (i) ought to be in writing (or by deed); but it may be
> > (a) oral [34];
> > (b) by conduct [35];
> > (c) by mere inactivity (*semble*) [36];
> > (d) signified on behalf of the person appointed trustee by counsel at the Bar [37];
>
> (ii) must be a disclaimer of the whole trust; it cannot be partial. [38]

If a *married woman* who has been appointed trustee of *land* intends to disclaim, she ought to do so by deed. [39]

If a person is appointed both executor and trustee and he proves the will, he thereby accepts the trust. But if he renounces probate, he does not thereby necessarily disclaim the trust. [40]

Section 4. Removal of Trustees

The court has a jurisdiction, independent of statute, to remove trustees: *Letterstedt* v. *Broers, infra.*

LETTERSTEDT v. BROERS

Privy Council (1884) 9 App.Cas. 371; 53 L.J.P.C. 44; 51 L.T. 169
(Lord Blackburn, Sir Robert P. Collier, Sir Richard Couch and Sir Arthur Hobhouse)

---

[34] *Bingham* v. *Clanmorris* (1828) 2 Moll. 253; *dubitante* Wood V.-C. in *Re Ellison* (1856) 2 Jur. 62.

[35] *Stacey* v. *Elph* (1833) 1 My. & K. 195; *Urch* v. *Walker* (1838) 3 My. & Cr. 702; *Re Birchall* (1889) 40 Ch.D. 436.

[36] *Re Clout and Frewer* [1924] 2 Ch. 230; preferring *Re Gordon* (1877) 6 Ch.D. 531 and *Re Birchall* (1889) 40 Ch.D. 436 to *Re Uniacke* (1844) 1 Jo. & Lat. 1 and *Re Needham* (1844) 1 Jo. & Lat. 34; *M'Kenna* v. *Eager* (1875) Ir.R. 9 C.L. 79; *White* v. *M'Dermott* (1872) Ir.R. 7 C.L. 1, 8; *Jago* v. *Jago* (1893) 68 L.T. 654; 172 L.T.J. 297.

[37] *Landbroke* v. *Bleaden* (1852) 16 Jur.(o.s.) 630; *Foster* v. *Dawber* (1860) 8 W.R. 646.

[38] *Re Lord and Fullerton* [1896] 1 Ch. 228; *cf. Malzy* v. *Edge* (1856) 4 W.R. 213.

[39] See the Law of Property Act 1925, s. 168; Snell, p. 201; Underhill, 12th ed., p. 248.

[40] *Mucklow* v. *Fuller* (1821) Jac. 198; *Ward* v. *Butler* (1824) 2 Moll. 533; Romilly M.R. in *Dix* v. *Burford* (1854) 19 Beav. 409, 412; and see *Booth* v. *Booth* (1838) 1 Beav. 125; *Re Gordon, Roberts* v. *Gordon* (1877) 37 L.T. 627.

The Board of Executors of Cape Town were the sole surviving executors and trustees of a will under which the appellant was a beneficiary. The appellant alleged misconduct in the administration of the trust, and claimed that the Board were unfit to be entrusted with the management of the estate and should be removed in favour of a new appointment. The Supreme Court of the Cape of Good Hope had refused the application to remove the Board. The beneficiary appealed.

LORD BLACKBURN: ". . . The whole of the matters which have been complained of, and the whole that, if this judgment stands, may yet have to be done by the Board, are matters which they had to do, as having accepted the burthen of carrying out the trusts which on the true construction of the will were imposed upon them, and so become trustees. What they had to do as executors merely, such as paying debts, collecting assets, etc., have long ago been over, and by the terms of the compromise the plaintiff cannot now say they have not been done properly. There may be some peculiarity in the Dutch colonial law, which made it proper to make the prayer in the way in which it was done to remove them from the office of executor; if so, it has not been brought to their Lordships' notice; the whole case has been argued here, and, as far as their Lordships can perceive, in the court below, as depending on the principles which should guide an English court of equity when called upon to remove old trustees and substitute new ones. It is not disputed that there is a jurisdiction 'in cases requiring such a remedy,' as is said in Story's *Equity Jurisprudence*, s. 1287, but there is very little to be found to guide us in saying what are the cases requiring such a remedy; so little that their Lordships are compelled to have recourse to general principles.

"Story says, section 1289: 'But in cases of positive misconduct, courts of equity have no difficulty in interposing to remove trustees who have abused their trust; it is not indeed every mistake or neglect of duty, or inaccuracy of conduct of trustees, which will induce courts of equity to adopt such a course. But the acts or omissions must be such as to endanger the trust property or to show a want of honesty, or a want of proper capacity to execute the duties, or a want of reasonable fidelity.'

"It seems to their Lordships that the jurisdiction which a court of equity has no difficulty in exercising under the circumstances indicated by Story is merely ancillary to its principal duty, to see that the trusts are properly executed. This duty is constantly being performed by the substitution of new trustees in the place of original trustees for a variety of reasons in non-contentious cases. And therefore, though it should appear that the charges of misconduct were either not made out, or were greatly exaggerated, so that the trustee was justified in resisting them, and the court might consider that in awarding costs, yet if satisfied that the continuance of the trustee would prevent the trusts being properly executed, the trustee might be removed. It must always be borne in mind that trustees exist for the benefit of those to whom the creator of the trust has given the trust estate.

" The reason why there is so little to be found in the books on this subject is probably that suggested by Mr. Davey in his argument. As soon as all questions of character are as far settled as the nature of the case admits, if it appears clear that the continuance of the trustee would be detrimental to the execution of the trusts, even if for no other reason than that human infirmity would prevent those beneficially interested, or those who act for them, from working in harmony with the trustee, and if there is no reason to the contrary from the intentions of the framer of the trust to give this trustee a benefit or otherwise, the trustee is always advised by his own counsel to resign, and does so. If, without any reasonable ground, he refused to do so, it seems to their Lordships that the court might think it proper to remove him; but cases involving the necessity of deciding this, if they ever arise, do so without getting reported.[41] It is to be lamented that the case was not considered in this light by the parties in the court below, for, as far as their Lordships can see, the Board would have little or no profit from continuing to be trustees, and as such coming into continual conflict with the appellant and her legal advisers, and would probably have been glad to resign, and get out of an onerous and disagreeable position. But the case was not so treated.

" In exercising so delicate a jurisdiction as that of removing trustees, their Lords do not venture to lay down any general rule beyond the very broad principle above enunciated, that their main guide must be the welfare of the beneficiaries. Probably it is not possible to lay down any more definite rule in a matter so essentially dependent on details often of great nicety.[42] . . .

" It is quite true that friction or hostility between trustees and the immediate possessor of the trust estate is not of itself a reason for the removal of the trustees. But where the hostility is grounded on the mode in which the trust has been administered, where it has been caused wholly or partially by substantial overcharges against the trust estate, it is certainly not to be disregarded.

" Looking, therefore, at the whole circumstances of this very peculiar case, the complete change of position, the unfortunate hostility that has arisen, and the difficult and delicate duties that may yet have to be performed, their Lordships can come to no other conclusion than that it is necessary, for the welfare of the beneficiaries, that the Board should no longer be trustees.

---

[41] Some do get reported : *infra*, note 43.

[42] " You must find," said Warrington J. in *Re Wrightson* [1908] 1 Ch. 789, 803, " something which induces the court to think either that the trust property will not be safe, or that the trust will not be properly executed in the interests of the beneficiaries."

"Probably if it had been put in this way below they would have consented. But for the benefit of the trust they should cease to be trustees, whether they consent or not. . . ."

The charge of misconduct was not proved. *Appeal allowed.*[43]

Section 5. Special types of trustee

Custodian trustees [44]

These are distinct from the usual managing trustees. They hold the trust property and the trust documents (*e.g.*, title deeds, share certificates) and all sums payable to or out of the income or capital of the trust property are paid to or by them except that dividends and other income derived from the trust property may be paid to such other persons as they direct, *e.g.*, the managing trustees or a beneficiary.[45] The day-to-day running of the trust is left to the managing trustees. The following may be appointed custodian trustees: the Public Trustee, the Official Custodian for Charities and trust corporations.[46]

Trust corporations

A trust corporation can act alone where otherwise two individual trustees would be required, *e.g.*, receipt of capital moneys on a sale of land. The following are trust corporations[47]: the Public Trustee, the Treasury Solicitor, the Official Solicitor, certain charitable corporations and corporations either appointed by the court in any particular case or entitled to act as custodian trustees under the Public Trustee Act 1906. Corporations so entitled include those constituted under United Kingdom law doing business

---

43 See also *Uzedale* v. *Ettrick* (1682) 2 Ch.Cas. 130 (a trustee's co-trustees unwilling to act with him); *Millard* v. *Eyre* (1793) 2 Ves.J. 94 (trustee absconding); *Buchanan* v. *Hamilton* (1801) 5 Ves. 722 (trustee going abroad indefinitely); *Howard* v. *Rhodes* (1837) 1 Keen 581 and *Palairet* v. *Carew* (1863) 32 Beav. 564 (trustee not performing his trust); *Passingham* v. *Sherborne* (1846) 9 Beav. 424 (trustee also lessee of trust property, though so authorised); *Re Harrison* (1852) 22 L.J.Ch. 69 (trustee not traceable); *Att.-Gen.* v. *Murdoch* (1856) 2 K. & J. 571 (trustees become unqualified to act, but refuse to retire); *Forster* v. *Davies* (1861) 4 De G.F. & J. 133, 139 and *Assets Co.* v. *Securities Corp.* (1895) 65 L.J.Ch. 74 (not sufficient ground for removal); *Reid* v. *Hadley* (1885) 2 T.L.R. 12 (neglect in administration); *Moore* v. *M'Glynn* [1894] 1 Ir.R. 74, 88–90 (trustee setting up a business competing with his trust); *Re Wrightson* [1908] 1 Ch. 789, 800–803 (general discussion).
  The *bankruptcy* of a trustee is as a general rule a ground for his removal. See Jessel M.R. in *Re Barker's Trusts* (1875) 1 Ch.D. 43; 169 L.T.J. 74. The following are decisions on the removal of a trustee on account of insolvency or bankruptcy, under the court's general jurisdiction: *Bainbrigge* v. *Blair* (*No.* 1) (1839) 1 Beav. 495; *Re Roche* (1842) 2 Dr. & War. 287, 289; *Charitable Donations* v. *Archbold* (1847) 11 Ir.Eq.R. 187; *Harris* v. *Harris* (*No.* 1) (1861) 29 Beav. 107; *Re Hopkins* (1881) 19 Ch.D. 61, 63, Jessel M.R.
  The following are decisions under the court's statutory power to remove a trustee on account of his bankruptcy: *Re Bridgman* (1860) 1 Dr. & Sm. 164; *Re Renshaw* (1869) L.R. 4 Ch. 783; *Re Barker's Trusts* (1875) 1 Ch.D. 43; *Re Adams* (1879) 12 Ch.D. 634; *Re Foster* (1886) 55 L.T. 479; *Re Betts* (1897) 41 S.J. 209; Trustee Act 1925, s. 41 (1).
44 Generally see S. G. Maurice (1960) 24 Conv.(N.S.) 196; P. Pearce (1972) 36 Conv.(N.S.) 260–261; Keeton's *Modern Developments in the Law of Trusts*, Chap. 3.
45 Public Trustee Act, s. 4 (2).
46 Public Trustee Rules 1912. r. 30, as substituted by The Public Trustee (Custodian Trustee) Rules 1971, S.I. 1971 No. 1894; *Re Brooke Bond & Co. Ltd.'s Trust Deed* [1963] Ch. 357.   47 *Ibid.*

in the United Kingdom and empowered to undertake trust business which are either incorporated by special Act or Royal Charter or else registered companies with an issued capital of at least £250,000 of which at least £100,000 has been paid up in cash.

The public trustee [48]

He was established in 1906 as a corporation sole available to deal with the difficulty persons might have in finding someone willing to act as trustee. However, he cannot accept charitable trusts, insolvent estates or, normally, trusts involving the carrying on of a business. He can act as personal representative, ordinary managing trustee, custodian trustee or judical trustee.

Judicial trustee

The Judicial Trustees Act 1896 established judicial trustees in order " to provide a middle course in cases where the administration of the estate by the ordinary trustees had broken down and it was not desired to put the estate to the expense of a full administration " by the court.[49] Judicial trustees can only be appointed by the court upon a summons in existing proceedings or an originating summons if there are no existing proceedings. Trouble-shooting accountants are often appointed to sort out the muddled situation. The judicial trustee is an officer of the court so that he can at any time obtain the court's directions as to the way in which he should act without the necessity of a formal application by summons though he has as much authority as ordinary trustees to act on his own initiative, and, for example, compromise claims.[50]

Section 6. Trusts do not fail for want of Trustees

If the settlor or testator failed to appoint trustees or if the trustees appointed refuse or are unable to act or have ceased to exist the trust does not fail [51] (unless its operation was conditional upon a specific trustee undertaking the trust [52]). The property reverts to the settlor or remains in the personal representatives of the testator to be held upon the trusts of the settlement or the will as the case may be.[53]

On the death of a sole or sole surviving trustee the trust property vests in his personal representatives subject to the trusts and by the Trustee Act 1925, s. 18 (2), they are capable of exercising or performing any power or trust which the deceased trustee could have exercised or performed. They

---

[48] The Committee of Enquiry into the Public Trustee Office (1972) Cmnd. 4913 recommended that it be wound up and merged with the Official Solicitor's Department but it is still going strong and continuing to accept new business. In July 1974 the Lord Chancellor announced that the government do not propose to take any action on the Committee's recommendations.

[49] *Per* Jenkins J. in *Re Ridsdell* [1947] Ch. 597, 605.

[50] *Re Ridsdell* [1947] Ch. 597.

[51] *Moggridge* v. *Thackwell* (1803) 7 Ves. 36 (affirmed 13 Ves. 416); *Re Willis* [1921] 1 Ch. 44; *Re Armitage* [1972] Ch. 438; *Re Morrison* (1967) 111 S.J. 758.

[52] *Re Lysaght* [1966] Ch. 191.

[53] *Mallot* v. *Wilson* [1903] 2 Ch. 494.

are not bound to accept the position and duties of trustees and may exercise their power of appointing new trustees under s. 36 with a right to payment of the costs thereof from the trust moneys.[54]   If need be the court may appoint new trustees under section 41 or itself execute the trust.[55]

---

[54] *Re Benett* [1906] 1 Ch. 216.
[55] *McPhail* v. *Doulton* [1971] A.C. 424 *supra*, p. 79; (A. J. Hawkins) (1967) 31 (Conv.(N.S.) 117.

CHAPTER 10

THE ADMINISTRATION OF A TRUST

Section 1. General Introduction

THE office of trustee is onerous. Equity imposes many duties [1] upon a trustee and they must all be strictly discharged with the utmost diligence in order to escape liability for any loss sustained by the trust as a result of any breach of the duties or liability to account to the trust for profits made by the trustee personally in breach of his duties. A trustee has even more discretions but in exercising those discretions the trustee merely has to act bona fide using as much diligence as " a man of ordinary prudence would exercise in the management of his own private affairs," [2] except that in selecting investments he must take as much care as a prudent man would take in making an investment for persons for whom he felt morally obliged to provide and ignore speculative investments which a prudent man might take a chance on occasionally. [3] If the appropriate standard of care is honestly taken but loss occurs the trustee will not be liable (e.g., for the dramatic depreciation of a trust holding of Rolls-Royce shares) nor will he be liable for profits that the trust would have made if he had been more dynamic and skilful (e.g., in manipulating a significant minority shareholding in a private company so as either to sell at a very high price or to take over the company and strip it of its assets).

If any doubts arise then the trustee should apply by originating summons to the Chancery Division for directions. As a last resort the trustee may under section 61 of the Trustee Act be excused liability wholly or partly for breach of trust if he acted " honestly and reasonably, and ought fairly to be excused for the breach of trust *and* for omitting to obtain the directions of the court in the matter in which he committed such breach." A paid trustee will be less likely to be excused than an unpaid trustee. [4]

Where there is more than one trustee, as is usually the case, each trustee is personally responsible for the acts performed in the administration of the trust and so should personally consider each act requiring to be done: it is no defence that one was a " sleeping trustee " blindly relying on one's co-trustees. [5] It is not possible to delegate a trustee's duties except where authorised under the trust instrument or by statute. [6] The trustees must act

---

[1] These duties may be relaxed by the trust instrument or by the court. Indeed, most properly drawn trust instruments considerably relax these duties.

[2] *Learoyd* v. *Whiteley* (1887) 12 App.Cas. 727, 737 *per* Lord Watson; see also *Re Lucking's W.T.* [1968] 1 W.L.R. 866, 875; *Speight* v. *Gaunt* (1883) 22 Ch.D. 727 affd. (1883) 9 App.Cas. 1.

[3] *Learoyd* v. *Whiteley* (*supra*).

[4] *Re Rosenthal* [1972] 1 W.L.R. 1273; *Re Pauling's S.T.* [1964] Ch. 303, 338, 339; *National Trustee Co. of Australasia* v. *General Finance Co.* [1905] A.C. 373. The fact that the trustee acted under the advice of his counsel or solicitor will be a significant factor: indeed, it will not be necessary to invoke s. 61 if such action amounts to proof of diligence where the alleged breach of trust is negligence.

[5] *Bahin* v. *Hughes* (1886) 31 Ch.D. 390; *Munch* v. *Cockerell* (1840) 5 Myl. & Cr. 178; *Re Turner* [1897] 1 Ch. 536; *Head* v. *Gould* [1898] 2 Ch. 250. There is no automatic vicarious liability for co-trustees' breaches, *e.g.*, *Re Lucking's W.T.* [1968] 1 W.L.R. 866, *infra*, p. 618.

[6] Underhill, pp. 427–442.

unanimously except where the settlement or the court otherwise directs or in the case of charitable trusts where the trustees may act by a majority.[7] It follows that if there is a trust to sell with power to postpone sale then the power is only effective so long as all trustees wish to postpone sale: once one wishes a sale the trust to sell must be carried out, all the trustees being under a duty to sell so long as the power to postpone sale is not effectively exercised unanimously.[8]

Upon accepting[9] a trusteeship in order to safeguard himself against claims for breach of trust the new trustee should ascertain the terms of the trust and check that he has been properly appointed. He should inspect all trust documents and ensure that all trust property is properly invested and is in the joint names of himself and his co-trustees.[10] It is often best to have title deeds or share certificates deposited at a bank in the joint names but in the absence of special circumstances the court will not order one trustee who has possession of the documents so to deposit them.[11] If appointed new trustee of an existing trust then it is necessary to investigate any suspicious circumstances which indicate a prior breach of trust so that action may be taken to recoup the trust fund if necessary.[12]

Equity is seen at its strictest in the duty it imposes upon a trustee not to allow himself to be put in a position where there may be a conflict between his position as trustee and his personal interest—as the next section shows. This overriding duty of loyalty to the trust must always be borne in mind by trustees.

Section 2. Conflict of Interest and Duty [13]

I. PURCHASE OF TRUST PROPERTY BY TRUSTEES

A purchase of trust property by a trustee is avoidable at the instance of any beneficiary unless authorised by the trust instrument or by the court or by section 68 of the Settled Land Act 1925 (purchases by tenant for life[14]) or made pursuant to a contract or option[15] arising before the trusteeship arose.

[7] *Luke* v. *South Kensington Hotel Ltd.* (1879) 11 Ch.D. 121; *Re 90 Thornhill Rd.* [1970] Ch. 261; Charitable Trusts Act 1869, ss. 12, 13; Charities Act 1960, ss. 28, 34.
[8] *Re Mayo* [1943] Ch. 302. However, the letter of the trust will not be enforced if so to do would defeat the spirit of the trust: *Jones* v. *Challenger* [1961] 1 Q.B. 176.
[9] Of course, no one is bound to accept office as trustee and office should be refused if one wishes to buy property owned by the trust or run a business likely to compete with a business owned by the trust or if one is likely to be in a position where it might be said that profits had been made through advantage being taken of the office.
[10] *Hallows* v. *Lloyd* (1888) 39 Ch.D. 686, 691; *Harvey* v. *Olliver* (1887) 57 L.T. 239; *Tiger* v. *Barclays Bank* [1952] W.N. 38; *Re Strahan* (1856) 8 De G.M. & G. 291; *Lewis* v. *Nobbs* (1878) 8 Ch.D. 591. For those clauses of property not vesting in the new trustee under Trustee Act 1925, s. 40, the ordinary modes of transferring the property will have to be utilised.
[11] *Re Sisson's Settlements* [1903] 1 Ch. 262. Special circumstances will, it is thought, be present if the existing trustee refuses to put property into the joint names of himself and the new trustee(s), *e.g.*, mortgages, shares and registered land which do not fall within the vesting declaration implied by Trustee Act 1925, s. 40. Bearer securities have to be deposited in the custody of a banker: Trustee Act 1925, s. 7.
[12] *Re Strahan* (1856) 8 De G.M. & G. 291; *Re Forest of Dean Coal Co.* (1878) 10 Ch.D. 250.
[13] See A. W. Scott, "The Trustee's Duty of Loyalty" (1936) 49 H.L.R. 521; Marshall, "Conflict of Interest and Duty" (1955) 8 C.L.P. 91; Gareth Jones, "Unjust Enrichment and the Fiduciary's Duty of Loyalty" (1968) 84 L.Q.R. 472.
[14] *Re Pennant's W.T.* [1970] Ch. 75.　　　[15] *Re Mulholland's W.T.* [1949] 1 All E.R. 460.

However, a purely nominal trustee who acquired no special knowledge as trustee and who took no part in preparing for a sale by public auction takes a valid title if he is the highest bidder: *Holder* v. *Holder, infra.*

HOLDER v. HOLDER

Court of Appeal [1968] Ch. 353; [1968] 2 W.L.R. 237; [1968] 1 All
   E.R. 665

The plaintiff beneficiary sought to rescind the sale of trust property to the third defendant in circumstances sufficiently appearing from the following extracts of the reserved judgments of Harman, Danckwerts and Sachs L.JJ.

HARMAN L.J.: " The cross-appeal raises far more difficult questions, and they are broadly three. First, whether the actions of the third defendant before probate made his renunciation ineffective. Second, whether on that footing he was disentitled from bidding at the sale. Third, whether the plaintiff is disentitled from taking this point because of his acquiescence.

" It was admitted at the Bar in the court below that the acts of the third defendant were enough to constitute intermeddling with the estate and that his renunciation was ineffective. On this footing he remained a personal representative even after probate had been granted to his co-executors and could have been obliged by a creditor or a beneficiary to re-assume the duties of an executor. The judge decided in favour of the plaintiff on this point because the third defendant at the time of the sale was himself still in a fiduciary position and, like any other trustee, could not purchase the trust property. I feel the force of this argument, but doubt its validity in the very special circumstances of this case. The reason for the rule is that a man may not be both vendor and purchaser; but the third defendant was never in that position here. He took no part in instructing the valuer who fixed the reserves or in the preparations for the auction. Everyone in the family knew that he was not a seller but a buyer. In this case the third defendant never assumed the duties of an executor. It is true that he concurred in signing a few cheques for trivial sums and endorsing a few insurance policies, but he never so far as appears interfered in any way with the administration of the estate. It is true he managed the farms, but he did that as tenant and not as executor. He acquired no special knowledge as executor. What he knew he knew as tenant of the farms.

" Another reason lying behind the rule is that there must never be a conflict of duty and interest, but in fact there was none here in the case of the third defendant, who made no secret throughout that he intended to buy. There is of course ample authority that a trustee cannot purchase. The leading cases are decisions of Lord Eldon L.C.

—*Ex p. Lacey*[16] and *Ex p. James*.[17] In the former case Lord Eldon L.C. expressed himself thus[18]:

> ' The rule I take to be this: not, that a trustee cannot buy from his *cestui que trust*, but, that he shall not buy from himself. If a trustee will so deal with his *cestui que trust*, that the amount of the transaction shakes off the obligation, that attaches upon him as trustee, then he may buy. If that case is rightly understood, it cannot lead to much mistake. The true interpretation of what is there reported does not break in upon the law as to trustees. The rule is this. A trustee, who is entrusted to sell and manage for others, undertakes in the same moment, in which he becomes a trustee, not to manage for the benefit and advantage of himself.'

" In *Ex p. James* Lord Eldon L.C. said this[19]:

> ' This doctrine as to purchases by trustees, assignees, and persons having a confidential character, stands much more upon general principle than upon the circumstances of any individual case. It rests upon this, that the purchase is not permitted in any case, however honest the circumstances, the general interests of justice requiring it to be destroyed in every instance.'

These are no doubt strong words, but it is to be observed that Lord Eldon was dealing with cases where the purchaser was at the time of sale acting for the vendors. In this case the third defendant was not so acting: his interference with the administration of the estate was of a minimal character, and the last cheque that he signed was in August before he executed the deed of renunciation. He took no part in the instructions for probate, nor in the valuations or fixing of the reserves. Everyone concerned knew of the renunciation and of the reason for it, namely that he wished to be a purchaser. Equally, everyone including the three firms of solicitors engaged assumed that the renunciation was effective and entitled the third defendant to bid. I feel great doubt whether the admission made at the Bar was correct, as did the judge, but assuming that it was right, the acts were only technically acts of intermeddling and I find no case where the circumstances are parallel. Of course, I feel the force of the judge's reasoning that if the third defendant remained an executor he is within the rule, but in a case where the reasons behind the rule do not exist I do not feel bound to apply it. My reasons are that the beneficiaries never looked to the third defendant to protect their interests. They all knew he was in the market as purchaser; that the price paid was a good one and probably higher than anyone not a sitting tenant would give.

---

16 (1802) 6 Ves. 625.
17 (1803) 8 Ves. 337.
18 (1802) 6 Ves. 625, 626.
19 (1803) 8 Ves. 337, 344.

Further, the first two defendants alone acted as executors and sellers: they alone could convey: they were not influenced by the third defendant in connection with the sales.

"I hold, therefore, that the rule does not apply in order to disentitle the third defendant to bid at the auction, as he did."

DANCKWERTS L.J.: "There is no allegation of fraud in the present case. The third defendant acted in complete innocence and did not know that he was regarded as debarred from purchasing the farms. He bought them at a public auction, in respect of which he took no part in regard to the arrangements for the auction, and the judge found [20] that the prices that he paid were good prices. They were well above the reserve prices. The third defendant and the two proving executors were at arm's length. There was no question of knowledge which the third defendant might have acquired as an executor. He had a great amount of knowledge of the farms acquired by him, while he was a tenant or when he helped his father in the carrying on of the farms, and he was the obvious person to purchase these farms and likely to offer the best price. I agree with Harman L.J. that there was no reason why he should not bid at the auction and purchase the farms.

"As regards the authorities, no case is at all near to the facts of this case. The principle that a trustee cannot purchase part of the trust estate goes back to the statement of it by Lord Eldon L.C. in 1802 in *Ex p. Lacey*.[21] Lord Eldon stated the principle in the most severe form. The reason given by Lord Eldon, that it is impossible to ascertain what knowledge the trustee may have, seems less persuasive in the light of Bowen L.J.'s famous dictum [22] that 'the state of a man's mind is as much a fact as the state of his digestion,' and the almost daily experience of any judge engaged in ascertaining the knowledge and intentions of a party to proceedings. The principle is repeated in *Ex p. James*.[23] The subject is dealt with in Snell's *Equity* (26th edn.), at p. 259, where it is pointed out that the true rule is not that a trustee may not purchase trust property; it is that a purchase of trust property by a trustee is voidable within a reasonable time at the instance of any beneficiary (citing *Ex p. James*, and *Re Bulmer, The Trustee and Inland Revenue Comrs.* v. *National Provincial Bank, Ltd.*).[24]

"It is said that it makes no difference, even though the sale may be fair and honest and may be made at a public auction (see Snell's *Equity*, p. 260); but the court may sanction such a purchase and, if the court can do that (see Snell, p. 219), there can be no more than a

---

[20] [1966] 3 W.L.R. 229, 237.
[21] (1802) 6 Ves. 625, 626.
[22] In *Edgington* v. *Fitzmaurice* (1885) 29 Ch.D. 459, 483.
[23] (1803) 8 Ves. 337.
[24] [1937] Ch. 499.

practice that the court should not allow a trustee to bid. In my view it is a matter for the discretion of the judge."

SACHS L.J.: " . . . the first issue is whether in the circumstances of this unusual case the third defendant remained after executing the deed of purported renunciation under that disability which normally attaches to an executor in relation to purchasing part of the estate or whether he was, as counsel for the third defendant submitted, so ' moribund' *qua executor* that the disability did not attach to him.

" The court having been informed that there was no authority touching anyone who had been in a position precisely parallel to that of the third defendant, reliance was placed by counsel for the plaintiff on the rule that no trustee and accordingly no executor could bid for or purchase property vested in him *qua* trustee or executor. This is the rule as enunciated by Lord Eldon L.C. in 1802 and 1803 in the leading cases, *Ex p. Lacey*[25] and *Ex p. James*,[26] from which Harman L.J. has already cited the relevant passages. These cases related to men who had been acting as assignees of a bankrupt's estate and who had thus gained considerable special knowledge of which they could make use at an auction or otherwise when purchasing that property: indeed at any rate one of them (*Ex p. James*) related to a professional man advising the assignees as such. For the reasons given by Harman L.J. in his judgment after citing those passages I, too, consider that the rule is not applicable in the present case, where the plaintiff was in practice ' moribund' *qua executor*, and was affirmatively established to have gained no helpful knowledge from his position as executor before he executed the deed which was intended to effect a renunciation.

" It is moreover a matter which may well be open to argument whether the above rule is, in any event, nowadays quite as rigid as was postulated by counsel for the plaintiff. It is clear that the court has jurisdiction to allow a trustee to bid for trust property (*Tennant* v. *Trenchard*[27]), and in addition it was conceded at the Bar that procedure exists by which a trustee or an executor can obtain the leave of the court in appropriate circumstances to purchase such property: and I understand that such leave has been given even where a beneficiary has objected.

" Moreover I agree with Danckwerts L.J. in his comments on that part of the foundation of the rule which stems from the alleged inability of a court to ascertain the state of mind of a trustee: and am inclined to the view that an irrebuttable presumption as to the state of his knowledge may no longer accord with the way in which the courts have now come to regard matters of this type. Thus the rigidity of the shackles imposed by the rule on the discretion of the court may perhaps before long be reconsidered as the courts tend to lean more

[25] (1802) 6 Ves. 625.
[26] (1803) 8 Ves. 337.   [27] (1869) 4 Ch.App. 537.

and more against such rigidity of rules as can cause patent injustice—such as was done in *Cockerell* v. *Chomeley*.[28] The rule, after all, appears on analysis to be one of practice as opposed to one going to the jurisdiction of the court."

Note

The prohibition against purchase by the trustee applies whether or not he himself fixes the price. Thus in *Wright* v. *Morgan*,[29] a testator left land on trust for sale with power to postpone sale for seven years and provided that it should be offered at a price to be fixed by valuers to one of his sons X, who was one of the trustees. X assigned his right (which was treated as an option and not a right of pre-emption) to his brother, Y, who was also one of the trustees but who was not authorised to purchase by the terms of the will. Y retired from the trust and purchased at a price fixed by the valuers, and it was held that the sale could be set aside. After all, Y as a trustee was one of those responsible for determining when the land was first to be offered for sale (and prices could fluctuate over the years) and for determining the terms of payment, *e.g.* cash or instalments with interest payable. If X had assigned to a stranger, Z, then Z could quite properly have purchased the land. *Quaere* if Y had assigned his right to Z. Of course, if X had exercised his right and had the land conveyed to him, then a subsequent conveyance to Y would have been proper.

The prohibition against purchase by the trustee is applicable where the sale is conducted at an auction held by the trustee himself,[30] since the trustee is in a position to discourage bidders. Further, where the sale is conducted, not by the trustee, but a third party, as, for example, where a trustee holds trust property subject to a mortgage and the mortgagee sells under his power of sale, the trustee is nevertheless not allowed to buy the property, since to hold otherwise might be to permit him to prefer his own interest to his duty,[31] and this is so whether or not he could have prevented the sale.[32] The rule is a strong one and is not circumvented by the device of the trustee selling to a third party to hold on trust for him.[33] But if there is no prior agreement and the sale is in all respects bona fide there is no objection to the trustee subsequently buying the trust property from the person to whom he sold it,[34] though if the trustee contracts to sell the property to X, a stranger, and before the conveyance is made he purchases the benefit of the contract

[28] (1830) 1 Russ. & M. 418.
[29] [1926] A.C. 788.
[30] *Whelpdale* v. *Cookson* (1747) 1 Ves.Sen. 9; stated from the Register's Book in *Campbell* v. *Walker* (1800) 5 Ves. 678, 682.
[31] A. W. Scott, " The Trustee's Duty of Loyalty " (1936) 49 H.L.R. 521, 529–530.
[32] *Griffith* v. *Owen* [1907] 1 Ch. 195, where it was held that the tenant for life of an equity of redemption could not purchase the property for himself from the mortgagee selling under his power of sale.
[33] *Michoud* v. *Girod* (1846) 4 How. 503 (U.S.).
[34] *Re Postlethwaite* (1888) 37 W.R. 200.

from X, the contract can be set aside.[35]   Further, if the trustee has retired from the trust with a view to purchasing the property the sale can be avoided,[36] but it is otherwise if at the date of his retirement he had no idea of making the purchase, unless the circumstances show that when he made the purchase he used information acquired by him while a trustee.[37] But a trustee who has disclaimed is not caught by the rule.[38]

Moreover, the rule is sufficiently strong and elastic to prevent a trustee from selling the trust property to a company of which he is the principal shareholder,[39] managing director or other principal officer,[40] or to a partnership of which he is a member.[41]   Further, the rule applies to trustees, whether individual or corporate, so that a trust corporation cannot in the absence of authorisation by the trust instrument or consent of the beneficiaries or approval of the court sell the trust property either to itself or to its subsidiaries.[42]

Where a sale takes place in breach of the rules outlined above, the beneficiaries have a number of remedies open to them. Thus they may claim any profit made by the trustee on a resale of the property. If the property has not been resold they can insist on a reconveyance or alternatively they can demand that it be offered for sale again. If on this occasion a higher price is bid than that which the trustee paid, it will be sold at that price. If not, the trustee may at the option of the beneficiaries be allowed to retain the property, and in the nature of things the beneficiaries will confer this doubtful favour upon him where the property has fallen in value since he purchased it. The right which the beneficiaries have to avoid the sale is an equitable one, and as such is liable to be lost through laches, but for laches to apply the beneficiaries must have full knowledge of the facts and must acquiesce in the situation for an unreasonably long period.[43]   Further, the right to have the sale set aside may be lost if the court in the exercise of its inherent jurisdiction sets the seal of its approval on the transaction, and it seems that not only may the court authorise a sale which is about to take place, but in a suitable case it may ratify one which has already occurred.[44]

The above presupposes that the sale has taken place without the consent of the beneficiaries. Where, however, the beneficiaries are *sui juris* they may authorise the sale, which will then stand, provided that the trustee made a full disclosure, and did not induce the sale by taking advantage of his

35 *Williams* v. *Scott* [1900] A.C. 499.
36 *Wright* v. *Morgan* [1926] A.C. 788.
37 *Re Boles and British Land Co.'s Contract* [1902] 1 Ch. 244.
38 *Stacey* v. *Elph* (1833) 1 Myl. & K. 195; but see *Clark* v. *Clark* (1884) 9 App.Cas. 733, 737 (P.C.).
39 *Silkstone & Haigh Moor Coal Co.* v. *Edey* [1900] 1 Ch. 167; *Farrar* v. *Farrars Ltd.* (1888) 40 Ch.D. 395. Sale to a trustee's wife is risky (see *Ferraby* v. *Hobson* (1847) 2 Ph. 255, 261) but perhaps not absolutely prohibited (see *Burrell* v. *Burrell's Trustees*, 1915 S.C. 33; (1949) 13 Conv.(N.S.) 248) though see *Re McNally* [1967] N.Z.L.R. 521.
40 *Eberhardt* v. *Christiana Window Glass Co.* (1911) 9 Del.Ch. 284 (U.S.).
41 *Colegate's Executor* v. *Colgate* (1873) 23 N.J.Eq. 372 (U.S.).
42 *Purchase* v. *Atlantic Safe Deposit and Trust Co.* (1913) 81 N.J.Eq. 344 (U.S.). *Quaere* whether a trust corporation can sell trust property to another corporation of which the directors are also directors of the trust corporation. See *Shanley* v. *Fidelity Union Trust Co.* (1927) 108 N.J.Eq. 564 (U.S.); *cf. Loud* v. *St. Louis Union Trust Co.* (1926) 313 Mo. 552 (U.S.).
43 *Infra*, p. 654; *Holder* v. *Holder* [1968] Ch. 353.
44 *Farmer* v. *Dean* (1863) 32 Beav. 327; *Campbell* v. *Walker* (1800) 5 Ves. 678.

relation to the beneficiaries or by other improper conduct, and the trans-action was in all respects fair and reasonable.[45] The onus of proof is on the trustee to show affirmatively that these conditions existed, but there is no objection to the consent of the beneficiaries being obtained after the sale to the trustees.[46]

Of course, a trustee may purchase his beneficiary's equitable interest under the trust (subject to making full disclosure and negativing undue influence) so as to acquire the trust property itself when he has acquired all the equitable interests.

II. PROFITS INCIDENTAL TO TRUSTEESHIP

To deter a trustee from putting himself where his personal interest may con-flict with his loyalty to the trust, if a trustee happens to make a profit by virtue of using trust property or his position as trustee he is not allowed to retain the profit.[47] He can be made to account for the profit and, if need be, the courts will normally be prepared to find that the profit belongs to the trust by virtue of a constructive trust.[48] Of course, an injunction also lies against any trustee who is in breach of or is about to break his duties to the trust.

As *Boardman* v. *Phipps* shows[49] (*supra*, p. 367, which should be read now) equity is very strict: the trustee must disgorge any benefit gained even though he acted honestly and in the trust's best interests, even though the trust benefited as well as he, even though the trust could not otherwise have obtained the benefit, and even though the benefit was obtained through the use of the trustee's own assets and in consequence of his personal skill and judgment. The rule applies to all fiduciaries (*e.g.*, directors, company pro-moters, partners) but in the case of partners it seems that the courts are more ready to accept that the profits made were not incidental to the partnership relation.[50]

Where the fiduciary acts dishonestly or otherwise obtains a benefit at his beneficiaries' expense there is no reason why the benefit should not be held as constructive trustee for the beneficiaries. However, where the fiduciary acts honestly in the best interests of his beneficiaries so as to make a profit for his beneficiaries and himself at the expense of third parties there

---

[45] *Coles* v. *Trecothick* (1804) 9 Ves. 234; *Morse* v. *Royal* (1806) 12 Ves. 355; *Gibson* v. *Jeyes* (1801) 6 Ves. 266; *cf. Fox* v. *Mackreth* (1788) 2 Bro.C.C. 400. These factors can make it difficult for the trustee to find a purchaser when he himself wishes to sell, as a purchaser will be bound by a beneficiary's equity to set aside the transaction if he has actual or constructive notice.

[46] See T. B. Ruoff, " Purchases in Breach of Trust: A Suggested Cure " (1954) 18 Conv.(N.S.) 528.

[47] *Bray* v. *Ford* [1896] A.C. 44, 51; *Parker* v. *McKenna* (1874) L.R. 10 Ch. 96, 124–125; *Phipps* v. *Boardman* [1967] 2 A.C. 46; Goff & Jones, Chap. 55.

[48] *Aberdeen Town Council* v. *Aberdeen University* (1877) 2 App.Cas. 544, 549; *Sugden* v. *Crossland* (1856) 3 Sm. & Giff. 192; *Re Payne's Settlement* (1886) 54 L.T. 840; *Phipps* v. *Boardman* [1967] 2 A.C. 46; *Cook* v. *Deeks* [1916] 1 A.C. 554.

[49] As also do *Regal (Hastings) Ltd.* v. *Gulliver* [1967] 2 A.C. 134; *Industrial De-velopment Consultants* v. *Cooley* [1972] 1 W.L.R. 443 (noted 89 L.Q.R. 187 and *cf. Re David Payne* [1904] 2 Ch. 648 as to information obtained by a director privately).

[50] *Aas* v. *Benham* [1891] 2 Ch. 244; *Trimble* v. *Goldberg* [1906] A.C. 494. See also *N.Z. Netherlands Society* v. *Kuys* [1973] 1 W.L.R. 1126 where a prima facie fiduciary obligation was held displaced by the Privy Council.

is much to be said [51] against the straightforward approach of the majority of the Lords in *Boardman* v. *Phipps*. Should not the court concentrate on the reasons behind equity's rule and ask itself [52] : (1) Has the fiduciary been unjustly enriched at his beneficiaries' expense? (2) Does policy demand, in the circumstances of the case, the imposition of a penal liability to account? [53]

Benefits may be retained if authorised by the trust instrument [54] (Company Articles,[55] Deed of Partnership) or if authorised after full disclosure to the beneficiaries being each *sui juris* and between them absolutely entitled to the trust property [56] (a majority of the shareholders unless a fraud on the minority is involved, all partners). A trustee does not escape liability by full disclosure to his co-trustees as they may well have too close a relationship with him to be sufficiently objective in regarding the interests of the beneficiaries. However, it would seem that someone employed by the trustees in a fiduciary position or a beneficiary with confidential information *qua* beneficiary may be able to escape liability by obtaining the informed consent of independent trustees—at least if the consent was in the best interests of the beneficiaries at the time.[57] Assistance towards this conclusion can be derived from contrasting the position of directors and promoters of companies. Promoters must make full disclosure either to an independent [58] board of directors or to the members of the company as a whole. Directors must make full disclosure to the members of the company as a whole [59] (unless authorised by the Articles, *e.g.*, article 84 (3) of Table ' A ' to the Companies Act 1948 to retain profits after disclosure to the board alone).

At this stage it is worthwhile remarking that irrespective of fiduciary or contractual relationships an equitable obligation of confidence may arise from the mere receipt of information in the knowledge that it was confidential. " The law on this subject . . . depends on the broad principle of equity that he who has received information in confidence shall not take unfair advantage of it. He must not make use of it to the prejudice of him who

---

51 Gareth Jones (1968) 84 L.Q.R. 472, emphasising the force of Lord Upjohn's speech particularly on the fact that there was no " real sensible possibility of conflict " and on the notion of information as trust " property." *Cf. North & South Trust Co.* v. *Berkeley* [1971] 1 W.L.R. 471, 489.

52 These two questions are those posed by Gareth Jones (*ibid.*). See the liberal approach in *Pine Pass Oil* v. *Pacific Petroleum* (1968) 70 D.L.R. (2d) 196: *Peso Silver Mines* v. *Copper* (1966) 58 D.L.R. (2d) noted (1967) 30 M.L.R. 450; *Manufacturers Trust Co.* v. *Becker* (1949) 338 U.S. 304; 70 Sup.Ct. 127; *Canadian Aero Service Ltd.* v. *Malley* (1973) 40 D.L.R. (3d) 371, noted (1974) 37 M.L.R. 414 (D. D. Prentice).

53 Gareth Jones points out that it is inappropriate for the plaintiff to have the proprietary claim (enabling the plaintiff to have priority over the defendant's general creditors and to trace not merely the property itself but also its fruits) if the fiduciary has acted honestly and the beneficiaries have suffered no loss.

54 *Re Llewellin* [1949] Ch. 225.

55 1948 Companies Act Table A Article 84.

56 *Boardman* v. *Phipps* [1967] 2 A.C. 46; *Costa Rica Rly.* v. *Forwood* [1901] Ch. 746.

57 This may explain certain dicta in *Boardman* v. *Phipps* [1967] 2 A.C. 46; [1965] Ch. 992 indicating that full disclosure to the trustees by the solicitor and the beneficiary might have sufficed. Further see *Mosser* v. *Darrow*, 71 S.Ct. 680 (1951), where the U.S.A. Supreme Court held a trustee accountable for profits he had authorised trust employees to make, and *per* Lord Upjohn at p. 375 *supra*.

58 Disclosure to cronies will not suffice: *Gluckstein* v. *Barnes* [1900] A.C. 240.

59 Gower's *Company Law*, 3rd ed., pp. 530–531, 535–539.

gave it without obtaining his consent "[60]: *Seager* v. *Copydex, infra.*
Moreover, " if the circumstances are such that any reasonable man standing
in the shoes of the recipient of the information would have realised that
upon reasonable grounds the information was being given to him in confidence, then this should suffice to impose upon him the equitable obligation
of conscience." [61] If the defendant consciously breaks the plaintiff's confidence then the courts will be ready to grant an injunction and to direct an
account of profits [62] or even impose a constructive trusteeship where the
plaintiff's information alone leads to the defendant dishonestly taking out a
patent.   However, if the defendant acted honestly but foolishly in believing
that he was not breaching confidence then damages [63] alone will be awarded
at least if the information imparted had only partially contributed to the
product marketed to produce the profits: *Seager* v. *Copydex.* Nonetheless,
if the information were the *sine qua non* and the defendant was foolish and
acting unreasonably in thinking that he was not breaching the plaintiff's
confidence there is much to be said for the view that the defendant should
be liable to account for his unjust enrichment.[64]

Re GEE, WOOD AND OTHERS v. STAPLES AND OTHERS

Chancery Division [1948] Ch. 284; [1948] L.J.R. 1400; 92 S.J. 232;
[1948] 1 All E.R. 498

The capital of a private company, Gee & Co. (Publishers) Ltd., was
£5,000 in £1 shares. Immediately before his death on December 2, 1937,
Alfred Lionel Gee (" the testator ") was the registered owner of 4,996
shares, of which he held 1,996 in his own right and 3,000 as sole
surviving executor of his father's will upon the trusts relating thereto.
The remaining four shares were held, one each, by the testator's sister,
Miss Gee; his second wife, who remarried after his death and at the
time of this action had become Mrs. Haynes; his daughter, Mrs. Hunter;
and Mr. Staples.

The testator appointed Mrs. Haynes, Mrs. Hunter and Mr. Staples
to be the executors and trustees of his will. After the death of the
testator Mr. Staples was appointed managing director of the company
by unanimous agreement of the executors and Miss Gee, who together
constituted all the registered shareholders. The appointment and
remuneration of Mr. Staples were subsequently confirmed by an annual
general meeting.

---

[60] *Per* Lord Denning in *Seager* v. *Copydex* [1967] 1 W.L.R. 923, 926; also *Fraser* v.
Evans [1969] 1 Q.B. 349, 353, " Even if he comes by it innocently, nevertheless,
once he gets to know that it was originally given in confidence, he can be
restrained from breaking that confidence." As to which see *Stevenson Jordan &
Harrison Ltd.* v. *Macdonald & Evans* (1951) 68 R.P.C. 190, 195; (1952) 69 R.P.C.
10, 16. Generally see Gareth Jones (1970) 86 L.Q.R. 463 and Law Com. W.P. No.
58.
[61] *Coco* v. *A. N. Clark (Engineers) Ltd.* [1969] R.P.C. 41, 48 *per* Megarry J.
[62] *Peter Pan Manufacturing Co.* v. *Corsets Silhouette Ltd.* [1964] 1 W.L.R. 96. An
injunction alone may suffice if the plaintiff is quick enough: *Cranleigh Precision
Engineering Ltd.* v. *Bryant* [1965] 1 W.L.R. 1293.
[63] For the principles of assessment see *Seager* v. *Copydex (No. 2)* [1969] 1 W.L.R.
809. Presumably awarded in lieu of injunction: Lord Cairns' Act 1858.
[64] Gareth Jones (1970) 86 L.Q.R. 463, 476.

The testator's will was proved on March 24, 1939, by all three executors, and the 3,000 shares, previously vested in the testator as executor of his father's will, were registered in the names of the beneficiaries entitled under that will. The testator was himself so entitled to 334 shares.

The company was in a very bad way at the time of the testator's death but it prospered under Mr. Staples' management to the point of declaring a dividend of 75 per cent. free of tax.

Mr. Staples received £15,721 as remuneration between the date of the testator's death and March 31, 1947. Some of the beneficiaries under the testator's will claimed that Mr. Staples was liable to account.

HARMAN J.: " ... [The claim] raises in a complicated form the vexed question of the liability of trustees who become salaried officers of companies in which their testator's estate is largely interested. . . .

" The allegation made against Mr. Staples is that he made use of his position of trust under the testator's will to obtain his remuneration, and it is this which needs examination. The cases on the subject are not numerous, nor do I find them very helpful. None of them deals with a position where more than one trust estate is involved. The principle that a trustee, in the absence of a special contract, cannot make a profit out of his trust, nor be paid for his time and trouble, is an old one, and is spoken of as established in *Robinson* v. *Pett.*[65] It is most clearly stated by Lord Herschell in *Bray* v. *Ford* [66] in these words: ' It is an inflexible rule of a court of equity that a person in a fiduciary position . . . is not, unless otherwise expressly provided, entitled to make a profit; he is not allowed to put himself in a position where his interest and duty conflict.' The difficulty of applying this principle arises where the payment is made not directly out of the trust estate, but by a third party or body, and, in particular, by a limited company. The modern cases begin with *Re Francis*,[67] from which it appears—though the case is not reported on this point—that Kekewich J. declined to allow trustees to retain for their own use remuneration received by them from a company in which the testator held substantially all the shares. The remuneration was voted at a general meeting, and appears to have been procured by the trustees by the exercise of the voting powers attached to the trust shares which had become registered in their names. This case was not cited in *Re Dover Coalfield Extension Ltd.*,[68] which has been sometimes thought to be inconsistent with it.[69] This, however, in my judgment is not so. The *Dover* case appears, when examined, to have been what Cozens-Hardy M.R. called it,[70] ' a very plain case.' The trustees there had become directors before they held

65 (1734) 3 P.Wms. 250, 261.
66 [1896] A.C. 44, 51.
67 (1905) 74 L.J.Ch. 198.
68 [1908] 1 Ch. 65.
69 See, *e.g.*, *Underhill on Trusts*, 9th ed., p. 353.
70 [1908] 1 Ch. 65, 69.

any trust shares. The trust shares were, by their own procurement, registered in their names in order to qualify them to continue as directors, but it was not by virtue of the use of these shares that they either became entitled or continued to earn their fees. Warrington J., however, in this case does suggest [71] that remuneration paid for acting as a director of a company can never be a profit for which a trustee needs to account, and it is this expression of opinion which is reflected in the headnote and has given rise to a good deal of misconception about the case. This view was not necessary to the decision and may be regarded as mere *obiter dictum*. It is, in my judgment, too wide, if applied to a case where either the use of the trust shares brings about the appointment, or there is no independent board of the employing company to strike a proper bargain with the employed trustee. Moreover, it leaves out of account the second leg of the principle stated by Lord Herschell in *Bray* v. *Ford*.[72] The beneficiaries are entitled to the advantage of the unfettered use by the trustee of his judgment as to the government of the company in which they are interested. This they do not get if his judgment is clouded by the prospect of the pecuniary advantage he may acquire if he makes use of the trust shares to obtain for himself a directorship carrying remuneration. *Re Lewis* [73] is again an instance where the trustee did not receive the remuneration by virtue of the use of his position as a trustee, but by an independent bargain with the firm employing him.

" There follow two cases on the other side of the line, first, *Williams* v. *Barton*,[74] where one of the trustees, a half-commission agent in the Stock Exchange, had persuaded his co-trustees to employ his firm to value the trust securities, thus increasing his commission from his firm and making a profit directly by the use of his position as a trustee. Russell J. held him accountable. Last, there is the decision of Cohen J. in *Re Macadam*,[75] where the cases are reviewed. There certain trustees had a power as such, and by virtue of the articles of the company, to appoint two directors of it. By the exercise of this power they appointed themselves and were held liable to account for the remuneration they received because they had acquired it by the direct use of their trust powers. Cohen J. felt (and I respectfully concur) that he ought to do nothing to weaken the principle, and he expressed the view that [76] ' the root of the matter . . . is: Did the trustee acquire the position in respect of which he drew the remuneration by virtue of his position as trustee? ' The judge also held [77] that the liability to account for a profit could not ' be confined to cases where the profit is derived directly from the trust estate.'

---

71 [1907] 2 Ch. 76, 83.
72 [1896] A.C. 44, 51.
73 (1910) 103 L.T. 495.
74 [1927] 2 Ch. 9.
75 [1946] Ch. 73.
76 *Ibid.* 82.
77 *Ibid.*

" I conclude from this review that a trustee who either uses a power vested in him as such to obtain a benefit, as in *Re Macadam*, or who (as in *Barton's* case) procures his co-trustees to give him, or those associated with him, remunerative employment, must account for the benefit obtained. Further, it appears to me that a trustee, who has the power, by the use of trust votes, to control his own appointment to a remunerative position, and refrains from using them, with the result that he is elected to the position of profit, would also be accountable. On the other hand, it appears not to be the law that every man who becomes a trustee, holding, as such, shares in a limited company, is made *ipso facto* accountable for remuneration received from that company independently of any use by him of the trust holding, whether by voting or refraining from so doing. For instance, A, who holds the majority of the shares in a limited company, becomes the trustee of the estate of B, a holder of a minority interest. This cannot, I think, disentitle A to use his own shares to procure his appointment as an officer of the company, nor compel him to disgorge the remuneration he so receives, for he cannot be disentitled to the use of his own voting powers, nor could the use of the trust votes in a contrary sense prevent the majority prevailing. Many other instances could be given of a similar kind of these, *Re Dover Coalfield Extension Ltd.* is really one. There the trustees did not earn their fees by virtue of the trust shares, though, no doubt, the holding of those shares was a qualification necessary for the continued earning of the fees. In so far as Warrington J. goes further than this, as he seems to do by suggesting that remuneration paid by a company could not be a ' profit,' it being a mere wage equivalent in value to the work done for it, I feel he goes too far. Certainly this view was not taken in *Re Macadam*. It would gravely encroach on the principle which Cohen J. [in that case] and Russell J. in *Williams* v. *Barton* felt to be so important.

" I turn now to an examination of the facts in this case to see what (if any) use was made of the trust shares in the appointment of Mr. Staples. In my judgment, when the facts are examined, no such use was made. After the death of the testator, only four persons remained on the register of this company, and they alone could attend meetings of it. As I have said before, the meeting [at which Mr. Staples was appointed managing director] was attended by all the corporators. Each of them held one share, and, as the resolutions were passed unanimously, they must be supposed to have voted in favour by the use of that share. If the corporators, as I think, held their shares beneficially, they were entitled to vote as they chose. If, on the other hand, they were nominees of the testator, there were still three of them whose votes outweighed the vote of Mr. Staples if it was his duty to vote against his own interest. In neither event did the trust shares come into the picture at all. If this be too narrow a view to take, and it is right for this purpose to look behind the register at the beneficial interests in the shares of the company, then it will be seen that the majority interest belonged to the estate of [the testator's father] and that the persons entitled to have his shares registered in their names . . . were in favour of the appointment and the payment of the stipulated remuneration. If then the shares in which the testator's estate was interested had all been used against the resolutions, they would still have been carried, and, therefore, the appointment was not procured by the use of the trust interest vested in the defendant executors, or any of them, by the will of the testator, in which alone the plaintiffs are interested. On the evidence tendered to me, I think it is clear that the persons present at this meeting had no notion that they were using trust votes, or that trust votes controlled the company. They merely met as the four corporators to decide the company's future and were entitled to come to the conclusion at which they arrived. . . ." [78]

Gareth Jones (1968) 84 L.Q.R. 472

Manufacturers Trust Co. v. *Becker* [79] concerned the fate of claims made on the liquidation of a corporation. Directors of the corporation [80] had acquired debentures at a discount, at prices varying from 3 per cent. to 14 per cent. of their face value. At the time of their purchase the corporation was a going concern but the market value of its property was insufficient to pay its outstanding debts. [81] The referee found that the purchases were made " without overreaching or failure to disclose any material fact to the selling bond holders," that the purchases " were not unfair to debtor, that at the time of respondents' purchases debtor was not in the field to settle its indebtedness on the debentures, and that the assistance rendered to debtor by respondents materially aided [it] in its grave financial situation." [82] The trustee for the debenture holders objected to the claims on the ground that the holders, being directors, could not profit from the purchase of claims against an insolvent corporation. The Supreme Court dismissed the trustee's objection, and allowed the claims in full.

Justice Clark, who delivered the opinion of the court, recognised

---

[78] See also *Re Llewellin* [1949] Ch. 225 (testator authorised trustees to use trust shares to secure appointment as directors: *held* he must be deemed to have authorised them to retain directors' fees).

[79] 338 U.S. 304, 70 S.Ct. 127 (1949).

[80] The facts of the case have been simplified in the text. The claims had in fact been bought by close relatives and an office associate of the directors. But the Supreme Court treated the acquisition as having been made by the directors themselves: see 338 U.S. 304, 310. And see *post*, note 86 for a further comment on this point.

[81] This distinction is fundamental to the court's decision. If the corporation has been in liquidation the court would have had to " reject any claim that would not be fair and equitable to other creditors ": see *Pepper* v. *Litton*, 308 U.S. 295, 60 S.Ct. 238 (1939). On going into liquidation, the company's assets are held on trust for its creditors and contributors: see *R. S. Hollins* v. *The Brierfield Coal & Iron Co.*, 150 U.S. 371, 383 *per* Justice Brewer (1893); *Re Calton Crescent Inc.*, 173 F. 2d 944, 950, *per* Swan J. (1949); *cited post*, p. 481. And *cf.* The English case of *I.R.C.* v. *Olive Mill Ltd.* [1963] 1 W.L.R. 712.

[82] 338 U.S. 304, 309.

" that equity must apply not only the doctrines of unjust enrichment when fiduciaries have yielded to the temptation of self-interest but also a standard of loyalty which will prevent a conflict of interests from arising." [83]   It was true that there was a possibility of " an inherent conflict of interests. . . .   It may [have been] necessary for them [the directors] to choose between a corporate policy of reorganisation which might be best for the corporation and one of liquidation which might yield more certain profits to them as note holding directors." [84]   On the other hand, the directors had acted in the utmost good faith with the interests of the corporation at heart.   There was " nothing to suggest that had the debentures been acquired by the *Becker* directors, they would have been unjustly enriched." [85]   Against " this potentiality of conflict " the court balanced the desirability of permitting the directors, in the circumstances of the case, to reinforce the financial position of the insolvent company; and concluded that the latter policy should prevail. [86]

In the *Becker* case, the fiduciaries, the directors, had acted in good faith, with the firm intention of assisting the corporation.   By pumping money into the corporation at a critical time in its history and thereby encouraging public confidence in its future, they acted in what was reasonably thought to be its best interests. [87]   Moreover, the profit was made not at the expense of the corporation, which always remained liable for the face value of the bonds to the holders whoever they might be, but at the expense of the selling bond holders.   The corporation suffered no real loss.   This consideration weighed heavily with the judges of the Federal Court of Appeals, Second Circuit, from whose judgment the trustee-in-bankruptcy had appealed. [88]

As Judge Swan said [89]:

> " After insolvency it may be said that the directors are fiduciaries for the group of creditors who will share in the insolvent's estate.   But the creditors who have retained their claims will suffer nothing whether or not the director is allowed to make a profit from his purchases.   If a wrong has been done to any of the group of *cestuis*, it is to those who sold their claims at a price less than the dividend they would have received had they retained them.   If they were suing for the wrong done them, they would have to show something equivalent to a fraudulent non-

---

[83] 338 U.S. 304, 312.

[84] This quotation is in fact taken from Justice Burton's dissenting opinion: 338 U.S. 304, 316. In his view, there was such a conflict.

[85] 338 U.S. 304, 311.

[86] If the court had held the other way, the question would have arisen as to the extent (if any) to which the relatives and the office associate should be identified with the directors: see *Re Franklin Building Co.*, 178 F. 2d 805 (1950), cert. denied 339 U.S. 978 (1950).

[87] *Cf. McGeoch Building Co.* v. *Dick & Reuteman Co.*, 253 Wis. 166, 33 N.W. 2d 252 (1948).

[88] *Sub nom. Re Calton Crescent Inc.*, 173 F. 2d 944 (1949).

[89] At p. 950.

disclosure.... Plainly if the contest for the director's profits was between the wronged *cestuis* and the unwronged *cestuis*, the former should prevail. Where it is between the unwronged *cestuis* and a director, if the former are allowed to prevail it can only be as a disciplinary measure against the director for wronging someone who has not complained of the wrong. ...

" In the case at bar, where there was no overreaching of the sellers, we are not convinced that the circumstances are such as to require imposition of the sanction."

Both the Supreme Court and the Court of Appeals refused, therefore, to create a conflict of interest where none in fact existed and, on the particular facts, to impose a penal liability on a fiduciary whose enrichment could not be said to be unjust.

In *Phipps* v. *Boardman*,[90] however, the majority of the House of Lords imposed such a liability on fiduciaries who had acted in the best interests of their principal, without inquiring whether it was necessary to do so. ...

In Canada, the Supreme Court has recently refused to declare that a director who had acted honestly and in perfect good faith was a trustee of a mining claim for his corporation, where the board of which he was a member had previously refused to take it up.[91] As Bull J.A. said in the lower court [92]:

" In this modern day and country when it is accepted as commonplace that substantially all business and commercial undertakings, regardless of size or importance, are carried on through the corporate vehicle with the attendant complexities involved by interlocking, subsidiary and associated corporations, I do not consider it enlightened to extend the application of these principles beyond their present limits. That the principles, and the strict rules applicable to trustees upon which they are based, are salutary cannot be disputed, but care should be taken to interpret them in the light of modern practice and way of life."

Similar reasoning persuaded the Michigan court to allow a director to retain a tax title when it would have been *ultra vires* the corporation to have bought it.[93]

Regal (Hastings) Ltd. v. *Gulliver*[94] is a good illustration of the approach of the English courts. The appellant company owned a

---

[90] [1967] 2 A.C. 46 (*sub nom. Boardman* v. *Phipps*); affirming the decision of the Court of Appeal ([1965] Ch. 992).

[91] *Peso Silver Mines Ltd.* v. *Cropper* (1966) 58 D.L.R. (2d) 1; affirming the judgment of the British Columbia Court of Appeal: 56 D.L.R. (2d) 117; 54 W.W.R. 329. *Cf. Lincoln Stores* v. *Grant*, 309 Mass. 417, 34 N.E. 2d 704 (1941), and *Canadian Western National Gas Co. Ltd.* v. *Central Gas Utilities, Ltd.* (1966) 58 W.W.R. 155.

[92] (1966) 56 D.L.R. (2d) 117, 154–155.

[93] *Thilco Timber* v. *Sawyer*, 236 Mich. 401 (1926). But *cf. Fine Industrial Commodities Ltd.* v. *Powling* (1954) 71 R.P.C. 253.

[94] The decision has now been reproduced in the *Law Reports*: [1967] 2 A.C. 134n.

cinema in Hastings and wanted to acquire two more cinemas, with a view to selling the property of the company as a going concern. For the purpose of acquiring the cinemas a subsidiary company was formed. The landlord was prepared to offer a lease of these properties but required the directors to guarantee the rent unless the paid-up capital of the subsidiary was £5,000. The appellant company, which was to hold all the shares of the subsidiary company, could only afford to subscribe for 2,000 shares; and the directors did not want to give personal guarantees for the rest. Accordingly the directors (on their own behalf and on behalf of certain third parties) and the company solicitor arranged to finance the transaction by personally taking up the other 3,000 shares. This arrangement was formalised by a resolution at a board meeting at which the solicitor was present, and the shares were duly paid up and allotted. The trial judge found that the directors and the solicitor had acted in perfect good faith and in the best interests of the appellant company. Shortly afterwards the proposed sale and purchase of the three cinemas as going concerns fell through. But it was replaced by another proposal which involved a sale of the shares in the appellant company and its subsidiary. This proposal was accepted. From the sale of their shares in the subsidiary, the directors and the solicitor made a profit of £2 16s. 1d. per share. In this action the appellant company, now controlled by the purchasers, sought to recover this profit from the former directors and the solicitor.

The House of Lords held that the directors, but not the solicitor, must disgorge their profits to the company, for the opportunity and special knowledge to acquire the shares had come to them *qua* fiduciaries. As Lord Russell of Killowen said [95]:

> " The rule of equity which insists on those who by use of a fiduciary position make a profit, being liable to account for that profit, in no way depends on fraud, or absence of bona fides; or upon such questions or considerations as whether the profit would or should otherwise have gone to the plaintiff, or whether the profiteer was under a duty to obtain the source of the profit for the plaintiff, or whether he took a risk or acted as he did for the benefit of the plaintiff, or whether the plaintiff has in fact been damaged or benefited by his action. The liability arises from the mere fact of a profit having, in the stated circumstances, been made. The profiteer, however, honest and well intentioned, cannot escape the risk of being called upon to account....
>
> " I am of the opinion that the directors standing in a fiduciary relationship to Regal [the appellant company] in regard to the exercise of their powers as directors, and having obtained these shares by reason and only by reason of the fact that they were directors of Regal and in the course of the execution of that

---

95 [1967] 2 A.C. 134, 145, 149.

office, are accountable for the profits which they have made out of them. The equitable rule laid down in *Keech* v. *Sandford* . . . and similar authorities applies to them in full force. It was contended that these cases were distinguishable by reason of the fact that it was impossible for Regal to get the shares owing to lack of funds, and that the directors in taking the shares were really acting as members of the public. I cannot accept this argument. It was impossible for the *cestui que trust* in *Keech* v. *Sandford* to obtain the lease, nevertheless the trustee was accountable. The suggestion that the directors were applying simply as members of the public is a travesty of the facts."

The solicitor, however, was not in a fiduciary position. Because he had taken the shares at the directors' request, he was not compelled to account for his profits. The chairman of the company who had bought his shares only as a nominee of third parties was also not liable to account to the appellant company. "Neither the shares nor the profit ever belonged to [him]." [96]

The company's claim lacked all merit.[97] As a result of the House of Lords' decision, the purchasers of the shares " receive[d] in one hand part of the sum which ha[d] been paid by the other. For the shares in Amalgamated [the subsidiary] they paid £3 16s. 1d. per share, yet part of that sum may be returned to the group, though not necessarily to the individual shareholders by reason of the enhancement in the value of the shares in Regal—an enhancement brought about as a result of the receipt by the company of the profit made by some of its former directors on the sale of Amalgamated shares." [98] Only Lord Porter, from whose speech this quotation is taken, chose to mention this point. He recognised that Regal, and hence its purchasers, had received an " unexpected windfall." But, he concluded,[99]

> " whether it be so or not, the principle that a person occupying a fiduciary relationship shall not make a profit by reason thereof is of such vital importance that the possible consequence in the present case is in fact as it is in law an immaterial consideration."

But did the House too easily assume that principle to be of " vital importance "? The critical issue was whether directors, acting in good faith, should be allowed to retain profits made from the sale of shares in circumstances where the company wanted to acquire them but was financially unable to do so. It may well be necessary in such a case to impose a prophylactic rule. As Judge Swan of the Court of Appeals, Second Circuit, pointed out in *Irving Trust Co.* v. *Deutsch*,[1] if

---

[96] At p. 151, *per* Lord Russell of Killowen.
[97] L. C. B. Gower, *Modern Company Law*, 2nd ed. (London 1957), p. 487.
[98] [1967] 2 A.C. 134, 152 *per* Lord Porter.
[99] At p. 152.
[1] 73 F. 2d 121, 124 (1934). But *cf. Zeckendorf* v. *Steinfeld*, 12 Ariz. 245, 100 P. 784 (1909); *Beaumont* v. *Folsom*, 136 Neb. 235, 285 N.W. 547 (1939).

directors could justify their conduct on the theory that their corporation was financially unable to undertake their venture,

" there will be a temptation to refrain from exerting their strongest efforts on behalf of the corporation since, if it does not meet the obligations, an opportunity of profit will be open to them [the directors] personally. . . .

" If the directors are uncertain whether the corporation can make the necessary outlays, they need not embark it upon the venture; if they do, they may not substitute themselves for the corporation any place along the line and divert possible benefits into their own pockets."

But directors are business men. In the Court of Appeal in *Regal (Hastings) Ltd.* v. *Gulliver,*[2] Lord Greene sympathised with the dilemma of the Regal directors:

" [A]s a matter of business . . . there was only one way left of raising the money, and that was putting it up themselves. . . . That being so, the only way in which [they] could secure that benefit for the company was by putting up the money themselves. Once that decision is held to be a bona fide one and fraud drops out of the case, it seems to me that there is only one conclusion, namely, that the [company's] appeal must be dismissed with costs."

The House of Lords rejected Lord Greene's reasoning and followed *Keech* v. *Sandford.*[3] Yet it is not easy to see why because Lord King decided in 1726 that a trustee could not renew a trust lease for his own benefit, it *must* follow that the Regal directors, acting honestly and in the best interests of the company should disgorge the profit from the sale of the shares. The relevant policy considerations were delicately balanced. But the House of Lords' unquestioning adherence to the inexorable rule of equity meant that they were never properly weighed against each other.

SEAGER v. COPYDEX

Court of Appeal [1967] 1 W.L.R. 923; [1967] 2 All E.R. 415 (Lord Denning M.R., Salmon and Winn L.JJ.)

LORD DENNING M.R. (in a reserved judgment): " Summarised, the facts are these—

" (i) The plaintiff invented the ' Klent ' carpet grip and took out a patent for it. He manufactured this grip and sold it. He was looking for a selling organisation to market it.

---

[2] The decision of the Court of Appeal is not reported. This quotation from Lord Greene's judgment was cited by Viscount Sankey in his speech in the House of Lords (at p. 381). It was adopted and followed in *Peso Silver Mines Ltd.* (*N.P.L.*) v. *Cropper* (1966) 58 D.L.R. (2d) 1.
[3] (1726) Cas.temp. King 61.

" (ii) The plaintiff negotiated with the defendant company with a view to their marketing the ' Klent ' grip. These negotiations were with Mr. Preston, the assistant manager, and Mr. Boon, the sales manager. These negotiations lasted more than a year, but came to nothing.

" (iii) In the course of those negotiations, the plaintiff disclosed to Mr. Preston and Mr. Boon all the features of the ' Klent ' grip. He also told them of an idea of his for an alternative carpet grip with a ' V ' tang and strong point. But they rejected it, saying that they were only interested in the ' Klent ' grip.

" (iv) Both Mr. Preston and Mr. Boon realised that the information was given to them in confidence. Neither of them had any engineering skills, nor had invented anything.

" (v) As soon as the negotiations looked like coming to nothing, the defendant company decided to make a carpet grip of their own, which was to be basically similar to the ' Klent ' grip, but with spikes which would not infringe the plaintiff's patent.

" (vi) The defendant company did in fact make a carpet grip which did not infringe the plaintiff's patent for a ' Klent ' grip. But it embodied the very idea of an alternative grip (of a ' V-tang ' with strong point) which the plaintiff mentioned to them in the course of the negotiations. They made an application to patent it, and gave the name of Mr. Preston as the true and first inventor.

" (vii) The defendant company gave this carpet grip the name ' Invisigrip ' which was the very name which the plaintiff says that he mentioned to Mr. Preston and Mr. Boon in the course of the negotiations.

" (viii) The defendant company say that their alternative grip was the result of their own ideas and was not derived in any way from any information given to them by the plaintiff. They say also that the name of ' Invisigrip ' was their own spontaneous idea.

" (ix) I have no doubt that the defendant company honestly believed the alternative grip was their own idea; but I think that they must unconsciously have made use of the information which the plaintiff gave them. The coincidences are too strong to permit of any other explanation.

" *The Law.* I start with one sentence in the judgment of Lord Greene M.R. in *Saltman Engineering Co. Ltd.* v. *Campbell Engineering Co. Ltd.*[4]:

> ' If a defendant is proved to have used confidential informa-
> tion, directly or indirectly obtained from the plaintiff, without the
> consent, express or implied, of the plaintiff, he will be guilty of an
> infringement of the plaintiff's rights.'

---

4 [1963] 3 All E.R. 413, 414; 65 R.P.C. 203, 213.

To this I add a sentence from the judgment of Roxburgh J. in *Terrapin Ltd.* v. *Builders' Supply Co. (Hayes) Ltd., Taylor Woodrow Ltd. & Swiftplan Ltd.*,[5] which was quoted and adopted as correct by Roskill J. in *Cranleigh Precision Engineering Co. Ltd.* v. *Bryant* [6]:

> ' As I understand it, the essence of this branch of the law, whatever the origin of it may be, is that a person who has obtained information in confidence is not allowed to use it as a springboard for activities detrimental to the person who made the confidential communication, and springboard it remains even when all the features have been published or can be ascertained by actual inspection by any member of the public.'

The law on this subject does not depend on any implied contract. It depends on the broad principle of equity that he who has received information in confidence shall not take unfair advantage of it. He must not make use of it to the prejudice of him who gave it without obtaining his consent. The principle is clear enough when the whole of the information is private. The difficulty arises when the information is in part public and in part private. As for instance in this case. A good deal of the information which the plaintiff gave to the defendant company was available to the public, such as the patent specification in the Patent Office, or the ' Klent ' grip, which he sold to anyone who asked. But there was a good deal of other information which was private, such as, the difficulties which had to be overcome in making a satisfactory grip; the necessity for a strong, sharp tooth; the alternative forms of tooth; and the like. When the information is mixed, being partly public and partly private, then the recipient must take special care to use only the material which is in the public domain. He should go to the public source and get it: or, at any rate, not be in a better position than if he had gone to the public source. He should not get a start over others by using the information which he received in confidence. At any rate, he should not get a start without paying for it. It may not be a case for injunction but only for damages, depending on the worth of the confidential information to him in saving him time and trouble.

" *Conclusion.* Applying these principles, I think that the plaintiff should succeed. On the facts which I have stated, he told the defendant company a lot about the making of a satisfactory carpet grip which was not in the public domain. They would not have got going so quickly except for what they had learned in their discussions with him. They got to know in particular that it was possible to make an alternative grip in the form of a ' V-tang ', provided the tooth was sharp enough and strong enough, and they were told about the special shape required. The judge thought that the information was not significant.

---

[5] [1960] R.P.C. 130.
[6] [1965] 1 W.L.R. 1293.

But I think it was. It was the springboard which enabled them to go on to devise the 'Invisigrip' and to apply for a patent for it. They were quite innocent of any intention to take advantage of him. They thought that, as long as they did not infringe his patent, they were exempt. In this they were in error. They were not aware of the law as to confidential information.

" I would allow the appeal and give judgment to the plaintiff for damages to be assessed. . . .

" The court grants neither an account of profits, nor an injunction, but only damages to be assessed by the master. Damages should be assessed on the basis of reasonable compensation for the use of the confidential information which was given to the defendant company." [7]

III. COMPETITION WITH THE TRUST

The general rule is that a trustee may not, after accepting a trust which comprises a business, set up a private business which competes or may compete with the business of the trust since, if he did so, his interest would conflict with his duty. Thus in *Re Thomson*,[8] the testator's estate included a yachtbroker's business which he bequeathed to his executors on trust to continue it. One of the executors claimed the right to set up a similar business in competition with the trust, but the court granted an injunction to restrain him. On the other hand, in the Irish case of *Moore* v. *M'Glynn*,[9] the court refused to restrain a trustee from setting up a competing business, but considered that it would be a good ground for removing him from his trusteeship. Chatterton V.-C. observed [10]: " I have not been referred to, nor am I aware of, any case deciding that an executor or trustee of a will carrying on the business of his testator is disabled from setting up a similar business in the same locality on his own account. . . . I am not prepared to hold that a trustee is guilty of a breach of trust in setting up for himself in a similar line of business in the neighbourhood, provided that he does not resort to deception or solicitation of custom from persons dealing at the old shop." Perhaps the distinction between this case and *Re Thomson* is that in the latter the business was highly specialised and the locality was very small so that the competition was inevitable whether or not there was solicitation of custom.

Any profits made in breach of duty should be held on trust for the beneficiaries as the profits are their profits which have been lost by the trustee's competition.[11] Whilst partners are under a statutory obligation [12] not to

---

[7] See *Seager* v. *Copydex (No. 2)* [1969] 1 W.L.R. 809 for the assessment of damages.

[8] [1930] 1 Ch. 203. Where at p. 215 Clauson J. said, " An executor and trustee having duties to discharge of a fiduciary nature towards the beneficiaries under the will shall not be allowed to enter into any engagement in which he has or can have a personal interest conflicting or which possibly may conflict with the interests of those whom he is bound to protect."

[9] [1894] 1 Ir.R. 74.

[10] *Ibid.* 89.

[11] Goff and Jones, p. 453 citing *Somerville* v. *Mackay* (1810) 16 Ves. 382; *Dean* v. *MacDowell* (1877) 8 Ch.D. 345, 353; *Trimble* v. *Goldberg* [1906] A.C. 494; Restatement of Restitution, para. 199.

[12] Partnership Act 1890, s. 30.

engage in competing business it seems that non-service directors are not so obliged but they must be very careful as to the information they disclose to rival companies.[13]

IV. GRATUITOUS ADMINISTRATION OF TRUST

Trustees must, in the absence of some special dispensation, administer the trust gratuitously for otherwise " the trust estate might be loaded and made of little value." [14]

The cases in which the trustee is entitled to payment for his services are:

First, in a suitable case the court has an inherent jurisdiction to authorise a trustee to receive remuneration.   In order to do so the court must be satisfied that the services of the trustee will be or have been of exceptional benefit to the estate.[15]   The court, when appointing a *corporation* (other than the Public Trustee) to act, also has a statutory jurisdiction [16] under section 42 of the Trustee Act 1925 to authorise it to charge for its services.

Secondly, if the settlement authorises the trustee to charge for his services he is entitled to be paid, but charging clauses are construed strictly in the sense that the onus is on the trustee to show that the charge which he proposes to make is covered by the terms of the settlement. Thus, if a solicitor-trustee is authorised to make " professional charges," even where the words " for his time and trouble " are added, he will not be allowed to charge for time and trouble expended other than in his position as solicitor.[17]   But where a will authorises the solicitor-trustee to make " the usual professional or *other proper and reasonable* charges for all business done and time expended in relation to the trusts of the will, *whether such business is usually within the business of a solicitor or not,*" the solicitor is permitted to charge for business not strictly of a professional nature transacted by him in relation to the trust,[18] though, apparently, not for work altogether outside his professional vocation.[19]   Even if not needed at first it is important always to insert a charging clause so that a professional trustee may be appointed if need be at some stage.

Thirdly, if the beneficiaries are all *sui juris* and between them absolutely entitled to the trust estate, they may authorise the trustee to be paid. If the

---

13 *London & Mashonaland Exploration Co.* v. *New Mashonaland Exploration Co.* [1891] W.N. 165 approved by Lord Blanesburgh in *Bell* v. *Lever Bros.* [1932] A.C. 161, 195; Gower's *Company Law*, 3rd ed. pp. 547–548.

14 *Robinson* v. *Pett* (1734) 3 P.Wms. 249, 251.

15 *Marshall* v. *Holloway* (1820) 2 Swans. 432; *Re Freeman* (1887) 37 Ch.D. 148; *Re Masters* [1953] 1 W.L.R. 81; *Re Macadam* [1946] Ch. 73; *Boardman* v. *Phipps* [1967] 2 A.C. 46; *Re Barbour's Settlement* [1974] 1 All E.R. 1188, 1192.

16 The Public Trustee has a statutory right to charge under the Public Trustee Act 1906, s. 7, as have custodian trustees acting as custodian trustees *only* under the Public Trustee Act 1906, s. 4: *Forster* v. *Williams Deacon's Bank* [1935] Ch. 359. Judicial trustees may charge under Judicial Trustees Act 1896, s. 1.

17 *Re Chapple* (1884) 27 Ch.D. 584.

18 *Re Ames* (1883) 25 Ch.D. 72.

19 *Clarkson* v. *Robinson* [1900] 2 Ch. 722. See charging clause in settlement in Chap. 1. It should be noted that if a will appoints a solicitor trustee and there is a charging clause the charges are treated as a legacy—except for tax purposes when they are earned income: *Dale* v. *I.R.C.* [1954] A.C. 11. It follows that the solicitor must not be an attesting witness (Wills Act 1837, s. 15) and that if the assets are insufficient the " legacy " will abate proportionally with the other legacies unless there is some provision giving it priority.

beneficiaries then sue the trustee for breach of trust in paying trust moneys to himself the trustee has their acquiescence as a defence unless undue influence was exercised by him.

Fourthly, the general rule of gratuitous service is particularly severe in the case of solicitor-trustees. Thus in *Christophers* v. *White*,[20] it was held that a solicitor-trustee's firm was not entitled to charge for professional services rendered to the trust by a partner in the firm even though the partner was not one of the trustees.[21] But where a solicitor-trustee employed his partner, as distinct from his firm, under an *express* agreement that the partner should be individually entitled to charges, these were allowed on the ground that where such an agreement is carried out there is no infringement of the rule that a trustee may not make his office a source of remuneration.[22] Moreover, the severity of the rule has been relaxed by the case of *Cradock* v. *Piper*,[23] in which a solicitor-trustee acted as solicitor for himself and his co-trustees in legal proceedings relating to the trust, and was held to be entitled to his usual charges. The rule is that unlike a sole trustee acting as solicitor to the trust, a solicitor-trustee acting in legal proceedings [24] for a body of trustees, of whom he himself is one, is entitled to his usual charges if the fact of his appearing for himself and his co-trustees jointly has not increased the costs which would have been incurred if he had appeared for those co-trustees only.

Fifthly, where the trust property is situate abroad and the law of the foreign country permits payment, the trustee is entitled to keep any remuneration which he has received. Thus in *Re Northcote*,[25] a testator who left assets both in this country and in the U.S.A. died domiciled in England, and the principal forum of administration was therefore English. The executors took out an English grant, and on doing so they were put on terms by the Revenue, the English effects being insufficient to pay the English duty, to undertake themselves personally to obtain a grant in New York in respect of the American assets. In due course they obtained such a grant, and got in the assets. Under the law of New York they were entitled to commission for so doing, and Harman J. held that they were under no duty to account for it to the beneficiaries.

Section 3. Investment of Trust Funds [26]

A trustee is under a duty to invest trust funds in investments, authorised expressly or impliedly by the trust instrument or authorised by the court under the Trustee Act 1925, s. 57 or the Variation of Trusts Act 1958 or authorised by the Trustee Investments Act 1961. A properly drawn trust instrument contains very wide express powers of investment so that there is no need to rely on the 1961 Act. Wills, however, quite often impliedly authorise the retention of a small range of investments by making certain investments the subject matter of a specific bequest. When investing a

---

[20] (1847) 10 Beav. 523.
[21] See also *Re Gates* [1933] Ch. 913 and *Re Hill* [1934] Ch. 623.
[22] *Clack* v. *Carlon* (1861) 30 L.J.Ch. 639.
[23] (1850) 1 Mac. & G. 664.
[24] Legal proceedings need not necessarily be hostile litigation but may be friendly proceedings in chambers: *Re Corsellis* (1887) 34 Ch.D. 675.
[25] [1949] 1 All E.R. 442; see also *Chambers* v. *Goldwin* (1802) 9 Ves. 271.
[26] See generally Keeton, *The Investment and Taxation of Trust Funds* (1964).

trustee is under paramount duties to keep an even hand between those beneficiaries interested in income and those interested in capital, to act honestly, and not to select investments of a speculative character even though they may appear a good bet to a prudent businessman. Of course, trustees may often take one or two chances for the benefit of their beneficiaries but if the gamble fails then they bear the loss unless they had (1) the consent of all the beneficiaries between them absolutely entitled to the trust funds and each *sui juris* or (2) an indemnity from a wealthy adult beneficiary or (3) the benefit of a clause in the trust instrument exonerating them from any liability for losses so long as they acted honestly.

I. THE TRUSTEE INVESTMENTS ACT 1961

New powers of investment of trustees

Section 1.—(1) A trustee may invest any property in his hands, whether at the time in a state of investment or not, in any manner specified in Part I or II of the First Schedule to this Act or, subject to the next following section, in any manner specified in Part III of that Schedule, and may also from time to time vary any such investments.

(2) The supplemental provisions contained in Part IV of that Schedule shall have effect for the interpretation and for restricting the operation of the said Parts I to III.

(3) No provision relating to the powers of the trustee contained in any instrument (not being an enactment or an instrument made under an enactment) made before the passing of this Act shall limit the powers conferred by this section, but those powers are exercisable only in so far as a contrary intention is not expressed in any Act or instrument made under an enactment whenever passed or made, and so relating or in any other instrument so relating which is made after the passing of this Act.

For the purposes of this subsection any rule of the law of Scotland whereby a testamentary writing may be deemed to be made on a date other than that on which it was actually executed shall be disregarded.

[Under the Trustee Act 1893, s. 1, the statutory power of investment was available to trustees unless they were *expressly forbidden* to exercise it in one or more respect; see *Re Maire* [27]; *Re Burke.*[28] Under the Trustee Act 1925, s. 69 (2), the power was available unless a *contrary intention* was expressed. The same effect was given to the latter words as to the former; see *Re Warren* [29]; *Re Rider's W.T.*[30] The new powers conferred by this Act are available to trustees unless a *contrary intention* is expressed in any statute or statutory instrument, whenever made, relating to the powers of trustees or in any other instrument so relating made after August 3, 1961.]

(4) In this Act "narrower-range investment" means an investment falling within Part I or II of the First Schedule to this Act and "wider-range investment" means an investment falling within Part III of that Schedule.

Restrictions on wider-range investment

Section 2.—(1) A trustee shall not have power by virtue of the foregoing section to make or retain any wider-range investment unless the trust fund

[27] (1905) 45 S.J. 383.
[28] [1908] 2 Ch. 248.
[29] [1939] Ch. 684. [30] [1958] 1 W.L.R. 974.

has been divided into two parts (hereinafter referred to as the narrower-range part and the wider-range part), the parts being, subject to the provisions of this Act, equal in value at the time of the division; and where such a division has been made no subsequent division of the same fund shall be made for the purposes of this section, and no property shall be transferred from one part of the fund to the other unless either—

(*a*) the transfer is authorised or required by the following provisions of this Act, or

(*b*) a compensating transfer is made at the same time.

In this section "compensating transfer", in relation to any transferred property, means a transfer in the opposite direction of property of equal value.

(2) Property belonging to the narrower-range part of a trust fund shall not by virtue of the foregoing section be invested except in narrower-range investments, and any property invested in any other manner which is or becomes comprised in that part of the trust fund shall either be transferred to the wider-range part of the fund, with a compensating transfer, or be reinvested in narrower-range investments as soon as may be.[31]

[Trustees *may* invest in wider-range investments, subject to two conditions: (a) the trust fund must have been divided into two parts of equal value without taking into account the "special range" part of the fund (as to which, see section 3 (3) and Schedule 2, *infra*); (b) the trustees must obtain and consider written expert advice about the particular investments (as to which, see, section 6 (2)–(5), *infra*). But even after such division trustees *may* invest the wider-range part in narrower-range investments: on the other hand they *must* always invest the narrower-range part in narrower-range investments or arrange for a compensating transfer.]

(3) Where any property accrues to a trust fund after the fund has been divided in pursuance of subsection (1) of this section, then—

(*a*) if the property accrues to the trustees as owner or former owner of property comprised in either part of the fund, it shall be treated as belonging to that part of the fund;

(*b*) in any other case, the trustee shall secure, by apportionment of the accruing property or the transfer of property from one part of the fund to the other, or both, that the value of each part of the fund is increased by the same amount.

Where a trustee acquires property in consideration of a money payment the acquisition of the property shall be treated for the purposes of this section as investment and not as the accrual of property to the trust fund, notwithstanding that the amount of the consideration is less than the value of the property acquired; and paragraph (*a*) of this subsection shall not include the case of a dividend or interest becoming part of a trust fund.

[Thus (i) a bonus issue in respect of shares in the wider-range part accrues to that part; (ii) a "rights" issue taken up by the trustees constitutes a new investment and the new shares belong to that part of the fund which paid for them; (iii) accumulations of income and gifts to the trustees on the trusts of the settlement have to be apportioned between the two parts of the fund.]

---

[31] Compare Trustee Act 1925, s. 4; Samuels (1962) 26 Conv.(N.S.) 353.

(4) Where in the exercise of any power or duty of a trustee property falls to be taken out of the trust fund, nothing in this section shall restrict his discretion as to the choice of property to be taken out.[32]

Relationship between Act and other powers of investment

Section 3.—(1) The powers conferred by section one of this Act are in addition to and not in derogation from any power conferred otherwise than by this Act of investment or postponing conversion exercisable by a trustee (hereinafter referred to as a " special power ").

(2) Any special power (however expressed) to invest property in any investment for the time being authorised by law for the investment of trust property, being a power conferred on a trustee before the passing of this Act or conferred on him under any enactment passed before the passing of this Act, shall have effect as a power to invest property in like manner and subject to the like provisions as under the foregoing provisions of this Act.

(3) In relation to property, including wider-range but not including narrower-range investments,—

(a) which a trustee is authorised to hold apart from—

(i) the provisions of section one of this Act or any of the provisions of Part I of the Trustee Act 1925 or any of the provisions of the Trusts (Scotland) Act 1921, or

(ii) any such power to invest in authorised investments as is mentioned in the foregoing subsection, or

(b) which became part of a trust fund in consequence of the exercise by the trustee, as owner of property falling within this subsection, of any power conferred by subsection (3) or (4) of section ten of the Trustee Act 1925 or paragraph (o) or (p) of subsection (1) of section four of the Trusts (Scotland) Act 1921,

the foregoing section shall have effect subject to the modifications set out in the Second Schedule to this Act.

[Subsections (1)–(3) of this section and Schedule 2, *infra,* contain the main rules where the trust includes " special-range " property. A trustee with a wide special power of investment (*e.g.,* to invest in all respects as if he was the beneficial owner of the trust fund) may not wish to use the Act at all. On the other hand a trustee with a limited special power of investment (*e.g.,* to invest in certain ordinary or preference shares not authorised under the Act, or in the purchase of land, may also wish to make use of the powers of investment conferred by the Act. If he does so wish, then in dividing the fund he will ignore the value of the special-range property (*e.g.,* preference shares) which will be carried to a separate part of the fund. If he sells other investments and buys preference shares, they also become special-range property: it appears that he may purchase them entirely out of the proceeds of sale of narrower-range investments or wider-range investments or partly one and partly the other in his absolute discretion. If he sells the preference shares he can put the proceeds of sale either in narrower-range or wider-range investments or partly in one and partly in the other but he must comply with the requirement that the values of each of these two parts of the fund must be increased by the same amount. Suppose the trustees sell the preference shares for £2,000 and at that date the value of the narrower-range part of the fund is £4,000 and of the wider-range part £5,000, including £1,000 worth of narrower-range invest-

---

[32] This enables a trustee to reduce the narrower range part effectively.

ments. The trustees can *either* split the £2,000 and invest £1,000 in narrower-range investments in the narrower-range part of the fund and the other £1,000 in wider-range investments in the wider-range part of the fund, *or* invest the whole £2,000 in wider-range investments and transfer the £1,000 worth of narrower-range investments from the wider-range part of the fund *or* invest £1,500 in wider-range investments and £500 in narrower-range investments together with a transfer of £500 worth of the narrower-range investments in the wider-range part of the fund.]

(4) The foregoing subsection shall not apply where the powers of the trustee to invest or postpone conversion have been conferred or varied—

(*a*) by an order of any court made within the period of ten years ending with the passing of this Act, or

(*b*) by any enactment passed, or instrument having effect under an enactment made, within that period, being an enactment or instrument relating specifically to the trusts in question, or

(*c*) by an enactment contained in a local Act of the present Session;

but the provisions of the Third Schedule to this Act shall have effect in a case falling within this subsection.

[One effect of this is that if the court has, within the period mentioned in the subsection, extended the powers of investment of the trustees, the extended powers are not to be regarded as special so as to constitute investments made by virtue of their exercise " special-range " property, and leave the remainder of the fund available for division into a narrower-range part and a wider-range part under the Act. Another effect can be illustrated by the following example: In 1958 the court authorised trustees to invest in shares of a kind now authorised by the Act. On August 3, 1961, the value of the trust fund was £10,000, of which the shares constituted £6,000. If the fund was divided, the narrower-range part would include £1,000 worth of shares, *i.e.,* wider-range investments. So long as that situation continued, the trustees could not use the powers under the Act (*e.g.,* to invest in units of a unit trust) but they could go on using the extended powers given them by the court.]

Interpretation of references to trust property and trust funds

Section 4.—(1) In this Act " property " includes real or personal property of any description, including money and things in action:

Provided that it does not include an interest in expectancy,[33] but the falling into possession of such an interest, or the receipt of proceeds of the sale thereof, shall be treated for the purposes of this Act as an accrual of property to the trust fund.

(2) So much of the property in the hands of a trustee shall for the purposes of this Act constitute one trust fund as is held on trusts which (as respects the beneficiaries or their respective interests or the purposes of the trust or as respects the powers of the trustee) are not identical with those on which any other property in his hands is held.

(3) Where property is taken out of a trust fund by way of appropriation so as to form a separate fund, and at the time of the appropriation the trust fund had (as to the whole or a part thereof) been divided in pursuance of subsection (1) of section two of this Act, or that subsection as modified by the Second Schedule to this Act, then if the separate fund is so divided the narrower-range and wider-range parts of the separate fund may be

---

[33] *Quaere* if this has any effect on the rule in *Howe* v. *Dartmouth* since s. 1 (1) is concerned only with " property ": Wolstenholme and Cherry's *Conveyancing Statutes,* Vol. 4 (13th ed. by J. T. Farrand), p. 114.

constituted so as either to be equal, or to bear to each other the same proportion as the two corresponding parts of the fund out of which it was so appropriated (the values of those parts of those funds being ascertained as at the time of appropriation), or some intermediate proportion.

[The following is an example. T1 and T2 hold a trust fund worth £10,000 on trust for X for life, with remainder to Y. T1 and T2 divide the fund into two equal parts and some years later decide to make an advancement in favour of Y in the form of a marriage settlement. At that date the narrower-range part of the fund has depreciated to £4,000 and the wider-range part has appreciated to £8,000. The amount to be advanced is £2,000. This sum could be drawn from the two parts of the parent fund either equally or in the proportions 1:2 or in any intermediate proportions.]

(4) In the application of this section to Scotland the following subsection shall be substituted for subsection (1) thereof:—

" (1) In this Act ' property' includes property of any description (whether heritable or moveable, corporeal or incorporeal) which is presently enjoyable, but does not include a future interest, whether vested or contingent."

Certain valuations to be conclusive for purposes of division of trust fund

Section 5.—(1) If for the purposes of section two or four of this Act or the Second Schedule thereto a trustee obtains, from a person reasonably believed by the trustee to be qualified to make it, a valuation in writing of any property, the valuation shall be conclusive in determining whether the division of the trust fund in pursuance of subsection (1) of the said section two, or any transfer or apportionment of property under that section or the said Second Schedule, has been duly made.

(2) The foregoing subsection applies to any such valuation notwithstanding that it is made by a person in the course of his employment as an officer or servant.

Duty of trustees in choosing investments

Section 6.—(1) In the exercise of his powers of investment a trustee shall have regard—

(*a*) to the need for diversification of investments of the trust, in so far as is appropriate to the circumstances of the trust;

(*b*) to the suitability to the trust of investments of the description of investment proposed and of the investment proposed as an investment of that description.

[In *Learoyd* v. *Whiteley* [34] Lord Watson stated the general equitable position thus " . . . the law requires of a trustee no higher degree of diligence in the execution of his office than a man of ordinary prudence would exercise in the management of his own private affairs. Yet he is not allowed the same discretion in investing the moneys of the trust as if he were a person *sui juris* dealing with his own estate. Business men of ordinary prudence may, and frequently do, select investments which are more or less of a speculative character; but it is the duty of a trustee to confine himself to the class of investments which are permitted by the trust, and likewise to avoid all investments of that class which are attended with hazard. So, so long as he acts in the honest observance of these limitations, the general rule already stated will apply."]

---

[34] (1887) 12 App.Cas. 727, 733.

(2) Before exercising any power conferred by section one of this Act to invest in a manner specified in Part II or III of the First Schedule to this Act, or before investing in any such manner in the exercise of a power falling within subsection (2) of section three of this Act, a trustee shall obtain and consider [35] proper advice on the question whether the investment is satisfactory having regard to the matters mentioned in paragraphs (*a*) and (*b*) of the foregoing subsection.

(3) A trustee retaining any investment made in the exercise of such a power as aforesaid shall determine at what intervals the circumstances, and in particular the nature of the investment, make it desirable to obtain such advice as aforesaid, and shall obtain and consider such advice accordingly.

(4) For the purposes of the two foregoing subsections, proper advice is the advice of a person who is reasonably believed by the trustee to be qualified by his ability in and practical experience of financial matters; and such advice may be given by a person notwithstanding that he gives it in the course of his employment as an officer or servant.

(5) A trustee shall not be treated as having complied with subsection (2) or (3) of this section unless the advice was given or has been subsequently confirmed in writing.

(6) Subsections (2) and (3) of this section shall not apply to one of two or more trustees where he is the person giving the advice required by this section to his co-trustee or co-trustees, and shall not apply where powers of a trustee are lawfully exercised by an officer or servant competent under subsection (4) of this section to give proper advice.

(7) Without prejudice to section eight of the Trustee Act 1925 or section thirty of the Trusts (Scotland) Act 1921 (which relate to valuation, and the proportion of the value to be lent, where a trustee lends on the security of property) the advice required by this section shall not include, in the case of a loan on the security of freehold or leasehold property in England and Wales or Northern Ireland or on heritable security in Scotland, advice on the suitability of the particular loan.

[For section 8 of the Trustee Act 1925, see *infra*, p. 500.]

. . . . . .

Saving for powers of court

Section 15. The enlargement of the investment powers of trustees by this Act shall not lessen any power of a court to confer wider powers of investment in trustees, or affect the extent to which any such power is to be exercised.

[The courts have indicated that they will not confer investment powers wider than those contained in the Act, unless there are special circumstances: see *Re Cooper's Settlement* [36]; *Re Kolb's W.T.* [37]; *Re Clarke's W.T.* [38]; and *Re University of London Charitable Trusts.* [39]]

. . . . . .

---

[35] Theoretically they must exercise their own judgment but in practice it would be difficult for them to justify refusing to follow the advice.

[36] [1962] Ch. 826.

[37] [1962] Ch. 531.

[38] [1961] 1 W.L.R. 1471.

[39] [1964] Ch. 282.

FIRST SCHEDULE

MANNER OF INVESTMENT

PART I

NARROWER-RANGE INVESTMENTS NOT REQUIRING ADVICE

Section 1

1. In Defence Bonds, National Savings Certificates and Ulster Savings Certificates, Ulster Development Bonds,[40] National Development Bonds [41] and British Savings Bonds.[42]

2. In deposits in the Post Office Savings Bank, ordinary deposits in a trustee savings bank and deposits in a bank or department thereof certified under subsection (3) of section nine of the Finance Act 1956.[43]

PART II

NARROWER-RANGE INVESTMENTS REQUIRING ADVICE

1. In securities issued by Her Majesty's Government in the United Kingdom, the Government of Northern Ireland or the Government of the Isle of Man, not being securities falling within Part I of this Schedule and being fixed-interest securities registered in the United Kingdom or the Isle of Man, Treasury Bills or Tax Reserve Certificates.

2. In any securities the payment of interest on which is guaranteed by Her Majesty's Government in the United Kingdom or the Government of Northern Ireland.

3. In fixed-interest securities issued in the United Kingdom by any public authority or nationalised industry or undertaking in the United Kingdom.

4. In fixed-interest securities issued in the United Kingdom by the government of any overseas territory within the Commonwealth or by any public or local authority within such a territory, being securities registered in the United Kingdom.

References in this paragraph to an overseas territory or to the government of such a territory shall be construed as if they occurred in the Overseas Service Act 1958.

5. In fixed-interest securities issued in the United Kingdom by the International Bank for Reconstruction and Development, or the Inter-American Development Bank,[44] being securities registered in the United Kingdom.

6. In debentures issued in the United Kingdom by a company incorporated in the United Kingdom, being debentures registered in the United Kingdom.

7. In stock of the Bank of Ireland.

8. In debentures issued by the Agricultural Mortgage Corporation Limited or the Scottish Agricultural Securities Corporation Limited.

9. In loans to any authority to which this paragraph applies charged on all or any of the revenues of the authority or on a fund into which all or any of those revenues are payable, in any fixed-interest securities issued in the United Kingdom by any such authority for the purpose of borrowing money so charged, and in deposits with any such authority by way of temporary loan made on the giving of a receipt for the loan by the treasurer or other similar officer of the authority and on the giving of an undertaking by the authority that, if requested to charge the loan as aforesaid, it will either comply with the request or repay the loan.

This paragraph applies to the following authorities, that is to say—

---

[40] Added as from December 5, 1962, by the Trustee Investments (Additional Powers) (No. 2) Order 1962 (S.I. 1962 No. 2611).

[41] Added as from May 15, 1964, by the Trustee Investments (Additional Powers) Order 1964 (S.I. 1964 No. 703).

[42] Trustee Investments (Additional Powers) Order 1968 (S.I. 1968 No. 470).

[43] *e.g.*, the Birmingham Municipal Bank (S.I. 1958 No. 923, as amended by S.I. 1959 No. 300).

[44] Added by S.I. 1964 No. 1404.

(*a*) any local authority in the United Kingdom;

(*b*) any authority all the members of which are appointed or elected by one or more local authorities in the United Kingdom;

(*c*) any authority the majority of the members of which are appointed or elected by one or more local authorities in the United Kingdom, being an authority which by virtue of any enactment has power to issue a precept to a local authority in England and Wales, or a requisition to a local authority in Scotland, or to the expenses of which, by virtue of any enactment, a local authority in the United Kingdom is or can be required to contribute;

(*d*) the Receiver for the Metropolitan Police District or a combined police authority (within the meaning of the Police Act 1946);

(*e*) the Belfast City and District Water Commissioners;

(*f*) the Great Ouse Water Authority.[45]

10. In debentures or in the guaranteed or preference stock of any incorporated company, being statutory water undertakers within the meaning of the Water Act 1945 or any corresponding enactment in force in Northern Ireland, and having during each of the ten years immediately preceding the calendar year in which the investment was made paid a dividend of not less than 5 per cent. on its ordinary shares.

11. In deposits by way of special investment in a trustee savings bank or in a department (not being a department certified under subsection (3) of section nine of the Finance Act 1956) of a bank any other department of which is so certified.

12. In deposits in a building society designated under section one of the House Purchase and Housing Act 1959.

13. In mortgages of freehold property in England and Wales or Northern Ireland and of leasehold property in those countries of which the unexpired term at the time of investment is not less than sixty years, and in loans on heritable security in Scotland.

14. In perpetual rent-charges charged on land in England and Wales or Northern Ireland and fee-farm rents (not being rent-charges) issuing out of such land, and in feu-duties or ground annuals in Scotland.

PART III

WIDER-RANGE INVESTMENTS

1. In any securities issued in the United Kingdom by a company incorporated in the United Kingdom, being securities registered in the United Kingdom and not being securities falling within Part II of this Schedule.

2. In shares in any building society designated under section one of the House Purchase and Housing Act 1959.

3. In any units, or other shares of the investments subject to the trusts, of a unit trust scheme in the case of which there is in force at the time of investment an order of the Board of Trade under section seventeen of the Prevention of Fraud (Investments) Act 1958 or of the Ministry of Commerce for Northern Ireland under section sixteen of the Prevention of Fraud (Investments) Act (Northern Ireland) 1940.

PART IV

SUPPLEMENTAL

1. The securities mentioned in Parts I to III of this Schedule do not include any securities where the holder can be required to accept repayment of the principal, or the payment of any interest, otherwise than in sterling.

2. The securities mentioned in paragraphs 1 to 8 of Part II, other than Treasury Bills or Tax Reserve Certificates, securities issued before the passing

---

[45] Added as from April 4, 1962, by the Trustee Investments (Additional Powers) Order 1962 (S.I. 1962 No. 658). For other additions, see Water Resources Act 1963, s. 136 (1) and Sched. 13, para. 16.

of this Act by the Government of the Isle of Man, securities falling within paragraph 4 of the said Part II issued before the passing of this Act or securities falling within paragraph 9 of that Part, and the securities mentioned in paragraph 1 of Part III of this Schedule do not include—

(a) securities the price of which is not quoted on a recognised stock exchange within the meaning of the Prevention of Fraud (Investments) Act 1958, or the Belfast stock exchange;

(b) shares or debenture stock not fully paid up (except shares or debenture stock which by the terms of issue are required to be fully paid up within nine months of the date of issue).

3. The securities mentioned in paragraph 6 of Part II and paragraph 1 of Part III of this Schedule do not include—

(a) shares or debentures of an incorporated company of which the total issued and paid up share capital is less than one million pounds;

(b) shares or debentures of an incorporated company which has not in each of the five years immediately preceding the calendar year in which the investment is made paid a dividend on all the shares issued by the company, excluding any shares issued after the dividend was declared and any shares which by their terms of issue did not rank for the dividend for that year.

For the purposes of sub-paragraph (b) of this paragraph a company formed—

(i) to take over the business of another company or other companies,

(ii) or to acquire the securities of, or control of, another company or other companies,

or for either of those purposes and for other purposes shall be deemed to have paid a dividend as mentioned in that sub-paragraph in any year in which such a dividend has been paid by the other company or all the other companies, as the case may be.

4. In this Schedule, unless the context otherwise requires, the following expressions have the meanings hereby respectively assigned to them, that is to say—

"debenture" includes debenture stock and bonds, whether constituting a charge on assets or not, and loan stock or notes;

"enactment" includes an enactment of the Parliament of Northern Ireland;

"fixed-interest securities" means securities which under their terms of issue bear a fixed rate of interest;

"local authority" in relation to the United Kingdom, means any of the following authorities—

(a) in England and Wales, the council of a county, a *county, metropolitan or other* [46] borough (including a borough which has been included in a rural district), an urban or rural district or a parish, the Common Council of the City of London [the Greater London Council] [47] and the Council of the Isles of Scilly;

(b) in Scotland, a local authority within the meaning of the Local Government (Scotland) Act 1947;

(c) in Northern Ireland, the council of a county, a county or other borough, or an urban or rural district;

"ordinary deposits" and "special investment" have the same meanings respectively as in the Trustee Savings Banks Act 1954;

"securities" includes shares, debentures, Treasury Bills and Tax Reserve Certificates;

"share" includes stock;

---

[46] Words in italics repealed as from April 1, 1965, by the London Government Act 1963, s. 93 (1) (b) and Sched. 18, Part II.

[47] Words in square brackets added as from April 1, 1965, by s. 83 (1) of and Sched. 17 to the above Act.

"Treasury Bills" includes Exchequer bills and other bills issued by Her Majesty's Government in the United Kingdom and Northern Ireland Treasury Bills.

5. It is hereby declared that in this Schedule "mortgage", in relation to freehold or leasehold property in Northern Ireland, includes a registered charge which, by virtue of subsection (4) of section forty of the Local Registration of Title (Ireland) Act 1891 or any other enactment, operates as a mortgage by deed.

6. References in this Schedule to an incorporated company are references to a company incorporated by or under any enactment and include references to a body of persons established for the purpose of trading for profit and incorporated by Royal Charter.

7. The references in paragraph 12 of Part II and paragraph 2 of Part III of this Schedule to a building society designated under section one of the House Purchase and Housing Act 1959 include references to a permanent society incorporated under the Building Societies Acts (Northern Ireland) 1874 to 1940 for the time being designated by the Registrar for Northern Ireland under subsection (2) of that section (which enables such a society to be so designated for the purpose of trustees' powers of investment specified in paragraph (*a*) of subsection (1) of that section).

Section 3

SECOND SCHEDULE

MODIFICATION OF S. 2 IN RELATION TO PROPERTY FALLING WITHIN S. 3 (3)

1. In this Schedule "special-range property" means property falling within subsection (3) of section three of this Act.

2.—(1) Where a trust fund includes special-range property, subsection (1) of section two of this Act shall have effect as if references to the trust fund were references to so much thereof as does not consist of special-range property, and the special-range property shall be carried to a separate part of the fund.

(2) Any property which—

    (*a*) being property belonging to the narrower-range or wider-range part of a trust fund, is converted into special-range property, or

    (*b*) being special-range property, accrues to a trust fund after the division of the fund or part thereof in pursuance of subsection (1) of section two of this Act or of that subsection as modified by sub-paragraph (1) of this paragraph,

shall be carried to such a separate part of the fund as aforesaid; and subsections (2) and (3) of the said section two shall have effect subject to this sub-paragraph.

3. Where property carried to such a separate part as aforesaid is converted into property other than special-range property,—

    (*a*) it shall be transferred to the narrower-range part of the fund or the wider-range part of the fund or apportioned between them, and

    (*b*) any transfer of property from one of those parts to the other shall be made which is necessary to secure that the value of each of those parts of the fund is increased by the same amount.

Section 3

THIRD SCHEDULE

PROVISIONS SUPPLEMENTARY TO S. 3 (4)

1. Where in a case falling within subsection (4) of section three of this Act, property belonging to the narrower-range part of a trust fund—

    (*a*) is invested otherwise than in a narrower-range investment, or (*b*) being so invested, is retained and not transferred or as soon as may be reinvested as mentioned in subsection (2) of section two of this Act,

then, so long as the property continues so invested and comprised in the narrow-range part of the fund, section one of this Act shall not authorise the making or retention of any wider-range investment.

2. Section four of the Trustee Act 1925 or section thirty-three of the Trusts (Scotland) Act 1921 (which relieve a trustee from liability for retaining an investment which has ceased to be authorised) shall not apply where an investment ceases to be authorised in consequence of the foregoing paragraph.

.   .   .   .   .

II. INVESTMENT IN MORTGAGES OF LAND

For the power, see paragraph 13 of Part II of Schedule 1 to the Trustee Investments Act 1961; *supra*, p. 497. It is doubtful whether this power has swept away the old restrictions prohibiting either a second, an equitable or a contributory mortgage so a prudent trustee should refuse to advance money on such types of mortgage. It would seem that a simple power to invest upon mortgage is not taken at its face value by courts of equity.[48]

The Trustee Act 1925

Loans and investments by trustees not chargeable as breaches of trust

Section 8.[49]—(1) A trustee lending money on the security of any property on which he can properly lend [50] shall not be chargeable with breach of trust by reason only of the proportion borne by the amount of the loan to the value of the property at the time when the loan was made, if it appears to the court—

    (*a*) that in making the loan the trustee was acting upon a report as to the value of the property made by a person whom he reasonably believed to be an able practical surveyor or valuer instructed and employed independently of any owner of the property, whether such surveyor or valuer carried on business in the locality where the property is situate or elsewhere; and

    (*b*) that the amount of the loan does not exceed two third parts of the value of the property as stated in the report; and

    (*c*) that the loan was made under the advice of the surveyor or valuer expressed in the report.

(2) A trustee lending money on the security of any leasehold property shall not be chargeable with breach of trust only upon the ground that in making such loan he dispensed either wholly or partly with the production or investigation of the lessor's title.

(3) A trustee shall not be chargeable with breach of trust only upon the ground that in effecting the purchase, or in lending money upon the security, of any property he has accepted a shorter title than the title which

---

[48] Underhill, p. 415.

[49] Re-enacting the Trustee Act 1893, s. 8, which re-enacted the Trustee Act 1888, s. 4. This section is not affected by the Trustee Investment Act 1961 : see s. 6 (7), *supra*, p. 495.

[50] On a sale of trust property trustees may leave on legal mortgage not more than two-thirds of the purchase price without having first obtained a report and without being liable for any loss incurred by reason only of the security being insufficient at the date of the legal mortgage : Trustee Act 1925, s. 10.

a purchaser is, in the absence of a special contract, entitled to require, if in the opinion of the court the title accepted be such as a person acting with prudence and caution would have accepted.

(4) This section applies to transfers of existing securities as well as to new securities and to investments made before as well as after the commencement of this Act.

Liability for loss by reason of improper investment

Section 9.[51]—(1) Where a trustee improperly advances trust money on a mortgage security which would at the time of the investment be a proper investment in all respects for a smaller sum than is actually advanced thereon, the security shall be deemed an authorised investment for the smaller sum, and the trustee shall only be liable to make good the sum advanced in excess thereof with interest.

(2) This section applies to investments made before as well as after the commencement of this Act.

SHAW v. CATES

Chancery Division [1909] 1 Ch. 389; 78 L.J.Ch. 226; 100 L.T. 146

Trustees in 1897 invested £4,400 on a mortgage of freehold house property (in which they had power to invest). The valuer employed, (Mr. Barton), who was also the mortgagor's rent-collector, made a report in which he stated the total value of the four properties which were contemplated, and recommended the safety of an advance of two-thirds. The trustees had not sufficient funds to make an advance of two-thirds of the total value, but, without consulting the valuer, made the advance of £4,400, which purported to be two-thirds of the value of the first two properties mentioned in the report, on the security of those two houses. The interest due on the sum advanced exceeded the existing income of these two properties, and nine years later the mortgagor ceased to pay it.

The plaintiff beneficiaries alleged that the investment was improper as being, from the nature of the property, a hazardous trust investment, and contended that, whether this were so or not, it was in any case an improper investment for the sum actually advanced. The defendant trustees claimed, first, that they were protected by section 8 (1) of the Trustee Act 1893; and, secondly, that they had acted honestly and reasonably, and might be wholly relieved of any liability under section 3 of the Judicial Trustees Act 1896,[52] or partially relieved under section 9 of the Trustee Act 1893. They argued, also, that the test was value, not valuation, *i.e.*, that if they could show without any valuation that the property was at the time of sufficient value, they were as well protected as if they had had a valuation. Furthermore, the test of reasonableness under section 3 of the Judicial Trustees Act 1896 could not depend

---

[51] Re-enacting the Trustee Act 1893, s. 9, which re-enacted the Trustee Act 1888, s. 5.
[52] Now s. 61 of the Trustee Act 1925; *infra*, p. 635.

on whether they had acted strictly within section 8 of the Trustee Act 1893, because that would make the Act of 1896 superfluous.

The learned judge was of opinion that the plaintiffs had not discharged the burden of showing that the investment was made on a security of too hazardous a nature to be accepted as a trust investment.

PARKER J.: ". . . Section 8 of the Trustee Act 1893 is a re-enactment of section 4 of the Trustee Act 1888. Prior to the Trustee Act 1888 the duties of trustees investing trust money on the security of freehold hereditaments were well known. They were entitled to rely on expert advice as to the value of the property, but if they did so, is was their duty to see that the expert was properly instructed—that he knew for whom and with what object he was advising, and that he was acting independently of the mortgagor, these being precautions which a prudent man of business might reasonably be expected to take in the conduct of his own affairs. Having thus been advised as to value, they had themselves to determine, and could not delegate it to a third party (even an expert) to determine, what amount they could prudently advance on the security in question. In determining this amount, however, they had for their guidance certain general rules laid down for the purpose by the courts. Thus it had been laid down that as a general rule a trustee ought not to advance more than two-thirds of the value of the property if it were freehold agricultural land, or more than one-half of the value if the property were house property or buildings used in trade, it being considered that a prudent man in the management of his own affairs would ordinarily require for his protection in the one case a margin of at least one-third of the value, and in the other case, having regard to the nature of the property, a larger margin, usually stated as one-half of the value. These rules, however, were not so stringent as not to admit of exceptions based upon special circumstances, and I think that the rule as to one-half margin of value, in the case at any rate of houses as distinguished from buildings used in trade, was somewhat less stringent than the rule as to one-third margin of value in the case of agricultural land. In either case the onus of justifying a departure from the rule would probably lie upon the trustee, though possibly the onus might be discharged more easily in the one case than in the other. It should be remembered that the rules were rules concerning the minimum margins which a prudent man would require for his protection, and could not be relied on as justifying an advance where a prudent man would, because of other circumstances, be likely to require a larger margin. In this connection all the circumstances had to be considered, including the character and situation of the property, and the actual income which the property might be producing at the time of the advance. The method of valuation adopted by the expert who had advised as to value might also, I think, be very material in considering the limit of protection which a prudent man ought to require, especially in the case of house property or buildings used for trade purposes. If, for example, the nature and character of the property had already been taken into account by the expert in arriving at the value, there would be less need to take them into acount in determining the limit of protection to be required.

" Section 4 of the Trustee Act 1888 somewhat modified the law as above stated. It provides as follows: [His Lordship read the section.] Since the Act, therefore, a trustee has been, and is, justified in acting on expert advice, not only as to the value of the property, but also as to the amount he may properly advance thereon, provided the advice be given in such manner, and by such person, as is contemplated in the section, and that, whatever be the nature of the property, the amount advanced is not more than two-thirds of its value. The principle involved seems to be that within the limits of what is often called the ' two-thirds ' rule a prudent man may, as to the amount which can properly be advanced on any proposed security, whether the property be agricultural land or houses or buildings used for trade purposes, rely on expert advice obtained with certain precautions, it being of course assumed that in giving the advice the expert will consider all the circumstances of the case, including the nature of the property, and will not advise a larger advance than under all the circumstances can be prudently made. I dissent entirely from the position taken up by some of the defendants' expert witnesses that when once they have ascertained the value of the property they are, whatever its nature and whatever method of valuation they have adopted, at least prima facie justified in advising an advance of two-thirds of its value. Such a position in my opinion defeats the object of the section by making what the legislature has recognised as the standard of the minimum protection which a prudent man will require into a standard of the normal risk which, whatever the nature of the property, a prudent man will be prepared to run; and it deprives the expert advice on which the trustee is to rely as to the margin of protection to be required of all its value. It is as true now as it was before the Act that the maximum sum which a prudent man can be advised to lend upon a mortgage depends on the nature of the property and upon all the circumstances of the case. If the property is liable to deteriorate or is specially subject to fluctuations in value, or depends for its value on circumstances the continual existence of which is precarious, a prudent man will now, as much as before the Act, require a larger margin for his protection than he would in the case of property attended by no such disadvantages, and an expert who does his duty will take this into consideration. . . .

" I have come to the conclusion that, under the circumstances which I have shortly stated, Mr. Barton's report is not such a report as was contemplated by the Act. To advise an advance of two-thirds of the value of four properties is not the same thing as advising an advance of two-thirds of the value of any one or more of the properties apart

from the others or other. This is more especially the case where one
of the properties is not at the date of the report an income-bearing
property. As I have already pointed out, the amount of income which
a property is producing is material in considering what amount can
properly be advanced thereon. . . .

"In my opinion the advance which was actually made was not the
advance which Mr. Barton advised, and his report, therefore, cannot
be relied on as within section 8 of the Trustee Act 1893. Again, I
do not think that Mr. Barton was in fact instructed and employed
independently of the mortgagor. He was suggested by the mortgagor,
instructed by the mortgagor's solicitors, referred to the mortgagor both
as to his fee and as to the properties he was to value, and was
accompanied by the mortgagor when he made his survey. I am not
suggesting that he was consciously influenced by the mortgagor or that
he acted otherwise than honestly in the matter, but I do not think that
he in fact fulfilled the conditions mentioned in the section as to his
instructions and employment. If, according to the true meaning of
the section, the belief of the trustees is the material point, I am unable
to hold that the trustees did reasonably believe that Mr. Barton was
instructed and employed independently of the mortgagor. They left
the instructions to be given by Beckingsale & Co.,[53] who were also the
mortgagor's solicitors, and after ascertaining that Mr. Barton was a
competent person took no further trouble in the matter. . . .

"If, apart from section 8 of the Trustee Act 1893, I ask myself
whether in the matter of this mortgage the trustees acted reasonably
and took all the precautions which a prudent man acting in his own
affairs might be expected to have taken, I can only answer the question
in the negative. In leaving Mr. Barton to be instructed by their
solicitors, whom they knew to be acting for the mortgagor, in taking no
means to see that he was properly instructed or that he was instructed
and employed independently of the mortgagor, in not themselves considering the surveyor's report when made, but leaving it to their
solicitors to decide whether the report might be acted on, in making
an advance not advised in the report to two-thirds of the value of two
only of the properties mentioned in the report, notwithstanding that
one of the properties consisted of unfinished houses—in all this it seems
to me that they failed to act as a prudent man might reasonably be
expected to act in the management of his own affairs.

"I am of opinion also that under the circumstances, however
honestly they acted—and no one has suggested or could suggest that
they did not act honestly—they cannot be said to have acted reasonably
within the meaning of section 3 of the Judicial Trustees Act 1896, if
only because they neglected to do what a reasonable man would do
in the prudent management of his own business.

"It remains, therefore, to consider whether the three houses com-

---

[53] Solicitors to one of the trustees.

prised in the mortgage were in fact of sufficient value to justify an advance of trust money to the amount of £4,400, and, if not, for what amount they might properly have been accepted as security by the trustees; for having decided that there was nothing hazardous in advancing trust moneys thereon the trustees are, in my opinion, entitled to the benefit of section 9 of the Trustee Act 1893.

"For the purpose of considering these questions it seems to me that the court ought to be guided by the same general considerations which would have guided it prior to the Trustee Act 1888. Section 8 of that Act,[54] merely protects trustees who within certain limits and under certain circumstances act on expert opinions as to the amount they may advance. It does not, as has been suggested, abrogate all distinction between agricultural land and houses or buildings used for trade in determining the margin of protection to be required by a prudent man, or indicate that a prudent man may, prima facie, be content in all cases with a margin of one-third the value of the property. At most it suggests that the extra margin of protection beyond one-third the value depends on the particular circumstances of each case, and assumes that whatever may be the nature of the property the expert employed will give the matter his bona fide consideration, advising with a view to the security of the trust money, and not only in such a way as to protect the trustees from liability for breach of trust. In cases not within the section it perhaps suggests that the rule which the courts had laid down in the case of houses and buildings used for trade is less stringent than the two-thirds rule laid down in the case of agricultural land, and this I believe to have been the case before the Act. As well since the Act as before it, it is therefore necessary to consider not only the value of the property proposed to be mortgaged, but also the margin of protection which a prudent man would require, remembering that the margin of protection to be required must depend on the nature of the property and all the circumstances of the case . . .

"Considering all the facts of this case, I have come to the conclusion that the largest sum for which the property could be considered a good security in 1897 is £3,400; and therefore, under section 9 of the Act, the trustees' liability is confined to making good the excess of the sum actually advanced over this amount and with interest. . . ."

Note

Another important case on section 8 of the Trustee Act 1925 is *Re Solomon*.[55] The judgment of Warrington J. brings out the following points in relation to the section:

(1) "By reason only of the proportion borne by the amount of the loan to the value of the property." As to this, Warrington J. said [56]:

---

[54] "Section 8" appears to be a misprint for section 4.
[55] [1912] 1 Ch. 261, before Warrington J., compromised in the Court of Appeal [1913] 1 Ch. 200.　　　　　　　　　　　　　　　[56] [1912] 1 Ch. 261, 279.

" Translated into simpler language, that means and means only, it seems to me, that they shall not be chargeable by reason only of their investing on an insufficient security."

(2) " Instructed and employed independently of any owner of the property." As to this, Warrington J. said [57] : " What is meant by ' instructed and employed independently of any owner of the property '? I think it means this: that the relation existing between employer and employed must exist as between the trustees and the valuer, and between them only— that the valuer must be entitled to look for his remuneration to the person who employs him, and, on the other hand, must be responsible to that person and to that person only for the due performance of his duty as valuer. When you have that, he is instructed and employed by the trustee, and he is instructed and employed by him independently of the owner." [58]

(3) " That the loan was made under the advice of the surveyor or valuer expressed in the report." The learned judge said [59] : " It is said that that condition has not been complied with because the surveyor and valuer in this case did not in so many words say ' I advise the trustees to advance so much money.' In my opinion, to so hold would be to cast away the substance for the shadow." The condition is satisfied if the surveyor indicates that the property is a sufficient security for the amount advanced.

(4) The business of taking into account the circumstances which affect the value of the property is the business of the valuer. " I agree," said Warrington J.,[60] " with what Parker J. said in *Shaw* v. *Cates*,[61] that it is the business of the expert to determine what are the facts and circumstances connected with the property which it is necessary for him to take into account in arriving at his valuation, and it will be properly assumed that, when the expert is directed to report on the value of the property, he will discover for himself those circumstances which bear on its value and will make his valuation in accordance with those circumstances."

(5) It is the valuer's duty to advise the trustee not only as to the actual value of the property, but also as to what proportion of that value may with safety be advanced.[62]

Warrington J. also questions [63] whether the valuer must *in fact* be instructed and employed independently of any owner of the property, or whether it is sufficient that the trustee reasonably believed him to be so instructed and employed. Kekewich J. had held, however, in *Re Walker*,[64] and had considered *obiter* in *Re Somerset*,[65] that the surveyor or valuer must in fact be instructed and employed independently.

If a trustee does not comply with all the requirements of the section, the effect is that he cannot claim the relief it affords; he is not thereby prevented from falling back on the general law or deprived of the benefit

[57] *Ibid.* 281.
[58] See also *Smith* v. *Stoneham* [1886] W.N. 178.
[59] [1912] 1 Ch. 261, 283.
[60] *Ibid.* 274.
[61] [1909] 1 Ch. 389, 398; *supra*, p. 503.
[62] [1912] 1 Ch. 261, 282.
[63] *Ibid.* 281.
[64] (1890) 62 L.T. 449, 452: the next case in the text, though not reproduced on this point.
[65] [1894] 1 Ch. 231, 253.

of some other statutory provision.[66]   "Section 8," observed Eve J. in
Palmer v. *Emerson*,[67] " is really a relieving section, and not a section which
imposes further obligations upon trustees." The section does, however, in
the case of investment of trust funds on mortgage, constitute a standard
by which reasonable conduct is to be judged.[68]

Re WALKER, WALKER v. WALKER

Chancery Division (1890) 59 L.J.Ch. 386; 62 L.T. 449

Trustees claimed the benefit of section 5 [69] of the Trustee Act 1888.

KEKEWICH J.: ". . .Then, as regards the fifth section of the Act,
a different question arises. That is a beneficial section, the object of
which is to provide that when a trustee has advanced more money on
mortgage of the property than was reasonably prudent, and the estate
fails, then he is not to be chargeable with the whole, but only with so
much as would have been a loss if you take the real value at the time
of investment, [and] not the value he put upon it. That is the substance
of it. Supposing, for instance, a man invests £100 on property that
would bear only £80; he is not to lose the whole £100 because of that.
That is a reasonable provision on behalf of trustees. But the whole
section depends on this: ' When a trustee shall have improperly
advanced trust money on a mortgage security which would, at the time
of the investment, have been a proper investment in all respects for
a less sum than was actually advanced thereon.' That I understand to
mean that the impropriety consists in the amount invested. If the
investment is otherwise improper—as, for instance, if a man invests on
mortgage of trade buildings when he is only entitled to invest on mortgage of agricultural land—he cannot claim the benefit of the section,
and say, ' I might take the value at two-thirds of the advance, although
not the whole.' He must *establish the propriety of the investment
independently of value*, and then he has the benefit of the section to
save him from any loss greater than that which would have been
incurred by advancing too large a sum on what otherwise would be a
proper security. . . ." [70]

III. INVESTMENTS IN PURCHASE OF LAND

The Settled Land Act 1925

Section 73.—(1) Capital money arising under this Act, subject to payment
of claims properly payable thereout and to the application thereof for any

---

[66] See *Re Dive* [1909] 1 Ch. 328, 342.
[67] [1911] 1 Ch. 758, 769.
[68] *Re Stuart* [1897] 2 Ch. 583 ; *infra*, p. 637.
[69] Re-enacted in s. 9 of the Trustee Act 1893 and s. 9 of the Trustee Act 1925, the text
  of which is set out *supra*, p. 501.
[70] On s. 9; see also *Shaw* v. *Cates* [1909] 1 Ch. 389; *supra*, p. 501; *Re Somerset*
  [1894] 1 Ch. 231, 253; *infra*, p. 648; *Re Turner* [1897] 1 Ch. 536, 541; *Palmer* v.
  Emerson [1911] 1 Ch. 758, 764; *Jones* v. *Julian* (1890) 25 L.R.Ir. 45.

special authorised object for which the capital money was raised, shall, when received, be invested or otherwise applied wholly in one, or partly in one and partly in another or others, of the following modes (namely): . . .

> (xi) In purchase of land in fee simple, or of leasehold land held for sixty years or more unexpired at the time of purchase, subject or not to any exception or reservation of or in respect of mines or minerals therein, or of or in respect of rights or powers relative to the working of mines or minerals therein, or in other land.

The Law of Property Act 1925

Section 28.—(1) Trustees for sale shall, in relation to land or to manorial incidents and to the proceeds of sale, have all the powers of a tenant for life and the trustees of a settlement under the Settled Land Act 1925, including in relation to the land the powers of management conferred by that Act during a minority; and (subject to any express trust to the contrary) all capital money arising under the said powers shall, unless paid or applied for any purpose authorised by the Settled Land Act 1925, be applicable in the same manner as if the money represented proceeds of sale arising under the trust for sale.

All land acquired under this subsection shall be conveyed to the trustees on trust for sale.

The powers conferred by this subsection shall be exercised with such consents (if any) as would have been required on a sale under the trust for sale, and when exercised shall operate to overreach any equitable interests or powers which are by virtue of this Act or otherwise made to attach to the net proceeds of sale as if created by a trust affecting those proceeds.

[Trustees for sale of land have power to invest the proceeds of sale in the purchase of other land provided they have not ceased to be trustees for sale by selling all their land: *Re Wakeman.*[71] Proceeds of sale of land remain such so long as they can be traced. Thus, if trustees hold Blackacre on trust for sale and sell part of it for £5,000, which they invest in shares, they can realise the shares and reinvest in the purchase of land: *Re Wellsted's W.T.*[72]]

IV. Interpretation of Investment Clauses

Re HARARI'S SETTLEMENT TRUSTS, WORDSWORTH v. FANSHAWE

Chancery Division [1949] L.J.R. 675; 93 S.J. 102; [1949] 1 All E.R. 430; [1949] W.N. 79

By a settlement dated June 16, 1938, the settlor, Sir Victor Harari, Pasha, transferred certain securities, none of them on the Trustee List, to trustees and directed: " The trustees shall hold the said investments so transferred to them as aforesaid upon trust that they may either allow the same to remain in their present state of investment so long as

---

[71] [1945] Ch. 177. Whether or not trustees ceased to be trustees for sale of land within s. 205 (1) (xxix) upon sale of all trust land was expressly reserved by Cohen L.J. in *Re Wellsted's W.T.* [1949] Ch. 296, 319.
[72] [1949] Ch. 296 (C.A.).

the trustees may think fit or may at any time or times with the consent
of the daughter [a beneficiary under the trust] realise the said investments or any of them or any part thereof respectively and shall with
the like consent invest the money produced thereby and also all capital
moneys which may be or become subject to the trusts of this settlement
in the names or under the control of the trustees in or upon such
investments as to them may seem fit with power with such consent to
vary or transpose any investments for or into others. . . ."

JENKINS J.: " I have to decide whether, on the true construction of
the few words in the settlement referring to investment, the trustees have
an unrestricted discretion to invest in such investments as they think
fit, whether they are or are not of a kind authorised by law for the
investment of trust funds, or whether such discretion as they have
should be construed as limited in its operation to the trustee range of
investments. . . .

" The question turns primarily on the meaning to be attached to the
words ' in or upon such investments as to them may seem fit.' Prima
facie those words mean what they say—that the trustees are not to be
limited in any way by any statutory range of investments, but can invest
in any investment which they may select as seeming to them a fit one
for the money subject to the trusts of the settlement. There is, however, a good deal of authority, which must be borne in mind, to the
effect that investment clauses should be strictly construed and should
not be construed as authorising investments outside the trustee range
unless they clearly and unambiguously indicate an intention to that
effect. [He referred to these authorities and continued.]

" That, I think, is a representative collection of the authorities bearing on this topic, and, having given them the best consideration I can,
it seems to me that I am left free to construe this settlement according
to what I consider to be the natural and proper meaning of the words
used in their context, and, so construing the words ' in or upon such
investments as to them may seem fit,' I see no justification for implying
any restriction. I think the trustees have power, under the plain meaning of those words, to invest in any investments which, to adopt
Kekewich J.'s observation, they ' honestly think ' are desirable investments for the investment of moneys subject to the trusts of the settlement. To hold otherwise would really be to read words into the
settlement which are not there. The wide construction which the
words themselves are, in my view, sufficient to bear is, I think, to some
extent, supported by the fact that the investments brought in, in the
first place, are non-trustee investments, and also to some small extent by
the reference in paragraph 2 [of the settlement] to ' investment money
or property representing ' the trust fund. There is nothing in those
words that one can say is really inconsistent with a limitation on the
range of investment to trustee investments, but there is, perhaps, more
likelihood of something which in common parlance would be described

as 'property' rather than an 'investment' coming into the hands of the trustees in the course of exercising their powers of investment if the range is the unrestricted one rather than the narrow one. The real ground, however, for my decision is the plain and ordinary meaning of the words 'in or upon such investments as to them may seem fit.' Having found nothing in the authorities to constrain me to construe those words otherwise than in accordance with their plain meaning, that is the meaning I propose to place on them.

"For these reasons, I will declare that the power given by the settlement in question to the trustees to invest trust moneys, with the consent therein mentioned, in or upon such investments as to them may seem fit, with power to vary or transpose any investments for or into others, enables investments to be made in any investments which seem fit to the trustees, whether or not they are investments authorised by law for the investment of trust funds." [73] *Declaration accordingly.*

Section 4. Delegation by a Trustee

(a) *Delegation of authority to do specific acts*

The general rule of equity is *delegatus non potest delegare.* "I must observe," said Langdale M.R. in *Turner* v. *Corney* [74]; "that trustees who take on themselves the management of property for the benefit of others have no right to shift their duty on other persons; and if they employ an agent, they remain subject to the responsibility towards their *cestuis que trust,* for whom they have undertaken the duty." The trustee was, however, justified in delegating if, in the circumstances, delegation was either reasonably necessary or in the ordinary course of affairs: *Ex p. Belchier,* [75] *Speight* v. *Gaunt, infra.* But even in cases where the employment of an agent was justified, the trustee had to exercise the care of a reasonable man of business in his choice of the agent and he could not employ an agent to do an act outside the scope of the agent's business: *Fry* v. *Tapson,* [76] *Rowland* v. *Witherden.* [77] If these conditions were satisfied the trustee would not be responsible for a loss arising through the default of the agent,

---

[73] See also *Re Douglas' Will Trusts* [1959] 1 W.L.R. 1212: "securities" held not to be confined to secured investments but to include "stocks and shares"; *Re Peczenic's Settlement* [1964] 1 W.L.R. 720. For an even wider investment clause than appeared in *Re Harari's Settlement Trusts, supra,* see *Re Power's Will Trusts* [1947] Ch. 572; 63 L.Q.R. 421 (R. E. M.). "All moneys requiring to be invested . . . may be invested by the trustee in any manner which he may in his absolute discretion think fit in all respects as if he were the sole beneficial owner of such moneys including the purchase of freehold property in England and Wales." *Held* by Jenkins J. not to authorise the purchase of a house with vacant possession for the occupation of the beneficiaries because that part of the purchase-money paid for the advantage of vacant possession would not be laid out in income-producing property for the sake of the income which it would yield. *Quaere* (a) would the result have been different if the clause had authorised "investment or other application of the money whether by way of investment or not"?; (b) does the conferment upon the trustee of a power to act "as if he were the sole beneficial owner" exempt him from the duty of care required of him by *Learoyd* v. *Whiteley* (1887) 12 App.Cas. 727 and s. 6 (1) of the Trustee Investments Act 1961? *Cf. Re Maberly* (1886) 33 Ch.D. 455. See also *Re Svenson-Taylor's S.T.* [1974] 3 All E.R. 396.
[74] (1841) 5 Beav. 515, 517.
[75] (1754) Amb. 218.
[76] (1884) 28 Ch.D. 268.   [77] (1851) 3 McN. & G. 568.

provided he exercised a proper supervision over the agent: *Matthews* v. *Brise*.[78] In this respect an express or statutory provision [79] exempting a trustee from liability for loss caused by the acts or defaults of an agent unless the loss occurred through the trustee's "wilful default" did not relieve the trustee of his duty to show the care of the reasonable man of business both in the appointment and in the supervision of agents: *Re Brier*.[80] A trustee was thus only liable for his own acts or defaults *e.g.*, negligent appointment, or negligent supervision. There was no automatic vicarious liability for the agent's acts or defaults in those cases where delegation to agents was permissible.

Re Vickery, infra, is a decision to the effect that section 23 (1) of the Trustee Act 1925, *infra*, has reversed the old law of delegation. Whereas formerly a trustee could not delegate unless it was either reasonably necessary or in the ordinary course of affairs, today it seems that he can delegate whether there is any necessity for it or not.

In so far as *Re Vickery* purports to decide more than this, and, in particular, that a trustee is no longer liable if he fails to exercise any supervision over the acts of his agents, it has been severely criticised, notably by Dr. Gareth Jones in his article on "Delegation by Trustees: A Reappraisal." [81] The main grounds of criticism are: first, that so wide an interpretation of section 23 (1) of the Trustee Act 1925 renders section 23 (3), *infra* (which, on any interpretation, is limited in its effect), "meaningless and unnecessary " [82]; secondly, that so far as delegation of specific acts (as opposed to delegation of discretions) is concerned it renders the effect of section 23 (2) and old section 25 nugatory, if the trustee is allowed in all cases to act under section 23 (1) and thus to protect himself by " the umbrella of an honest appointment " [83]; thirdly, that Maugham J.'s restriction in *Re Vickery* of liability for "wilful default " to cases of intentional or reckless breach of duty, while correct for cases outside the law of trusts, had no relevance to the " law as to the employment of agents by trustees," [84] in respect of which the phrase "wilful default " always included " lack of reasonable care ": "wilful default " in section 30 (1) of the Trustee Act 1925, *infra*, should bear the same meaning as it did in the earlier legislation which the section replaced [85]; fourthly, the Trustee Act, as a whole, is primarily a consolidating Act,[86] and its provisions should therefore be interpreted in such a way as not to effect any substantial changes in the law: section 23 (1) should, therefore, protect the trustee whether or not there was any legal or moral necessity for the delegation, but only where he has appointed the agent in good faith

---

[78] (1845) 10 Jur.(o.s.) 105.

[79] *Underwood* v. *Stevens* (1816) 1 Mer. 712; s. 30 (1) of the Trustee Act 1925, *infra*, p. 519, replacing s. 24 of the Trustee Act 1893, which in turn replaced s. 31 of the Law of Property Amendment Act 1859; *infra*, p. 521.

[80] (1884) 26 Ch.D. 238, 243 (*per* Lord Selborne L.C.). Also *Re Chapman* [1896] 2 Ch. 763, 776 *per* Lindley L.J., " Wilful default which includes want of ordinary prudence on the part of the trustees must be proved."

[81] (1959) 22 M.L.R. 381; see also (1931) 47 L.Q.R. 463 (Holdsworth); *ibid.* 330 (H. Potter).

[82] (1931) 47 L.Q.R. 330 (H. Potter).

[83] Jones, *loc. cit.*, note 25, p. 390.

[84] *Re City Equitable Fire Insurance* [1925] Ch. 407, *per* Romer J. 439; *cf. Re Munton* [1927] 1 Ch. 262, *per* Astbury J. at 274.

[85] Jones, *loc. cit.*, note 25, p. 393. See pp. 625–627, *infra*.

[86] *Re Turner's Will Trusts* [1937] Ch. 15, *per* Romer J. at 24.

and taken reasonable care in the supervision of his activities [87]; fifthly, section 23 (1) has not altered the liability of the trustee *for his own acts* or defaults: is he not guilty of a default if he fails to take reasonable care in supervising the activities of agents appointed by him? [88] If section 23 (1) had altered the liability of a trustee for his own acts or defaults so as to excuse him once he had made an honest appointment this could hardly be reconciled with section 30 (1) making it clear that a trustee is liable for his agent's acts or defaults if he has been guilty of " wilful default."

It is noteworthy that in *Re Lucking's Will Trusts*,[89] Cross J. (as he then was) obiter treated *Re Vickery* as only deciding (a) that section 23 (1) empowered the trustee's appointment of the solicitor or agent and (b) that the trustee would be excused liability by virtue of section 30 (1) unless guilty of " wilful default " which he was not in the circumstances. So restricted, *Re Vickery* is unexceptional except for its interpretation of " wilful default." In *Re Lucking's Will Trusts* a company, of which the trustee was a director with a substantial interest, honestly appointed the trustee's old army friend, Lt.-Col. Dewar O.B.E., to manage the company's business. Since the manager was appointed by the company and not by the trustees section 23 (1) and section 30 (1) were inapplicable. On *Speight* v. *Grant* [90] principles the trustee was liable in the events that happened for failing to supervise the manager properly.

(b) *Delegation of discretions*

Discretions may now be delegated under section 23 (2) (for things to be done outside the United Kingdom) and under section 25 as substantially amended by section 9 of the Powers of Attorney Act 1971 (allowing a general power to delegate whereas previously it was dependent on the trustee leaving the United Kingdom for more than one month). Whereas under section 25 (5) a trustee is automatically vicariously liable for the acts or defaults of his agent a trustee's liability is personal only under section 23 (2).

Under section 29 of the Law of Property Act 1925 trustees for sale of land may revocably in writing delegate the powers of leasing, accepting surrenders of leases and management to any person of full age beneficially entitled in possession to the net rents and profits.[91] By section 29 (3) the trustees are under no automatic vicarious liability for the beneficiary's acts or defaults: their personal liability, however, remains, *e.g.*, if they do not revoke the delegation when it has become obvious that the beneficiary is completely unfitted to exercise the powers revocably delegated to him.

---

[87] Jones, *loc. cit.*, note 25, pp. 393–394.   *Sed quaere*: is this ground of criticism affected by the fact that s. 23 (1) re-enacts s. 125 (1) of the Law of Property Act 1922, Part IV of which, wherein s. 125 (1) appears, is headed " *Amendment of the Trustee Acts* ".   On the other hand, it can be argued that whilst the main part of s. 23 (1) alters the law the last clause " shall not be responsible for the default of any such agent if employed in good faith " was added to emphasise that despite the new unlimited scope for employing agents there was still to be no automatic vicarious liability.   This leaves untouched the question of the trustee's liability for his own defaults.

[88] Jones, *loc. cit.*, note 25, pp. 394–395.

[89] [1968] 1 W.L.R. 866, *infra*, p. 618.

[90] (1883) 9 App.Cas. 1.

[91] Such a person may obtain the court's assistance under the Law of Property Act 1925, s. 30, to compel a delegation.

SPEIGHT v. GAUNT [92]

Court of Appeal (1883) 22 Ch.D. 727 (Jessel M.R., Lindley and Bowen
   L.JJ.); affirmed, 9 App.Cas. 1; 53 L.J.Ch. 419; 50 L.T. 330;
   48 J.P. 84; 32 W.R. 435 (Earl of Selborne L.C., Lords Blackburn, Watson and Fitzgerald)

A trustee (the defendant) employed a broker (Mr. Cooke) for the
purpose of investing £15,000 of trust funds in corporation stocks.
Cooke (who was chosen as the broker on the suggestion of the beneficiaries) had previously been in partnership with his late father under
the name of John Cooke & Son, a firm of high repute. The broker
brought the trustee a bought-note stating that he required the money
to pay for the corporation stocks on the following day, which was the
next settling-day. Cheques for the necessary amount were drawn in
favour of and handed to the broker, who left the bought-note with
the trustee's cashier. Four days later the trustee asked the broker
whether the securities had been acquired, to which the broker answered
that there had not been time; and when the trustee made inquiries of
the broker on further occasions he was from time to time put off with
similar excuses. The broker had in fact appropriated the cheques to
his own use a day or two after they had been handed to him; and a
month afterwards he filed a petition on which he was adjudicated
bankrupt.

The *cestuis que trust* claimed a declaration that the defendant trustee
had committed a breach of trust with respect to this transaction and
was personally liable to make good the loss. They argued that the
trust funds handed to the broker should have been paid to the corporations' bankers pending the acquisition of the securities, instead of being
made payable to the broker by means of cheques drawn in his favour.
The defendant contended that he could not be fixed with liability unless
it were shown that he had not acted as a prudent man of business
would have acted on his own behalf; that it was the regular course of
business for investors, on receiving the bought-note, to give their broker
a cheque for the amount, the cheque being retained by the broker in
the interval between purchase and transfer; and that he, the defendant,
had followed the regular course of business. Evidence was given that
the form of the bought-note would indicate to brokers, but probably
not to the public in general, that the securities were to be acquired not
in the market but direct from the corporations.

---

[92] For cases on the employment of agents by trustees (and executors), see *Knight* v.
Plymouth (1747) 1 Dick. 120, *Rowth* v. *Howell* (1797) 3 Ves. 565 and *France* v.
Woods (1829) Tam. 172 (banker); *Macnamara* v. *Jones* (1784) 2 Dick. 587 and *Re
Bird* (1873) 28 L.T. 658 (solicitor); *Henderson* v. *M'Iver* (1818) 3 Madd. 275 and
Re Bennett, Jones v. *Bennett* [1896] 1 Ch. 778 (accountant); *Wilkinson* v. *Wilkinson*
(1825) 2 Sim. & St. 237 and *Re Muffett* (1887) 3 T.L.R. 605 (rent-collector); *Ex p.
Turner* (1828) 1 Mont. & Mac. 52 and *Edmonds* v. *Peake* (1843) 7 Beav. 239
(auctioneer); *Jones* v. *Powell* (1843) 6 Beav. 488 (stockbroker); *Weiss* v. *Dill* (1834)
3 My. & K. 26, *Hopkinson* v. *Roe* (1838) 1 Beav. 180 and *Re Brier* (1884) 26 Ch.D.
238 (debt-collector).

Bacon V.-C. held the trustee liable to make good the loss, inasmuch as he had not acted prudently in drawing cheques in favour of the broker (instead of in favour of the corporations) on the strength of a " scrap of paper " (the bought-note). The trustee appealed.

JESSEL M.R.: ". . . In the first place, I think we ought to consider what is the liability of a trustee who undertakes an office which requires him to make an investment on behalf of his *cestui que trust*. It seems to me that on general principles a trustee ought to conduct the business of the trust in the same manner that an ordinary prudent man of business would conduct his own, and that beyond that there is no liability or obligation on the trustee. In other words, a trustee is not bound because he is a trustee to conduct business in other than the ordinary and usual way in which similar business is conducted by mankind in transactions of their own. It never could be reasonable to make a trustee adopt further and better precautions than an ordinary prudent man of business would adopt, or to conduct the business in any other way. If it were otherwise, no one would be a trustee at all. He is not paid for it. He says, ' I take all reasonable precautions, and all the precautions which are deemed reasonable by prudent men of business, and beyond that I am not required to go.' Now what are the usual pre-cautions taken by men of business when they make an investment? If the investment is an investment made on the Stock Exchange through a stock-broker, the ordinary course of business is for the investor to select a stockbroker in good credit and in a good position, having regard to the sum to be invested, and to direct him to make the investment—that is, to purchase on the Stock Exchange of a jobber or another broker the investment required. In the ordinary course, all that the broker can do is to enter into a contract—usually it is for the next account-day. Of course you may, by special bargain, make it for cash or for any other day, but the ordinary course is for the next account-day. Before the account-day arrives the purchasing stockbroker requests his principal to pay him the money, because on the account-day he is himself liable to pay over the money to the vendor, whether a jobber or broker, and therefore he must have it ready for the account-day, and according to the usual course of business he sends a copy of the purchasing note to the principal stating when the money is required to be paid, and he obtains the money from him a day or two before the account-day. When he gets it he pays it over, if it is a single transaction, to the vendor, and if it is one of a number of transactions he makes out an account with his vendor and pays over or receives from him the balance on the transactions. It by no means follows, therefore, that he pays over to the vendor the sum received, indeed there may be a number of transactions, and if the balance is the other way, then he has to receive money on the account, but he must in any case have the money in order to keep himself out of cash advances. It is after payment, and very often a considerable time after payment, that is, several days, that he gets the securities perfected. If they are shares or stock in a company, or railway or other company, it may be a considerable time before the transfers are lodged at the office, and it is not until the matter is ready for completion that he gets the transfer and the certificates. But in all cases, except in the case of consols, and a few other such stocks, there is some interval between the payment of the purchase-money and the obtaining of the security, or of the investment purchased.

"If, therefore, a trustee has made a proper selection of a broker, and has paid him the money on the bought-note, and, by reason of the default of the broker, the money is lost, it does not appear to me in that case that the trustee can be liable. Indeed it was not argued in this court that he would be liable, and I have said what I have said upon the subject more on account of an observation reported to have been made by Vice-Chancellor Bacon in the court below than because of any argument that was addressed to us upon the point . . .

"I now come to the point upon which the case was decided and on which it was argued before us. I must say as I read the pleadings that the law is stated in conformity with that which I have been laying down. The accusation against the trustee is one of negligence. It is called 'gross negligence,' that does not matter, negligence is the charge made against the trustee, and the question is whether he has been guilty of negligence. Now where you have, as you have in this case, an innocent man—that is, innocent at any rate as to any moral guilt—who was sincerely anxious to do his best for the trust fund, and as to whom, as was stated by the Vice-Chancellor in the court below, there was really nothing that he could be reproached with unless it were carelessness, I think the court is bound to look carefully at the pleadings to see what he is charged with, and not to allow the charge to be extended beyond the pleadings. I shall not decide the case upon that ground, because, as will be seen presently, even if I had thought the plaintiffs were at liberty to go beyond the pleadings, I should have come to the same conclusion as I have upon the pleadings.

"Now the Vice-Chancellor said this about Mr. Gaunt, in which I think he was fully justified, and I merely quote it to show that my view of these cases against trustees is rather corroborated by the observations which I am about to read. My view has always been this, that where you have an honest trustee fairly anxious to perform his duty and to do as he thinks best for the estate, you are not to strain the law against him to make him liable for doing that which he has done and which he believes is right in the execution of his duty, without you have a plain case made against him. In other words, you are not to exercise your ingenuity, which it appears to me the Vice-Chancellor has done, for the purpose of finding reasons for fixing a trustee with liability; but you are rather to avoid all such hypercriticism of documents and acts and to give the trustee the benefit of any doubt or ambiguity which may appear in any document, so as to relieve him from the liability with which it is sought to fix him.

"I think it is the duty of the court in these cases where there is a question of nicety as to construction or otherwise to lean to the side of the honest trustee, and not to be anxious to find fine and extraordinary reasons for fixing him with any liability upon the contract. You are to endeavour as far as possible, having regard to the whole transaction, to avoid making an honest man who is not paid for the performance of an unthankful office liable for the failure of other people from whom he receives no benefit.[93] I think that is the view which has been taken by modern judges, and some of the older cases in which a different view has been taken would now be repudiated with indignation. It appears to me that the Vice-Chancellor has adopted an entirely different view. I think he has inferred that which is not fairly to be inferred in this case; and even if he were right it could only be inferred by taking one of two views, and we ought not to take the adverse view if the other view, being equally as good, can be adopted . . ."

Held, by the Court of Appeal, that the trustee was not liable, inasmuch as he had acted in accordance with the regular course of business. The beneficiaries' appeal to the House of Lords was dismissed.[94]

The Trustee Act 1925

Power to employ agents

Section 23.—(1) Trustees or personal representatives may, instead of acting personally, employ and pay an agent, whether a solicitor, banker, stockbroker, or other person, to transact any business or do any act required to be transacted or done in the execution of the trust, or the administration of the testator's or intestate's estate, including the receipt and payment of money, and shall be entitled to be allowed and paid all charges and expenses so incurred, and shall not be responsible for the default of any such agent if employed in good faith.[95]

(2) Trustees or personal representatives may appoint any person to act as their agent or attorney for the purpose of selling, converting, collecting,

---

[93] Bowen L.J. expressly left this point open: (1883) 22 Ch.D. 727, 766. In the House of Lords, Lord Fitzgerald did not accept Jessel M.R.'s view: (1883) 9 App.Cas. 1, 31.

[94] Other cases which illustrate the application of the principle of *Speight* v. *Gaunt, supra*, are *Warner* v. *Torkington* (1835) 4 L.J.Ch. 193; *Re Godfrey* (1883) 23 Ch.D. 483; *Re Pearson* (1884) 51 L.T. 692; *Bullock* v. *Bullock* (1886) 56 L.J.Ch. 221; *Walcott* v. *Lyons* (1886) 54 L.T. 786; *Rae* v. *Meek* (1889) 14 App.Cas. 558, 573; *Jobson* v. *Palmer* [1893] 1 Ch. 71, 76; *Rochfort* v. *Seaton* [1896] 1 Ir.R. 18; *Shepherd* v. *Harris* (1905) 74 L.J.Ch. 574; *Little* v. *County Down Infirmary* [1918] 1 Ir.R. 221.

[95] In *Green* v. *Whitehead* [1930] 1 Ch. 38, X and Y were trustees for sale of land, which they contracted to sell to Z. Y gave A a power to sell and convey " my property." Z refused to take a conveyance from X and A. Eve J. held that Z's refusal was justified: Y had made a complete delegation of the office of trustee which was not possible under s. 23 (1). His decision was affirmed by the Court of Appeal on the grounds that the power conferred by Y upon A extended only to property of which Y was beneficial owner; Hanworth M.R. thought that but for this, the delegation would have been valid: see Jones, *loc. cit.*, p. 387, citing the report at 46 T.L.R. 11.

getting in, and executing and perfecting assurances of, or managing or cultivating, or otherwise administering any property, real or personal, moveable or immoveable, subject to the trust or forming part of the testator's or intestate's estate, in any place outside the United Kingdom or executing or exercising any discretion or trust or power vested in them in relation to any such property, with such ancillary powers, and with and subject to such provisions and restrictions as they may think fit, including a power to appoint substitutes, and shall not, by reason only of their having made such appointment, be responsible for any loss arising thereby.[96]

(3) Without prejudice to such general power of appointing agents as aforesaid—

(a) A trustee may appoint a solicitor to be his agent to receive and give a discharge for any money or valuable consideration or property receivable by the trustee under the trust, by permitting the solicitor to have the custody of, and to produce, a deed having in the body thereof or endorsed thereon a receipt for such money or valuable consideration or property, the deed being executed, or the endorsed receipt being signed, by the person entitled to give a receipt for that consideration;

(b) A trustee shall not be chargeable with breach of trust by reason only of his having made or concurred in making any such appointment; and the production of any such deed by the solicitor shall have the same statutory validity and effect as if the person appointing the solicitor had not been a trustee;

(c) A trustee may appoint a banker or solicitor to be his agent to receive and give a discharge for any money payable to the trustee under or by virtue of a policy of insurance, by permitting the banker or solicitor to have the custody of and to produce the policy of insurance with a receipt signed by the trustee and a trustee shall not be chargeable with a breach of trust by reason only of his having made or concurred in making any such appointment:

Provided that nothing in this subsection shall exempt a trustee from any liability which he would have incurred if this Act and any enactment replaced by this Act had not been passed, in case he permits any such money, valuable consideration, or property to remain in the hands or under the control of the banker or solicitor for a period longer than is reasonably necessary to enable the banker or solicitor, as the case may be, to pay or transfer the same to the trustee.

This subsection applies whether the money or valuable consideration or property was or is received before or after the commencement of this Act.[97]

Power to delegate trusts

25.[98]—[(1) Notwithstanding any rule of law or equity to the contrary, a trustee may, by power of attorney, delegate for a period not exceeding

---

[96] This subsection is new. It was not applicable in *Green* v. *Whitehead, supra*, because the property in that case was situated in England.
[97] This subsection reproduces with amendments s. 17 of the Trustee Act 1893, which replaced s. 2 of the Trustee Act 1888.
[98] By the Powers of Attorney Act 1971, s. 2, no instrument creating a power of attorney, and no copy of any such instrument shall be deposited or filed at the

twelve months [99] the execution or exercise of all or any of the trusts, powers and discretions vested in him as trustee either alone or jointly with any other person or persons.

(2) The persons who may be donees of a power of attorney under this section include a trust corporation but not (unless a trust corporation) the only other co-trustee of the donor of the power.

(3) An instrument creating a power of attorney under this section shall be attested by at least one witness.

(4) Before or within seven days after giving a power of attorney under this section the donor shall give written notice thereof (specifying the date on which the power comes into operation and its duration, the donee of the power, the reason why the power is given and, where some only are delegated, the trusts, powers and discretions delegated) to—

(a) each person (other than himself) if any, who under any instrument creating the trust has power (whether alone or jointly) to appoint a new trustee; and

(b) each of the other trustees, if any;

but failure to comply with this subsection shall not, in favour of a person dealing with the donee of the power, invalidate any act done or instrument executed by the donee.

(5) The donor of a power of attorney given under this section shall be liable for the acts or defaults of the donee in the same manner as if they were the acts or defaults of the donor.] [1]

[(6)] [2] For the purpose of executing or exercising the trusts or powers delegated to him, the donee may exercise any of the powers conferred on the donor as trustee by statute or by the instrument creating the trust, including power, for the purpose of the transfer of any inscribed stock, himself to delegate to an attorney power to transfer but not including the power of delegation conferred by this section.

[(7)] [3] The fact that it appears from any power of attorney given under this section, or from any evidence required for the purposes of any such power of attorney or otherwise, that in dealing with any stock the donee of the power is acting in the execution of a trust shall not be deemed for any purpose to affect any person in whose books the stock is inscribed or registered with any notice of the trust.

[(8) This section applies to a personal representative, tenant for life and statutory owner as it applies to a trustee except that subsection (4) shall apply as if it required the notice there mentioned to be given—

---

central office of the Supreme Court or at the Land Registry under this section, although any right to search for, inspect, copy, or obtain an office copy of, any such document deposited or filed before October 1, 1971, remains unaffected. Similarly, s. 9 applies whenever the trusts, powers or discretions in question arose but does not invalidate anything done by virtue of this section.

[99] If no period at all were specified would the power be valid for one year from its date applying the *Mogridge* v. *Clapp* [1892] 3 Ch. 382 principle recently applied in *Re Pennant's W.T.* [1970] Ch. 75?

[1] These subsections were substituted for the former subss. (1) to (8) by the Powers of Attorney Act 1971, s. 9 (1) and (2).

[2] The former subss. (9) and (10) now stand as subss. (6) and (7): *ibid.*, s. 9 (1) and (3).

[3] *Ibid.*

(*a*) in the case of a personal representative, to each of the other personal representatives, if any, except any executor who has renounced probate;

(*b*) in the case of a tenant for life, to the trustees of the settlement and to each person, if any, who together with the person giving the notice constitutes the tenant for life;

(*c*) in the case of a statutory owner, to each of the persons, if any, who together with the person giving the notice constitute the statutory owner and, in the case of a statutory owner by virtue of section 23 (1) (*a*) of the Settled Land Act 1925, to the trustees of the settlement.] [4]

Implied indemnity of trustees

Section 30.—(1) A trustee shall be chargeable only for money and securities actually received by him notwithstanding his signing any receipt for the sake of conformity, and shall be answerable and accountable only for his own acts, receipts, neglects, or defaults, and not for those of any other trustee, nor for any banker, broker, or other person with whom any trust money or securities may be deposited, nor for the insufficiency or deficiency of any securities, nor for any loss,[5] unless the same happens through his own wilful default.

Re VICKERY, VICKERY v. STEPHENS

Chancery Division [1931] 1 Ch. 572; 100 L.J.Ch. 138

" The plaintiffs were the two sons of a testatrix, entitled in equal shares to her estate undisposed of by her will, including £214 14s. 5d. in the Post Office Savings Bank and £62 4s. in Savings Certificates. The defendant, as sole executor of the testatrix, employed [in May 1927] to wind up her estate a solicitor [Mr. Jennens] who, unknown to him, had at one time been suspended from practice, and who obtained from the first plaintiff the Post Office Savings Bank deposit book and the Savings Certificates. The defendant heard for the first time of the solicitor's suspension [approximately] three months later, when the first plaintiff told him of it. Under the defendant's written authority, a warrant valued at £62 4s. had been issued [in respect of the Savings Certificates] in favour of the solicitor's firm, and the first plaintiff wrote to the defendant objecting to his having taken that course. Later, the first plaintiff asked the defendant to employ another solicitor, but the defendant did not do so, as the solicitor was then promising to settle the matter. Ultimately the solicitor absconded, and the sums of £214 14s. 5d. and £62 4s. were not recovered." [6]

---

[4] This subsection was substituted for the former subs. (11): *ibid.*

[5] The *ejusdem generis* rule applies to this as made clear by Maugham J. in *Re Vickery, infra*, so that the loss must flow from the depositing of trust money or securities: a person employed by a trustee to manage an unincorporated business owned by the trust is not a person with whom trust money or securities are deposited within the meaning of s. 30: *Re Lucking's W.T.* [1968] 1 W.L.R. 866, *infra*, p. 618.

[6] Headnote. The defendant did in fact put the matter in the hands of another solicitor in December 1927.

In this action the plaintiffs claimed a declaration that the defendant had committed a breach of trust in allowing the two sums to be received and retained for over a month by the solicitor, and that he was liable to replace the loss with interest. The defendant relied mainly on sections 23 (1) and 30 (1) of the Trustee Act 1925.

MAUGHAM J. (after stating the facts): " The question that arises is whether in the circumstances, and in view of my findings as to the facts, the defendant is liable to make good these sums with interest by reason of his negligence either in employing Jennens to receive the sums, or in permitting those sums to remain in his hands, in the circumstances of the case, for a longer period than was necessary.

"In considering this question the court has to bear in mind in particular two sections of the Trustee Act 1925. Section 23 (1) is as follows: [His Lordship read the subsection, and continued:] This subsection is new and, in my opinion, authorised the defendant in signing the authorities to Jennens & Jennens to collect the two sums in question,[7] for I do not think it can be doubted that the defendant acted in good faith in employing Jennens for the purpose. It will be observed that the subsection has no proviso or qualification to it such as we find in relation to section 23 (3). It is hardly too much to say that it revolutionises the position of a trustee or an executor so far as regards the employment of agents. He is no longer required to do any actual work himself, but he may employ a solicitor or other agent to do it, *whether there is any real necessity for the employment or not.* No doubt he should use his discretion in selecting an agent, and should employ him only to do acts within the scope of the usual business of the agent; but, as will be seen, a question arises whether even in these respects he is personally liable for a loss due to the employment of the agent unless he has been guilty of wilful default.

" Section 23 (3) is in the following terms: [His Lordship read the subsection, and continued:] This subsection is a reproduction with amendments of section 17 of the Trustee Act 1893, which replaced section 2 of the Trustee Act 1888. It will be observed that paragraph (*a*) of the subsection relates to the production of a deed having indorsed thereon a receipt for money or other property, and that paragraph (*c*) refers to the receipt of money payable to the trustee under a policy of insurance.[8] In these cases, no doubt, there is no reason why the banker or the solicitor should do anything more than receive the money and pay the same to the trustee or as he shall direct. The proviso must, I think, be limited to these two cases; and, of course, it is not intended to preclude a trustee from keeping trust funds at his bank pending investment or other proper use of them; and it has nothing to

---

[7] It is not definitely stated in any other part of the report that the defendant had signed more than one authority.

[8] On the subsection referred to, see *Re Sheppard* [1911] 1 Ch. 50 and *Wyman* v. *Paterson* [1900] A.C. 271, 280–281.

do, in my opinion, with the case I have to decide, in which the powers given by paragraphs (*a*) and (*c*) were not utilised by the defendant. There was no doubt a good reason for not making the proviso extend to subsection (1) of section 23, since in many cases, where, for example, a banker or other agent is employed by a trustee to receive money, the money cannot at once be conveniently paid to the trustee, but has to be employed by the banker or other agent in a number of ways.

" I have now to consider section 30 (1) of the Trustee Act 1925, a section which replaces section 24 of the Trustee Act 1893, which in its turn re-enacted Lord Cranworth's Act,[9] s. 31. It is in the following terms: [His Lordship read the subsection, and continued:] Reliance has been placed on the words concluding the subsection, ' nor for any other loss, unless the same happens through his own wilful default.' To avoid misconception I wish to say that, having regard to the numerous decisions since the enactment of Lord Cranworth's Act in relation to the liability of trustees for innocent breaches of trust, it is impossible now to hold that the words ' for any other loss ' are quite general, with the result that no trustee is ever liable for breach of trust unless the breach is occasioned by his own wilful default. In my opinion the words are confined to losses for which it is sought to make the trustee liable, occasioned by his signing receipts for the sake of conformity, or by reason of the wrongful acts or defaults of another trustee or of an agent with whom trust money or securities have been deposited, or for the insufficiency or deficiency of securities or some other analogous loss. It may be noted that if the phrase is not so limited it is difficult to see how there could have been any need for section 3 of the Judicial Trustees Act 1896, now re-enacted as section 61 of the Trustee Act 1925, or for section 29 of that Act [10]; nor would it be possible to explain the numerous cases before 1896 where trustees were made liable for honest mistakes either of construction or fact: see, for example, *Learoyd* v. *Whiteley*,[11] *National Trustees Co. of Australasia* v. *General Finance Co. of Australasia*,[12] and cases there cited.

" On the other hand, since section 30 (1) expressly refers to the defaults of bankers, brokers, or other persons with whom any trust money or other securities may be deposited, I am unable—dealing here with the more limited case—to escape the conclusion that the trustee cannot be made liable for the default of such a person unless the loss happens through the ' wilful default ' of the trustee. Before considering the meaning of the words ' wilful default ' in this connection, I would observe that in the case of *Re Brier* [13] the Court of Appeal, consisting of Lord Selborne L.C. and Cotton and Fry L.JJ., gave effect to Lord Cranworth's Act, s. 31, and held the trustees and executors not liable inasmuch as it had not been established that the

---

[9] Law of Property Amendment Act 1859.
[10] Exoneration of trustees in respect of certain powers of attorney.
[11] (1887) 12 App.Cas. 727.
[12] [1905] A.C. 373.   [13] (1884) 26 Ch.D. 238.

loss occasioned by the agent's insolvency (in a case where, as the law
then required, it was shown that the employment of the agent was a
proper one) was due to the wilful default of the trustees and executors.

"Now the meaning of the phrase 'wilful default' has been expounded by the Court of Appeal in the case of *Re Trusts of Leeds City
Brewery Ltd.'s Deed* [14] and in the case of *Re City Equitable Fire Insurance Co.* [15] It should be noted that in both those cases the indemnity,
given to the trustees in the first case and to the directors and officers of
the company in the second case, was worded in a general form, so that
it could not be contended that they were liable for any matter or thing
done or omitted unless it could be shown that the loss so occasioned
arose from their own wilful default. This, as I have said, is not true
of an ordinary executor or trustee; but the exposition of the phrase
'wilful default' is not the less valuable. The Court of Appeal held,
following in the case of *Re City Equitable Fire Insurance Co.* the
decision of Romer J., that a person is not guilty of wilful neglect or
default unless he is conscious that, in doing the act which is complained
of or in omitting to do the act which it is said he ought to have done,
he is committing a breach of his duty, or is recklessly careless whether
it is a breach of his duty or not. I accept with respect what Warrington L.J. said—namely, that in the case of trustees there are definite
and precise rules of law as to what a trustee may or may not do in the
execution of his trust, and that a trustee in general is not excused in
relation to a loss occasioned by a breach of trust merely because he
honestly believed that he was justified in doing the act in question.
But for the reasons which I have given I think that, where an executor
employs a solicitor or other agent to receive money belonging to the
estate in reliance on section 23 (1) of the Trustee Act 1925, he will not
be liable for a loss of the money occasioned by the misconduct of the
agent unless the loss happens through the wilful default of the executor,
using those words as implying, as the Court of Appeal have decided,
either a consciousness of negligence or breach of duty, or a recklessness
in the performance of a duty . . ."

After reviewing the circumstances, his Lordship came to the conclusion that the defendant had been guilty only of an error of judgment,
and held, therefore, that he was not liable. [16]

---

[14] [1925] Ch. 532n.
[15] [1925] Ch. 407.
[16] With reference to the relative positions where a testator requests or directs his
trustees to employ a designated person in some capacity or other in the administration of the trust, see A. W. Scott in (1928) 41 H.L.R. 709. The English and Irish
cases are *Hibbert* v. *Hibbert* (1808) 3 Mer. 681; *Friswell* v. *Moore* (1819), cited 5
Cl. & F. 142, *semble*; *Kilbee* v. *Sneyd* (1828) 2 Moll. 186, 199-200; *Williams* v.
Corbet (1837) 8 Sim. 349; *Shaw* v. *Lawless* (1838) 5 Cl. & F. 129; *Finden* v.
Stephens (1846) 1 Coop.t.Cott. 318; *Belaney* v. *Kelly* (1871) 24 L.T. 738; *Foster*
v. *Elsley* (1881) 19 Ch.D. 518.

Section 5. Deviations from the Terms of a Trust

In case it is overlooked it is, of course, possible to change the structure of fixed or discretionary interests under a settlement if there is an overriding power in this behalf conferred by the settlement, *e.g.*, upon the trustees, or the life tenant (or settlor) with the consent of the trustees.

I. WHERE THE BENEFICIARIES ARE SUI JURIS

If property is given to a person of full age *any* restriction on his enjoyment of it is inconsistent with his absolute interest.[17] Hence a beneficiary *sui juris* and entitled *absolutely* can call for a transfer: *Saunders* v. *Vautier, infra*; and he may do so even if the settlor purports to remove this right.[18] So also *several* beneficiaries who are all *sui juris* and between them entitled absolutely may call for a transfer, if they act together.[19] Even beneficiaries who are entitled *in succession* can combine to call for a transfer, provided they are *sui juris* and are collectively entitled absolutely.[20] The rule in *Saunders* v. *Vautier, infra*, operates also in favour of a charity.[21] But it does not apply where other persons have an interest in the accumulations of income which the beneficiaries are seeking to stop.[22] Nor does it give beneficiaries the right to control the trustee in the exercise of any discretion conferred upon him by statute or the trust instrument.[23]

SAUNDERS v. VAUTIER [24]

Master of the Rolls (1841) 4 Beav. 115; Cr. & Ph. 240; 10 L.J.Ch. 354

A testator bequeathed his stock on trust to accumulate the dividends until V. should attain the age of twenty-five, and then to transfer the principal, together with the accumulated dividends, to V. V., having attained twenty-one, claimed to have the fund transferred to him. It was contended for him that he had " a vested interest, and that as the accumulation and postponement of payment was for his benefit alone, he might waive it and call for an immediate transfer of the fund."

---

17 *Weatherall* v. *Thornburgh* (1878) 8 Ch.D. 261, 270 (Cotton L.J.).
18 *Stokes* v. *Cheek* (1860) 28 Beav. 620.
19 *Re Sandeman* [1937] 1 All E.R. 368; *Magrath* v. *Morehead* (1871) L.R. 12 Eq. 491.
20 *Leng* v. *Hodges* (1822) Jac. 585; *Barton* v. *Briscoe* (1822) Jac. 603; *Brown* v. *Pringle* (1845) 4 Hare 124; *Haynes* v. *Haynes* (1866) 35 L.J.Ch. 303; *Re Millner* (1872) L.R. 14 Eq. 245; *Anson* v. *Potter* (1879) 13 Ch.D. 141; *Re White* [1901] 1 Ch. 570; *Re Thornhill* [1904] W.N. 112.
21 *Wharton* v. *Masterman* [1895] A.C. 186; but see *Re Levy* [1960] Ch. 346. Whilst an indefinite gift of income to an individual carries the right to the capital, this is not necessarily so in the case of a similar gift to charity, for such a gift can be enjoyed by the charity in perpetuity.
22 *Berry* v. *Geen* [1938] A.C. 575.
23 *Re Brockbank* [1948] Ch. 206, *supra*, p. 451; see also *Re George Whichelow Ltd.* [1954] 1 W.L.R. 5; *cf. Butt* v. *Kelson* [1952] Ch. 197, 207. See M. Jump [1974] B.T.R. 68.
24 See also *Barnes* v. *Rowley* (1797) 3 Ves. 305; *Woodmeston* v. *Walker* (1831) 2 Russ. & M. 197; *Josselyn* v. *Josselyn* (1837) 9 Sim. 63; *Rocke* v. *Rocke* (1845) 9 Beav. 66; *Ford* v. *Batley* (1853) 17 Beav. 303; *Re Browne* (1859) 27 Beav. 324; *Stokes* v. *Cheek* (1860) 28 Beav. 620; *Hunt-Foulston* v. *Furber* (1876) 3 Ch.D. 285; *Parkes* v. *Royal Botanic Society* (1908) 24 T.L.R. 508; *Re Marshall* [1914] 1 Ch. 192; Trustee Act 1925, s. 51 (1) (ii) (*d*).

LORD LANGDALE M.R.: " I think that principle has been repeatedly acted upon; and where a legacy is directed to accumulate for a certain period, or where the payment is postponed the legatee, if he has an absolute indefeasible interest in the legacy, is not bound to wait until the expiration of that period, but may require payment the moment he is competent to give a valid discharge."

On a question raised, with reference to a previous order for maintenance, as to whether there was a vested interest in V. before he attained twenty-five, the petition stood over, with liberty to apply to the Lord Chancellor.

Held, by the Lord Chancellor, the fund was intended wholly for the benefit of V., although the enjoyment of it was postponed: it vested immediately, and he could now claim the transfer.[25]

II. WHERE THE BENEFICIARIES ARE NOT SUI JURIS

A. *Introductory* [26]

The decision of the House of Lords in *Chapman* v. *Chapman* [27] in 1954 made it clear that the court did not possess plenary powers to alter a trust because alteration was thought to be advantageous to infant or unborn beneficiaries except in certain limited cases. Some of these exceptions related to acts done by the trustees in regard to the trust property in the administration of the trust, while others went beyond this and conferred a limited power to remould the beneficial interests when this was to the advantage of the beneficiaries.

(a) *Exceptions relating to acts done in administration of trust*

(i) *Salvage.* This group of cases involved the alienation of infants' property and established the proposition that the court could sanction a mortgage or sale of part of an infant's beneficial interest for the benefit of the part retained in cases of absolute necessity.[28]

(ii) *Emergency.* This exception can be regarded as an extension of the salvage cases. The salvage cases required proof of absolute necessity. The principle of the emergency cases was somewhat wider and enabled the court to sanction departure from the terms of a trust where an emergency had arisen which the settlor had not foreseen and which required to be dealt with by the conferment of extraordinary powers on the trustees.[29]

(iii) *Expediency*—Section 57 of the Trustee Act 1925. Section 57 of the Trustee Act 1925 rested the jurisdiction on expediency—a basis which, it is conceived, is wider than that of salvage or emergency. The section provides:

---

[25] Joyce J., in *Re Couturier* [1907] 1 Ch. 470, 473, points out the distinction between giving a person a *vested* interest and postponing the enjoyment to a certain age, and giving him an interest *contingent* on his attaining a certain age.
[26] See O. R. Marshall, " Deviations from the Terms of a Trust " (1954) 17 M.L.R. 420; "The Scope of S. 53 of the Trustee Act 1925 " (1957) 21 Conv.(N.S.) 448.
[27] [1954] A.C. 429. The variation of the trust sought in that case has now been effected under the Variation of Trusts Act 1958, *infra*, p. 531: see *Re Chapman's Settlement Trusts (No. 2)* [1959] 1 W.L.R. 372.
[28] See *Re Jackson* (1882) 21 Ch.D. 786; *Conway* v. *Fenton* (1888) 40 Ch.D. 512; *cf. Re De Teissier* [1893] 1 Ch. 153; *Re Montagu* [1897] 2 Ch. 8.
[29] *Re New* [1901] 1 Ch. 534; *Re Tollemache* [1903] 1 Ch. 457.

" Where in the management or administration of any property vested in trustees, any sale, lease, mortgage, surrender, release or other disposition or any purchase, investment, acquisition, expenditure, or other transaction is in the opinion of the court *expedient*, but the same cannot be effected by reason of the absence of any power for that purpose vested in the trustees by the trust instrument, if any, or by law, the court may by order confer upon the trustees, either generally or in any particular instance, the necessary power for the purpose, in such terms, and subject to such provisions and conditions, if any, as the court may think fit and may direct in what manner any money authorised to be expended, and the costs of any transaction, are to be paid or borne as between capital and income."

The object of the section is to enable the court to authorise specific dealings with the trust property which it might not have been able to do on the basis of salvage or emergency, but it was no part of the legislative aim to disturb the rule that the court will not rewrite a trust.[30]

This is an overriding section, the provisions of which are read into every settlement.[31] The powers of the court are limited only by expediency, though the proposed transaction must be for the benefit not of one beneficiary but of the whole trust.[32] The power has been used to authorise the sale of chattels settled on trusts which prevent sale,[33] the sale of land where a consent requisite to sale has been refused,[34] the partitioning of land where there was no power to partition,[35] and the blending of two charitable funds into one.[36] Apparently, trustees could not obtain from the court a general extension of their investment powers, although they could apply for a particular investment to be specially authorised.[37]

(iv) *Conversion.* This group of cases arose out of the differences that used to exist between real and personal property both in regard to succession on intestacy (realty going to the heirs-at-law and personalty to the next-of-kin) and also to the power of testamentary disposition (personalty could be disposed of by will at the age of seventeen, but realty not until twenty-one). The general rule was that trustees for an infant could not change the nature of an estate from realty to personalty, or vice versa, because that would prejudice succession and also the power of disposition.[38]

---

[30] *Re Downshire* [1953] Ch. 218.
[31] *Re Mair* [1935] Ch. 562.
[32] *Re Craven's Estate (No. 2)* [1937] Ch. 431.
[33] *Re Hope's Will Trust* [1929] 2 Ch. 136.
[34] *Re Beale's Settlement Trusts* [1932] 2 Ch. 15.
[35] *Re Thomas* [1930] 1 Ch. 194.
[36] *Re Harvey* [1941] 3 All E.R. 284; for other cases on s. 57, see *Municipal and General Securities Ltd.* v. *Lloyds Bank Ltd.* [1950] Ch. 212; *Re Pratt* [1943] 2 All E.R. 375; *Re Basden* [1943] 2 All E.R. 11.
[37] See *Re Powell-Cotton's Resettlement* [1956] 1 W.L.R. 23. The court had an inherent jurisdiction to authorise a general extension in case of trustees of charity. See *Re Royal Society's Charitable Trusts* [1956] Ch. 87; 19 M.L.R. 93 (S. F. C. Milsom); *cf. Re Shipwrecked Fishermen and Mariners' Royal Benevolent Society* [1959] Ch. 220; *Re Kolb's W.T.* [1962] Ch. 531. Since the coming into force of the Variation of Trusts Act 1958, *infra,* all trustees may apply for extended investment powers under that Act and should not do so under s. 57 of the Trustee Act, *supra;* see *Re Coates' Trusts* [1959] 1 W.L.R. 375, 378. Investment powers will not be enlarged in the absence of special circumstances since the passing of the Trustee Investments Act 1961; *supra,* p. 495.
[38] See *Witter* v. *Witter* (1730) 3 P.Wms. 99.

But the rule grew up that the court itself could sanction a change where it was for the benefit of the infant,[39] though the court would usually insert in its order a proviso that the estate should remain notionally unchanged in equity during the minority of the infant.[40] The same principle was applied in the case of lunatics.[41]

(b) *Exceptions relating to the remoulding of the beneficial interests*

(i) *Maintenance.*[42] Where a settlor made a provision for a family but postponed the enjoyment, either for a particular purpose or generally for the increase of the estate, it was assumed that he did not intend that the children should be left unprovided for, or in a state of such moderate means that they could not be educated properly for the position which he intended them to have, and the court accordingly broke in upon the accumulation and provided maintenance for the children. The exercise of this jurisdiction resulted in an alteration of beneficial interests since income was applied in maintaining beneficiaries notwithstanding the fact that the settlor had directed that it should be accumulated or applied in reduction of incumbrances. The jurisdiction was not confined to cases of emergency or necessity.[43]

(ii) *Compromise.* It has long been clear that where the rights of the beneficiaries under a trust are the subject of doubt or dispute, the court has jurisdiction on behalf of all interested parties, whether adult, infant or unborn, to sanction a compromise by substituting certainty for doubt.[44] The issue in *Re Downshire, Re Blackwell* and *Re Chapman* before the Court of Appeal,[45] and in the last-named case [46] before the House of Lords, was whether the court had jurisdiction to do the same with regard to rights which were admittedly not in dispute. Their Lordships emphatically rejected the view that the courts had so ample a jurisdiction; but Lord Cohen, alone, was prepared to give an extended meaning to the word " compromise." In his opinion, even where there was no dispute, the court could sanction arrangements between tenants for life on the one hand and remaindermen on the other; but it could not vary the rights of a class *inter se* which the settlor had directed should be treated in a particular way.

(iii) *Section 64 of the Settled Land Act* 1925. Section 64 (1) of the Settled Land Act 1925 provides that any transaction affecting or concerning the settled land, or any part thereof, or any other land (not being a transaction otherwise authorised by the Act, or by the settlement) which in the opinion of the court would be for the benefit of the settled land, or any

---

[39] *Earl of Winchester* v. *Norcliffe* (1686) 1 Vern. 435; *Pierson* v. *Shire* (1739) 1 Atk. 480; *Inwood* v. *Twine* (1762) Amb. 417.

[40] *Bridges* v. *Bridges* (1752), noted (1887) 12 App.Cas. 693; *Ashburton* v. *Ashburton* (1801) 6 Ves. 6; *Ex p. Phillips* (1812) 19 Ves. 118. The age of majority is now 18 under the Family Law Reform Act 1969.

[41] *Ex p. Annandale* (1749) Amb. 80; *Ex p. Grimstone* (1772) Amb. 706; *Att.-Gen.* v. *Ailesbury* (1887) 12 App.Cas. 672.

[42] *Havelock* v. *Havelock* (1880) 17 Ch.D. 807; *Re Collins* (1886) 32 Ch.D. 229; *Revel* v. *Watkinson* (1748) 1 Ves.Sen. 93; *Re Walker* [1901] 1 Ch. 879; *Greenwell* v. *Greenwell* (1800) 5 Ves. 194; *Cavendish* v. *Mercer* (1776) 5 Ves. 195n.; *Errat* v. *Barlow* (1807) 14 Ves. 202.

[43] See *Haley* v. *Bannister* (1820) 4 Madd. 275.

[44] *Brooke* v. *Mostyn* (1864) 2 De G.J. & S. 415; *Re Barbour's Settlement* [1974] 1 All E.R. 1188.

[45] [1953] Ch. 218.

[46] [1954] A.C. 429.

part thereof, or the persons interested under the settlement, may, under an order of the court, be effected by a tenant for life, if it is one which could have been validly effected by an absolute owner. " Transaction " is defined by subsection (2) to include " any sale, extinguishment of manorial incidents, exchange, assurance, grant, lease, surrender, reconveyance, release, reservation or other disposition, any purchase or other acquisition, any covenant, contract, or option, and any application of capital money . . . and any compromise or other dealing or arrangement. . . ."

Roxburgh J. in *Re Downshire* [47] thought that the section did nothing more than authorise, with the sanction of the court, the carrying out of transactions in the nature of practical steps of an administrative character; it did not authorise the remoulding of beneficial interests. On appeal Lord Evershed M.R. and Romer L.J. expressed the view that the jurisdiction conferred by the section was more ample.[48] " Transaction " is a word of very wide import, and is defined by the section itself to include " compromise, and any other dealing or other arrangement." Practical steps of an administrative character are provided for by section 71 of the Settled Land Act. Therefore it was improbable that section 64 was meant to act merely as a supplement to section 71. Nor was the fact that the transaction has to be effected by the tenant for life an indication that a restricted meaning should be given to the word " transaction," since section 75 (2) of the Act permitted the tenant for life to give directions to the trustees with regard to the application of capital moneys. The factors limiting the scope of the section were, first, that the transaction must be for the benefit either of the settled land or of the persons interested under the settlement, though not necessarily of both; secondly, it must affect or concern the settled land, or any other land whether settled or not, and whether within or without England; and, thirdly, when it concerns settled land, it must have an effect which is real and substantial by ordinary common-sense standards as distinct from one which is oblique or remote and merely incidental.[49] It has since been held that the powers conferred by section 64 are also available to trustees for sale.[50]

(iv) *Section 53 of the Trustee Act* 1925. Section 53 of the Trustee Act provides that where an infant is beneficially entitled to *any* property the court may with a view to the *application* of the capital or income thereof for the maintenance, education or *benefit* of the infant make an order appointing a person to convey such property upon such terms as the court may think fit. The effect of this section may be summarised as follows: Where—

(a) an infant is beneficially entitled to any interest in property, whether real or personal;

(b) the interest itself is not under the settlement applicable for his maintenance, education or benefit, nor is it producing any income which is so applicable;

---

[47] *Sub nom. Re D's Settled Estates* [1952] W.N. 428, 432.

[48] [1953] Ch. 218.

[49] For other cases on the section, see *Re Scarisbrick* [1944] Ch. 229; *Re Mount Edgcumbe* [1950] Ch. 615; *Re White-Popham* [1936] Ch. 725.

[50] *Re Simmons' Trusts* [1956] Ch. 125.

(c) a proposal is made that the court should authorise a "conveyance "[51] of the infant's interest with a view to the application of the capital or income, arising out of such conveyance, for the maintenance, education or benefit of the infant;

then the court has jurisdiction to sanction the proposal upon such terms as it thinks fit. More particularly, the sale of an infant's contingent reversionary interest to the life-tenant in order to minimise liability to estate duty is made with a view to, and is, an application of the proceeds of sale for the infant's benefit, if these amount to more than he would be likely to receive if no sale took place, and if they are to be settled upon [52] and not paid outright to him.[53]

B. *The Variation of Trusts Act 1958* [54]

The decision in *Chapman* v. *Chapman* [55] was criticised by the Law Reform Committee whose report [56] led to the passing of the Variation of Trusts Act 1958, *infra*.

Essentially, the Act enables the court on behalf of persons who cannot themselves give their approval (*e.g.*, because unborn, unascertainable or infant) to approve arrangements varying or revoking beneficial and administrative provisions under trusts so long as such arrangements are for the benefit of the individual persons in question. Exceptionally, in the case of persons with contingent discretionary interests under protective trusts, where the interest of the protected beneficiary has not failed or determined, the court can give an approval on behalf of (and against the will of) ascertained adults and no benefit to them is required.[57] Jurisdiction extends to foreign settlements where the property and the trustees are within the physical jurisdiction [58] and to the approval of an arrangement substituting a foreign settlement for an English one [59] if the beneficiaries have a genuine foreign connection.[60]

However, it does not extend beyond a variation to a completely new

---

[51] Including a mortgage: *Re Gower's Settlement* [1934] Ch. 365; *Re Bristol's Settled Estates* [1965] 1 W.L.R. 469.
[52] *Re Meux's Will Trusts* [1957] 3 W.L.R. 377; *Re Lansdowne's W.T.* [1967] 1 All E.R. 888.
[53] *Re Heyworth's Contingent Reversionary Interest* [1956] Ch. 364. Other exceptions under this head which are outside the scope of this note are the *cy-près* jurisdiction of the court in relation to charitable trusts and the statutory jurisdiction of the Family Division of the High Court to vary ante-nuptial and post-nuptial settlements. See Matrimonial Causes Act 1973, s. 24.
[54] See [1958] B.T.R. 235 (J. A. Brightman); [1960] B.T.R. 42 (Leolin Price); [1959] C.L.J. 166 (S. J. Bailey); (1963) 27 Conv.(N.S.) 6 (D. M. E. Evans); (1969) 33 Conv.(N.S.) 113, 183 (J. W. Harris); Harris, *Variation of Trusts* (Sweet and Maxwell 1975).
[55] [1954] A.C. 429.
[56] (1957) Cmnd. 310; [1958] C.L.J. 1 (S. J. Bailey).
[57] s. 1 (1) (d) and proviso thereto in Variation of Trusts Act 1958.
[58] *Re Ker's S.T.* [1963] Ch. 553; *Re Paget's Settlement* [1965] 1 W.L.R. 1046.
[59] *Re Seale's Marriage Settlement* [1961] Ch. 574; *Re Windeatt's W.T.* [1969] 1 W.L.R. 692, *supra*, p. 454.
[60] *Re Weston's Settlement* [1969] 1 Ch. 223 where the Court of Appeal refused to make the settlement a Jersey settlement for the reason *inter alia* that it doubted whether the beneficiaries, having only moved to Jersey three months before making the application, would stay in Jersey very long after the approval of the arrangement, if approved, and the saving of the liability to capital gains tax of £163,000.

resettlement as pointed out by Megarry J. in *Re Holt's Settlement, infra.*
Later, in *Re Ball's Settlement* [61] Megarry J. enunciated a substratum test for
ascertaining upon which side of this jurisdictional line a proposed arrangement falls [62]: " If an arrangement changes the whole substratum of the
trust, then it may well be that it cannot be regarded merely as varying that
trust. But if, an arrangement, whilst leaving the substratum, effectuates the
purpose of the trust by other means, it may still be possible to regard that
arrangement as merely varying the original trusts, even though the means
employed are wholly different and even though the form is completely
changed." In the case a settlement conferred a life interest on the settlor
(subject to a power of appointment in favour of his sons and grandchildren)
and the capital was in default of appointment to be divided between the
two sons of the settlor or their issue *per stirpes* if either son predeceased the
settlor. The approved arrangement revoked the beneficial and administrative
provisions of the settlement and replaced them with new provisions whereby
each half of the trust fund was held on trust for one of the sons for life
and, subject thereto, for such of that son's children equally as were born
before a certain date. This jurisdictional limit is thus unlikely in practice to
cause much difficulty.

" Benefit " may be financial, moral or social [63] or the facilitation of the
administration of the settlement.[64] Unfortunately, the reported cases all
too often show, as one commentator puts it,[65] " that benefit and the measure
of it is simply what the court says it is." The court may, however, sanction
a proposed arrangement which involves an element of risk to infant or
unborn beneficiaries if the risk is one which an adult might well be prepared
to take.[66] It will not sanction an arrangement involving an appointment
made under a special power considered to be a fraud on the power.[67]

Application is by originating summons supported by affidavits to which
a draft scheme of arrangement will be exhibited. The proper plaintiffs are
the adult beneficiaries and not the trustees.[68] The trustees are supposed to
be " watch-dogs " concerned with the interests of those who may possibly
be adversely affected by the arangement proposed. The defendant should be
the trustees, the settlor, any beneficiary not a plaintiff, and any person
who may be interested under the trusts as being at a future date or on the
happening of a future event a person of any specified description or a
member of any specified class (*e.g.,* next-of-kin of S, still alive) who would
be of that description or of that class if the said date had fallen or the said
event had happened (*e.g.,* S's death) at the date of the application to the

---

[61] [1968] 1 W.L.R. 899; (1968) 84 L.Q.R. 459.

[62] [1968] 1 W.L.R. 899, 904.

[63] *Re Towler's S.T.* [1964] Ch. 158; *Re Holt's Settlement, infra,* p. 533; *Re Weston's Settlement* [1969] 1 Ch. 223; *Re Remnant's S.T.* [1970] Ch. 560, but *cf. Re Tinker's Settlement* [1960] 1 W.L.R. 1011. See also G. R. Bretten (1968) 32 Conv.(N.S.) 194.

[64] *Re University of London Charitable Trusts* [1964] Ch. 282; *Re Seale's Marriage Settlement* [1961] Ch. 574.

[65] R. H. M. Cotterell (1971) 34 M.L.R. 98.

[66] *Re Cohen's W.T.* [1959] 1 W.L.R. 865; (1960) 76 L.Q.R. (R. E. M.); *Re Holt's Settlement, infra,* p. 533.

[67] *Re Brook's Settlement* [1968] 1 W.L.R. 1661, *infra,* p. 597; S. M. Cretney (1969) 32 M.L.R. 317.

[68] *Re Druce's S.T.* [1962] 1 W.L.R. 145; trustees should only act as plaintiffs where they are satisfied that the proposed arrangement is beneficial and that no bene-ficiary is willing to make the application.

court.[69] No other persons who might eventually fulfil that description or be members of that class (*e.g.*, distant relatives who might be next-of-kin if the nearer relatives conveniently died) need be made parties, nor need possible objects of a power of appointment which has not actually been exercised in their favour, or persons whose only interest is under discretionary trusts in a protective trust where the interest of the protected beneficiary has not failed or determined.

The variation takes effect as soon as the order of the court is made without any further instrument,[70] and the order may well be liable to stamp duty.[71]

A controversial question is whether it is the order of the court or the arrangement which that order approves which has the effect of varying the trusts.[72] The former view was taken in *Re Hambleden's W.T.*[73] The latter view is supported by dicta of Lords Reid and Wilberforce in *Re Holmden's Settlement.*[74] In particular, Lord Reid said,[75]

> " Under the Variation of Trusts Act 1958 the court does not itself amend or vary the trusts of the original settlement. The beneficiaries are not bound by variations because a court has made the variation. Each beneficiary is bound because he has consented to the variation. If he was not of full age when the arrangement was made he is bound because the court was authorised by the Act of 1958 to approve of it on his behalf and did so by making an order. If he was of full age and did not in fact consent he is not affected by the order of the court and he is not bound. So the arrangement must be regarded as an arrangement made by the beneficiaries themselves. The court merely acted on behalf of or as representing those beneficiaries who were not in a position to give their own consent and approval."

In *Re Holt's Settlement, infra,* decided before *Re Holmden's Settlement*[76] was reported, Megarry J. rejected the view taken in *Re Hambleden's W.T.*,[77] canvassed the difficulties arising from such rejection and accepted counsel's submission that,[78] " when the adults by their counsel assented to the arrangement and the court on behalf of the infants by order approved the arrangement then there was an arrangement which varied the trusts." The variation is thus effected by the consent of all parties on *Saunders* v. *Vautier*[79] principles, the court supplying the consents of the unborn, the unascertained and infants, and new trusts replace the old so that since July 16, 1964, the Perpetuities and Accumulations Act 1964 has been available to provide new perpetuity and accumulation periods for trusts varied under

---

69 Rules of Supreme Court, Order 93.
70 *Re Holmden's Settlement* [1968] A.C. 685; *Re Holt's Settlement* [1969] 1 Ch. 100, *infra,* p. 533.
71 Practice Note [1966] 1 W.L.R. 345; *Re Holt's Settlement, supra.*
72 Underhill, pp. 307–308; Pettit, pp. 305–306; Maudsley & Burn, pp. 590–591; J. W. Harris (1969) 33 Conv.(N.S.) 195–201.
73 [1960] 1 W.L.R. 82.
74 [1968] A.C. 685, 701, 702, 710, 713.
75 *Ibid.* at 701–702.
76 [1968] A.C. 685.
77 [1960] 1 W.L.R. 82.
78 [1969] 1 Ch. 100, 115.
79 *Supra,* p. 523.

the Variation of Trusts Act.[80] There are dicta in *Re Holmden's Settlement* [81] for and against such a view on the availability of the 1964 Act.

Variations fail to satisfy section 53 (1) (*c*) of the Law of Property Act 1925 which requires writing *signed* by all the beneficiaries (or their agents lawfully authorised in writing) unless the Variation of Trusts Act 1958 can be said to have provided an implied statutory exception to these requirements, for the alternative means of escape via a constructive trust within section 53 (2) is difficult to reconcile with *Oughred* v. *I.R.C.*[82]

Re Holt's Settlement's reliance on the arrangement taking place on *Saunders* v. *Vautier* principles may have capital gains tax repercussions, as it affords scope for the view that there is a moment in time when the property is held for all the beneficiaries absolutely, so that they are absolutely entitled as against the trustees within section 25 (3) of the Finance Act 1965. So far it appears that the Revenue have not been prepared to take this point, accepting, instead, dicta of Lords Hodson and Guest in *Re Holmden's Settlement* [83] indicating that the old settlement continues with new substituted provisions [84] rather than being replaced by a new settlement at the direction of all beneficiaries acting in their own right or by court order.

Variation of Trusts Act 1958

Section 1.—(1) Where property, whether real or personal, is held on trusts arising, whether before or after the passing of this Act, under any will, settlement or other disposition, the court may if it thinks fit by order approve [85] on behalf of—

(*a*) any person having, directly or indirectly, an interest, whether vested or contingent, under the trusts who by reason of infancy or other incapacity is incapable of assenting, or

(*b*) any person (whether ascertained or not) who may become entitled, directly or indirectly, to an interest under the trusts as being at a future date or on the happening of a future event a person of any specified description or a member of any specified class of persons, so however that this paragraph shall not include any person who would be of that description, or a member of that class, as the case may be, if the said date had fallen or the said event had happened at the date of the application to the court,[86] or

(*c*) any person unborn, or

(*d*) any person [87] in respect of any discretionary interest of his under

---

[80] So held in *Re Holt's Settlement, infra,* p. 533. It is thought that as it is the court that orders variations under Matrimonial Causes Act 1973, s. 24, such orders in the Family Division, like the exercise of special powers, are subject to the periods laid down in the original settlement.

[81] [1968] A.C. 685, 701, 702, 713 and 705, 710 respectively. See also *Spens* v. *I.R.C.* [1970] 1 W.L.R. 1173, 1183, 1184.

[82] [1960] A.C. 206, *supra,* p. 57. See J. W. Harris (1969) 33 Conv.(N.S.) 197–199 on the difficulties.   [83] [1968] A.C. 655, 705, 710.

[84] Disposals or part disposals by original beneficiaries of their equitable interests do not give rise to chargeable gains : Finance Act 1965, Sched. 7, para. 13.

[85] See *Re Hambleden's Will Trusts* [1960] 1 W.L.R. 82 (Wynn-Parry J.) and *Re Holt's Settlement, infra,* p. 533.

[86] This refers *inter alia* to the potential next-of-kin of a living person, who must make up their own minds whether or not to give their consent : *Re Suffert's Settlement* [1961] Ch. 1. See J. W. Harris (1969) 33 Conv.(N.S.) 116–119.

[87] Including an unascertained or unborn person : *Re Turner's Will Trusts* [1960] Ch. 122; (1959) 75 L.Q.R. 451 (R. E. M.). Thus approval may be given without the need to show " benefit."

protective trusts where the interest of the principal beneficiary has not failed or determined,

any arrangement [88] (by whomsoever proposed,[89] and whether or not there is any other person beneficially interested who is capable of assenting thereto) varying or revoking all or any of the trusts, or enlarging [90] the powers of the trustees of managing or administering any of the property subject to the trusts:

Providing that except [91] by virtue of paragraph (d) of this subsection the court shall not approve an arrangement on behalf of any person unless the carrying out thereof would be for the benefit [92] of that person.

(2) In the foregoing subsection "protective trusts" means the trusts specified in paragraphs (i) and (ii) of subsection (1) of section thirty-three of the Trustee Act 1925 or any like trusts, "the principal beneficiary" has the same meaning as in the said subsection (1) and "discretionary interest" means an interest arising under the trust specified in paragraph (ii) of the said subsection (1) or any like trust.

(3) [93] The jurisdiction [94] conferred by subsection (1) of this section shall

---

[88] The arrangement need not be in the nature of a contract between parties: *Re Steed's W.T.* [1959] Ch. 354; but must not amount to a completely new settlement: *Re T's S.T.* [1964] Ch. 158; *Re Ball's S.T.* [1968] 1 W.L.R. 899; and it must be practical and businesslike: *Re Van Jenisen's W.T.* [1964] 1 W.L.R. 449.

[89] As to who should be parties, see *Re Clitheroe's S.T.* [1959] 1 W.L.R. 1159; *Re Tinker's Settlement* [1960] 1 W.L.R. 1011; *Re Longman's S.T.* [1962] 1 W.L.R. 455; *Re Druce's S.T.* [1962] 1 W.L.R. 363; *Re Moncrieff's S.T.* [1962] 1 W.L.R. 455; *Re Munro's S.T.* [1963] 1 W.L.R. 145; *Re Courtauld's Settlement* [1965] 1 W.L.R. 1385.

[90] *e.g.*, conferring wider investment powers: see *Re Coates' Trusts* [1959] 1 W.L.R. 375; *Re Byng's Will Trusts* [1959] 1 W.L.R. 375; *Re Allen's Settlement Trusts* [1960] 1 W.L.R. 6; *Re Royal Naval and Royal Marine Children's Homes, Portsmouth* [1959] 1 W.L.R. 755. Investment powers will not now be extended beyond those conferred by the Trustee Investments Act 1961, unless there are special circumstances; *supra*, p. 495.

[91] Even in the excepted case the court must exercise its discretion judicially: *Re Burney's Settlement* [1961] 1 W.L.R. 545; *Re Baker's S.T.* [1964] 1 W.L.R. 336.

[92] In *Re Cohen's W.T.* [1959] 1 W.L.R. 865, 868 Danckwerts J. said that the court could take a risk on behalf of an infant if it was a risk an adult would be prepared to take. This was criticised at (1960) 76 L.Q.R. 22 (R. E. M.). In a case of the same name [1965] 1 W.L.R. 1229, Stamp J. stressed, however, that (i) the court had to be satisfied that there was a benefit in the case of each individual infant and not merely of the whole class to which the infant belonged; and (ii) while the court need not be satisfied that each individual infant is bound to be better off than he would otherwise have been, it must be sure that he is making a bargain which is a reasonable one which an adult would be prepared to make. Jurisdiction has been exercised to vary beneficial interests, usually to reduce liability to tax (*Re Clitheroe's S.T.* [1959] 1 W.L.R. 1159; *Re Holmden's S.T.* [1966] Ch. 511; *Re Drewe's Settlement* [1966] 1 W.L.R. 1518; *Re Sainsbury's Settlement* [1967] 1 W.L.R. 476 and to incorporate desirable administrative provisions (*e.g.*, power of advancement in a pre-1926 settlement: *Re Lister's W.T.* [1962] 1 W.L.R. 1441). But the court will not approve an arrangement which is a fraud on a power (*Re Robertson's W.T.*) [1960] 1 W.L.R. 1050 or is contrary to public policy (*Re Michelham's W.T.* [1964] Ch. 550). Nor will the court use the Act as a justification for rectifying a settlement on the basis of mistake (*Re Tinker's Settlement* [1960] 1 W.L.R. 1011) or for making an order which can be made without the aid of the Act (*Re Pettifor's W.T.* [1966] Ch. 257).

[93] As amended by the County Courts Act 1959, s. 204, Sched. 3, and the Mental Health Act 1959, s. 149, Sched. 7.

[94] Jurisdiction not limited to trusts created under English law. See *Re Paget's Settlement* [1965] 1 W.L.R. 1046 (New York trust); *Re Ker's S.T.* [1963] Ch. 553 (Northern Ireland trust); *Re Seale's Marriage Settlement* [1961] Ch. 574 (substitution of a Canadian trust for an English trust). Contrast *Re Weston's Settlement* [1969] 1 Ch. 223.

be exercisable by the High Court, except that the question whether the carrying out of any arrangement would be for the benefit of a person falling within paragraph (*a*) of the said subsection (1) shall be determined by order of the authority having jurisdiction under Part VIII of the Mental Health Act 1959 if that person is a patient within the meaning of the said Part VIII.

(4) [95]

(5) Nothing in the foregoing provisions of this section shall apply to trusts affecting property settled by Act of Parliament.

(6) [96] Nothing in this section shall be taken to limit the powers conferred by section sixty-four of the Settled Land Act 1925, section fifty-seven of the Trustee Act 1925, or the powers of the authority having jurisdiction under Part VIII of the Mental Health Act 1959.

2.—(1) This Act shall not extend to Scotland.

(2) The foregoing section shall not extend to Northern Ireland, but, notwithstanding anything in the Government of Ireland Act 1920, the Parliament of Northern Ireland shall have power to make laws for purposes similar to any of the purposes of the foregoing section.

Re HOLT'S SETTLEMENT

Chancery Division [1969] 1 Ch. 100; [1968] 2 W.L.R. 653; [1968] 1 All E.R. 470

MEGARRY J.: " This is an originating summons under the Variation of Trusts Act 1958. It concerns a settlement of pure personalty which was made *inter vivos* on December 22, 1959. The trusts are simple. They consist of a life interest for Mrs. Wilson (the settlor's daughter), and subject thereto trusts for all her children who attain the age of 21 years and if more than one in equal shares. The settlement makes no disposition of the ultimate interest if there is no such child, and so there would be a resulting trust to the settlor. Mrs. Wilson is now about 35 years old and has three children aged some 10, 7 and 6 years respectively. The sum settled in 1959 was £15,000, but the capital is now worth something like £320,000, so that its value has increased by more than 20 times.

" In broad terms the arrangement proposed is that Mrs. Wilson should surrender her life interest in one-half of the income of the trust fund. This surrender would reduce the impact of income tax and surtax upon her and her husband, and increase the value of the children's interests under the trusts. It is also proposed that the children should have the vesting of their interests deferred until they are aged 30 years respectively, and that half the income of their respective shares should be accumulated until they attain the age of 25 or die, or until the earlier expiration of 21 years from the date

---

[95] Repealed by s. 204 of and Sched. 3 to the County Court Act 1959; see now ss. 52 (1) (*b*) and 53 thereof.

[96] As amended by the Mental Health Act 1959, s. 149, Sched. 7.

of the order. The reason given for this is that if Mrs. Wilson surrendered her life interest in half, the present children (assuming no more to be born) would under the trusts as they stand each at the age of 21 become entitled to capital worth some £75,000 and enjoy an income of some £3,750 a year. Not surprisingly, Mrs. Wilson says in her affidavit:

> ' I would be strongly opposed to this. Nor is it only a question of capital, for I would consider it equally undesirable for my children to receive an income of, say, £3,750 per annum at that stage. I believe it to be most important that young people should be reasonably advanced in a career and settled in life before they are in receipt of an income sufficient to make them independent of the need to work."

" Two main questions have been debated before me. I propose to consider these now, and to deal separately with certain details of the proposed arrangement. These questions are: first, does an order under the Act of 1958 *ipso facto* vary the terms of the trust without the execution of the arrangement or any other document by or on behalf of any beneficiary, apart from those on whose behalf section 1 (1) of the Act empowers the court to approve the arrangement? Secondly, if after the commencement of the Perpetuities and Accumulations Act 1964, a variation is made in trusts constituted before the commencement of that Act, can that variation take advantage of the changes in the rules against perpetuities and accumulations which that Act has made?

"Under the first head, the basic issue is whether an order under the Act of 1958 by itself varies the terms of the trust. Put rather differently, the question is whether the Act does no more than empower the court to supply on behalf of the infants, unborn persons and others mentioned in section 1 (1) that binding approval which they cannot give, leaving the other beneficiaries to provide their own approvals in some other document which will bind them. In the present case the arrangement was drafted on the assumption that the order of the court will *ipso facto* vary the terms of the trusts; for the ' operative date ' is defined as being the date of the order approving this arrangement, and the perpetuity period and the accumulation period (which are made use of in the terms of the trusts) each commences on the operative date.

" The only authority directly on the point which has been cited to me is the decision in *In re Hambleden's Will Trusts.*[97] I do not think I need read the provisions of the trusts in that case. It was a summons under the Act of 1958, and the judgment of Wynn-Parry J. as reported is very short. The report does, however, include certain interlocutory observations. Wynn-Parry J. made it clear that his view was that the

---

[97] [1960] 1 W.L.R. 82.

order of the court *ipso facto* varied the trusts. He had had cited to him the decision of Vaisey J. in *In re Joseph's Will Trusts*,[98] where that learned judge had inserted words in the order of the court which authorised and directed the trustees to carry the arrangement into effect. Wynn-Parry J. said[99]:

> 'I do not agree with that decision. I take the view that I have no jurisdiction to make an order including words directing the trustees to carry the arrangement into effect, and those words should be deleted from the draft minutes. Nothing is required except the approval of the court to the arrangement. If that approval is given the trusts are *ipso facto* altered, and the trustees are bound thereafter to give effect to the arrangement.'

Later in the course of the argument he said: 'If I approve an arrangement, I alter the trusts. *Res ipsa loquitur*.' Again, a little later he said: 'If I approve an arrangement, I vary the trusts.' His judgment [1] I will recite in its entirety:

> 'Very well. I hold that the effect of my approval is effective for all purposes to vary the trusts. Thereafter, the trusts are the trusts as varied. I approve the minutes of order, with the slight alterations which have been referred to, and the arrangement in the schedule.'

"If that were a decision of the Court of Appeal I could venerate and obey, even without fully comprehending. But the decision is at first instance, and so is of persuasive and not binding authority. It is my misfortune not to be persuaded by such assertions, even though fourfold, when made without explanation. I bear in mind that *In re Joseph's Will Trusts* [2] was a decision of a very experienced judge of the same Division. In his judgment Vaisey J. referred [3] to two decisions of Lord Jenkins when sitting as a judge of the Chancery Division, in one of which Lord Jenkins had directed an addition to be made to his order of the same nature as that made by Vaisey J. in *In re Joseph's Will Trusts*,[4] whereas in the other Lord Jenkins had not directed any such addition. But, as Vaisey J. pointed out,[5] we do not know the facts in either of those cases.

"In that state of the authorities I must go back to the words of the Act of 1958. Section 1 (1) provides:

> 'Where property, whether real or personal, is held on trusts arising, whether before or after the passing of this Act, under any will, settlement or other disposition, the court may if it thinks fit by order approve on behalf of . . .'

---

[98] [1959] 1 W.L.R. 1019.
[99] [1960] 1 W.L.R. 82, 85.
[1] *Ibid.* 86.
[2] [1959] 1 W.L.R. 1019.
[3] *Ibid.* 1021.
[4] [1959] 1 W.L.R. 1019.
[5] *Ibid.* 1021.

At that point I pause; for there is then set out in paragraphs (*a*) to (*d*) a number of persons who, being infants or unborn or unascertained, are not in a position to provide their own binding assents to any arrangement. In relation to the Act I shall use the term ' infants ' as a compendious expression to embrace all those who are specified in paragraphs (*a*) to (*d*); and by parity of reasoning I shall use the word ' adults ' for all other beneficiaries. Returning, then, to the subsection it continues:

> ' . . . [the infants] any arrangement . . . varying or revoking all or any of the trusts, or enlarging the powers of the trustees or managing or administering any of the property subject to the trusts: . . .'

Then there is an important proviso requiring that no arrangement shall be approved on behalf of any person (apart from the persons mentioned in paragraph (*d*)) unless the carrying out thereof would be for the benefit of that person.

"I have been much assisted in this case by the arguments of counsel. I will not attempt to ascribe to each the precise portions of the various arguments as they have emerged: I will simply express my gratitude collectively to all four. The argument against the doctrine of *ipso facto* variation as laid down in *In re Hambleden's Will Trusts* [6] (an argument for which counsel do not bear the sole responsibility) is somewhat as follows. It starts with the well-known mischief which the Act was designed to meet, a mischief confirmed by the House of Lords decision in *Chapman* v. *Chapman.* [7] If under a trust every possible beneficiary was under no disability and concurred in the rearrangement or termination of the trusts, then under the doctrine of *Saunders* v. *Vautier* [8] those beneficiaries could dispose of the trust property as they thought fit; for in equity the property was theirs. Yet if any beneficiary was an infant, or an unborn or unascertained person, it was held that the court had no general inherent or other jurisdiction to concur in any such arrangement on behalf of that beneficiary. Accordingly, some while after the decision of the House of Lords to this effect the Act of 1958 conferred on the court the power contained in section 1. But, proceeds the argument, that Act did no more than allow the court to provide the binding assent which the infant himself could not provide; and the wording of the Act shows this to be so. The Act merely provides that the court may if it thinks fit by order ' approve ' on behalf of the infants ' any arrangement . . . varying or revoking all or any of the trusts,' so that all Parliament has done is to empower the court to provide the binding approval of an arrangement which the infants themselves could not give.

---

[6] [1960] 1 W.L.R. 82.
[7] [1954] A.C. 429.
[8] (1841) 4 Beav. 115.

" The argument continues by pointing a contrast between the wording of section 1 (1) and two other statutory provisions which may fairly be said to have been present to the draftsman's mind; for they are mentioned in section 1 (6). These provisions are section 64 of the Settled Land Act 1925 and section 57 of the Trustee Act 1925. Section 64 provides:

' Any transaction affecting or concerning the settled land . . . which in the opinion of the court would be for the benefit of the settled land . . . may, under an order of the court, be effected by a tenant for life. . . .'

" Section 57 of the Trustee Act 1925 provides that in certain circumstances where the court considers it expedient ' the court may by order confer upon the trustees . . . the necessary power for the purpose,' that is, the purpose previously set out in the section. In each of these cases, the statute authorises the court to make an order conferring a power to do something which otherwise could not be done. This, it is pointed out, is very different from a provision which in terms confers no power but merely authorises the court to approve an arrangement on behalf of infants.

" It is said that there is no escape from this conclusion merely by saying that where an arrangement is approved under the Act of 1958 the adults provide the necessary concurrence in assenting by their counsel to the arrangement; for section 53 (1) (*c*) of the Law of Property Act 1925 stands in the way. This provides that:

' a disposition of an equitable interest or trust subsisting at the time of the disposition, must be in writing signed by the person disposing of the same, or by his agent thereunto lawfully authorised in writing or by will.'

Where the arrangement is put into effect there is a disposition of an equitable interest, so that unless there is some document signed by the adult beneficiaries, or by some agent authorised by them in writing, the requirements of section 53 (1) (*c*) are not satisfied. This contention is supported by a reference to the decision by the House of Lords in *Grey* v. *Inland Revenue Commissioners* [9] that an oral direction by a beneficiary to his trustees to hold property on certain trusts is a disposition, and that ' disposition ' must be given its ordinary wide meaning. It is further said that as there is here a transaction under which a moiety of a life interest will pass from Mrs. Wilson to her children, this is a fortiori a ' disposition.' I may add that there is the minor point that the common form of order under the Act does not normally recite that all the adults have consented to the transaction, though where the insertion of such a recital is required by the parties, the registrars insert it.

---

[9] [1960] A.C. 1.

" Let me say at once that there would seem to be no great difficulty in averting the consequences of this argument for the future. The adults could either execute the arrangement or, perhaps more conveniently, give written authority to their solicitors or counsel to execute it on their behalf. The latter course would usually be the more convenient, because not infrequently changes (often minor) have to be made to the arrangement put before the court. It is, however, a fact that many thousands of orders must have been made in the past on the footing of *In re Hambleden's Will Trusts.*[10] If the argument is right, there is the very real difficulty that those orders will, perhaps in most cases, perhaps only in some, have effected no variation of the trusts. This is a consideration which is particularly awkward in that a question of jurisdiction is involved; for if the court has no jurisdiction to make an order which itself varies the trusts, and orders have been made on the footing that the orders do *ipso facto* vary the trusts, then it seems at least arguable that such orders were made without jurisdiction. It has also been pointed out that the Inland Revenue has for some while acted upon the decision, and that orders of the court have been stamped on the footing that they *ipso facto* vary the terms of the trusts. Yet again, it is plain that present practice is convenient. It avoids the burden which usually, perhaps, would not be very great, but in individual cases might be substantial, of getting the necessary signatures of the adults either to the document itself or to written authorities. I bear all those considerations in mind; nevertheless, it seems to me that there is very considerable force in the argument that has been advanced. The decision in *In re Hambleden's Will Trusts* [11] provides authority to the contrary but no explanation of the grounds for the decision. Accordingly, a substantial part of the argument in this case has been directed to the discovery of some basis upon which the convenient practice of *In re Hambleden's Will Trusts* can be rested.

" In attempting to summarise Mr. Godfrey's argument for the settlor, I am sure I shall fail to do it justice. As I understood it, he submitted that the decision in *In re Hambleden's Will Trusts* was quite wrong but that in effect this did not matter. All that the court has to do, he said, is to approve the arrangement (*i.e.*, the proposal made), and there was no question of the court approving anything which in law amounted to a disposition. The arrangement was not a disposition but merely a bargain or proposal, which was not within the ambit of section 53 (1) (c) of the Law of Property Act 1925. The court, he urged, was not concerned to see that the adults consented and certainly not that they executed any disposition. There might thus be no disposition at all; but the persons specified by section 1 (1) of the Act of 1958 would be bound by the order of the court approving the arrangement, and the other beneficiaries could not in practice go

[10] [1960] 1 W.L.R. 82.
[11] [1960] 1 W.L.R. 82.

back on what their counsel had assented to, at any rate so far as it had been acted upon. The result would be that, although there would be no new equitable interests actually created under the arrangement, all the beneficiaries would by a species of estoppel be treated as if they had those interests. I hope that Mr. Godfrey will forgive me if I say that I find this argument somewhat unattractive. In particular, I find it very hard to believe that Parliament intended the court to approve on behalf of infants arrangements which depended for their efficacy upon the uncertainties of estoppel. I bear in mind, too, the wide meaning which *Grey* v. *Inland Revenue Commissioners* [12] gave to the word ' disposition ' in section 53 (1) (*c*).

" Mr. Brookes, for the trustees, boldly asserted that, when correctly read, the Act of 1958 indirectly did what *In re Hambleden's Will Trusts* [13] said it did. He went back to the words of section 1 (1), and emphasised that the power of the court was a power exercisable ' by order ' and that that power was a power to approve an arrangement ' varying or revoking ' all or any of the trusts. In emphasising those phrases, he said that the right way to read the section was to say that the power of the court was merely a power to make an order approving an arrangement which in fact varied or revoked the trusts, and not an arrangement which failed to do any such thing. When the adults by their counsel assented to the arrangement, and the court on behalf of the infants by order approved the arrangement, then there was an arrangement which varied or revoked the trust. So the order of the court both conferred jurisdiction and exercised it. His escape from section 53 (1) (*c*) had a similar dexterity about it: by conferring an express power on the court to do something by order, Parliament in the Act of 1958 had provided by necessary implication an exception from section 53 (1) (*c*). He buttressed his contention by a reference to *In re Joseph's Will Trusts.* [14] Vaisey J. there accepted that the order which he made, directing the trustees to carry the order of the court into effect, was neither contemplated by the Act nor expressly authorised by it. Rather than read into the Act words that are not there, said Mr. Brookes, one should construe the Act as authorising an order which is efficacious to achieve its avowed object. He pointed to the long title of the Act which reads: ' An Act to extend the jurisdiction of courts of law to vary trusts in the interests of beneficiaries and sanction dealings with trust property.'

" I hope that Mr. Brookes, too, will pardon me if I say that I did not find his argument compelling. Indeed, at times I think it tended to circularity. But I find it tempting; and I yield. It is not a construction which I think the most natural. But it is not an impossible construction; it accords with the long title; it accords with the practice

[12] [1960] A.C. 1.
[13] [1960] 1 W.L.R. 82.
[14] [1959] 1 W.L.R. 1019.

which has been relied upon for many years in some thousands of cases; and it accords with considerations of convenience. The point is technical, and I do not think that I am doing more than straining a little at the wording in the interests of legislative efficacy.

"However, that is not all. Mr. Millett, for Mrs. Wilson, the tenant for life, provided another means of escape from section 53 (1) (c) in his helpful reply. Where, as here, the arrangement consists of an agreement made for valuable consideration, and that agreement is specifically enforceable, then the beneficial interests pass to the respective purchasers on the making of the agreement. Those interests pass by virtue of the species of constructive trust made familiar by contracts for the sale of land, whereunder the vendor becomes a constructive trustee for the purchaser as soon as the contract is made, albeit the constructive trust has special features about it. Section 53 (2), he continued, provides that ' This section does not affect the creation or operation of resulting, implied or constructive trusts.' Accordingly, because the trust was constructive, section 53 (1) (c) was excluded. He supported this contention by the House of Lords decision in *Oughtred* v. *Inland Revenue Commissioners.*[15] He relied in particular upon passages in the speeches[16] of Lord Radcliffe and Lord Cohen, albeit that they were dissenting on the main point for decision. He pointed out that although Lord Jenkins (with whom Lord Keith concurred) had not decided the point, he had assumed for the purposes of his speech that it was correct,[17] and that the rejection of the contention by Lord Denning[18] was in a very brief passage. Mr. Millett accepts that if there were to be some subsequent deed of family arrangement which would carry out the bargain, then this deed might well be caught by section 53 (1) (c); but that, he said, cannot affect the ' arrangement,' and the parties might well be willing to let matters rest on that. It seems to me that there is considerable force in this argument in cases where the agreement is specifically enforceable, and in its essentials I accept it. At all events it supports the conclusion that in such cases the practice established by *In re Hambleden's Will Trusts*[19] is right. For this and the other reasons that I have given, though with some hesitation, I accordingly hold this to be the case.

"Finally, before turning to the second main point, I should mention that in this case the arrangement carries out its purpose by revoking all the existing trusts and establishing a new set of trusts. That being so, it is said that some difficulty arises on the wording of section 1 (1) of the Act of 1958. This merely empowers the court to approve an arrangement ' varying or revoking all or any of the trusts,'

---

[15] [1960] A.C. 206; *supra*, p. 57.
[16] [1960] A.C. 206, 227, 231.
[17] *Ibid.* 239.
[18] *Ibid.* 233. See *supra*, p. 60.
[19] [1960] 1 W.L.R. 82.

and so, it is said, the court cannot approve an arrangement which, instead of merely ' revoking ' or merely ' varying,' proceeds to revoke and then to set up new trusts, thereby producing an effect equivalent to the process of settlement and resettlement. The section, it is argued, says nothing of establishing new trusts for old. As a matter of principle, however, I do not really think that there is anything in this point, at all events in this case. Here the new trusts are in many respects similar to the old. In my judgment, the old trusts may fairly be said to have been varied by the arrangement whether the variation is effected directly, by leaving some of the old words standing and altering others, or indirectly, by revoking all the old words and then setting up new trusts partly, though not wholly, in the likeness of the old. One must not confuse machinery with substance; and it is the substance that matters. Comparing the position before and after the arrangement takes effect, I am satisfied that the result is a variation of the old trusts, even though effected by the machinery of revocation and resettlement.

" Mr. Brookes pressed me with the decision in *In re T.'s Settlement Trusts.*[20] He accepts that the point is not a mere matter of form, that is, whether in form there is a mere series of variations of the existing trusts, or whether in form there is a revocation and declaration of new trusts; but he says that the form gives some indication as to whether there is a mere variation or not. For myself, I cannot see much force in this; for so much depends on the individual draftsman who prepares the arrangement. One draftsman may choose to effect the arrangement by a series of variations of the existing trusts. Another may prefer to effect precisely the same variations by the formally more radical process of revocation and new declaration. In any event, *In re T.'s Settlement Trusts* seems to me to be an entirely different case. There the infant was within 18 days of attaining her majority and obtaining an absolute interest in the trust property. The existing trusts were at their very end, and what in substance was proposed was to make a new settlement of what was on the point of becoming an absolute unfettered interest. Further, although Wilberforce J. rejected the wider proposal put before him, he did in fact make some variation in the trusts; and I cannot read the case as going so far as I think Mr. Brookes would take it. It is not, of course, for the court to draw the line in any particular place between what is a variation and what, on the other hand, is a completely new settlement. A line may, perhaps, one day emerge from a sufficiently ample series of reported decisions; but for the present all that is necessary for me to say is whether the particular case before me is on the right side or the wrong side of any reasonable line that could be drawn. In this case I am satisfied that

---

[20] [1964] Ch. 158.

the arrangement proposed falls on the side of the line which bears the device ' variation.'

" I can now turn to the second main point, namely, that under the Perpetuities and Accumulations Act 1964. The settlement in this case was made prior to the commencement of that Act, and any variation will be made after that commencement. Section 15 (5) provides that ' The foregoing sections of this Act shall apply . . .' (and there is then an exception with which I am not concerned) '. . . only in relation to instruments taking effect after the commencement of this Act. . . .' There follows a reference to instruments made in the exercise of a special power of appointment. The Act received the Royal Assent on July 16, 1964, so that this is the date of its commencement.

" The kind of question that arises is this. Suppose an instrument taking effect in 1959, as the original trusts did in this case, and a variation made under the Act of 1958 which merely alters a few words: will such a variation allow the Act of 1964 to apply to the trusts in their revised form? Again, suppose that, as here, there is a revocation of the old trusts and a declaration of new trusts, so that in form there is a new start, although in substance merely a variation: does this alter the position? Could something be done by the second method which cannot be done by a method which in form as well as in substance is a mere variation? Is it possible to have a variation under the Act of 1958 once every generation, and then with each variation start afresh with a relaxed perpetuity rule and a new accumulation period bounteously provided by the Act of 1964?

" Mr. Millett boldly answered ' Yes ' to this last question, and harked back to those spacious days when strict settlements of land were common, and once a generation there was a process of settlement and resettlement, with all the old entails securely barred and new entails established. He pointed out that on each resettlement the settlors in effect changed, and that often there would be a similar result on a variation under the Act of 1958. When the settlement was first made the original settlor was the settlor; but when the first variation came to be made, then if there was any alteration in the beneficial interests (as distinct from the mere conferring of additional administrative powers *quoad* those beneficial interests) the beneficiaries concerned would be the settlors, transferring their interests to be held on new trusts. Thus in effect there would be a new start each time. Mr. Millett drew my attention to the decision of Plowman J. in *In re Lloyd's Settlement*,[21] where, he said, this in effect was done. In that case a settlement *inter vivos* was made on March 21, 1958 (March 21, 1959, in the headnote and March 31, 1958, in the statement of facts seem to be erroneous). The settlement directed an accumulation, and in the result the only appropriate accumulation period was that of the

21 [1967] 2 W.L.R. 1078.

settlor's life. The effect was to expose the trust property to estate
duty risks in respect of an interest which would pass on the settlor's
death, and accordingly in 1966 a variation of the trusts was sought
under the Act of 1958. By then the Act of 1964 had come into effect.
Under the trusts as varied by the arrangement, accumulation was
directed for a period of 21 years from the date of the settlement; and
this period is one which was made available for the first time by the
Act of 1964. Accordingly, under the Act of 1958 a settlement made
prior to the Act of 1964 was varied after that Act in a way which took
advantage of the provisions of that Act. The case is shortly reported,
setting out the facts at some length, the cases cited in the argument,
and the order made; but unfortunately there is no statement of the
reasons of the learned judge. Nevertheless it seems to me that the
variation in fact there made supports Mr. Millett's contention.

" Mr. Millett also referred me to *Lewin on Trusts*, 16th ed. (1964),
at p. 741, where an argument which is in accord with Mr. Millett's
submission is advanced by the learned editor (the passage cannot have
been the work of the late Mr. Lewin). I would only observe that there
appears on page 742 to have been a slip in the statement of *Pilkington*
v. *Inland Revenue Commissioners* [22]; for the reference in the text
should, it seems, be to a power of advancement rather than to a power
of appointment, and the citation of the case is also erroneous. For
myself, I find any analogy with powers of appointment and powers of
advancement unsatisfactory. The mischief attacked by the rule against
perpetuities in the case of powers of appointment, and now, since
Pilkington v. *Inland Revenue Commissioners*,[23] in the case of powers
of advancement as well, is that the property is tied up *ab initio*. The
power is conferred by the settlement, and the person exercising the
power can do so only within pre-ordained limits. The power indeed
' belongs ' to the old settlement, if I may respectfully adopt the
language of Lord Radcliffe in the *Pilkington* case.[24] Under the Act
of 1958, there are no such limits. The property, as it seems to me, is
freely disposable. Under an arrangement approved by the court the
trusts may be brought wholly to an end. On the other hand, they may
be varied; and there is no limit, other than the discretion of the court
and the agreement of the parties, to the variation which may be made.
Any variation owes its authority not to anything in the initial settlement but to the statute and the consent of the adults coming, as it
were, *ab extra*. This certainly seems to be so in any case not within
the Act where a variation or resettlement is made under the doctrine
of *Saunders* v. *Vautier* [25] by all the adults joining together; and I can-

---

[22] [1964] A.C. 612.
[23] [1964] A.C. 612.
[24] *Ibid.* 642.
[25] 4 Beav. 115.

not see any real difference in principle in a case where the court exercises its jurisdiction on behalf of the infants under the Act of 1958. It seems to me that the arrangement, coupled with the order of the court, constitute an ' instrument,' or, since the singular includes the plural, ' instruments,' which take effect after July 15, 1964. Whether the documents are regarded as separate instruments or as together constituting one composite instrument, the effect is produced by the complex of documents; and what takes effect after July 15, 1964, is the result of this complex of documents. In my judgment, therefore, it is permissible to insert provisions deriving their validity from the Act of 1964 into an arrangement approved under the Act of 1958.

" That, I think, suffices to dispose of the two substantial points; and I should perhaps say that I have been astute to do so without resort to the Fourth [26] and Sixth [27] Reports of the Law Reform Committee or the discussions which led to those reports, despite their relationship to the Acts of 1964 and 1958 respectively. I propose now to consider the merits of the arrangement put forward.

" I can deal with the merits of this application quite shortly. It seems to me that, subject to one reservation, the arrangement proposed is for the benefit of each of the beneficiaries contemplated by section 1 (1) of the Act of 1958. The financial detriment to the children is that the absolute vesting of their interests will be postponed from age 21 to age 30. As against that, they will obtain very substantial financial benefits, both in the acceleration of their interests in a moiety of the trust fund and in the savings of estate duty to be expected in a case such as this. Where the advantages of the scheme are overwhelming, any detailed evaluation, or ' balance-sheet ' of advantages and disadvantages, seems to me to be unnecessary; but I can imagine cases under the Act where it may be important that an attempt should be made to put in evidence a detailed evaluation of the financial and other consequences of the changes proposed to be made, so that it may be seen whether on balance there is a sufficient advantage to satisfy the proviso to section 1 (1). But this is not such a case, and I say no more about it. I should, however, state that I fully concur in the view taken by Mrs. Wilson that, speaking in general terms, it is most important that young children ' should be reasonably advanced in a career and settled in life before they are in receipt of an income sufficient to make them independent of the need to work.' The word ' benefit ' in the proviso to section 1 (1) is, I think, plainly not confined to financial benefit, but may extend to moral or social benefit, as is shown by *In re T.'s Settlement Trusts.* [28]

" The point that at one stage troubled me concerns the unborn issue. Mr. Brookes, as in duty bound, put before me a contention that

[26] 1956, Cmnd. 18.
[27] 1957, Cmnd. 310.
[28] [1964] Ch. 158.

it was possible to conceive of an unborn infant who would be so circumstanced that a proposed rearrangement would be entirely to his disadvantage. He postulated the case of a child born to Mrs. Wilson next year, and of Mrs. Wilson dying in childbirth, or shortly after the child's birth. In such a case, he said, the benefit of the acceleration of interest resulting from Mrs. Wilson surrendering the moiety of her life interest would be minimal, and there would be no saving of estate duty. All that would happen in regard to such an infant would be that the vesting of his interest would be postponed from age 21 to age 30; and the only possible advantage in that would be the non-financial moral or social advantage to which I have just referred. In support of this contention he referred me to the decision of Stamp J. in *In re Cohen's Settlement Trusts.*[29] There, the scheme originally proposed was not approved by the court because there was a possibility of there being a beneficiary who would get no advantage whatsoever from the proposed arrangement; it would merely be to his detriment.

" Mr. Millett, however, points out that there is an essential distinction between that case and this; for there, whatever the surrounding circumstances, the unborn person contemplated could not benefit from the arrangement. In the present case, he says, all that Mr. Brookes has done is to put forward the case of an infant who might be born next year; and it would be a result of the surrounding circumstances, and not of the time of birth or the characteristics of the infant, that that infant might derive no benefit from the arrangement proposed. Mr. Millett referred me to *In re Cohen's Will Trusts,*[30] where Danckwerts J. held that in exercising the jurisdiction under the Act of 1958 the court must, on behalf of those persons for whom it was approving the arrangement, take the sort of risk which an adult would be prepared to take. Accordingly, says Mr. Millett, Mr. Brookes' special infant to be born next year was in the position that although there was the chance that its mother would die immediately afterwards, there was also the alternative chance that its mother would survive its birth for a substantial period of time. In the latter event, which was the more probable, the advantages of the arrangement would accrue to the infant. In short, he distinguishes the decision of Stamp J. in *In re Cohen's Settlement Trusts*[31] on the footing that that was the case of an unborn person whose prospects were hopeless, whatever the events whereas in the present case the hypothetical unborn person has the normal prospects of events occurring which will either improve or not improve his position. Such an unborn person falls, he says, into the category of unborn persons on whose behalf the court should be prepared to take a risk if the arrangement appears on the whole to be for their benefit.

---

[29] [1965] 1 W.L.R. 1229.
[30] [1959] 1 W.L.R. 865.
[31] [1965] 1 W.L.R. 1229.

" It seems to me that this is a proper distinction to make, and I accept it. Accordingly, I hold that the arrangement is for the benefit of the classes of persons specified in section 1 (1) of the Act, and I approve it." *Order accordingly. Direction that order contain recital of consent of adults.*

Section 6. The Trustee's Duty of Impartiality

It is the trustees' duty to balance the conflicting interests of life tenants interested in income and remaindermen interested in capital and certain rules have evolved to guide trustees and, in some cases, to provide what is to be done if the rules have been broken.[32]

I. THE RULE IN ALLHUSEN *v.* WHITTELL [33]

Take a case where a testator has left his residuary estate to A for life remainder to B absolutely and in accordance with the general law debts, funeral and testamentary expenses and legacies have to be paid out of the residue. It would be unfair to apply all the income of the gross residue towards payment of debts, expenses and legacies, so favouring B. Similarly, it would be unfair to apply capital only towards such payments, so favouring A. The rule in *Allhusen* v. *Whittell* thus treats the payments as coming partly from income and partly from capital. It requires that sum to be ascertained which together with interest for the year succeeding death would amount to the total expended on payment of debts, expenses and legacies: the sum so ascertained will be borne by B and the excess of the total expenditure over that sum will be borne by A. The rate of interest to be taken depends on the ratio subsisting between the actual net income after tax [34] for the year succeeding death and the gross capital of the estate. The rule assumes payment at the end of the executor's year and should be modified if payment is significantly before or after that year.[35] Exact calculations are not required: rough and ready bona fide calculations will suffice.[36] In practice many wills exclude the rule (as any contrary intention displaces it).[37] Moreover, the rule is often ignored, especially as few beneficiaries know about the rule and most beneficiaries are so pleased to receive the testator's bounty that they do not " look a gift horse in the mouth." [38]

II. THE DUTY TO CONVERT

Once the net residue to which A and B are entitled has been ascertained there are still further problems. The residue may comprise wasting, hazardous or other unauthorised investments producing a high income for

---

[32] Generally, see Josling's *Apportionments for Executors and Trustees*, 3rd ed. (Oyez Publications); also the Chapter by John Flower in *Debits, Credits, Finance & Profits* edited by Edey and Yamey (Sweet & Maxwell, 1974).

[33] (1887) L.R. 4 Eq. 295. For a good general statement of the Rule see *per* Romer L.J. in *Corbett* v. *I.R.C.* [1938] 1 K.B. 567.

[34] *Re Oldham* [1927] W.N. 113.

[35] *Re McEwen* [1913] 2 Ch. 704; *Re Wills* [1915] 1 Ch. 769.

[36] *Re Wills* [1915] 1 Ch. 769, 779.

[37] *Re Ullswater* [1952] Ch. 105 holding that a common form clause for excluding the rule in *Howe* v. *Dartmouth* failed to exclude the rule in *Allhusen* v. *Whittell.*

[38] (1946) 10 Conv.(N.S.) 125 (George and George).

A and making B worry whether the capital will have depreciated considerably by the time he receives it. Alternatively, the residue may comprise some reversionary (or other non-income producing asset) such that A receives no income whilst the capital value of the reversionary interest increases all the time as the life tenant grows older and older. The rule in *Howe* v. *Dartmouth* [39] thus lays down that where there is a residuary bequest of personal property to be enjoyed by persons in succession then unauthorised investments (such as wasting and hazardous assets, reversionary interests and other non-income producing assets) are held upon an implied trust to sell them and to invest the proceeds in authorised investments.

N.B. (1) The rule only applies to personalty not realty as it is presumed that realty is meant to be enjoyed *in specie*. [40]

(2) It only applies to residuary bequests not specific bequests since a specific bequest of assets makes those assets authorised for purposes of retention.

(3) It only applies to wills not deeds as deeds necessarily deal with specific property. [41]

(4) The rule being based on the presumed intention of the testator (that all persons are to be benefited so that the assets should be converted into permanent investments of a recognised character) may be excluded expressly or by provisions in the will which show that the testator's intentions were inconsistent with an application of the rule. [42] The onus of proof is on the person seeking to show that the rule has been excluded, *e.g.*, by provisions indicating that the life tenant is to enjoy the property *in specie*: *Re Evans' W.T.*, *infra*.

(5) The rule, implying a trust for sale, obviously cannot apply where there is an express trust for sale. [43]

Where there is an express trust for sale of residuary personalty, it is necessary to ascertain whether the property subject to the trust is meant to be enjoyed *in specie* until sale for, if so, then the life tenant will properly receive all the rents, profits, dividends etc. in accordance with the testator's intention. [44] Otherwise under the rule in *Gibson* v. *Bott* [45] an apportionment will be necessary to balance the interests of the life tenant and the remainderman till the date of sale.

---

[39] (1802) 7 Ves. 137; S. J. Bailey (1943) 7 Conv.(N.S.) 128, 191.

[40] *Re Woodhouse* [1941] Ch. 332.

[41] *Re Van Straubenzee* [1901] 2 Ch. 779.

[42] *Re Pitcairn* [1896] 2 Ch. 199 (discretionary power to sell when trustees deem expedient inconsistent with any duty to sell); *Alcock* v. *Sloper* (1833) 2 My. & K. 699; *Re Barratt* [1925] Ch. 550; *Re Nicholson* [1909] 2 Ch. 111.

[43] On an intestacy a trust for sale arises under the Administration of Estates Act 1925, s. 33.

[44] An express power to postpone sale will normally be treated as inserted as incidental or ancillary to the trust for sale for the purpose of achieving an advantageous sale of the property for the benefit of all interested under the trust. Exceptionally, it may be treated as an independent power inserted for the benefit of the life tenant to enable the property to be enjoyed *in specie* so excluding the rule in *Gibson* v. *Bott* (1802) 7 Ves. 137: *Re Inman* [1915] 1 Ch. 187. However, for the period until such power is consciously exercised by the trustees there is a duty to apportion; *Re Rowlls* [1900] 2 Ch. 107; *Re Guinness Settlement* [1966] 1 W.L.R. 1355.

[45] (1802) 7 Ves. 137.

Re EVANS' WILL TRUSTS, PICKERING v. EVANS

Chancery Division [1921] 2 Ch. 309; 91 L.J.Ch. 29

EVE J.: " At the date of his death, on July 25, 1914, the testator was possessed of the copyright in certain literary works of which his aunt, Mrs. Puddicombe, was the authoress. Some of these works were being published under agreements with publishers, securing royalties to the testator as owner of the copyright. By his will he gave and bequeathed all his real and personal estate, other than certain specified property, to trustees upon trust to pay the income thereof to his wife until her decease or second marriage, and from and after her decease or second marriage he appointed, devised, and bequeathed the whole of his real and personal estate unto his trustees upon trust to divide the same into three equal shares, and to pay the income of one-third to a sister, of a second third to another sister, and of the remaining third to a brother, with remainder in each case to the children of the life-tenant as therein mentioned. The question is whether the tenant for life is entitled to receive and retain for her own use the whole of the royalties payable by the publishers under the agreements I have mentioned, and the answer involves the inquiry whether the rule in *Howe* v. *Lord Dartmouth* is to be applied, or whether I can find in the will any sufficient indication of an intention that the rule shall not be applied. According to James L.J. in *Macdonald* v. *Irvine*,[46] ' it is quite clear that the rule must be applied unless, upon the fair construction of the will, you find a sufficient indication of intention that it is not to be applied; the burden in every case being upon the person who says the rule of the Court of Chancery ought not to be applied in the particular case.' In *Pickering* v. *Pickering* [47] Lord Cottenham in explaining the rule says this: ' Very nice distinctions have been taken, and must have been taken, in determining whether the tenant for life is to have the income of the property in the state in which it is at the date of the testator's death, or the income of the produce of the conversion of the property. The principle upon which all the cases on the subject turn is clear enough, although its application is not always very easy. All that *Howe* v. *Lord Dartmouth* decided—and that was not the first decision to the same effect—is that, where the residue or bulk of the property is left *en masse*, and it is given to several persons in succession as tenants for life and remaindermen, it is the duty of the court to carry into effect the apparent intention of the testator. How is the apparent intention to be ascertained, if the testator has given no particular directions? If, although he has given no directions at all, yet he has carved out parts of the property to be enjoyed in strict settlement by certain persons, it is evident that the property must be put in

---

[46] (1878) 8 Ch.D. 101, 124.
[47] (1839) 3 My. & Cr. 289, 298.

such a state as will allow of its being so enjoyed. That cannot be, unless it is taken out of a temporary fund and put into a permanent fund. But that is merely an inference from the mode in which the property is to be enjoyed, if no direction is given as to how the property is to be managed. It is equally clear that, if a person gives certain property *specifically* to one person for life, with remainder over afterwards, then, although there is a danger that one object of his bounty will be defeated by the tenancy for life lasting as long as the property endures, yet there is a manifestation of intention which the court cannot overlook.' In this case it cannot be suggested that I have the state of things contemplated in the concluding sentence I have quoted from Lord Cottenham's judgment. What I have to deal with is a gift of the residuary real and personal property *en masse*. Prima facie therefore the case is one to which the rule ought to be applied. Does the fact that the testator after the determinable life interest given to his widow appoints, devises and bequeaths the whole of his residuary real and personal estate to trustees upon trust to divide the same into three parts manifest an intention on his part to exclude the application of the rule? I do not think it does. There is no other phrase or direction in the will indicative of any such intention, and I am not prepared to hold that the mere trust, on the determination of the limited interest, to divide the residuary estate is, by itself, a sufficient manifestation of an intention that the rule is not to apply. I think, on the true construction of the will, the rule ought to be applied; and that the interest of the testator in the copyrights comprised in the agreements I have mentioned must be valued at the expiration of one year from the date of his death, and the tenant for life be paid interest at 4 per cent. on the value so ascertained, commencing from the date of the death. . . ." [48]

III. Duty to Apportion

Even if there is a duty to convert it does not follow that pending conversion the tenant for life will get an apportioned part of the income only. The duty to apportion may itself be excluded by an intention of specific enjoyment. The rules are:

(i) If the property is realty, then, if a duty to convert exists, it must be express. The tenant for life gets the actual income, unless the will directs an apportionment, or there is an improper postponement of conversion: *Wentworth* v. *Wentworth*.[49]

(ii) If the property is personalty of the prescribed kind [50] and there is an express trust for conversion the tenant for life gets an apportionment only unless the will expressly or impliedly gives him the

---

[48] This is the rule of apportionment (*infra*, p. 553).

[49] [1900] A.C. 163 : testator gave trustees power to postpone sale of realty for 21 years. Trustees improperly postponed for longer. *Held* by the Privy Council the tenant for life entitled to a reasonable percentage yield based upon the value of the property estimated as at the expiration of the period of 21 years.

[50] Residuary comprising wasting, hazardous or unauthorised investments or reversionary interests.

actual income: *Re Chaytor, infra.* A mere trust for conversion with an ancillary power to postpone conversion does not of itself give the income of the property before conversion *in specie* to the life tenant.[51] More is required in the way of showing an intention that the power was intended not for the more convenient realisation of the estate but for the special benefit of the life tenant.[52] Even then until the trustees consciously exercise this power for the life tenant's benefit the life tenant is entitled to an apportioned income and not the actual income.[53]

(iii) If the property is personalty of the prescribed kind and there is no express trust for conversion and no intention of specific enjoyment, a duty to convert arises under the rule in *Howe* v. *Dartmouth*, and there will be apportionment.[54]

There is, of course, no duty to apportion income of property invested in authorised investments. The effect of the extension by the Trustee Investments Act 1961 of the powers of investment of trustees upon the rule in *Howe* v. *Dartmouth* is not absolutely clear. It would seem that whilst the rule will not apply to special-range property, narrower-range property not requiring advice, and narrower-range and wider-range property requiring advice for the period after advice to retain them has been properly obtained,[55] the rule may possibly apply to narrower-range and wider-range property requiring advice for the period before advice to retain them has been sought.[56] If retention of such property were then advised, the rule would cease to apply though if sale and reinvestment were recommended the rule would continue to apply until such sale.

Re CHAYTOR, CHAYTOR v. HORN

Chancery Division [1905] 1 Ch. 233; 74 L.J.Ch. 106; 92 L.T. 290; 53 W.R. 251

A testator directed as follows: " I devise and bequeath all my real and personal estate not hereby otherwise disposed of unto and to the use of my trustees upon trust to sell and convert into money the same, with power to postpone such sale and conversion as long as my trustees shall think proper and to retain any investments subsisting at my death, whether of the kind hereinafter authorised or not, and out of the moneys produced by such sale and conversion and out of such part of my estate as shall consist of money to pay my funeral and testamentary expenses and debts and the legacies bequeathed by this my will or any codicil hereto, and at the discretion of my trustees to invest the residue of the said moneys, with power for my trustees from time to time at their dis-

---

51 *Re Chaytor, infra; Re Slater* (1915) 113 L.T. 691, 693.
52 *Re Inman.*
53 *Re Rowlls* [1900] 2 Ch. 107; *Re Fisher* [1943] Ch. 377 (intestacy trust for sale); *Re Hey's S.T.* [1945] Ch. 294; *Re Guinness' Settlement* [1966] 1 W.L.R. 1355.
54 If there is an intention of specific enjoyment then there is no duty to convert and no question of apportionment arises.
55 This presupposes that the fund has been divided in accordance with s. 2 (1) of the Act of 1961.
56 For an analogous situation, see *Re Guinness' Settlement* [1966] 1 W.L.R. 1355.

cretion to vary such investments, and to stand possessed of the residuary trust moneys and the investments for the time being representing the same (hereinafter called ' the residuary trust funds ') upon the trusts following, that is to say, in trust to pay the income thereof to my said wife during her life if she shall so long continue my widow," with remainder after her second marriage or death on trust for the testator's children. Part of the property consisted of unauthorised securities bearing a high dividend, of which the trustees sold some, and decided to postpone the conversion of the remainder. The trustees paid the widow, not the full income of the shares retained, but a percentage of the capitalised value as at the death of the testator, *i.e.*, they apportioned. This summons (which was adjourned into court) was taken out by the tenant for life to determine whether she was entitled to the income *in specie* of the retained shares pending conversion.

WARRINGTON J.: "The question I have to decide is whether the tenant for life in this case is entitled *in specie* to the entire income of certain unauthorised securities which the trustees are retaining at present until an opportunity of conversion arises, or whether, under the trusts of the will which I have to deal with, she is only entitled to interest at a certain rate on the value of those securities . . .

"As regards the unauthorised securities, there is no express gift of the income of the funds or items of property forming part of the testator's estate during postponement of conversion; but I am invited by Mr. Carson [57] to find such a gift by construction in the will. In the first place, what is the general principle which is applied in such a case as this, where there is an express trust for conversion and a power to retain securities of every kind, authorised and unauthorised, and there is no express gift of the income pending conversion? As I understand it, the general rule is that the tenant for life is entitled to the income of authorised securities, but not entitled to the income of unauthorised securities. In the latter case he is only entitled to interest, which is now fixed at the rate of 3 per cent. on their value at the testator's death.[58] That certainly was the rule adopted by Kekewich J. in *Re Thomas*.[59] In the first paragraph of his judgment he says: 'I am not prepared to hold that where there is a direction for conversion of personal estate, followed by a power of retention of existing securities in the absolute discretion of the trustees, and then there are trusts for tenants for life, and afterwards for remaindermen, the power of retention necessarily gives the tenants for life the enjoyment *in specie* of the securities retained by the trustees in the exercise of their discretion ' . . . That is the general rule. Is there anything to take this case out of that rule? In my judgment, so far from that, the words of this will are adverse to

---

[57] Counsel for the widow.
[58] Now 4 per cent.: *Re Beech* [1920] 1 Ch. 40; *Re Baker* [1924] 2 Ch. 271; *Re Owen* [1912] 1 Ch. 519; *Re Fawcett* [1940] Ch. 402; *Re Parry* [1947] Ch. 23. This figure seems out-dated: see p. 553, *infra*.
[59] [1891] 3 Ch. 482.

the contention of the tenant for life. The trustees are to sell and convert
the real and personal estate. They may retain any investments subsisting
at the testator's death as long as they think proper. The only trusts in
favour of beneficiaries are trusts of the 'residuary trust funds,' which
are defined to be the 'residuary trust moneys'—that is, the proceeds
of conversion—' and the investments for the time being representing the
same '—that is, representing the proceeds of conversion. I take that to
mean that the tenant for life is entitled to the income of the trust moneys
—that is, the proceeds of conversion and the income of the investments
made with those moneys. That, of course, includes the income of any
authorised investments which are retained (for that is the same as if
the trustees had sold them and reinvested the proceeds of sale in the
same securities), but does not include the income of securities which
do not represent 'trust funds' at all, but are items of property which
are retained by the trustees only until they could realise them. In order
that the tenant for life should not lose income altogether, the court
steps in and says for the proper administration of the estate the value of
these investments at the testator's death shall be taken as the value of
the proceeds of sale. As these unauthorised securities cannot be kept
as part of the estate, the tenant for life gets the income of them as
notionally converted at the testator's death. That appears to be the rule
laid down with the object of preventing the discretion of the trustees
from operating to the prejudice of the tenant for life or the remainderman. It is applied in both ways. That, in my opinion, is the true
construction of this will.

"Then I am asked, if I cannot find an express gift, to find an implied
gift of this income to the tenant for life. That argument also fails.
There is no express gift—that is, there is no gift in terms of the income
of these unauthorised securities, and I am unable to find an implied
gift. But whether I find a gift or not, it is said that the rule to be applied
is not the one I have mentioned, but a rule which distinguishes between
unauthorised securities which are of a wasting nature and unauthorised
securities which are not wasting. Many cases have been cited, but in
all of them, in one form or another, what was given was the income of
the estate, and not, as in the words of this will, the income of the
residuary trust funds. It seems that the distinction between those cases
and this is that the question in those cases was whether the rule of
Howe v. *Earl of Dartmouth* ought to be applied. In this case there is
an *express* trust for conversion, and the income of the *proceeds* is given
to the widow [60] . . . ."

Held, therefore, the tenant for life was not entitled to the income
in specie of the retained shares pending conversion, there being no
express or implied gift to her of the income *in specie*.[61]

---

[60] His Lordship dissented from the decision in *Bulkeley* v. *Stephens* (1863) 3 N.R. 105.
[61] So also in the following cases there was an express trust for conversion of personalty, with a power to postpone conversion (or a power to retain)—*Lambert* v.
Rendle (1863) 3 N.R. 247; *Cooper* v. *Laroche* (1869) 38 L.J.Ch. 591; *Re Carter*

IV. The Method of Apportionment

If the tenant for life is entitled to an apportionment only it will be calculated [62] as follows:

(a) Where there is for the benefit of the estate as a whole a power to postpone conversion and the trustees postpone:

(i) The subject-matter being wasting or unauthorised property, the tenant for life is entitled, as from the testator's death, to the current percentage [63] of a notional conversion estimated as at the death, plus interest on the difference (if any) between that percentage and the income actually produced: *Re Owen*,[64] *Re Parry*.[65] Valuation is at the date of death as no other date is appropriate in view of the power to postpone sale.

(ii) The subject-matter being reversionary interests or other non-income producing property (*e.g.*, outstanding estate), the mode of apportionment is that adopted in *Re Chesterfield's Trusts, infra.*

(b) Where there is no power to postpone sale but an immediate sale would be disadvantageous to the estate:

(i) The subject-matter being wasting or unauthorised property, the tenant for life is entitled, as from the testator's death to the current percentage [62] of a notional conversion estimated as at the expiration of the executor's year, *i.e.*,[66] one year from the death, plus interest on the difference (if any) between that percentage and the income actually produced: *Re Fawcett, infra.*

(ii) The subject-matter being reversionary interests or other non-income-producing property, the mode of apportionment is apparently as in *Re Chesterfield's Trusts, infra.*

Re FAWCETT

Chancery Division [1940] Ch. 402; 109 L.J.Ch. 124

The testatrix bequeathed her residuary estate, which comprised several unauthorised investments, to trustees upon trust to invest it

---

[62] (1892) 41 W.R. 140; *Re Berry* [1962] Ch. 97; *Morley* v. *Mendham* (1856) 2 Jur. 998; *Johnston* v. *Moore* (1858) 27 L.J.Ch. 453; *Lambert* v. *Lambert* (1872) 27 L.T. 59; *Waters* v. *Waters* (1875) 32 L.T. 306n.; *Lean* v. *Lean* (1875) 32 L.T. 305; *Re Chancellor* (1884) 26 Ch.D. 42; *Re Thomas* [1891] 3 Ch. 482; *Re Crowther* [1895] 2 Ch. 56; *Re Morgan, Vachell* v. *Morgan* [1914] 1 Ch. 910; *Re Godfree* [1914] 2 Ch. 110; *Re Slater* (1915) 113 L.T. 691; *Re Inman* [1915] 1 Ch. 187; *Re Aste* (1918) 87 L.J.Ch. 660; *Re Bate* [1938] 4 All E.R. 218. In the first four there was held to be no gift to the tenant for life of the income *in specie* pending conversion.

[62] For calculations see J. F. Josling's *Apportionments for Executors and Trustees*, 3rd ed. (1968); Rowland's *Trust Account*, 3rd ed., 1964, Ranking Spicer & Pegler's *Executorship Law and Accounts*, 21st ed.

[63] Semble 4 per cent. It is surprising that no one has asked for directions from the court as to whether or not a higher rate is now proper: *cf.* interest rate on legacies increased from 4 per cent. to 5 per cent. by S.I. 1972 No. 1898, r. 6, and 7½ per cent. interest on damages in *Cremer* v. *General Carriers S.A.* [1974] 1 W.L.R. 341. Furthermore, in *Wallersteiner* v. *Moir, The Times*, January 29, 1975 (a breach of fiduciary duty case) Bank of England minimum lending rate was used as a base.

[64] [1912] 1 Ch. 519.   [65] [1947] Ch. 23.

[66] If sale takes place before the end of the executor's year then the actual sale price is taken: *Re Fawcett, infra.*

and divide the income equally among her nephews and nieces for their respective lives and then for their children.

FARWELL J. (in a reserved judgment): " The rule in *Howe* v. *Lord Dartmouth* [67] is founded on the judgment of Lord Eldon L.C. in the case of that name. It was made for the purpose of holding, as far as possible, an even hand between those whose interests are in capital and those whose interests are in income, in respect of investments which are not authorised by law for the investment of trust funds. In the present case, so far as the construction of this will is concerned, it is, I think, clear that there is a trust for sale so far as the unauthorised investments are concerned. There is no express trust for sale but there is a trust to invest and that must mean to invest in trustee securities. Accordingly there is an implied trust for sale of any investments which are not authorised by law for the investment of trust funds. It is also to be noticed that there is no power to postpone the sale in question. The rule in *Howe* v. *Lord Dartmouth*, in my judgment, was based upon the equitable idea of treating that which ought to be done as having been done, and accordingly in the early cases the general rule was that the tenant for life was entitled to whatever the investments, if they were sold and re-invested in Consols, would produce. To that extent, and to that extent only, he was entitled to payment on account of income. In more recent years the practice has generally been to give to the tenant for life interest at 4 per cent. upon the capital value of the unauthorised investment. The reason for the alteration in the rule was, I think, due to the fact that the range of authorised investments has been very greatly extended in comparatively recent years, and accordingly the Court took the view that a rate of interest which might be higher than that which was produced by Consols would be a reasonable rate to allow to tenants for life, since there was, at any rate, some possibility that trust funds could be invested in securities returning such income. The general, although not the universal, rule is now to allow 4 per cent., and I see no reason in the present case to depart from that modern practice. In order to give effect to the rule it appears to me that in a case of this kind it is the duty of the trustees to have the unauthorised investments valued as at the end of the first year after the testatrix's death. During that year the executors are given time to deal with the estate as a whole. At the end of it comes the time when, in my judgment, any unauthorised investments which they still retain should be valued and the tenant for life becomes entitled to be paid 4 per cent. on the valuation of the whole of the unauthorised investments. To that extent these tenants for life are entitled to receive income in each year and that income, 4 per cent. on the capital value of the unauthorised investments, must be paid out of the actual income received from the unauthorised

---

[67] 7 Ves. 137.

investments; that is to say, the trustes will receive the whole of the dividends which the unauthorised investments pay and there will be no apportionment. Those dividends will be applied in the first instance in paying, so far as they go, 4 per cent. on the capital value of the unauthorised investments. If the income received on the unauthorised investments is more than sufficient to pay the 4 per cent., then the balance will be added to the capital and it will form part of the whole fund in the hands of the trustees. If, on the other hand, the income actually received from the unauthorised investments is not sufficient to pay 4 per cent. in each year to the tenants for life, they will not be entitled to immediate recoupment out of the capital, but when the unauthorised investments are sold the trustees will then have in their hands a fund representing the proceeds of sale of the unauthorised investments, together with any surplus income which may have accrued in the earlier years; out of those proceeds of sale the tenants for life will be entitled to be recouped so as to provide them with the full 4 per cent. during the whole period and they will be entitled to be refunded the deficit calculated at 4 per cent. simple interest but less tax. In that way it appears to me the rule can be worked out satis-factorily as between capital and income and the balance will be held as evenly as possible between those two opposing interests. No doubt the duty of the trustees is to realise the unauthorised securities as soon as conveniently may be, but until that has been done that, in my view, is the right way of dealing with the matter. The fact that there may be some investments which are of little or no value and which produce no income does not affect the position if the whole of the unauthorised investments are treated as one whole, and the value of the whole of those investments is ascertained and the income received from the whole of those investments is received by the trustees and applied in the way which I have stated.

" That being the general principle upon which, in my view, the trustees should act in this case, I think the questions raised in the summons can be answered without much difficulty.

" I should add this. It must be observed that in the present case, as I have already pointed out, there is no power to postpone the sale, and the judgment which I have given does not necessarily apply in a case where there is an express power to postpone; other considera-tions may arise in such a case, but where there is no power to postpone and there is a trust for sale and re-investment in trustee securities the judgment which I have given indicates the right way in which the administration of the estate should be proceeded with.

" Accordingly I will make a declaration, in answer to question 1 of the summons, that on the true construction of the will of the testa-trix there was and is a trust for sale as to all unauthorised investments and that the rule in *Howe* v. *Lord Dartmouth* ought to have been and

ought to be applied with reference to her residuary estate as between
capital and income.

" In answer to question 2 of the summons I will make a declaration
that (*a*) in the case of unauthorised investments which were still
retained unsold at the end of one year from the death of the testatrix
the life tenants were and are entitled to interest at the rate of 4 per
cent. per annum on the value of such investments taken at the end of
such year but commencing from the date of the death and running on
until the realisation of such investments respectively; (*b*) in the case of
unauthorised investments realised during the first year after the death
of the testatrix the life tenants are entitled to interest at the rate
aforesaid on the net proceeds of such realisation respectively from the
date of the death down to the respective dates of completions of such
realisations; (*c*) the unauthorised investments for the time being unsold
ought to be taken en bloc as one aggregate for the purposes of the
rule in *Howe* v. *Lord Dartmouth*; (*d*) in applying that rule the Apportionment Act 1870 ought not to be applied in the income accounts at
the death of the testatrix or at the beginning or end of any accounting
period with reference to the income of unauthorised investments; (*e*)
any excess of income from unauthorised investments beyond the
interest payable in respect of such investments to the life tenants ought
to be invested in authorised investments as part of the capital with the
other authorised investments, and accordingly the whole of the actual
subsequent income of such invested excess income is payable as
income; (*f*) the interest so payable in respect of unauthorised investments was and is payable out of moneys being income from unauthorised investments or, so far as such income is insufficient, being
proceeds of realisation of such investments, and any interest so payable
for the time being in arrear is payable (but calculated as simple interest
only) out of subsequent income from unauthorised investments which
are for the time being retained and out of the proceeds of sale of such
investments as and when realised, but neither any excess income from
unauthorised investments, which at the end of any accounting period
is available under head (*e*) for investment in authorised investments,
nor any proceeds of realisation of unauthorised investments not
required at the date of realisation to pay interest payable as aforesaid
for the time being in arrear and accordingly available to be invested
in authorised investments, were or are applicable towards payment of
subsequently accruing interest as aforesaid in respect of unauthorised
investments then still retained."

Note

Assume that the testator died on January 1, 1970, and that it is now
January 1, 1972. It is estimated that a sale of the unauthorised securities at
the death of the testator would have produced £1,000. The tenant for life
is entitled to the current percentage—say, 4 per cent.—of that sum, *i.e.,* £80.

The income in fact produced during the two years is £100. The difference of £20—being the difference between the percentage on the notional conversion and the income actually produced—forms part of the capital. The interest on that £20 when invested henceforth goes to income. If the tenant for life actually received the whole of the £100, he has received £20 more than he was entitled to, so that an adjustment will be made out of subsequent payments; and if the tenant for life dies before a complete adjustment, the balance may apparently be recouped out of his estate.[68]

The difference might also be the other way round. The percentage on the notional conversion is £80, but the income actually produced and actually received by the tenant for life might have been only £50, so that he has received £30 *less* than the sum he was entitled to. Here also an adjustment will be made. The deficiency in the income payable to the tenant for life is primarily payable out of any excess income produced by the unauthorised assets in a subsequent accounting period, and, failing that, out of the proceeds of sale of the unauthorised assets. Any excess income received in a previous year cannot be resorted to in order to make good the deficiency, as such excess income must be regarded as capital and invested accordingly.[69]

Re EARL OF CHESTERFIELD'S TRUSTS

Chancery Division (1883) 24 Ch.D. 643; 52 L.J.Ch. 958; 49 L.T. 261; 32 W.R. 361

A testator who died on December 1, 1871, devised and bequeathed his residuary estate to trustees on trust for conversion, with a discretionary power to postpone conversion, for the benefit of one for life, with remainders over. This residue included outstanding personal estate consisting of (*inter alia*) a mortgage debt with arrears of interest. The trustees postponed the conversion of the outstanding estate, which eventually fell in (with interest) a number of years later.

Held, following *Beavan* v. *Beavan*,[70] that the property was to be apportioned between capital and income " by ascertaining the respective sums which, put out at £4 per cent. per annum on December 1, 1871 . . . and accumulating at compound interest calculated at that rate with yearly rests, and deducting income tax, would, with the accumulations of interest, have produced, at the respective dates of receipt, the amounts actually received; and that the aggregate of the sums so ascertained ought to be treated as principal and be applied accordingly, and the residue should be treated as income." [71]

---

[68] *Cf. Hood* v. *Clapham* (1854) 19 Beav. 90.
[69] See *Re Fawcett* [1940] Ch. 402.
[70] (1883) 24 Ch.D. 649n.
[71] So also *Wilkinson* v. *Duncan* (1857) 23 Beav. 469; *Beavan* v. *Beavan* (1883) 24 Ch.D. 649n.; *Flower, Matheson* v. *Goodwyn* (1890) 62 L.T. 216; reversed on a point of construction (1890) 63 L.T. 201; *Re Godden* [1893] 1 Ch. 292; *Re Goodenough* [1895] 2 Ch. 537; *Re Morley* [1895] 2 Ch. 738; *Rowlls* v. *Bebb* [1900] 2 Ch. 107; *Re Hollebone* [1919] 2 Ch. 93; *Re Baker* [1924] 2 Ch. 271; *Re Hey's S.T.* [1945] Ch. 294; *Re Guinness's Settlement* [1966] 1 W.L.R. 1355; *cf. Re Hengler* [1893] 1 Ch. 586.

Note

A testator who dies on December 1, 1871, bequeaths his residuary personalty
on trust for conversion, with a power of postponement, for A for life,
remainder to B. Part of this residue consists of a reversionary interest under
a marriage settlement of which the tenant for. life is the testator's wife, and
the remainderman the testator. The testator's trustees postpone, and it is
assumed, in order to eliminate the necessity of calculating with yearly rests
(compound interest), that the wife dies exactly one year after the testator,
whereupon the reversionary interest falls in and produces £1,038. Of this
sum £1,000 goes to capital for B, and £38 goes to income for A; for the
sum which, with interest at 4 per cent. from December 1, 1871, to December 1, 1872, minus income tax at one shilling in the pound,[72] would produce
£1,038 is £1,000. Henceforth A receives the income of this £1,000 when
invested. Calculation becomes involved if a lengthy period has elapsed
between the testator's death and the apportionment, for after the first year
of calculation there is interest upon interest. The position would be the
same if the trustees had sold the reversionary interest at the end of the
year for £1,038. As the £38 passing to A is part of the £1,038 capital it is
not liable to income tax: the notional tax deducted in the calculation enures
for B's benefit. As reversionary interests fetch relatively little owing to the
imponderable factors involved, it is best if possible to wait till they fall into
possession.[73]

The same method of apportionment applies to a *contingent* reversionary
interest.[74] But it does not apply where the interest is vested in possession,
but the income therefrom is temporarily charged in favour of a third
party,[75] and it does not apply to realty.[76] On the other hand, it can apply
where the sum to be apportioned includes both principal and interest.[77]

V. APPORTIONMENT IN RELATION TO LEASEHOLDS

Leaseholds for 60 years or more unexpired are authorised investments,[78] so
no question of apportionment arises. Lesser leaseholds are unauthorised so
there will be a duty to convert under the rule in *Howe* v. *Dartmouth* unless
there is some positive indication in the will that the rents are to be enjoyed
in specie. In *Re Trollope's W.T.*[79] Tomlin J. said *obiter* that " so far as leaseholds held in trust for sale are concerned the rule of *Howe* v. *Dartmouth* is
gone " but, as that quotation shows,[80] he was presupposing the existence of
a trust for sale which can only be implied by an application of the *Howe* v.
Dartmouth rule. His reference to *Howe* v. *Dartmouth* (like the references

---

[72] A hypothetical case with a hypothetical rate of tax.
[73] As administrators are directed to do under an intestacy by the Administration of
Estates Act 1925, s. 33 (1). See also Finance Act 1965, Sched. 7, para. 13 (2).
[74] *Re Hobson* (1885) 55 L.J.Ch. 422.
[75] *Re Holliday* [1947] Ch. 402.
[76] *Re Woodhouse* [1941] Ch. 332.
[77] *Re Chance's W.T.* [1962] Ch. 593 (the aggregate of principal sums payable out of
the compensation fund established under the Town and Country Planning Act 1947,
as subsequently amended, together with the interest thereon held to be apportionable
in accordance with the rule).
[78] *Re Gough* [1957] Ch. 323; Settled Land Act 1925, s. 73 (xi); Law of Property Act
1925, s. 28 (1).
[79] [1927] 1 Ch. 596, 601.
[80] Also the preceding paragraph of his judgment.

of so many judges) [81] seems to be a reference not to the duty to convert under *Howe* v. *Dartmouth* but to the apportionment rules that apply once an implied trust for sale has arisen.

The apportionment rules for leaseholds have been altered by subsection (2) of section 28 of the Law of Property Act 1925: " Subject to any direction to the contrary in the *disposition on trust for sale* or in the *settlement of the proceeds of sale*, the net rents and profits of the land until sale . . . shall be paid or applied . . . in like manner as the income of investments representing the purchase money would be payable or applicable if a sale had been made and the proceeds had been duly invested." Thus, in the case of a disposition on trust for sale of land or a settlement of the proceeds of sale of land, the tenant for life is, pending conversion, entitled *in specie*, unless there is a contrary direction. By subsection (5) of the section it is provided: " This section applies to dispositions on trust for sale coming into operation either before or after the commencement or by virtue of this Act." Accordingly, in *Re Brooker*,[82] Lawrence J. held that where a residuary bequest in 1903 upon express trust for sale included leaseholds the life tenants were entitled to the rent, *in specie* as from January 1, 1926. Furthermore, in *Re Berton* [83] Clauson L.J. (sitting at first instance) held that where a residuary bequest of leaseholds was made directly to two persons equally for their respective lives so as to take effect by virtue of sections 34 and 35 Law of Property Act 1925 as a trust for sale for the persons as tenants in common, then section 28 (2) applied to entitle the life tenants to the rents *in specie*. Since section 28 (2) applies in the case of express trusts for sale and trusts for sale implied by statute it seems [84] that it should apply to trusts for sale implied by *Howe* v. *Dartmouth* although in previous editions of this text [85] the following view was taken. " A *Howe* v. *Dartmouth* trust for sale is probably not a 'disposition on trust for sale,' notwithstanding that by section 205 (1) (ii) of the Act the word 'disposition' in the Act includes a bequest of property contained in a will; for a *Howe* v. *Dartmouth* trust for sale is not a bequest of property on trust for sale, but a bequest of property on which a trust for sale is engrafted by operation of law. Again, a 'settlement of the proceeds of sale' presupposes an *express* trust for sale. It is submitted, therefore, that section 28 does not affect the *Howe* v. *Dartmouth* rule."

In case it might be thought that section 28 (2) scandalously enables a life tenant to receive all the rents during the last 10 or 12 years of an unauthorised lease, leaving nothing for the remainderman, it should be remembered that the trustees have an overriding duty to keep an even hand between the beneficiaries. They would be in breach of this duty [86] if they

---

[81] *e.g.*, Clauson L.J. in *Re Berton* [1939] Ch. 200; Pennycuick J. in *Re Berry* [1962] Ch. 97.

[82] [1926] W.N. 93.

[83] [1939] Ch. 200. S. J. Bailey, " Leaseholds and the Rule in *Howe* v. *The Earl of Dartmouth* " (1932) 4 C.L.J. 357; 164 L.T.J. 326.

[84] Snell, p. 219.

[85] 5th ed., p. 418.

[86] *e.g.*, *Beauclerk* v. *Ashburnham* (1845) 8 Beav. 322; 14 L.J.Ch. 241 where trustees were *authorised and required* by and with the consent and direction in writing of the life tenant to invest in leaseholds. Obviously, the trustees could not object to investment in leaseholds as such, but they had a discretion whether or not to agree to a particular investment proposed " because it must be agreed at once that it would not be fit for them to lay out the trust moneys in a low, bad and deteriorating situation " *per* Lord Langdale M.R. at 8 Beav. 328. It should be noted that

retained the leases till they expired or for any longer period than reasonably necessary to sell the depreciating leases. It would also seem that the remainderman could specifically invoke section 30 of the Law of Property Act for the court to compel the trustees to sell or he could take advantage of his inherent right to call for conversion.[87]

PROBLEM

Discuss the purpose and effect of the following clause in a will:

" I give all my property of whatsoever kind and wheresoever situate of which I have any power of testamentary disposition and not otherwise disposed of by this my will or by any codicil hereto to my trustees upon the following trusts:

Upon trust to sell, call in and convert the same into money with power to postpone such sale, calling in and conversion for so long as they in the exercise of their absolute discretion shall think fit without being liable for loss and so that the income of my real, leasehold and personal estate howsoever constituted and invested (including the income of property required for the payment of debts and other payments in due course of administration in payment whereof the proceeds of such sale, calling in and conversion are hereinafter directed to be applied) shall as from my death be treated as income and that a reversionary or future interest shall not be sold prior to falling into possession unless my trustees shall see special reason for such earlier sale and that the net rents and profits of my real and leasehold estate for the time being remaining unsold after payment thereout of all outgoings which my trustees shall consider to be properly payable out of income shall go and be applied as if the same were income of authorised investments of such proceeds of an actual sale thereof and no property not actually producing income shall be treated as producing income."

VI. OTHER APPORTIONMENT INSTANCES [88]

Losses on realisation of authorised securities, e.g., mortgages, debentures. Where a trust security turns out to be insufficient, then the proceeds of the security are divisible between income and capital in shares bearing the same proportion to each other as the arrears of interest and capital: *Re Atkinson.*[89]

Losses on realisation of unauthorised investments made by the trustees. If the personal remedy against the trustees is worthless, then the life tenant cannot be compelled to refund income received by him over the current percentage (4 per cent.) to make up the capital.[90] Otherwise the loss is borne rateably by dividing the sum realised (including both the proceeds of

---

executors in realising the estate and paying off liabilities have a duty to consider the interest of the estate as a whole and are under no duty to consider the effect between the beneficiaries so as to hold the balance evenly between them: *Re Hayes' W.T.* [1971] 1 W.L.R. 758.

[87] *Thornton* v. *Ellis* (1852) 15 Beav. 193; *Wightwick* v. *Lord* (1857) 6 H.L.C. 217.

[88] Generally see Josling's *Apportionments for Executors and Trustees*, 3rd ed. (Oyez Publications).

[89] [1904] 2 Ch. 160; *Re Morris's W.T.* [1960] 1 W.L.R. 1210. For the position where trustee mortgagees foreclose, see Law of Property Act 1925, s. 31; *Re Horn's Estate* [1924] 2 Ch. 222.

[90] *Re Bird* [1901] 1 Ch. 916.

sale and any income received before sale) in the proportion which the income which the life tenant ought to have received had the unauthorised investment not been made bears to the value of the sum wrongly invested, but the life tenant must bring into hotchpot [91] all the income actually received during the currency of the unauthorised investment: *Re Bird*. If no loss of capital has been sustained, then the remainderman is not entitled to have the capital increased by adding to it the difference between the income actually paid to the life tenant and the current percentage.[92]

General apportionment rule. By section 2 of the Apportionment Act 1870 " all rents, annuities, dividends and other periodical payments in the nature of income . . . shall . . . be considered as accruing from day to day and shall be apportionable in respect of time accordingly."

Stocks or shares bought or sold cum dividend. By the rule in *Bulkeley* v. *Stephens* [93] there is no apportionment here unless a really glaring injustice would otherwise be caused.

Capitalised profits of companies. Where a company instead of distributing its profits by way of dividend capitalises those profits by issuing bonus shares, debentures or redeemable loan stock, the company's decision binds those interested under trusts so that those interested in capital benefit: Rule in *Bouch* v. *Sproule*.[94] Of course, if the issue of shares is a rights issue (entitling current shareholders to subscribe new capital in proportion to their existing share holdings) the new shares, being bought with capital moneys, form part of capital.

Section 7. The Trust Property

I. REDUCTION OF TRUST PROPERTY INTO POSSESSION

The Trustee Act 1925

Power to compound liabilities

Section 15. A personal representative or two or more trustees acting together, or, subject to the restrictions [95] imposed in regard to receipts by a sole trustee not being a trust corporation, a sole acting trustee where by the instrument, if any, creating the trust, or by statute, a sole trustee is authorised to execute the trusts and powers reposed in him, may, if and as he or they think fit—

    (*a*) accept any property, real or personal, before the time at which it is made transferable or payable; or

    (*b*) sever and apportion any blended trust funds or property; or

    (*c*) pay or allow any debt or claim on any evidence that he or they think sufficient; or

    (*d*) accept any composition or any security, real or personal, for any debt or for any property, real or personal, claimed; or

    (*e*) allow any time of payment of any debt; or

---

[91] *Stroud* v. *Gwyer* (1860) 28 Beav. 130, 141; *Re Appleby* [1903] 1 Ch. 565.
[92] *Slade* v. *Chaine* [1908] 1 Ch. 522; *Re Hoyles* [1912] 1 Ch. 67.
[93] [1896] 2 Ch. 241; *Re Henderson* [1940] Ch. 368.
[94] (1887) 12 App.Cas. 385; *Hill* v. *Permanent Trustee Co. of New South Wales Ltd.* [1930] A.C. 720.
[95] See s. 27 of the Law of Property Act 1925; s. 14 of the Trustee Act 1925.

(*f*) compromise, compound, abandon, submit to arbitration, or otherwise settle any debt, account, claim or thing whatever relating to
the testator's or intestate's estate or to the trust;

and for any of those purposes may enter into, give, execute, and do such
agreements, instruments of composition or arrangement, releases, and other
things as to him or them seem expedient, without being responsible for any
loss occasioned by any act or thing so done by him or them in good faith.

Note

This section replaces, with amendments and additions, section 21 of the Trustee
Act 1893 which replaced section 37 of the Conveyancing Act 1881. In *Re
Brogden*[96] the Court of Appeal laid it down that trustees must demand payment
of funds due to the trust, and take legal proceedings, if necessary, to enforce
payment if the demand is not complied with within a reasonable time, unless
they reasonably believe that such action would be fruitless. In this case the
breach of trust occurred before the Conveyancing Act 1881 came into force. In
Re Owens[97] Jessel M.R. said *obiter*: " [Section 37 of the Conveyancing Act
1881] may have a revolutionary effect on this branch of the law. It looks as
if the only question left would be whether the executors [or trustees] have acted
in good faith or not." But Eve J. in *Re Greenwood*[98] put a strict interpretation
on the section by holding that it involved the exercise of an *active discretion* on
the part of the trustee, with the result that if loss arises from the neglect, carelessness or supineness of the trustee, the case is outside the section altogether.

Reversionary interests, valuations and audit

Section 22.—(1) Where trust property includes any share or interest in
property not vested in the trustees, or the proceeds of the sale of any such
property, or any other thing in action, the trustees on the same falling into
possession, or becoming payable or transferable may—

(*a*) agree or ascertain the amount or value thereof or any part thereof
in such manner as they may think fit;

(*b*) accept in or towards satisfaction thereof, at the market or current
value, or upon any valuation or estimate of value which they may
think fit, any authorised investments;

(*c*) allow any deductions for duties, costs, charges and expenses which
they may think proper or reasonable;

(*d*) execute any release in respect of the premises so as effectually to
discharge all accountable parties from all liability in respect of any
matters coming within the scope of such release;

without being responsible in any such case for any loss occasioned by any
act or thing so done by them in good faith.

(2) The trustees shall not be under any obligation and shall not be
chargeable with any breach of trust by reason of any omission—

(*a*) to place any distringas notice or apply for any stop or other like
order upon any securities or other property out of or on which
such share or interest or other thing in action as aforesaid is
derived, payable or charged; or

(*b*) to take any proceedings on acount of any act, default, or neglect
on the part of the persons in whom such securities or other property

96 (1888) 38 Ch.D. 546.
97 (1882) 47 L.T. 61, 64.
98 (1911) 105 L.T. 509.

      or any of them or any part thereof are for the time being, or had
      at any time been, vested;

unless and until required in writing so to do by some person, or the
guardian of some person, beneficially interested under the trust, and unless
also due provision is made to their satisfaction for payment of the costs
of any proceedings required to be taken:

Provided that nothing in this subsection shall relieve the trustees of the
obligation to get in and obtain payment or transfer of such share or interest
or other thing in action on the same falling into possession.

(3) Trustees may, for the purpose of giving effect to the trust, or any of
the provisions of the instrument, if any, creating the trust or of any statute,
from time to time (by duly qualified agents) ascertain and fix the value of
any trust property in such manner as they think proper, and any valuation
so made in good faith shall be binding upon all persons interested under
the trust.

(4) Trustees may, in their absolute discretion, from time to time, but not
more than once in every three years unless the nature of the trust or any
special dealings with the trust property make a more frequent exercise of
the right reasonable, cause the accounts of the trust property to be examined
or audited by an independent accountant, and shall, for that purpose,
produce such vouchers and give such information to him as he may require;
and the costs of such examination or audit, including the fee of the auditor,
shall be paid out of the capital or income of the trust property, or partly
in one way and partly in the other, as the trustees, in their absolute discretion, think fit, but, in default of any direction by the trustees to the
contrary in any special case, costs attributable to capital shall be borne by
capital and those attributable to income by income.

Public Trustee Act 1906

Investigation and audit of trust accounts

Section 13.—(1) Subject to rules under this Act and unless the court otherwise orders, the condition and acounts of any trust shall, on an application
being made and notice thereof given in the prescribed manner by any trustee
or beneficiary, be investigated and audited by such solicitor or public accountant as may be agreed on by the applicant and the trustees or, in default
of agreement, by the public trustee or some person appointed by him:

Provided that (except with the leave of the court) such an investigation
or audit shall not be required within twelve months after any such previous
investigation or audit, and that a trustee or beneficiary shall not be appointed
under this section to make an investigation or audit.

(2) The person making the investigation or audit (hereinafter called the
auditor) shall have a right of access to the books, acounts, and vouchers of
the trustees, and to any securities and documents of title held by them on
account of the trust, and may require from them such information and
explanation as may be necessary for the performance of his duties, and upon
the completion of the investigation and audit shall forward to the applicant
and to every trustee a copy of the accounts, together with a report thereon,
and a certificate signed by him to the effect that the accounts exhibit a true
view of the state of the affairs of the trust and that he has had the securities

of the trust fund investments produced to and verified by him (or as the case may be) that such accounts are deficient in such respects as may be specified in such certificate.

(3) Every beneficiary under the trust shall, subject to rules under this Act, be entitled at all reasonable times to inspect and take copies of the accounts, report, and certificate, and, at his own expense, to be furnished with copies thereof or extracts therefrom.

Note

Trustees must keep proper accounts and have them ready for inspection and examination.[99] If a trustee causes expense through neglect or refusal to furnish or keep accounts he has to bear that expense personally.[1] In general, beneficiaries have a right to investigate the accounts of their trustees.[2]

II. DUTY TO GIVE INFORMATION

Re LONDONDERRY'S SETTLEMENT, PEAT AND OTHERS v. WALSH

Court of Appeal [1965] Ch. 918; [1965] 2 W.L.R. 229; 108 S.J. 896; [1964] 3 All E.R. 855 (Harman, Danckwerts and Salmon L.JJ.)

On December 5, 1934, the seventh Marquess of Londonderry settled a trust fund upon trusts as to the capital for members of a specified class in such shares and generally in such manner as the trustees with the consent of certain named persons, called " the appointors," might in writing from time to time appoint. There were provisions in default of that appointment.

The settlement then directed the trustees to hold the income until disposal of the capital upon trust for such member or members of the same class as the trustees might from time to time within twelve months after the receipt of such income with the written consent of the appointors determine and subject thereto upon trust to pay an annuity of £5,000 to the settlor's wife and subject thereto to pay the income to the settlor's eldest son and after his death to the settlor's other children.

The settlor's wife and eldest son having died, the settlor's daughter, Lady Helen Maglona Walsh, became entitled to share in the income of the trust fund under the above gift of income in default of appointment. There were other children of the marriage.

The trustees had from time to time appointed considerable sums to various beneficiaries and in December 1962 they unanimously decided

---

[99] *Eglin* v. *Sanderson* (1862) 3 Giff. 434, 440; *Pearse* v. *Green* (1819) 1 Jac. & W. 135, 140. Where funds are given to parents to provide for the maintenance and education of their infant children the parents are under no duty to keep accounts to show the precise manner in which the funds have been spent provided that the infants have been maintained by the parents: *Browne* v. *Paull* (1850) 1 Sim.(N.S.) 92; *Re Rogers* [1944] Ch. 297 revealing that in such cases the funds are treated as a beneficial gift to the parents subject to an equitable charge for the maintenance and education of the infant children.

[1] *Re Skinner* [1904] 1 Ch. 289. *Cf. Heugh* v. *Scard* (1875) 33 L.T. 659.

[2] *Re Fish* [1893] 2 Ch. 413, 425.

with the consent of the appointors to make further substantial appointments of capital with a view to bringing the settlement to an end. The
settlor's daughter was dissatisfied with the amounts proposed to be
appointed to her and asked the trustees to supply her with copies of
various documents relating to the settlement. The trustees supplied
copies of the appointments and of the accounts up to date but refused
to disclose any other documents. The settlor's daughter remained
dissatisfied.

Accordingly on January 30, 1964, the trustees issued a summons,
to which the settlor's daughter was defendant, asking which, if any,
of the following documents the trustees were bound to disclose: (a) the
minutes of the meetings of the trustees of the settlement; (b) agendas
and other documents prepared for the purposes of the meetings or
otherwise for the consideration of the trustees; (c) correspondence
relating to the administration of the trust property or otherwise to the
execution of the trusts and passing between (i) the trustees and the
appointors; (ii) the trustees and the appointors on the one hand and
the solicitors to the trustees on the other; and (iii) the trustees and
the appointors on the one hand and the beneficiaries on the other.

Plowman J.[3] made a declaration that the trustees were bound to
disclose all the documents in the categories set out above.

HARMAN L.J.: " I have found this a difficult case. It raises what in
my judgment is a novel question on which there is no authority exactly
in point although several cases have been cited to us somewhere near it.
The court is really required here to resolve two principles that come
into conflict, or at least apparent conflict. The first is that . . . trustees
exercising a discretionary power are not bound to disclose to their
beneficiaries the reasons actuating them in coming to a decision. This
is a long-standing principle and rests largely, I think, on the view that
nobody could be called upon to accept a trusteeship involving the
exercise of a discretion unless, in the absence of bad faith, he were
not liable to have his motives or his reasons called in question either
by the beneficiaries or by the court. To this there is added a rider,
namely, that if trustees do give reasons, their soundness can be considered by the court. . . .

" It would seem on the face of it that there is no reason why this
principle should be confined to decisions orally arrived at and should
not extend to a case, like the present, where, owing to the complexity
of the trust and the large sums involved, the trustees, who act subject
to the consent of another body called the appointors, have brought into
existence various written documents, including, in particular, agenda
for and minutes of their meetings from time to time held in order to
consider distributions made of the fund and its income. It is here

---

[3] [1964] Ch. 594.

that the conflicting principle is said to emerge. All these documents, it is argued, came into existence for the purposes of the trust and are in the possession of the trustees as such and are, therefore, trust documents, the property of the beneficiaries, and as such open to them to inspect. . . .

" The judge, though he felt the strength of the trustees' submission that it was undesirable to wash family linen in public which would be productive only of family strife and also odium for the trustees and embarrassment in the performance of their duties, felt constrained by a decision of Kindersley V.-C. in *Talbot* v. *Marshfield*,[4] reported in (among other places) 2 Drewry & Smale. It now appears, however, in the light of documents obtained from the Record Office and the other reports of the case, notably in the *Weekly Reporter*[5] and *Law Reports* 4 *Equity*,[6] that this case was not at all in point. It was an action by beneficiaries against trustees who had a discretionary power, by making advancements to the tenants for life, to deprive the remaindermen. The matter came on first as a motion for an order on the trustees to pay into court. In the course of the hearing of that motion, the trustees stated their reasons for the action they proposed to take and were cross-examined. The court refused to order payment into court, whereupon the trustees distributed and the action proceeded as an action to administer the estate upon the footing of wilful default. There was an application for discovery and it was upon the hearing of this application that Kindersley V.-C. gave his decision. He ordered[7] the trustees to disclose a case to counsel and opinion taken by the trustees before the action was started and also a number of letters showing the trustees' intentions and their action in distributing other parts of the fund.

" The case and opinion were, of course, trust papers, having come into existence *ante litem motam*. Counsel was advising the trustees as to their rights and duties and every beneficiary must be entitled to seek advice of that sort. It is paid for out of the trust money and is the property of the beneficiaries. As to the letters, the trustees' objection seems to have been that as they were with beneficiaries of other shares in which the plaintiff was not interested, they were not relevant and need not be disclosed. This was overruled, as is not surprising, for the action was an action to administer the estate and the dealings of the trustees with all the shares was called in question. No point was taken that the trustees' exercise of their discretion was confidential. They had in fact already been cross-examined about it. I find nothing in this decision which helps us here.

" Apart from this, the defendant relied on certain observations in *O'Rourke* v. *Darbishire*.[8] The decision was that the plaintiff was not

---

[4] (1865) 2 Drew. & Sm. 549.
[5] 13 W.R. 885.
[6] (1867) L.R. 4 Eq. 661.
[7] 13 W.R. 885, 886.   [8] [1920] A.C. 581.

entitled to the production of what were called the ' trust documents,' and I find Lord Parmoor making this observation [9]: ' A *cestui que trust*, in an action against his trustees, is generally entitled to the production for inspection of all documents relating to the affairs of the trust. It is not material for the present purpose whether this right is to be regarded as a paramount proprietary right in the *cestui que trust*, or as a right to be enforced under the law of discovery.' Lord Wrenbury says [10]: ' If the plaintiff is right in saying that he is a beneficiary, and if the documents are documents belonging to the executors as executors, he has a right to access to the documents which he desires to inspect upon what has been called in the judgments in this case a proprietary right. The beneficiary is entitled to see all the trust documents because they are trust documents and because he is a beneficiary. They are in a sense his own. Action or no action, he is entitled to access to them. This has nothing to do with discovery. The right to discovery is a right to see someone else's documents. A proprietary right is a right to access to documents which are your own. No question of professional privilege arises in such a case. Documents containing professional advice taken by the executors as trustees contain advice taken by trustees for their *cestuis que trust*, and the beneficiaries are entitled to see them because they are beneficiaries.'

" General observations of this sort give very little guidance, for first they beg the question what are trust documents, and secondly their Lordships were not considering the point here that papers are asked for which bear on the question of the exercise of the trustees' discretion. In my judgment category (a) . . . *viz.*, the minutes of the meetings of the trustees . . . ; and part of (b), *viz.*, agenda prepared for trustees' meetings, are, in the absence of an action impugning the trustees' good faith, documents which a beneficiary cannot claim the right to inspect. If the defendant is allowed to examine these, she will know at once the very matters which the trustees are not bound to disclose to her, namely, their motives and reasons. Trustees who wish to preserve their rights in this respect must either commit nothing to paper or destroy everything from meeting to meeting. Indeed, if the defendant be right, I doubt if the last course is open, for she must succeed, if at all, on the ground that the papers belong to her, and if so, the trustees have no right to destroy them.

" I would hold that even if documents of this type ought properly to be described as trust documents, they are protected for the special reason which protects the trustees' deliberations on a discretionary matter from disclosure. If necessary, I hold that this principle overrides the ordinary rule. This is, in my judgment, no less in the true interest of the beneficiary than of the trustees. Again, if one of the

---

[9] *Ibid.* 619.
[10] *Ibid.* 626.

trustees commits to paper his suggestions and circulates them among his co-trustees; or if inquiries are made in writing as to the circumstances of a member of the class; I decline to hold that such documents are trust documents the property of the beneficiaries. . . . On the other hand, if the solicitor advising the trustees commits to paper an *aide-mémoire* summarising the state of the fund or of the family and reminding the trustees of past distributions and future possibilities, I think that must be a document which any beneficiary must be at liberty to inspect. It seems to me, therefore, that category (b) [as set out *supra*, p. 565] embraces documents on both sides of the line.

" As to (c) [as set out *supra*, p. 565] I cannot think that communications passing between individual trustees and appointors are documents in which beneficiaries have a proprietary right. On the other hand, as to category (ii) [as set out *supra*, p. 565], in general the letters of the trustees' solicitors to the trustees do seem to me to be trust documents in which the beneficiaries have a property. As to category (iii) [as set out *supra*, p. 565], I do not think letters to or from an individual beneficiary ought to be open to inspection by another beneficiary. . . ." [11]

SALMON L.J.: " The category of trust documents has never been comprehensively defined. Nor could it be—certainly not by me. Trust documents do, however, have these characteristics in common: (1) they are documents in the possession of the trustees as trustees; (2) they contain information about the trust which the beneficiaries are entitled to know; (3) the beneficiaries have a proprietary interest in the documents and, accordingly, are entitled to see them. If any parts of a document contain information which the beneficiaries are not entitled to know, I doubt whether such parts can truly be said to be integral parts of a trust document. Accordingly, any part of a document that lacked the second characteristic to which I have referred would automatically be excluded from the document in its character as a trust document.

" I agree with my Lords that the appeal should be allowed."

R. E. Megarry (1965) 81 L.Q.R. 196

" It seems safe to say that the last of *Re Londonderry's Settlement* has not been heard. Perhaps the most obvious point which may arise is whether a beneficiary who is determined to discover all he can about the grounds upon which a discretion has been exercised may not achieve this by instituting litigation alleging that the trustees have exercised their discretion in some improper way, and then obtaining discovery of documents in those proceedings, as in *Talbot* v. *Marshfield* (1865) 2 Drew. & Sm. 549. Will the courts permit the bonds of secrecy to be invaded by the simple process of commencing hostile litigation against the trustees? It is not easy to see how the

---

[11] See also *Re Cowin* (1886) 33 Ch.D. 179; *Re Bosworth* (1889) 55 L.J.Ch. 432; *Re Dartnall* [1895] 1 Ch. 474; *Tiger* v. *Barclays Bank Ltd.* [1952] W.N. 38; *Hawkesley* v. *May* [1956] 1 Q.B. 304; generally (1965) 81 L.Q.R. 192 (R. E. M.).

courts can prevent this. True, questions of relevance may obviously arise; but on discovery the test of relevance is wide. The classical statement is that of Brett L.J.: an applicant is entitled to discovery of any document ' which may fairly lead him to a train of inquiry ' that may ' either directly or indirectly enable the party requiring the affidavit either to advance his own case or to damage the case of his adversary ' (*Compagnie Financière et Commerciale du Pacifique* v. *Peruvian Guano Co.* (1882) 11 Q.B.D. 55 at 63). Indeed, the formal order of the court, . . . seems to recognise this possibility.

"The other main point which plainly needs further exploration is the ambit of the term ' trust documents.' The negative proposition is now plain: not all documents held by trustees as such are ' trust documents.' But even after a detailed examination of the judgments it is difficult to frame any positive proposition with any degree of confidence. Nor does the formal order of the court (see at p. 938) lessen the difficulty; indeed, it contributes its own quota of problems. The order states that without prejudice to any right of the defendant to discovery in any subsequent proceedings against the trustees, and subject to any order of the court in any particular circumstances, there are four categories of documents which the trustees are not bound to disclose to the defendant. The first of these categories is ' The agenda of the meetings of the trustees of the settlement '; the second and third categories consist of correspondence of the trustees *inter se* and with the beneficiaries; and the fourth category consists of minutes of the meetings of the trustees and other documents disclosing their deliberations as to the manner in which they should exercise their discretion or disclosing their reasons for any particular exercise of their discretion, or the materials therefor. It is thus only the minutes and the other documents in the fourth category which appear to be qualified by words relating to disclosure of the trustees' reasons for exercising their discretion in a particular way; the freedom from disclosure seems to apply to all agenda and correspondence, whether or not they would reveal any such reasons or the material on which they were based. Nor does the order make it plain how it applies to documents in the fourth category which not only disclose confidential matters but also deal with other points as well; the inclusion of any confidential matter seems to confer exemption upon the entire document, and not merely upon the confidential matter. The order did, however, declare that the trustees were bound to disclose to the defendant any written advice from their solicitors or counsel as to the manner in which the trustees were in law entitled to exercise their discretion.

"Putting all the material together, it seems at present to be difficult to say more than that all documents held by trustees *qua* trustees are prima facie trust documents, but that there is a class of exceptions from this rule which is ill-defined but includes confidential documents which the beneficiaries ought not to see. For greater precision than that we must await further decisions by the courts. The Court of Appeal has taken a firm step in the right direction; but that is all."

III. Distribution of Trust Property

A. *Maintenance*

The Trustee Act 1925

Power to apply income for maintenance and to accumulate surplus income during a minority [12]

Section 31.—(1) Where any property is held by trustees in trust for any person for any interest whatsoever, whether vested or contingent, then, subject to any prior interests [13] or charges affecting that property—

(i) during the infancy of any such person, if his interest so long continues, the trustees may, at their sole discretion, pay to his parent or guardian, if any, or otherwise apply for or towards his maintenance, education, or benefit, the whole or such part, if any, of the income of that property as may, in all the circumstances, be reasonable, whether or not there is—

   (a) any other fund applicable to the same purpose; or
   (b) any person bound by law to provide for his maintenance or education; and

(ii) if such person on attaining the age of [eighteen] [14] years has not a vested [15] interest in such income, the trustees shall [16] thenceforth pay the income of that property and of any accretion thereto under subsection (2) of this section to him, until he either attains a vested interest therein or dies, or until failure of his interest:

Provided that, in deciding whether the whole or any part of the income of the property is during a minority to be paid or applied for the purposes aforesaid, the trustees shall have regard to the age of the infant and his requirements and generally to the circumstances of the case, and in particular to what other income, if any, is applicable for the same purposes; and where trustees have notice that the income of more than one fund is

---

[12] See B. S. Ker, "Trustees' Power of Maintenance" (1953) 17 Conv.(N.S.) 273 and Wolstenholme & Cherry's *Conveyancing Statutes* Vol. 4 (13th ed., by J. T. Farrand).

[13] If there is a prior direction to set apart and accumulate income, the trustees have no power to apply intermediate income for maintenance under this section: *Re Reade-Revell* [1930] 1 Ch. 52, but the court may do so under its inherent jurisdiction: *Re Walker* [1901] 1 Ch. 879; *supra*, p. 526.

[14] Substituted by the Family Law Reform Act 1969, s. 1 (3), Sched. 1, Pt. I. For interests under any instruments made before Jan. 1, 1970, 21 years remain the relevant age: Sched. III, para. 5 (1). In such a case money may be paid direct to the beneficiary once he attains 18 instead of to his parent or guardian, Sched. III, para. 5 (2).

[15] The section does not apply if the person has a vested interest, even if it is liable to be divested: *Re McGeorge* [1963] Ch. 544.

[16] The word "shall" prima facie imports a "duty" as distinct from a "power." In this context, however, it imports a "power" which can be overridden by the expression of a contrary intention: see s. 69 (2) of the Trustee Act 1925; *Re Turner's Will Trusts* [1937] Ch. 15. Provisions made by the settlor or testator if inconsistent with the statutory power amount to contrary intention, *e.g.*, a direction to accumulate: *Re Erskine's S.T.* [1971] 1 W.L.R. 162, *Re Henderson's Trusts* [1969] 1 W.L.R. 651, 659. But if there is no contrary intention the trustees appear to be under a duty to pay the income to the beneficiary on his attaining the age of 18: *Re Jones' Will Trusts* [1947] Ch. 48. Even though the beneficiary may not be entitled to the capital till attaining 30 years of age the fact that he is entitled to the income will render the capital liable to estate duty. Accordingly, it is common expressly to oust this right to income until the right to capital has arisen but care must be taken not to infringe the rule against accumulations.

applicable for those purposes, then, so far as practicable, unless the entire income of the funds is paid or applied as aforesaid or the court otherwise directs, a proportionate part only of the income of each fund shall be so paid or applied.

(2) During the infancy of any such person, if his interest so long continues, the trustees shall accumulate [17] all the residue of that income in the way of compound interest by investing the same and the resulting income thereof from time to time in authorised investments, and shall hold those accumulations as follows:

    (i) If any such person—

          (*a*) attains the age of [eighteen] [18] years, or marries under that age, and his interest in such income during his infancy or until his marriage is a vested interest; or

          (*b*) on attaining the age of [eighteen] [19] years or on marriage under that age becomes entitled to the property from which such income arose in fee simple, absolute or determinable,[20] or absolutely,[21] or for an entailed interest;

    the trustees shall hold the accumulations in trust for such person absolutely, but without prejudice to any provision with respect thereto contained in any settlement by him made under any statutory powers during his infancy, and so that the receipt of such person after marriage, and though still an infant, shall be a good discharge; and

    (ii) In any other case the trustees shall, notwithstanding that such person had a vested interest in such income, hold the accumulations as an accretion to the capital of the property from which such accumulations arose,[22] and as one fund with such capital for all purposes, and so that, if such property is settled land, such accumulations shall be held upon the same trusts as if the same were capital money arising therefrom;

but the trustees may, at any time during the infancy of such person if his interest so long continues, apply those accumulations, or any part thereof, as if they were income arising in the then current year.

(3) This section applies in the case of a contingent interest only if the limitation or trust carries the intermediate income [23] of the property, but it applies to a future or contingent legacy by the parent of, or a person standing *in loco parentis* to, the legatee, if and for such period as, under the general law, the legacy carries interest for the maintenance of the legatee, and in any such case as last aforesaid the rate of interest shall (if

---

[17] See A. M. Pritchard [1973] C.L.J. 246.

[18] See n. 14 *supra*.

[19] See n. 14 *supra*.

[20] It seems this means a determinable fee in the strict sense distinct from a fee simple on condition: *Re Sharp's S.T.* [1973] Ch. 331.

[21] This applies exclusively to personalty and requires the interest in personalty to be indefeasible so that there is an odd distinction between realty and personalty: *Re Sharp's S.T.* (*supra*).

[22] Thus accumulations subject to an overriding power of appointment form an accretion to the respective shares of the beneficiaries subject to the overriding power: *Re Sharp's S.T.* [1973] Ch. 331 following *Re Joel's W.T.* [1967] Ch. 14.

[23] As to this, see s. 175 of the Law of Property Act 1925, *infra*; (1963) 79 L.Q.R. 184 (P. V. B.).

the income available is sufficient, and subject to any rules of court to the contrary) be five pounds per centum per annum.

(4) This section applies to a vested annuity in like manner as if the annuity were the income of property held by trustees in trust to pay the income thereof to the annuitant for the same period for which the annuity is payable, save that in any case accumulations made during the infancy of the annuitant shall be held in trust for the annuitant or his personal representatives absolutely.

(5) This section does not apply where the instrument, if any, under which the interest arises came into operation before the commencement of this Act.[24]

The Law of Property Act 1925

Contingent and future testamentary gifts carry intermediate income

Section 175.—(1) A contingent or future specific devise or bequest of property, whether real or personal, and a contingent residuary devise of freehold land, and a specific or residuary devise of freehold land to trustees upon trust for persons whose interests are contingent or executory shall, subject to the statutory provisions relating to accumulations, carry the intermediate income of that property from the death of the testator, except so far as such income, or part thereof, may be otherwise expressly disposed of.

(2) This section applies only to wills coming into operation after the commencement of this Act.

Note

Section 31 of the Trustee Act 1925, *supra*, enables income to be applied for the maintenance of an infant whose interest is vested unless the income is disposed of in favour of someone else or directed to be accumulated.[25] But if the infant's interest is contingent, income cannot be so applied unless the limitation or trust carries the intermediate income. The rules in regard to this are as follows:

1. A contingent gift by will of residuary personalty carries with it all the income which it produces after the testator's death: *Re Adams*.[26] If the income is accumulated until the contingency occurs, the rules in sections 164–166 of the Law of Property Act 1925, and section 13 of the Perpetuities and Accumulations Act 1964, which limit the period of accumulation, must be complied with: *Countess of Bective* v. *Hodgson*.[27] On the other hand, a residuary bequest, whether vested or contingent, which is expressly deferred to a future date does not carry intermediate income: *Re Oliver*[28]; *Re Gillett's Will Trusts*[29]; *Re Geering*.[30]

2. A contingent residuary devise of freehold land and a residuary devise of freehold land to trustees upon trust for persons, whose interests are contingent, carry the intermediate income which they produce: s. 175 of the Law of Property Act 1925, *supra*.

---

24 The section applies to an appointment made after 1925 under a power created before 1926: *Re Dickinson's Settlements* [1939] Ch. 27. S. 43 of the Conveyancing Act 1881, which was more limited in its scope than the present section, applies to instruments coming into operation before 1926.

25 *Re Turner's W.T.* [1937] Ch. 15; *Re Ransome* [1957] Ch. 348; *Re Reade-Revell* [1930] 1 Ch. 52; *Re Stapleton* [1946] 1 All E.R. 323.

26 [1893] 1 Ch. 329, 334.

27 (1864) 10 H.L.C. 656.

28 [1947] 2 All E.R. 162, 166.

29 [1950] Ch. 102.

30 [1964] Ch. 136.

3. A contingent or future specific bequest of personalty carries the intermediate income: *ibid.*

4. So does a contingent or future specific devise of realty: *Re McGeorge*,[31] *infra.*

5. But a general or pecuniary contingent legacy does not carry intermediate income: *Re Raine*,[32] unless *either*

(a) The testator was the father of, or *in loco parentis* to, the infant legatee. The gift must be made direct to the infant and not to trustees for him: *Re Pollock*.[33] If the legacy is contingent, the contingency must have reference to the infancy of the legatee, *i.e.*, must not be the attaining of an age greater than eighteen: *Re Abrahams*.[34] Finally no other fund must be set aside for the maintenance of the infant: *Re West*.[35] In this case, the legacy carries interest at 5 per cent.: s. 31 (3) of the Trustee Act 1925, *supra*; *or*

(b) The testator shows an intention that the income shall be used for the maintenance: *Re Churchill*,[36] or education: *Re Selby-Walker*,[37] of the infant. In this case the testator need not be the parent of the legatee: the contingency may be the attaining of an age greater than twenty-one: *Re Jones*[37a]; and the rate of interest is 5 per cent.[38]; *or*

(c) The testator directs the legacy to be set apart from the rest of his estate for the benefit of the legatee: *Re Medlock*,[39] cf. *Re Judkin's Trusts*.[40] In this case, also, the rate of interest is 5 per cent.

Intermediate income is, however, carried from the date when the legacy itself is payable.[41]

Tax considerations should always be borne in mind. Income applied for an infant unmarried child of the settlor is treated as the settlor's income.[42] Moreover, any sum paid out of trust funds to the settlor's child is treated as income and not capital to an amount equal to the total undistributed income of the trust to that date.[43] The 1974 Labour Government intends to reintroduce the rule applicable from 1969–72 that all the income of an infant unmarried child not regularly working is to be aggregated with the parents' income.[44]

Re McGEORGE

Chancery Division [1963] Ch. 544; [1963] 2 W.L.R. 767; 107 S.J. 253; [1963] 1 All E.R. 519

A testator devised land to his daughter and declared that " the devise . . . shall not take effect until after the death of my wife should she survive me." The testator also provided that if the daughter should die during the lifetime of the wife leaving issue, then the issue on attaining twenty-one were to " take by substitution the aforesaid devise in favour of " the daughter. The testator bequeathed his residuary

---

[31] [1963] Ch. 544.
[32] [1929] 1 Ch. 716.
[33] [1943] Ch. 338.
[34] [1911] 1 Ch. 108.
[35] [1913] 2 Ch. 345.
[36] [1909] 2 Ch. 431.
[37] [1949] 2 All E.R. 178.
[37a] [1932] 1 Ch. 108.
[38] R.S.C., Ord. 44, r. 19 as amended by S.I. 1972 No. 1898, r. 6.
[39] (1886) 55 L.J.Ch. 738.
[40] (1884) 25 Ch.D. 743.
[41] *Re Hall* [1951] W.N. 231; *Re Raine* [1929] 1 Ch. 716.
[42] ss. 437–444 Income and Corporation Taxes Act 1970.
[43] s. 438 (2) (3) (*ibid.*).
[44] See Income and Corporation Taxes, s. 43, for the former provisions.

estate on trust for his wife for life and after her death to be divided equally between his son and daughter.

CROSS J. held that the declaration that the devise should not take effect until a future time deferred its vesting in possession until that time but not its vesting in interest, read the terms of section 175 of the Law of Property Act 1925, *supra*, and continued:

" The devise is, it is said, a future specific devise within the meaning of the section; the testator has not made any express disposition of the income accruing from it between his death and the death of his widow, and so that income is carried by the gift. At first sight it is hard to see how Parliament could have enacted a section which produces such a result. If a testator gives property to A after the death of B, then whether or not he disposes of the income accruing during B's life he is at all events showing clearly that A is not to have it. Yet if the future gift to A is absolute and the intermediate income is carried with it by force of this section, A can claim to have the property transferred to him at once, since no one else can be interested in it. The section, that is to say, will have converted a gift in remainder into a gift in possession in defiance of the testator's wishes. The explanation for the section taking the form which it does is, I think, probably as follows. It has long been established that a gift of residuary personalty to a legatee in being on a contingency or to an unborn person at birth carried the intermediate income so far as the law would allow it to be accumulated, but that rule had been held, for reasons depending on the old land law, not to apply to gifts of real property, and it was apparently never applied to specific dispositions of personalty. Section 175 of the Law of Property Act 1925 was plainly intended to extend the rule to residuary devises and to specific gifts whether of realty or of personalty. It is now established, at all events so far as courts of first instance are concerned, that the old rule does not apply to residuary bequests whether vested or contingent which are expressly deferred to a future date which must come sooner or later (see *Re Oliver*,[45] *Re Gillett's Will Trusts*[46] and *Re Geering*[47]). There is a good reason for this distinction. If a testator gives property to X contingently on his attaining the age of thirty it is reasonable to assume, in the absence of a direction to the contrary, that the testator would wish X, if he attains thirty, to have the income produced by the property between the testator's death and the happening of the contingency. If, on the other hand, he gives property to X for any sort of interest after the death of A, it is reasonable to assume that he does not wish X to have the income accruing during A's lifetime unless he directs that he is to have it. This distinction between an immediate gift on a contingency and a gift which is expressly deferred was not drawn until after the Law of Property Act 1925 was passed. There were statements in textbooks and even in

---

[45] [1947] L.J.R. 1400.
[46] [1950] Ch. 102.   [47] [1964] Ch. 136.

judgments to the effect that the rule applied to deferred as well as to contingent gifts of residuary personalty.[48] The legislature, when it extended this rule to residuary devises and specific gifts, must, I think, have adopted this erroneous view of the law. I would have liked, if I could, to construe the reference to 'future specific devises' and 'executory interest' in section 175 (1) of the Act of 1925 in such a way as to make it consistent with the recent cases on the scope of the old rule applicable to residuary bequests. To do that, however, would be to rectify the Act, not to construe it, and I see no escape from the conclusion that whereas before 1926 a specific gift or a residuary devise which was not vested in possession did not prima facie carry intermediate income at all, now such a gift may carry intermediate income in circumstances in which a residuary bequest would not carry it.

" It was argued in this case that the fact that the will contained a residuary gift constituted an express disposition of the income of the land in question which prevented the section from applying. I am afraid that I cannot accept this submission. I have little doubt that the testator expected the income of the land to form part of the income of residue during his widow's lifetime, but he has made no express disposition of it. I agree with what was said in this connection by Eve J. in *Re Raine*.[49] As the devise is not vested indefeasibly in the daughter but is subject to defeasance during the mother's lifetime the intermediate income which the gift carries by virtue of section 175 ought prima facie to be accumulated to see who eventually becomes entitled to it. It was, however, submitted by counsel for the daughter that she could claim payment of it under section 31 (1) of the Trustee Act 1925. [His Lordship summarised the subsection, and continued:] There are, as I see it, two answers to the daughter's claim. The first— and narrower—answer is that her interest in the income of the devised land is a vested interest. It is a future interest liable to be divested but it is not contingent. Therefore section 31 (1) does not apply to it. The second—and wider—answer is that the whole framework of section 31 shows that it is inapplicable to a future gift of this sort and that a will containing such a gift expresses a contrary intention within section 69 (2) which prevents the subsection from applying. By deferring the enjoyment of the devise until after the widow's death the testator has expressed the intention that the daughter shall not have the immediate income. It is true that as he has not expressly disposed of it in any other way, section 175 of the Law of Property Act 1925 defeats that intention to the extent of making the future devise carry the income, so that the daughter will get it eventually, if she survives her mother or dies before her leaving no children to take

---

[48] See *Jarman on Wills* (7th ed.), p. 1006.
[49] [1929] 1 Ch. 716, 719.

by substitution. Even if, however, the words of section 31 (1) of the Trustee Act 1925 fitted the case, there would be no warrant for defeating the testator's intention still further by reading section 31 (1) into the will and thus giving the daughter an interest in possession in the income during her mother's lifetime. In the result, the income ... must be accumulated, in my judgment, for twenty-one years if the widow so long lives."

B. *Advancement* [50]

The power of advancement in section 32 of the Trustee Act 1925 is much used as a way of reducing the size of a trust fund thereby reducing the ultimate liability to estate duty. However, in the Court of Appeal's words in *Re Pauling's S.T.*,[51] " Being a fiduciary power, it seems to us quite clear that the power can be exercised only if it is for the benefit of the child or remoter issue to be advanced or, as was said during argument, it is thought to be ' a good thing ' for the advanced person to have a share of capital before his or her due time. That this must be so, we think, follows from a consideration of the fact that the parties to a settlement intend the normal trusts to take effect, and that a power of advancement be exercised only if there is some good reason for it. That good reason must be beneficial to the person to be advanced; the power cannot be exercised capriciously or with some other benefit in view.[52] The trustees, before exercising the power have to weigh on the one side the benefit to the proposed advancee, and on the other hand the rights of those who are or may hereafter become interested under the trusts of the settlement."

It is no objection to an advancement that someone other than a beneficiary under the settlement is benefited so long as the beneficiary receives the primary benefit as a whole, *e.g.*,[53] receiving a life interest in the advanced moneys with remainder to his widow for life, remainder to his children equally. In such a case the beneficiary will often not have been alive at the date of the creation of the settlement so that great care must be taken to ensure that the rule against remoteness is not infringed, for the perpetuity period relevant to the exercise of the power of advancement runs from the date of the settlement and not from the date of the exercise of the power [54]: *Pilkington* v. *I.R.C., infra.* If part of the exercise of the power of advancement is void for remoteness *and* the resultant effect of the intended advancement is such that it could not reasonably be regarded as being beneficial to the beneficiary intended to be advanced, then the advancement fails for it cannot be authorised as within the powers of the trustees under section 32: otherwise the part of the advancement not void for remoteness will

---

50 See D. W. M. Waters, " The ' New ' Power of Advancement " (1958) 22 Conv.(N.S.) 413; (1959) 23 Conv.(N.S.) 27, 423; Wolstenholme & Cherry's *Conveyancing Statutes*, Vol. 4 (13th ed. by J. T. Farrand).
51 [1964] Ch. 303.
52 *e.g.*, an advancement to an 18-year-old beneficiary so that he can let his father have it all for some purpose of the father.
53 *Pilkington* v. *I.R.C., infra*, p. 578.
54 The exercise of a power of advancement is treated as the exercise of a special power so that the Perpetuities and Accumulations Act 1964 is of no avail unless the original settlement was created after July 15, 1964: s. 15 (5) of the Perpetuities and Accumulations Act 1964.

stand as within the trustees' powers,[55] *e.g.,* C's life interest stands where the advancement is to C for life with remainders to his issue where the remainders are void for remoteness. The fact that in such a case no effective beneficial trusts of capital are created does not mean that there has been no payment or application of capital as required by section 32: the transfer of capital to the trustees of the sub-settlement for C for life is an application of capital within section 32.[56]

The Trustee Act 1925

Section 32.—(1) Trustees may [57] at any time or times pay or apply any capital money [58] subject to a trust, for the advancement or benefit, in such manner as they may, in their absolute discretion, think fit, of any person entitled to the capital [59] of the trust property or of any share thereof, whether absolutely or contingently on his attaining any specified age or on the occurrence of any other event, or subject to a gift over on his death under any specified age or on the occurrence of any other event, and whether in possession or in remainder or reversion, and such payment or application may be made notwithstanding that the interest of such person is liable to be defeated by the exercise of a power of appointment or revocation, or to be diminished by the increase of the class to which he belongs:

Provided that—

(a) the money so paid or applied for the advancement or benefit of any person shall not exceed altogether in amount one-half [60] of the presumptive or vested share or interest of that person in the trust property; and

(b) if that person is or becomes absolutely and indefeasibly entitled

---

[55] *Re Abraham's W.T.* [1969] 1 Ch. 463 as cut down by the interpretation of the Court of Appeal in *Re Hastings-Bass* [1974] 2 All E.R. 193.

[56] *Re Hastings-Bass* [1974] 2 All E.R. 193. At p. 203 the court laid down the general proposition, " where by the terms of a trust (as under s. 32) a trustee is given a discretion as to some matter under which he acts in good faith, the court should not interfere with his action notwithstanding that it does not have the full effect intended unless (1) what he has achieved is unauthorised by the power conferred on him or (2) it is clear that he would not have acted as he did (a) had he not taken into account considerations which he should not have taken into account or (b) had he not failed to take into account considerations which he ought to have taken into account."

[57] The section confers a power: it does not impose a duty: hence it cannot be utilised if the settlement contains a contrary intention: see *Inland Revenue Commissioners* v. *Bernstein* [1960] Ch. 444 (Danckwerts J.); [1961] Ch. 399 (C.A.); *Re Henderson's Trusts* [1969] 1 W.L.R. 651; *Re Evans Settlement* [1967] 1 W.L.R. 1294. Whilst a duty to accumulate is necessarily inconsistent with the power of maintenance it is not necessarily inconsistent with the power of advancement: *I.R.C.* v. *Bernstein* [1961] Ch. 399.

[58] Assets can be transferred *in specie*: *Re Collard's W.T.* [1961] Ch. 293 noted (1961) 77 L.Q.R. 161.

[59] The section does not apply where the beneficiary is given only an interest in income: *Re Winch's Settlement* [1917] 1 Ch. 633.

[60] If A and B are the two beneficiaries contingently equally entitled to a trust fund of £200,000 and B receives the maximum advancement of £50,000 does this mean that the power can no longer be exercised in his favour or if the fund remaining appreciates to £250,000 can B maintain that the fund is now notionally worth £250,000 plus his advanced £50,000 so that an advancement of half of half of £300,000, *i.e.,* £75,000, may be made to him so that he may receive a further £25,000 on top of the £50,000 he has already received? What if B had originally received only £40,000?

to a share in the trust property the money so paid or applied shall be brought into account as part of such share; and

(c) no such payment or application shall be made so as to prejudice any person entitled to any prior life or other interest,[61] whether vested or contingent, in the money paid or applied unless such person is in existence and of full age and consents in writing to such payment or application.

(2) This section applies only where the trust property consists of money [62] or securities or of property held upon trust for sale calling in and conversion, and such money or securities, or the proceeds of such sale calling in and conversion are not by statute or in equity considered as land, or applicable as capital money for the purposes of the Settled Land Act 1925.

(3) This section does not apply to trusts constituted or created before the commencement of this Act.

PILKINGTON AND ANOTHER v. INLAND REVENUE COMMISSIONERS

House of Lords [1964] A.C. 612; [1962] 3 W.L.R. 1051; 106 S.J. 834; [1962] 3 All E.R. 622; 40 T.C. 416 (Viscount Radcliffe, Lords Reid, Jenkins, Hodson and Devlin)

By his will dated December 14, 1934, the testator, William Norman Pilkington, who died on February 8, 1935, left his residuary estate to trustees on trust, in the events which happened, for his nephew, Richard Godfrey Pilkington (hereinafter called "Richard"), upon protective trusts during his life with a provision that any consent which he might give to the exercise of any applicable form of advancement should not cause a forfeiture of his life interest. After Richard's death the trustees were to hold the residuary estate upon trust for such of Richard's children or remoter issue at such age in such shares and with such trusts for their respective benefit and such provisions for their respective advancement and maintenance and education as Richard should by deed or will without transgressing the rule against perpetuities appoint. In default of appointment the trustees were to hold the residuary estate on trust for such of Richard's children as, being male, attained the age of twenty-one, or, being female, attained that age or married under it. and, if more than one, in equal shares.

The testator's will did not confer any express power of advancement

---

[61] An object of a discretionary trust is not entitled to such a prior interest as to render his consent requisite: *Re Beckett's Settlement* [1940] Ch. 279 but where income is held on the protective trusts in Trustee Act 1925, s. 33, and there has been no forfeiture the " principal beneficiary " has a prior interest within para. (c) his consent not incurring a forfeiture: *Re Harris' Settlement* (1940) 162 L.T. 358; *Re Rees' W.T.* [1954] Ch. 202.

[62] If the trust is a testamentary one and the testator dies after 1925, the power contained in s. 32 of the Act, *supra*, is available to the trustees: *Re Taylor's Will Trusts* (1950) 66 T.L.R.(Pt. 2) 507. *Aliter* if the trusts arose under a special power of appointment created before 1926 but exercised after 1925: *Re Batty* [1952] Ch. 280; criticised (1952) 68 L.Q.R. 319 (J. H. C. M., citing *Re Stimpson* [1931] 2 Ch. 77).

upon the trustees, but, by implication, the power of advancement
under section 32 of the Trustee Act 1925, *supra*, was applicable.

Richard had three children, of whom the defendant Penelope Margaret Pilkington (hereinafter called " Miss Penelope ") was one.

Richard's father, Guy Reginald Pilkington (hereinafter called " the
settlor "), proposed to make a settlement, to be executed by himself,
Richard and the trustees of the testator's will, upon the following trusts:
(i) Until Miss Penelope attained the age of twenty-one the trustees of
the settlement were to have power to apply income for her maintenance
whether or not there was any other income available for that purpose
and were to accumulate and capitalise surplus income; (ii) If Miss
Penelope attained the age of twenty-one the trustees were to be under a
duty to pay the income to her until she reached the age of thirty or
died under that age; (iii) If Miss Penelope attained the age of thirty the
trustees were to hold the capital of the trust fund upon trust for her
absolutely; (iv) If Miss Penelope died under the age of thirty, leaving
a child or children who attained the age of twenty-one, the trustees
were to hold the trust fund and the income thereof in trust for such
child or children, and, if more than one, in equal shares.

Subject to these trusts, the trustees of the settlement were to hold the
trust fund in trust equally for all of Richard's children (other than
Miss Penelope) who, being male, attained the age of twenty-one, or,
being female, attained that age or married under it.

In the case of the failure of the trust, the fund was to be held on
the trusts of the testator's will which would take effect after Richard's
death as if he had died without having been married.

The proposed settlement provided that the power of maintenance
contained in section 31 of the Trustee Act 1925, subject to certain
modifications, and the power of advancement contained in section 32
of the Act in an unmodified form, should be available to the trustees.

The trustees of the testator's will took out an originating summons
for the determination of the question whether they as such trustees
could lawfully exercise the powers conferred on them in relation to the
expectant interest of the defendant Miss Penelope, in the testator's
residuary estate by applying (with the consent of the defendant Richard,
her father) some part not exceeding one-half of the capital of such
interest in such manner as to make it subject to the trusts, powers and
provisions of the settlement proposed to be executed by the plaintiff, the
settlor, or whether such application would be improper and unauthorised.
Danckwerts J.[63] held that the exercise of the power of advancement in
this way would not be objectionable; but his decision was reversed by
the Court of Appeal.[64] Richard and Miss Penelope appealed.

VISCOUNT RADCLIFFE: " The word ' advancement ' itself meant in
this context the establishment in life of the beneficiary who was the

---

[63] [1959] Ch. 699.
[64] [1961] Ch. 466.

object of the power or at any rate some step that would contribute to the furtherance of his establishment. Thus it was found in such phrases as ' preferment or advancement ' (*Lowther* v. *Bentinck* [65]), ' business, profession, or employment or . . . advancement or preferment in the world ' (*Roper-Curzon* v. *Roper-Curzon* [66]) and ' placing out or advancement in life ' (*Re Breeds' Will* [67]). Typical instances of expenditure for such purposes under the social conditions of the nineteenth century were an apprenticeship or the purchase of a commission in the Army or of an interest in business. In the case of a girl there could be advancement on marriage (*Lloyd* v. *Cocker* [68]). Advancement had, however, to some extent a limited range of meaning, since it was thought to convey the idea of some step in life of permanent significance, and accordingly, to prevent uncertainties about the permitted range of objects for which moneys could be raised and made available, such words as ' or otherwise for his or her benefit ' were often added to the word ' advancement '. It was always recognised that these added words were ' large words ' (see Jessel M.R. in *Re Breeds' Will* [69]) and indeed in another case (*Lowther* v. *Bentinck* [70]) the same judge spoke of preferment and advancement as being ' both large words ' but of ' benefit ' as being the ' largest of all." So, too, Kay J. in *Re Brittlebank*.[71] Recent judges have spoken in the same terms—see Farwell J. in *Re Halsted's Will Trusts* [72] and Danckwerts J. in *Re Moxon's Will Trusts*.[73] This wide construction of the range of the power, which evidently did not stand upon niceties of distinction provided that the proposed application could fairly be regarded as for the benefit of the beneficiary who was the object of the power, must have been carried into the statutory power created by section 32, since it adopts without qualification the accustomed wording ' for the advancement or benefit in such manner as they may in their absolute discretion think fit.'

" So much for ' advancement,' which I now use for brevity to cover the combined phrase ' advancement or benefit.' It means any use of the money which will improve the material situation of the beneficiary. It is important, however, not to confuse the idea of ' advancement ' with the idea of advancing the money out of the beneficiary's expectant interest. The two things have only a casual connection with each other. The one refers to the operation of finding money by way of anticipation of an interest not yet absolutely vested in possession or, if so vested, belonging to an infant: the other refers to the status of the beneficiary and the improvement of his situation. The power to carry out the operation of anticipating an interest is not conferred by the word ' advancement ' but by those other words

---

[65] (1874) L.R. 19 Eq. 166.
[66] (1871) L.R. 11 Eq. 452.
[68] (1860) 27 Beav. 645.
[70] (1874) L.R. 19 Eq. 166, 169.
[72] [1937] 2 All E.R. 570, 571.

[67] (1875) 1 Ch.D. 226.
[69] (1875) 1 Ch.D. 226, 228.
[71] (1881) 30 W.R. 99, 100.
[73] [1958] 1 W.L.R. 165, 168.

of the section which expressly authorise the payment or application
of capital money for the benefit of a person entitled ' whether absolutely or contingently on his attaining any specified age or on the
occurrence of any other event, or subject to a gift over on his death
under any specified age or on the occurrence of any other event, and
whether in possession or in remainder or reversion,' etc.

"I think, with all respect to the Commissioners, a good deal of
their argument is infected with some of this confusion. To say, for
instance, that there cannot be a valid exercise of a power of advancement that results in a deferment of the vesting of the beneficiary's
absolute title (Miss Penelope, it will be remembered, is to take at
thirty under the proposed settlement instead of at twenty-one under
the will) is in my opinion to play upon words. The element of anticipation consists in the raising of money for her now before she has
any right to receive anything under the existing trusts: the advancement consists in the application of that money to form a trust fund,
the provisions of which are thought to be for her benefit. I have
not forgotten, of course, the references to powers of advancement which
are found in such cases as *Re Joicey*,[74] *Re May's Settlement*[75] and
Re Mewburn's Settlement,[76] to which our attention was called, or the
answer supplied by Cotton L.J. in *Re Aldridge*[77] to his own question
' What is advancement? '; but I think that it will be apparent from
what I have already said that the description that he gives (it cannot
be a definition) is confined entirely to the aspect of anticipation or
acceleration which renders the money available and not to any description
or limitation of the purposes for which it can then be applied.

"I have not been able to find in the words of section 32, to which
I have now referred, anything which in terms or by implication restricts
the width of the manner or purpose of advancement. It is true
that, if this settlement is made, Miss Penelope's children, who are
not objects of the power, are given a possible interest in the event of
her dying under thirty leaving surviving issue. But if the disposition
itself, by which I mean the whole provision made, is for her benefit,
it is no objection to the exercise of the power that other persons
benefit incidentally as a result of the exercise. Thus a man's creditors
may in certain cases get the most immediate advantage from an advancement made for the purpose of paying them off, as in *Lowther* v. *Bentinck*;
and a power to raise money for the advancement of a wife may cover
a payment made direct to her husband in order to set him up in
business (*Re Kershaw's Trusts*[78]). The exercise will not be bad,
therefore, on this ground.

---

[74] [1915] 2 Ch. 115 (C.A.).
[75] [1926] Ch. 136.
[76] [1934] Ch. 112.
[77] (1886) 55 L.T. 554, 556 (C.A.): " It is a payment to persons who are presumably
entitled to, or have a vested or contingent interest in, an estate or a legacy, before
the time fixed by the will for their obtaining the absolute interest in a portion or
the whole of that to which they would be entitled."   [78] (1868) L.R. 6 Eq. 322.

" Nor in my opinion will it be bad merely because the moneys are
to be tied up in the proposed settlement. If it could be said that the
payment or application permitted by section 32 cannot take the form
of a settlement in any form but must somehow pass direct into or
through the hands of the object of the power, I could appreciate the
principle upon which the Commissioners' objection was founded. But
can that principle be asserted? Anyone can see, I think, that there
can be circumstances in which, while it is very desirable that some
money should be raised at once for the benefit of an owner of an
expectant or contingent interest, it would be very undesirable that the
money should not be secured to him under some arrangement that
will prevent him having the absolute disposition of it. I find it very
difficult to think that there is something at the back of section 32
which makes such an advancement impossible. Certainly neither
Danckwerts J. nor the members of the Court of Appeal in this case
took the view. Both Lord Evershed M.R. and Upjohn L.J.[79] explicitly
accept the possibility of a settlement being made in exercise of a
power of advancement. Farwell J. authorised one in *Re Halsted's
Will Trusts*,[80] a case in which the trustees had left their discretion to the
court. The trustees should raise the money and ' have ' it ' settled,'
he said. So, too, Harman J. in *Re Ropner's Settlement Trusts*[81]
authorised the settlement of an advance provided for an infant, saying
that the child could not ' consent or request the trustees to make the
advance, but the transfer of a part of his contingent share to the trustees
of a settlement for him must advance his interest and thus be for his
benefit . . .' All this must be wrong in principle if a power of
advancement cannot cover an application of the moneys by way of
settlement.

" The truth is, I think, that the propriety of requiring a settlement of moneys found for advancement was recognised as long ago
as 1871 in *Roper-Curzon* v. *Roper-Curzon* and, so far as I know, it
has not been impugned since. Lord Romilly M.R.'s decision passed
into the textbooks and it must have formed the basis of a good deal
of subsequent practice. True enough, as counsel for the Commissioners
has reminded us, the beneficiary in that case was an adult who was
offering to execute the post-nuptial settlement required: but I find
it impossible to read Lord Romilly's words as amounting to anything
less than a decision that he would permit an advancement under the
power only on the terms that the money was to be secured by settlement. That was what the case was about. If, then, it is a proper
exercise of a power of advancement for trustees to stipulate that the
money shall be settled, I cannot see any difference between having it
settled that way and having it settled by themselves paying it to
trustees of a settlement which is in the desired form.

---

[79] [1961] Ch. 466, 481, 486.
[80] [1937] 2 All E.R. 570, 572. [81] [1956] 1 W.L.R. 902, 906.

"It is not as if anyone were contending for a principle that a power of advancement cannot be exercised 'over the head' of a beneficiary, that is, unless he actually asks for the money to be raised and consents to its application. From some points of view that might be a satisfactory limitation, and no doubt it is the way in which an advancement takes place in the great majority of cases. But, if application and consent were necessary requisites of advancement, that would cut out the possibility of making any advancement for the benefit of a person under age, at any rate without the institution of court proceedings and formal representation of the infant: and it would mean, moreover, that the trustees of an adult could not in any circumstances insist on raising money to pay his debts, however much the operation might be to his benefit, unless he agreed to that course. Counsel for the Commissioners did not contend before us that the power of advancement was inherently limited in this way: and I do not think that such a limitation would accord with the general understanding. Indeed its 'paternal' nature is well shown by the fact that it is often treated as being peculiarly for the assistance of an infant.

"The Commissioners' objections seem to be concentrated upon such propositions as that the proposed transaction is 'nothing less than a resettlement' and that a power of advancement cannot be used so as to alter or vary the trusts created by the settlement from which it is derived. Such a transaction, they say, amounts to using the power of advancement as a way of appointing or declaring new trusts different from those of the settlement. The reason why I do not find that these propositions have any compulsive effect upon my mind is that they seem to me merely vivid ways of describing the substantial effect of that which is proposed to be done and they do not in themselves amount to convincing arguments against doing it. Of course, whenever money is raised for advancement on terms that it is to be settled on the beneficiary, the money only passes from one settlement to be caught up in the other. It is therefore the same thing as a resettlement. But, unless one is to say that such moneys can never be applied by way of settlement, an argument which, as I have shown, has few supporters and is contrary to authority, it merely describes the inevitable effect of such an advancement to say that it is nothing less than a resettlement. Similarly, if it is part of the trusts and powers created by one settlement that the trustees of it should have power to raise money and make it available for a beneficiary upon new trusts approved by them, then they are in substance given power to free the money from one trust and to subject it to another. So be it: but, unless they cannot require a settlement of it at all, the transaction they carry out is the same thing in effect as an appointment of new trusts.

"In the same way I am unconvinced by the argument that the trustees would be improperly delegating their trust by allowing the money raised to pass over to new trustees under a settlement conferring new powers on the latter. In fact I think that the whole issue of delegation is here beside the mark. The law is not that trustees cannot delegate: it is that trustees cannot delegate unless they have authority to do so. If the power of advancement which they possess is so read as to allow them to raise money for the purpose of having it settled, then they do have the necessary authority to let the money pass out of the old settlement into the new trusts. No question of delegation of their powers or trusts arises. If, on the other hand, their power of advancement is read so as to exclude settled advances, *cadit quaestio.*

"I ought to note for the record (1) that the transaction envisaged does not actually involve the raising of money, since the trustees propose to appropriate a block of shares in the family's private limited company as the trust investment, and (2) there will not be any actual transfer, since the trustees of the proposed settlement and the will trustees are the same persons. As I have already said, I do not attach any importance to these factors, nor, I think, do the Commissioners. To transfer or appropriate outright is only to do by short cut what could be done in a more roundabout way by selling the shares to a consenting party, paying the money over to the new settlement with appropriate instructions and arranging for it to be used in buying back the shares as the trust investment. It cannot make any difference to follow the course taken in *Re Collard's Will Trusts* [82] and deal with the property direct. On the other point, so long as there are separate trusts, the property effectually passes out of the old settlement into the new one, and it is of no relevance that, at any rate for the time being, the persons administering the new trusts are the same individuals.

"I have not yet referred to the ground which was taken by the Court of Appeal as their reason for saying that the proposed settlement was not permissible. To put it shortly, they held that the statutory power of advancement could not be exercised unless the benefit to be conferred was 'personal to the person concerned, in the sense of being related to his or her own real or personal needs.' [83] Or, to use other words of the learned Master of the Rolls, [84] the exercise of the power 'must be an exercise done to meet the circumstances as they present themselves in regard to a person within the scope of the section, whose circumstances call for that to be done which the trustees think fit to do.' Upjohn L.J. [85] expressed himself in virtually the same terms.

"My Lords, I differ with reluctance from the views of judges so learned and experienced in matters of this sort: but I do not find it possible to import such restrictions into the words of the statutory power which itself does not contain them. First, the suggested qualification, that the considerations or circumstances must be 'personal' to the beneficiary, seems to me uncontrollably vague as a guide to general administration. What distinguishes a personal need from any

---

[82] [1961] Ch. 293.
[84] [1961] Ch. 466, 481.
[83] *Ibid.* 484.
[85] *Ibid.*

other need to which the trustees in their discretion think it right to attend in the beneficiary's interest? And, if the advantage of preserving the funds of a beneficiary from the incidence of death duty is not an advantage personal to that beneficiary, I do not see what is. Death duty is a present risk that attaches to the settled property in which Miss Penelope has her expectant interest, and even accepting the validity of the supposed limitation, I would not have supposed that there was anything either impersonal or unduly remote in the advantage to be conferred upon her of some exemption from that risk. I do not think, therefore, that I can support the interpretation of the power of advancement that has commended itself to the Court of Appeal, and, with great respect, I think that the judgments really amount to little more than a decision that in the opinion of the members of that court this was not a case in which there was any occasion to exercise the power. That would be a proper answer from a court to which trustees had referred their discretion with a request for its directions; but it does not really solve any question where, as here, they retain their discretion and merely ask whether it is impossible for them to exercise it.

" To conclude, therefore, on this issue, I am of opinion that there is no maintainable reason for introducing into the statutory power of advancement a qualification that would exclude the exercise in the case now before us. It would not be candid to omit to say that, though I think that that is what the law requires, I am uneasy at some of the possible applications of this liberty, when advancements are made for the purposes of settlement or on terms that there is to be a settlement. It is quite true, as the Commissioners have pointed out, that you might have really extravagant cases of resettlements being forced on beneficiaries in the name of advancement, even a few months before an absolute vesting in possession would have destroyed the power. I have tried to give due weight to such possibilities, but when all is said I do not think that they ought to compel us to introduce a limitation of which no one, with all respect, can produce a satisfactory definition. First, I do not believe that it is wise to try to cut down an admittedly wide and discretionary power, enacted for general use, through fear of its being abused in certain hypothetical instances. And moreover, as regards this fear, I think that it must be remembered that we are speaking of a power intended to be in the hands of trustees chosen by a settlor because of his confidence in their discretion and good sense and subject to the external check that no exercise can take place without the consent of a prior life-tenant; and that there does remain at all times a residual power in the court to restrain or correct any purported exercise that can be shown to be merely wanton or capricious and not to be attributable to a genuine discretion. I think, therefore, that, although extravagant possibilities exist, they may be more menacing in argument than in real life. . . ."

[However, their Lordships also held that the power of advancement under section 32 was to be regarded in the same way as a special
power of appointment so far as the application of the rule against
perpetuities was concerned so that the proposed advancement was
void.[86]]

C. *Payment of Trust Funds to Beneficiaries*

Trustees must pay trust moneys to the right beneficiaries, for otherwise
it is a breach of trust. In *Eaves* v. *Hickson*,[87] trustees were induced by
a forgery to pay trust funds to persons not entitled, and Romilly M.R.
held that, as between trustee and beneficiary, the loss fell on the former.[88]

Section 61 of the Trustee Act 1925, *infra,* is now available as a defence
to a trustee who honestly and reasonably makes a wrongful payment
through circumstances similar to those in *Eaves* v. *Hickson,* or through an
erroneous construction of the instrument of trust,[89] but section 30 (1) of
the Act, *supra,* is not.[90]

Before paying trust funds to an alleged *assignee* from a beneficiary a
trustee must investigate the assignee's title. If he relies merely on the
alleged assignee's statement, he is not acting reasonably, even if the assignee
happens also to be solicitor to the trust.[91] But although the trustee must
investigate the assignee's title, he cannot require actual delivery up to him
of the assignee's document of title.[92]

If a trustee, through inadvertence or a mistake of construction or of
fact, has overpaid one beneficiary at the expense of another, and the
court is administering the estate, it will adjust accounts out of future
payments.[93] If the estate is not being administered by the court, an
adjustment can be made with the court's assistance; and might presumably
be made without any application to the court. If the underpaid beneficiary
can identify the fund erroneously paid, he has, in addition, the remedy
of following it into the hands of the overpaid beneficiary or an assignee
(except a bona fide purchaser).[94]

---

86 As to express powers, see also *Taylor* v. *Taylor* (1875) L.R. 20 Eq. 155; *Re
Blockley* (1885) 29 Ch.D. 250; *Re Scott* [1903] 1 Ch. 1; *Re Livesey* [1953] 1
W.L.R. 1114; *Re Williams' W.T.* [1953] Ch. 138; *Re Stranger* (1891) 60 L.J.Ch.
326; *Re Vestey's Settlement* [1951] Ch. 209; on the meaning of "advancement":
Re Hayward [1957] Ch. 528. See also *Re Wills' W.T.* [1959] Ch. 1 (a settlement
on very young children which might save estate duty in certain events held to be
for their benefit); *Re Clore's S.T.* [1966] 1 W.L.R. 955 (advancement permitted for
the purpose of making charitable gifts which the beneficiary considered himself to
be under a moral obligation to make); *Re Pauling's S.T.* [1964] Ch. 303 (trustees
must be satisfied that the proposed advance is for the benefit of the beneficiary and
must see that it is applied for the purpose for which it was made).
87 (1861) 30 Beav. 136.
88 See also *Ashby* v. *Blackwell* (1765) 2 Eden 299, 302; *Sheridan* v. *Joyce* (1844) 7
Ir.Eq.R. 115; *Boulton* v. *Beard* (1853) 3 De G.M. & G. 608; *Sporle* v. *Barnaby*
(1864) 10 Jur. 1142; *cf. Leslie* v. *Baillie* (1843) 2 Y. & C.C.C. 91.
89 *Re Smith, Smith* v. *Thompson* (1902) 71 L.J.Ch. 411; *National Trustees' Case*
[1905] A.C. 381; *Re Allsop* [1914] 1 Ch. 1.
90 *Re Windsor Co.* [1929] 1 Ch. 151, 161, 166, 170.
91 *Davis* v. *Hutchings* [1907] 1 Ch. 356.
92 *Re Palmer* [1907] 1 Ch. 486; see *Warter* v. *Anderson* (1853) 11 Hare 301.
93 *Dibbs* v. *Goren* (1849) 11 Beav. 483. Goff and Jones, pp. 86–87.
94 See *Livesey* v. *Livesey* (1827) 3 Russ. 287; *Brooksbank* v. *Smith* (1836) 2 Y. &
C.Ex. 58; *Downes* v. *Bullock* (1858) 25 Beav. 54, 62; *Harris* v. *Harris* (*No.
2*) (1861) 29 Beav. 110; explained in [1911] 1 Ch. 509; *Re Ainsworth* [1915] 2 Ch.

But if a *trustee-beneficiary* underpays *himself*, then, as held in *Re Horne*,[95] he suffers by his mistake.

IV. STATUTORY AND JUDICIAL PROTECTION OF TRUSTEES IN RESPECT OF THE DISTRIBUTION OF THE TRUST PROPERTY

The Trustee Act 1925

Protection against liability in respect of rents and covenants

Section 26.[96]—(1) Where a personal representative or trustee liable as such [97] for—

(a) any rent, covenant, or agreement reserved by or contained in any lease; or

(b) any rent, covenant or agreement payable under or contained in any grant made in consideration of a rentcharge; or

(c) any indemnity given in respect of any rent, covenant or agreement referred to in either of the foregoing paragraphs:

satisfies all liabilities under the lease or grant which may have accrued, or been claimed, up to the date of the conveyance hereinafter mentioned, and where necessary, sets apart a sufficient fund to answer any future claim that may be made in respect of any fixed and ascertained sum which the lessee or grantee agreed to lay out on the property demised or granted, although the period for laying out the same may not have arrived, then and in any such case the personal representative or trustee may convey the property demised or granted to a purchaser, legatee, devisee or other person entitled to call for a conveyance thereof and thereafter—

(i) he may distribute the residuary real and personal estate of the deceased testator or intestate, or, as the case may be, the trust estate (other than the fund, if any, set apart as aforesaid) to or amongst the persons entitled thereto, without appropriating any part, or any further part, as the case may be, of the estate of the deceased or of the trust estate to meet any future liability under the said lease or grant;

(ii) notwithstanding such distribution, he shall not be personally liable in respect of any subsequent claim under the said lease or grant.

(2) This section operates without prejudice to the right of the lessor or grantor, or the persons deriving title under the lessor or grantor, to follow the assets of the deceased or the trust property into the hands of the persons

---

96; *Re Musgrave* [1916] 2 Ch. 417; *Re Reading* [1916] W.N. 262; *Re Wooldridge* [1920] W.N. 78; but see *Re Winslow* (1890) 45 Ch.D. 249, *Warren* v. *Warren* (1895) 72 L.T. 628 and *Re Sharp* [1906] 1 Ch. 793. *Re Diplock* [1948] Ch. 465; *Ministry of Health* v. *Simpson* [1951] A.C. 251.

95 [1905] 1 Ch. 76.

96 This section replaces and extends ss. 27 and 28 of the Law of Property Amendment Act 1859. It is printed as amended by the Schedule to the Law of Property (Amendment) Act 1926.

97 The protection of the section avails a personal representative or trustee in respect of his liability *as such*. Personal liability, unprotected by the section, is incurred if the personal representative or trustee takes possession of the leaseholds: *Re Owers, Public Trustee* v. *Death (No. 2)* [1941] Ch. 389; *Re Bennett, Midland Bank Executor and Trustee Co. Ltd.* v. *Fletcher* [1943] 1 All E.R. 467; *Youngmin* v. *Heath* [1974] 1 W.L.R. 135, 138.

amongst whom the same may have been respectively distributed, and applies notwithstanding anything to the contrary in the will or other instrument, if any, creating the trust.

(3) In this section " lease " includes an underlease and an agreement for a lease or underlease and any instrument giving any such indemnity as aforesaid or varying the liabilities under the lease; " grant " applies to a grant whether the rent is created by limitation, grant, reservation, or otherwise, and includes an agreement for a grant and any instrument giving any such indemnity as aforesaid or varying the liabilities under the grant; " lessee " and " grantee " include persons respectively deriving title under them.

Protection by means of advertisements

Section 27.[98]—(1) With a view to the conveyance to or distribution among the persons entitled to any real or personal property, the trustees of a settlement or of a disposition on trust for sale or personal representatives, may give notice by advertisement in the Gazette, and in a daily London newspaper, and also, if the property includes land not situated in London in a daily or weekly newspaper circulating in the district in which the land is situated, and such other like notices, including notices elsewhere than in England and Wales, as would, in any special case, have been directed by a court of competent jurisdiction in an action for administration, of their intention to make such conveyance or distribution as aforesaid, and requiring any person interested [99] to send to the trustees or personal representatives within the time, not being less than two months, fixed in the notice or, where more than one notice is given, in the last of the notices, particulars of his claim in respect of the property or any part thereof to which the notice relates.

(2) At the expiration of the time fixed by the notice the trustees or personal representatives may convey or distribute the property or any part thereof to which the notice relates, to or among the persons entitled thereto, having regard only to the claims, whether formal or not, of which the trustees or personal representatives then had notice and shall not, as respects the property so conveyed or distributed, be liable to any person of whose claim the trustees or personal representatives have not had notice at the time of conveyance or distribution; but nothing in this section—

(a) prejudices the right of any person to follow the property, or any property representing the same, into the hands of any person, other than a purchaser, who may have received it; or

(b) frees the trustees or personal representatives from any obligation to make searches or obtain official certificates of search similar to those which an intending purchaser would be advised to make or obtain.

(3) This section applies notwithstanding anything to the contrary in the will or other instrument, if any, creating the trust.

---

[98] This section replaces s. 29 of the Law of Property Amendment Act 1859, which applied only to personal representatives. It is printed as amended by the Schedule to the Law of Property (Amendment) Act 1926. For the form which the advertisement should take, see *Re Aldhous* [1955] 1 W.L.R. 459.

[99] Protection is afforded against belated claims of creditors, next of kin or beneficiaries under a will: *Re Aldhous* [1955] 1 W.L.R. 459, 462.

Payment into court by trustees

Section 63.[1]—(1) Trustees, or the majority of trustees, having in their hands or under their control money or securities belonging to a trust, may pay the same into court; and the same shall, subject to rules of court, be dealt with according to the orders of the court.

(2) The receipt or certificate of the proper officer shall be a sufficient discharge to trustees for the money or securities so paid into court.

(3) Where money or securities are vested in any persons as trustees, and the majority are desirous of paying the same into court, but the concurrence of the other or others cannot be obtained, the court may order the payment into court to be made by the majority without the concurrence of the other or others.

(4) Where any such money or securities are deposited with any banker, broker, or other depositary, the court may order payment or delivery of the money or securities to the majority of the trustees for the purpose of payment into court.

(5) Every transfer payment and delivery made in pursuance of any such order shall be valid and take effect as if the same had been made on the authority by the act of all the persons entitled to the money and securities so transferred, paid, or delivered.

A. J. Hawkins (1968) 84 *L.Q.R.* 65

" Payment into court, no matter how unjustified, was always effective, to give the trustees a good discharge. As Kindersley V.-C. said in *Re Lloyd's Trusts*,[2] ' The intention of the Trustee Act was for the present relief of trustees.' Relief might prove expensive, but it appears to have been effective to the extent that trustees were relieved of the burden of future administration. The sanction against unjustifiable payment into court was a disallowance of the cost incurred in paying in. Trustees were later condemned in the cost incurred in the payment out to the beneficiaries. In the early cases they were not entitled to costs of the payment in if their actions had been vexatious.[3] Later, they had to justify their actions by showing doubt as to the identity of the beneficiaries, the extent of their interest or their inability to give receipts.[4] ' The legislature did not intend that where the trust was clear, a trustee should pay the fund into court. A trustee cannot pay money into court merely to get rid of a trust he has undertaken to perform, and the Act would lead to greater oppression if it were otherwise.'[5] Further-

---

[1] This section replaces s. 42 of the Trustee Act 1893, which replaced ss. 1 and 2 of the Trustees' Relief Act 1847. Unless trustees have reasonable cause, they may be made liable for the costs of paying funds into, and getting them out of, court. " It is quite evident," said Kindersley V.-C. in *Re Waring* (1852) 21 L.J.Ch. 784, 785, " that the intention of the legislature in passing the Trustees Relief Act was only to enable the trustees to pay into court a legacy or share of a trust fund under peculiar circumstances. The object was to relieve trustees; that is, to relieve them from the position of having in their hands money which they do not know what to do with: as, for instance, where a legacy is given to A B, and the trustees cannot find the A B to whom it is made payable, or where trustees cannot take upon themselves the responsibility of distributing a fund." In case of doubt as to the claim, share or identity of a beneficiary the practice today is to submit the matter to the court for determination by an originating summons under Ord. 85, r. 2, and Ord. 5, rr. 1 and 4, of the Rules of the Supreme Court.

[2] (1854) 2 W.R. 371.

[3] *Re Lane's Trust* (1854) 3 W.R. 134.

[4] *Re Knight's Trusts* (1859) 27 Beav. 45.   [5] *Ibid.* Romilly M.R. at p. 49.

more the trustees' doubts should be bona fide. This appears to have meant such doubts as would assail and disturb a practical lawyer, rather than ruffle the academic conscience of eminent conveyancers.[6] What is the effect of payment in? Clearly, payment into court does operate as a discharge of trustees. In other words, by paying in the trustees retire from the trust.[7] They will, of course, still be liable for any breaches of trust in the past,[8] and responsible for any money that should come into their hands in the future.[9] Apparently, they also remain trustees for the purposes of receiving notices relating to dealings with the trust funds.[10] Subject to these two matters, however, new trustees can be appointed, either by the persons nominated as appointors in the trust instrument,[11] or by the court." [12]

Order 85

(R.S.C. 1965)

Administration and Similar Actions

Interpretation (O. 85, r. 1).

1. In this Order "administration action" means an action for the administration under the direction of the Court of the estate of a deceased person or for the execution under the direction of the Court of a trust.

Determination of questions, etc., without administration (O. 85, r. 2).

2.—(1) An action may be brought for the determination of any question or for any relief which could be determined or granted, as the case may be, in an administration action and a claim need not be made in the action for the administration or execution under the direction of the Court of the estate or trust in connection with which the question arises or the relief is sought.

(2) Without prejudice to the generality of paragraph (1), an action may be brought for the determination of any of the following questions: —

    (a) any question arising in the administration of the estate of a deceased person or in the execution of a trust;

    (b) any question as to the composition of any class of persons having a claim against the estate of a deceased person or a beneficial interest in the estate of such a person or in any property subject to a trust;

    (c) any question as to the rights or interests of a person claiming to be a creditor of the estate of a deceased person or to be entitled under a will or on the intestacy of a deceased person or to be beneficially entitled under a trust.

---

[6] In *Re Knight's Trusts* (1859) 27 Beav. 45, the fact that trustees acted on counsel's opinion was regretted but made no difference to their liability. In *Re Cull's Trusts* (1875) L.R. 20 Eq. 561, the particular trustees were protected having taken counsel's opinion, but Jessel M.R. added " the next set of trustees who come before me having so acted must pay costs."

[7] *Re Williams' Settlement* (1858) 4 K. & J. 87.

[8] *Barker* v. *Peile* (1865) 2 Dr. & Sm. 340.

[9] *Re Nettlefold's Trusts* (1888) 59 L.T.(N.S.) 315.

[10] *Thompson* v. *Tomkins* (1862) 2 Dr. & Sm. 8 and see also *Warburton* v. *Hill* (1854) Kay 470.

[11] *Re Bailey's Trust* (1854) 3 W.R. 31.

[12] 13 & 14 Vict. c. 60, ss. 32 and 33, replaced with significant changes by ss. 25 and 37 of the Trustee Act 1893. See now ss. 41 and 43 of the Trustee Act 1925.

(3) Without prejudice to the generality of paragraph (1), an action may be brought for any of the following reliefs : —

    (*a*) an order requiring an executor, administrator or trustee to furnish and, if necessary, verify accounts;

    (*b*) an order requiring the payment into court of money held by a person in his capacity as executor, administrator or trustee;

    (*c*) an order directing a person to do or abstain from doing a particular act in his capacity as executor, administrator or trustee;

    (*d*) an order approving any sale, purchase, compromise or other transaction by a person in his capacity as executor, administrator or trustee;

    (*e*) an order directing any act to be done in the administration of the estate of a deceased person or in the execution of a trust which the Court could order to be done if the estate or trust were being administered or executed, as the case may be, under the direction of the Court.

Parties

3.—(1) All the executors or administrators of the estate or trustees of the trust, as the case may be, to which an administration action or such an action as is referred to in rule 2 relates must be parties to the action, and where the action is brought by executors, administrators or trustees, any of them who does not consent to being joined as a plaintiff must be made a defendant.

(2) Notwithstanding anything in Order 15, rule 4 (2), and without prejudice to the powers of the Court under that Order, all the persons having a beneficial interest in or claim against the estate or having a beneficial interest under the trust, as the case may be, to which such an action as is mentioned in paragraph (1) relates need not be parties to the action; but the plaintiff may make such of those persons, whether all or any one or more of them, parties as, having regard to the nature of the relief or remedy claimed in the action, he thinks fit.

R. E. Megarry (1966) 82 L.Q.R. 306

" The facts in *Re Allen-Meyrick's Will Trusts* ([1966] 1 W.L.R. 499; [1966] 1 All E.R. 740), were simple and elegant. A testatrix gave her residue to trustees in trust to apply the income thereof ' in their absolute discretion for the maintenance of my . . . husband,' and subject to the exercise of this discretion, she gave the residue in trust for her two godchildren equally. The trustees had made certain payments for the benefit of the husband, who was bankrupt, but had been unable to agree whether any further income should be so applied. In these circumstances, the trustees sought to surrender their discretion to the court, and also sought to have it determined whether their discretion still existed in relation to past accumulations of income.

" It is well settled that trustees confronted by a particular problem may surrender their discretion to the court, and so be relieved both of the agony of decision and the responsibility for the result. But it is another matter where it is sought to surrender discretion which is not merely present and confined but prospective and indefinite. The Court of Chancery had a long history of administrative jurisdiction; but it exercised this jurisdiction not on its own investigations but on facts duly put before it in evidence by those concerned. It is not surprising, therefore, that Buckley, J. refused to accept the proffered general surrender of discretion. Whenever a specific problem arose upon specific facts, the aid of the court could be sought; but that was all. As regard past accumulations of income, the position was simple. The whole of the property, capital and income, belonged to the two godchildren except in so far as the trustees had effectually exercised their discretionary power to apply income to the husband. Trustees must, of course, be unanimous in exercising any powers vested in them, and so if within a reasonable time of receiving any income they had failed to exercise their discretion in favour of the husband, it ceased to be exercisable, and the godchildren became entitled to it. The principles are old, the facts new, and the result satisfactory."

It might be added that in cases where it is likely that there will be further disagreements necessitating expensive applications to the court it is best for the trustees to retire to allow the appointment of more compatible trustees.

Section 8. Judicial Control of Trustees

Whilst trustees have to discharge their duties they only have to consider the exercise of powers conferred upon them.[13] Thus in *Tempest* v. *Lord Camoys, infra,* nothing could be done when one of the trustees bona fide considered that it would not be in the interests of the trust to exercise a power of purchasing land by purchasing Bracewell Hall. However, if a trustee's attitude is that he is not going to bother about using any powers to benefit B as B does not deserve any consideration, *e.g.,* because B married without his consent the court will intervene: *Klug* v. *Klug.*[14] In that case legacy duty had to be paid by a beneficiary in four equal instalments but the beneficiary's income was insufficient to pay these instalments. Neville J. said,[15] " When the summons was previously before me, I decided that the trustees could in the exercise of their discretion under the powers of advancement, if they thought fit, advance out of capital a sum sufficient to pay this legacy duty. The public trustee thinks that their discretion should be so exercised, but his co-trustee, the mother, declines to join him in so doing, not because she has considered whether or not it would be for her daughter's welfare, that the advance should be made, but because her daughter has married without her consent, and her letters show, in my opinion, that she has not exercised her discretion at all. . . . In such circumstances, it is the duty of the court to interfere and to direct a sum to be raised out of capital sufficient to pay off . . . the legacy duty."

Once powers are exercised, then the court will not intervene [16] unless it can be shown that the particular purported exercise of the powers is

---

[13] A. J. Hawkins (1967) 31 Conv.(N.S.) 117; A. K. Kiralfy (1953) 17 Conv.(N.S.) 285.
[14] [1918] 2 Ch. 67.   [15] *Ibid.* at 71.
[16] *Re Charteris* [1917] 2 Ch. 379; *Re Steed's W.T.* [1960] Ch. 407; *Re Hastings-Bass* [1974] 2 All E.R. 193 which indicates in its interpretation of *Re Abraham's W.T.* [1969] 1 Ch. 463 that in the special case where some rule of law (*e.g.,* rule against remoteness) has altered the consequences of the exercise of a power of the trustees so drastically that the trustees cannot reasonably be supposed to have addressed their minds to the questions relevant to the true effect of the transaction then the exercise of the power will be void.

unauthorised by the powers or that the trustees acted in bad faith, oppressively, corruptly or with improper motive.[17] In this respect there is the doctrine of a fraud on a power[18] if the donee of a special power of appointment (*e.g.*, A, where there is a trust for A for life then to such of his children as he shall appoint and in default of appointment for his children equally) exercises it other than bona fide for the purpose for which it was given him, *e.g.*, if he exercises it for a corrupt or foreign purpose or pursuant to a bargain to benefit non-objects of the power. The doctrine in modern times has become particularly relevant where for fiscal reasons the life tenant donee of the power has wished to appoint to certain adult (or infant) beneficiaries in order that the trust property can then be divided up between them. The strict view is laid down in *Re Brook's Settlement, infra*, though certain judges[19] have taken a more liberal line in answering the question of fact "was the appointment made for the ulterior purpose, or partly for the ulterior purpose, of enabling a division of the trust fund?" If a fraud on the power is involved then the appointment is void but the appointor can still make a fresh appointment.[20] Purchasers from appointees to whom "fraudulent" appointments have been made have a limited amount of protection under section 157 of the Law of Property Act 1925.

The doctrine of fraud on a power does not apply to releases of powers as they simply benefit those entitled in default of appointment, who have all along had the property vested in them subject only to divestment upon an exercise of the power. Thus in *Re Somes*[21] where a father had a power of appointment in favour of a daughter or her issue, the daughter also being entitled in default of appointment, the father was able to release his power so that his daughter could mortgage the property to secure a sum of £10,000 to be paid to the father for his own purposes.[22]

It should be noted that whilst powers given to individuals in their private capacity can be released, powers given to trustees as fiduciaries cannot be released[23] (except under an express authority in the trust instrument or under the Variation of Trusts Act 1958) though the trustees' beneficiaries can validly release the trustees from their duties towards them, *e.g.*, so as even to cease to be objects of a discretionary trust: *Re Gulbenkian's Trusts (No. 2).*[24]

In the case of discretionary trusts the trustees, of course, have a duty to exercise their discretion by distributing income (or capital) in some sort of proportions to the beneficiaries or if there is power to accumulate by deciding

---

[17] This is very difficult to prove especially if the trustees, as they are entitled to do, refuse to give any reasons for their acts: see *Re Londonderry's Settlement, supra*, p. 564 and comment of R. E. M. thereon (1965) 81 L.Q.R. 196.

[18] Snell, pp. 556–560.

[19] *e.g.*, Megarry J. in *Re Wallace's Settlements* [1968] 1 W.L.R. 711 and Templeman J. in unreported cases. See also S. M. Cretney (1969) 32 M.L.R. 317, J. G. Monroe [1968] B.T.R. 424, Potter & Monroe's *Tax Planning*, 7th ed., pp. 258–259.

[20] *Topham* v. *Duke of Portland* (1869) 5 Ch.App. 40; *Re Chadwick's Trusts* [1939] 1 All E.R. 850.

[21] [1896] 1 Ch. 250.

[22] Similarly the doctrine of fraud on a power does not apply to the revocation of a revocable appointment even though the revoking appointor thereby intends to obtain a benefit: *Re Greaves* [1954] Ch. 434.

[23] This is basically the position but the borderlines are difficult to draw though an attempt was made in *Re Wills' Trust Deeds* [1964] Ch. 219. See A. J. Hawkins (1968) 84 L.Q.R. 64.

[24] [1970] Ch. 408.

to accumulate the income.[25] If the trustees neglect or refuse to discharge their duty then the court will have the settlor's intentions carried out "by appointing new trustees or by authorising or directing representative persons of the classes of beneficiaries to prepare a scheme for distribution, or even, should the proper basis for distribution appear, by itself directing the trustees so to distribute." [26]

Exceptionally, where the trustees are trustees for sale of land then the court has a vast discretion under section 30 of the Law of Property Act though it will not enforce the letter of a trust for sale if so to do would defeat the purpose of the trust.[27] The section provides: "If the trustees for sale refuse to sell or to exercise any of the powers conferred by either of the last two sections,[28] or any requisite consent cannot be obtained, any person interested may apply to the court for a vesting or other order for giving effect to the proposed transaction or for an order directing the trustees for sale to give effect thereto, and the court may make such order as it thinks fit." [29] Trustees must sell at the best price reasonably obtainable so that even if negotiations have so far advanced that ordinary commercial morality would preclude the trustees from honourably withdrawing from a projected sale they must not reject a better offer without first probing it with a view to acceptance.[30]

It should be noted that the jurisdiction of the court cannot be ousted by provisions in the trust instrument giving the trustees power to determine all questions arising in the execution of the trusts under the instrument.[31]

TEMPEST v. LORD CAMOYS [32]

Court of Appeal (1882) 21 Ch.D. 571; 51 L.J.Ch. 785; 48 L.T. 13; 31 W.R. 326 (Jessel M.R., Brett and Cotton L.JJ.)

The headnote summarises the facts as follows: "A testator gave his trustees a power to be exercised at their absolute discretion of selling

---

25 For the exercise of trustees' discretions after a general administration order of the court see 84 L.Q.R. pp. 68–73 (A. J. Hawkins).

26 *Per* Lord Wilberforce in *McPhail* v. *Doulton* [1971] A.C. 424, 451; A. J. Hawkins (1967) 31 Conv.(N.S.) 117.

27 *Jones* v. *Challenger* [1961] 1 Q.B. 176; *Bull* v. *Bull* [1955] 1 Q.B. 234. This is generally treated as a land law topic so see Megarry & Wade, 3rd ed., pp. 426–427, Cheshire, 22th ed., p. 176, Wolstenholme & Cherry's *Conveyancing Statutes*, 13th ed., Vol. 1, pp. 89–90.

28 Section 28 confers very wide powers equivalent to those of a tenant for life under the Settled Land Act 1925 whilst s. 29 enables the trustees to delegate their powers of management and leasing and accepting surrenders of leases.

29 No such possibility exists for settled land: *Re 90, Thornhill Rd., Tolworth* [1970] Ch. 261 (nothing can be done if joint tenants for life disagree bona fide as to exercise of power of sale).

30 *Buttle* v. *Saunders* [1950] 2 All E.R. 193.

31 *Re Wynn* [1952] Ch. 271; *Re Coxen* [1948] Ch. 747 especially 761, 762; *cf. Dundee General Hospitals Board* v. *Walker* [1952] 1 All E.R. 896.

32 See also *French* v. *Davidson* (1818) 3 Madd. 396; *Collins* v. *Vining* (1837) C.P. Coop. 472; *Costabadie* v. *Costabadie* (1847) 6 Hare 410; *Kekewich* v. *Marker* (1851) 3 Mac. & G. 311, 326; *Re Wilkes* (1851) 3 Mac. & G. 440; *Re Coe* (1858) 4 K. & J. 199; *Gray* v. *Gray* (1862) 13 Ir.Ch.R. 404; *Brophy* v. *Bellamy* (1873) L.R. 8 Ch. 798; *Gisborne* v. *Gisborne* (1877) 2 App.Cas. 300; *Tabor* v. *Brooks* (1878) 10 Ch.D. 273; *Re Roper* (1879) 11 Ch.D. 272; *Camden* v. *Murray* (1880) 16 Ch.D. 161, 170; *Re Blake* (1885) 29 Ch.D. 913, 917; *Re Courtier* (1886) 34 Ch.D. 136; *Re Wainwright* (1889) 5 T.L.R. 301; *Re Burrage* (1890) 62 L.T. 752; *Re Bryant* [1894] 1 Ch. 324; *Moore* v. *M'Glynn* [1894] 1 Ir.R. 74, 86; *Re Boys*

real estates, with a declaration that the proceeds should be applied, at the like discretion, in the purchase of other real estates. He also gave them power at their absolute discretion to raise money by mortgage for the purchase of real estates. A suit having been instituted for the execution of the trusts of the will, and a sum of money, the proceeds of the sale of real estate, having been paid into court, one of the trustees proposed to purchase a large estate and to apply the fund in court in part-payment of the purchase-money, and to raise the remainder of the purchase-money by mortgage of the purchased estate. The other trustee refused to concur in the purchase."

Some of the beneficiaries being in favour of the proposal, a petition was presented for the purpose of having the purchase carried out. It was contended that it was desirable to purchase at a moderate price—£60,000, there being some £30,000 in court—an estate which had previously been in the family for a long while. The dissentient trustee, Mr. Fleming, objected that the transaction would not be a prudent exercise of the power. Chitty J. held, in accordance with *Gisborne* v. *Gisborne*,[33] that the court had no power to interfere with Mr. Fleming's bona fide exercise of his discretion. The petitioners appealed.

JESSEL M.R.: " It is very important that the law of the court on this subject should be understood. It is settled law that when a testator has given a pure discretion to trustees as to the exercise of a power, the court does not enforce the exercise of a power against the wish of the trustees, but it does prevent them from exercising it improperly. The court says that the power, if exercised at all, is to be properly exercised. This may be illustrated by the case of persons having a power of appointing new trustees. Even after a decree in a suit for administering the trusts has been made they may still exercise the power, but the court will see that they do not appoint improper persons.

" But in all cases where there is a trust or duty coupled with the power the court will then compel the trustees to carry it out in a proper manner and within a reasonable time. In the present case there was a power which amounts to a trust to invest the fund in question in the purchase of land. The trustees would not be allowed by the court to disregard that trust, and if Mr. Fleming had refused to invest the money in land at all the court would have found no difficulty in interfering. But that is a very different thing from saying that the court ought to take from the trustees their uncontrolled discretion as to the particular time for the investment and the particular property which should be purchased. In this particular case it appears to me that the testator in his will has carefully distinguished between what is to be at the discretion of his trustees and what is obligatory on them.

" There is another difficulty in this case. The estate proposed to be

(1896) 41 S.J. 111; *Re Horsnaill* [1909] 1 Ch. 631; *Re Kipping* [1914] 1 Ch. 62; *Re Charteris* [1917] 2 Ch. 379, 391; but see *Walker* v. *Walker* (1820) 5 Madd. 424.
33 (1877) 2 App.Cas. 300.

purchased will cost £60,000, and only £30,000 is available for the purchase, and the trustees will have to borrow the remaining £30,000. There is power to raise money by mortgage at the absolute discretion of the trustees, and assuming that such a transaction as this is within the power, and that the trustees can mortgage the estate before they have actually bought it, there is no trust to mortgage, it is purely discretionary. The court cannot force Mr. Fleming to take the view that it is proper to mortgage the estate in this way; he may well have a different opinion from the other trustee. Here again the court cannot interfere with his discretion. The appeal must therefore be dismissed."
Appeal dismissed.

Re BELOVED WILKES' CHARITY

Lord Chancellor (1851) 3 Mac. & G. 440

Charitable trustees had to select a boy to be educated at Oxford for the Anglican Ministry, preference to be given to boys from four named parishes if in the trustees' judgment a fit and proper candidate therefrom could be found. Without giving any reasons, but stating that they had acted impartially, the trustees selected Charles Joyce who did not come from the named parishes but who had a brother who was a Minister who had put forward Charles' merits to the trustees. The court was asked to set aside the selection, and to select William Gale, whose father was a respectable farmer residing in one of the specified parishes.

Held. In the absence of evidence that the trustees had exercised their discretion unfairly or dishonestly, the Court would not interfere.

LORD TRURO L.C.: " The question, therefore, is, whether it was the duty of the trustees to enter into particulars, or whether the law is not, that trustees who are appointed to execute a trust according to discretion, that discretion to be influenced by a variety of circumstances (as, in this instance, by those particular circumstances which should be connected with the fitness of a lad to be brought up as a minister of the Church of England), are not bound to go into a detail of the grounds upon which they come to their conclusion, their duty being satisfied by shewing that they have considered the circumstances of the case, and have come to their conclusion accordingly. Without occupying time by going into a lengthened examination of the decisions, the result of them appears to me so clear and reasonable, that it will be sufficient to state my conclusion in point of law to be, that in such cases as I have mentioned it is to the discretion of the trustees that the execution of the trust is confided, that discretion being exercised with an entire absence of indirect motive, with honesty of intention, and with a fair consideration of the subject. The duty of supervision on the part of this Court will thus be confined to the question of the honesty, integrity, and fairness with which the deliberation has been conducted, and will not be extended to the accuracy of the conclusion arrived at, except in particular cases. If, however, as stated by Lord Ellenborough in *The King* v. *The Archbishop of Canterbury* ((1812) 15 East 117), trustees think fit to state a reason, and the reason is one which does not justify their conclusion, then the Court may say that they have acted by mistake and in error, and that it will correct their decision; but if, without entering into details, they simply state, as in many cases it would be most prudent and judicious for them to do, that they have met and considered and come to a conclusion, the Court has then no means of saying that they have failed in their duty, or to consider the accuracy of their conclusion.[34] It seems, therefore, to me, that having in the present case to look to the motives of the trustees as developed in the affidavits, no ground exists for imputing bad motives. The Petitioners, indeed, candidly state, on the face of their petition, that they do not impute such motives, they merely charge the trustees with a miscarriage as regards the duty which they had to perform. I cannot, therefore, deal with the case as if the petition had contained a statement of a different kind, and if I could, still I should say, having read the affidavits, that I see nothing whatever which can lay the foundation for any judicial conclusion that the trustees intentionally and from bad motives failed in their duty, if they failed at all."

Re BROOK'S SETTLEMENT

Chancery Division [1968] 1 W.L.R. 1661; [1968] 3 All E.R. 416

STAMP J., read the following judgment: " Under a settlement of personalty made on October 25, 1934, by the plaintiff's father, the late Reginald James Brook, a share of the trust fund is now held on trust whereunder the plaintiff is entitled to a protected life interest in possession. At the date of the issue of the originating summons, the fund comprising the plaintiff's share stood settled, subject to his protected life interest, on trust for such of the plaintiff's children and remoter issue as the plaintiff should by deed or by will or codicil appoint and in default of and subject to any such appointment on trust for such of the plaintiff's children as being male attained the age of twenty-one or being female attained that age or married, if more than one in equal shares. There was a provision for hotchpot and a gift over, which cannot now take effect because one of the plaintiff's children the defendant, Richard Brook, has attained the age of twenty-one, and a power to the plaintiff to appoint a life interest to a surviving wife, the existence and terms of which are not relevant for the purpose of this judgment. The plaintiff has two children, namely the defendant, Richard Brook, and a daughter, the defendant, Ann Brook, who is under the age of twenty-one and unmarried The plaintiff is forty-

---

[34] See *Re Londonderry's Settlement* [1965] Ch. 918, *supra*, p. 564.

nine and, of course, under the trusts of the settlement as they stood when the originating summons was issued, any future child of his who attained the age of twenty-one or being a daughter married under that age would, in default of appointment, have taken a share of the fund on the death of the plaintiff.

" By the originating summons which was issued under the Variation of Trusts Act, 1958, on February 28, 1968, the plaintiff asks that the court may approve on behalf of the infant defendant, Ann Brook, and on behalf of all persons who may become interested under the discretionary trust to arise in the event of a forfeiture of the plaintiff's life interest, a variation of the trust of the settlement affecting the fund constituting the plaintiff's share. By the effect of the proposed variation a part of the fund would be held on trust for the plaintiff absolutely, the *quid pro quo* being in effect the release of the remainder of the fund from the protected life interest of the plaintiff and the consequent acceleration of the interests of those entitled in reversion expectant on the determination of that protected life interest.

" The proposed variation, however, and this is the point at which the difficulty arises, proceeds on the footing that the two existing children are alone entitled to a share in the capital of the fund and the part of the fund which is to be freed from the protected life interest of the plaintiff is, under the proposed variation, to be held on trust, in effect, for them to the exclusion of after-born children. The court is not asked to approve the variation on behalf of after-born children. Plainly this would not do because even if the court could properly have approved the variation on the ground that it was for the benefit of Miss Ann Brook, the interest of after-born children would not be bound and the trustees could not have given effect to the variation. Nor could this court have bound the interest of after-born children because as the proposed variation stood, and still stands, they are to take nothing. The thing had apparently gone awry because it had been assumed that before the application came before the court, perhaps before the summons was issued, the plaintiff would, in exercise of his power of appointment, have made an appointment in favour of his two existing children thereby defeating the interests of any after-born child. The plaintiff indicated in his affidavit in support of the summons an intention so to do if the court approved of the variation: which is not the same thing and would not have removed the difficulty. When the plaintiff's counsel considered the matter a few days before the hearing he, of course, appreciated the difficulty; and in reliance, perhaps, on a recent decision of this court in *Re Wallace's Settlements* [35] an appointment was executed by the plaintiff of the whole of the plaintiff's share in favour of his two existing children. The question then arises was this appointment an effective appointment

[35] [1968] 1 W.L.R. 711.

or was it a fraud on the power of appointment? This is a question which must be decided because, until it is decided, the trustees of the settlement will not know to whom the fund belongs; and counsel for the trustees in accordance with his duty on behalf of the trustees, was bound to argue, as he did, that the appointment was a fraud on the power.

" I start to consider the question by referring to what were described by Vaisey J. in *Re Greaves' Will Trusts, Public Trustee* v. *Ash* [36] as ' the classic pronouncments of the highest authorities ' on the subject. First of all there is the speech of Lord Westbury L.C. in *Duke of Portland* v. *Lady Topham.* [37] He said this:

> ' Without dwelling on the matter further, in as much as your lordships concur in opinion, I think we must all feel that the settled principles of the law must be upheld, namely, that the donee, the appointor under the power, shall, at the time of the exercise of that power, and for any purpose for which it is used, act with good faith and sincerity, and with an entire and single view to the real purpose and object of the power, and not for the purpose of accomplishing or carrying into effect any bye or sinister object (I mean sinister in the sense of its being beyond the purpose and intent of the power) which he may desire to effect in the exercise of the power. I think it would be endangering the whole of the established principles of our law upon this subject if we were to permit a transaction of this kind to stand, or to hold that it is a transaction which can be reconciled with the faithful, sincere, just, and honest exercise of the power committed to the appointor, and which he is to exercise as a trustee.'

Lord St. Leonards' speech was to the same effect when he said this [38]:

> ' The rules on this subject are so well settled that it is quite unnecessary to go through any authorities on the subject. A party having a power like this must fairly and honestly execute it without having any ulterior object to be accomplished. He cannot carry into execution any indirect object, or acquire any benefit for himself, directly or indirectly. It may be subject to limitations and directions, but it must be a pure, straightforward, honest dedication of the property as property, to the person to whom he affects or attempts to give it in that character.'

See also the judgment of the Privy Council in *Vatcher* v. *Paull* [39]:

> ' The term " fraud " in connection with frauds on a power does not necessarily denote any conduct on the part of the appointor amounting to fraud in the common law meaning of the

---

[36] [1954] Ch. 434, 439.
[37] (1864) 11 H.L.Cas. 32, 54.
[38] (1864) 11 H.L.Cas. 32, 55.
[39] [1915] A.C. 372, 378.

terms or any conduct which could be properly termed dishonest or immoral. It merely means that the power has been exercised for a purpose, or with an intention, beyond the scope of or not justified by the instrument creating the power. Perhaps the most common instance of this is where the exercise is due to some bargain between the appointor and appointee, whereby the oppointor, or some other person not an object of the power, is to derive a benefit. It is enough that the appointor's purpose and intention is to secure a benefit for himself, or some other person not an object of the power. In such a case the appointment is invalid, unless the court can clearly distinguish between the quantum of the benefit bona fide intended to be conferred on the appointee, and the quantum of the benefit intended to be derived by the appointor or to be conferred on a stranger.'

If the authorities rested there it might have been thought to follow that an appointment by a life tenant, the purpose of which, or one of the purposes of which, was to enable a division of the trust fund between appointor and appointee, thereby excluding the other objects of the power and those entitled in default of appointment, would *ipso facto* be a fraudulent exercise of the power. So to hold would have been to apply the doctrine of fraud on the power strictly. It is, however, to be observed that the exercise of a fiduciary power of appointment does not become a fraud on the power because in fact it confers a benefit on a person who is not an object of the power, but because the purpose, or one of the purposes, of the appointment is not to benefit the appointee who is an object of the power but is an ulterior purpose. The fact that a person who is not an object of the power does obtain a benefit is no doubt often evidence that that was the purpose or one of the purposes of the appointment. That is not always so, however, and the distinction between the effect of the appointment and its purpose remains. Since the purpose of an appointment by a father who, in exercise of a fiduciary power, appoints a fund to his daughter to enable her to settle it on the trusts of her marriage settlement is to benefit the daughter and it has no other purpose, such an appointment is not a fraud on the power notwithstanding that the daughter's husband and children will obtain a benefit. In the cases to which I must make reference hereafter, the courts have tended to make this distinction and to hold that an appointment made by a tenant for life is not *ipso facto* made for a purpose outside the scope of the power although in fact the appointor himself is intended to take part of the appointed property. A step in that direction was taken in *Re Merton's Settlement, Public Trustee* v. *Wilson* [40] and *Re Robertson's Will Trusts,*[41] where the appointments, although made in anticipation of a

---

[40] [1953] 2 All E.R. 707.
[41] [1960] 1 W.L.R. 1050.

division of the trust fund between appointor and appointee, were held not to be tainted because they were transactions separate from and independent of the scheme for the division of the trust funds and it was no part of the purpose of the appointor in making the appointment to put part of the appointed fund in the hands of the appointor or to produce a situation in which the other objects of the power or those entitled in default of appointment would be precluded from objecting to the division.

" Before coming to the cases which I think take the matter somewhat further I observe first that the question whether an appointment is made for the ulterior purpose, or partly for the ulterior purpose, of enabling a division of a trust fund or without any such ulterior purpose is one of fact; secondly, that the protestation that the appointor had no such ulterior purpose but that the appointment was a separate and independent transaction made irrespective of the scheme of division, is more easily acceptable if the apparent ulterior purpose—here a division of the trust fund under which the appointor takes part— could from the appointor's point of view have been better or equally well achieved had there been no appointment. In the present case counsel for the infant defendant, found no difficulty in submitting that the division proposed is one which is for her benefit; but had there been no appointment it is at least less clear, because after-born children will not have the same advantage of acceleration, that the proposed division, under which the plaintiff is to have a half share of the fund, could have been supported as beneficial to any after-born child of the plaintiff. It appears, moreover, from what counsel told me, that in the course of the negotiations and discussions leading up to the formulation of the proposed variation it became apparent, as in my experience is very often the case, that the plaintiff wished to obtain as much as he could fairly do on the division and the fact that he might be able to receive less if there was no appointment was very present in the minds of his advisers. It was not argued, and I could not find, that the appointment here was a transaction separate and distinct from the division of the trust fund sought to be achieved or had not, to use a phrase taken from the judgment of Megarry J., in *Re Wallace's Settlements*,[42] to which I will refer in a moment, ' become embrangled with the arrangements.' [43]

" It was, however, submitted in reliance on *Re Wallace's Settlements*, that where you find that under the scheme for the division of the fund contemplated by the appointing tenant for life and the appointee, the tenant for life is to take no more than the equivalent of the market value of his life interest, there is no such benefit to the tenant for life as to render the appointment *ipso facto* a fraud on the

---

[42] [1968] 1 W.L.R. 711.
[43] [1968] 1 W.L.R. 711, 719.

power. It was for the purpose of considering the implications of this submission that I reserved my judgment.

" The facts in *Re Wallace's Settlements* were not quite the same as the facts of this case, but there is a clear finding in *Re Wallace's Settlements* that the appointments there in question were not fraudulent. The considerations which led Megarry J. to conclude that the extent to which the appointments there had become embrangled with the arrangements for the variation of the trusts had not tainted the appointments, were I think these: first, that as regards such advantages as there might be in the certainty and flexibility of capital as opposed to the limitations of an inalienable and defeasible life interest, the judge was satisfied that in relation to other material circumstances of the life tenants there was no real advantage to either of them: secondly, that, on the facts of the cases there before him, the prospects of the life interests determining in the lifetime of either life tenant seemd to him to be negligible; and, thirdly, the excess of the actuarial value of the protected life interests, which was what each life tenant was to receive under the division, over the market value of the life interests, had those life interests not been protected, was negligible; so that the life tenants under the two settlements were receiving no more than the value to them of their life interests. In effect, therefore, Megarry J. took the view that the receipt by the life tenant of part of the capital of the appointed fund, if of no more value to him than the market value of his protected life interest if sold as an unprotected life interest, was not a benefit to the tenant for life, or at least not such a benefit as was referred to by Lord St. Leonards in *Duke of Portland* v. *Lady Topham*.[44] In so holding, the judge followed decisions of the Court of Session to which he referred and in which the Court of Session placed reliance on a late decision of Lord Romilly M.R., in *Re Huish's Charity*.[45]

" Consistently with *Portland* v. *Topham*[46] and *Vatcher* v. *Paull*,[47] *Re Wallace's Settlements*[48] and the cases in the Court of Session which it followed, can in my judgment go no further than this: that if you find an appointment such as is here in question and, on the contemplated division of the fund, the appointor takes no more of the appointed fund than the value of his life interest, the appointment is not invalidated by the mere fact that it is made in contemplation of the division. It does not in my judgment, however follow that an appointment made by one entitled to a life interest not with an entire and single object of benefiting the appointee, but with a view also to having part of the capital of the appointed fund to spend, would be unobjectionable if the capital to be received was less than the market

---

44 (1864) 11 H.L.Cas. 32, 55.
45 (1870) L.R. 10 Eq. 5.
46 (1864) 11 H.L.Cas. 32, 55.
47 [1915] A.C. 372.
48 [1968] 1 W.L.R. 711.

value of the life interest. The question must be one of fact. If my view of the earlier high authorities is correct and it is the purpose and the object of the appointment which is the test of its validity or invalidity, it must, I think, follow that, an appointment made partly for the purpose of enabling part of the capital of the appointed fund, however small, to be put in the pocket of the appointor is a fraud on the power: for if that be part of the motive for the appointment there is not the absence of an ulterior object necessary to support it. Nor do I find it easy to accept that, in an age when income tax and surtax rests so heavily on the recipients of income, the advantage of having the capital equivalent of the value of a life interest is not a benefit, or may not prompt an appointment which would not otherwise be made thereby excluding other objects of the power and those entitled in default of appointment. If, however, one finds that just before the issue of the originating summons or, as in this case, just before its hearing, that an appointment has been made and that the court is being invited to approve on behalf of some person a variation of the trusts of a settlement under which part of the appointed fund is to be paid or transferred to the appointor, then in the absence of evidence that the appointment was a separate transaction or would have been made irrespective of the division, it may be—for I find nothing in *Re Wallace's Settlements* to suggest that this is not so—that the proper prima facie inference is that the appointment was not made 'with the entire and single view' that the appointee should have the property. Suppose a fund be settled on A for life and after his death on trust for such of his three children in such shares as he shall appoint and in default of appointment on trust for those same named children in equal shares. Then suppose that the tenant for life partly in order to avoid estate duty, partly in order to put a capital sum into his own pocket and partly in order to benefit one of the three children, makes an appointment in favour of that child with a view to a division of the fund between himself and that child. I cannot doubt that in that case the appointment constitutes a fraudulent appointment as against the other two children who might have been willing to give him only a lesser price. Moreover in my view it would be none the less a fraudulent appointment if the amount received by the tenant for life was less than the amount which he could have obtained by selling his life interest on the market. I have come to the conclusion, however, in accordance with the recent authorities, that the mere fact that the tenant for life makes the appointment as part of a scheme for the division of the appointed fund does not *ipso facto* show that the appointment was made for an ulterior purpose not permitted by the instrument creating the power; at least in a case where the part of the appointed fund to be taken by the appointor is not more valuable than the life interest which the appointor gives up. If that were the position here I would, but subject to the caution at the end of this judgment, hold that the appointment which I have to consider was not a fraud on the power and make the order asked for.

" The facts of this case are, however, in my judgment clearly distinguishable from the facts in *Re Wallace's Settlements* and the cases on which Megarry J. rested his judgment in that case: for here, first, the known effect of the appointment was to produce, by defeating the interests of future children, a state of affairs under which the court might be expected to approve a division more favourable to the tenant for life than would have been the case if the division had had to be shown to be for the benefit of the after-born children: and secondly, because of the fact that the tenant for life here was anxious to obtain all he could on the division. As counsel for the trustees pointed out, prima facie an appointment should be treated as made for the object which it achieved and I am constrained to hold that one of the objects of this appointment was to obtain a benefit for the appointor which he might not otherwise have had, and was a fraud on the power."

Section 9. Indemnity of Trustees [49]

I. INDEMNITY AGAINST THE TRUST PROPERTY [50]

The Trustee Act 1925

Section 30.— . . . (2) [51] A trustee may reimburse himself or pay or discharge out of the trust premises all expenses incurred in or about the execution of the trusts or powers.

This has always been the rule of equity in respect of expenses properly incurred [52] in the administration of the trust: *Stott* v. *Milne, infra; aliter* in respect of expenses or costs improperly incurred through unreasonable conduct on the part of the trustee: *Re Chapman*,[53] *infra.* If litigation is contemplated trustees should safeguard themselves by obtaining a Beddoe's

---

[49] See generally A. W. Scott, " Liabilities Incurred in the Administration of Trusts " (1915) 28 H.L.R. 725; Stone " A Theory of Liability of Trust Estates for the Contracts and Torts of the Trustee " (1922) 22 Col.L.R. 527. As to a trustee's indemnity (a) in respect of liabilities incurred in carrying on (with authority) his testator's business, see Murray, " Indemnity of Executor " (1893) 9 L.Q.R. 331; *Re Oxley* [1914] 1 Ch. 604; (b) in respect of damages he has paid for a tort committed in the course of the administration of the trust, see *Bennett* v. *Wyndham* (1862) 4 De G.F. & J. 259; *Re Raybould* [1900] 1 Ch. 199.

[50] For indemnity against the beneficiaries personally, see Part II of this Section, *infra*, p. 608; for indemnity against the beneficiary's beneficial interest under s. 62 of the Trustee Act 1925, see *infra*, p. 641; for a trustee's indemnity against his co-trustee, see *infra*, p. 662.

[51] This subsection replaces s. 24 of the Trustee Act 1893. See also s. 11 (2) of the Trustee Act 1925 and s. 100 of the Settled Land Act 1925.

[52] The trustee need not satisfy the liability before claiming indemnity; he may in the first instance discharge the liability by making the payments direct from the trust estate: see *Lacey* v. *Hill* (1874) L.R. 18 Eq. 182; *Re National Financial Co.* (1868) L.R. 3 Ch. 791; *Hobbs* v. *Wayet* (1887) 36 Ch.D. 256; *Re Blundell* (1888) 40 Ch.D. 370.

[53] See also *Re Beddoe* [1893] 1 Ch. 547, 558; *Re England* [1918] 1 Ch. 24; *Ecclesiastical Commissioners* v. *Pinney* [1900] 2 Ch. 736, 742, 743; *Hosegood* v. *Pedler* (1896) 66 L.J.Q.B. 18; *cf. Jesse* v. *Lloyd* (1883) 48 L.T. 656; *Re Dargie* [1953] 1 W.L.R. 991. A trustee may apparently restrict, by contract, his right of indemnity against the trust estate: *Gillam* v. *Morrison* (1847) 1 De G. & Sm. 421.

Order from the court: this entitles them to be reimbursed the costs no matter how the litigation results.[54] Persons having claims against the trustees *qua* trustees can be subrogated to the trustees' right and obtain the benefit of the trustees' lien for expenses.[55]

STOTT v. MILNE [56]

Court of Appeal (1884) 25 Ch.D. 710; 50 L.T. 742 (Lord Selborne L.C., Cotton and Lindley L.JJ.)

The defendant trustees had brought two actions, on the advice of counsel, and without the knowledge of the plaintiff beneficiary, against third parties for wrongs alleged to have been done to the trust estate. The actions were compromised on trial. The trustees found themselves out of pocket after having paid, from the income of the trust, the balance of the costs in one of the actions. The plaintiff (tenant for life) brought the present action, before the Vice-Chancellor of the Lancaster Palatine Court, claiming payment to him of income received by the trustees, he being willing to concur in an arrangement to pay costs (if satisfied that they were properly chargeable) out of corpus only.

Held, by the Vice-Chancellor, that the actions having been brought by the trustees without the concurrence or knowledge of the beneficiary, the costs were not chargeable against income. Secondly, the actions having been brought on the advice of counsel, costs were chargeable against corpus. Thirdly, the trustees must pay the plaintiff his cost of the present action.

This decision was reversed by the Court of Appeal on the first and third points, and affirmed on the second, but on the following grounds:

EARL OF SELBORNE L.C.: " I feel no doubt that the trustees acted bona fide and reasonably in bringing the actions. The property was peculiarly circumstanced, it was not large, but was available for building purposes, and anything done by tenants or neighbours which would give any other persons rights over it might cause a material depreciation in its value. The trustees therefore had an anxious duty to perform, which was not rendered less anxious by the course taken by the plaintiff. In 1872, he, being desirous of avoiding actions, gave the trustees an indemnity for not bringing any; but he afterwards changed his mind, withdrew the indemnity, and gave the trustees notice that he should

---

[54] *Re Beddoe* [1893] 1 Ch. 541; *Re Yorke* [1911] Ch. 370; *Re England's S.T.* [1918] 1 Ch. 24.

[55] *Stannier* v. *Evans* (1886) 34 Ch.D. 470; *Re Firth* [1902] 1 Ch. 344; *Re Oxley* [1914] 1 Ch. 604.

[56] See also *Worrall* v. *Harford* (1802) 8 Ves. 4; *Morison* v. *Morison* (1855) 7 De G. M. & G. 214; *Spackman* v. *Holbrook* (1860) 2 L.T. 367; *Re Exhall Co.* (1866) 35 Beav. 449; *Re Pooley Co.* (1869) 21 L.T. 690; *Travis* v. *Illingworth* [1868] W.N. 206; *Courtney* v. *Rumley* (1871) Ir.R. 6 Eq. 99, 106 *et seq.*; *Walters* v. *Wood-bridge* (1878) 7 Ch.D. 504; *Re Pumfrey* (1882) 22 Ch.D. 255; *Budgett* v. *Budgett* (1894) 43 W.R. 167; *Rowley* v. *Ginnever* [1897] 2 Ch. 503; *Jennings* v. *Mather* [1902] 1 K.B. 1; *Re Smith's Estate, Bilham* v. *Smith* [1937] Ch. 636; *Darke* v. *Williamson* (1858) 25 Beav. 622.

hold them liable if they did not take proper steps to protect the estate. Under these circumstances we ought to be clearly satisfied that the actions were improper before we reverse the decisions that the cost of them were properly payable out of the estate. I think, however, that the reason given in the decree for allowing them is not sufficient, and ought to be varied, because it states merely that they were commenced under the advice of counsel. Now, I cannot say that because an action is advised by counsel it is always and necessarily one which trustees may properly bring. The advice of counsel is not an absolute indemnity to trustees in bringing an action, though it may go a long way towards it. The actions were compromised before trial. That the result of the first action was beneficial to the estate is clear. Whether the estate was benefited by the second action is disputed, but I am disposed to think that it was. Looking at the whole circumstances, at the manifest bona fides of the trustees, and at the opinion of the Vice-Chancellor that the costs ought to be allowed, I am of opinion that the direction for payment of them out of the corpus must be sustained.

" Then as to the second appeal, the Vice-Chancellor has ordered the trustees to pay the costs up to the hearing. This is a severe order, which can only be justified by misconduct on their part, and I cannot find any misconduct which would justify it. The only thing urged against them is that they retained the cost of the actions out of the income, and they are alleged also to have insisted that the tenant for life should bear them. But did they so insist in any such way as to amount to misconduct? I think not. On referring to the correspondence, we find that the trustees before this action expressed themselves ready to concur in any reasonable arrangement as to the raising and paying the costs. Under these circumstances it would be very harsh to make them pay costs because they refused to part with the income until the costs of the former actions had been paid. If they had had no right to retain their costs out of the income the case would have stood very differently, and perhaps the Vice-Chancellor thought that they had not; but if he was of that opinion I cannot agree with him. The right of trustees to indemnity against all costs and expenses properly incurred by them in the execution of the trust is a first charge on all the trust property, both income and corpus. The trustees, therefore, had a right to retain the costs out of the income until provision could be made for raising them out of the corpus. I am of opinion that their costs of this action ought to be raised and paid out of the estate in the same way as the costs of the former actions."

Re CHAPMAN, FREEMAN v. PARKER [57]

Court of Appeal (1895) 72 L.T. 66; 11 T.L.R. 177; 39 S.J. 217 (Lord Herschell L.C., Lindley and Smith L.JJ.)

In accordance with the terms of his trust a trustee (Mr. Parker) paid the income to a beneficiary but, after fifteen years, began to suspect that

---

[57] See also *Hide* v. *Haywood* (1740) 2 Atk. 126; *Mosley* v. *Ward* (1805) 11 Ves. 581;

the beneficiary, whom he had never seen, had died, and that the person who had been receiving the income was an impostor. He therefore required evidence to satisfy him that the recipient was the beneficiary entitled. The evidence which was given failed to satisfy him. A summons was taken out by the recipient to compel him to pay the income.

North J. held that the defendant trustee had acted unreasonably, and ordered him to pay the income to the plaintiff and the costs of the application. The defendant appealed against the order as to costs.

LORD HERSCHELL L.C.: "This is an appeal from a judgment of North J., by which he ordered the appellant to pay over certain dividends and the costs of the proceedings. The appeal is only from the latter part of the order, namely, as to the costs. The appellant contends that not only ought he not to have been ordered to pay the costs, but that he should be allowed to receive them. The law which, in my opinion, is applicable to the case may be shortly stated. I think that a trustee is bound to act reasonably. I do not dissent from Mr. Parker's proposition that what is reasonable must be measured by the responsibility which the law imposes on a trustee. I do not think that a trustee is bound to run any risks. I think that he is entitled to satisfy himself by all reasonable inquiry and investigation, because, if he pays money to any person who is not properly entitled to receive it, he may be held liable. But if he sees risk where none in fact exists, and if he refuses to be satisfied by evidence which would satisfy all reasonable men, then I think that he must bear all the expenses which his conduct causes, and cannot throw that expense upon any particular beneficiary or upon the trust estate. The appellant contends that the trustee is the only judge of what is reasonable, and that he is entitled to be satisfied in such a way as he considers proper. I must entirely dissent from that proposition. The appellant asked how the court could decide whether a trustee had been acting reasonably, and suggested that that point must be left to the trustee himself. But the courts have every day in a variety of cases to determine whether men are acting reasonably; and I can see no ground why they should not determine what is reasonable in the case of a trustee, just as in any other case. So much for the law. I pass now to the facts. [His Lordship reviewed the evidence which had been furnished to the trustee of the identity of the plaintiff, stating that it was overwhelmingly in favour of the plaintiff, and that he did not think that any other human being would have displayed such phenomenal scepticism, and continued:] One word I will add, as to the appellant's conduct. I do not

---

Holcombe v. *Jones* (1831) 1 L.J.Ch. 46; *Baker* v. *Carter* (1835) 1 Y. & C.Ex. 250; *Howard* v. *Rhodes* (1837) 1 Keen 581; *Noble* v. *Meymott* (1851) 14 Beav. 471, 480; *Byrne* v. *Norcott* (1851) 13 Beav. 336, 346; *Att.-Gen.* v. *Murdoch* (1856) 2 K. & J. 571; *Beer* v. *Tapp* (1862) 6 L.T. 269; *Palairet* v. *Carew* (1863) 32 Beav. 564, 569; *Talbot* v. *Marshfield* (1867) L.R. 4 Eq. 661, 673; *Att.-Gen.* v. *Stroud* (1868) 19 L.T. 545; *Griffin* v. *Brady* (1869) 18 W.R. 130; *Re Wiseman* (1870) 18 W.R. 574; *Bell* v. *Turner* (1877) 47 L.J.Ch. 75; *Re Cabburn* (1882) 46 L.T. 848; *Re Weall* (1889) 42 Ch.D. 674; *Easton* v. *Landor* (1892) 62 L.J.Ch. 164.

believe that he acted dishonestly, or that he had any personal ends to
serve. I think that it was sheer unreasonableness on his part. Sometimes
a man gets an idea into his head, and nothing will shake him. That is
the case with the appellant. The question is what is to be done? It would
be a most lamentable state of the law if the costs occasioned by this
unreasonable conduct should fall either on the beneficiary or on the trust
estate. I think that the proper order is that the appellant should pay all
the costs, to be taxed as between solicitor and client. It may be
unfortunate that the appellant, having acted honestly, should be compelled to pay the costs; but it would be still more unfortunate if they
should be allowed to fall on the beneficiary or on the trust estate. I
think that the judgment of North J. must be affirmed, with costs."
Appeal dismissed.[58]

II. INDEMNITY AGAINST THE BENEFICIARY PERSONALLY

A trustee's right of indemnity in respect of expenses properly incurred—
e.g., in respect of costs, a call on shares, solicitor's, stockbroker's or auctioneer's charges—is a right of indemnity against the trust *estate,* not
against the beneficiary. Hence, *e.g.,* the trustees of an ordinary club are
entitled to be indemnified by the club property, not by the club members.[59]
But in the following circumstances a trustee's indemnity extends beyond
the estate to the *beneficiary* personally:

First, where he (the trustee) accepted the trust at the request of the
beneficiary.[60]

Secondly, where the beneficiary was the creator of the trust.[61]

Thirdly, where the beneficiary is a *sole* beneficiary *sui juris* and entitled
absolutely: *Hardoon* v. *Belilios, infra.*[62]

Fourthly, there is apparently also a personal indemnity against *several*

---

[58] In the following cases the trustee was visited with costs, as having acted unreasonably in withholding payment—*Jones* v. *Lewis* (1786) 1 Cox 199; *Thorby* v. *Yeats*
(1842) 6 Jur.(o.s.) 939; *Campbell* v. *Home* (1842) 1 Y. & C.C.C. 664; *Penfold* v.
Bouch (1844) 4 Hare 271; *Hampshire* v. *Bradley* (1845) 2 Coll. 34; *Firmin* v.
Pulham (1848) 2 De G. & Sm. 99; *Cockcroft* v. *Sutcliffe* (1856) 4 W.R. 339; *Price*
v. *Loaden* (1856) 21 Beav. 508; *Smith* v. *Bolden* (1863) 33 Beav. 262; *Southwell* v.
Martin (1869) 21 L.T. 135; *De Burgh* v. *M'Clintock* (1883) 11 L.R.Ir. 220; *Cop-
pinger* v. *Shekleton* (1885) 15 L.R.Ir. 461.
  On the other hand, in the following cases the trustee was held to have had
reasonable doubts and therefore relieved of costs—*Taylor* v. *Glanville* (1818) 3
Madd. 176; *Angier* v. *Stannard* (1834) 3 My. & K. 566; *Poole* v. *Pass* (1839) 1
Beav. 600; *King* v. *King* (1857) 1 De G. & J. 663; *Martin* v. *Wilson* [1913] 1 Ir.R.
470.
  Matters of personal feeling between trustee and beneficiary are not taken into
account on a question of costs: see *Moore* v. *Prance* (1851) 9 Hare 299.
[59] *Wise* v. *Perpetual Trustee Co.* [1903] A.C. 139, a decision criticised in (1903) 19
L.Q.R. 386, but approved in (1903) 3 Col.L.R. 407. The club rules, however, may
make the members personally liable.
[60] *Jervis* v. *Wolferstan* (1874) L.R. 18 Eq. 18; but see Lord Blackburn in *Fraser* v.
Murdoch (1881) 6 App.Cas. 855, 872.
[61] *Matthews* v. *Ruggles-Brise* [1911] 1 Ch. 194. In that case it was also held that
where a beneficiary is personally liable to indemnify his trustee, an assignment by
him of his beneficial interest does not affect that liability as it stood at the date of
the assignment.
[62] See also *Re Universal Corp.* (1868) 16 W.R. 451; *Re National Financial Co.* (1868)
L.R. 3 Ch. 791; *Hemming* v. *Maddick* (1872) L.R. 7 Ch. 395; *Brown* v. *Black*
(1873) L.R. 8 Ch. 929.

beneficiaries, provided they are *sui juris* and collectively entitled absolutely, certainly if the expense was incurred at the request of all of them.[63]

HARDOON v. BELILIOS

Privy Council [1901] A.C. 118; 70 L.J.P.C. 9; 83 L.T. 573; 49 W.R. 209; 17 T.L.R. 126 (Lords Hobhouse, Robertson, Lindley, Sir Francis Jeune and Sir Ford North)

On April 3, 1891, fifty £10 shares in the Bank of China, Japan, and the Straits Ltd. were placed in the name of the plaintiff, Hardoon, by his employers, Benjamin & Kelly, who were sharebrokers. The plaintiff never had any beneficial interest in the shares.

The plaintiff's provisional certificate of title to the shares and a blank transfer signed by him were held by Benjamin & Kelly, who paid the application and allotment money and first call. The certificate and transfer were afterwards acquired by one Coxon, who acted on behalf of a syndicate which had been formed to speculate in shares and was financed by the defendant, Belilios. The certificate and transfer were pledged by Coxon with the defendant as security for the advances made by the defendant.

In October 1891 the plaintiff's provisional certificate was exchanged for an ordinary certificate which was handed to the defendant. In March 1892 the plaintiff received the dividends on the shares which he handed to the defendant at the defendant's request. On October 1892 the syndicate was wound up and the defendant became the absolute beneficial owner of the shares.

In November 1893 a call of £1 per share was made, payable by four instalments of 5s. each. The first three of these instalments were, at the plaintiff's request, paid by the defendant to the plaintiff and by the plaintiff to the Bank of China, Japan, and the Straits Ltd. In his books the defendant debited the plaintiff with these payments but there was no evidence that the plaintiff knew of this.

On April 10, 1894, the plaintiff asked the defendant to accept a transfer of the shares, but the defendant refused. In June 1894 the defendant, at the plaintiff's request, paid the fourth instalment of the call of 5s. but debited the plaintiff with the amount as before. Shortly afterwards, the defendant declined a request from the plaintiff's solicitors to have the shares transferred out of the plaintiff's name.

In December 1894 the Bank of China, Japan, and the Straits Ltd. went into liquidation, the liquidator made calls upon the plaintiff for £402 12s. 11d., and, on the plaintiff's failure to pay, judgment was given against him for that amount.

The plaintiff brought an action claiming an indemnity from the defendant in respect of the calls made upon the plaintiff in the winding up of the Bank of China, Japan, and the Straits Ltd.

---

[63] *Buchan* v. *Ayre* [1915] 2 Ch. 474, 477.

The Chief Justice of Hongkong nonsuited the plaintiff on the ground
that he had failed to prove any contract by the defendant to indemnify
him either express or implied. The plaintiff appealed to the Full Court,
which dismissed his appeal, on the ground that, although the defendant
had become beneficial owner of the shares, the relation of trustee and
cestui que trust had not been created between the plaintiff and defendant,
with the result that the defendant had not become liable to indemnify
the plaintiff.

The plaintiff appealed to the Judicial Committee of the Privy Council.

LORD LINDLEY: " It appears from the evidence as it stands that the
defendant became in October 1892 the sole beneficial owner of these
shares, the legal title to which was vested in the plaintiff. Assuming this
to be established, their Lordships are at a loss to understand what more
was required to create the relation of trustee and *cestui que trust* between
the plaintiff and the defendant. The facts that they never stood in the
relation of vendor and purchaser, that there was no contract between
them, that the defendant never requested the plaintiff to become his
trustee, are quite immaterial. All that is necessary to establish the
relation of trustee and *cestui que trust* is to prove that the legal title was
in the plaintiff and the equitable title in the defendant. This might be
proved in many ways. The mode of proof is quite immaterial. Being
proved, no matter how, the relation of trustee and *cestui que trust* was
thereby established.

" No one can be made the beneficial owner of shares against his will.
Any attempt to make him so can be defeated by disclaimer. But the
moment the defendant accepted the beneficial ownership of these shares
he became the plaintiff's *cestui que trust*, and the plaintiff had no option
in the matter.

" The next step is to consider on what principle an absolute beneficial
owner of the trust property can throw upon his trustee the burdens incidental to its ownership. The plainest principles of justice require that the
cestui que trust who gets all the benefit of the property should bear its
burdens unless he can show some good reason why his trustee should
bear them himself. The obligation is equitable and not legal, and the
legal decisions negativing it, unless there is some contract or custom
imposing the obligation, are wholly irrelevant and beside the mark.
Even where trust property is settled on tenants for life and children, the
right of their trustee to be indemnified out of the whole trust estate
against any liabilities arising out of any part of it is clear and indisputable; although if that which was once one large trust estate has been converted by the trustees into several smaller distinct trust estates, the
liabilities incidental to one of them cannot be thrown on the beneficial
owners of the others. This was decided in *Fraser* v. *Murdoch*,[64] which
was referred to in argument. But where the only *cestui que trust* is a

---

[64] (1881) 6 App.Cas. 855.

person *sui juris,* the right of the trustee to indemnity by him against liabilities incurred by the trustee by his retention of the trust property has never been limited to the trust property; it extends further, and imposes upon the *cestui que trust* a personal obligation enforceable in equity to indemnify his trustee. This is no new principle, but is as old as trusts themselves. . . .

" Where, as in *Balsh* v. *Hyham,*[65] a trustee seeks indemnity in respect of transactions in which he need not have engaged and which were not within the scope of his trust, he must prove that his *cestui que trust* either authorised or ratified such transactions. But if he has incurred liability within the scope of his trust, and for the benefit of his *cestui que trust, Ex p. Chippendale*[66] shows that nothing more is required.

" When a trustee seeks indemnity from his *cestui que trust* against liabilities arising from the mere fact of ownership, there is neither principle nor authority for saying that the trustee need prove any request from his *cestui que trust* to incur such liability. In the case supposed the trust involves such liabilities, and the trustee, whilst he remains such, cannot get rid of them. He is subject to them as legal owner; but in equity they fall on the equitable owner unless there are good reasons why they should not.

" . . . The fact that the defendant did not create the trust on which the plaintiff held the shares when they were first placed in his name affords the defendant no defence to this action. Although the defendant did not create the trust, he accepted a transfer of the beneficial ownership in the shares, first as mortgagee and afterwards as sole beneficial owner, with full knowledge of the fact that they were registered in the plaintiff's name as trustee for their original purchasers and their assigns, whoever they might be. By this acceptance the defendant became the plaintiff's *cestui que trust;* and the plaintiff could not prevent it or effectually dispute his trusteeship for the defendant. By this acceptance the defendant created the trust for himself. Having done so, the defendant as the beneficial owner of the shares demanded from the plaintiff and obtained dividends declared in respect of them. The defendant also paid calls made upon them, although he attempted to protect himself from any admission of liability by entering these payments in his books as made on behalf of the plaintiff. Lastly, when asked by the plaintiff to procure a transfer of the shares out of the plaintiff's name, the defendant refused to do so, and thereby compelled the plaintiff to continue to hold them as his trustee. It is idle after this to rely on the fact that the defendant did not create the trust in the first instance, and idle to talk of renunciation or disclaimer of these shares by the defendant. He cannot now get rid of the trust for himself which he created by becoming beneficial owner of the shares, and which trust he has recognised since as subsisting.

---

[65] (1728) 2 P.Wms. 453.   [66] (1853) 4 D.M. & G. 19.

"It is quite unnecessary to consider in this case the difficulties which would arise if these shares were held by the plaintiff on trust for tenants for life, or for infants, or upon special trusts limiting the right to indemnity. In those cases there is no beneficiary who can be justly expected or required personally to indemnify the trustee against the whole of the burdens incident to his legal ownership; and the trustee accepts the trust knowing that under such circumstances and in the absence of special contract his right to indemnity cannot extend beyond the trust estate, *i.e.*, beyond the respective interests of his *cestuis que trustent*.[67] In this case their Lordships have only to deal with a person *sui juris* beneficially entitled to shares which he cannot disclaim. The obligation of such a person to indemnify his trustee against calls upon them [68] appears to their Lordships indisputable in a court of equity unless, of course, there is some contract or other circumstance which excludes such obligation. Here there is none. Whether the plaintiff in this case could sue Benjamin & Kelly on any promise by them to indemnify him need not be discussed. Such a right, if it exists, in no way affects the obligation of the defendant as the plaintiff's *cestui que trust*. But it is obvious that any payment to the plaintiff by Benjamin & Kelly or by the defendant in respect of the calls would reduce the amount which the plaintiff could recover from the defendant or from them as the case might be.

"For these reasons their Lordships will advise Her Majesty to allow the appeal, and to reverse the judgments appealed from with costs; and the defendant will pay the costs of this appeal." *Appeal allowed.*

PROBLEMS

1. Alan and Brian are brothers. They are trustees of a trust fund and directors of a private company in which they are majority shareholders. In good faith they sell to the trust for £30,000 a number of shares in the company which they had themselves bought for £15,000. The price paid by the trust was the proper market value of the shares. Since the sale the shares have appreciated in value to £45,000. The brothers continue as directors of the company and continue to be paid directors' fees. An adult beneficiary is seeking to take advantage of any rights he may have. Advise the brothers.

2. David, Eric and Ferdinand are trustees of a fund whose portfolio of investments includes some 10,000 shares out of an issued 30,000 shares in a private company. The fund is held upon protective trusts for Ferdinand during his life and after his death for George and Harry equally. Ian, who is the trustees' solicitor, discussed with them the possibility of their acquiring a sufficient number of shares in the company to give them a majority holding. The trustees refused for though they had power to retain their existing shares they had no power to invest in further shares in any private companies. Ian told them that they had a chance of applying successfully to the

---

[67] This should be *cestuis que trust*: see C. Sweet (1910) 26 L.Q.R. 196.
[68] Apparently a misprint for " him."

court for such a power but the trustees considered that it would not be worth it. However, they told Ian that if he wished he could personally go ahead and try and obtain control for himself for as far as they could see this could only enhance the value of the trust's shareholding.

Ian then acquired all the remaining shares in the company, disposed of some of its assets, reorganised the business and increased the value of the shares from £1 each to £4 each. In the meantime, Ferdinand had become bankrupt and David and Eric removed him from his trusteeship on the ground of his unfitness to act (without replacing him) and refused to apply any income for his benefit.

How far is Ian entitled to keep the profit on these transactions?

How far is the conduct of David and Eric legally justified?

Can Ferdinand call for the correspondence which passed between David and Eric, on the one hand, and Ian, on the other, relating to his removal from office and to the decision not to pay him any money?

3. Terence died having bequeathed all his residuary personalty to his executors and trustees upon trust for Arthur for life, remainder to Brian absolutely. A charging clause in the will authorised any executor or trustee thereof being a person engaged in any profession to be paid all usual professional charges for services performed in connection with proving the will and executing the trusts.

Advise the executors and trustees who happen to be stockbrokers, as to the scope of the charging clause and their responsibilities towards Arthur and Brian in relation to:

  (i) the incidence of debts, expenses and legacies;
  (ii) some shares in a private company which form part of Terence's residuary personalty;
  (iii) a leasehold flat held on a lease with only seven years to run which is sub-let to a weekly tenant at £8 per week;
  (iv) a reversionary interest in a fund of personalty which is held on trust for Terence's mother (still alive) for life and thereafter for Terence absolutely.

4. Instructing solicitors act for 24-year old David Rockechild who is beneficially interested under a settlement made by his grandfather on 1st April 1966. Sir Malcolm Place and Sir Frank Haddock are the trustees of the settlement (with the broadest possible powers of investment) currently holding investments worth about £100,000 upon trust for Alan Rockechild for life, with overriding power for the trustees to appoint that upon or before Alan Rockechild's death the capital be distributed to any one or more of Alan's children in such shares as the trustees in their absolute discretion may think fit, but with remainder in default of appointment to Alan's three children, Brian, Charles and David equally if they attain 30 years of age.

In the settlement the settlor had covenanted with the trustees to transfer a further £50,000 to them nine years from the date of the settlement but when the time came he refused to perform his covenant. The trustees have refused to take any action over this flagrant breach of covenant.

Furthermore, the settlor's wife recently sent her cheque for £10,000 to the trustees to be held on the trusts of the settlement. Unfortunately, she died two days after the cheque was received, by which time the cheque had not been presented. Her executors have refused to pay the £10,000 and the trustees have meekly accepted this.

Worst of all, the trustees have recently refused to pay an already agreed advancement of money to David in the following circumstances. David is a qualified Chartered Accountant and he was offered the opportunity to buy his way into a good accountancy practice for £12,000. His father and the trustees recognised that this was a very worthwhile opportunity so arrangements were made for David to call upon the trustees to receive the moneys under an exercise of the statutory power of advancement.

When David arrived he was told that he would have to sign a particular document before he could have the moneys. Upon examining the document he discovered it to be a deed already signed by his father and his brothers consenting to certain share transactions carried out in 1967 and authorising the trustees to retain any profits made by them in respect of those transactions.

Apparently, at tea at an Annual General Meeting of Quickgains Ltd. attended by the trustees as representatives of the settlement, which had a not insubstantial shareholding, the trustees had obtained some confidential information about some prospective profitable contracts that might lead to a take-over bid in a year or so from one of the directors who was an old friend of theirs. The trustees discussed this information with Alan, Brian and Charles (for David, the youngest son by 5 years, was away at boarding school) and they all agreed that it would be worth risking investing a further £10,000 (but no more) of trust moneys in the company and that the trustees could spend as much of their own moneys as they wished once the £10,000 trust moneys had been invested.

The trustees invested the £10,000 and then their own moneys and the shares had quadrupled in value between 1967 and 1972 when the trust shareholding was sold upon the written advice of the trust's stockbrokers.

When pressed by David the trustees refused to disclose how much of their own moneys had been invested in Quickgains Ltd., how much profit they had made or when or if they had sold their shares. The trustees merely pointed out that David should be very grateful for the profits which they had enabled the trust to make. However, David refused to sign the deed whereupon the trustees refused to advance any moneys to him. They also pointed out that if he did not be sensible like his father and his brothers and sign the deed, then it might well be that the power of appointment might be exercised in a way that might not be favourable to him. Two days later David received a letter from his father saying that as the father's personal circumstances had changed he was no longer prepared to consent to any advancement being made to David. Instructing solicitors imagine that the trustees put the father up to this.

Consider what courses of action may be available to David.

CHAPTER 11

LIABILITY FOR BREACH OF TRUST

Section 1. The Test of Liability

A TRUSTEE is liable for a breach of trust if he fails to do what his duty requires or if he does what he is not entitled to do. Breaches may be grossly fraudulent or innocently technical.[1]

TOWNLEY v. SHERBORNE

Lord Keeper (1634) Bridg.J. 35; Toth. 88; Cro.Car. 312

Mr. Townley joined, for conformity, with his co-trustee in signing receipts during the three first half-years for rents forming part of the trust. Townley did not in fact receive any of the rents, but allowed them to remain in the hands of his co-trustee, who became insolvent.[2]

Held, the trustee Townley was not liable for any loss by reason only of having signed the receipts,[3] but (*semble*) was liable for a breach of trust in having left the rents in the hands of his co-trustee for an unreasonable time without inquiry, inasmuch as this was an act which prejudiced the trust.

Note

The difficulty arises when the active hand in the breach of trust was the hand of a co-trustee.[4] This resolves itself into the question: To what extent, if any, is a trustee liable for the acts or defaults of his co-trustee? Here, apart from miscellaneous instances, the cases seem to revolve mainly around four sets of circumstances, in which a trustee is guilty of an act or a default prejudicial to the trust:

1. If he leaves a matter in the hands of his co-trustee without inquiry.[5]

---

[1] Snell, p. 272; *Townley* v. *Sherborne, infra*; *Fellows* v. *Mitchell* (1705) 1 P.Wms. 81; *Brice* v. *Stokes* (1805) 11 Ves. 319; *Marriott* v. *Kinnersley* (1830) Tam. 470; *Gregory* v. *Gregory* (1836) 2 Y. & C.Ex. 313; *Williams* v. *Nixon* (1840) 2 Beav. 472; *Terrell* v. *Matthews* (1841) 11 L.J.Ch. 31; *Dix* v. *Burford* (1854) 19 Beav. 409; *Burrows* v. *Walls* (1855) 5 De G.M. & G. 233; *Griffiths* v. *Porter* (1858) 25 Beav. 236; *Brumridge* v. *Brumridge* (1858) 27 Beav. 5; *Horton* v. *Brocklehurst* (1858) 29 Beav. 504; *Barnard* v. *Bagshaw* (1862) 3 De G.J. & S. 355, 359; *Re Munton* [1927] 1 Ch. 262; *cf. Re Gasquoine* [1894] 1 Ch. 470 and *Lowe* v. *Shields* [1902] 1 Ir.R. 320 (executors).

[2] The report in Cro.Car. 312, and that in Bridg.J. 35, appear to conflict on the question whether Townley had received any of the rents during the first year-and-a-half.

[3] *Blakely* v. *Blakely* (1855) 3 W.R. 288; *Re Fryer* (1857) 5 W.R. 552; Trustee Act 1925, s. 30 (1); *supra*, p. 519.

[4] See the cases cited in note 1, *supra*.

[5] *Chambers* v. *Minchin* (1802) 7 Ves. 186; *Shipbrook* v. *Hinchinbrook* (1810) 16 Ves. 477; *Hanbury* v. *Kirkland* (1829) 3 Sim. 265; *Broadhurst* v. *Balguy* (1841) 1 Y. & C.C.C. 16; *Thompson* v. *Finch* (1856) 8 De G.M. & G. 560; *Mendes* v. *Guedalla* (1862) 8 Jur. 878; *Hale* v. *Adams* (1873) 21 W.R. 400; *Wynne* v. *Tempest* (1897) 13 T.L.R. 360; *Re Second East Dulwich* (1899) 68 L.J.Ch. 196; *Re Lucking's W.T., infra.*

2. If he stands by while a breach of trust, of the facts of which he is cognisant, is being committed by his co-trustee.[6] In the words of Lord Cottenham in *Styles* v. *Guy*,[7] it is the duty of executors and trustees " to watch over, and, if necessary, to correct, the conduct of each other."

3. If he allows trust funds to remain in the sole control of his co-trustee.[8] " The duty of trustees," said Kay J. in *Re Flower*,[9] " is to prevent one of themselves having the exclusive control over the money, and certainly not, by any act of theirs, to enable one of themselves to have the exclusive control of it." Hence the decision in *Att.-Gen.* v. *Randall*,[10] where Lord Talbot is reported to have said that he saw " no reason why trustees may not make one of themselves their cashier, where there is no fraud," is inconsistent with later authority.

4. Apparently also if, becoming aware of a breach of trust committed or contemplated by his co-trustee, he takes no steps to obtain redress.[11]

What is the general principle of these decisions in which a trustee is held liable for a breach of trust when the active hand was not his own, but that of his co-trustee? It appears to be that he is *himself* guilty of an act or a default prejudicial to the trust. It is in fact a rule of equity that a trustee is not liable for the acts or defaults of his co-trustee: he is liable for *his own* acts or defaults, *his own* acts of commission *or of omission*; for in the eye of equity there is no difference in substance between an active and a passive breach of trust.[12] But the rule seems always to have been a somewhat poor measure of protection, for a trustee can be guilty, in many unsuspected ways, of an act or a default which in the eye of equity constitutes a breach of trust. It is only an *exceptionally strong* protective clause in the instrument of trust which will keep him outside the range of equitable liability.[13]

A trustee is not liable for breach of trust merely by retiring from the trust in circumstances in which he is aware that his retirement will facilitate the commission of a breach of trust by his successor in office. To make him liable in such a case it must be shown that he retired *with the object of* facilitating that breach of trust which was in fact committed by his successor.[14]

The question now arises whether legislation has affected the law represented by the cases cited above.[15] Prima facie section 31 of the Act of

---

[6] *Booth* v. *Booth* (1838) 1 Beav. 125; *Gough* v. *Smith* [1872] W.N. 18.

[7] (1849) 1 Mac. & G. 422, 433.

[8] *English* v. *Willats* (1831) 1 L.J.Ch. 84; *Ex p. Booth* (1831) Mont. 248; *Child* v. *Giblett* (1834) 3 L.J.Ch. 124; *Curtis* v. *Mason* (1843) 12 L.J.Ch. 442; *Hewett* v. *Foster* (1843) 6 Beav. 259; *Wigglesworth* v. *Wigglesworth* (1852) 16 Beav. 269; *Byass* v. *Gates* (1854) 2 W.R. 487; *Trutch* v. *Lamprell* (1855) 20 Beav. 116; *Cowell* v. *Gatcombe* (1859) 27 Beav. 568; *Williams* v. *Higgins* (1868) 17 L.T. 525; *Rodbard* v. *Cooke* (1877) 25 W.R. 555; *Lewis* v. *Nobbs* (1878) 8 Ch.D. 591.

[9] (1884) 27 Ch.D. 592, 597. See also *Magnus* v. *Queensland National Bank* (1888) 37 Ch.D. 466.

[10] (1734) 2 Eq.Cas.Abr. 742.

[11] *Boardman* v. *Mosman* (1779) 1 Bro.C.C. 68; Lord Westbury in *Wilkins* v. *Hogg* (1861) 8 Jur. 25, 26.

[12] See Lord Langdale's observations in *Ghost* v. *Waller* (1846) 9 Beav. 497, 499, 500.

[13] See *Wilkins* v. *Hogg* (1861) 8 Jur. 25; *Pass* v. *Dundas* (1880) 43 L.T. 665; *cf. Birls* v. *Betty* (1821) 6 Madd. 90.

[14] *Head* v. *Gould* [1898] 2 Ch. 250, and cases there cited; *Kingdom* v. *Castleman* (1877) 36 L.T. 141.

[15] See s. 31 of the Law of Property Amendment Act 1859 (repealed) of which the substance is now to be found in s. 30 (1) of the Trustee Act 1925; *supra*, p. 519. The important words are the concluding ones, " wilful default."

1859 diminished, and section 30 of the Act of 1925 diminishes, the area of equitable liability by abolishing those breaches of trust which are both passive and innocent; and the majority of the cases mentioned above were cases in which a trustee was held liable for a breach of trust both passive and innocent in character. Against this, however, it is arguable, first, that since the statute was not pleaded in any of these cases which were decided after 1859—with the exception of *Re Munton* [16]—the reason must presumably have been that it would not have made any difference if it had been pleaded. Secondly, there is in *Re Brier* [17] a statement of Lord Selborne on section 31 of the Act of 1859 which appears (so far) to settle the matter: "The statute incorporated, generally, into instruments creating trusts the common indemnity clause which was usually inserted in such instruments. *It does not substantially alter the law as it was administered by courts of equity.*" Section 31 of the Act of 1859 was in fact merely a reproduction of the common indemnity clause, which was present in many of the cases cited above, but seems to have been a poor measure of protection: so poor, indeed, that one is tempted to believe that its practical value lay in beguiling a prospective trustee into accepting the trust. A good example will be found in *Underwood* v. *Stevens,* [18] where a clause in a will which provided that the executor-trustees should not be responsible for any loss unless it occurred through their "wilful default" was not even *mentioned* in a judgment which made one of the executor-trustees liable for a breach of trust in having, in good faith, allowed trust funds to be in the sole control of his co-executor-trustee; *and* notwithstanding misrepresentations by that co-executor-trustee as to the circumstances attending the transactions in question. It appears true to say, in fact, that the common indemnity clause did not shield a trustee from the passive innocent breach of trust; and if all that the statute has done is to incorporate the clause into instruments of trust, it would seem to follow that the general law is unaltered. [19]

However, the interpretation put upon the expression "wilful default" in *Re Vickery* [20] as meaning a consciousness of committing a breach of duty or a recklessness as to whether or not a breach was being committed turns the scales in favour of trustees where losses occur within section 30 of the Trustee Act 1925. It is doubtful whether such an interpretation will stand a determined onslaught in future litigation as the interpretation is based on company law cases and is out of line with the pre-1925 trust cases which establish that "wilful default includes want of ordinary prudence." [21]

Trustees liable for a breach of trust are liable jointly and severally. This means that the beneficiaries may call upon any two or more of the trustees jointly, or any one of them severally (separately), to discharge the liability. [22]

---

[16] [1927] 1 Ch. 262.   [17] (1884) 26 Ch.D. 238, 243.

[18] (1816) 1 Mer. 712.

[19] See Bogert, "The Liability of an Inactive Co-trustee" (1921) 34 H.L.R. 483, 496, *supra*, pp. 511–512.

[20] [1931] 1 Ch. 572; *supra*, p. 519.

[21] *Re Chapman* [1896] 2 Ch 763, 776 *per* Lindley L.J.; Gareth Jones (1959) 22 M.L.R. 381.

[22] See *Edwards* v. *Hood-Barrs* [1905] 1 Ch. 20; *Keble* v. *Thompson* (1790) 3 Bro.C.C. 112; *Wilson* v. *Moore* (1833) 1 My. & K. 126, 143; *Cowper* v. *Stoneham* (1893) 68 L.T. 18; *Re Ingham* (1885) 52 L.T. 714.

Ordinarily, between trustees who are jointly and severally liable for a breach of trust there is a right of contribution.[23] That is, as between the trustees themselves the liability must be shared. But where there " has existed a relation between a trustee and his co-trustee which will justify the court in treating his co-trustee as solely liable "—as where he acted under the *guidance* of his *solicitor* co-trustee—or where his co-trustee " has himself got the benefit of the breach of trust," a right of *indemnity* against that co-trustee comes into play.[23] That is, as between the trustee and his co-trustee the former can, in these special circumstances, shift the entire liability onto the shoulders of his co-trustee. Contribution and indemnity are thus mutually exclusive; contribution between trustees exists ordinarily: indemnity between them arises only in special circumstances.

Re LUCKING'S WILL TRUSTS

Chancery Division [1968] 1 W.L.R. 866; [1967] 3 All E.R. 726

Mr. L's father ran a prosperous company in Chester before dying in 1949 some five years before his wife. She left her residuary estate to Mr. L upon trusts giving him (and his children after his death) a three-quarters interest, and her niece, the plaintiff, a one-eighth interest absolutely and a life interest in another eighth. Of the company's 10,000 £1 shares, 6,980 belonged to the trust, 2,920 to Mr. L, and 100 to Mr. L's wife.

In October 1954, Mr. and Mrs. L, as the directors, appointed an old army friend of Mr. L, Lt. Col. Dewar O.B.E., to manage the business and be a director since Mr. L was a barrister practising in London. In 1956 Mr. L appointed Mr. Block, a solicitor, to be co-trustee.

Lt. Col. Dewar for his personal use overdrew £15,000 on the company's confidential No. 2 account (requiring two directors' signatures). Mr. L had signed blank cheques. Dewar was dismissed in 1961, subsequently became bankrupt and no part of his indebtedness was recovered.

The plaintiff sued both trustees for breach of trust.

CROSS J. (in a reserved judgment): " . . . After some months it became the practice for Mr. Dewar to send cheques in blank for Mr. Lucking to sign. Mr. Dewar lived in Scotland in order to be near his wife's parents, who were old, and because his children were being educated there, and was allowed hotel and travelling expenses; these amounted respectively to about £400 and £300 annually. There was delay over the auditing of the company's accounts for 1955 and 1956, which was attributable partly to obstruction by Mr. Dewar. In these years travelling expenses charged to the company greatly increased: Mr. Dewar's hotel expenses increased; the gross profits of the company increased, but the net profits did not increase proportionately. More-

---

[23] *Infra*, Sect. 5.

over Mr. Dewar had drawn in 1955 and 1956 in excess of entitlement, and the aggregate excess (£2,800) was shown in the accounts for those years as a ' loan to a director,' without specifying to whom. Mr. Lucking accepted an explanation of this from Mr. Dewar. These accounts were not prepared and approved by the board until the summer of 1957. A copy of the accounts were supplied to Mr. Block, but he was not told that the loan was to Mr. Dewar, and did not know at this time that Mr. Dewar was a director. In 1957 the profits increased. Mr. Dewar again overdrew his salary and commission, bringing the amount of his loan up to £4,133 by the end of 1957. The 1958 and 1959 accounts were delayed until the summer and autumn of 1960; the cause of the delay being that Mr. Dewar did not produce the No. 2 account and his cash book for inspection by the auditors. Mr. Lucking continued to sign blank cheques during the first half of 1959. By the summer of 1960 Mr. Lucking was aware that both the accountants and the bank manager were worried about the position (the bank overdraft of the company in April, 1960, was £19,000) and were suspicious of Mr. Dewar. When the 1958 accounts were completed, Mr. Dewar's loan had risen to £7,000. At about that time (August, 1958) Mr. Lucking believed that Mr. Dewar was good for the money owing from him to the company (then some £8,000 in all). Mr. Lucking was well aware that the large sums paid and spent by Mr. Dewar absorbed a large part of the company's profits. Mr. Dewar agreed that his salary should be reduced for 1959, that his hotel expenses should not be charged and that his out-of-pocket expenses should be reduced to £500. As a result his indebtedness to the company, as at the end of 1959, increased to £11,530, which figure was shown in the accounts before the board at the end of November, 1960. Mr. Dewar stated at the directors' meeting then that he had paid £4,000 in reduction of the loan. This was untrue and, in fact, he had increased his indebtedness by further drawings in 1960. Mr. Lucking did not check whether the £4,000 had been repaid, and did not cease to send blank cheques to Mr. Dewar. In the spring of 1961 Mr. Lucking realised that Mr. Dewar had not repaid the £4,000. Mr. Dewar was not dismissed until October, 1961, and subsequently he became bankrupt. After writing off the loan to Mr. Dewar and a quantity of stock purchased by him which was unsaleable, the company's balance sheet at December 31, 1961, showed assets worth £42,000 and liabilities of about £37,000. When Mr. Dewar came to the company there had been a balance on profit and loss account of £18,000.''

His Lordship continued: " Those being the facts, what of the law? The claim is for breach of trust alleged to have been committed by both trustees as holders of 70 per cent. of the shares in the company, not a claim against Mr. Lucking for breach of his duty to the company as one of its directors. The plaintiff, who is simply one of the persons beneficially interested under the trust of the shares, could not, of course, have brought such proceedings against Mr. Lucking. The most that she could have done in that direction would have been to have brought proceedings for execution of the trust and in them to have asked the court to remove the existing trustees and to direct new trustees to take action against Mr. Lucking for misfeasance. What success, if any, the plaintiff would have had if she had taken that course I need not enquire, for she has not taken it.

" Counsel for the defendants first submitted that the court could not, without defying the principle of *Salomon* v. *Salomon & Co., Ltd.*,[24] hold shareholders as such liable for mismanagement of the company's affairs. Secondly, he submitted that if this court was prepared in a case like this to go behind the screen interposed between the business and the trust by the separate existence of the company, it could only do so in one of two ways. One was by treating the trust asset as a major share in a business instead of a majority shareholding in a company which owned a business. This would mean that the liability of the trustees would be the same as that of trustees who carried on an unincorporated business under a power in the trust instrument and appointed an agent—here, it would be Mr. Dewar—to manage it for them. The other way would be to overlook the fact that the duty of directors is owed to the company whereas the duty of trustees holding a controlling interest is owed to their beneficiaries and to treat the trustees as owing the same duty to the beneficiaries as they would have owed to the company had they both been non-executive directors with Mr. Dewar as the managing director. Counsel further submitted that whichever way one looked at the matter the defendants could only be liable for ' wilful default ' as defined in *Re City Equitable Fire Insurance Co., Ltd.*[25] That is to say that they would not be liable unless they were conscious that, in doing the act which is complained of or in omitting to do the act which it is said they ought to have done, they were committing a breach of duty or were recklessly careless whether it was a breach of their duty or not.

" As I do not propose to defy *Salomon's* case and neglect the independent existence of the company, it is not necessary for me to explore either of the suggested analogies in detail. I would, however, say that I do not agree that, if I were to look at the case in either of the ways suggested, the result would be that the defendants would be liable only for ' wilful default.' In support of the proposition that a trustee who is carrying on an unincorporated business is only liable for negligence in his supervision of a manager employed by him if the negligence amounts to ' wilful default,' counsel relied on the decision of Maugham J. in *Re Vickery, Vickery* v. *Stephens*.[26] In that case an executor employed a solicitor to obtain payment of sums of money

---

[24] [1897] A.C. 22.
[25] [1925] Ch. 407.
[26] [1931] 1 Ch. 572, *supra*, p. 519.

due to the estate and furnished him with documents of title for the purpose. The solicitor made away with the money and it was said that having regard to what the executor had learnt of the reputation of the solicitor in question he ought to have cancelled the authority given him before the money got into his hands. Maugham J. held that section 23 of the Trustee Act 1925 empowered the executor to employ the solicitor for the purpose in question in the first instance; and he held further that as section 30 of the Act provided, *inter alia*, that a trustee should not be liable for the defaults of any person with whom any trust money or securities might be deposited unless the resulting loss happens through his own wilful default, the executor in the case before him would only be liable if he were guilty of wilful default. I see no reason whatever to think that Maugham J. would have considered that a person employed by a trustee to manage a business owned by the trust was a person with whom trust money or securities were deposited within the meaning of section 30. In support of the proposition that directors are only liable for ' wilful default ' counsel referred to the *City Equitable* case; but there one of the company's articles provided that directors should only be liable for ' wilful default.' Romer J. made it clear in his judgment [27] that, but for that article, he would have held some of the directors liable in some matters for negligence falling short of ' wilful default.' In my view, ' wilful default ' does not enter into the picture in this case at all. The conduct of the defendant trustees is, I think, to be judged by the standard applied in *Re Speight, Speight* v. *Gaunt*,[28] namely, that a trustee is only bound to conduct the business of the trust in such a way as an ordinary prudent man would conduct a business of his own.

" Now what steps, if any, does a reasonably prudent man who finds himself a majority shareholder in a private company take with regard to the management of the company's affairs? He does not, I think, content himself with such information as to the management of the company's affairs as he is entitled to as shareholder, but ensures that he is represented on the board. He may be prepared to run the business himself as managing director or, at least, to become a non-executive director while having the business managed by someone else. Alternatively, he may find someone who will act as his nominee on the board and report to him from time to time as to the company's affairs. In the same way, as it seems to me, trustees holding a controlling interest ought to ensure so far as they can that they have such information as to the progress of the company's affairs as directors would have. If they sit back and allow the company to be run by the minority shareholder and receive no more information than shareholders are entitled to, they do so at their risk if things go wrong. In this case, of course, the trust was represented on the board by Mr. Lucking. As

[27] [1925] Ch. 407, 500.
[28] (1883) 22 Ch.D. 727.

I see it, however, one ought not to regard him as performing a duty to the trust which it was incumbent on the trustees to perform personally, so that Mr. Block became automatically responsible for any deficiencies in Mr. Lucking, as does a passive trustee who allows his co-trustee to exercise alone discretions which it is their duty to exercise jointly. If these trustees had decided, as they might have done, to be represented on the board by a nominee they would have been entitled to rely on the information given them by that nominee as to the way in which the company's affairs were being managed even though such information was inaccurate or inadequate, unless they had some reason to suspect that it was inaccurate or inadequate. Mr. Block, as I see it, cannot have been in a worse position because his co-trustee was the trust's representative on the board than he would have been if the trust's representative had not been a trustee at all. The position of Mr. Lucking, on the other hand, as I see it, was quite different. He cannot say that what he knew or ought to have known about the company's affairs he knew or ought to have known simply as a director with a duty to the company and no one else. He was in the position he was partly as a representative of the trust and, if and so far as he failed in his duty to the company, he also failed in his duty to the trust. To hold this is not, as I see it, inconsistent with any principle to be found in *Salomon's* case.[29]

" Finally, I must ask myself how these principles are to be applied to the facts of this case. It is not suggested that it was not proper for the company to appoint Mr. Dewar to be manager of its business on the terms contained in the service agreement; nor can it be suggested that Mr. Lucking failed to follow the fortunes of the company under Mr. Dewar's management. Mr. Dewar sent him the trading figures regularly and discussed with him regularly the profit ratios, the introduction of new lines, and so on. Mr. Lucking formed, and still retains, a high opinion of Mr. Dewar as manager, so far as the trading side of the business went. He says that he was responsible for introducing various lines which have proved a great success and for training Mr. Poland, who has in fact proved a very satisfactory manager. It may be that looking back now Mr. Lucking, for obvious reasons, exaggerates Mr. Dewar's virtues as a manager. It is certainly a fact that he caused the company to buy a quantity of stock which became unsaleable, and in respect of which, indeed, the plaintiff made a claim in the action, although she dropped it during the hearing. Again, it is a fact that he incurred very heavy advertising and travelling expenses, quite apart from his journeys to and from Stirling, and that the business appears to be prospering under a much less expensive manager. I am not, however, prepared to say that Mr. Lucking had no grounds for thinking that Mr. Dewar was proving a successful manager, and I am not

---

[29] [1897] A.C. 22.

prepared to hold that his allowing him to have hotel expenses in Chester and travelling expenses to and from Chester as well as his salary (which represented an additional remuneration of, perhaps, some £750 a year) constituted a breach of trust. It may very well have been an unnecessary concession and an error of judgment, but not in my judgment a breach of trust. If Mr. Lucking is not liable for it, then *a fortiori* Mr. Block, who was not told of it by Mr. Lucking, is not liable for it.

" I turn now to the overdrawings. The first point which the plaintiff makes with regard to them is that Mr. Lucking ought never to have allowed Mr. Dewar to draw on the No. 2 account with cheques which he signed in blank, but ought to have seen the amounts and the payees before signing the cheques. In this connection one should, I think, distinguish between the period before and the period after Mr. Lucking saw the 1955 and the 1956 accounts which first showed him that Mr. Dewar was overdrawing substantially. Of course, to sign cheques in blank is a notoriously dangerous course; but it is fair to say that the No. 2 account was not set up as an account over the drawings on which Mr. Lucking was expected to exercise any particular super-vision. The reason for setting it up was so that Miss Higham and other members of the staff should not see what payments were made to the management. Mr. Dewar could have drawn a cheque in favour of some creditors of his on the No. 1 account, the ordinary trading account. Indeed, in the later stages of his career he drew such cheques, and Miss Higham countersigned such cheques without query. ' Why then,' says Mr. Lucking, ' should I not have signed blank cheques on this No. 2 account? Business must be conducted on a basis of trust and I would have been perfectly willing to have allowed this No. 2 account to be operated by Mr. Dewar alone had he requested me to do so.'

" Although I think that it was unfortunate that he ever did sign blank cheques and that his doing so was probably the start of this trouble by encouraging Mr. Dewar in a course on which he might otherwise not have started, yet I am not prepared to say that in the circumstances of this case it was a breach of trust so long as Mr. Lucking had no reason to think that Mr. Dewar was abusing the con-fidence reposed in him. In my judgment, however, the position changed altogether when Mr. Lucking realised—in the summer of 1957—that Mr. Dewar was overdrawing at a rate of some £1,400 a year on top of his salary and his expenses and travel allowance. I do not say that Mr. Lucking ought to have leaped there and then to the conclusion that Mr. Dewar was dishonest and that he would be unable to pay what he owed. That is £2,800 to the end of 1956 and, perhaps, some £500 or so more to October, 1957; but Mr. Lucking saw—or if he did not, ought to have seen—that Mr. Dewar was very careless in matters of account, and in my judgment it was negligent of him to retain Mr. Dewar as manager without imposing any check on his drawings. He told me that to have done so—to have refused to sign blank cheques and to have inspected the pass book—would have argued distrust; that he only kept Mr. Dewar because he trusted him completely and, trusting him completely, he would not take safeguards against him. Mr. Lucking, as the history shows, pushed his trust in Mr. Dewar to extremes. It even survived the realisation that he had lied to Mr. Guy. I cannot help thinking that Mr. Lucking would have acted differently if the plaintiff, instead of having only a sixth interest in the company had had five-sixths interest. Mr. Lucking, quite naturally, tended to look on the business as his own. With his own property a man may well say: ' I will trust my friend even though there are circumstances which might make some stranger suspicious of him. I would rather be cheated than spy on him.' But a trustee cannot take that line and, although Mr. Lucking owned a third of the shares and had a life interest in three-quarters of the other two-thirds, his obligations as trustee to the other persons interested were just as great as though he had no beneficial interest at all. Although I have sympathy for Mr. Lucking, I feel bound to hold that he is liable to the other beneficiaries for such loss as was suffered by the trust share-holding for his failing adequately to supervise Mr. Dewar's drawings after the summer of 1957.

" I turn now to consider the position of Mr. Block with regard to the overdrawings. As I have said I do not look on him as a passive trustee who has allowed his co-trustee to decide for him matters on which they ought to have exercised a joint discretion. He was entitled to rely on what Mr. Lucking told him about the company's affairs as being accurate and adequate, unless he had some positive reason to think the contrary. Mr. Lucking told him nothing about the over-drawings by Mr. Dewar until September, 1960. It is said that he was put on enquiry by the entries ' loan to director ' in the accounts for 1955, 1956 and 1957; but he did not know that this was a loan to Mr. Dewar. He thought that it was a loan to Mr. Lucking and having regard to the size of Mr. Lucking's interest in the company and from what Mr. Block knew of him I do not think that he was guilty of negligence in not raising the question. In September, 1960, he was told that Mr. Dewar owed the company some £7,000 or £8,000 representing overdrawings, but he was told at the same time that he was about to repay £4,000 and that Mr. Lucking was satisfied that the rest would be repaid shortly and it was arranged that he should see Mr. Dewar, which he did on December 1. I think that on this occasion he must have been told that the loan—largely owing to Mr. Dewar having forgone part of his salary and expenses—had increased to £11,000, but he was told that £4,000 had already been repaid and that the rest soon would be. I do not think that he was obliged to doubt the fact of this repayment or to ask Mr. Lucking whether he had checked it. Looking back after the event, one can see that a good deal of money might have been saved if Mr. Block had not relied so entirely on what Mr. Lucking told him. I have little doubt that if he had known all that Mr. Lucking knew about the history of the loans Mr. Block would have taken steps to stop any further overdrawings: but I am not prepared to hold that in this case he was guilty of any breach of trust. He heard no more of Mr. Dewar until October 1961, and then did all that he could to obtain repayment. In the event I think that this action fails against Mr. Block.

"It remains to consider by how much the trust shares have decreased in value by what I have held to be the breaches of trust of Mr. Lucking. The total overdrawings were £15,890, but the company succeeded in slightly reducing this by treating £666 as the part of Mr. Dewar's salary attributable to the period from October to December 1961 which they could treat as expenses. One should therefore deduct some £200 for tax to get at the net overdrawings.

" On the other hand, the plaintiff says, with force, that there should be added something in respect of the increase in interest on overdraft which the company suffered—on varying amounts from 1955 to 1961—by reason of their overdrawings. On the other side there are two considerations to be borne in mind. First that one does not know whether if Mr. Lucking had made a stand against the overdrawings in 1957 the £3,000 then owing would have been repaid and, secondly, that the loss with which I am concerned is not the total loss to the company, but the decrease in value in the trust shares in consequence of it, which may well not be proportional. Neither side wanted an enquiry, but wanted me, if I should decide that there was a liability, to fix the quantities myself as best I could on the material before me. The result must, in the nature of the case, be rough and ready, but I assess the damage to the trust shares at £12,000. The plaintiff has suffered one-eighth of this loss—*i.e.*, £1,500—personally, and has also suffered as life tenant of a further one-eighth." *Declaration accordingly.*

Gareth Jones (1959) 22 M.L.R. 390

The learned judge's definition of " wilful default " as a conscious or reckless breach of duty on the part of the trustee cannot be supported; the words should have been construed, in their pre-1926 sense, so as to include want of reasonable care. His Lordship purported to follow the judgment of Romer J. in the *Re City Equitable* case. In that decision, Romer J. was called upon, *inter alia*, to construe a set of articles of association, and in particular, a clause which was in terms similar to the indemnity clause (s. 24) of the Trustee Act 1893. It was inevitable, therefore, that counsel should rely [30] on the *Re Brier* [31] line of cases, which had impliedly interpreted " wilful

---

[30] *Re City Equitable, loc. cit.,* p. 424.
[31] (1884) 26 Ch.D. 238.

default " to include lack of reasonable care, as well as a conscious act of
commission or recklessness on the part of the trustee. Romer J. rejected
this argument. He pointed out that these cases did not involve a consideration of these precise words and that, in the *Re Brier* line of cases, the court
was concerned with the " law as to the employment of agents by trustees." [32]
Directors and auditors were not trustees in the strict sense of the word and
there is little resemblance between their duties and the " duties of a trustee
of a will or a marriage settlement." His Lordship preferred to follow a
number of company law decisions, which were authority for a *Derry* v.
Peek [33] definition of " wilful default."

> " An act, or an omission to do an act, is wilful where the person of
> whom we are speaking knows what he is doing and intends to do what
> he is doing. But if that act or omission amounts to a breach of his duty,
> and therefore to negligence, is the person guilty of wilful negligence?
> In my opinion that question must be answered in the negative unless he
> knows that he is committing, and intends to commit, a breach of this
> duty, or is recklessly careless in the sense of not caring whether his act
> or omission is or is not a breach of duty." [34]

This definition was later accepted by Astbury J. in *Re Munton*,[35] a decision
which was concerned with the liability of a trustee for the acts or defaults
of his agent. The learned judge held that a retiring trustee was not guilty
of a breach of trust in executing a power of attorney authorising a broker
to sell stock and receive the purchase price, the broker having, without
authority, handed over the proceeds of sale to a co-trustee who had mis-
appropriated them. The reasoning of the learned judge is, with respect, a
little difficult to follow. The following passage is significant:

> " The indemnity clauses, containing the exception of wilful default,
> in the Trustee Acts, may or may not have added anything to the
> previous law, but in *Re City Equitable Fire Insurance Co. Ltd.*, the
> whole question of wilful default as regards a fiduciary agent is dealt
> with at great length. Warrington L.J. says: ' Romer J. was quite right
> in arriving at the conclusion that a person is not guilty of " wilful
> neglect or default " unless he is conscious that in doing the act which
> is complained of, or in omitting to do the act which it is said he ought
> to have done, he is committing a breach of his duty, and also, as he
> said, recklessly careless whether it is a breach of the duty or not. . . .'
> " The plaintiff's counsel say that the *City Equitable* case has made no
> change in the law as regards an ordinary trustee's liability. I do not
> propose to discuss that. I have read the passage representing the
> general result of the decision and it seems to me to apply to the present
> case." [36]

The question was not raised in the Court of Appeal and their Lordships did
not comment on these observations of Astbury J.

It is submitted, with respect, that the translation of the definition of
" wilful default " in *Re City Equitable* to section 30 (1) of the Trustee Act

---

[32] At p. 439. Maugham J. in *Re Vickery* recognised this distinction but found the
exposition of Romer J. of " wilful default " none the less valuable (at p. 583).
[33] (1889) 14 App.Cas. 337.   [34] At p. 434.
[35] [1927] 1 Ch. 262.   [36] At p. 274.

1925 was completely unjustified. Romer J. was construing a particular set of
articles of association and the decision on the facts of *Re City Equitable* was
to have no application to the case of trustees, *stricto sensu*. This, indeed,
was the view of Warrington L.J., in the Court of Appeal, in that case, and
his approval of Romer J.'s definition, quoted by Astbury J. in the above passage, was a strictly limited approval. The following extract from the learned
Lord Justice's judgment is relevant.[37]

> "With all respect to counsel who cited those trustees cases to us, I
> think there is great danger of being misled if we attempt to apply
> decisions as to the duties of trustees to a case as to the conduct of
> persons in the position of auditors in this case. In the case of trustees
> there are certain definite and precise rules of law as to what a trustee
> may or may not do in the execution of his trust, and it is no answer for
> a trustee to say, if, for example, he invests the trust property in his
> hands in a security which the law regards as an unauthorised security:
> ' I honestly believed that I was justified in doing that.' No honest belief
> will justify him in committing that which is a breach of such a rule of
> law, and therefore the question which we have to determine in expressing
> a view on the construction of such words in a contract like the present
> is not solved by seeing how the question has been determined in a case
> relating to the duties of a trustee."

In effect, neither Romer J. nor the Court of Appeal in *Re City Equitable*
intended to derogate from the pre-1926 decisions, which, impliedly if not
expressly interpreted the words " wilful default," within section 24 of the
1893 Act, so as to include lack of reasonable care. Section 30 (1) is a mere
re-enactment of section 24 of the Trustee Act 1893 and like that section
should, it is submitted, render the trustee liable if he failed to act with
reasonable care.

Section 2. Extent of Liability

As a general rule the measure of liability for breach of trust is the loss
caused to the estate.[38] The following are instances of the application of
that rule. A trustee cannot set off profits made on breaches of trust against
losses made on breaches of trust.[39]

I. UNAUTHORISED INVESTMENTS

KNOTT v. COTTEE

Master of the Rolls (1852) 16 Beav. 77; 16 Jur.(o.s.) 752

A testator who died in January 1844 directed his executor-trustees
to invest in " the public or Government stocks or funds of Great
Britain, or upon real security in England or Wales." In 1845 and

---

[37] *Re City Equitable, loc. cit.*, pp. 523–524.
[38] *Newton* v. *Reid* (1831) 9 L.J.Ch.(o.s.) 273; *Macdonnell* v. *Harding* (1834) 4 L.J.Ch.
10; *Fowler* v. *Reynal* (1849) 13 L.T.(o.s.) 203; *Lunham* v. *Blundell* (1857) 6 W.R.
49; *Devaynes* v. *Robinson* (1857) 5 W.R. 509; *Cook* v. *Addison* (1869) 20 L.T.
212; *Gough* v. *Etty* (1869) 20 L.T. 358; *Briggs* v. *Massey* (1882) 30 W.R. 325;
quaere, as to *Gibbins* v. *Taylor* (1856) 4 W.R. 432.
[39] *Dimes* v. *Scott* (1828) 4 Russ. 195.

1846, the defendant executor-trustee invested part of the estate in Exchequer bills, which in 1846 were ordered into court, and in the same year sold at a loss. By a decree made in 1848, the court declared that the investment in Exchequer bills was improper. If, however, the investment had been retained, its realisation at the time of the decree of 1848 would have resulted in a profit.

Held, " that the executor ought to be charged with the *amount improperly invested*, and credited with the produce of the Exchequer bills in 1846."

ROMILLY M.R.: " Here is an executor who had a direct and positive trust to perform, which was, to invest the money upon government stocks or funds, or upon real securities, and accumulate at compound interest all the balances after maintaining the children. He has made certain investments, which the court has declared to be improper. The case must either be treated as if these investments had not been made, or had been made for his own benefit out of his own moneys, and that he had at the same time retained moneys of the testator in his hands. I think, therefore, that there must be a reference back, to ascertain what balances the executor retained from time to time, it being clear that he has retained some balances. . . .

" I cannot concur in the argument that the court must charge him as if the money had been invested in consols. If that were so, the court must charge him the other way where the funds have fallen, which it never does. There was a conflict of decision as to how a trustee was to be charged, where the investment might either be made in the funds or on real security. The decisions of Lord Langdale and Sir John Leach were opposed.[40] The case, however, of *Robinson* v. *Robinson* [41] has settled the rule, and I have adopted it in a former case. I stated my reasons for doing so.

" As to the mode of charging the executor in respect of the Exchequer bills, I treat the laying out in Exchequer bills in this way: The persons interested were entitled to earmark them, as being bought with the testator's assets, in the same manner as if the executor had bought a house with the trust funds; and though they do not recognise the investment, they had a right to make it available for what was due; and though part of the property of the executor, it was specifically applicable to the payment. When the Exchequer bills were sold and produced £3,955, the court must consider the produce as a sum of money refunded by the executor to the testator's estate on that day; and on taking the account, the master must give credit for this amount as on the day on which the Exchequer bills were sold. . . ." [42]

---

[40] See an examination of authorities in *Robinson* v. *Robinson* (1851) 1 De G.M. & G. 247.

[41] (1851) 1 De G.M. & G. 247.

[42] See also *Widdowson* v. *Duck* (1817) 2 Mer. 494; *Marsh* v. *Hunter* (1822) 6 Madd. 295. Where an investment is improper only in so far as it is an over-investment in a mortgage otherwise proper, see s. 9 of the Trustee Act 1925, *supra*, p. 501.

Note

If a trustee of a trust to which the rule in *Howe* v. *Earl of Dartmouth,
supra,* p. 546, does *not* apply invests in an unauthorised investment, and
pays the income therefrom to the tenant for life, and the capital is intact
or has been replaced, the remainderman has no equity to make the trustee
pay into capital any excess of income actually received over income which
would have been received on an authorised investment.[43] In the words of
Cozens-Hardy M.R. in *Slade* v. *Chaine,*[44] there is neither a loss to the
capital of the trust, nor a profit to the trustee by the breach of trust. It is
immaterial that the trustee happens also to be himself the tenant for life.[45]
Suppose, however, that the capital has diminished, and the trustee could
not replace the whole of the balance. " If the trustee were not solvent, the
reduced amount which he was able to pay and did pay would no doubt
have to be apportioned as between corpus and income." [46] These cases
also illustrate the proposition that a technical breach of trust grounds no
liability unless there is actual loss.

If a trustee makes an unauthorised investment, the beneficiaries may,
if they choose, and if they are all *sui juris,* adopt the investment as part
of the trust.[47] The difficulty is as to the *extent* of their remedy. If they
decide to adopt the investment, but it has caused a loss to the estate, can
they also require the trustee to replace that loss? According to *Re Lake,*[48]
they apparently can. But Wood V.-C. in *Thornton* v. *Stokill* [49] seems to
have held that if they adopt the investment, it settles the matter. Certainly
if they *reject* it, they can have it sold and require any loss to be replaced.
If, however, the investment is of an *authorised* nature, they have no option
of adopting or rejecting it, for it is necessarily part of the trust.[50]

II. IMPROPER RETENTION OF UNAUTHORISED INVESTMENTS [51]

FRY v. FRY

Master of the Rolls (1859) 27 Beav. 144; 28 L.J.Ch. 591; 34 L.T.(o.s.)
51; 5 Jur. 1047

A testator who died in March 1834, after devising his residuary real
estate to two trustees on trust to pay the rents (except those of the
Langford Inn) to his wife during her widowhood, with remainder over,
and bequeathing his residuary personal estate upon trust for conversion
for his wife during her widowhood, with remainder over, directed the
trustees: "And as for and concerning all that messuage or dwelling-

---

43 *Stroud* v. *Gwyer* (1860) 28 Beav. 130; *Re Appleby* [1903] 1 Ch. 565, 566; *Slade* v.
   Chaine [1908] 1 Ch. 522. See *supra,* pp. 560–561.
44 [1908] 1 Ch. 522, 533.
45 *Re Hoyles* [1912] 1 Ch. 67.
46 Buckley L.J. in *Slade* v. *Chaine* [1908] 1 Ch. 522, 536; *Re Bird* [1901] 1 Ch. 916.
47 *Re Patten* (1883) 52 L.J.Ch. 787; *Re Jenkins* [1903] 2 Ch. 362; *Wright* v. *Morgan*
   [1926] A.C. 788, 799.
48 [1903] 1 K.B. 439; and see *Ex p. Biddulph* (1849) 3 De G. & Sm. 587.
49 (1855) 1 Jur. 751. See also *Re Cape Breton* (1885) 29 Ch.D. 795.
50 *Re Salmon* (1889) 42 Ch.D. 351.
51 The assumption being that the investment has depreciated; otherwise any gain
   belongs of course to the trust. See Arden M.R. in *Piety* v. *Stace* (1799) 4 Ves. 620,
   622, 623.

house called Langford Inn . . . upon trust, as soon as convenient after his decease, to sell and dispose of the same, either by auction or private sale, and for the most money that could be reasonably obtained for the same." In April 1836 the trustees advertised the Langford Inn for sale for £1,000. They refused an offer of £900, made in 1837. One of the trustees died in 1842. A railway opened in 1843 caused the property to depreciate in value through the diversion of traffic. The property was again advertised for sale in 1845, but no offer was received. The other trustee died in 1856. Langford Inn was still unsold, and could not be sold except at a low price.

Held, by Romilly M.R., the trustees had committed a breach of trust by reason of their negligence in not selling the property for so many years, that the property must be sold, and that the estates of the trustees were "liable to make good the deficiency between the amount which should be produced by the sale of the inn and the sum of £900, in case the purchase-money thereof should not amount to that sum." [52]

Note

It was held by the Court of Appeal in *Re Chapman, Cocks* v. *Chapman*,[53] and in *Rawsthorne* v. *Rowley*,[54] that a trustee is not liable for a loss arising through the retention of an *authorised* investment unless he was guilty of *wilful default*.[55] This requires proof of want of ordinary prudence on the part of the trustee.[56]   Section 4 of the Trustee Act 1925 now provides: "A trustee shall not be liable for breach of trust by reason *only* of his continuing to hold an investment which has ceased to be an investment authorised by the trust instrument or by the general law." This provision is inapplicable in cases governed by section 3 (4) of the Trustee Investments Act 1961.   Moreover, where investments requiring advice are made under that Act, the trustees must from time to time obtain and consider advice on whether the retention of the investment is satisfactory having regard to the need for diversification and the suitability of the investments.[57]

III. IMPROPER REALISATION OF PROPER INVESTMENTS

PHILLIPSON v. GATTY

Vice-Chancellor (1848) 6 Hare 26; affirmed (1850) 7 Hare 516; 2 H. & Tw. 459; 12 L.T.(o.s.) 445; 13 Jur.(o.s.) 318

The trustees of a sum of consols, who had power to convert and

---

[52] See also *Taylor* v. *Tabrum* (1833) 6 Sim. 281; *Robinson* v. *Robinson* (1851) 1 De G.M. & G. 247; *Bate* v. *Hooper* (1855) 5 De G.M. & G. 338; *Sculthorpe* v. *Tipper* (1871) L.R. 13 Eq. 232; *Dunning* v. *Gainsborough* (1885) 54 L.J.Ch. 991. *Cf. Edwards* v. *Edmunds* (1876) 34 L.T. 522, where the trustee was held justified by the terms of the will in retaining, and *Buxton* v. *Buxton* (1835) 1 My. & Cr. 80, where an executor-trustee was not charged with the loss occasioned by a delay in realising, on the ground of his having exercised a vigilant discretion.
[53] [1896] 2 Ch. 763.   [54] [1909] 1 Ch. 409n.
[55] See also *Baud* v. *Fardell* (1855) 4 W.R. 40; *Henderson* v. *Hunter* (1843) 1 L.T.(o.s.) 359, 385; *Robinson* v. *Murdoch* (1881) 45 L.T. 417; Joyce J. in *Re Oddy* (1910) 104 L.T. 128, 131; *Re Godwin* (1918) 87 L.J.Ch. 645.
[56] *Per* Lindley L.J. [1896] 2 Ch. 763, 776.
[57] s. 6 (3) (4) (5) of the Trustee Investments Act 1961; *supra*, p. 495.

reinvest in the public funds or upon real security, realised part of the stock and invested in an *un*authorised investment.

WIGRAM V.-C.: ". . . Then comes another material question—are the trustees to replace the stock, or the money produced by the sale? Mr. Wood argued that they were liable to make good the money only, distinguishing the sale, which he said was lawful, from the investment, which I have decided to have been a breach of trust. My opinion is, that the trustees must replace the stock. There was no authority to sell, except with a view to the reinvestment; and here the sale was made with a view to the investment I have condemned. It was all one transaction, and the sale and investment must stand or fall together. . . ."

Held, therefore, the trustees must replace the stock improperly realised. *Affirmed on appeal.*[58]

Note

Where, *e.g.,* a trustee improperly realises a trustee security, the proceeds being £300 and to purchase the same amount of stock would now require £325, the beneficiary may require the trustee to do so. On the other hand, if the stock has depreciated and it would require only £275 to repurchase the same amount, the beneficiary may choose to take the equivalent of the proceeds of the improper realisation, £300.

The above example is a simple case of the improper realisation of a proper investment; but it is not exactly what occurred in *Phillipson* v. *Gatty, supra.* There the trustee had power to realise and reinvest, and after realisation he reinvested in an improper investment. This, however, was in contemplation of law one transaction, and was equivalent to the improper realisation of a proper investment, so that the trustee was liable to replace the original investment, or its value in a sum of money. The principle of *Phillipson* v. *Gatty, supra,* is evidently applied strictly, as in *Re Massingberd.*[59] In that case there was a trust of consols, with a power to convert and reinvest, and the trustee converted and reinvested in an improper investment. The improper investment was itself realised *without* loss, but as consols stood (at the time the case was decided) at a price higher than when they were sold, the remainderman successfully called upon the trustee to restore an amount of consols as they stood originally. There was, *e.g.,* a trust fund of £1,000 consols, with a power to convert and reinvest in certain securities. On Monday, the trustee realised the trust fund, the proceeds being £1,000, and purchased therewith an unauthorised investment. On Tuesday, the unauthorised investment was sold, the proceeds being £1,000. On Wednesday, the beneficiary called upon the trustee to restore the trust property to its original state (or its equivalent in a sum of money). In order to do so, the trustee had to find £1,100, for between Monday and Wednesday consols had appreciated.[60]

---

[58] See also *Harrison* v. *Harrison* (1740) 2 Atk. 121; *Powlet* v. *Herbert* (1791) 1 Ves.J. 297; *Pocock* v. *Reddington* (1801) 5 Ves. 794; *Bateman* v. *Davis* (1818) 3 Madd. 98; *O'Brien* v. *O'Brien* (1828) 1 Moll. 533; *Kellaway* v. *Johnson* (1842) 5 Beav. 319.
[59] (1890) 63 L.T. 296.
[60] See also *Lander* v. *Weston* (1855) 3 Drew. 389.

IV. NON-INVESTMENT OF TRUST FUNDS

A trustee ought not to leave trust moneys uninvested for an unreasonable length of time. If he unnecessarily retains trust moneys which he ought to have invested, he is chargeable with interest.[61]

While an investment is being sought, however, a trustee has a statutory power to pay trust moneys into a deposit or other account.[62] Cases prior to the Act, and decided under the general law, have held that the moneys must not be left in the bank for an unreasonable length of time.[63]

If a trustee, having been *directed* to invest in a *specific* investment, *makes no investment at all,* and the price of the specified investment rises, he may be required to purchase so much of that investment as would have been obtained by a purchase at the proper time.[64] This applies equally where he is directed to invest in a specific investment and he makes some investment other than the one specified.[65] But if he is directed to invest in a specified *range* of investments, and he makes no investment at all, he is chargeable only with the trust fund itself, and not with the amount of one or other of the investments which might have been purchased.[66] The reason was stated by Wigram V.-C. in *Shepherd* v. *Mouls*[67] as follows: "The discretion given to the trustees to select an investment among several securities makes it impossible to ascertain the amount of the loss (if any) which has arisen to the trust from the omission to invest, except, perhaps, in the possible case (which has not occurred here) of a particular security having been offered to the trustees, in conformity with the terms of the trust."[68]

V. TRUST FUNDS IN TRADE

If a trustee in breach of trust lends funds to a third party who takes with notice of the trust and employs the trust funds in trade, the beneficiaries cannot claim from the third party a share of the profits. *E.g.,* a trustee in breach of trust lends £1,000 of trust moneys to X, who takes with notice of the trust and employs the fund in his trade. The agreement between the trustee and X provides that X is to pay interest at the rate of 5 per cent. By employing this fund of £1,000 in his trade, X makes a profit during the first year of £100. The beneficiaries cannot claim from X a share of that profit; all that they can require is that he replace, with interest, the fund which he borrowed. The difficulty is to ascertain from the authorities

---

61 *Littlehales* v. *Gascoyne* (1790) 3 Bro.C.C. 73; *Rocke* v. *Hart* (1805) 11 Ves. 58; *Raphael* v. *Boehm* (1805) 11 Ves. 92; *Holgate* v. *Haworth* (1853) 17 Beav. 259; *Att.-Gen.* v. *Alford* (1855) 4 De G.M. & G. 843; *Stafford* v. *Fiddon* (1857) 23 Beav. 386; *Chugg* v. *Chugg* [1874] W.N. 185; *Re Jones, Jones* v. *Searle* (1883) 49 L.T. 91.

62 Trustee Act 1925, s. 11 (1).

63 *Moyle* v. *Moyle* (1831) 2 Russ. & M. 710; *Cann* v. *Cann* (1884) 33 W.R. 40.

64 *Byrchall* v. *Bradford* (1822) 6 Madd. 235.

65 *Pride* v. *Fooks* (1840) 2 Beav. 430, 432.

66 *Shepherd* v. *Mouls* (1845) 4 Hare 500.

67 *Ibid.* 504.

68 In accordance with *Shepherd* v. *Mouls* are *Rees* v. *Williams* (1847) 1 De G. & Sm. 314 and *Fisher* v. *Gilpin* (1869) 38 L.J.Ch. 230. But *contra* are *Hockley* v. *Bantock* (1826) 1 Russ. 141; *Watts* v. *Girdlestone* (1843) 6 Beav. 188; *Ames* v. *Parkinson* (1844) 7 Beav. 379; and *Ouseley* v. *Anstruther* (1847) 10 Beav. 453; *cf. Aspland* v. *Watte* (1855) 25 L.T. 231.

whether the same rule applies if X had notice, not merely that the funds were trust funds, but also *that the loan was itself a breach of trust*. In this latter case, it would seem that X is a constructive trustee, that he may not " traffic in his trust," and must therefore account for profit; but the point is not absolutely certain.[69] Certainly if the instrument of trust authorises a loan of trust funds to a third party, and such a loan is made, the beneficiaries have still less of a right to claim profits.[70]

On the other hand, if it is the trustee himself who in breach of trust employs trust funds in *his own* trade, the beneficiaries may, instead of taking interest, require him to account for the profit. Thus, if in breach of trust he employs £1,000 of trust moneys in his own trade and thereby makes a profit during the first year of £100, the beneficiaries (in calling upon him to replace the fund of £1,000) may, instead of taking interest on that sum, claim the profit of £100.[71]

Even if the trust funds so employed by the trustee in his own trade were mixed up with his private moneys, so that the fund used by him was a mixed one, the beneficiaries may still claim a proportionate share of the profits.[72] But it is either the one or the other, *either* interest *or* profit. They cannot, even if they find it advantageous to do so, claim interest for part of the time and profit for the other part.[73]

VI. SUMMARY OF INCOME POSITION

If the life tenant has lost income owing to the trustee's default he is entitled to interest on the capital moneys. The position is well summarised in Snell as follows.

Snell's Principles of Equity, 27th ed., p. 277

The rate of interest is in the discretion of the court, and is now usually 4 per cent.[74]; but the court will charge more than 4 per cent. in the following cases.

    (i) Where the trustee has actually received more than 4 per cent. Here he is accountable for the interest actually received.[75]

    (ii) Where he ought to have received more, as where he has improperly called in a mortgage carying 5 per cent. interest. In this case he is charged with the interest he ought to have received.

    (iii) Where he must be presumed to have received more, as where he has traded with the money. Here the *cestui que trust* can claim either 5 per cent. interest (which is usually but not always compound

---

[69] *Stroud* v. *Gwyer* (1860) 28 Beav. 130; *Vyse* v. *Foster* (1874) L.R. 7 H.L. 318; *Smith* v. *Nelson* (1905) 92 L.T. 313.

[70] *Parker* v. *Bloxam* (1855) 20 Beav. 295, 302–304.

[71] *Newton* v. *Bennet* (1784) 1 Bro.C.C. 359; *Ex p. Watson* (1814) 2 V. & B. 414; *Walker* v. *Woodward* (1826) 1 Russ. 107, 111; *Att.-Gen.* v. *Solly* (1829) 2 Sim. 518; *Wedderburn* v. *Wedderburn* (1838) 4 My. & Cr. 41, 46; *Jones* v. *Foxall* (1852) 15 Beav. 388; *Williams* v. *Powell* (1852) 15 Beav. 461; *Macdonald* v. *Richardson* (1858) 1 Giff. 81; *Townend* v. *Townend* (1859) 1 Giff. 201; *Re Davis, Davis* v. *Davis* [1902] 2 Ch. 314.

[72] *Docker* v. *Somes* (1834) 2 My. & K. 655; *Edinburgh T.C.* v. *Lord Advocate* (1879) 4 App.Cas. 823.

[73] *Heathcote* v. *Hulme* (1819) 1 Jac. & W. 122.

[74] *Re Davy* [1908] 1 Ch. 61. But see *supra*, p. 553, n. 63 where it will be seen that the Bank of England's minimum lending rate may now be appropriate.

[75] *Re Emmet's Estate* (1881) 17 Ch.D. 142.

interest [76]) or else, at his option, the profits actually made by the
trustee [77]; but the *cestui que trust* has no right to claim such profits
from a trader to whom the money has been improperly lent, even
though the borrower knew that the money lent was trust money.[78]

(iv) Where the trustee is guilty of fraud or serious misconduct. In this
case the court may charge him with 5 per cent. compound interest
with yearly [79] or even half-yearly rests,[80] though half-yearly rests
are rarely directed.[81]

Section 3. Impounding the Trustee's Beneficial Interest

Rule in *Re Dacre* [82]

If a beneficiary is also trustee, but is in default to the estate in his character
of trustee, he is not entitled to receive any further part of his beneficial
interest until his default is made good. His beneficial interest may also be
applied in satisfaction of his liability. X is a trustee, for himself for life,
remainder to Y. X commits a breach of trust, and has not yet satisfied his
liability. Until he does so, he cannot receive any further part of his beneficial interest, and that interest may be applied in satisfaction of his
liability. The rule holds good where X's beneficial interest is *derivative*
as well as where it is original. *E.g.*, X holds on trust for several beneficiaries, of which he is not himself one. He is in default to the estate
in his character of trustee. One of the beneficiaries dies, and then X
becomes entitled to that beneficiary's share as intestate successor or as
legatee or devisee. X is now derivatively a beneficiary, and the rule applies
as stated above.

What is the position of an *assignee* from the trustee-beneficiary X? The
assignee is in the same position as his assignor, *i.e.*, he takes subject to the
equity available against the trustee-beneficiary.[83] He takes subject to that
equity even if the trustee-beneficiary's default to the estate was *subsequent*
to the assignment.[84]

It can, in fact, be most unsafe to take an assignment of the beneficial
interest of a trustee-beneficiary, especially if that interest is reversionary.
But it was held in *Re Towndrow* [85] that the rule does not apply to a case
in which the trustee-beneficiary's liability relates to one trust and his
beneficial interest is derived from another trust, even though he is trustee
of both trusts and both trusts are created by the same instrument. The

---

[76] Contrast, *e.g.*, *Jones* v. *Foxall* (1852) 15 Beav. 388 and *Williams* v. *Powell* (1852)
   15 Beav. 461 (compound) with *Burdick* v. *Garrick* (1870) 5 Ch.App. 233 (simple).
[77] *Vyse* v. *Foster* (1872) 8 Ch.App. 309 at 329 (affd. L.R. 7 H.L. 318); *Re Davis*,
   Davis v. *Davis* [1902] 2 Ch. 314; *Gordon* v. *Gonda* [1955] 1 W.L.R. 885.
[78] *Stroud* v. *Gwyer* (1860) 28 Beav. 130.
[79] See *Re Barclay* [1899] 1 Ch. 674.
[80] *Re Emmet's Estate* (1881) 17 Ch.D. 142.
[81] See *Burdick* v. *Garrick* (1870) 5 Ch.App. 233.
[82] [1916] 1 Ch. 344; *Jacubs* v. *Rylance* (1874) L.R. 17 Eq. 341; *Re Brown* (1886) 32
   Ch.D. 597.
[83] *Irby* v. *Irby* (*No. 3*) (1858) 25 Beav. 632.
[84] *Morris* v. *Livie* (1842) 1 Y. & C.C.C. 380; *Cole* v. *Muddle* (1852) 10 Hare 186;
   Barnett v. *Sheffield* (1852) 1 De G.M. & G. 371; *Wilkins* v. *Sibley* (1863) 4 Giff.
   442; *Re Hervey* (1889) 61 L.T. 429; *Doering* v. *Doering* (1889) 42 Ch.D. 203;
   Hall V.-C. in *Re Knapman* (1881) 18 Ch.D. 300, 307.
[85] [1911] 1 Ch. 662.

rule in *Re Dacre* therefore applies only where the default relates to, and the beneficial interest is derived from, the same trust.

Section 4. Statutory Protection

I. Power of the Court to Relieve Trustees from Personal Liability

The Trustee Act 1925

Section 61.[86] If it appears to the court that a trustee, whether appointed by the court or otherwise, is or may be personally liable for any breach of trust, whether the transaction alleged to be a breach of trust occurred before or after the commencement of this Act, but has acted honestly and reasonably, and ought fairly to be excused for the breach of trust and for omitting to obtain the directions of the court in the matter in which he committed such breach, then the court may relieve him either wholly or partly from personal liability for the same.

PERRINS v. BELLAMY

Chancery Division [1898] 2 Ch. 521 (Kekewich J.); affirmed [1899] 1 Ch. 797; 68 L.J.Ch. 397; 80 L.T. 478; 47 W.R. 417; 43 S.J. 437 (Lindley M.R., Rigby and Romer L.JJ.)

By a voluntary settlement of October 1879, a settlor assigned seventeen leasehold houses to trustees on trust for his wife for life, remainder to his two daughters (of whom the plaintiff was one) for their lives, remainder to children. There was no clause which authorised the trustees to sell the property. In October 1882 the settlor executed a deed which purported to give the trustees a power of sale. The settlor died in 1888, his widow in 1895. The trustees then consulted their solicitors on the question of raising estate duty, and were advised that there was a power to sell, impliedly by the settlement of 1879, and expressly by the deed of 1882; whereupon they employed a surveyor, who reported that the leaseholds were undesirable as trust property. All the houses were sold by auction in May 1895, but the purchasers of four of them declined to complete, on the ground that the trustees had no power to sell. On a summons taken out by one of these purchasers in November 1895 it was held by Kekewich J. that the trustees had no power to sell, that the purchaser's deposit should be returned with interest, and that the trustees should pay the costs of the summons. The plaintiff declined to accede to a proposition which was subsequently made that the sale should be

---

[86] Re-enacting s. 3 of the Judicial Trustees Act 1896. For an exhaustive survey, see Sheridan, "Excusable Breaches of Trust" (1955) 19 Conv.(N.S.) 420; also Lord Maugham, "Excusable Breaches of Trust" (1898) 14 L.Q.R. 159. For other examples of statutory protection, see the Trustee Act 1925, ss. 8 and 9, *supra*, pp. 500–501.

For similar protection of officers of a company, see s. 448 of the Companies Act 1948.

effected by the tenants for life under the Settled Land Acts, so that the four houses remained unsold.

The plaintiff and her children commenced this action in May 1897 against the trustees, claiming a declaration that the defendants had committed a breach of trust in contracting to sell the property, and were liable for any loss arising therefrom. It was contended for them (the plaintiffs) that the trustees' defence, based on section 3 of the Judicial Trustees Act, 1896, failed on the ground that they ought to have obtained the direction of the court.

KEKEWICH J.: "There has been here a distinct breach of trust. It is impossible for the trustees, in view of my previous decision, to contend in this court that they had any power, express or implied, to sell these leaseholds. Nevertheless, they have sold them, and by so doing they have committed a breach of trust. How the responsibility for that breach of trust is to be enforced, and what is the limit and extent of the remedies of the *cestuis que trust*, is a separate question. Broadly speaking, these trustees have committed a breach of trust, and they are responsible for it. But then the statute comes in, and the very foundation for the application of the statute is that the trustee whose conduct is in question ' is or may be personally liable for any breach of trust.' I am bound to look at the rest of the section by the light of these words, and with the view that, in cases falling within the section, the breach of trust is not of itself to render the trustee personally liable. Leaving out the intervening words, which merely make the section retrospective, I find when in general the trustee is to be relieved from personal liability. He is not to be held personally liable if he ' has acted honestly and reasonably, and ought fairly to be excused for the breach of trust.' In this case, as in the large majority of cases of breach of trust which come before the court, the word ' honestly ' may be left out of consideration. Cases do unfortunately occur from time to time in which trustees, and even solicitors in whom confidence has been reposed, run away with the money of their *cestuis que trust*, and where such flagrant dishonesty occurs breach of trust becomes a minor consideration. In the present case there is no imputation or ground for imputation of any dishonesty whatever. The legislature has made the absence of all dishonesty a condition precedent to the relief of the trustee from liability. But that is not the gist of the section. The gist is in the words ' reasonably, and ought fairly to be excused for the breach of trust.' How much the latter words add to the force of the word ' reasonably ' I am not at present prepared to say. I suppose, however, that in the view of the legislature there might be cases in which a trustee, though he had acted reasonably, ought not fairly to be excused for the breach of trust. Indeed, I am not sure that some of the evidence adduced in this case was not addressed to a view of that kind, as, for instance, the evidence by which it was attempted to show that these trustees, though they acted reasonably in selling the property, ought not fairly to be excused because the plaintiff,

Mrs. Perrin, objected to their selling, and her objection was brought to their notice. In the section the copulative ' and ' is used, and it may well be argued that in order to bring a case within the section it must be shown not merely that the trustee has acted ' reasonably ' but also that he ought ' fairly ' to be excused for the breach of trust. I venture, however, to think that, in general and in the absence of special circumstances, a trustee who has acted ' reasonably ' ought to be relieved, and that it is not incumbent on the court to consider whether he ought ' fairly ' to be excused, unless there is evidence of a special character showing that the provisions of the section ought not to be applied in his favour. I need not pursue that subject further, because in the present case I find no ground whatever for saying that these trustees, if they acted reasonably, ought not to be excused. The question, and the only question, is whether they acted ' reasonably.' In saying that, I am not unmindful of the words of the section which follow, and which require that it should be shown that the trustee ought ' fairly ' to be excused, not only ' for the breach of trust,' but also ' for omitting to obtain the directions of the court in the matter in which he committed such breach of trust.' I find it difficult to follow that. I do not see how the trustee can be excused for the breach of trust without being also excused for the omission referred to, or how he can be excused for the omission without also being excused for the breach of trust. If I am at liberty to guess, I should suppose that these words were added by way of amendment, and crept into the statute without due regard being had to the meaning of the context. The fact that a trustee has omitted to obtain the directions of the court has never been held to be a ground for holding him personally liable, though it may be a reason guiding the court in the matters of costs, or in deciding whether he has acted reasonably or otherwise, and especially so in these days when questions of difficulty, even as regards the legal estate, can be decided economically and expeditiously on originating summons. But if the court comes to the conclusion that a trustee has acted reasonably, I cannot see how it can usefully proceed to consider, as an independent matter, the question whether he has or has not omitted to obtain the directions of the court . . ."

Held, in the circumstances the trustees had acted (honestly and) reasonably and should be relieved of personal liability under section 3 of the Judicial Trustees Act of 1896. *Affirmed on appeal.*

Re STUART, SMITH v. STUART

Chancery Division [1897] 2 Ch. 583; 66 L.J.Ch. 780; 77 L.T. 128; 46 W.R. 41; 41 S.J. 714

The defendant, Mr. Box, being one of the executor-trustees of a will which contained a power to invest in leasehold mortgages, invested trust funds in 1881, 1888 and 1890, on four separate mortgages of leasehold houses and cottages. One of the mortgages was a second mortgage, on which the defendant had also obtained no valuation; this security proved to be valueless. With regard to the other three mortgages the defendant acted on the valuations of surveyors employed by the solicitor to the trust, Mr. Muskett (who had previously been the testator's solicitor). Muskett acted also as solicitor to the mortgagors.[87] Of these other three mortgages, the valuation in two of them stated the amount for which the property was a good security without stating the value of the property itself, while in the remaining mortgage more than two-thirds of the value of the property as stated in the valuation was advanced. These other three mortgages proved to be insufficient.

It was contended for the defendant that he had acted honestly and reasonably, even with regard to the mortgage on which he advanced more than two-thirds, on the ground that in that case he had nevertheless left a margin of £500, having exceeded the two-thirds margin by about £200 only. It was also to be observed that the solicitor had previously acted for the testator and that he had afterwards been employed by the trustees in numerous transactions (about twenty-seven), of which only four were now impeached. Furthermore, non-compliance with all the requirements mentioned in section 8 of the Trustee Act 1893 [88] did not disentitle a trustee from claiming relief under section 3 of the Judicial Trustees Act 1896, for otherwise a trustee could never have recourse to the Act of 1896 in the case of an insufficient mortgage investment.[89]

STIRLING J.: " The effect of section 3 of the Judicial Trustees Act 1896 appears to me to be this. The law as it stood at the passing of the Act is not altered, but a jurisdiction is given to the court under special circumstances, the court being satisfied as to the several matters mentioned in the section, to relieve the trustee of the consequences of a breach of trust as regards his personal liability. But the court must first be satisfied that the trustee has acted honestly and reasonably. As to the honesty of the trustee in this case there is no question; but that is not the only condition to be satisfied, and the question arises whether the other conditions are satisfied. I quite agree that this section applies to a trustee making an improper investment of the trust funds as well as to any other breach of trust. This matter has been considered by Byrne J. in *Re Turner*,[90] where he says this: ' I think that the section relied on is meant to be acted upon freely and fairly in the exercise of judicial discretion, but I think that the court ought to be satisfied, before exercising the very large powers conferred upon it, by sufficient evidence, that the trustee acted reasonably. I do not think that I have sufficient evidence in this case that he so acted; in fact, it does not appear from the

---

87 See observations of the Lord Chancellor in *Waring* v. *Waring* (1852) 3 Ir.Ch.R. 331, 337 on the employment of the same solicitor for both mortgagor and mortgagee; and *Crampton* v. *Walker* (1893) 31 L.R.Ir. 437, 453–454.
88 Now s. 8 of the Act of 1925; *supra*, p. 500.
89 *Re Turner* [1897] 1 Ch. 536.
90 [1897] 1 Ch. 536, 542.

letters that Mr. Turner acted in respect of this mortgage as he would probably have acted had it been a transaction of his own. I think that if he was—and he well may have been—a businesslike man, he would not, before lending his money, have been satisfied without some further inquiry as to the means of the mortgagor and as to the nature and value of the property upon which he was about to advance his money.' That has since been approved by the Court of Appeal; and I willingly adopt what is there laid down as a guide to me in this matter. In my opinion the burden lies on the trustee who asks the court to exercise the jurisdiction conferred by this section to show that he has acted reasonably; and, certainly, it is fair in dealing with such a question to consider whether Mr. Box would have acted with reference to these investments as he did if he had been lending money of his own. Now, in his affidavit Mr. Box states that these mortgages were assented to by him partly by reason of the confidence he placed in Mr. Muskett as the long-trusted solicitor of the testator, and by reason of the valuations of the surveyor employed by Mr. Muskett. It is not suggested that any blame attaches to Mr. Box for employing Mr. Muskett as his solicitor, and it is fair to say that Mr. Muskett appears to have been employed both by the trustees and by the testator in a large number of transactions. Those in which he was employed by the trustees amounted to twenty-seven, and of these four only are challenged. Still, I think a man dealing with his own money would not act upon the opinion of his solicitor alone in a question as to the value of property proposed as a security, though, no doubt, he might do so as to any question of title or of law which may be involved. However, Mr. Box does not tell us what advice either as to questions of value or as to questions of law was given to him by Mr. Muskett. For aught that appears in Mr. Box's affidavit he may have had full advice as to the rules laid down by the court with reference to investments by trustees; and he certainly was not entirely ignorant of how the duties of a trustee ought to be performed; for he tells us that in 1889 he had a proper trust account opened in the joint names of himself and his co-trustee, and that, on discovering about the same time that Mr. Muskett had negotiated mortgages in his own name as mortgagor for sums amounting to £1,800, he called in the mortgages and obtained payment of what was owing. It is quite true that Mr. Box did not rely solely on Mr. Muskett's opinion, but relied also on certain valuations of surveyors employed by Mr. Muskett as regards three of the mortgages, and these valuations are produced; as regards the fourth no valuation was produced, and it was really not contended that Mr. Box ought to be relieved as to that. As to the valuations which have been produced, they do not satisfy the requirements of section 4 of the Trustee Act 1888, which has now been replaced by section 8 of the Trustee Act 1893. It was contended, and in my opinion rightly contended, that this was not necessarily a fatal obstacle to the application of the section. Still, I think that those requirements cannot be left out of consideration. The legislature in

1888 dealt with the duties of trustees with regard to investments, and laid down certain rules for their guidance which in some respects relaxed those previously existing and are in themselves reasonable, and they appear to me to constitute a standard by which reasonable conduct is to be judged. One of the requirements of these Acts is that in making a loan the trustee shall act on a valuation made by a person whom the trustee ' reasonably believed ' to be an able practical surveyor or valuer ' instructed and employed independently of any owner of the property.' In point of fact, Mr. Muskett acted in respect of these mortgages on behalf of the mortgagors, and the surveyors on whose valuations Mr. Box acted were not employed independently of the mortgagors. Apparently Mr. Box was not aware until 1889 that Mr. Muskett had acted for the mortgagors; but it is remarkable that in an affidavit intended to be used for the purpose of defending himself against the claims of the beneficiaries he does not state that at the dates of the advances he believed the surveyors were instructed or employed independently of the mortgagors; still less does he give his reasons for his belief, if it existed. The proper inference seems to be that he did not so believe; and, if so, he does not explain why he nevertheless acted on the valuations. I confess that I do not think that if Mr. Box had been dealing with money of his own he would under these circumstances have advanced it without further inquiry. Another requirement prescribes that the amount of the loan shall not exceed two-thirds of the value of the property stated in the valuation. In two out of the three valuations no value is stated: all that is given is the amount for which the valuer considered the property a good security. In the third the value is given, but the amount lent exceeded by £200 that value. No special circumstances are put forward in explanation. Having regard to all these circumstances, I think that I have not before me sufficient materials to enable me to relieve the trustee from the consequences of the breaches of trust with which he has been fixed by the master's certificate."

Held, therefore, the trustee ought not to be relieved of liability under section 3 of the Judicial Trustees Act 1896.[91]

---

[91] See further, on the honest and reasonable trustee's *tabula in naufragio*, the following: *National Trustees Co.* v. *General Finance Co.* [1905] A.C. 373, 380–382; *Davis* v. *Hutchings* [1907] 1 Ch. 356; *Shaw* v. *Cates* [1909] 1 Ch. 389, 405; *Re Dive* [1909] 1 Ch. 328, 342; *Palmer* v. *Emerson* [1911] 1 Ch. 758, 769; *Re Greenwood* (1911) 105 L.T. 509, 515; *Re Allsop* [1914] 1 Ch. 1; *Re Brookes* [1914] 1 Ch. 558; *Re Pawson* [1917] 1 Ch. 541; *Khoo Tek Kheong* v. *Ch'ng Joo Tuan Neoh* [1934] A.C. 529, 536–537; *Holland* v. *Administrator of German Property* (1937) 156 L.T. 373; *Re Mackay* [1911] 1 Ch. 300; *Re Gee* [1948] Ch. 284, 297; *Re Wightwick's Will Trusts* [1950] Ch. 260. The court is reluctant to grant relief to a paid trustee under this section, but is not debarred from doing so if the circumstances warrant it: *National Trustees Co. of Australasia Ltd.* v. *General Finance Co. of Australasia Ltd.* [1905] A.C. 373; *Re Windsor Steam Coal Co. (1901) Ltd.* [1929] 1 Ch. 151; *Re Pauling's S.T.* [1964] Ch. 303; *Re Rosenthal* [1972] 1 W.L.R. 1273; *Hawksley* v. *May* [1956] 1 Q.B. 304.

II. POWER OF THE COURT TO MAKE BENEFICIARY INDEMNIFY TRUSTEE FOR BREACH OF TRUST

Trustee Act 1925

Section 62.[92]—(1) Where a trustee commits a breach of trust at the instigation or request or with the consent in writing [93] of a beneficiary, the court may, if it thinks fit, make such order as to the court seems just, for impounding all or any part of the interest of the beneficiary in the trust estate by way of indemnity to the trustee [94] or persons claiming through him.[95]

(2) This section applies to breaches of trust committed as well before as after the commencement of this Act.

Note

Independently of section 62 of the Trustee Act 1925, *supra*, a beneficiary who is *sui juris* [96] and knowingly [97] concurs in a breach of trust cannot afterwards complain of it against the trustee, whether he has obtained any personal benefit from it or not: *Fletcher* v. *Collis, infra.* It is not necessary that the beneficiary should know that what he is concurring in is a breach of trust so long as he fully understands what he is concurring in: *Holder* v. *Holder, infra.* If, however, another beneficiary called upon the trustee to make good the breach of trust, the court always had jurisdiction to order the trustee to be indemnified out of the interest of the beneficiary who, being *sui juris*, either instigated, requested or concurred in the breach. A motive of personal benefit on the part of the beneficiary was sufficient to invoke the jurisdiction in cases of instigation [98] or request [99]; but personal benefit actually derived by the beneficiary was necessary in cases of concurrence.[1]

---

[92] The section is printed as amended by the Married Women (Restraint upon Anticipation) Act 1949. It replaces s. 45 of the Trustee Act 1893, which re-enacted in substance s. 6 of the Trustee Act 1888.

[93] The requirement of writing only refers to consent and not instigation or request: *Re Somerset, infra.*

[94] An order for indemnity can be made in favour of a former trustee: *Re Pauling's S.T. (No. 2)* [1963] Ch. 576, *infra.*

[95] Would the section be available (a) if one trustee wished to impound an instigating life tenant's interest whilst the other trustee, the father of the life tenant, did not or (b) if the sole trustee had fled the country leaving no assets behind and the remainderman claimed to be subrogated to the trustee's right to impound the instigating life tenant's income?

[96] See *Wilkinson* v. *Parry* (1828) 4 Russ. 272, 276; *cf. Overton* v. *Bannister* (1844) 3 Hare 503. A beneficiary cannot fraudulently rely on his incapacity.

[97] *Re Pauling's S.T.* [1964] Ch. 303. This case shows that even if a beneficiary is of full age he can still sue if he was under the undue influence of his parents who were clearly profiting from the trustee's breaches.

[98] *Trafford* v. *Boehm* (1746) 3 Atk. 440, 442; *Raby* v. *Ridehalgh* (1855) 7 De G.M. & G. 104.

[99] *Fuller* v. *Knight* (1843) 6 Beav. 205; *M'Gachen* v. *Dew* (1851) 15 Beav. 84; *Hanchett* v. *Briscoe* (1856) 22 Beav. 496.

[1] *Montford* v. *Cadogan* (1816) 19 Ves. 635; *Cocker* v. *Quayle* (1830) 1 Russ. & M. 535, 538; *Booth* v. *Booth* (1838) 1 Beav. 125; *Williams* v. *Allen (No. 2)* (1863) 32 Beav. 650; *Blyth* v. *Fladgate* [1891] 1 Ch. 337, 363. It makes no difference that the concurring beneficiary became a beneficiary after the date of his concurrence: *Evans* v. *Benyon* (1887) 37 Ch.D. 329, 344. These factors of motive and actual benefit appear to be relevant still in assisting the court determining whether all or any part of the beneficial interest should be impounded: see *per* Kay L.J. in *Chillingworth* v. *Chambers* [1896] 1 Ch. 685, 707.

In order to succeed in claiming an indemnity, the trustee had to show that the beneficiary knew the facts which constituted the breach of trust although it was not necessary to show that the beneficiary knew that these facts amounted in law to a breach of trust: *Re Somerset, infra.*[2]

Section 62 of the Trustee Act 1925, *supra,* enlarges the jurisdiction by giving the court a discretionary power to impound the interest of a beneficiary who consents in writing[3] to a breach of trust, whether or not he derived a personal benefit, or who instigates or requests a breach of trust, whether or not he had a motive of personal benefit. In short, the section is applicable where a beneficiary instigates, or requests, or consents in writing to, a breach of trust.

The section provides for impounding the interest of the " beneficiary in the trust estate." In *Ricketts* v. *Ricketts*[4] there was a marriage settlement for a mother for her life, remainder to her son. The son, on his marriage, assigned his reversionary interest under that settlement to the trustees of his own marriage settlement, under which latter settlement he was a beneficiary for life. Notice of the assignment was given to the trustees of the first settlement. By that assignment the son divested himself of his character of beneficiary under the first settlement, and substituted in his place the trustees of the second settlement. Afterwards the son instigated the trustees of the first settlement to commit a breach of trust in his favour by applying trust capital in discharging his debts, and when those trustees proceeded against him under the section for an indemnity, they discovered that he was not a beneficiary against whom they could proceed. Their beneficiary was now to be found in the trustees of the second settlement, who were trustees for the son who instigated the breach of trust to pay off his debts. He was not a " beneficiary in the trust estate."

FLETCHER v. COLLIS

Court of Appeal [1905] 2 Ch. 24; 74 L.J.Ch. 502; 92 L.T. 749; 53 W.R. 516; 49 S.J. 499 (Vaughan Williams, Romer and Stirling L.JJ.)

By a marriage settlement of 1881 securities were settled on trust for the husband for life, remainder to the wife for life, remainder to children. At the request of the wife and with the (written) consent of the husband, the trustee in 1885 sold out the whole of the trust fund and handed the proceeds to the wife, who spent them. In June 1891 the husband was adjudicated bankrupt. In August 1891 the present action was commenced by the *remaindermen* against the trustee to make him replace the loss, but proceedings were stayed on an undertaking by the trustee, on the security of (*inter alia*) certain policies on his life, to make good the trust fund. By means of payments by the trustee and of the policies which fell in on his death in 1902, the whole of the trust fund was replaced, together with interest from August 1891.

The personal representative of the deceased trustee then took out a summons in this action for a declaration that she was entitled, during

[2] See also *Rehden* v. *Wesley* (1861) 29 Beav. 213, 215.
[3] *Griffith* v. *Hughes* [1892] 3 Ch. 105.
[4] (1891) 64 L.T. 263.

the life of the husband, to the income of the trust fund replaced by the deceased trustee. It was argued for her (before the Court of Appeal) that a beneficiary who concurs in a breach of trust cannot afterwards complain of it against his trustee. The capital had in fact been replaced by the trustee at the instance of the remaindermen, but since the husband himself had by virtue of his concurrence no claim against the trustee, the income of the capital so replaced should (during the life of the husband) go to her as personal representative of the trustee who replaced it.

For the husband's trustee in bankruptcy, who resisted the claim of the personal representative, it was contended that the authorities showed that mere concurrence by a beneficiary does not preclude him from complaining against his trustee: it must be shown that he (the beneficiary) also derived a personal benefit from the breach of trust, which was not the case here.

ROMER L.J.: " There was one proposition of law urged by the counsel on behalf of the respondents before us to which I accede. It is this: If a beneficiary claiming under a trust does not *instigate* or *request* a breach of trust, is not the active moving party towards it, but merely *consents* to it, *and* he obtains no personal benefit from it, then his interest in the trust estate would not be impoundable in order to indemnify the trustee liable to make good loss occasioned by the breach. I think this is what was meant and referred to by Chitty J. in his judgment in *Sawyer* v. *Sawyer*,[5] where he says: ' It strikes me as a novelty in law, and a proposition not founded on principle, to say that the person who merely consents is bound to do more than what he says he consents to do. It does not mean that he makes himself personally liable, nor does he render any property liable to make it good.' But that proposition of law must be taken to be subject to the following right of the trustee as between himself and the beneficiaries. In the case I have before referred to in respect to the general proposition, the beneficiary who knowingly consented to the breach could not, if of full contracting age and capacity, and in the absence of special circumstances, afterwards be heard to say that the conduct of the trustee in committing the breach of trust was, as against him the particular beneficiary, improper, so as to make the trustee liable to the beneficiary for any damage suffered in respect of that beneficiary's interest in the trust estate by reason of the loss occasioned by the breach, and of course if satisfactorily proved the consent of the beneficiary to the breach need not be in writing.

" I will illustrate what I have said by a concrete case, not only to make my meaning perfectly plain, but also because the illustration will have a bearing upon the case now before us. Take a simple case of a trust under a settlement, say, of £3,000, for a tenant for life, and after the death of the tenant for life for certain remaindermen. Suppose the

---

[5] (1885) 28 Ch.D. 595, 598.

trustee commits a breach of trust and sells out £1,000, and pays it over to some third person, so that the *cestui que trust* does not benefit by it himself, and suppose that the tenant for life, being of full age and *sui juris*, knows of that act of the trustee and consents to it. What would be the position of the trustee in reference to that breach of trust if he were made liable at the instance of the remaindermen for the loss accruing to the trust estate by the breach of trust, assuming the £1,000 to have been lost? The remaindermen would have the right of saying, so far as their interest in remainder is concerned, the capital must be made good by the trustee; but the tenant for life who consented could not himself have brought an action against the trustee to make him liable for the loss of income suffered by the tenant for life by reason of the breach of trust as to the £1,000. On the other hand, the trustee would not have had a right, as against the *cestui que trust*, the tenant for life, to have impounded the tenant for life's interest on the remaining £2,000 of the trust fund in order to indemnify himself. Now suppose the remaindermen having brought an action to make good the breach of trust against the trustee, and the tenant for life is a co-plaintiff, a defence is put in by the trustee raising his right as against the tenant for life seeking relief in respect of the loss of income, but admitting the right of the remaindermen: what would the court in such a case do if the question between the tenant for life and the trustee had to be tried out, and the tenant for life was found to have consented knowingly to the breach of trust? To my mind the right thing for the court to do would have been clear. It might order the £1,000 to be paid into court by the trustee; but, pending the life of the tenant for life, it might also order the income to be paid to the trustee, because the income of the £1,000 would have been out of the pocket of the trustee just as much as the corpus from which it proceeded, and not to have given that relief to the trustee would have been to ignore his right, and to have acceded to the claim of the tenant for life in the action by him that I have indicated. Now suppose that the tenant for life is not a plaintiff, but co-defendant with the trustee, so that the question cannot be tried out at the trial as between the tenant for life and the trustee: what might the court do, if so advised, in that case? It might order the £1,000 to be paid into court by the trustee, and it might reserve the question of the right as between the tenant for life and the trustee to the income to be determined at some later period. It will be found that that illustration is pertinent to the case that is now before us. In such a case when the question as to income arose the trustee would be able to say: ' The remaindermen are clearly not entitled to the income on the trust fund I have replaced, if the tenant for life is not entitled to it as against me. I replaced it; it is my money, and I am entitled to it '; and, therefore, when the question came to be tried out ultimately as between the tenant for life and the trustee, if that income was still under the control of the court, the court would again have the right to say to the trustee who replaced the corpus: ' The income is yours in the absence of the right of the beneficiary, the tenant for life, to claim as against you to make you liable for that income.'

" Now that right of a trustee which I have been dealing with, the right to resist the claim by the beneficiary to make good as against him the income, has clearly not been affected either by section 6 of the Trustee Act of 1888, or by section 45 of the Trustee Act of 1893. As I pointed out in *Bolton* v. *Curre*,[6] those sections were intended to and did *extend* the powers of the court for the benefit of the trustee. They clearly extended the powers of the court so far as concerns the case of a married woman restrained from anticipation; but they also extended them in another respect by giving power to the court to impound any part of the interest in the trust property of any beneficiary who consented to a breach of trust, provided that consent was in writing. But clearly there was nothing in those sections which was intended to, and nothing in my opinion which operated so as to, deprive the trustee of the right I previously indicated, namely, the right of saying as against a beneficiary who has consented to a breach of trust that the beneficiary cannot make him, the trustee, personally liable to recoup, to the beneficiary who consented, the loss accruing to that beneficiary by the breach of trust committed with his consent. The beneficiary, if he consented to the breach of trust, could not be heard to make that a ground of complaint or a ground of action as against the trustee. Of course, the right I have indicated of a trustee as against the consenting beneficiary might possibly be lost if not raised by the trustee before it was too late. Probably—I say probably, for I have not to decide the question—if a trustee in such a case were to hand over the funds out of his own pocket to new trustees without reserving his right in any way as against the tenant for life, it might be—I will say no more—that he might be held to have lost his right to claim the income after he had parted with the fund. It might be so, and other cases might be given; but so long as his right can be claimed by him it is a right which must be recognised by the court, and given full effect to when it is insisted upon at the proper time.

" Now that being the law, so far as it is necessary to deal with it for the purpose of the present case, I will say a few words about the facts of this case; and I ask myself, looking at those facts, this question: Is not this matter that we have to deal with on this appeal in substance one where a beneficiary who has consented to a breach of trust is now for his own benefit calling upon the trustee to make good the loss accruing to the beneficiary by reason of the breach? I think it is. . . ."

Held, therefore, by the Court of Appeal that the personal representative of the deceased trustee was entitled, during the life of the husband tenant for life, to the income of the fund replaced by the trustee.

---

[6] [1895] 1 Ch. 544, 549.

HOLDER v. HOLDER

Court of Appeal [1968] Ch. 353; [1968] 2 W.L.R. 237; [1968] 1 All
    E.R. 665

The plaintiff was seeking to set aside a sale made to the third
defendant by the first two defendant trustees when the third defendant
was technically a trustee. The facts have already been set out at p. 467
and Harman L.J. with whom Danckwerts and Sachs L.JJ. expressly
agreed on this point dealt as follows with the defence of the plaintiff's
consent or acquiescence.

HARMAN L.J.: " . . . There arises a further defence, namely, that of
acquiescence, and this requires some further recital of the facts.

" Completion of the sale was due for Michaelmas, 1961, but by that
time the third defendant was not in a position to find the purchase
money. The proving executors served a notice to complete in October,
1961, and, the validity of this notice being questioned, served a further
notice in December. In February 1962 the plaintiff's solicitor pressed
the defendants to forfeit the third defendant's deposit and this was a
right given by the contract of sale and is an affirmation of it. Further,
in May, 1962, the plaintiff issued a writ for a common decree of
administration against the proving executors, seeking thus to press
them to complete the contract and wind up the estate. The contract
was in fact completed in June, 1962, and in the same month £2,000 on
account was paid to and accepted by the plaintiff as his share and he
thereupon took no further steps with his action. In order to complete,
the third defendant borrowed £21,000 from the Agricultural Mortgage
Corporation with interest at 7½ per cent. He also borrowed £3,000
from his mother with interest at 6½ per cent., and a like sum from his
sister at a similar rate of interest. In November 1962 the third
defendant demanded possession of Glebe Farm house from the plaintiff, who at that time changed his solicitors, and it was suggested by the
new solicitors in February 1963 that the third defendant was disqualified from bidding at the auction. This was the first time any such
suggestion had been made by anyone. The writ was not issued till a
year later.

" I have found this question a difficult one. The plaintiff knew
all the relevant facts but he did not realise nor was he advised till 1963
that the legal result might be that he could object to his brother's
purchase because he continued to be a personal representative. There
is no doubt strong authority for the proposition that a man is not
bound by acquiescences until he knows his legal rights. In *Cockerell*
v. *Cholmeley* [7] Sir John Leach M.R. said this:

    ' It has been argued that the defendant, being aware of the
    facts of the case in the lifetime of Sir Henry Englefield, has, by his

---

[7] (1830) 1 Russ. & M. 418, 425.

silence, and by being a party to the application to Parliament, confirmed the title of the plaintiffs. In equity it is considered, as good sense requires it should be, that no man can be held by any act of his to confirm a title, unless he was fully aware at the time, not only of the fact upon which the defect of title depends, but of the consequence in point of law; and here there is no proof that the defendant, at the time of the acts referred to, was aware of the law on the subject. . . .'

There, however, the judge was asked to set aside a legal right. In *Willmott* v. *Barber* [8] Fry J. said this:

'A man is not to be deprived of his legal rights unless he has acted in such a way as would make it fraudulent for him to set up those rights. What, then, are the elements or requisites necessary to constitute fraud of that description? In the first place the plaintiff must have made a mistake as to his legal rights. Secondly, the plaintiff must have expended some money or must have done some act (not necessarily upon the defendant's land) on the faith of his mistaken belief. Thirdly, the defendant, the possessor of the legal right, must know of the existence of his own right which is inconsistent with the right claimed by the plaintiff. If he does not know of it he is in the same position as the plaintiff, and the doctrine of acquiescence is founded upon conduct with a knowledge of your legal rights.'

On the other hand, in *Stafford* v. *Stafford* [9] Knight Bruce L.J. said this:

'Generally, when the facts are known from which a right arises, the right is presumed to be known. . . .'

"Like the judge, I should desire to follow the conclusion of Wilberforce J. who reviewed the authorities in *Re Pauling's Settlement Trusts, Younghusband* v. *Coutts & Co.*[10]; and this passage was mentioned without dissent in the same case in the Court of Appeal[11]:

'The result of these authorities appears to me to be that the court has to consider all the circumstances in which the concurrence of the *cestui que trust* was given with a view to seeing whether it is fair and equitable that, having given his concurrence, he should afterwards turn round and sue the trustees: that, subject to this, it is not necessary that he should know that what he is concurring in is a breach of trust, provided that he fully understands what he is concurring in, and that it is not necessary that he should himself have directly benefited by the breach of trust.'

There is, therefore, no hard and fast rule that ignorance of a legal

---

[8] (1880) 15 Ch.D. 96, 105.
[9] (1857) 1 De G. & J. 193, 202.
[10] [1961] 3 All E.R. 713, 730.
[11] [1964] Ch. 303.

right is a bar, but the whole of the circumstances must be looked at to see whether it is just that the complaining beneficiary should succeed against the trustee.

" On the whole I am of opinion that in the circumstances of this case it would not be right to allow the plaintiff to assert his right (assuming he has one) because with full knowledge of the facts he affirmed the sale. He has had £2,000 as a result. He has caused the third defendant to embark on liabilities which he cannot recoup. There can in fact be no *restitutio in integrum* which is a necessary element in rescission.

" The plaintiff is asserting an equitable and not a legal remedy. He has by his conduct disentitled himself to it. It is extremely doubtful whether the order if worked out would benefit anyone. I think we should not assent to it, on general equitable principles."

Re SOMERSET, SOMERSET v. EARL POULETT

Court of Appeal [1894] 1 Ch. 231; 63 L.J.Ch. 41; 69 L.T. 744; 42 W.R. 145; 10 T.L.R. 46; 38 S.J. 39; 7 R. 34 (Lindley, A. L. Smith and Davey L.JJ.)

The defendants were the three surviving trustees of a settlement made in 1875 on the marriage of the plaintiff, Mr. Somerset. By that settlement securities were settled on trust either to retain the investments or, with the consent in writing of the plaintiff and his wife or of the survivor, to convert and reinvest in (*inter alia*) Government, real or leasehold securities in England, Wales or Ireland (subject or not to prior incumbrances), on the usual trusts (the plaintiff and his wife successively for life, remainder to children). The trust investments included Russian and Brazilian bonds, and in 1876 the plaintiff became desirous of having these investments realised and reinvested on a mortgage at 4 per cent. of an estate in Hawkestone. The owner of the Hawkestone estate, Lord Hill, made it a condition of the proposed mortgage that his solicitors, Messrs. Wilde, Berger & Co., should act for all parties. The plaintiff was acquainted with the Hawkestone estate, was anxious to effect the mortgage, and took an active part in the preliminary negotiations, while the defendants were apparently unacquainted with the estate, were not particularly in favour of the proposed investment, and relied on the advice of their co-trustee (since deceased), who was a barrister with a wide experience of landed estates. A temporary advance on the estate having been made by the trustees, the solicitors instructed Messrs. Farebrother, Ellis, Clark & Co. in June 1878 to make a valuation, as follows: " The whole of the above properties are held by yearly tenants and are subject to mortgages to clients of ours for £20,700 at 4 per cent.[12] The mortgagees are desirous of advancing a further sum upon the same security. Messrs. Farebrother, Ellis, Clark & Co. are requested to

---

[12] The figure of £20,700 appears to be a misprint for £12,200.

inspect the above farms and report as to the value of them. They are also requested to advise the mortgagees, who are trustees of a marriage settlement, what additional sum they may properly advance to Viscount Hill upon the security above-mentioned. . . . It is desired by both mortgagor and mortgagees that as much money shall be advanced as you can advise will be properly secured. . . ." Sir John Ellis, of the firm of valuers, valued the estate at £42,750, his report stating that the actual rental was £1,180, and that the tithe and land tax of about £111 were payable by the landlord; and a letter was written by Sir John Ellis's firm to the solicitors (and enclosed with the report) as follows: ' We have not stated any amount which we think might be advanced, as to a very great extent it depends on the circumstances of the parties. . . . We think, however, that fully three-fourths might be advanced."

In July 1878 the solicitors wrote to the plaintiff as follows: " The land belonging to Lord Hill, upon which it is proposed to invest a portion of your settlement money, has been surveyed by a valuer, and, according to his report, the sum of £30,000 may be advanced. £12,200 of this sum has already been advanced, and we now enclose an authority to the trustees for the signatures of yourself and Mrs. Somerset to enable them to sell out sufficient of the securities to raise the remaining sum of £17,800." Lord Hill, however, was dissatisfied with the valuation and report, being desirous of borrowing £35,000, in order to pay off other advances to him at a higher rate of interest. Accordingly Sir John Ellis was again consulted and a letter was received from him by the solicitors, as follows: " We have again considered the value of the properties referred to in our report to you of July 8 instant, and looking at the great value that is attached to the several farms, from the position in which they are placed with reference to other lands, and to the largely increased rent which there is no doubt they would command, if his Lordship would allow fresh arrangements to be made with the tenants, we think there is no doubt but that they represent a sufficient security for an advance of thirty-five thousand pounds (£35,000) to his Lordship."

In May and August of 1878 the trustees advanced with the consent in writing of the plaintiff and his wife, the sum of £34,612, being the whole amount of the trust fund available for the purpose, on the security of three mortgages of the Hawkestone estate at 4 per cent. The interest on the mortgages was punctually paid by the mortgagor direct to the plaintiff until August 1890, but the interest due in February 1891 was not paid.

The plaintiff (whose wife had died in 1889) and his infant children (the remaindermen) brought this action against the defendants for a declaration that the mortgage investment was a breach of trust, alleging that the Hawkestone estate was an insufficient and improper security. The defendants contended (*inter alia*) that if they were held liable to make good the £34,612 or any part thereof they were entitled, under section 6 of the Trustee Act 1888, and under the general law, to be indemnified by the plaintiff's life interest. It was argued for them that the beneficiary's consent in writing is sufficient to bring a case within the section, without evidence of knowledge on his part that the investment was a breach of trust. Here the investment was made at the plaintiff's instigation and with his consent in writing, and he was aware of the circumstances, for he took an active part in negotiating the investment.

Held, by Kekewich J., that the investment was a proper investment except in so far as the trustees had advanced too much, so that they were liable for a breach of trust in respect only of the amount excessively advanced: Trustee Act 1888, s. 5.[13] The learned judge considered that the largest sum which in the circumstances the trustees could properly have advanced was £26,000. *Held*, further, that the trustees were entitled to have the plaintiff's life interest impounded by way of indemnity under the Trustee Act 1888, s. 6; as to which the plaintiff appealed.

LINDLEY L.J.: ". . . The second question is whether, in order to indemnify the trustees, the court ought to impound the income of the trust funds during the life of the appellant. This question turns on the construction of section 6, and on the conduct of the parties. [His Lordship then read section 6, and continued:]

" Did the trustees commit the breach of trust for which they have been made liable at the instigation or request, or with the consent in writing, of the appellant? The section is intended to protect trustees, and ought to be construed so as to carry out that intention. But the section ought not, in my opinion, to be construed as if the word ' investment ' had been inserted instead of ' breach of trust.' An enactment to that effect would produce great injustice in many cases. In order to bring a case within this section the *cestui que trust* must instigate, or request or consent in writing to some act or omission which is itself a breach of trust, and not to some act or omission which only becomes a breach of trust by reason of want of care on the part of the trustees. If a *cestui que trust* instigates, requests or consents in writing to an investment not in terms authorised by the power of investment, he clearly falls within the section; and in such a case his ignorance or forgetfulness of the terms of the power would not, I think, protect him—at all events, not unless he could give some good reason why it should, *e.g.*, that it was caused by the trustee. But if all that a *cestui que trust* does is to instigate, request or consent in writing to an investment which is authorised by the terms of the power, the case is, I think, very different. He has a right to expect that the trustees will act with proper care in making the investment, and if they do not they cannot throw the consequences on him unless they can show that he instigated, requested or consented in writing to their non-performance of their duty in this respect. This is, in my opinion, the true construction of this section.

---

[13] s. 9 of the Act of 1925; *supra*, p. 501. Other points arose in this case not material for the present purpose.

" As regards the necessity for a writing, I agree with the decision of Mr. Justice Kekewich in *Griffith* v. *Hughes*,[14] that an instigation or request need not be in writing, and that the words ' in writing ' apply only to the consent.

" I pass now to the facts. It is, in my opinion, perfectly clear that the appellant instigated, requested and consented in writing to the investment by the trustees of the trust money on a mortgage of Lord Hill's estate. This, indeed, was not disputed. But the evidence does not, that I can see, go further than this. He certainly never instigated, requested or consented in writing to an investment on the property without inquiry; still less, if upon inquiry the rents payable in respect of the lands mortgaged were found to be less than the interest payable on the mortgage.

" Whether the appellant knew the rental is a very important question. Mr. Justice Kekewich has found that he did. But the evidence does not, in my opinion, warrant this inference. The appellant certainly knew a good deal about the property; and Colonel Hill [his father-in-law], to whom he very much trusted, most likely knew more than the appellant himself. There was also a proposal from Lord Hill, which the appellant once had, but which was lost. This might have shown the rental. But the appellant positively denies that he knew the rental, and says that Mr. Haste, the mortgagor's agent, told him it was £1,700 a year, whilst in fact it was only £1,070 net. It was contended that Messrs. Wilde, Berger & Co., who were the solicitors of the mortgagor and of the trustees, were also the solicitors of the appellant, and that through them he must be treated as having known of the valuation and the rental, and all other material facts. But to affect him with this notice would be extremely unjust, for the facts, a knowledge of which the court is asked to impute to him, were clearly kept from him. The solicitors obtained the valuation for and on behalf of the trustees; they obtained the second opinion of the valuers for the benefit of the borrower, and for the protection of the trustees. In obtaining the valuation and opinion the solicitors were not acting for or on behalf of the appellant; and, considering that they never disclosed the valuation or opinion to the appellant, and never informed him of their effect, he cannot, in my opinion, be held to have known them. It is important to observe that the statute does not make a *cestui que trust* responsible for a breach of trust simply because he had actual or constructive notice of it; he must have instigated or requested it, or have consented to it in writing. Even if the knowledge of his solicitors could be imputed to him for some purposes, it is not true in fact that the appellant did by himself or his agent instigate, request or consent in writing to the breach of trust.[15]

---

[14] [1892] 3 Ch. 105.

[15] On this point A. L. Smith L.J. observed (at p. 270): " In my opinion, upon the true reading of this section, a trustee, in order to obtain the benefit conferred thereby, must establish that the beneficiary knew the facts which rendered what he was

Even if the appellant had constructive notice through his solicitors of the valuation, the court, in exercising the power conferred upon it by the statute, would, in my opinion, be acting unjustly, and not justly, if, under the circumstances of this case, it held the appellant liable to indemnify the trustees. The court would be treating the appellant as having done more than he did, and I can see no justification for such a course. It must be borne in mind that the plaintiff was not seeking to benefit himself at the expense of the remaindermen as in *Raby* v. *Ridehalgh*.[16] He was seeking a better security for the trust money for the benefit of everyone interested in it . . ."

Held, therefore, by the Court of Appeal that the defendants were not entitled to have the plaintiff's life interest impounded by way of indemnity.[17]

Re PAULING'S SETTLEMENT TRUST (No. 2)

Chancery Division [1963] Ch. 576; [1963] 2 W.L.R. 838; [1963] 1 All E.R. 857

Coutts & Co. were held liable for breach of trust in respect of a number of advances of capital to the children of the life tenant, Mrs. Younghusband. The bank claimed to be entitled to impound the life interest. The plaintiffs sought the appointment of two new trustees in place of the bank who opposed this as it might negate their right to impound.

Wilberforce J. appointed new trustees as this would not affect the right to impound.

WILBERFORCE J.: . . . Next I come to a separate series of objections which raise some difficult questions of law. The defendants, as I have already mentioned, have a claim to impound the life interest of Mrs. Younghusband now vested in the Guardian Assurance Co. Ltd. in order to recoup themselves against any money which they may be ordered to repay. What is said by the defendants is that that right to impound would be prejudiced if new trustees were appointed now and the trust fund handed over to them. That involves a consideration as to what is the nature of the right to impound which exists in favour of a trustee who has committed a breach of trust at the instigation of a beneficiary. I have to consider both the ordinary right which exists

---

instigating, requesting or consenting to in writing a breach of trust." Davey L.J. observed (at p. 274): " . . . in order to bring the case within the section the beneficiary must have requested the trustee to depart from and go outside the terms of his trust. It is not, of course, necessary that the beneficiary should know the investment to be in law a breach of trust; but he must, I think, know the facts which constitute the breach of trust."

16 (1855) 7 De G.M. &. G. 104.

17 In accordance with this case is *Mara* v. *Browne* [1895] 2 Ch. 69, 92–93, where North J. held that the trustee was not entitled to impound the interest of the beneficiary (a married woman restrained from anticipation), for the beneficiary, though she had consented in writing, had not consented to those acts which constituted the breach of trust. *Mara* v. *Browne* was taken to the Court of Appeal—[1896] 1 Ch. 199— but in the view which the court took of the circumstances the point did not arise.

in equity apart from statute and also the further statutory right which has been conferred by section 62 of the Trustee Act 1925 both of which are invoked by the defendants as plaintiffs in the Chancery action now pending. It seems to me that it is not possible to maintain, as is the defendants' contention here, that a trustee, having committed a breach of trust, is entitled to remain as a trustee until it has exercised its right to impound the income of the beneficiary in order to recoup itself. That seems to me an impossible proposition. It is quite true that, in the reported authorities, there is no case where the right to impound has been exercised by a former trustee as distinct from an existing trustee, but it seems to me in principle that it is impossible to contend that the right to impound is limited to the case where the trustee seeking the right is an actual trustee. The nature of the right to impound seems to me to turn on two things: first, that the money paid back to capital is in its origin the money of the trustee, and that when it comes to considering who should get the income of it, the trustee who has provided the money has a better right to it than the tenant for life who has instigated the breach of trust. The alternative way of putting the matter is that the trustee in breach of trust is in some way subrogated to the rights of the beneficiary. He stands in his position in order that he may be indemnified. That seems to me the way in which it was put by the Lords Justices in *Raby* v. *Ridehalgh*.[18] It does not seem to me that there is any support in authority or in principle for saying that the right depends upon the actual possession of the trust fund, and it appears to me that the analogy which has been sought to be drawn with the executor's right to retain is a false one and does not apply to this case. So much for the equitable right to impound as opposed to the statutory right.

" As regards the statutory right, that depends on the language of section 62 of the Trustee Act 1925, and at first sight it might look as if that right only exists in favour of a person who is actually a trustee. But, on consideration, that seems to me to be a misconstruction of the section. In the first place, the same objection against limiting the right in that way applies to the statutory jurisdiction. It seems to me an absurdity that it is required as a condition of exercising the right to obtain an impounding order, that the trustee who, *ex hypothesi*, is in breach of trust, must remain the trustee in order to acquire a right of indemnity. Further, it seems to me on the authorities, and, indeed, on the very terms of the section, that the section is giving an additional right, among other things, to deal with the case of a married woman beneficiary; that the statutory right is extending the equitable right and not limiting it, and that it is not right to read the section so as to apply only to a person who was formerly a trustee. The section begins with the words: ' Where a trustee commits a breach of trust,' thereby indicating that at the time the breach of trust is committed the person

---

18 (1855) 7 De G.M. & G. 104.

in question must be a trustee. Then further down in the section there is a reference to a trustee and that appears to me to be merely a reference back to the same person as the person who committed the breach of trust and not as an indication that the person in question must be a trustee at the date of the order. I would add to that, that here the writ which has been issued in the Chancery Division was issued at a time when the defendants were trustees, and, therefore, at the date of the writ the requirement of being a trustee was fulfilled. So that, although I entirely appreciate that the defendants may be anxious not to lose their right to impound the income of the tenant for life, that right could not, in my view, be prejudiced by appointing new trustees at this stage."

III. Statutes of Limitation

The effect of the Limitation Act 1939 [19] in respect of the law of trusts may be summarised as follows:

The doctrine of " laches " [20] is expressly preserved by the Act, section 29 of which provides that " nothing in the Act shall affect any equitable jurisdiction to refuse relief on the ground of acquiescence or otherwise." The doctrine is available " where it would be practically unjust to give a remedy, either because the party has, by his conduct, done that which might fairly be regarded as equivalent to a waiver of it, or where by his conduct and neglect he has, though perhaps not waiving that remedy, yet put the other party in a situation in which it would not be reasonable to place him if the remedy were afterwards asserted." [21]

The field of operation of the doctrine is much narrowed by the inclusion in the Act of cases which were previously not the subject of a statutory limitation, but which had been dealt with under this equitable doctrine. Accordingly, today it is the statutory period which operates against a *cestui que trust* in respect of a claim against the trustee for a breach of trust [22] and not the equitable doctrine of " laches." But there are cases under the Act [23] in which the liability of the trustee is subject to no *statutory* period of limitation at all, *e.g.*, a claim against trustees for property retained by them. In such a case it is submitted that the right of the *cestui que trust* would be barred by an unreasonably long period of delay. [24]

---

[19] " It was drafted by a very eminent Chancery lawyer, but nonetheless it . . . gives considerable difficulties of interpretation whenever the court is concerned with its application ": *per* Danckwerts J. in *Baker* v. *Medway Supplies* [1958] 2 All E.R. 532, 535. It consolidates with amendments certain earlier enactments: *Beaman* v. *A.R.T.S.* [1949] 1 K.B. 550, 556 (C.A.); *Phillips-Higgins* v. *Harper* [1954] 1 Q.B. 411, 417 (Pearson J.); *Baker* v. *Medway Supplies, supra.* Generally see Preston and Newsom's *Limitation of Actions*, 3rd ed., 1953, Chap. 5; Franks' *Limitation of Actions* (1959), pp. 62–80. The old position is set out on pp. 481–484 of the 5th ed. of this work.

[20] Snell, pp. 35–36; Tiley's *Casebook on Equity*, pp. 151 *et seq.*; Z. Chafee (1949) 47 Mich.L.R. 877, 1065.

[21] *Per* Lord Selborne L.C. in *Lindsay Petroleum Co.* v. *Hurd* (1874) L.R. 5 P.C. 221, 239–240. See also *Holder* v. *Holder* [1968] Ch. 353.

[22] See Limitation Act 1939, s. 19 (2); *Re Pauling's S.T.* [1964] Ch. 303.

[23] *Ibid.* s. 19 (1).

[24] See *McDonnel* v. *White* (1865) 11 H.L.C. 271; *Sleeman* v. *Wilson* (1871) L.R. 13 Eq. 36.

The ability of equity to act by analogy to the statute is expressly recognised and preserved, for section 2 (7) of the Act provides that the six-year period, which is laid down by the section for certain actions in contract and tort, is not to apply to " any claim for specific performance of a contract or for an injunction or for *other equitable relief* " save in so far as a court of equity may apply it by analogy. But the analogous application of section 2 (7) is limited to claims for which no express provision is to be found elsewhere in the statute.[25]

Thus it was held in *Re Diplock* [26] that even if the claims in equity were analogous to the common law action for money had and received (which they were not), they were also " actions in respect of a claim to the personal estate of a deceased person " for which under section 20 of the Act the relevant period of limitation was one of twelve years from the date when the right to receive the share or interest accrued; accordingly, there was no scope for applying any other period by way of analogy or otherwise.

The equitable rule that time would not run against the plaintiff in cases of fraud and mistake is now adopted by the Act, section 26 of which provides:

" Where in the case of *any action* for which a period of limitation is prescribed by this Act, either:

(a) the action is based upon the fraud of the defendant or his agent or of any person through whom he claims or his agent, or

(b) the right of action is concealed by the fraud of any such person as aforesaid, or

(c) the action is for relief from the consequences of mistake,

the period of limitation shall not begin to run until the plaintiff has discovered the fraud or mistake, as the case may be, or could with reasonable diligence have discovered it." [27] [There follows a proviso protecting transactions without notice of the fraud having been committed or the mistake having been made, as the case may be.]

As Lord Denning has said,[28] " The word ' fraud ' here is not used in the common law sense. It is used in the equitable sense to denote conduct by the defendant or his agent [29] such that it would be against conscience for him to avail himself of the lapse of time. The cases show that if a man knowingly commits a wrong in such circumstances that it is unlikely to be found out for many a long day, he cannot rely on the statute as a bar to the claim. In order to show that he ' concealed ' the right of action ' by fraud,' it is not necessary to show that he took active steps to conceal his wrong-doings. . . . It is sufficient that he *knowingly* committed it and did not tell anything about it . . . To this word knowingly there must be added ' reck-

---

[25] A case like *Re Robinson* [1911] 1 Ch. 502 would be decided today in accordance with the provisions of s. 19 (2) of the Limitation Act 1939, and not by the use of any analogy to the statute.

[26] [1948] Ch. 465, 502–516; when the case reached the House of Lords, *sub nom. Ministry of Health* v. *Simpson* [1951] A.C. 251, their Lordships approved the views of the Court of Appeal on the applicability of s. 20 of the Limitation Act, and it therefore became unnecessary to express an opinion on the applicability of s. 26 thereof.

[27] See *Kitchen* v. *R.A.F. Association* [1958] 1 W.L.R. 563 (C.A.) (solicitor's negligence); *Baker* v. *Medway Supplies* [1958] 1 W.L.R. 1216 (fraudulent conversion of money).

[28] *King* v. *Victor Parsons & Co.* [1973] 1 W.L.R. 29, 33.

[29] See *Archer* v. *Moss* [1971] 1 Q.B. 406 for agents including independent contractors.

lessly.'[30] Like the man who . . . is aware that what he is doing may well be a wrong . . . but he takes the risk of it being so. He refrains from further enquiry lest it should prove to be correct; and says nothing about it. The court will not allow him to get away with conduct of that kind. It may be that he has no dishonest motive; but that does not matter. He has kept the plaintiff out of the knowledge of his right of action; and that is enough: see *Kitchen* v. *Royal Air Force Association.*"[31] The fraud required to bring a claim within section 26 (*b*), *supra*, need not be such as to give rise to an independent cause of action, and the fraudulent concealment may be simultaneous with the act which gives rise to the right of action.[32] "It may acquire its character as such from the very manner in which that act is performed."[33] It was decided in *Phillips-Higgins* v. *Harper*[34] that section 26 (*c*) of the Act does not apply to the case of a right of action concealed from the plaintiff by a mistake. Its scope is limited to actions where a mistake has been made and has had certain consequences and the plaintiff is seeking to be relieved from those consequences, *e.g.*, actions to recover money paid under a mistake; to rescind or rectify contracts on the ground of mistake; to reopen accounts settled in consequence of mistakes. It applies, in fact, only where mistake is an essential ingredient of the cause of action,[35] and it does not help a plaintiff to ascertain the amount still due to him after the ordinary period of limitation has expired. The anomalous result is that a person who has by mistake paid too much can take advantage of the section, but the person who has by mistake received too little cannot avail himself of it.

The extinction of the liability of a trustee in respect of trust property is provided for by section 19 of the Act, which reads as follows:

"(1) No period of limitation prescribed by this Act shall apply to an action by a beneficiary under a trust, being an action—

(*a*) in respect of any fraud or fraudulent breach of trust to which the trustee was a party or privy[36]; or

(*b*) to recover from the trustee trust property or the proceeds thereof in the possession of the trustee, or previously received by the trustee and converted to his use.

(2) Subject as aforesaid an action by a beneficiary to recover trust property or in respect of any breach of trust, not being an action for which a period of limitation is prescribed by any other provision of this Act,[37] shall not be brought after the expiration of six years from the date

---

30 *Beaman* v. *A.R.T.S. Ltd.* [1949] 1 K.B. 550.   31 [1958] 1 W.L.R. 563.

32 *Beaman* v. *A.R.T.S. Ltd.* [1949] 1 K.B. 550 (C.A.); applying *Bulli Coal Mining Co.* v. *Osborne* [1899] A.C. 351; and *Re McCallum* [1901] 1 Ch. 143.

33 *Per* Lord Greene M.R. at p. 559; see also *Shaw* v. *Shaw* [1954] 2 Q.B. 429; *Clark* v. *Woor* [1965] 1 W.L.R. 650, *Archer* v. *Moss* [1971] 1 Q.B. 406.

34 [1954] 1 Q.B. 411.

35 *Sed quaere.* In *Re Diplock, supra,* note 26, the mistake was not an essential ingredient of the cause of action, yet the Court of Appeal held s. 26 (*c*) to be applicable.

36 Does this apply both to proceedings against a trustee who has been guilty of fraud and to a person who was not the original trustee but who acquired the trust property or payment which was fraudulently made out of the trust property? *Semble* it applies to both: *Baker* v. *Medway Supplies* [1958] 1 W.L.R. 1216.

37 Where personal representatives have become trustees upon completing administration of an estate the relationship between s. 19 (2) and s. 20 is unclear. It would seem that the breadth of s. 20 has changed the law so that a 12-year period is applicable, s. 19 (2) excluding " an action for which a period of limitation is pre-

on which the right of action accrued: Provided that the right of action shall not be deemed to have accrued to any beneficiary entitled to a future interest in the trust property until the interest fell into possession.

(3) No beneficiary as against whom there would be a good defence under this Act shall derive any greater or other benefit from a judgment or order obtained by any other beneficiary than he could have obtained if he had brought the action and this Act had been pleaded in defence."

The following observations may be made upon the effect of the section.

There is no longer any distinction drawn between express and other trustees, since the word " trustee " is defined by reference to section 68 (17) of the Trustee Act 1925. This definition excludes the duties incident to an estate conveyed by way of mortgage,[38] but includes implied and constructive trusts. And it has been held to include the directors of a company,[39] but not trustees in bankruptcy[40] nor apparently the liquidators of companies in voluntary liquidation.[41]

The section is limited to actions by *beneficiaries* in respect of trust property. It is thought, however, that a newly appointed trustee would have the same rights as the beneficiaries themselves against the surviving trustees.[42]

Perpetual liability is confined under this section as under the 1888 Act to cases of (a) fraudulent[43] breaches of trust and (b) of retention or conversion of the trust property. It appears from *Thorne* v. *Heard*[44] that the negligence of a trustee, resulting in his solicitor embezzling the trust funds, was insufficient to render the trustee " party or privy " to the fraud.

With regard to the latter the Law of Property Act 1925 has had some unexpected results. In *Re Landi*[45] X and Y were tenants in common of leasehold premises acquired by them in 1923. On December 31, 1925, by virtue of section 34 of the Law of Property Act 1925, the legal estate became vested in them as joint tenants on trust for sale for themselves as tenants in common in equity. X had been in possession of the whole of the rents and profits from 1923 to 1935, and it was held that in respect of the period from January 1, 1926, onwards he was liable to account to Y for a moiety of the rents and profits by reason of the fact that he had become a statutory trustee.

---

scribed by any other provision of this Act ". *Re Diplock* [1948] Ch. 465, 511–513, *Ministry of Health* v. *Simpson* [1951] A.C. 251, 276–277.

[38] But a prior mortgagee of land exercising his power of sale seems to be a trustee of the surplus for subsequent mortgagees after meeting his own claims. See *Thorne* v. *Heard* [1894] 1 Ch. 599; [1895] A.C. 495; *Re Bell* (1886) 34 Ch.D. 462; but see *Banner* v. *Berridge* (1881) 18 Ch.D. 254.

[39] *Re Lands Allotment Co.* [1894] 1 Ch. 616, 631, 638, 643 and *Whitwam* v. *Watkin* (1898) 78 L.T. 188. In *Tintin Exploration Syndicate Ltd.* v. *Sandys* (1947) 177 L.T. 412 Roxburgh J. said *obiter* that the classification of trusts under the old law was still applicable. In *Baker* v. *Medway Supplies* [1958] 1 W.L.R. 1216 it was assumed that it did not.

[40] *Re Cornish* [1896] 1 Q.B. 99.

[41] *Re Windsor Steam Coal Co.* (*1901*) *Ltd.* [1928] Ch. 609; affd. on a different ground [1929] 1 Ch. 151.

[42] See *Re Bowden* (1890) 45 Ch.D. 444, a case decided under the 1888 Act which was not limited to actions by beneficiaries.

[43] See *North American Land Co.* v. *Watkins* [1904] 1 Ch. 242; [1904] 2 Ch. 233; *Vane* v. *Vane* (1872) L.R. 8 Ch. 383.

[44] [1895] A.C. 495.

[45] [1939] Ch. 828. See (1971) 35 Conv.(N.S.) 6 (G. Battersby).

Re Milking Pail Farm Trusts [46] goes even further, for in that case
it was held that a mortgagee of land held by the mortgagors as tenants
in common before 1926 had not lost his title despite a lapse of some
thirteen years, since after 1925 the land had become vested in the mortgagors on the statutory trusts which include under section 35 of the Law
of Property Act 1925 a trust to discharge incumbrances.

The section speaks of property " previously received by the trustee and
converted to his use." In *Re Howlett* [47] it was contended that this referred
to an *actual* receipt of property, but Danckwerts J. held that it included
a *notional* receipt, and so he was able to charge a trustee who had occupied
trust property for some twenty years with an occupation rent. To fall foul
of section 19 (1) the trustees retention or conversion must be wrongful in
some way.[48]

Section 19 (2) of the Act prescribes a six-year period of limitation for
cases not falling within section 19 (1) or within any other provision of the
Act. This subsection will therefore protect a trustee from liability for more
than six years' arrears of income.[49] His liability with regard to the capital
will on the other hand usually be perpetual, since he will either have it in
his possession, or have converted it to his use. But if he can show that he
has parted with it innocently the six-year period is the appropriate one
to limit his liability. The recipient will be subject to a perpetual liability
unless he is a bona fide purchaser for value without notice.

The proviso to section 19 (2) protects reversionary interests by enacting
that time shall not run against a beneficiary until his interest has fallen
into possession.[50] Even before that date a remainderman can sue for
breach of trust. In such a case if the prior beneficiary is himself barred the
trustees must nevertheless replace the fund at the suit of the remainderman,
but during the continuance of the prior beneficiary's interest they will be
entitled to the income of the property: for a judgment recovered by one
beneficiary is not to improve the position of one who is already barred.[51]

Section 5. Liability of Trustees *inter se*

Since trustees are jointly and severally liable one trustee may be compelled
to replace the whole loss or more than his share of the loss. In such a case
he will have a right of contribution from the others unless he was a fraudulent trustee. Exceptionally, a trustee can obtain a complete indemnity so as
to throw the whole loss on his co-trustee if (a) his co-trustee has exclusively
benefited from the breach of trust or is alone morally guilty or (b) his co-
trustee is a solicitor or Chancery barrister whose advice and control caused

---

[46] [1940] Ch. 990; criticised (1941) 57 L.Q.R. 27 on the ground that the relationship
of mortgagor-mortgagee is essentially different from that of trustee-beneficiary.
Also criticised by Preston & Newsom, p. 151.

[47] [1949] Ch. 767.

[48] *Re Gurney* [1893] 1 Ch. 590; *Re Page* [1893] 1 Ch. 304; *Re Fountaine* [1909] 2
Ch. 382.

[49] Subject, of course, to the exceptional cases of perpetual liability, viz., fraud, and
retention or conversion of the trust property; see A. K. Kiralfy (1949) 13 Conv.
(N.S.) 276.

[50] Consent by a life-tenant to an advance in favour of a remainderman does not
amount to a release of the life interest so as to convert the remainderman's interest
into an interest in possession: *Re Pauling's S.T.* [1964] Ch. 303.

[51] *Re Somerset* [1894] 1 Ch. 231; s. 19 (3) of the Limitation Act 1939; *Mara* v. *Browne*
[1895] 2 Ch. 69 reversed on another point [1896] 1 Ch. 199.

his passive participation in the breach of trust or (c) his co-trustee has a beneficial interest liable to impounding under general equitable principles or section 62 of the Trustee Act which is large enough to satisfy the loss: *Chillingworth* v. *Chambers*.[52] In respect of the unsatisfied loss in this last instance the trustee is left to his right of contribution against the co-trustee.

I. CONTRIBUTION

LINGARD v. BROMLEY

Master of the Rolls (1812) 1 V. & B. 114

A loss to the estate of a bankrupt was incurred through the joint act of three assignees in bankruptcy, of whom the plaintiff was one, and the defendants the other two. An order was made against the three to replace the loss. The plaintiff made good the loss in full.

Held, the plaintiff was entitled to contribution from his co-assignees.[53]

BAHIN v. HUGHES

Court of Appeal (1886) 31 Ch.D. 390; 55 L.J.Ch. 472; 54 L.T. 188; 34 W.R. 311; 2 T.L.R. 276 (Cotton, Bowen and Fry L.JJ.)

A testator, Robert Hughes, bequeathed a legacy of £2,000 to his three daughters—Eliza Hughes, Mrs. Burden and Mrs. Edwards—on trust to invest in specified securities and in real securities in England and Wales. Eliza Hughes, who was the active trustee, and Mr. Burden invested the fund on the (unauthorised) security of leasehold properties, an investment discovered by Mr. Burden. Mrs. Edwards had been informed of the proposal, but her concurrence was not obtained. The security proving insufficient, the tenant for life and remaindermen brought this action against Eliza Hughes, Mr. Edwards (whose wife had died) and Mr. and Mrs. Burden, claiming that the defendants were liable to make good the trust fund.[54] Edwards served a third party notice on Eliza Hughes claiming to be indemnified by her, on the ground that she had assumed the role of sole trustee, that the investment had been made

---

52 [1896] 1 Ch. 685, *infra*.
53 See also *Worthington* v. *Pakenham* (1851) 17 L.T.(o.s.) 224; *Prime* v. *Savelle* [1867] W.N. 227; *Bacon* v. *Camphausen* (1888) 58 L.T. 851; Romilly M.R. in *Birks* v. *Micklethwait* (1864) 33 Beav. 409, 411; *Robinson* v. *Harkin* [1896] 2 Ch. 415; *Fletcher* v. *Green* (1864) 33 Beav. 426, 430; *Re Stuart, Smith* v. *Stuart* [1897] 2 Ch. 583, 593. In *Jackson* v. *Dickinson* [1903] 1 Ch. 947 a trustee's right of contribution was enforced against the estate of his deceased co-trustee; in *Robinson* v. *Evans* (1843) 7 Jur.(o.s.) 738 by the estate of a deceased trustee against the surviving trustees. Apparently, a fraudulent trustee has no right of contribution against his co-trustee even if the latter is also fraudulent: see *Att.-Gen.* v. *Wilson* (1840) Cr. & Ph. 1, 28, *sed quaere* in view of s. 6 of the Law Reform (Married Women and Tortfeasors) Act 1935; see, however, Winfield (1948) 64 L.Q.R. 46, 47.
54 Prior to s. 18 of the Married Women's Property Act of 1882 (which did not apply to the present case) a married woman could not act as trustee without the participation of her husband (Mr. Edwards); he was necessarily a trustee through her trusteeship, and was responsible for her breaches of trust. Cotton L.J. in the present case (31 Ch.D. 394), and Fry L.J., *infra*, p. 661.

at her instigation, and that she had represented to Mrs. Edwards that the mortgage was a proper and sufficient security.

Held, by Kay J., that the defendants were jointly and severally liable to replace the £2,000, and that the defendant Edwards had no right of indemnity against Eliza Hughes. Edwards appealed.

COTTON L.J.: ". . . We come to another and more difficult question, namely, how far Mr. Edwards can, as against Miss Hughes, have indemnity for the loss, on the ground that she was the acting trustee, that she and Mrs. Burden took upon themselves to invest this money, and that although both she and Mr. Edwards are liable to the beneficiaries, she is liable to Mr. Edwards, who left the matter in her hands. On going into the authorities, there are very few cases in which one trustee, who has been guilty with a co-trustee of breach of trust and held answerable, has successfully sought indemnity as against his co-trustee. *Lockhart* v. *Reilly* [55] and *Thompson* v. *Finch* [56] are the only cases which appear to be reported. Now, in *Lockhart* v. *Reilly* [57] it appears from the report of the case in the *Law Journal* that the trustee by whom the loss was sustained had been not only trustee, but had been and was a solicitor, and acting as solicitor for himself and his co-trustee, and it was on his advice that Lockhart had relied in making the investment which gave rise to the action of the *cestui que trust*. The Lord Chancellor (Lord Cranworth) refers to the fact that he was a solicitor, and makes the remark: ' The whole thing was trusted to him. He was the solicitor, and, independently of the consideration that one cannot help seeing it was done with a view of favouring his own family, yet if that had not been so, the co-trustee leaves it with the solicitor-trustee, by whose negligence (I use no harsher word) all this evil, in a great degree, has arisen.' Therefore the Lord Chancellor, in giving his decision, relies upon the fact of the trustee being a solicitor. In *Thompson* v. *Finch* [58] a right was conceded to prove against the estate of the deceased trustee for the full loss sustained; but it appears that in this case also he was a solicitor, and that he really took this money to himself, for he mixed it with his own money, and invested it on a mortgage; and therefore it was held that the trustee was entitled to indemnity from the estate of the co-trustee, who was a solicitor. This was affirmed in the Court of Appeal; and the Court of Appeal took so strong a view of the conduct of the solicitor that both of the judges concurred in thinking that he ought to be called on to show cause why he should not be struck off the rolls. Of course, where one trustee has got the money into his own hands, and made use of it, he will be liable to his co-trustee to give him an indemnity. Now I think it wrong to lay down any limitation of the circumstances under which one trustee would be held liable to the other for indemnity,

55 (1856) 25 L.J.Ch. 697.
56 (1856) 25 L.J.Ch. 681.
57 (1856) 25 L.J.Ch. 697, 702.
58 (1856) 25 L.J.Ch. 681.

both having been held liable to the *cestui que trust*; but so far as cases have gone at present, relief has only been granted against a trustee who has himself got the benefit of the breach of trust, or between whom and his co-trustees there has existed a relation which will justify the court in treating him as solely liable for the breach of trust. . . .

" Miss Hughes was the active trustee and Mr. Edwards did nothing, and in my opinion it would be laying down a wrong rule to hold that where one trustee acts honestly, though erroneously, the other trustee is to be held entitled to indemnity who by doing nothing neglects his duty more than the acting trustee. That Miss Hughes made an improper investment is true, but she acted honestly, and intended to do the best she could, and believed that the property was sufficient security for the money, although she made no inquiries about their being leasehold houses. In my opinion the money was lost just as much by the default of Mr. Edwards as by the innocent though erroneous action of his co-trustee, Miss Hughes. All the trustees were in the wrong, and every one is equally liable to indemnify the beneficiaries."

FRY L.J.: " It appears to me that on the first point arising in this appeal there is no case at all. It appears that in a certain trust the wife of the defendant Mr. Edwards was one of the trustees, and that he has been rendered liable for breaches of trust committed by her, which liability he repudiates by alleging that a husband is not responsible for all but only for some, of the breaches of trust which a wife may commit. I rather understand that he draws a distinction between active and passive breaches of trust, but it was admitted by Mr. Smith that there is no authority for such distinction, and I can see no principle in law for such a distinction. The law of England, which has long existed, is that the husband is responsible for the breaches of trust of his wife. Upon the second point I also agree with my brother Lord Justice Cotton. This part of the appeal is based upon some notion that one trustee is liable to indemnify his co-trustee against loss or injury from his acts, but I cannot think that such liability exists, for if it did exist the books would be full of authorities bearing upon the point, and the courts would be crowded with litigation on the subject. It is well known that the authorities are extremely few, and the authorities which do exist do not favour the appellant's contention. It has been pointed out by Lord Justice Cotton that in each of the two cases cited the trustee who was held to be secondarily liable, and who had a right of indemnity, had been misled by his co-trustee, who was the solicitor to the trust, and had been proved to have been guilty of negligence in his duty as such solicitor. In my judgment the courts ought to be very jealous of raising any such implied liability as is insisted on, because if such existed it would act as an opiate upon the consciences of the trustees; so that instead of the *cestui que trust* having the benefit of several acting trustees, each trustee would be looking to the other or others for a right of indemnity, and so neglect the performance of his duties. Such a doctrine would be against the policy of the court in relation to trusts.

"In the present case, in my judgment, the loss which has happened is the result of the combination of the action of Miss Hughes with the inaction of Mr. Edwards. If Miss Hughes has made a mistake, it was through simple ignorance and want of knowledge, and if on the other hand Mr. Edwards had used all the diligence which he ought to have done, I doubt whether any loss would have been incurred. The money might have been recovered before the property went down in value. I think, therefore, that it is not possible for Mr. Edwards to obtain any relief, and I concur with my brethren that this appeal must be dismissed with costs." *Appeal dismissed.*

II. INDEMNITY

Re PARTINGTON, PARTINGTON v. ALLEN

Chancery Division (1887) 57 L.T. 654; 3 T.L.R. 828; 4 T.L.R. 4

The learned judge has held that the trustee, Mrs. Partington, and her solicitor co-trustee, Mr. Allen, were jointly and severally liable towards their beneficiaries in respect of a breach of trust consisting of improper mortgage investments. Mrs. Partington claimed to be indemnified by her co-trustee.

STIRLING J.: ". . . The facts in this case seem to me to be these: Mr. Allen, by his own bills of costs, appears to have acted as solicitor on behalf of the mortgagees, namely, himself and his co-trustee, Mrs. Partington, and he has charged, as I understand it, in those bills of costs the full scale fees allowed both for negotiating the loan, and for deducing the title, and for preparing and completing the mortgage. Therefore he appears to me to have taken upon himself to act, in the words of one of the rules, as solicitor engaged in the whole business relating to the mortgage. By undertaking to negotiate the loan he undertook to procure a borrower from the trustees who was able to give a satisfactory security—that is, a security which would not only be sufficient as regards the legal title, but also ample in point of value to secure the fund which was to be advanced by the trustees, and therefore which would be such a security as the trustees could properly accept. I have already decided that the actual investments were not such as the trustees ought to have accepted, and, therefore, Mr. Allen, having undertaken this duty as solicitor, has failed to perform it. Next, I have got to consider the question, has he communicated what he did to Mrs. Partington in such a way as to enable her to exercise her judgment upon the investments, and so make them, really and in truth, her acts as well as his own? I think not. First of all, I held that the investments were improper because Mr. Allen did not make the necessary inquiries for the purpose of verifying the statements made by the proposed mortgagors as to the nature of the security which they were to give. Secondly, because he did not give proper instructions to the valuers on the footing of the real nature of the property being explained to them; and, thirdly, that the valuations which he obtained were not such as ought to have been acted upon by him and his co-trustee as trustees, having regard to the rule of convenience and practice which has been laid down by the court, and which he was not only bound to know, but which he actually knew. As to the first two points, it does not seem to me, upon the evidence, that there is anything to show he ever communicated to his co-trustee at all either the real state of the property, or that he did not make inquiries or that he communicated the instructions which he gave to the valuers. As to the third point, namely, whether he told his co-trustee the nature of the rule which has been laid down, or advised her as to the valuation, there is a conflict of evidence, and undoubtedly it would have been much more satisfactory if the matter had been further inquired into, and possibly if a cross-examination had been taken before myself. But both parties are desirous that I should decide the question on the present materials, and therefore I have formed the best opinion which I can upon the point. Now the case stands in this way. [His Lordship then reviewed the evidence, and continued:] On the evidence before me I come to the conclusion that Mr. Allen did not advise Mrs. Partington with reference to these valuations, or as to any apparent impropriety in them. Then that being so, what do we find? Mr. Allen acts as solicitor, and he has undertaken, as I have said, to procure a proper investment such as trustees might accept. He fails to do so. In truth Mrs. Partington, who had a control over the trust fund by reason of it standing in her name jointly with Mr. Allen, signs cheques and parts with the control over the trust fund on the faith that these were proper investments which had been looked into by Mr. Allen as solicitor, and were fit and proper investments for the trustees. What arises out of that as regards mutual liability? That, as has been pointed out, has been discussed in the case of *Bahin* v. *Hughes*,[59] and, as I read the judgment of the Court of Appeal in that case, they came to the conclusion that if there is a relationship existing between the co-trustees which will justify the court in treating one of them as solely responsible for the breach of trust, then the other trustee is entitled to indemnity from him in respect of that breach of trust. Cotton L.J. says this: 'So far as cases have gone at present, relief has only been granted against a trustee who has himself got the benefit of the breach of trust, or between whom and his co-trustees there has existed a relation which will justify the court in treating him as solely liable for the breach of trust.' He discussed the cases that had previously occurred of *Lockhart* v. *Reilly* [60] and *Thompson* v. *Finch*,[61] pointing out that in *Lockhart* v. *Reilly* the co-trustee was a solicitor, and in the other he not only was a solicitor, but

---

[59] (1886) 31 Ch.D. 390, 398.
[60] (1856) 25 L.J.Ch. 697.
[61] (1856) 25 L.J.Ch. 681.

had taken the money for himself and mixed it with his own and invested it on mortgage. Fry L.J. says: ' It has been pointed out by Cotton L.J. that in each of the two cases cited the trustee who was held to be secondarily liable, and who had a right of indemnity, had been *misled* by his co-trustee who was the solicitor to the trust, and had been proved to have been guilty of negligence in his duty as such solicitor.' I think those circumstances which are pointed out by Fry L.J. occur here. The trustee, Mrs. Partington, appears to me to have been misled by her co-trustee by reason of his not giving her full information as to the nature of the investments which he was asking her to advance the money upon, and I think he has been guilty of negligence also in his duty as a solicitor . . ."

Held, therefore, the trustee, Mrs. Partington, had a right of indemnity against her co-trustee.

HEAD v. GOULD

Chancery Division [1898] 2 Ch. 250; 67 L.J.Ch. 480; 78 L.T. 739; 46 W.R. 597; 14 T.L.R. 444; 42 S.J. 553

Several points fell to be decided in this case, but for the purposes of a trustee's claim of indemnity against his co-trustee the facts may be sufficiently stated as follows:

Miss Head and Mr. Gould were appointed new trustees of certain marriage settlements (the beneficial interests being the same under both settlements), and thenceforth Gould acted as solicitor to the trusts. Miss Head was one of the remaindermen under these settlements, the tenant for life being her mother. The new trustees sold a house forming part of the trust, and in breach of trust handed the proceeds of sale to the tenant for life. Part of the trust property consisted also of certain policies on the life of Mrs. Head, policies which Mrs. Head had mortgaged to the trust by way of security for advances of trust capital which the former trustees had made to her at her urgent request for the purpose of assisting the family. These policies were (in breach of trust) surrendered by the new trustees with the concurrence of Mrs. Head.

Miss Head claimed to be indemnified by her co-trustee, Gould, under circumstances which appear from the judgment:

KEKEWICH J.: ". . . It will be convenient here at once to deal with the claim made by Miss Head against her co-trustee, Gould. By her third party notice she seeks to be indemnified by him against loss by reason of the breaches of trust, on the ground that the loss and mis-application (if any) of the trust funds, or any part thereof, were occasioned entirely by his acts or defaults, and that he assumed to act as solicitor to the trust estate and as the sole trustee thereof, and exercised control of the administration of the trust funds, and that whatever was done by herself in connection with the trust was at his instigation and in reliance upon his advice.

" This is a serious charge, and if it had been proved would have
entitled her to the relief claimed according to well-known and well-
recognised principles. Mr. Gover, in support of the claim, relied on the
decision of Byrne J. in *Re Turner* [62]; but it is to be observed that the
learned judge did no more than follow *Lockhart* v. *Reilly*, [63] and act
upon the principles there enunciated and to which I have alluded. There
is before me no evidence bringing the case within those principles, or
showing that the charge which is correctly formulated on them is consistent with the facts. My conclusion from such evidence as there is
before the court is distinctly adverse to the claim. I know that, before
the appointment of herself and Gould as trustees, Miss Head was an
active party to the importunities of her mother which induced the former
trustees to commit a breach of trust for their benefit, and that she looked
to the change of trustees as a means of, in some way or other, obtaining
further advances. I know, further, that she was well acquainted with
the position of the trust, and that it was all-important to maintain the
policies and to appropriate the rents of the house to that purpose. She
now affects to ignore all that has been done since her appointment,
and professes not to remember having executed the several instruments
which must have been executed by her for the sale of the house and the
surrender of the policies, or the receipt of moneys arising therefrom.
With regret, and under a painful sense of duty, I am bound to say that
I do not credit her testimony. True it is that the defendant, Gould, is a
solicitor, and that he was appointed a trustee for that very reason. True
no doubt, also, that the legal business was managed by him, and I do
not propose to absolve him from any responsibility attaching to him
on that ground; but I do not myself think that Byrne J. or any other
judge ever intended to hold that a man is bound to indemnify his
co-trustee against loss *merely* because he was a solicitor, when that
co-trustee was an active participator in the breach of trust complained
of, and is not proved to have participated merely in consequence of the
advice and control of the solicitor . . ."

Held, therefore, the trustee, Miss Head, had no claim of indemnity
against her co-trustee. [64]

Chillingworth v. *Chambers* [65]

The decision of the Court of Appeal in the above case has been said to lie
on the border between contribution and indemnity. It is to the effect that
a *trustee-beneficiary* who has participated in, and, as between himself and

---

[62] [1897] 1 Ch. 536.
[63] (1856) 25 L.J.Ch. 697.
[64] On indemnity between trustees, see also *Thompson* v. *Finch* (1856) 25 L.J.Ch. 681;
Lockhart v. *Reilly* (1857) 1 De G. & J. 464, 476, 477; *Costello* v. *O'Rorke* (1869)
Ir.R. 3 Eq. 172; *Price* v. *Price* (1880) 42 L.T. 626; *Blyth* v. *Fladgate* [1891] 1 Ch.
337, 364, 365; *Re Turner, Barker* v. *Ivimey* [1897] 1 Ch. 536, 544; *Re Linsley* [1904]
2 Ch. 785; *Belemore* v. *Watson* (1885) 1 T.L.R. 241. In light of *Rondel* v. *Worsley*
[1969] 1 A.C. 191 it seems likely that Chancery barristers will be dealt with on the
same footing as solicitors.
[65] [1896] 1 Ch. 685. See *Re Dacre* [1916] 1 Ch. 344, *supra*, p. 634.

his co-trustee, benefited exclusively by, a breach of trust for which he and his co-trustee are equally to blame must indemnify his co-trustee to the extent of his beneficial interest. X and Y were trustees. X was also a beneficiary, his share being (say) £500. X and Y, with the object of increasing the rate of dividend, invested trust funds in a mortgage which was held to be a breach of trust. As between X and Y, X benefited exclusively by this breach of trust; at any rate, he was so treated by the Court of Appeal. The mortgage was eventually realised at a loss of £400, the whole of which was in fact made good out of X's beneficial share (the trust fund now being in court). X's claim of contribution against Y, that Y should share the loss with him, failed; for X was held liable to indemnify his co-trustee Y to the extent of his beneficial interest. Since X's beneficial interest (£500) exceeded the actual loss (£400), the result was that Y managed to shift the whole of that loss onto X. Strictly speaking, Y did not shift the loss onto X; he shifted it onto X's beneficial interest.

Lindley L.J. summed up the position between X and Y as follows [66]: " To the extent to which the [trustee-beneficiary's] right as trustee is neutralised by his obligation as *cestui que trust* he will have no right to contribution." The trustee-beneficiary's right as trustee is a right of contribution from his co-trustee. His obligation as *cestui que trust* is to indemnify that trustee out of his beneficial interest, for where a beneficiary is an active party in a breach of trust committed with a view towards his benefit he is liable to indemnify his trustee out of his beneficial interest.[67]

Lindley L.J. continued: " But except so far as it is thus neutralised his right of contribution will remain." If, therefore, X's beneficial interest had been £300, and not £500, that £300 would have been used up in indemnifying Y as to three-quarters of the loss of £400, but the remaining £100 would have been shared between them.

In considering *Chillingworth* v. *Chambers*[68] it is of advantage to approach the matter in three stages:

First, the set of circumstances which brings it into operation, *viz.*, a trustee-beneficiary and his co-trustee have between them committed a breach of trust from which the former benefited and the latter did not;

Secondly, the trustee-beneficiary's obligation to indemnify which arises from his character of beneficiary, the rule being that a beneficiary who participates in a breach of trust committed with a view towards his benefit must indemnify his trustees out of his beneficial interest; and

Thirdly, the trustee-beneficiary's right of contribution which arises from his character of trustee.

It would seem that, in order to bring the rule in *Chillingworth* v. *Chambers* into operation, it is not necessary that the trustee-beneficiary *actually benefit* from the breach of trust. The decisions on this particular point establish that it is quite sufficient if a beneficiary participates in a breach of trust with *a motive of personal benefit*.[69] Thus simplified, the

---

[66] *Ibid.* 698.   [67] *Supra*, pp. 641–642.

[68] [1896] 1 Ch. 685.

[69] *Supra*, p. 641; and see s. 62 of the Trustee Act, 1925. In *Chillingworth* v. *Chambers* Lindley L.J. at 700 considered personal benefit immaterial though Kay L.J. at 707 was not prepared so to commit himself as the plaintiff in the circumstances had received a personal benefit. They were concerned only with liability to impound on general equitable principles as the action was pending before section 6 of the Trustee Act 1888 was enacted: see *per* Kay L.J. at 707.

decision in *Chillingworth* v. *Chambers* decides only one new point, *viz.,* that where a right of contribution *qua* trustee conflicts with an obligation to indemnify *qua* beneficiary, the obligation to indemnify must be discharged before the right of contribution may be exercised.

Just as *Chillingworth* v. *Chambers* was based on liability *qua* beneficiary to have a beneficial interest impounded under the old law so it would appear that its principles have been extended by section 62 of the Trustee Act 1925 which extends the law on impounding beneficial interests.

In *Chillingworth* v. *Chambers* it was also held that it made no difference that the trustee-beneficiary was not a beneficiary at the time the breach of trust was committed, but became a beneficiary *after* that date. This part of the decision was based on the analogy of *Evans* v. *Benyon,*[70] where it was held that the rule that a beneficiary who concurs in a breach of trust cannot complain of it against his trustee holds good even if the beneficiary was not a beneficiary at the time of his concurrence, but became a beneficiary after that date.

PROBLEMS

1. Would it have made any difference in *Re Lucking's W.T.* if the business had been unincorporated or if Mr. Lucking's co-trustee had been a layman who had exercised no supervision over the business because Mr. Lucking was a practising Chancery barrister who had led his co-trustee to rely on him implicitly?

2. Ted and Tom are trustees of a £50,000 fund held on trust for Ted himself, Arthur, Brian, Charles and David in equal shares contingent upon each attaining 30 years of age. To allay any suspicions of the other beneficiaries Ted takes little part in running the trust affairs, relying to a large extent on Tom, a 50-year old solicitor.

Tom and Arthur consider that it would be desirable to buy shares in Exploration Syndicate Co. Ltd. but realise that the trustees have no power to do so under the Trustee Investments Act 1961, the will creating the trust conferring no express powers of investment. Nevertheless, Tom writes to Ted telling him that his City connections lead him to consider it a very good idea to buy shares in Exploration Syndicate Co. Ltd. For this purpose they can call in £15,000 deposited with the Countrywide Building Society bringing in a net 7½ per cent. interest. Ted replies by letter, " If you wish us to invest that £15,000 in the Exploration Syndicate Co. Ltd. that is all right by me."

Tom then wrote to Brian, Charles and David, " Ted and I as trustees are considering investing £15,000 of the trust funds in buying shares in the Exploration Syndicate Co. Ltd. That is quite a lot of money but we would consider it well spent in such shares. However, before we go ahead we would like to have your consent. Arthur has already consented and we look forward to receiving replies from you and the other beneficiaries quite soon."

Brian and David replied briefly consenting. Charles replied, " I am quite happy for the £15,000 to be invested in the shares proposed. Of course, I assume they are authorised investments." The beneficiaries, Ted, Arthur,

---

[70] (1887) 37 Ch.D. 329, 344; *supra*, p. 641, note.

Brian, Charles and David were then respectively aged 29, 27, 25, 23 and 17 years. After the replies had been received the £15,000 was invested in buying the proposed shares.

Three years later the company collapsed and the whole £15,000 was lost, the shares only having produced a net 2 per cent. yield in the first year and nothing thereafter.

Advise the trustees on their position *vis-à-vis* (1) the beneficiaries and (2) themselves.

3. Look at the fourth problem at the end of Chapter 10. If David does there take action against the trustees, what repercussions might follow in respect of David's father and brothers?

INDEX

Trustees—*cont.*
 judicial control of, 592–604
 jurisdiction of court
  attempted ouster, 594
 lack of
  trusts do not fail for, 463–464
 land purchase, 507–508
 liability
  inter se, 658–668
  limitation, 656–658
 mental patient, 452–453
 minor, 448
 misconduct
  removal for, 459–462
 name
  use in proceedingss, 171
 number, 448
 payment, 488–489
  solicitor-trustee, 489
 payment into court by, 589–590
 personal responsibility, 465
 powers
  advancement, 576–586. *See also*
   Advancement.
 compound liabilities, to, 561–562
  compromise, to, 561–562
  court's jurisdiction, 595
  failure to exercise, 592
  fraud on a power, 593
  investment, of, 489–500
  land purchase, 507–508
  maintenance of minor, 570–576
  mortgage advance, 500–507
  release, 562, 593
 proceedings against settlor, 156
 proceedings by
  settlor, against, 150–151
 profit, 473–487
  disclosure, 474
  retention, 474
 protection
  advertisements, by, 588
  rents and covenants, 587–588
 prudence, 630
 purchase of land by, 507–508
  statutory power, 507–508
 purchase of trust property, 466–473
 relationship with beneficiaries, 3
 removal
  beneficiaries, by, 451
  court's jurisdiction, 459–462
 retirement, 458–459
 sale of trust property to
  acquiescence, 646–648
 solicitors as, 384
 surrender of discretion, 591–592
 trust corporation, 462–463
 unanimity, 465–466
 unincorporated association, of, 131
 valuation, 562, 563
 vesting of trust property in, 457–458
 want of
  trusts do not fail for, 463–464
 wilful default
  meaning, 620
   criticism, 625

Trust for Sale,
 enforcement
  court's powers, 594
 sale price, 594
Trust Fund,
 apportionment of income, 549–553
  authorised investments, from, 550
   See also Apportionment.
 assignee from beneficiary
  payment to, 586
 aduit, 563
 bank account, in, 632
 conversion of residue, 546–549
 costs out of, 605
 debts paid from
  capital and income apportionment,
   546
 duties of trustee, 489–490
 income
  apportionment, 549–553
 investigation, 563
 investment of, 489–510
  interpretation of investment clause,
   508–510
  investments, 496–499
  court's powers, 495
  mortgages, in, 500–507
  powers, 492–493
  powers of trustees, 490
  purchase of land, 507–508
  special-range property, 492, 499
 legacies paid from
  capital and income apportionment,
   546
 loss to, 627–634
 mixed with other money
  entitlement, 437–447
 narrower-range investments.
  not requiring advice, 496
  requiring advice, 496–497
 overpayment, 586
 payment
  assignee from beneficiary, to, 586
  beneficiary, to, 586–596
  overpayment, 586
  underpayment
   trustee-beneficiary, to, 587
 protection of trustee, 490
 trade, in, 632–633
 transfer, 490–492
 unauthorised investment, 627–630
  quantification of loss, 627–629
 underpayment
  trustee-beneficiary, to, 587
 valuation, 562, 563
  division, for, 494
 vesting in trustees, 457–458
 under-range investments, 497
  restrictions on, 490–492
Trust Powers, 82
 definition, 74
 mere powers compared, 74
Trust Property,
 indemnity of trustee against, 604–608
Trusts,
 abstract impersonal purposes, 108
 administration. *See* Administration
  of trusts.